CRAFTING AND EXECUTING STRATEGY

The Quest for Competitive Advantage

Concepts and Cases

CRAFTING AND EXECUTING STRATEGY

The Quest for Competitive Advantage

Concepts and Cases | 23RD EDITION

Arthur A. Thompson
The University of Alabama

Margaret A. Peteraf
Dartmouth College

John E. Gamble
Texas A&M University–Corpus Christi

A.J. Strickland III
The University of Alabama

CRAFTING & EXECUTING STRATEGY: THE QUEST FOR COMPETITIVE ADVANTAGE:
CONCEPTS AND CASES, TWENTY THIRD EDITION

Published by McGraw Hill LLC, 1325 Avenue of the Americas, New York, NY 10121. Copyright ©2022 by McGraw Hill LLC. All rights reserved. Printed in the United States of America. Previous editions ©2020, 2018, and 2016. No part of this publication may be reproduced or distributed in any form or by any means, or stored in a database or retrieval system, without the prior written consent of McGraw Hill LLC, including, but not limited to, in any network or other electronic storage or transmission, or broadcast for distance learning.

Some ancillaries, including electronic and print components, may not be available to customers outside the United States.

This book is printed on acid-free paper.

3 4 5 6 7 8 9 LKV 24 23 22

ISBN 978-1-260-73517-8 (bound edition)
MHID 1-260-73517-6 (bound edition)
ISBN 978-1-264-25013-4 (loose-leaf edition)
MHID 1-264-25013-4 (loose-leaf edition)

Director: *Michael Ablassmeir*
Product Development Manager: *Michele Janicek*
Product Developer: *Anne Ehrenworth*
Executive Marketing Manager: *Debbie Clare*
Content Project Managers: *Melissa M. Leick; Keri Johnson*
Buyer: *Sandy Ludovissy*
Designer: *Matt Diamond*
Content Licensing Specialist: *Sarah Flynn*
Cover Image: *Image Source/Getty Images*
Compositor: *SPi Global*

All credits appearing on page or at the end of the book are considered to be an extension of the copyright page.

Library of Congress Cataloging-in-Publication Data

Names: Thompson, Arthur A., 1940- author.
Title: Crafting and executing strategy : the quest for competitive
    advantage : concepts and cases / Arthur A. Thompson [and three others].
Description: 23rd edition. | New York, NY : McGraw-Hill Education, [2022] |
    Includes bibliographical references and index.
Identifiers: LCCN 2020036767 | ISBN 9781260735178 (paperback)
Subjects: LCSH: Strategic planning. | Strategic planning—Case studies.
Classification: LCC HD30.28 .T53 2022 | DDC 658.4/012—dc23
LC record available at https://lccn.loc.gov/2020036767

mheducation.com/highered

To our families and especially our spouses:
Hasseline, Paul, Heather, and Kitty.

About the Authors

Courtesy of Arthur A. Thompson, Jr.

Arthur A. Thompson, Jr., earned his BS and PhD degrees in economics from The University of Tennessee, spent three years on the economics faculty at Virginia Tech, and served on the faculty of The University of Alabama's College of Commerce and Business Administration for 24 years. In 1974 and again in 1982, Dr. Thompson spent semester-long sabbaticals as a visiting scholar at the Harvard Business School.

His areas of specialization are business strategy, competition and market analysis, and the economics of business enterprises. In addition to publishing over 30 articles in some 25 different professional and trade publications, he has authored or co-authored five textbooks and six computer-based simulation exercises. His textbooks and strategy simulations have been used at well over 1,000 college and university campuses worldwide.

Dr. Thompson and his wife of 58 years have two daughters, two grandchildren, and a Yorkshire Terrier.

Courtesy of Margaret A. Peteraf

Margaret A. Peteraf is the Leon E. Williams Professor of Management Emerita at the Tuck School of Business at Dartmouth College. She is an internationally recognized scholar of strategic management, with a long list of publications in top management journals. She has earned myriad honors and prizes for her contributions, including the 1999 Strategic Management Society Best Paper Award recognizing the deep influence of her work on the field of Strategic Management. Professor Peteraf is a fellow of the Strategic Management Society and the Academy of Management. She served previously as a member of the Board of Governors of both the Society and the Academy of Management and as Chair of the Business Policy and Strategy Division of the Academy. She has also served in various editorial roles and on numerous editorial boards, including the *Strategic Management Journal,* the *Academy of Management Review,* and *Organization Science.* She has taught in Executive Education programs in various programs around the world and has won teaching awards at the MBA and Executive level.

Professor Peteraf earned her PhD, MA, and MPhil at Yale University and held previous faculty appointments at Northwestern University's Kellogg Graduate School of Management and at the University of Minnesota's Carlson School of Management.

John E. Gamble is a Professor of Management and Dean of the College of Business at Texas A&M University–Corpus Christi. His teaching and research for 25 years has focused on strategic management at the undergraduate and graduate levels. He has conducted courses in strategic management in Germany since 2001, which have been sponsored by the University of Applied Sciences in Worms.

Courtesy of Richard's Photography, LLC.

Dr. Gamble's research has been published in various scholarly journals and he is the author or co-author of more than 75 case studies published in an assortment of strategic management and strategic marketing texts. He has done consulting on industry and market analysis for clients in a diverse mix of industries.

Professor Gamble received his PhD, MA, and BS degrees from The University of Alabama and was a faculty member in the Mitchell College of Business at the University of South Alabama before his appointment to the faculty at Texas A&M University–Corpus Christi.

Dr. A. J. (Lonnie) Strickland is the Thomas R. Miller Professor of Strategic Management at the Culverhouse School of Business at The University of Alabama. He is a native of north Georgia, and attended the University of Georgia, where he received a BS degree in math and physics; Georgia Institute of Technology, where he received an MS in industrial management; and Georgia State University, where he received his PhD in business administration.

Courtesy of Dr. A. J. (Lonnie) Strickland

Lonnie's experience in consulting and executive development is in the strategic management arena, with a concentration in industry and competitive analysis. He has developed strategic planning systems for numerous firms all over the world. He served as Director of Marketing and Strategy at BellSouth, has taken two companies to the New York Stock Exchange, is one of the founders and directors of American Equity Investment Life Holding (AEL), and serves on numerous boards of directors. He is a very popular speaker in the area of strategic management.

Lonnie and his wife, Kitty, have been married for over 49 years. They have two children and two grandchildren. Each summer, Lonnie and his wife live on their private game reserve in South Africa where they enjoy taking their friends on safaris.

Preface

By offering the most engaging, clearly articulated, and conceptually sound text on strategic management, *Crafting and Executing Strategy* has been able to maintain its position as the leading textbook in strategic management for over 35 years. With this latest edition, we build on this strong foundation, maintaining the attributes of the book that have long made it the most teachable text on the market, while updating the content, sharpening its presentation, and providing enlightening new illustrations and examples.

The distinguishing mark of the 23rd edition is its enriched and enlivened presentation of the material in each of the 12 chapters, providing an as up-to-date and engrossing discussion of the core concepts and analytical tools as you will find anywhere. As with each of our new editions, there is an accompanying lineup of exciting new cases that bring the content to life and are sure to provoke interesting classroom discussions, deepening students' understanding of the material in the process.

While this 23rd edition retains the 12-chapter structure of the prior edition, every chapter—indeed every paragraph and every line—has been reexamined, refined, and refreshed. New content has been added to keep the material in line with the latest developments in the theory and practice of strategic management. In other areas, coverage has been trimmed to keep the book at a more manageable size. Scores of new examples have been added, along with many new Illustration Capsules, to enrich understanding of the content and to provide students with a ringside view of strategy in action. The result is a text that cuts straight to the chase in terms of what students really need to know and gives instructors a leg up on teaching that material effectively. It remains, as always, solidly mainstream and balanced, mirroring *both* the penetrating insight of academic thought and the pragmatism of real-world strategic management.

A standout feature of this text has always been the tight linkage between the content of the chapters and the cases. The lineup of cases that accompany the 23rd edition is outstanding in this respect—a truly appealing mix of strategically relevant and thoughtfully crafted cases, certain to engage students and sharpen their skills in applying the concepts and tools of strategic analysis. Many involve high-profile companies that the students will immediately recognize and relate to; all are framed around key strategic issues and serve to add depth and context to the topical content of the chapters. We are confident you will be impressed with how well these cases work in the classroom and the amount of student interest they will spark.

For some years now, growing numbers of strategy instructors at business schools worldwide have been transitioning from a purely text-case course structure to a more robust and energizing text-case-simulation course structure. Incorporating a competition-based strategy simulation has the strong appeal of providing class members with *an immediate and engaging opportunity to apply the concepts and analytical tools covered in the chapters and to become personally involved in crafting and executing a strategy for a virtual company that they have been assigned to manage and that competes head-to-head with companies run by other class members.* Two widely used and pedagogically effective online strategy simulations, *The Business Strategy Game* and *GLO-BUS,* are optional companions for this text. Both simulations were created by Arthur Thompson, one of the text authors, and, like the cases, are closely linked to the content of each chapter in the text. The Exercises for Simulation Participants, found at the end of each chapter and integrated into the Connect package for the text, provide clear guidance to class members in applying the concepts and analytical tools covered in the chapters to the issues and decisions that they have to wrestle with in managing their simulation company.

To assist instructors in assessing student achievement of program learning objectives, in line with AACSB requirements, the 23rd edition includes a set of Assurance of Learning Exercises at the end of each chapter that link to the specific learning objectives appearing at the beginning of each chapter and highlighted throughout the text. An important instructional feature of the 23rd edition is its more closely *integrated* linkage of selected chapter-end Assurance of Learning Exercises and cases to Connect™. Your students will be able to use Connect™ to (1) complete chapter-specific activities, including selected Assurance of Learning Exercises appearing at the end of each of the 12 chapters as well as video and comprehension cases, (2) complete chapter-end quizzes, (3) complete suggested assignment questions for 14 of the 27 cases in this edition and (4) complete assignment questions for simulation users. All Connect exercises are automatically graded (with the exception of select Exercises for Simulation Participants), thereby enabling you to easily assess the learning that has occurred.

In addition, both of the companion strategy simulations have a built-in Learning Assurance Report that quantifies how well each member of your class performed on nine skills/learning measures *versus tens of thousands of other students worldwide* who completed the simulation in the past 12 months. We believe the chapter-end Assurance of Learning Exercises, the all-new online and automatically graded Connect™ exercises, and the Learning Assurance Report generated at the conclusion of *The Business Strategy Game* and *GLO-BUS* simulations provide you with easy-to-use, empirical measures of student learning in your course. All can be used in conjunction with other instructor-developed or school-developed scoring rubrics and assessment tools to comprehensively evaluate course or program learning outcomes and measure compliance with AACSB accreditation standards.

Taken together, the various components of the 23rd edition package and the supporting set of instructor resources provide you with enormous course design flexibility and a powerful kit of teaching/learning tools. We've done our very best to ensure that the elements constituting the 23rd edition will work well for you in the classroom, help you economize on the time needed to be well prepared for each class, and cause students to conclude that your course is one of the very best they have ever taken—from the standpoint of both enjoyment and learning.

DIFFERENTIATING FEATURES OF THE 23RD EDITION

Nine standout features strongly differentiate this text and the accompanying instructional package from others in the field:

1. *We provide the clearest discussion of business models to be found anywhere.* By introducing this often-misunderstood concept right in the first chapter and defining it precisely, we give students a leg up on grasping this important concept. Follow-on discussions in the next eight chapters drive the concept home. Illustration capsules and cases show how a new business model can enable a company to compete successfully even against well-established rivals. In some cases, a new business model can even be the agent for disrupting an existing industry.

2. *Our integrated coverage of the two most popular perspectives on strategic management—positioning theory and resource-based theory—is unsurpassed by any other leading strategy text.* Principles and concepts from both the positioning perspective and the resource-based perspective are prominently and comprehensively integrated into our coverage of crafting both single-business and multibusiness strategies. By highlighting the relationship between a firm's resources and capabilities to the activities it conducts along its value chain, we show explicitly how these two perspectives relate to one another. Moreover, in Chapters 3 through 8 it is emphasized repeatedly that a company's strategy must be matched *not only* to its external market circumstances *but also* to its internal resources and competitive capabilities.

3. *With this new edition, we provide the clearest, easiest to understand presentation of the value-price-cost framework.* In recent years, this framework has become an essential aid to teaching students how companies create economic value in the course of conducting business. We show how this simple framework informs the concept of the business model as well as the all-important concept of competitive advantage. In Chapter 5, we add further clarity by showing in pictorial fashion how the value-price-cost framework relates to the different sources of competitive advantage that underlie the five generic strategies.

4. *Our coverage of cooperative strategies and the role that interorganizational activity can play in the pursuit of competitive advantage is similarly distinguished.* The topics of the value net, ecosystems, strategic alliances, licensing, joint ventures, and other types of collaborative relationships are featured prominently in a number of chapters and are integrated into other material throughout the text. We show how strategies of this nature can contribute to the success of single-business companies as well as multibusiness enterprises, whether with respect to firms operating in domestic markets or those operating in the international realm.

5. *The attention we give to international strategies, in all their dimensions, make this textbook an indispensable aid to understanding strategy formulation and execution in an increasingly connected, global world.* Our treatment of this topic as one of the most critical elements of the *scope* of a company's activities brings home to students the connection between the topic of international strategy with other topics concerning firm scope, such as multibusiness (or corporate) strategy, outsourcing, insourcing, and vertical integration.

6. *With a standalone chapter devoted to these topics, our coverage of business ethics, corporate social responsibility, and environmental sustainability goes well beyond that offered by any other leading strategy text.* Chapter 9, "Ethics, Corporate Social Responsibility, Environmental Sustainability, and Strategy," fulfills the important functions of (1) alerting students to the role and importance of ethical and socially

responsible decision making and (2) addressing the accreditation requirement of the AACSB International that business ethics be visibly and thoroughly embedded in the core curriculum. Moreover, discussions of the roles of values and ethics are integrated into portions of other chapters, beginning with the first chapter, to further reinforce why and how considerations relating to ethics, values, social responsibility, and sustainability should figure prominently into the managerial task of crafting and executing company strategies.

7. *Long known as an important differentiator of this text, the case collection in the 23rd edition is truly unrivaled* from the standpoints of student appeal, teachability, and suitability for drilling students in the use of the concepts and analytical treatments in Chapters 1 through 12. The 27 cases included in this edition are the very latest, the best, and the most on target that we could find. The ample information about the cases in the Instructor's Manual makes it effortless to select a set of cases each term that will capture the interest of students from start to finish.

8. *The text is now optimized for hybrid and online delivery through robust assignment and assessment content integrated into Connect™.* This will enable professors to gauge class members' prowess in accurately completing (a) additional exercises and selected chapter-end exercises, (b) chapter-end quizzes, (c) exercises for simulation participants, and (d) exercises for 14 of the cases in this edition.

9. *Two cutting-edge and widely used strategy simulations—The Business Strategy Game and GLO-BUS—are optional companions to the 23rd edition.* These give you an unmatched capability to employ a text-case-simulation model of course delivery.

ORGANIZATION, CONTENT, AND FEATURES OF THE 23RD-EDITION TEXT CHAPTERS

- Chapter 1 serves as a brief, general introduction to the topic of strategy, focusing on the central questions of *"What is strategy?"* and *"Why is it important?"* As such, it serves as the perfect accompaniment for your opening-day lecture on what the course is all about and why it matters. Using the example of Apple, Inc., to drive home the concepts in this chapter, we introduce students to what we mean by "competitive advantage" and the key features of business-level strategy. Describing strategy making as a process, we explain why a company's strategy is partly planned and partly reactive and why a strategy tends to co-evolve with its environment over time. As part of this strategy making process, we discuss the importance of ethics in choosing among strategic alternatives. We introduce the concept of a business model and offer a clear definition along with an illustration capsule that provides examples from the real world of business. We explain why a viable business model must provide both an attractive value proposition for the company's customers and a formula for making profits for the company. A key feature of this chapter is a depiction of how the value-price-cost framework can be used to frame this discussion. We show how the mark of a winning strategy is its ability to pass three tests: (1) the *fit test* (for internal and external fit), (2) the *competitive advantage test,* and (3) the *performance test.* And we explain why good company performance depends not only upon a sound strategy but upon solid strategy execution as well.

- Chapter 2 presents a more complete overview of the strategic management process, covering topics ranging from the role of vision, mission, and values to what constitutes good corporate governance. It makes a great assignment for the second day of class and provides a smooth transition into the heart of the course.

It introduces students to such core concepts as strategic versus financial objectives, the balanced scorecard, strategic intent, and business-level versus corporate-level strategies. It explains why *all managers are on a company's strategy-making, strategy-executing team* and why a company's strategic plan is a collection of strategies devised by different managers at different levels in the organizational hierarchy. The chapter concludes with a section on the role of the board of directors in the strategy-making, strategy-executing process and examines the conditions that have led to recent high-profile corporate governance failures. The illustration capsule on Volkswagen's emissions scandal brings this section to life.

- The next two chapters introduce students to the two most fundamental perspectives on strategy making: the positioning view, exemplified by Michael Porter's classic "five forces model of competition," and the resource-based view. Chapter 3 provides *what has long been the clearest, most straightforward discussion of the five forces framework to be found in any text on strategic management.* It also offers a set of complementary analytical tools for conducting competitor analysis, identifying strategic groups along with the mobility barriers that limit movement among them, and demonstrates the importance of tailoring strategy to fit the circumstances of a company's industry and competitive environment. The chapter includes a discussion of the value net framework, which is useful for conducting analysis of how cooperative as well as competitive moves by various parties contribute to the creation and capture of value in an industry.

- Chapter 4 presents the resource-based view of the firm, showing why resource and capability analysis is such a powerful tool for sizing up a company's competitive assets. It offers a simple framework for identifying a company's resources and capabilities and explains how the VRIN framework can be used to determine whether they can provide the company with a sustainable competitive advantage over its competitors. Other topics covered in this chapter include dynamic capabilities, SWOT analysis, value chain analysis, benchmarking, and competitive strength assessments, thus enabling a solid appraisal of a company's cost position and customer value proposition vis-á-vis its rivals. *An important feature of this chapter is a table showing how key financial and operating ratios are calculated and how to interpret them.* Students will find this table handy in doing the number crunching needed to evaluate whether a company's strategy is delivering good financial performance.

- Chapter 5 sets forth the basic approaches available for competing and winning in the marketplace in terms of the five generic competitive strategies— broad low-cost, broad differentiation, best-cost, focused differentiation, and focused low cost. It demonstrates pictorially the link between generic strategies, the value-price-cost framework, and competitive advantage. The chapter also describes when each of the five approaches works best and what pitfalls to avoid. Additionally, it explains the role of *cost drivers* and *uniqueness drivers* in reducing a company's costs and enhancing its differentiation, respectively.

- Chapter 6 focuses on *other strategic actions* a company can take to complement its competitive approach and maximize the power of its overall strategy. These include a variety of offensive or defensive competitive moves, and their timing, such as blue-ocean strategies and first-mover advantages and disadvantages. It also includes choices concerning the breadth of a company's activities (or its *scope* of operations along an industry's entire value chain), ranging from horizontal mergers and acquisitions, to vertical integration, outsourcing, and strategic alliances. This material serves to segue into the scope issues covered in the next two chapters on international and diversification strategies.

- Chapter 7 takes up the topic of how to compete in international markets. It begins with a discussion of why differing market conditions across countries must necessarily influence a company's strategic choices about how to enter and compete in foreign markets. It presents five major strategic options for expanding a company's geographic scope and competing in foreign markets: export strategies, licensing, franchising, establishing a wholly owned subsidiary via acquisition or "greenfield" venture, and alliance strategies. It includes coverage of topics such as Porter's Diamond of National Competitive Advantage, multi-market competition, and the choice between multidomestic, global, and transnational strategies. This chapter explains the impetus for sharing, transferring, or accessing valuable resources and capabilities across national borders in the quest for competitive advantage, connecting the material to that on the resource-based view from Chapter 4. The chapter concludes with a discussion of the unique characteristics of competing in developing-country markets.

- Chapter 8 concerns strategy making in the multibusiness company, introducing the topic of corporate-level strategy with its special focus on diversification. The first portion of this chapter describes when and why diversification makes good strategic sense, the different means of diversifying a company's business lineup, and the pros and cons of related versus unrelated diversification strategies. The second part of the chapter looks at how to evaluate the attractiveness of a diversified company's business lineup, how to decide whether it has a good diversification strategy, and what strategic options are available for improving a diversified company's future performance. The evaluative technique integrates material concerning both industry analysis and the resource-based view, in that it considers the relative attractiveness of the various industries the company has diversified into, the company's competitive strength in each of its lines of business, and the extent to which its different businesses exhibit both *strategic fit* and *resource fit*.

- Although the topic of ethics and values comes up at various points in this textbook, Chapter 9 brings more direct attention to such issues and may be used as a stand-alone assignment in either the early, middle, or late part of a course. It concerns the themes of ethical standards in business, approaches to ensuring consistent ethical standards for companies with international operations, corporate social responsibility, and environmental sustainability. The contents of this chapter are sure to give students some things to ponder, rouse lively discussion, and help to make students more *ethically aware* and conscious of *why all companies should conduct their business in a socially responsible and sustainable manner.*

- The next three chapters (Chapters 10, 11, and 12) comprise a module on strategy execution that is presented in terms of a 10-step action framework. Chapter 10 provides an overview of this framework and then explores the first three of these tasks: (1) *staffing the organization* with people capable of executing the strategy well, (2) *building the organizational capabilities* needed for successful strategy execution, and (3) *creating an organizational structure* supportive of the strategy execution process.

- Chapter 11 discusses five additional managerial actions that advance the cause of good strategy execution: (1) *allocating resources* to enable the strategy execution process, (2) ensuring that *policies and procedures* facilitate rather than impede strategy execution, (3) using *process management tools* and *best practices* to drive continuous improvement in the performance of value chain activities, (4) installing *information and operating systems* that help company personnel carry out their strategic roles, and (5) using *rewards and incentives* to encourage good strategy execution and the achievement of performance targets.

- Chapter 12 completes the 10-step framework with a consideration of the importance of *creating a healthy* corporate *culture* and *exercising effective leadership* in promoting good strategy execution. The recurring theme throughout the final three chapters is that executing strategy involves deciding on the specific actions, behaviors, and conditions needed for a smooth strategy-supportive operation and then following through to get things done and deliver results. The goal here is to ensure that students understand that the strategy-executing phase is a *make-things-happen and make-them-happen-right* kind of managerial exercise—one that is critical for achieving operating excellence and reaching the goal of strong company performance.

In this latest edition, we have put our utmost effort into ensuring that the 12 chapters are consistent with the latest and best thinking of academics and practitioners in the field of strategic management and provide the topical coverage required for both undergraduate and MBA-level strategy courses. The ultimate test of the text, of course, is the positive pedagogical impact it has in the classroom. If this edition sets a more effective stage for your lectures and does a better job of helping you persuade students that the discipline of strategy merits their rapt attention, then it will have fulfilled its purpose.

THE CASE COLLECTION

The 27-case lineup in this edition is flush with interesting companies and valuable lessons for students in the art and science of crafting and executing strategy. There's a good blend of cases from a length perspective—about two-thirds of the cases are under 15 pages yet offer plenty for students to chew on; and the remainder are detail-rich cases that call for more sweeping analysis.

At least 25 of the 27 cases involve companies, products, people, or activities that students will have heard of, know about from personal experience, or can easily identify with. The lineup includes at least 20 cases that will deepen student understanding of the special demands of competing in industry environments where product life cycles are short and competitive maneuvering among rivals is quite active. Twenty-three of the cases involve situations in which company resources and competitive capabilities play as large a role in the strategy-making, strategy executing scheme of things as industry and competitive conditions do. Scattered throughout the lineup are 20 cases concerning non-U.S. companies, globally competitive industries, and/or cross-cultural situations. These cases, in conjunction with the globalized content of the text chapters, provide abundant material for linking the study of strategic management tightly to the ongoing globalization of the world economy. You'll also find 8 cases dealing with the strategic problems of family-owned or relatively small entrepreneurial businesses and 24 cases involving public companies and situations where students can do further research on the Internet.

The "Guide to Case Analysis" follows the last case. It contains sections on what a case is, why cases are a standard part of courses in strategy, preparing a case for class discussion, doing a written case analysis, doing an oral presentation, and using financial ratio analysis to assess a company's financial condition. We suggest having students read this guide before the first class discussion of a case.

A number of cases have accompanying YouTube video segments which are listed in Section 3 of the Instructor's Manual, in a separate Video Library within the Instructor's Resources, and in the Teaching Note for each case.

THE TWO STRATEGY SIMULATION SUPPLEMENTS:
THE BUSINESS STRATEGY GAME AND *GLO-BUS*

The Business Strategy Game and *GLO-BUS: Developing Winning Competitive Strategies*—two competition-based strategy simulations that are delivered online and that feature automated processing and grading of performance—are being marketed by the publisher as companion supplements for use with the 23rd edition (and other texts in the field).

- *The Business Strategy Game* is the world's most popular strategy simulation, having been used by nearly 3,600 different instructors for courses involving close to one million students at 1,300 university campuses in 76 countries. It features global competition in the athletic footwear industry, a product/market setting familiar to students everywhere and one whose managerial challenges are easily grasped. A freshly updated and much-enhanced version of *The Business Strategy Game* was introduced in August 2018.

- *GLO-BUS*, a newer and somewhat simpler strategy simulation first introduced in 2004 and freshly revamped in 2016 to center on competition in two exciting product categories—wearable miniature action cameras and unmanned camera-equipped drones suitable for multiple commercial purposes, has been used by 2,100 different instructors for courses involving nearly 360,000 students at 800+ university campuses in 53 countries.

How the Strategy Simulations Work

In both *The Business Strategy Game (BSG)* and *GLO-BUS*, class members are divided into teams of one to five persons and assigned to run a company that competes head-to-head against companies run by other class members. In both simulations, companies compete in a global market arena, selling their products in four geographic regions—Europe-Africa, North America, Asia-Pacific, and Latin America. Each management team is called upon to craft a strategy for their company and make decisions relating to production operations, workforce compensation, pricing and marketing, social responsibility/citizenship, and finance.

Company co-managers are held accountable for their decision making. Each company's performance is scored on the basis of earnings per share, return-on-equity investment, stock price, credit rating, and image rating. Rankings of company performance, along with a wealth of industry and company statistics, are available to company co-managers after each decision round to use in making strategy adjustments and operating decisions for the next competitive round. You can be certain that the market environment, strategic issues, and operating challenges that company co-managers must contend with are *very tightly linked* to what your class members will be reading about in the text chapters. The circumstances that co-managers face in running their simulation company embrace the very concepts, analytical tools, and strategy options they encounter in the text chapters (this is something you can quickly confirm by skimming through some of the Exercises for Simulation Participants that appear at the end of each chapter).

We suggest that you schedule one or two practice rounds and anywhere from four to 10 regular (scored) decision rounds (more rounds are better than fewer rounds). Each decision round represents a year of company operations and will entail roughly two hours of time for company co-managers to complete. In traditional 13-week, semester-long courses, there is merit in scheduling one decision round per week. In courses that run five to 10 weeks, it is wise to schedule two decision rounds per week for the last several weeks of the term (sample course schedules are provided for courses of varying length and varying numbers of class meetings).

When the instructor-specified deadline for a decision round arrives, the simulation server automatically accesses the saved decision entries of each company, determines the competitiveness and buyer appeal of each company's product offering relative to the other companies being run by students in your class, and then awards sales and market shares to the competing companies, geographic region by geographic region. The unit sales volumes awarded to each company *are totally governed by*

- How its prices compare against the prices of rival brands.
- How its product quality compares against the quality of rival brands.
- How its product line breadth and selection compare.
- How its advertising effort compares.
- And so on, for a total of 11 competitive factors that determine unit sales and market shares.

The competitiveness and overall buyer appeal of each company's product offering *in comparison to the product offerings of rival companies* is all-decisive—this algorithmic feature is what makes *BSG* and *GLO-BUS* "competition-based" strategy simulations. Once each company's sales and market shares are awarded based on the competitiveness and buyer appeal of its respective overall product offering vis-à-vis those of rival companies, the various company and industry reports detailing the outcomes of the decision round are then generated. Company co-managers can access the results of the decision round 15 to 20 minutes after the decision deadline.

The Compelling Case for Incorporating Use of a Strategy Simulation

There are *three exceptionally important benefits* associated with using a competition-based simulation in strategy courses taken by seniors and MBA students:

- *A three-pronged text-case-simulation course model delivers significantly more teaching-learning power than the traditional text-case model.* Using *both* cases and a strategy simulation to drill students in thinking strategically and applying what they read in the text chapters is a stronger, more effective means of helping them connect theory with practice and develop better business judgment. What cases do that a simulation cannot is give class members broad exposure to a variety of companies and industry situations and insight into the kinds of strategy-related problems managers face. But what a competition-based strategy simulation does far better than case analysis is thrust class members squarely into *an active, hands-on managerial role* where they are totally responsible for assessing market conditions, determining how to respond to the actions of competitors, forging a long-term direction and strategy for their company, and making all kinds of operating decisions. Because they are held fully accountable for their decisions and their company's performance, *co-managers are strongly motivated* to dig deeply into company operations, probe for ways to be more cost-efficient and competitive, and ferret out strategic moves and decisions calculated to boost company performance. *Consequently, incorporating both case assignments and a strategy simulation to develop the skills of class members in thinking strategically and applying the concepts and tools of strategic analysis turns out to be more pedagogically powerful than relying solely on case assignments—there's stronger retention of the lessons learned and better achievement of course learning objectives.*

To provide you with quantitative evidence of the learning that occurs with using *The Business Strategy Game* or *GLO-BUS,* there is a built-in Learning Assurance Report showing how well each class member performs on nine skills/learning measures versus tens of thousands of students worldwide who have completed the simulation in the past 12 months.

- *The competitive nature of a strategy simulation arouses positive energy and steps up the whole tempo of the course by a notch or two.* Nothing sparks class excitement quicker or better than the concerted efforts on the part of class members at each decision round to achieve a high industry ranking and avoid the perilous consequences of being outcompeted by other class members. Students really enjoy taking on the role of a manager, running their own company, crafting strategies, making all kinds of operating decisions, trying to outcompete rival companies, and getting immediate feedback on the resulting company performance. Lots of back-and-forth chatter occurs when the results of the latest simulation round become available and co-managers renew their quest for strategic moves and actions that will strengthen company performance. Co-managers become *emotionally invested* in running their company and figuring out what strategic moves to make to boost their company's performance. Interest levels climb. All this stimulates learning and causes students to see the practical relevance of the subject matter and the benefits of taking your course.

As soon as your students start to say, "Wow! Not only is this fun but I am learning a lot," *which they will,* you have won the battle of engaging students in the subject matter and moved the value of taking your course to a much higher plateau in the business school curriculum. This translates into *a livelier, richer learning experience from a student perspective and better instructor-course evaluations.*

- *Use of a fully automated online simulation reduces the time instructors spend on course preparation, course administration, and grading.* Since the simulation exercise involves a 20- to 30-hour workload for student teams (roughly two hours per decision round times 10 to 12 rounds, plus optional assignments), simulation adopters often compensate by trimming the number of assigned cases from, say, 10 to 12 to perhaps 4 to 6. This significantly reduces the time instructors spend reading cases, studying teaching notes, and otherwise getting ready to lead class discussion of a case or grade oral team presentations. Course preparation time is further cut because you can use several class days to have students bring their laptops to class or meet in a computer lab to work on upcoming decision rounds or a three-year strategic plan (in lieu of lecturing on a chapter or covering an additional assigned case). Not only does use of a simulation permit assigning fewer cases, but it also permits you to eliminate at least one assignment that entails considerable grading on your part. Grading one less written case or essay exam or other written assignment saves enormous time. With *BSG* and *GLO-BUS,* grading is effortless and takes only minutes; once you enter percentage weights for each assignment in your online grade book, a suggested overall grade is calculated for you. You'll be pleasantly surprised—and quite pleased—at how little time it takes to gear up for and administer *The Business Strategy Game* or *GLO-BUS.*

In sum, incorporating use of a strategy simulation turns out to be *a win–win proposition for both students and instructors.* Moreover, a very convincing argument can be made that a competition-based strategy simulation is *the single most effective teaching/learning tool that instructors can employ to teach the discipline of business and competitive strategy, to make learning more enjoyable, and to promote better achievement of course learning objectives.*

A Bird's-Eye View of *The Business Strategy Game*

The setting for *The Business Strategy Game (BSG)* is the global athletic footwear industry (there can be little doubt in today's world that a globally competitive strategy simulation is *vastly superior* to a simulation with a domestic-only setting). Global market demand for footwear grows at the rate of seven to nine percent annually for the first five years and five to seven percent annually for the second five years. However, market growth rates vary by geographic region—North America, Latin America, Europe-Africa, and Asia-Pacific.

Companies begin the simulation producing branded and private-label footwear in two plants, one in North America and one in Asia. They have the option to establish production facilities in Latin America and Europe-Africa. Company co-managers exercise control over production costs on the basis of the styling and quality they opt to manufacture, plant location (wages and incentive compensation vary from region to region), the use of best practices and Six Sigma programs to reduce the production of defective footwear and to boost worker productivity, and compensation practices.

All newly produced footwear is shipped in bulk containers to one of four geographic distribution centers. All sales in a geographic region are made from footwear inventories in that region's distribution center. Costs at the four regional distribution centers are a function of inventory storage costs, packing and shipping fees, import tariffs paid on incoming pairs shipped from foreign plants, and exchange rate impacts. At the start of the simulation, import tariffs average $4 per pair in North America, $6 in Europe-Africa, $8 per pair in Latin America, and $10 in the Asia-Pacific region. Instructors have the option to alter tariffs as the game progresses.

Companies market their brand of athletic footwear to footwear retailers worldwide and to individuals buying online at the company's website. Each company's sales and market share in the branded footwear segments hinge on its competitiveness on 13 factors: attractive pricing, footwear styling and quality, product line breadth, advertising, use of mail-in rebates, appeal of celebrities endorsing a company's brand, success in convincing footwear retailers to carry its brand, number of weeks it takes to fill retailer orders, effectiveness of a company's online sales effort at its website, and brand reputation. Sales of private-label footwear hinge solely on being the low-price bidder.

All told, company co-managers make as many as 57 types of decisions each period that cut across production operations (up to 11 decisions per plant, with a maximum of four plants), the addition of facility space, equipment, and production improvement options (up to eight decisions per plant), worker compensation and training (up to six decisions per plant), shipping and distribution center operations (five decisions per geographic region), pricing and marketing (up to nine decisions in four geographic regions), bids to sign celebrities (two decision entries per bid), financing of company operations (up to eight decisions), and corporate social responsibility and environmental sustainability (up to eight decisions). Plus, there are 10 entries for each region pertaining to assumptions about the upcoming-year actions and competitive efforts of rival companies that factor directly into the forecasts of a company's unit sales, revenues, and market share in each of the four geographic regions.

Each time company co-managers make a decision entry, an assortment of on-screen calculations instantly shows the projected effects on unit sales, revenues, market shares, unit costs, profit, earnings per share, ROE, and other operating statistics. The on-screen calculations help team members evaluate the relative merits of one decision entry versus another and put together a promising strategy.

Companies can employ any of the five generic competitive strategy options in selling branded footwear—low-cost leadership, differentiation, best-cost provider, focused low cost, and focused differentiation. They can pursue essentially the same strategy worldwide or craft slightly or very different strategies for the Europe-Africa, Asia-Pacific, Latin America, and North America markets. They can strive for competitive advantage based on more advertising, a wider selection of models, more appealing styling/quality, bigger rebates, and so on.

Any well-conceived, well-executed competitive approach is capable of succeeding, provided it is not overpowered by the strategies of competitors or defeated by the presence of too many copycat strategies that dilute its effectiveness. The challenge for each company's management team is to craft and execute a competitive strategy that produces good performance on five measures: earnings per share, return on equity investment, stock price appreciation, credit rating, and brand image.

All activity for *The Business Strategy Game* takes place at www.bsg-online.com.

A Bird's-Eye View of *GLO-BUS*

In *GLO-BUS,* class members run companies that are in a neck-and-neck race for global market leadership in two product categories: (1) wearable video cameras smaller than a teacup that deliver stunning video quality and have powerful photo capture capabilities (comparable to those designed and marketed by global industry leader GoPro and numerous others) and (2) sophisticated camera-equipped copter drones that incorporate a company designed and assembled action-capture camera and that are sold to commercial enterprises for prices in the $850 to 2,000+ range. Global market demand for action cameras grows at the rate of six to eight percent annually for the first five years and four to six percent annually for the second five years. Global market demand for commercial drones grows briskly at rates averaging 18 percent for the first two years, then gradually slows over eight years to a rate of four to six percent.

Companies assemble action cameras and drones of varying designs and performance capabilities at a Taiwan facility and ship finished goods directly to buyers in North America, Asia-Pacific, Europe-Africa, and Latin America. Both products are assembled usually within two weeks of being received and are then shipped to buyers no later than two to three days after assembly. Companies maintain no finished goods inventories and all parts and components are delivered by suppliers on a just-in-time basis (which eliminates the need to track inventories and simplifies the accounting for plant operations and costs).

Company co-managers determine the quality and performance features of the cameras and drones being assembled. They impact production costs by raising/lowering specifications for parts/components and expenditures for product R&D, adjusting work force compensation, spending more/less on worker training and productivity improvement, lengthening/shortening warranties offered (which affects warranty costs), and how cost-efficiently they manage assembly operations. They have options to manage/control selling and certain other costs as well.

Each decision round, company co-managers make some 50 types of decisions relating to the design and performance of the company's two products (21 decisions, 10 for cameras and 11 for drones), assembly operations and workforce compensation (up to eight decision entries for each product), pricing and marketing (seven decisions for cameras and five for drones), corporate social responsibility and citizenship (up to six decisions), and the financing of company operations (up to eight decisions). In addition, there are 10 entries for cameras and seven entries for drones involving assumptions about the competitive actions of rivals; these entries help company co-managers to make more accurate forecasts of their company's unit sales (so they have a good idea of how many cameras and drones will need to be assembled each year to fill customer orders). Each time co-managers make a decision entry, an assortment of on-screen calculations instantly shows the projected effects on unit sales, revenues, market shares, total profit, earnings per share, ROE, costs, and other operating outcomes. All of these on-screen calculations help co-managers evaluate the relative merits of one decision entry versus another. Company managers can try out as many different decision combinations as they wish in stitching the separate decision entries into a cohesive whole that is projected to produce good company performance.

Competition in action cameras revolves around 11 factors that determine each company's unit sales/market share:

1. How each company's average wholesale price to retailers compares against the all-company average wholesale prices being charged in each geographic region.
2. How each company's camera performance and quality compares against industry-wide camera performance/quality.
3. How the number of week-long sales promotion campaigns a company has in each region compares against the regional average number of weekly promotions.
4. How the size of each company's discounts off the regular wholesale prices during sales promotion campaigns compares against the regional average promotional discount.
5. How each company's annual advertising expenditures compare against regional average advertising expenditures.
6. How the number of models in each company's camera line compares against the industry-wide average number of models.
7. The number of retailers stocking and merchandising a company's brand in each region.
8. Annual expenditures to support the merchandising efforts of retailers stocking a company's brand in each region.
9. The amount by which a company's expenditures for ongoing improvement and updating of its company's website in a region is above/below the all-company regional average expenditure.
10. How the length of each company's camera warranties compare against the warranty periods of rival companies.
11. How well a company's brand image/reputation compares against the brand images/reputations of rival companies.

Competition among rival makers of commercial copter drones is more narrowly focused on just nine sales-determining factors:

1. How a company's average retail price for drones at the company's website in each region compares against the all-company regional average website price.
2. How each company's drone performance and quality compares against the all-company average drone performance/quality.
3. How the number of models in each company's drone line compares against the industry-wide average number of models.

4. How each company's annual expenditures to recruit/support third-party online electronics retailers in merchandising its brand of drones in each region compares against the regional average.

5. The amount by which a company's price discount to third-party online retailers is above/below the regional average discounted price.

6. How well a company's expenditures for search engine advertising in a region compares against the regional average.

7. How well a company's expenditures for ongoing improvement and updating of its website in a region compares against the regional average.

8. How the length of each company's drone warranties in a region compares against the regional average warranty period.

9. How well a company's brand image/reputation compares against the brand images/reputations of rival companies.

Each company typically seeks to enhance its performance and build competitive advantage via its own custom-tailored competitive strategy based on more attractive pricing, greater advertising, a wider selection of models, more appealing performance/quality, longer warranties, a better image/reputation, and so on. The greater the differences in the overall competitiveness of the product offerings of rival companies, the bigger the differences in their resulting sales volumes and market shares. Conversely, the smaller the overall competitive differences in the product offerings of rival companies, the smaller the differences in sales volumes and market shares. This algorithmic approach is what makes *GLO-BUS* a "competition-based" strategy simulation and accounts for why *the sales and market share outcomes for each decision round are always unique to the particular strategies and decision combinations employed by the competing companies.*

As with *BSG, all the various generic competitive strategy options*—low-cost leadership, differentiation, best-cost provider, focused low-cost, and focused differentiation—*are viable choices for pursuing competitive advantage and good company performance.* A company can have a strategy aimed at being the clear market leader in either action cameras or drones or both. It can focus its competitive efforts on one or two or three geographic regions or strive to build strong market positions in all four geographic regions. It can pursue essentially the same strategy worldwide or craft customized strategies for the Europe-Africa, Asia-Pacific, Latin America, and North America markets. Just as with *The Business Strategy Game, most any well-conceived, well-executed competitive approach is capable of succeeding, provided it is not overpowered by the strategies of competitors or defeated by the presence of too many copycat strategies that dilute its effectiveness.*

The challenge for each company's management team is to craft and execute a competitive strategy that produces good performance on five measures: earnings per share, return on equity investment, stock price appreciation, credit rating, and brand image.

All activity for *GLO-BUS* occurs at www.glo-bus.com.

Special Note: The time required of company co-managers to complete each decision round in *GLO-BUS* is typically about 15 to 30 minutes less than for *The Business Strategy Game* because

(a) there are only 8 market segments (versus 12 in *BSG*),

(b) co-managers have only one assembly site to operate (versus potentially as many as four plants in *BSG,* one in each geographic region), and

(c) newly assembled cameras and drones are shipped directly to buyers, eliminating the need to manage finished goods inventories and operate distribution centers.

Administration and Operating Features of the Two Simulations

The Internet delivery and user-friendly designs of both *BSG* and *GLO-BUS* make them incredibly easy to administer, even for first-time users. And the menus and controls are so similar that you can readily switch between the two simulations or use one in your undergraduate class and the other in a graduate class. If you have not yet used either of the two simulations, you may find the following of particular interest:

- Setting up the simulation for your course is done online and takes about 10 to 15 minutes. Once setup is completed, no other administrative actions are required beyond those of moving participants to a different team (should the need arise) and monitoring the progress of the simulation (to whatever extent desired).

- Participant's Guides are delivered electronically to class members at the website—students can read the guide on their monitors or print out a copy, as they prefer.

- There are two to four minute Video Tutorials scattered throughout the software (including each decision screen and each page of each report) that provide on-demand guidance to class members who may be uncertain about how to proceed.

- Complementing the Video Tutorials are detailed and clearly written Help sections explaining "all there is to know" about (a) each decision entry and the relevant cause-effect relationships, (b) the information on each page of the Industry Reports, and (c) the numbers presented in the Company Reports. *The Video Tutorials and the Help screens allow company co-managers to figure things out for themselves, thereby curbing the need for students to ask the instructor "how things work."*

- Team members running the same company who are logged in simultaneously on different computers at different locations can click a button to enter Collaboration Mode, enabling them to work collaboratively from the same screen in viewing reports and making decision entries, and click a second button to enter Audio Mode, letting them talk to one another and hold an online meeting.

  ○ When in "Collaboration Mode," each team member sees the same screen at the same time as all other team members who are logged in and have joined Collaboration Mode. If one team member chooses to view a particular decision screen, that same screen appears on the monitors for all team members in Collaboration Mode.

  ○ Each team member controls their own color-coded mouse pointer (with their first-name appearing in a color-coded box linked to their mouse pointer) and can make a decision entry or move the mouse to point to particular on-screen items.

  ○ A decision entry change made by one team member is seen by all, in real time, and all team members can immediately view the on-screen calculations that result from the new decision entry.

  ○ If one team member wishes to view a report page and clicks on the menu link to the desired report, that same report page will immediately appear for the other team members engaged in collaboration.

  ○ Use of Audio Mode capability requires that each team member work from a computer with a built-in microphone (if they want to be heard by their team members) and speakers (so they may hear their teammates) or else have a headset with a microphone that they can plug into their desktop or laptop. A headset is recommended for best results, but most laptops now are equipped with a built-in microphone and speakers that will support use of our new voice chat feature.

- Real-time VoIP audio chat capability among team members who have entered both the Audio Mode and the Collaboration Mode is a tremendous boost in functionality that enables team members to go online simultaneously on computers at different locations and conveniently and effectively collaborate in running their simulation company.

- In addition, instructors have the capability to join the online session of any company and speak with team members, thus circumventing the need for team members to arrange for and attend a meeting in the instructor's office. Using the standard menu for administering a particular industry, instructors can connect with the company desirous of assistance. Instructors who wish not only to talk but also to enter Collaboration (highly recommended because all attendees are then viewing the same screen) have a red-colored mouse pointer linked to a red box labeled Instructor.

Without a doubt, the Collaboration and Voice-Chat capabilities are hugely valuable for students enrolled in online and distance-learning courses where meeting face-to-face is impractical or time-consuming. Likewise, the instructors of online and distance-learning courses will appreciate having the capability to join the online meetings of particular company teams when their advice or assistance is requested.

- Both simulations work equally well for online courses and in-person classes.
- Participants and instructors are notified via e-mail when the results are ready (usually about 15 to 20 minutes after the decision round deadline specified by the instructor/game administrator).
- Following each decision round, participants are provided with a complete set of reports—a six-page Industry Report, a Competitive Intelligence report for each geographic region that includes strategic group maps and a set of Company Reports (income statement, balance sheet, cash flow statement, and assorted production, marketing, and cost statistics).
- Two "open-book" multiple-choice tests of 20 questions are built into each simulation. The quizzes, which you can require or not as you see fit, are taken online and automatically graded, with scores reported instantaneously to participants and automatically recorded in the instructor's electronic grade book. Students are automatically provided with three sample questions for each test.
- Both simulations contain a three-year strategic plan option that you can assign. Scores on the plan are automatically recorded in the instructor's online grade book.
- At the end of the simulation, you can have students complete online peer evaluations (again, the scores are automatically recorded in your online grade book).
- Both simulations have a Company Presentation feature that enables each team of company co-managers to easily prepare PowerPoint slides for use in describing their strategy and summarizing their company's performance in a presentation to either the class, the instructor, or an "outside" board of directors.
- *A Learning Assurance Report provides you with hard data concerning how well your students performed vis-à-vis students playing the simulation worldwide over the past 12 months.* The report is based on nine measures of student proficiency, business know-how, and decision-making skill and can also be used in evaluating the extent to which your school's academic curriculum produces the desired degree of student learning insofar as accreditation standards are concerned.

For more details on either simulation, please consult Section 2 of the Instructor's Manual accompanying this text or register as an instructor at the simulation websites (www.bsg-online.com and www.glo-bus.com) to access even more comprehensive information. You should also consider signing up for one of the webinars that the simulation authors conduct several times each month (sometimes several times weekly) to demonstrate how the software works, walk you through the various features and menu options, and answer any questions. You have an open invitation to call the senior author of this text at (205) 722-9145 to arrange a personal demonstration or talk about how one of the simulations might work in one of your courses. We think you'll be quite impressed with the cutting-edge capabilities that have been programmed into *The Business Strategy Game* and *GLO-BUS,* the simplicity with which both simulations can be administered, and their exceptionally tight connection to the text chapters, core concepts, and standard analytical tools.

RESOURCES AND SUPPORT MATERIALS FOR THE 23RD EDITION

For Students

Key Points Summaries   At the end of each chapter is a synopsis of the core concepts, analytical tools, and other key points discussed in the chapter. These chapter-end synopses, along with the core concept definitions and margin notes scattered throughout each chapter, help students focus on basic strategy principles, digest the messages of each chapter, and prepare for tests.

Two Sets of Chapter-End Exercises   Each chapter concludes with two sets of exercises. The *Assurance of Learning Exercises* are useful for helping students prepare for class discussion and to gauge their understanding of the material. The *Exercises for Simulation Participants* are designed expressly for use in class which incorporate the use of a simulation. These exercises explicitly connect the chapter content to the simulation company the students are running. Even if they are not assigned by the instructor, they can provide helpful practice for students as a study aid.

Connect™   The 23rd edition takes full advantage of Connect™, a personalized teaching and learning tool. The Connect™ package for this edition includes several robust and valuable features that simplify the task of assigning and grading three types of exercises for students:

- Autograded chapter quizzes that students can take to measure their grasp of the material presented in each of the 12 chapters.
- A variety of interactive exercises for each of the 12 chapters that drill students in the use and application of the concepts and tools of strategic analysis, including selected Assurance of Learning Exercises and newly integrated Exercises for Simulation Participants.
- Case Exercises for 14 of the 27 cases in this edition that require students to work through answers to a select number of the assignment questions for the case. These exercises have multiple components and are tailored to match the circumstances presented in each case, calling upon students to do whatever strategic thinking and

strategic analysis are called for to arrive at pragmatic, analysis-based action recommendations for improving company performance.

All Connect™ exercises are automatically graded (with the exception of a few select Exercises for Simulation Participants that entail answers in the form of short essays), thereby simplifying the task of evaluating each class member's performance and monitoring the learning outcomes. The progress-tracking function built into Connect™ enables you to

- View scored work immediately and track individual or group performance with assignment and grade reports.
- Access an instant view of student or class performance relative to learning objectives.
- Collect data and generate reports required by many accreditation organizations, such as AACSB International.

SmartBook 2.0® SmartBook 2.0 is the first and only adaptive reading experience designed to change the way students read and learn. It creates a personalized reading experience by highlighting the most impactful concepts a student needs to learn at that moment in time. As a student engages with SmartBook, the reading experience continuously adapts by highlighting content based on what the student knows and doesn't know. This ensures that the focus is on the content he or she needs to learn, while simultaneously promoting long-term retention of material. Use SmartBook's real-time reports to quickly identify the concepts that require more attention from individual students–or the entire class. The end result? Students are more engaged with course content, can better prioritize their time, and come to class ready to participate.

For Instructors

Assurance of Learning Aids Each chapter begins with a set of Learning Objectives, which are tied directly to the material in the text meant to address these objectives with helpful signposts. At the conclusion of each chapter, there is a set of *Assurance of Learning Exercises* that can be used as the basis for class discussion, oral presentation assignments, short written reports, and substitutes for case assignments. Similarly, there is a set of *Exercises for Simulation Participants* that are designed expressly for use by adopters who have incorporated use of a simulation and want to go a step further in tightly and explicitly connecting the chapter content to the simulation company their students are running. New to this edition is the incorporation of these assignable Exercises for Simulation Participants within Connect. The questions in both sets of exercises (along with those Illustration Capsules that qualify as "mini-cases") can be used to round out the rest of a 75-minute class period should your lecture on a chapter last for only 50 minutes.

Instructor Library The Connect Instructor Library is your repository for additional resources to improve student engagement in and out of class. You can select and use any asset that enhances your lecture.

Instructor's Manual The accompanying IM contains:
- A section on suggestions for organizing and structuring your course.
- Sample syllabi and course outlines.

- A set of lecture notes on each chapter.
- Answers to the chapter-end Assurance of Learning Exercises.
- A test bank for all 12 chapters.
- A comprehensive case teaching note for each of the 27 cases. These teaching notes are filled with suggestions for using the case effectively, have very thorough, analysis-based answers to the suggested assignment questions for the case, and contain an epilogue detailing any important developments since the case was written.

Test Builder   The accompanying Test Bank, which contains over 900 multiple choice and short answer/essay questions, is available in Connect™ via Test Builder.

Test Builder is a cloud-based tool that enables instructors to format tests that can be printed or administered within an LMS. Test Builder offers a modern, streamlined interface for easy content configuration that matches course needs, without requiring a download. Test Builder provides a secure interface for better protection of content and allows for just-in-time updates to flow directly into assessments.

PowerPoint Slides   To facilitate delivery preparation of your lectures and to serve as chapter outlines, you'll have access to approximately 500 colorful and professional-looking slides displaying core concepts, analytical procedures, key points, and all the figures in the text chapters.

CREATE™   is McGraw-Hill's custom-publishing program where you can access full-length readings and cases that accompany *Crafting and Executing Strategy: The Quest for a Competitive Advantage* (http://create.mheducation.com/thompson). Through Create™, you will be able to select from 30 readings that go specifically with this text-book. These include cases and readings from Harvard, MIT, and much more! You can assemble your own course and select the chapters, cases, and readings that work best for you. Also, you can choose from several ready-to-go, author-recommended complete course solutions. Among the pre-loaded solutions, you'll find options for undergrad, MBA, accelerated, and other strategy courses.

The Business Strategy Game and *GLO-BUS Online Simulations*   Using one of the two companion simulations is a powerful and constructive way of emotionally connecting students to the subject matter of the course. We know of no more effective way to arouse the competitive energy of students and prepare them for the challenges of real-world business decision making than to have them match strategic wits with classmates in running a company in head-to-head competition for global market leadership.

ACKNOWLEDGMENTS

We heartily acknowledge the contributions of the case researchers whose case-writing efforts appear herein and the companies whose cooperation made the cases possible. To each one goes a very special thank-you. We cannot overstate the importance of timely, carefully researched cases in contributing to a substantive study of strategic management issues and practices.

A great number of colleagues and students at various universities, business acquaintances, and people at McGraw-Hill provided inspiration, encouragement, and counsel during the course of this project. Like all text authors in the strategy field, we are intellectually indebted to the many academics whose research and writing have blazed new trails and advanced the discipline of strategic management. In addition, we'd like to thank the following reviewers who provided seasoned advice and splendid suggestions over the years for improving the chapters:

Robert B. Baden, Edward Desmarais, Stephen F. Hallam, Joy Karriker, Wendell Seaborne, Joan H. Bailar, David Blair, Jane Boyland, William J. Donoher, Stephen A. Drew, Jo Anne Duffy, Alan Ellstrand, Susan Fox-Wolfgramm, Rebecca M. Guidice, Mark Hoelscher, Sean D. Jasso, Xin Liang, Paul Mallette, Dan Marlin, Raza Mir, Mansour Moussavi, James D. Spina, Monica A. Zimmerman, Dennis R. Balch, Jeffrey R. Bruehl, Edith C. Busija, Donald A. Drost, Randall Harris, Mark Lewis Hoelscher, Phyllis Holland, James W. Kroeger, Sal Kukalis, Brian W. Kulik, Paul Mallette, Anthony U. Martinez, Lee Pickler, Sabine Reddy, Thomas D. Schramko, V. Seshan, Charles Strain, Sabine Turnley, S. Stephen Vitucci, Andrew Ward, Sibin Wu, Lynne Patten, Nancy E. Landrum, Jim Goes, Jon Kalinowski, Rodney M. Walter, Judith D. Powell, Seyda Deligonul, David Flanagan, Esmerlda Garbi, Mohsin Habib, Kim Hester, Jeffrey E. McGee, Diana J. Wong, F. William Brown, Anthony F. Chelte, Gregory G. Dess, Alan B. Eisner, John George, Carle M. Hunt, Theresa Marron-Grodsky, Sarah Marsh, Joshua D. Martin, William L. Moore, Donald Neubaum, George M. Puia, Amit Shah, Lois M. Shelton, Mark Weber, Steve Barndt, J. Michael Geringer, Ming-Fang Li, Richard Stackman, Stephen Tallman, Gerardo R. Ungson, James Boulgarides, Betty Diener, Daniel F. Jennings, David Kuhn, Kathryn Martell, Wilbur Mouton, Bobby Vaught, Tuck Bounds, Lee Burk, Ralph Catalanello, William Crittenden, Vince Luchsinger, Stan Mendenhall, John Moore, Will Mulvaney, Sandra Richard, Ralph Roberts, Thomas Turk, Gordon Von Stroh, Fred Zimmerman, S. A. Billion, Charles Byles, Gerald L. Geisler, Rose Knotts, Joseph Rosenstein, James B. Thurman, Ivan Able, W. Harvey Hegarty, Roger Evered, Charles B. Saunders, Rhae M. Swisher, Claude I. Shell, R. Thomas Lenz, Michael C. White, Dennis Callahan, R. Duane Ireland, William E. Burr II, C. W. Millard, Richard Mann, Kurt Christensen, Neil W. Jacobs, Louis W. Fry, D. Robley Wood, George J. Gore, and William R. Soukup.

We owe a debt of gratitude to Professors Catherine A. Maritan, Jeffrey A. Martin, Richard S. Shreve, and Anant K. Sundaram for their helpful comments on various chapters. We'd also like to thank the following students of the Tuck School of Business for their assistance with the revisions: Alen A. Ameni, Dipti Badrinath, Stephanie K. Berger, Courtney D. Bragg, Katie Coster, Jacob Crandall, Robin Daley, Kathleen T. Durante, Shawnda Lee Duvigneaud, Isaac E. Freeman, Vedrana B. Greatorex, Brittany J. Hattingh, Sadé M. Lawrence, Heather Levy, Margaret W. Macauley, Ken Martin, Brian R. McKenzie, Mathew O'Sullivan, Sara Paccamonti, Byron Peyster, Jeremy Reich, Carry S. Resor, Edward J. Silberman, David Washer, and Lindsey Wilcox. And we'd like to acknowledge the help of Dartmouth students Avantika Agarwal, Charles K. Anumonwo, Maria Hart, Meaghan I. Haugh, Artie Santry, as well as Tuck staff member Doreen Aher.

As always, we value your recommendations and thoughts about the book. Your comments regarding coverage and contents will be taken to heart, and we always are grateful for the time you take to call our attention to printing errors, deficiencies, and other shortcomings. Please e-mail us at athompso@cba.ua.edu, margaret.a.peteraf@tuck.dartmouth.edu, john.gamble@tamucc.edu, or astrickl@cba.ua.edu.

Arthur A. Thompson

Margaret A. Peteraf

John E. Gamble

A. J. Strickland

The Business Strategy Game or *GLO-BUS* Simulation Exercises

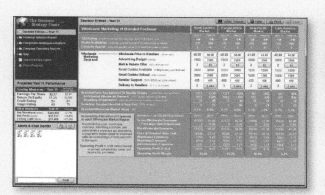

The Business Strategy Game or GLO-BUS Simulation Exercises
Either one of these text supplements involves teams of students managing companies in a head-to-head contest for global market leadership. Company co-managers have to make decisions relating to product quality, production, workforce compensation and training, pricing and marketing, and financing of company operations. The challenge is to craft and execute a strategy that is powerful enough to deliver good financial performance despite the competitive efforts of rival companies. Each company competes in North America, Latin America, Europe-Africa, and Asia-Pacific. *Fanatic Studio/Getty Images*

Instructors: Student Success Starts with You

Tools to enhance your unique voice

Want to build your own course? No problem. Prefer to use our turnkey, prebuilt course? Easy. Want to make changes throughout the semester? Sure. And you'll save time with Connect's auto-grading too.

65%
Less Time Grading

Laptop: McGraw Hill; Woman/dog: George Doyle/Getty Images

Study made personal

Incorporate adaptive study resources like SmartBook® 2.0 into your course and help your students be better prepared in less time. Learn more about the powerful personalized learning experience available in SmartBook 2.0 at **www.mheducation.com/highered/connect/smartbook**

Affordable solutions, added value

Make technology work for you with LMS integration for single sign-on access, mobile access to the digital textbook, and reports to quickly show you how each of your students is doing. And with our Inclusive Access program you can provide all these tools at a discount to your students. Ask your McGraw Hill representative for more information.

Padlock: Jobalou/Getty Images

Solutions for your challenges

A product isn't a solution. Real solutions are affordable, reliable, and come with training and ongoing support when you need it and how you want it. Visit **www. supportateverystep.com** for videos and resources both you and your students can use throughout the semester.

Checkmark: Jobalou/Getty Images

Students: Get Learning that Fits You

Effective tools for efficient studying

Connect is designed to make you more productive with simple, flexible, intuitive tools that maximize your study time and meet your individual learning needs. Get learning that works for you with Connect.

Study anytime, anywhere

Download the free ReadAnywhere app and access your online eBook or SmartBook 2.0 assignments when it's convenient, even if you're offline. And since the app automatically syncs with your eBook and SmartBook 2.0 assignments in Connect, all of your work is available every time you open it. Find out more at **www.mheducation.com/readanywhere**

> *"I really liked this app—it made it easy to study when you don't have your textbook in front of you."*
>
> - Jordan Cunningham,
>   Eastern Washington University

Everything you need in one place

Your Connect course has everything you need—whether reading on your digital eBook or completing assignments for class, Connect makes it easy to get your work done.

Calendar: owattaphotos/Getty Images

Learning for everyone

McGraw Hill works directly with Accessibility Services Departments and faculty to meet the learning needs of all students. Please contact your Accessibility Services Office and ask them to email accessibility@mheducation.com, or visit **www.mheducation.com/about/accessibility** for more information.

Top: Jenner Images/Getty Images, Left: Hero Images/Getty Images, Right: Hero Images/Getty Images

Brief Contents

Contents

PART 2   Cases in Crafting and Executing Strategy

Section A: Crafting Strategy in Single-Business Companies

PART 1

Concepts and Techniques for Crafting and Executing Strategy

chapter 1

What Is Strategy and Why Is It Important?

Learning Objectives

After reading this chapter, you should be able to:

LO 1-1 Understand what is meant by a company's *strategy* and why it needs to differ from competitors' strategies.

LO 1-2 Grasp the concept of a *sustainable competitive advantage*.

LO 1-3 Identify the five most basic strategic approaches for setting a company apart from its rivals.

LO 1-4 Understand why a company's strategy tends to evolve.

LO 1-5 Identify what constitutes a viable business model.

LO 1-6 Identify the three tests of a winning strategy.

Gary Waters/Ikon Images/Superstock

Strategy is about setting yourself apart from the competition.

Michael Porter—*Professor and consultant*

Strategy means making clear-cut choices about how to compete.

Jack Welch—*Former CEO of General Electric*

I believe that people make their own luck by great preparation and good strategy.

Jack Canfield—*Corporate trainer and entrepreneur*

According to *The Economist,* a leading publication on business, economics, and international affairs, "In business, strategy is king. Leadership and hard work are all very well and luck is mighty useful, but it is strategy that makes or breaks a firm."[1] Luck and circumstance can explain why some companies are blessed with initial, short-lived success. But only a well-crafted, well-executed, constantly evolving strategy can explain why an elite set of companies somehow manage to rise to the top and stay there, year after year, pleasing their customers, shareholders, and other stakeholders alike in the process. Companies such as Apple, Disney, Starbucks, Alphabet (parent company of Google), Berkshire Hathaway, General Electric, and Amazon come to mind—but long-lived success is not just the province of U.S. companies. Diverse kinds of companies, both large and small, from many different countries have been able to sustain strong performance records, including Denmark's Lego Group, the United Kingdom's HSBC (in banking), Dubai's Emirates Airlines, Switzerland's Rolex China Mobile (in telecommunications), and India's Tata Steel.

In this opening chapter, we define the concept of strategy and describe its many facets. We introduce you to the concept of competitive advantage and explore the tight linkage between a company's strategy and its quest for competitive advantage. We will also explain why company strategies are partly proactive and partly reactive, why they evolve over time, and the relationship between a company's strategy and its business model. We conclude the chapter with a discussion of what sets a winning strategy apart from others and why that strategy should also pass the test of moral scrutiny. By the end of this chapter, you will have a clear idea of why the tasks of crafting and executing strategy are core management functions and why excellent execution of an excellent strategy is the most reliable recipe for turning a company into a standout performer over the long term.

WHAT DO WE MEAN BY *STRATEGY*?

A company's **strategy** is the set of coordinated actions that its managers take in order to outperform the company's competitors and achieve superior profitability. The objective of a well-crafted strategy is not merely temporary competitive success and profits in the short run, but rather the sort of lasting success that can support growth and secure the company's future over the long term. Achieving this entails making a managerial commitment to a coherent array of well-considered choices about how to compete.[2] These include

- *How* to position the company in the marketplace.
- *How* to attract customers.
- *How* to compete against rivals.
- *How* to achieve the company's performance targets.
- *How* to capitalize on opportunities to grow the business.
- *How* to respond to changing economic and market conditions.

● LO 1-1

Understand what is meant by a company's *strategy* and why it needs to differ from competitors' strategies.

In most industries, companies have considerable freedom in choosing the *hows* of strategy.[3] Some companies strive to achieve lower costs than rivals, while others aim for product superiority or more personalized customer service dimensions that rivals cannot match. Some companies opt for wide product lines, while others concentrate their energies on a narrow product lineup. Some deliberately confine their operations to local or regional markets; others opt to compete nationally, internationally (several countries), or globally (all or most of the major country markets worldwide). Choices of how best to compete against rivals have to be made in light of the firm's resources and capabilities and in light of the competitive approaches rival companies are employing.

Strategy Is about Competing Differently

Mimicking the strategies of successful industry rivals—with either copycat product offerings or maneuvers to stake out the same market position—rarely works. Rather, every company's strategy needs to have some distinctive element that draws in customers and provides a competitive edge. Strategy, at its essence, is about competing differently—doing what rival firms *don't* do or what rival firms *can't* do.[4] This does not mean that the key elements of a company's strategy have to be 100 percent different, but rather that they must differ in at least *some important respects*. A strategy stands a better chance of succeeding when it is predicated on actions, business approaches, and competitive moves aimed at (1) appealing to buyers in ways that *set a company apart from its rivals* and (2) staking out a market position that is not crowded with strong competitors.

Strategy is about competing differently from rivals—doing what competitors don't do or, even better, doing what they can't do!

A company's strategy provides direction and guidance, in terms of not only what the company *should* do but also what it *should not* do. Knowing what not to do can be as important as knowing what to do, strategically. At best, making the wrong strategic moves will prove a distraction and a waste of company resources. At worst, it can bring about unintended long-term consequences that put the company's very survival at risk.

Figure 1.1 illustrates the broad types of actions and approaches that often characterize a company's strategy in a particular business or industry. For a more concrete example, see Illustration Capsule 1.1 describing the elements of Apple, Inc.'s successful strategy.

FIGURE 1.1 Identifying a Company's Strategy—What to Look For

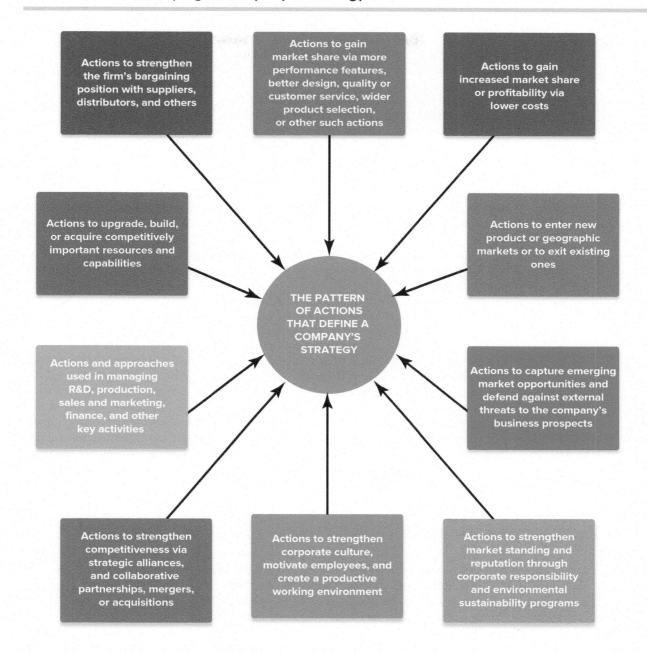

Strategy and the Quest for Competitive Advantage

The heart and soul of any strategy are the actions in the marketplace that managers take to gain a competitive advantage over rivals. A company has a **competitive advantage** whenever it has some type of edge over rivals in attracting buyers and coping with competitive forces. A competitive advantage is essential for realizing greater marketplace success and higher profitability over the long term.

● **LO 1-2**

Grasp the concept of a *sustainable competitive advantage.*

There are many routes to competitive advantage, but they all involve one of two basic mechanisms. Either they provide the customer with a product or service that the customer values more highly than others (higher perceived value), or they produce their product or service more efficiently (lower costs). Delivering superior value or delivering value more efficiently—whatever form it takes—nearly always requires performing value chain activities differently than rivals and building capabilities that are not readily matched. In Illustration Capsule 1.1, it is evident that Apple, Inc. has gained a competitive advantage over its rivals in the technological device industry through its efforts to create "must-have," exciting new products, that are beautifully designed, technologically advanced, easy to use, and sold in appealing stores that offer a fun experience, knowledgeable staff, and excellent service. By differentiating itself in this manner from its competitors Apple has been able to charge prices for its products that are well above those of its rivals and far exceed the low cost of its inputs. Its expansion policies have allowed the company to make it easy for customers to find an Apple store in almost any high-quality mall or urban shopping district, further enhancing the brand and cementing customer loyalty. A creative *distinctive* strategy such as that used by Apple is a company's most reliable ticket for developing a competitive advantage over its rivals. If a strategy is not distinctive, then there can be no competitive advantage, since no firm would be meeting customer needs better or operating more efficiently than any other.

If a company's competitive edge holds promise for being *sustainable* (as opposed to just temporary), then so much the better for both the strategy and the company's future profitability. What makes a competitive advantage **sustainable** (or durable), as opposed to temporary, are elements of the strategy that give buyers lasting reasons to prefer a company's products or services over those of competitors—*reasons that competitors are unable to nullify, duplicate, or overcome despite their best efforts.* In the case of Apple, the company's unparalleled name recognition, its reputation for technically superior, beautifully designed, "must-have" products, and the accessibility of the appealing, consumer-friendly stores with knowledgeable staff, make it difficult for competitors to weaken or overcome Apple's competitive advantage. Not only has Apple's strategy provided the company with a sustainable competitive advantage, but it has made Apple, Inc. one of the most admired companies on the planet.

Five of the most frequently used and dependable strategic approaches to setting a company apart from rivals, building strong customer loyalty, and gaining a competitive advantage are

1. *A low-cost provider strategy*—achieving a cost-based advantage over rivals. Walmart and Southwest Airlines have earned strong market positions because of the low-cost advantages they have achieved over their rivals. Low-cost provider strategies can produce a durable competitive edge when rivals find it hard to match the low-cost leader's approach to driving costs out of the business.

2. *A broad differentiation strategy*—seeking to differentiate the company's product or service from that of rivals in ways that will appeal to a broad spectrum of buyers. Successful adopters of differentiation strategies include Apple (innovative products), Johnson & Johnson in baby products (product reliability), Rolex (luxury and prestige), and BMW (engineering design and performance). One way to sustain this type of competitive advantage is to be sufficiently innovative to thwart the efforts of clever rivals to copy or closely imitate the product offering.

CORE CONCEPT

A company achieves a **competitive advantage** when it provides buyers with superior value compared to rival sellers or offers the same value at a lower cost to the firm. The advantage is **sustainable** if it persists despite the best efforts of competitors to match or surpass this advantage.

● **LO 1-3**

Identify the five most basic strategic approaches for setting a company apart from rivals.

Apple Inc. is one of the most profitable companies in the world, with revenues of more than $265 billion. For more than 10 consecutive years, it has ranked number one on Fortune's list of the "World's Most Admired Companies." Given the worldwide popularity of its products and services, along with its reputation for superior technological innovation and design capabilities, this is not surprising. The key elements of Apple's successful strategy include:

- *Designing and developing its own operating systems, hardware, application software, and services.* This allows Apple to bring the best user experience to its customers through products and solutions with innovative design, superior ease-of-use, and seamless integration across platforms. The ability to use services like iCloud across devices incentivizes users to join Apple's technological ecosystem and has been critical to fostering brand loyalty.

- *Continuously investing in research and development (R&D) and frequently introducing products.* Apple has invested heavily in R&D, spending upwards of $11 billion a year, to ensure a continual and timely injection of competitive products, services, and technologies into the marketplace. Its successful products and services include the Mac, iPod, iPhone, iPad, Apple Watch, Apple TV, and Apple Music. It is currently investing in an Apple electric car and Apple solar energy.

- *Strategically locating its stores and staffing them with knowledgeable personnel.* By operating its own Apple stores and positioning them in high-traffic locations, Apple is better equipped to provide its customers with the optimal buying experience. The stores' employees are well versed in the value of the hardware and software integration and demonstrate the unique solutions available on its products. This high-quality sale and after-sale supports allows Apple to continuously attract new and retain existing customers.

- *Expanding Apple's reach domestically and internationally.* Apple operates more than 500 retail stores across

PUGUN SJ/Shutterstock

24 countries. During fiscal year 2019, 60 percent of Apple's revenue came from international sales.

- *Maintaining a quality brand image, supported by premium pricing.* Although the computer industry is incredibly price competitive, Apple has managed to sustain a competitive edge by focusing on its inimitable value proposition and deliberately keeping a price premium—thus creating an aura of prestige around its products.

- *Committing to corporate social responsibility and sustainability through supplier relations.* Apple's strict Code of Conduct requires its suppliers to comply with several standards regarding safe working conditions, fair treatment of workers, and environmentally safe manufacturing.

- *Cultivating a diverse workforce rooted in transparency.* Apple believes that diverse teams make innovation possible and is dedicated to incorporating a broad range of perspectives in its workforce. Every year, Apple publishes data showing the representation of women and different race and ethnicity groups across functions.

Note: Developed with Shawnda Lee Duvigneaud
Sources: Apple 10-K, Company website.

---

3. *A focused low-cost strategy*—concentrating on a narrow buyer segment (or market niche) and outcompeting rivals by having lower costs and thus being able to serve niche members at a lower price. Private-label manufacturers of food, health and beauty products, and nutritional supplements use their low-cost advantage to offer supermarket buyers lower prices than those demanded by producers of branded

products. IKEA's emphasis on modular furniture, ready for assembly, makes it a focused low-cost player in the furniture market.

4. *A focused differentiation strategy*—concentrating on a narrow buyer segment (or market niche) and outcompeting rivals by offering buyers customized attributes that meet their specialized needs and tastes better than rivals' products. Lululemon, for example, specializes in high-quality yoga clothing and the like, attracting a devoted set of buyers in the process. Tesla, Inc., with its electric cars, LinkedIn specializing in the business and employment aspects of social networking, and Goya Foods in Hispanic specialty food products provide some other examples of this strategy.

5. *A best-cost provider strategy*—giving customers more value for the money by satisfying their expectations on key quality features, performance, and/or service attributes while beating their price expectations. This approach is a hybrid strategy that blends elements of low-cost provider and differentiation strategies; the aim is to have lower costs than rivals while simultaneously offering better differentiating attributes. Target is an example of a company that is known for its hip product design (a reputation it built by featuring limited edition lines by designers such as Rodarte, Victoria Beckham, and Jason Wu), as well as a more appealing shopping ambience for discount store shoppers. Its dual focus on low costs as well as differentiation shows how a best-cost provider strategy can offer customers great value for the money.

Winning a *sustainable* competitive edge over rivals with any of the preceding five strategies generally hinges as much on building competitively valuable expertise and capabilities that rivals cannot readily match as it does on having a distinctive product offering. Clever rivals can nearly always copy the attributes of a popular product or service, but for rivals to match the experience, know-how, and specialized capabilities that a company has developed and perfected over a long period of time is substantially harder to do and takes much longer. The success of the Swatch in watches, for example, was driven by impressive design, marketing, and engineering capabilities, while Apple has demonstrated outstanding product innovation capabilities in digital music players, smartphones, and e-readers. Hyundai has become the world's fastest-growing automaker as a result of its advanced manufacturing processes and unparalleled quality control systems. Capabilities such as these have been hard for competitors to imitate or best.

● **LO 1-4**

Understand why a company's strategy tends to evolve.

Why a Company's Strategy Evolves over Time

The appeal of a strategy that yields a sustainable competitive advantage is that it offers the potential for a more enduring edge than a temporary advantage over rivals. But sustainability is a relative term, with some advantages lasting longer than others. And regardless of how sustainable a competitive advantage may appear to be at a given point in time, conditions change. Even a substantial competitive advantage over rivals may crumble in the face of drastic shifts in market conditions or disruptive innovations. Therefore, managers of every company must be willing and ready to modify the strategy in response to changing market conditions, advancing technology, unexpected moves by competitors, shifting buyer needs, emerging market opportunities, and new ideas for improving the strategy. Most of the time, a company's strategy evolves incrementally as management fine-tunes various pieces of the strategy and adjusts the strategy in response to unfolding events.[5] However, on occasion, major strategy shifts are called for, such as when the strategy is clearly failing or when industry conditions change in dramatic ways. Industry environments characterized by high-velocity change require companies to repeatedly adapt their strategies.[6] For example, companies in industries with rapid-fire advances in technology like 3-D printing, shale fracking, and genetic engineering often find it essential to adjust key elements of their strategies several times a year. When the technological change is drastic enough to "disrupt" the entire industry, displacing market leaders and altering market boundaries, companies may find it necessary to "reinvent" entirely their approach to providing value to their customers.

Regardless of whether a company's strategy changes gradually or swiftly, the important point is that the task of crafting strategy is not a one-time event but always a work in progress. Adapting to new conditions and constantly evaluating what is working well enough to continue and what needs to be improved are normal parts of the strategy-making process, resulting in an *evolving strategy*.[7]

A Company's Strategy Is Partly Proactive and Partly Reactive

The evolving nature of a company's strategy means that the typical company strategy is a blend of (1) *proactive,* planned initiatives to improve the company's financial performance and secure a competitive edge and (2) *reactive* responses to unanticipated developments and fresh market conditions. The biggest portion of a company's current strategy flows from previously initiated actions that have proven themselves in the marketplace and newly launched initiatives aimed at edging out rivals and boosting financial performance. This part of management's action plan for running the company is its **deliberate strategy,** consisting of proactive strategy elements that are both planned and realized as planned (while other planned strategy elements may not work out and are abandoned in consequence)—see Figure 1.2.[8]

But managers must always be willing to supplement or modify the proactive strategy elements with as-needed reactions to unanticipated conditions. Inevitably, there will be occasions when market and competitive conditions take an unexpected turn that calls for some kind of strategic reaction. Hence, *a portion of a company's strategy is always developed on the fly,* coming as a response to fresh strategic maneuvers on the part of rival firms, unexpected shifts in customer requirements, fast-changing technological developments, newly appearing market opportunities, a changing political or economic climate, or other unanticipated happenings in the surrounding environment. These adaptive strategy adjustments make up the firm's **emergent strategy.** A company's strategy *in toto* (its **realized strategy**) thus tends to be a *combination* of proactive and reactive elements, with certain strategy elements being *abandoned* because they have become obsolete or ineffective. A company's realized strategy can be observed in the pattern of its actions over time, which is a far better indicator than any of its strategic plans on paper or any public pronouncements about its strategy.

Strategy and Ethics: Passing the Test of Moral Scrutiny

In choosing among strategic alternatives, company managers are well advised to embrace actions that can pass the test of moral scrutiny. Just keeping a company's strategic actions within the bounds of what is legal does not mean the strategy is

Changing circumstances and ongoing management efforts to improve the strategy cause a company's strategy to evolve over time—a condition that makes the task of crafting strategy a *work in progress,* not a one-time event.

A company's strategy is shaped partly by management analysis and choice and partly by the necessity of adapting and learning by doing.

CORE CONCEPT

A company's **deliberate strategy** consists of *proactive* strategy elements that are planned; its **emergent strategy** consists of *reactive* strategy elements that emerge as changing conditions warrant.

A strategy cannot be considered ethical just because it involves actions that are legal. To meet the standard of being ethical, a strategy must entail actions and behavior that can pass moral scrutiny in the sense of *not being* deceitful, unfair or harmful to others, disreputable, or unreasonably damaging to the environment.

FIGURE 1.2   A Company's Strategy Is a Blend of Proactive Initiatives and Reactive Adjustments

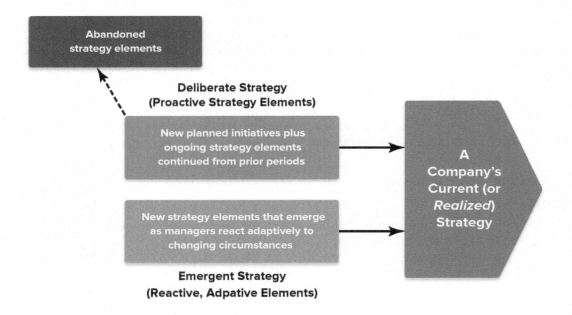

ethical. Ethical and moral standards are not fully governed by what is legal. Rather, they involve issues of "right" versus "wrong" and duty—what one should do. A strategy is ethical only if it does not entail actions that cross the moral line from "can do" to "should not do." For example, a company's strategy *definitely* crosses into the "should not do" zone and cannot pass moral scrutiny if it entails actions and behaviors that are deceitful, unfair or harmful to others, disreputable, or unreasonably damaging to the environment. A company's strategic actions cross over into the "should not do" zone and are likely to be deemed unethical when (1) they reflect badly on the company or (2) they adversely impact the legitimate interests and well-being of shareholders, customers, employees, suppliers, the communities where it operates, and society at large or (3) they provoke public outcries about inappropriate or "irresponsible" actions, behavior, or outcomes.

Admittedly, it is not always easy to categorize a given strategic behavior as ethical or unethical. Many strategic actions fall in a gray zone and can be deemed ethical or unethical depending on how high one sets the bar for what qualifies as ethical behavior. For example, is it ethical for advertisers of alcoholic products to place ads in media having an audience of as much as 50 percent underage viewers? Is it ethical for companies to employ undocumented workers who may have been brought to the United States as children? Is it ethical for Nike, Under Armour, and other makers of athletic wear to pay a university athletic department large sums of money as an "inducement" for the university's athletic teams to use their brand of products? Is it ethical for pharmaceutical manufacturers to charge higher prices for life-saving drugs in some countries than they charge in others? Is it ethical for a company to ignore the damage done to the environment by its operations in a particular country, even though they are in compliance with current environmental regulations in that country?

Senior executives with strong ethical convictions are generally proactive in linking strategic action and ethics; they forbid the pursuit of ethically questionable business opportunities and insist that all aspects of company strategy are in accord with high ethical standards. They make it clear that all company personnel are expected to act with integrity, and they put organizational checks and balances into place to monitor behavior, enforce ethical codes of conduct, and provide guidance to employees regarding any gray areas. Their commitment to ethical business conduct is genuine, not hypocritical lip service.

The reputational and financial damage that unethical strategies and behavior can do is substantial. When a company is put in the public spotlight because certain personnel are alleged to have engaged in misdeeds, unethical behavior, fraudulent accounting, or criminal behavior, its revenues and stock price are usually hammered hard. Many customers and suppliers shy away from doing business with a company that engages in sleazy practices or turns a blind eye to its employees' illegal or unethical behavior. Repulsed by unethical strategies or behavior, wary customers take their business elsewhere and wary suppliers tread carefully. Moreover, employees with character and integrity do not want to work for a company whose strategies are shady or whose executives lack character and integrity. Consequently, solid business reasons exist for companies to shun the use of unethical strategy elements. Besides, immoral or unethical actions are just plain wrong.

A COMPANY'S STRATEGY AND ITS BUSINESS MODEL

At the core of every sound strategy is the company's **business model.** A business model is management's blueprint for delivering a valuable product or service to customers in a manner that will generate revenues sufficient to cover costs and yield an attractive profit.[9] The two elements of a company's business model are (1) its *customer value proposition* and (2) its *profit formula.* The customer value proposition lays out the company's approach to satisfying buyer wants and needs at a price customers will consider a good value. The profit formula describes the company's approach to determining a cost structure that will allow for acceptable profits, given the pricing tied to its customer value proposition. Figure 1.3 illustrates the elements of the business model in terms of what is known as the *value-price-cost framework.*[10] As the framework indicates,

● LO 1-5

Identify what constitutes a viable business model.

FIGURE 1.3   **The Business Model and the Value-Price-Cost Framework**

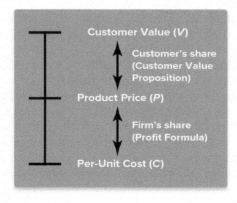

the customer value proposition can be expressed as $V - P$, which is essentially the customers' perception of how much value they are getting for the money. The profit formula, on a per-unit basis, can be expressed as $P - C$. Plainly, from a customer perspective, the greater the value delivered (V) and the lower the price (P), the more attractive is the company's value proposition. On the other hand, the lower the costs (C), given the customer value proposition ($V - P$), the greater the ability of the business model to be a moneymaker. Thus, the profit formula reveals how efficiently a company can meet customer wants and needs and deliver on the value proposition. The nitty-gritty issue surrounding a company's business model is whether it can execute its customer value proposition profitably. Just because company managers have crafted a strategy for competing and running the business does not automatically mean that the strategy will lead to profitability—it may or it may not.

Aircraft engine manufacturer Rolls-Royce employs an innovative "power-by-the-hour" business model that charges airlines leasing fees for engine use, maintenance, and repairs based on actual hours flown. The company retains ownership of the engines and is able to minimize engine maintenance costs through the use of sophisticated sensors that optimize maintenance and repair schedules. Gillette's business model in razor blades involves selling a "master product"—the razor—at an attractively low price and then making money on repeat purchases of razor blades that can be produced cheaply and sold at high profit margins. Printer manufacturers like Hewlett-Packard, Canon, and Epson pursue much the same business model as Gillette—selling printers at a low (virtually break-even) price and making large profit margins on the repeat purchases of ink cartridges and other printer supplies. McDonald's invented the business model for fast food—providing value to customers in the form of economical quick-service meals at clean, convenient locations. Its profit formula involves such elements as standardized cost-efficient store design, stringent specifications for ingredients, detailed operating procedures for each unit, sizable investment in human resources and training, and heavy reliance on advertising and in-store promotions to drive volume. Illustration Capsule 1.2 describes three contrasting business models in radio broadcasting.

WHAT MAKES A STRATEGY A WINNER?

Three tests can be applied to determine whether a strategy is a *winning strategy:*

1. ***The Fit Test:*** *How well does the strategy fit the company's situation?* To qualify as a winner, a strategy has to be well matched to industry and competitive conditions, a company's best market opportunities, and other pertinent aspects of the business environment in which the company operates. No strategy can work well unless it exhibits good *external fit* with respect to prevailing market conditions. At the same time, a winning strategy must be tailored to the company's resources and competitive capabilities and be supported by a complementary set of functional activities (i.e., activities in the realms of supply chain management, operations, sales and marketing, and so on). That is, it must also exhibit *internal fit* and be compatible with a company's ability to execute the strategy in a competent manner. Unless a strategy exhibits good fit with both the external and internal aspects of a company's overall situation, it is likely to be an underperformer and fall short of producing winning results. Winning strategies also exhibit *dynamic fit* in the sense that they evolve over time in a manner that maintains close and effective alignment with the company's situation even as external and internal conditions change.[11]

Pandora, SiriusXM, and Over-the-Air Broadcast Radio: Three Contrasting Business Models

Vivien Killilea/Stringer/Getty Images

	Pandora	SiriusXM	Over-the-Air Radio Broadcasters
Customer value proposition	• Through free-of-charge Internet radio service, allowed PC, tablet computer, and smartphone users to create up to 100 personalized music and comedy stations. • Utilized algorithms to generate playlists based on users' predicted music preferences. • Offered programming interrupted by brief, occasional ads; eliminated advertising for Pandora One subscribers.	• For a monthly subscription fee, provided satellite-based music, news, sports, national and regional weather, traffic reports in limited areas, and talk radio programming. • Also offered subscribers streaming Internet channels and the ability to create personalized commercial-free stations for online and mobile listening. • Offered programming interrupted only by brief, occasional ads.	• Provided free-of-charge music, national and local news, local traffic reports, national and local weather, and talk radio programming. • Included frequent programming interruption for ads.
Profit formula	*Revenue generation:* Display, audio, and video ads targeted to different audiences and sold to local and national buyers; subscription revenues generated from an advertising-free option called Pandora One. *Cost structure:* Fixed costs associated with developing software for computers, tablets, and smartphones. Fixed and variable costs related to operating data centers to support streaming network, content royalties, marketing, and support activities.	*Revenue generation:* Monthly subscription fees, sales of satellite radio equipment, and advertising revenues. *Cost structure:* Fixed costs associated with operating a satellite-based music delivery service and streaming Internet service. Fixed and variable costs related to programming and content royalties, marketing, and support activities.	*Revenue generation:* Advertising sales to national and local businesses. *Cost structure:* Fixed costs associated with terrestrial broadcasting operations. Fixed and variable costs related to local news reporting, advertising sales operations, network affiliate fees, programming and content royalties, commercial production activities, and support activities.

(Continued)

Pandora	SiriusXM	Over-the-Air Radio Broadcasters
Profit margin: Profitability dependent on generating sufficient advertising revenues and subscription revenues to cover costs and provide attractive profits.	*Profit margin:* Profitability dependent on attracting a sufficiently large number of subscribers to cover costs and provide attractive profits.	*Profit margin:* Profitability dependent on generating sufficient advertising revenues to cover costs and provide attractive profits.

A **winning strategy** must pass three tests:
1. The fit test
2. The competitive advantage test
3. The performance test

2. *The Competitive Advantage Test: Is the strategy helping the company achieve a competitive advantage? Is the competitive advantage likely to be sustainable?* Strategies that fail to achieve a competitive advantage over rivals are unlikely to produce superior performance. And unless the competitive advantage is sustainable, superior performance is unlikely to last for more than a brief period of time. Winning strategies enable a company to achieve a competitive advantage over key rivals that is long-lasting. The bigger and more durable the competitive advantage, the more powerful it is.

3. *The Performance Test: Is the strategy producing superior company performance?* The mark of a winning strategy is strong company performance. Two kinds of performance indicators tell the most about the caliber of a company's strategy: (1) competitive strength and market standing and (2) profitability and financial strength. Above-average financial performance or gains in market share, competitive position, or profitability are signs of a winning strategy.

Strategies—either existing or proposed—that come up short on one or more of the preceding tests are plainly less desirable than strategies passing all three tests with flying colors. New initiatives that don't seem to match the company's internal and external situations should be scrapped before they come to fruition, while existing strategies must be scrutinized on a regular basis to ensure they have good fit, offer a competitive advantage, and are contributing to above-average performance or performance improvements. Failure to pass one or more of the three tests should prompt managers to make immediate changes in an existing strategy.

WHY CRAFTING AND EXECUTING STRATEGY ARE IMPORTANT TASKS

Crafting and executing strategy are top-priority managerial tasks for two big reasons. First, a clear and reasoned strategy is management's prescription for doing business, its road map to competitive advantage, its game plan for pleasing customers, and its formula for improving performance. High-performing enterprises are nearly always the product of astute, creative, and proactive strategy making. Companies don't get to the top of the industry rankings or stay there with flawed strategies, copycat strategies, or timid attempts to try to do better. Only a handful of companies can boast of hitting home runs in the marketplace due to lucky breaks or the good fortune of having stumbled into the right market at the right time with the right product. Even if this is the case, success will not be lasting unless the companies subsequently craft a strategy that capitalizes on their luck, builds on what is working, and discards the rest. So there can be little argument that the process of crafting a company's strategy matters—and matters a lot.

Second, even the best-conceived strategies will result in performance shortfalls if they are not executed proficiently. The processes of crafting and executing strategies must go hand in hand if a company is to be successful in the long term. The chief executive officer of one successful company put it well when he said

> In the main, our competitors are acquainted with the same fundamental concepts and techniques and approaches that we follow, and they are as free to pursue them as we are. More often than not, the difference between their level of success and ours lies in the relative thoroughness and self-discipline with which we and they develop and execute our strategies for the future.

Good Strategy + Good Strategy Execution = Good Management

Crafting and executing strategy are thus core management tasks. Among all the things managers do, nothing affects a company's ultimate success or failure more fundamentally than how well its management team charts the company's direction, develops competitively effective strategic moves, and pursues what needs to be done internally to produce good day-in, day-out strategy execution and operating excellence. Indeed, *good strategy and good strategy execution are the most telling and trustworthy signs of good management.* The rationale for using the twin standards of good strategy making and good strategy execution to determine whether a company is well managed is therefore compelling: *The better conceived a company's strategy and the more competently it is executed, the more likely the company will be a standout performer in the marketplace.* In stark contrast, a company that lacks clear-cut direction, has a flawed strategy, or can't execute its strategy competently is a company whose financial performance is probably suffering, whose business is at long-term risk, and whose management is sorely lacking.

THE ROAD AHEAD

Throughout the chapters to come and in Part 2 of this text, the spotlight is on the foremost question in running a business enterprise: *What must managers do, and do well, to make a company successful in the marketplace?* The answer that emerges is that doing a good job of managing inherently requires good strategic thinking and good management of the strategy-making, strategy-executing process.

> How well a company performs is directly attributable to the caliber of its strategy and the proficiency with which the strategy is executed.

The mission of this book is to provide a solid overview of what every business student and aspiring manager needs to know about crafting and executing strategy. We will explore what good strategic thinking entails, describe the core concepts and tools of strategic analysis, and examine the ins and outs of crafting and executing strategy. The accompanying cases will help build your skills in both diagnosing how well the strategy-making, strategy-executing task is being performed and prescribing actions for how the strategy in question or its execution can be improved. The strategic management course that you are enrolled in may also include a strategy simulation exercise in which you will run a company in head-to-head competition with companies run by your classmates. Your mastery of the strategic management concepts presented in the following chapters will put you in a strong position to craft a winning strategy for your company and figure out how to execute it in a cost-effective and profitable manner. As you progress through the chapters of the text and the activities assigned during the term, we hope to convince you that first-rate capabilities in crafting and executing strategy are essential to good management.

As you tackle the content and accompanying activities of this book, ponder the following observation by the essayist and poet Ralph Waldo Emerson: "Commerce is a game of skill which many people play, but which few play well." If your efforts help you become a savvy player and better equip you to succeed in business, the time and energy you spend here will indeed prove worthwhile.

KEY POINTS

1. A company's strategy is the set of coordinated actions that its managers take in order to outperform its competitors and achieve superior profitability.

2. The success of a company's strategy depends upon *competing differently* from rivals and gaining a competitive advantage over them.

3. A company achieves a *competitive advantage* when it provides buyers with superior value compared to rival sellers or produces its products or services more efficiently. The advantage is *sustainable* if it persists despite the best efforts of competitors to match or surpass this advantage.

4. A company's strategy typically evolves over time, emerging from a blend of (1) proactive deliberate actions on the part of company managers to improve the strategy and (2) reactive emergent responses to unanticipated developments and fresh market conditions.

5. A company's business model sets forth the logic for how its strategy will create value for customers and at the same time generate revenues sufficient to cover costs and realize a profit. Thus, it contains two crucial elements: (1) the *customer value proposition*—a plan for satisfying customer wants and needs at a price customers will consider good value, and (2) the *profit formula*—a plan for a cost structure that will enable the company to deliver the customer value proposition profitably. These elements are illustrated by the value-price-cost framework.

6. A winning strategy will pass three tests: (1) *fit* (external, internal, and dynamic consistency), (2) *competitive advantage* (durable competitive advantage), and (3) *performance* (outstanding financial and market performance).

7. Ethical strategies must entail actions and behavior that can pass the test of moral scrutiny in the sense of *not being* deceitful, unfair or harmful to others, disreputable, or unreasonably damaging to the environment.

8. Crafting and executing strategy are core management functions. How well a company performs and the degree of market success it enjoys are directly attributable to the caliber of its strategy and the proficiency with which the strategy is executed.

ASSURANCE OF LEARNING EXERCISES

1. Based on your experiences and/or knowledge of Apple's current products and services, does Apple's strategy (as described in Illustration Capsule 1.1) seem to set it apart from rivals? Does the strategy seem to be keyed to a cost-based advantage, differentiating features, serving the unique needs of a niche, or some combination of these? What is there about Apple's strategy that can lead to sustainable competitive advantage?

   connect
   LO 1-1, LO 1-2, LO 1-3

2. Elements of Amazon's strategy have evolved in meaningful ways since the company's founding in 1994. After reviewing the company's history and all of the links at the company's investor relations site **ir.aboutamazon.com** prepare a one- to two-page report that discusses how its strategy has evolved. Your report should also assess how well Amazon's strategy passes the three tests of a winning strategy.

   LO 1-4, LO 1-6

3. Go to **investor.siriusxm.com** and check whether Sirius XM's recent financial reports indicate that its business model is working. Are its subscription fees increasing or declining? Are its revenue stream advertising and equipment sales growing or declining? Does its cost structure allow for acceptable profit margins?

   connect
   LO 1-5

EXERCISES FOR SIMULATION PARTICIPANTS

connect

Three basic questions must be answered by managers of organizations of all sizes as they begin the process of crafting strategy:

- What is our present situation?
- Where do we want to go from here?
- How are we going to get there?

After you have read the Participant's Guide or Player's Manual for the strategy simulation exercise that you will participate in during this academic term, you and your co-managers should come up with brief one- or two-paragraph answers to these three questions *prior to* entering your first set of decisions. While your answer to the first of the six questions can be developed from your reading of the manual, the remaining questions will require a collaborative discussion among the members of your company's management team about how you intend to manage the company you have been assigned to run.

1. Your company's strategy in the business simulation for this course should include choices about what types of issues?

   LO 1-1

2. What is your company's current situation? A substantive answer to this question should cover the following issues:

   LO 1-6

   - Does your company appear to be in sound financial condition?
   - What problems does your company have that need to be addressed?

3. Why will your company matter to customers? A complete answer to this question should say something about each of the following: How will you goals or aspirations do you have for your company?

   LO 1-3

   - How will you create customer value?
   - What will be distinctive about the company's products or services?
   - How will capabilities and resources be deployed to deliver customer value?

LO 1-5   **4.** What are the primary elements of your company's business model?

- Describe your customer value proposition.
- Discuss the profit formula tied to your business model.
- What level of revenues is required for your company's business model to become a moneymaker?

LO 1-6   **5.** How will you build and sustain competitive advantage?

- Which of the basic strategic and competitive approaches discussed in this chapter do you think makes the most sense to pursue?
- What kind of competitive advantage over rivals will you try to achieve?
- How do you envision that your strategy might evolve as you react to the competitive moves of rival firms?
- Does your strategy have the ability to pass the three tests of a winning strategy? Explain.

LO 1-1, 1-2, 1-6   **6.** Why will strategy execution be important to your company's success?

ENDNOTES

[1] B. R, "Strategy," *The Economist,* October 19, 2012, www.economist.com/blogs/schumpeter/2012/10/z-business-quotations-1 (accessed January 4, 2014).

[2] Jan Rivkin, "An Alternative Approach to Making Strategic Choices," Harvard Business School case 9-702-433, 2001.

[3] Michael E. Porter, "What Is Strategy?" *Harvard Business Review* 74, no. 6 (November–December 1996), pp. 65–67.

[4] Ibid.

[5] Eric T. Anderson and Duncan Simester, "A Step-by-Step Guide to Smart Business Experiments," *Harvard Business Review* 89, no. 3 (March 2011).

[6] Shona L. Brown and Kathleen M. Eisenhardt, *Competing on the Edge: Strategy as Structured Chaos* (Boston, MA: Harvard Business School Press, 1998).

[7] Cynthia A. Montgomery, "Putting Leadership Back into Strategy," *Harvard Business Review* 86, no. 1 (January 2008).

[8] Henry Mintzberg and J. A. Waters, "Of Strategies, Deliberate and Emergent," *Strategic Management Journal* 6 (1985); Costas Markides, "Strategy as Balance: From 'Either-Or' to 'And,' " *Business Strategy Review* 12, no. 3 (September 2001).

[9] Mark W. Johnson, Clayton M. Christensen, and Henning Kagermann, "Reinventing Your Business Model," *Harvard Business Review* 86, no. 12 (December 2008); Joan Magretta, "Why Business Models Matter," *Harvard Business Review* 80, no. 5 (May 2002).

[10] A. Brandenburger and H. Stuart, "Value-Based Strategy," *Journal of Economics and Management Strategy* 5 (1996), pp. 5–24; D. Hoopes, T. Madsen, and G. Walker, "Guest Editors' Introduction to the Special Issue: Why Is There a Resource-Based View? Toward a Theory of Competitive Heterogeneity," *Strategic Management Journal* 24 (2003), pp. 889–992; M. Peteraf and J. Barney, "Unravelling the Resource-Based Tangle," *Managerial and Decision Economics* 24 (2003), pp. 309–323.

[11] Rivkin, "An Alternative Approach to Making Strategic Choices."

chapter 2

Charting a Company's Direction

Its Vision, Mission, Objectives, and Strategy

Learning Objectives

After reading this chapter, you should be able to:

LO 2-1 Understand why it is critical for managers to have a clear strategic vision of where the company needs to head.

LO 2-2 Explain the importance of setting both strategic and financial objectives.

LO 2-3 Explain why the strategic initiatives taken at various organizational levels must be tightly coordinated.

LO 2-4 Recognize what a company must do to execute its strategy proficiently.

LO 2-5 Comprehend the role and responsibility of a company's board of directors in overseeing the strategic management process.

Pamela Hamilton/Getty Images

Sound strategy starts with having the right goal.

Michael Porter—*Professor and consultant*

Purpose must be deliberately conceived and chosen, and then pursued.

Clayton Christensen—*Professor and consultant*

A vision without a strategy remains an illusion.

Lee Bolman—*Author and leadership consultant*

Crafting and executing strategy are the heart and soul of managing a business enterprise. But exactly what is involved in developing a strategy and executing it proficiently? What goes into charting a company's strategic course and long-term direction? Is any analysis required? Does a company need a strategic plan? What are the various components of the strategy-making, strategy-executing process and to what extent are company personnel—aside from senior management—involved in the process?

This chapter presents an overview of the ins and outs of crafting and executing company strategies. The focus is on management's direction-setting responsibilities—charting a strategic course, setting performance targets, and choosing a strategy capable of producing the desired outcomes. We explain why strategy-making is a task for a company's entire management team and which kinds of strategic decisions tend to be made at which levels of management. The chapter concludes with a look at the roles and responsibilities of a company's board of directors and how good corporate governance protects shareholder interests and promotes good management.

WHAT DOES THE STRATEGY-MAKING, STRATEGY-EXECUTING PROCESS ENTAIL?

Crafting and executing a company's strategy is an ongoing process that consists of five interrelated stages:

1. *Developing a strategic vision* that charts the company's long-term direction, a *mission statement* that describes the company's purpose, and a set of *core values* to guide the pursuit of the vision and mission.
2. *Setting objectives* for measuring the company's performance and tracking its progress in moving in the intended long-term direction.
3. *Crafting a strategy* for advancing the company along the path management has charted and achieving its performance objectives.
4. *Executing the chosen strategy* efficiently and effectively.
5. *Monitoring developments, evaluating performance, and initiating corrective adjustments* in the company's vision and mission statement, objectives, strategy, or approach to strategy execution in light of actual experience, changing conditions, new ideas, and new opportunities.

> **CORE CONCEPT**
>
> A **strategic inflection point** is the point at which the extent of industry change requires management to consider changing the company's strategic vision.

Figure 2.1 displays this five-stage process, which we examine next in some detail. The first three stages of the strategic management process involve making a strategic plan. **A strategic plan** maps out where a company is headed, establishes strategic and financial targets, and outlines the basic business model, competitive moves, and approaches to be used in achieving the desired business results.[1] We explain this more fully at the conclusion of our discussion of stage 3, later in this chapter.

The five-stage process model illustrates the need for management to evaluate a number of external and internal factors in deciding upon a strategic direction, appropriate objectives, and approaches to crafting and executing strategy (see Table 2.1). Management's decisions that are made in the strategic management process must be shaped by the prevailing economic conditions and competitive environment and the company's own internal resources and competitive capabilities. These strategy-shaping conditions will be the focus of Chapters 3 and 4.

The model shown in Figure 2.1 also illustrates the need for management to evaluate the company's performance on an ongoing basis. Any indication that the company is failing to achieve its objectives calls for corrective adjustments in one of the first four stages of the process. The company's implementation efforts might have fallen short, and new tactics must be devised to fully exploit the potential of the company's strategy. If management determines that the company's execution efforts are sufficient, it should challenge the assumptions underlying the company's business model and strategy, and make alterations to better fit competitive conditions and the company's internal capabilities. If the company's strategic approach to competition is rated as sound, then perhaps management set overly ambitious targets for the company's performance.

The evaluation stage of the strategic management process shown in Figure 2.1 also allows for a change in the company's vision, but this should be necessary only when it becomes evident to management that the industry has changed in a significant way that renders the vision obsolete. Such occasions can be referred to as strategic inflection points. When a company reaches a strategic inflection point, management has tough decisions to make about the company's direction because abandoning an established

FIGURE 2.1   The Strategy-Making, Strategy-Executing Process

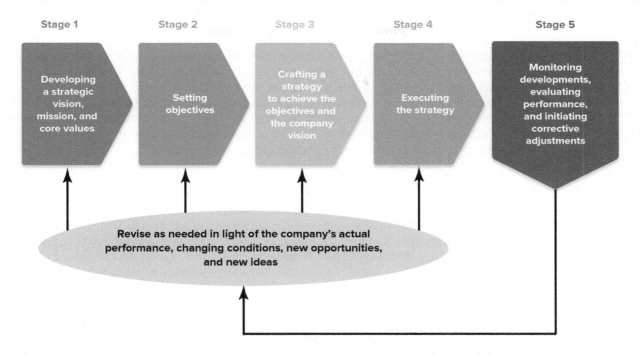

TABLE 2.1   Factors Shaping Decisions in the Strategy-Making, Strategy-Execution Process

External Considerations
- Does sticking with the company's present strategic course present attractive opportunities for growth and profitability?
- What kind of competitive forces are industry members facing, and are they acting to enhance or weaken the company's prospects for growth and profitability?
- What factors are driving industry change, and what impact on the company's prospects will they have?
- How are industry rivals positioned, and what strategic moves are they likely to make next?
- What are the key factors of future competitive success, and does the industry offer good prospects for attractive profits for companies possessing those capabilities?

Internal Considerations
- Does the company have an appealing customer value proposition?
- What are the company's competitively important resources and capabilities, and are they potent enough to produce a sustainable competitive advantage?
- Does the company have sufficient business and competitive strength to seize market opportunities and nullify external threats?
- Are the company's costs competitive with those of key rivals?
- Is the company competitively stronger or weaker than key rivals?

course carries considerable risk. However, responding to unfolding changes in the marketplace in a timely fashion lessens a company's chances of becoming trapped in a stagnant or declining business or letting attractive new growth opportunities slip away.

STAGE 1: DEVELOPING A STRATEGIC VISION, MISSION STATEMENT, AND SET OF CORE VALUES

Very early in the strategy-making process, a company's senior managers must wrestle with the issue of what directional path the company should take. Can the company's prospects be improved by changing its product offerings, or the markets in which it participates, or the customers it aims to serve? Deciding to commit the company to one path versus another pushes managers to draw some carefully reasoned conclusions about whether the company's present strategic course offers attractive opportunities for growth and profitability or whether changes of one kind or another in the company's strategy and long-term direction are needed.

Developing a Strategic Vision

Top management's views about the company's long-term direction and what product-market-customer business mix seems optimal for the road ahead constitute a **strategic vision** for the company. A strategic vision delineates management's aspirations for the company's future, providing a panoramic view of "where we are going" and a convincing rationale for why this makes good business sense. A strategic vision thus points an organization in a particular direction, charts a strategic path for it to follow, builds commitment to the future course of action, and molds organizational identity. A clearly articulated strategic vision communicates management's aspirations to stakeholders (customers, employees, stockholders, suppliers, etc.) and helps steer the energies of company personnel in a common direction. The vision of Google's cofounders Larry Page and Sergey Brin "to organize the world's information and make it universally accessible and useful" provides a good example. In serving as the company's guiding light, it has captured the imagination of stakeholders and the public at large, served as the basis for crafting the company's strategic actions, and aided internal efforts to mobilize and direct the company's resources.

Well-conceived visions are *distinctive* and *specific* to a particular organization; they avoid generic, feel-good statements like "We will become a global leader and the first choice of customers in every market we serve."[2] Likewise, a strategic vision proclaiming management's quest "to be the most innovative" or "to be recognized as the best company in the industry" offers scant guidance about a company's long-term direction or the kind of company that management is striving to build.

A surprising number of the vision statements found on company websites and in annual reports are vague and unrevealing, saying very little about the company's future direction. Some could apply to almost any company in any industry. Many read like a public relations statement—high-sounding words that someone came up with because it is fashionable for companies to have an official vision statement.[3] An example is Hilton Hotel's vision "to fill the earth with light and the warmth of hospitality," which simply borders on the incredulous. The real purpose of a vision statement is to serve as a management tool for giving the organization a sense of direction.

For a strategic vision to function as a valuable management tool, it must convey what top executives want the business to look like and provide managers at all organizational levels with a reference point in making strategic decisions and preparing the company for the future. It must say something definitive about how the company's leaders intend to position the company beyond where it is today.

TABLE 2.2 Wording a Vision Statement—the Dos and Don'ts

The Dos	The Don'ts
Be graphic. Paint a clear picture of where the company is headed and the market position(s) the company is striving to stake out.	**Don't be vague or incomplete.** Never skimp on specifics about where the company is headed or how the company intends to prepare for the future.
Be forward-looking and directional. Describe the strategic course that will help the company prepare for the future.	**Don't dwell on the present.** A vision is not about what a company once did or does now; it's about "where we are going."
Keep it focused. Focus on providing managers with guidance in making decisions and allocating resources.	**Don't use overly broad language.** Avoid all-inclusive language that gives the company license to pursue any opportunity.
Have some wiggle room. Language that allows some flexibility allows the directional course to be adjusted as market, customer, and technology circumstances change.	**Don't state the vision in bland or uninspiring terms.** The best vision statements have the power to motivate company personnel and inspire shareholder confidence about the company's future.
Be sure the journey is feasible. The path and direction should be within the realm of what the company can accomplish; over time, a company should be able to demonstrate measurable progress in achieving the vision.	**Don't be generic.** A vision statement that could apply to companies in any of several industries (or to any of several companies in the same industry) is not specific enough to provide any guidance.
Indicate why the directional path makes good business sense. The directional path should be in the long-term interests of stakeholders (especially shareholders, employees, and suppliers).	**Don't rely on superlatives.** Visions that claim the company's strategic course is the "best" or "most successful" usually lack specifics about the path the company is taking to get there.
Make it memorable. A well-stated vision is short, easily communicated, and memorable. Ideally, it should be reducible to a few choice lines or a one-phrase slogan.	**Don't run on and on.** A vision statement that is not concise and to the point will tend to lose its audience.

Sources: John P. Kotter, *Leading Change* (Boston: Harvard Business School Press, 1996); Hugh Davidson, *The Committed Enterprise* (Oxford: Butterworth Heinemann, 2002); Michel Robert, *Strategy Pure and Simple II* (New York: McGraw-Hill, 1992).

Table 2.2 provides some dos and don'ts in composing an effectively worded vision statement. Illustration Capsule 2.1 provides a critique of the strategic visions of several prominent companies.

Communicating the Strategic Vision

A strategic vision offers little value to the organization unless it's effectively communicated down the line to lower-level managers and employees. A vision cannot provide direction for middle managers or inspire and energize employees unless everyone in the company is familiar with it and can observe senior management's commitment to the vision. It is particularly important for executives to provide a compelling rationale for a dramatically *new* strategic vision and company direction. When company

Examples of Strategic Visions—How Well Do They Measure Up?

Philip Arno Photography/Shutterstock

Vision Statement	Effective Elements	Shortcomings
Whole Foods Whole Foods Market is a dynamic leader in the quality food business. We are a mission-driven company that aims to set the standards of excellence for food retailers. We are building a business in which high standards permeate all aspects of our company. Quality is a state of mind at Whole Foods Market. Our motto—Whole Foods, Whole People, Whole Planet— emphasizes that our vision reaches far beyond just being a food retailer. Our success in fulfilling our vision is measured by customer satisfaction, team member happiness and excellence, return on capital investment, improvement in the state of the environment and local and larger community support. Our ability to instill a clear sense of interdependence among our various stakeholders (the people who are interested and benefit from the success of our company) is contingent upon our efforts to communicate more often, more openly, and more compassionately. Better communication equals better understanding and more trust.	• Forward-looking • Graphic • Focused • Makes good business sense	• Long • Not memorable
Keurig Dr. Pepper A leading producer and distributor of hot and cold beverages to satisfy every consumer need, anytime and anywhere.	• Easy to communicate • Focused	• Not distinctive • Not forward-looking
Nike NIKE, Inc. fosters a culture of invention. We create products, services and experiences for today's athlete* while solving problems for the next generation. *If you have a body, you are an athlete.	• Forward-looking • Flexible	• Vague • Not focused

Note: Developed with Frances C. Thunder.

Source: Company websites (accessed online February 12, 2016).

personnel don't understand or accept the need for redirecting organizational efforts, they are prone to resist change. Hence, explaining the basis for the new direction, addressing employee concerns head-on, calming fears, lifting spirits, and providing updates and progress reports as events unfold all become part of the task in mobilizing support for the vision and winning commitment to needed actions.

Winning the support of organization members for the vision nearly always requires putting "where we are going and why" in writing, distributing the statement organizationwide, and having top executives personally explain the vision and its rationale to as many people as feasible. Ideally, executives should present their vision for the company in a manner that reaches out and grabs people. An engaging and convincing strategic vision has enormous motivational value—for the same reason that a stonemason is more inspired by the opportunity to build a great cathedral for the ages than a house. Thus, executive ability to paint a convincing and inspiring picture of a company's journey to a future destination is an important element of effective strategic leadership.

Expressing the Essence of the Vision in a Slogan   The task of effectively conveying the vision to company personnel is assisted when management can capture the vision of where to head in a catchy or easily remembered slogan. A number of organizations have summed up their vision in a brief phrase. Instagram's vision is "Capture and share the world's moments," while Charles Schwab's is simply "Helping investors help themselves." Habitat for Humanity's aspirational vision is "A world where everyone has a decent place to live." Even Scotland Yard has a catchy vision, which is to "make London the safest major city in the world." Creating a short slogan to illuminate an organization's direction and using it repeatedly as a reminder of "where we are headed and why" helps rally organization members to maintain their focus and hurdle whatever obstacles lie in the company's path.

Why a Sound, Well-Communicated Strategic Vision Matters   A well-thought-out, forcefully communicated strategic vision pays off in several respects: (1) It crystallizes senior executives' own views about the firm's long-term direction; (2) it reduces the risk of rudderless decision making; (3) it is a tool for winning the support of organization members to help make the vision a reality; (4) it provides a beacon for lower-level managers in setting departmental objectives and crafting departmental strategies that are in sync with the company's overall strategy; and (5) it helps an organization prepare for the future. When top executives are able to demonstrate significant progress in achieving these five benefits, the first step in organizational direction setting has been successfully completed.

Developing a Company Mission Statement

The defining characteristic of a strategic vision is what it says about the company's *future strategic course*—"the direction we are headed and the shape of our business in the future." It is aspirational. In contrast, a **mission statement** describes the enterprise's *present business and purpose*—"who we are, what we do, and why we are here." It is purely descriptive. Ideally, a company mission statement (1) identifies the company's products and/or services, (2) specifies the buyer needs that the company seeks to satisfy and the customer groups or markets that it serves, and (3) gives the company its own identity. The mission statements that one finds in company annual reports or posted on company websites are typically quite brief; some do a better job than others of conveying what the enterprise's current business operations and purpose are all about.

The distinction between a strategic vision and a mission statement is fairly clear-cut: A **strategic vision** portrays a company's aspirations for its *future* ("where we are going"), whereas a company's **mission** describes the scope and purpose of its *present* business ("who we are, what we do, and why we are here").

Consider, for example, the mission statement of FedEx Corporation, which has long been known for its overnight shipping service, but also for pioneering the package tracking system now in general use:

> The FedEx Corporation offers express and fast delivery transportation services, delivering an estimated 3 million packages daily all around the globe. Its services include overnight courier, ground, heavy freight, document copying, and logistics services.

Note that FedEx's mission statement does a good job of conveying "who we are, what we do, and why we are here," but it provides no sense of "where we are headed." This is as it should be, since a company's vision statement is that which speaks to the future.

Another example of a well-stated mission statement with ample specifics about what the organization does is that of St. Jude Children's Research Hospital: "to advance cures, and means of prevention, for pediatric catastrophic diseases through research and treatment. Consistent with the vision of our founder Danny Thomas, no child is denied treatment based on race, religion or a family's ability to pay." Twitter's mission statement, while short, still captures the essence of what the company is about: "To give everyone the power to create and share ideas and information instantly, without barriers." An example of a not-so-revealing mission statement is that of JetBlue: "To inspire humanity—both in the air and on the ground." It says nothing about the company's activities or business makeup and could apply to many companies in many different industries. A person unfamiliar with JetBlue could not even discern from its mission statement that it is an airline, without reading between the lines. Coca-Cola, which markets more than 500 beverage brands in over 200 countries, also has an uninformative mission statement: "to refresh the world; to inspire moments of optimism and happiness; to create value and make a difference." The usefulness of a mission statement that cannot convey the essence of a company's business activities and purpose is unclear.

All too often, companies couch their mission in terms of making a profit, like Dean Foods with its mission "To maximize long-term stockholder value." This, too, is flawed.

> To be well worded, a company mission statement must employ language specific enough to distinguish its business makeup and purpose from those of other enterprises and give the company its own identity.

Profit is more correctly an *objective* and a *result* of what a company does. Moreover, earning a profit is the obvious intent of every commercial enterprise. Companies such as Gap, Inc., Edward Jones, Honda, The Boston Consulting Group, Citigroup, DreamWorks Animation, and Intuit are all striving to earn a profit for shareholders; but plainly the fundamentals of their businesses are substantially different when it comes to "who we are and what we do." It is management's answer to "make a profit doing what and for whom?" that reveals the substance of a company's true mission and business purpose.

Linking the Vision and Mission with Company Values

Companies commonly develop a set of values to guide the actions and behavior of company personnel in conducting the company's business and pursuing its strategic vision and mission. By **values** (or **core values,** as they are often called) we mean certain designated beliefs, traits, and behavioral norms that management has determined should guide the pursuit of its vision and mission. Values relate to such things as fair treatment, honor and integrity, ethical behavior, innovativeness, teamwork, a passion for top-notch quality or superior customer service, social responsibility, and community citizenship.

> **CORE** CONCEPT
>
> A company's **values** are the beliefs, traits, and behavioral norms that company personnel are expected to display in conducting the company's business and pursuing its strategic vision and mission.

Most companies articulate four to eight core values that company personnel are expected to display and that are supposed to be mirrored in how the company conducts its business. Build-A-Bear Workshop, with its cuddly Teddy bears and stuffed animals, credits six core values with creating its highly acclaimed working environment: (1) Reach, (2) Learn, (3) Di-bear-sity (4) Colla-bear-ate, (5) Give, and (6) Cele-bear-ate. Zappos prides itself on its 10 core values, which employees are expected to embody:

1. Deliver WOW Through Service
2. Embrace and Drive Change
3. Create Fun and a Little Weirdness
4. Be Adventurous, Creative, and Open-Minded
5. Pursue Growth and Learning
6. Build Open and Honest Relationships with Communication
7. Build a Positive Team and Family Spirit
8. Do More with Less
9. Be Passionate and Determined
10. Be Humble

Do companies practice what they preach when it comes to their professed values? Sometimes no, sometimes yes—it runs the gamut. At one extreme are companies with window-dressing values; the values are given lip service by top executives but have little discernible impact on either how company personnel behave or how the company operates. Such companies have value statements because they are in vogue and make the company look good. The limitation of these value statements becomes apparent whenever corporate misdeeds come to light. Prime examples include Volkswagen, with its emissions scandal, and Uber, facing multiple allegations of misbehavior and a criminal probe of illegal operations. At the other extreme are companies whose executives are committed to grounding company operations on sound values and principled ways of doing business. Executives at these companies deliberately seek to ingrain the designated core values into the corporate culture—the core values thus become an integral part of the company's DNA and what makes the company tick. At such values-driven companies, executives "walk the talk" and company personnel are held accountable for embodying the stated values in their behavior.

At companies where the stated values are real rather than cosmetic, managers connect values to the pursuit of the strategic vision and mission in one of two ways. In companies with long-standing values that are deeply entrenched in the corporate culture, senior managers are careful to craft a vision, mission, strategy, and set of operating practices that match established values; moreover, they repeatedly emphasize how the value-based behavioral norms contribute to the company's business success. If the company changes to a different vision or strategy, executives make a point of explaining how and why the core values continue to be relevant. Few companies with sincere commitment to established core values ever undertake strategic moves that conflict with ingrained values. In new companies, top management has to consider what values and business conduct should characterize the company and then draft a value statement that is circulated among managers and employees for discussion and possible modification. A final value statement that incorporates the desired behaviors and that connects to the vision and mission is then officially adopted. Some companies combine their vision, mission, and values into a single statement or document, circulate it to all organization members, and in many instances post the vision, mission, and value statement on the company's website. Illustration Capsule 2.2 describes how the success of TOMS Shoes has been largely driven by the nature of its mission, linked to the vision and core values of its founder.

TOMS Shoes was founded in 2006 by Blake Mycoskie after a trip to Argentina where he witnessed many children with no access to shoes in areas of extreme poverty. Mycoskie returned to the United States and founded TOMS Shoes with the purpose of matching every pair of shoes purchased by customers with a new pair of shoes to give to a child in need, a model he called One for One®. In contrast to many companies that begin with a product and then articulate a mission, Mycoskie started with the mission and then built a company around it. Although the company has since expanded their product portfolio, its mission remains essentially the same:

With every product you purchase, TOMS will help a person in need. One for One.®

TOMS's mission is ingrained in their business model. While Mycoskie could have set up a nonprofit organization to address the problem he witnessed, he was certain he didn't want to rely on donors to fund giving to the poor; he wanted to create a business that would fund the giving itself. With the one-for-one model, TOMS built the cost of giving away a pair of shoes into the price of each pair they sold, enabling the company to make a profit while still giving away shoes to the needy.

Much of TOMS's success (and ability to differentiate itself in a competitive marketplace) is attributable to the appeal of its mission and origin story. Mycoskie first got TOMS shoes into a trendy store in LA because he told them the story of why he founded the company, which got picked up by the LA Times and quickly spread. As the company has expanded communication channels, they continue to focus on leading with the story of their mission to ensure that customers know they are doing more than just buying a product.

As TOMS expanded to other products, they stayed true to the one-for-one business model, adapting it

Shutterstock/Teresa Schaeffer

to each new product category. In 2011, the company launched TOMS Eyewear, where every purchase of glasses helps restore sight to an individual. They've since launched TOMS Roasting Co. that helps support access to safe water with every purchase of coffee, TOMS Bags where purchases fund resources for safe birth, and TOMS High Road Backpack Collection where purchases provide training for bullying prevention.

By ingraining the mission in the company's business model, TOMS has been able to truly live up to Mycoskie's aspiration of a mission with a company, funding giving through a for-profit business. TOMS even ensured that the business model will never change; when Mycoskie sold 50 percent of the company to Bain Capital in 2014, part of the transaction protected the one-for-one business model forever. TOMS is a successful example of a company that proves a commitment to core values can spur both revenue growth and giving back.

Note: Developed with Carry S. Resor

Sources: TOMS Shoes website, accessed February 2018, http://www.toms.com/about-toms; Lebowitz, Shana, *Business Insider,* "TOMS Blake Mycoskie Talks Growing a Business While Balancing Profit with Purpose," June 15, 2016, http://www.businessinsider.com/toms-blake-mycoskie-talks-growing-a-business-while-balancing-profit-with-purpose-2016-6; Mycoskie, Blake, *Harvard Business Review,* "The Founder of TOMS on Reimaging the Company's Mission," from January–February 2016 issue, https://hbr.org/2016/01/the-founder-of-toms-on-reimagining-the-companys-mission.

STAGE 2: SETTING OBJECTIVES

The managerial purpose of setting **objectives** is to convert the vision and mission into specific performance targets. Objectives reflect management's aspirations for company performance in light of the industry's prevailing economic and competitive conditions and the company's internal capabilities. Well-stated objectives must be *specific,* as well as *quantifiable* or *measurable.* As Bill Hewlett, cofounder of Hewlett-Packard, shrewdly observed, "You cannot manage what you cannot measure. . . . And what gets measured gets done."[4] Concrete, measurable objectives are managerially valuable for three reasons: (1) They focus organizational attention and align actions throughout the organization, (2) they serve as *yardsticks* for tracking a company's performance and progress, and (3) they motivate employees to expend greater effort and perform at a high level. For company objectives to serve their purpose well, they must also meet three other criteria: they must contain a deadline for achievement and they must be challenging, yet achievable.

Setting Stretch Objectives

The experiences of countless companies teach that one of the best ways to promote outstanding company performance is for managers to set performance targets high enough to *stretch an organization to perform at its full potential and deliver the best possible results.* Challenging company personnel to go all out and deliver "stretch" gains in performance pushes an enterprise to be more inventive, to exhibit more urgency in improving both its financial performance and its business position, and to be more intentional and focused in its actions. Employing stretch goals can help create an exciting work environment and attract the best people. In many cases, stretch objectives spur exceptional performance and help build a firewall against contentment with modest gains in organizational performance.

There is a difference, however, between stretch goals that are clearly reachable with enough effort, and those that are well beyond the organization's current capabilities, regardless of the level of effort. Extreme stretch goals, involving radical expectations, fail more often than not. And failure to meet such goals can kill motivation, erode employee confidence, and damage both worker and company performance. CEO Marissa Mayer's inability to return Yahoo to greatness is a case in point.

Extreme stretch goals can work as envisioned under certain circumstances. High profile success stories at companies such as Southwest Airlines, 3M, SpaceX, and General Electric provide evidence. But research suggests that success of this sort depends upon two conditions being met: (1) the company must have ample resources available, and (2) its recent performance must be strong. Under any other circumstances, managers would be well advised not to pursue overly ambitious stretch goals.[5]

What Kinds of Objectives to Set

Two distinct types of performance targets are required: those relating to financial performance and those relating to strategic performance. **Financial objectives** communicate management's goals for financial performance. **Strategic objectives** are goals concerning a company's marketing standing and competitive position. A company's set of financial and strategic objectives should include both near-term and longer-term performance targets. Short-term (quarterly or annual) objectives focus

● LO 2-2

Explain the importance of setting both strategic and financial objectives.

CORE CONCEPT

Objectives are an organization's performance targets—the specific results management wants to achieve.

Well-chosen **objectives** are:
- specific
- measurable
- time-limited
- challenging
- achievable

CORE CONCEPT

Stretch objectives set performance targets high enough to *stretch* an organization to perform at its full potential and deliver the best possible results. **Extreme stretch goals** are warranted only under certain conditions.

CORE CONCEPT

Financial objectives communicate management's goals for financial performance. **Strategic objectives** lay out target outcomes concerning a company's market standing, competitive position, and future business prospects.

attention on delivering performance improvements in the current period and satisfy shareholder expectations for near-term progress. Longer-term targets (three to five years off) force managers to consider what to do *now* to put the company in position to perform better later. Long-term objectives are critical for achieving optimal long-term performance and stand as a barrier to a nearsighted management philosophy and an undue focus on short-term results. When trade-offs have to be made between achieving long-term objectives and achieving short-term objectives, long-term objectives should take precedence (unless the achievement of one or more short-term performance targets has unique importance). Examples of commonly used financial and strategic objectives are listed in Table 2.3. Illustration Capsule 2.3 provides selected financial and strategic objectives of three prominent companies.

The Need for a Balanced Approach to Objective Setting

The importance of setting and attaining financial objectives is obvious. Without adequate profitability and financial strength, a company's long-term health and ultimate survival are jeopardized. Furthermore, subpar earnings and a weak balance sheet alarm shareholders and creditors and put the jobs of senior executives at risk. In consequence, companies often focus most of their attention on financial outcomes. However, good financial performance, by itself, is not enough. Of equal or greater importance is a company's strategic performance—outcomes that indicate whether a company's market position and competitiveness are deteriorating, holding steady, or improving. *A stronger market standing and greater competitive vitality—especially when accompanied by competitive advantage—is what enables a company to improve its financial performance.*

Moreover, financial performance measures are really *lagging indicators* that reflect the results of past decisions and organizational activities.[6] But a company's past or current financial performance is not a reliable indicator of its future prospects—poor financial performers often turn things around and do better, while good financial

TABLE 2.3   Common Financial and Strategic Objectives

Financial Objectives	Strategic Objectives
• An *x* percent increase in annual revenues	• Winning an *x* percent market share
• Annual increases in after-tax profits *of x* percent	• Achieving lower overall costs than rivals
• Annual increases in earnings per share of *x* percent	• Overtaking key competitors on product performance, quality, or customer service
• Annual dividend increases of *x* percent	• Deriving *x* percent of revenues from the sale of new products introduced within the past five years
• Profit margins of *x* percent	
• An *x* percent return on capital employed (ROCE) or return on shareholders' equity (ROE) investment	• Having broader or deeper technological capabilities than rivals
	• Having a wider product line than rivals
• Increased shareholder value in the form of an upward-trending stock price	• Having a better-known or more powerful brand name than rivals
• Bond and credit ratings of *x*	• Having stronger national or global sales and distribution capabilities than rivals
• Internal cash flows of *x* dollars to fund new capital investment	• Consistently getting new or improved products to market ahead of rivals

JETBLUE

Produce above average industry margins by offering a quality product at a competitive price; generate revenues of over $6.6 billion, up 3.4 percent year over year; earn a net income of $759 million, an annual increase of 12.0 percent; further develop fare options, a co-branded credit card, and the Mint franchise; commit to achieving total cost savings of $250 to $300 million by 2020; kickoff multi-year cabin restyling program; convert all core A321 aircraft from 190 to 200 seats; target growth in key cities like Boston, plan to grow 150 flights a day to 200 over the coming years; grow toward becoming the carrier of choice in South Florida; organically grow west coast presence by expanding Mint offering to more transcontinental routes; optimize fare mix to increase overall average fare.

LULULEMON ATHLETICA, INC.

Optimize and strategically grow square footage in North America; explore new concepts such as stores that are tailored to each community; build a robust digital ecosystem with key investments in customer relationship management, analytics, and capabilities to elevate guest experience across all touch points; continue to expand the brand globally through international expansion, open 11 new stores in Asia and Europe, which include the first stores in China, South Korea, and Switzerland—operating a total of 50+ stores across nine countries outside of North America; increase revenue $4 billion by 2020; increase total comparable sales, which includes comparable store sales and direct to consumer, by 6 percent increase gross profit as a percentage of net revenue, or gross margin, by 51.2 percent; increase income from operations for fiscal 2016 by 14 percent.

Eric Broder Van Dyke/Shutterstock

GENERAL MILLS

Generate low single-digit organic net sales growth and high single-digit growth in earnings per share. Deliver double-digit returns to shareholders over the long term. To drive future growth, focus on Consumer First strategy to gain a deep understanding of consumer needs and respond quickly to give them what they want; more specifically: (1) grow cereal globally with a strong line-up of new products, including new flavors of iconic Cheerios, (2) innovate in fast growing segments of the yogurt category to improve performance and expand the yogurt platform into new cities in China; (3) expand distribution and advertising for high performing brands, such as Häagen-Dazs and Old El Paso; (4) build a more agile organization by streamlining support functions, allowing for more fluid use of resources and idea sharing around the world; enhancing e-commerce know-how to capture more growth in this emerging channel; and investing in strategic revenue management tools to optimize promotions, prices and mix of products to drive sales growth.

Note: Developed with Kathleen T. Durante

Sources: Information posted on company websites.

---

performers can fall upon hard times. The best and most reliable *leading indicators* of a company's future financial performance and business prospects are strategic outcomes that indicate whether the company's competitiveness and market position are stronger or weaker. The accomplishment of strategic objectives signals that the company is well positioned to sustain or improve its performance. For instance, if a company is achieving ambitious strategic objectives such that its competitive strength and market position are on the rise, then there's reason to expect that its *future* financial performance will be better than its current or past performance. If a company is losing ground to competitors and its market position is slipping—outcomes that reflect weak strategic performance—then its ability to maintain its present profitability is highly suspect.

Consequently, it is important to use a performance measurement system that strikes a *balance* between financial and strategic objectives.[7] The most widely used framework of this sort is known as the **Balanced Scorecard**.[8] This is a method for linking financial performance objectives to specific strategic objectives that derive from a company's business model. It maps out the key objectives of a company, with performance indicators, along four dimensions:

- Financial: listing financial objectives
- Customer: objectives relating to customers and the market
- Internal process: objectives relating to productivity and quality
- Organizational: objectives concerning human capital, culture, infrastructure, and innovation

Done well, this can provide a company's employees with clear guidelines about how their jobs are linked to the overall objectives of the organization, so they can contribute most productively and collaboratively to the achievement of these goals. The balanced scorecard methodology continues to be ranked as one of the most popular management tools.[9] Over 50 percent of companies in the United States, Europe, and Asia report using a balanced scorecard approach to measuring strategic and financial performance.[10] Organizations that have adopted the balanced scorecard approach include 7-Eleven, Ann Taylor Stores, Allianz Italy, Wells Fargo Bank, Ford Motor Company, Verizon, ExxonMobil, Pfizer, DuPont, Royal Canadian Mounted Police, U.S. Army Medical Command, and over 30 colleges and universities.[11] Despite its popularity, the balanced scorecard is not without limitations. Importantly, it may not capture some of the most important priorities of a particular organization, such as resource acquisition or partnering with other organizations. Further, as with most strategy tools, its value depends on implementation and follow through as much as on substance.

Setting Objectives for Every Organizational Level

Objective setting should not stop with top management's establishing companywide performance targets. Company objectives need to be broken down into performance targets for each of the organization's separate businesses, product lines, functional departments, and individual work units. Employees within various functional areas and operating levels will be guided much better by specific objectives relating directly to their departmental activities than broad organizational-level goals. Objective setting is thus a *top-down process* that must extend to the lowest organizational levels. This means that each organizational unit must take care to set performance targets that support—rather than conflict with or negate—the achievement of companywide strategic and financial objectives.

The ideal situation is a team effort in which each organizational unit strives to produce results that contribute to the achievement of the company's performance targets and strategic vision. Such consistency signals that organizational units know their strategic role and are on board in helping the company move down the chosen strategic path and produce the desired results.

STAGE 3: CRAFTING A STRATEGY

As indicated in Chapter 1, the task of stitching a strategy together entails addressing a series of "hows": *how* to attract and please customers, *how* to compete against rivals, *how* to position the company in the marketplace, *how* to respond to changing market conditions, *how* to capitalize on attractive opportunities to grow the business, and *how* to achieve strategic and financial objectives. Choosing among the alternatives available in a way that coheres into a viable business model requires an understanding of the basic principles of strategic management. Fast-changing business environments demand astute entrepreneurship searching for opportunities to do new things or to do existing things in new or better ways.

In choosing among opportunities and addressing the hows of strategy, strategists must embrace the risks of uncertainty and the discomfort that naturally accompanies such risks. Bold strategies involve making difficult choices and placing bets on the future. Good strategic planning is not about eliminating risks, but increasing the odds of success.

This places a premium on astute entrepreneurship searching for opportunities to do new things or to do existing things in new or better ways.[12] The faster a company's business environment is changing, the more critical it becomes for its managers to be good entrepreneurs in diagnosing the direction and force of the changes underway and in responding with timely adjustments in strategy. Strategy makers have to pay attention to early warnings of future change and be willing to experiment with dare-to-be-different ways to establish a market position in that future. When obstacles appear unexpectedly in a company's path, it is up to management to adapt rapidly and innovatively. *Masterful strategies come from doing things differently from competitors where it counts—out-innovating them, being more efficient, being more imaginative, adapting faster—rather than running with the herd.* Good strategy making is therefore inseparable from good business entrepreneurship. One cannot exist without the other.

● **LO 2-3**

Explain why the strategic initiatives taken at various organizational levels must be tightly coordinated.

Strategy Making Involves Managers at All Organizational Levels

A company's senior executives obviously have lead strategy-making roles and responsibilities. The chief executive officer (CEO), as captain of the ship, carries the mantles of chief direction setter, chief objective setter, chief strategy maker, and chief strategy implementer for the total enterprise. Ultimate responsibility for *leading* the strategy-making, strategy-executing process rests with the CEO. And the CEO is always fully accountable for the results the strategy produces, whether good or bad. In some enterprises, the CEO or owner functions as chief architect of the strategy, personally deciding what the key elements of the company's strategy will be, although he or she may seek the advice of key subordinates and board members. A CEO-centered approach to strategy development is characteristic of small owner-managed companies and some large corporations that were founded by the present CEO or that have a CEO with strong strategic leadership skills. Elon Musk at Tesla Motors and SpaceX, Mark Zuckerberg at Facebook, Jeff Bezos at Amazon, Jack Ma of Alibaba, Warren Buffett at Berkshire Hathaway, and Marillyn Hewson at Lockheed Martin are examples of high-profile corporate CEOs who have wielded a heavy hand in shaping their company's strategy.

In most corporations, however, strategy is the product of more than just the CEO's handiwork. Typically, other senior executives—business unit heads, the chief financial officer, and vice presidents for production, marketing, and other functional departments—have influential strategy-making roles and help fashion the chief strategy components. Normally, a company's chief financial officer is in charge of devising and implementing an appropriate financial strategy; the production vice president takes the lead in developing the company's production strategy; the marketing vice president orchestrates sales and marketing strategy; a brand manager is in charge of the strategy for a particular brand in the company's product lineup; and so on. Moreover, the strategy-making efforts of top managers are complemented by advice and counsel from the company's board of directors; normally, all major strategic decisions are submitted to the board of directors for review, discussion, perhaps modification, and official approval.

> In most companies, crafting and executing strategy is a *collaborative team effort* in which every manager has a role for the area he or she heads; it is rarely something that only high-level managers do.

But strategy making is by no means solely a *top* management function, the exclusive province of owner-entrepreneurs, CEOs, high-ranking executives, and board members. The more a company's operations cut across different products, industries, and geographic areas, the more that headquarters executives have little option but to delegate considerable strategy-making authority to down-the-line managers in charge of particular subsidiaries, divisions, product lines, geographic sales offices, distribution centers, and plants. On-the-scene managers who oversee specific operating units can be reliably counted on to have more detailed command of the strategic issues for the particular operating unit under their supervision since they have more intimate knowledge of the prevailing market and competitive conditions, customer requirements and expectations, and all the other relevant aspects affecting the several strategic options available. Managers with day-to-day familiarity of, and authority over, a specific operating unit thus have a big edge over headquarters executives in making wise strategic choices for their unit. The result is that, in most of today's companies, crafting and executing strategy is a *collaborative team effort* in which *every company manager plays a strategy-making role*—ranging from minor to major—for the area he or she heads.

> The larger and more diverse the operations of an enterprise, the more points of strategic initiative it has and the more levels of management that have a significant strategy-making role.

Take, for example, a company like General Electric, a $213 billion global corporation with nearly 300,000 employees, operations in over 180 countries, and businesses that include jet engines, lighting, power generation, medical imaging and diagnostic equipment, locomotives, industrial automation, aviation services, and financial services. While top-level headquarters executives may well be personally involved in shaping GE's *overall* strategy and fashioning *important* strategic moves, they simply cannot know enough about the situation in every GE organizational unit to direct every strategic move made in GE's worldwide organization. Rather, it takes involvement on the part of GE's whole management team—top executives, business group heads, the heads of specific business units and product categories, and key managers in plants, sales offices, and distribution centers—to craft the thousands of strategic initiatives that end up composing the whole of GE's strategy.

A Company's Strategy-Making Hierarchy

In diversified companies like GE, where multiple and sometimes strikingly different businesses have to be managed, crafting a full-fledged strategy involves four distinct types of strategic actions and initiatives. Each of these involves different facets of the company's overall strategy and calls for the participation of different types of managers, as shown in Figure 2.2.

FIGURE 2.2   A Company's Strategy-Making Hierarchy

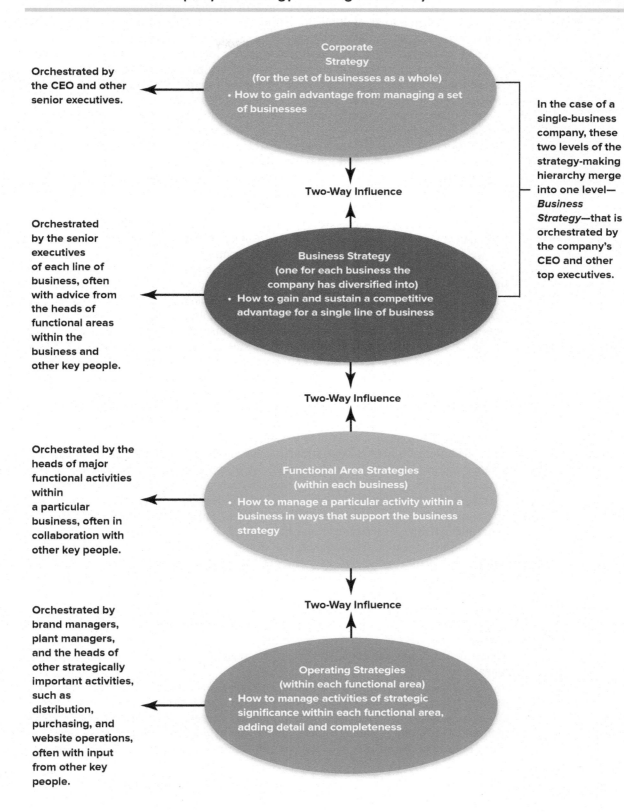

Orchestrated by the CEO and other senior executives.

Corporate Strategy
(for the set of businesses as a whole)
• How to gain advantage from managing a set of businesses

In the case of a single-business company, these two levels of the strategy-making hierarchy merge into one level—*Business Strategy*—that is orchestrated by the company's CEO and other top executives.

Two-Way Influence

Orchestrated by the senior executives of each line of business, often with advice from the heads of functional areas within the business and other key people.

Business Strategy
(one for each business the company has diversified into)
• How to gain and sustain a competitive advantage for a single line of business

Two-Way Influence

Orchestrated by the heads of major functional activities within a particular business, often in collaboration with other key people.

Functional Area Strategies
(within each business)
• How to manage a particular activity within a business in ways that support the business strategy

Two-Way Influence

Orchestrated by brand managers, plant managers, and the heads of other strategically important activities, such as distribution, purchasing, and website operations, often with input from other key people.

Operating Strategies
(within each functional area)
• How to manage activities of strategic significance within each functional area, adding detail and completeness

As shown in Figure 2.2, **corporate strategy** is orchestrated by the CEO and other senior executives and establishes an overall strategy for managing a *set of businesses* in a diversified, multibusiness company. Corporate strategy concerns how to improve the combined performance of the set of businesses the company has diversified into by capturing cross-business synergies and turning them into competitive advantage. It addresses the questions of what businesses to hold or divest, which new markets to enter, and how to best enter new markets (by acquisition, creation of a strategic alliance, or through internal development, for example). Corporate strategy and business diversification are the subjects of Chapter 8, in which they are discussed in detail.

Business strategy is concerned with strengthening the market position, building competitive advantage, and improving the performance of a single line of business. Business strategy is primarily the responsibility of business unit heads, although corporate-level executives may well exert strong influence; in diversified companies it is not unusual for corporate officers to insist that business-level objectives and strategy conform to corporate-level objectives and strategy themes. The business head has at least two other strategy-related roles: (1) seeing that lower-level strategies are well conceived, consistent, and adequately matched to the overall business strategy; and (2) keeping corporate-level officers (and sometimes the board of directors) informed of emerging strategic issues.

Functional-area strategies concern the approaches employed in managing particular functions within a business—like research and development (R&D), production, procurement of inputs, sales and marketing, distribution, customer service, and finance. A company's marketing strategy, for example, represents the managerial game plan for running the sales and marketing part of the business. A company's product development strategy represents the game plan for keeping the company's product lineup in tune with what buyers are looking for.

Functional strategies flesh out the details of a company's business strategy. Lead responsibility for functional strategies within a business is normally delegated to the heads of the respective functions, with the general manager of the business having final approval. Since the different functional-level strategies must be compatible with the overall business strategy and with one another to have beneficial impact, there are times when the general business manager exerts strong influence on the content of the functional strategies.

Operating strategies concern the relatively narrow approaches for managing key operating units (e.g., plants, distribution centers, purchasing centers) and specific operating activities with strategic significance (e.g., quality control, materials purchasing, brand management, Internet sales). A plant manager needs a strategy for accomplishing the plant's objectives, carrying out the plant's part of the company's overall manufacturing game plan, and dealing with any strategy-related problems that exist at the plant. A company's advertising manager needs a strategy for getting maximum audience exposure and sales impact from the ad budget. Operating strategies, while of limited scope, add further detail and completeness to functional strategies and to the overall business strategy. Lead responsibility for operating strategies is usually delegated to frontline managers, subject to the review and approval of higher-ranking managers.

Even though operating strategy is at the bottom of the strategy-making hierarchy, its importance should not be downplayed. A major plant that fails in its strategy to achieve production volume, unit cost, and quality targets can damage the company's reputation for quality products and undercut the achievement of company sales and profit objectives. Frontline managers are thus an important part of an organization's strategy-making team. One cannot reliably judge the strategic importance of a given action simply by the strategy level or location within the managerial hierarchy where it is initiated.

> A company's strategy is at full power only when its many pieces are united.

In single-business companies, the uppermost level of the strategy-making hierarchy is the business strategy, so a single-business company has three levels of strategy: business strategy, functional-area strategies, and operating strategies. Proprietorships, partnerships, and owner-managed enterprises may have only one or two strategy-making levels since it takes only a few key people to craft and oversee the firm's strategy. The larger and more diverse the operations of an enterprise, the more points of strategic initiative it has and the more levels of management that have a significant strategy-making role.

Uniting the Strategy-Making Hierarchy

The components of a company's strategy up and down the strategy hierarchy should be cohesive and mutually reinforcing, fitting together like a jigsaw puzzle. *Anything less than a unified collection of strategies weakens the overall strategy and is likely to impair company performance.*[13] It is the responsibility of top executives to achieve this unity by clearly communicating the company's vision, mission, objectives, and major strategy components to down-the-line managers and key personnel. Midlevel and frontline managers cannot craft unified strategic moves without first understanding the company's long-term direction and knowing the major components of the corporate and/or business strategies that their strategy-making efforts are supposed to support and enhance. Thus, as a general rule, strategy making must start at the top of the organization, then proceed downward from the corporate level to the business level, and then from the business level to the associated functional and operating levels. Once strategies up and down the hierarchy have been created, lower-level strategies must be scrutinized for consistency with and support of higher-level strategies. Any strategy conflicts must be addressed and resolved, either by modifying the lower-level strategies with conflicting elements or by adapting the higher-level strategy to accommodate what may be more appealing strategy ideas and initiatives bubbling up from below.

A Strategic Vision + Mission + Objectives + Strategy = A Strategic Plan

Developing a strategic vision and mission, setting objectives, and crafting a strategy are basic direction-setting tasks. They map out where a company is headed, delineate its strategic and financial targets, articulate the basic business model, and outline the competitive moves and operating approaches to be used in achieving the desired business results. Together, these elements constitute a **strategic plan** for coping with industry conditions, competing against rivals, meeting objectives, and making progress along the chosen strategic course.[14] Typically, a strategic plan includes a commitment to allocate resources to carrying out the plan and specifies a time period for achieving goals.

> **CORE** CONCEPT
>
> A company's **strategic plan** lays out its direction, business model, competitive strategy, and performance targets for some specified period of time.

In companies that do regular strategy reviews and develop explicit strategic plans, the strategic plan usually ends up as a written document that is circulated to most managers. Near-term performance targets are the part of the strategic plan most often communicated to employees more generally and spelled out explicitly. A number of companies summarize key elements of their strategic plans in the company's annual report to shareholders, in postings on their websites, or in statements provided to the business media; others, perhaps for reasons of competitive sensitivity, make only vague, general statements about their strategic plans.[15] In small, privately owned companies it is rare for strategic plans to exist in written form. Small-company strategic plans tend to reside in the thinking and directives of owner-executives; aspects of the plan are revealed in conversations with company personnel about where to head, what to accomplish, and how to proceed.

STAGE 4: EXECUTING THE STRATEGY

LO 2-4

Recognize what a company must do to achieve operating excellence and to execute its strategy proficiently.

Managing the implementation of a strategy is easily the most demanding and time-consuming part of the strategic management process. Converting strategic plans into actions and results tests a manager's ability to direct organizational change, motivate company personnel, build and strengthen competitive capabilities, create and nurture a strategy-supportive work climate, and meet or beat performance targets. Initiatives to put the strategy in place and execute it proficiently must be launched and managed on many organizational fronts.

Management's action agenda for executing the chosen strategy emerges from assessing what the company will have to do to achieve the financial and strategic performance targets. Each company manager has to think through the answer to the question "What needs to be done in my area to execute my piece of the strategic plan, and what actions should I take to get the process under way?" How much internal change is needed depends on how much of the strategy is new, how far internal practices and competencies deviate from what the strategy requires, and how well the present work culture supports good strategy execution. Depending on the amount of internal change involved, full implementation and proficient execution of the company strategy (or important new pieces thereof) can take several months to several years.

In most situations, managing the strategy execution process includes the following principal aspects:

- Creating a strategy-supporting structure.
- Staffing the organization to obtain needed skills and expertise.
- Developing and strengthening strategy-supporting resources and capabilities.
- Allocating ample resources to the activities critical to strategic success.
- Ensuring that policies and procedures facilitate effective strategy execution.
- Organizing the work effort along the lines of best practice.
- Installing information and operating systems that enable company personnel to perform essential activities.
- Motivating people and tying rewards directly to the achievement of performance objectives.
- Creating a company culture conducive to successful strategy execution.
- Exerting the internal leadership needed to propel implementation forward.

Good strategy execution requires diligent pursuit of operating excellence. It is a job for a company's whole management team. Success hinges on the skills and cooperation of operating managers who can push for needed changes in their organizational units and consistently deliver good results. Management's handling of the strategy implementation process can be considered successful if things go smoothly enough that the company meets or beats its strategic and financial performance targets and shows good progress in achieving management's strategic vision. In Chapters 10, 11, and 12, we discuss the various aspects of the strategy implementation process more fully.

STAGE 5: EVALUATING PERFORMANCE AND INITIATING CORRECTIVE ADJUSTMENTS

The fifth component of the strategy management process—monitoring new external developments, evaluating the company's progress, and making corrective adjustments—is the trigger point for deciding whether to continue or change the company's vision and mission, objectives, strategy, business model and/or strategy execution methods.[16] As long as the company's strategy continues to pass the three tests of a winning strategy discussed in Chapter 1 (good fit, competitive advantage, strong performance), company executives may decide to stay the course. Simply fine-tuning the strategic plan and continuing with efforts to improve strategy execution are sufficient.

But whenever a company encounters disruptive changes in its environment, questions need to be raised about the appropriateness of its direction and strategy. If a company experiences a downturn in its market position or persistent shortfalls in performance, then company managers are obligated to ferret out the causes—do they relate to poor strategy, poor strategy execution, or both?—and take timely corrective action. A company's direction, objectives, business model, and strategy have to be revisited anytime external or internal conditions warrant.

Likewise, managers are obligated to assess which of the company's operating methods and approaches to strategy execution merit continuation and which need improvement. Proficient strategy execution is always the product of much organizational learning. It is achieved unevenly—coming quickly in some areas and proving troublesome in others. Consequently, top-notch strategy execution entails vigilantly searching for ways to improve and then making corrective adjustments whenever and wherever it is useful to do so.

> A company's vision, mission, objectives, strategy, and approach to strategy execution are never final; reviewing whether and when to make revisions is an ongoing process.

CORPORATE GOVERNANCE: THE ROLE OF THE BOARD OF DIRECTORS IN THE STRATEGY-CRAFTING, STRATEGY-EXECUTING PROCESS

Although senior managers have the *lead responsibility* for crafting and executing a company's strategy, it is the duty of a company's board of directors to exercise strong oversight and see that management performs the various tasks involved in each of the five stages of the strategy-making, strategy-executing process in a manner that best serves the interests of shareholders and other stakeholders, including the company's customers, employees, and the communities in which the company operates.[17] A company's board of directors has four important obligations to fulfill:

● **LO 2-5**

Comprehend the role and responsibility of a company's board of directors in overseeing the strategic management process.

1. *Oversee the company's financial accounting and financial reporting practices.* While top executives, particularly the company's CEO and CFO (chief financial

officer), are primarily responsible for seeing that the company's financial statements fairly and accurately report the results of the company's operations, board members have a *legal obligation* to warrant the accuracy of the company's financial reports and protect shareholders. It is their job to ensure that generally accepted accounting principles (GAAP) are used properly in preparing the company's financial statements and that proper financial controls are in place to prevent fraud and misuse of funds. Virtually all boards of directors have an audit committee, always composed entirely of *outside directors* (*inside directors* hold management positions in the company and either directly or indirectly report to the CEO). The members of the audit committee have the lead responsibility for overseeing the decisions of the company's financial officers and consulting with both internal and external auditors to ensure accurate financial reporting and adequate financial controls.

2. *Critically appraise the company's direction, strategy, and business approaches.* Board members are also expected to guide management in choosing a strategic direction and to make independent judgments about the validity and wisdom of management's proposed strategic actions. This aspect of their duties takes on heightened importance when the company's strategy is failing or is plagued with faulty execution, and certainly when there is a precipitous collapse in profitability. But under more normal circumstances, many boards have found that meeting agendas become consumed by compliance matters with little time left to discuss matters of strategic importance. The board of directors and management at Philips Electronics hold annual two- to three-day retreats devoted exclusively to evaluating the company's long-term direction and various strategic proposals. The company's exit from the semiconductor business and its increased focus on medical technology and home health care resulted from management-board discussions during such retreats.[18]

3. *Evaluate the caliber of senior executives' strategic leadership skills.* The board is always responsible for determining whether the current CEO is doing a good job of strategic leadership (as a basis for awarding salary increases and bonuses and deciding on retention or removal).[19] Boards must also exercise due diligence in evaluating the strategic leadership skills of other senior executives in line to succeed the CEO. When the incumbent CEO steps down or leaves for a position elsewhere, the board must elect a successor, either going with an insider or deciding that an outsider is needed to perhaps radically change the company's strategic course. Often, the outside directors on a board visit company facilities and talk with company personnel personally to evaluate whether the strategy is on track, how well the strategy is being executed, and how well issues and problems are being addressed by various managers. For example, independent board members at GE visit operating executives at each major business unit once a year to assess the company's talent pool and stay abreast of emerging strategic and operating issues affecting the company's divisions. Home Depot board members visit a store once per quarter to determine the health of the company's operations.[20]

4. *Institute a compensation plan for top executives that rewards them for actions and results that serve stakeholder interests, and most especially those of shareholders.* A basic principle of corporate governance is that the owners of a corporation (the shareholders) delegate operating authority and managerial control to top management in return for compensation. In their role as *agents* of shareholders, top executives have a clear and unequivocal duty to make decisions and operate the

company in accord with shareholder interests. (This does not mean disregarding the interests of other stakeholders—employees, suppliers, the communities in which the company operates, and society at large.) Most boards of directors have a compensation committee, composed entirely of directors from *outside* the company, to develop a salary and incentive compensation plan that rewards senior executives for boosting the company's *long-term* performance on behalf of shareholders. The compensation committee's recommendations are presented to the full board for approval. But during the past 10 years, many boards of directors have done a poor job of ensuring that executive salary increases, bonuses, and stock option awards are tied tightly to performance measures that are truly in the long-term interests of shareholders. Rather, compensation packages at many companies have increasingly rewarded executives for short-term performance improvements—most notably, for achieving quarterly and annual earnings targets and boosting the stock price by specified percentages. This has had the perverse effect of causing company managers to become preoccupied with actions to improve a company's near-term performance, often motivating them to take unwise business risks to boost short-term earnings by amounts sufficient to qualify for multimillion-dollar compensation packages (that many see as obscenely large). The focus on short-term performance has proved damaging to long-term company performance and shareholder interests— witness the huge loss of shareholder wealth that occurred at many financial institutions during the banking crisis of 2008–2009 because of executive risk-taking in subprime loans, credit default swaps, and collateralized mortgage securities. As a consequence, the need to overhaul and reform executive compensation has become a hot topic in both public circles and corporate boardrooms. Illustration Capsule 2.4 discusses how weak governance at Volkswagen contributed to the 2015 emissions cheating scandal, which cost the company billions of dollars and the trust of its stakeholders.

> **CORE CONCEPT**
>
> A company's **stakeholders** include its stockholders, employees, suppliers, the communities in which the company operates, and society at large.

Every corporation should have a strong independent board of directors that (1) is well informed about the company's performance, (2) guides and judges the CEO and other top executives, (3) has the courage to curb management actions the board believes are inappropriate or unduly risky, (4) certifies to shareholders that the CEO is doing what the board expects, (5) provides insight and advice to management, and (6) is intensely involved in debating the pros and cons of key decisions and actions.[21] Boards of directors that lack the backbone to challenge a strong-willed or "imperial" CEO or that rubber-stamp almost anything the CEO recommends without probing inquiry and debate abdicate their fiduciary duty to represent and protect shareholder interests.

> Effective corporate governance requires the board of directors to oversee the company's strategic direction, evaluate its senior executives, handle executive compensation, and oversee financial reporting practices.

In 2015, Volkswagen admitted to installing "defeat devices" on at least 11 million vehicles with diesel engines. These devices enabled the cars to pass emission tests, even though the engines actually emitted pollutants up to 40 times above what is allowed in the United States. Current estimates are that it will cost the company at least €7 billion to cover the cost of repairs and lawsuits. Although management must have been involved in approving the use of cheating devices, the Volkswagen supervisory board has been unwilling to accept any responsibility. Some board members even questioned whether it was the board's responsibility to be aware of such problems, stating "matters of technical expertise were not for us" and "the scandal had nothing, not one iota, to do with the advisory board." Yet governing boards do have a responsibility to be well informed, to provide oversight, and to become involved in key decisions and actions. So what caused this corporate governance failure? Why is this the third time in the past 20 years that Volkswagen has been embroiled in scandal?

The key feature of Volkswagen's board that appears to have led to these issues is a lack of independent directors. However, before explaining this in more detail it is important to understand the German governance model. German corporations operate two-tier governance structures, with a management board, and a separate supervisory board that does not contain any current executives. In addition, German law requires large companies to have at least 50 percent supervisory board representation from workers. This structure is meant to provide more oversight by independent board members and greater involvement by a wider set of stakeholders.

In Volkswagen's case, these objectives have been effectively circumvented. Although Volkswagen's supervisory board does not include any current management, the chairmanship appears to be a revolving door of former senior executives. Ferdinand Piëch, the chair during the scandal, was CEO for 9 years prior to becoming

Vytautas Kielaitis/Shutterstock

chair in 2002. Martin Winterkorn, the recently ousted CEO, was expected to become supervisory board chair prior to the scandal. The company continues to elevate management to the supervisory board even though they have presided over past scandals. Hans Dieter Poetsch, the newly appointed chair, was part of the management team that did not inform the supervisory board of the EPA investigation for two weeks.

VW also has a unique ownership structure where a single family, Porsche, controls more than 50 percent of voting shares. Piëch, a family member and chair until 2015, forced out CEOs and installed unqualified family members on the board, such as his former nanny and current wife. He also pushed out independent-minded board members, such as Gerhard Cromme, author of Germany's corporate governance code. The company has lost numerous independent directors over the past 10 years, leaving it with only one non-shareholder, non-labor representative. Although Piëch has now been removed, it is unclear that Volkswagen's board has solved the underlying problem. Shareholders have seen billions of dollars wiped away and the Volkswagen brand tarnished. As long as the board continues to lack independent directors, change will likely be slow.

Note: Developed with Jacob M. Crandall.

Sources: "Piëch under Fire," *The Economist*, December 8, 2005; Chris Bryant and Richard Milne, "Boardroom Politics at Heart of VW Scandal," *Financial Times*, October 4, 2015; Andreas Cremer and Jan Schwartz, "Volkswagen Mired in Crisis as Board Members Criticize Piech," Reuters, April 24, 2015; Richard Milne, "Volkswagen: System Failure," *Financial Times*, November 4, 2015.

KEY POINTS

The strategic management process consists of five interrelated and integrated stages:

1. *Developing a strategic vision* of the company's future, a *mission statement* that defines the company's current purpose, and a set of *core values* to guide the pursuit of the vision and mission. This stage of strategy making provides direction for the company, motivates and inspires company personnel, aligns and guides actions throughout the organization, and communicates to stakeholders management's aspirations for the company's future.

2. *Setting objectives* to convert the vision and mission into performance targets that can be used as yardsticks for measuring the company's performance. Objectives need to spell out *how much* of *what kind* of performance *by when.* Two broad types of objectives are required: *financial objectives* and *strategic objectives.* A *balanced scorecard* approach for measuring company performance entails setting both financial objectives and strategic objectives. *Stretch objectives* can spur exceptional performance and help build a firewall against complacency and mediocre performance. Extreme stretch objectives, however, are only warranted in limited circumstances.

3. *Crafting a strategy* to achieve the objectives and move the company along the strategic course that management has charted. A single business enterprise has three levels of strategy—business strategy for the company as a whole, functional-area strategies (e.g., marketing, R&D, logistics), and operating strategies (for key operating units, such as manufacturing plants). In diversified, multibusiness companies, the strategy-making task involves four distinct types or levels of strategy: corporate strategy for the company as a whole, business strategy (one for each business the company has diversified into), functional-area strategies within each business, and operating strategies. Thus, strategy making is an inclusive collaborative activity involving not only senior company executives but also the heads of major business divisions, functional-area managers, and operating managers on the frontlines.

4. *Executing the chosen strategy* and converting the strategic plan into action. Management's agenda for executing the chosen strategy emerges from assessing what the company will have to do to achieve the targeted financial and strategic performance. Management's handling of the strategy implementation process can be considered successful if things go smoothly enough that the company meets or beats its strategic and financial performance targets and shows good progress in achieving management's strategic vision.

5. *Monitoring developments, evaluating performance, and initiating corrective adjustments* in light of actual experience, changing conditions, new ideas, and new opportunities. This stage of the strategy management process is the trigger point for deciding whether to continue or change the company's vision and mission, objectives, business model strategy, and/or strategy execution methods.

The sum of a company's strategic vision, mission, objectives, and strategy constitutes a *strategic plan* for coping with industry conditions, outcompeting rivals, meeting objectives, and making progress toward aspirational goals.

Boards of directors have a duty to shareholders as well as other stakeholders to play a vigilant role in overseeing management's handling of a company's strategy-making, strategy-executing process. This entails four important obligations: (1) Ensure that the company issues accurate financial reports and has adequate financial controls; (2) critically appraise the company's direction, strategy, and strategy execution; (3) evaluate the caliber of senior executives' strategic leadership skills; and (4) institute a compensation plan for top executives that rewards them for actions and results that serve stakeholder interests, most especially those of shareholders.

ASSURANCE OF LEARNING EXERCISES

LO 2-1

1. Using the information in Table 2.2, critique the adequacy and merit of the following vision statements, listing effective elements and shortcomings. Rank the vision statements from best to worst once you complete your evaluation.

Vision Statement	Effective Elements	Shortcomings
American Express • We work hard every day to make American Express the world's most respected service brand.		
Hilton Hotels Corporation Our vision is to be the first choice of the world's travelers. Hilton intends to build on the rich heritage and strength of our brands by: • Consistently delighting our customers • Investing in our team members • Delivering innovative products and services • Continuously improving performance • Increasing shareholder value • Creating a culture of pride • Strengthening the loyalty of our constituents		
MasterCard • A world beyond cash.		
BASF We are "The Chemical Company" successfully operating in all major markets. • Our customers view BASF as their partner of choice. • Our innovative products, intelligent solutions and services make us the most competent worldwide supplier in the chemical industry. • We generate a high return on assets. • We strive for sustainable development. • We welcome change as an opportunity. • We, the employees of BASF, together ensure our success.		

Sources: Company websites and annual reports.

2. Go to the company investor relations websites for Starbucks (**investor.starbucks.com**), Pfizer (**www.pfizer.com/investors**), and Salesforce (**investor.salesforce.com**) to find examples of strategic and financial objectives. List four objectives for each company, and indicate which of these are strategic and which are financial.

LO 2-2

3. Go to the investor relations website for Walmart (**investors.walmartstores.com**) and review past presentations Walmart has made during various investor conferences by clicking on the Events option in the navigation bar. Prepare a one- to two-page report that outlines what Walmart has said to investors about its approach to strategy execution. Specifically, what has management discussed concerning staffing, resource allocation, policies and procedures, information and operating systems, continuous improvement, rewards and incentives, corporate culture, and internal leadership at the company?

LO 2-4

4. Based on the information provided in Illustration Capsule 2.4, describe the ways in which Volkswagen did not fulfill the requirements of effective corporate governance. In what ways did the board of directors sidestep its obligations to protect shareholder interests? How could Volkswagen better select its board of directors to avoid mistakes such as the emissions scandal in 2015?

LO 2-5

EXERCISES FOR SIMULATION PARTICIPANTS

1. Which of the five stages of the strategy formulation, strategy execution process apply to your company in the simulation?

LO 2-5

2. Meet with your co-managers and prepare a strategic vision statement for your company. It should be at least one sentence long and no longer than a brief paragraph. When you are finished, check to see if your vision statement meets the conditions for an effectively worded strategic vision set forth in Table 2.2. If not, then revise it accordingly. What would be a good slogan that captures the essence of your strategic vision and that could be used to help communicate the vision to company personnel, shareholders, and other stakeholders?

LO 2-1

3. What are your company's financial objectives? What are your company's strategic objectives?

LO 2-2

4. What are the three to four key elements of your company's strategy?

LO 2-3

5. The strategy execution process for your company in the business simulation includes which principle aspects?

LO 2-4

ENDNOTES

[1] Gordon Shaw, Robert Brown, and Philip Bromiley, "Strategic Stories: How 3M Is Rewriting Business Planning," *Harvard Business Review* 76, no. 3 (May–June 1998); David J. Collis and Michael G. Rukstad, "Can You Say What Your Strategy Is?" *Harvard Business Review* 86, no. 4 (April 2008) pp. 82–90.
[2] Hugh Davidson, *The Committed Enterprise: How to Make Vision and Values Work*

(Oxford: Butterworth Heinemann, 2002); W. Chan Kim and Renée Mauborgne, "Charting Your Company's Future," *Harvard Business Review* 80, no. 6 (June 2002), pp. 77–83; James C. Collins and Jerry I. Porras, "Building Your Company's Vision," *Harvard Business Review* 74, no. 5 (September–October 1996), pp. 65–77; Jim Collins and Jerry Porras, *Built to Last: Successful Habits of Visionary Companies*

(New York: HarperCollins, 1994); Michel Robert, *Strategy Pure and Simple II: How Winning Companies Dominate Their Competitors* (New York: McGraw-Hill, 1998).
[3] Davidson, *The Committed Enterprise,* pp. 20 and 54.
[4] As quoted in Charles H. House and Raymond L. Price, "The Return Map: Tracking Product Teams," *Harvard Business Review* 60, no. 1 (January–February 1991), p. 93.

[5] Sitkin, S., Miller, C. and See, K., "The Stretch Goal Paradox", *Harvard Business Review,* 95, no. 1 (January–February, 2017, pp. 92–99.

[6] Robert S. Kaplan and David P. Norton, *The Strategy-Focused Organization* (Boston: Harvard Business School Press, 2001); Robert S. Kaplan and David P. Norton, *The Balanced Scorecard: Translating Strategy into Action* (Boston: Harvard Business School Press, 1996).

[7] Kaplan and Norton, *The Strategy-Focused Organization;* Kaplan and Norton, *The Balanced Scorecard;* Kevin B. Hendricks, Larry Menor, and Christine Wiedman, "The Balanced Scorecard: To Adopt or Not to Adopt," *Ivey Business Journal* 69, no. 2 (November–December 2004), pp. 1–7; Sandy Richardson, "The Key Elements of Balanced Scorecard Success," *Ivey Business Journal* 69, no. 2 (November–December 2004), pp. 7–9.

[8] Kaplan and Norton, *The Balanced Scorecard.*

[9] Ibid.

[10] Ibid.

[11] Information posted on the website of the Balanced Scorecard Institute, **balancedscorecard .org** (accessed October, 2015).

[12] Henry Mintzberg, Bruce Ahlstrand, and Joseph Lampel, *Strategy Safari: A Guided Tour through the Wilds of Strategic Management* (New York: Free Press, 1998); Bruce Barringer and Allen C. Bluedorn, "The Relationship between Corporate Entrepreneurship and Strategic Management," *Strategic Management Journal* 20 (1999), pp. 421–444; Jeffrey G. Covin and Morgan P. Miles, "Corporate Entrepreneurship and the Pursuit of Competitive Advantage," *Entrepreneurship: Theory and Practice* 23, no. 3 (Spring 1999), pp. 47–63; David A. Garvin and Lynne C. Levesque, "Meeting the Challenge of Corporate Entrepreneurship," *Harvard Business Review* 84, no. 10 (October 2006), pp. 102–112.

[13] Joseph L. Bower and Clark G. Gilbert, "How Managers' Everyday Decisions Create or Destroy Your Company's Strategy," *Harvard Business Review* 85, no. 2 (February 2007), pp. 72–79.

[14] Gordon Shaw, Robert Brown, and Philip Bromiley, "Strategic Stories: How 3M Is Rewriting Business Planning," *Harvard Business Review* 76, no. 3 (May–June 1998), pp. 41–50.

[15] David Collis and Michael Rukstad, "Can You Say What Your Stratgey Is?" *Harvard Business Review*, May 2008, pp. 82–90.

[16] Cynthia A. Montgomery, "Putting Leadership Back into Strategy," *Harvard Business Review* 86, no. 1 (January 2008), pp. 54–60.

[17] Jay W. Lorsch and Robert C. Clark, "Leading from the Boardroom," *Harvard Business Review* 86, no. 4 (April 2008), pp. 105–111.

[18] Ibid.

[19] Stephen P. Kaufman, "Evaluating the CEO," *Harvard Business Review* 86, no. 10 (October 2008), pp. 53–57.

[20] Ibid.

[21] David A. Nadler, "Building Better Boards," *Harvard Business Review* 82, no. 5 (May 2004), pp. 102–105; Cynthia A. Montgomery and Rhonda Kaufman, "The Board's Missing Link," *Harvard Business Review* 81, no. 3 (March 2003), pp. 86–93; John Carver, "What Continues to Be Wrong with Corporate Governance and How to Fix It," *Ivey Business Journal* 68, no. 1 (September–October 2003), pp. 1–5. See also Gordon Donaldson, "A New Tool for Boards: The Strategic Audit," *Harvard Business Review* 73, no. 4 (July–August 1995), pp. 99–107.

chapter 3

Evaluating a Company's External Environment

Learning Objectives

After reading this chapter, you should be able to:

LO 3-1 Recognize the factors in a company's broad macro-environment that may have strategic significance.

LO 3-2 Use analytic tools to diagnose the competitive conditions in a company's industry.

LO 3-3 Map the market positions of key groups of industry rivals.

LO 3-4 Determine whether an industry's outlook presents a company with sufficiently attractive opportunities for growth and profitability.

Fanatic Studio/Getty Images

No matter what it takes, the goal of *strategy* is to beat the competition.

    Kenichi Ohmae—*Consultant and author*

Companies that solely focus on competition will die. Those that focus on value creation will thrive.

    Edward de Bono—*Author and consultant*

Continued innovation is the best way to beat the competition.

    Thomas A Edison—*Inventor and Businessman*

In Chapter 2, we learned that the strategy formulation, strategy execution process begins with an appraisal of the company's present situation. Two facets of a company's situation are especially pertinent: (1) its external environment—most notably, the competitive conditions of the industry in which the company operates; and (2) its internal environment—particularly the company's resources and organizational capabilities.

Insightful diagnosis of a company's external and internal environments is a prerequisite for managers to succeed in crafting a strategy that is an excellent *fit* with the company's situation—the first test of a winning strategy. As depicted in Figure 3.1, strategic thinking begins with an appraisal of the company's external and internal environments (as a basis for deciding on a long-term direction and developing a strategic vision). It then moves toward an evaluation of the most promising alternative business models, and strategies and finally culminates in choosing a specific strategy.

This chapter presents the concepts and analytic tools for zeroing in on those aspects of a company's external environment that should be considered in making strategic choices. Attention centers on the broad environmental context, the specific market arena in which a company operates, the drivers of change, the positions and likely actions of rival companies, and key success factors. In Chapter 4, we explore the methods of evaluating a company's internal circumstances and competitive capabilities.

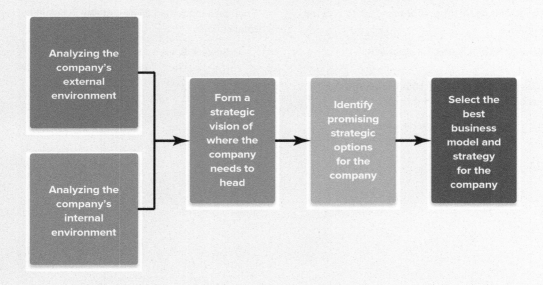

ASSESSING THE COMPANY'S INDUSTRY AND COMPETITIVE ENVIRONMENT

Thinking strategically about a company's industry and competitive environment entails using some well-validated concepts and analytical tools to get clear answers to seven questions:

1. Do macro-environmental factors and industry characteristics offer sellers opportunities for growth and attractive profits?
2. What kinds of competitive forces are industry members facing, and how strong is each force?
3. What forces are driving industry change, and what impact will these changes have on competitive intensity and industry profitability?
4. What market positions do industry rivals occupy—who is strongly positioned and who is not?
5. What strategic moves are rivals likely to make next?
6. What are the key factors of competitive success?
7. Does the industry outlook offer good prospects for profitability?

Analysis-based answers to these questions are prerequisites for a strategy offering good fit with the external situation. The remainder of this chapter is devoted to describing the methods of obtaining solid answers to these seven questions.

ANALYZING THE COMPANY'S MACRO-ENVIRONMENT

A company's external environment includes the immediate industry and competitive environment and a broader "macro-environment" (see Figure 3.2). This macro-environment comprises six principal components: political factors; economic conditions in the firm's general environment (local, country, regional, worldwide); sociocultural forces; technological factors; environmental factors (concerning the natural environment); and legal/regulatory conditions. Each of these components has the potential to affect the firm's more immediate industry and competitive environment, although some are likely to have a more important effect than others. An analysis of the impact of these factors is often referred to as **PESTEL analysis,** an acronym that

FIGURE 3.2 The Components of a Company's Macro-Environment

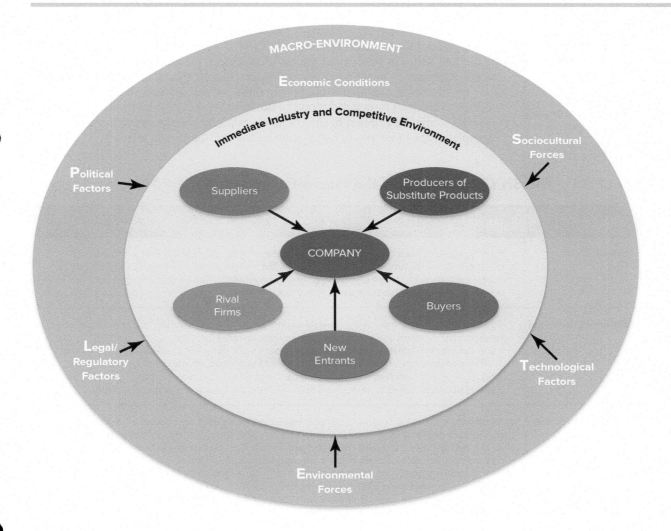

serves as a reminder of the six components involved (Political, Economic, Sociocultural, Technological, Environmental, Legal/regulatory).

Since macro-economic factors affect different industries in different ways and to different degrees, it is important for managers to determine which of these represent the most *strategically relevant factors* outside the firm's industry boundaries. By *strategically relevant,* we mean important enough to have a bearing on the decisions the company ultimately makes about its long-term direction, objectives, strategy, and business model. The impact of the outer-ring factors depicted in Figure 3.2 on a company's choice of strategy can range from big to small. Those factors that are likely to a bigger impact deserve the closest attention. But even factors that have a low impact on the company's business situation merit a watchful eye since their level of impact may change.

For example, when stringent new federal banking regulations are announced, banks must rapidly adapt their strategies and lending practices to be in compliance. Cigarette producers must adapt to new antismoking ordinances, the decisions of governments to impose higher cigarette taxes, the growing cultural stigma attached to smoking and newly emerging e-cigarette technology. The homebuilding industry is affected by such macro-influences as trends in household incomes and buying power, rules and regulations that make it easier or harder for homebuyers to obtain mortgages, changes in mortgage interest rates, shifting preferences of families for renting versus owning a home, and shifts in buyer preferences for homes of various sizes, styles, and price ranges. Companies in the food processing, restaurant, sports, and fitness industries have to pay special attention to changes in lifestyles, eating habits, leisure-time preferences, and attitudes toward nutrition and fitness in fashioning their strategies. Table 3.1 provides a brief description of the components of the macro-environment and some examples of the industries or business situations that they might affect.

TABLE 3.1   The Six Components of the Macro-Environment

Component	Description
Political factors	Pertinent political factors include matters such as tax policy, fiscal policy, tariffs, the political climate, and the strength of institutions such as the federal banking system. Some political policies affect certain types of industries more than others. An example is energy policy, which clearly affects energy producers and heavy users of energy more than other types of businesses.
Economic conditions	Economic conditions include the general economic climate and specific factors such as interest rates, exchange rates, the inflation rate, the unemployment rate, the rate of economic growth, trade deficits or surpluses, savings rates, and per-capita domestic product. Some industries, such as construction, are particularly vulnerable to economic downturns but are positively affected by factors such as low interest rates. Others, such as discount retailing, benefit when general economic conditions weaken, as consumers become more price-conscious.
Sociocultural forces	Sociocultural forces include the societal values, attitudes, cultural influences, and lifestyles that impact demand for particular goods and services, as well as demographic factors such as the population size, growth rate, and age distribution. Sociocultural forces vary by locale and change over time. An example is the trend toward healthier lifestyles, which can shift spending toward exercise equipment and health clubs and away from alcohol and snack foods. The demographic effect of people living longer is having a huge impact on the health care, nursing homes, travel, hospitality, and entertainment industries.

(continued)

TABLE 3.1   *(continued)*

Component	Description
Technological factors	Technological factors include the pace of technological change and technical developments that have the potential for wide-ranging effects on society, such as genetic engineering, nanotechnology, and solar energy technology. They include institutions involved in creating new knowledge and controlling the use of technology, such as R&D consortia, university-sponsored technology incubators, patent and copyright laws, and government control over the Internet. Technological change can encourage the birth of new industries, such as drones, virtual reality technology, and connected wearable devices. They can disrupt others, as cloud computing, 3-D printing, and big data solution have done, and they can render other industries obsolete (film cameras, music CDs).
Environmental forces	These include ecological and environmental forces such as weather, climate, climate change, and associated factors like flooding, fire, and water shortages. These factors can directly impact industries such as insurance, farming, energy production, and tourism. They may have an indirect but substantial effect on other industries such as transportation and utilities. The relevance of environmental considerations stems from the fact that some industries contribute more significantly than others to air and water pollution or to the depletion of irreplaceable natural resources, or to inefficient energy/resource usage, or are closely associated with other types of environmentally damaging activities (unsustainable agricultural practices, the creation of waste products that are not recyclable or biodegradable). Growing numbers of companies worldwide, in response to stricter environmental regulations and also to mounting public concerns about the environment, are implementing actions to operate in a more environmentally and ecologically responsible manner.
Legal and regulatory factors	These factors include the regulations and laws with which companies must comply, such as consumer laws, labor laws, antitrust laws, and occupational health and safety regulation. Some factors, such as financial services regulation, are industry-specific. Others affect certain types of industries more than others. For example, minimum wage legislation largely impacts low-wage industries (such as nursing homes and fast food restaurants) that employ substantial numbers of relatively unskilled workers. Companies in coal-mining, meat-packing, and steel-making, where many jobs are hazardous or carry high risk of injury, are much more impacted by occupational safety regulations than are companies in industries such as retailing or software programming.

As the events surrounding the coronavirus pandemic of 2020 made abundantly clear, there is a class of macro-level external factors that is not included as part of PESTEL analysis. This is the set of factors that occurs more irregularly and unpredictably, unlike the categories within PESTEL that can be expected to affect firms in an ongoing and more foreseeable manner. This additional set of factors can be thought of as **societal shocks** to the macro-environment; they include terrorism (whether by domestic or foreign agents), civil war, foreign invasion or occupation, and epidemics and pandemics. Societal shocks such as these also affect different industries and companies to varying degrees, but they are much harder for companies to anticipate and prepare for since they often begin with little warning. The coordinated terrorist attacks by al-Qaeda against the United States now referred to as 9/11 (since they occurred on September 11, 2001) offer an example. These attacks had a significant economic impact, not only within the United States, but on world markets as well. New York City's businesses suffered enormously, particularly those located

The Differential Effects of the Coronavirus Pandemic of 2020

While the world had suffered through a number of other pandemics, including the Spanish Flu (which caused somewhere between 20 to 50 million deaths in 1918–1919), the Coronavirus pandemic of 2020 was predicted to be even more devastating. Not only was the world now more interconnected due to globalization, but the disease causing the pandemic, known as Covid-19, was easily transmissible. By April 1, 2020, there were already more than 31,000 deaths worldwide, despite the fact that the disease had not yet peaked in some of the world's most populous countries.

The virus was new to the world and identified as such in early January, 2020. First appearing in Wuhan, a Chinese city of 11 million, it spread around the globe rapidly, reaching at least 170 countries by the end of March. Different countries were affected by the pandemic at different rates and handled the crisis in different ways. Nations that were particularly hard hit by Covid-19 include China, Italy (with 1/3 of the deaths as of April 1, 2020), Spain, France, Iran, and the United States. Italy's high death rate may be explained in part due to demographics, since its much older population was more susceptible to the disease. But in contrast to South Korea, which utilized extensive testing to identify and control the spread of the disease, Italy failed to test widely. The United States also found itself with insufficient test kits to implement South Korea's strategy, a situation exacerbated by the Trump administration's downplaying the seriousness of the threat until March.

The economic impact of the pandemic was catastrophic, despite a $2 trillion U.S. fiscal stimulus package and similar measures elsewhere designed to combat its economic consequences. Emerging markets seemed destined to absorb much of the hit, as international investment dried up, tourism collapsed, and demand for commodities fell. But even wealthy nations were not immune from dire consequences, although different sectors and industries were affected to varying degrees. In the United States, the hospitality and transportation industries were hard hit, along with retail, oil and gas,

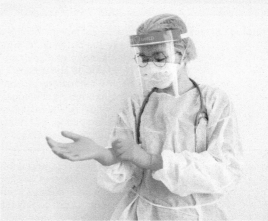

Shutterstock / theskaman306

live sports and other forms of entertainment. Small businesses and low-margin industries, with little ability to weather a significant downturn, were particularly vulnerable. Some industries, such as health care, online retail, and delivery services found themselves facing demand in excess of their capabilities, especially in light of supply chain breakdowns. A number of large companies responded to the crisis by switching to the production of supplies needed for managing the crisis. GM, Ford, and other automakers aided the efforts to produce critically needed ventilators, while distilleries such as Tito's Handmade Vodka and Dillon's Distillery began making hand sanitizers. Fashion companies, such as Inditex (with its Zara brand) and Los Angeles Apparel, turned their production capabilities toward making hospital gowns and face masks. Virtually no company was unaffected by the pandemic, but those which quickly adopted practices to remain nimble, control costs, minimize job losses, support their workers and suppliers, and join in the effort to combat the crisis were best positioned to weather it.

Sources: "Timeline: How the new coronavirus spread, Aljazeera news, March 29, 2020; "These companies are switching gears to help address coronavirus shortages", by Chloe Hadavas, Slate, March 23, 2020; SlateStatista.com (accessed April 1, 2020).

within and nearby the World Trade Center complex. Industries suffering an outsized effect include the airline industry, which had to cut back travel capacity by nearly 20%, and the export industry. Illustration Capsule 3.1 illustrates how another such societal shock—the coronavirus pandemic of 2020—affected industries, businesses, geographies, and countries differentially.

As company managers scan the external environment, they must be alert for potentially important outer-ring developments (whether in the form of societal shocks or among the components of PESTEL analysis), assess their impact and influence, and adapt the company's direction and strategy as needed. However, the factors in a company's environment having the *greatest* strategy-shaping impact typically pertain to the company's immediate industry and competitive environment. Consequently, it is on a company's industry and competitive environment (depicted in the center of Figure 3.2) that we concentrate the bulk of our attention in this chapter.

ASSESSING THE COMPANY'S INDUSTRY AND COMPETITIVE ENVIRONMENT

After gaining an understanding of the industry's general economic characteristics, attention should be focused on the competitive dynamics of the industry. This entails using some well-validated concepts and analytic tools. These include the five forces framework, the value net, driving forces, strategic groups, competitor analysis, and key success factors. Proper use of these analytic tools can provide managers with the understanding needed to craft a strategy that fits the company's situation within their industry environment. The remainder of this chapter is devoted to describing how managers can use these tools to inform and improve their strategic choices.

LO 3-2

Use analytic tools to diagnose the competitive conditions in a company's industry.

The Five Forces Framework

The character and strength of the competitive forces operating in an industry are never the same from one industry to another. The most powerful and widely used tool for diagnosing the principal competitive pressures in a market is the *five forces framework.*[1] This framework, depicted in Figure 3.3, holds that competitive pressures on companies within an industry come from five sources. These include (1) competition from *rival sellers,* (2) competition from *potential new entrants* to the industry, (3) competition from producers of *substitute products,* (4) *supplier* bargaining power, and (5) *customer* bargaining power.

Using the five forces model to determine the nature and strength of competitive pressures in a given industry involves three steps:

- *Step 1:* For each of the five forces, identify the different parties involved, along with the specific factors that bring about competitive pressures.
- *Step 2:* Evaluate how strong the pressures stemming from each of the five forces are (strong, moderate, or weak).
- *Step 3:* Determine whether the five forces, overall, are supportive of high industry profitability.

Competitive Pressures Created by the Rivalry among Competing Sellers

The strongest of the five competitive forces is often the rivalry for buyer patronage among competing sellers of a product or service. The intensity of rivalry among competing sellers within an industry depends on a number of identifiable factors. Figure 3.4 summarizes these factors, identifying those that intensify or weaken rivalry among direct competitors in an industry. A brief explanation of why these factors affect the degree of rivalry is in order:

FIGURE 3.3 The Five Forces Model of Competition: A Key Analytic Tool

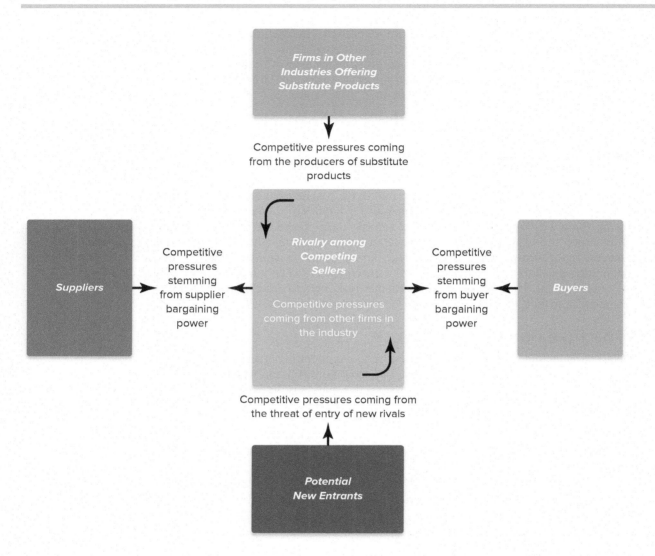

Sources: Adapted from M. E. Porter, "How Competitive Forces Shape Strategy," *Harvard Business Review* 57, no. 2 (1979), pp. 137–145; M. E. Porter, "The Five Competitive Forces That Shape Strategy," *Harvard Business Review* 86, no. 1 (2008), pp. 80–86.

- *Rivalry increases when buyer demand is growing slowly or declining.* Rapidly expanding buyer demand produces enough new business for all industry members to grow without having to draw customers away from rival enterprises. But in markets where buyer demand is slow-growing or shrinking, companies eager to gain more business are likely to engage in aggressive price discounting, sales promotions, and other tactics to increase their sales volumes at the expense of rivals, sometimes to the point of igniting a fierce battle for market share.

- *Rivalry increases as it becomes less costly for buyers to switch brands.* The less costly (or easier) it is for buyers to switch their purchases from one seller to another, the easier it is for sellers to steal customers away from rivals. When the cost of

FIGURE 3.4 Factors Affecting the Strength of Rivalry

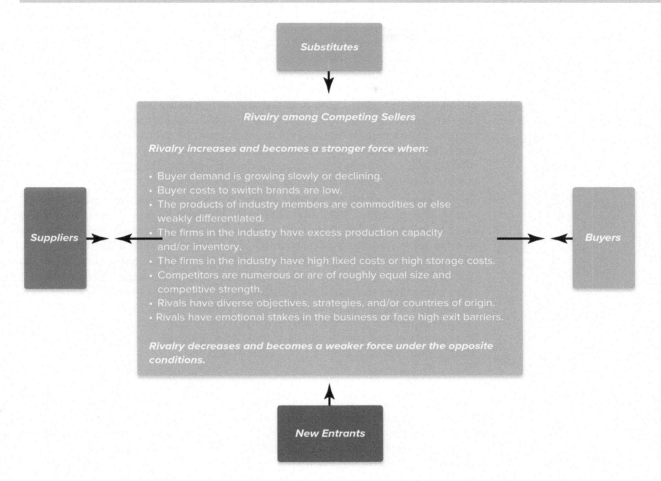

switching brands is higher, buyers are less prone to brand switching and sellers have protection from rivalrous moves. Switching costs include not only monetary costs but also the time, inconvenience, and psychological costs involved in switching brands. For example, retailers may not switch to the brands of rival manufacturers because they are hesitant to sever long-standing supplier relationships or incur the additional expense of retraining employees, accessing technical support, or testing the quality and reliability of the new brand. Consumers may not switch brands because they become emotionally attached to a particular brand (e.g. if you identify with the Harley motorcycle brand and lifestyle).

• *Rivalry increases as the products of rival sellers become less strongly differentiated.* When the offerings of rivals are identical or weakly differentiated, buyers have less reason to be brand-loyal—a condition that makes it easier for rivals to convince buyers to switch to their offerings. Moreover, when the products of different sellers are virtually identical, shoppers will choose on the basis of price, which can result in fierce price competition among sellers. On the other hand, strongly differentiated product offerings among rivals breed high brand loyalty on the part of buyers who view the attributes of certain brands as more appealing or better suited to their needs.

- *Rivalry is more intense when industry members have too much inventory or significant amounts of idle production capacity, especially if the industry's product entails high fixed costs or high storage costs.* Whenever a market has excess supply (overproduction relative to demand), rivalry intensifies as sellers cut prices in a desperate effort to cope with the unsold inventory. A similar effect occurs when a product is perishable or seasonal, since firms often engage in aggressive price cutting to ensure that everything is sold. Likewise, whenever fixed costs account for a large fraction of total cost so that unit costs are significantly lower at full capacity, firms come under significant pressure to cut prices whenever they are operating below full capacity. Unused capacity imposes a significant cost-increasing penalty because there are fewer units over which to spread fixed costs. The pressure of high fixed or high storage costs can push rival firms into offering price concessions, special discounts, and rebates and employing other volume-boosting competitive tactics.

- *Rivalry intensifies as the number of competitors increases and they become more equal in size and capability.* When there are many competitors in a market, companies eager to increase their meager market share often engage in price-cutting activities to drive sales, leading to intense rivalry. When there are only a few competitors, companies are more wary of how their rivals may react to their attempts to take market share away from them. Fear of retaliation and a descent into a damaging price war leads to restrained competitive moves. Moreover, when rivals are of comparable size and competitive strength, they can usually compete on a fairly equal footing—an evenly matched contest tends to be fiercer than a contest in which one or more industry members have commanding market shares and substantially greater resources than their much smaller rivals.

- *Rivalry becomes more intense as the diversity of competitors increases in terms of long-term directions, objectives, strategies, and countries of origin.* A diverse group of sellers often contains one or more mavericks willing to try novel or rule-breaking market approaches, thus generating a more volatile and less predictable competitive environment. Globally competitive markets are often more rivalrous, especially when aggressors have lower costs and are intent on gaining a strong foothold in new country markets.

- *Rivalry is stronger when high exit barriers keep unprofitable firms from leaving the industry.* In industries where the assets cannot easily be sold or transferred to other uses, where workers are entitled to job protection, or where owners are committed to remaining in business for personal reasons, failing firms tend to hold on longer than they might otherwise—even when they are bleeding red ink. Deep price discounting typically ensues, in a desperate effort to cover costs and remain in business. This sort of rivalry can destabilize an otherwise attractive industry.

The previous factors, taken as whole, determine whether the rivalry in an industry is relatively strong, moderate, or weak. When rivalry is *strong,* the battle for market share is generally so vigorous that the profit margins of most industry members are squeezed to bare-bones levels. When rivalry is *moderate,* a more normal state, the maneuvering among industry members, while lively and healthy, still allows most industry members to earn acceptable profits. When rivalry is *weak,* most companies in the industry are relatively well satisfied with their sales growth and market shares and rarely undertake offensives to steal customers away from one another. Weak rivalry means that there is no downward pressure on industry profitability due to this particular competitive force.

The Choice of Competitive Weapons

Competitive battles among rival sellers can assume many forms that extend well beyond lively price competition. For example, competitors may resort to such marketing tactics as special sales promotions, heavy advertising, rebates, or low-interest-rate financing to drum up additional sales. Rivals may race one another to differentiate their products by offering better performance features or higher quality or improved customer service or a wider product selection. They may also compete through the rapid introduction of next-generation products, the frequent introduction of new or improved products, and efforts to build stronger dealer networks, establish positions in foreign markets, or otherwise expand distribution capabilities and market presence. Table 3.2 displays the competitive weapons that firms often employ in battling rivals, along with their primary effects with respect to price (P), cost (C), and value (V)—the elements of an effective business model and the value-price-cost framework, discussed in Chapter 1.

Competitive Pressures Associated with the Threat of New Entrants

New entrants into an industry threaten the position of rival firms since they will compete fiercely for market share, add to the number of industry rivals, and add to the industry's production capacity in the process. But even the *threat* of new entry puts added competitive pressure on current industry members and thus functions as an important competitive force. This is because credible threat of entry often prompts industry members to lower their prices and initiate defensive actions in an attempt

TABLE 3.2 Common "Weapons" for Competing with Rivals

Types of Competitive Weapons	Primary Effects
Discounting prices, holding clearance sales	Lowers price (P), increases total sales volume and market share, lowers profits if price cuts are not offset by large increases in sales volume
Offering coupons, advertising items on sale	Increases sales volume and total revenues, lowers price (P), increases unit costs (C), may lower profit margins per unit sold ($P - C$)
Advertising product or service characteristics, using ads to enhance a company's image	Boosts buyer demand, increases product differentiation and perceived value (V), increases total sales volume and market share, but may increase unit costs (C) and lower profit margins per unit sold
Innovating to improve product performance and quality	Increases product differentiation and value (V), boosts buyer demand, boosts total sales volume, likely to increase unit costs (C)
Introducing new or improved features, increasing the number of styles to provide greater product selection	Increases product differentiation and value (V), strengthens buyer demand, boosts total sales volume and market share, likely to increase unit costs (C)
Increasing customization of product or service	Increases product differentiation and value (V), increases buyer switching costs, boosts total sales volume, often increases unit costs (C)
Building a bigger, better dealer network	Broadens access to buyers, boosts total sales volume and market share, may increase unit costs (C)
Improving warranties, offering low-interest financing	Increases product differentiation and value (V), increases unit costs (C), increases buyer switching costs, boosts total sales volume and market share

to deter new entrants. Just how serious the threat of entry is in a particular market depends on (1) whether entry barriers are high or low, and (2) the expected reaction of existing industry members to the entry of newcomers.

Whether Entry Barriers Are High or Low   The strength of the threat of entry is governed to a large degree by the height of the industry's entry barriers. High barriers reduce the threat of potential entry, whereas low barriers enable easier entry. Entry barriers are high under the following conditions:[2]

- *There are sizable economies of scale in production, distribution, advertising, or other activities.* When incumbent companies enjoy cost advantages associated with large-scale operations, outsiders must either enter on a large scale (a costly and perhaps risky move) or accept a cost disadvantage and consequently lower profitability.

- *Incumbents have other hard to replicate cost advantages over new entrants.* Aside from enjoying economies of scale, industry incumbents can have cost advantages that stem from the possession of patents or proprietary technology, exclusive partnerships with the best and cheapest suppliers, favorable locations, and low fixed costs (because they have older facilities that have been mostly depreciated). Learning-based cost savings can also accrue from experience in performing certain activities such as manufacturing or new product development or inventory management. The extent of such savings can be measured with learning/experience curves. The steeper the learning/experience curve, the bigger the cost advantage of the company with the largest *cumulative* production volume. The microprocessor industry provides an excellent example of this:

    Manufacturing unit costs for microprocessors tend to decline about 20 percent each time cumulative production volume doubles. With a 20 percent experience curve effect, if the first 1 million chips cost $100 each, once production volume reaches 2 million, the unit cost would fall to $80 (80 percent of $100), and by a production volume of 4 million, the unit cost would be $64 (80 percent of $80).[3]

- *Customers have strong brand preferences and high degrees of loyalty to seller.* The stronger the attachment of buyers to established brands, the harder it is for a newcomer to break into the marketplace. In such cases, a new entrant must have the financial resources to spend enough on advertising and sales promotion to overcome customer loyalties and build its own clientele. Establishing brand recognition and building customer loyalty can be a slow and costly process. In addition, if it is difficult or costly for a customer to switch to a new brand, a new entrant may have to offer a discounted price or otherwise persuade buyers that its brand is worth the switching costs. Such barriers discourage new entry because they act to boost financial requirements and lower expected profit margins for new entrants.

- *Patents and other forms of intellectual property protection are in place.* In a number of industries, entry is prevented due to the existence of intellectual property protection laws that remain in place for a given number of years. Often, companies have a "wall of patents" in place to prevent other companies from entering with a "me too" strategy that replicates a key piece of technology.

- *There are strong "network effects" in customer demand.* In industries where buyers are more attracted to a product when there are many other users of the product, there are said to be "network effects," since demand is higher the larger the network of users. Video game systems are an example because users prefer to have the same systems as their friends so that they can play together on systems they all know and can share games. When incumbents have a large existing base of users, new entrants with otherwise comparable products face a serious disadvantage in attracting buyers.

- *Capital requirements are high.* The larger the total dollar investment needed to enter the market successfully, the more limited the pool of potential entrants. The most obvious capital requirements for new entrants relate to manufacturing facilities and equipment, introductory advertising and sales promotion campaigns, working capital to finance inventories and customer credit, and sufficient cash to cover startup costs.

- *There are difficulties in building a network of distributors/dealers or in securing adequate space on retailers' shelves.* A potential entrant can face numerous distribution-channel challenges. Wholesale distributors may be reluctant to take on a product that lacks buyer recognition. Retailers must be recruited and convinced to give a new brand ample display space and an adequate trial period. When existing sellers have strong, well-functioning distributor–dealer networks, a newcomer has an uphill struggle in squeezing its way into existing distribution channels. Potential entrants sometimes have to "buy" their way into wholesale or retail channels by cutting their prices to provide dealers and distributors with higher markups and profit margins or by giving them big advertising and promotional allowances. As a consequence, a potential entrant's own profits may be squeezed unless and until its product gains enough consumer acceptance that distributors and retailers are willing to carry it.

- *There are restrictive regulatory policies.* Regulated industries like cable TV, telecommunications, electric and gas utilities, radio and television broadcasting, liquor retailing, nuclear power, and railroads entail government-controlled entry. Government agencies can also limit or even bar entry by requiring licenses and permits, such as the medallion required to drive a taxicab in New York City. Government-mandated safety regulations and environmental pollution standards also create entry barriers because they raise entry costs. Recently enacted banking regulations in many countries have made entry particularly difficult for small new bank startups—complying with all the new regulations along with the rigors of competing against existing banks requires very deep pockets.

- *There are restrictive trade policies.* In international markets, host governments commonly limit foreign entry and must approve all foreign investment applications. National governments commonly use tariffs and trade restrictions (antidumping rules, local content requirements, quotas, etc.) to raise entry barriers for foreign firms and protect domestic producers from outside competition.

The Expected Reaction of Industry Members in Defending against New Entry
A second factor affecting the threat of entry relates to the ability and willingness of industry incumbents to launch strong defensive maneuvers to maintain their positions and make it harder for a newcomer to compete successfully and profitably. Entry candidates may have second thoughts about attempting entry if they conclude that existing firms will mount well-funded campaigns to hamper (or even defeat) a newcomer's attempt to gain a market foothold big enough to compete successfully. Such campaigns can include any of the "competitive weapons" listed in Table 3.2, such as ramping up advertising expenditures, offering special price discounts to the very customers a newcomer is seeking to attract, or adding attractive new product features (to match or beat the newcomer's product offering). Such actions can raise a newcomer's cost of entry along with the risk of failing, making the prospect of entry less appealing. The result is that even the expectation on the part of new entrants that industry incumbents will contest a newcomer's entry may

be enough to dissuade entry candidates from going forward. Microsoft can be counted on to fiercely defend the position that Windows enjoys in computer operating systems and that Microsoft Office has in office productivity software. This may well have contributed to Microsoft's ability to continuously dominate this market space.

However, there are occasions when industry incumbents have nothing in their competitive arsenal that is formidable enough to either discourage entry or put obstacles in a newcomer's path that will defeat its strategic efforts to become a viable competitor. In the restaurant industry, for example, existing restaurants in a given geographic market have few actions they can take to discourage a new restaurant from opening or to block it from attracting enough patrons to be profitable. A fierce competitor like Nike was unable to prevent newcomer Under Armour from rapidly growing its sales and market share in sports apparel. Furthermore, there are occasions when industry incumbents can be expected to refrain from taking or initiating any actions specifically aimed at contesting a newcomer's entry. In large industries, entry by small startup enterprises normally poses no immediate or direct competitive threat to industry incumbents and their entry is not likely to provoke defensive actions. For instance, a new online retailer with sales prospects of maybe $5 to $10 million annually can reasonably expect to escape competitive retaliation from much larger online retailers selling similar goods. The less that a newcomer's entry will adversely impact the sales and profitability of industry incumbents, the more reasonable it is for potential entrants to expect industry incumbents to refrain from reacting defensively.

> Even high entry barriers may not suffice to keep out certain kinds of entrants: those with resources and capabilities that enable them to leap over or bypass the barriers.

Figure 3.5 summarizes the factors that cause the overall competitive pressure from potential entrants to be strong or weak. An analysis of these factors can help managers determine whether the threat of entry into their industry is high or low, *in general.* But certain kinds of companies—those with sizable financial resources, proven competitive capabilities, and a respected brand name—may be able to hurdle an industry's entry barriers even when they are high.[4] For example, when Honda opted to enter the U.S. lawn-mower market in competition against Toro, Snapper, Craftsman, John Deere, and others, it was easily able to hurdle entry barriers that would have been formidable to other newcomers because it had long-standing expertise in gasoline engines and a reputation for quality and durability in automobiles that gave it instant credibility with homeowners. As a result, Honda had to spend relatively little on inducing dealers to handle the Honda lawn-mower line or attracting customers. Similarly, Samsung's brand reputation in televisions, DVD players, and other electronics products gave it strong credibility in entering the market for smartphones—Samsung's Galaxy smartphones are now a formidable rival of Apple's iPhone.

> High entry barriers and weak entry threats today do not always translate into high entry barriers and weak entry threats tomorrow.

It is also important to recognize that the barriers to entering an industry can become stronger or weaker over time. For example, once key patents preventing new entry in the market for functional 3-D printers expired, the way was open for new competition to enter this industry. On the other hand, new strategic actions by incumbent firms to increase advertising, strengthen distributor–dealer relations, step up R&D, or improve product quality can erect higher roadblocks to entry.

Competitive Pressures from the Sellers of Substitute Products

Companies in one industry are vulnerable to competitive pressure from the actions of companies in a closely adjoining industry whenever buyers view the products of the two industries as good substitutes. Substitutes do *not* include other brands within your

FIGURE 3.5   Factors Affecting the Threat of Entry

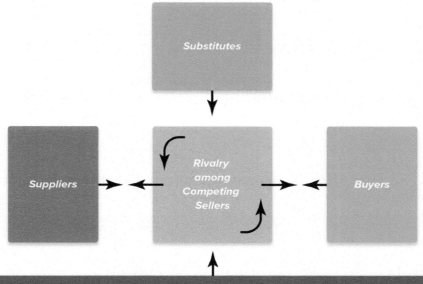

Substitutes

Suppliers

Rivalry among Competing Sellers

Buyers

Competitive Pressures from Potential Entrants

Threat of entry is a stronger force when (1) incumbents are unlikely to make retaliatory moves against new entrants and (2) entry barriers are low. Entry barriers are high (and threat of entry is low) when
- Incumbents have large cost advantages over potential entrants due to
  - High economies of scale
  - Significant experience-based cost advantages or learning curve effects
  - Other cost advantages (e.g., favorable access to inputs, technology, location, or low fixed costs)
- Customers with strong brand preferences and/or loyalty to incumbent sellers
- Patents and other forms of intellectual property protection
- Strong network effects
- High capital requirements
- Limited new access to distribution channels and shelf space
- Restrictive government policies
- Restrictive trade policies

industry; this type of pressure comes from *outside* the industry. Substitute products from outside the industry are those that can perform the same or similar functions for the consumer as products within your industry. For instance, the producers of eyeglasses and contact lenses face competitive pressures from the doctors who do corrective laser surgery. Similarly, the producers of sugar experience competitive pressures from the producers of sugar substitutes (high-fructose corn syrup, agave syrup, and artificial sweeteners). Internet providers of news-related information have put brutal competitive pressure on the publishers of newspapers. The makers of smartphones, by building ever better cameras into their cell phones, have cut deeply into the sales of producers of handheld digital cameras—most smartphone owners now use their phone to take pictures rather than carrying a digital camera for picture-taking purposes.

As depicted in Figure 3.6, three factors determine whether the competitive pressures from substitute products are strong or weak. Competitive pressures are stronger when

1. *Good substitutes are readily available and attractively priced.* The presence of readily available and attractively priced substitutes creates competitive pressure by placing a ceiling on the prices industry members can charge without risking sales erosion. This price ceiling, at the same time, puts a lid on the profits that industry members can earn unless they find ways to cut costs.

2. *Buyers view the substitutes as comparable or better in terms of quality, performance, and other relevant attributes.* The availability of substitutes inevitably invites customers to compare performance, features, ease of use, and other attributes besides price. The users of paper cartons constantly weigh the price-performance trade-offs

FIGURE 3.6   Factors Affecting Competition from Substitute Products

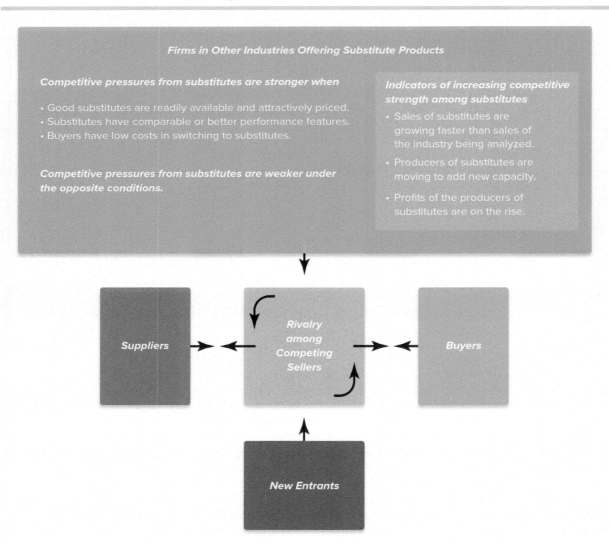

with plastic containers and metal cans, for example. Movie enthusiasts are increasingly weighing whether to go to movie theaters to watch newly released movies or wait until they can watch the same movies streamed to their home TV by Netflix, Amazon Prime, cable providers, and other on-demand sources.

3. *The costs that buyers incur in switching to the substitutes are low.* Low switching costs make it easier for the sellers of attractive substitutes to lure buyers to their offerings; high switching costs deter buyers from purchasing substitute products.

Some signs that the competitive strength of substitute products is increasing include (1) whether the sales of substitutes are growing faster than the sales of the industry being analyzed, (2) whether the producers of substitutes are investing in added capacity, and (3) whether the producers of substitutes are earning progressively higher profits.

But before assessing the competitive pressures coming from substitutes, company managers must identify the substitutes, which is less easy than it sounds since it involves (1) determining where the industry boundaries lie and (2) figuring out which other products or services can address the same basic customer needs as those produced by industry members. Deciding on the industry boundaries is necessary for determining which firms are direct rivals and which produce substitutes. This is a matter of perspective—there are no hard-and-fast rules, other than to say that other brands of the same basic product constitute rival products and not substitutes. Ultimately, it's simply the buyer who decides what can serve as a good substitute.

Competitive Pressures Stemming from Supplier Bargaining Power

Whether the suppliers of industry members represent a weak or strong competitive force depends on the degree to which suppliers have sufficient *bargaining power* to influence the terms and conditions of supply in their favor. Suppliers with strong bargaining power are a source of competitive pressure because of their ability to charge industry members higher prices, pass costs on to them, and limit their opportunities to find better deals. For instance, Microsoft and Intel, both of which supply PC makers with essential components, have been known to use their dominant market status not only to charge PC makers premium prices but also to leverage their power over PC makers in other ways. The bargaining power of these two companies over their customers is so great that both companies have faced antitrust charges on numerous occasions. Prior to a legal agreement ending the practice, Microsoft pressured PC makers to load only Microsoft products on the PCs they shipped. Intel has defended itself against similar antitrust charges, but in filling orders for newly introduced Intel chips, it continues to give top priority to PC makers that use the biggest percentages of Intel chips in their PC models. Being on Intel's list of preferred customers helps a PC maker get an early allocation of Intel's latest chips and thus allows the PC maker to get new models to market ahead of rivals.

Small-scale retailers often must contend with the power of manufacturers whose products enjoy well-known brand names, since consumers expect to find these products on the shelves of the retail stores where they shop. This provides the manufacturer with a degree of pricing power and often the ability to push hard for favorable shelf displays. Supplier bargaining power is also a competitive factor in industries where unions have been able to organize the workforce (which supplies labor). Air pilot unions, for example, have employed their bargaining power to increase pilots' wages and benefits in the air transport industry. The growing clout of the largest healthcare union in the United States has led to better wages and working conditions in nursing homes.

As shown in Figure 3.7, a variety of factors determine the strength of suppliers' bargaining power. Supplier power is stronger when

- *Demand for suppliers' products is high and the products are in short supply.* A surge in the demand for particular items shifts the bargaining power to the suppliers of those products; suppliers of items in short supply have pricing power.

- *Suppliers provide differentiated inputs that enhance the performance of the industry's product.* The more valuable a particular input is in terms of enhancing the performance or quality of the products of industry members, the more bargaining leverage suppliers have. In contrast, the suppliers of commodities are in a weak bargaining position, since industry members have no reason other than price to prefer one supplier over another.

- *It is difficult or costly for industry members to switch their purchases from one supplier to another.* Low switching costs limit supplier bargaining power by enabling industry members to change suppliers if any one supplier attempts to raise prices by more than the costs of switching. Thus, the higher the switching costs of industry members, the stronger the bargaining power of their suppliers.

- *The supplier industry is dominated by a few large companies and it is more concentrated than the industry it sells to.* Suppliers with sizable market shares and strong demand for the items they supply generally have sufficient bargaining power to charge high prices and deny requests from industry members for lower prices or other concessions.

FIGURE 3.7   Factors Affecting the Bargaining Power of Suppliers

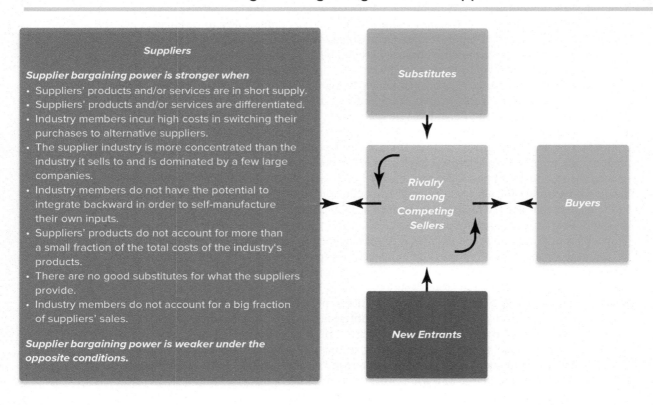

- *Industry members are incapable of integrating backward to self-manufacture items they have been buying from suppliers.* As a rule, suppliers are safe from the threat of self-manufacture by their customers until the volume of parts a customer needs becomes large enough for the customer to justify backward integration into self-manufacture of the component. When industry members can threaten credibly to self-manufacture suppliers' goods, their bargaining power over suppliers increases proportionately.

- *Suppliers provide an item that accounts for no more than a small fraction of the costs of the industry's product.* The more that the cost of a particular part or component affects the final product's cost, the more that industry members will be sensitive to the actions of suppliers to raise or lower their prices. When an input accounts for only a small proportion of total input costs, buyers will be less sensitive to price increases. Thus, suppliers' power increases when the inputs they provide do *not* make up a large proportion of the cost of the final product.

- *Good substitutes are not available for the suppliers' products.* The lack of readily available substitute inputs increases the bargaining power of suppliers by increasing the dependence of industry members on the suppliers.

- *Industry members are not major customers of suppliers.* As a rule, suppliers have less bargaining leverage when their sales to members of the industry constitute a big percentage of their total sales. In such cases, the well-being of suppliers is closely tied to the well-being of their major customers, and their dependence upon them increases. The bargaining power of suppliers is stronger, then, when they are *not* bargaining with major customers.

In identifying the degree of supplier power in an industry, it is important to recognize that different types of suppliers are likely to have different amounts of bargaining power. Thus, the first step is for managers to identify the different types of suppliers, paying particular attention to those that provide the industry with important inputs. The next step is to assess the bargaining power of each type of supplier separately.

Competitive Pressures Stemming from Buyer Bargaining Power and Price Sensitivity

Whether buyers are able to exert strong competitive pressures on industry members depends on (1) the degree to which buyers have bargaining power and (2) the extent to which buyers are price-sensitive. Buyers with strong bargaining power can limit industry profitability by demanding price concessions, better payment terms, or additional features and services that increase industry members' costs. Buyer price sensitivity limits the profit potential of industry members by restricting the ability of sellers to raise prices without losing revenue due to lost sales.

As with suppliers, the leverage that buyers have in negotiating favorable terms of sale can range from weak to strong. Individual consumers seldom have much bargaining power in negotiating price concessions or other favorable terms with sellers. However, their price sensitivity varies by individual and by the type of product they are buying (whether it's a necessity or a discretionary purchase, for example). Similarly, small businesses usually have weak bargaining power because of the small-size orders they place with sellers. Many relatively small wholesalers and retailers join buying groups to pool their purchasing power and approach manufacturers for better terms than could be gotten individually. Large business buyers, in contrast, can have considerable bargaining power. For example, large retail chains like

Walmart, Best Buy, Staples, and Home Depot typically have considerable bargaining power in purchasing products from manufacturers, not only because they buy in large quantities, but also because of manufacturers' need for access to their broad base of customers. Major supermarket chains like Kroger, Albertsons, Hannaford, and Aldi have sufficient bargaining power to demand promotional allowances and lump-sum payments (called *slotting fees*) from food products manufacturers in return for stocking certain brands or putting them in the best shelf locations. Motor vehicle manufacturers have strong bargaining power in negotiating to buy original-equipment tires from tire makers such as Bridgestone, Goodyear, Michelin, Continental, and Pirelli, partly because they buy in large quantities and partly because consumers are more likely to buy replacement tires that match the tire brand on their vehicle at the time of its purchase. The starting point for the analysis of buyers as a competitive force is to identify the different types of buyers along the value chain—then proceed to analyzing the bargaining power and price sensitivity of each type separately. It is important to recognize that *not all buyers of an industry's product have equal degrees of bargaining power with sellers, and some may be less sensitive than others to price, quality, or service differences.*

Figure 3.8 summarizes the factors determining the strength of buyer power in an industry. The top of this chart lists the factors that increase buyers' bargaining power,

FIGURE 3.8   Factors Affecting the Power of Buyers

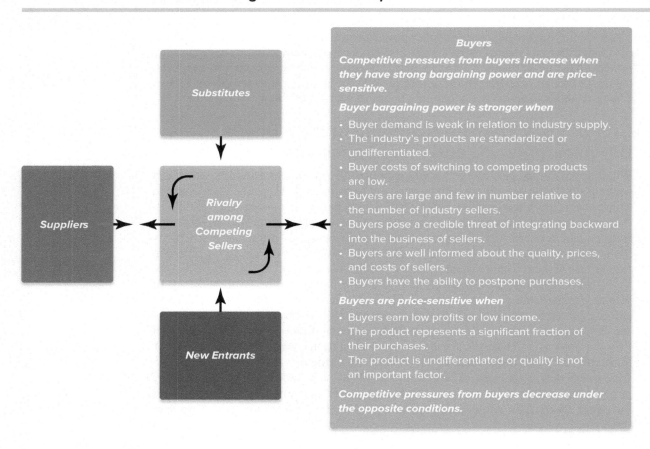

which we discuss next. Note that the first five factors are the mirror image of those determining the bargaining power of suppliers.

Buyer bargaining power is stronger when

- *Buyer demand is weak in relation to the available supply.* Weak or declining demand and the resulting excess supply create a "buyers' market," in which bargain-hunting buyers have leverage in pressing industry members for better deals and special treatment. Conversely, strong or rapidly growing market demand creates a "sellers' market" characterized by tight supplies or shortages—conditions that put buyers in a weak position to wring concessions from industry members.

- *Industry goods are standardized or differentiation is weak.* In such circumstances, buyers make their selections on the basis of price, which increases price competition among vendors.

- *Buyers' costs of switching to competing brands or substitutes are relatively low.* Switching costs put a cap on how much industry producers can raise prices or reduce quality before they will lose the buyer's business.

- *Buyers are large and few in number relative to the number of sellers.* The larger the buyers, the more important their business is to the seller and the more sellers will be willing to grant concessions.

- *Buyers pose a credible threat of integrating backward into the business of sellers.* Beer producers like Anheuser Busch InBev SA/NV (whose brands include Budweiser, Molson Coors, and Heineken) have partially integrated backward into metal-can manufacturing to gain bargaining power in obtaining the balance of their can requirements from otherwise powerful metal-can manufacturers.

- *Buyers are well informed about the product offerings of sellers (product features and quality, prices, buyer reviews) and the cost of production (an indicator of markup).* The more information buyers have, the better bargaining position they are in. The mushrooming availability of product information on the Internet (and its ready access on smartphones) is giving added bargaining power to consumers, since they can use this to find or negotiate better deals. Apps such as ShopSavvy and BuyVia are now making comparison shopping even easier.

- *Buyers have discretion to delay their purchases or perhaps even not make a purchase at all.* Consumers often have the option to delay purchases of durable goods (cars, major appliances), or decline to buy discretionary goods (massages, concert tickets) if they are not happy with the prices offered. Business customers may also be able to defer their purchases of certain items, such as plant equipment or maintenance services. This puts pressure on sellers to provide concessions to buyers so that the sellers can keep their sales numbers from dropping off.

Whether Buyers Are More or Less Price-Sensitive   Low-income and budget-constrained consumers are almost always price-sensitive; bargain-hunting consumers are highly price-sensitive by nature. Most consumers grow more price-sensitive as the price tag of an item becomes a bigger fraction of their spending budget. Similarly, business buyers besieged by weak sales, intense competition, and other factors squeezing their profit margins are price-sensitive. Price sensitivity also grows among businesses as the cost of an item becomes a bigger fraction of their cost structure. Rising prices of frequently purchased items heighten the price sensitivity of all types of buyers. On the other hand, the price sensitivity of all types of buyers decreases the more that the quality of the product matters.

The following factors increase buyer price sensitivity and result in greater competitive pressures on the industry as a result:

- *Buyer price sensitivity increases when buyers are earning low profits or have low income.* Price is a critical factor in the purchase decisions of low-income consumers and companies that are barely scraping by. In such cases, their high price sensitivity limits the ability of sellers to charge high prices.

- *Buyers are more price-sensitive if the product represents a large fraction of their total purchases.* When a purchase eats up a large portion of a buyer's budget or represents a significant part of his or her cost structure, the buyer cares more about price than might otherwise be the case.

- *Buyers are more price-sensitive when the quality of the product is not uppermost in their considerations.* Quality matters little when products are relatively undifferentiated, leading buyers to focus more on price. But when quality affects performance, or can reduce a business buyer's other costs (by saving on labor, materials, etc.), price will matter less.

Is the Collective Strength of the Five Competitive Forces Conducive to Good Profitability?

Assessing whether each of the five competitive forces gives rise to strong, moderate, or weak competitive pressures sets the stage for evaluating whether, overall, the strength of the five forces is conducive to good profitability. Is any of the competitive forces sufficiently powerful to undermine industry profitability? Can companies in this industry reasonably expect to earn decent profits in light of the prevailing competitive forces?

The most extreme case of a "competitively unattractive" industry occurs when all five forces are producing strong competitive pressures: Rivalry among sellers is vigorous, low entry barriers allow new rivals to gain a market foothold, competition from substitutes is intense, and both suppliers and buyers are able to exercise considerable leverage. Strong competitive pressures coming from all five directions drive industry profitability to unacceptably low levels, frequently producing losses for many industry members and forcing some out of business. But an industry can be competitively unattractive without all five competitive forces being strong. In fact, *intense competitive pressures from just one of the five forces may suffice to destroy the conditions for good profitability and prompt some companies to exit the business.*

> **CORE CONCEPT**
>
> The strongest of the five forces determines the extent of the downward pressure on an industry's profitability.

As a rule, *the strongest competitive forces determine the extent of the competitive pressure on industry profitability.* Thus, in evaluating the strength of the five forces overall and their effect on industry profitability, managers should look to the strongest forces. Having more than one strong force will not worsen the effect on industry profitability, but it does mean that the industry has multiple competitive challenges with which to cope. In that sense, an industry with three to five strong forces is even more "unattractive" as a place to compete. Especially intense competitive conditions due to multiple strong forces seem to be the norm in tire manufacturing, apparel, and commercial airlines, three industries where profit margins have historically been thin.

In contrast, when the overall impact of the five competitive forces is moderate to weak, an industry is "attractive" in the sense that the *average* industry member can reasonably expect to earn good profits and a nice return on investment. The ideal competitive environment for earning superior profits is one in which both suppliers and customers have limited power, there are no good substitutes, high barriers block further entry, and rivalry among present sellers is muted. Weak competition is the best of all possible worlds for also-ran companies because even they can usually eke out a decent profit—if a company can't make a decent profit when competition is weak, then its business outlook is indeed grim.

Matching Company Strategy to Competitive Conditions

Working through the five forces model step by step not only aids strategy makers in assessing whether the intensity of competition allows good profitability but also promotes sound strategic thinking about how to better match company strategy to the specific competitive character of the marketplace. Effectively matching a company's business strategy to prevailing competitive conditions has two aspects:

> A company's strategy is strengthened the more it provides insulation from competitive pressures, shifts the competitive battle in the company's favor, and positions the firm to take advantage of attractive growth opportunities.

1. Pursuing avenues that shield the firm from as many of the different competitive pressures as possible.
2. Initiating actions calculated to shift the competitive forces in the company's favor by altering the underlying factors driving the five forces.

But making headway on these two fronts first requires identifying competitive pressures, gauging the relative strength of each of the five competitive forces, and gaining a deep enough understanding of the state of competition in the industry to know which strategy buttons to push.

COMPLEMENTORS AND THE VALUE NET

Not all interactions among industry participants are necessarily competitive in nature. Some have the potential to be cooperative, as the value net framework demonstrates. Like the five forces framework, the value net includes an analysis of buyers, suppliers, and substitutors (see Figure 3.9). But it differs from the five forces framework in several important ways.

First, the analysis focuses on the interactions of industry participants with a particular company. Thus, it places that firm in the center of the framework, as Figure 3.9 shows. Second, the category of "competitors" is defined to include not only the focal firm's direct competitors or industry rivals but also the sellers of substitute products and potential entrants. Third, the value net framework introduces a new category of industry participant that is not found in the five forces framework— that of "complementors." **Complementors** are the producers of complementary products, which are products that enhance the value of the focal firm's products when they are used together. Some examples include snorkels and swim fins or shoes and shoelaces.

> **CORE** CONCEPT
>
> **Complementors** are the producers of complementary products, which are products that enhance the value of the focal firm's products when they are used together.

The inclusion of complementors draws particular attention to the fact that success in the marketplace need not come at the expense of other industry participants. Interactions among industry participants may be cooperative in nature rather than competitive. In the case of complementors, an increase in sales for them is likely to increase the sales of the focal firm as well. But the value net framework also encourages managers to consider other forms of cooperative interactions and realize that value is created jointly by all industry participants. For example, a company's success in the marketplace depends on establishing a reliable supply chain for its inputs, which implies the need for cooperative relations with its suppliers. Often a firm works

FIGURE 3.9   The Value Net

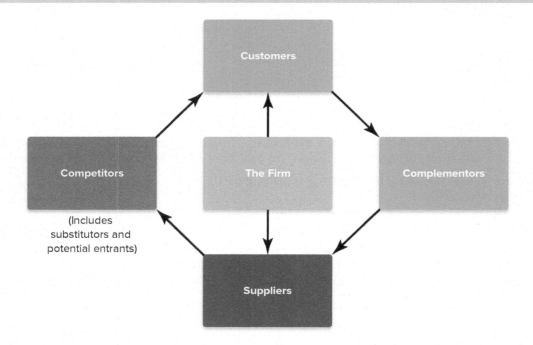

hand in hand with its suppliers to ensure a smoother, more efficient operation for both parties. Newell-Rubbermaid, and Procter & Gamble for example, work cooperatively as suppliers to companies such as Walmart, Target, and Kohl's. Even direct rivals may work cooperatively if they participate in industry trade associations or engage in joint lobbying efforts. Value net analysis can help managers discover the potential to improve their position through cooperative as well as competitive interactions.

INDUSTRY DYNAMICS AND THE FORCES DRIVING CHANGE

While it is critical to understand the nature and intensity of competitive and cooperative forces in an industry, it is equally critical to understand that the intensity of these forces is fluid and subject to change. All industries are affected by new developments and ongoing trends that alter industry conditions, some more speedily than others. The popular hypothesis that industries go through a life cycle of takeoff, rapid growth, maturity, market saturation and slowing growth, followed by stagnation or decline is but one aspect of industry change—many other new developments and emerging trends cause industry change.[5] Any strategies devised by management will therefore play out in a dynamic industry environment, so it's imperative that managers consider the factors driving industry change and how they might affect the industry environment. Moreover, with early notice, managers may be able to influence the direction or scope of environmental change and improve the outlook.

Industry and competitive conditions change because forces are enticing or pressuring certain industry participants (competitors, customers, suppliers, complementors) to alter their actions in important ways. The most powerful of the change agents are called **driving forces** because they have the biggest influences in reshaping the industry landscape and altering competitive conditions. Some driving forces originate in the outer ring of the company's macro-environment (see Figure 3.2), but most originate in the company's more immediate industry and competitive environment.

> **CORE** CONCEPT
>
> **Driving forces** are the major underlying causes of change in industry and competitive conditions.

Driving-forces analysis has three steps: (1) identifying what the driving forces are; (2) assessing whether the drivers of change are, on the whole, acting to make the industry more or less attractive; and (3) determining what strategy changes are needed to prepare for the impact of the driving forces. All three steps merit further discussion.

Identifying the Forces Driving Industry Change

Many developments can affect an industry powerfully enough to qualify as driving forces. Some drivers of change are unique and specific to a particular industry situation, but most drivers of industry and competitive change fall into one of the following categories:

- *Changes in an industry's long-term growth rate.* Shifts in industry growth up or down have the potential to affect the balance between industry supply and buyer demand, entry and exit, and the character and strength of competition. Whether demand is growing or declining is one of the key factors influencing the intensity of rivalry in an industry, as explained earlier. But the strength of this effect will depend on how changes in the industry growth rate affect entry and exit in the industry. If entry barriers are low, then growth in demand will attract new entrants, increasing the number of industry rivals and changing the competitive landscape.

- *Increasing globalization.* Globalization can be precipitated by such factors as the blossoming of consumer demand in developing countries, the availability of lower-cost foreign inputs, and the reduction of trade barriers, as has occurred recently in many parts of Latin America and Asia. Significant differences in labor costs among countries give manufacturers a strong incentive to locate plants for labor-intensive products in low-wage countries and use these plants to supply market demand across the world. Wages in China, India, Vietnam, Mexico, and Brazil, for example, are much lower than those in the United States, Germany, and Japan. The forces of globalization are sometimes such a strong driver that companies find it highly advantageous, if not necessary, to spread their operating reach into more and more country markets. Globalization is very much a driver of industry change in such industries as energy, mobile phones, steel, social media, public accounting, commercial aircraft, electric power generation equipment, and pharmaceuticals.

- *Emerging new Internet capabilities and applications.* Mushrooming use of high-speed Internet service and Voice-over-Internet-Protocol (VoIP) technology, growing acceptance of online shopping, and the exploding popularity of Internet applications ("apps") have been major drivers of change in industry after industry. The Internet has allowed online discount stock brokers, such as E*TRADE, and TD Ameritrade to mount a strong challenge against full-service firms such as Edward Jones and Merrill Lynch. The newspaper industry has yet to figure out a strategy for surviving the advent of online news.

Massive open online courses (MOOCs) facilitated by organizations such as Coursera, edX, and Udacity are profoundly affecting higher education. The "Internet of things" will feature faster speeds, dazzling applications, and billions of connected gadgets performing an array of functions, thus driving further industry and competitive changes. But Internet-related impacts vary from industry to industry. The challenges are to assess precisely how emerging Internet developments are altering a particular industry's landscape and to factor these impacts into the strategy-making equation.

- *Shifts in who buys the products and how the products are used.* Shifts in buyer demographics and the ways products are used can greatly alter competitive conditions. Longer life expectancies and growing percentages of relatively well-to-do retirees, for example, are driving demand growth in such industries as cosmetic surgery, assisted living residences, and vacation travel. The burgeoning popularity of streaming video has affected broadband providers, wireless phone carriers, and television broadcasters, and created opportunities for such new entertainment businesses as Hulu and Netflix.

- *Technological change and manufacturing process innovation.* Advances in technology can cause disruptive change in an industry by introducing substitutes or can alter the industry landscape by opening up whole new industry frontiers. For instance, revolutionary change in autonomous system technology has put Google, Tesla, Apple, and every major automobile manufacturer into a race to develop viable self-driving vehicles.

- *Product innovation.* An ongoing stream of product innovations tends to alter the pattern of competition in an industry by attracting more first-time buyers, rejuvenating industry growth, and/or increasing product differentiation, with concomitant effects on rivalry, entry threat, and buyer power. Product innovation has been a key driving force in the smartphone industry, which in an ever more connected world is driving change in other industries. Philips Lighting Hue bulbs now allow homeowners to use a smartphone app to remotely turn lights on and off, blink if an intruder is detected, and create a wide range of white and color ambiances. Wearable action-capture cameras and unmanned aerial view drones are rapidly becoming a disruptive force in the digital camera industry by enabling photography shots and videos not feasible with handheld digital cameras.

- *Marketing innovation.* When firms are successful in introducing new ways to market their products, they can spark a burst of buyer interest, widen industry demand, increase product differentiation, and lower unit costs—any or all of which can alter the competitive positions of rival firms and force strategy revisions. Consider, for example, the growing propensity of advertisers to place a bigger percentage of their ads on social media sites like Facebook and Twitter.

- *Entry or exit of major firms.* Entry by a major firm thus often produces a new ball game, not only with new key players but also with new rules for competing. Similarly, exit of a major firm changes the competitive structure by reducing the number of market leaders and increasing the dominance of the leaders who remain.

- *Diffusion of technical know-how across companies and countries.* As knowledge about how to perform a particular activity or execute a particular manufacturing technology spreads, products tend to become more commodity-like. Knowledge diffusion can occur through scientific journals, trade publications, onsite plant tours, word of mouth among suppliers and customers, employee migration, and Internet sources.

- *Changes in cost and efficiency.* Widening or shrinking differences in the costs among key competitors tend to dramatically alter the state of competition. Declining costs of producing tablets have enabled price cuts and spurred tablet sales (especially lower-priced models) by making them more affordable to lower-income households worldwide. Lower cost e-books are cutting into sales of costlier hardcover books as increasing numbers of consumers have laptops, iPads, Kindles, and other brands of tablets.

- *Reductions in uncertainty and business risk.* Many companies are hesitant to enter industries with uncertain futures or high levels of business risk because it is unclear how much time and money it will take to overcome various technological hurdles and achieve acceptable production costs (as is the case in the solar power industry). Over time, however, diminishing risk levels and uncertainty tend to stimulate new entry and capital investments on the part of growth-minded companies seeking new opportunities, thus dramatically altering industry and competitive conditions.

- *Regulatory influences and government policy changes.* Government regulatory actions can often mandate significant changes in industry practices and strategic approaches—as has recently occurred in the world's banking industry. New rules and regulations pertaining to government-sponsored health insurance programs are driving changes in the health care industry. In international markets, host governments can drive competitive changes by opening their domestic markets to foreign participation or closing them to protect domestic companies.

- *Changing societal concerns, attitudes, and lifestyles.* Emerging social issues as well as changing attitudes and lifestyles can be powerful instigators of industry change. Growing concern about the effects of climate change has emerged as a major driver of change in the energy industry. Concerns about the use of chemical additives and the nutritional content of food products have been driving changes in the restaurant and food industries. Shifting societal concerns, attitudes, and lifestyles alter the pattern of competition, favoring those players that respond with products targeted to the new trends and conditions.

> The most important part of driving-forces analysis is to determine whether the collective impact of the driving forces will increase or decrease market demand, make competition more or less intense, and lead to higher or lower industry profitability.

While many forces of change may be at work in a given industry, *no more than three or four* are likely to be true driving forces powerful enough to qualify as the *major determinants* of why and how the industry is changing. Thus, company strategists must resist the temptation to label every change they see as a driving force. Table 3.3 lists the most common driving forces.

TABLE 3.3   The Most Common Drivers of Industry Change

- Changes in the long-term industry growth rate
- Increasing globalization
- Emerging new Internet capabilities and applications
- Shifts in buyer demographics
- Technological change and manufacturing process innovation
- Product and marketing innovation
- Entry or exit of major firms
- Diffusion of technical know-how across companies and countries
- Changes in cost and efficiency
- Reductions in uncertainty and business risk
- Regulatory influences and government policy changes
- Changing societal concerns, attitudes, and lifestyles

Assessing the Impact of the Forces Driving Industry Change

The second step in driving-forces analysis is to determine whether the prevailing change drivers, on the whole, are acting to make the industry environment more or less attractive. Three questions need to be answered:

> The real payoff of driving-forces analysis is to help managers understand what strategy changes are needed to prepare for the impacts of the driving forces.

1. Are the driving forces, on balance, acting to cause demand for the industry's product to increase or decrease?
2. Is the collective impact of the driving forces making competition more or less intense?
3. Will the combined impacts of the driving forces lead to higher or lower industry profitability?

Getting a handle on the collective impact of the driving forces requires looking at the likely effects of each factor separately, since the driving forces may not all be pushing change in the same direction. For example, one driving force may be acting to spur demand for the industry's product while another is working to curtail demand. Whether the net effect on industry demand is up or down hinges on which change driver is the most powerful.

Adjusting the Strategy to Prepare for the Impacts of Driving Forces

The third step in the strategic analysis of industry dynamics—where the real payoff for strategy making comes—is for managers to draw some conclusions about *what strategy adjustments will be needed to deal with the impacts of the driving forces.* But taking the "right" kinds of actions to prepare for the industry and competitive changes being wrought by the driving forces first requires accurate diagnosis of the forces driving industry change and the impacts these forces will have on both the industry environment and the company's business. To the extent that managers are unclear about the drivers of industry change and their impacts, or if their views are off-base, the chances of making astute and timely strategy adjustments are slim. So driving-forces analysis is not something to take lightly; it has practical value and is basic to the task of thinking strategically about where the industry is headed and how to prepare for the changes ahead.

STRATEGIC GROUP ANALYSIS

● ● ● ●

● **LO 3-3**

Map the market positions of key groups of industry rivals.

Within an industry, companies commonly sell in different price/quality ranges, appeal to different types of buyers, have different geographic coverage, and so on. Some are more attractively positioned than others. Understanding which companies are strongly positioned and which are weakly positioned is an integral part of analyzing an industry's competitive structure. The best technique for revealing the market positions of industry competitors is **strategic group mapping.**

Using Strategic Group Maps to Assess the Market Positions of Key Competitors

A **strategic group** consists of those industry members with similar competitive approaches and positions in the market. Companies in the same strategic group can resemble one another in a variety of ways. They may have comparable product-line breadth, sell in the same price/quality range, employ the same distribution channels, depend on identical technological approaches, compete in much the same geographic areas, or offer buyers essentially the same product attributes or similar services and technical assistance.[6] Evaluating strategy options entails examining what strategic groups exist, identifying the companies within each group, and determining if a competitive "white space" exists where industry competitors are able to create and capture altogether new demand. As part of this process, the number of strategic groups in an industry and their respective market positions can be displayed on a strategic group map.

The procedure for constructing a *strategic group map* is straightforward:

- Identify the competitive characteristics that delineate strategic approaches used in the industry. Typical variables used in creating strategic group maps are price/quality range (high, medium, low), geographic coverage (local, regional, national, global), product-line breadth (wide, narrow), degree of service offered (no frills, limited, full), use of distribution channels (retail, wholesale, Internet, multiple), degree of vertical integration (none, partial, full), and degree of diversification into other industries (none, some, considerable).
- Plot the firms on a two-variable map using pairs of these variables.
- Assign firms occupying about the same map location to the same strategic group.
- Draw circles around each strategic group, making the circles proportional to the size of the group's share of total industry sales revenues.

This produces a two-dimensional diagram like the one for the U.S. pizza chain industry in Illustration Capsule 3.2.

Several guidelines need to be observed in creating strategic group maps. First, the two variables selected as axes for the map should *not* be highly correlated; if they are, the circles on the map will fall along a diagonal and reveal nothing more about the relative positions of competitors than would be revealed by comparing the rivals on just one of the variables. For instance, if companies with broad product lines use multiple distribution channels while companies with narrow lines use a single distribution channel, then looking at the differences in distribution-channel approaches adds no new information about positioning.

Second, the variables chosen as axes for the map should reflect important differences among rival approaches—when rivals differ on both variables, the locations of the rivals will be scattered, thus showing how they are positioned differently. Third, the variables used as axes don't have to be either quantitative or continuous; rather, they can be discrete variables, defined in terms of distinct classes and combinations. Fourth, drawing the sizes of the circles on the map proportional to the combined sales of the firms in each strategic group allows the map to reflect the relative sizes of each strategic group. Fifth, if more than two good variables can be used as axes for the map, then it is wise to draw several maps to give different exposures to the competitive positioning relationships present in the industry's structure—there is not necessarily one best map for portraying how competing firms are positioned.

CORE CONCEPT

Strategic group mapping is a technique for displaying the different market or competitive positions that rival firms occupy in the industry.

CORE CONCEPT

A **strategic group** is a cluster of industry rivals that have similar competitive approaches and market positions.

The Value of Strategic Group Maps

Strategic group maps are revealing in several respects. The most important has to do with identifying which industry members are close rivals and which are distant rivals. Firms in the same strategic group are the closest rivals; the next closest rivals

Strategic group maps reveal which companies are close competitors and which are distant competitors.

ILLUSTRATION CAPSULE 3.2

Comparative Market Positions of Selected Companies in the Pizza Chain Industry: A Strategic Group Map Example

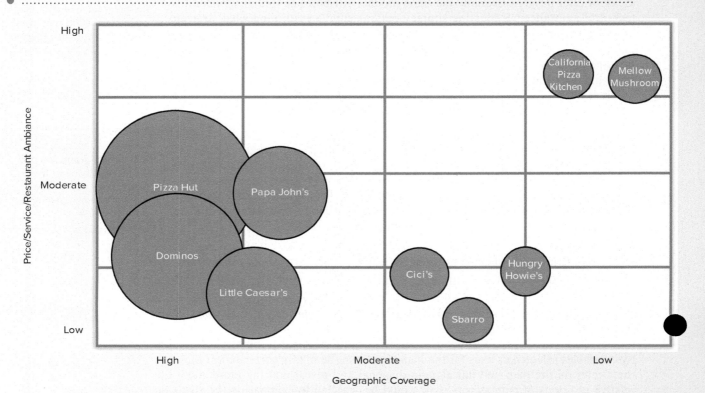

Note: Circles are drawn roughly proportional to the sizes of the chains, based on revenues.

are in the immediately adjacent groups. Often, firms in strategic groups that are far apart on the map hardly compete at all. For instance, Walmart's clientele, merchandise selection, and pricing points are much too different to justify calling Walmart a close competitor of Neiman Marcus or Saks Fifth Avenue. For the same reason, the beers produced by Yuengling are really not in competition with the beers produced by Pabst.

The second thing to be gleaned from strategic group mapping is that *not all positions on the map are equally attractive.*[7] Two reasons account for why some positions can be more attractive than others:

1. *Prevailing competitive pressures from the industry's five forces may cause the profit potential of different strategic groups to vary.* The profit prospects of firms in different strategic groups can vary from good to poor because of differing degrees of competitive rivalry within strategic groups, differing pressures from potential entrants to each group, differing degrees of exposure to competition from substitute products outside the industry, and differing degrees of supplier or customer bargaining power from group to group. For instance, in the ready-to-eat cereal industry, there are significantly higher entry barriers (capital requirements, brand loyalty, etc.) for

the strategic group comprising the large branded-cereal makers than for the group of generic-cereal makers or the group of small natural-cereal producers. Differences among the branded rivals versus the generic cereal makers make rivalry stronger within the generic-cereal strategic group. Among apparel retailers, the competitive battle between Marshall's and TJ MAXX is more intense (with consequently smaller profit margins) than the rivalry among Prada, Burberry, Gucci, Armani, and other high-end fashion retailers.

2. *Industry driving forces may favor some strategic groups and hurt others.* Likewise, industry driving forces can boost the business outlook for some strategic groups and adversely impact the business prospects of others. In the energy industry, producers of renewable energy, such as solar and wind power, are gaining ground over fossil fuel-based producers due to improvements in technology and increased concern over climate change. Firms in strategic groups that are being adversely impacted by driving forces may try to shift to a more favorably situated position. If certain firms are known to be trying to change their competitive positions on the map, then attaching arrows to the circles showing the targeted direction helps clarify the picture of competitive maneuvering among rivals.

> Some strategic groups are more favorably positioned than others because they confront weaker competitive forces and/or because they are more favorably impacted by industry driving forces.

Thus, part of strategic group map analysis always entails drawing conclusions about where on the map is the "best" place to be and why. Which companies/strategic groups are destined to prosper because of their positions? Which companies/strategic groups seem destined to struggle? What accounts for why some parts of the map are better than others? Since some strategic groups are more attractive than others, one might ask why less well-positioned firms do not simply migrate to the more attractive position. The answer is that **mobility barriers** restrict movement between groups in the same way that entry barriers prevent easy entry into attractive industries. The most profitable strategic groups may be protected from entry by high mobility barriers.

> **CORE** CONCEPT
>
> **Mobility barriers** restrict firms in one strategic group from entering another more attractive strategic group in the same industry.

COMPETITOR ANALYSIS AND THE SOAR FRAMEWORK

Unless a company pays attention to the strategies and situations of competitors and has some inkling of what moves they will be making, it ends up flying blind into competitive battle. As in sports, scouting the opposition is an essential part of game plan development. Gathering competitive intelligence about the strategic direction and likely moves of key competitors allows a company to prepare defensive countermoves, to craft its own strategic moves with some confidence about what market maneuvers to expect from rivals in response, and to exploit any openings that arise from competitors' missteps. The question is where to look for such information, since rivals rarely reveal their strategic intentions openly. If information is not directly available, what are the best indicators?

> Studying competitors' past behavior and preferences provides a valuable assist in anticipating what moves rivals are likely to make next and outmaneuvering them in the marketplace.

Michael Porter's **SOAR Framework for Competitor Analysis** points to four indicators of a rival's likely strategic moves and countermoves. These include a rival's *Strategy, Objectives, Assumptions* about itself and the industry, and *Resources and capabilities,* as shown in Figure 3.10. A strategic profile of a competitor that provides good clues to its behavioral proclivities can be constructed by characterizing the rival along these four dimensions. By "behavioral proclivities," we mean what competitive moves a rival is likely to make and how they are likely to react to the competitive moves of your company—its

FIGURE 3.10   The SOAR Framework for Competitor Analysis

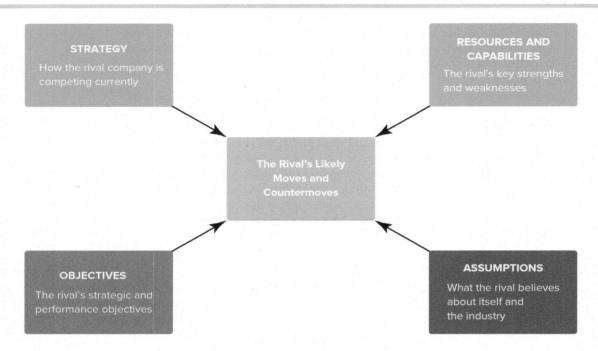

probable actions and reactions. By listing all that you know about a competitor (or a set of competitors) with respect to each of the four elements of the SOAR framework, you are likely to gain some insight about how the rival will behave in the near term. And knowledge of this sort can help you to predict how this will affect you, and how you should position yourself to respond. That is, what should you do to protect yourself or gain advantage now (in advance); and what should you do in response to your rivals next moves?

Current Strategy   To succeed in predicting a competitor's next moves, company strategists need to have a good understanding of each rival's current strategy, as an indicator of its pattern of behavior and best strategic options. Questions to consider include: How is the competitor positioned in the market? What is the basis for its competitive advantage (if any)? What kinds of investments is it making (as an indicator of its growth trajectory)?

Objectives   An appraisal of a rival's objectives should include not only its financial performance objectives but strategic ones as well (such as those concerning market share). What is even more important is to consider the extent to which the rival is meeting these objectives and whether it is under pressure to improve. Rivals with good financial performance are likely to continue their present strategy with only minor fine-tuning. Poorly performing rivals are virtually certain to make fresh strategic moves.

Resources and Capabilities   A rival's strategic moves and countermoves are both enabled and constrained by the set of resources and capabilities the rival has at hand. Thus, a rival's resources and capabilities (and efforts to acquire new resources and capabilities) serve as a strong signal of future strategic actions (and reactions to your company's moves). Assessing a rival's resources and capabilities involves sizing up not only its strengths in this respect but its weaknesses as well.

Assumptions   How a rival's top managers think about their strategic situation can have a big impact on how the rival behaves. Banks that believe they are "too big to fail," for example, may take on more risk than is financially prudent. Assessing a rival's assumptions entails considering its assumptions about itself as well as about the industry it participates in.

Information regarding these four analytic components can often be gleaned from company press releases, information posted on the company's website (especially the presentations management has recently made to securities analysts), and such public documents as annual reports and 10-K filings. Many companies also have a competitive intelligence unit that sifts through the available information to construct up-to-date strategic profiles of rivals.[8]

Doing the necessary detective work can be time-consuming, but scouting competitors well enough to anticipate their next moves allows managers to prepare effective countermoves (perhaps even beat a rival to the punch) and to take rivals' probable actions into account in crafting their own best course of action. Despite the importance of gathering such information, these activities should never cross the bounds of ethical impropriety (see Illustration Capsule 3.3).

KEY SUCCESS FACTORS

An industry's **key success factors (KSFs)** are those competitive factors that most affect industry members' ability to survive and prosper in the marketplace: the particular strategy elements, product attributes, operational approaches, resources, and competitive capabilities that spell the difference between being a strong competitor and a weak competitor—and between profit and loss. KSFs by their very nature are so important to competitive success that *all firms* in the industry must pay close attention to them or risk becoming an industry laggard or failure. To indicate the significance of KSFs another way, how well the elements of a company's strategy measure up against an industry's KSFs determines whether the company can meet the basic criteria for surviving and thriving in the industry. Identifying KSFs, in light of the prevailing and anticipated industry and competitive conditions, is therefore always a top priority in analytic and strategy-making considerations. Company strategists need to understand the industry landscape well enough to separate the factors most important to competitive success from those that are less important.

Key success factors vary from industry to industry, and even from time to time within the same industry, as change drivers and competitive conditions change. But regardless of the circumstances, an industry's key success factors can always be deduced by asking the same three questions:

1.   On what basis do buyers of the industry's product choose between the competing brands of sellers? That is, what product attributes and service characteristics are crucial?

2.   Given the nature of competitive rivalry prevailing in the marketplace, what resources and competitive capabilities must a company have to be competitively successful?

3.   What shortcomings are almost certain to put a company at a significant competitive disadvantage?

> **CORE** CONCEPT
>
> **Key success factors** are the strategy elements, product and service attributes, operational approaches, resources, and competitive capabilities that are essential to surviving and thriving in the industry.

Only rarely are there more than five key factors for competitive success. And even among these, two or three usually outrank the others in importance. Managers should therefore bear in mind the purpose of identifying key success factors—to determine which factors are most important to competitive success—and resist the temptation to label a factor that has only minor importance as a KSF.

In the beer industry, for example, although there are many types of buyers (wholesale, retail, end consumer), it is most important to understand the preferences and buying behavior of the beer drinkers. Their purchase decisions are driven by price, taste, convenient access, and marketing. Thus, the KSFs include a *strong network of wholesale distributors* (to get the company's brand stocked and favorably displayed in retail outlets, bars, restaurants, and stadiums, where beer is sold) and *clever advertising* (to induce beer drinkers to buy the company's brand and thereby pull beer sales through the established wholesale and retail channels). Because there is a potential for strong buyer power on the part of large distributors and retail chains, competitive success depends on some mechanism to offset that power, of which advertising (to create demand pull) is one. Thus, the KSFs also include *superior product differentiation* (as in microbrews) or *superior firm size and branding capabilities* (as in national brands). The KSFs also include *full utilization of brewing capacity* (to keep manufacturing costs low and offset the high costs of advertising, branding, and product differentiation).

Correctly diagnosing an industry's KSFs also raises a company's chances of crafting a sound strategy. The key success factors of an industry point to those things that every firm in the industry needs to attend to in order to retain customers and weather the competition. If the company's strategy cannot deliver on the key success factors of its industry, it is unlikely to earn enough profits to remain a viable business.

THE INDUSTRY OUTLOOK FOR PROFITABILITY

Each of the frameworks presented in this chapter—PESTEL, five forces analysis, driving forces, strategy groups, competitor analysis, and key success factors—provides a useful perspective on an industry's outlook for future profitability. Putting them all together provides an even richer and more nuanced picture. Thus, the final step in evaluating the industry and competitive environment is to use the results of each of the analyses performed to determine whether the industry presents the company with strong prospects for competitive success and attractive profits. The important factors on which to base a conclusion include

● LO 3-4

Determine whether an industry's outlook presents a company with sufficiently attractive opportunities for growth and profitability.

- How the company is being impacted by the state of the macro-environment.
- Whether strong competitive forces are squeezing industry profitability to subpar levels.
- Whether the presence of complementors and the possibility of cooperative actions improve the company's prospects.
- Whether industry profitability will be favorably or unfavorably affected by the prevailing driving forces.
- Whether the company occupies a stronger market position than rivals.
- Whether this is likely to change in the course of competitive interactions.
- How well the company's strategy delivers on the industry key success factors.

As a general proposition, *the anticipated industry environment is fundamentally attractive if it presents a company with good opportunity for above-average profitability; the industry outlook is fundamentally unattractive if a company's profit prospects are unappealingly low.*

However, it is a mistake to think of a particular industry as being equally attractive or unattractive to all industry participants and all potential entrants.[9] Attractiveness is relative, not absolute, and conclusions one way or the other have to be drawn from the perspective of a particular company. For instance, a favorably positioned competitor may see ample opportunity to capitalize on the vulnerabilities of weaker rivals even though industry conditions are otherwise somewhat dismal. At the same time, industries attractive to insiders may be unattractive to outsiders because of the difficulty of challenging current market leaders or because they have more attractive opportunities elsewhere.

When a company decides an industry is fundamentally attractive and presents good opportunities, a strong case can be made that it should invest aggressively to capture the opportunities it sees and to improve its long-term competitive position in the business. When a strong competitor concludes an industry is becoming less attractive, it may elect to simply protect its present position, investing cautiously—if at all—and looking for opportunities in other industries. A competitively weak company in an unattractive industry may see its best option as finding a buyer, perhaps a rival, to acquire its business.

> The degree to which an industry is attractive or unattractive is not the same for all industry participants and all potential entrants.

KEY POINTS

Thinking strategically about a company's external situation involves probing for answers to the following questions:

1. *What are the strategically relevant factors in the macro-environment, and how do they impact an industry and its members?* Industries differ significantly as to how they are affected by conditions and developments in the broad macro-environment. Using PESTEL analysis to identify which of these factors is strategically relevant is the first step to understanding how a company is situated in its external environment.

2. *What kinds of competitive forces are industry members facing, and how strong is each force?* The strength of competition is a composite of five forces: (1) rivalry within

the industry, (2) the threat of new entry into the market, (3) inroads being made by the sellers of substitutes, (4) supplier bargaining power, and (5) buyer power. All five must be examined force by force, and their collective strength evaluated. One strong force, however, can be sufficient to keep average industry profitability low. Working through the five forces model aids strategy makers in assessing how to insulate the company from the strongest forces, identify attractive arenas for expansion, or alter the competitive conditions so that they offer more favorable prospects for profitability.

3. *What cooperative forces are present in the industry, and how can a company harness them to its advantage?* Interactions among industry participants are not only competitive in nature but cooperative as well. This is particularly the case when complements to the products or services of an industry are important. The Value Net framework assists managers in sizing up the impact of cooperative as well as competitive interactions on their firm.

4. *What factors are driving changes in the industry, and what impact will they have on competitive intensity and industry profitability?* Industry and competitive conditions change because certain forces are acting to create incentives or pressures for change. The first step is to identify the three or four most important drivers of change affecting the industry being analyzed (out of a much longer list of potential drivers). Once an industry's change drivers have been identified, the analytic task becomes one of determining whether they are acting, individually and collectively, to make the industry environment more or less attractive.

5. *What market positions do industry rivals occupy—who is strongly positioned and who is not?* Strategic group mapping is a valuable tool for understanding the similarities, differences, strengths, and weaknesses inherent in the market positions of rival companies. Rivals in the same or nearby strategic groups are close competitors, whereas companies in distant strategic groups usually pose little or no immediate threat. The lesson of strategic group mapping is that some positions on the map are more favorable than others. The profit potential of different strategic groups may not be the same because industry driving forces and competitive forces likely have varying effects on the industry's distinct strategic groups. Moreover, mobility barriers restrict movement between groups in the same way that entry barriers prevent easy entry into attractive industries.

6. *What strategic moves are rivals likely to make next?* Anticipating the actions of rivals can help a company prepare effective countermoves. Using the SOAR Framework for Competitor Analysis is helpful in this regard.

7. *What are the key factors for competitive success?* An industry's key success factors (KSFs) are the particular strategy elements, product attributes, operational approaches, resources, and competitive capabilities that all industry members must have in order to survive and prosper in the industry. For any industry, they can be deduced by answering three basic questions: (1) On what basis do buyers of the industry's product choose between the competing brands of sellers, (2) what resources and competitive capabilities must a company have to be competitively successful, and (3) what shortcomings are almost certain to put a company at a significant competitive disadvantage?

8. *Is the industry outlook conducive to good profitability?* The last step in industry analysis is summing up the results from applying each of the frameworks employed in answering questions 1 to 7: PESTEL, five forces analysis, Value Net, driving forces, strategic group mapping, competitor analysis, and key success factors.

Applying multiple lenses to the question of what the industry outlook looks like offers a more robust and nuanced answer. If the answers from each framework, seen as a whole, reveal that a company's profit prospects in that industry are above-average, then the industry environment is basically attractive *for that company.* What may look like an attractive environment for one company may appear to be unattractive from the perspective of a different company.

Clear, insightful diagnosis of a company's external situation is an essential first step in crafting strategies that are well matched to industry and competitive conditions. To do cutting-edge strategic thinking about the external environment, managers must know what questions to pose and what analytic tools to use in answering these questions. This is why this chapter has concentrated on suggesting the right questions to ask, explaining concepts and analytic approaches, and indicating the kinds of things to look for.

ASSURANCE OF LEARNING EXERCISES

1. Prepare a brief analysis of the organic food industry using the information provided by the Organic Trade Association at **www.ota.com** and the *Organic Report* magazine at **theorganicreport.com.** That is, based on the information provided on these websites, draw a five forces diagram for the organic food industry and briefly discuss the nature and strength of each of the five competitive forces.

   LO 3-2

2. Based on the strategic group map in Illustration Capsule 3.2, which pizza chains are Hungry Howie's closest competitors? With which strategic group does California Pizza Kitchen compete the least, according to this map? Why do you think no Pizza chains are positioned in the area above the Pizza Hut's strategic group?

   Mc Graw Hill connect®

   LO 3-3

3. The National Restaurant Association publishes an annual industry fact book that can be found at **www.restaurant.org.** Based on information in the latest report, does it appear that macro-environmental factors and the economic characteristics of the industry will present industry participants with attractive opportunities for growth and profitability? Explain.

   LO 3-1, LO 3-4

EXERCISES FOR SIMULATION PARTICIPANTS

Mc Graw Hill connect®

1. Which of the factors listed in Table 3.1 might have the most strategic relevance for your industry?

   LO 3-1

2. Which of the five competitive forces is creating the strongest competitive pressures for your company?

   LO 3-2

3. What are the "weapons of competition" that rival companies in your industry can use to gain sales and market share? See Table 3.2 to help you identify the various competitive factors.

   LO 3-3

4. What are the factors affecting the intensity of rivalry in the industry in which your company is competing? Use Figure 3.4 and the accompanying discussion to help you in pinpointing the specific factors most affecting competitive intensity. Would you characterize the rivalry and jockeying for better market position, increased sales, and market share among the companies in your industry as fierce, very strong, strong, moderate, or relatively weak? Why?

   LO 3-4

LO 3-2   **5.** Are there any driving forces in the industry in which your company is competing? If so, what impact will these driving forces have? Will they cause competition to be more or less intense? Will they act to boost or squeeze profit margins? List at least two actions your company should consider taking in order to combat any negative impacts of the driving forces.

LO 3-3   **6.** Draw a strategic group map showing the market positions of the companies in your industry. Which companies do you believe are in the most attractive position on the map? Which companies are the most weakly positioned? Which companies do you believe are likely to try to move to a different position on the strategic group map?

LO 3-4   **7.** What do you see as the key factors for being a successful competitor in your industry? List at least three.

LO 3-4   **8.** Does your overall assessment of the industry suggest that industry rivals have sufficiently attractive opportunities for growth and profitability? Explain.

ENDNOTES

[1] Michael E. Porter, *Competitive Strategy* (New York: Free Press, 1980); Michael E. Porter, "The Five Competitive Forces That Shape Strategy," *Harvard Business Review* 86, no. 1 (January 2008), pp. 78–93.

[2] J. S. Bain, *Barriers to New Competition* (Cambridge, MA: Harvard University Press, 1956); F. M. Scherer, *Industrial Market Structure and Economic Performance* (Chicago: Rand McNally, 1971).

[3] Ibid.

[4] C. A. Montgomery and S. Hariharan, "Diversified Expansion by Large Established Firms," *Journal of Economic Behavior & Organization* 15, no. 1 (January 1991).

[5] For a more extended discussion of the problems with the life-cycle hypothesis, see Porter, *Competitive Strategy,* pp. 157–162.

[6] Mary Ellen Gordon and George R. Milne, "Selecting the Dimensions That Define Strategic Groups: A Novel Market-Driven Approach," *Journal of Managerial Issues* 11, no. 2 (Summer 1999), pp. 213–233.

[7] Avi Fiegenbaum and Howard Thomas, "Strategic Groups as Reference Groups: Theory, Modeling and Empirical Examination of Industry and Competitive Strategy," *Strategic Management Journal* 16 (1995), pp. 461–476; S. Ade Olusoga, Michael P. Mokwa, and Charles H. Noble, "Strategic Groups, Mobility Barriers, and Competitive Advantage," *Journal of Business Research* 33 (1995), pp. 153–164.

[8] Larry Kahaner, *Competitive Intelligence* (New York: Simon & Schuster, 1996).

[9] B. Wernerfelt and C. Montgomery, "What Is an Attractive Industry?" *Management Science* 32, no. 10 (October 1986), pp. 1223–1230.

chapter 4

Evaluating a Company's Resources, Capabilities, and Competitiveness

Learning Objectives

After reading this chapter, you should be able to:

LO 4-1 Evaluate how well a company's strategy is working.

LO 4-2 Assess the company's strengths and weaknesses in light of market opportunities and external threats.

LO 4-3 Explain why a company's resources and capabilities are critical for gaining a competitive edge over rivals.

LO 4-4 Understand how value chain activities affect a company's cost structure and customer value proposition.

LO 4-5 Explain how a comprehensive evaluation of a company's competitive situation can assist managers in making critical decisions about their next strategic moves.

PhotoDisc Imaging/Getty Images

Crucial, of course, is having a difference that matters in the industry.

Cynthia Montgomery—*Professor and author*

If you don't have a competitive advantage, don't compete.

Jack Welch—*Former CEO of General Electric*

Organizations succeed in a competitive marketplace over the long run because they can do certain things their customers value better than can their competitors.

Robert Hayes, Gary Pisano, and David Upton—
Professors and consultants

Chapter 3 described how to use the tools of industry and competitor analysis to assess a company's external environment and lay the groundwork for matching a company's strategy to its external situation. This chapter discusses techniques for evaluating a company's internal situation, including its collection of resources and capabilities and the activities it performs along its value chain. Internal analysis enables managers to determine whether their strategy is likely to give the company a significant competitive edge over rival firms (given external conditions). Combined with external analysis, it facilitates an understanding of how to reposition a firm to take advantage of new opportunities and to cope with emerging competitive threats. The analytic spotlight will be trained on six questions:

1. How well is the company's present strategy working?

2. What are the company's strengths and weaknesses in relation to the market opportunities and external threats?

3. What are the company's most important resources and capabilities, and will they give the company a lasting competitive advantage over rival companies?

4. How do a company's value chain activities impact its cost structure and customer value proposition?

5. Is the company competitively stronger or weaker than key rivals?

6. What strategic issues and problems merit front-burner managerial attention?

In probing for answers to these questions, five analytic tools—resource and capability analysis, SWOT analysis, value chain analysis, benchmarking, and competitive strength assessment—will be used. All five are valuable techniques for revealing a company's competitiveness and for helping company managers match their strategy to the company's particular circumstances. Accordingly, this will enable the company to pass the first of the three tests of a *winning strategy* (the Fit Test), as discussed in Chapter 1.

QUESTION 1: HOW WELL IS THE COMPANY'S PRESENT STRATEGY WORKING?

• **LO 4-1**

Evaluate how well a company's strategy is working.

Before evaluating how well a company's present strategy is working, it is best to start with a clear view of what the strategy entails. The first thing to examine is the company's competitive approach. What moves has the company made recently to attract customers and improve its market position—for instance, has it cut prices, improved the design of its product, added new features, stepped up advertising, entered a new geographic market, or merged with a competitor? Is it striving for a competitive advantage based on low costs or a better product offering? Is it concentrating on serving a broad spectrum of customers or a narrow market niche? The company's functional strategies in R&D, production, marketing, finance, human resources, information technology, and so on further characterize company strategy, as do any efforts to establish alliances with other enterprises. Figure 4.1 shows the key components of a single-business company's strategy.

A determination of the effectiveness of this strategy requires a more in-depth type of analysis. The two best indicators of how well a company's strategy is working are (1) whether the company is recording gains in financial strength and profitability, and (2) whether the company's competitive strength and market standing are improving. Persistent shortfalls in meeting company performance targets and weak marketplace performance relative to rivals are reliable warning signs that the company has a weak

FIGURE 4.1   Identifying the Components of a Single-Business Company's Strategy

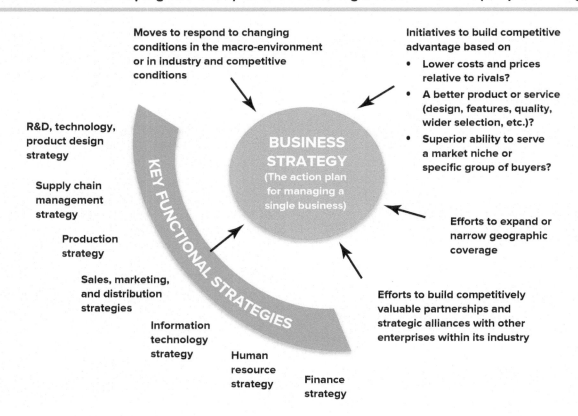

strategy, suffers from poor strategy execution, or both. Specific indicators of how well a company's strategy is working include

- Trends in the company's sales and earnings growth.
- Trends in the company's stock price.
- The company's overall financial strength.
- The company's customer retention rate.
- The rate at which new customers are acquired.
- Evidence of improvement in internal processes such as defect rate, order fulfillment, delivery times, days of inventory, and employee productivity.

The stronger a company's current overall performance, the more likely it has a well-conceived, well-executed strategy. The weaker a company's financial performance and market standing, the more its current strategy must be questioned and the more likely the need for radical changes. Table 4.1 provides a compilation of the financial ratios most commonly used to evaluate a company's financial performance and balance sheet strength.

> Sluggish financial performance and second-rate market accomplishments almost always signal weak strategy, weak execution, or both.

TABLE 4.1   Key Financial Ratios: How to Calculate Them and What They Mean

Ratio	How Calculated	What It Shows
Profitability ratios		
1. Gross profit margin	$$\frac{\text{Sales revenues} - \text{Cost of goods sold}}{\text{Sales revenues}}$$	Shows the percentage of revenues available to cover operating expenses and yield a profit.
2. Operating profit margin (or return on sales)	$$\frac{\text{Sales revenues} - \text{Operating expenses}}{\text{Sales revenues}}$$ _or_ $$\frac{\text{Operating income}}{\text{Sales revenues}}$$	Shows the profitability of current operations without regard to interest charges and income taxes. Earnings before interest and taxes is known as _EBIT_ in financial and business accounting.
3. Net profit margin (or net return on sales)	$$\frac{\text{Profits after taxes}}{\text{Sales revenues}}$$	Shows after-tax profits per dollar of sales.
4. Total return on assets	$$\frac{\text{Profits after taxes} + \text{Interest}}{\text{Total assets}}$$	A measure of the return on total investment in the enterprise. Interest is added to after-tax profits to form the numerator, since total assets are financed by creditors as well as by stockholders.
5. Net return on total assets (ROA)	$$\frac{\text{Profits after taxes}}{\text{Total assets}}$$	A measure of the return earned by stockholders on the firm's total assets.
6. Return on stockholders' equity (ROE)	$$\frac{\text{Profits after taxes}}{\text{Total stockholders' equity}}$$	The return stockholders are earning on their capital investment in the enterprise. A return in the 12% to 15% range is average.
7. Return on invested capital (ROIC)—sometimes referred to as return on capital employed (ROCE)	$$\frac{\text{Profits after taxes}}{\text{Long-term debt} + \text{Total stockholders' equity}}$$	A measure of the return that shareholders are earning on the monetary capital invested in the enterprise. A higher return reflects greater bottom-line effectiveness in the use of long-term capital.

(continued)

TABLE 4.1   *(continued)*

Ratio	How Calculated	What It Shows
Liquidity ratios		
1. Current ratio	$\dfrac{\text{Current assets}}{\text{Current liabilities}}$	Shows a firm's ability to pay current liabilities using assets that can be converted to cash in the near term. Ratio should be higher than 1.0.
2. Working capital	Current assets − Current liabilities	The cash available for a firm's day-to-day operations. Larger amounts mean the company has more internal funds to (1) pay its current liabilities on a timely basis and (2) finance inventory expansion, additional accounts receivable, and a larger base of operations without resorting to borrowing or raising more equity capital.
Leverage ratios		
1. Total debt-to-assets ratio	$\dfrac{\text{Total debt}}{\text{Total assets}}$	Measures the extent to which borrowed funds (both short-term loans and long-term debt) have been used to finance the firm's operations. A low ratio is better—a high fraction indicates overuse of debt and greater risk of bankruptcy.
2. Long-term debt-to-capital ratio	$\dfrac{\text{Long-term debt}}{\text{Long-term debt} + \text{Total stockholders' equity}}$	A measure of creditworthiness and balance sheet strength. It indicates the percentage of capital investment that has been financed by both long-term lenders and stockholders. A ratio below 0.25 is preferable since the lower the ratio, the greater the capacity to borrow additional funds. Debt-to-capital ratios above 0.50 indicate an excessive reliance on long-term borrowing, lower creditworthiness, and weak balance sheet strength.
3. Debt-to-equity ratio	$\dfrac{\text{Total debt}}{\text{Total stockholders' equity}}$	Shows the balance between debt (funds borrowed both short term and long term) and the amount that stockholders have invested in the enterprise. The further the ratio is below 1.0, the greater the firm's ability to borrow additional funds. Ratios above 1.0 put creditors at greater risk, signal weaker balance sheet strength, and often result in lower credit ratings.
4. Long-term debt-to-equity ratio	$\dfrac{\text{Long-term debt}}{\text{Total stockholders' equity}}$	Shows the balance between long-term debt and stockholders' equity in the firm's *long-term* capital structure. Low ratios indicate a greater capacity to borrow additional funds if needed.
5. Times-interest-earned (or coverage) ratio	$\dfrac{\text{Operating income}}{\text{Interest expenses}}$	Measures the ability to pay annual interest charges. Lenders usually insist on a minimum ratio of 2.0, but ratios above 3.0 signal progressively better creditworthiness.
Activity ratios		
1. Days of inventory	$\dfrac{\text{Inventory}}{\text{Cost of goods sold} \div 365}$	Measures inventory management efficiency. Fewer days of inventory are better.

(continued)

TABLE 4.1   *(continued)*

Ratio	How Calculated	What It Shows
2. Inventory turnover	$\dfrac{\text{Cost of goods sold}}{\text{Inventory}}$	Measures the number of inventory turns per year. Higher is better.
3. Average collection period	$\dfrac{\text{Accounts receivable}}{\text{Total sales} \div 365}$ *or* $\dfrac{\text{Accounts receivable}}{\text{Average daily sales}}$	Indicates the average length of time the firm must wait after making a sale to receive cash payment. A shorter collection time is better.

Other important measures of financial performance

1. Dividend yield on common stock	$\dfrac{\text{Annual dividends per share}}{\text{Current market price per share}}$	A measure of the return that shareholders receive in the form of dividends. A "typical" dividend yield is 2% to 3%. The dividend yield for fast-growth companies is often below 1%; the dividend yield for slow-growth companies can run 4% to 5%.
2. Price-to-earnings (P/E) ratio	$\dfrac{\text{Current market price per share}}{\text{Earnings per share}}$	P/E ratios above 20 indicate strong investor confidence in a firm's outlook and earnings growth; firms whose future earnings are at risk or likely to grow slowly typically have ratios below 12.
3. Dividend payout ratio	$\dfrac{\text{Annual dividends per share}}{\text{Earnings per share}}$	Indicates the percentage of after-tax profits paid out as dividends.
4. Internal cash flow	After-tax profits + Depreciation	A rough estimate of the cash a company's business is generating after payment of operating expenses, interest, and taxes. Such amounts can be used for dividend payments or funding capital expenditures.
5. Free cash flow	After-tax profits + Depreciation − Capital expenditures − Dividends	A rough estimate of the cash a company's business is generating after payment of operating expenses, interest, taxes, dividends, and desirable reinvestments in the business. The larger a company's free cash flow, the greater its ability to internally fund new strategic initiatives, repay debt, make new acquisitions, repurchase shares of stock, or increase dividend payments.

QUESTION 2: WHAT ARE THE COMPANY'S STRENGTHS AND WEAKNESSES IN RELATION TO THE MARKET OPPORTUNITIES AND EXTERNAL THREATS?

An examination of the financial and other indicators discussed previously can tell you how well a strategy is working, but they tell you little about the underlying reasons—*why* it's working or not. The simplest and most easily applied tool for gaining some insight into the reasons for the success of a strategy or lack thereof is known as

SWOT analysis. SWOT is an acronym that stands for a company's internal **S**trengths and **W**eaknesses, market **O**pportunities, and external **T**hreats. Another name for SWOT analysis is Situational Analysis. A first-rate SWOT analysis can help explain why a strategy is working well (or not) by taking a good hard look a company's strengths in relation to its weaknesses and in relation to the strengths and weaknesses of competitors. Are the company's strengths great enough to make up for its weaknesses? Has the company's strategy built on these strengths and shielded the company from its weaknesses? Do the company's strengths exceed those of its rivals or have they been overpowered? Similarly, a SWOT analysis can help determine whether a strategy has been effective in fending off external threats and positioning the firm to take advantage of market opportunities.

SWOT analysis has long been one of the most popular and widely used diagnostic tools for strategists. It is used fruitfully by organizations that range in type from large corporations to small businesses, to government agencies to non-profits such as churches and schools. Its popularity stems in part from its ease of use, but also because it can be used not only to evaluate the efficacy of a strategy, but also as the basis for crafting a strategy from the outset that capitalizes on the company's strengths, overcomes its weaknesses, aims squarely at capturing the company's best opportunities, and defends against competitive and macro-environmental threats. Moreover, a SWOT analysis can help a company with a strategy that is working well in the present determine whether the company is in a position to pursue new market opportunities and defend against emerging threats to its future well-being.

> **CORE** CONCEPT
>
> **SWOT analysis,** or Situational Analysis, is a popular, easy-to-use tool for sizing up a company's strengths and weaknesses, its market opportunities, and external threats.

> Basing a company's strategy on its most competitively valuable strengths gives the company its best chance for market success.

Identifying a Company's Internal Strengths

An internal **strength** is something a company is good at doing or an attribute that enhances its competitiveness in the marketplace.

One way to appraise a company's strengths is to ask: What activities does the company perform well? This question directs attention to the company's skill level in performing key pieces of its business—such as supply chain management, R&D, production, distribution, sales and marketing, and customer service. A company's skill or proficiency in performing different facets of its operations can range from the extreme of having minimal ability to perform an activity (perhaps having just struggled to do it the first time) to the other extreme of being able to perform the activity better than any other company in the industry.

When a company's proficiency rises from that of mere ability to perform an activity to the point of being able to perform it consistently well and at acceptable cost, it is said to have a **competence**—a true *capability,* in other words. If a company's competence level in some activity domain is superior to that of its rivals it is known as a **distinctive competence.** A **core competence** is a proficiently performed internal activity that is *central* to a company's strategy and is typically distinctive as well. A core competence is a more competitively valuable strength than a competence because of the activity's key role in the company's strategy and the contribution it makes to the company's market success and profitability. Often, core competencies can be leveraged to create new markets or new product demand, as the engine behind a company's growth. Procter and Gamble has a core competence in brand management, which has led to an ever-increasing portfolio of market-leading consumer products, including Charmin, Tide, Crest, Tampax, Olay, Febreze, Luvs, Pampers,

> **CORE** CONCEPT
>
> A **competence** is an activity that a company has learned to perform with proficiency.

> A **distinctive competence** is a capability that enables a company to perform a particular set of activities better than its rivals.

and Swiffer. Nike has a core competence in designing and marketing innovative athletic footwear and sports apparel. Kellogg has a core competence in developing, producing, and marketing breakfast cereals.

Identifying Company Internal Weaknesses

An internal **weakness** is something a company lacks or does poorly (in comparison to others) or a condition that puts it at a disadvantage in the marketplace. It can be thought of as a competitive deficiency. A company's internal weaknesses can relate to (1) inferior or unproven skills, expertise, or intellectual capital in competitively important areas of the business, or (2) deficiencies in competitively important physical, organizational, or intangible assets. Nearly all companies have competitive deficiencies of one kind or another. Whether a company's internal weaknesses make it competitively vulnerable depends on how much they matter in the marketplace and whether they are offset by the company's strengths.

Table 4.2 lists many of the things to consider in compiling a company's strengths and weaknesses. Sizing up a company's complement of strengths and deficiencies is akin to constructing a *strategic balance sheet,* where strengths represent *competitive assets* and weaknesses represent *competitive liabilities.* Obviously, the ideal condition is for the company's competitive assets to outweigh its competitive liabilities by an ample margin!

> **CORE CONCEPT**
>
> A **core competence** is an activity that a company performs proficiently and that is also central to its strategy and competitive success.

> **CORE CONCEPT**
>
> A company's **strengths** represent its competitive assets; its **weaknesses** are shortcomings that constitute competitive liabilities.

Identifying a Company's Market Opportunities

Market opportunity is a big factor in shaping a company's strategy. Indeed, managers can't properly tailor strategy to the company's situation without first identifying its market opportunities and appraising the growth and profit potential each one holds. Depending on the prevailing circumstances, a company's opportunities can be plentiful or scarce, fleeting or lasting, and can range from wildly attractive to marginally interesting or unsuitable.

Newly emerging and fast-changing markets sometimes present stunningly big or "golden" opportunities, but it is typically hard for managers at one company to peer into "the fog of the future" and spot them far ahead of managers at other companies.[1] But as the fog begins to clear, golden opportunities are nearly always seized rapidly— and the companies that seize them are usually those that have been staying alert with diligent market reconnaissance and preparing themselves to capitalize on shifting market conditions swiftly. Table 4.2 displays a sampling of potential market opportunities.

Identifying External Threats

Often, certain factors in a company's external environment pose *threats* to its profitability and competitive well-being. Threats can stem from such factors as the emergence of cheaper or better technologies, the entry of lower-cost competitors into a company's market stronghold, new regulations that are more burdensome to a company than to its competitors, unfavorable demographic shifts, and political upheaval in a foreign country where the company has facilities.

External threats may pose no more than a moderate degree of adversity (all companies confront some threatening elements in the course of doing business), or they may be imposing enough to make a company's situation look tenuous. On rare occasions, market shocks can give birth to a *sudden-death* threat that throws a

> Simply making lists of a company's strengths, weaknesses, opportunities, and threats is not enough; the payoff from SWOT analysis comes from the conclusions about a company's situation and the implications for strategy improvement that flow from the four lists.

TABLE 4.2   What to Look for in Identifying a Company's Strengths, Weaknesses, Opportunities, and Threats

Strengths and Competitive Assets	Weaknesses and Competitive Deficiencies
• Ample financial resources to grow the business • Strong brand-name image or reputation • Distinctive core competencies • Cost advantages over rivals • Attractive customer base • Proprietary technology, superior technological skills, important patents • Strong bargaining power over suppliers or buyers • Superior product quality • Wide geographic coverage and/or strong global distribution capability • Alliances and/or joint ventures that provide access to valuable technology, competencies, and/or attractive geographic markets	• No distinctive core competencies • Lack of attention to customer needs • Inferior product quality • Weak balance sheet, too much debt • Higher costs than competitors • Too narrow a product line relative to rivals • Weak brand image or reputation • Lack of adequate distribution capability • Lack of management depth • A plague of internal operating problems or obsolete facilities • Too much underutilized plant capacity

Market Opportunities	External Threats
• Meet sharply rising buyer demand for the industry's product • Serve additional customer groups or market segments • Expand into new geographic markets • Expand the company's product line to meet a broader range of customer needs • Enter new product lines or new businesses • Take advantage of falling trade barriers in attractive foreign markets • Take advantage of an adverse change in the fortunes of rival firms • Acquire rival firms or companies with attractive technological expertise or competencies • Take advantage of emerging technological developments to innovate • Enter into alliances or other cooperative ventures	• Increased intensity of competition • Slowdowns in market growth • Likely entry of potent new competitors • Growing bargaining power of customers or suppliers • A shift in buyer needs and tastes away from the industry's product • Adverse demographic changes that threaten to curtail demand for the industry's product • Adverse economic conditions that threaten critical suppliers or distributors • Changes in technology—particularly disruptive technology that can undermine the company's distinctive competencies • Restrictive foreign trade policies • Costly new regulatory requirements • Tight credit conditions • Rising prices on energy or other key inputs

company into an immediate crisis and a battle to survive. Many of the world's major financial institutions were plunged into unprecedented crisis in 2008–2009 by the aftereffects of high-risk mortgage lending, inflated credit ratings on subprime mortgage securities, the collapse of housing prices, and a market flooded with mortgage-related investments (collateralized debt obligations) whose values suddenly evaporated. It is management's job to identify the threats to the company's future prospects and to evaluate what strategic actions can be taken to neutralize or lessen their impact.

What Do the SWOT Listings Reveal?

SWOT analysis involves more than making four lists. In crafting a new strategy, it offers a strong foundation for understanding how to position the company to build on its strengths in seizing new business opportunities and how to mitigate external threats by shoring up its competitive deficiencies. In assessing the effectiveness of an existing strategy, it can be used to glean insights regarding the company's overall business situation (thus the name Situational Analysis); and it can help translate these insights into recommended strategic actions. Figure 4.2 shows the steps involved in gleaning insights from SWOT analysis.

The beauty of SWOT analysis is its simplicity; but this is also its primary limitation. For a deeper and more accurate understanding of a company's situation, more sophisticated tools are required. Chapter 3 introduced you to a set of tools for analyzing a company's external situation. In the rest of this chapter, we look more deeply at a company's internal situation, beginning with the company's resources and capabilities.

FIGURE 4.2   The Steps Involved in SWOT Analysis: Identify the Four Components of SWOT, Draw Conclusions, Translate Implications into Strategic Actions

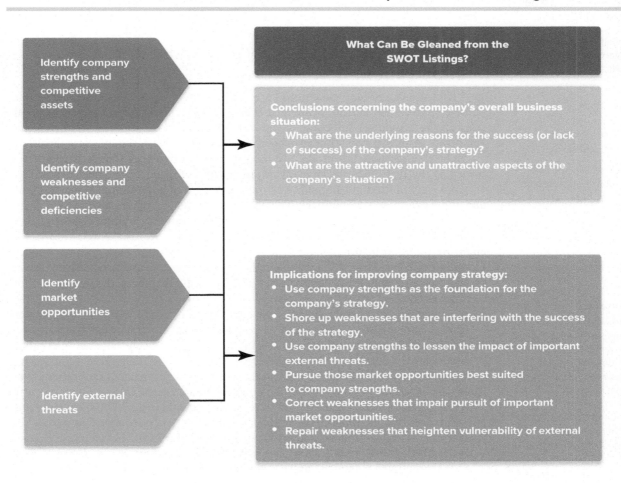

QUESTION 3: WHAT ARE THE COMPANY'S MOST IMPORTANT RESOURCES AND CAPABILITIES, AND WILL THEY GIVE THE COMPANY A LASTING COMPETITIVE ADVANTAGE?

> **CORE** CONCEPT
>
> A company's resources and capabilities represent its **competitive assets** and are determinants of its competitiveness and ability to succeed in the marketplace.

An essential element of a company's internal environment is the nature of resources and capabilities. A company's resources and capabilities are its **competitive assets** and determine whether its competitive power in the marketplace will be impressively strong or disappointingly weak. Companies with second-rate competitive assets nearly always are relegated to a trailing position in the industry.

Resource and capability analysis provides managers with a powerful tool for sizing up the company's competitive assets and determining whether they can provide the foundation necessary for competitive success in the marketplace. This is a two-step process. The first step is to identify the company's resources and capabilities. The second step is to examine them more closely to ascertain which are the most competitively important and whether they can support a sustainable competitive advantage over rival firms.[2] This second step involves applying the *four tests of a resource's competitive power*.

> **Resource and capability analysis** is a powerful tool for sizing up a company's competitive assets and determining whether the assets can support a sustainable competitive advantage over market rivals.

Identifying the Company's Resources and Capabilities

A firm's resources and capabilities are the fundamental building blocks of its competitive strategy. In crafting strategy, it is essential for managers to know how to take stock of the company's full complement of resources and capabilities. But before they can do so, managers and strategists need a more precise definition of these terms.

> • **LO 4-3**
>
> Explain why a company's resources and capabilities are critical for gaining a competitive edge over rivals.

In brief, a **resource** is a productive input or competitive asset that is owned or controlled by the firm. Firms have many different types of resources at their disposal that vary not only in kind but in quality as well. Some are of a higher quality than others, and some are more competitively valuable, having greater potential to give a firm a competitive advantage over its rivals. For example, a company's brand is a resource, as is an R&D team—yet some brands such as Coca-Cola and Xerox are well known, with enduring value, while others have little more name recognition than generic products. In similar fashion, some R&D teams are far more innovative and productive than others due to the outstanding talents of the individual team members, the team's composition, its experience, and its chemistry.

> **CORE** CONCEPT
>
> A **resource** is a competitive asset that is owned or controlled by a company; a **capability** (or **competence**) is the capacity of a firm to perform some internal activity competently. Capabilities are developed and enabled through the deployment of a company's resources.

A **capability** (or **competence**) is the capacity of a firm to perform some internal activity competently. Capabilities or competences also vary in form, quality, and competitive importance, with some being more competitively valuable than others. American Express displays superior capabilities in brand management and marketing; Starbucks's employee management, training, and real estate capabilities are the drivers behind its rapid growth; Microsoft's competences are in developing operating systems for computers and user software like Microsoft Office®. *Organizational capabilities are developed and enabled through the deployment of a company's resources.*[3] For example, Nestlé's brand management capabilities for its 2,000 + food, beverage, and pet care brands draw on the knowledge of the company's brand managers, the expertise of its marketing department, and the company's relationships with retailers in nearly

200 countries. W. L. Gore's product innovation capabilities in its fabrics and medical and industrial product businesses result from the personal initiative, creative talents, and technological expertise of its associates and the company's culture that encourages accountability and creative thinking.

Types of Company Resources   A useful way to identify a company's resources is to look for them within categories, as shown in Table 4.3. Broadly speaking, resources can be divided into two main categories: **tangible** and **intangible** resources. Although *human resources* make up one of the most important parts of a company's resource base, we include them in the intangible category to emphasize the role played by the skills, talents, and knowledge of a company's human resources.

Tangible resources are the most easily identified, since tangible resources are those that can be *touched* or *quantified* readily. Obviously, they include various types of *physical resources* such as manufacturing facilities and mineral resources, but they also include a company's *financial resources, technological resources,* and *organizational resources* such as the company's communication and control systems. Note that technological resources are included among tangible resources, *by convention,* even though some types, such as copyrights and trade secrets, might be more logically categorized as intangible.

Intangible resources are harder to discern, but they are often among the most important of a firm's competitive assets. They include various sorts of *human assets and intellectual capital,* as well as a company's *brands, image, and reputational assets.*

TABLE 4.3   Types of Company Resources

Tangible resources

- *Physical resources:* land and real estate; manufacturing plants, equipment, and/or distribution facilities; the locations of stores, plants, or distribution centers, including the overall pattern of their physical locations; ownership of or access rights to natural resources (such as mineral deposits)
- *Financial resources:* cash and cash equivalents; marketable securities; other financial assets such as a company's credit rating and borrowing capacity
- *Technological assets:* patents, copyrights, production technology, innovation technologies, technological processes
- *Organizational resources:* IT and communication systems (satellites, servers, workstations, etc.); other planning, coordination, and control systems; the company's organizational design and reporting structure

Intangible resources

- *Human assets and intellectual capital:* the education, experience, knowledge, and talent of the workforce, cumulative learning, and tacit knowledge of employees; collective learning embedded in the organization, the intellectual capital and know-how of specialized teams and work groups; the knowledge of key personnel concerning important business functions; managerial talent and leadership skill; the creativity and innovativeness of certain personnel
- *Brands, company image, and reputational assets:* brand names, trademarks, product or company image, buyer loyalty and goodwill; company reputation for quality, service, and reliability; reputation with suppliers and partners for fair dealing
- *Relationships:* alliances, joint ventures, or partnerships that provide access to technologies, specialized know-how, or geographic markets; networks of dealers or distributors; the trust established with various partners
- *Company culture and incentive system:* the norms of behavior, business principles, and ingrained beliefs within the company; the attachment of personnel to the company's ideals; the compensation system and the motivation level of company personnel

While intangible resources have no material existence on their own, they are often embodied in something material. Thus, the skills and knowledge resources of a firm are embodied in its managers and employees; a company's brand name is embodied in the company logo or product labels. Other important kinds of intangible resources include a company's *relationships* with suppliers, buyers, or partners of various sorts, and the *company's culture and incentive system.*

Listing a company's resources category by category can prevent managers from inadvertently overlooking some company resources that might be competitively important. At times, it can be difficult to decide exactly how to categorize certain types of resources. For example, resources such as a work group's specialized expertise in developing innovative products can be considered to be technological assets or human assets or intellectual capital and knowledge assets; the work ethic and drive of a company's workforce could be included under the company's human assets or its culture and incentive system. In this regard, it is important to remember that *it is not exactly how a resource is categorized that matters but, rather, that all of the company's different types of resources are included in the inventory.* The real purpose of using categories in identifying a company's resources is *to ensure that none of a company's resources go unnoticed when sizing up the company's competitive assets.*

Identifying Organizational Capabilities   Organizational capabilities are more complex entities than resources; indeed, they are built up through the use of resources and draw on some combination of the firm's resources as they are exercised. Virtually all organizational capabilities are *knowledge-based, residing in people and in a company's intellectual capital, or in organizational processes and systems, which embody tacit knowledge.* For example, Amazon's speedy delivery capabilities rely on the knowledge of its fulfillment center managers, its relationship with the United Parcel Service, and the experience of its merchandisers to correctly predict inventory flow. Bose's capabilities in auditory system design arise from the talented engineers that form the R&D team as well as the company's strong culture, which celebrates innovation and beautiful design.

Because of their complexity, organizational capabilities are harder to categorize than resources and more challenging to search for as a result. There are, however, two approaches that can make the process of uncovering and identifying a firm's capabilities more systematic. The first method takes the completed listing of a firm's resources as its starting point. Since organizational capabilities are built from resources and utilize resources as they are exercised, a firm's resources can provide a strong set of clues about the types of capabilities the firm is likely to have accumulated. This approach simply involves looking over the firm's resources and considering whether (and to what extent) the firm has built up any related capabilities. So, for example, a fleet of trucks, the latest RFID tracking technology, and a set of large automated distribution centers may be indicative of sophisticated capabilities in logistics and distribution. R&D teams composed of top scientists with expertise in genomics may suggest organizational capabilities in developing new gene therapies or in biotechnology more generally.

The second method of identifying a firm's capabilities takes a functional approach. Many organizational capabilities relate to fairly specific functions; these draw on a limited set of resources and typically involve a single department or organizational unit. Capabilities in injection molding or continuous casting or metal stamping are manufacturing-related; capabilities in direct selling, promotional pricing, or database marketing all connect to the sales and marketing functions; capabilities in basic research, strategic innovation, or new product development link to a company's R&D

function. This approach requires managers to survey the various functions a firm performs to find the different capabilities associated with each function.

A problem with this second method is that many of the most important capabilities of firms are inherently *cross-functional*. Cross-functional capabilities draw on a number of different kinds of resources and are multidimensional in nature—they spring from the effective collaboration among people with different types of expertise working in different organizational units. Warby Parker draws from its cross-functional design process to create its popular eyewear. Its design capabilities are not just due to its creative designers, but are the product of their capabilities in market research and engineering as well as their relations with suppliers and manufacturing companies. Cross-functional capabilities and other complex capabilities involving numerous linked and closely integrated competitive assets are sometimes referred to as **resource bundles.**

It is important not to miss identifying a company's resource bundles, since they can be the most competitively important of a firm's competitive assets. Resource bundles can sometimes pass the four tests of a resource's competitive power (described below) even when the individual components of the resource bundle cannot. Although PetSmart's supply chain and marketing capabilities are matched well by rival Petco, the company continues to outperform competitors through its customer service capabilities (including animal grooming and veterinary and day care services). Nike's bundle of styling expertise, marketing research skills, professional endorsements, brand name, and managerial know-how has allowed it to remain number one in the athletic footwear and apparel industry for more than 20 years.

Assessing the Competitive Power of a Company's Resources and Capabilities

To assess a company's competitive power, one must go beyond merely identifying its resources and capabilities to probe its *caliber.*[4] Thus, the second step in resource and capability analysis is designed to ascertain which of a company's resources and capabilities are competitively superior and to what extent they can support a company's quest for a sustainable competitive advantage over market rivals. When a company has competitive assets that are central to its strategy and superior to those of rival firms, they can support a competitive advantage, as defined in Chapter 1. If this advantage proves durable despite the best efforts of competitors to overcome it, then the company is said to have a *sustainable* **competitive advantage.** While it may be difficult for a company to achieve a sustainable competitive advantage, it is an important strategic objective because it imparts a potential for attractive and long-lived profitability.

The Four Tests of a Resource's Competitive Power The competitive power of a resource or capability is measured by how many of four specific tests it can pass.[5] These tests are referred to as the **VRIN tests for sustainable competitive advantage**—*VRIN* is a shorthand reminder standing for *Valuable, Rare, Inimitable,* and *Nonsubstitutable.* The first two tests determine whether a resource or capability can support a competitive advantage. The last two determine whether the competitive advantage can be sustained.

1. *Is the resource or organizational capability competitively **Valuable?*** To be competitively valuable, a resource or capability must be directly relevant to the company's strategy, making the company a more effective competitor. Unless the resource or capability contributes to the effectiveness of the company's strategy, it cannot pass

this first test. An indicator of its effectiveness is whether the resource enables the company to strengthen its business model by improving its customer value proposition and/or profit formula (see Chapter 1). Google failed in converting its technological resources and software innovation capabilities into success for Google Wallet, which incurred losses of more than $300 million before being abandoned in 2016. While these resources and capabilities have made Google the world's number-one search engine, they proved to be less valuable in the mobile payments industry.

2.   *Is the resource or capability* **Rare**—*is it something rivals lack?* Resources and capabilities that are common among firms and widely available cannot be a source of competitive advantage. All makers of branded cereals have valuable marketing capabilities and brands, since the key success factors in the ready-to-eat cereal industry demand this. They are not rare. However, the brand strength of Oreo cookies is uncommon and has provided Kraft Foods with greater market share as well as the opportunity to benefit from brand extensions such as Golden Oreos, Oreo Thins, and Mega Stuf Oreos. A resource or capability is considered rare if it is held by only a small percentage of firms in an industry or specific competitive domain. Thus, while general management capabilities are not rare in an absolute sense, they are relatively rare in some of the less developed regions of the world and in some business domains.

3.   *Is the resource or capability* **Inimitable**—*is it hard to copy?* The more difficult and more costly it is for competitors to imitate a company's resource or capability, the more likely that it can also provide a *sustainable* competitive advantage. Resources and capabilities tend to be difficult to copy when they are unique (a fantastic real estate location, patent-protected technology, an unusually talented and motivated labor force), when they must be built over time in ways that are difficult to imitate (a well-known brand name, mastery of a complex process technology, years of cumulative experience and learning), and when they entail financial outlays or large-scale operations that few industry members can undertake (a global network of dealers and distributors). Imitation is also difficult for resources and capabilities that reflect a high level of *social complexity* (company culture, interpersonal relationships among the managers or R&D teams, trust-based relations with customers or suppliers) and *causal ambiguity,* a term that signifies the hard-to-disentangle nature of the complex resources, such as a web of intricate processes enabling new drug discovery. Hard-to-copy resources and capabilities are important competitive assets, contributing to the longevity of a company's market position and offering the potential for sustained profitability.

4.   *Is the resource or capability* **Nonsubstitutable**—*is it invulnerable to the threat of substitution from different types of resources and capabilities?* Even resources that are competitively valuable, rare, and costly to imitate may lose much of their ability to offer competitive advantage if rivals possess equivalent substitute resources. For example, manufacturers relying on automation to gain a cost-based advantage in production activities may find their technology-based advantage nullified by rivals' use of low-wage offshore manufacturing. Resources can contribute to a sustainable competitive advantage only when resource substitutes aren't on the horizon.

The vast majority of companies are not well endowed with standout resources or capabilities, capable of passing all four tests with high marks. Most firms have a mixed bag of resources—one or two quite valuable, some good, many satisfactory to mediocre. Resources and capabilities that are valuable pass the first of the four tests. As key contributors to the effectiveness of the strategy, they are relevant to the firm's competitiveness but are no guarantee of competitive advantage. They may offer no more than competitive parity with competing firms.

Passing both of the first two tests requires more—it requires resources and capabilities that are not only valuable but also rare. This is a much higher hurdle that can be cleared only by resources and capabilities that are *competitively superior.* Resources and capabilities that are competitively superior are the company's true strategic assets. They provide the company with a competitive advantage over its competitors, if only in the short run.

To pass the last two tests, a resource must be able to maintain its competitive superiority in the face of competition. It must be resistant to imitative attempts and efforts by competitors to find equally valuable substitute resources. Assessing the availability of substitutes is the most difficult of all the tests since substitutes are harder to recognize, but the key is to look for resources or capabilities held by other firms or being developed that *can serve the same function* as the company's core resources and capabilities.[6]

Very few firms have resources and capabilities that can pass all four tests, but those that do enjoy a sustainable competitive advantage with far greater profit potential. Costco is a notable example, with strong employee incentive programs and capabilities in supply chain management that have surpassed those of its warehouse club rivals for over 35 years. Lincoln Electric Company, less well known but no less notable in its achievements, has been the world leader in welding products for over 100 years as a result of its unique piecework incentive system for compensating production workers and the unsurpassed worker productivity and product quality that this system has fostered.

A Company's Resources and Capabilities Must Be Managed Dynamically   Even companies like Costco and Lincoln Electric cannot afford to rest on their laurels. Rivals that are initially unable to replicate a key resource may develop better and better substitutes over time. Resources and capabilities can depreciate like other assets if they are managed with benign neglect. Disruptive changes in technology, customer preferences, distribution channels, or other competitive factors can also destroy the value of key strategic assets, turning resources and capabilities "from diamonds to rust."[7]

Resources and capabilities must be continually strengthened and nurtured to sustain their competitive power and, at times, may need to be broadened and deepened to allow the company to position itself to pursue emerging market opportunities.[8] Organizational resources and capabilities that grow stale can impair competitiveness unless they are refreshed, modified, or even phased out and replaced in response to ongoing market changes and shifts in company strategy. Management's challenge in managing the firm's resources and capabilities dynamically has two elements: (1) attending to the ongoing modification of existing competitive assets, and (2) casting a watchful eye for opportunities to develop totally new kinds of capabilities.

The Role of Dynamic Capabilities   Companies that know the importance of recalibrating and upgrading their most valuable resources and capabilities ensure that these activities are done on a continual basis. By incorporating these activities into their routine managerial functions, they gain the experience necessary to be able to do them consistently well. At that point, their ability to freshen and renew their competitive assets becomes a capability in itself—a **dynamic capability.** A dynamic capability is the ability to modify, deepen, or augment the company's existing resources and capabilities.[9] This includes the capacity to improve existing resources and capabilities incrementally, in the way that Toyota aggressively upgrades the company's capabilities in fuel-efficient hybrid engine technology and constantly fine-tunes its famed Toyota production system. Likewise, management at BMW developed new organizational capabilities in hybrid engine design that allowed the company to launch its highly touted i3 and i8 plug-in hybrids. A dynamic capability

> A company requires a dynamically evolving portfolio of resources and capabilities to sustain its competitiveness and help drive improvements in its performance.

CORE CONCEPT

A **dynamic capability** is an ongoing capacity of a company to modify its existing resources and capabilities or create new ones.

also includes the capacity to add new resources and capabilities to the company's competitive asset portfolio. One way to do this is through alliances and acquisitions. An example is General Motor's partnership with Korean electronics firm LG Corporation, which enabled GM to develop a manufacturing and engineering platform for producing electric vehicles. This enabled GM to beat the likes of Tesla and Nissan to market with the first affordable all-electric car with good driving range—the Chevy Bolt EV.

QUESTION 4: HOW DO VALUE CHAIN ACTIVITIES IMPACT A COMPANY'S COST STRUCTURE AND CUSTOMER VALUE PROPOSITION?

● **LO 4-4**

Understand how value chain activities can affect a company's cost structure and customer value proposition.

Company managers are often stunned when a competitor cuts its prices to "unbelievably low" levels or when a new market entrant introduces a great new product at a surprisingly low price. While less common, new entrants can also storm the market with a product that ratchets the quality level up so high that customers will abandon competing sellers even if they have to pay more for the new product. This is what seems to have happened with Apple's iPhone 7 and iMac computers.

Regardless of where on the quality spectrum a company competes, it must remain competitive in terms of its customer value proposition in order to stay in the game. Patagonia's value proposition, for example, remains attractive to customers who value quality, wide selection, and corporate environmental responsibility over cheaper outerwear alternatives. Since its inception in 1925, the *New Yorker*'s customer value proposition has withstood the test of time by providing readers with an amalgam of well-crafted and topical writing.

> The greater the amount of customer value that a company can offer profitably relative to close rivals, the less competitively vulnerable the company becomes.

Recall from our discussion of the Customer Value Proposition in Chapter 1: The value (V) provided to the customer depends on how well a customer's needs are met for the price paid (V-P). How well customer needs are met depends on the perceived quality of a product or service as well as on other, more tangible attributes. The greater the amount of customer value that the company can offer profitably compared to its rivals, the less vulnerable it will be to competitive attack. For managers, the key is to keep close track of how *cost-effectively* the company can deliver value to customers relative to its competitors. If it can deliver the same amount of value with lower expenditures (or more value at the same cost), it will maintain a competitive edge.

> The higher a company's costs are above those of close rivals, the more competitively vulnerable the company becomes.

Two analytic tools are particularly useful in determining whether a company's costs and customer value proposition are competitive: value chain analysis and benchmarking.

The Concept of a Company Value Chain

CORE CONCEPT

A company's **value chain** identifies the primary activities and related support activities that create customer value.

Every company's business consists of a collection of activities undertaken in the course of producing, marketing, delivering, and supporting its product or service. All the various activities that a company performs internally combine to form a **value chain**—so called because the underlying intent of a company's activities is ultimately to *create value for buyers*.

As shown in Figure 4.3, a company's value chain consists of two broad categories of activities: the *primary activities* foremost in creating value for customers and the requisite *support activities* that facilitate and enhance the performance of the

FIGURE 4.3 A Representative Company Value Chain

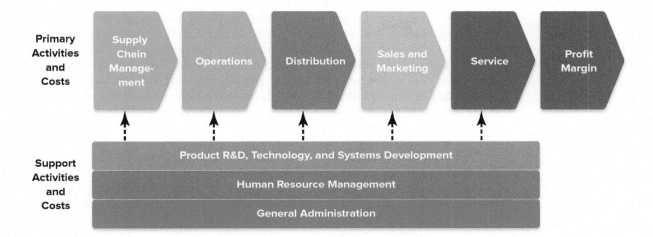

PRIMARY ACTIVITIES

- **Supply Chain Management**—Activities, costs, and assets associated with purchasing fuel, energy, raw materials, parts and components, merchandise, and consumable items from vendors; receiving, storing, and disseminating inputs from suppliers; inspection; and inventory management.

- **Operations**—Activities, costs, and assets associated with converting inputs into final product form (production, assembly, packaging, equipment maintenance, facilities, operations, quality assurance, environmental protection).

- **Distribution**—Activities, costs, and assets dealing with physically distributing the product to buyers (finished goods warehousing, order processing, order picking and packing, shipping, delivery vehicle operations, establishing and maintaining a network of dealers and distributors).

- **Sales and Marketing**—Activities, costs, and assets related to sales force efforts, advertising and promotion, market research and planning, and dealer/distributor support.

- **Service**—Activities, costs, and assets associated with providing assistance to buyers, such as installation, spare parts delivery, maintenance and repair, technical assistance, buyer inquiries, and complaints.

SUPPORT ACTIVITIES

- **Product R&D, Technology, and Systems Development**—Activities, costs, and assets relating to product R&D, process R&D, process design improvement, equipment design, computer software development, telecommunications systems, computer-assisted design and engineering, database capabilities, and development of computerized support systems.

- **Human Resource Management**—Activities, costs, and assets associated with the recruitment, hiring, training, development, and compensation of all types of personnel; labor relations activities; and development of knowledge-based skills and core competencies.

- **General Administration**—Activities, costs, and assets relating to general management, accounting and finance, legal and regulatory affairs, safety and security, management information systems, forming strategic alliances and collaborating with strategic partners, and other "overhead" functions.

Source: Based on the discussion in Michael E. Porter, *Competitive Advantage* (New York: Free Press, 1985), pp. 37–43.

primary activities.[10] The kinds of primary and secondary activities that constitute a company's value chain vary according to the specifics of a company's business; hence, the listing of the primary and support activities in Figure 4.3 is illustrative rather than definitive. For example, the primary activities at a hotel operator like Starwood Hotels and Resorts mainly consist of site selection and construction, reservations, and hotel operations (check-in and check-out, maintenance and housekeeping, dining and room service, and conventions and meetings); principal support activities that drive costs and impact customer value include hiring and training hotel staff and handling general administration. Supply chain management is a crucial activity for Boeing and Amazon but is not a value chain component at Facebook, WhatsApp, or Goldman Sachs. Sales and marketing are dominant activities at GAP and Match.com but have only minor roles at oil-drilling companies and natural gas pipeline companies. Customer delivery is a crucial activity at Domino's Pizza and Blue Apron but insignificant at Starbucks and Dunkin Donuts.

With its focus on value-creating activities, the value chain is an ideal tool for examining the workings of a company's customer value proposition and business model. It permits a deep look at the company's cost structure and ability to offer low prices. It reveals the emphasis that a company places on activities that enhance differentiation and support higher prices, such as service and marketing. It also includes a profit margin component (P-C), since profits are necessary to compensate the company's owners and investors, who bear risks and provide capital. Tracking the profit margin along with the value-creating activities is critical because unless an enterprise succeeds in delivering customer value profitably (with a sufficient return on invested capital), it can't survive for long. Attention to a company's profit formula in addition to its customer value proposition is the essence of a sound business model, as described in Chapter 1.

Illustration Capsule 4.1 shows representative costs for various value chain activities performed by Everlane, Inc., an American clothing retailer that sells primarily online.

Comparing the Value Chains of Rival Companies   Value chain analysis facilitates a comparison of how rivals, activity by activity, deliver value to customers. Even rivals in the same industry may differ significantly in terms of the activities they perform. For instance, the "operations" component of the value chain for a manufacturer that makes all of its own parts and components and assembles them into a finished product differs from the "operations" of a rival producer that buys the needed parts and components from outside suppliers and performs only assembly operations. How each activity is performed may affect a company's relative cost position as well as its capacity for differentiation. Thus, even a simple comparison of how the activities of rivals' value chains differ can reveal competitive differences.

A Company's Primary and Secondary Activities Identify the Major Components of Its Internal Cost Structure   The combined costs of all the various primary and support activities constituting a company's value chain define its internal cost structure. Further, the cost of each activity contributes to whether the company's overall cost position relative to rivals is favorable or unfavorable. The roles of value chain analysis and benchmarking are to develop the data for comparing a company's costs activity by activity against the costs of key rivals and to learn which internal activities are a source of cost advantage or disadvantage.

Evaluating a company's cost-competitiveness involves using what accountants call *activity-based costing* to determine the costs of performing each value chain activity.[11] The degree to which a company's total costs should be broken down into costs for

Everlane, Inc. prides itself on producing casual clothing, designed to last, in ethically managed factories, under a policy of what they call "radical transparency". From the start, they have made their cost and margin breakdowns readily available on their website. Below is such a breakdown for a pair of their slim-fit denim jeans:

M4OS Photos/Alamy Stock Photo

Materials (11 oz. denim - 98% cotton; 2% elastane	$12.78	
Hardware (metal fasteners, trim)	2.15	
Labor	7.50	
Cost of Goods		**22.43**
Shipping	1.90	
Import Duties	3.70	
Total Cost		**28.03**
Everlane Retail Price		**68.00**
Everlane Profit Margin (Retail Price – Total Cost)	39.97	
Average Traditional Retailer's Price		**140.00**

Source: Everlane.com/about (accessed 2/08/20).

specific activities depends on how valuable it is to know the costs of specific activities versus broadly defined activities. At the very least, cost estimates are needed for each broad category of primary and support activities, but cost estimates for more specific activities within each broad category may be needed if a company discovers that it has a cost disadvantage vis-à-vis rivals and wants to pin down the exact source or activity causing the cost disadvantage. However, a company's own *internal costs* may be insufficient to assess whether its product offering and customer value proposition are competitive with those of rivals. Cost and price differences among competing companies can have their origins in activities performed by suppliers or by distribution allies involved in getting the product to the final customers or end users of the product, in which case the company's entire *value chain system* becomes relevant.

> A company's cost-competitiveness depends not only on the costs of internally performed activities (its own value chain) but also on costs in the value chains of its suppliers and distribution-channel allies.

The Value Chain System

A company's value chain is embedded in a larger system of activities that includes the value chains of its suppliers and the value chains of whatever wholesale distributors and retailers it utilizes in getting its product or service to end users. This *value chain system* (sometimes called a vertical chain) has implications that extend far beyond the company's costs. It can affect attributes like product quality that enhance differentiation and have importance for the company's customer value proposition, as well as its profitability.[12] Suppliers' value chains are relevant because suppliers perform activities and incur costs in creating and delivering the purchased inputs utilized in a company's own value-creating activities. The costs, performance features, and quality of these inputs influence a company's own costs and product differentiation capabilities.

Anything a company can do to help its suppliers drive down the costs of their value chain activities or improve the quality and performance of the items being supplied can enhance its own competitiveness—a powerful reason for working collaboratively with suppliers in managing supply chain activities.[13] For example, automakers have encouraged their automotive parts suppliers to build plants near the auto assembly plants to facilitate just-in-time deliveries, reduce warehousing and shipping costs, and promote close collaboration on parts design and production scheduling.

Similarly, the value chains of a company's distribution-channel partners are relevant because (1) the costs and margins of a company's distributors and retail dealers are part of the price the ultimate consumer pays and (2) the quality of the activities that such distribution allies perform affect sales volumes and customer satisfaction. For these reasons, companies that don't sell directly to the end consumer work closely with their distribution allies (including their direct customers) to perform value chain activities in mutually beneficial ways. For instance, motor vehicle manufacturers have a competitive interest in working closely with their automobile dealers to promote higher sales volumes and better customer satisfaction with dealers' repair and maintenance services. Producers of kitchen cabinets are heavily dependent on the sales and promotional activities of their distributors and building supply retailers and on whether distributors and retailers operate cost-effectively enough to be able to sell at prices that lead to attractive sales volumes.

As a consequence, *accurately assessing a company's competitiveness entails scrutinizing the nature and costs of value chain activities throughout the entire value chain system for delivering its products or services to end-use customers.* A typical value chain system that incorporates the value chains of suppliers, business buyers, and other forward-channel allies (if any) is shown in Figure 4.4. As was the case with company value chains, the specific activities constituting value chain systems vary significantly from industry to industry. The primary value chain system activities in the pulp and paper industry (timber farming, logging, pulp mills, and papermaking) differ from the primary value chain system activities in the home appliance industry (parts and components manufacture, assembly, wholesale distribution, retail sales) and yet again from the computer software industry (programming, disk loading, marketing, distribution). Some value chains may also include strategic partners whose activities may likewise affect both the value and cost of the end product.

FIGURE 4.4   A Representative Value Chain System

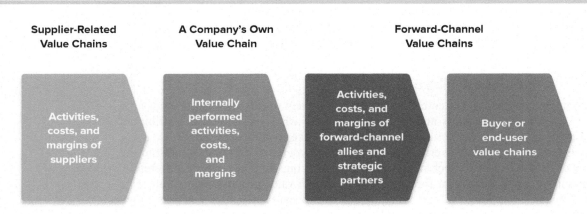

Supplier-Related Value Chains	A Company's Own Value Chain	Forward-Channel Value Chains	
Activities, costs, and margins of suppliers	Internally performed activities, costs, and margins	Activities, costs, and margins of forward-channel allies and strategic partners	Buyer or end-user value chains

Source: Based in part on the single-industry value chain displayed in Michael E. Porter, *Competitive Advantage* (New York: Free Press, 1985), p. 35.

Benchmarking: A Tool for Assessing the Costs and Effectiveness of Value Chain Activities

Benchmarking entails comparing how different companies perform various value chain activities—how materials are purchased, how inventories are managed, how products are assembled, how fast the company can get new products to market, how customer orders are filled and shipped—and then making cross-company comparisons of the costs and effectiveness of these activities.[14] The comparison is often made between companies in the same industry, but benchmarking can also involve comparing how activities are done by companies in other industries. The objectives of benchmarking are simply to identify the best means of performing an activity and to emulate those best practices. It can be used to benchmark the activities of a company's internal value chain or the activities within an entire value chain system.

A **best practice** is a method of performing an activity or business process that consistently delivers superior results compared to other approaches.[15] To qualify as a legitimate best practice, the method must have been employed by at least one enterprise and shown to be *consistently more effective* in lowering costs, improving quality or performance, shortening time requirements, enhancing safety, or achieving some other highly positive operating outcome. Best practices thus identify a path to operating excellence with respect to value chain activities.

Xerox pioneered the use of benchmarking to become more cost-competitive, quickly deciding not to restrict its benchmarking efforts to its office equipment rivals but to extend them to *any company regarded as "world class"* in performing *any activity* relevant to Xerox's business. Other companies quickly picked up on Xerox's approach. Toyota managers got their idea for just-in-time inventory deliveries by studying how U.S. supermarkets replenished their shelves. Southwest Airlines reduced the turnaround time of its aircraft at each scheduled stop by studying pit crews on the auto racing circuit. More than 80 percent of Fortune 500 companies reportedly use benchmarking for comparing themselves against rivals on cost and other competitively important measures. Illustration Capsule 4.2 describes benchmarking practices in the solar industry.

The tough part of benchmarking is not whether to do it but, rather, how to gain access to information about other companies' practices and costs. Sometimes benchmarking can be accomplished by collecting information from published reports, trade groups, and industry research firms or by talking to knowledgeable industry analysts, customers, and suppliers. Sometimes field trips to the facilities of competing or noncompeting companies can be arranged to observe how things are done, compare practices and processes, and perhaps exchange data on productivity and other cost components. However, such companies, even if they agree to host facilities tours and answer questions, are unlikely to share competitively sensitive cost information. Furthermore, comparing two companies' costs may not involve comparing apples to apples if the two companies employ different cost accounting principles to calculate the costs of particular activities.

However, a third and fairly reliable source of benchmarking information has emerged. The explosive interest of companies in benchmarking costs and identifying best practices has prompted consulting organizations (e.g., Accenture, A. T. Kearney, Benchnet—The Benchmarking Exchange, and Best Practices, LLC) and several associations (e.g., the QualServe Benchmarking Clearinghouse, and the Strategic Planning Institute's Council on Benchmarking) to gather benchmarking data, distribute information about best practices, and provide comparative cost data without identifying the names of particular companies. Having an independent group gather the information and report it in a manner that disguises the names of

> **CORE CONCEPT**
>
> **Benchmarking** is a potent tool for improving a value chain activities that is based on learning how other companies perform them and borrowing their "best practices."

> **CORE CONCEPT**
>
> A **best practice** is a method of performing an activity that consistently delivers superior results compared to other approaches.

> Benchmarking the costs of company activities against those of rivals provides hard evidence of whether a company is cost-competitive.

ILLUSTRATION
CAPSULE 4.2   Benchmarking in the Solar Industry

The cost of solar power production is dropping rapidly, leading to lower solar power prices for consumers and an expanding market for solar companies. According to the Solar Energy Industries Association, over 11 gigawatts (GW) of solar serving electric utilities were installed in 2016—enough to supply power for approximately 1.8 million households. Simultaneously, the solar landscape is becoming more competitive. As of 2017, 46 firms had installed a cumulative total of over 45 GW of solar serving electric utilities in the United States.

As competition grows, benchmarking plays an increasingly critical role in assessing a solar company's relative costs and price positioning compared to other firms. This is often measured using the all-in installation and production costs per kilowatt hour generated by a solar asset, called the "Levelized Cost of Energy" (LCOE). Kilowatt hours are the units of electricity that are sold to consumers.

In 2008, SunPower—one of the largest solar firms in the United States—used benchmarking to target a 50 percent decrease in its solar LCOE by 2012. This early benchmarking strategy helped the company to defend against new market entrants offering lower prices. But in the ensuing years, between 2009 and 2014, the overall industry solar LCOE fell by 78 percent, leading the company to conclude that an even more aggressive approach was needed to manage downward pricing pressure. Over the course of 2017, SunPower's quarterly earnings calls highlighted efforts to compete on benchmark prices by simplifying its company structure; divesting from non-core assets; and diversifying beyond the low-cost, large-scale utility solar market and into residential and commercial solar where it could compete more easily on price.

Geniusksy/Shutterstock

Continuing to anticipate and adapt to falling solar prices requires reliable industry data on benchmark costs. The National Renewable Energy Laboratory (NREL) Quarterly U.S. Solar Photovoltaic System Cost Benchmark breaks down industry solar costs by inputs, including solar modules, structural hardware, and electrical components, as well as soft costs like labor and land expenses. This enables firms like SunPower to assess how their component costs compare to benchmarks and informs SunPower's outlook for how solar prices will continue to fall over time.

For solar to play a major role in U.S. power generation, costs must keep decreasing. As solar companies race toward lower costs, benchmarking will continue to be a core strategic tool in determining pricing and market positioning.

Note: Developed with Mathew O'Sullivan.

Sources: Solar Power World, "Top 500 Solar Contractors" (2017); SunPower, "The Drivers of the Levelized Cost of Electricity for Utility-Scale Photovoltaics" (2008); Lazard, "Levelized Cost of Energy Analysis, Version 8.0" (2014).

individual companies protects competitively sensitive data and lessens the potential for unethical behavior on the part of company personnel in gathering their own data about competitors. The ethical dimension of benchmarking is discussed in Illustration Capsule 4.3.

Industry associations are another source of data that may be used for benchmarking purposes. In the cement industry, for example, the Portland Cement Association publishes key plant level data for the industry that enables companies to understand whether their own plants are cost leaders or laggards. Benchmarking data is also provided by some government agencies; data of this sort plays an important role in electricity pricing, for example.

Because discussions between benchmarking partners can involve competitively sensitive data, conceivably raising questions about possible restraint of trade or improper business conduct, the Strategic Planning Institute's Council on Benchmarking and the Global Benchmarking Network urge all individuals and organizations involved in benchmarking to abide by a code of conduct grounded in ethical business behavior. The code is based on the following principles:

- **Principle of Legality.** Avoid discussions or actions that might lead to or imply an interest in restraint of trade: market or customer allocation schemes, price fixing, dealing arrangements, bid rigging, bribery, or misappropriation. Do not discuss costs with competitors if costs are an element of pricing.

- **Principle of Exchange.** Be willing to provide the same level of information that you request, in any benchmarking exchange.

- **Principle of Confidentiality.** Treat benchmarking interchange as something confidential to the individuals and organizations involved. Information obtained must not be communicated outside the partnering organizations without prior consent of participating benchmarking partners.

An organization's participation in a study should not be communicated externally without their permission.

- **Principle of Use.** Use information obtained through benchmarking partnering only for the purpose of improvement of operations within the partnering companies themselves. External use or communication of a benchmarking partner's name with their data or observed practices requires permission of that partner. Do not, as a consultant or client, extend one company's benchmarking study findings to another without the first company's permission.

- **Principle of First Party Contact.** Initiate contacts, whenever possible, through a benchmarking contact designated by the partner company. Obtain mutual agreement with the contact on any hand off of communication or responsibility to other parties.

- **Principle of Third Party Contact.** Obtain an individual's permission before providing their name in response to a contact request.

- **Principle of Preparation.** Demonstrate commitment to the efficiency and effectiveness of the benchmarking process with adequate preparation at each process step; particularly, at initial partnering contact.

Source: BPIR.com (Business Performance Improvement Resource), https://www.bpir.com/benchmarking-code-of-conduct-bpir.com/menu-id-56.html (accessed 2/08/20).

Strategic Options for Remedying a Cost or Value Disadvantage

The results of value chain analysis and benchmarking may disclose cost or value disadvantages relative to key rivals. Such information is vital in crafting strategic actions to eliminate any such disadvantages and improve profitability. Information of this nature can also help a company find new avenues for enhancing its competitiveness through lower costs or a more attractive customer value proposition. There are three main areas in a company's total value chain system where company managers can try to improve its efficiency and effectiveness in delivering customer value: (1) a company's own internal activities, (2) suppliers' part of the value chain system, and (3) the forward-channel portion of the value chain system.

Improving Internally Performed Value Chain Activities   Managers can pursue any of several strategic approaches to reduce the costs of internally performed value chain activities and improve a company's cost-competitiveness. They can *implement best practices* throughout the company, particularly for high-cost activities. They can *redesign the product and/or some of its components* to eliminate high-cost components or facilitate speedier and more economical manufacture or assembly. They can *relocate* *high-cost activities* (such as manufacturing) to geographic areas where they can be performed more cheaply or *outsource activities* to lower-cost vendors or contractors.

To improve the effectiveness of the company's customer value proposition and enhance differentiation, managers can take several approaches. They can *adopt best practices for quality, marketing, and customer service.* They can *reallocate resources to activities that address buyers' most important purchase criteria,* which will have the biggest impact on the value delivered to the customer. They can *adopt new technologies that spur innovation, improve design, and enhance creativity.* Additional approaches to managing value chain activities to lower costs and/or enhance customer value are discussed in Chapter 5.

Improving Supplier-Related Value Chain Activities   Supplier-related cost disadvantages can be attacked by pressuring suppliers for lower prices, switching to lower-priced substitute inputs, and collaborating closely with suppliers to identify mutual cost-saving opportunities.[16] For example, just-in-time deliveries from suppliers can lower a company's inventory and internal logistics costs and may also allow suppliers to economize on their warehousing, shipping, and production scheduling costs—a win–win outcome for both. In a few instances, companies may find that it is cheaper to integrate backward into the business of high-cost suppliers and make the item in-house instead of buying it from outsiders.

Similarly, a company can enhance its customer value proposition through its supplier relationships. Some approaches include selecting and retaining suppliers that meet higher-quality standards, providing quality-based incentives to suppliers, and integrating suppliers into the design process. Fewer defects in parts from suppliers not only improve quality throughout the value chain system but can lower costs as well since less waste and disruption occur in the production processes.

Improving Value Chain Activities of Distribution Partners   Any of three means can be used to achieve better cost-competitiveness in the forward portion of the industry value chain:

1. Pressure distributors, dealers, and other forward-channel allies to reduce their costs and markups.
2. Collaborate with them to identify win–win opportunities to reduce costs—for example, a chocolate manufacturer learned that by shipping its bulk chocolate in liquid form in tank cars instead of as 10-pound molded bars, it could not only save its candy bar manufacturing customers the costs associated with unpacking and melting but also eliminate its own costs of molding bars and packing them.
3. Change to a more economical distribution strategy, including switching to cheaper distribution channels (selling direct via the Internet) or integrating forward into company-owned retail outlets.

The means to enhancing differentiation through activities at the forward end of the value chain system include (1) engaging in cooperative advertising and promotions with forward allies (dealers, distributors, retailers, etc.), (2) creating exclusive arrangements with downstream sellers or utilizing other mechanisms that increase their incentives to enhance delivered customer value, and (3) creating and enforcing standards for downstream activities and assisting in training channel partners in business practices. Harley-Davidson, for example, enhances the shopping experience and perceptions of buyers by selling through retailers that sell Harley-Davidson motorcycles exclusively and meet Harley-Davidson standards. The bottlers of Pepsi and Coca Cola engage in cooperative promotional activities with large grocery chains such as Kroger, Publix, and Safeway.

Translating Proficient Performance of Value Chain Activities into Competitive Advantage

A company that does a *first-rate job* of managing the activities of its value chain or value chain system *relative to competitors* stands a good chance of profiting from its competitive advantage. A company's value-creating activities can offer a competitive advantage in one of two ways (or both):

1. They can contribute to greater efficiency and lower costs relative to competitors.
2. They can provide a basis for differentiation, so customers are willing to pay relatively more for the company's goods and services.

Achieving a cost-based competitive advantage requires determined management efforts to be cost-efficient in performing value chain activities. Such efforts have to be ongoing and persistent, and they have to involve each and every value chain activity. The goal must be continuous cost reduction, not a one-time or on-again–off-again effort. Companies like Dollar General, Nucor Steel, Irish airline Ryanair, T.J.Maxx, and French discount retailer Carrefour have been highly successful in managing their value chains in a low-cost manner.

Ongoing and persistent efforts are also required for a competitive advantage based on differentiation. Superior reputations and brands are built up slowly over time, through continuous investment and activities that deliver consistent, reinforcing messages. Differentiation based on quality requires vigilant management of activities for quality assurance throughout the value chain. While the basis for differentiation (e.g., status, design, innovation, customer service, reliability, image) may vary widely among companies pursuing a differentiation advantage, companies that succeed do so on the basis of a commitment to coordinated value chain activities aimed purposefully at this objective. Examples include Rolex (status), Braun (design), Room and Board (craftsmanship), Zappos and L.L. Bean (customer service), Salesforce.com and Tesla (innovation), and FedEx (reliability).

How Value Chain Activities Relate to Resources and Capabilities There is a close relationship between the value-creating activities that a company performs and its resources and capabilities. An organizational capability or competence implies a *capacity* for action; in contrast, a value-creating activity *initiates* the action. With respect to resources and capabilities, activities are "where the rubber hits the road." When companies engage in a value-creating activity, they do so by drawing on specific company resources and capabilities that underlie and enable the activity. For example, brand-building activities depend on human resources, such as experienced brand managers (including their knowledge and expertise in this arena), as well as organizational capabilities in advertising and marketing. Cost-cutting activities may derive from organizational capabilities in inventory management, for example, and resources such as inventory tracking systems.

Because of this correspondence between activities and supporting resources and capabilities, value chain analysis can complement resource and capability analysis as another tool for assessing a company's competitive advantage. Resources and capabilities that are *both valuable and rare* provide a company with *what it takes* for competitive advantage. For a company with competitive assets of this sort, the potential is there. When these assets are deployed in the form of a value-creating activity, that potential is realized due to their competitive superiority. Resource analysis is one tool for identifying competitively superior resources and capabilities. But their value and the competitive superiority of that value can be assessed

Value chain analysis and benchmarking provide the type of data needed to assess objectively whether a company's resources and capabilities are competitively superior.

> Performing value chain activities with capabilities that permit the company to either outmatch rivals on differentiation or beat them on costs will give the company a competitive advantage.

objectively only *after* they are deployed. Value chain analysis and benchmarking provide the type of data needed to make that objective assessment.

There is also a dynamic relationship between a company's activities and its resources and capabilities. Value-creating activities are more than just the embodiment of a resource's or capability's potential. They also contribute to the formation and development of organizational capabilities. The road to competitive advantage begins with management efforts to build organizational expertise in performing certain competitively important value chain activities. With consistent practice and continuous investment of company resources, these activities rise to the level of a reliable organizational capability or a competence. To the extent that top management makes the growing capability a cornerstone of the company's strategy, this capability becomes a core competence for the company. Later, with further organizational learning and gains in proficiency, the core competence may evolve into a distinctive competence, giving the company superiority over rivals in performing an important value chain activity. Such superiority, if it gives the company significant competitive clout in the marketplace, can produce an attractive competitive edge over rivals. Whether the resulting competitive advantage is on the cost side or on the differentiation side (or both) will depend on the company's choice of which types of competence-building activities to engage in over this time period.

QUESTION 5: IS THE COMPANY COMPETITIVELY STRONGER OR WEAKER THAN KEY RIVALS?

> ● **LO 4-5**
>
> Explain how a comprehensive evaluation of a company's competitive situation can assist managers in making critical decisions about their next strategic moves.

Using resource analysis, value chain analysis, and benchmarking to determine a company's competitiveness on value and cost is necessary but not sufficient. A more comprehensive assessment needs to be made of the company's *overall* competitive strength. The answers to two questions are of particular interest: First, how does the company rank relative to competitors on each of the important factors that determine market success? Second, all things considered, does the company have a *net* competitive advantage or disadvantage versus major competitors?

An easy-to-use method for answering these two questions involves developing quantitative strength ratings for the company and its key competitors on each industry key success factor and each competitively pivotal resource, capability, and value chain activity. Much of the information needed for doing a competitive strength assessment comes from previous analyses. Industry and competitive analyses reveal the key success factors and competitive forces that separate industry winners from losers. Benchmarking data and scouting key competitors provide a basis for judging the competitive strength of rivals on such factors as cost, key product attributes, customer service, image and reputation, financial strength, technological skills, distribution capability, and other factors. Resource and capability analysis reveals which of these are competitively important, given the external situation, and whether the company's competitive advantages are sustainable. SWOT analysis provides a more general forward-looking picture of the company's overall situation.

Step 1 in doing a competitive strength assessment is to make a list of the industry's key success factors and other telling measures of competitive strength or weakness (6 to 10 measures usually suffice). Step 2 is to assign weights to each of the measures of competitive strength based on their perceived importance. (The sum of the weights for each measure must add up to 1.) Step 3 is to calculate weighted strength ratings by scoring each competitor on each strength measure (using a 1-to-10 rating scale, where 1 is very weak and 10 is very strong) and multiplying the assigned rating by the assigned weight. Step 4 is to sum the weighted strength ratings on each factor to get an overall measure of competitive strength for each company being rated. Step 5 is to use the overall strength ratings to draw conclusions about the size and extent of the company's net competitive advantage or disadvantage and to take specific note of areas of strength and weakness.

Table 4.4 provides an example of competitive strength assessment in which a hypothetical company (ABC Company) competes against two rivals. In the example,

TABLE 4.4   A Representative Weighted Competitive Strength Assessment

| Key Success Factor/Strength Measure | Importance Weight | Competitive Strength Assessment (rating scale: 1 = very weak, 10 = very strong) | | | | | |
| | | ABC Co. | | Rival 1 | | Rival 2 | |
		Strength Rating	Weighted Score	Strength Rating	Weighted Score	Strength Rating	Weighted Score
Quality/product performance	0.10	8	0.80	5	0.50	1	0.10
Reputation/ image	0.10	8	0.80	7	0.70	1	0.10
Manufacturing capability	0.10	2	0.20	10	1.00	5	0.50
Technological skills	0.05	10	0.50	1	0.05	3	0.15
Dealer network/ distribution capability	0.05	9	0.45	4	0.20	5	0.25
New product innovation capability	0.05	9	0.45	4	0.20	5	0.25
Financial resources	0.10	5	0.50	10	1.00	3	0.30
Relative cost position	0.30	5	1.50	10	3.00	1	0.30
Customer service capabilities	0.15	5	0.75	7	1.05	1	0.15
Sum of importance weights	**1.00**						
Overall weighted competitive strength rating			**5.95**		**7.70**		**2.10**

relative cost is the most telling measure of competitive strength, and the other strength measures are of lesser importance. The company with the highest rating on a given measure has an implied competitive edge on that measure, with the size of its edge reflected in the difference between its weighted rating and rivals' weighted ratings. For instance, Rival 1's 3.00 weighted strength rating on relative cost signals a considerable cost advantage over ABC Company (with a 1.50 weighted score on relative cost) and an even bigger cost advantage over Rival 2 (with a weighted score of 0.30). The measure-by-measure ratings reveal the competitive areas in which a company is strongest and weakest, and against whom.

The overall competitive strength scores indicate how all the different strength measures add up—whether the company is at a net overall competitive advantage or disadvantage against each rival. The higher a company's *overall weighted strength rating,* the stronger its *overall competitiveness* versus rivals. The bigger the difference between a company's overall weighted rating and the scores of *lower-rated* rivals, the greater is its implied *net competitive advantage.* Thus, Rival 1's overall weighted score of 7.70 indicates a greater net competitive advantage over Rival 2 (with a score of 2.10) than over ABC Company (with a score of 5.95). Conversely, the bigger the difference between a company's overall rating and the scores of *higher-rated* rivals, the greater its implied *net competitive disadvantage.* Rival 2's score of 2.10 gives it a smaller net competitive disadvantage against ABC Company (with an overall score of 5.95) than against Rival 1 (with an overall score of 7.70).

> High-weighted competitive strength ratings signal a strong competitive position and possession of competitive advantage; low ratings signal a weak position and competitive disadvantage.

Strategic Implications of Competitive Strength Assessments

In addition to showing how competitively strong or weak a company is relative to rivals, the strength ratings provide guidelines for designing wise offensive and defensive strategies. For example, if ABC Company wants to go on the offensive to win additional sales and market share, such an offensive probably needs to be aimed directly at winning customers away from Rival 2 (which has a lower overall strength score) rather than Rival 1 (which has a higher overall strength score). Moreover, while ABC has high ratings for technological skills (a 10 rating), dealer network/distribution capability (a 9 rating), new product innovation capability (a 9 rating), quality/product performance (an 8 rating), and reputation/image (an 8 rating), these strength measures have low importance weights—meaning that ABC has strengths in areas that don't translate into much competitive clout in the marketplace. Even so, it outclasses Rival 2 in all five areas, plus it enjoys substantially lower costs than Rival 2 (ABC has a 5 rating on relative cost position versus a 1 rating for Rival 2)—and relative cost position carries the highest importance weight of all the strength measures. ABC also has greater competitive strength than Rival 3 regarding customer service capabilities (which carries the second-highest importance weight). Hence, because ABC's strengths are in the very areas where Rival 2 is weak, ABC is in a good position to attack Rival 2. Indeed, ABC may well be able to persuade a number of Rival 2's customers to switch their purchases over to its product.

> A company's competitive strength scores pinpoint its strengths and weaknesses against rivals and point directly to the kinds of offensive and defensive actions it can use to exploit its competitive strengths and reduce its competitive vulnerabilities.

But ABC should be cautious about cutting price aggressively to win customers away from Rival 2, because Rival 1 could interpret that as an attack by ABC to win away Rival 1's customers as well. And Rival 1 is in far and away the best position to compete on the basis of low price, given its high rating on relative cost in an industry where low costs are competitively important (relative cost carries an importance weight of 0.30).

Rival 1's strong relative cost position vis-à-vis both ABC and Rival 2 arms it with the ability to use its lower-cost advantage to thwart any price cutting on ABC's part. Clearly ABC is vulnerable to any retaliatory price cuts by Rival 1—Rival 1 can easily defeat both ABC and Rival 2 in a price-based battle for sales and market share. If ABC wants to defend against its vulnerability to potential price cutting by Rival 1, then it needs to aim a portion of its strategy at lowering its costs.

The point here is that a competitively astute company should utilize the strength scores in deciding what strategic moves to make. When a company has important competitive strengths in areas where one or more rivals are weak, it makes sense to consider offensive moves to exploit rivals' competitive weaknesses. When a company has important competitive weaknesses in areas where one or more rivals are strong, it makes sense to consider defensive moves to curtail its vulnerability.

QUESTION 6: WHAT STRATEGIC ISSUES AND PROBLEMS MERIT FRONT-BURNER MANAGERIAL ATTENTION?

The final and most important analytic step is to zero in on exactly what strategic issues company managers need to address—and resolve—for the company to be more financially and competitively successful in the years ahead. This step involves drawing on the results of both industry analysis and the evaluations of the company's internal situation. The task here is to get a clear fix on exactly what strategic and competitive challenges confront the company, which of the company's competitive shortcomings need fixing, and what specific problems merit company managers' front-burner attention. *Pinpointing the specific issues that management needs to address sets the agenda for deciding what actions to take next to improve the company's performance and business outlook.*

The "priority list" of issues and problems that have to be wrestled with can include such things as *how* to stave off market challenges from new foreign competitors, *how* to combat the price discounting of rivals, *how* to reduce the company's high costs, *how* to sustain the company's present rate of growth in light of slowing buyer demand, *whether* to correct the company's competitive deficiencies by acquiring a rival company with the missing strengths, *whether* to expand into foreign markets, *whether* to reposition the company and move to a different strategic group, *what to do* about growing buyer interest in substitute products, and *what to do* to combat the aging demographics of the company's customer base. The priority list thus always centers on such concerns as "how to . . . ," "what to do about . . . ," and "whether to . . ." The purpose of the priority list is to identify the specific issues and problems that management needs to address, not to figure out what specific actions to take. Deciding what to do—which strategic actions to take and which strategic moves to make—comes later (when it is time to craft the strategy and choose among the various strategic alternatives).

If the items on the priority list are relatively minor—which suggests that the company's strategy is mostly on track and reasonably well matched to the company's overall situation—company managers seldom need to go much beyond fine-tuning the present strategy. If, however, the problems confronting the company are serious and indicate the present strategy is not well suited for the road ahead, the task of crafting a better strategy needs to be at the top of management's action agenda.

> Compiling a "priority list" of problems creates an agenda of strategic issues that merit prompt managerial attention.

> A good strategy must contain ways to deal with all the strategic issues and obstacles that stand in the way of the company's financial and competitive success in the years ahead.

KEY POINTS

There are six key questions to consider in evaluating a company's ability to compete successfully against market rivals:

1. *How well is the present strategy working?* This involves evaluating the strategy in terms of the company's financial performance and market standing. The stronger a company's current overall performance, the less likely the need for radical strategy changes. The weaker a company's performance, the more its current strategy must be questioned.

2. *What is the company's overall situation, in terms of its internal strengths and weaknesses in relation to its market opportunities and external threats?* The answer to this question comes from performing a SWOT analysis. A company's strengths and competitive assets are strategically relevant because they are the most logical and appealing building blocks for strategy; internal weaknesses are important because they may represent vulnerabilities that need correction. External opportunities and threats come into play because a good strategy necessarily aims at capturing a company's most attractive opportunities and at defending against threats to its well-being.

3. *What are the company's most important resources and capabilities and can they give the company a sustainable advantage?* A company's resources can be identified using the tangible/intangible typology presented in this chapter. Its capabilities can be identified either by starting with its resources to look for related capabilities or looking for them within the company's different functional domains.

   The answer to the second part of the question comes from conducting the four tests of a resource's competitive power—the VRIN tests. If a company has resources and capabilities that are competitively *valuable* and *rare,* the firm will have a competitive advantage over market rivals. If its resources and capabilities are also hard to copy *(inimitable),* with no good substitutes *(nonsubstitutable),* then the firm may be able to sustain this advantage even in the face of active efforts by rivals to overcome it.

4. *Are the company's cost structure and value proposition competitive?* One telling sign of whether a company's situation is strong or precarious is whether its costs are competitive with those of industry rivals. Another sign is how the company compares with rivals in terms of differentiation—how effectively it delivers on its customer value proposition. Value chain analysis and benchmarking are essential tools in determining whether the company is performing particular functions and activities well, whether its costs are in line with those of competitors, whether it is differentiating in ways that really enhance customer value, and whether particular internal activities and business processes need improvement. They complement resource and capability analysis by providing data at the level of individual activities that provide more objective evidence of whether individual resources and capabilities, or bundles of resources and linked activity sets, are competitively superior.

5. *On an overall basis, is the company competitively stronger or weaker than key rivals?* The key appraisals here involve how the company matches up against key rivals on industry key success factors and other chief determinants of competitive success and whether and why the company has a *net* competitive advantage or disadvantage. Quantitative competitive strength assessments, using the method presented in Table 4.4, indicate where a company is competitively strong and weak and provide insight into the company's ability to defend or enhance its market position. As a rule, a company's competitive strategy should be built around its competitive strengths and should aim at shoring up areas where it is competitively vulnerable.

When a company has important competitive strengths in areas where one or more rivals are weak, it makes sense to consider offensive moves to exploit rivals' competitive weaknesses. When a company has important competitive weaknesses in areas where one or more rivals are strong, it makes sense to consider defensive moves to curtail its vulnerability.

6. *What strategic issues and problems merit front-burner managerial attention?* This analytic step zeros in on the strategic issues and problems that stand in the way of the company's success. It involves using the results of industry analysis as well as resource and value chain analysis of the company's competitive situation to identify a "priority list" of issues to be resolved for the company to be financially and competitively successful in the years ahead. Actually deciding on a strategy and what specific actions to take is what comes after developing the list of strategic issues and problems that merit front-burner management attention.

Like good industry analysis, solid analysis of the company's competitive situation vis-à-vis its key rivals is a valuable precondition for good strategy making.

ASSURANCE OF LEARNING EXERCISES

1. Using the financial ratios provided in Table 4.1 and following the financial statement information presented for Urban Outfitters, Inc., calculate the following ratios for Urban Outfitters for both 2018 and 2019:

LO 4-1

   a. Gross profit margin
   b. Operating profit margin
   c. Net profit margin
   d. Times-interest-earned (or coverage) ratio
   e. Return on stockholders' equity
   f. Return on assets
   g. Debt-to-equity ratio
   h. Days of inventory
   i. Inventory turnover ratio
   j. Average collection period

   Based on these ratios, did Urban Outfitter's financial performance improve, weaken, or remain about the same from 2018 to 2019?

Consolidated Income Statements for Urban Outfitters, Inc., 2018–2019 (in thousands, except per share data)

	2018	2019
Net sales (total revenue)	$3,616,014	$3,950,623
Cost of sales	2,440,507	2,603,911
Selling, general, and administrative	915,615	965,399

(continued)

	2018	2019
Operating income	$259,892	$381,313
Other income (expense)		
Other expenses	(4,840)	(6,325)
Interest income and other, net	6,314	10,565
Income before income taxes	261,366	385,553
Provision for income taxes	153,103	87,550
Net income	$108,263	$298,003
Basic earnings per share	$ 0.97	$ 2.75
Diluted earnings per share	$ 0.96	$ 2.72

Source: Urban Outfitters, Inc., 2019.

Consolidated Balance Sheets for Urban Outfitters, Inc., 2018–2019 (in thousands, except per share data)

	January 31, 2018	January 31, 2019
Assets		
Current Assets		
Cash and cash equivalents	$ 282,220	$ 358,260
Short-term investments	165,125	279,232
Receivables, net	76,962	80,461
Merchandise inventories	351,395	370,507
Prepaid expenses and other current assets	103,055	114,296
Total current assets	978,757	1,202,756
Net property and equipment	813,768	796,029
Deferred income taxes and Other assets	160,255	161,730
Total assets	$1,952,780	$2,160,515
Liabilities and Shareholders' Equity		
Current Liabilities		
Accounts payable	$ 128,246	$ 144,414
Accrued salaries and benefits	36,058	54,799
Accrued expenses and Other current liabilities	195,910	187,431
Total current liabilities	360,214	$ 386,644

(continued)

	January 31, 2018	January 31, 2019
Long-term debt	0	0
Deferred rent and other liabilities	284,773	291,663
Total liabilities	671,417	651,877
Commitments and Contingencies		
Equity		
Preferred stock $.0001 par value; 10,000,000 shares authorized; no shares issued and outstanding	0	0
Common stock $.0001 par value; 200,000,000 shares authorized; 105,642,283 and 108,248,568 shares issued and outstanding	11	11
Additional paid-in capital	$ 0	$ 684
Retained earnings	1,489,087	1,300,208
Total stockholders' equity	1,489,098	1,300,90
Total Liabilities and Equity	$2,160,515	$1,952,780

Source: Urban Outfitters, Inc., 2019 10-K.

2. Cinnabon, famous for its cinnamon rolls, is an American chain commonly located in high traffic areas, such as airports and malls. They operate more than 1,200 bakeries in more than 48 countries. How many of the four tests of the competitive power of a resource does the store network pass? Using your general knowledge of this industry, perform a SWOT analysis. Explain your answers.   **LO 4-2, LO 4-3**

3. Review the information in Illustration Capsule 4.1 concerning Everlane's average costs of producing and selling a pair of denim jeans, and compare this with the representative value chain depicted in Figure 4.3. Then answer the following questions:
   LO 4-4

   a. Which of the company's costs correspond to the primary value chain activities depicted in Figure 4.3?

   b. Which of the company's costs correspond to the support activities described in Figure 4.3?

   c. What value chain activities might be important in securing or maintaining Everlane's advantage? Explain your answer.

4. Using the methodology illustrated in Table 4.3 and your knowledge as an automobile owner, prepare a competitive strength assessment for General Motors and its rivals Ford, Chrysler, Toyota, and Honda. Each of the five automobile manufacturers should be evaluated on the key success factors and strength measures of cost-competitiveness, product-line breadth, product quality and reliability, financial resources and profitability, and customer service. What does your competitive strength assessment disclose about the overall competitiveness of each automobile manufacturer? What factors account most for Toyota's competitive success? Does Toyota have competitive weaknesses that were disclosed by your analysis? Explain.   **LO 4-5**

EXERCISES FOR SIMULATION PARTICIPANTS

LO 4-1 **1.** Using the formulas in Table 4.1 and the data in your company's latest financial statements, calculate the following measures of financial performance for your company:
  a. Operating profit margin
  b. Total return on total assets
  c. Current ratio
  d. Working capital
  e. Long-term debt-to-capital ratio
  f. Price-to-earnings ratio

LO 4-1 **2.** On the basis of your company's latest financial statements and all the other available data regarding your company's performance that appear in the industry report, list the three measures of financial performance on which your company did best and the three measures on which your company's financial performance was worst.

LO 4-1 **3.** What hard evidence can you cite that indicates your company's strategy is working fairly well (or perhaps not working so well, if your company's performance is lagging that of rival companies)?

LO 4-2, LO 4-3 **4.** What internal strengths and weaknesses does your company have? What external market opportunities for growth and increased profitability exist for your company? What external threats to your company's future well-being and profitability do you and your co-managers see? What does the preceding SWOT analysis indicate about your company's present situation and future prospects—where on the scale from "exceptionally strong" to "alarmingly weak" does the attractiveness of your company's situation rank?

LO 4-2, LO 4-3 **5.** Does your company have any core competencies? If so, what are they?

LO 4-4 **6.** What are the key elements of your company's value chain? Refer to Figure 4.3 in developing your answer.

LO 4-5 **7.** Using the methodology presented in Table 4.4, do a weighted competitive strength assessment for your company and two other companies that you and your co-managers consider to be very close competitors.

ENDNOTES

[1] Donald Sull, "Strategy as Active Waiting," *Harvard Business Review* 83, no. 9 (September 2005), pp. 121–126.
[2] Birger Wernerfelt, "A Resource-Based View of the Firm," *Strategic Management Journal* 5, no. 5 (September–October 1984), pp. 171–180; Jay Barney, "Firm Resources and Sustained Competitive Advantage," *Journal of Management* 17, no. 1 (1991), pp. 99–120.
[3] R. Amit and P. Schoemaker, "Strategic Assets and Organizational Rent," *Strategic Management Journal* 14 (1993).
[4] Jay B. Barney, "Looking Inside for Competitive Advantage," *Academy of Management Executive* 9, no. 4 (November

1995), pp. 49–61; Christopher A. Bartlett and Sumantra Ghoshal, "Building Competitive Advantage through People," *MIT Sloan Management Review* 43, no. 2 (Winter 2002), pp. 34–41; Danny Miller, Russell Eisenstat, and Nathaniel Foote, "Strategy from the Inside Out: Building Capability-Creating Organizations," *California Management Review* 44, no. 3 (Spring 2002), pp. 37–54.
[5] M. Peteraf and J. Barney, "Unraveling the Resource-Based Tangle," *Managerial and Decision Economics* 24, no. 4 (June–July 2003), pp. 309–323.
[6] Margaret A. Peteraf and Mark E. Bergen, "Scanning Dynamic Competitive Landscapes: A Market-Based and Resource-Based

Framework," *Strategic Management Journal* 24 (2003), pp. 1027–1042.
[7] C. Montgomery, "Of Diamonds and Rust: A New Look at Resources," in C. Montgomery (ed.), *Resource-Based and Evolutionary Theories of the Firm* (Boston: Kluwer Academic, 1995), pp. 251–268.
[8] Constance E. Helfat and Margaret A. Peteraf, "The Dynamic Resource-Based View: Capability Lifecycles," *Strategic Management Journal* 24, no. 10 (2003).
[9] D. Teece, G. Pisano, and A. Shuen, "Dynamic Capabilities and Strategic Management," *Strategic Management Journal* 18, no. 7 (1997), pp. 509–533; K. Eisenhardt and J. Martin, "Dynamic Capabilities: What Are They?"

Strategic Management Journal 21, no. 10–11 (2000), pp. 1105–1121; M. Zollo and S. Winter, "Deliberate Learning and the Evolution of Dynamic Capabilities," *Organization Science* 13 (2002), pp. 339–351; C. Helfat et al., *Dynamic Capabilities: Understanding Strategic Change in Organizations* (Malden, MA: Blackwell, 2007).

[10] Michael Porter in his 1985 best seller *Competitive Advantage* (New York: Free Press).

[11] John K. Shank and Vijay Govindarajan, *Strategic Cost Management* (New York: Free Press, 1993), especially chaps. 2–6,

10, and 11; Robin Cooper and Robert S. Kaplan, "Measure Costs Right: Make the Right Decisions," *Harvard Business Review* 66, no. 5 (September–October, 1988), pp. 96–103; Joseph A. Ness and Thomas G. Cucuzza, "Tapping the Full Potential of ABC," *Harvard Business Review* 73, no. 4 (July–August 1995), pp. 130–138.

[12] Porter, *Competitive Advantage,* p. 34.

[13] Hau L. Lee, "The Triple-A Supply Chain," *Harvard Business Review* 82, no. 10 (October 2004), pp. 102–112.

[14] Gregory H. Watson, *Strategic Benchmarking: How to Rate Your Company's Performance*

against the World's Best (New York: Wiley, 1993); Robert C. Camp, *Benchmarking: The Search for Industry Best Practices That Lead to Superior Performance* (Milwaukee: ASQC Quality Press, 1989); Dawn Iacobucci and Christie Nordhielm, "Creative Benchmarking," *Harvard Business Review* 78 no. 6 (November–December 2000), pp. 24–25.

[15] www.businessdictionary.com/definition/best-practice.html (accessed December 2, 2009).

[16] Reuben E. Stone, "Leading a Supply Chain Turnaround," *Harvard Business Review* 82, no. 10 (October 2004), pp. 114–121.

chapter 5

The Five Generic Competitive Strategies

Learning Objectives

After reading this chapter, you should be able to:

LO 5-1 Understand what distinguishes each of the five generic strategies and explain why some of these strategies work better in certain kinds of competitive conditions than in others.

LO 5-2 Recognize the major avenues for achieving a competitive advantage based on lower costs.

LO 5-3 Identify the major avenues to a competitive advantage based on differentiating a company's product or service offering from the offerings of rivals.

LO 5-4 Explain the attributes of a best-cost strategy—a hybrid of low-cost and differentiation strategies.

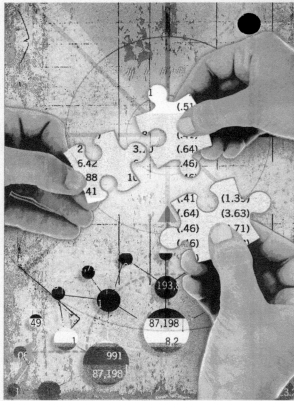

Roy Scott/Media Bakery

It's all about strategic positioning and competition.

Michele Hutchins—*Consultant*

Strategic positioning means performing different activities from rivals or performing similar activities in different ways.

Michael E. Porter—*Professor, author, and cofounder of Monitor Consulting*

I learnt the hard way about positioning in business, about catering to the right segments.

Shaffi Mather—*Social entrepreneur*

A company can employ any of several basic approaches to gaining a competitive advantage over rivals, but they all involve *delivering more value* to customers than rivals or *delivering value more efficiently* than rivals (or both). More value for customers can mean a good product at a lower price, a superior product worth paying more for, or a best-value offering that represents an attractive combination of price, features, service, and other appealing attributes. Greater efficiency means delivering a given level of value to customers at a lower cost to the company. But whatever approach to delivering value the company takes, it nearly always requires performing value chain activities differently than rivals and building competitively valuable resources and capabilities that rivals cannot readily match or outdo.

This chapter describes the five *generic competitive strategy options*. Each of the five generic strategies represents a distinctly different approach to competing in the marketplace. Which of the five to employ is a company's first and foremost choice in crafting an overall strategy and beginning its quest for competitive advantage.

TYPES OF GENERIC COMPETITIVE STRATEGIES

● **LO 5-1**

Understand what distinguishes each of the five generic strategies and explain why some of these strategies work better in certain kinds of competitive conditions than in others.

A company's competitive strategy lays out the specific efforts of the company to position itself in the marketplace, please customers, ward off competitive threats, and achieve a particular kind of competitive advantage. The chances are remote that any two companies—even companies in the same industry—will employ competitive strategies that are exactly alike in every detail. However, when one strips away the details to get at the real substance, the two biggest factors that distinguish one competitive strategy from another boil down to (1) whether a company's market target is broad or narrow and (2) whether the company is pursuing a competitive advantage linked to lower costs or differentiation. These two factors give rise to four distinct competitive strategy options, plus one hybrid option, as shown in Figure 5.1 and listed next.[1]

1. *A broad, low-cost strategy*—striving to achieve broad lower overall costs than rivals on comparable products that attract a broad spectrum of buyers, usually by underpricing rivals.

2. *A broad differentiation strategy*—seeking to differentiate the company's product offering from rivals' with attributes that will appeal to a broad spectrum of buyers.

3. *A focused low-cost strategy*—concentrating on the needs and requirements of a narrow buyer segment (or market niche) and striving to meet these needs at lower costs than rivals (thereby being able to serve niche members at a lower price).

4. *A focused differentiation strategy*—concentrating on a narrow buyer segment (or market niche) and offering niche members customized attributes that meet their tastes and requirements better than rivals' products.

FIGURE 5.1   The Five Generic Competitive Strategies

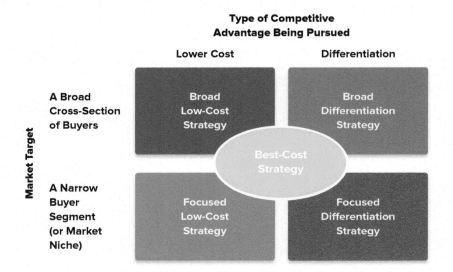

Source: This is an expanded version of a three-strategy classification discussed in Michael E. Porter, *Competitive Strategy* (New York: Free Press, 1980).

5. *A best-cost strategy*—striving to incorporate upscale product attributes at a lower cost than rivals. Being the "best-cost" producer of an upscale, multifeatured product allows a company to *give customers more value for their money* by underpricing rivals whose products have similar upscale, multifeatured attributes. This competitive approach is a *hybrid* strategy that *blends elements of the previous four options* in a unique and often effective way. It may be focused or broad in its appeal.

The remainder of this chapter explores the ins and outs of these five generic competitive strategies and how they differ.

BROAD LOW-COST STRATEGIES

Striving to achieve lower costs than rivals targeting a broad spectrum of buyers is an especially effective competitive approach in markets with many price-sensitive buyers. A company achieves **low-cost leadership** when it becomes the industry's lowest-cost producer rather than just being one of perhaps several competitors with comparatively low costs. But a low-cost producer's foremost strategic objective is *meaningfully* lower costs than rivals—*not necessarily the absolutely lowest possible cost.* In striving for a cost advantage over rivals, company managers must incorporate features and services that buyers consider essential. A product offering that is too frills-free can be viewed by consumers as offering little value regardless of its pricing.

> ● **LO 5-2**
>
> Recognize the major avenues for achieving a competitive advantage based on lower costs.

A company has two options for translating a low-cost advantage over rivals into superior profit performance. Option 1 is to use the lower-cost edge to underprice competitors and attract price-sensitive buyers in great enough numbers to increase total profits. Option 2 is to maintain the present price, be content with the present market share, and use the lower-cost edge to raise total profits by earning a higher profit margin on each unit sold.

> **CORE** CONCEPT
>
> The essence of a **broad, low-cost strategy** is to produce goods or services for a broad base of buyers at a lower cost than rivals.

While many companies are inclined to exploit a low-cost advantage by using option 1 (attacking rivals with lower prices), this strategy can backfire if rivals respond with retaliatory price cuts (in order to protect their customer base and defend against a loss of sales). A rush to cut prices can often trigger a price war that lowers the profits of all price discounters. The bigger the risk that rivals will respond with matching price cuts, the more appealing it becomes to employ the second option for using a low-cost advantage to achieve higher profitability.

The Two Major Avenues for Achieving a Cost Advantage

To achieve a low-cost edge over rivals, a firm's cumulative costs across its overall value chain must be lower than competitors' cumulative costs. There are two major avenues for accomplishing this:[2]

> A low-cost advantage over rivals can translate into superior profitability through lower price and higher market share or higher profit margins.

1. Perform internal value chain activities and/or value chain system activities more cost-effectively than rivals.
2. Revamp the firm's overall value chain to eliminate or bypass some cost-producing activities.

Cost-Efficient Management of Value Chain Activities   For a company to do a more cost-effective job of managing its value chain than rivals, managers must diligently search out cost-saving opportunities in every part of the value chain.

> **CORE** CONCEPT
>
> A **cost driver** is a factor that has a strong influence on a company's costs.

No activity can escape cost-saving scrutiny, and all company personnel must be expected to use their talents and ingenuity to come up with innovative and effective ways to keep down costs. Particular attention must be paid to a set of factors known as **cost drivers** that have a strong effect on a company's costs and can be used as levers to lower costs. Figure 5.2 shows the most important cost drivers. Cost-cutting approaches that demonstrate an effective use of the cost drivers include

1. *Capturing all available economies of scale.* Economies of scale stem from an ability to lower unit costs by increasing the scale of operation. Economies of scale may be available at different points along a company's value chain (both internally and elsewhere along its value chain system). Often, a large plant is more economical to operate than a small one, particularly if it can be operated round the clock robotically. Economies of scale may be available due to a large warehouse operation on the input side or a large distribution center on the output side. In global industries, selling a mostly standard product worldwide tends to lower unit costs as opposed to making separate products (each at lower scale) for each country market. There are economies of scale in advertising as well. For example, Anheuser-Busch InBev SA/NV could afford to pay the $5.6 million cost of a 30-second Super Bowl ad in 2020 because the cost could be spread out over the hundreds of millions of units of Budweiser that the company sells.

FIGURE 5.2   Cost Drivers: The Keys to Driving Down Company Costs

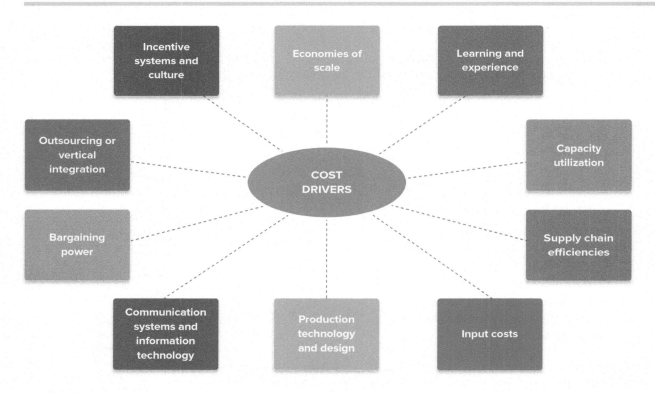

Source: Adapted from Michael E. Porter, *Competitive Advantage: Creating and Sustaining Superior Performance* (New York: Free Press, 1985).

2. *Taking full advantage of experience and learning-curve effects.* The cost of performing an activity can decline over time as the learning and experience of company personnel build. Learning and experience economies can stem from debugging and mastering newly introduced technologies, using the experiences and suggestions of workers to install more efficient plant layouts and assembly procedures, and the added speed and effectiveness that accrues from repeatedly picking sites for and building new plants, distribution centers, or retail outlets.

3. *Operating facilities at full capacity.* Whether a company is able to operate at or near full capacity has a big impact on unit costs when its value chain contains activities associated with substantial fixed costs. Higher rates of capacity utilization allow depreciation and other fixed costs to be spread over a larger unit volume, thereby lowering fixed costs per unit. The more capital-intensive the business and the higher the fixed costs as a percentage of total costs, the greater the unit-cost penalty for operating at less than full capacity.

4. *Improving supply chain efficiency.* Partnering with suppliers to streamline the ordering and purchasing process, to reduce inventory carrying costs via just-in-time inventory practices, to economize on shipping and materials handling, and to ferret out other cost-saving opportunities is a much-used approach to cost reduction. A company with a distinctive competence in cost-efficient supply chain management, such as Colgate-Palmolive or Unilever (leading consumer products companies), can sometimes achieve a sizable cost advantage over less adept rivals.

5. *Substituting lower-cost inputs wherever there is little or no sacrifice in product quality or performance.* If the costs of certain raw materials and parts are "too high," a company can switch to using lower-cost items or maybe even design the high-cost components out of the product altogether.

6. *Using the company's bargaining power vis-à-vis suppliers or others in the value chain system to gain concessions.* Home Depot, for example, has sufficient bargaining clout with suppliers to win price discounts on large-volume purchases.

7. *Using online systems and sophisticated software to achieve operating efficiencies.* For example, sharing data and production schedules with suppliers, coupled with the use of enterprise resource planning (ERP) and manufacturing execution system (MES) software, can reduce parts inventories, trim production times, and lower labor requirements.

8. *Improving process design and employing advanced production technology.* Often, production costs can be cut by (1) using design for manufacture (DFM) procedures and computer-assisted design (CAD) techniques that enable more integrated and efficient production methods, (2) investing in highly automated robotic production technology, and (3) shifting to a mass-customization production process. Dell's highly automated PC assembly plant in Austin, Texas, is a prime example of the use of advanced product and process technologies. Many companies are ardent users of total quality management (TQM) systems, business process reengineering, Six Sigma methodology, and other business process management techniques that aim at boosting efficiency and reducing costs.

9. *Being alert to the cost advantages of outsourcing or vertical integration.* Outsourcing the performance of certain value chain activities can be more economical than performing them in-house if outside specialists, by virtue of their expertise and volume, can perform the activities at lower cost. On the other hand, there can be times when integrating into the activities of either suppliers or distribution-channel allies

can lower costs through greater production efficiencies, reduced transaction costs, or a better bargaining position.

10. *Motivating employees through incentives and company culture.* A company's incentive system can encourage not only greater worker productivity but also cost-saving innovations that come from worker suggestions. The culture of a company can also spur worker pride in productivity and continuous improvement. Companies that are well known for their cost-reducing incentive systems and culture include Nucor Steel, which characterizes itself as a company of "20,000 teammates," Southwest Airlines, and DHL Express (rival of FedEx).

Revamping of the Value Chain System to Lower Costs   Dramatic cost advantages can often emerge from redesigning the company's value chain system in ways that eliminate costly work steps and entirely bypass certain cost-producing value chain activities. Such value chain revamping can include

- *Selling direct to consumers and bypassing the activities and costs of distributors and dealers.* To circumvent the need for distributors and dealers, a company can create its own direct sales force, which adds the costs of maintaining and supporting a sales force but may be cheaper than using independent distributors and dealers to access buyers. Alternatively, they can conduct sales operations at the company's website, since the costs for website operations and shipping may be substantially cheaper than going through distributor-dealer channels). Costs in the wholesale and retail portions of the value chain frequently represent 35 to 50 percent of the final price consumers pay, so establishing a direct sales force or selling online may offer big cost savings.

- *Streamlining operations by eliminating low-value-added or unnecessary work steps and activities.* At Walmart, some items supplied by manufacturers are delivered directly to retail stores rather than being routed through Walmart's distribution centers and delivered by Walmart trucks. In other instances, Walmart unloads incoming shipments from manufacturers' trucks arriving at its distribution centers and loads them directly onto outgoing Walmart trucks headed to particular stores without ever moving the goods into the distribution center. Many supermarket chains have greatly reduced in-store meat butchering and cutting activities by shifting to meats that are cut and packaged at the meatpacking plant and then delivered to their stores in ready-to-sell form.

- *Reducing materials-handling and shipping costs by having suppliers locate their plants or warehouses close to the company's own facilities.* Having suppliers locate their plants or warehouses close to a company's own plant facilitates just-in-time deliveries of parts and components to the exact workstation where they will be used in assembling the company's product. This not only lowers incoming shipping costs but also curbs or eliminates the company's need to build and operate storerooms for incoming parts and to have plant personnel move the inventories to the workstations as needed for assembly.

Illustration Capsule 5.1 describes the path that Vanguard has followed in achieving its position as the low-cost leader of the investment management industry.

Examples of Companies That Revamped Their Value Chains to Reduce Costs
Nucor Corporation, the most profitable steel producer in the United States and one of the largest steel producers worldwide, drastically revamped the value chain process for

Vanguard's Path to Becoming the Low-Cost Leader in Investment Management

Vanguard is now one of the world's largest investment management companies. It became an industry giant by leading the way in low-cost passive index investing. In active trading, an investment manager is compensated for making an educated decision on which stocks to sell and which to buy. This incurs both transactional and management fees. In contrast, passive index portfolios aim to mirror the movements of a major market index like the S&P 500, Dow Jones Industrial Average, or NASDAQ. Passive portfolios incur fewer fees and can be managed with lower operating costs. A measure used to compare operating costs in this industry is known as the expense ratio, which is the percentage of an investment that goes toward expenses. In 2019, Vanguard's expense ratio was less than 14 percent of the industry's average expense ratio. Vanguard was the first to capitalize on what was at the time an underappreciated fact: over long horizons, well-managed index funds, with their lower costs and fees, typically outperform their actively trading competitors.

Vanguard provides low-cost investment options for its clients in several ways. By creating funds that track index(es) over a long horizon, the client does not incur transaction and management fees normally charged in actively managed funds. Possibly more important, Vanguard was created with a unique client-owner structure. When you invest with Vanguard you become an owner of Vanguard. This structure effectively cut out traditional shareholders who seek to share in profits. Under client ownership, any returns in excess of operating costs are returned to the clients/investors.

Vanguard keeps its costs low in several other ways. One notable one is its focus on its employees and organizational structure. The company prides itself on low turnover rates (8 percent) and very flat organizational

Keith Srakocic/AP Images

structure. In several instances Vanguard has been able to capitalize on being a fast follower. They launched several product lines after their competitors introduced those products. Being a fast follower allowed them to develop superior products and reach scale more quickly—both further lowering their cost structure.

The low-cost structure has not come at the expense of performance. Vanguard now has 410 funds, over 30 million investors, has surpassed $5.5 trillion in AUM (assets under management), and is growing faster than all its competitors combined. When *Money* published its January 2020 list of recommended investment funds, 44 percent of the funds listed were Vanguard funds.

Vanguard's low-cost strategy has been so successful that industry experts now refer to The Vanguard Effect. This refers to the pressure that this investment management giant has put on competitors to lower their fees in order to compete with Vanguard's low-cost value proposition.

Note: Developed with Vedrana B. Greatorex.

Sources: https://www.nytimes.com/2017/04/14/business/mutfund/vanguard-mutual-index-funds-growth.html; https://investor.vanguard.com; Sunderam, A., Viceira, L., & Ciechanover, A. (2016) *The Vanguard Group, Inc. in 2015: Celebrating 40.* HBS No. 9-216-026. Boston, MA: Harvard Business School Publishing; Money.com; About Vanguard.com/Fast Facts About Vanguard.

manufacturing steel products by using relatively inexpensive electric arc furnaces and continuous casting processes. Using electric arc furnaces to melt recycled scrap steel eliminated many of the steps used by traditional steel mills that made their steel products from iron ore, coke, limestone, and other ingredients using costly coke ovens, basic oxygen blast furnaces, ingot casters, and multiple types of finishing facilities—plus Nucor's value chain system required far fewer employees. As a consequence, Nucor produces steel with a far lower capital investment, a far smaller workforce, and far lower operating costs than traditional steel mills. Nucor's strategy to replace the

> Success in achieving a low-cost edge over rivals comes from out-managing rivals in finding ways to perform value chain activities faster, more accurately, and more cost-effectively.

traditional steelmaking value chain with its simpler, quicker value chain approach has made it one of the world's lowest-cost producers of steel, allowing it to take a huge amount of market share away from traditional steel companies and earn attractive profits. This approach has allowed the company to remain steadily profitable even as a flood of illegally subsidized imports wreaked havoc on the rest of the North American steel market.

Southwest Airlines has achieved considerable cost savings by reconfiguring the traditional value chain of commercial airlines, thereby permitting it to offer travelers lower fares. Its mastery of fast turnarounds at the gates (about 25 minutes versus 45 minutes for rivals) allows its planes to fly more hours per day. This translates into being able to schedule more flights per day with fewer aircraft, allowing Southwest to generate more revenue per plane on average than rivals. Southwest does not offer assigned seating, baggage transfer to connecting airlines, or first-class seating and service, thereby eliminating all the cost-producing activities associated with these features. The company's fast and user-friendly online reservation system facilitates e-ticketing and reduces staffing requirements at telephone reservation centers and airport counters. Its use of automated check-in equipment reduces staffing requirements for terminal check-in. The company's carefully designed point-to-point route system minimizes connections, delays, and total trip time for passengers, allowing about 75 percent of Southwest passengers to fly nonstop to their destinations and at the same time reducing Southwest's costs for flight operations.

The Keys to a Successful Broad Low-Cost Strategy

A low-cost producer is in the best position to win the business of price-sensitive buyers, set the floor on market price, and still earn a profit.

While broad, low-cost companies are champions of frugality, they seldom hesitate to spend aggressively on resources and capabilities *that promise to drive costs out of the business.* Indeed, having competitive assets of this type and ensuring that they remain competitively superior is essential for achieving competitive advantage as a broad, low-cost leader. Walmart, for example, has been an early adopter of state-of-the-art technology throughout its operations; however, the company *carefully estimates the cost savings of new technologies before it rushes to invest in them.* By continuously investing in complex, cost-saving technologies that are hard for rivals to match, Walmart has sustained its low-cost advantage for over 45 years.

Uber and Lyft, employing a formidable low-cost provider strategy and an innovative business model, have stormed their way into hundreds of locations across the world, totally disrupting and seemingly forever changing competition in the taxi markets where they have a presence. And, most significantly, the ultra-low fares charged by Uber and Lyft have resulted in dramatic increases in the demand for taxi services, particularly those provided by these two low-cost providers. Other companies noted for their successful use of broad low-cost strategies include Spirit Airlines, EasyJet, and Ryanair in airlines; Briggs & Stratton in small gasoline engines; Huawei in networking and telecommunications equipment; Bic in ballpoint pens; Stride Rite in footwear; and Poulan in chain saws.

When a Low-Cost Strategy Works Best

A low-cost strategy becomes increasingly appealing and competitively powerful when

1. *Price competition among rival sellers is vigorous.* Low-cost leaders are in the best position to compete offensively on the basis of price, to gain market share at the expense of rivals, to win the business of price-sensitive buyers, to remain profitable despite strong price competition, and to survive price wars.

2. *The products of rival sellers are essentially identical and readily available from many eager sellers.* Look-alike products and/or overabundant product supply set the stage for lively price competition; in such markets, it is the less efficient, higher-cost companies whose profits get squeezed the most.

3. *There are few ways to achieve product differentiation that have value to buyers.* When the differences between product attributes or brands do not matter much to buyers, buyers are nearly always sensitive to price differences, and industry-leading companies tend to be those with the lowest-priced brands.

4. *Buyers incur low costs in switching their purchases from one seller to another.* Low switching costs give buyers the flexibility to shift purchases to lower-priced sellers having equally good products or to attractively priced substitute products. A low-cost leader is well positioned to use low price to induce potential customers to switch to its brand.

5. *Buyers are price-sensitive or have the power to bargain down prices.* When buyers are focused primarily on price or have substantial bargaining power, then a low-cost strategy becomes something of a necessity!

Pitfalls to Avoid in Pursuing a Low-Cost Strategy

Perhaps the biggest mistake a low-cost producer can make is getting carried away with overly aggressive price cutting. *Higher unit sales and market shares do not automatically translate into higher profits.* Reducing price results in earning a lower profit margin on each unit sold. Thus, reducing price improves profitability *only if* the lower price increases unit sales enough to offset the loss in revenues due to the lower per unit profit margin. A simple numerical example tells the story: Suppose a firm selling 1,000 units at a price of $10, a cost of $9, and a profit margin of $1 opts to cut price 5 percent to $9.50—which reduces the firm's profit margin to $0.50 per unit sold. If unit costs remain at $9, then it takes a 100 percent sales increase to 2,000 units just to offset the narrower profit margin and get back to total profits of $1,000. Hence, whether a price cut will result in higher or lower profitability depends on how big the resulting sales gains will be and how much, if any, unit costs will fall as sales volumes increase.

A second pitfall is *relying on cost reduction approaches that can be easily copied by rivals.* If rivals find it relatively easy or inexpensive to imitate the leader's low-cost methods, then the leader's advantage will be too short-lived to yield a valuable edge in the marketplace.

> Reducing price does not lead to higher total profits unless the added gains in unit sales are large enough to offset the loss in revenues due to lower margins per unit sold.

A third pitfall is *becoming too fixated on cost reduction.* Low costs cannot be pursued so zealously that a firm's offering ends up being too feature-poor to generate buyer appeal. Furthermore, a company driving hard to push down its costs has to guard against ignoring declining buyer sensitivity to price, increased buyer interest in added features or service, or new developments that alter how buyers use the product. Otherwise, it risks losing market ground if buyers start opting for more upscale or feature-rich products.

Even if these mistakes are avoided, a low-cost strategy still entails risk. An innovative rival may discover an even lower-cost value chain approach. Important cost-saving technological breakthroughs may suddenly emerge. And if a low-cost producer has heavy investments in its present means of operating, then it can prove costly to quickly shift to the new value chain approach or a new technology.

> A low-cost producer's product offering must always contain enough attributes to be attractive to prospective buyers—low price, by itself, is not always appealing to buyers.

BROAD DIFFERENTIATION STRATEGIES

Differentiation strategies are attractive whenever buyers' needs and preferences are too diverse to be fully satisfied by a standardized product offering. Successful product differentiation requires careful study to determine what attributes buyers will find appealing, valuable, and worth paying for.[3] Then the company must incorporate a combination of these desirable features into its product or service that will be different enough to stand apart from the product or service offerings of rivals. A broad differentiation strategy achieves its aim when a wide range of buyers find the company's offering more appealing than that of rivals and worth a somewhat higher price.

Successful differentiation allows a firm to do one or more of the following:

CORE CONCEPT

The essence of a **broad differentiation strategy** is to offer unique product attributes that a wide range of buyers find appealing and worth paying more for.

- Command a premium price for its product.
- Increase unit sales (because additional buyers are won over by the differentiating features).
- Gain buyer loyalty to its brand (because buyers are strongly attracted to the differentiating features and bond with the company and its products).

Differentiation enhances profitability whenever a company's product can command a sufficiently higher price or generate sufficiently bigger unit sales *to more than cover the added costs of achieving the differentiation.* Company differentiation strategies fail when buyers don't place much value on the brand's uniqueness and/or when a company's differentiating features are easily matched by its rivals.

Companies can pursue differentiation from many angles: a unique taste (Red Bull, Listerine); multiple features (Microsoft Office, Apple Watch); wide selection and one-stop shopping (Home Depot, Alibaba.com); superior service (Ritz-Carlton, Nordstrom); spare parts availability (John Deere; Morgan Motors); engineering design and performance (Mercedes, BMW); high fashion design (Prada, Gucci); product reliability (Whirlpool, LG, and Bosch in large home appliances); quality manufacture (Michelin); technological leadership (3M Corporation in bonding and coating products); a full range of services (Charles Schwab in stock brokerage); and wide product selection (Campbell's soups; Frito-Lay snack foods.).

Managing the Value Chain in Ways that Enhance Differentiation

CORE CONCEPT

A **value driver** is a factor that is particularly effective in creating differentiation.

Differentiation is not something in marketing and advertising departments, nor is it limited to the catchalls of quality and service. Differentiation opportunities can exist in activities all along a company's value chain and value chain system. The most systematic approach that managers can take, however, involves focusing on the **value drivers,** a set of factors—analogous to cost drivers—that are particularly effective in creating differentiation. Figure 5.3 contains a list of important value drivers. Ways that managers can enhance differentiation based on value drivers include the following:

1. *Create product features and performance attributes that appeal to a wide range of buyers.* The physical and functional features of a product have a big influence on differentiation, including features such as added user safety or enhanced environmental protection. Styling and appearance are big differentiating factors in the apparel and motor vehicle industries. Size and weight matter in binoculars and mobile devices.

FIGURE 5.3   Value Drivers: The Keys to Creating a Differentiation Advantage

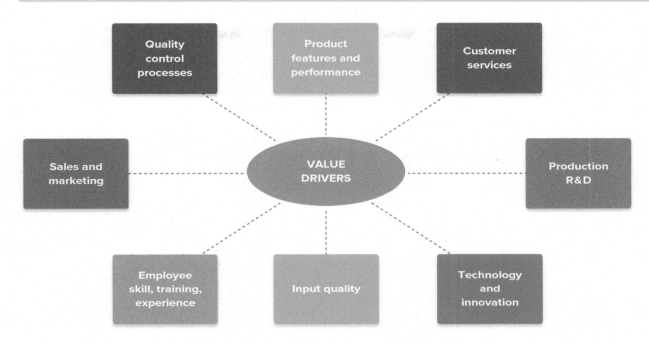

Source: Adapted from Michael E. Porter, *Competitive Advantage: Creating and Sustaining Superior Performance* (New York: Free Press, 1985).

Most companies employing broad differentiation strategies make a point of incorporating innovative and novel features in their product or service offering, especially those that improve performance and functionality.

2. *Improve customer service or add extra services.* Better customer services, in areas such as delivery, returns, and repair, can be as important in creating differentiation as superior product features. Examples include superior technical assistance to buyers, higher-quality maintenance services, more and better product information provided to customers, more and better training materials for end users, better credit terms, quicker order processing, and greater customer convenience.

3. *Invest in production-related R&D activities.* Engaging in production R&D may permit custom-order manufacture at an efficient cost, provide wider product variety and selection through product "versioning," or improve product quality. Many manufacturers have developed flexible manufacturing systems that allow different models and product versions to be made on the same assembly line. Being able to provide buyers with made-to-order products can be a potent differentiating capability.

4. *Strive for innovation and technological advances.* Successful innovation is the route to more frequent first-on-the-market victories and is a powerful differentiator. If the innovation proves hard to replicate, through patent protection or other means, it can provide a company with a first-mover advantage that is sustainable.

5. *Pursue continuous quality improvement.* Quality control processes reduce product defects, prevent premature product failure, extend product life, make it economical to offer longer warranty coverage, improve economy of use, result in more end-user

convenience, or enhance product appearance. Companies whose quality management systems meet certification standards, such as the ISO 9001 standards, can enhance their reputation for quality with customers.

6. *Increase marketing and brand-building activities.* Marketing and advertising can have a tremendous effect on the value perceived by buyers and therefore their willingness to pay more for the company's offerings. They can create differentiation even when little tangible differentiation exists otherwise. For example, blind taste tests show that even the most loyal Pepsi or Coke drinkers have trouble telling one cola drink from another.[4] Brands create customer loyalty, which increases the perceived "cost" of switching to another product.

7. *Seek out high-quality inputs.* Input quality can ultimately spill over to affect the performance or quality of the company's end product. Starbucks, for example, gets high ratings on its coffees partly because it has very strict specifications on the coffee beans purchased from suppliers.

8. *Emphasize human resource management activities that improve the skills, expertise, and knowledge of company personnel.* A company with high-caliber intellectual capital often has the capacity to generate the kinds of ideas that drive product innovation, technological advances, better product design and product performance, improved production techniques, and higher product quality. Well-designed incentive compensation systems can often unleash the efforts of talented personnel to develop and implement new and effective differentiating attributes.

Revamping the Value Chain System to Increase Differentiation   Just as pursuing a cost advantage can involve the entire value chain system, the same is true for a differentiation advantage. Activities performed upstream by suppliers or downstream by distributors and retailers can have a meaningful effect on customers' perceptions of a company's offerings and its value proposition. Approaches to enhancing differentiation through changes in the value chain system include

- *Coordinating with downstream channel allies to enhance customer value.* Coordinating with downstream partners such as distributors, dealers, brokers, and retailers can contribute to differentiation in a variety of ways. Methods that companies use to influence the value chain activities of their channel allies include setting standards for downstream partners to follow, providing them with templates to standardize the selling environment or practices, training channel personnel, or cosponsoring promotions and advertising campaigns. Coordinating with retailers is important for enhancing the buying experience and building a company's image. Coordinating with distributors or shippers can mean quicker delivery to customers, more accurate order filling, and/or lower shipping costs. The Coca-Cola Company considers coordination with its bottler-distributors so important that it has at times taken over a troubled bottler to improve its management and upgrade its plant and equipment before releasing it again.[5]

- *Coordinating with suppliers to better address customer needs.* Collaborating with suppliers can also be a powerful route to a more effective differentiation strategy. Coordinating and collaborating with suppliers can improve many dimensions affecting product features and quality. This is particularly true for companies that engage only in assembly operations, such as Dell in PCs and Ducati in motorcycles. Close coordination with suppliers can also enhance differentiation by speeding up new product development cycles or speeding delivery to end customers. Strong relationships with suppliers can also mean that the company's supply requirements are prioritized when industry supply is insufficient to meet overall demand.

Delivering Superior Value via a Broad Differentiation Strategy

Differentiation strategies depend on meeting customer needs in unique ways or creating new needs through activities such as innovation or persuasive advertising. The objective is to offer customers something that rivals can't—at least in terms of the level of satisfaction. There are four basic routes to achieving this aim:

The first route is to incorporate product attributes and user features that *lower the buyer's overall costs* of using the company's product. This is the least obvious and most overlooked route to a differentiation advantage. It is a differentiating factor since it can help *business buyers* be more competitive in their markets and more profitable. Producers of materials and components often win orders for their products by reducing a buyer's raw-material waste (providing cut-to-size components), reducing a buyer's inventory requirements (providing just-in-time deliveries), using online systems to reduce a buyer's procurement and order processing costs, and providing free technical support. This route to differentiation can also appeal to *individual consumers* who are looking to economize on their overall costs of consumption. Making a company's product more economical for a consumer to use can be done by incorporating energy-efficient features (energy-saving appliances and lightbulbs help cut buyers' utility bills; fuel-efficient vehicles cut buyer costs for gasoline) and/or by increasing maintenance intervals and product reliability to lower buyer costs for maintenance and repairs.

A second route is to incorporate *tangible* features that increase customer satisfaction with the product, such as product specifications, functions, and styling. This can be accomplished by including attributes that add functionality; enhance the design; save time for the user; are more reliable; or make the product cleaner, safer, quieter, simpler to use, more portable, more convenient, or longer-lasting than rival brands. Smartphone manufacturers are in a race to introduce next-generation devices capable of being used for more purposes and having simpler menu functionality.

A third route to a differentiation-based competitive advantage is to incorporate *intangible* features that enhance buyer satisfaction in noneconomic ways. Toyota's Prius and GM's Chevy Bolt appeal to environmentally conscious motorists not only because these drivers want to help reduce global carbon dioxide emissions but also because they identify with the image conveyed. Bentley, Ralph Lauren, Louis Vuitton, Burberry, Cartier, and Coach have differentiation-based competitive advantages linked to buyer desires for status, image, prestige, upscale fashion, superior craftsmanship, and the finer things in life. Intangibles that contribute to differentiation can extend beyond product attributes to the reputation of the company and to customer relations or trust.

> Differentiation can be based on *tangible* or *intangible* attributes.

The fourth route is to *signal the value* of the company's product offering to buyers. The value of certain differentiating features is rather easy for buyers to detect, but in some instances buyers may have trouble assessing what their experience with the product will be. Successful differentiators go to great lengths to make buyers knowledgeable about a product's value and employ various signals of value. Typical signals of value include a high price (in instances where high price implies high quality and performance), more appealing or fancier packaging than competing products, ad content that emphasizes a product's standout attributes, the quality of brochures and sales presentations, and the luxuriousness and ambience of a seller's facilities. The nature of a company's facilities are important for high-end retailers and other types of companies whose facilities are frequented by customers; they make potential buyers aware of the professionalism, appearance, and personalities of the seller's employees and/or make potential buyers realize that a company has prestigious customers. Signaling value is particularly important (1) when the nature of differentiation is based on intangible features and is therefore subjective or hard to quantify, (2) when buyers are making a first-time purchase and are unsure what their experience with the product will be, (3) when repurchase is infrequent, and (4) when buyers are unsophisticated.

Regardless of the approach taken, achieving a successful differentiation strategy requires, first, that the company have capabilities in areas such as customer service, marketing, brand management, and technology that can create and support differentiation. That is, the resources, competencies, and value chain activities of the company must be well matched to the requirements of the strategy. For the strategy to result in competitive advantage, the company's competencies must also be sufficiently unique in delivering value to buyers that they help set its product offering apart from those of rivals. They must be competitively superior. There are numerous examples of companies that have differentiated themselves on the basis of distinctive capabilities. Health care facilities like M.D. Anderson, Mayo Clinic, and Cleveland Clinic have specialized expertise and equipment for treating certain diseases that most hospitals and health care providers cannot afford to emulate. When a major news event occurs, many people turn to Fox News and CNN because they have the capabilities to get reporters on the scene quickly, break away from their regular programming (without suffering a loss of advertising revenues associated with regular programming), and devote extensive air time to newsworthy stories.

| Easy-to-copy differentiating features cannot produce sustainable competitive advantage. |

The most successful approaches to differentiation are those that are difficult for rivals to duplicate. Indeed, this is the route to a sustainable competitive advantage based on differentiation. While resourceful competitors can, in time, clone almost any tangible product attribute, socially complex intangible attributes such as company reputation, long-standing relationships with buyers, and image are much harder to imitate. Differentiation that creates switching costs that lock in buyers also provides a route to sustainable advantage. For example, if a buyer makes a substantial investment in learning to use one type of system, that buyer is less likely to switch to a competitor's system. (This has kept many users from switching away from Microsoft Office products, despite the fact that there are other applications with superior features.) As a rule, differentiation yields a longer-lasting and more profitable competitive edge when it is based on a well-established brand image, patent-protected product innovation, complex technical superiority, a reputation for superior product quality and reliability, relationship-based customer service, and unique competitive capabilities.

When a Differentiation Strategy Works Best

Differentiation strategies tend to work best in market circumstances where

- *Buyer needs and uses of the product are diverse.* Diverse buyer preferences allow industry rivals to set themselves apart with product attributes that appeal to particular buyers. For instance, the diversity of consumer preferences for menu selection, ambience, pricing, and customer service gives restaurants exceptionally wide latitude in creating a differentiated product offering. Other industries with diverse buyer needs include magazine publishing, automobile manufacturing, footwear, and kitchen appliances.

- *There are many ways to differentiate the product or service that have value to buyers.* Industries in which competitors have opportunities to add features to products and services are well suited to differentiation strategies. For example, hotel chains can differentiate on such features as location, size of room, range of guest services, in-hotel dining, and the quality and luxuriousness of bedding and furnishings. Similarly, cosmetics producers are able to differentiate based on prestige and image, formulations that fight the signs of aging, UV light protection, exclusivity of retail locations, the inclusion of antioxidants and natural ingredients, or prohibitions against animal testing. Basic commodities, such as chemicals, mineral deposits, and agricultural products, provide few opportunities for differentiation.

- *Few rival firms are following a similar differentiation approach.* The best differentiation approaches involve trying to appeal to buyers on the basis of attributes that rivals are not emphasizing. A differentiator encounters less head-to-head rivalry when it goes its own separate way in creating value and does not try to out-differentiate rivals on the very same attributes. When many rivals base their differentiation efforts on the same attributes, the most likely result is weak brand differentiation and "strategy overcrowding"—competitors end up chasing much the same buyers with much the same product offerings.

- *Technological change is fast-paced and competition revolves around rapidly evolving product features.* Rapid product innovation and frequent introductions of next-version products heighten buyer interest and provide space for companies to pursue distinct differentiating paths. In smartphones and wearable Internet devices, drones for hobbyists and commercial use, automobile lane detection sensors, and battery-powered cars, rivals are locked into an ongoing battle to set themselves apart by introducing the best next-generation products. Companies that fail to come up with new and improved products and distinctive performance features quickly lose out in the marketplace.

Pitfalls to Avoid in Pursuing a Differentiation Strategy

Differentiation strategies can fail for any of several reasons. *A differentiation strategy keyed to product or service attributes that are easily and quickly copied is always suspect.* Rapid imitation means that no rival achieves differentiation, since whenever one firm introduces some value-creating aspect that strikes the fancy of buyers, fast-following copycats quickly reestablish parity. This is why a firm must seek out sources of value creation that are time-consuming or burdensome for rivals to match if it hopes to use differentiation to win a sustainable competitive edge.

> Any differentiating feature that works well is a magnet for imitators.

Differentiation strategies can also falter when buyers see little value in the unique attributes of a company's product. Thus, even if a company succeeds in setting its product apart from those of rivals, its strategy can result in disappointing sales and profits if the product does not deliver adequate perceived value to buyers. Anytime many potential buyers look at a company's differentiated product offering with indifference, the company's differentiation strategy is in deep trouble.

The third big pitfall is overspending on efforts to differentiate the company's product offering, thus eroding profitability. Company efforts to achieve differentiation nearly always raise costs—often substantially, since marketing and R&D are expensive undertakings. The key to profitable differentiation is either to keep the unit cost of achieving differentiation below the price premium that the differentiating attributes can command (thus increasing the profit margin per unit sold) or to offset thinner profit margins per unit by selling enough additional units to increase total profits. If a company goes overboard in pursuing costly differentiation, it could be saddled with unacceptably low profits or even losses.

Other common mistakes in crafting a differentiation strategy include

- *Offering only trivial improvements in quality, service, or performance features vis-à-vis rivals' products.* Trivial differences between rivals' product offerings may not be visible or important to buyers. If a company wants to generate the fiercely loyal customer following needed to earn superior profits and open up a differentiation-based competitive advantage over rivals, then its strategy must result in *strong rather than weak product differentiation.* In markets where differentiators do no better than achieve weak product differentiation, customer loyalty is weak, the costs of brand switching are low, and no one company has enough of a differentiation edge to command a price premium over rival brands.

- *Over-differentiating so that product quality, features, or service levels exceed the needs of most buyers.* A dazzling array of features and options not only drives up product price but also runs the risk that many buyers will conclude that a less deluxe and lower-priced brand is a better value since they have little occasion to use the deluxe attributes.

- *Charging too high a price premium.* While buyers may be intrigued by a product's deluxe features, they may nonetheless see it as being overpriced relative to the value delivered by the differentiating attributes. A company must guard against turning off would-be buyers with what is perceived as "price gouging." Normally, the bigger the price premium for the differentiating extras, the harder it is to keep buyers from switching to the lower-priced offerings of competitors.

FOCUSED (OR MARKET NICHE) STRATEGIES

What sets focused strategies apart from broad low-cost and broad differentiation strategies is concentrated attention on a narrow piece of the total market. The target segment, or niche, can be in the form of a geographic segment (such as New England), or a customer segment (such as young urban creatives or "yuccies"), or a product segment (such as a class of models or some version of the overall product type). Community Coffee, the largest family-owned specialty coffee retailer in the United States, has a geographic focus on the state of Louisiana and communities across the Gulf of Mexico. Community holds only a small share of the national coffee market but has recorded sales in excess of $100 million and has won a strong following in the Southeastern United States. Examples of firms that concentrate on a well-defined market niche keyed to a particular product or buyer segment include Zipcar (hourly and daily car rental in urban areas), Airbnb and HomeAway (owner of VRBO) (by-owner lodging rental), Fox News Channel and HGTV (cable TV), Blue Nile (online jewelry), Tesla Motors (electric cars), and CGA, Inc. (a specialist in providing insurance to cover the cost of lucrative hole-in-one prizes at golf tournaments). Microbreweries, local bakeries, bed-and-breakfast inns, and retail boutiques have also scaled their operations to serve narrow or local customer segments.

A Focused Low-Cost Strategy

A focused low-cost strategy aims at securing a competitive advantage by serving buyers in the target market niche at a lower cost (and usually lower price) than those of rival competitors. This strategy has considerable attraction when a firm can lower costs significantly by limiting its customer base to a well-defined buyer segment. The avenues to achieving a cost advantage over rivals also serving the target market niche are the same as those for broad low-cost leadership—use the cost drivers to perform value chain activities more

Clinícas del Azúcar's Focused Low-Cost Strategy

Though diabetes is a manageable condition, it is the leading cause of death in Mexico. Over 14 million adults (14 percent of all adults) suffer from diabetes, 3.5 million cases remain undiagnosed, and more than 80,000 die due to related complications each year. The key driver behind this public health crisis is limited access to affordable, high-quality care. Approximately 90 percent of the population cannot access diabetes care due to financial and time constraints; private care can cost upwards of $1,000 USD per year (approximately 45 percent of Mexico's population has an annual income less than $2,000 USD) while average wait times alone at public clinics surpass five hours. Clinícas del Azúcar (CDA), however, is quickly scaling a solution that uses a *focused low-cost strategy* to provide affordable and convenient care to low-income patients.

Rob Marmion/Shutterstock

By relentlessly focusing only on the needs of its target population, CDA has reduced the cost of diabetes care by more than 70 percent and clinic visit times by over 80 percent. The key has been the use of proprietary technology and a streamlined care system. First, CDA leverages evidence-based algorithms to diagnose patients for a fraction of the costs of traditional diagnostic tests. Similarly, its mobile outreach significantly reduces the costs of supporting patients in managing their diabetes after leaving CDA facilities. Second, CDA has redesigned the care process to implement a streamlined "patient process flow" that eliminates the need for multiple referrals to other care providers and brings together the necessary professionals and equipment into one facility. Consequently, CDA has become a one-stop shop for diabetes care, providing every aspect of diabetes treatment under one roof.

The bottom line: CDA's cost structure allows it to keep its prices for diabetes treatment very low, saving patients both time and money. Patients choose from three different care packages, ranging from preventive to comprehensive care, paying an annual fee that runs between approximately $70 and $200 USD. Given this increase in affordability and convenience, CDA estimates that it has saved its patients over $2 million USD in medical costs and will soon increase access to affordable, high-quality care for 10 to 80 percent of the population. These results have attracted investment from major funders including Endeavor, Echoing Green, and the Clinton Global Initiative. As a result, CDA and others expect CDA to grow from five clinics serving approximately 5,000 patients to more than 50 clinics serving over 100,000 patients throughout Mexico by 2020.

Note: Developed with David B. Washer.

Sources: www.clinicasdelazucar.com; "Funding Social Enterprises Report," *Echoing Green,* June 2014; Jude Webber, "Mexico Sees Poverty Climb Despite Rise in Incomes," *Financial Times* online, July 2015, www.ft.com/intl/cms/s/3/98460bbc-31e1-11e5-8873-775ba7c2ea3d.html#axzz3zz8grtec; "Javier Lozano," Schwab Foundation for Social Entrepreneurship online, 2016, www.schwabfound.org/content/javier-lozano.

efficiently than rivals and search for innovative ways to bypass nonessential value chain activities. The only real difference between a broad low-cost strategy and a focused low-cost strategy is the size of the buyer group to which a company is appealing—the former involves a product offering that appeals to almost all buyer groups and market segments, whereas the latter aims at just meeting the needs of buyers in a narrow market segment.

Budget motel chains, like Motel 6, Sleep Inn, and Super 8, cater to price-conscious travelers who just want to pay for a clean, no-frills place to spend the night. Illustration Capsule 5.2 describes how Clinícas del Azúcar's focus on lowering the costs of diabetes care is allowing it to address a major health issue in Mexico.

Focused low-cost strategies are fairly common. Costco, BJ's, and Sam's Club sell large lots of goods at wholesale prices to small businesses and bargain-hunters. Producers of private-label goods are able to achieve low costs in product development, marketing, distribution, and advertising by concentrating on making generic items imitative of name-brand merchandise and selling directly to retail chains wanting a low-priced store brand. The Perrigo Company Plc has become a leading manufacturer of over-the-counter health care products and self-care, with 2018 sales of nearly $5 billion, by focusing on producing private-label brands for retailers such as Walmart, CVS, Walgreens, Rite Aid, and Safeway.

A Focused Differentiation Strategy

Focused differentiation strategies involve offering superior products or services tailored to the unique preferences and needs of a narrow, well-defined group of buyers. Successful use of a focused differentiation strategy depends on (1) the existence of a buyer segment that is looking for special product or service attributes and (2) a firm's ability to create a product or service offering that stands apart from that of rivals competing in the same target market niche.

Companies like Molton Brown in bath, body, and beauty products, Bugatti in high-performance automobiles, and Four Seasons Hotels in lodging employ successful differentiation-based focused strategies targeted at upscale buyers wanting products and services with world-class attributes. Indeed, most markets contain a buyer segment willing to pay a big price premium for the very finest items available, thus opening the strategic window for some competitors to pursue differentiation-based focused strategies aimed at the very top of the market pyramid. Whole Foods Market, which was acquired by Amazon in 2017, became the largest organic and natural foods supermarket chain in the United States by catering to health-conscious consumers who prefer organic, natural, minimally processed, and locally grown foods. Whole Foods prides itself on stocking the highest-quality organic and natural foods it can find; the company defines quality by evaluating the ingredients, freshness, taste, nutritive value, appearance, and safety of the products it carries. Illustration Capsule 5.3 describes how Canada Goose has become a popular winter apparel brand with a focused differentiation strategy.

When a Focused Low-Cost or Focused Differentiation Strategy Is Attractive

A focused strategy aimed at securing a competitive edge based on either low costs or differentiation becomes increasingly attractive as more of the following conditions are met:

- The target market niche is big enough to be profitable and offers good growth potential.
- Industry leaders have chosen not to compete in the niche—in which case focusers can avoid battling head to head against the industry's biggest and strongest competitors.
- It is costly or difficult for multisegment competitors to meet the specialized needs of niche buyers and at the same time satisfy the expectations of their mainstream customers.
- The industry has many different niches and segments, thereby allowing a focuser to pick the niche best suited to its resources and capabilities. Also, with more niches there is room for focusers to concentrate on different market segments and avoid competing in the same niche for the same customers.
- Few if any rivals are attempting to specialize in the same target segment—a condition that reduces the risk of segment overcrowding.

Canada Goose's Focused Differentiation Strategy

Open up a winter edition of *People* and you will probably see photos of a celebrity sporting a Canada Goose parka. Recognizable by a distinctive red, white, and blue arm patch, the brand's parkas have been spotted on movie stars like Emma Stone and Bradley Cooper, on New York City streets, and on the cover of *Sports Illustrated*. Lately, Canada Goose has become extremely successful thanks to a focused differentiation strategy that enables it to thrive within its niche in the $1.2 trillion fashion industry. By targeting upscale buyers and providing a uniquely functional and stylish jacket, Canada Goose can charge nearly $1,000 per jacket and never need to put its products on sale.

While Canada Goose was founded in 1957, its recent transition to a focused differentiation strategy allowed it to rise to the top of the luxury parka market. In 2001, CEO Dani Reiss took control of the company and made two key decisions. First, he cut private-label and non-outerwear production in order to focus on the branded outerwear portion of Canada Goose's business. Second, Reiss decided to remain in Canada despite many North American competitors moving production to Asia to increase profit margins. Fortunately for him, these two strategy decisions have led directly to the company's current success. While other luxury brands, like Moncler, are priced similarly, no competitor's products fulfill the promise of handling harsh winter weather quite like a Canada Goose "Made in Canada" parka. The Canadian heritage, use of down sourced from rural Canada, real coyote fur (humanely trapped), and promise to provide warmth in sub-25°F

Galit Rodan/Bloomberg/Getty Images

temperatures have let Canada Goose break away from the pack when it comes to selling parkas. The company's distinctly Canadian product has made it a hit among buyers, which is reflected in the willingness to pay a steep premium for extremely high-quality and warm winter outerwear.

Since Canada Goose's shift to a focused differentiation strategy, the company has seen a boom in revenue and appeal across the globe. Prior to Reiss's strategic decisions in 2001, Canada Goose had annual revenue of about $3 million. Within a decade, the company had experienced over 4,000 percent growth in annual revenue; by the end of 2019, revenues from purchases in more than 50 countries had exceeded $830 million. At this pace, it looks like Canada Goose will remain a hot commodity as long as winter temperatures remain cold.

Note: Developed with Arthur J. Santry.

Sources: Drake Bennett, "How Canada Goose Parkas Migrated South," *Bloomberg Businessweek,* March 13, 2015, www.bloomberg.com; Hollie Shaw, "Canada Goose's Made-in-Canada Marketing Strategy Translates into Success," *Financial Post,* May 18, 2012, www.financialpost.com; "The Economic Impact of the Fashion Industry," *The Economist,* June 13, 2015, www.maloney.house.gov; and company website (accessed January 26, 2020).

The advantages of focusing a company's entire competitive effort on a single market niche are considerable, especially for smaller and medium-sized companies that may lack the breadth and depth of resources to tackle going after a broader customer base with a more complex set of needs. YouTube became a household name by concentrating on short video clips posted online. Papa John's, Little Caesars, and Domino's Pizza have created impressive businesses by focusing on the home delivery segment.

The Risks of a Focused Low-Cost or Focused Differentiation Strategy

Focusing carries several risks. One is the chance that competitors outside the niche will find effective ways to match the focused firm's capabilities in serving the target niche—perhaps by coming up with products or brands specifically designed to appeal to buyers in the target niche or by developing expertise and capabilities that offset the focuser's strengths. In the lodging business, large chains like Marriott and Hilton have launched multibrand strategies that allow them to compete effectively in several lodging segments simultaneously. Hilton has flagship hotels with a full complement of services and amenities that allow it to attract travelers and vacationers going to major resorts; it has Waldorf Astoria, Conrad Hotels & Resorts, Hilton Hotels & Resorts, and DoubleTree hotels that provide deluxe comfort and service to business and leisure travelers; it has Homewood Suites, Embassy Suites, and Home2 Suites designed as a "home away from home" for travelers staying five or more nights; and it has nearly 700 Hilton Garden Inn and 2,100 Hampton by Hilton locations that cater to travelers looking for quality lodging at an "affordable" price. Tru by Hilton is the company's newly introduced brand focused on value-conscious travelers seeking basic accommodations. Hilton has also added Curio Collection, Tapestry Collection, and Canopy by Hilton hotels that offer stylish, distinctive decors and personalized services that appeal to young professionals seeking distinctive lodging alternatives. Multibrand strategies are attractive to large companies such as Hilton precisely because they enable a company to enter a market niche and siphon business away from companies that employ a focus strategy.

A second risk of employing a focused strategy is the potential for the preferences and needs of niche members to shift over time toward the product attributes desired by buyers in the mainstream portion of the market. An erosion of the differences across buyer segments lowers entry barriers into a focuser's market niche and provides an open invitation for rivals in adjacent segments to begin competing for the focuser's customers. A third risk is that the segment may become so attractive that it is soon inundated with competitors, intensifying rivalry and splintering segment profits. And there is always the risk for segment growth to slow to such a small rate that a focuser's prospects for future sales and profit gains become unacceptably dim.

BEST-COST (HYBRID) STRATEGIES

To profitably employ a best-cost strategy, a company *must have the capability to incorporate upscale attributes into its product offering at a lower cost than rivals.* When a company can incorporate more appealing features, good to excellent product performance or quality, or more satisfying customer service into its product offering *at a lower cost than rivals,* then it enjoys "best-cost" status—it is the low-cost provider of a product or service with *upscale attributes.* A best-cost producer can use its low-cost advantage to underprice rivals whose products or services have similarly upscale attributes and still earn attractive profits. As Figure 5.1 indicates, **best-cost strategies** are a hybrid of low-cost and differentiation strategies, incorporating features of both simultaneously. They may address either a broad or narrow (focused) customer base. This permits companies to aim squarely at the sometimes great mass of value-conscious buyers looking for a better product or service at a somewhat lower price. Value-conscious buyers frequently shy away from both cheap low-end

> **CORE** CONCEPT
>
> **Best-cost strategies** are a *hybrid* of low-cost and differentiation strategies, incorporating features of both simultaneously.

products and expensive high-end products, but they are quite willing to pay a "fair" price for extra features and functionality they find appealing and useful. The essence of a best-cost strategy is giving customers *more value for the money* by satisfying buyer desires for appealing features and charging a lower price for these attributes compared to rivals with similar-caliber product offerings.[6]

A best-cost strategy is different from a low-cost strategy because the additional attractive attributes entail additional costs (which a low-cost producer can avoid by offering buyers a basic product with few frills). Moreover, the two strategies aim at a distinguishably different market target. *The target market for a best-cost producer is value-conscious buyers*—buyers who are looking for appealing extras and functionality at a comparatively low price, regardless of whether they represent a broad or more focused segment of the market. Value-hunting buyers (as distinct from *price-conscious buyers* looking for a basic product at a bargain-basement price) often constitute a very sizable part of the overall market for a product or service. A best-cost strategy differs from a differentiation strategy because it entails the ability to produce upscale features at a lower cost than other high-end producers. This implies the ability to profitably offer the buyer more value for the money.

Best-cost producers need not offer the highest end products and services (although they may); often the quality levels are simply better than average. Positioning of this sort permits companies to aim squarely at the sometimes great mass of value-conscious buyers looking for a better product or service at an economical price. Value-conscious buyers frequently shy away from both cheap low-end products and expensive high-end products, but they are quite willing to pay a "fair" price for extra features and functionality they find appealing and useful. The essence of a best-cost strategy is the ability to provide *more value for the money* by satisfying buyer desires for better quality while charging a lower price compared to rivals with similar-caliber product offerings.

Toyota has employed a classic best-cost strategy for its Lexus line of motor vehicles. It has designed an array of high-performance characteristics and upscale features into its Lexus models to make them comparable in performance and luxury to Mercedes, BMW, Audi, Jaguar, Cadillac, and Lincoln models. To signal its positioning in the luxury market segment, Toyota established a network of Lexus dealers, separate from Toyota dealers, dedicated to providing exceptional customer service. Most important, though, Toyota has drawn on its considerable know-how in making high-quality vehicles at low cost to produce its high-tech upscale-quality Lexus models at substantially lower costs than other luxury vehicle makers have been able to achieve in producing their models. To capitalize on its lower manufacturing costs, Toyota prices its Lexus models below those of comparable Mercedes, BMW, Audi, and Jaguar models to induce value-conscious luxury car buyers to purchase a Lexus instead. The price differential has typically been quite significant. For example, in 2017, a well-equipped Lexus RX 350 (a midsized SUV) had a sticker price of $54,370, whereas the sticker price of a comparably equipped Mercedes GLE-class SUV was $62,770 and the sticker price of a comparably equipped BMW X5 SUV was $66,670.

When a Best-Cost Strategy Works Best

A best-cost strategy works best in markets where product differentiation is the norm and an attractively large number of value-conscious buyers can be induced to purchase midrange products rather than cheap, basic products or expensive, top-of-the-line products. In markets such as these, a best-cost producer needs to position itself *near the*

● LO 5-4

Explain the attributes of a best-cost strategy—a hybrid of low-cost and differentiation strategies.

Over the last 50 years, Trader Joe's has built a cult-like following by offering a limited selection of highly popular private-label products at great prices, under the Trader Joe's brand. By pursuing a *focused best-cost* strategy, Trader Joe's has been able to thrive in the notoriously low-margin grocery business. Today, Trader Joe's earns over $2,000 of annual sales per square foot—nearly double that of Whole Foods.

One key to Trader Joe's success, and a major part of its strategy, is its unique approach to product selection. By selling mainly private label goods under its own brand, Trader Joe's keeps its costs low, enabling it to offer lower prices. By being very selective about the particular products that it carries, it has also managed to ensure that its brand is associated with very high quality. The company's policy is to swiftly replace any product that does not prove popular with another more appealing product. This has paid off: when you ask U.S. consumers which grocery store represents quality, Trader Joe's tops the list. On a recent YouGov Brand Index poll, nearly 40 percent of consumers ranked Trader Joe's best for quality—the highest among its competitors. While Trader Joe's offers far fewer stock-keeping units (SKUs) than a typical grocery store—only 4,000 SKUs as compared to 50,000 + in a Kroger or Safeway—the upside for customers is that this also helps to keep costs and prices low. It results in higher inventory turns (a key measure of efficiency in retail), lower inventory costs, and lower rents since stores in any given location can be smaller.

Ken Wolter/Shutterstock

Trader Joe's also intentionally locates its stores in areas with value-focused customers who appreciate quality. Trader Joe's identifies potential sites for expansion by evaluating demographic information. This enables Trader Joe's to focus on serving young educated singles and couples who may not be able to afford more expensive groceries but prefer organics and ready-to-eat products. Given that it occupies smaller sized retail spaces, Trader Joe's can locate in walkable areas and urban centers, the very same neighborhoods in which its chosen customer base lives. Because of its focused best-cost strategy, it is unlikely that the company's loyal customers will quit lining up to buy its tasty corn salsa or organic cold brew coffee any time soon.

Note: Developed with Stephanie K. Berger.

Sources: Company website; Beth Kowitt, "Inside the Secret World of Trader Joe's," *Fortune* (August 2010); Elain Watson, "Quirky, Cult-life, Aspirational, but Affordable: The Rise and Rise of Trader Joes," Food Navigator USA (April 2014; Janie Ryan, "The Surprising Secrets Behind Trader Joe's Supply Chain", Elementum.com, (December 13, 2018).

middle of the market with either a medium-quality product at a below-average price or a high-quality product at an average or slightly higher price. But as the Lexus example shows, a firm with the capabilities to produce top-of-the-line products more efficiently than its rivals, would also do well to pursue a best-cost strategy. Best-cost strategies also work well in recessionary times, when masses of buyers become more value-conscious and are attracted to economically priced products and services with more appealing attributes. However, unless a company has the resources, know-how, and capabilities to incorporate upscale product or service attributes at a lower cost than rivals, adopting a best-cost strategy is ill-advised. Illustration Capsule 5.4 describes how Trader Joe's has applied the principles of a focused best-cost strategy to thrive in the competitive grocery store industry.

The Risk of a Best-Cost Strategy

A company's biggest vulnerability in employing a best-cost strategy is getting squeezed between the strategies of firms using low-cost and high-end differentiation strategies. Low-cost producers may be able to siphon customers away with the appeal of a lower price (despite less appealing product attributes). High-end differentiators may be able to steal customers away with the appeal of better product attributes (even though their products carry a higher price tag). Thus, to be successful, a firm employing a best-cost strategy must achieve significantly lower costs in providing upscale features so that it can outcompete high-end differentiators on the basis of a *significantly* lower price. Likewise, it must offer buyers *significantly* better product attributes to justify a price above what low-cost leaders are charging. In other words, it must offer buyers a more attractive customer value proposition.

THE CONTRASTING FEATURES OF THE GENERIC COMPETITIVE STRATEGIES

Deciding which generic competitive strategy should serve as the framework on which to hang the rest of the company's strategy is not a trivial matter. Each of the five generic competitive strategies *positions* the company differently in its market and competitive environment. Each establishes a *central theme* for how the company will endeavor to outcompete rivals. Each creates some boundaries or guidelines for maneuvering as market circumstances unfold and as ideas for improving the strategy are debated. Each entails differences in terms of product line, production emphasis, marketing emphasis, and means of maintaining the strategy, as shown in Table 5.1.

> A company's competitive strategy should be well matched to its internal situation and predicated on leveraging its collection of competitively valuable resources and capabilities.

Thus, a choice of which generic strategy to employ spills over to affect many aspects of how the business will be operated and the manner in which value chain activities must be managed. Deciding which generic strategy to employ is perhaps the most important strategic commitment a company makes—it tends to drive the rest of the strategic actions a company decides to undertake.

Successful Generic Strategies Are Resource-Based

For a company's competitive strategy to succeed in delivering good performance and gain a competitive edge over rivals, it has to be well matched to a company's internal situation and underpinned by an appropriate set of resources, know-how, and competitive capabilities. To succeed in employing a low-cost strategy, a company must have the resources and capabilities to keep its costs below those of its competitors. This means having the expertise to cost-effectively manage value chain activities better than rivals by leveraging the cost drivers more effectively, and/or having the innovative capability to bypass certain value chain activities being performed by rivals. To succeed in a differentiation strategy, a company must have the resources and capabilities to leverage value drivers more effectively than rivals and incorporate attributes into its product offering that a broad range of buyers will find appealing. Successful focus strategies (both low cost and differentiation) require the capability to do an outstanding job of satisfying the needs and expectations of niche buyers. Success in employing a best-cost strategy requires the resources and capabilities to incorporate upscale product or service attributes at a lower cost than rivals. *For all types of generic strategies, success in sustaining the competitive edge depends on having resources and capabilities that rivals have trouble duplicating and for which there are no good substitutes.*

TABLE 5.1 Distinguishing Features of the Five Generic Competitive Strategies

	Broad Low-Cost	Broad Differentiation	Focused Low-Cost	Focused Differentiation	Best-Cost
Strategic target	• A broad cross-section of the market.	• A broad cross-section of the market.	• A narrow market niche where buyer needs and preferences are distinctively different.	• A narrow market niche where buyer needs and preferences are distinctively different.	• A broad or narrow range of value-conscious buyers.
Basis of competitive strategy	• Lower overall costs than competitors.	• Ability to offer buyers something attractively different from competitors' offerings.	• Lower overall cost than rivals in serving niche members.	• Attributes that appeal specifically to niche members.	• Ability to incorporate upscale features and attributes at lower costs than rivals.
Product line	• A good basic product with few frills (acceptable quality and limited selection).	• Many product variations, wide selection; emphasis on differentiating features.	• Features and attributes tailored to the tastes and requirements of niche members.	• Features and attributes tailored to the tastes and requirements of niche members.	• Items with appealing attributes and assorted features; better quality, not necessarily best.
Production emphasis	• A continuous search for cost reduction without sacrificing acceptable quality and essential features.	• Build in whatever differentiating features buyers are willing to pay for; strive for product superiority.	• A continuous search for cost reduction for products that meet basic needs of niche members.	• Small-scale production or custom-made products that match the tastes and requirements of niche members.	• Build in appealing features and better quality at lower cost than rivals.
Marketing emphasis	• Low prices, good value. • Try to make a virtue out of product features that lead to low cost.	• Tout differentiating features. • Charge a premium price to cover the extra costs of differentiating features.	• Communicate attractive features of a budget-priced product offering that fits niche buyers' expectations.	• Communicate how product offering does the best job of meeting niche buyers' expectations.	• Emphasize delivery of best value for the money.
Keys to maintaining the strategy	• Strive to manage costs down, year after year, in every area of the business.	• Stress continuous improvement in products or services and constant innovation to stay ahead of imitative competitors.	• Stay committed to serving the niche at the lowest overall cost; don't blur the firm's image by entering other market segments or adding other products to widen market appeal.	• Stay committed to serving the niche better than rivals; don't blur the firm's image by entering other market segments or adding other products to widen market appeal.	• Stress continuous improvement in products or services and constant innovation, along with continuous efforts to improve efficiency.
Resources and capabilities required	• Capabilities for driving costs out of the value chain system. • *Examples:* large-scale automated plants, an efficiency-oriented culture, bargaining power.	• Capabilities concerning quality, design, intangibles, and innovation. • *Examples:* marketing capabilities, R&D teams, technology.	• Capabilities to lower costs on niche goods. • *Examples:* lower input costs for the specific product desired by the niche, batch production capabilities.	• Capabilities to meet the highly specific needs of niche members. • *Examples:* custom production, close customer relations.	• Capabilities to simultaneously deliver lower cost and higher-quality/differentiated features. • *Examples:* TQM practices, mass customization.

150

Generic Strategies and the Three Different Approaches to Competitive Advantage

Just as a company's resources and capabilities underlie its choice of generic strategy, its generic strategy determines its approach to gaining a competitive advantage. There are three such approaches. Clearly, low-cost strategies aim for a cost advantage over rivals, differentiation strategies strive to create relatively more perceived value for consumers, while best-cost strategies aim to do better than the average rival on both dimensions. Whether the strategy is broad based or focused makes no difference as to the basic approach employed (see Figure 5.1).

Exactly how this works is best understood with the use of the value-price-cost framework, first introduced in Chapter 1 in the context of different kinds of business models. Figure 5.4 illustrates the three basic approaches to competitive advantage in terms of the value-price-cost framework. The left figure in the diagram represents an average competitor's cost (C) of producing a good, how highly the customer values it (V), and its price (P). The difference between the good's value to the customer (V) and its cost (C) is the total economic value (V-C) produced by the average competitor. And as explained in Chapter 4, a company has a competitive advantage over another if its strategy generates *more total economic value.* It is this excess in total economic value over rivals that allows the company to offer customers a better value proposition or earn larger profits (or both). The dashed yellow lines facilitate a comparison of the average competitor's costs (C) and perceived value (V) with the costs and value produced by each of the three basic types of generic strategies (low cost, differentiation, best cost). In this way, it also facilitates a comparison of the total economic value generated by each of the three representative generic strategies in relation to the average competitor, thereby shedding light on the nature of each strategy's competitive advantage.

FIGURE 5.4   Three Approaches to Competitive Advantage and the Value-Price-Cost Framework

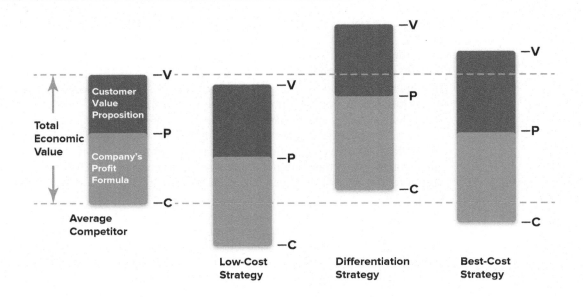

As Figure 5.4 shows, a low-cost generic strategy aims to achieve lower costs than an average competitor, at the sacrifice of some of the perceived value to the consumer. If the decrease in costs is less than the decrease in perceived value, then the total economic value (V-C) for the low-cost leader will be greater than the total economic value produced by its average rival and the low-cost leader will have a competitive advantage. This is clearly the case for the example of a low-cost strategy depicted in Figure 5.4. As is common with low-cost strategies, the example company has chosen to charge a lower price than its average rival. The result is that even with a lower V, the low-cost leader offers the consumer a more attractive (larger) consumer value proposition (depicted in mauve) and finds itself with a better profit formula (depicted in blue).

In contrast, the example of a differentiation strategy shows that costs might well exceed those of the average competitor. But with a successful differentiation strategy, that disadvantage is more than made up for by the rise in the perceived value (V) of the differentiated good, giving the differentiator a clear competitive advantage over the average rival (greater V-C). And while the price charged in this example is a good deal higher in comparison with the average rival's price, this differentiation strategy enables both a larger consumer value proposition (in mauve) as well as greater profits (in blue).

The depiction of a best-cost strategy shows a company pursuing the middle ground of offering neither the most highly valued goods in the market nor the lowest costs. But in comparison with the average rival, it does better on both scores, resulting in more total economic value (V-C) and a substantial competitive advantage. Once again, the example shows both a larger customer value proposition as well as a more attractive profit formula.

The last thing to note is that the generic strategies depicted in Figure 5.4 are examples of *successful* generic strategies. Being successful with a generic strategy depends on much more than positioning. It depends on the competitive context (the company's external situation) and on the company's internal situation, including its complement of resources and capabilities. Importantly, it also depends on how well the strategy is executed—the topic of this text's three concluding chapters.

KEY POINTS

1. Deciding which of the five generic competitive strategies to employ—broad low-cost, broad differentiation, focused low-cost, focused differentiation, or best-cost—is perhaps the most important strategic commitment a company makes. It tends to drive the remaining strategic actions a company undertakes and sets the whole tone for pursuing a competitive advantage over rivals.

2. In employing a broad low-cost strategy and trying to achieve a low-cost advantage over rivals, a company must do a better job than rivals of cost-effectively managing value chain activities and/or it must find innovative ways to eliminate cost-producing activities. An effective use of cost drivers is key. Low-cost strategies work particularly well when price competition is strong and the products of rival sellers are virtually identical, when there are not many ways to differentiate, when buyer switching costs are low, and when buyers are price-sensitive or have the power to bargain down prices.

3. Broad differentiation strategies seek to produce a competitive edge by incorporating attributes that set a company's product or service offering apart from rivals in ways that buyers consider valuable and worth paying for. This depends on the appropriate use of value drivers. Successful differentiation allows a firm to (1) command a premium price for its product, (2) increase unit sales (if additional

buyers are won over by the differentiating features), and/or (3) gain buyer loyalty to its brand (because some buyers are strongly attracted to the differentiating features and bond with the company and its products). Differentiation strategies work best when buyers have diverse product preferences, when few other rivals are pursuing a similar differentiation approach, and when technological change is fast-paced and competition centers on rapidly evolving product features. A differentiation strategy is doomed when competitors are able to quickly copy the appealing product attributes, when a company's differentiation efforts fail to interest many buyers, and when a company overspends on efforts to differentiate its product offering or tries to overcharge for its differentiating extras.

4. A focused strategy delivers competitive advantage either by achieving lower costs than rivals in serving buyers constituting the target market niche or by developing a specialized ability to offer niche buyers an appealingly differentiated offering that meets their needs better than rival brands do. A focused strategy based on either low cost or differentiation becomes increasingly attractive when the target market niche is big enough to be profitable and offers good growth potential, when it is costly or difficult for multisegment competitors to meet the specialized needs of the target market niche and at the same time satisfy the expectations of their mainstream customers, when there are one or more niches that present a good match for a focuser's resources and capabilities, and when few other rivals are attempting to specialize in the same target segment.

5. Best-cost strategies create competitive advantage on the basis of their capability to incorporate attractive or upscale attributes at a lower cost than rivals. Best-cost strategies can be either broad or focused. A best-cost strategy works best in broad or narrow market segments with value-conscious buyers desirous of purchasing better products and services for less money.

6. In all cases, competitive advantage depends on having competitively superior resources and capabilities that are a good fit for the chosen generic strategy. A sustainable advantage depends on maintaining that competitive superiority with resources, capabilities, and value chain activities that rivals have trouble matching and for which there are no good substitutes.

ASSURANCE OF LEARNING EXERCISES

1. Best Buy is the largest consumer electronics retailer in the United States, with fiscal 2019 sales of nearly $43 billion. The company competes aggressively on price with such rivals as Costco, Sam's Club, Walmart, and Target, but it is also known by consumers for its first-rate customer service. Best Buy customers have commented that the retailer's sales staff is exceptionally knowledgeable about the company's products and can direct them to the exact location of difficult-to-find items. Best Buy customers also appreciate that demonstration models of PC monitors, digital media players, and other electronics are fully powered and ready for in-store use. Best Buy's Geek Squad tech support and installation services are additional customer service features that are valued by many customers.

    LO 5-1, LO 5-2, LO 5-3, LO 5-4

    How would you characterize Best Buy's competitive strategy? Should it be classified as a low-cost strategy? A differentiation strategy? A best-cost strategy? Also, has the company chosen to focus on a narrow piece of the market, or does it appear to pursue a broad market approach? Explain your answer.

LO 5-2

2. Illustration Capsule 5.1 discusses Vanguard's position as the low-cost leader in the investment management industry. Based on information provided in the capsule, explain how Vanguard built its low-cost advantage in the industry and why a low-cost strategy can succeed in the industry.

LO 5-1, LO 5-2,
LO 5-3, LO 5-4

3. USAA is a Fortune 500 insurance and financial services company with 2018 annual sales exceeding $30 billion. The company was founded in 1922 by 25 Army officers who decided to insure each other's vehicles and continues to limit its membership to active-duty and retired military members, officer candidates, and adult children and spouses of military-affiliated USAA members. The company has received countless awards, including being listed among *Fortune*'s World's Most Admired Companies in 2014 through 2019 and 100 Best Companies to Work For in 2010 through 2019. You can read more about the company's history and strategy at **www.usaa.com.**

   How would you characterize USAA's competitive strategy? Should it be classified as a low-cost strategy? A differentiation strategy? A best-cost strategy? Also, has the company chosen to focus on a narrow piece of the market, or does it appear to pursue a broad market approach? Explain your answer.

LO 5-3

4. Explore Kendra Scott's website at **www.kendrascott.com** and see if you can identify at least three ways in which the company seeks to differentiate itself from rival jewelry firms. Is there reason to believe that Kendra Scott's differentiation strategy has been successful in producing a competitive advantage? Why or why not?

EXERCISES FOR SIMULATION PARTICIPANTS

LO 5-1, LO 5-2,
LO 5-3, LO 5-4

1. Which one of the five generic competitive strategies can best be utilized to compete successfully in the business simulation by your company?
2. Which rival companies appear to be employing a low-cost strategy?
3. Which rival companies appear to be employing a differentiation strategy?
4. Which rival companies appear to be employing a best-cost strategy?
5. Which cost drivers and/or value drivers are important for creating superior total economic value in the business simulation?
6. What is your company's action plan to achieve a sustainable competitive advantage over rival companies? List at least three (preferably more than three) specific kinds of decision entries on specific decision screens that your company has made or intends to make to win this kind of competitive edge over rivals.

ENDNOTES

[1] Michael E. Porter, *Competitive Strategy: Techniques for Analyzing Industries and Competitors* (New York: Free Press, 1980), chap. 2; Michael E. Porter, "What Is Strategy?" *Harvard Business Review* 74, no. 6 (November–December 1996).
[2] Michael E. Porter, *Competitive Advantage: Creating and Sustaining Superior Performance* (New York: Free Press, 1985).

[3] Richard L. Priem, "A Consumer Perspective on Value Creation," *Academy of Management Review* 32, no. 1 (2007), pp. 219–235.
[4] jrscience.wcp.muohio.edu/nsfall01/FinalArticles/Final-IsitWorthitBrandsan.html.
[5] D. Yoffie, "Cola Wars Continue: Coke and Pepsi in 2006," Harvard Business School case 9-706-447.

[6] Peter J. Williamson and Ming Zeng, "Value-for-Money Strategies for Recessionary Times," *Harvard Business Review* 87, no. 3 (March 2009), pp. 66–74.

chapter 6

Strengthening a Company's Competitive Position

Strategic Moves, Timing, and Scope of Operations

Learning Objectives

After reading this chapter, you should be able to:

LO 6-1 Understand whether, how, and when to deploy offensive or defensive strategic moves.

LO 6-2 Identify when being a first mover, a fast follower, or a late mover is most advantageous.

LO 6-3 Explain the strategic benefits and risks of expanding a company's horizontal scope through mergers and acquisitions.

LO 6-4 Explain the advantages and disadvantages of extending the company's scope of operations via vertical integration.

LO 6-5 Recognize the conditions that favor farming out certain value chain activities to outside parties.

LO 6-6 Understand how to capture the benefits and minimize the drawbacks of strategic alliances and partnerships.

Fanatic Studio/Getty Images

Whenever you look at any potential merger or acquisition, you look at the potential to create value for your shareholders.

> Dilip Shanghvi—*Founder and managing director of Sun Pharmaceuticals*

Alliances have become an integral part of contemporary strategic thinking.

> Fortune Magazine

The important thing about outsourcing . . . is that it becomes a very powerful tool to leverage talent, improve productivity, and reduce work cycles.

> Azim Premji—*Chairman of Wipro Limited (India's third-largest outsourcer)*

Once a company has settled on which of the five generic competitive strategies to employ, attention turns to what *other strategic actions* it can take to complement its competitive approach and maximize the power of its overall strategy. The first set of decisions concerns whether to undertake offensive or defensive competitive moves, and the timing of such moves. The second set concerns expanding or contracting the breadth of a company's activities (or its *scope* of operations along an industry's entire value chain). All in all, the following measures to strengthen a company's competitive position must be considered:

- Whether to go on the offensive and initiate aggressive strategic moves to improve the company's market position.
- Whether to employ defensive strategies to protect the company's market position.

- When to undertake new strategic initiatives— whether advantage or disadvantage lies in being a first mover, a fast follower, or a late mover.
- Whether to bolster the company's market position by merging with or acquiring another company in the same industry.
- Whether to integrate backward or forward into more stages of the industry value chain system.
- Which value chain activities, if any, should be outsourced.
- Whether to enter into strategic alliances or partnership arrangements with other enterprises.

This chapter presents the pros and cons of each of these strategy-enhancing measures.

LAUNCHING STRATEGIC OFFENSIVES TO IMPROVE A COMPANY'S MARKET POSITION

● LO 6-1

Understand whether, how, and when to deploy offensive or defensive strategic moves.

No matter which of the five generic competitive strategies a firm employs, there are times when a company should *go on the offensive* to improve its market position and performance. **Strategic offensives** are called for when a company spots opportunities to gain profitable market share at its rivals' expense or when a company has no choice but to try to whittle away at a strong rival's competitive advantage. Companies like Facebook, Amazon, Apple, and Google play hardball, aggressively pursuing competitive advantage and trying to reap the benefits a competitive edge offers—a leading market share, excellent profit margins, and rapid growth.[1] The best offensives tend to incorporate several principles: (1) focusing relentlessly on building competitive advantage and then striving to convert it into a sustainable advantage, (2) applying resources where rivals are least able to defend themselves, (3) employing the element of surprise as opposed to doing what rivals expect and are prepared for, and (4) displaying a capacity for swift and decisive actions to overwhelm rivals.[2]

Sometimes a company's best strategic option is to seize the initiative, go on the attack, and launch a strategic offensive to improve its market position.

Choosing the Basis for Competitive Attack

As a rule, challenging rivals on competitive grounds where they are strong is an uphill struggle.[3] Offensive initiatives that exploit competitor weaknesses stand a better chance of succeeding than do those that challenge competitor strengths, especially if the weaknesses represent important vulnerabilities and weak rivals can be caught by surprise with no ready defense.

Strategic offensives should exploit the power of a company's strongest competitive assets—its most valuable resources and capabilities such as a better-known brand name, a more efficient production or distribution system, greater technological capability, or a superior reputation for quality. But a consideration of the company's strengths should not be made without also considering the rival's strengths and weaknesses. A strategic offensive should be based on those areas of strength where the company has its greatest competitive advantage over the targeted rivals.

The best offensives use a company's most powerful resources and capabilities to attack rivals in the areas where they are competitively weakest.

If a company has especially good customer service capabilities, it can make special sales pitches to the customers of those rivals that provide subpar customer service. Likewise, it may be beneficial to pay special attention to buyer segments that a rival is neglecting or is weakly equipped to serve. The best offensives use a company's most powerful resources and capabilities to attack rivals in the areas where they are weakest.

Ignoring the need to tie a strategic offensive to a company's competitive strengths and what it does best is like going to war with a popgun—the prospects for success are dim. For instance, it is foolish for a company with relatively high costs to employ a price-cutting offensive. Likewise, it is ill-advised to pursue a product innovation offensive without having proven expertise in R&D and new product development.

The principal offensive strategy options include the following:

1. *Offering an equally good or better product at a lower price.* Lower prices can produce market share gains if competitors don't respond with price cuts of their own and if the challenger convinces buyers that its product is just as good or better. However, such a strategy increases total profits only if the gains in additional unit sales are enough to offset the impact of thinner margins per unit sold. Price-cutting offensives should be initiated only by companies that have *first achieved a cost advantage.*[4] British airline EasyJet used this strategy successfully against rivals such as

British Air, Alitalia, and Air France by first cutting costs to the bone and then targeting leisure passengers who care more about low price than in-flight amenities and service.[5] Spirit Airlines is using this strategy in the U.S. airline market.

2. *Leapfrogging competitors by being first to market with next-generation products.* In technology-based industries, the opportune time to overtake an entrenched competitor is when there is a shift to the next generation of the technology. Eero got its whole-home Wi-Fi system to market nearly one year before Linksys and Netgear developed competing systems, helping it build a sizable market share and develop a reputation for cutting-edge innovation in Wi-Fi systems.

3. *Pursuing continuous product innovation to draw sales and market share away from less innovative rivals.* Ongoing introductions of new and improved products can put rivals under tremendous competitive pressure, especially when rivals' new product development capabilities are weak. But such offensives can be sustained only if a company can keep its pipeline full with new product offerings that spark buyer enthusiasm.

4. *Pursuing disruptive product innovations to create new markets.* While this strategy can be riskier and more costly than a strategy of continuous innovation, it can be a game changer if successful. Disruptive innovation involves perfecting a new product with a few trial users and then quickly rolling it out to the whole market in an attempt to get many buyers to embrace an altogether new and better value proposition quickly. Examples include online universities, Twitter, Venmo, CampusBookRentals, and Waymo (Alphabet's self-driving tech company).

5. *Adopting and improving on the good ideas of other companies (rivals or otherwise).* The idea of warehouse-type home improvement centers did not originate with Home Depot cofounders Arthur Blank and Bernie Marcus; they got the "big-box" concept from their former employer, Handy Dan Home Improvement. But they were quick to improve on Handy Dan's business model and take Home Depot to the next plateau in terms of product-line breadth and customer service. Offensive-minded companies are often quick to adopt any good idea (not nailed down by a patent or other legal protection) and build on it to create competitive advantage for themselves.

6. *Using hit-and-run or guerrilla warfare tactics to grab market share from complacent or distracted rivals.* Options for "guerrilla offensives" include occasionally lowballing on price (to win a big order or steal a key account from a rival), surprising rivals with sporadic but intense bursts of promotional activity (offering a discounted trial offer to draw customers away from rival brands), or undertaking special campaigns to attract the customers of rivals plagued with a strike or problems in meeting buyer demand.[6] Guerrilla offensives are particularly well suited to small challengers that have neither the resources nor the market visibility to mount a full-fledged attack on industry leaders.

7. *Launching a preemptive strike to secure an industry's limited resources or capture a rare opportunity.*[7] What makes a move preemptive is its one-of-a-kind nature—whoever strikes first stands to acquire competitive assets that rivals can't readily match. Examples of preemptive moves include (1) securing the best distributors in a particular geographic region or country; (2) obtaining the most favorable site at a new interchange or intersection, in a new shopping mall, and so on; (3) tying up the most reliable, high-quality suppliers via exclusive partnerships, long-term contracts, or acquisition; and (4) moving swiftly to acquire the assets of distressed rivals at bargain prices. To be successful, a preemptive move doesn't have to totally block rivals from following; it merely needs to give a firm a prime position that is not easily circumvented.

How long it takes for an offensive action to yield good results varies with the competitive circumstances.[8] It can be short if buyers respond immediately (as can occur with a dramatic cost-based price cut, an imaginative ad campaign, or a disruptive innovation). Securing a competitive edge can take much longer if winning consumer acceptance of the company's product will take some time or if the firm may need several years to debug a new technology or put a new production capacity in place. But how long it takes for an offensive move to improve a company's market standing—and whether the move will prove successful—depends in part on whether market rivals recognize the threat and begin a counterresponse. Whether rivals will respond depends on whether they are capable of making an effective response and if they believe that a counterattack is worth the expense and the distraction.[9]

Choosing Which Rivals to Attack

Offensive-minded firms need to analyze which of their rivals to challenge as well as how to mount the challenge. The following are the best targets for offensive attacks:[10]

- *Market leaders that are vulnerable.* Offensive attacks make good sense when a company that leads in terms of market share is not a true leader in terms of serving the market well. Signs of leader vulnerability include unhappy buyers, an inferior product line, aging technology or outdated plants and equipment, a preoccupation with diversification into other industries, and financial problems. Caution is well advised in challenging strong market leaders—there's a significant risk of squandering valuable resources in a futile effort or precipitating a fierce and profitless industrywide battle for market share.
- *Runner-up firms with weaknesses in areas where the challenger is strong.* Runner-up firms are an especially attractive target when a challenger's resources and capabilities are well suited to exploiting their weaknesses.
- *Struggling enterprises that are on the verge of going under.* Challenging a hard-pressed rival in ways that further sap its financial strength and competitive position can weaken its resolve and hasten its exit from the market. In this type of situation, it makes sense to attack the rival in the market segments where it makes the most profits, since this will threaten its survival the most.
- *Small local and regional firms with limited capabilities.* Because small firms typically have limited expertise and resources, a challenger with broader and/or deeper capabilities is well positioned to raid their biggest and best customers—particularly those that are growing rapidly, have increasingly sophisticated requirements, and may already be thinking about switching to a supplier with a more full-service capability.

Blue-Ocean Strategy—a Special Kind of Offensive

CORE CONCEPT

A blue-ocean strategy offers growth in revenues and profits by discovering or inventing new industry segments that create altogether new demand.

A **blue-ocean strategy** seeks to gain a dramatic competitive advantage by abandoning efforts to beat out competitors in existing markets and, instead, *inventing a new market segment that allows a company to create and capture altogether new demand.*[11] This strategy views the business universe as consisting of two distinct types of market space. One is where industry boundaries are well defined, the competitive rules of the game are understood, and companies try to outperform rivals by capturing a bigger share of existing demand. In such markets, intense competition constrains a company's prospects for rapid growth and superior profitability since rivals move quickly to either imitate or counter the successes of competitors. The second type of market space is a "blue ocean," where the industry does not really exist yet, is untainted by competition, and offers wide-open opportunity for profitable and rapid growth if a company can create new demand with a new type of product offering. The "blue ocean" represents wide-open opportunity, offering smooth sailing in uncontested waters for the company first to venture out upon it.

A terrific example of such blue-ocean market space is the online auction industry that eBay created and now dominates. Other companies that have created blue-ocean market spaces include NetJets in fractional jet ownership, Drybar in hair blowouts, Tune Hotels in limited service "backpacker" hotels, Uber and Lyft in ride-sharing services, and Cirque du Soleil in live entertainment. Cirque du Soleil "reinvented the circus" by pulling in a whole new group of customers—adults and corporate clients—who not only were noncustomers of traditional circuses (like Ringling Brothers) but also were willing to pay several times more than the price of a conventional circus ticket to have a "sophisticated entertainment experience" featuring stunning visuals and star-quality acrobatic acts. Australian winemaker Casella Wines used a blue ocean strategy to find some uncontested market space for its Yellow Tail brand. By creating a product designed to appeal to wider market—one that also includes beer and spirit drinkers—Yellow Tail was able to unlock substantial new demand, becoming the fastest growing wine brand in U.S. history. Illustration Capsule 6.1 discusses the way that Etsy used a blue ocean strategy to open up new competitive space in online retailing.

Blue-ocean strategies provide a company with a great opportunity in the short run but they don't guarantee a company's long-term success, which depends more on whether a company can protect the market position it opened up and sustain its early advantage. Gilt Groupe serves as an example of a company that opened up new competitive space in online luxury retailing only to see its blue-ocean waters ultimately turn red. Its competitive success early on prompted an influx of fast followers into the luxury flash-sale industry, including HauteLook, RueLaLa, Lot18, and MyHabit.com. The new rivals not only competed for online customers, who could switch costlessly from site to site (since memberships were free), but also competed for unsold designer inventory. Once valued at over $1 billion, Gilt Groupe was finally sold to Hudson's Bay, the owner of Sak's Fifth Avenue, for just $250 million in 2016.

DEFENSIVE STRATEGIES—PROTECTING MARKET POSITION AND COMPETITIVE ADVANTAGE

In a competitive market, all firms are subject to offensive challenges from rivals. The purposes of defensive strategies are to lower the risk of being attacked, weaken the impact of any attack that occurs, and induce challengers to aim their efforts at other rivals. While defensive strategies usually don't enhance a firm's competitive advantage, they can definitely help fortify the firm's competitive position, protect its most valuable resources and capabilities from imitation, and defend whatever competitive advantage it might have. Defensive strategies can take either of two forms: actions to block challengers or actions to signal the likelihood of strong retaliation.

Etsy's Blue Ocean Strategy in Online Retailing of Handmade Crafts

Etsy, the online artisanal marketplace, was the inspirational idea of three New York entrepreneurs who saw that eBay had become too large and ineffective for craftsman and artisans who wished to sell their one-of-a-kind products online. While eBay's timed auction format made for an exciting experience for bargain-hunting consumers, Etsy in contrast promoted its ability to connect thoughtful consumers with artisans selling unique hand-crafted items. Typical Etsy buyers valued craftsmanship and wanted to know how items were made and who made them. The ability to develop a direct relationship with the seller was important to many Etsy buyers who enjoyed a personalized shopping experience. Purchases made by Etsy buyers ranged from $5 ornaments to $50 hand-made clothing items to $2,000 custom-made coffee tables.

Etsy thrived in what was initially uncontested competitive space. In 2015, to the surprise of many, theirs was the largest venture capital backed IPO (Initial Public Offering) to have come out of New York City. By 2018, they had 39 million active buyers and 2.1 million crafters and artisans offering their products. The company's gross merchandise sales totaled more than $3.9 billion that same year. Etsy charged sellers a 3.5 percent transaction fee and a 20-cent listing fee and generated additional revenue from payment processing fees and the sales of shipping labels. The company's revenues had grown from $74.6 million in 2012 to $603.7 million in 2018.

Piotr Swat/Shutterstock

The tremendous success of the company's Blue Ocean Strategy had not gone unnoticed. Amazon announced in May 2016 that it would launch a site featuring artisan goods named Handmade. Amazon believed that its free 2-day shipping to Prime members would give it an advantage over Etsy. Etsy's share price took a steep dive in 2016, but by late 2019, the company's stock was back up to nearly three times its IPO first-day closing price of $22.24. The strength of its strategy and the quality of its execution would determine if Etsy would be able to continue to thrive despite well-funded new entrants into its specialty online retailing sector.

Note: Developed with Rochelle R. Brunson and Marlene M. Reed.

Blocking the Avenues Open to Challengers

> Good defensive strategies can help protect a competitive advantage but rarely are the basis for creating one.

The most frequently employed approach to defending a company's present position involves actions that restrict a challenger's options for initiating a competitive attack. There are any number of obstacles that can be put in the path of would-be challengers. A defender can introduce new features, add new models, or broaden its product line to close off gaps and vacant niches to opportunity-seeking challengers. It can thwart rivals' efforts to attack with a lower price by maintaining its own lineup of economy-priced options. It can discourage buyers from trying competitors' brands by lengthening warranties, making early announcements about impending new products or price changes, offering free training and support services, or providing coupons and sample giveaways to buyers most prone to experiment. It can induce potential buyers to reconsider switching. It can challenge the quality or safety of rivals' products. Finally, a defender can grant volume discounts or better financing terms to dealers and distributors to discourage them from experimenting with other suppliers, or it can convince them to handle its product line *exclusively* and force competitors to use other distribution outlets.

Signaling Challengers That Retaliation Is Likely

The goal of signaling challengers that strong retaliation is likely in the event of an attack is either to dissuade challengers from attacking at all or to divert them to less threatening options. Either goal can be achieved by letting challengers know the battle will cost more than it is worth. Signals to would-be challengers can be given by

- Publicly announcing management's commitment to maintaining the firm's present market share.
- Publicly committing the company to a policy of matching competitors' terms or prices.
- Maintaining a war chest of cash and marketable securities.
- Making an occasional strong counterresponse to the moves of weak competitors to enhance the firm's image as a tough defender.

To be an effective defensive strategy, however, signaling needs to be accompanied by a *credible commitment* to follow through.

> To be an effective defensive strategy signaling needs to be accompanied by a *credible commitment* to follow through.

TIMING A COMPANY'S STRATEGIC MOVES

When to make a strategic move is often as crucial as *what* move to make. Timing is especially important when **first-mover advantages and disadvantages** exist. Under certain conditions, being first to initiate a strategic move can have a high payoff in the form of a competitive advantage that later movers can't dislodge. Moving first is no guarantee of success, however, since first movers also face some significant disadvantages. Indeed, there are circumstances in which it is more advantageous to be a fast follower or even a late mover. Because the timing of strategic moves can be consequential, it is important for company strategists to be aware of the nature of first-mover advantages and disadvantages and the conditions favoring each type of move.[12]

> **CORE** CONCEPT
>
> Because of **first-mover advantages and disadvantages,** competitive advantage can spring from *when* a move is made as well as from what move is made.

The Potential for First-Mover Advantages

Market pioneers and other types of first movers typically bear greater risks and greater development costs than firms that move later. If the market responds well to its initial move, the pioneer will benefit from a monopoly position (by virtue of being first to market) that enables it to recover its investment costs and make an attractive profit. If the firm's pioneering move gives it a competitive advantage that can be sustained even after other firms enter the market space, its first-mover advantage will be greater still. The extent of this type of advantage, however, will depend on whether and how fast follower firms can piggyback on the pioneer's success and either imitate or improve on its move.

> ● **LO 6-2**
>
> Identify when being a first mover, a fast follower, or a late mover is most advantageous.

There are six such conditions in which first-mover advantages are most likely to arise:

1. *When pioneering helps build a firm's reputation and creates strong brand loyalty.* Customer loyalty to an early mover's brand can create a tie that binds, limiting the success of later entrants' attempts to poach from the early mover's customer base and steal market share. For example, Open Table's early move as an online restaurant-reservation service built a strong brand that has since fueled its expansion worldwide.

2. *When a first mover's customers will thereafter face significant switching costs.* Switching costs can protect first movers when consumers make large investments in learning how to use a specific company's product or in purchasing complementary products that are also brand-specific. Switching costs can also arise from loyalty programs or long-term contracts that give customers incentives to remain with an initial provider. FreshDirect, for example, offers its grocery-delivery customers bigger savings, the longer they keep their service subscription.

3. *When property rights protections thwart rapid imitation of the initial move.* In certain types of industries, property rights protections in the form of patents, copyrights, and trademarks prevent the ready imitation of an early mover's initial moves. First-mover advantages in pharmaceuticals, for example, are heavily dependent on patent protections, and patent races in this industry are common. In other industries, however, patents provide limited protection and can frequently be circumvented. Property rights protections also vary among nations, since they are dependent on a country's legal institutions and enforcement mechanisms.

4. *When an early lead enables the first mover to reap scale economies or move down the learning curve ahead of rivals.* If significant scale-based advantages are available to an early mover, later entrants (with a smaller market share) will face relatively higher production costs. This disadvantage will make it even harder for later entrants to gain share and overcome the first-mover scale advantage. When there is a steep learning curve and when learning can be kept *proprietary,* a first mover can benefit from volume-based cost advantages that grow ever larger as its experience accumulates and its scale of operations increases. This type of first-mover advantage is self-reinforcing and, as such, can preserve a first mover's competitive advantage over long periods of time. Honda's advantage in small multiuse motorcycles has been attributed to such an effect.

5. *When a first mover can set the technical standard for the industry.* In many technology-based industries, the market will converge around a single technical standard. By establishing the industry standard, a first mover can gain a powerful advantage that, like experience-based advantages, builds over time. The lure of such an advantage, however, can result in standard wars among early movers, as each strives to set the industry standard. The key to winning such wars is to enter early on the basis of strong fast-cycle product development capabilities, gain the support of key customers and suppliers, employ penetration pricing, and make allies of the producers of complementary products.

6. *When strong network effects compel increasingly more consumers to choose the first mover's product or service.* As we described in Chapter 3, network effects are at work whenever consumers benefit from having other consumers use the same product or service that they use—a benefit that increases with the number of consumers using the product. An example is FaceTime. The more that people you know have FaceTime on their phones or devices, the more that you are able to have a video conversation with them if you also have FaceTime—a benefit that grows with the number of users in your circle. Network effects can also occur with respect to suppliers. eBay has enjoyed a considerable first-mover advantage for years, not just because of early brand name recognition but also because of powerful network

ILLUSTRATION
CAPSULE 6.2   Tinder Swipes Right for First-Mover Success

Tinder, a simple, swipe-based dating app, entered the market in 2012 with a bang, gaining over a million monthly active users in less than a year. While other dating apps were already in existence, Tinder started the swiping phenomenon, thereby easing the process of finding love online and making the use of dating apps commonplace. By 2014, Tinder was processing over a billion swipes daily and users were spending an average of an hour and a half on the app each day. (Today, the average user spends about an hour on Facebook, Instagram, Snapchat, and Twitter—combined.)

Tinder's fast start had much to do with the fact that it was easy-to-use, without the time-consuming questionnaires of other dating services, and fun, with a game-like aspect that many called addictive. In addition, Tinder was rolled out on college campuses using viral marketing techniques that helped it to quickly gain acceptance among social circles such as fraternities and sororities, in which "key influencers" boosted its popularity to the point where it reached a critical mass. But its sustained success has had more to do with the fact that it has been able to reap the benefits of a first mover advantage, as the first major entrant into the field of mobile dating.

In the dating service industry, efficacy is wholly dependent on network effects (where users of an app benefit increasingly as the number of users of that same app increases). By focusing first on ensuring high usage among local social domains, Tinder benefited from strong local network effects. As its popularity spread, users increasingly found Tinder to be the most attractive app to use, since so many others were using it—thereby strengthening the network effect advantage, and drawing ever more people to download the Tinder app. With increased volume, Tinder gained other classic

BigTunaOnline/Shutterstock

first mover advantages, such as enhanced reputational benefits, learning curve efficiencies, and increased interest from investors. By 2019, Tinder had nearly 8 million users, making the app the most popular online dating app in the United States.

Tinder's first mover advantage has not kept others from entering the mobile dating market. In fact, Tinder's phenomenal success has led to a surge in new entrants, with many imitating the Tinder's most popular features. Despite this, Tinder's first mover advantage has proven protective in many ways. Tinder's user base far outstrips the user base of rivals. And while other apps have been trying to play catch up, Tinder has been introducing new subscription products and other paid features to turn its market share advantage into a profitability advantage. As it stands, most analysts see Tinder as the mobile dating application with the highest commercial potential. And with a valuation of $3B and the distinction of Apple's *top-grossing* app in August 2017, it seems that Tinder is here to stay.

Note: Developed with Lindsey Wilcox and Charles K. Anumonwo.

Sources: https://www.inc.com/issie-lapowsky/how-tinder-is-winning-the-mobile-dating-wars.html; http://www.adweek.com/digital/mediakix-time-spent-social-media-infographic/; www.pewresearch.org/fact-tank/2016/02/29/5-facts-about-online-dating/; https://www.forbes.com/sites/stevenbertoni/2017/08/31/tinder-hits-3-billion-valuation-after-match-group-converts-options/#653a516f34f9; company website; J. Clement. Statista, November 22, 2019.

effects on the supply and demand side. The more suppliers choose to auction their items on eBay, the more attractive it is for others to do so as well, since the greater number of items being auctioned attracts more and more potential buyers, which in turn attracts more and more items being auctioned. Strong network effects are self-reinforcing and may lead to a winner-take-all situation for the first mover.

Illustration Capsule 6.2 describes how Tinder achieved a first-mover advantage in the field of mobile dating.

The Potential for Late-Mover Advantages or First-Mover Disadvantages

In some instances there are advantages *to being an adept follower* rather than a first mover. Late-mover advantages (or *first-mover disadvantages*) arise in four instances:

- When the costs of pioneering are high relative to the benefits accrued and imitative followers can achieve similar benefits with far lower costs. This is often the case when second movers can learn from a pioneer's experience and avoid making the same costly mistakes as the pioneer.

- When an innovator's products are somewhat primitive and do not live up to buyer expectations, thus allowing a follower with better-performing products to win disenchanted buyers away from the leader.

- When rapid market evolution (due to fast-paced changes in either technology or buyer needs) gives second movers the opening to leapfrog a first mover's products with more attractive next-version products.

- When market uncertainties make it difficult to ascertain what will eventually succeed, allowing late movers to wait until these needs are clarified.

- When customer loyalty to the pioneer is low and a first mover's skills, know-how, and actions are easily copied or even surpassed.

- When the first mover must make a risky investment in complementary assets or infrastructure (and these may be enjoyed at low cost or risk by followers).

To Be a First Mover or Not

In weighing the pros and cons of being a first mover versus a fast follower versus a late mover, it matters whether the race to market leadership in a particular industry is a 10-year marathon or a 2-year sprint. In marathons, a slow mover is not unduly penalized—first-mover advantages can be fleeting, and there's ample time for fast followers and sometimes even late movers to catch up.[13] Thus, the speed at which the pioneering innovation is likely to catch on matters considerably as companies struggle with whether to pursue an emerging market opportunity aggressively (as a first mover) or cautiously (as a late mover). For instance, it took 5.5 years for worldwide mobile phone use to grow from 10 million to 100 million, and it took close to 10 years for the number of at-home broadband subscribers to grow to 100 million worldwide. The lesson here is that there is a market penetration curve for every emerging opportunity. Typically, the curve has an inflection point at which all the pieces of the business model fall into place, buyer demand explodes, and the market takes off. The inflection point can come early on a fast-rising curve (like the use of e-mail and watching movies streamed over the Internet) or farther up on a slow-rising curve (as with battery-powered motor vehicles, solar and wind power, and textbook rental for college students). Any company that seeks competitive advantage by being a first mover thus needs to ask some hard questions:

- Does market takeoff depend on the development of complementary products or services that currently are not available?
- Is new infrastructure required before buyer demand can surge?
- Will buyers need to learn new skills or adopt new behaviors?
- Will buyers encounter high switching costs in moving to the newly introduced product or service?
- Are there influential competitors in a position to delay or derail the efforts of a first mover?

When the answers to any of these questions are yes, then a company must be careful not to pour too many resources into getting ahead of the market opportunity—the race is likely going to be closer to a 10-year marathon than a 2-year sprint.[14] On the other hand, if the market is a winner-take-all type of market, where powerful first-mover advantages insulate early entrants from competition and prevent later movers from making any headway, then it may be best to move quickly despite the risks.

STRENGTHENING A COMPANY'S MARKET POSITION VIA ITS SCOPE OF OPERATIONS

Apart from considerations of competitive moves and their timing, there is another set of managerial decisions that can affect the strength of a company's market position. These decisions concern the scope of a company's operations—the breadth of its activities and the extent of its market reach. Decisions regarding the **scope of the firm** focus on which activities a firm will perform internally and which it will not.

Consider, for example, Ralph Lauren Corporation. In contrast to Rambler's Way, a sustainable clothing company with a small chain of retail stores, Ralph Lauren designs, markets, and distributes fashionable apparel and other merchandise to approximately 13,000 major department stores and specialty retailers throughout the world. In addition, it operates nearly 500 retail stores, more than 650 concession-based shops within shops, and 10 e-commerce sites. Scope decisions also concern which segments of the market to serve—decisions that can include geographic market segments as well as product and service segments. Almost 50 percent of Ralph Lauren's sales are made outside North America, and its product line includes apparel, fragrances, home furnishings, eyewear, watches and jewelry, and handbags and other leather goods. Its lineup of brands includes Polo Ralph Lauren, Club Monaco, Chaps, and Double RL, as well as its Ralph Lauren Collection brands.

Decisions such as these, in essence, determine where the boundaries of a firm lie and the degree to which the operations within those boundaries cohere. They also have much to do with the direction and extent of a business's growth. In this chapter, we discuss different types of decisions regarding the scope of the company in relation to a company's business-level strategy. In the next two chapters, we develop two additional dimensions of a firm's scope; Chapter 7 focuses on international expansion—a matter of extending the company's geographic scope into foreign markets; Chapter 8 takes up the topic of corporate strategy, which concerns diversifying into a mix of different businesses. *Scope issues are at the very heart of corporate-level strategy.*

Several dimensions of firm scope have relevance for business-level strategy in terms of their capacity to strengthen a company's position in a given market. These include the firm's **horizontal scope,** which is the range of product and service segments that the firm serves within its product or service market. Mergers and acquisitions involving other market participants provide a means for a company to expand its horizontal scope. Expanding the firm's vertical scope by means of vertical integration can also affect the success of its market strategy. **Vertical scope** is the extent to which the firm engages in the various activities that make up the industry's entire value chain system, from initial activities such as raw-material production all the way to retailing and after-sale service activities. **Outsourcing** decisions concern another dimension of scope since they involve narrowing the firm's boundaries with respect to its participation in value chain activities. We discuss the pros and cons of each of

CORE CONCEPT

The **scope of the firm** refers to the range of activities that the firm performs internally, the breadth of its product and service offerings, the extent of its geographic market presence, and its mix of businesses.

CORE CONCEPT

Horizontal scope is the range of product and service segments that a firm serves within its focal market.

CORE CONCEPT

Vertical scope is the extent to which a firm's internal activities encompass the range of activities that make up an industry's entire value chain system, from raw-material production to final sales and service activities.

these options in the sections that follow. Because **strategic alliances and partnerships** provide an alternative to vertical integration and acquisition strategies and are sometimes used to facilitate outsourcing, we conclude this chapter with a discussion of the benefits and challenges associated with *cooperative arrangements* of this nature.

HORIZONTAL MERGER AND ACQUISITION STRATEGIES

● LO 6-3

Explain the strategic benefits and risks of expanding a company's horizontal scope through mergers and acquisitions.

Mergers and acquisitions are much-used strategic options to strengthen a company's market position. A *merger* is the combining of two or more companies into a single corporate entity, with the newly created company often taking on a new name. An *acquisition* is a combination in which one company, the acquirer, purchases and absorbs the operations of another, the acquired. The difference between a merger and an acquisition relates more to the details of ownership, management control, and financial arrangements than to strategy and competitive advantage. The resources and competitive capabilities of the newly created enterprise end up much the same whether the combination is the result of an acquisition or a merger.

Horizontal mergers and acquisitions, which involve combining the operations of firms *within the same product or service market,* provide an effective means for firms to rapidly increase the scale and horizontal scope of their core business. For example, the merger of AMR Corporation (parent of American Airlines) with US Airways has increased the airlines' scale of operations and extended their reach geographically to create the world's largest airline.

Merger and acquisition strategies typically set sights on achieving any of five objectives:[15]

1. *Creating a more cost-efficient operation out of the combined companies.* When a company acquires another company in the same industry, there's usually enough overlap in operations that less efficient plants can be closed or distribution and sales activities partly combined and downsized. Likewise, it is usually feasible to squeeze out cost savings in administrative activities, again by combining and downsizing such administrative activities as finance and accounting, information technology, human resources, and so on. The combined companies may also be able to reduce supply chain costs because of greater bargaining power over common suppliers and closer collaboration with supply chain partners. By helping consolidate the industry and remove excess capacity, such combinations can also reduce industry rivalry and improve industry profitability.

2. *Expanding a company's geographic coverage.* One of the best and quickest ways to expand a company's geographic coverage is to acquire rivals with operations in the desired locations. Since a company's size increases with its geographic scope, another benefit is increased bargaining power with the company's suppliers or buyers. Greater geographic coverage can also contribute to product differentiation by enhancing a company's name recognition and brand awareness. The vacation rental marketplace, HomeAway, Inc., relied on an aggressive horizontal acquisition strategy to expand internationally, as well as to extend its reach across the United States. It now offers vacation rentals in 190 countries through its 50 websites in 23 languages. Travel company Expedia has since acquired HomeAway, thus extending its reach horizontally into the vacation rental product category—an objective described in the next point.

3. *Extending the company's business into new product categories.* Many times a company has gaps in its product line that need to be filled in order to offer customers a more effective product bundle or the benefits of one-stop shopping. For example, customers might prefer to acquire a suite of software applications from a single vendor that can offer more integrated solutions to the company's problems. Acquisition can be a quicker and more potent way to broaden a company's product line than going through the exercise of introducing a company's own new product to fill the gap. In 2018, Keurig Green Mountain vastly expanded its range of beverage offerings by acquiring the Dr Pepper Snapple Group in an $18.7 billion deal.

4. *Gaining quick access to new technologies or other resources and capabilities.* Making acquisitions to bolster a company's technological know-how or to expand its skills and capabilities allows a company to bypass a time-consuming and expensive internal effort to build desirable new resources and capabilities. Over the course of its history, Cisco Systems has purchased over 200 companies to give it more technological reach and product breadth, thereby enhancing its standing as the world's largest provider of hardware, software, and services for creating and operating Internet networks.

5. *Leading the convergence of industries whose boundaries are being blurred by changing technologies and new market opportunities.* In fast-cycle industries or industries whose boundaries are changing, companies can use acquisition strategies to hedge their bets about the direction that an industry will take, to increase their capacity to meet changing demands, and to respond flexibly to changing buyer needs and technological demands. The convergence of the pharmacy industry with health insurers and the benefits management industry led to the merger between Cigna and Express Scripts as well as that between CVS and Aetna in 2018.

Illustration Capsule 6.3 describes how Walmart employed a horizontal acquisition strategy to expand into the e-commerce domain.

Why Mergers and Acquisitions Sometimes Fail to Produce Anticipated Results

Despite many successes, mergers and acquisitions do not always produce the hoped-for outcomes.[16] Cost savings may prove smaller than expected. Gains in competitive capabilities may take substantially longer to realize or, worse, may never materialize at all. Efforts to mesh the corporate cultures can stall due to formidable resistance from organization members. Key employees at the acquired company can quickly become disenchanted and leave; the morale of company personnel who remain can drop to disturbingly low levels because they disagree with newly instituted changes. Differences in management styles and operating procedures can prove hard to resolve. In addition, the managers appointed to oversee the integration of a newly acquired company can make mistakes in deciding which activities to leave alone and which activities to meld into their own operations and systems.

A number of mergers and acquisitions have been notably unsuccessful. Google's $12.5 billion acquisition of struggling smartphone manufacturer Motorola Mobility in 2012 turned out to be minimally beneficial in helping to "supercharge Google's Android ecosystem" (Google's stated reason for making the acquisition). When Google's attempts to rejuvenate Motorola's smartphone business by spending over $1.3 billion on new

Walmart's Expansion into E-Commerce via Horizontal Acquisition

As the boundaries between traditional retailing and online retailing have begun to blur, Walmart has responded by expanding its presence in e-commerce via horizontal acquisition. In 2016, Walmart acquired Jet.com, an innovative U.S. e-commerce start-up that was designed to compete with Amazon. Jet sells everything from household goods and electronics to beauty products, apparel, and toys from more than 2,400 retailer and brand partners. Jet.com rewards customers for ordering multiple items, using a debit card instead of a credit card, or choosing a no-returns option; it passes its cost savings on to customers in the form of lower prices. The low-price approach of Jet.com fit well with Walmart's low-price strategy. In addition, Walmart hoped that the acquisition would help it to accelerate its growth in e-commerce, provide quick access to some valuable e-commerce knowledge and capabilities, increase its breadth of online product offerings, and attract new customer segments.

Walmart, like other brick and mortar retailers, was facing a myriad of issues caused by changing customer expectations. Consumers increasingly valued large assortments of products, a convenient shopping experience, and low prices. Price sensitivity was increasing due to the ease of comparing prices online. As a traditional retailer, Walmart was facing stiff competition from Amazon, the world's largest and fastest growing e-commerce company. Amazon's seemingly endless inventory of goods, excellent customer service, expertise in search engine marketing, and appeal to a wide consumer demographic added pressure on the overall global retail industry.

The acquisition of Jet built on the foundation already in place for Walmart to respond to the external pressure and continue growing as an omni-channel retailer (i.e., bricks and mortar, online, or mobile). After investing heavily in their own online channel,

Sundry Photography/Shutterstock

Walmart.com, the company was looking for other ways to attract customers by lowering prices, broadening their product assortment, and offering the simplest, most convenient shopping experience. Jet's breadth of products, access to millennial and higher-income customer segments, and best in-class pricing algorithm would accelerate Walmart's progress across all of these priorities.

Since the acquisition, Jet has continued to expand its own offerings with private-label groceries, further increasing competition with Amazon's AmazonFresh grocery business. More recently, Walmart made several other acquisitions of online apparel companies, thereby strengthening Jet's apparel offerings and further expanding Walmart's presence in e-commerce. These include ShoeBuy (a competitor of Amazon-owned Zappos), Bonobos in menswear, Moosejaw in outdoor gear and apparel, and Modcloth in vintage and indie womenswear. While Walmart's e-commerce sales still pale in comparison to Amazon, this represents a promising start for Walmart, as the retail industry continues to transform.

Note: Developed with Dipti Badrinath.

Sources: http://www.businessinsider.com/jet-walmart-weapon-vs-amazon-2017-9; https://news.walmart.com/2016/08/08/walmart-agrees-to-acquire-jetcom-one-of-the-fastest-growing-e-commerce-companies-in-the-us; https://www.fool.com/investing/2017/10/03/1-year-later-wal-marts-jetcom-acquisition-is-an-un.aspx; https://blog.walmart.com/business/20160919/five-big-reasons-walmart-bought-jetcom.

product R&D and revamping Motorola's product line resulted in disappointing sales and huge operating losses, Google sold Motorola Mobility to China-based PC maker Lenovo for $2.9 billion in 2014 (however, Google retained ownership of Motorola's extensive patent portfolio). The jury is still out on whether Lenovo's acquisition of Motorola will prove to be a moneymaker.

VERTICAL INTEGRATION STRATEGIES

Expanding the firm's vertical scope by means of a vertical integration strategy provides another possible way to strengthen the company's position in its core market. A **vertically integrated firm** is one that participates in multiple stages of an industry's value chain system. Thus, if a manufacturer invests in facilities to produce component parts that it had formerly purchased from suppliers, or if it opens its own chain of retail stores to bypass its former distributors, it is engaging in vertical integration. A good example of a vertically integrated firm is Maple Leaf Foods, a major Canadian producer of fresh and processed meats whose best-selling brands include Maple Leaf and Schneiders. Maple Leaf Foods participates in hog and poultry production, with company-owned hog and poultry farms; it has its own meat-processing and rendering facilities; it packages its products and distributes them from company-owned distribution centers; and it conducts marketing, sales, and customer service activities for its wholesale and retail buyers but does not otherwise participate in the final stage of the meat-processing vertical chain—the retailing stage.

A vertical integration strategy can expand the firm's range of activities *backward* into sources of supply and/or *forward* toward end users. When Tiffany & Co., a manufacturer and retailer of fine jewelry, began sourcing, cutting, and polishing its own diamonds, it integrated backward along the diamond supply chain. Mining giant De Beers Group and Canadian miner Aber Diamond integrated forward when they entered the diamond retailing business.

A firm can pursue vertical integration by starting its own operations in other stages of the vertical activity chain or by acquiring a company already performing the activities it wants to bring in-house. Vertical integration strategies can aim at *full integration* (participating in all stages of the vertical chain) or *partial integration* (building positions in selected stages of the vertical chain). Firms can also engage in *tapered integration* strategies, which involve a mix of in-house and outsourced activity in any given stage of the vertical chain. Oil companies, for instance, supply their refineries with oil from their own wells as well as with oil that they purchase from other producers—they engage in tapered backward integration. Coach, Inc., the maker of Coach handbags and accessories, engages in tapered forward integration since it operates full-price and factory outlet stores but also sells its products through third-party department store outlets.

The Advantages of a Vertical Integration Strategy

Under the right conditions, a vertical integration strategy can add materially to a company's technological capabilities, strengthen the firm's competitive position, and boost its profitability.[17] But it is important to keep in mind that vertical integration has no real payoff strategy-wise or profit-wise unless the extra investment can be justified by compensating improvements in company costs, differentiation, or competitive strength.

Integrating Backward to Achieve Greater Competitiveness   It is harder than one might think to generate cost savings or improve profitability by integrating backward

LO 6-4

Explain the advantages and disadvantages of extending the company's scope of operations via vertical integration.

CORE CONCEPT

A vertically integrated firm is one that performs value chain activities along more than one stage of an industry's value chain system.

CORE CONCEPT

Backward integration
involves entry into activities
previously performed by suppliers or other enterprises
positioned along earlier
stages of the industry value
chain system; forward integration involves entry into
value chain system activities
closer to the end user.

into activities such as the manufacture of parts and components (which could otherwise be purchased from suppliers with specialized expertise in making the parts and
components). For **backward integration** to be a cost-saving and profitable strategy, a
company must be able to (1) achieve the same scale economies as outside suppliers
and (2) match or beat suppliers' production efficiency with no drop-off in quality.
Neither outcome is easily achieved. To begin with, a company's in-house requirements are often too small to reach the optimum size for low-cost operation. For
instance, if it takes a minimum production volume of 1 million units to achieve scale
economies and a company's in-house requirements are just 250,000 units, then it
falls far short of being able to match the costs of outside suppliers (which may readily find buyers for 1 million or more units). Furthermore, matching the production
efficiency of suppliers is fraught with problems when suppliers have considerable
production experience, when the technology they employ has elements that are hard
to master, and/or when substantial R&D expertise is required to develop next-version
components or keep pace with advancing technology in components production.

That said, occasions still arise when a company can gain or extend a competitive
advantage by performing a broader range of industry value chain activities internally
rather than having such activities performed by outside suppliers. There are several
ways that backward vertical integration can contribute to a cost-based competitive
advantage. When there are few suppliers and when the item being supplied is a major
component, vertical integration can lower costs by limiting supplier power. Vertical
integration can also lower costs by facilitating the coordination of production flows
and avoiding bottlenecks and delays that disrupt production schedules. Furthermore,
when a company has proprietary know-how that it wants to keep from rivals, then in-
house performance of value-adding activities related to this know-how is beneficial
even if such activities could otherwise be performed by outsiders.

Apple decided to integrate backward into producing its own chips for iPhones,
chiefly because chips are a major cost component, suppliers have bargaining power, and
in-house production would help coordinate design tasks and protect Apple's proprietary
iPhone technology. International Paper Company backward integrates into pulp mills
that it sets up near its paper mills and reaps the benefits of coordinated production flows,
energy savings, and transportation economies. It does this, in part, because outside suppliers are generally unwilling to make a site-specific investment for a buyer.

Backward vertical integration can support a differentiation-based competitive
advantage when performing activities internally contributes to a better-quality product or service offering, improves the caliber of customer service, or in other ways
enhances the performance of the final product. On occasion, integrating into more
stages along the industry value chain system can add to a company's differentiation
capabilities by allowing it to strengthen its core competencies, better master key skills
or strategy-critical technologies, or add features that deliver greater customer value.
Spanish clothing maker Inditex has backward integrated into fabric making, as well
as garment design and manufacture, for its successful Zara brand. By tightly controlling the process and postponing dyeing until later stages, Zara can respond quickly to
changes in fashion trends and supply its customers with the hottest items. Amazon and
Netflix backward integrated by establishing Amazon Studios and Netflix Originals to
produce high-quality original content for their streaming services.

Integrating Forward to Enhance Competitiveness   Like backward integration,
forward integration can enhance competitiveness and contribute to competitive advantage on the cost side as well as the differentiation (or value) side. On the cost side,

forward integration can lower costs by increasing efficiency and reducing or eliminating the bargaining power of companies that had wielded such power further along the value system chain. It can allow manufacturers to gain better access to end users, improve market visibility, and enhance brand name awareness. For example, Harley-Davidson's and Ducati's company-owned retail stores are essentially little museums, filled with iconography, that provide an environment conducive to selling not only motorcycles and gear but also memorabilia, clothing, and other items featuring the brand. Insurance companies and brokerages like Allstate and Edward Jones have the ability to make consumers' interactions with local agents and office personnel a differentiating feature by focusing on building relationships.

In many industries, independent sales agents, wholesalers, and retailers handle competing brands of the same product and have no allegiance to any one company's brand—they tend to push whatever offers the biggest profits. To avoid dependence on distributors and dealers with divided loyalties, Goodyear has integrated forward into company-owned and franchised retail tire stores. Consumer-goods companies like Coach, Under Armour, Pepperidge Farm, Bath & Body Works, Nike, Tommy Hilfiger, and Ann Taylor have integrated forward into retailing and operate their own branded stores in factory outlet malls, enabling them to move overstocked items, slow-selling items, and seconds.

Some producers have opted to integrate forward by selling directly to customers at the company's website. Indochino in custom men's suits, Warby Parker in eyewear, and Everlane in sustainable apparel are examples. Bypassing regular wholesale and retail channels in favor of direct sales and Internet retailing can have appeal if it reinforces the brand and enhances consumer satisfaction or if it lowers distribution costs, produces a relative cost advantage over certain rivals, and results in lower selling prices to end users. In addition, sellers are compelled to include the Internet as a retail channel when a sufficiently large number of buyers in an industry prefer to make purchases online. However, a company that is vigorously pursuing online sales to consumers at the same time that it is also heavily promoting sales to consumers through its network of wholesalers and retailers is *competing directly against its distribution allies*. Such actions constitute *channel conflict* and create a tricky route to negotiate. A company that is actively trying to expand online sales to consumers is signaling a weak strategic commitment to its dealers *and* a willingness to cannibalize dealers' sales and growth potential. The likely result is angry dealers and loss of dealer goodwill. Quite possibly, a company may stand to lose more sales by offending its dealers than it gains from its own online sales effort. Consequently, in industries where the strong support and goodwill of dealer networks is essential, companies may conclude that it is important to avoid channel conflict and that *their websites should be designed to partner with dealers rather than compete against them.*

The Disadvantages of a Vertical Integration Strategy

Vertical integration has some substantial drawbacks beyond the potential for channel conflict.[18] The most serious drawbacks to vertical integration include the following concerns:

- Vertical integration raises a firm's capital investment in the industry, thereby *increasing business risk* (what if industry growth and profitability unexpectedly go sour?).
- Vertically integrated companies are often *slow to adopt technological advances or more efficient production methods* when they are saddled with older technology or facilities. A company that obtains parts and components from outside suppliers can

always shop the market for the newest, best, and cheapest parts, whereas a vertically integrated firm with older plants and technology may choose to continue making suboptimal parts rather than face the high costs of writing off undepreciated assets.

- Vertical integration can result in *less flexibility in accommodating shifting buyer preferences*. It is one thing to eliminate use of a component made by a supplier and another to stop using a component being made in-house (which can mean laying off employees and writing off the associated investment in equipment and facilities). Integrating forward or backward locks a firm into relying on its own in-house activities and sources of supply. Most of the world's automakers, despite their manufacturing expertise, have concluded that purchasing a majority of their parts and components from best-in-class suppliers results in greater design flexibility, higher quality, and lower costs than producing parts or components in-house.

- Vertical integration *may not enable a company to realize economies of scale* if its production levels are below the minimum efficient scale. Small companies in particular are likely to suffer a cost disadvantage by producing in-house.

- Vertical integration poses all kinds of *capacity-matching problems*. In motor vehicle manufacturing, for example, the most efficient scale of operation for making axles is different from the most economic volume for radiators, and different yet again for both engines and transmissions. Building the capacity to produce just the right number of axles, radiators, engines, and transmissions in-house—and doing so at the lowest unit costs for each—poses significant challenges and operating complications.

- Integration forward or backward typically *calls for developing new types of resources and capabilities*. Parts and components manufacturing, assembly operations, wholesale distribution and retailing, and direct sales via the Internet represent different kinds of businesses, operating in different types of industries, with different key success factors. Many manufacturers learn the hard way that company-owned wholesale and retail networks require skills that they lack, fit poorly with what they do best, and detract from their overall profit performance. Similarly, a company that tries to produce many components in-house is likely to find itself very hard-pressed to keep up with technological advances and cutting-edge production practices for each component used in making its product.

In today's world of close working relationships with suppliers and efficient supply chain management systems, relatively few companies can make a strong economic case for integrating backward into the business of suppliers. The best materials and components suppliers stay abreast of advancing technology and best practices and are adept in making good quality items, delivering them on time, and keeping their costs and prices as low as possible.

Weighing the Pros and Cons of Vertical Integration

All in all, therefore, a strategy of vertical integration can have both strengths and weaknesses. The tip of the scales depends on (1) whether vertical integration can enhance the performance of strategy-critical activities in ways that lower cost, build expertise, protect proprietary know-how, or increase differentiation; (2) what impact vertical integration will have on investment costs, flexibility, and response times; (3) what administrative costs will be incurred by coordinating operations across more vertical chain activities; and (4) how difficult it will be for the company to acquire the set of skills and capabilities needed to operate in another stage of the vertical chain. *Vertical integration strategies have merit according to which capabilities and value-adding activities*

Tesla's Vertical Integration Strategy

Unlike many vehicle manufacturers, Tesla embraces vertical integration from component manufacturing all the way through vehicle sales and servicing. The majority of the company's $11.8 billion in 2017 revenue came from electric vehicle sales and leasing, with the remainder coming from servicing those vehicles and selling residential battery packs and solar energy systems.

At its core an electric vehicle manufacturer, Tesla uses both backward and forward vertical integration to achieve multiple strategic goals. In order to drive innovation in a critical part of its supply chain, Tesla has invested in a "gigafactory" that manufacturers the batteries that are essential for a long-lasting electric vehicle. According to Tesla's former VP of Production, in-house manufacturing of key components and new parts that require frequent updates has enabled the company to learn quickly and launch new versions faster. Moreover, having closer relationships between engineering and manufacturing gives Tesla greater control over product design. Tesla uses forward vertical integration to improve the customer experience by owning the distribution and servicing of the vehicles it builds. Their network of dealerships allows Tesla to sell directly to consumers and handle maintenance needs without relying on third parties that sometimes have competing priorities.

Beyond vertically integrating the manufacture and distribution of their electric vehicles, Tesla uses the strategy to build the ecosystem that is necessary to support further adoption of their vehicles. As many consumers perceive electric cars to have limited range and long charging times that prevent long-distance travel, Tesla is building a network of Supercharger stations to overcome this pain point. By investing in this development themselves, Tesla does not need to wait for another company to deliver the critical infrastructure

Hadrian/Shutterstock

that drivers demand before they switch from traditional gasoline-powered cars. Similarly, Tesla sells solar power generation and storage products that make it easier for customers to make the switch to transportation powered by sustainable energy.

While Tesla's mission to accelerate the world's transition to sustainable energy has required large investments throughout the value chain, this strategy has not been without challenges. Unlike batteries, seats are of limited strategic importance, yet Tesla decided to manufacture their Model 3 seats in house. While there is no indication that the seats were the source of major production delays in 2017, diverting resources to develop new manufacturing capabilities could have added to the problem. Although Tesla's vertical integration strategy is not without downsides, it has enabled the firm to quickly roll out innovative new products and launch the network that is required for widespread vehicle adoption. Investors have rewarded Tesla for this bold strategy by lifting its valuation to $80 billion by the start of 2020, higher than the other major American automakers.

Note: Developed with Edward J. Silberman.

Sources: Tesla 2017 Annual Report; G. Reichow, "Tesla's Secret Second Floor," *Wired*, October 18,2017, https://www.wired.com/story/teslas-secret-second-floor/; A. Sage, "Tesla's Seat Strategy Goes Against the Grain. . . For Now," *Reuters*, October 26, 2017, https://www.reuters.com/article/us-tesla-seats/teslas-seat-strategy-goes-against-the-grain-for-now-idUSKBN1CV0DS; Yahoo Finance.

truly need to be performed in-house and which can be performed better or cheaper by outsiders. Absent solid benefits, integrating forward or backward is not likely to be an attractive strategy option.

Electric automobile maker Tesla, Inc. has made vertical integration a central part of its strategy, as described in Illustration Capsule 6.4.

OUTSOURCING STRATEGIES: NARROWING THE SCOPE OF OPERATIONS

● **LO 6-5**

Recognize the conditions that favor farming out certain value chain activities to outside parties.

CORE CONCEPT

Outsourcing involves contracting out certain value chain activities that are normally performed in-house to outside vendors.

In contrast to vertical integration strategies, outsourcing strategies narrow the scope of a business's operations, in terms of what activities are performed internally. **Outsourcing** involves contracting out certain value chain activities that are normally performed in-house to outside vendors.[19] Many PC makers, for example, have shifted from assembling units in-house to outsourcing the entire assembly process to manufacturing specialists, which can operate more efficiently due to their greater scale, experience, and bargaining power over components makers. Nearly all name-brand apparel firms have in-house capability to design, market, and distribute their products but they outsource all fabric manufacture and garment-making activities. Starbucks finds purchasing coffee beans from independent growers far more advantageous than having its own coffee-growing operation, with locations scattered across most of the world's coffee-growing regions.

Outsourcing certain value chain activities makes strategic sense whenever

- *An activity can be performed better or more cheaply by outside specialists.* A company should generally *not* perform any value chain activity internally that can be performed more efficiently or effectively by outsiders—the chief exception occurs when a particular activity is strategically crucial and internal control over that activity is deemed essential. Dolce & Gabbana, for example, outsources the manufacture of its brand of sunglasses to Luxottica—a company considered to be the world's best sunglass manufacturing company, known for its Oakley, Oliver Peoples, and Ray-Ban brands. Colgate-Palmolive, for instance, has reduced its information technology operational costs by more than 10 percent annually through an outsourcing agreement with IBM.

- *The activity is not crucial to the firm's ability to achieve sustainable competitive advantage.* Outsourcing of support activities such as maintenance services, data processing, data storage, fringe-benefit management, and website operations has become commonplace. Many smaller companies, for example, find it advantages to outsource HR activities such as benefit administration, training, recruiting, hiring and payroll to specialists, such as XcelHR, Insperity, Paychex, and Aon Hewitt.

- *The outsourcing improves organizational flexibility and speeds time to market.* Outsourcing gives a company the flexibility to switch suppliers in the event that its present supplier falls behind competing suppliers. Moreover, seeking out new suppliers with the needed capabilities already in place is frequently quicker, easier, less risky, and cheaper than hurriedly retooling internal operations to replace obsolete capabilities or trying to install and master new technologies.

- *It reduces the company's risk exposure to changing technology and buyer preferences.* When a company outsources certain parts, components, and services, its suppliers must bear the burden of incorporating state-of-the-art technologies and/or undertaking redesigns and upgrades to accommodate a company's plans to introduce next-generation products. If what a supplier provides falls out of favor with buyers, or is rendered unnecessary by technological change, it is the supplier's business that suffers rather than the company's.

- *It allows a company to concentrate on its core business, leverage its key resources, and do even better what it already does best.* A company is better able to enhance its own capabilities when it concentrates its full resources and energies on performing only those activities. United Colors of Benetton and Sisley, for example, outsource the production of handbags and other leather goods while devoting their energies to the clothing lines for which they are known. Apple outsources production of its iPod, iPhone, and iPad models to Chinese contract manufacturer Foxconn and concentrates in-house on design, marketing, and innovation. Hewlett-Packard and IBM have sold some of their manufacturing plants to outsiders and contracted to repurchase the output instead from the new owners.

The Risk of Outsourcing Value Chain Activities

The biggest danger of outsourcing is that a company will farm out the wrong types of activities and thereby hollow out its own capabilities.[20] For example, in recent years companies eager to reduce operating costs have opted to outsource such strategically important activities as product development, engineering design, and sophisticated manufacturing tasks—the very capabilities that underpin a company's ability to lead sustained product innovation. While these companies have apparently been able to lower their operating costs by outsourcing these functions to outsiders, *their ability to lead the development of innovative new products is weakened because so many of the cutting-edge ideas and technologies for next-generation products come from outsiders.*

> A company must guard against outsourcing activities that hollow out the resources and capabilities that it needs to be a master of its own destiny.

Another risk of outsourcing comes from the lack of direct control. It may be difficult to monitor, control, and coordinate the activities of outside parties via contracts and arm's-length transactions alone. Unanticipated problems may arise that cause delays or cost overruns and become hard to resolve amicably. Moreover, contract-based outsourcing can be problematic because outside parties lack incentives to make investments specific to the needs of the outsourcing company's internal value chain.

Companies like Cisco Systems are alert to these dangers. Cisco guards against loss of control and protects its manufacturing expertise by designing the production methods that its contract manufacturers must use. Cisco keeps the source code for its designs proprietary, thereby controlling the initiation of all improvements and safeguarding its innovations from imitation. Further, Cisco has developed online systems to monitor the factory operations of contract manufacturers around the clock so that it knows immediately when problems arise and can decide whether to get involved.

STRATEGIC ALLIANCES AND PARTNERSHIPS

Strategic alliances and cooperative partnerships provide one way to gain some of the benefits offered by vertical integration, outsourcing, and horizontal mergers and acquisitions while minimizing the associated problems. Companies frequently engage in cooperative strategies as an alternative to vertical integration or horizontal mergers and acquisitions. Increasingly, companies are also employing strategic alliances and partnerships to extend their scope of operations via international expansion and diversification strategies, as we describe in Chapters 7 and 8. Strategic alliances and cooperative arrangements are now a common means of narrowing a company's scope of operations as well, serving as a useful way to manage outsourcing (in lieu of traditional, purely price-oriented contracts).

LO 6-6

Understand how to capture the benefits and minimize the drawbacks of strategic alliances and partnerships.

For example, oil and gas companies engage in considerable vertical integration—but Shell Oil Company and Pemex (Mexico's state-owned petroleum company) have found that joint ownership of their Deer Park Refinery in Texas lowers their investment costs and risks in comparison to going it alone. The colossal failure of the Daimler–Chrysler merger formed an expensive lesson for Daimler AG about what can go wrong with horizontal mergers and acquisitions; the Renault–Nissan–Mitsubishi Alliance has proved more successful in developing the capabilities for the manufacture of plug-in electric vehicles and introducing the Nissan Leaf.

Many companies employ strategic alliances to manage the problems that might otherwise occur with outsourcing—Cisco's system of alliances guards against loss of control, protects its proprietary manufacturing expertise, and enables the company to monitor closely the assembly operations of its partners while devoting its energy to designing new generations of the switches, routers, and other Internet-related equipment for which it is known.

A **strategic alliance** is a formal agreement between two or more separate companies in which they agree to work collaboratively toward some strategically relevant objective. Typically, they involve shared financial responsibility, joint contribution of resources and capabilities, shared risk, shared control, and mutual dependence. They may be characterized by cooperative marketing, sales, or distribution; joint production; design collaboration; or projects to jointly develop new technologies or products. They can vary in terms of their duration and the extent of the collaboration; some are intended as long-term arrangements, involving an extensive set of cooperative activities, while others are designed to accomplish more limited, short-term objectives.

Collaborative arrangements may entail a contractual agreement, but they commonly stop short of formal ownership ties between the partners (although sometimes an alliance member will secure minority ownership of another member).

A special type of strategic alliance involving ownership ties is the **joint venture.** A joint venture entails forming a *new corporate entity that is jointly owned* by two or more companies that agree to share in the revenues, expenses, and control of the newly formed entity. Since joint ventures involve setting up a mutually owned business, they tend to be more durable but also riskier than other arrangements. In other types of strategic alliances, the collaboration between the partners involves a much less rigid structure in which the partners retain their independence from one another. If a strategic alliance is not working out, a partner can choose to simply walk away or reduce its commitment to collaborating at any time.

An alliance becomes "strategic," as opposed to just a convenient business arrangement, when it serves any of the following purposes:[21]

1. It facilitates achievement of an important business objective (like lowering costs or delivering more value to customers in the form of better quality, added features, and greater durability).
2. It helps build, strengthen, or sustain a core competence or competitive advantage.
3. It helps remedy an important resource deficiency or competitive weakness.
4. It helps defend against a competitive threat, or mitigates a significant risk to a company's business.
5. It increases bargaining power over suppliers or buyers.
6. It helps open up important new market opportunities.
7. It speeds the development of new technologies and/or product innovations.

Strategic cooperation is a much-favored approach in industries where new technological developments are occurring at a furious pace along many different paths and where advances in one technology spill over to affect others (often blurring industry boundaries). Whenever industries are experiencing high-velocity technological

---

CORE CONCEPT

A **strategic alliance** is a formal agreement between two or more separate companies in which they agree to work cooperatively toward some common objective.

CORE CONCEPT

A **joint venture** is a partnership involving the establishment of an independent corporate entity that the partners own and control jointly, sharing in its revenues and expenses.

advances in many areas simultaneously, firms find it virtually essential to have cooperative relationships with other enterprises to stay on the leading edge of technology, even in their own area of specialization. In industries like these, alliances are all about fast cycles of learning, gaining quick access to the latest round of technological know-how, and developing dynamic capabilities. In bringing together firms with different skills and knowledge bases, alliances open up learning opportunities that help partner firms better leverage their own resources and capabilities.[22]

In 2017, Daimler entered into an agreement with automotive supplier Robert Bosch GmbH to develop self-driving taxis that customers can hail with a smartphone app; the objective is to make this a reality in urban areas by the beginning of the next decade.

Microsoft has been partnering with a variety of companies to advance technology in the healthcare industry. Its 2017 alliance with PAREXEL, a clinical research organization, aims to use their combined capabilities to accelerate drug development and bring new therapies to patients sooner. In 2018, it joined forces with immuno-sequencing company Adaptive Biotechnologies to find ways to detect cancers and other diseases earlier using Microsoft's artificial intelligence capabilities.

Because of the varied benefits of strategic alliances, many large corporations have become involved in 30 to 50 alliances, and a number have formed hundreds of alliances. Hoffmann-La Roche, a multinational healthcare company, has set up Roche Partnering to manage their more than 190 alliances. Companies that have formed a host of alliances need to manage their alliances like a portfolio—terminating those that no longer serve a useful purpose or that have produced meager results, forming promising new alliances, and restructuring existing alliances to correct performance problems and/or redirect the collaborative effort.

> Companies that have formed a host of alliances need to manage their alliances like a portfolio.

> The best alliances are highly selective, focusing on particular value chain activities and on obtaining a specific competitive benefit. They enable a firm to build on its strengths and to learn.

Capturing the Benefits of Strategic Alliances

The extent to which companies benefit from entering into alliances and partnerships seems to be a function of six factors:[23]

1. *Picking a good partner.* A good partner must bring complementary strengths to the relationship. To the extent that alliance members have nonoverlapping strengths, there is greater potential for synergy and less potential for coordination problems and conflict. In addition, a good partner needs to share the company's vision about the overall purpose of the alliance and to have specific goals that either match or complement those of the company. Strong partnerships also depend on good chemistry among key personnel and compatible views about how the alliance should be structured and managed.

2. *Being sensitive to cultural differences.* Cultural differences among companies can make it difficult for their personnel to work together effectively. Cultural differences can be problematic among companies from the same country, but when the partners have different national origins, the problems are often magnified. Unless there is respect among all the parties for cultural differences, including those stemming from different local cultures and local business practices, productive working relationships are unlikely to emerge.

3. *Recognizing that the alliance must benefit both sides.* Information must be shared as well as gained, and the relationship must remain forthright and trustful. If either partner plays games with information or tries to take advantage of the other, the resulting friction can quickly erode the value of further collaboration. Open, trustworthy behavior on both sides is essential for fruitful collaboration.

4. *Ensuring that both parties live up to their commitments.* Both parties have to deliver on their commitments for the alliance to produce the intended benefits. The division of work has to be perceived as fairly apportioned, and the caliber of the benefits received on both sides has to be perceived as adequate.

5. *Structuring the decision-making process so that actions can be taken swiftly when needed.* In many instances, the fast pace of technological and competitive changes dictates an equally fast decision-making process. If the parties get bogged down in discussions or in gaining internal approval from higher-ups, the alliance can turn into an anchor of delay and inaction.

6. *Managing the learning process and then adjusting the alliance agreement over time to fit new circumstances.* One of the keys to long-lasting success is adapting the nature and structure of the alliance to be responsive to shifting market conditions, emerging technologies, and changing customer requirements. Wise allies are quick to recognize the merit of an evolving collaborative arrangement, where adjustments are made to accommodate changing conditions and to overcome whatever problems arise in establishing an effective working relationship.

Most alliances that aim at sharing technology or providing market access turn out to be temporary, lasting only a few years. This is not necessarily an indicator of failure, however. Strategic alliances can be terminated after a few years simply because they have fulfilled their purpose; indeed, many alliances are intended to be of limited duration, set up to accomplish specific short-term objectives. Longer-lasting collaborative arrangements, however, may provide even greater strategic benefits. Alliances are more likely to be long-lasting when (1) they involve collaboration with partners that do not compete directly, such as suppliers or distribution allies; (2) a trusting relationship has been established; and (3) both parties conclude that continued collaboration is in their mutual interest, perhaps because new opportunities for learning are emerging.

The Drawbacks of Strategic Alliances and Their Relative Advantages

While strategic alliances provide a way of obtaining the benefits of vertical integration, mergers and acquisitions, and outsourcing, they also suffer from some of the same drawbacks. Anticipated gains may fail to materialize due to an overly optimistic view of the potential or a poor fit in terms of the combination of resources and capabilities. When outsourcing is conducted via alliances, there is no less risk of becoming dependent on other companies for essential expertise and capabilities—indeed, this may be the Achilles' heel of such alliances. Moreover, there are additional pitfalls to collaborative arrangements. The greatest danger is that a partner will gain access to a company's proprietary knowledge base, technologies, or trade secrets, enabling the partner to match the company's core strengths and costing the company its hard-won competitive advantage. This risk is greatest when the alliance is among industry rivals or when the alliance is for the purpose of collaborative R&D, since this type of partnership requires an extensive exchange of closely held information.

The question for managers is when to engage in a strategic alliance and when to choose an alternative means of meeting their objectives. The answer to this question depends on the relative advantages of each method and the circumstances under which each type of organizational arrangement is favored.

The principal advantages of strategic alliances over vertical integration or horizontal mergers and acquisitions are threefold:

1. They lower investment costs and risks for each partner by facilitating resource pooling and risk sharing. This can be particularly important when investment needs and uncertainty are high, such as when a dominant technology standard has not yet emerged.

2. They are more flexible organizational forms and allow for a more adaptive response to changing conditions. Flexibility is essential when environmental conditions or technologies are changing rapidly. Moreover, strategic alliances under such circumstances may enable the development of each partner's dynamic capabilities.

3. They are more rapidly deployed—a critical factor when speed is of the essence. Speed is of the essence when there is a winner-take-all type of competitive situation, such as the race for a dominant technological design or a race down a steep experience curve, where there is a large first-mover advantage.

The key advantages of using strategic alliances rather than arm's-length transactions to manage outsourcing are (1) the increased ability to exercise control over the partners' activities and (2) a greater willingness for the partners to make relationship-specific investments. Arm's-length transactions discourage such investments since they imply less commitment and do not build trust.

On the other hand, there are circumstances when other organizational mechanisms are preferable to alliances and partnering. Mergers and acquisitions are especially suited for situations in which strategic alliances or partnerships do not go far enough in providing a company with access to needed resources and capabilities. Ownership ties are more permanent than partnership ties, allowing the operations of the merger or acquisition participants to be tightly integrated and creating more in-house control and autonomy. Other organizational mechanisms are also preferable to alliances when there is limited property rights protection for valuable know-how and when companies fear being taken advantage of by opportunistic partners.

While it is important for managers to understand when strategic alliances and partnerships are most likely (and least likely) to prove useful, it is also important to know how to manage them.

How to Make Strategic Alliances Work

A surprisingly large number of alliances never live up to expectations. Even though the number of strategic alliances increases by about 25 percent annually, about 60 to 70 percent of alliances continue to fail each year.[24] The success of an alliance depends on how well the partners work together, their capacity to respond and adapt to changing internal and external conditions, and their willingness to renegotiate the bargain if circumstances so warrant. A successful alliance requires real in-the-trenches collaboration, not merely an arm's-length exchange of ideas. Unless partners place a high value on the contribution each brings to the alliance and the cooperative arrangement results in valuable win–win outcomes, it is doomed to fail.

While the track record for strategic alliances is poor on average, many companies have learned how to manage strategic alliances successfully and routinely defy this average. Samsung Group, which includes Samsung Electronics, successfully manages an ecosystem of over 1,300 partnerships that enable productive activities from global procurement to local marketing to collaborative R&D. Companies that have greater success in managing their strategic alliances and partnerships often credit the following factors:

- *They create a system for managing their alliances.* Companies need to manage their alliances in a systematic fashion, just as they manage other functions. This means setting up a process for managing the different aspects of alliance management from partner selection to alliance termination procedures. To ensure that the system is followed on a routine basis by all company managers, many companies create a set of explicit procedures, process templates, manuals, or the like.

- *They build relationships with their partners and establish trust.* Establishing strong interpersonal relationships is a critical factor in making strategic alliances work since such relationships facilitate opening up channels of communication, coordinating activity, aligning interests, and building trust.

- *They protect themselves from the threat of opportunism by setting up safeguards.* There are a number of means for preventing a company from being taken advantage of by an untrustworthy partner or unwittingly losing control over key assets. Contractual safeguards, including noncompete clauses, can provide other forms of protection.

- *They make commitments to their partners and see that their partners do the same.* When partners make credible commitments to a joint enterprise, they have stronger incentives for making it work and are less likely to "free-ride" on the efforts of other partners. Because of this, equity-based alliances tend to be more successful than nonequity alliances.[25]

- *They make learning a routine part of the management process.* There are always opportunities for learning from a partner, but organizational learning does not take place automatically. Whatever learning occurs cannot add to a company's knowledge base unless the learning is incorporated systematically into the company's routines and practices.

Finally, managers should realize that alliance management is an organizational capability, much like any other. It develops over time, out of effort, experience, and learning. For this reason, it is wise to begin slowly, with simple alliances designed to meet limited, short-term objectives. Short-term partnerships that are successful often become the basis for much more extensive collaborative arrangements. Even when strategic alliances are set up with the hope that they will become long-term engagements, they have a better chance of succeeding if they are phased in so that the partners can learn how they can work together most fruitfully.

KEY POINTS

1. Once a company has settled on which of the five generic competitive strategies to employ, attention turns to how strategic choices regarding (1) competitive actions, (2) timing of those actions, and (3) scope of operations can complement its competitive approach and maximize the power of its overall strategy.

2. Strategic offensives should, as a general rule, be grounded in a company's strategic assets and employ a company's strengths to attack rivals in the competitive areas where they are weakest.

3. Companies have a number of offensive strategy options for improving their market positions: using a cost-based advantage to attack competitors on the basis of price or value, leapfrogging competitors with next-generation technologies, pursuing continuous product innovation, adopting and improving the best ideas of others, using hit-and-run tactics to steal sales away from unsuspecting rivals, and launching preemptive strikes. A blue-ocean type of offensive strategy seeks to gain a dramatic new competitive advantage by inventing a new industry or distinctive market

segment that renders existing competitors largely irrelevant and allows a company to create and capture altogether new demand in the absence of direct competitors.

4. The purposes of defensive strategies are to lower the risk of being attacked, weaken the impact of any attack that occurs, and influence challengers to aim their efforts at other rivals. Defensive strategies to protect a company's position usually take one of two forms: (1) actions to block challengers or (2) actions to signal the likelihood of strong retaliation.

5. The timing of strategic moves also has relevance in the quest for competitive advantage. Company managers are obligated to carefully consider the advantages or disadvantages that attach to being a first mover versus a fast follower versus a late mover.

6. Decisions concerning the scope of a company's operations—which activities a firm will perform internally and which it will not—can also affect the strength of a company's market position. The *scope of the firm* refers to the range of its activities, the breadth of its product and service offerings, the extent of its geographic market presence, and its mix of businesses. Companies can expand their scope horizontally (more broadly within their focal market) or vertically (up or down the industry value chain system that starts with raw-material production and ends with sales and service to the end consumer). Horizontal mergers and acquisitions (combinations of market rivals) provide a means for a company to expand its horizontal scope. Vertical integration expands a firm's vertical scope.

7. Horizontal mergers and acquisitions typically have any of five objectives: lowering costs, expanding geographic coverage, adding product categories, gaining new technologies or other resources and capabilities, and preparing for the convergence of industries.

8. Vertical integration, forward or backward, makes most strategic sense if it strengthens a company's position via either cost reduction or creation of a differentiation-based advantage. Otherwise, the drawbacks of vertical integration (increased investment, greater business risk, increased vulnerability to technological changes, less flexibility in making product changes, and the potential for channel conflict) are likely to outweigh any advantages.

9. Outsourcing involves contracting out pieces of the value chain formerly performed in-house to outside vendors, thereby narrowing the scope of the firm. Outsourcing can enhance a company's competitiveness whenever (1) an activity can be performed better or more cheaply by outside specialists; (2) the activity is not crucial to the firm's ability to achieve sustainable competitive advantage; (3) the outsourcing improves organizational flexibility, speeds decision making, and cuts cycle time; (4) it reduces the company's risk exposure; and (5) it permits a company to concentrate on its core business and focus on what it does best.

10. Strategic alliances and cooperative partnerships provide one way to gain some of the benefits offered by vertical integration, outsourcing, and horizontal mergers and acquisitions while minimizing the associated problems. They serve as an alternative to vertical integration and mergers and acquisitions, and as a supplement to outsourcing, allowing more control relative to outsourcing via arm's-length transactions.

11. Companies that manage their alliances well generally (1) create a system for managing their alliances, (2) build relationships with their partners and establish trust, (3) protect themselves from the threat of opportunism by setting up safeguards, (4) make commitments to their partners and see that their partners do the same, and (5) make learning a routine part of the management process.

ASSURANCE OF LEARNING EXERCISES

connect

LO 6-1, LO 6-2,
LO 6-3

1. Live Nation Entertainment operates music venues, provides management services to music artists, and promotes more than 35,000 shows and 100 festivals in 40 countries annually. The company acquired House of Blues, merged with Ticketmaster, and acquired concert and festival promoters in the United States, Australia, and Great Britain. How has the company used horizontal mergers and acquisitions to strengthen its competitive position? Are these moves primarily offensive or defensive? Has either Live Nation or Ticketmaster achieved any type of advantage based on the timing of its strategic moves?

connect

LO 6-4

2. Tesla, Inc. has rapidly become a stand-out among American car companies. Illustration Capsule 6.4 describes how Tesla has made vertical integration a central part of its strategy. What value chain segments has Tesla chosen to enter and perform internally? How has vertical integration and integration of its ecosystem aided the organization in building competitive advantage? Has vertical integration strengthened its market position? Explain why or why not.

LO 6-5

3. Perform an Internet search to identify at least two companies in different industries that have entered into outsourcing agreements with firms with specialized services. In addition, describe what value chain activities the companies have chosen to outsource. Do any of these outsourcing agreements seem likely to threaten any of the companies' competitive capabilities?

LO 6-6

4. Using your university library's business research resources, find two examples of how companies have relied on strategic alliances or joint ventures to substitute for horizontal or vertical integration.

EXERCISES FOR SIMULATION PARTICIPANTS

LO 6-1, LO 6-2

1. Has your company relied more on offensive or defensive strategies to achieve your rank in the industry? What options for being a first mover does your company have? Do any of these first-mover options hold competitive advantage potential?

LO 6-3

2. What would be an advantage of a horizontal merger within the industry?

LO 6-4

3. What are the pros and cons of vertical integration in the industry?

LO 6-5

4. What do you see as pros and cons of outsourcing in the business simulation?

ENDNOTES

[1] George Stalk, Jr., and Rob Lachenauer, "Hardball: Five Killer Strategies for Trouncing the Competition," *Harvard Business Review* 82, no. 4 (April 2004); Richard D'Aveni, "The Empire Strikes Back: Counterrevolutionary Strategies for Industry Leaders," *Harvard Business Review* 80, no. 11 (November 2002); David J. Bryce and Jeffrey H. Dyer, "Strategies to Crack Well-Guarded Markets," *Harvard Business Review* 85, no. 5 (May 2007).

[2] George Stalk, "Playing Hardball: Why Strategy Still Matters," *Ivey Business Journal* 69, no.2 (November–December 2004), pp. 1–2; W. J. Ferrier, K. G. Smith, and C. M. Grimm, "The Role of Competitive Action in Market Share Erosion and Industry Dethronement: A Study of Industry Leaders and Challengers," *Academy of Management Journal* 42, no. 4 (August 1999), pp. 372–388.

[3] David B. Yoffie and Mary Kwak, "Mastering Balance: How to Meet and Beat a Stronger Opponent," *California Management Review* 44, no. 2 (Winter 2002), pp. 8–24.
[4] Ian C. MacMillan, Alexander B. van Putten, and Rita Gunther McGrath, "Global Gamesmanship," *Harvard Business Review* 81, no. 5 (May 2003); Ashkay R. Rao, Mark E. Bergen, and Scott Davis, "How to Fight a Price War," *Harvard Business Review* 78, no. 2 (March–April 2000).

[5] D. B. Yoffie and M. A. Cusumano, "Judo Strategy–the Competitive Dynamics of Internet Time," *Harvard Business Review* 77, no. 1 (January–February 1999), pp. 70–81.

[6] Ming-Jer Chen and Donald C. Hambrick, "Speed, Stealth, and Selective Attack: How Small Firms Differ from Large Firms in Competitive Behavior," *Academy of Management Journal* 38, no. 2 (April 1995), pp. 453–482; William E. Rothschild, "Surprise and the Competitive Advantage," *Journal of Business Strategy* 4, no. 3 (Winter 1984), pp. 10–18.

[7] Ian MacMillan, "Preemptive Strategies," *Journal of Business Strategy* 14, no. 2 (Fall 1983), pp. 16–26.

[8] Ian C. MacMillan, "How Long Can You Sustain a Competitive Advantage?" in Liam Fahey (ed.), *The Strategic Planning Management Reader* (Englewood Cliffs, NJ: Prentice Hall, 1989), pp. 23–24.

[9] Kevin P. Coyne and John Horn, "Predicting Your Competitor's Reactions," *Harvard Business Review* 87, no. 4 (April 2009), pp. 90–97.

[10] Philip Kotler, *Marketing Management,* 5th ed. (Englewood Cliffs, NJ: Prentice Hall, 1984).

[11] W. Chan Kim and Renée Mauborgne, "Blue Ocean Strategy," *Harvard Business Review* 82, no. 10 (October 2004), pp. 76–84.

[12] Jeffrey G. Covin, Dennis P. Slevin, and Michael B. Heeley, "Pioneers and Followers: Competitive Tactics, Environment, and Growth," *Journal of Business Venturing* 15, no. 2 (March 1999), pp. 175–210; Christopher A. Bartlett and Sumantra Ghoshal, "Going Global: Lessons from Late-Movers," *Harvard Business Review* 78, no. 2 (March-April 2000), pp. 132–145.

[13] Costas Markides and Paul A. Geroski, "Racing to Be 2nd: Conquering the Industries of the Future," *Business Strategy Review* 15, no. 4 (Winter 2004), pp. 25–31.

[14] Fernando Suarez and Gianvito Lanzolla, "The Half-Truth of First-Mover Advantage," *Harvard Business Review* 83, no. 4 (April 2005), pp. 121–127.

[15] Joseph L. Bower, "Not All M&As Are Alike– and That Matters," *Harvard Business Review* 79, no. 3 (March 2001); O. Chatain and P. Zemsky, "The Horizontal Scope of the Firm: Organizational Tradeoffs vs. Buyer-Supplier Relationships," *Management Science* 53, no. 4 (April 2007), pp. 550–565.

[16] Jeffrey H. Dyer, Prashant Kale, and Harbir Singh, "When to Ally and When to Acquire," *Harvard Business Review* 82, no. 4 (July– August 2004), pp. 109–110.

[17] John Stuckey and David White, "When and When Not to Vertically Integrate," *Sloan Management Review* (Spring 1993), pp. 71–83.

[18] Thomas Osegowitsch and Anoop Madhok, "Vertical Integration Is Dead, or Is It?" *Business Horizons* 46, no. 2 (March–April 2003), pp. 25–35.

[19] Ronan McIvor, "What Is the Right Outsourcing Strategy for Your Process?" *European Management Journal* 26, no. 1 (February 2008), pp. 24–34.

[20] Gary P. Pisano and Willy C. Shih, "Restoring American Competitiveness," *Harvard Business Review* 87, no. 7-8 (July–August 2009), pp. 114–125; Jérôme Barthélemy, "The Seven Deadly Sins of Outsourcing," *Academy of Management Executive* 17, no. 2 (May 2003), pp. 87–100.

[21] Jason Wakeam, "The Five Factors of a Strategic Alliance," *Ivey Business Journal* 68, no. 3 (May–June 2003), pp. 1–4.

[22] A. Inkpen, "Learning, Knowledge Acquisition, and Strategic Alliances," *European Management Journal* 16, no. 2 (April 1998), pp. 223–229.

[23] *Advertising Age,* May 24, 2010, p. 14.

[24] Patricia Anslinger and Justin Jenk, "Creating Successful Alliances," *Journal of Business Strategy* 25, no. 2 (2004), pp. 18–23; Rosabeth Moss Kanter, "Collaborative Advantage: The Art of the Alliance," *Harvard Business Review* 72, no. 4 (July–August 1994), pp. 96-108; Gary Hamel, Yves L. Doz, and C. K. Prahalad, "Collaborate with Your Competitors– and Win," *Harvard Business Review* 67, no. 1 (January–February 1989), pp. 133–139.

[25] Y. G. Pan and D. K. Tse, "The Hierarchical Model of Market Entry Modes," *Journal of International Business Studies* 31, no. 4 (2000), pp. 535–554.

chapter **7**

Strategies for Competing in International Markets

Learning Objectives

After reading this chapter, you should be able to:

LO 7-1 Identify the primary reasons companies choose to compete in international markets.

LO 7-2 Understand how and why differing market conditions across countries influence a company's strategy choices in international markets.

LO 7-3 Identify the differences among the five primary modes of entry into foreign markets

LO 7-4 Identify the three main strategic approaches for competing internationally.

LO 7-5 Explain how companies are able to use international operations to improve overall competitiveness.

LO 7-6 Identify the unique characteristics of competing in developing-country markets.

Fanatic Studio/Getty Images

Our key words now are globalization, new products and businesses, and speed.

Tsutomu Kanai—*Former chair and president of Hitachi*

You have no choice but to operate in a world shaped by globalization and the information revolution. There are two options: Adapt or die.

Andy Grove—*Former chair and CEO of Intel*

What counts in global competition is the right strategy.

Heinrich von Pierer—*Former CEO of Siemens AG*

Any company that aspires to industry leadership in the 21st century must think in terms of global, not domestic, market leadership. The world economy is globalizing at an accelerating pace as ambitious, growth-minded companies race to build stronger competitive positions in the markets of more and more countries, as countries previously closed to foreign companies open up their markets, and as information technology shrinks the importance of geographic distance. The forces of globalization are changing the competitive landscape in many industries, offering companies attractive new opportunities and at the same time introducing new competitive threats. Companies in industries where these forces are greatest are therefore under considerable pressure to come up with a strategy for competing successfully in international markets.

This chapter focuses on strategy options for expanding beyond domestic boundaries and competing in the markets of either a few or a great many countries. In the process of exploring these options, we introduce such concepts as the Porter diamond of national competitive advantage; and discuss the specific market circumstances that support the adoption of multidomestic, transnational, and global strategies. The chapter also includes sections on cross-country differences in cultural, demographic, and market conditions; strategy options for entering foreign markets; the importance of locating value chain operations in the most advantageous countries; and the special circumstances of competing in developing markets such as those in China, India, Brazil, Russia, and eastern Europe.

WHY COMPANIES DECIDE TO ENTER FOREIGN MARKETS

● **LO 7-1**

Identify the primary reasons companies choose to compete in international markets.

A company may opt to expand outside its domestic market for any of five major reasons:

1. *To gain access to new customers.* Expanding into foreign markets offers potential for increased revenues, profits, and long-term growth; it becomes an especially attractive option when a company encounters dwindling growth opportunities in its home market. Companies often expand internationally to extend the life cycle of their products, as Honda has done with its classic 50-cc motorcycle, the Honda Cub (which is still selling well in developing markets, more than 60 years after it was first introduced in Japan). A larger target market also offers companies the opportunity to earn a return on large investments more rapidly. This can be particularly important in R&D-intensive industries, where development is fast-paced or competitors imitate innovations rapidly.

2. *To achieve lower costs through economies of scale, experience, and increased purchasing power.* Many companies are driven to sell in more than one country because domestic sales volume alone is not large enough to capture fully economies of scale in product development, manufacturing, or marketing. Similarly, firms expand internationally to increase the rate at which they accumulate experience and move down the learning curve. International expansion can also lower a company's input costs through greater pooled purchasing power. The relatively small size of country markets in Europe and limited domestic volume explains why companies like Michelin, BMW, and Nestlé long ago began selling their products all across Europe and then moved into markets in North America and Latin America.

3. *To gain access to low-cost inputs of production.* Companies in industries based on natural resources (e.g., oil and gas, minerals, rubber, and lumber) often find it necessary to operate in the international arena since raw-material supplies are located in different parts of the world and can be accessed more cost-effectively at the source. Other companies enter foreign markets to access low-cost human resources; this is particularly true of industries in which labor costs make up a high proportion of total production costs.

4. *To further exploit its core competencies.* A company may be able to extend a market-leading position in its domestic market into a position of regional or global market leadership by leveraging its core competencies further. H&M Group is capitalizing on its considerable expertise in fashion retailing to expand its reach internationally. By 2020, it had more than 5000 retail stores operating in 74 countries, and was continuing to expand its global reach. Companies can often leverage their resources internationally by replicating a successful business model, using it as a basic blueprint for international operations, as Starbucks and McDonald's have done.[1]

5. *To gain access to resources and capabilities located in foreign markets.* An increasingly important motive for entering foreign markets is to acquire resources and capabilities that may be unavailable in a company's home market. Companies often make acquisitions abroad or enter into cross-border alliances to gain access to capabilities that complement their own or to learn from their partners.[2] In other cases, companies choose to establish operations in other countries to utilize local distribution networks, gain local managerial or marketing expertise, or acquire specialized technical knowledge.

In addition, companies that are the suppliers of other companies often expand internationally when their major customers do so, to meet their customers' needs abroad and retain their position as a key supply chain partner. For example, when motor vehicle companies have opened new plants in foreign locations, big automotive parts suppliers have frequently opened new facilities nearby to permit timely delivery of their parts and components to the plant. Similarly, Newell-Rubbermaid, one of Walmart's biggest suppliers of household products, has followed Walmart into foreign markets.

WHY COMPETING ACROSS NATIONAL BORDERS MAKES STRATEGY MAKING MORE COMPLEX

Crafting a strategy to compete in one or more countries of the world is inherently more complex for five reasons. First, different countries have different home-country advantages in different industries; competing effectively requires an understanding of these differences. Second, there are location-based advantages to conducting particular value chain activities in different parts of the world. Third, different political and economic conditions make the general business climate more favorable in some countries than in others. Fourth, companies face risk due to adverse shifts in currency exchange rates when operating in foreign markets. And fifth, differences in buyer tastes and preferences present a challenge for companies concerning customizing versus standardizing their products and services.

● LO 7-2

Understand how and why differing market conditions across countries influence a company's strategy choices in international markets.

Home-Country Industry Advantages and the Diamond Model

Certain countries are known for their strengths in particular industries. For example, Chile has competitive strengths in industries such as copper, fruit, fish products, paper and pulp, chemicals, and wine. Japan is known for competitive strength in consumer electronics, automobiles, semiconductors, steel products, and specialty steel. Where industries are more likely to develop competitive strength depends on a set of factors that describe the nature of each country's business environment and vary from country to country. Because strong industries are made up of strong firms, the strategies of firms that expand internationally are usually grounded in one or more of these factors. The four major factors are summarized in a framework developed by Michael Porter and known as the *Diamond of National Competitive Advantage* (see Figure 7.1).[3]

Demand Conditions   The demand conditions in an industry's home market include the relative size of the market, its growth potential, and the nature of domestic buyers' needs and wants. Differing population sizes, income levels, and other demographic factors give rise to considerable differences in market size and growth rates from country to country. Industry sectors that are larger and more important in their home market tend to attract more resources and grow faster than others. For example, owing to widely differing population demographics and income levels, there is a far bigger market for luxury automobiles in the United States and Germany than in Argentina, India, Mexico, and China. At the same time, in developing markets like India, China, Brazil, and Malaysia, market growth potential is far higher than it is in the more mature economies of Britain, Denmark, Canada, and Japan. The potential for market growth

FIGURE 7.1   The Diamond of National Competitive Advantage

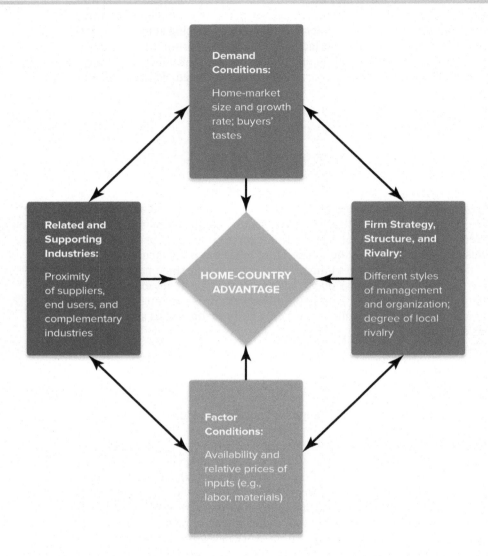

Source: Adapted from Michael E. Porter, "The Competitive Advantage of Nations," *Harvard Business Review,* March–April 1990, pp. 73–93.

in automobiles is explosive in China, where 2017 sales of new vehicles amounted to 28.9 million, surpassing U.S. sales of 17.2 million and making China the world's largest market for the eighth year in a row.[4] Demanding domestic buyers for an industry's products spur greater innovativeness and improvements in quality. Such conditions foster the development of stronger industries, with firms that are capable of translating a home-market advantage into a competitive advantage in the international arena.

Factor Conditions   Factor conditions describe the availability, quality, and cost of raw materials and other inputs (called *factors of production*) that firms in an industry require for producing their products and services. The relevant factors of production vary from industry to industry but can include different types of labor, technical or managerial knowledge, land, financial capital, and natural resources. Elements of a country's infrastructure may be included as well, such as its transportation, communication, and banking systems. For instance, in India there are efficient, well-developed national channels for distributing groceries, personal care items, and other packaged products to the country's 13 million retailers, (as of 2020) whereas in China distribution is primarily local and there is a limited national network for distributing most products. Competitively strong industries and firms develop where relevant factor conditions are favorable.

Related and Supporting Industries   Robust industries often develop in locales where there is a cluster of related industries, including others within the same value chain system (e.g., suppliers of components and equipment, distributors) and the makers of complementary products or those that are technologically related. The sports car makers Ferrari and Maserati, for example, are located in an area of Italy known as the "engine technological district," which includes other firms involved in racing, such as Ducati Motorcycles, along with hundreds of small suppliers. The advantage to firms that develop as part of a related-industry cluster comes from the close collaboration with key suppliers and the greater knowledge sharing throughout the cluster, resulting in greater efficiency and innovativeness.

Firm Strategy, Structure, and Rivalry   Different country environments foster the development of different styles of management, organization, and strategy. For example, strategic alliances are a more common strategy for firms from Asian or Latin American countries, which emphasize trust and cooperation in their organizations, than for firms from North America, where individualism is more influential. In addition, countries vary in terms of the competitive rivalry of their industries. Fierce rivalry in home markets tends to hone domestic firms' competitive capabilities and ready them for competing internationally.

> The Diamond Framework can be used to
> 1. predict from which countries foreign entrants are most likely to come
> 2. decide which foreign markets to enter first
> 3. choose the best country location for different value chain activities

For an industry in a particular country to become competitively strong, all four factors must be favorable for that industry. When they are, the industry is likely to contain firms that are capable of competing successfully in the international arena. Thus the diamond framework can be used to reveal the answers to several questions that are important for competing on an international basis. First, it can help predict *where foreign entrants into an industry are most likely to come from.* This can help managers prepare to cope with new foreign competitors, since the framework also reveals something about the basis of the new rivals' strengths. Second, it can reveal the countries in which foreign rivals are likely to be weakest and thus can help managers decide *which foreign markets to enter first.* And third, because it focuses on the attributes of a country's business environment that allow firms to flourish, it reveals something about the advantages of conducting particular business activities in that country. Thus the diamond framework is an aid to deciding *where to locate different value chain activities most beneficially*—a topic that we address next.

Opportunities for Location-Based Advantages

Increasingly, companies are locating different value chain activities in different parts of the world to exploit location-based advantages that vary from country to country. This is particularly evident with respect to the location of manufacturing activities. Differences in wage rates, worker productivity, energy costs, and the like create sizable variations in manufacturing costs from country to country. By locating its plants in certain countries, firms in some industries can reap major manufacturing cost advantages because of lower input costs (especially labor), relaxed government regulations, the proximity of suppliers and technologically related industries, or unique natural resources. In such cases, the low-cost countries become principal production sites, with most of the output being exported to markets in other parts of the world. Companies that build production facilities in low-cost countries (or that source their products from contract manufacturers in these countries) gain a competitive advantage over rivals with plants in countries where costs are higher. The competitive role of low manufacturing costs is most evident in low-wage countries like China, India, Pakistan, Cambodia, Vietnam, Mexico, Brazil, Guatemala, the Philippines, and several countries in Africa and eastern Europe that have become production havens for manufactured goods with high labor content (especially textiles and apparel). Hourly compensation for manufacturing workers in 2016 averaged about $3.27 in India, $2.06 in the Philippines, $3.60 in China, $3.91 in Mexico, $9.82 in Taiwan, $8.60 in Hungary, $7.98 in Brazil, $10.96 in Portugal, $22.98 in South Korea, $23.67 in New Zealand, $26.46 in Japan, $30.08 in Canada, $39.03 in the United States, $43.18 in Germany, and $60.36 in Switzerland.[5] China emerged as the manufacturing capital of the world in large part because of its low wages—virtually all of the world's major manufacturing companies now have facilities in China.

For other types of value chain activities, input quality or availability are more important considerations. Tiffany & Co. entered the mining industry in Canada to access diamonds that could be certified as "conflict free" and not associated with either the funding of African wars or unethical mining conditions. Many U.S. companies locate call centers in countries such as India and Ireland, where English is spoken and the workforce is well educated. Other companies locate R&D activities in countries where there are prestigious research institutions and well-trained scientists and engineers. Likewise, concerns about short delivery times and low shipping costs make some countries better locations than others for establishing distribution centers.

The Impact of Government Policies and Economic Conditions in Host Countries

Cross-country variations in government policies and economic conditions affect both the opportunities available to a foreign entrant and the risks of operating within the host country. The governments of some countries are eager to attract foreign investments, and thus they go all out to create a business climate that outsiders will view as favorable. Governments eager to spur economic growth, create more jobs, and raise living standards for their citizens usually enact policies aimed at stimulating business innovation and capital investment; Ireland is a good example. They may provide such incentives as reduced taxes, low-cost loans, site location and site development assistance, and government-sponsored training for workers to encourage companies to construct production and distribution facilities. When new business-related issues or developments arise, "pro-business" governments make a practice of seeking advice and counsel from business leaders. When tougher business-related regulations are deemed appropriate, they endeavor to make the transition to more costly and stringent regulations somewhat business-friendly rather than adversarial.

On the other hand, governments sometimes enact policies that, from a business perspective, make locating facilities within a country's borders less attractive. For example, the nature of a company's operations may make it particularly costly to achieve compliance with a country's environmental regulations. Some governments provide subsidies and low-interest loans to domestic companies to enable them to better compete against foreign companies. To discourage foreign imports, governments may enact deliberately burdensome procedures and requirements regarding customs inspection for foreign goods and may impose tariffs or quotas on imports. Additionally, they may specify that a certain percentage of the parts and components used in manufacturing a product be obtained from local suppliers, require prior approval of capital spending projects, limit withdrawal of funds from the country, and require partial ownership of foreign company operations by local companies or investors. There are times when a government may place restrictions on exports to ensure adequate local supplies and regulate the prices of imported and locally produced goods. Such government actions make a country's business climate less attractive and in some cases may be sufficiently onerous as to discourage a company from locating facilities in that country or even selling its products there.

A country's business climate is also a function of the political and economic risks associated with operating within its borders. **Political risks** have to do with the instability of weak governments, growing possibilities that a country's citizenry will revolt against dictatorial government leaders, the likelihood of new onerous legislation or regulations on foreign-owned businesses, and the potential for future elections to produce corrupt or tyrannical government leaders. In industries that a government deems critical to the national welfare, there is sometimes a risk that the government will nationalize the industry and expropriate the assets of foreign companies. In 2012, for example, Argentina nationalized the country's top oil producer, YPF, which was owned by Spanish oil major Repsol. In 2015, they nationalized all of the Argentine railway network, some of which had been in private hands. Other political risks include the loss of investments due to war or political unrest, regulatory changes that create operating uncertainties, security risks due to terrorism, and corruption. **Economic risks** have to do with instability of a country's economy and monetary system—whether inflation rates might skyrocket or whether uncontrolled deficit spending on the part of government or risky bank lending practices could lead to a breakdown of the country's monetary system and prolonged economic distress. In some countries, the threat of piracy and lack of protection for intellectual property are also sources of economic risk. Another is fluctuations in the value of different currencies—a factor that we discuss in more detail next.

> **CORE** CONCEPT
>
> **Political risks** stem from instability or weakness in national governments and hostility to foreign business. **Economic risks** stem from instability in a country's monetary system, economic and regulatory policies, and the lack of property rights protections.

The Risks of Adverse Exchange Rate Shifts

When companies produce and market their products and services in many different countries, they are subject to the impacts of sometimes favorable and sometimes unfavorable changes in currency exchange rates. The rates of exchange between different currencies can vary by as much as 20 to 40 percent annually, with the changes occurring sometimes gradually and sometimes swiftly. *Sizable shifts in exchange rates pose significant risks for two reasons:*

1. They are hard to predict because of the variety of factors involved and the uncertainties surrounding when and by how much these factors will change.

2. They create uncertainty regarding which countries represent the low-cost manufacturing locations and which rivals have the upper hand in the marketplace.

To illustrate the economic and competitive risks associated with fluctuating exchange rates, consider the case of a U.S. company that has located manufacturing facilities in Brazil (where the currency is *reals*—pronounced "ray-alls") and that exports most of the Brazilian-made goods to markets in the European Union (where the currency is euros). To keep the numbers simple, assume that the exchange rate is 4 Brazilian reals for 1 euro and that the product being made in Brazil has a manufacturing cost of 4 Brazilian reals (or 1 euro). Now suppose that the exchange rate shifts from 4 reals per euro to 5 reals per euro (meaning that the real has declined in value and that the euro is stronger). Making the product in Brazil is now more cost-competitive because a Brazilian good costing 4 reals to produce has fallen to only 0.8 euro at the new exchange rate (4 reals divided by 5 reals per euro = 0.8 euro). This clearly puts the producer of the Brazilian-made good *in a better position to compete* against the European makers of the same good. On the other hand, should the value of the Brazilian real grow stronger in relation to the euro—resulting in an exchange rate of 3 reals to 1 euro—the same Brazilian-made good formerly costing 4 reals (or 1 euro) to produce now has a cost of 1.33 euros (4 reals divided by 3 reals per euro = 1.33 euros), putting the producer of the Brazilian-made good in a weaker competitive position vis-à-vis the European producers. Plainly, the attraction of manufacturing a good in Brazil and selling it in Europe is far greater when the euro is strong (an exchange rate of 1 euro for 5 Brazilian reals) than when the euro is weak and exchanges for only 3 Brazilian reals.

But there is one more piece to the story. When the exchange rate changes from 4 reals per euro to 5 reals per euro, not only is the cost-competitiveness of the Brazilian manufacturer stronger relative to European manufacturers of the same item but the Brazilian-made good that formerly cost 1 euro and now costs only 0.8 euro can also be sold to consumers in the European Union for a lower euro price than before. In other words, the combination of a stronger euro and a weaker real acts to *lower the price of Brazilian-made goods* in all the countries that are members of the European Union, which is likely to *spur sales of the Brazilian-made good in Europe and boost Brazilian exports to Europe.* Conversely, should the exchange rate shift from 4 reals per euro to 3 reals per euro—which makes the Brazilian manufacturer less cost-competitive with European manufacturers of the same item—the Brazilian-made good that formerly cost 1 euro and now costs 1.33 euros will sell for a higher price in euros than before, thus weakening the demand of European consumers for Brazilian-made goods and acting to reduce Brazilian exports to Europe. Brazilian exporters are likely to experience (1) rising demand for their goods in Europe whenever the Brazilian real grows weaker relative to the euro and (2) falling demand for their goods in Europe whenever the real grows stronger relative to the euro. Consequently, from the standpoint of a company with Brazilian manufacturing plants, *a weaker Brazilian real is a favorable exchange rate shift* and *a stronger Brazilian real is an unfavorable exchange rate shift.*

It follows from the previous discussion that shifting exchange rates have a big impact on the ability of domestic manufacturers to compete with foreign rivals. For example, U.S.-based manufacturers locked in a fierce competitive battle with low-cost foreign imports benefit from a *weaker* U.S. dollar. There are several reasons why this is so:

- Declines in the value of the U.S. dollar against foreign currencies raise the U.S. dollar costs of goods manufactured by foreign rivals at plants located in the countries whose currencies have grown stronger relative to the U.S. dollar. A *weaker* dollar acts to reduce or eliminate whatever cost advantage foreign manufacturers may have had over U.S. manufacturers (and helps protect the manufacturing jobs of U.S. workers).

- A *weaker* dollar makes foreign-made goods more expensive in dollar terms to U.S. consumers—this curtails U.S. buyer demand for foreign-made goods, stimulates greater demand on the part of U.S. consumers for U.S.-made goods, and reduces U.S. imports of foreign-made goods.

- A *weaker* U.S. dollar enables the U.S.-made goods to be sold at lower prices to consumers in countries whose currencies have grown stronger relative to the U.S. dollar—such lower prices boost foreign buyer demand for the now relatively cheaper U.S.-made goods, thereby stimulating exports of U.S.-made goods to foreign countries and creating more jobs in U.S.-based manufacturing plants.

- A *weaker* dollar has the effect of increasing the dollar value of profits a company earns in foreign-country markets where the local currency is stronger relative to the dollar. For example, if a U.S.-based manufacturer earns a profit of €10 million on its sales in Europe, those €10 million convert to a larger number of dollars when the dollar grows weaker against the euro.

A weaker U.S. dollar is therefore an economically favorable exchange rate shift for manufacturing plants based in the United States. A decline in the value of the U.S. dollar strengthens the cost-competitiveness of U.S.-based manufacturing plants and boosts buyer demand for U.S.-made goods. When the value of the U.S. dollar is expected to remain weak for some time to come, foreign companies have an incentive to build manufacturing facilities in the United States to make goods for U.S. consumers rather than export the same goods to the United States from foreign plants where production costs in dollar terms have been driven up by the decline in the value of the dollar. Conversely, a *stronger* U.S. dollar is an *unfavorable exchange rate shift* for U.S.-based manufacturing plants because it makes such plants less cost-competitive with foreign plants and weakens foreign demand for U.S.-made goods. A strong dollar also weakens the incentive of foreign companies to locate manufacturing facilities in the United States to make goods for U.S. consumers. The same reasoning applies to companies that have plants in countries in the European Union where euros are the local currency. A weak euro versus other currencies enhances the cost-competitiveness of companies manufacturing goods in Europe vis-à-vis foreign rivals with plants in countries whose currencies have grown stronger relative to the euro; a strong euro versus other currencies weakens the cost-competitiveness of companies with plants in the European Union.

> Fluctuating exchange rates pose significant economic risks to a company's competitiveness in foreign markets. Exporters are disadvantaged when the currency of the country where goods are being manufactured grows stronger relative to the currency of the importing country.

> Domestic companies facing competitive pressure from lower-cost imports benefit when their government's currency grows *weaker* in relation to the currencies of the countries where the lower-cost imports are being made.

Cross-Country Differences in Demographic, Cultural, and Market Conditions

Buyer tastes for a particular product or service sometimes differ substantially from country to country. In France, consumers prefer top-loading washing machines, whereas in most other European countries consumers prefer front-loading machines. People in Hong Kong prefer compact appliances, but in Taiwan large appliances are more popular. Ice cream flavors like matcha, black sesame, and red beans have more appeal to East Asian customers than they have for customers in the United States and in Europe. Sometimes, product designs suitable in one country are inappropriate in another because of differing local standards—for example, in the United States electrical devices run on 110-volt electric systems, but in some European countries the standard is a 240-volt electric system, necessitating the use of different electrical designs and components. Cultural influences can also affect consumer demand for a product. For instance, in South Korea many parents are reluctant to purchase PCs even when they can afford them because of concerns that their children will be distracted from their schoolwork by surfing the Web, playing PC-based video games, and becoming Internet "addicts."[6]

Consequently, companies operating in an international marketplace have to wrestle with *whether and how much to customize their offerings in each country market to match local buyers' tastes and preferences or whether to pursue a strategy of offering a mostly standardized product worldwide.* While making products that are closely matched to local tastes makes them more appealing to local buyers, customizing a company's products country by country may raise production and distribution costs due to the greater variety of designs and components, shorter production runs, and the complications of added inventory handling and distribution logistics. Greater standardization of a global company's product offering, on the other hand, can lead to scale economies and learning-curve effects, thus reducing per-unit production costs and contributing to the achievement of a low-cost advantage. *The tension between the market pressures to localize a company's product offerings country by country and the competitive pressures to lower costs is one of the big strategic issues that participants in foreign markets have to resolve.*

STRATEGIC OPTIONS FOR ENTERING INTERNATIONAL MARKETS

● LO 7-3

Identify the differences among the five primary modes of entry into foreign markets.

Once a company decides to expand beyond its domestic borders, it must consider the question of how to enter foreign markets. There are five primary *modes of entry* to choose among:

1. Maintain a home-country production base and *export* goods to foreign markets.
2. *License* foreign firms to produce and distribute the company's products abroad.
3. Employ a *franchising* strategy in foreign markets.
4. Establish a *subsidiary* in a foreign market via acquisition or internal development.
5. Rely on *strategic alliances* or joint ventures with foreign companies.

Which mode of entry to employ depends on a variety of factors, including the nature of the firm's strategic objectives, the firm's position in terms of whether it has the full range of resources and capabilities needed to operate abroad, country-specific factors such as trade barriers, and the transaction costs involved (the costs of contracting with a partner and monitoring its compliance with the terms of the contract, for example). The options vary considerably regarding the level of investment required and the associated risks—but higher levels of investment and risk generally provide the firm with the benefits of greater ownership and control.

Export Strategies

Using domestic plants as a production base for exporting goods to foreign markets is an excellent initial strategy for pursuing international sales. It is a conservative way to test the international waters. The amount of capital needed to begin exporting is often minimal; existing production capacity may well be sufficient to make goods for export. With an export-based entry strategy, a manufacturer can limit its involvement in foreign markets by contracting with foreign wholesalers experienced in importing to handle the entire distribution and marketing function in their countries or regions of the world. If it is more advantageous to maintain control over these functions, however, a manufacturer can establish its own distribution and sales organizations in some or all of the target foreign markets. Either way, a home-based production and export strategy helps the firm minimize its direct investments in foreign countries. Such strategies are commonly favored by Chinese, Korean, and Italian companies—products are designed and manufactured at home and then distributed through local channels in the importing countries. The primary functions performed abroad relate chiefly to establishing a network of distributors and perhaps conducting sales promotion and brand-awareness activities.

Whether an export strategy can be pursued successfully over the long run depends on the relative cost-competitiveness of the home-country production base. In some industries, firms gain additional scale economies and learning-curve benefits from centralizing production in plants whose output capability exceeds demand in any one country market; exporting enables a firm to capture such economies. However, an export strategy is vulnerable when (1) manufacturing costs in the home country are substantially higher than in foreign countries where rivals have plants, (2) the costs of shipping the product to distant foreign markets are relatively high, (3) adverse shifts occur in currency exchange rates, and (4) importing countries impose tariffs or erect other trade barriers. Unless an exporter can keep its production and shipping costs competitive with rivals' costs, secure adequate local distribution and marketing support of its products, and effectively hedge against unfavorable changes in currency exchange rates, its success will be limited.

Licensing Strategies

Licensing as an entry strategy makes sense when a firm with valuable technical know-how, an appealing brand, or a unique patented product has neither the internal organizational capability nor the resources to enter foreign markets. Licensing also has the advantage of avoiding the risks of committing resources to country markets that are unfamiliar, politically volatile, economically unstable, or otherwise risky. By licensing the technology, trademark, or production rights to foreign-based firms, a company can generate income from royalties while shifting the costs and risks of entering foreign markets to the licensee. One downside of the licensing alternative is that the partner who bears the risk is also likely to be the biggest beneficiary from any upside gain. Disney learned this lesson when it relied on licensing agreements to open its first foreign theme park, Tokyo Disneyland. When the venture proved wildly successful, it was its licensing partner, the Oriental Land Company, and not Disney who reaped the windfall. Another disadvantage of licensing is the risk of providing valuable technological know-how to foreign companies and thereby losing some degree of control over its use; monitoring licensees and safeguarding the company's proprietary know-how can prove quite difficult in some circumstances. But if the royalty potential is considerable and the companies to which the licenses are being granted are trustworthy and reputable, then licensing can be a very attractive option. Many software and pharmaceutical companies use licensing strategies to participate in foreign markets.

Franchising Strategies

While licensing works well for manufacturers and owners of proprietary technology, franchising is often better suited to the international expansion efforts of service and retailing enterprises. McDonald's, Yum! Brands (the parent of Pizza Hut, KFC, Taco Bell, and WingStreet), the UPS Store, Roto-Rooter, 7-Eleven, and Hilton Hotels have all used franchising to build a presence in foreign markets. Franchising has many of the same advantages as licensing. The franchisee bears most of the costs and risks of establishing foreign locations; a franchisor has to expend only the resources to recruit, train, support, and monitor franchisees. The big problem a franchisor faces is maintaining quality control; foreign franchisees do not always exhibit strong commitment to consistency and standardization, especially when the local culture does not stress the same kinds of quality concerns. A question that can arise is whether to allow foreign franchisees to make modifications in the franchisor's product offering so as to better satisfy the tastes and expectations of local buyers. Should McDonald's give franchisees in each nation some leeway in what products they put on their menus? Should franchised KFC units in China be permitted to substitute spices that appeal to Chinese consumers? Or should the same menu offerings be rigorously and unvaryingly required of all franchisees worldwide?

Foreign Subsidiary Strategies

CORE CONCEPT

A **greenfield venture** (or internal startup) is a subsidiary business that is established by setting up the entire operation from the ground up.

Very often companies electing to compete internationally prefer to have direct control over all aspects of operating in a foreign market. Companies that want to participate in direct performance of all essential value chain activities typically establish a wholly owned subsidiary, either by acquiring a local company or by establishing its own new operating organization from the ground up. A subsidiary business that is established internally from scratch is called an *internal startup* or a **greenfield venture.**

Acquiring a local business is the quicker of the two options; it may be the least risky and most cost-efficient means of hurdling such entry barriers as gaining access to local distribution channels, building supplier relationships, and establishing working relationships with government officials and other key constituencies. Buying an ongoing operation allows the acquirer to move directly to the task of transferring resources and personnel to the newly acquired business, redirecting and integrating the activities of the acquired business into its own operation, putting its own strategy into place, and accelerating efforts to build a strong market position.

One thing an acquisition-minded firm must consider is whether to pay a premium price for a successful local company or to buy a struggling competitor at a bargain price. If the buying firm has little knowledge of the local market but ample capital, it is often better off purchasing a capable, strongly positioned firm. However, when the acquirer sees promising ways to transform a weak firm into a strong one and has the resources and managerial know-how to do so, a struggling company can be the better long-term investment.

Entering a new foreign country via a greenfield venture makes sense when a company already operates in a number of countries, has experience in establishing new subsidiaries and overseeing their operations, and has a sufficiently large pool of resources and capabilities to rapidly equip a new subsidiary with the personnel and what it needs otherwise to compete successfully and profitably. Four more conditions combine to make a greenfield venture strategy appealing:

- When creating an internal startup is cheaper than making an acquisition.
- When adding new production capacity will not adversely impact the supply–demand balance in the local market.
- When a startup subsidiary has the ability to gain good distribution access (perhaps because of the company's recognized brand name).
- When a startup subsidiary will have the size, cost structure, and capabilities to compete head-to-head against local rivals.

Greenfield ventures in foreign markets can also pose problems, just as other entry strategies do. They represent a costly capital investment, subject to a high level of risk. They require numerous other company resources as well, diverting them from other uses. They do not work well in countries without strong, well-functioning markets and institutions that protect the rights of foreign investors and provide other legal protections. Moreover, an important disadvantage of greenfield ventures relative to other means of international expansion is that they are the slowest entry route—particularly if the objective is to achieve a sizable market share. On the other hand, successful greenfield ventures may offer higher returns to compensate for their high risk and slower path.

Collaborative strategies involving alliances or joint ventures with foreign partners are a popular way for companies to edge their way into the markets of foreign countries.

Alliance and Joint Venture Strategies

Strategic alliances, joint ventures, and other cooperative agreements with foreign companies are a widely used means of entering foreign markets.[7] A company can benefit immensely from a foreign partner's familiarity with local government regulations, its knowledge of the buying habits and product preferences of consumers, its distribution-channel relationships, and so on.[8] Both Japanese and American companies are actively forming alliances with European companies to better compete in the 28-nation European Union (and the five countries that are candidates to become EU members). Many U.S. and European companies are allying with Asian companies in their efforts to enter markets in China, India, Thailand, Indonesia, and other Asian countries.

Another reason for cross-border alliances is to capture economies of scale in production and/or marketing. By joining forces in producing components, assembling models, and marketing their products, companies can realize cost savings not achievable with their own small volumes. A third reason to employ a collaborative strategy is to share distribution facilities and dealer networks, thus mutually strengthening each partner's access to buyers. A fourth benefit of a collaborative strategy is the learning and added expertise that comes from performing joint research, sharing technological know-how, studying one another's manufacturing methods, and understanding how to tailor sales and marketing approaches to fit local cultures and traditions. A fifth benefit is that cross-border allies can direct their competitive energies more toward mutual rivals and less toward one another; teaming up may help them close the gap on leading companies. And, finally, alliances can be a particularly useful way for companies across the world to gain agreement on important technical standards—they have been used to arrive at standards for assorted PC devices, Internet-related technologies, high-definition televisions, and mobile phones.

Cross-border alliances enable a growth-minded company to widen its geographic coverage and strengthen its competitiveness in foreign markets; at the same time, they offer flexibility and allow a company to retain some degree of autonomy and operating control.

Cross-border alliances are an attractive means of gaining the aforementioned types of benefits (as compared to merging with or acquiring foreign-based companies) because they allow a company to preserve its independence (which is not the case with a merger) and avoid using scarce financial resources to fund acquisitions. Furthermore, an alliance offers the flexibility to readily disengage once its purpose has been served or if the benefits prove elusive, whereas mergers and acquisitions are more permanent arrangements.[9]

Alliances may also be used to pave the way for an intended merger; they offer a way to test the value and viability of a cooperative arrangement with a foreign partner before making a more permanent commitment. Illustration Capsule 7.1 shows how Walgreens pursued this strategy with Alliance Boots in order to facilitate its expansion abroad.

Walgreens Boots Alliance, Inc.: Entering Foreign Markets via Alliance Followed by Merger

Walgreens pharmacy began in 1901 as a single store on the South Side of Chicago and grew to become the largest chain of pharmacy retailers in America. Walgreens was an early pioneer of the "self-service" pharmacy and found success by moving quickly to build a vast domestic network of stores after the Second World War. This growth-focused strategy served Walgreens well up until the beginning of the 21st century, by which time it had nearly saturated the U.S. market. By 2014, 75 percent of Americans lived within five miles of a Walgreens. The company was also facing threats to its core business model. Walgreens relies heavily on pharmacy sales, which generally are paid for by someone other than the patient, usually the government or an insurance company. As the government and insurers started to make a more sustained effort to cut costs, Walgreens's core profit center was at risk. To mitigate these threats, Walgreens looked to enter foreign markets.

Walgreens found an ideal international partner in Alliance Boots. Based in the UK, Alliance Boots had a global footprint with 3,300 stores across 10 countries. A partnership with Alliance Boots had several strategic advantages, allowing Walgreens to gain swift entry into foreign markets as well as complementary assets and expertise. First, it gave Walgreens access to new markets beyond the saturated United States for its retail pharmacies. Second, it provided Walgreens with a new revenue stream in wholesale drugs. Alliance Boots held a vast European distribution network for wholesale drug sales; Walgreens could leverage that network and expertise to build a similar model in the United States. Finally, a merger with Alliance Boots would strengthen Walgreens's existing business by increasing the company's market position and therefore bargaining power

Jonathan Weiss/Shutterstock

with drug companies. In light of these advantages, Walgreens moved quickly to partner with and later acquire Alliance Boots and merged both companies in 2014 to become Walgreens Boots Alliance. Walgreens Boots Alliance, Inc. is now one of the world's largest drug purchasers, able to negotiate from a strong position with drug companies and other suppliers to realize economies of scale in its current businesses.

The market has thus far responded favorably to the merger. Walgreens Boots Alliance's stock has more than doubled in value since the first news of the partnership in 2012. However, the company is still struggling to integrate and faces new risks such as currency fluctuation in its new combined position. Yet as the pharmaceutical industry continues to consolidate, Walgreens is in an undoubtedly stronger position to continue to grow in the future thanks to its strategic international acquisition.

Note: Developed with Katherine Coster.

Sources: Company 10-K Form, 2015, investor.walgreensbootsalliance.com/secfiling.cfm?filingID=1140361-15-38791&CIK=1618921; L. Capron and W. Mitchell, "When to Change a Winning Strategy," *Harvard Business Review,* July 25, 2012, hbr.org/2012/07/when-to-change-a-winning-strat; T. Martin and R. Dezember, "Walgreen Spends $6.7 Billion on Alliance Boots Stake," *The Wall Street Journal,* June 20, 2012.

The Risks of Strategic Alliances with Foreign Partners Alliances and joint ventures with foreign partners have their pitfalls, however. Sometimes a local partner's knowledge and expertise turns out to be less valuable than expected (because its knowledge is rendered obsolete by fast-changing market conditions or because its operating practices are archaic). Cross-border allies typically must overcome language and cultural barriers and figure out how to deal with diverse (or conflicting) operating practices. The transaction costs of working out a mutually agreeable arrangement and monitoring partner compliance with the terms of the arrangement can be high. The communication, trust building, and coordination costs are not trivial in terms of management time.[10] Often, partners soon discover they have conflicting objectives and strategies, deep differences of opinion about how to proceed, or important differences in corporate values and ethical standards. Tensions build, working relationships cool, and the hoped-for benefits never materialize.[11] It is not unusual for there to be little personal chemistry among some of the key people on whom the success or failure of the alliance depends—the rapport such personnel need to work well together may never emerge. And even if allies are able to develop productive personal relationships, they can still have trouble reaching mutually agreeable ways to deal with key issues or launching new initiatives fast enough to stay abreast of rapid advances in technology or shifting market conditions.

One worrisome problem with alliances or joint ventures is that a firm may risk losing some of its competitive advantage if an alliance partner is given full access to its proprietary technological expertise or other competitively valuable capabilities. There is a natural tendency for allies to struggle to collaborate effectively in competitively sensitive areas, thus spawning suspicions on both sides about forthright exchanges of information and expertise. It requires many meetings of many people working in good faith over a period of time to iron out what is to be shared, what is to remain proprietary, and how the cooperative arrangements will work.

Even if the alliance proves to be a win–win proposition for both parties, there is the danger of becoming overly dependent on foreign partners for essential expertise and competitive capabilities. Companies aiming for global market leadership need to develop their own resources and capabilities in order to be masters of their destiny. Frequently, experienced international companies operating in 50 or more countries across the world find less need for entering into cross-border alliances than do companies in the early stages of globalizing their operations.[12] Companies with global operations make it a point to develop senior managers who understand how "the system" works in different countries, plus they can avail themselves of local managerial talent and know-how by simply hiring experienced local managers and thereby detouring the hazards of collaborative alliances with local companies. One of the lessons about cross-border partnerships is that they are more effective in helping a company establish a beachhead of new opportunity in world markets than they are in enabling a company to achieve and sustain global market leadership.

INTERNATIONAL STRATEGY: THE THREE MAIN APPROACHES

Broadly speaking, a firm's **international strategy** is simply its strategy for competing in two or more countries simultaneously. Typically, a company will start to compete internationally by entering one or perhaps a select few foreign markets—selling its products or services in countries where there is a ready market for them. But as it expands further internationally, it will have to confront head-on two conflicting pressures: the demand for responsiveness to local needs versus the prospect of efficiency gains from offering a standardized product globally. Deciding on the competitive approach to best address these competing pressures is perhaps the foremost strategic issue that must be addressed when a company is operating in two or more foreign markets.[13] Figure 7.2 shows a company's three options for resolving this issue: choosing a *multidomestic, global,* or *transnational* strategy.

● LO 7-4

Identify the three main strategic approaches for competing internationally.

CORE CONCEPT

An **international strategy** is a strategy for competing in two or more countries simultaneously.

FIGURE 7.2   Three Approaches for Competing Internationally

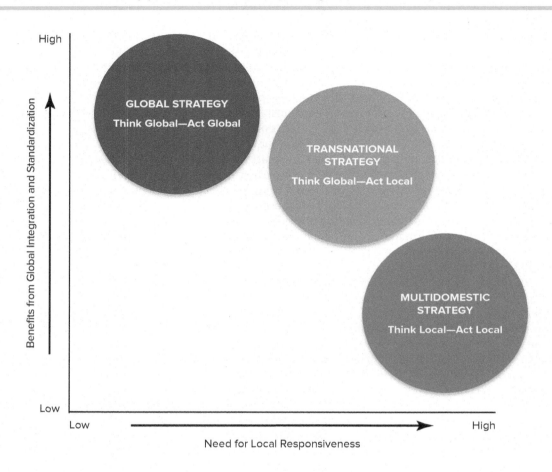

Multidomestic Strategies—a "Think-Local, Act-Local" Approach

A **multidomestic strategy** is one in which a company varies its product offering and competitive approach from country to country in an effort to meet differing buyer needs and to address divergent local-market conditions. It involves having plants produce different product versions for different local markets and adapting marketing and distribution to fit local customs, cultures, regulations, and market requirements. In the food products industry, it is common for companies to vary the ingredients in their products and sell the localized versions under local brand names to cater to country-specific tastes and eating preferences. Government requirements for gasoline additives that help reduce carbon monoxide, smog, and other emissions are almost never the same from country to country. BP utilizes localized strategies in its gasoline and service station business segment because of these cross-country formulation differences and because of customer familiarity with local brand names. For example, the company markets gasoline in the United States under its BP and Arco brands, but markets gasoline in Germany, Belgium, Poland, Hungary, and the Czech Republic under the Aral brand. Castrol, a BP-owned specialist in oil lubricants, produces over 3,000 different formulas of lubricants to meet the requirements of different climates, vehicle types and uses, and equipment applications that characterize different country markets.

In essence, a multidomestic strategy represents a **think-local, act-local** approach to international strategy. A think-local, act-local approach to strategy making is most appropriate when the need for local responsiveness is high due to significant cross-country differences in demographic, cultural, and market conditions and when the potential for efficiency gains from standardization is limited, as depicted in Figure 7.2. A think-local, act-local approach is possible only when decision making is decentralized, giving local managers considerable latitude for crafting and executing strategies for the country markets they are responsible for. Giving local managers decision-making authority allows them to address specific market needs and respond swiftly to local changes in demand. It also enables them to focus their competitive efforts, stake out attractive market positions vis-à-vis local competitors, react to rivals' moves in a timely fashion, and target new opportunities as they emerge.[14]

Despite their obvious benefits, think-local, act-local strategies have three big drawbacks:

1. They hinder transfer of a company's capabilities, knowledge, and other resources across country boundaries, since the company's efforts are not integrated or coordinated across country boundaries. This can make the company less innovative overall.

2. They raise production and distribution costs due to the greater variety of designs and components, shorter production runs for each product version, and complications of added inventory handling and distribution logistics.

3. They are not conducive to building a single, worldwide competitive advantage. When a company's competitive approach and product offering vary from country to country, the nature and size of any resulting competitive edge also tends to vary. At the most, multidomestic strategies are capable of producing a group of local competitive advantages of varying types and degrees of strength.

Global Strategies—a "Think-Global, Act-Global" Approach

A **global strategy** contrasts sharply with a multidomestic strategy in that it takes a standardized, globally integrated approach to producing, packaging, selling, and delivering the company's products and services worldwide. Companies employing a global strategy sell the same products under the same brand names everywhere, utilize much the same distribution channels in all countries, and compete on the basis of the same capabilities and marketing approaches worldwide. Although the company's strategy or product offering may be adapted in minor ways to accommodate specific situations in a few host countries, the company's fundamental competitive approach (low cost, differentiation, best cost, or focused) remains very much intact worldwide and local managers stick close to the global strategy.

A **think-global, act-global** approach prompts company managers to integrate and coordinate the company's strategic moves worldwide and to expand into most, if not all, nations where there is significant buyer demand. It puts considerable strategic emphasis on building a *global* brand name and aggressively pursuing opportunities to transfer ideas, new products, and capabilities from one country to another. Global strategies are characterized by relatively centralized value chain activities, such as production and distribution. While there may be more than one manufacturing plant and distribution center to minimize transportation costs, for example, they tend to be few

> **CORE** CONCEPT
>
> A **global strategy** is one in which a company employs the same basic competitive approach in all countries where it operates, sells standardized products globally, strives to build global brands, and coordinates its actions worldwide with strong headquarters control. It represents a **think-global, act-global** approach.

in number. Achieving the efficiency potential of a global strategy requires that resources and best practices be shared, value chain activities be integrated, and capabilities be transferred from one location to another as they are developed. These objectives are best facilitated through centralized decision making and strong headquarters control.

Because a global strategy cannot accommodate varying local needs, it is an appropriate strategic choice when there are pronounced efficiency benefits from standardization and when buyer needs are relatively homogeneous across countries and regions. A globally standardized and integrated approach is especially beneficial when high volumes significantly lower costs due to economies of scale or added experience (moving the company further down a learning curve). It can also be advantageous if it allows the firm to replicate a successful business model on a global basis efficiently or engage in higher levels of R&D by spreading the fixed costs and risks over a higher-volume output. It is a fitting response to industry conditions marked by global competition.

Consumer electronics companies such as Apple, Nokia, and Motorola Mobility tend to employ global strategies. The development of universal standards in technology is one factor supporting the use of global strategies. So is the rise of global accounting and financial reporting standards. Whenever country-to-country differences are small enough to be accommodated within the framework of a global strategy, a global strategy is preferable because a company can more readily unify its operations and focus on establishing a brand image and reputation that are uniform from country to country. Moreover, with a global strategy a company is better able to focus its full resources on securing a sustainable low-cost or differentiation-based competitive advantage over both domestic rivals and global rivals.

There are, however, several drawbacks to global strategies: (1) They do not enable firms to address local needs as precisely as locally based rivals can; (2) they are less responsive to changes in local market conditions, in the form of either new opportunities or competitive threats; (3) they raise transportation costs and may involve higher tariffs; and (4) they involve higher coordination costs due to the more complex task of managing a globally integrated enterprise.

Transnational Strategies—a "Think-Global, Act-Local" Approach

A **transnational strategy** (sometimes called *glocalization*) incorporates elements of both a globalized and a localized approach to strategy making. This type of middle-ground strategy is called for when there are relatively high needs for local responsiveness as well as appreciable benefits to be realized from standardization, as Figure 7.2 suggests. A transnational strategy encourages a company to use a **think-global, act-local** approach to balance these competing objectives.

> **CORE CONCEPT**
>
> **transnational strategy** is a **think-global, act-local** approach that incorporates elements of both multidomestic and global strategies.

Often, companies implement a transnational strategy with mass-customization techniques that enable them to address local preferences in an efficient, semi-standardized manner. McDonald's, KFC, and Starbucks have discovered ways to customize their menu offerings in various countries without compromising costs, product quality, and operating effectiveness. Unilever is responsive to local market needs regarding its consumer products, while realizing global economies of scale in certain functions. Otis Elevator found that a transnational strategy delivers better results than a global strategy when it is competing in countries like China, where local needs are highly differentiated. By switching from its customary single-brand approach to a multibrand strategy aimed at serving different segments of the market, Otis was able to double its market share in China and increased its revenues sixfold over a nine-year period.[15]

As a rule, most companies that operate internationally endeavor to employ as global a strategy as customer needs and market conditions permit. Electronic Arts (EA) has two major design studios—one in Vancouver, British Columbia, and one in Los Angeles—and smaller design studios in locations including San Francisco, Orlando, London, and Tokyo. This dispersion of design studios helps EA design games that are specific to different cultures—for example, the London studio took the lead in designing the popular FIFA Soccer game to suit European tastes and to replicate the stadiums, signage, and team rosters; the U.S. studio took the lead in designing games involving NFL football, NBA basketball, and NASCAR racing.

A transnational strategy is far more conducive than other strategies to transferring and leveraging subsidiary skills and capabilities. But, like other approaches to competing internationally, transnational strategies also have significant drawbacks:

1. They are the most difficult of all international strategies to implement due to the added complexity of varying the elements of the strategy to situational conditions.
2. They place large demands on the organization due to the need to pursue conflicting objectives simultaneously.
3. Implementing the strategy is likely to be a costly and time-consuming enterprise, with an uncertain outcome.

Illustration Capsule 7.2 explains how Four Seasons Hotels has been able to compete successfully on the basis of a transnational strategy.

Table 7.1 provides a summary of the pluses and minuses of the three approaches to competing internationally.

TABLE 7.1 Advantages and Disadvantages of Multidomestic, Global, and Transnational Strategies

	Advantages	Disadvantages
Multidomestic (think local, act local)	• Can meet the specific needs of each market more precisely • Can respond more swiftly to localized changes in demand • Can target reactions to the moves of local rivals • Can respond more quickly to local opportunities and threats	• Hinders resource and capability sharing or cross-market transfers • Has higher production and distribution costs • Is not conducive to a worldwide competitive advantage
Global (think global, act global)	• Has lower costs due to scale and scope economies • Can lead to greater efficiencies due to the ability to transfer best practices across markets • Increases innovation from knowledge sharing and capability transfer • Offers the benefit of a global brand and reputation	• Cannot address local needs precisely • Is less responsive to changes in local market conditions • Involves higher transportation costs and tariffs • Has higher coordination and integration costs
Transnational (think global, act local)	• Offers the benefits of both local responsiveness and global integration • Enables the transfer and sharing of resources and capabilities across borders • Provides the benefits of flexible coordination	• Is more complex and harder to implement • Entails conflicting goals, which may be difficult to reconcile and require trade-offs • Involves more costly and time-consuming implementation

Four Seasons Hotels: Local Character, Global Service

Four Seasons Hotels is a Toronto, Canada–based manager of luxury hotel properties. With more than 100 properties located in many of the world's most popular tourist destinations and business centers, Four Seasons commands a following of many of the world's most discerning travelers. In contrast to its key competitor, Ritz-Carlton, which strives to create one uniform experience globally, Four Seasons Hotels has gained market share by deftly combining local architectural and cultural experiences with globally consistent luxury service.

When moving into a new market, Four Seasons always seeks out a local capital partner. The understanding of local custom and business relationships this financier brings is critical to the process of developing a new Four Seasons hotel. Four Seasons also insists on hiring a local architect and design consultant for each property, as opposed to using architects or designers it's worked with in other locations. While this can be a challenge, particularly in emerging markets, Four Seasons has found it is worth it in the long run to have a truly local team.

The specific layout and programming of each hotel is also unique. For instance, when Four Seasons opened its hotel in Mumbai, India, it prioritized space for large banquet halls to target the Indian wedding market. In India, weddings often draw guests numbering in the thousands. When moving into the Middle East, Four Seasons designed its hotels with separate prayer rooms for men and women. In Bali, where destination weddings are common, the hotel employs a "weather shaman" who, for some guests, provides reassurance that the weather will cooperate for their special day. In all cases, the objective is to provide a truly local experience.

When staffing its hotels, Four Seasons seeks to strike a fine balance between employing locals who have

Chris Lawrence/Alamy Stock Photo

an innate understanding of the local culture alongside expatriate staff or "culture carriers" who understand the DNA of Four Seasons. It also uses global systems to track customer preferences and employs globally consistent service standards. Four Seasons claims that its guests experience the same high level of service globally but that no two experiences are the same.

While it is much more expensive and time-consuming to design unique architectural and programming experiences, doing so is a strategic trade-off Four Seasons has made to achieve the local experience demanded by its high-level clientele. Likewise, it has recognized that maintaining globally consistent operation processes and service standards is important too. Four Seasons has struck the right balance between thinking globally and acting locally—the marker of a truly transnational strategy. As a result, the company has been rewarded with an international reputation for superior service and a leading market share in the luxury hospitality segment.

Note: Developed with Brian R. McKenzie.

Sources: Four Seasons annual report and corporate website; interview with Scott Woroch, executive vice president of development, Four Seasons Hotels, February 22, 2014.

INTERNATIONAL OPERATIONS AND THE QUEST FOR COMPETITIVE ADVANTAGE

There are three important ways in which a firm can gain competitive advantage (or offset domestic disadvantages) by expanding outside its domestic market. First, it can use location to lower costs or achieve greater product differentiation. Second, it can transfer competitively valuable resources and capabilities from one country to another or share them across international borders to extend its competitive advantages. And third, it can benefit from cross-border coordination opportunities that are not open to domestic-only competitors.

● **LO 7-5**

Explain how companies are able to use international operations to improve overall competitiveness.
....

Using Location to Build Competitive Advantage

To use location to build competitive advantage, a company must consider two issues: (1) whether or not to concentrate some of the activities it performs in only a few select countries of those in which they operate and if so (2) in which countries to locate particular activities.

> Companies that compete internationally can pursue competitive advantage in world markets by locating their value chain activities in whatever nations prove most advantageous.

When to Concentrate Activities in a Few Locations   It is advantageous for a company to concentrate its activities in a limited number of locations when

- *The costs of manufacturing or other activities are significantly lower in some geographic locations than in others.* For example, much of the world's athletic footwear is manufactured in Asia (China, Vietnam, and Indonesia) because of low labor costs; much of the production of circuit boards for PCs is located in Taiwan because of both low costs and the high-caliber technical skills of the Taiwanese labor force.

- *Significant scale economies exist in production or distribution.* The presence of significant economies of scale in components production or final assembly means that a company can gain major cost savings from operating a few super-efficient plants as opposed to a host of small plants scattered across the world. Makers of digital cameras and LED TVs located in Japan, South Korea, and Taiwan have used their scale economies to establish a low-cost advantage in this way. Achieving low-cost leadership status often requires a company to have the largest worldwide manufacturing share (as distinct from brand share or market share), with production centralized in one or a few giant plants. Some companies even use such plants to manufacture units sold under the brand names of rivals to further boost production-related scale economies. Likewise, a company may be able to reduce its distribution costs by establishing large-scale distribution centers to serve major geographic regions of the world market (e.g., North America, Latin America, Europe and the Middle East, and the Asia-Pacific region).

- *Sizable learning and experience benefits are associated with performing an activity.* In some industries, learning-curve effects can allow a manufacturer to lower unit costs, boost quality, or master a new technology *more quickly* by concentrating production in a few locations. The key to riding down the learning curve is to concentrate production in a few locations to increase the cumulative volume at a plant (and thus the experience of the plant's workforce) as rapidly as possible.

- *Certain locations have superior resources, allow better coordination of related activities, or offer other valuable advantages.* Companies often locate a research unit or a sophisticated production facility in a particular country to take advantage of its pool of technically trained personnel. Adidas located its first robotic "speedfactory" in Germany to benefit from its superior technological resources and to allow greater oversight from the company's headquarters (which are in Germany). Where just-in-time inventory practices yield big cost savings and/or where an assembly firm has long-term partnering arrangements with its key suppliers, parts manufacturing plants may be clustered around final-assembly plants. A customer service center or sales office may be opened in a particular country to help cultivate strong relationships with pivotal customers located nearby. Airbus established a major assembly site for their commercial aircraft in Alabama since the United States is a major market.

When to Disperse Activities across Many Locations   In some instances, dispersing activities across locations is more advantageous than concentrating them. Buyer-related activities—such as distribution, marketing, and after-sale service—usually must take place close to buyers. This makes it necessary to physically locate the capability to perform such activities in every country or region where a firm has major customers. For example, firms that make mining and oil-drilling equipment maintain operations in many locations around the world to support customers' needs for speedy equipment repair and technical assistance. Large public accounting firms have offices in numerous countries to serve the foreign operations of their international corporate clients. Dispersing activities to many locations is also competitively important when high transportation costs, diseconomies of large size, and trade barriers make it too expensive to operate from a central location. Many companies distribute their products from multiple locations to shorten delivery times to customers. In addition, dispersing activities helps hedge against the risks of fluctuating exchange rates, supply interruptions (due to strikes, natural disasters, or transportation delays), and adverse political developments. Such risks are usually greater when activities are concentrated in a single location.

Even though global firms have strong reason to disperse buyer-related activities to many international locations, such activities as materials procurement, parts manufacture, finished-goods assembly, technology research, and new product development can frequently be decoupled from buyer locations and performed wherever advantage lies. Components can be made in Mexico; technology research done in Frankfurt; new products developed and tested in Phoenix; and assembly plants located in Spain, Brazil, Taiwan, or South Carolina, for example. Capital can be raised wherever it is available on the best terms.

Sharing and Transferring Resources and Capabilities across Borders to Build Competitive Advantage

When a company has competitively valuable resources and capabilities, it may be able to leverage them further by expanding internationally. If its resources retain their value in foreign contexts, then entering new foreign markets can extend the company's resource-based competitive advantage over a broader domain. For example, companies like Tiffany, Cartier, and Rolex have utilized their powerful brand names to extend their differentiation-based competitive advantages into markets far beyond their home-country origins. In each of these cases, the luxury brand name represents a valuable competitive asset that can readily be *shared* by all of the company's international stores, enabling them to attract buyers and gain a higher degree of market penetration over a wider geographic area than would otherwise be possible.

Another way for a company to extend its competitive advantage internationally is to *transfer* technological know-how or other important resources and capabilities from its operations in one country to its operations in other countries. For instance, if a company discovers ways to assemble a product faster and more cost-effectively at one plant, then that know-how can be transferred to its assembly plants in other countries. Whirlpool's efforts to link its product R&D and manufacturing operations in North America, Latin America, Europe, and Asia allowed it to accelerate the discovery of innovative appliance features, coordinate the introduction of these features in the appliance products marketed in different countries, and create a cost-efficient worldwide supply chain. Whirlpool's conscious efforts to integrate and coordinate its various operations around the world have helped it achieve operational excellence and speed product innovations to market. Walmart is expanding its international operations with a strategy that involves transferring its considerable resource capabilities in distribution and discount retailing to its retail units in 28 foreign countries.

Cross-border sharing or transferring resources and capabilities provides a cost-effective way for a company to leverage its core competencies more fully and extend its competitive advantages into a wider array of geographic markets. The cost of sharing or transferring already developed resources and capabilities across country borders is low in comparison to the time and considerable expense it takes to create them. Moreover, deploying them abroad spreads the fixed development costs over a greater volume of unit sales, thus contributing to low unit costs and a potential cost-based competitive advantage in recently entered geographic markets. Even if the shared or transferred resources or capabilities have to be adapted to local-market conditions, this can usually be done at low additional cost.

Consider the case of Walt Disney's theme parks as an example. The success of the theme parks in the United States derives in part from core resources such as the Disney brand name and characters like Mickey Mouse that have universal appeal and worldwide recognition. These resources can be freely shared with new theme parks as Disney expands internationally. Disney can also replicate its theme parks in new countries cost-effectively since it has already borne the costs of developing its core resources, park attractions, basic park design, and operating capabilities. The cost of replicating its theme parks abroad is relatively low, even if the parks need to be adapted to a variety of local country conditions. Thus, in establishing Disney parks in Tokyo, Paris, Hong Kong, and Shanghai, Disney has been able to leverage the differentiation advantage conferred by resources such as the Disney name and the park attractions. And by moving into new foreign markets, it has augmented its competitive advantage further through the efficiency gains that come from cross-border resource sharing and low-cost capability transfer and business model replication.

Sharing and transferring resources and capabilities across country borders may also contribute to the development of broader or deeper competencies and capabilities—helping a company achieve *dominating depth* in some competitively valuable area. For example, the reputation for quality that Honda established worldwide began in motorcycles but enabled the company to command a position in both automobiles and outdoor power equipment in multiple-country markets. A one-country customer base is often too small to support the resource buildup needed to achieve such depth; this is particularly true in a developing or protected market, where competitively powerful resources are not required. By deploying capabilities across a larger international domain, a company can gain the experience needed to upgrade them to a higher performance standard. And by facing a more challenging set of international competitors, a company may be spurred to develop a stronger set of competitive capabilities. Moreover, by entering international markets, firms may be able to augment their capability set by learning from international rivals, cooperative partners, or acquisition targets.

However, cross-border resource sharing and transfers of capabilities are not guaranteed recipes for competitive success. For example, whether a resource or capability can confer a competitive advantage abroad depends on the conditions of rivalry in each particular market. If the rivals in a foreign-country market have superior resources and capabilities, then an entering firm may find itself at a competitive disadvantage even if it has a resource-based advantage domestically and can transfer the resources at low cost. In addition, since lifestyles and buying habits differ internationally, resources and capabilities that are valuable in one country may not have value in another. Sometimes a popular or well-regarded brand in one country turns out to have little competitive clout against local brands in other countries.

Benefiting from Cross-Border Coordination

Companies that compete on an international basis have another source of competitive advantage relative to their purely domestic rivals: They are able to benefit from coordinating activities across different countries' domains.[16] For example, an international manufacturer can shift production from a plant in one country to a plant in another to take advantage of exchange rate fluctuations, to cope with components shortages, or to profit from changing wage rates or energy costs. Production schedules can be coordinated worldwide; shipments can be diverted from one distribution center to another if sales rise unexpectedly in one place and fall in another. By coordinating their activities, international companies may also be able to enhance their leverage with host-country governments or respond adaptively to changes in tariffs and quotas. Efficiencies can also be achieved by shifting workloads from where they are unusually heavy to locations where personnel are underutilized.

CROSS-BORDER STRATEGIC MOVES

While international competitors can employ any of the offensive and defensive moves discussed in Chapter 6, there are two types of strategic moves that are particularly suited for companies competing internationally. The first is an offensive move that an international competitor is uniquely positioned to make, due to the fact that it may have a strong or protected market position in more than one country. The second type of move is a type of defensive action involving multiple markets.

Waging a Strategic Offensive

CORE CONCEPT

Cross-market subsidization—supporting competitive offensives in one market with resources and profits diverted from operations in another market—can be a powerful competitive weapon.

One advantage to being an international competitor is the possibility of having more than one significant and possibly protected source of profits. This may provide the company with the financial strength to engage in strategic offensives in selected country markets. The added financial capability afforded by multiple profit sources gives an international competitor the financial strength to wage an offensive campaign against a domestic competitor whose only source of profit is its home market. The international company has the flexibility of lowballing its prices or launching high-cost marketing campaigns in the domestic company's home market and grabbing market share at the domestic company's expense. Razor-thin margins or even losses in these markets can be subsidized with the healthy profits earned in its markets abroad—a practice called **cross-market subsidization.**

The international company can adjust the depth of its price cutting to move in and capture market share quickly, or it can shave prices slightly to make gradual market inroads (perhaps over a decade or more) so as not to threaten domestic firms precipitously and trigger protectionist government actions. If the domestic company retaliates with matching price cuts or increased marketing expenses, it thereby exposes its entire revenue stream and profit base to erosion; its profits can be squeezed substantially and its competitive strength sapped, even if it is the domestic market leader.

> A company is said to be *dumping* when it sells its goods in foreign markets at prices that are
> 1. well below the prices at which it normally sells them in its home market or
> 2. well below its full costs per unit.

When taken to the extreme, cut-rate pricing attacks by international competitors may draw charges of unfair "dumping." A company is said to be *dumping* when it sells its goods in foreign markets at prices that are (1) well below the prices at which it normally sells them in its home market or (2) well below its full costs per unit. Almost all governments can be expected to retaliate against perceived dumping practices by imposing special tariffs on goods being imported from the countries of the guilty companies. Indeed, as the trade among nations has mushroomed over the past 10 years, most governments have joined the World Trade Organization (WTO), which promotes fair trade practices among nations and actively polices dumping. Companies deemed guilty of dumping frequently come under pressure from their own government to cease and desist, especially if the tariffs adversely affect innocent companies based in the same country or if the advent of special tariffs raises the specter of an international trade war.

Defending against International Rivals

Cross-border tactics involving multiple country markets can also be used as a means of defending against the strategic moves of rivals with multiple profitable markets of their own. If a company finds itself under competitive attack by an international rival in one country market, one way to respond is to conduct a counterattack against the rival in one of its key markets in a different country—preferably where the rival is least protected and has the most to lose. This is a possible option when rivals compete against one another in much the same markets around the world and engage in *multimarket competition.*

> *Multimarket competition* refers to a situation where rivals compete against one another in many of the same markets.

For companies with at least one major market, having a presence in a rival's key markets can be enough to deter the rival from making aggressive attacks. The reason for this is that the combination of market presence in the rival's key markets and a highly profitable market elsewhere can send a signal to the rival that the company could quickly ramp up production (funded by the profit center) to mount a competitive counterattack if the rival attacks one of the company's key markets.

> **CORE** CONCEPT
>
> When the same companies compete against one another in multiple geographic markets, the threat of cross-border counterattacks may be enough to encourage **mutual restraint** among international rivals.

When international rivals compete against one another in multiple-country markets, this type of deterrence effect can restrain them from taking aggressive action against one another, due to the fear of a retaliatory response that might escalate the battle into a cross-border competitive war. **Mutual restraint** of this sort tends to stabilize the competitive position of multimarket rivals against one another. And while it may prevent each firm from making any major market share gains at the expense of its rival, it also protects against costly competitive battles that would be likely to erode the profitability of both companies without any compensating gain.

STRATEGIES FOR COMPETING IN THE MARKETS OF DEVELOPING COUNTRIES

● LO 7-6

Identify the unique characteristics of competing in developing-country markets.

Companies racing for global leadership have to consider competing in developing-economy markets like China, India, Brazil, Indonesia, Thailand, Poland, Mexico, and Russia—countries where the business risks are considerable but where the opportunities for growth are huge, especially as their economies develop and living standards climb toward levels in the industrialized world.[17] In today's world, a company that aspires to international market leadership (or to sustained rapid growth) cannot ignore the market opportunities or the base of technical and managerial talent such countries offer. For example, in 2018, China was the world's second-largest economy (behind the United States), based on the purchasing power of its population of over 1.4 billion people. China's growth in demand for consumer goods has made it the fifth largest market for luxury goods, with sales greater than those in developed markets such as Germany, Spain, and the United Kingdom. Thus, no company that aspires to global market leadership can afford to ignore the strategic importance of establishing competitive market positions in the so-called BRIC countries (Brazil, Russia, India, and China), as well as in other parts of the Asia-Pacific region, Latin America, and eastern Europe.

Tailoring products to fit market conditions in developing countries, however, often involves more than making minor product changes and becoming more familiar with local cultures. McDonald's has had to offer vegetable burgers in parts of Asia and to rethink its prices, which are often high by local standards and affordable only by the well-to-do. Kellogg has struggled to introduce its cereals successfully because consumers in many less developed countries do not eat cereal for breakfast. Single-serving packages of detergents, shampoos, pickles, cough syrup, and cooking oils are very popular in India because they allow buyers to conserve cash by purchasing only what they need immediately. Thus, many companies find that trying to employ a strategy akin to that used in the markets of developed countries is hazardous.[18] Experimenting with some, perhaps many, local twists is usually necessary to find a strategy combination that works.

Strategy Options for Competing in Developing-Country Markets

There are several options for tailoring a company's strategy to fit the sometimes unusual or challenging circumstances presented in developing-country markets:

- *Prepare to compete on the basis of low price.* Consumers in developing markets are often highly focused on price, which can give low-cost local competitors the edge unless a company can find ways to attract buyers with bargain prices as well as better products. For example, in order to enter the market for laundry detergents in India, Unilever had to develop a low-cost detergent (named Wheel), construct new low-cost production facilities, package the detergent in single-use amounts so that it could be sold at a very low unit price, distribute the product to local merchants by handcarts, and craft an economical marketing campaign that included painted signs on buildings and demonstrations near stores. The new brand quickly captured $100 million in sales and by 2014 was the top detergent brand in India-based dollar sales. Unilever replicated the strategy in India with low-priced packets of shampoos and deodorants and in South America with a detergent brand-named Ala.

- *Modify aspects of the company's business model to accommodate the unique local circumstances of developing countries.* For instance, Honeywell had sold industrial products and services for more than 100 years outside the United States and Europe using a foreign subsidiary model that focused international activities on sales only. When Honeywell entered China, it discovered that industrial customers in that country considered how many key jobs foreign companies created in China, in addition to the quality and price of the product or service when making purchasing decisions. Honeywell added about 150 engineers, strategists, and marketers in China to demonstrate its commitment to bolstering the Chinese economy. Honeywell replicated its "East for East" strategy when it entered the market for industrial products and services in India. Within 10 years of Honeywell establishing operations in China and three years of expanding into India, the two emerging markets accounted for 30 percent of the firm's worldwide growth.

- *Try to change the local market to better match the way the company does business elsewhere.* An international company often has enough market clout to drive major changes in the way a local country market operates. When Japan's Suzuki entered India, it triggered a quality revolution among Indian auto parts manufacturers. Local component suppliers teamed up with Suzuki's vendors in Japan and worked with Japanese experts to produce higher-quality products. Over the next two decades, Indian companies became proficient in making top-notch components for vehicles, won more prizes for quality than companies in any country other than Japan, and broke into the global market as suppliers to many automakers in Asia and other parts of the world. Mahindra and Mahindra, one of India's premier automobile manufacturers, has been recognized by a number of organizations for its product quality. Among its most noteworthy awards was its number-one ranking by J.D. Power Asia Pacific for new-vehicle overall quality.

- *Stay away from developing markets where it is impractical or uneconomical to modify the company's business model to accommodate local circumstances.* Home Depot expanded successfully into Mexico, but it has avoided entry into other developing countries because its value proposition of good quality, low prices, and attentive customer service relies on (1) good highways and logistical systems to minimize store inventory costs, (2) employee stock ownership to help motivate store personnel to provide good customer service, and (3) high labor costs for housing construction and home repairs that encourage homeowners to engage in do-it-yourself projects. Relying on these factors in North American markets has worked spectacularly for Home Depot, but the company found that it could not count on these factors in China, from which it withdrew in 2012.

Company experiences in entering developing markets like Brazil, Russia, India, and China indicate that profitability seldom comes quickly or easily. Building a market for the company's products can often turn into a long-term process that involves reeducation of consumers, sizable investments in advertising to alter tastes and buying habits, and upgrades of the local infrastructure (transportation systems, distribution channels, etc.). In such cases, a company must be patient, work within the system to improve the infrastructure, and lay the foundation for generating sizable revenues and profits once conditions are ripe for market takeoff.

> Profitability in developing markets rarely comes quickly or easily—new entrants have to adapt their business models to local conditions, which may not always be possible.

DEFENDING AGAINST GLOBAL GIANTS: STRATEGIES FOR LOCAL COMPANIES IN DEVELOPING COUNTRIES

If opportunity-seeking, resource-rich international companies are looking to enter developing-country markets, what strategy options can local companies use to survive? As it turns out, the prospects for local companies facing global giants are by no means grim. Studies of local companies in developing markets have disclosed five strategies that have proved themselves in defending against globally competitive companies[19]:

1. *Develop business models that exploit shortcomings in local distribution networks or infrastructure.* In many instances, the extensive collection of resources possessed by the global giants is of little help in building a presence in developing markets. The lack of well-established local wholesaler and distributor networks, telecommunication systems, consumer banking, or media necessary for advertising makes it difficult for large internationals to migrate business models proved in developed markets to emerging markets. Emerging markets sometimes favor local companies whose managers are familiar with the local language and culture and are skilled in selecting large numbers of conscientious employees to carry out labor-intensive tasks. Shanda, a Chinese producer of massively multiplayer online role-playing games (MMORPGs), overcame China's lack of an established credit card network by selling prepaid access cards through local merchants. The company's focus on online games also protects it from shortcomings in China's software piracy laws. An India-based electronics company carved out a market niche for itself by developing an all-in-one business machine, designed especially for India's millions of small shopkeepers, that tolerates the country's frequent power outages.

2. *Utilize keen understanding of local customer needs and preferences to create customized products or services.* When developing-country markets are largely made up of customers with strong local needs, a good strategy option is to concentrate on customers who prefer a local touch and to accept the loss of the customers attracted to global brands.[20] A local company may be able to astutely exploit its local orientation—its familiarity with local preferences, its expertise in traditional products, its long-standing customer relationships. A small Middle Eastern cell phone manufacturer competes successfully against industry giants Samsung, Apple, Nokia, and Motorola by selling a model designed especially for Muslims—it is loaded with the Koran, alerts people at prayer times, and is equipped with a compass that points them toward Mecca. Shenzhen-based Tencent has become the leader in instant messaging in China through its unique understanding of Chinese behavior and culture.

3. *Take advantage of aspects of the local workforce with which large international companies may be unfamiliar.* Local companies that lack the technological capabilities of foreign entrants may be able to rely on their better understanding of the local labor force to offset any disadvantage. Focus Media is China's largest outdoor advertising firm and has relied on low-cost labor to update its more than 170,000 LCD displays and billboards in over 90 cities in a low-tech manner, while international companies operating in China use electronically networked screens that

allow messages to be changed remotely. Focus uses an army of employees who ride to each display by bicycle to change advertisements with programming contained on a USB flash drive or DVD. Indian information technology firms such as Infosys Technologies and Satyam Computer Services have been able to keep their personnel costs lower than those of international competitors EDS and Accenture because of their familiarity with local labor markets. While the large internationals have focused recruiting efforts in urban centers like Bangalore and Delhi, driving up engineering and computer science salaries in such cities, local companies have shifted recruiting efforts to second-tier cities that are unfamiliar to foreign firms.

4. *Use acquisition and rapid-growth strategies to better defend against expansion-minded internationals.* With the growth potential of developing markets such as China, Indonesia, and Brazil obvious to the world, local companies must attempt to develop scale and upgrade their competitive capabilities as quickly as possible to defend against the stronger international's arsenal of resources. Most successful companies in developing markets have pursued mergers and acquisitions at a rapid-fire pace to build first a nationwide and then an international presence. Hindalco, India's largest aluminum producer, has followed just such a path to achieve its ambitions for global dominance. By acquiring companies in India first, it gained enough experience and confidence to eventually acquire much larger foreign companies with world-class capabilities.[21] When China began to liberalize its foreign trade policies, Lenovo (the Chinese PC maker) realized that its long-held position of market dominance in China could not withstand the onslaught of new international entrants such as Dell and HP. Its acquisition of IBM's PC business allowed Lenovo to gain rapid access to IBM's globally recognized PC brand, its R&D capability, and its existing distribution in developed countries. This has allowed Lenovo not only to hold its own against the incursion of global giants into its home market but also to expand into new markets around the world.[22]

5. *Transfer company expertise to cross-border markets and initiate actions to contend on an international level.* When a company from a developing country has resources and capabilities suitable for competing in other country markets, launching initiatives to transfer its expertise to foreign markets becomes a viable strategic option. Televisa, Mexico's largest media company, used its expertise in Spanish culture and linguistics to become the world's most prolific producer of Spanish-language soap operas. By continuing to upgrade its capabilities and learn from its experience in foreign markets, a company can sometimes transform itself into one capable of competing on a worldwide basis, as an emerging global giant. Sundaram Fasteners of India began its foray into foreign markets as a supplier of radiator caps to General Motors—an opportunity it pursued when GM first decided to outsource the production of this part. As a participant in GM's supplier network, the company learned about emerging technical standards, built its capabilities, and became one of the first Indian companies to achieve QS 9000 quality certification. With the expertise it gained and its recognition for meeting quality standards, Sundaram was then able to pursue opportunities to supply automotive parts in Japan and Europe.

Illustration Capsule 7.3 discusses the strategy behind the success of WeChat (China's most popular messenger app), in keeping out international social media rivals.

WeChat's Strategy for Defending against International Social Media Giants in China

WeChat, a Chinese social media and messenger app similar to Whatsapp, allows users to chat, post photos, shop online, and share information as well as music. It has continued to add new features, such as WeChat Games and WePay, which allow users to send money electronically, much like Venmo. The company now serves more than a billion active users, a testament to the success of its strategy.

WeChat has also had incredible success keeping out international rivals. Due to censorship and regulations in China, Chinese social media companies have an inherent advantage over foreign competitors. However, this is not why WeChat has become an indispensable part of Chinese life.

WeChat has been able to surpass international rivals because, by better understanding Chinese customer needs, it can anticipate their desires. WeChat added features that allow users to check traffic cameras during rush hour, purchase tickets to movies, and book doctor appointments all on the app. Booking appointments with doctors is a feature that is wildly popular with the Chinese customer base due to common scheduling difficulties. Essentially, WeChat created its own distribution network for sought after information and goods in busy Chinese cities.

WeChat also has an understanding of local customs that international rivals can't match. In order to promote WePay, WeChat created a Chinese New Year lottery-like promotion in which users could win virtual "red envelopes" on the app. Red envelopes of money are traditionally given on Chinese New Year as presents. WePay was able to grow users from 30 to 100 million in the month following the

BigTunaOnline/Shutterstock

promotion due to the popularity of the New Year's feature. By 2020, many of WeChat's over one billion active users were also using WePay. WeChat continues to allow users to send red envelopes and has continued New Year's promotions in subsequent years with success. Even Chinese companies have been bested by WeChat. Rival founder of Alibaba, Jack Ma, admitted the promotion put WeChat ahead of his company, saying it was a "pearl harbor attack" on his company. Chinese tech experts noted that the promotion was Ma's nightmare because it pushed WeChat to the forefront of Chinese person-to-person payments.

WeChat's strategy of continually developing new features also keeps the competition at bay. As China's "App for Everything," it now permeates all walks of life in China in a way that will likely continue to keep foreign competitors out.

Note: Developed with Meaghan I. Haugh.

Sources: Guilford, Gwynn. "WeChat's Little Red Envelopes Are Brilliant Marketing for Mobile Payments." *Quartz,* January 29, 2014; Pasternack, Alex. "How Social Cash Made WeChat the App for Everything," *Fast Company,* January 3, 2017; "WeChat's World," *The Economist,* August 6, 2016; Stanciu, Tudor. "Why WeChat City Services Is a Game-Changing Move for Smartphone Adoption," *TechCrunch,* April 24, 2015.

KEY POINTS

1. Competing in international markets allows a company to (1) gain access to new customers; (2) achieve lower costs through greater economies of scale, learning, and increased purchasing power; (3) gain access to low-cost inputs of production; (4) further exploit its core competencies; and (5) gain access to resources and capabilities located outside the company's domestic market.

2. Strategy making is more complex for five reasons: (1) Different countries have *home-country advantages* in different industries; (2) there are location-based advantages to performing different value chain activities in different parts of the world; (3) varying political and economic risks make the business climate of some countries more favorable than others; (4) companies face the risk of adverse shifts in exchange rates when operating in foreign countries; and (5) differences in buyer tastes and preferences present a conundrum concerning the trade-off between customizing and standardizing products and services.

3. The strategies of firms that expand internationally are usually grounded in home-country advantages concerning demand conditions; factor conditions; related and supporting industries; and firm strategy, structure, and rivalry, as described by the Diamond of National Competitive Advantage framework.

4. There are five strategic options for entering foreign markets. These include maintaining a home-country production base and *exporting* goods to foreign markets, *licensing* foreign firms to produce and distribute the company's products abroad, employing a *franchising* strategy, establishing a foreign *subsidiary via an acquisition or greenfield venture,* and using *strategic alliances or other collaborative partnerships.*

5. A company must choose among three alternative approaches for competing internationally: (1) a *multidomestic strategy*—a *think-local, act-local* approach to crafting international strategy; (2) a *global strategy*—a *think-global, act-global* approach; and (3) a combination *think-global, act-local* approach, known as a *transnational strategy.* A multidomestic strategy (think local, act local) is appropriate for companies that must vary their product offerings and competitive approaches from country to country in order to accommodate different buyer preferences and market conditions. The global strategy (think global, act global) works best when there are substantial cost benefits to be gained from taking a standardized, globally integrated approach and there is little need for local responsiveness. A transnational strategy (think global, act local) is called for when there is a high need for local responsiveness as well as substantial benefits from taking a globally integrated approach. In this approach, a company strives to employ the same basic competitive strategy in all markets but still customizes its product offering and some aspect of its operations to fit local market circumstances.

6. There are three general ways in which a firm can gain competitive advantage (or offset domestic disadvantages) in international markets. One way involves locating various value chain activities among nations in a manner that lowers costs or achieves greater product differentiation. A second way draws on an international competitor's ability to extend its competitive advantage by cost-effectively sharing, replicating, or transferring its most valuable resources and capabilities across borders. A third looks for benefits from cross-border coordination that are unavailable to domestic-only competitors.

7. Two types of strategic moves are particularly suited for companies competing internationally. The first involves waging strategic offenses in international markets through *cross-subsidization*—a practice of supporting competitive offensives in one

market with resources and profits diverted from operations in another market. The second is a defensive move used to encourage *mutual restraint* among competitors when there is international *multimarket competition* by signaling that each company has the financial capability for mounting a strong counterattack if threatened. For companies with at least one highly profitable or well defended market, having a presence in a rival's key markets can be enough to deter the rival from making aggressive attacks.

8. Companies racing for global leadership have to consider competing in developing markets like the BRIC countries—Brazil, Russia, India, and China—where the business risks are considerable but the opportunities for growth are huge. To succeed in these markets, companies often have to (1) compete on the basis of low price, (2) modify aspects of the company's business model to accommodate local circumstances, and/or (3) try to change the local market to better match the way the company does business elsewhere. Profitability is unlikely to come quickly or easily in developing markets, typically because of the investments needed to alter buying habits and tastes, the increased political and economic risk, and/or the need for infrastructure upgrades. And there may be times when a company should simply stay away from certain developing markets until conditions for entry are better suited to its business model and strategy.

9. Local companies in developing-country markets can seek to compete against large international companies by (1) developing business models that exploit shortcomings in local distribution networks or infrastructure, (2) utilizing a superior understanding of local customer needs and preferences or local relationships, (3) taking advantage of competitively important qualities of the local workforce with which large international companies may be unfamiliar, (4) using acquisition strategies and rapid-growth strategies to better defend against expansion-minded international companies, or (5) transferring company expertise to cross-border markets and initiating actions to compete on an international level.

ASSURANCE OF LEARNING EXERCISES

LO 7-1, LO 7-3   1. L'Oréal markets over 500 brands of products in all sectors of the beauty business in 140 countries. The company's international strategy involves manufacturing these products in 43 plants located around the world. L'Oréal's international strategy is discussed in its operations section of the company's website (www .loreal.com/careers/who-you-can-be/operations) and in its press releases, annual reports, and presentations. Why has the company chosen to pursue a foreign subsidiary strategy? Are there strategic advantages to global sourcing and production in the cosmetics, fragrances, and hair care products industry relative to an export strategy?

connect

LO 7-1, LO 7-3   2. Alliances, joint ventures, and mergers with foreign companies are widely used as a means of entering foreign markets. Such arrangements have many purposes, including learning about unfamiliar environments, and the opportunity to access the complementary resources and capabilities of a foreign partner. Illustration Capsule 7.1 provides an example of how Walgreens used a strategy of entering foreign markets via alliance, followed by a merger with the same entity. What was this entry strategy designed to achieve, and why would this make sense for a company like Walgreens?

3. Assume you are in charge of developing the strategy for an international company selling products in some 50 different countries around the world. One of the issues you face is whether to employ a multidomestic strategy, a global strategy, or a transnational strategy.

    LO 7-2, LO 7-4

    a. If your company's product is mobile phones, which of these strategies do you think it would make better strategic sense to employ? Why?

    b. If your company's product is dry soup mixes and canned soups, would a multidomestic strategy seem to be more advisable than a global strategy or a transnational strategy? Why or why not?

    c. If your company's product is large home appliances such as washing machines, ranges, ovens, and refrigerators, would it seem to make more sense to pursue a multidomestic strategy, a global strategy, or a transnational strategy? Why?

4. Using your university library's business research resources and Internet sources, identify and discuss three key strategies that General Motors is using to compete in China.

    LO 7-5, LO 7-6

EXERCISES FOR SIMULATION PARTICIPANTS

The following questions are for simulation participants whose companies operate in an international market arena. If your company competes only in a single country, then skip the questions in this section.

1. To what extent, if any, have you and your co-managers adapted your company's strategy to take shifting exchange rates into account? In other words, have you undertaken any actions to try to minimize the impact of adverse shifts in exchange rates?

    LO 7-2

2. To what extent, if any, have you and your co-managers adapted your company's strategy to take geographic differences in import tariffs or import duties into account?

    LO 7-2

3. What are the attributes of each of the following approaches to competing in international markets?

    • Multidomestic or think-local, act-local approach.

    • Global or think-global, act-global approach.

    • Transnational or think-global, act-local approach.

    Explain your answer and indicate two or three chief elements of your company's strategy for competing in two or more different geographic regions.

ENDNOTES

[1] Sidney G. Winter and Gabriel Szulanski, "Getting It Right the Second Time," *Harvard Business Review* 80, no. 1 (January 2002), pp. 62–69.
[2] P. Dussauge, B. Garrette, and W. Mitchell, "Learning from Competing Partners: Outcomes and Durations of Scale and Link Alliances in Europe, North America and Asia," *Strategic Management Journal* 21, no. 2 (February 2000), pp. 99–126; K. W. Glaister and P. J. Buckley, "Strategic Motives for International Alliance Formation," *Journal of Management Studies* 33, no. 3 (May 1996), pp. 301–332.
[3] Michael E. Porter, "The Competitive Advantage of Nations," *Harvard Business Review,* March–April 1990, pp. 73–93.
[4] Tom Mitchell and Avantika Chilkoti, "China Car Sales Accelerate Away from US and Brazil in 2013," *Financial Times,* January 9, 2014, www.ft.com/cms/s/0/8c649078-78f8-11e3-b381-00144feabdc0.html#axzz2rpEqjkZO.
[5] U.S. Department of Labor, Bureau of Labor Statistics, "International Comparisons of Hourly Compensation Costs in Manufacturing 2012," August 9, 2013. (The numbers for India and China are estimates.)

[6] Sangwon Yoon, "South Korea Targets Internet Addicts; 2 Million Hooked," *Valley News,* April 25, 2010, p. C2.

[7] Joel Bleeke and David Ernst, "The Way to Win in Cross-Border Alliances," *Harvard Business Review* 69, no. 6 (November–December 1991), pp. 127–133; Gary Hamel, Yves L. Doz, and C. K. Prahalad, "Collaborate with Your Competitors–and Win," *Harvard Business Review* 67, no. 1 (January–February 1989), pp. 134–135.

[8] K. W. Glaister and P. J. Buckley, "Strategic Motives for International Alliance Formation," *Journal of Management Studies* 33, no. 3 (May 1996), pp. 301–332.

[9] Jeffrey H. Dyer, Prashant Kale, and Harbir Singh, "When to Ally and When to Acquire," *Harvard Business Review* 82, no. 7–8 (July–August 2004).

[10] Yves Doz and Gary Hamel, *Alliance Advantage: The Art of Creating Value through Partnering* (Harvard Business School Press, 1998); Rosabeth Moss Kanter, "Collaborative Advantage: The Art of the Alliance," *Harvard Business Review* 72, no. 4 (July–August 1994), pp. 96–108.

[11] Jeremy Main, "Making Global Alliances Work," *Fortune,* December 19, 1990, p. 125.

[12] C. K. Prahalad and Kenneth Lieberthal, "The End of Corporate Imperialism," *Harvard Business Review* 81, no. 8 (August 2003), pp. 109–117.

[13] Pankaj Ghemawat, "Managing Differences: The Central Challenge of Global Strategy," *Harvard Business Review* 85, no. 3 (March 2007).

[14] C. A. Bartlett and S. Ghoshal, *Managing across Borders: The Transnational Solution,* 2nd ed. (Boston: Harvard Business School Press, 1998).

[15] Lynn S. Paine, "The China Rules," *Harvard Business Review* 88, no. 6 (June 2010), pp. 103–108.

[16] C. K. Prahalad and Yves L. Doz, *The Multinational Mission: Balancing Local Demands and Global Vision* (New York: Free Press, 1987).

[17] David J. Arnold and John A. Quelch, "New Strategies in Emerging Markets," *Sloan Management Review* 40, no. 1 (Fall 1998), pp. 7–20.

[18] Tarun Khanna, Krishna G. Palepu, and Jayant Sinha, "Strategies That Fit Emerging Markets," *Harvard Business Review* 83, no. 6 (June 2005), p. 63; Arindam K. Bhattacharya and David C. Michael, "How Local Companies Keep Multinationals at Bay," *Harvard Business Review* 86, no. 3 (March 2008), pp. 94–95.

[19] Tarun Khanna and Krishna G. Palepu, "Emerging Giants: Building World-Class Companies in Developing Countries," *Harvard Business Review* 84, no. 10 (October 2006), pp. 60–69.

[20] Niroj Dawar and Tony Frost, "Competing with Giants: Survival Strategies for Local Companies in Emerging Markets," *Harvard Business Review* 77, no. 1 (January–February 1999), p. 122; Guitz Ger, "Localizing in the Global Village: Local Firms Competing in Global Markets," *California Management Review* 41, no. 4 (Summer 1999), pp. 64–84.

[21] N. Kumar, "How Emerging Giants Are Rewriting the Rules of M&A," *Harvard Business Review,* May 2009, pp. 115–121.

[22] H. Rui and G. Yip, "Foreign Acquisitions by Chinese Firms: A Strategic Intent Perspective," *Journal of World Business* 43 (2008), pp. 213–226.

chapter **8**

Corporate Strategy

Diversification and the Multibusiness Company

Learning Objectives

After reading this chapter, you should be able to:

LO 8-1   Explain when and how business diversification can enhance shareholder value.

LO 8-2   Describe how related diversification strategies can produce cross-business strategic fit capable of delivering competitive advantage.

LO 8-3   Identify the merits and risks of unrelated diversification strategies.

LO 8-4   Use the analytic tools for evaluating a company's diversification strategy.

LO 8-5   Understand the four main corporate strategy options a diversified company can employ to improve company performance.

Richard Schneider/Getty Images

I suppose my formula might be: dream, diversify, and never miss an angle.

Walt Disney—Founder of the Walt Disney Company

Make winners out of every business in your company. Don't carry losers.

Jack Welch—Legendary CEO of General Electric

Fit between a parent and its businesses is a two-edged sword: A good fit can create value; a bad one can destroy it.

Andrew Campbell, Michael Goold, and Marcus Alexander—Academics, authors, and consultants

This chapter moves up one level in the strategy-making hierarchy, from strategy making in a single-business enterprise to strategy making in a diversified, multibusiness enterprise. Because a diversified company is a collection of individual businesses, the strategy-making task is more complicated. In a one-business company, managers have to come up with a plan for competing successfully in only a single industry environment—the result is what Chapter 2 labeled as *business strategy* (or *business-level strategy*). But in a diversified company, the strategy-making challenge involves assessing multiple industry environments and developing a *set of business strategies,* one for each industry arena in which the diversified company operates. And top executives at a diversified company must still go one step further and devise a companywide (or *corporate*) strategy for improving the performance of the company's overall business lineup and for making a rational whole out of its diversified collection of individual businesses.

In the first part of this chapter, we describe what crafting a diversification strategy entails, when and why diversification makes good strategic sense, the various approaches to diversifying a company's business lineup, and the pros and cons of related versus unrelated diversification strategies. The second part of the chapter looks at how to evaluate the attractiveness of a diversified company's business lineup, how to decide whether it has a good diversification strategy, and the strategic options for improving a diversified company's future performance.

WHAT DOES CRAFTING A DIVERSIFICATION STRATEGY ENTAIL?

The task of crafting a diversified company's overall *corporate strategy* falls squarely in the lap of top-level executives and involves three distinct facets:

1. *Picking new industries to enter and deciding on the means of entry.* Pursuing a diversification strategy requires that management decide which new industries to enter and then, for each new industry, whether to enter by starting a new business from the ground up, by acquiring a company already in the target industry, or by forming a joint venture or strategic alliance with another company. The choice of industries depends upon on the strategic rationale (or justification) for diversifying and the type of diversification being pursued—important issues that we discuss more fully in sections to follow.

2. *Pursuing opportunities to leverage cross-business value chain relationships, where there is strategic fit, into competitive advantage.* The task here is to determine whether there are opportunities to strengthen a diversified company's businesses by such means as transferring competitively valuable resources and capabilities from one business to another, combining the related value chain activities of different businesses to achieve lower costs, sharing resources, such as the use of a powerful and well-respected brand name or an R&D facility, across multiple businesses, and encouraging knowledge sharing and collaborative activity among the businesses.

3. *Initiating actions to boost the combined performance of the corporation's collection of businesses.* Strategic options for improving the corporation's overall performance include (1) sticking closely with the existing business lineup and pursuing opportunities presented by these businesses, (2) broadening the scope of diversification by entering additional industries, (3) retrenching to a narrower scope of diversification by divesting either poorly performing businesses or those that no longer fit into management's long-range plans, and (4) broadly restructuring the entire company by divesting some businesses, acquiring others, and reorganizing, to put a whole new face on the company's business lineup.

The demanding and time-consuming nature of these three tasks explains why corporate executives generally refrain from becoming immersed in the details of crafting and executing business-level strategies. Rather, the normal procedure is to delegate lead responsibility for business strategy to the heads of each business, giving them the latitude to develop strategies suited to the particular industry environment in which their business operates and holding them accountable for producing good financial and strategic results.

WHEN TO CONSIDER DIVERSIFYING

As long as a company has plentiful opportunities for profitable growth in its present industry, there is no urgency to pursue diversification. But growth opportunities are often limited in mature industries and markets where buyer demand is flat or declining. In addition, changing industry conditions—new technologies, inroads being made by substitute products, fast-shifting buyer preferences, or intensifying competition—can undermine a company's ability to deliver ongoing gains in revenues and profits.

Consider, for example, what mobile phone companies and marketers of Voice over Internet Protocol (VoIP) have done to the revenues of long-distance providers such as AT&T, British Telecommunications, and NTT in Japan. Thus, diversifying into new industries always merits strong consideration whenever a single-business company encounters diminishing market opportunities and stagnating sales in its principal business.

The decision to diversify presents wide-ranging possibilities. A company can diversify into closely related businesses or into totally unrelated businesses. It can diversify its present revenue and earnings base to a small or major extent. It can move into one or two large new businesses or a greater number of small ones. It can achieve diversification by acquiring an existing company, starting up a new business from scratch, or forming a joint venture with one or more companies to enter new businesses. In every case, however, the decision to diversify must start with a strong economic justification for doing so.

BUILDING SHAREHOLDER VALUE: THE ULTIMATE JUSTIFICATION FOR DIVERSIFYING

Diversification must do more for a company than simply spread its business risk across various industries. In principle, diversification cannot be considered wise or justifiable unless it results in *added long-term economic value for shareholders*—value that shareholders cannot capture on their own by purchasing stock in companies in different industries or investing in mutual funds to spread their investments across several industries. A move to diversify into a new business stands little chance of building shareholder value without passing the following three **Tests of Corporate Advantage**[1]:

> **LO 8-1**
>
> Explain when and how business diversification can enhance shareholder value.

1. *The industry attractiveness test.* The industry to be entered through diversification must be structurally attractive (in terms of the five forces), have resource requirements that match those of the parent company, and offer good prospects for growth, profitability, and return on investment.

2. *The cost of entry test.* The cost of entering the target industry must not be so high as to exceed the potential for good profitability. A catch-22 can prevail here, however. The more attractive an industry's prospects are for growth and good long-term profitability, the more expensive it can be to enter. Entry barriers for startup companies are likely to be high in attractive industries—if barriers were low, a rush of new entrants would soon erode the potential for high profitability. And buying a well-positioned company in an appealing industry often entails a high acquisition cost that makes passing the cost of entry test less likely. Since the owners of a successful and growing company usually demand a price that reflects their business's profit prospects, it's easy for such an acquisition to fail the cost of entry test.

3. *The better-off test.* Diversifying into a new business must offer potential for the company's existing businesses and the new business to perform better together under a single corporate umbrella than they would perform operating as independent, stand-alone businesses—an effect known as **synergy.** For example, let's say that company A diversifies by purchasing company B in another industry. If A and B's consolidated profits in the years to come prove no greater than what each could have earned on its own, then A's diversification won't provide

> **CORE CONCEPT**
>
> To add shareholder value, a move to diversify into a new business must pass the three **Tests of Corporate Advantage:**
> **1.** The industry attractiveness test
> **2.** The cost of entry test
> **3.** The better-off test

> **CORE CONCEPT**
>
> Creating added value for shareholders via diversification requires building a multibusiness company in which the whole is greater than the sum of its parts; such $1 + 1 = 3$ effects are called **synergy.**

its shareholders with any added value. Company A's shareholders could have achieved the same $1 + 1 = 2$ result by merely purchasing stock in company B. Diversification does not result in added long-term value for shareholders unless it produces a $1 + 1 = 3$ effect, whereby the businesses *perform better together as part of the same firm than they could have performed as independent companies.*

Diversification moves must satisfy all three tests to grow shareholder value over the long term. Diversification moves that can pass only one or two tests are suspect.

APPROACHES TO DIVERSIFYING THE BUSINESS LINEUP

The means of entering new businesses can take any of three forms: acquisition, internal startup, or joint ventures with other companies.

Diversifying by Acquisition of an Existing Business

Acquisition is a popular means of diversifying into another industry. Not only is it quicker than trying to launch a new operation, but it also offers an effective way to hurdle such entry barriers as acquiring technological know-how, establishing supplier relationships, achieving scale economies, building brand awareness, and securing adequate distribution. Acquisitions are also commonly employed to access resources and capabilities that are complementary to those of the acquiring firm and that cannot be developed readily internally. Buying an ongoing operation allows the acquirer to move directly to the task of building a strong market position in the target industry rather than getting bogged down in trying to develop the knowledge, experience, scale of operation, and market reputation necessary for a startup entrant to become an effective competitor.

> **CORE CONCEPT**
>
> An **acquisition premium,** or control premium, is the amount by which the price offered exceeds the pre-acquisition market value or stock price of the target company.

However, acquiring an existing business can prove quite expensive. The costs of acquiring another business include not only the acquisition price but also the costs of performing the due diligence to ascertain the worth of the other company, the costs of negotiating the purchase transaction, and the costs of integrating the business into the diversified company's portfolio. If the company to be acquired is a successful company, the acquisition price will include a hefty *premium* over the preacquisition value of the company for the right to control the company. For example, the $1.2 billion that luxury fashion company Michael Kors paid to acquire luxury accessories brand Jimmy Choo included a 36.5 percent premium over Jimmy Choo's share price before being put up for sale. Premiums are paid in order to convince the shareholders and managers of the target company that it is in their financial interests to approve the deal. The average premium paid by U.S. companies over the last 15 years was more often in the 20 to 25 percent range.

While acquisitions offer an enticing means for entering a new business, many fail to deliver on their promise.[2] Realizing the potential gains from an acquisition requires a successful integration of the acquired company into the culture, systems, and structure of the acquiring firm. This can be a costly and time-consuming operation. Acquisitions can also fail to deliver long-term shareholder value if the acquirer overestimates the potential gains and pays a premium in excess of the realized gains. High integration costs and excessive price premiums are two reasons that an acquisition might fail the cost of entry test. Firms with significant experience in making acquisitions are better able to avoid these types of problems.[3]

Entering a New Line of Business through Internal Development

Achieving diversification through *internal development* involves starting a new business subsidiary from scratch. Internal development has become an increasingly important way for companies to diversify and is often referred to as **corporate venturing** or *new venture development*. Although building a new business from the ground up is generally a time-consuming and uncertain process, it avoids the pitfalls associated with entry via acquisition and may allow the firm to realize greater profits in the end. It may offer a viable means of entering a new or emerging industry where there are no good acquisition candidates.

Entering a new business via internal development, however, poses some significant hurdles. An internal new venture not only has to overcome industry entry barriers but also must invest in new production capacity, develop sources of supply, hire and train employees, build channels of distribution, grow a customer base, and so on, unless the new business is quite similar to the company's existing business. The risks associated with internal startups can be substantial, and the likelihood of failure is often high. Moreover, the culture, structures, and organizational systems of some companies may impede innovation and make it difficult for corporate entrepreneurship to flourish.

Generally, internal development of a new business has appeal only when (1) the parent company already has in-house most of the resources and capabilities it needs to piece together a new business and compete effectively; (2) there is ample time to launch the business; (3) the internal cost of entry is lower than the cost of entry via acquisition; (4) adding new production capacity will not adversely impact the supply–demand balance in the industry; and (5) incumbent firms are likely to be slow or ineffective in responding to a new entrant's efforts to crack the market.

Using Joint Ventures to Achieve Diversification

Entering a new business via a joint venture can be useful in at least three types of situations.[4] First, a joint venture is a good vehicle for pursuing an opportunity that is too complex, uneconomical, or risky for one company to pursue alone. Second, joint ventures make sense when the opportunities in a new industry require a broader range of competencies and know-how than a company can marshal on its own. Many of the opportunities in satellite-based telecommunications, biotechnology, and network-based systems that blend hardware, software, and services call for the coordinated development of complementary innovations and the tackling of an intricate web of financial, technical, political, and regulatory factors simultaneously. In such cases, pooling the resources and competencies of two or more companies is a wiser and less risky way to proceed. Third, companies sometimes use joint ventures to diversify into a new industry when the diversification move entails having operations in a foreign country. However, as discussed in Chapters 6 and 7, partnering with another company can have significant drawbacks due to the potential for conflicting objectives, disagreements over how to best operate the venture, culture clashes, and so on. Joint ventures are generally the least durable of the entry options, usually lasting only until the partners decide to go their own ways.

CORE CONCEPT

Corporate venturing (or *new venture development*) is the process of developing new businesses as an outgrowth of a company's established business operations. It is also referred to as *corporate entrepreneurship* or *intrapreneurship* since it requires entrepreneurial-like qualities within a larger enterprise.

Choosing a Mode of Entry

The choice of how best to enter a new business—whether through internal development, acquisition, or joint venture—depends on the answers to four important questions:

- Does the company have all of the resources and capabilities it requires to enter the business through internal development, or is it lacking some critical resources?
- Are there entry barriers to overcome?
- Is speed an important factor in the firm's chances for successful entry?
- Which is the least costly mode of entry, given the company's objectives?

The Question of Critical Resources and Capabilities   If a firm has all the resources it needs to start up a new business or will be able to easily purchase or lease any missing resources, it may choose to enter the business via internal development. However, if missing critical resources cannot be easily purchased or leased, a firm wishing to enter a new business must obtain these missing resources through either acquisition or joint venture. Bank of America acquired Merrill Lynch to obtain critical investment banking resources and capabilities that it lacked. The acquisition of these additional capabilities complemented Bank of America's strengths in corporate banking and opened up new business opportunities for the company. Firms often acquire other companies as a way to enter foreign markets where they lack local marketing knowledge, distribution capabilities, and relationships with local suppliers or customers. McDonald's acquisition of Burghy, Italy's only national hamburger chain, offers an example.[5] If there are no good acquisition opportunities or if the firm wants to avoid the high cost of acquiring and integrating another firm, it may choose to enter via joint venture. This type of entry mode has the added advantage of spreading the risk of entering a new business, an advantage that is particularly attractive when uncertainty is high. De Beers's joint venture with the luxury goods company LVMH provided De Beers not only with the complementary marketing capabilities it needed to enter the diamond retailing business but also with a partner to share the risk.

The Question of Entry Barriers   The second question to ask is whether entry barriers would prevent a new entrant from gaining a foothold and succeeding in the industry. If entry barriers are low and the industry is populated by small firms, internal development may be the preferred mode of entry. If entry barriers are high, the company may still be able to enter with ease if it has the requisite resources and capabilities for overcoming high barriers. For example, entry barriers due to reputational advantages may be surmounted by a diversified company with a widely known and trusted corporate name. But if the entry barriers cannot be overcome readily, then the only feasible entry route may be through acquisition of a well-established company. While entry barriers may also be overcome with a strong complementary joint venture, this mode is the more uncertain choice due to the lack of industry experience.

The Question of Speed   Speed is another determining factor in deciding how to go about entering a new business. Acquisition is a favored mode of entry when speed is of the essence, as is the case in rapidly changing industries where fast movers can secure long-term positioning advantages. Speed is important in industries where early movers gain experience-based advantages that grow ever larger over time as they move down the learning curve. It is also important in technology-based industries where there is a race to establish an industry standard or leading technological platform. But, in other cases, it can be better to enter a market after the uncertainties about technology or consumer preferences have been resolved and learn from the missteps of early entrants. In these cases, when it is more advantageous to be a second-mover, joint venture or internal development may be preferred.

The Question of Comparative Cost   The question of which mode of entry is most cost-effective is a critical one, given the need for a diversification strategy to pass the cost of entry test. Acquisition can be a high-cost mode of entry due to the need to pay a premium over the share price of the target company. When the premium is high, the price of the deal will exceed the worth of the acquired company as a stand-alone business by a substantial amount. Whether it is worth it to pay that high a price will depend on how much extra value will be created by the new combination of companies in the form of synergies. Moreover, the true cost of an acquisition must include the **transaction costs** of identifying and evaluating potential targets, negotiating a price, and completing other aspects of deal making. Often, companies pay hefty fees to investment banking firms, lawyers, and others to advise them and assist with the deal-making process. Finally, the true cost must take into account the costs of integrating the acquired company into the parent company's portfolio of businesses.

> **CORE CONCEPT**
>
> **Transaction costs** are the costs of completing a business agreement or deal, over and above the price of the deal. They can include the costs of searching for an attractive target, the costs of evaluating its worth, bargaining costs, and the costs of completing the transaction.

Joint ventures may provide a way to conserve on such entry costs. But even here, there are organizational coordination costs and transaction costs that must be considered, including settling on the terms of the arrangement. If the partnership doesn't proceed smoothly and is not founded on trust, these costs may be significant.

CHOOSING THE DIVERSIFICATION PATH: RELATED VERSUS UNRELATED BUSINESSES

Once a company decides to diversify, it faces the choice of whether to diversify into **related businesses, unrelated businesses,** or some mix of both. Businesses are said to be *related* when their value chains exhibit competitively important cross-business commonalities. By this we mean that there is a close correspondence between the businesses in terms of *how they perform* key value chain activities and *the resources and capabilities each needs* to perform those activities. The big appeal of related diversification is the opportunity to build shareholder value by leveraging these cross-business commonalities into competitive advantages for the individual businesses, thus allowing the company as a whole to perform better than just the sum of its businesses. Businesses are said to be *unrelated* when the resource requirements and key value chain activities are so dissimilar that no competitively important cross-business commonalities exist.

> **CORE CONCEPT**
>
> **Related businesses** possess competitively valuable cross-business value chain and resource commonalities; **unrelated businesses** have dissimilar value chains and resource requirements, with no competitively important cross-business commonalities at the value chain level.

The next two sections explore the ins and outs of related and unrelated diversification.

DIVERSIFICATION INTO RELATED BUSINESSES

A related diversification strategy involves building the company around businesses where there is good *strategic fit across corresponding value chain activities.* **Strategic fit** exists whenever one or more activities constituting the value chains of different businesses are sufficiently similar to present opportunities for cross-business sharing or transferring of the resources and capabilities that enable these activities.[6] That is to say, it implies the existence of competitively important cross-business commonalities. Prime examples of such opportunities include:

- *Transferring specialized expertise, technological know-how, or other competitively valuable strategic assets from one business's value chain to another's.* Google's ability to transfer software developers and other information technology specialists from other business applications to the development of its Android mobile operating system and Chrome operating system for PCs aided considerably in the success of these new internal ventures.

  - *Sharing costs between businesses by combining their related value chain activities into a single operation.* For instance, it is often feasible to manufacture the products of different businesses in a single plant, use the same warehouses for shipping and distribution, or have a single sales force for the products of different businesses if they are marketed to the same types of customers.

  - *Exploiting the common use of a well-known brand name.* For example, Yamaha's name in motorcycles gave the company instant credibility and recognition in entering the personal-watercraft business, allowing it to achieve a significant market share without spending large sums on advertising to establish a brand identity for the WaveRunner. Likewise, Apple's reputation for producing easy-to-operate computers was a competitive asset that facilitated the company's diversification into digital music players, smartphones, and connected watches.

- *Sharing other resources (besides brands) that support corresponding value chain activities across businesses.* When Disney acquired Marvel Comics, management saw to it that Marvel's iconic characters, such as Spiderman, Iron Man, and the Black Widow, were shared with many of the other Disney businesses, including its theme parks, retail stores, motion picture division, and video game business. (Disney's characters, starting with Mickey Mouse, have always been among the most valuable of its resources.) Automobile companies like Ford share resources such as their relationships with suppliers and dealer networks across their lines of business.

- *Engaging in cross-business collaboration and knowledge sharing to create new competitively valuable resources and capabilities.* Businesses performing closely related value chain activities may seize opportunities to join forces, share knowledge and talents, and collaborate to create altogether new capabilities (such as virtually defect-free assembly methods or increased ability to speed new products to market) that will be mutually beneficial in improving their competitiveness and business performance.

Related diversification is based on value chain matchups with respect to *key* value chain activities—those that play a central role in each business's strategy and that link to its industry's key success factors. Such matchups facilitate the sharing or transfer of the resources and capabilities that enable the performance of these activities and underlie each business's quest for competitive advantage. By facilitating the sharing or transferring of such important competitive assets, related diversification can elevate each business's prospects for competitive success.

The resources and capabilities that are leveraged in related diversification are **specialized resources and capabilities.** By this we mean that they have very *specific* applications; their use is restricted to a limited range of business contexts in which these applications are competitively relevant. Because they are adapted for particular applications, specialized resources and capabilities must be utilized by particular types of businesses operating in specific kinds of industries to have value; they have limited utility outside this designated range of industry and business applications. This is in contrast to **general resources and capabilities** (such as general management capabilities, human resource management capabilities, and general accounting services), which can be applied usefully across a wide range of industry and business types.

L'Oréal is the world's largest beauty products company, with almost $30 billion in revenues and a successful strategy of related diversification built on leveraging a highly specialized set of resources and capabilities. These include 18 dermatologic and cosmetic research centers, R&D capabilities and scientific knowledge concerning skin and hair care, patents and secret formulas for hair and skin care products, and robotic applications developed specifically for testing the safety of hair and skin care products. These resources and capabilities are highly valuable for businesses focused on products for human skin and hair—they are *specialized* to such applications, and, in consequence, they are of little or no value beyond this restricted range of applications. To leverage these resources in a way that maximizes their potential value, L'Oréal has diversified into cosmetics, hair care products, skin care products, and fragrances (but not food, transportation, industrial services, or any application area far from the narrow domain in which its specialized resources are competitively relevant). L'Oréal's businesses are related to one another on the basis of its value-generating specialized resources and capabilities and the cross-business linkages among the value chain activities that they enable.

Corning's most competitively valuable resources and capabilities are specialized to applications concerning fiber optics and specialty glass and ceramics. Over the course of its 165-year history, it has developed an unmatched understanding of fundamental glass science and related technologies in the field of optics. Its capabilities now span a variety of sophisticated technologies and include expertise in domains such as custom glass composition, specialty glass melting and forming, precision optics, high-end transmissive coatings, and optomechanical materials. Corning has leveraged these specialized capabilities into a position of global leadership in five related market segments: display technologies based on glass substrates; environmental technologies using ceramic substrates and filters; optical communications, providing optical fiber, cable and connectivity solutions; life sciences supporting research and drug discovery; and specialty materials employing advanced optics and specialty glass solutions. The market segments into which Corning has diversified are all related by their reliance on Corning's specialized capability set and by the many value chain activities that they have in common as a result.

General Mills has diversified into a closely related set of food businesses on the basis of its capabilities in the realm of "kitchen chemistry" and food production technologies. Its four U.S. retail divisions—meals and baking, cereal, snacks, and yogurt—include brands such as Old El Paso, Cascadian Farm Lucky Charms and General Mills brand cereals, Nature Valley, Annie's Organic, Pillsbury and Betty Crocker, and Yoplait yogurt. Earlier it had diversified into restaurant businesses on the mistaken notion that all food businesses were related. By exiting these businesses in the mid-1990s, the company was able to improve its overall profitability and strengthen its position in its remaining businesses. The lesson from its experience—and a takeaway for the managers of any diversified company—is that *it is not product relatedness that defines a well-crafted related diversification strategy*. Rather, *the businesses must be related in terms of their key value chain activities and the specialized resources and capabilities that enable these activities.*[7] An example is Citizen Watch Company, whose products appear to be different (watches, machine tools, and flat panel displays) but are related in terms of their common reliance on miniaturization know-how and advanced precision technologies.

While companies pursuing related diversification strategies may also have opportunities to share or transfer their *general* resources and capabilities (e.g., information systems; human resource management practices; accounting and tax services; budgeting, planning, and financial reporting systems; expertise in legal and regulatory affairs; and fringe-benefit management systems), *the most competitively valuable opportunities for resource sharing or transfer always come from leveraging their specialized resources and capabilities.* The reason for this is that specialized resources and capabilities drive the key value-creating activities that both connect the businesses (at points along their value chains where there is strategic fit) and link to the key success factors in the markets where they are competitively relevant. Figure 8.1 illustrates the range of opportunities to share and/or transfer specialized resources and capabilities among the value chain activities of related businesses. It is important to recognize that *even though general resources and capabilities may be also shared by multiple business units, such resource sharing alone cannot form the backbone of a strategy keyed to related diversification.* Illustration Capsule 8.1 provides examples of a few successful firms with related diversification strategies.

Identifying Cross-Business Strategic Fit along the Value Chain

Cross-business strategic fit can exist anywhere along the value chain—in R&D and technology activities, in supply chain activities and relationships with suppliers, in manufacturing, in sales and marketing, in distribution activities, or in customer service activities.[8]

FIGURE 8.1   Related Businesses Provide Opportunities to Benefit from Competitively Valuable Strategic Fit

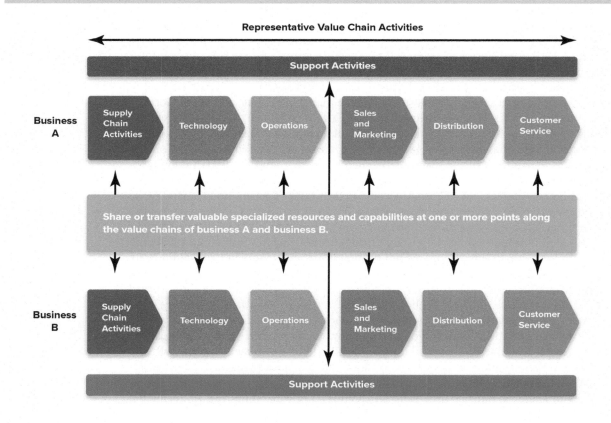

Examples of Companies Pursuing a Related Diversification Strategy

INDITEX

Inditex began as a small family business making women's clothing, but it has since evolved into one of the world's largest and most successful fashion retailers. The company is not just a retailer, however—it is involved with all aspects of producing fashion: design, manufacture, distribution, and retail. Its growth has been driven by acquisition as well as by internal growth and development. By 2020, Inditex included eight distinct brands or lines of business: Zara, Zara Home, Pull&Bear, Massimo Dutti, Berksha (which includes the BSK and Man brands), Stradivarius, Oysho (women's lingerie, beachwear, and sport), and Uterqüe (accessories, leatherwear).

NEWS CORP

News Corp was created in 2013 when News Corporation was split into two independent companies: 21st Century Fox and News Corp. This move allowed News Corp to focus on the newspaper and publishing businesses, while 21st Century Fox retained the other parts of News Corporation (mainly television and film). News Corp characterizes itself today as a mass media company. The companies in its network include The New York Post, Harper Collins Publishers, News Corp Australia, News UK, News America Marketing, Storyful (a social media newswire), Dow Jones and Move (a provider of real estate information). News Corp Australia actually includes a broad portfolio of national, metropolitan, regional, and community newspapers; while News UK has similar breadth. Despite the general disruption in the newspaper industry due to Internet-related developments, News Corp recently announced record-setting subscriber performances at Dow Jones and the Wall Street Journal—two of their most important holdings.

KIMBERLY-CLARK CORPORATION

Kimberly-Clark is a Texas based multinational in the personal care industry, producing mostly paper-based consumer products. Its products include iconic brands such as Kleenex, Huggies, Pull-Ups, Cottonelle, Scott, Viva, Kotex, and Depend. The company has organized its products into five related lines of business: Adult Care, Baby and Child Care, Family Care, Feminine Care, and K-C Professional. Its products are recognized and trusted around the world—distributed across more than 175 countries. With its sharp focus on the consumer and financial discipline,

(top): Shutterstock/Ientamart; (middle): Edith38/Shutterstock; (bottom): Neilson Barnard/Staff/Getty Images

Kimberly-Clark has managed to sustain its record of solid performance and growth even during recessionary periods, since the types of products it offers are always in demand. Its outlook for 2020 and beyond continues to look rosy.

Sources: Company websites, Wikipedia; https://www.businesswire.com/news/home/20200207005506/en/News-Corp-Announces-Record-Setting-Subscriber-Performances-Dow; https://finance.yahoo.com/news/kimberly-clarks-impressive-momentum-continue-130001056.html, accessed February 10, 2020.

Strategic Fit in Supply Chain Activities   Businesses with strategic fit with respect to their supply chain activities can perform better together because of the potential for transferring skills in procuring materials, sharing resources and capabilities in logistics, collaborating with common supply chain partners, and/or increasing leverage with shippers in securing volume discounts on incoming parts and components. Dell's strategic partnerships with leading suppliers of microprocessors, circuit boards, disk drives, memory chips, flat-panel displays, wireless capabilities, long-life batteries, and other PC-related components have been an important element of the company's strategy to diversify into servers, data storage devices, networking components, plasma TVs, and printers—products that include many components common to PCs and that can be sourced from the same strategic partners that provide Dell with PC components.

Strategic Fit in R&D and Technology Activities   Businesses with strategic fit in R&D or technology development perform better together than apart because of potential cost savings in R&D, shorter times in getting new products to market, and more innovative products or processes. Moreover, technological advances in one business can lead to increased sales for both. Technological innovations have been the driver behind the efforts of cable TV companies to diversify into high-speed Internet access (via the use of cable modems) and, further, to explore providing local and long-distance telephone service to residential and commercial customers either through a single wire or by means of Voice over Internet Protocol (VoIP) technology. These diversification efforts have resulted in companies such as DISH Network and Comcast (through its XFINITY subsidiary) offering TV, Internet, and phone bundles.

Manufacturing-Related Strategic Fit   Cross-business strategic fit in manufacturing-related activities can be exploited when a diversifier's expertise in quality control and cost-efficient production methods can be transferred to another business. When Emerson Electric diversified into the chain-saw business, it transferred its expertise in low-cost manufacture to its newly acquired Beaird-Poulan business division. The transfer drove Beaird-Poulan's new strategy—to be the low-cost provider of chainsaw products—and fundamentally changed the way Beaird-Poulan chain saws were designed and manufactured. Another benefit of production-related value chain commonalities is the ability to consolidate production into a smaller number of plants and significantly reduce overall production costs. When snowmobile maker Bombardier diversified into motorcycles, it was able to set up motorcycle assembly lines in the manufacturing facility where it was assembling snowmobiles. When Smucker's acquired Procter & Gamble's Jif peanut butter business, it was able to combine the manufacture of the two brands of peanut butter products while gaining greater leverage with vendors in purchasing its peanut supplies.

Strategic Fit in Sales and Marketing Activities   Various cost-saving opportunities spring from diversifying into businesses with closely related sales and marketing activities. When the products are sold directly to the same customers, sales costs can often be reduced by using a single sales force instead of having two different salespeople call on the same customer. The products of related businesses can be promoted at the same website and included in the same media ads and sales brochures. There may be opportunities to reduce costs by consolidating order processing and billing and by using common promotional tie-ins. When global power toolmaker Black & Decker acquired Vector Products, it was able to use its own global sales force to sell the newly acquired

Vector power inverters, vehicle battery chargers, and rechargeable spotlights because the types of customers that carried its power tools (discounters like Kmart, home centers, and hardware stores) also stocked the types of products produced by Vector.

A second category of benefits arises when different businesses use similar sales and marketing approaches. In such cases, there may be competitively valuable opportunities to transfer selling, merchandising, advertising, and product differentiation skills from one business to another. Procter & Gamble's product lineup includes Pampers diapers, Olay beauty products, Tide laundry detergent, Crest toothpaste, Charmin toilet tissue, Gillette razors and blades, Vicks cough and cold products Oral-B toothbrushes, and Head & Shoulders shampoo. All of these have different competitors and different supply chain and production requirements, but they all move through the same wholesale distribution systems, are sold in common retail settings to the same shoppers, and require the same marketing and merchandising skills.

Distribution-Related Strategic Fit   Businesses with closely related distribution activities can perform better together than apart because of potential cost savings in sharing the same distribution facilities or using many of the same wholesale distributors and retail dealers. When Conair Corporation acquired Allegro Manufacturing's travel bag and travel accessory business, it was able to consolidate its own distribution centers for hair dryers and curling irons with those of Allegro, thereby generating cost savings for both businesses. Likewise, since Conair products and Allegro's neck rests, ear plugs, luggage tags, and toiletry kits were sold by the same types of retailers (discount stores, supermarket chains, and drugstore chains), Conair was able to convince many of the retailers not carrying Allegro products to take on the line.

Strategic Fit in Customer Service Activities   Strategic fit with respect to customer service activities can enable cost savings or differentiation advantages, just as it does along other points of the value chain. For example, cost savings may come from consolidating after-sale service and repair organizations for the products of closely related businesses into a single operation. Likewise, different businesses can often use the same customer service infrastructure. For instance, an electric utility that diversifies into natural gas, water, appliance repair services, and home security services can use the same customer data network, the same call centers and local offices, the same billing and accounting systems, and the same customer service infrastructure to support all of its products and services. Through the transfer of best practices in customer service across a set of related businesses or through the sharing of resources such as proprietary information about customer preferences, a multi-business company can also create a differentiation advantage through higher-quality customer service.

Strategic Fit, Economies of Scope, and Competitive Advantage

Strategic fit in the value chain activities of a diversified corporation's different businesses opens up opportunities for **economies of scope**—a concept distinct from *economies of scale*. Economies of *scale* are cost savings that accrue directly from a larger-sized operation—for example, unit costs may be lower in a large plant than in a small plant. In contrast, economies of scope are cost savings that flow from operating in multiple businesses (a larger *scope* of

CORE CONCEPT

Economies of scope are cost reductions that flow from operating in multiple businesses (a larger scope of operation). This is in contrast to economies of scale, which accrue from a larger-sized operation.

operation). *They stem directly from strategic fit along the value chains of related businesses,* which in turn enables the businesses to share resources or to transfer them from business to business at low cost. Significant scope economies are open only to firms engaged in related diversification, since they are the result of related businesses performing R&D together, transferring managers from one business to another, using common manufacturing or distribution facilities, sharing a common sales force or dealer network, using the same established brand name, and the like. *The greater the cross-business economies associated with resource sharing and transfer, the greater the potential for a related diversification strategy to give the individual businesses of a multibusiness enterprise a cost advantage over rivals.*

From Strategic Fit to Competitive Advantage, Added Profitability, and Gains in Shareholder Value   The cost advantage from economies of scope is due to the fact that resource sharing allows a multibusiness firm to spread resource costs across its businesses and to avoid the expense of having to acquire and maintain duplicate sets of resources—one for each business. But related diversified companies can benefit from strategic fit in other ways as well.

Sharing or transferring valuable specialized assets among the company's businesses can help each business perform its value chain activities more proficiently. This translates into competitive advantage for the businesses in one or two basic ways: (1) The businesses can contribute to greater efficiency and lower costs relative to their competitors, and/or (2) they can provide a basis for differentiation so that customers are willing to pay relatively more for the businesses' goods and services. In either or both of these ways, a firm with a well-executed related diversification strategy can boost the chances of its businesses attaining a competitive advantage.

The greater the relatedness among a diversified company's businesses, the bigger a company's window for converting strategic fit into competitive advantage. The strategic and business logic is compelling: Capturing the benefits of strategic fit along the value chains of its related businesses gives a diversified company a clear path to achieving competitive advantage over undiversified competitors and competitors whose own diversification efforts don't offer equivalent strategic-fit benefits.[9] Such competitive advantage potential provides a company with a dependable basis for earning profits and a return on investment that exceeds what the company's businesses could earn as stand-alone enterprises. Converting the competitive advantage potential into greater profitability is what fuels $1 + 1 = 3$ gains in shareholder value—the necessary outcome for satisfying the *better-off test* and proving the business merit of a company's diversification effort.

> Diversifying into related businesses where competitively valuable strategic-fit benefits can be captured puts a company's businesses in position to perform better financially as part of the company than they could have performed as independent enterprises, thus providing a clear avenue for increasing shareholder value and satisfying the better-off test.

There are five things to bear in mind here:

1. Capturing cross-business strategic-fit benefits via a strategy of related diversification builds shareholder value in ways that shareholders cannot undertake by simply owning a portfolio of stocks of companies in different industries.

2. The capture of cross-business strategic-fit benefits is possible only via a strategy of related diversification.

3. The greater the relatedness among a diversified company's businesses, the bigger the company's window for converting strategic fit into competitive advantage for its businesses.

4. The benefits of cross-business strategic fit come from the transferring or sharing of competitively valuable resources and capabilities among the businesses—resources

The Kraft–Heinz Merger: Pursuing the Benefits of Cross-Business Strategic Fit

The $62.6 billion merger between Kraft and Heinz that was finalized in the summer of 2015 created the third largest food and beverage company in North America and the fifth largest in the world. It was a merger predicated on the idea that the strategic fit between these two companies was such that they could create more value as a combined enterprise than they could as two separate companies. As a combined enterprise, Kraft Heinz would be able to exploit its cross-business value chain activities and resource similarities to more efficiently produce, distribute, and sell profitable processed food products.

Kraft and Heinz products share many of the same raw materials (milk, sugar, salt, wheat, etc.), which allows the new company to leverage its increased bargaining power as a larger business to get better deals with suppliers, using strategic fit in supply chain activities to achieve lower input costs and greater inbound efficiencies. Moreover, because both of these brands specialized in prepackaged foods, there is ample manufacturing-related strategic fit in production processes and packaging technologies that allow the new company to trim and streamline manufacturing operations.

Their distribution-related strategic fit will allow for the complete integration of distribution channels and transportation networks, resulting in greater outbound efficiencies and a reduction in travel time for products moving from factories to stores. The Kraft Heinz Company is currently looking to leverage Heinz's global platform to expand Kraft's products internationally. By utilizing Heinz's already highly developed global distribution network and brand familiarity (key specialized resources), Kraft can more easily expand into the global

Hayden Stirling/Shutterstock

market of prepackaged and processed food. Because these two brands are sold at similar types of retail stores (supermarket chains, wholesale retailers, and local grocery stores), they are now able to claim even more shelf space with the increased bargaining power of the combined company.

Strategic fit in sales and marketing activities will allow the company to develop coordinated and more effective advertising campaigns. Toward this aim, the Kraft Heinz Company is moving to consolidate its marketing capabilities under one marketing firm. Also, by combining R&D teams, the Kraft Heinz Company could come out with innovative products that may appeal more to the growing number of on-the-go and health-conscious buyers in the market. Many of these potential and predicted synergies for the Kraft Heinz Company have yet to be realized, since merger integration activities always take time.

Note: Developed with Maria Hart.

Sources: www.forbes.com/sites/paulmartyn/2015/03/31/heinz-and-kraft-merger-makes-supply-management-sense/; fortune.com/2015/03/25/kraft-mess-how-heinz-deal-helps/; www.nytimes.com/2015/03/26/business/dealbook/kraft-and-heinz-to-merge.html?_r=2; company websites (accessed December 3, 2015).

and capabilities that are *specialized* to certain applications and have value only in specific types of industries and businesses.

5. The benefits of cross-business strategic fit are not automatically realized when a company diversifies into related businesses; *the benefits materialize only after management has successfully pursued internal actions to capture them.*

Illustration Capsule 8.2 describes the merger of Kraft Foods Group, Inc. with the H. J. Heinz Holding Corporation, in pursuit of the strategic-fit benefits of a related diversification strategy.

DIVERSIFICATION INTO UNRELATED BUSINESSES

A willingness to diversify
into any business in any
industry is unlikely to result
in successful unrelated
diversification. The key to
success even for unrelated
diversification is to create economic value for
shareholders.

Achieving cross-business strategic fit is not a motivation for unrelated diversification. Companies that pursue a strategy of unrelated diversification often exhibit a willingness to diversify into *any business in any industry* where senior managers see an opportunity to realize consistently good financial results. Such companies are frequently labeled *conglomerates* because their business interests range broadly across diverse industries. Companies engaged in unrelated diversification nearly always enter new businesses by acquiring an established company rather than by forming a startup subsidiary within their own corporate structures or participating in joint ventures.

With a strategy of unrelated diversification, an acquisition is deemed to have potential if it passes the industry-attractiveness and cost of entry tests and if it has good prospects for attractive financial performance. Thus, with an unrelated diversification strategy, company managers spend much time and effort screening acquisition candidates and evaluating the pros and cons of keeping or divesting existing businesses, using such criteria as

- Whether the business can meet corporate targets for profitability and return on investment.
- Whether the business is in an industry with attractive growth potential.
- Whether the business is big enough to contribute *significantly* to the parent firm's bottom line.

But the key to successful unrelated diversification is to go beyond these considerations and *ensure that the strategy passes the better-off test as well.* This test requires more than just growth in revenues; it requires *growth in profits*—beyond what could be achieved by a mutual fund or a holding company that owns shares of the businesses without adding any value. Unless the combination of businesses is more profitable together under the corporate umbrella than they are apart as independent businesses, *the strategy cannot create economic value for shareholders.* And unless it does so, there is *no real justification for unrelated diversification,* since top executives have a fiduciary responsibility to maximize long-term shareholder value for the company's owners (its shareholders). Illustration Capsule 8.3 provides some examples of successful companies with unrelated diversification.

Building Shareholder Value via Unrelated Diversification

Given the absence of cross-business strategic fit with which to create competitive advantages, building shareholder value via unrelated diversification ultimately hinges on the ability of the parent company to improve its businesses (and make the combination *better off*) via other means. Critical to this endeavor is the role that the parent company plays as a *corporate parent.*[10] To the extent that a company has strong *parenting capabilities*—capabilities that involve nurturing, guiding, grooming, and governing constituent businesses—a corporate parent can propel its businesses forward and help them gain ground over their market rivals. Corporate parents also contribute to the competitiveness of their unrelated businesses by sharing or transferring *general resources and capabilities* across the businesses—competitive assets that have utility in *any type* of industry and that can be leveraged across a wide range of business types as a result. Examples of the kinds of general resources that a corporate parent leverages in unrelated diversification include the corporation's reputation, credit rating, and

Examples of Companies Pursuing an Unrelated Diversification Strategy

TATA

The Tata group is a global enterprise with total revenues exceeding $115 billion in 2020. It is organized into 11 "verticals," which are essentially industry domains. The verticals include Information Technology, Steel, Automotive, Consumer and Retail, Infrastructure, Financial Services, Aerospace and Defense, Tourism and Travel, Telecom and Media, and Trading and Investments. Within these 11 verticals are 30 or more independently managed companies. The most well-known of these include: Tata Motors, Tata Steel, Tata Chemicals, Titan (jewelry and eyewear), Tata Power, Tata Communications, Tata Consumer Products, Tata Capital, Tata Consultancy Services, and Indian Hotels.

BERKSHIRE HATHAWAY

Berkshire Hathaway is an American conglomerate with a long and successful history, often attributed to the sage investment and acquisition strategy of its Chairman and CEO, Warren Buffet. Its holdings include an insurance group, an energy group, a financial products group, and a diverse group covering manufacturing, service, and retailing. Companies that are wholly owned by Berkshire Hathaway include GEICO, Dairy Queen, Duracell, Fruit of the Loom, Burlington Northern Sante Fe Railway, and Helzberg Diamonds. It owns a significant share of a number of other companies, including Bank of America, Southwest Airlines, Kraft Heinz, American Express, and Coca Cola.

YAMAHA CORPORATION

The Yamaha Corporation no longer includes Yamaha Motor Co. (the motorcycle, snowmobile, boat, and motorized product maker), although it is still a major shareholder. But even without Yamaha Motor, the Yamaha Corporation still produces a wide array of products. It is the world's largest producer of all types of musical instruments, along

(top): The India Today Group/Contributor/Getty Images; (middle): Ranta Images/Shutterstock; (bottom): Gwenael_LE_VOT/Getty Images

with arguably related audio equipment and communication devices. But, in addition, it is involved in the production of industrial robots, home appliances, sporting goods, industrial machinery and components, specialty metals, golf products, resorts, and semiconductors.

Sources: Company websites, Wikipedia, accessed February 14, 2020.

access to financial markets; governance mechanisms; management training programs; a corporate ethics program; a central data and communications center; shared administrative resources such as public relations and legal services; and common systems for functions such as budgeting, financial reporting, and quality control.

The Benefits of Astute Corporate Parenting   One of the most important ways that corporate parents contribute to the success of their businesses is by offering high-level oversight and guidance.[11] The top executives of a large diversified corporation have among them many years of accumulated experience in a variety of business settings and can often contribute expert problem-solving skills, creative strategy suggestions, and first-rate advice and guidance on how to improve competitiveness and financial performance to the heads of the company's various business subsidiaries. This is especially true in the case of newly acquired, smaller businesses. Particularly astute high-level guidance from corporate executives can help the subsidiaries perform better than they would otherwise be able to do through the efforts of the business unit heads alone. The outstanding leadership of Royal Little, the founder of Textron, was a major reason that the company became an exemplar of the unrelated diversification strategy while he was CEO. Little's bold moves transformed the company from its origins as a small textile manufacturer into a global powerhouse known for its Bell helicopters, Cessna aircraft, and a host of other strong brands in a wide array of industries. Norm Wesley, a former CEO of the conglomerate Fortune Brands, is similarly credited with driving the sharp rise in the company's stock price while he was at the helm. Under his leadership, Fortune Brands became the $7 billion maker of products ranging from spirits (e.g., Jim Beam bourbon and rye, Gilbey's gin and vodka, Courvoisier cognac) to golf products (e.g., Titleist golf balls and clubs, FootJoy golf shoes and apparel, Scotty Cameron putters) to hardware (e.g., Moen faucets, American Lock security devices). (Fortune Brands has since been converted into two separate entities, Beam Inc. and Fortune Brands Home & Security.)

Corporate parents can also create added value for their businesses by providing them with other types of general resources that lower the operating costs of the individual businesses or that enhance their operating effectiveness. The administrative resources located at a company's corporate headquarters are a prime example. They typically include legal services, accounting expertise and tax services, and other elements of the administrative infrastructure, such as risk management capabilities, information technology resources, and public relations capabilities. Providing individual businesses with general support resources such as these creates value by *lowering companywide overhead costs,* since each business would otherwise have to duplicate the centralized activities.

Corporate brands that do not connote any specific type of product are another type of general corporate resource that can be shared among unrelated businesses. General Electric, for example, successfully applied its GE brand to such unrelated products and businesses as medical products and health care (GE Healthcare), jet engines (GE Aviation), and power and water technologies (GE Power and Water). Corporate brands that are applied in this fashion are sometimes called **umbrella brands.** Utilizing a well-known corporate name (GE) in a diversified company's individual businesses has the potential not only to lower costs (by spreading the fixed cost of developing and maintaining the brand over many businesses) but also to enhance each business's customer value proposition by linking its products to a name that consumers trust. In similar fashion, a corporation's reputation for well-crafted products, for product reliability, or for trustworthiness can lead to greater customer willingness to

---

purchase the products of a wider range of a diversified company's businesses. Incentive systems, financial control systems, and a company's culture are other types of general corporate resources that may prove useful in enhancing the daily operations of a diverse set of businesses. The parenting activities of corporate executives may also include recruiting and hiring talented managers to run individual businesses.

We discuss two other commonly employed ways for corporate parents to add value to their unrelated businesses next.

Judicious Cross-Business Allocation of Financial Resources By reallocating surplus cash flows from some businesses to fund the capital requirements of other businesses—in essence, having the company serve as an *internal capital market*—corporate parents may also be able to create value. Such actions can be particularly important in times when credit is unusually tight (such as in the wake of the worldwide banking crisis that began in 2008) or in economies with less well developed capital markets. Under these conditions, with strong financial resources a corporate parent can add value by shifting funds from business units generating excess cash (more than they need to fund their own operating requirements and new capital investment opportunities) to other, cash-short businesses with appealing growth prospects. A parent company's ability to function as its own internal capital market enhances overall corporate performance and increases shareholder value to the extent that (1) its top managers have better access to information about investment opportunities internal to the firm than do external financiers or (2) it can provide funds that would otherwise be unavailable due to poor financial market conditions.

Acquiring and Restructuring Undervalued Companies Another way for parent companies to add value to unrelated businesses is by acquiring weakly performing companies at a bargain price and then *restructuring* their operations in ways that produce sometimes dramatic increases in profitability. **Restructuring** refers to overhauling and streamlining the operations of a business—combining plants with excess capacity, selling off underutilized assets, reducing unnecessary expenses, revamping its product offerings, consolidating administrative functions to reduce overhead costs, and otherwise improving the operating efficiency and profitability of a company. Restructuring generally involves transferring seasoned managers to the newly acquired business, either to replace the top layers of management or to step in temporarily until the business is returned to profitability or is well on its way to becoming a major market contender.

> **CORE** CONCEPT
>
> **Restructuring** refers to overhauling and streamlining the activities of a business—combining plants with excess capacity, selling off underutilized assets, reducing unnecessary expenses, and otherwise improving the productivity and profitability of a company.

Restructuring is often undertaken when a diversified company acquires a new business that is performing well below levels that the corporate parent believes are achievable. Diversified companies that have proven *turnaround capabilities* in rejuvenating weakly performing companies can often apply these capabilities in a relatively wide range of unrelated industries. Newell Brands (whose diverse product line includes Rubbermaid food storage, Sharpie pens, Graco strollers and car seats, Goody hair accessories, Calphalon cookware, and Yankee Candle—all businesses with different value chain activities) developed such a strong set of turnaround capabilities that the company was said to "Newellize" the businesses it acquired.

Successful unrelated diversification strategies based on restructuring require the parent company to have considerable expertise in identifying underperforming target companies and in negotiating attractive acquisition prices so that each acquisition passes the cost of entry test. The capabilities in this regard of Lord James Hanson and Lord Gordon White, who headed up the storied British conglomerate Hanson Trust, played a large part in Hanson Trust's impressive record of profitability.

The Path to Greater Shareholder Value through Unrelated Diversification

For a strategy of unrelated diversification to produce companywide financial results above and beyond what the businesses could generate operating as standalone entities, corporate executives must do three things to pass the three Tests of Corporate Advantage:

1. Diversify into industries where the businesses can produce consistently good earnings and returns on investment (to satisfy the industry-attractiveness test).
2. Negotiate favorable acquisition prices (to satisfy the cost of entry test).
3. Do a superior job of corporate parenting via high-level managerial oversight and resource sharing, financial resource allocation and portfolio management, and/or the restructuring of underperforming businesses (to satisfy the better-off test).

> **CORE CONCEPT**
>
> A diversified company has a **parenting advantage** when it is more able than other companies to boost the combined performance of its individual businesses through high-level guidance, general oversight, and other corporate-level contributions.

The best corporate parents understand the nature and value of the kinds of resources at their command and know how to leverage them effectively across their businesses. Those that are able to create more value in their businesses than other diversified companies have what is called a **parenting advantage.** When a corporation has a parenting advantage, its top executives have the best chance of being able to craft and execute an unrelated diversification strategy that can satisfy all three Tests of Corporate Advantage and truly enhance long-term economic shareholder value.

The Drawbacks of Unrelated Diversification

Unrelated diversification strategies have two important negatives that undercut the pluses: very demanding managerial requirements and limited competitive advantage potential.

Demanding Managerial Requirements   Successfully managing a set of fundamentally different businesses operating in fundamentally different industry and competitive environments is a challenging and exceptionally difficult proposition.[12] Consider, for example, that corporations like General Electric, ITT, Mitsubishi, and Bharti Enterprises have dozens of business subsidiaries making hundreds and sometimes thousands of products. While headquarters executives can glean information about an industry from third-party sources, ask lots of questions when making occasional visits to the operations of the different businesses, and do their best to learn about the company's different businesses, they still remain heavily dependent on briefings from business unit heads and on "managing by the numbers"—that is, keeping a close track on the financial and operating results of each subsidiary. Managing by the numbers works well enough when business conditions are normal and the heads of the various business units are capable of consistently meeting their numbers. But problems arise if things start to go awry in a business and corporate management has to get deeply involved in the problems of a business it does not know much about. Because every business tends to encounter rough sledding at some juncture, unrelated diversification is thus a somewhat risky strategy from a managerial perspective.[13] Just one or two unforeseen problems or big strategic mistakes—which are much more likely without close corporate oversight—can cause a precipitous drop in corporate earnings and crash the parent company's stock price.

Hence, competently overseeing a set of widely diverse businesses can turn out to be much harder than it sounds. In practice, comparatively few companies have proved that they have top-management capabilities that are up to the task. There are far more companies whose corporate executives have failed at delivering consistently good financial results with an unrelated diversification strategy than there are companies with corporate executives who have been successful.[14] Unless a company truly has a parenting advantage, the odds are that the result of unrelated diversification will be $1 + 1 = 2$ or even less.

Limited Competitive Advantage Potential   The second big negative is that *unrelated diversification offers only a limited potential for competitive advantage beyond what each individual business can generate on its own.* Unlike a related diversification strategy, unrelated diversification provides no cross-business strategic-fit benefits that allow each business to perform its key value chain activities in a more efficient and effective manner. A cash-rich corporate parent pursuing unrelated diversification can provide its subsidiaries with much-needed capital, may achieve economies of scope in activities relying on general corporate resources, may extend an umbrella brand and may even offer some managerial know-how to help resolve problems in particular business units, but otherwise it has little to add in the way of enhancing the competitive strength of its individual business units. In comparison to the highly specialized resources that facilitate related diversification, the general resources that support unrelated diversification tend to be relatively low value, for the simple reason that they are more common. Unless they are of exceptionally high quality (such as GE's world-renowned general management capabilities and umbrella brand or Newell Rubbermaid's turnaround capabilities), resources and capabilities that are general in nature are less likely to provide a significant source of competitive advantage for the businesses of diversified companies. Without the competitive advantage potential of strategic fit in competitively important value chain activities, consolidated performance of an unrelated group of businesses may not be very much more than the sum of what the individual business units could achieve if they were independent, in most circumstances.

> Relying solely on leveraging general resources and the expertise of corporate executives to wisely manage a set of unrelated businesses is a much weaker foundation for enhancing shareholder value than is a strategy of related diversification.

Misguided Reasons for Pursuing Unrelated Diversification

Companies sometimes pursue unrelated diversification for reasons that are entirely misguided. These include the following:

- *Risk reduction.* Spreading the company's investments over a set of diverse industries to spread risk cannot create long-term shareholder value since the company's shareholders can more flexibly (and more efficiently) reduce their exposure to risk by investing in a diversified portfolio of stocks and bonds.
- *Growth.* While unrelated diversification may enable a company to achieve rapid or continuous growth, firms that pursue growth for growth's sake are unlikely to maximize shareholder value. Only *profitable growth*—the kind that comes from creating added value for shareholders—can justify a strategy of unrelated diversification.
- *Stabilization.* Managers sometimes pursue broad diversification in the hope that market downtrends in some of the company's businesses will be partially offset by cyclical upswings in its other businesses, thus producing somewhat less earnings volatility. In actual practice, however, there's no convincing evidence that the consolidated profits of firms with unrelated diversification strategies are more stable or less subject to reversal in periods of recession and economic stress than the profits of firms with related diversification strategies.

- *Managerial motives.* Unrelated diversification can provide benefits to managers such as higher compensation (which tends to increase with firm size and degree of diversification) and reduced their unemployment risk. Pursuing diversification for these reasons will likely reduce shareholder value and violate managers' fiduciary responsibilities.

Because unrelated diversification strategies *at their best* have only a limited potential for creating long-term economic value for shareholders, it is essential that managers not compound this problem by taking a misguided approach toward unrelated diversification, in pursuit of objectives that are more likely to destroy shareholder value than create it.

> Only profitable growth—the kind that comes from creating added value for shareholders—can justify a strategy of unrelated diversification.

COMBINATION RELATED–UNRELATED DIVERSIFICATION STRATEGIES

There's nothing to preclude a company from diversifying into both related and unrelated businesses. Indeed, in actual practice the business makeup of diversified companies varies considerably. Some diversified companies are really *dominant-business enterprises*—one major "core" business accounts for 50 to 80 percent of total revenues and a collection of small related or unrelated businesses accounts for the remainder. Some diversified companies are *narrowly diversified* around a few (two to five) related or unrelated businesses. Others are *broadly diversified* around a wide-ranging collection of related businesses, unrelated businesses, or a mixture of both. A number of multibusiness enterprises have diversified into unrelated areas but have a collection of related businesses within each area—thus giving them a business portfolio consisting of *several unrelated groups of related businesses.* There's ample room for companies to customize their diversification strategies to incorporate elements of both related and unrelated diversification, as may suit their own competitive asset profile and strategic vision. *Combination related-unrelated diversification strategies have particular appeal for companies with a mix of valuable competitive assets, covering the spectrum from general to specialized resources and capabilities.*

Figure 8.2 shows the range of alternatives for companies pursuing diversification.

EVALUATING THE STRATEGY OF A DIVERSIFIED COMPANY

• LO 8-4

Use the analytic tools for evaluating a company's diversification strategy.

Strategic analysis of diversified companies builds on the concepts and methods used for single-business companies. But there are some additional aspects to consider and a couple of new analytic tools to master. The procedure for evaluating the pluses and minuses of a diversified company's strategy and deciding what actions to take to improve the company's performance involves six steps:

1. Assessing the attractiveness of the industries the company has diversified into, both individually and as a group.

2. Assessing the competitive strength of the company's business units and drawing a nine-cell matrix to simultaneously portray industry attractiveness and business unit competitive strength.

FIGURE 8.2   Three Strategy Options for Pursuing Diversification

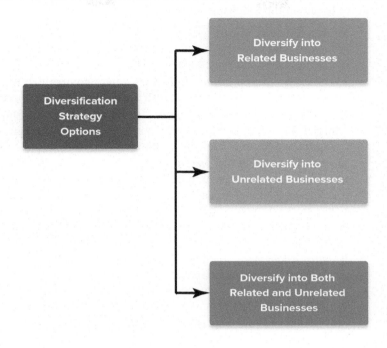

3. Evaluating the extent of cross-business strategic fit along the value chains of the company's various business units.
4. Checking whether the firm's resources fit the requirements of its present business lineup.
5. Ranking the performance prospects of the businesses from best to worst and determining what the corporate parent's priorities should be in allocating resources to its various businesses.
6. Crafting new strategic moves to improve overall corporate performance.

The core concepts and analytic techniques underlying each of these steps merit further discussion.

Step 1: Evaluating Industry Attractiveness

A principal consideration in evaluating the caliber of a diversified company's strategy is the attractiveness of the industries in which it has business operations. Several questions arise:

1. Does each industry the company has diversified into represent a good market for the company to be in—does it pass the industry-attractiveness test?
2. Which of the company's industries are most attractive, and which are least attractive?
3. How appealing is the whole group of industries in which the company has invested?

The more attractive the industries (both individually and as a group) that a diversified company is in, the better its prospects for good long-term performance.

Calculating Industry-Attractiveness Scores   A simple and reliable analytic tool for gauging industry attractiveness involves calculating quantitative industry-attractiveness scores based on the following measures:

- *Market size and projected growth rate.* Big industries are more attractive than small industries, and fast-growing industries tend to be more attractive than slow-growing industries, other things being equal.
- *The intensity of competition.* Industries where competitive pressures are relatively weak are more attractive than industries where competitive pressures are strong.
- *Emerging opportunities and threats.* Industries with promising opportunities and minimal threats on the near horizon are more attractive than industries with modest opportunities and imposing threats.
- *The presence of cross-industry strategic fit.* The more one industry's value chain and resource requirements match up well with the value chain activities of other industries in which the company has operations, the more attractive the industry is to a firm pursuing related diversification. However, cross-industry strategic fit is not something that a company committed to a strategy of unrelated diversification considers when it is evaluating industry attractiveness.
- *Resource requirements.* Industries in which resource requirements are within the company's reach are more attractive than industries in which capital and other resource requirements could strain corporate financial resources and organizational capabilities.
- *Social, political, regulatory, and environmental factors.* Industries that have significant problems in such areas as consumer health, safety, or environmental pollution or those subject to intense regulation are less attractive than industries that do not have such problems.
- *Industry profitability.* Industries with healthy profit margins and high rates of return on investment are generally more attractive than industries with historically low or unstable profits.

Each attractiveness measure is then assigned a weight reflecting its relative importance in determining an industry's attractiveness, since not all attractiveness measures are equally important. The intensity of competition in an industry should nearly always carry a high weight (say, 0.20 to 0.30). Strategic-fit considerations should be assigned a high weight in the case of companies with related diversification strategies; but for companies with an unrelated diversification strategy, strategic fit with other industries may be dropped from the list of attractiveness measures altogether. The importance weights must add up to 1.

Finally, each industry is rated on each of the chosen industry-attractiveness measures, using a rating scale of 1 to 10 (where a *high* rating signifies *high* attractiveness, and a *low* rating signifies *low* attractiveness). *Keep in mind here that the more intensely competitive an industry is, the lower the attractiveness rating for that industry.* Likewise, the more the resource requirements associated with being in a particular industry are beyond the parent company's reach, the lower the attractiveness rating. On the other hand, the presence of good cross-industry strategic fit should be given a very high attractiveness rating, since there is good potential for competitive advantage and added shareholder value. Weighted attractiveness scores are then calculated by multiplying the industry's rating on each measure by the corresponding weight. For example, a rating of 8 times a weight of 0.25 gives a weighted attractiveness score of 2. The sum of the weighted scores for all the attractiveness measures provides an overall industry-attractiveness score. This procedure is illustrated in Table 8.1.

TABLE 8.1   Calculating Weighted Industry-Attractiveness Scores

Industry-Attractiveness Measure	Importance Weight	Industry-Attractiveness Assessments					
		Industry A		Industry B		Industry C	
		Attractiveness Rating*	Weighted Score	Attractiveness Rating*	Weighted Score	Attractiveness Rating*	Weighted Score
Market size and projected growth rate	0.10	8	0.80	3	0.30	5	0.50
Intensity of competition	0.25	8	2.00	2	0.50	5	1.25
Emerging opportunities and threats	0.10	6	0.60	5	0.50	4	0.40
Cross-industry strategic fit	0.30	8	2.40	2	0.60	3	0.90
Resource requirements	0.10	5	0.50	5	0.50	4	0.40
Social, political, regulatory, and environmental factors	0.05	8	0.40	3	0.15	7	1.05
Industry profitability	0.10	5	0.50	4	0.40	6	0.60
Sum of importance weights	**1.00**						
Weighted overall industry-attractiveness scores			**7.20**		**2.95**		**5.10**

Rating scale: 1 = very unattractive to company; 10 = very attractive to company.

Interpreting the Industry-Attractiveness Scores   Industries with a score much below 5 probably do not pass the attractiveness test. If a company's industry-attractiveness scores are all above 5, it is probably fair to conclude that the group of industries the company operates in is attractive as a whole. But the group of industries takes on a decidedly lower degree of attractiveness as the number of industries with scores below 5 increases, especially if industries with low scores account for a sizable fraction of the company's revenues.

For a diversified company to be a strong performer, a substantial portion of its revenues and profits must come from business units with relatively high attractiveness scores. It is particularly important that a diversified company's principal businesses be in industries with a good outlook for growth and above-average profitability. Having a big fraction of the company's revenues and profits come from industries with slow growth, low profitability, intense competition, or other troubling conditions tends to drag overall company performance down. Business units in the least attractive industries are potential candidates for divestiture, unless they are positioned strongly enough to overcome the unattractive aspects of their industry environments or they are a strategically important component of the company's business makeup.

Step 2: Evaluating Business Unit Competitive Strength

The second step in evaluating a diversified company is to appraise the competitive strength of each business unit in its respective industry. Doing an appraisal of each business unit's strength and competitive position in its industry not only reveals its chances for success in its industry but also provides a basis for ranking the units from competitively strongest to competitively weakest and sizing up the competitive strength of all the business units as a group.

Calculating Competitive-Strength Scores for Each Business Unit   Quantitative measures of each business unit's competitive strength can be calculated using a procedure similar to that for measuring industry attractiveness. The following factors are used in quantifying the competitive strengths of a diversified company's business subsidiaries:

- *Relative market share.* A business unit's *relative market share* is defined as the ratio of its market share to the market share held by the largest rival firm in the industry, with market share measured in unit volume, not dollars. For instance, if business A has a market-leading share of 40 percent and its largest rival has 30 percent, A's relative market share is 1.33. (Note that only business units that are market share leaders in their respective industries can have relative market shares greater than 1.) If business B has a 15 percent market share and B's largest rival has 30 percent, B's relative market share is 0.5. *The further below 1 a business unit's relative market share is, the weaker its competitive strength and market position vis-à-vis rivals.*

- *Costs relative to competitors' costs.* Business units that have low costs relative to those of key competitors tend to be more strongly positioned in their industries than business units struggling to maintain cost parity with major rivals. The only time a business unit's competitive strength may not be undermined by having higher costs than rivals is when it has incurred the higher costs to strongly differentiate its product offering and its customers are willing to pay premium prices for the differentiating features.

- *Ability to match or beat rivals on key product attributes.* A company's competitiveness depends in part on being able to satisfy buyer expectations with regard to features, product performance, reliability, service, and other important attributes.

- *Brand image and reputation.* A widely known and respected brand name is a valuable competitive asset in most industries.

- *Other competitively valuable resources and capabilities.* Valuable resources and capabilities, including those accessed through collaborative partnerships, enhance a company's ability to compete successfully and perhaps contend for industry leadership.

- *Ability to benefit from strategic fit with other business units.* Strategic fit with other businesses within the company enhances a business unit's competitive strength and may provide a competitive edge.
- *Ability to exercise bargaining leverage with key suppliers or customers.* Having bargaining leverage signals competitive strength and can be a source of competitive advantage.
- *Profitability relative to competitors.* Above-average profitability on a consistent basis is a signal of competitive advantage, whereas consistently below-average profitability usually denotes competitive disadvantage.

After settling on a set of competitive-strength measures that are well matched to the circumstances of the various business units, the company needs to assign weights indicating each measure's importance. As in the assignment of weights to industry-attractiveness measures, the importance weights must add up to 1. Each business unit is then rated on each of the chosen strength measures, using a rating scale of 1 to 10 (where a *high* rating signifies competitive *strength,* and a *low* rating signifies competitive *weakness*). In the event that the available information is too limited to confidently assign a rating value to a business unit on a particular strength measure, it is usually best to use a score of 5—this avoids biasing the overall score either up or down. Weighted strength ratings are calculated by multiplying the business unit's rating on each strength measure by the assigned weight. For example, a strength score of 6 times a weight of 0.15 gives a weighted strength rating of 0.90. The sum of the weighted ratings across all the strength measures provides a quantitative measure of a business unit's overall competitive strength. Table 8.2 provides sample calculations of competitive-strength ratings for three businesses.

Interpreting the Competitive-Strength Scores   Business units with competitive-strength ratings above 6.7 (on a scale of 1 to 10) are strong market contenders in their industries. Businesses with ratings in the 3.3-to-6.7 range have moderate competitive strength vis-à-vis rivals. Businesses with ratings below 3.3 have a competitively weak standing in the marketplace. If a diversified company's business units all have competitive-strength scores above 5, it is fair to conclude that its business units are all fairly strong market contenders in their respective industries. But as the number of business units with scores below 5 increases, there's reason to question whether the company can perform well with so many businesses in relatively weak competitive positions. This concern takes on even more importance when business units with low scores account for a sizable fraction of the company's revenues.

Using a Nine-Cell Matrix to Simultaneously Portray Industry Attractiveness and Competitive Strength   The industry-attractiveness and business-strength scores can be used to portray the strategic positions of each business in a diversified company. Industry attractiveness is plotted on the vertical axis and competitive strength on the horizontal axis. A nine-cell grid emerges from dividing the vertical axis into three regions (high, medium, and low attractiveness) and the horizontal axis into three regions (strong, average, and weak competitive strength). As shown in Figure 8.3, scores of 6.7 or greater on a rating scale of 1 to 10 denote high industry attractiveness, scores of 3.3 to 6.7 denote medium attractiveness, and scores below 3.3 signal low attractiveness. Likewise, high competitive strength is defined as scores greater than 6.7, average strength as scores of 3.3 to 6.7, and low strength as scores below 3.3. *Each business unit*

TABLE 8.2   Calculating Weighted Competitive-Strength Scores for a Diversified Company's Business Units

		Competitive-Strength Assessments					
		Business A in Industry A		Business B in Industry B		Business C in Industry C	
Competitive-Strength Measures	Importance Weight	Strength Rating*	Weighted Score	Strength Rating*	Weighted Score	Strength Rating*	Weighted Score
Relative market share	0.15	10	1.50	2	0.30	6	0.90
Costs relative to competitors' costs	0.20	7	1.40	4	0.80	5	1.00
Ability to match or beat rivals on key product attributes	0.05	9	0.45	5	0.25	8	0.40
Ability to benefit from strategic fit with sister businesses	0.20	8	1.60	4	0.80	8	0.80
Bargaining leverage with suppliers/customers	0.05	9	0.45	2	0.10	6	0.30
Brand image and reputation	0.10	9	0.90	4	0.40	7	0.70
Other valuable resources/capabilities	0.15	7	1.05	2	0.30	5	0.75
Profitability relative to competitors	0.10	5	0.50	2	0.20	4	0.40
Sum of importance weights	**1.00**						
Weighted overall competitive strength scores			**7.85**		**3.15**		**5.25**

*Rating scale: 1 = very weak; 10 = very strong.

is plotted on the nine-cell matrix according to its overall attractiveness score and strength score, and then it is shown as a "bubble." The size of each bubble is scaled to the percentage of revenues the business generates relative to total corporate revenues. The bubbles in Figure 8.3 were located on the grid using the three industry-attractiveness scores from Table 8.1 and the strength scores for the three business units in Table 8.2.

The locations of the business units on the attractiveness–strength matrix provide valuable guidance in deploying corporate resources. Businesses positioned in the three cells in the upper left portion of the attractiveness–strength matrix (like business A) have both favorable industry attractiveness and competitive strength.

Next in priority come businesses positioned in the three diagonal cells stretching from the lower left to the upper right (like business C). Such businesses usually merit intermediate priority in the parent's resource allocation ranking. However, some

FIGURE 8.3   A Nine-Cell Industry-Attractiveness–Competitive-Strength Matrix

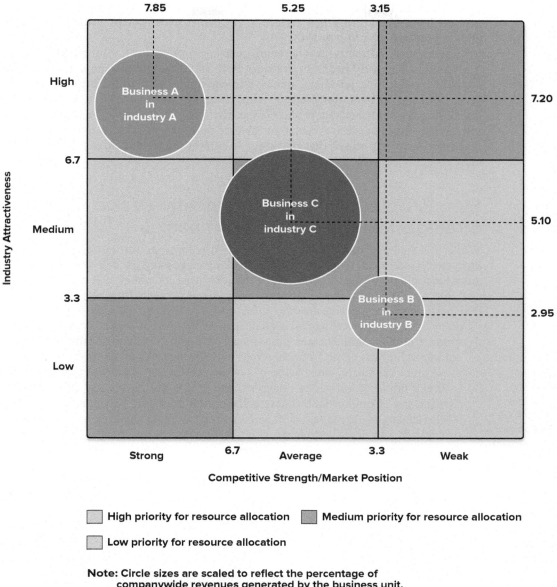

High priority for resource allocation   Medium priority for resource allocation

Low priority for resource allocation

Note: Circle sizes are scaled to reflect the percentage of
companywide revenues generated by the business unit.

businesses in the medium-priority diagonal cells may have brighter or dimmer prospects than others. For example, a small business in the upper right cell of the matrix, despite being in a highly attractive industry, may occupy too weak a competitive position in its industry to justify the investment and resources needed to turn it into a strong market contender.

Businesses in the three cells in the lower right corner of the matrix (like business B) have comparatively low industry attractiveness and minimal competitive strength, making them weak performers with little potential for improvement. At best, they have the lowest claim on corporate resources and may be good candidates for being divested (sold to other companies). However, there are occasions when a business located in the three lower-right cells generates sizable positive cash flows. It may make sense to retain such businesses and divert their cash flows to finance expansion of business units with greater potential for profit growth.

The nine-cell attractiveness–strength matrix provides clear, strong logic for why a diversified company needs to consider both industry attractiveness and business strength in allocating resources and investment capital to its different businesses. A good case can be made for concentrating resources in those businesses that enjoy higher degrees of attractiveness and competitive strength, being very selective in making investments in businesses with intermediate positions on the grid, and withdrawing resources from businesses that are lower in attractiveness and strength unless they offer exceptional profit or cash flow potential.

Step 3: Determining the Competitive Value of Strategic Fit in Diversified Companies

While this step can be bypassed for diversified companies whose businesses are all unrelated (since, by design, strategic fit is lacking), assessing the degree of strategic fit across a company's businesses is central to evaluating its related diversification strategy. But more than just checking for the presence of strategic fit is required here. *The real question is how much competitive value can be generated from whatever strategic fit exists.* Are the cost savings associated with economies of scope likely to give one or more individual businesses a cost-based advantage over rivals? How much competitive value will come from the cross-business transfer of skills, technology, or intellectual capital or the sharing of competitive assets? Can leveraging a potent umbrella brand or corporate image strengthen the businesses and increase sales significantly? Could cross-business collaboration to create new competitive capabilities lead to significant gains in performance? Without significant cross-business strategic fit and dedicated company efforts to capture the benefits, one has to be skeptical about the potential for a diversified company's businesses to perform better together than apart.

Figure 8.4 illustrates the process of comparing the value chains of a company's businesses and identifying opportunities to exploit competitively valuable cross-business strategic fit.

Step 4: Checking for Good Resource Fit

The businesses in a diversified company's lineup need to exhibit good **resource fit.** In firms with a related diversification strategy, good resource fit exists *when the firm's businesses have well-matched specialized resource requirements at points along their value chains* that are critical for the businesses' market success. Matching resource requirements are important in related diversification because they facilitate resource sharing and low-cost resource transfer. In companies pursuing unrelated diversification, resource fit exists when the company has solid *parenting capabilities or resources of a general nature that it can share or transfer to its component businesses.* Firms pursuing related diversification and firms with combination related–unrelated diversification strategies can also benefit from leveraging corporate parenting capabilities

CORE CONCEPT

A company pursuing related diversification exhibits **resource fit** when its businesses have matching specialized resource requirements along their value chains; a company pursuing unrelated diversification has resource fit when the parent company has adequate corporate resources (parenting and general resources) to support its businesses' needs and add value.

and other general resources. Another dimension of resource fit that concerns all types of multibusiness firms is whether they have resources sufficient to support their group of businesses without being spread too thin.

Financial Resource Fit The most important dimension of financial resource fit concerns whether a diversified company can generate the internal cash flows sufficient to fund the capital requirements of its businesses, pay its dividends, meet its debt obligations, and otherwise remain financially healthy. (Financial resources, including the firm's ability to borrow or otherwise raise funds, are a type of general resource.) While additional capital can usually be raised in financial markets, it is important for a diversified firm to have a healthy **internal capital market** that can support the financial requirements of its business lineup. The greater the extent to which a diversified company is able to fund investment in its businesses through internally generated cash flows rather than from equity issues or borrowing, the more powerful its financial resource fit and the less dependent the firm is on external financial resources. This can provide a competitive advantage over single business rivals when credit market conditions are tight, as they have been in the United States and abroad in recent years.

FIGURE 8.4 Identifying the Competitive Advantage Potential of Cross-Business Strategic Fit

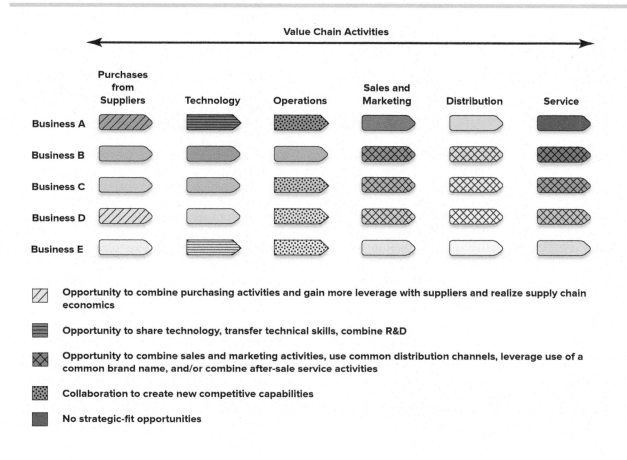

A **portfolio approach** to ensuring financial fit among a firm's businesses is based on the fact that different businesses have different cash flow and investment characteristics. For example, business units in rapidly growing industries are often **cash hogs**—so labeled because the cash flows they are able to generate from internal operations aren't big enough to fund their operations and capital requirements for growth. To keep pace with rising buyer demand, rapid-growth businesses frequently need sizable annual capital investments—for new facilities and equipment, for new product development or technology improvements, and for additional working capital to support inventory expansion and a larger base of operations. Because a cash hog's financial resources must be provided by the corporate parent, corporate managers have to decide whether it makes good financial and strategic sense to keep pouring new money into a cash hog business.

In contrast, business units with leading market positions in mature industries may be **cash cows** in the sense that they generate substantial cash surpluses over what is needed to adequately fund their operations. Market leaders in slow-growth industries often generate sizable positive cash flows *over and above what is needed for growth and reinvestment* because their industry-leading positions tend to generate attractive earnings and because the slow-growth nature of their industry often entails relatively modest annual investment requirements. Cash cows, although not attractive from a growth standpoint, are valuable businesses from a financial resource perspective. The surplus cash flows they generate can be used to pay corporate dividends, finance acquisitions, and provide funds for investing in the company's promising cash hogs. It makes good financial and strategic sense for diversified companies to keep cash cows in a healthy condition, fortifying and defending their market position so as to preserve their cash-generating capability and have an ongoing source of financial resources to deploy elsewhere. General Electric considers its advanced materials, equipment services, and appliance and lighting businesses to be cash cow businesses.

Viewing a diversified group of businesses as a collection of cash flows and cash requirements (present and future flows) can be helpful in understanding what the financial ramifications of diversification are and why having businesses with good financial resource fit can be important. For instance, *a diversified company's businesses exhibit good financial resource fit when the excess cash generated by its cash cow businesses is sufficient to fund the investment requirements of promising cash hog businesses.* Ideally, investing in promising cash hog businesses over time results in growing the hogs into self-supporting *star businesses* that have strong or market-leading competitive positions in attractive, high-growth markets and high levels of profitability. Star businesses are often the cash cows of the future. When the markets of star businesses begin to mature and their growth slows, their competitive strength should produce self-generated cash flows that are more than sufficient to cover their investment needs. The "success sequence" is thus cash hog to young star (but perhaps still a cash hog) to self-supporting star to cash cow. While the practice of viewing a diversified company in terms of cash cows and cash hogs has declined in popularity, it illustrates one approach to analyzing financial resource fit and allocating financial resources across a portfolio of different businesses.

Aside from cash flow considerations, there are two other factors to consider in assessing whether a diversified company's businesses exhibit good financial fit:

- *Do any of the company's individual businesses present financial challenges with respect to contributing adequately to achieving companywide performance targets?* A business exhibits poor financial fit if it soaks up a disproportionate share of the company's financial resources, while making subpar or insignificant contributions to the bottom line. Too many underperforming businesses reduce the company's overall performance and ultimately limit growth in shareholder value.

- *Does the corporation have adequate financial strength to fund its different businesses and maintain a healthy credit rating?* A diversified company's strategy fails the resource-fit test when the resource needs of its portfolio unduly stretch the company's financial health and threaten to impair its credit rating. Many of the world's largest banks, including Royal Bank of Scotland, Citigroup, and HSBC, recently found themselves so undercapitalized and financially overextended that they were forced to sell off some of their business assets to meet regulatory requirements and restore public confidence in their solvency.

Nonfinancial Resource Fit Just as a diversified company must have adequate financial resources to support its various individual businesses, it must also have a big enough and deep enough pool of managerial, administrative, and other parenting capabilities to support all of its different businesses. The following two questions help reveal whether a diversified company has sufficient nonfinancial resources:

- *Does the parent company have (or can it develop) the specific resources and capabilities needed to be successful in each of its businesses?* Sometimes the resources a company has accumulated in its core business prove to be a poor match with the competitive capabilities needed to succeed in the businesses into which it has diversified. For instance, BTR, a multibusiness company in Great Britain, discovered that the company's resources and managerial skills were quite well suited for parenting its industrial manufacturing businesses but not for parenting its distribution businesses (National Tyre Services and Texas-based Summers Group). As a result, BTR decided to divest its distribution businesses and focus exclusively on diversifying around small industrial manufacturing. For companies pursuing related diversification strategies, a mismatch between the company's competitive assets and the key success factors of an industry can be serious enough to warrant divesting businesses in that industry or not acquiring a new business. In contrast, when a company's resources and capabilities are a good match with the key success factors of industries it is not presently in, it makes sense to take a hard look at acquiring companies in these industries and expanding the company's business lineup.

- *Are the parent company's resources being stretched too thinly by the resource requirements of one or more of its businesses?* A diversified company must guard against overtaxing its resources and capabilities, a condition that can arise when (1) it goes on an acquisition spree and management is called on to assimilate and oversee many new businesses very quickly or (2) it lacks sufficient resource depth to do a creditable job of transferring skills and competencies from one of its businesses to another. The broader the diversification, the greater the concern about whether corporate executives are overburdened by the demands of competently parenting so many different businesses. Plus, the more a company's diversification strategy is tied to transferring know-how or technologies from existing businesses to newly acquired businesses, the more time and money that has to be put into developing a deep-enough resource pool to supply these businesses with the resources and capabilities they need to be successful.[15] Otherwise, its resource pool ends up being spread too thinly across many businesses, and the opportunity for achieving $1 + 1 = 3$ outcomes slips through the cracks.

Step 5: Ranking Business Units and Assigning a Priority for Resource Allocation

Once a diversified company's strategy has been evaluated from the perspective of industry attractiveness, competitive strength, strategic fit, and resource fit, the next step is to use this information to rank the performance prospects of the businesses from best to worst. Such ranking helps top-level executives assign each business a priority for resource support and capital investment.

The locations of the different businesses in the nine-cell industry-attractiveness–competitive-strength matrix provide a solid basis for identifying high-opportunity businesses and low-opportunity businesses. Normally, competitively strong businesses in attractive industries have significantly better performance prospects than competitively weak businesses in unattractive industries. Also, the revenue and earnings outlook for businesses in fast-growing industries is normally better than for businesses in slow-growing industries. As a rule, *business subsidiaries with the brightest profit and growth prospects, attractive positions in the nine-cell matrix, and solid strategic and resource fit should receive top priority for allocation of corporate resources.* However, in ranking the prospects of the different businesses from best to worst, it is usually wise to also take into account each business's past performance in regard to sales growth, profit growth, contribution to company earnings, return on capital invested in the business, and cash flow from operations. While past performance is not always a reliable predictor of future performance, it does signal whether a business is already performing well or has problems to overcome.

Allocating Financial Resources　Figure 8.5 shows the chief strategic and financial options for allocating a diversified company's financial resources. Divesting businesses

FIGURE 8.5　The Chief Strategic and Financial Options for Allocating a Diversified Company's Financial Resources

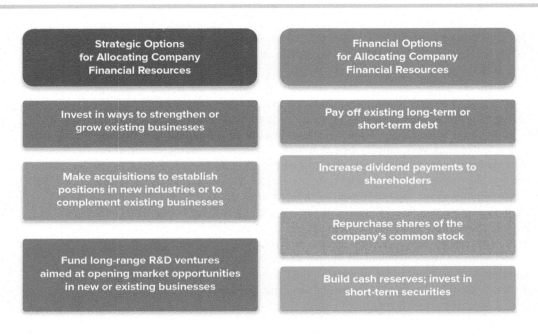

Strategic Options for Allocating Company Financial Resources

Invest in ways to strengthen or grow existing businesses

Make acquisitions to establish positions in new industries or to complement existing businesses

Fund long-range R&D ventures aimed at opening market opportunities in new or existing businesses

Financial Options for Allocating Company Financial Resources

Pay off existing long-term or short-term debt

Increase dividend payments to shareholders

Repurchase shares of the company's common stock

Build cash reserves; invest in short-term securities

with the weakest future prospects and businesses that lack adequate strategic fit and/or resource fit is one of the best ways of generating additional funds for redeployment to businesses with better opportunities and better strategic and resource fit. Free cash flows from cash cow businesses also add to the pool of funds that can be usefully redeployed. *Ideally,* a diversified company will have sufficient financial resources to strengthen or grow its existing businesses, make any new acquisitions that are desirable, fund other promising business opportunities, pay off existing debt, and periodically increase dividend payments to shareholders and/or repurchase shares of stock. But, as a practical matter, a company's financial resources are limited. Thus, to make the best use of the available funds, top executives must steer resources to those businesses with the best prospects and either divest or allocate minimal resources to businesses with marginal prospects—this is why ranking the performance prospects of the various businesses from best to worst is so crucial. *Strategic* uses of corporate financial resources should usually take precedence over strictly financial considerations (see Figure 8.5) unless there is a compelling reason to strengthen the firm's balance sheet or better reward shareholders.

Step 6: Crafting New Strategic Moves to Improve Overall Corporate Performance

The conclusions flowing from the five preceding analytic steps set the agenda for crafting strategic moves to improve a diversified company's overall performance. The strategic options boil down to four broad categories of actions (see Figure 8.6):

● **LO 8-5**

Understand the four main corporate strategy options a diversified company can employ to improve company performance.

1. Sticking closely with the existing business lineup and pursuing the opportunities these businesses present.
2. Broadening the company's business scope by making new acquisitions in new industries.
3. Divesting certain businesses and retrenching to a narrower base of business operations.
4. Restructuring the company's business lineup and putting a whole new face on the company's business makeup.

Sticking Closely with the Present Business Lineup   The option of sticking with the current business lineup makes sense when the company's existing businesses offer attractive growth opportunities and can be counted on to create economic value for shareholders. As long as the company's set of existing businesses have good prospects and are in alignment with the company's diversification strategy, then major changes in the company's business mix are unnecessary. Corporate executives can concentrate their attention on getting the best performance from each of the businesses, steering corporate resources into the areas of greatest potential and profitability. The specifics of "what to do" to wring better performance from the present business lineup have to be dictated by each business's circumstances and the preceding analysis of the corporate parent's diversification strategy.

Broadening a Diversified Company's Business Base   Diversified companies sometimes find it desirable to build positions in new industries, whether related or unrelated. Several motivating factors are in play. One is sluggish growth that makes the potential revenue and profit boost of a newly acquired business look attractive. A second is the potential for transferring resources and capabilities to other related or complementary businesses.

FIGURE 8.6   A Company's Four Main Strategic Alternatives after It Diversifies

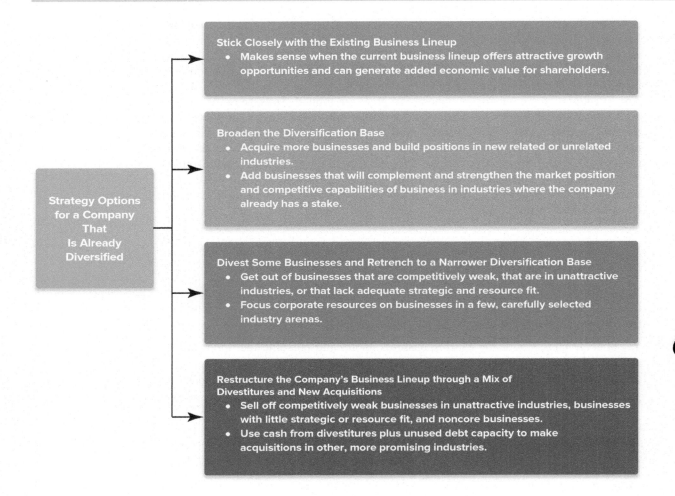

Strategy Options for a Company That Is Already Diversified

Stick Closely with the Existing Business Lineup
- Makes sense when the current business lineup offers attractive growth opportunities and can generate added economic value for shareholders.

Broaden the Diversification Base
- Acquire more businesses and build positions in new related or unrelated industries.
- Add businesses that will complement and strengthen the market position and competitive capabilities of business in industries where the company already has a stake.

Divest Some Businesses and Retrench to a Narrower Diversification Base
- Get out of businesses that are competitively weak, that are in unattractive industries, or that lack adequate strategic and resource fit.
- Focus corporate resources on businesses in a few, carefully selected industry arenas.

Restructure the Company's Business Lineup through a Mix of Divestitures and New Acquisitions
- Sell off competitively weak businesses in unattractive industries, businesses with little strategic or resource fit, and noncore businesses.
- Use cash from divestitures plus unused debt capacity to make acquisitions in other, more promising industries.

A third is rapidly changing conditions in one or more of a company's core businesses, brought on by technological, legislative, or demographic changes. For instance, the passage of legislation in the United States allowing banks, insurance companies, and stock brokerages to enter each other's businesses spurred a raft of acquisitions and mergers to create full-service financial enterprises capable of meeting the multiple financial needs of customers. A fourth, and very important, motivating factor for adding new businesses is to complement and strengthen the market position and competitive capabilities of one or more of the company's present businesses. Procter & Gamble's acquisition of Gillette strengthened and extended P&G's reach into personal care and household products—Gillette's businesses included Oral-B toothbrushes, Gillette razors and razor blades, Duracell batteries, Braun shavers, small appliances (coffeemakers, mixers, hair dryers, and electric toothbrushes), and toiletries. Johnson & Johnson has used acquisitions to diversify far beyond its well-known Band-Aid and baby care businesses and become a major player in pharmaceuticals, medical devices, and medical diagnostics.

Another important avenue for expanding the scope of a diversified company is to grow by extending the operations of existing businesses into additional country markets, as discussed in Chapter 7. Expanding a company's geographic scope may offer an exceptional competitive advantage potential by facilitating the full capture of economies of scale and learning- and experience-curve effects. In some businesses, the volume of sales needed to realize full economies of scale and/or benefit fully from experience-curve effects exceeds the volume that can be achieved by operating within the boundaries of just one or several country markets, especially small ones.

Retrenching to a Narrower Diversification Base   A number of diversified firms have had difficulty managing a diverse group of businesses and have elected to exit some of them. Selling a business outright to another company is far and away the most frequently used option for divesting a business. In 2017, Samsung Electronics sold its printing business to HP, Inc. in order better focus on its core smartphone, television, and memory chip businesses. But sometimes a business selected for divestiture has ample resources and capabilities to compete successfully on its own. In such cases, a corporate parent may elect to *spin off* the unwanted business as a financially and managerially independent company, either by selling shares to the public via an initial public offering or by distributing shares in the new company to shareholders of the corporate parent. eBay spun off PayPal in 2015 at a valuation of $45 billion—a value 30 times more than what eBay paid for the company in a 2002 acquisition. In 2018, pesticide maker FMC Corp. spun off its lithium business to boost profitability by focusing on its core business.

> A **spin-off** is an independent company created when a corporate parent divests a business either by selling shares to the public via an initial public offering or by distributing shares in the new company to shareholders of the corporate parent.

Retrenching to a narrower diversification base is usually undertaken when top management concludes that its diversification has ranged too far afield and that the company can improve long-term performance by concentrating on a smaller number of businesses. But there are other important reasons for divesting one or more of a company's present businesses. Sometimes divesting a business has to be considered because market conditions in a once-attractive industry have badly deteriorated. A business can become a prime candidate for divestiture because it lacks adequate strategic or resource fit, because it is a cash hog with questionable long-term potential, or because remedying its competitive weaknesses is too expensive relative to the likely gains in profitability. Sometimes a company acquires businesses that, down the road, just do not work out as expected even though management has tried its best. Subpar performance by some business units is bound to occur, thereby raising questions of whether to divest them or keep them and attempt a turnaround. Other business units, despite adequate financial performance, may not mesh as well with the rest of the firm as was originally thought. For instance, PepsiCo divested its group of fast-food restaurant businesses (Kentucky Fried Chicken, Pizza Hut, and Taco Bell) to focus on its core soft-drink and snack-food businesses, where their specialized resources and capabilities could add more value.

On occasion, a diversification move that seems sensible from a strategic-fit standpoint turns out to be a poor *cultural fit*.[16] When several pharmaceutical companies diversified into cosmetics and perfume, they discovered their personnel had little respect for the "frivolous" nature of such products compared to the far nobler task of developing miracle drugs to cure the ill. The absence of shared values and cultural compatibility between the medical research and chemical-compounding expertise of the pharmaceutical companies and the fashion and marketing orientation of the cosmetics business was the undoing of what otherwise was diversification into businesses

Diversified companies need to divest low-performing businesses or businesses that don't fit in order to concentrate on expanding existing businesses and entering new ones where opportunities are more promising.

CORE CONCEPT

Companywide restructuring *(corporate restructuring)* involves making major changes in a diversified company by divesting some businesses and/or acquiring others, so as to put a whole new face on the company's business lineup.

with technology-sharing potential, product development fit, and some overlap in distribution channels.

A useful guide to determine whether or when to divest a business subsidiary is to ask, "If we were not in this business today, would we want to get into it now?" When the answer is no or probably not, divestiture should be considered. Another signal that a business should be divested occurs when it is worth more to another company than to the present parent; in such cases, shareholders would be well served if the company sells the business and collects a premium price from the buyer for whom the business is a valuable fit.

Restructuring a Diversified Company's Business Lineup Restructuring a diversified company on a companywide basis *(corporate restructuring)* involves divesting some businesses and/or acquiring others, so as to put a whole new face on the company's business lineup.[17] Performing radical surgery on a company's business lineup is appealing when its financial performance is being squeezed or eroded by

- A serious mismatch between the company's resources and capabilities and the type of diversification that it has pursued.
- Too many businesses in slow-growth, declining, low-margin, or otherwise unattractive industries.
- Too many competitively weak businesses.
- The emergence of new technologies that threaten the survival of one or more important businesses.
- Ongoing declines in the market shares of one or more major business units that are falling prey to more market-savvy competitors.
- An excessive debt burden with interest costs that eat deeply into profitability.
- Ill-chosen acquisitions that haven't lived up to expectations.

On occasion, corporate restructuring can be prompted by special circumstances—such as when a firm has a unique opportunity to make an acquisition so big and important that it has to sell several existing business units to finance the new acquisition or when a company needs to sell off some businesses in order to raise the cash for entering a potentially big industry with wave-of-the-future technologies or products. As businesses are divested, corporate restructuring generally involves aligning the remaining business units into groups with the best strategic fit and then redeploying the cash flows from the divested businesses to either pay down debt or make new acquisitions to strengthen the parent company's business position in the industries it has chosen to emphasize.

Over the past decade, corporate restructuring has become a popular strategy at many diversified companies, especially those that had diversified broadly into many different industries and lines of business. Google is a prime example, having acquired over 200 businesses of varying types within the past 20 years. This rapid expansion led to a corporate restructuring in 2015 that created a new holding company called Alphabet, Inc. into which businesses other than Internet services were moved, each to be managed by its own CEO. Google remained the umbrella company for its core Internet service businesses, such as YouTube, Waze, the Android mobile operating system, and Google Search. Ultimately, Google was also folded into Alphabet and became its largest subsidiary. This restructuring allowed Google

Restructuring Strategically at VF Corporation

Over its 120 year history, VF Corporation has become one of the world's largest apparel, footwear, and accessories companies through an aggressive acquisition strategy. Brands that they have acquired include North Face, Timberland, Wrangler, Lee, Jan Sport, Nautica, Eagle Creek, Smart Wool, and Altra Footwear. In recent years, however, the company's top managers began to notice that different segments of their business had diverging management requirements, due to differing distribution channels, customer needs, and growth patterns. The solution was to restructure the company, which was characterized as very much a strategic move, since there was an absence of good strategic fit among these two different types of businesses.

In 2019, the company split itself into two separate organizations, moving VF's Jeanswear organization into an independent, publicly traded company (a type of move known as a *spin-off*). The new company was named Kontoor Brands, Inc., and included the Wrangler, Lee, and Rock & Republic brands, along with the VF Outlet business. VF Corporation, also known as VFC, would retain the more dynamic, faster-moving active-lifestyle brands. The split was hoped to enable the faster growing segments retained within VFC to pursue opportunities that

Soundaholic studio/Shutterstock

are less relevant to the concerns of the more staid sister business of Kontoor. It would also enable the brands within VFC to respond in a more nimble way to the rapid changes that tend to characterize the world of fashion. While there are always risks and uncertainties that come along with spin-offs, such as the risk of disruption of the businesses, and the temporary diversion of management resources, the full year 2019 revenue was up by 13 percent, and the prospects going forward looked rosy.

Sources: Company website; https://www.thestreet.com/investing/stocks/v-f-corp-ceo-why-we-just-made-one-of-the-biggest-decisions-in-our-company-history-14681383, accessed February 4, 2020.

---

to slim down a bit and focus more on its core businesses, while allowing the more unrelated companies greater independence under Alphabet. The restructuring has purportedly accomplished much of its aims, reaching $1 trillion market value by January 2020. Other seemingly successful restructuring efforts include Disney's reorganization into four business units to help it capitalize on growth opportunities, Hulu's steps to streamline while accommodating further growth, and the Wall Street Journal's efforts to shift toward a more digital strategy.

Illustration Capsule 8.4 discusses how VF Corporation, maker of North Face and other popular "lifestyle" apparel brands, has used a restructuring strategy to rationalize its management of different types of companies.

KEY POINTS

1. The purpose of diversification is to build shareholder value. Diversification builds shareholder value only when a diversified group of businesses can perform better under the auspices of a single corporate parent than they would as independent, standalone businesses. The goal is to achieve not just a $1 + 1 = 2$ result but rather to realize important $1 + 1 = 3$ performance benefits—an effect known as *synergy*. For a move to diversify into a new business to have a reasonable prospect of adding shareholder value, it must be capable of passing the three Tests of Corporate Advantage: the industry attractiveness test, the cost-of-entry test, and the better-off test.

2. Entry into new businesses can take any of three forms: acquisition, internal startup, or joint venture. The choice of which is best depends on the firm's resources and capabilities, the industry's entry barriers, the importance of speed, and relative costs.

3. There are two fundamental approaches to diversification—into related businesses and into unrelated businesses. The rationale for *related* diversification is to benefit from *strategic fit:* diversify into businesses with commonalities across their respective value chains, and then capitalize on the strategic fit by sharing or transferring the resources and capabilities across matching value chain activities to gain competitive advantages.

4. *Unrelated* diversification strategies surrender the competitive advantage potential of strategic fit at the value chain level in return for the potential that can be realized from superior corporate parenting or the sharing and transfer of general resources and capabilities. An outstanding corporate parent can benefit its businesses through (1) providing high-level oversight and making available other corporate resources, (2) allocating financial resources across the business portfolio (under certain circumstances), and (3) restructuring underperforming acquisitions.

5. Related diversification provides a stronger foundation for creating shareholder value than does unrelated diversification, since the *specialized resources and capabilities* that are leveraged in related diversification tend to be more valuable competitive assets than the *general resources and capabilities* underlying unrelated diversification, which in most cases are relatively common and easier to imitate.

6. Analyzing how good a company's diversification strategy is consists of a six-step process:

   Step 1: *Evaluate the long-term attractiveness of the industries into which the firm has diversified.* Determining industry attractiveness involves developing a list of industry-attractiveness measures, each of which might have a different importance weight.

   Step 2: *Evaluate the relative competitive strength of each of the company's business units.* The purpose of rating the competitive strength of each business is to gain a clear understanding of which businesses are strong contenders in their industries, which are weak contenders, and what the underlying reasons are for their strength or weakness. The conclusions about industry attractiveness can be joined with the conclusions about competitive strength by drawing a nine-cell industry-attractiveness–competitive-strength matrix that helps identify the prospects of each business and the level of priority each business should be given in allocating corporate resources and investment capital.

   Step 3: *Check for the competitive value of cross-business strategic fit.* A business is more attractive strategically when it has value chain relationships with the other business units that offer the potential to (1) combine operations to realize economies of scope, (2) transfer technology, skills, know-how, or other resource capabilities from one business to another, (3) leverage the use of a trusted brand name or other resources that enhance differentiation, (4) share other competitively valuable resources among the company's businesses, and (5) build new resources and competitive capabilities via cross-business collaboration. Cross-business strategic fit represents a significant avenue for producing competitive advantage beyond what any one business can achieve on its own.

Step 4: *Check whether the firm's resources fit the resource requirements of its present business lineup.* In firms with a related diversification strategy, resource fit exists when the firm's businesses have matching resource requirements at points along their value chains that are critical for the businesses' market success. In companies pursuing unrelated diversification, resource fit exists when the company has solid parenting capabilities or resources of a general nature that it can share or transfer to its component businesses. When there is financial resource fit among the businesses of any type of diversified company, the company can generate internal cash flows sufficient to fund the capital requirements of its businesses, pay its dividends, meet its debt obligations, and otherwise remain financially healthy.

Step 5: *Rank the performance prospects of the businesses from best to worst, and determine what the corporate parent's priority should be in allocating resources to its various businesses.* The most important considerations in judging business unit performance are sales growth, profit growth, contribution to company earnings, and the return on capital invested in the business. Normally, strong business units in attractive industries should head the list for corporate resource support.

Step 6: *Craft new strategic moves to improve overall corporate performance.* This step draws on the results of the preceding steps as the basis for selecting one of four different strategic paths for improving a diversified company's performance: (1) Stick closely with the existing business lineup and pursue opportunities presented by these businesses, (2) broaden the scope of diversification by entering additional industries, (3) retrench to a narrower scope of diversification by divesting poorly performing businesses, or (4) broadly restructure the business lineup with multiple divestitures and/or acquisitions.

ASSURANCE OF LEARNING EXERCISES

1. See if you can identify the value chain relationships that make the businesses of the following companies related in competitively relevant ways. In particular, you should consider whether there are cross-business opportunities for (1) transferring skills and technology, (2) combining related value chain activities to achieve economies of scope, and/or (3) leveraging the use of a well-respected brand name or other resources that enhance differentiation.

LO 8-1, LO 8-2,
LO 8-3, LO 8-4

Bloomin' Brands
* Outback Steakhouse
* Carrabba's Italian Grill
* Bonefish Grill (market-fresh fine seafood)
* Fleming's Prime Steakhouse & Wine Bar

L'Oréal
* Maybelline, Lancôme, Helena Rubinstein, essie, Kiehl's and Shu Uemura cosmetics
* L'Oréal and Soft Sheen/Carson hair care products

- Redken, Matrix, L'Oréal Professional, and Kerastase Paris professional hair care and skin care products
- Ralph Lauren and Giorgio Armani fragrances
- Biotherm skin care products
- La Roche-Posay and Vichy Laboratories dermo-cosmetics

Johnson & Johnson

- Baby products (powder, shampoo, oil, lotion)
- Band-Aids and other first-aid products
- Women's health and personal care products (Stayfree, Carefree, Sure & Natural)
- Neutrogena, and Aveeno skin care products
- Nonprescription drugs (Tylenol, Motrin, Pepcid AC, Mylanta, Monistat)
- Prescription drugs
- Prosthetic and other medical devices
- Surgical and hospital products
- Acuvue contact lenses

LO 8-1, LO 8-2, LO 8-3, LO 8-4

2. Peruse the business group listings for 3M Company shown as follows and listed at its website. How would you characterize the company's corporate strategy—related diversification, unrelated diversification, or a combination related–unrelated diversification strategy? Explain your answer.

- Consumer products—for the home and office including Post-it® and Scotch®
- Electronics and Energy—technology solutions for customers in electronics and energy markets
- Health Care—products for health care professionals
- Industrial—abrasives, adhesives, specialty materials and filtration systems
- Safety and Graphics—safety and security products; graphic solutions

Mc Graw Hill connect
LO 8-1, LO 8-2, LO 8-3, LO 8-4, LO 8-5

3. ITT is a technology-oriented engineering and manufacturing company with the following business divisions and products:

- Industrial Process Division—industrial pumps, valves, and monitoring and control systems; aftermarket services for the chemical, oil and gas, mining, pulp and paper, power, and biopharmaceutical markets
- Motion Technologies Division—durable brake pads, shock absorbers, and damping technologies for the automotive and rail markets
- Interconnect Solutions—connectors and fittings for the production of automobiles, aircraft, railcars and locomotives, oil field equipment, medical equipment, and industrial equipment
- Control Technologies—energy absorption and vibration dampening equipment, transducers and regulators, and motion controls used in the production of robotics, medical equipment, automobiles, subsea equipment, industrial equipment, aircraft, and military vehicles

Based on the previous listing, would you say that ITT's business lineup reflects a strategy of related diversification, unrelated diversification, or a combination of related and unrelated diversification? What benefits are generated from any strategic fit existing between ITT's businesses? Also, what types of companies should ITT consider acquiring that might improve shareholder value? Justify your answer.

EXERCISES FOR SIMULATION PARTICIPANTS

1. In the event that your company has the opportunity to diversify into other products or businesses of your choosing, what would be the advantages of opting to pursue related diversification, unrelated diversification, or a combination of both? Explain why.   **LO 8-1, LO 8-2, LO 8-3**

2. What strategic-fit benefits might be captured by transferring resources and competitive capabilities to newly acquired related businesses.

3. If your company opted to pursue a strategy of related diversification, what industries or product categories could it diversify into that would allow it to achieve economies of scope? Name at least two or three such industries or product categories, and indicate the specific kinds of cost savings that might accrue from entry into each.   **LO 8-1, LO 8-2**

4. If your company opted to pursue a strategy of unrelated diversification, what industries or product categories could it diversify into that would allow it to capitalize on using its present brand name and corporate image to good advantage in the newly entered businesses or product categories? Name at least two or three such industries or product categories, and indicate the *specific benefits* that might be captured by transferring your company's umbrella brand name to each.   **LO 8-1, LO 8-3**

ENDNOTES

[1] Michael E. Porter, "From Competitive Advantage to Corporate Strategy," *Harvard Business Review* 45, no. 3 (May–June 1987), pp. 46–49.

[2] A. Shleifer and R. Vishny, "Takeovers in the 60s and the 80s—Evidence and Implications," *Strategic Management Journal* 12 (Winter 1991), pp. 51–59; T. Brush, "Predicted Change in Operational Synergy and Post-Acquisition Performance of Acquired Businesses," *Strategic Management Journal* 17, no. 1 (1996), pp. 1–24; J. P. Walsh, "Top Management Turnover Following Mergers and Acquisitions," *Strategic Management Journal* 9, no. 2 (1988), pp. 173–183; A. Cannella and D. Hambrick, "Effects of Executive Departures on the Performance of Acquired Firms," *Strategic Management Journal* 14 (Summer 1993), pp. 137–152; R. Roll, "The Hubris Hypothesis of Corporate Takeovers," *Journal of Business* 59, no. 2 (1986), pp. 197–216; P. Haspeslagh and D. Jemison, *Managing Acquisitions* (New York: Free Press, 1991).

[3] M.L.A. Hayward, "When Do Firms Learn from Their Acquisition Experience? Evidence from 1990–1995," *Strategic Management Journal* 23, no. 1 (2002), pp. 21–29; G. Ahuja and R. Katila, "Technological Acquisitions and the Innovation Performance of Acquiring Firms: A Longitudinal Study," *Strategic Management Journal* 22, no. 3 (2001), pp. 197–220; H. Barkema and F. Vermeulen, "International Expansion through Start-Up or Acquisition: A Learning Perspective," *Academy of Management Journal* 41, no. 1 (1998), pp. 7–26.

[4] Yves L. Doz and Gary Hamel, *Alliance Advantage: The Art of Creating Value through Partnering* (Boston: Harvard Business School Press, 1998), chaps. 1 and 2.

[5] J. Glover, "The Guardian," March 23, 1996, www.mcspotlight.org/media/press/guardpizza_23mar96.html.

[6] Michael E. Porter, *Competitive Advantage* (New York: Free Press, 1985), pp. 318–319, 337–353; Porter, "From Competitive Advantage to Corporate Strategy," pp. 53–57; Constantinos C. Markides and Peter J. Williamson, "Corporate Diversification and Organization Structure: A Resource-Based View," *Academy of Management Journal* 39, no. 2 (April 1996), pp. 340–367.

[7] David J. Collis and Cynthia A. Montgomery, "Creating Corporate Advantage," *Harvard Business Review* 76, no. 3 (May–June 1998), pp. 72–80; Markides and Williamson, "Corporate Diversification and Organization Structure."

[8] Jeanne M. Liedtka, "Collaboration across Lines of Business for Competitive Advantage," *Academy of Management Executive* 10, no. 2 (May 1996), pp. 20–34.

[9] Kathleen M. Eisenhardt and D. Charles Galunic, "Coevolving: At Last, a Way to Make Synergies Work," *Harvard Business Review* 78, no. 1 (January–February 2000), pp. 91–101; Constantinos C. Markides and Peter J. Williamson, "Related Diversification, Core Competences and Corporate Performance," *Strategic Management Journal* 15 (Summer 1994), pp. 149–165.

[10] A. Campbell, M. Goold, and M. Alexander, "Corporate Strategy: The Quest for Parenting Advantage," *Harvard Business Review* 73, no. 2 (March–April 1995), pp. 120–132.

[11] Cynthia A. Montgomery and B. Wernerfelt, "Diversification, Ricardian Rents, and Tobin-Q," *RAND Journal of Economics* 19, no. 4 (1988), pp. 623–632.

[12] Patricia L. Anslinger and Thomas E. Copeland, "Growth through Acquisitions: A Fresh Look," *Harvard Business Review* 74, no. 1 (January–February 1996), pp. 126–135.

[13] M. Lubatkin and S. Chatterjee, "Extending Modern Portfolio Theory," *Academy of Management Journal* 37, no.1 (February 1994), pp. 109–136.

[14] Lawrence G. Franko, "The Death of Diversification? The Focusing of the World's Industrial Firms, 1980–2000," *Business Horizons* 47, no. 4 (July–August 2004), pp. 41–50.

[15] David J. Collis and Cynthia A. Montgomery, "Competing on Resources: Strategy in the 90s," *Harvard Business Review* 73, no. 4 (July–August 1995), pp. 118–128.

[16] Peter F. Drucker, *Management: Tasks, Responsibilities, Practices* (New York: Harper & Row, 1974), p. 709.

[17] Lee Dranikoff, Tim Koller, and Anton Schneider, "Divestiture: Strategy's Missing Link," *Harvard Business Review* 80, no. 5 (May 2002), pp. 74–83.

chapter 9

Ethics, Corporate Social Responsibility, Environmental Sustainability, and Strategy

Learning Objectives

After reading this chapter, you should be able to:

LO 9-1 Understand why the standards of ethical behavior in business are no different from ethical standards in general.

LO 9-2 Recognize conditions that give rise to unethical business strategies and behavior.

LO 9-3 Identify the costs of business ethics failures.

LO 9-4 Understand the concepts of corporate social responsibility and environmental sustainability and how companies balance these duties with economic responsibilities to shareholders.

Richard Schneider/Getty Images

A well-run business must have high and consistent standards of ethics.

> Richard Branson—*Founder of Virgin Atlantic Airlines and Virgin Group*

When sustainability is viewed as being a matter of survival for your business, I believe you can create massive change.

> Cameron Sinclair—*Head of social innovation at Airbnb*

Clearly, in capitalistic or market economies, a company has a responsibility to make a profit and grow the business. Managers of public companies have a fiduciary duty to operate the enterprise in a manner that creates value for the company's shareholders—a legal obligation. Just as clearly, a company and its personnel are duty-bound to obey the law otherwise and comply with governmental regulations. But does a company also have a duty to go beyond legal requirements and hold all company personnel responsible for conforming to high ethical standards? Does it have an obligation to contribute to the betterment of society, independent of the needs and preferences of the customers it serves? Should a company display a social conscience by devoting a portion of its resources to bettering society? Should its strategic initiatives be screened for possible negative effects on future generations of the world's population?

This chapter focuses on whether a company, in the course of trying to craft and execute a strategy that delivers value to both customers and shareholders, also has a duty to (1) act in an ethical manner; (2) be a committed corporate citizen and allocate some of its resources to improving the well-being of employees, the communities in which it operates, and society as a whole; and (3) adopt business practices that conserve natural resources, protect the interests of future generations, and preserve the well-being of the planet.

WHAT DO WE MEAN BY *BUSINESS ETHICS?*

● **LO 9-1**

Understand why the standards of ethical behavior in business are no different from ethical standards in general.

Ethics concerns principles of right or wrong conduct. **Business ethics** is the application of ethical principles and standards to the actions and decisions of business organizations and the conduct of their personnel.[1] *Ethical principles in business are not materially different from ethical principles in general.* Why? Because business actions have to be judged in the context of society's standards of right and wrong, not with respect to a special set of ethical standards applicable only to business situations. If dishonesty is considered unethical and immoral, then dishonest behavior in business—whether it relates to customers, suppliers, employees, shareholders, competitors, or government—qualifies as equally unethical and immoral. If being ethical entails not deliberately harming others, then businesses are ethically obliged to recall a defective or unsafe product swiftly, regardless of the cost. If society deems bribery unethical, then it is unethical for company personnel to make payoffs to government officials to win government contracts or bestow favors to customers to win or retain their business. In short, ethical behavior in business situations requires adhering to generally accepted norms about right or wrong conduct. As a consequence, company managers have an obligation—indeed, a duty—to observe ethical norms when crafting and executing strategy.

WHERE DO ETHICAL STANDARDS COME FROM—ARE THEY UNIVERSAL OR DEPENDENT ON LOCAL NORMS?

Notions of right and wrong, fair and unfair, moral and immoral are present in all societies and cultures. But there are three distinct schools of thought about the extent to which ethical standards travel across cultures and whether multinational companies can apply the same set of ethical standards in any and all locations where they operate.

The School of Ethical Universalism

According to the school of **ethical universalism,** the most fundamental conceptions of right and wrong are *universal* and transcend culture, society, and religion.[2] For instance, being truthful (not lying and not being deliberately deceitful) strikes a chord of what's right in the peoples of all nations. Likewise, demonstrating integrity of character, not cheating or harming people, and treating others with decency are concepts that resonate with people of virtually all cultures and religions.

Common moral agreement about right and wrong actions and behaviors across multiple cultures and countries gives rise to universal ethical standards that apply to members of all societies, all companies, and all businesspeople. These universal ethical principles set forth the traits and behaviors that are considered virtuous and that a good person is supposed to believe in and to display. Thus, adherents of the school of ethical universalism maintain that it is entirely appropriate to expect all members of society (including all personnel of all companies worldwide) to conform to these universal ethical standards.[3] For example, people in most societies would concur that it is unethical for companies to knowingly expose workers to toxic chemicals and hazardous materials or to sell products known to be unsafe or harmful to the users.

The strength of ethical universalism is that it draws on the collective views of multiple societies and cultures to put some clear boundaries on what constitutes ethical and unethical business behavior, regardless of the country or culture in which a company's personnel are conducting activities. This means that with respect to basic moral standards that do not vary significantly according to local cultural beliefs, traditions, or religious convictions, a multinational company can develop a code of ethics that it applies more or less evenly across its worldwide operations. It can avoid the slippery slope that comes from having different ethical standards for different company personnel depending on where in the world they are working.

The School of Ethical Relativism

While undoubtedly there are some universal moral prescriptions (like being truthful and trustworthy), there are also observable variations from one society to another as to what constitutes ethical or unethical behavior. Indeed, differing religious beliefs, social customs, traditions, core values, and behavioral norms frequently give rise to different standards about what is fair or unfair, moral or immoral, and ethically right or wrong. For instance, European and American managers often establish standards of business conduct that protect human rights such as freedom of movement and residence, freedom of speech and political opinion, and the right to privacy. In China, where societal commitment to basic human rights is weak, human rights considerations play a small role in determining what is ethically right or wrong in conducting business activities. In Japan, managers believe that showing respect for the collective good of society is a more important ethical consideration. In Muslim countries, managers typically apply ethical standards compatible with the teachings of Muhammad. Consequently, the school of **ethical relativism** holds that a "one-size-fits-all" template for judging the ethical appropriateness of business actions and the behaviors of company personnel is totally inappropriate. Rather, the underlying thesis of ethical relativism is that whether certain actions or behaviors are ethically right or wrong depends on the ethical norms of the country or culture in which they take place. For businesses, this implies that when there are cross-country or cross-cultural differences in ethical standards, it is appropriate for *local ethical standards to take precedence over what the ethical standards may be in a company's home market.*[4] In a world of ethical relativism, there are few absolutes when it comes to business ethics, and thus few ethical absolutes for consistently judging the ethical correctness of a company's conduct in various countries and markets.

> **CORE** CONCEPT
>
> The school of **ethical relativism** holds that differing religious beliefs, customs, and behavioral norms across countries and cultures give rise to *differing of standards concerning what is ethically right or wrong.* These differing standards mean that whether business-related actions are right or wrong depends on the prevailing local ethical standards.

This need to contour local ethical standards to fit local customs, local notions of fair and proper individual treatment, and local business practices gives rise to multiple sets of ethical standards. It also poses some challenging ethical dilemmas. Consider the following two examples.

The Use of Underage Labor   In industrialized nations, the use of underage workers is considered taboo. Social activists are adamant that child labor is unethical and that companies should neither employ children under the age of 18 as full-time employees nor source any products from foreign suppliers that employ underage workers. Many countries have passed legislation forbidding the use of underage labor or, at a minimum, regulating the employment of people under the age of 18. However, in Eretria, Uzbekistan, Myanmar, Somalia, Zimbabwe, Afghanistan, Sudan, North Korea, Yemen, and more than 50 other countries, it is customary to view children as potential, even necessary, workers. In other countries, like China, India, Russia, and Brazil, child

> Under ethical relativism, there can be no one-size-fits-all set of authentic ethical norms against which to gauge the conduct of company personnel.

labor laws are often poorly enforced.[5] As of 2016, the International Labor Organization estimated that there were about 152 million child laborers age 5 to 17 and that some 73 million of them were engaged in hazardous work.[6]

While exposing children to hazardous work and long work hours is unquestionably deplorable, the fact remains that poverty-stricken families in many poor countries cannot subsist without the work efforts of young family members; sending their children to school instead of having them work is not a realistic option. If such children are not permitted to work (especially those in the 12-to-17 age group)—due to pressures imposed by activist groups in industrialized nations—they may be forced to go out on the streets begging or to seek work in parts of the "underground" economy such as drug trafficking and prostitution.[7] So, if all businesses in countries where employing underage workers is common succumb to the pressures to stop employing underage labor, then have they served the best interests of the underage workers, their families, and society in general? In recognition of this issue, organizations opposing child labor are targeting certain forms of child labor such as enslaved child labor and hazardous work. IKEA is an example of a company that has worked hard to prevent any form of child labor by its suppliers. Its practices go well beyond standards and safeguards to include measures designed to address the underlying social problems of the communities in which their suppliers operate.

The Payment of Bribes and Kickbacks   A particularly thorny area facing multinational companies is the degree of cross–country variability in paying bribes.[8] In many countries in eastern Europe, Africa, Latin America, and Asia, it is customary to pay bribes to government officials in order to win a government contract, obtain a license or permit, or facilitate an administrative ruling.[9] In some developing nations, it is difficult for any company, foreign or domestic, to move goods through customs without paying off low-level officials. Senior managers in China and Russia often use their power to obtain kickbacks when they purchase materials or other products for their companies.[10] Likewise, in many countries it is normal to make payments to prospective customers in order to win or retain their business. Some people stretch to justify the payment of bribes and kickbacks on grounds that bribing government officials to get goods through customs or giving kickbacks to customers to retain their business or win new orders is simply a payment for services rendered, in the same way that people tip for service at restaurants.[11] But while this is a clever rationalization, it rests on moral quicksand.

Companies that forbid the payment of bribes and kickbacks in their codes of ethical conduct and that are serious about enforcing this prohibition face a particularly vexing problem in countries where bribery and kickback payments are an entrenched local custom. Complying with the company's code of ethical conduct in these countries is very often tantamount to losing business to competitors that have no such scruples—an outcome that penalizes ethical companies and ethical company personnel (who may suffer lost sales commissions or bonuses). On the other hand, the payment of bribes or kickbacks not only undercuts the company's code of ethics but also risks breaking the law. The Foreign Corrupt Practices Act (FCPA) prohibits U.S. companies from paying bribes to government officials, political parties, political candidates, or others in all countries where they do business. The Organization for Economic Cooperation and Development (OECD) has antibribery standards that criminalize the bribery of foreign public officials in international business transactions—all 35 OECD member countries and seven nonmember countries have adopted these standards.

Despite laws forbidding bribery to secure sales and contracts, the practice persists. As of January 2017, 443 individuals and 158 entities were sanctioned under criminal proceedings for foreign bribery by the OECD. At least 125 of the sanctioned individuals were sentenced to prison. In 2017, in the midst of a national opioid drug crisis, the executive chairman of Insys Therapeutics was arrested for bribing doctors to overprescribe the company's opioid products. In the same year, oil services giant Halliburton agreed to pay $29.2 million to settle charges brought against it by the Security and Exchange Commission's Foreign Corrupt Practices Act Enforcement Division; one of their executives had to pay a $75,000 penalty. The global snack company Cadbury Limited/Mondelez International had to pay a $13 million penalty for violations that included illicit payments to get approvals for a new chocolate factory in India. Other well-known companies caught up in recent bribery cases include JPMorgan; pharmaceutical companies GlaxoSmithKline, Novartis, and AstraZeneca; casino company Las Vegas Sands; and aircraft manufacturer Embraer.

Why Ethical Relativism Is Problematic for Multinational Companies   Relying on the principle of ethical relativism to determine what is right or wrong poses major problems for multinational companies trying to decide which ethical standards to enforce companywide. It is a slippery slope indeed to resolve conflicting ethical standards for operating in different countries without any kind of higher-order moral compass. Consider, for example, the ethical inconsistency of a multinational company that, in the name of ethical relativism, declares it impermissible to engage in kickbacks unless such payments are customary and generally overlooked by legal authorities. It is likewise problematic for a multinational company to declare it ethically acceptable to use underage labor at its plants in those countries where child labor is allowed but ethically inappropriate to employ underage labor at its plants elsewhere. If a country's culture is accepting of environmental degradation or practices that expose workers to dangerous conditions (toxic chemicals or bodily harm), should a multinational company lower its ethical bar in that country but rule the very same actions to be ethically wrong in other countries?

> Codes of conduct based on ethical relativism can be *ethically problematic* for multinational companies by creating a maze of conflicting ethical standards.

Business leaders who rely on the principle of ethical relativism to justify conflicting ethical standards for operating in different countries have little moral basis for establishing or enforcing ethical standards companywide. Rather, when a company's ethical standards vary from country to country, the clear message being sent to employees is that the company has no ethical standards or convictions of its own and prefers to let its standards of ethical right and wrong be governed by the customs and practices of the countries in which it operates. Applying multiple sets of ethical standards without some kind of higher-order moral compass is scarcely a basis for holding company personnel to high standards of ethical behavior. And it can lead to prosecutions of both companies and individuals alike when there are conflicting sets of laws.

Ethics and Integrative Social Contracts Theory

Integrative social contracts theory provides a middle position between the opposing views of ethical universalism and ethical relativism.[12] According to this theory, the ethical standards a company should try to uphold are governed by both (1) a limited number of universal ethical principles that are widely recognized as putting legitimate ethical boundaries on behaviors in *all* situations and (2) the circumstances of local cultures, traditions, and values that further prescribe what constitutes ethically permissible behavior. The universal ethical principles are based on the collective views of multiple cultures and societies and combine to form a "social contract" that all individuals, groups, organizations, and businesses in all situations have a duty to observe. *Within the boundaries of this social contract,* local cultures or groups can specify what *other* actions may or may not be ethically permissible. While this

> ### CORE CONCEPT
>
> According to **integrated social contracts theory**, universal ethical principles based on the collective views of multiple societies form a "social contract" that all individuals and organizations have a duty to observe in all situations. *Within the boundaries of this social contract,* local cultures or groups can specify what *additional* actions may or may not be ethically permissible.

system leaves some "moral free space" for the people in a particular country (or local culture, or profession, or even a company) to make specific interpretations of what other actions may or may not be permissible, *universal ethical norms always take precedence*. Thus, local ethical standards can be *more* stringent than the universal ethical standards but *never less so*. For example, both the legal and medical professions have standards regarding what kinds of advertising are ethically permissible that extend beyond the universal norm that advertising not be false or misleading.

The strength of integrated social contracts theory is that it accommodates the best parts of ethical universalism and ethical relativism. Moreover, integrative social contracts theory offers managers in multinational companies clear guidance in resolving cross-country ethical differences: Those parts of the company's code of ethics that involve universal ethical norms must be enforced worldwide, but within these boundaries there is room for ethical diversity and the opportunity for host-country cultures to exert *some* influence over the moral and ethical standards of business units operating in that country.

A good example of the application of integrative social contracts theory to business involves the payment of bribes and kickbacks. Yes, bribes and kickbacks are common in some countries. But the fact that bribery flourishes in a country does not mean it is an authentic or legitimate ethical norm. Virtually all of the world's major religions (e.g., Buddhism, Christianity, Confucianism, Hinduism, Islam, Judaism, Sikhism, and Taoism) and all moral schools of thought condemn bribery and corruption. Therefore, a multinational company might reasonably conclude that there is a universal ethical principle to be observed here—one of refusing to condone bribery and kickbacks on the part of company personnel no matter what the local custom is and no matter what the sales consequences are.

> According to integrated social contracts theory, adherence to universal or "first-order" ethical norms should always take precedence over local or "second-order" norms.

> In instances involving *universally applicable* ethical norms (like paying bribes), there can be *no compromise* on what is ethically permissible and what is not.

HOW AND WHY ETHICAL STANDARDS IMPACT THE TASKS OF CRAFTING AND EXECUTING STRATEGY

Many companies have acknowledged their ethical obligations in official codes of ethical conduct. In the United States, for example, the Sarbanes-Oxley Act, passed in 2002, requires that companies whose stock is publicly traded have a code of ethics or else explain in writing to the SEC why they do not. But the senior executives of ethically principled companies understand that there's a big difference between having a code of ethics because it is mandated and having ethical standards that truly provide guidance for a company's strategy and business conduct.[13] They know that *the litmus test of whether a company's code of ethics is cosmetic is the extent to which it is embraced in crafting strategy and in operating the business day to day.* Executives committed to high standards make a point of considering three sets of questions whenever a new strategic initiative or policy or operating practice is under review:

- Is what we are proposing to do fully compliant with our code of ethical conduct? Are there any areas of ambiguity that may be of concern?

- Is there any aspect of the strategy (or policy or operating practice) that gives the appearance of being ethically questionable?

- Is there anything in the proposed action that customers, employees, suppliers, stockholders, competitors, community activists, regulators, or the media might consider ethically objectionable?

Unless questions of this nature are posed—either in open discussion or by force of habit in the minds of company managers—there's a risk that strategic initiatives and/or the way daily operations are conducted will become disconnected from the company's code of ethics. If a company's executives believe strongly in living up to the company's ethical standards, they will unhesitatingly reject strategic initiatives and operating approaches that don't measure up. However, in companies with a cosmetic approach to ethics, any linkage of the professed standards to its strategy and operating practices stems mainly from a desire to avoid the risk of embarrassment and possible disciplinary action for approving actions that are later deemed unethical and perhaps illegal.

While most company managers are careful to ensure that a company's strategy is within the bounds of what is *legal*, evidence indicates they are not always so careful to ensure that all elements of their strategies and operating activities are within the bounds of what is considered *ethical*. In recent years, there have been revelations of ethical misconduct on the part of managers at such companies as Samsung, Kobe Steel, credit rating firm Equifax, United Airlines, several leading investment banking firms, and a host of mortgage lenders. Sexual harassment allegations plagued many companies in 2017, including film company Weinstein Company LLC and entertainment giant 21st Century Fox. The consequences of crafting strategies that cannot pass the test of moral scrutiny are manifested in sizable fines, devastating public relations hits, sharp drops in stock prices that cost shareholders billions of dollars, criminal indictments, and convictions of company executives. The fallout from all these scandals has resulted in heightened management attention to legal and ethical considerations in crafting strategy.

● **LO 9-2**

Recognize conditions that give rise to unethical business strategies and behavior.

DRIVERS OF UNETHICAL BUSINESS STRATEGIES AND BEHAVIOR

Apart from the "business of business is business, not ethics" kind of thinking apparent in recent high-profile business scandals, three other main drivers of unethical business behavior also stand out[14]:

- Faulty oversight, enabling the unscrupulous pursuit of personal gain and self-interest.
- Heavy pressures on company managers to meet or beat short-term performance targets.
- A company culture that puts profitability and business performance ahead of ethical behavior.

Faulty Oversight, Enabling the Unscrupulous Pursuit of Personal Gain and Self-Interest   People who are obsessed with wealth accumulation, power, status, and their own self-interest often push aside ethical principles in their quest for personal gain. Driven by greed and ambition, they exhibit few qualms in skirting the rules or doing whatever is necessary to achieve their goals. A general disregard for business ethics can prompt all kinds of unethical strategic maneuvers and behaviors at companies. The numerous scandals that have tarnished the reputation of ridesharing company Uber and forced the resignation of its CEO is a case in point, as described in Illustration Capsule 9.1.

Responsible corporate governance and oversight by the company's corporate board is necessary to guard against self-dealing and the manipulation of information to

The peer-to-peer ridesharing company Uber has been credited with transforming the transportation industry, upending the taxi market, and changing the way consumers travel from place to place. But its lack of attention to ethics has resulted in numerous scandals, a tarnished reputation, a loss of market share to rival companies, and the ouster of its co-founder Travis Kalanick from his position as the company's CEO. The ethical lapses for which Uber has been criticized include the following:

- **Sexual harassment and a toxic workplace culture.** In June 2017, Uber fired over 20 employees as a result of an investigation that uncovered widespread sexual harassment that had been going on for years at the company. Female employees who had reported incidents of sexual harassment were subjected to retaliation by their managers, and reports of the incidents to senior executives resulted in inaction.

- **Price gouging during crises.** During emergency situations such as Hurricane Sandy and the 2017 London Bridge attack, Uber added high surcharges to the cost of their services. This drew much censure, particularly since its competitors offered free or reduced cost rides during those same times.

- **Data breaches and violations of user privacy.** Since 2014, the names, email addresses, and license information of over 700,000 drivers and the personal information of over 65 million users have been disclosed as a result of data breaches. Moreover, in 2016 the company paid a hacker $100,000 in ransom to prevent the dissemination of personal driver and user data that had been breached, but it failed to publicly disclose the situation for over six months.

- **Inadequate attention to consumer safety.** Substandard vetting practices at Uber came to light after one of its drivers was arrested as the primary suspect in a mass shooting in Kalamazoo, Michigan, and after a series of reports alleging sexual assault and misconduct by its drivers. Uber's concern for safety was further questioned

TY Lim/Shutterstock

when a pedestrian was tragically struck and killed by one of its self-driving vehicles in 2018.

- **Unfair competitive practices.** When nascent competitor Gett launched in New York City, Uber employees ordered and cancelled hundreds of rides to waste driver's time and then offered the drivers cash to drop Gett and join Uber. Uber has been accused of employing similar practices against Lyft.

The ethical violations at Uber have not been without economic consequence. They contributed to a significant market share loss to Lyft, Uber's closest competitor in the United States. In January 2017, when Uber was thought to have gouged its prices during protests against legislation banning immigrants from specific countries, its market share dropped 5 percentage points in a week. While Uber's ethical dilemmas are not the sole contributor to Lyft's increase in market share and expansion rate, the negative perceptions of Uber's brand from its unethical actions has afforded its competitors significant opportunities for brand and market share growth. And without a real change in Uber's culture and corporate governance practices, there is a strong likelihood that ethical scandals involving Uber will continue to surface.

Note: Developed with Alen A. Amini.

Sources: https://www.recode.net/2017/8/31/16227670/uber-lyft-market-share-deleteuber-decline-users; https://www.inc.com/associated-press/lyft-thrives-while-rival-uber-tries-to-stabilize-regain-control-2017.html; https://www.entrepreneur.com/article/300789.

disguise such actions by a company's managers. **Self-dealing** occurs when managers take advantage of their position to further their own private interests rather than those of the firm. As discussed in Chapter 2, the duty of the corporate board (and its compensation and audit committees in particular) is to guard against such actions. A strong, independent board is necessary to have proper oversight of the company's financial practices and to hold top managers accountable for their actions.

A particularly egregious example of the lack of proper oversight is the scandal over mortgage lending and banking practices that resulted in a crisis for the U.S. residential real estate market and heartrending consequences for many home buyers. This scandal stemmed from consciously unethical strategies at many banks and mortgage companies to boost the fees they earned on home mortgages by deliberately lowering lending standards to approve so-called subprime loans for home buyers whose incomes were insufficient to make their monthly mortgage payments. Once these lenders earned their fees on these loans, they repackaged the loans to hide their true nature and auctioned them off to unsuspecting investors, who later suffered huge losses when the high-risk borrowers began to default on their loan payments. (Government authorities later forced some of the firms that auctioned off these packaged loans to repurchase them at the auction price and bear the losses themselves.) A lawsuit by the attorneys general of 49 states charging widespread and systematic fraud ultimately resulted in a $26 billion settlement by the five largest U.S. banks (Bank of America, Citigroup, JPMorgan Chase, Wells Fargo, and Ally Financial). Included in the settlement were new rules designed to increase oversight and reform policies and practices among the mortgage companies. The settlement includes what are believed to be a set of robust monitoring and enforcement mechanisms that should help prevent such abuses in the future.[15]

> **CORE** CONCEPT
>
> **Self-dealing** occurs when managers take advantage of their position to further their own private interests rather than those of the firm.

Heavy Pressures on Company Managers to Meet Short-Term Performance Targets When key personnel find themselves scrambling to meet the quarterly and annual sales and profit expectations of investors and financial analysts, they often feel enormous pressure to *do whatever it takes* to protect their reputation for delivering good results. Executives at high-performing companies know that investors will see the slightest sign of a slowdown in earnings growth as a red flag and drive down the company's stock price. In addition, slowing growth or declining profits could lead to a downgrade of the company's credit rating if it has used lots of debt to finance its growth. The pressure to "never miss a quarter"—to not upset the expectations of analysts, investors, and creditors—prompts nearsighted managers to engage in short-term maneuvers to make the numbers, regardless of whether these moves are really in the best long-term interests of the company. Sometimes the pressure induces company personnel to continue to stretch the rules until the limits of ethical conduct are overlooked.[16] Once ethical boundaries are crossed in efforts to "meet or beat their numbers," the threshold for making more extreme ethical compromises becomes lower.

To meet its demanding profit target, Wells Fargo put such pressure on its employees to hit sales quotas that many employees responded by fraudulently opening customer accounts. In 2017, after the practices came to light, the bank was forced to return $2.6 million to customers and pay $186 million in fines to the government. Wells Fargo's reputation took a big hit, its stock price plummeted, and its CEO lost his job.

Company executives often feel pressured to hit financial performance targets because their compensation depends heavily on the company's performance. Over the last two decades, it has become fashionable for boards of directors to grant lavish bonuses, stock option awards, and other compensation benefits to executives for meeting specified performance targets. So outlandishly large were these rewards that executives had strong personal incentives to bend the rules and engage in behaviors that allowed the targets to be met. Much of the accounting manipulation at the root of recent corporate scandals has entailed situations in which executives benefited enormously from misleading accounting or other shady activities that allowed them to hit the numbers and receive incentive awards ranging from $10 million to more than $1 billion for hedge fund managers.

The fundamental problem with **short-termism**—the tendency for managers to focus excessive attention on short-term performance objectives—is that it doesn't create value for customers or improve the firm's competitiveness in the marketplace; that is, it sacrifices the activities that are the most reliable drivers of higher profits and added shareholder value in the long run. Cutting ethical corners in the name of profits carries exceptionally high risk for shareholders—the steep stock price decline and tarnished brand image that accompany the discovery of scurrilous behavior leave shareholders with a company worth much less than before—and the rebuilding task can be arduous, taking both considerable time and resources.

> **CORE CONCEPT**
>
> **Short-termism** is the tendency for managers to focus excessively on short-term performance objectives at the expense of longer-term strategic objectives. It has negative implications for the likelihood of ethical lapses as well as company performance in the longer run.

A Company Culture That Puts Profitability and Business Performance Ahead of Ethical Behavior   When a company's culture spawns an ethically corrupt or amoral work climate, people have a company-approved license to ignore "what's right" and engage in any behavior or strategy they think they can get away with. Such cultural norms as "Everyone else does it" and "It is okay to bend the rules to get the job done" permeate the work environment. At such companies, ethically immoral people are certain to play down observance of ethical strategic actions and business conduct. Moreover, cultural pressures to utilize unethical means if circumstances become challenging can prompt otherwise honorable people to behave unethically. A perfect example of a company culture gone awry on ethics is Enron, a now-defunct but infamous company found guilty of one of the most sprawling business frauds in U.S. history.[17]

Enron's leaders pressured company personnel to be innovative and aggressive in figuring out how to grow current earnings—*regardless of the methods.* Enron's annual "rank and yank" performance evaluation process, in which the lowest-ranking 15 to 20 percent of employees were let go, made it abundantly clear that bottom-line results were what mattered most. The name of the game at Enron became devising clever ways to boost revenues and earnings, even if this sometimes meant operating outside established policies (and legal limits). In fact, outside-the-lines behavior was celebrated if it generated profitable new business.

A high-performance–high-rewards climate came to pervade the Enron culture, as the best workers (determined by who produced the best bottom-line results) received impressively large incentives and bonuses. On Car Day at Enron, an array of luxury sports cars arrived for presentation to the most successful employees. Understandably, employees wanted to be seen as part of Enron's star team and partake in the benefits granted to Enron's best and brightest employees. The high monetary rewards, the ambitious and hard-driving people whom the company hired and promoted, and the competitive, results-oriented culture combined to give Enron a reputation not only for trampling competitors but also for internal ruthlessness. The company's win-at-all-costs mindset nurtured a culture that gradually and then more rapidly fostered the erosion of ethical standards, eventually making a mockery of the company's stated values of integrity and respect. When it became evident that Enron was a house of cards propped up by deceitful accounting and myriad unsavory practices, the company imploded in a matter of weeks—one of the biggest bankruptcies of all time, costing investors $64 billion in losses.

In contrast, when high ethical principles are deeply ingrained in the corporate culture of a company, culture can function as a powerful mechanism for communicating ethical behavioral norms and gaining employee buy-in to the company's moral standards, business principles, and corporate values. In such cases, the ethical principles embraced in the company's code of ethics and/or in its statement of corporate values are seen as integral to the company's identity, self-image, and ways of operating. The message that ethics matters—and matters a lot—resounds loudly and clearly throughout the organization and in its strategy and decisions.

WHY SHOULD COMPANY STRATEGIES BE ETHICAL?

There are two reasons why a company's strategy should be ethical: (1) because a strategy that is unethical is morally wrong and reflects badly on the character of the company and its personnel, and (2) because an ethical strategy can be good business and serve the self-interest of shareholders.

The Moral Case for an Ethical Strategy

Managers do not dispassionately assess what strategic course to steer—how strongly committed they are to observing ethical principles and standards definitely comes into play in making strategic choices. Ethical strategy making is generally the product of managers who are of strong moral character (i.e., who are trustworthy, have integrity, and truly care about conducting the company's business honorably). Managers with high ethical principles are usually advocates of a corporate code of ethics and strong ethics compliance, and they are genuinely committed to upholding corporate values and ethical business principles. They demonstrate their commitment by displaying the company's stated values and living up to its business principles and ethical standards. They understand the difference between merely adopting value statements and codes of ethics and ensuring that they are followed strictly in a company's actual strategy and business conduct. As a consequence, ethically strong managers consciously opt for strategic actions that can pass the strictest moral scrutiny—they display no tolerance for strategies with ethically controversial components.

● LO 9-3

Identify the costs of business ethics failures.

The Business Case for Ethical Strategies

In addition to the moral reasons for adopting ethical strategies, there may be solid business reasons. Pursuing unethical strategies and tolerating unethical conduct not only damages a company's reputation but also may result in a wide-ranging set of other costly consequences. Figure 9.1 shows the kinds of costs a company can incur when unethical behavior on its part is discovered, the wrongdoings of company personnel are headlined in the media, and it is forced to make amends for its behavior. The more egregious are a company's ethical violations, the higher the costs and the bigger the damage to its reputation (and to the reputations of the company personnel involved). In high-profile instances, the costs of ethical misconduct can easily run into the hundreds of millions and even billions of dollars, especially if they provoke widespread public outrage and many people were harmed. The penalties levied on executives caught in wrongdoing can skyrocket as well, as the 150-year prison term sentence of infamous financier and Ponzi scheme perpetrator Bernie Madoff illustrates.

The fallout of a company's ethical misconduct goes well beyond the costs of making amends for the misdeeds. Customers shun companies caught up in highly publicized

FIGURE 9.1   The Costs Companies Incur When Ethical Wrongdoing Is Discovered

Visible Costs	Internal Administrative Costs	Intangible or Less Visible Costs
• Government fines and penalties • Civil penalties arising from class-action lawsuits and other litigation aimed at punishing the company for its offense and the harm done to others • The costs to shareholders in the form of a lower stock price (and possibly lower dividends)	• Legal and investigative costs incurred by the company • The costs of providing remedial education and ethics training to company personnel • The costs of taking corrective actions • Administrative costs associated with ensuring future compliance	• Customer defections • Loss of reputation • Lost employee morale and higher degrees of employee cynicism • Higher employee turnover • Higher recruiting costs and difficulty in attracting talented employees • Adverse effects on employee productivity • The costs of complying with often harsher government regulations

Source: Adapted from Terry Thomas, John R. Schermerhorn, and John W. Dienhart, "Strategic Leadership of Ethical Behavior," *Academy of Management Executive* 18, no. 2 (May 2004), p. 58.

ethical scandals. Rehabilitating a company's shattered reputation is time-consuming and costly. Companies with tarnished reputations have difficulty in recruiting and retaining talented employees. Most ethically upstanding people are repulsed by a work environment where unethical behavior is condoned; they don't want to get entrapped in a compromising situation, nor do they want their personal reputations tarnished by the actions of an unsavory employer. Creditors are unnerved by the unethical actions of a borrower because of the potential business fallout and subsequent higher risk of default on loans.

> Shareholders suffer major damage when a company's unethical behavior is discovered. Making amends for unethical business conduct is costly, and it takes years to rehabilitate a tarnished company reputation.

All told, a company's unethical behavior can do considerable damage to shareholders in the form of lost revenues, higher costs, lower profits, lower stock prices, and a diminished business reputation. To a significant degree, therefore, ethical strategies and ethical conduct are *good business.* Most companies understand the value of operating in a manner that wins the approval of suppliers, employees, investors, and society at large. Most businesspeople recognize the risks and adverse fallout attached to the discovery of unethical behavior. Hence, companies have an incentive to employ strategies that can pass the test of being ethical. Even if a company's managers are not personally committed to high ethical standards, they have good reason to operate within ethical bounds, if only to (1) avoid the risk of embarrassment, scandal, disciplinary action, fines, and possible jail time for unethical conduct on their part; and (2) escape being held accountable for lax enforcement of ethical standards and unethical behavior by personnel under their supervision. Illustration Capsule 9.2 discusses PepsiCo's commitment to high ethical standards and their approach to putting their ethical principles into practice.

PepsiCo is one of the world's leading food and beverage companies with over $65 billion in net revenue, coming from iconic brands such as Lays and Ruffles potato chips, Quaker Oatmeal, Tropicana juice, Mountain Dew, and Diet Pepsi. The company is also known for its dedication to ethical business practices, having ranked consistently as among the World's Most Ethical Companies by business ethics think tank *Ethicsphere* ever since the award program was initiated. PepsiCo's Global Code of Conduct plays a pivotal role in ensuring that PepsiCo's employees, managers, and directors around the world are complying with the company's high ethical standards. It provides specific guidance concerning how to make decisions, how to treat others, and how to conduct business globally, organized around four key operating principles: (1) respect in the workplace, (2) integrity in the marketplace, (3) ethics in business activities, and (4) responsibility to shareholders. Essentially, the Code of Conduct lays out a set of behavioral norms that has come to define the company's culture.

Even with a strong ethical culture, implementing a code of conduct across a global organization of over 263,000 employees is challenging. To assist, PepsiCo set up a Global Compliance & Ethics Department with primary responsibility for promoting, monitoring, and enforcing the code. Employees at all levels are required to participate in annual Code of Conduct training, through online courses as well as in-person, manager-led workshops. Compliance training also takes place in a more targeted fashion, based on role and geography, concerning such issues as bribery. Other types of communications throughout the year, such as internal newsletter articles and messaging from the leadership, reinforce the annual training.

monticello/Shutterstock

Employees are encouraged to seek guidance when faced with an ethical dilemma. They are also encouraged to raise concerns and are obligated to report any Code violations. A variety of channels have been set up for them to do this, including a hotline operated by an independent third party. All reports of suspected violations are reviewed in accordance with company policies designed to foster consistency of the investigative process and corrective actions (which may include termination of employment). PepsiCo has also established an annual peer-nominated Ethical Leadership Award designed to recognize instances of exceptional ethical conduct by employees.

The leadership at PepsiCo believes that their commitment to ethical principles has helped the company in attracting and retaining the best people. Indeed, PepsiCo has been listed as among the Top Attractors of talent globally. In addition, the company has regularly been listed as among the World's Most Respected Companies (Barron) and the World's Most Admired Companies (Fortune).

Sources: Company website; https://ethisphere.com/pepsico-performance-purpose/.

STRATEGY, CORPORATE SOCIAL RESPONSIBILITY, AND ENVIRONMENTAL SUSTAINABILITY

The idea that businesses have an obligation to foster social betterment, a much-debated topic over the past 50 years, took root in the 19th century when progressive companies in the aftermath of the industrial revolution began to provide workers with housing and other amenities. The notion that corporate executives should balance the interests of all stakeholders—shareholders, employees, customers, suppliers, the communities in

Understand the concepts of corporate social responsibility and environmental sustainability and how companies balance these duties with economic responsibilities to shareholders.

CORE CONCEPT

Corporate social responsibility (CSR) refers to a company's *duty* to operate in an honorable manner, provide good working conditions for employees, encourage workforce diversity, be a good steward of the environment, and actively work to better the quality of life in the local communities where it operates and in society at large.

which they operate, and society at large—began to blossom in the 1960s. Some years later, a group of chief executives of America's 200 largest corporations, calling themselves the Business Roundtable, came out in strong support of the concept of **corporate social responsibility (CSR):**

> Balancing the shareholder's expectations of maximum return against other priorities is one of the fundamental problems confronting corporate management. The shareholder must receive a good return but the legitimate concerns of other constituencies (customers, employees, communities, suppliers and society at large) also must have the appropriate attention. . . . [Leading managers] believe that by giving enlightened consideration to balancing the legitimate claims of all its constituents, a corporation will best serve the interest of its shareholders.

Today, corporate social responsibility is a concept that resonates in western Europe, the United States, Canada, and such developing nations as Brazil and India.

The Concepts of Corporate Social Responsibility and Good Corporate Citizenship

The essence of socially responsible business behavior is that a company should balance strategic actions to benefit shareholders against the *duty* to be a good corporate citizen. The underlying thesis is that company managers should display a *social conscience* in operating the business and specifically take into account how management decisions and company actions affect the well-being of employees, local communities, the environment, and society at large.[18] Acting in a socially responsible manner thus encompasses more than just participating in community service projects and donating money to charities and other worthy causes. Demonstrating social responsibility also entails undertaking actions that earn trust and respect from all stakeholders—operating in an honorable and ethical manner, striving to make the company a great place to work, demonstrating genuine respect for the environment, and trying to make a difference in bettering society. As depicted in Figure 9.2, corporate responsibility programs commonly include the following elements:

- *Striving to employ an ethical strategy and observe ethical principles in operating the business.* A sincere commitment to observing ethical principles is a necessary component of a CSR strategy simply because unethical conduct is incompatible with the concept of good corporate citizenship and socially responsible business behavior.

- *Making charitable contributions, supporting community service endeavors, engaging in broader philanthropic initiatives, and reaching out to make a difference in the lives of the disadvantaged.* Some companies fulfill their philanthropic obligations by spreading their efforts over a multitude of charitable and community activities—for instance, Cisco, LinkedIn, IBM, and Google support a broad variety of community, art, and social welfare programs. Others prefer to focus their energies more narrowly. McDonald's concentrates on sponsoring the Ronald McDonald House program (which provides a home away from home for the families of seriously ill children receiving treatment at nearby hospitals). Genentech and many pharmaceutical companies run prescription assistance programs to provide expensive medications at little or no cost to needy patients. Companies frequently reinforce their philanthropic efforts by encouraging employees to support charitable causes and participate in community affairs, often through programs that match employee contributions.

- *Taking actions to protect the environment and, in particular, to minimize or eliminate any adverse impact on the environment stemming from the company's own business activities.*

FIGURE 9.2   The Five Components of a Corporate Social Responsibility Strategy

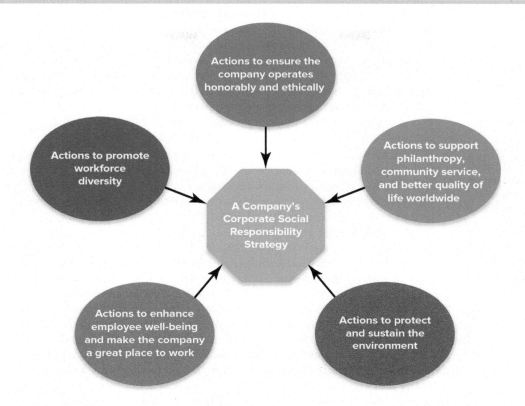

Source: Adapted from material in Ronald Paul Hill, Debra Stephens, and Iain Smith, "Corporate Social Responsibility: An Examination of Individual Firm Behavior," *Business and Society Review* 108, no. 3 (September 2003), p. 348.

Corporate social responsibility as it applies to environmental protection entails actively striving to be a good steward of the environment. This means using the best available science and technology to reduce environmentally harmful aspects of the company's operations *below the levels required by prevailing environmental regulations.* It also means putting time and money into improving the environment in ways that extend beyond a company's own industry boundaries—such as participating in recycling projects, adopting energy conservation practices, and supporting efforts to clean up local water supplies. Häagen-Dazs, a maker of all-natural ice creams, started a social media campaign to raise awareness about the dangers associated with the decreasing honeybee population; it donates a portion of its profits to research on this issue. The Walt Disney Company has created strict environmental targets for themselves and created the "Green Standard" to inspire employees to reduce their environmental impact.

- *Creating a work environment that enhances the quality of life for employees.* Numerous companies exert extra effort to enhance the quality of life for their employees at work and at home. This can include onsite day care, flexible work schedules, workplace exercise facilities, special leaves for employees to care for sick family members, work-at-home opportunities, career development programs and education opportunities, showcase plants and offices, special safety programs, and the like.

- *Building a diverse workforce with respect to gender, race, national origin, and other aspects that different people bring to the workplace.* Most large companies in the United States have established workforce diversity programs, and some go the extra mile to ensure that their workplaces are attractive to ethnic minorities and inclusive of all groups and perspectives. At some companies, the diversity initiative extends to suppliers—sourcing items from small businesses owned by women or members of ethnic minorities, for example. The pursuit of workforce diversity can also be good business. At Coca-Cola, where strategic success depends on getting people all over the world to become loyal consumers of the company's beverages, efforts to build a public persona of inclusiveness for people of all races, religions, nationalities, interests, and talents have considerable strategic value.

> **CORE** CONCEPT
>
> A company's **CSR strategy** is defined by the specific combination of socially beneficial activities the company opts to support with its contributions of time, money, and other resources.

The particular combination of socially responsible endeavors a company elects to pursue defines its **corporate social responsibility (CSR) strategy.** The specific components emphasized in a CSR strategy vary from company to company and are typically linked to a company's core values. Few companies have managed to integrate CSR as fully and seamlessly throughout their organization as Burt's Bees; there a special committee is dedicated to leading the organization to attain its CSR goals with respect to three primary areas: natural well-being, humanitarian responsibility, and environmental sustainability. General Mills also centers its CSR strategy around three themes: nourishing lives (via healthier and easier-to-prepare foods), nourishing communities (via charitable donations to community causes and volunteerism for community service projects), and nourishing the environment (via efforts to conserve natural resources, reduce energy and water usage, promote recycling, and otherwise support environmental sustainability).[19] Starbucks's CSR strategy includes four main elements (ethical sourcing, community service, environmental stewardship, and farmer support), all of which have touch points with the way that the company procures its coffee—a key aspect of its product differentiation strategy. Some companies use other terms, such as *corporate citizenship, corporate responsibility,* or *sustainable responsible business (SRB)* to characterize their CSR initiatives. Illustration Capsule 9.3 describes Warby Parker's approach to corporate social responsibility—an approach that ensures that social responsibility is reflected in all of the company's actions and endeavors.

Although there is wide variation in how companies devise and implement a CSR strategy, communities of companies concerned with corporate social responsibility (such as CSR Europe) have emerged to help companies share best CSR practices. Moreover, a number of reporting standards have been developed, including ISO 26000—a new internationally recognized standard for social responsibility set by the International Standards Organization (ISO).[20] Companies that exhibit a strong commitment to corporate social responsibility are often recognized by being included on lists such as *Corporate Responsibility* magazine's "100 Best Corporate Citizens" or *Corporate Knights* magazine's "Global 100 Most Sustainable Corporations."

Corporate Social Responsibility and the Triple Bottom Line   CSR initiatives undertaken by companies are frequently directed at improving the company's *triple bottom line (TBL)*—a reference to three types of performance metrics: *economic, social,* and *environmental.* The goal is for a company to succeed simultaneously in all three dimensions, as illustrated in Figure 9.3.[21] The three dimensions of performance are often referred to in terms of the "three pillars" of "people, planet, and profit." The term *people* refers to the various social initiatives that make up CSR strategies, such as corporate giving, community involvement, and company efforts to improve the lives of its internal

Warby Parker: Combining Corporate Social Responsibility with Affordable Fashion

Since its founding in 2010, Warby Parker has succeeded in selling over one million pairs of high-fashion glasses at a discounted price of $95—roughly 80 percent below the average $500 price tag on a comparable pair of eyeglasses from another producer. With more than 70 stores in the United States, the company has built a brand recognized universally as one of the strongest in the world; it consistently posts a net promoter score (a measure of how likely someone would be to recommend the product) of close to 90—higher than companies like Zappos and Apple.

Under its Buy a Pair, Give a Pair program, nearly more than five million pairs of glasses have been distributed to needy people in more than 50 countries. Warby Parker also supports partners, like Vision Spring, enabling them to provide basic eye exams and teach community members how to manufacture and sell glasses at very low prices, thereby providing vocational training and improving the standard of living in these communities. The average impact on a recipient of a pair of donated glasses was a 20 percent increase in personal income and a 35 percent increase in productivity.

Efforts to be a responsible company expand beyond Warby Parker's international partnerships. The company voluntarily evaluates itself against benchmarks in the fields of "environment," "workers," "customers," "community," and "governance," demonstrating a nearly unparalleled dedication to outcomes outside of profit. The company is widely seen as an employer of choice and regularly attracts top talent for all roles across the organization. It holds to an extremely high environmental standard, running an entirely carbon neutral operation.

While socially impactful actions matter at Warby Parker, the company is mindful of the critical role of its suppliers as well. Both founders spent countless hours coordinating partnerships with dedicated suppliers to ensure quality, invested deeply in building a lean

Interim Archives/Contributor/Getty Images

manufacturing operation to minimize cost, and sought to build an organization that would keep buyers happy. The net effect is a very economically healthy company—they post around $3,000 in sales per square foot, second only to Apple stores—with financial stability to pursue responsibilities outside of customer satisfaction.

The strong fundamentals put in place by the firm's founders blend responsibility into its DNA and attach each piece of commercial success to positive outcomes in the world. The company was recently recognized as number one on *Fast Company*'s "Most Innovative Companies" list and continues to build loyal followers—both of its products and its CSR efforts—as it expands.

Note: Developed with Jeremy P. Reich.

Sources: Warby Parker and "B Corp" websites; Max Chafkin, "Warby Parker Sees the Future of Retail," *Fast Company,* February 17, 2015 (accessed February 22, 2016); Jenni Avins, "Warby Parker Proves Customers Don't Have to Care about Your Social Mission," *Quartz,* December 29, 2014 (accessed February 14, 2016).

and external stakeholders. *Planet* refers to a firm's ecological impact and environmental practices. The term *profit* has a broader meaning with respect to the triple bottom line than it does otherwise. It encompasses not only the profit a firm earns for its shareholders but also the economic impact that the company has on society more generally, in terms of the overall value that it creates and the overall costs that it imposes on society. For example, Procter & Gamble's Swiffer cleaning system, one of the company's

FIGURE 9.3   The Triple Bottom Line: Excelling on Three Measures of Company Performance

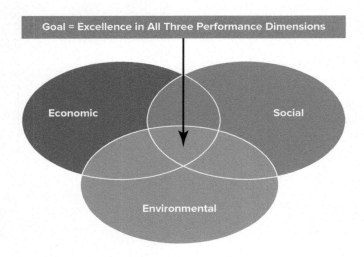

Source: Developed with help from Amy E. Florentino.

best-selling products, not only offers an earth-friendly design but also outperforms less ecologically friendly alternatives in terms of its broader economic impact: It reduces demands on municipal water sources, saves electricity that would be needed to heat mop water, and doesn't add to the amount of detergent making its way into waterways and waste treatment facilities. Nike sees itself as bringing people, planet, and profits into balance by producing innovative new products in a more sustainable way, recognizing that sustainability is key to its future profitability. TOMS shoes, which donates a pair of shoes to a child in need in over 50 different countries for every pair purchased, has also built its strategy around maintaining a well-balanced triple bottom line.

Many companies now make a point of citing the beneficial outcomes of their CSR strategies in press releases and issue special reports for consumers and investors to review. Southwest Airlines makes reporting an important part of its commitment to corporate responsibility; the company posts its annual Southwest Airlines One Report on its website that describes its initiatives and accomplishments with respect to each of the three pillars of triple bottom line performance—people, planet, profit. Triple-bottom-line reporting is emerging as an increasingly important way for companies to make the results of their CSR strategies apparent to stakeholders and for stakeholders to hold companies accountable for their impact on society. The use of standard reporting frameworks and metrics, such as those developed by the Global Reporting Initiative, promotes greater transparency and facilitates benchmarking CSR efforts across firms and industries.

Investment firms have created mutual funds consisting of companies that are excelling on the basis of the triple bottom line in order to attract funds from environmentally and socially aware investors. The Dow Jones Sustainability World Index is made up of the top 10 percent of the 2,500 companies listed in the Dow Jones World Index in terms of economic performance, environmental performance, and social performance. Companies are evaluated in these three performance areas, using indicators such as corporate governance, climate change mitigation, and labor practices. Table 9.1 shows a sampling of the companies selected for the Dow Jones Sustainability World Index in 2013.

TABLE 9.1   A Selection of Companies Recognized for Their Triple-Bottom-Line Performance in 2013

Name	Market Sector	Country
Peugeot SA	Automobiles & Components	France
Westpac Banking Group	Banks	Australia
CNH Industrial NV	Capital Goods	Great Britain
SGS SA	Commercial & Professional Services	Switzerland
LG Electronics Inc.	Consumer Durables & Apparel	South Korea
InterContinental Hotels Group	Consumer Services	Great Britain
UBS Group AB	Diversified Financials	Switzerland
Thai Oil PCL	Energy	Thailand
METRO AG	Food & Staples Retailing	Germany
Coca-Cola HBC AG	Food, Beverage & Tobacco	Switzerland
Abbott Laboratories	Health Care Equipment & Services	United States
Henkel AG & Co. KGaA	Household & Personal Products	Germany
Allianz SE	Insurance	Germany
Grupo Argos SA	Materials	Colombia
Pearson PLC	Media	Great Britain
Roche Holding AG	Pharmaceuticals, Biotechnology & Life Sciences	Switzerland
Mirvac Group	Real Estate	Australia
Industria de Diseno Textil SA	Retailing	Spain
Advanced Semiconductor Engineering Inc.	Semiconductors & Semiconductor Equipment	Taiwan
Amadeus IT Group SA	Software & Services	Spain
Konica Minolta Inc.	Technology Hardware & Equipment	Japan
Koninklijke KPN NV	Telecommunication Services	Netherlands
Royal Mail PLC	Transportation	Great Britain
Red Electric Corp SA	Utilities	Spain

Source: Adapted from RobecoSAM AG, www.sustainability-indices.com/review/industry-group-leaders-2017.jsp (accessed March 4, 2018).

What Do We Mean by *Sustainability* and *Sustainable Business Practices?*

The term *sustainability* is used in a variety of ways. In many firms, it is synonymous with corporate social responsibility; it is seen by some as a term that is gradually replacing *CSR* in the business lexicon. Indeed, sustainability reporting and TBL reporting are often one and the same, as illustrated by the Dow Jones Sustainability World Index, which tracks the same three types of performance measures that constitute the triple bottom line.

More often, however, the term takes on a more focused meaning, concerned with the relationship of a company to its *environment* and its use of *natural resources,* including land, water, air, plants, animals, minerals, fossil fuels, and biodiversity. It is widely recognized that the world's natural resources are finite and are being consumed and degraded at rates that threaten their capacity for renewal. Since corporations are the biggest users of natural resources, managing and maintaining these resources is critical for the long-term economic interests of corporations.

For some companies, this issue has direct and obvious implications for the continued viability of their business model and strategy. Pacific Gas and Electric has begun measuring the full carbon footprint of its supply chain to become not only a "greener" company but a more efficient energy producer.[22] Beverage companies such as Coca-Cola and PepsiCo are having to rethink their business models because of the prospect of future worldwide water shortages. For other companies, the connection is less direct, but all companies are part of a business ecosystem whose economic health depends on the availability of natural resources. In response, most major companies have begun to change *how* they do business, emphasizing the use of **sustainable business practices,** defined as those capable of meeting the needs of the present without compromising the ability to meet the needs of the future. Many have also begun to incorporate a consideration of environmental sustainability into their strategy-making activities.

Environmental sustainability strategies entail deliberate and concerted actions to operate businesses in a manner that protects natural resources and ecological support systems, guards against outcomes that will ultimately endanger the planet, and is therefore sustainable for centuries.[23] One aspect of environmental sustainability is keeping use of the Earth's natural resources within levels that can be replenished via the use of sustainable business practices. In the case of some resources (like crude oil, freshwater, and edible fish from the oceans), scientists say that use levels either are already unsustainable or will be soon, given the world's growing population and propensity to consume additional resources as incomes and living standards rise. Another aspect of sustainability concerns containing the adverse effects of greenhouse gases and other forms of air pollution to reduce their impact on undesirable climate and atmospheric changes. Other aspects of sustainability include greater reliance on sustainable energy sources; greater use of recyclable materials; the use of sustainable methods of growing foods (to reduce topsoil depletion and the use of pesticides, herbicides, fertilizers, and other chemicals that may be harmful to human health or ecological systems); habitat protection; environmentally sound waste management practices; and increased attempts to decouple environmental degradation and economic growth (according to scientists, economic growth has historically been accompanied by declines in the well-being of the environment).

Unilever, a diversified producer of processed foods, personal care, and home cleaning products, is among the many committed corporations pursuing sustainable business practices. The company tracks 11 sustainable agricultural indicators in its processed-foods business and has launched a variety of programs to improve the environmental performance of its suppliers. Examples of such programs include special low-rate financing for tomato suppliers choosing to switch to water-conserving irrigation systems and training programs in India that have allowed contract cucumber growers to reduce pesticide use by 90 percent while improving yields by 78 percent. Unilever has also

CORE CONCEPT

Sustainable business practices are those that meet the needs of the present without compromising the ability to meet the needs of the future.

CORE CONCEPT

A company's **environmental sustainability strategy** consists of its deliberate actions to protect the environment, provide for the longevity of natural resources, maintain ecological support systems for future generations, and guard against ultimate endangerment of the planet.

reengineered many internal processes to improve the company's overall performance on sustainability measures. For example, the company has reduced water usage in the production of their products by 37 percent since 2008 through the implementation of sustainability initiatives. Unilever has also redesigned packaging for many of its products to conserve natural resources and reduce the volume of consumer waste. The company's Suave shampoo bottles were reshaped to save almost 150 tons of plastic resin per year, which is the equivalent of 15 million fewer empty bottles making it to landfills annually. As the producer of Lipton Tea, Unilever is the world's largest purchaser of tea leaves; the company committed to sourcing all of its tea from Rainforest Alliance Certified farms, due to its comprehensive triple-bottom-line approach toward sustainable farm management. Illustration Capsule 9.4 sheds more light on Unilever's focus on sustainability.

Crafting Corporate Social Responsibility and Sustainability Strategies

While CSR and environmental sustainability strategies take many forms, those that both provide valuable social benefits *and* fulfill customer needs in a superior fashion may also contribute to a company's competitive advantage.[24] For example, while carbon emissions may be a generic social concern for financial institutions such as Wells Fargo, Ford's sustainability strategy for reducing carbon emissions has produced both competitive advantage and environmental benefits. Its Ford Fusion hybrid is among the least polluting automobiles The Ford Explorer plug-in hybrid SUV launched in Europe in 2019 provides 7-passenger seating capacity and has a 40-kilometer zero-emission city driving range. The development of hybrid models like the Fusion and the Explorer have helped Ford gain the loyalty of fuel-conscious buyers and given the company a new green image. Keurig Green Mountain (now part of Keurig Dr. Pepper) is committed to caring for the environment while also improving the livelihoods in coffee-growing communities. Their focus is on three primary solutions: (1) helping farmer improve their farming techniques; (2) addressing local water scarcity and planning for climate change; and (3) strengthening farmers' organizations. Its consumers are aware of these efforts and purchase Green Mountain coffee, in part, to encourage such practices.

CSR strategies and environmental sustainability strategies are more likely to contribute to a company's competitive advantage if they are linked to a company's competitively important resources and capabilities or value chain activities. Thus, it is common for companies engaged in natural resource extraction, electric power production, forestry and paper products manufacture, motor vehicles production, and chemical production to place more emphasis on addressing environmental concerns than, say, software and electronics firms or apparel manufacturers. Companies whose business success is heavily dependent on maintaining high employee morale or attracting and retaining the best and brightest employees are somewhat more prone to stress the well-being of their employees and foster a positive, high-energy workplace environment that elicits the dedication and enthusiastic commitment of employees, thus putting real meaning behind the claim "Our people are our greatest asset." EY, the third largest global accounting firm, has been on Fortune's list of 100 Best Companies to Work for every year for the last 20 years. It has long been known for respecting differences, fostering individuality, and promoting inclusiveness so that its more than 245,000 employees in over 150 countries can feel valued, engaged, and empowered in developing creative ways to serve the firm's clients.

At Whole Foods Market, a $16 billion supermarket chain specializing in organic and natural foods, its environmental sustainability strategy is evident in almost every

> CSR strategies and environmental sustainability strategies that both provide valuable social benefits *and* fulfill customer needs in a superior fashion can lead to competitive advantage. Corporate social agendas that address only social issues may help boost a company's reputation for corporate citizenship but are unlikely to improve its competitive strength in the marketplace.

Unilever's Focus on Sustainability

With over 53.7 billion euros in revenue in 2017, Unilever is one of the world's largest companies. The global consumer goods giant has products that are used by over 2 billion people on any given day. It manufactures iconic global brands like Dove, Axe, Hellman's, Heartbrand, and many others. What it is also known for, however, is its commitment to sustainability, leading GlobeScan's Global Sustainability Survey for sustainable companies with a score 2.5 times higher than its closest competitor.

Unilever implemented its sustainability plan in as transparent and explicit way as possible, evidenced by the Unilever Sustainable Living Plan (USLP). The USLP was released in 2010 by CEO Paul Polman, stating that the company's goal was to double the size of the business while halving its environmental footprint by 2020. Importantly, the USLP has remained a guiding force for the company, which dedicates significant resources and time to pursuing its sustainability goals. The plan is updated each year with targets and goals, as well as an annual progress report.

According to Polman, Unilever's focus on sustainability isn't just charity, but is really an act of self-interest. The company's most recent annual report states "growth and sustainability are not in conflict. In fact, in our experience, sustainability drives growth." Polman insists that this is the modern-day way to maximize profits, and that doing so is simply rational business thinking.

To help implement this plan, Unilever has instituted a corporate accountability plan. Each year, Unilever benchmarks its progress against three leading indices: the UN Global Compact, the Global Reporting Initiative's Index, and the UN Millennium Development Goals. In its annual sustainability report, the company details its progress

GeoPic/Alamy Stock Photo

toward its many sustainability goals. By 2018, Unilever had helped more than 601 million people to improve their health and hygiene habits and had enabled over 716,000 small farmers to improve their agricultural practices and/or their incomes.

Unilever has also created new business practices to reach even more ambitious targets. Unilever set up a central corporate team dedicated to spreading best sustainability practices from one factory or business unit to the rest of the company, a major change from the siloed manner in which the company previously operated. Moreover, the company set up a "small actions, big differences" fund to invest in innovative ideas that help the company achieve its sustainability goal. To reduce emissions from the overall footprint of its products and extend its sustainability efforts to its entire supply chain, it has worked with its suppliers to source sustainable agricultural products, improving from 14 percent sustainable in 2010 to 56 percent in 2017.

Note: Developed with Byron G. Peyster.

Sources: www.globescan.com/component/edocman/?view=document&id=179&Itemid=591; www.fastcocreate.com/3051498/behind-the-brand/why-unilever-is-betting-big-on-sustainability; www.economist.com/news/business/21611103-second-time-its-120-year-history—unilever-trying-redefine-what-it-means-be; *company website (accessed March 13, 2016).*

segment of its company value chain and is a big part of its differentiation strategy. The company's procurement policies encourage stores to purchase fresh fruits and vegetables from local farmers and screen processed-food items for more than 400 common ingredients that the company considers unhealthy or environmentally unsound. Spoiled food items are sent to regional composting centers rather than landfills, and all cleaning products used in its stores are biodegradable. The company also has created the Animal Compassion Foundation to develop natural and humane ways of raising farm animals and has converted all of its vehicles to run on biofuels.

Not all companies choose to link their corporate environmental or social agendas to their value chain, their business model, or their industry. For example, the Clorox Company Foundation supports programs that serve youth, focusing its giving on non-profit civic organizations, schools, and colleges. However, unless a company's social responsibility initiatives become part of the way it operates its business every day, the initiatives are unlikely to catch fire and be fully effective. As an executive at Royal Dutch/Shell put it, corporate social responsibility "is not a cosmetic; it must be rooted in our values. It must make a difference to the way we do business."[25] The same is true for environmental sustainability initiatives.

The Moral Case for Corporate Social Responsibility and Environmentally Sustainable Business Practices

The moral case for why businesses should act in a manner that benefits all of the company's stakeholders—not just shareholders—boils down to "It's the right thing to do." Ordinary decency, civic-mindedness, and contributions to society's well-being should be expected of any business.[26] In today's social and political climate, most business leaders can be expected to acknowledge that socially responsible actions are important and that businesses have a duty to be good corporate citizens. But there is a complementary school of thought that business operates on the basis of an implied social contract with the members of society. According to this contract, society grants a business the right to conduct its business affairs and agrees not to unreasonably restrain its pursuit of a fair profit for the goods or services it sells. In return for this "license to operate," a business is obligated to act as a responsible citizen, do its fair share to promote the general welfare, and avoid doing any harm. Such a view clearly puts a moral burden on a company to operate honorably, provide good working conditions to employees, be a good environmental steward, and display good corporate citizenship.

> Every action a company takes can be interpreted as a statement of what it stands for.

The Business Case for Corporate Social Responsibility and Environmentally Sustainable Business Practices

Whatever the moral arguments for socially responsible business behavior and environmentally sustainable business practices, there are definitely good business reasons why companies should be public-spirited and devote time and resources to social responsibility initiatives, environmental sustainability, and good corporate citizenship:

- *Such actions can lead to increased buyer patronage.* A strong visible social responsibility or environmental sustainability strategy gives a company an edge in appealing to consumers who prefer to do business with companies that are good corporate citizens. Ben & Jerry's, Whole Foods Market, Stonyfield Farm, TOMS, Keurig Green Mountain, and Patagonia have definitely expanded their customer bases because of their visible and well-publicized activities as socially conscious companies. More and more companies are also recognizing the cash register payoff of social responsibility strategies that reach out to people of all cultures and demographics (women, retirees, and ethnic groups).

- *A strong commitment to socially responsible behavior reduces the risk of reputation-damaging incidents.* Companies that place little importance on operating in a socially responsible manner are more prone to scandal and embarrassment. Consumer, environmental, and human rights activist groups are quick to criticize businesses whose behavior they consider to be out of line, and they are adept at getting their message into the media and onto the Internet. Pressure groups can generate widespread adverse publicity, promote boycotts, and influence like-minded or sympathetic buyers to avoid an offender's products.

Research has shown that product boycott announcements are associated with a decline in a company's stock price.[27] When a major oil company suffered damage to its reputation on environmental and social grounds, the CEO repeatedly said that the most negative impact the company suffered—and the one that made him fear for the future of the company—was that bright young graduates were no longer attracted to working for the company. For many years, Nike received stinging criticism for not policing sweatshop conditions in the Asian factories that produced Nike footwear, a situation that caused Nike cofounder and chair Phil Knight to observe that "Nike has become synonymous with slave wages, forced overtime, and arbitrary abuse."[28] In response, Nike began an extensive effort to monitor conditions in the 800 factories of the contract manufacturers that produced Nike shoes. As Knight said, "Good shoes come from good factories and good factories have good labor relations." Nonetheless, Nike has continually been plagued by complaints from human rights activists that its monitoring procedures are flawed and that it is not doing enough to correct the plight of factory workers. As this suggests, a damaged reputation is not easily repaired.

- *Socially responsible actions and sustainable business practices can lower costs and enhance employee recruiting and workforce retention.* Companies with deservedly good reputations for social responsibility and sustainable business practices are better able to attract and retain employees, compared to companies with tarnished reputations. Some employees just feel better about working for a company committed to improving society. This can contribute to lower turnover and better worker productivity. Other direct and indirect economic benefits include lower costs for staff recruitment and training. For example, Starbucks is said to enjoy much lower rates of employee turnover because of its full-benefits package for both full-time and part-time employees, management efforts to make Starbucks a great place to work, and the company's socially responsible practices. Sustainable business practices are often concomitant with greater operational efficiencies. For example, when a U.S. manufacturer of recycled paper, taking eco-efficiency to heart, discovered how to increase its fiber recovery rate, it saved the equivalent of 20,000 tons of waste paper—a factor that helped the company become the industry's lowest-cost producer. By helping two-thirds of its employees to stop smoking and by investing in a number of wellness programs for employees, Johnson & Johnson saved $250 million on its health care costs over a 10-year period.[29]

- *Opportunities for revenue enhancement may also come from CSR and environmental sustainability strategies.* The drive for sustainability and social responsibility can spur innovative efforts that in turn lead to new products and opportunities for revenue enhancement. Electric cars such as the Chevy Bolt and the Nissan Leaf are one example. In many cases, the revenue opportunities are tied to a company's core products. PepsiCo and Coca-Cola, for example, have expanded into the juice business to offer a healthier alternative to their carbonated beverages. General Electric has created a profitable new business in wind turbines. In other cases, revenue enhancement opportunities come from innovative ways to reduce waste and use the by-products of a company's production. Tyson Foods now produces jet fuel for B-52 bombers from the vast amount of animal waste resulting from its meat product business. Staples has become one of the largest nonutility corporate producers of renewable energy in the United States due to its installation of solar power panels in all of its outlets (and the sale of what it does not consume in renewable energy credit markets).

*   *Well-conceived CSR strategies and sustainable business practices are in the best long-term interest of shareholders.* When CSR and sustainability strategies increase buyer patronage, offer revenue-enhancing opportunities, lower costs, increase productivity, and reduce the risk of reputation-damaging incidents, they contribute to the economic value created by a company and improve its profitability. A two-year study of leading companies found that improving environmental compliance and developing environmentally friendly products can enhance earnings per share, profitability, and the likelihood of winning contracts. The stock prices of companies that rate high on social and environmental performance criteria have been found to perform 35 to 45 percent better than the average of the 2,500 companies that constitute the Dow Jones Global Index.[30] A review of 135 studies indicated there is a positive, but small, correlation between good corporate behavior and good financial performance; only two percent of the studies showed that dedicating corporate resources to social responsibility harmed the interests of shareholders.[31] Furthermore, socially responsible business behavior helps avoid or preempt legal and regulatory actions that could prove costly and otherwise burdensome. In some cases, it is possible to craft corporate social responsibility strategies that contribute to competitive advantage and, at the same time, deliver greater value to society. For instance, Walmart, by working with its suppliers to reduce the use of packaging materials and revamping the routes of its delivery trucks to cut out 100 million miles of travel, saved $200 million in costs (which enhanced its cost-competitiveness vis-à-vis rivals) and lowered carbon emissions.[32] Thus, a social responsibility strategy that packs some punch and is more than rhetorical flourish can produce outcomes that are in the best interest of shareholders.

In sum, companies that take social responsibility and environmental sustainability seriously can improve their business reputations and operational efficiency while also reducing their risk exposure and encouraging loyalty and innovation. Overall, companies that take special pains to protect the environment (beyond what is required by law), are active in community affairs, and are generous supporters of charitable causes and projects that benefit society are more likely to be seen as good investments and as good companies to work for or do business with. Shareholders are likely to view the business case for social responsibility as a strong one, particularly when it results in the creation of more customer value, greater productivity, lower operating costs, and lower business risk—all of which should increase firm profitability and enhance shareholder value even as the company's actions address broader stakeholder interests.

Companies are, of course, sometimes rewarded for bad behavior—a company that is able to shift environmental and other social costs associated with its activities onto society as a whole can reap large short-term profits. The major cigarette producers for many years were able to earn greatly inflated profits by shifting the health-related costs of smoking onto others and escaping any

Socially responsible strategies that create value for customers and lower costs can improve company profits and shareholder value at the same time that they address other stakeholder interests.

There's little hard evidence indicating shareholders are disadvantaged in any meaningful way by a company's actions to be socially responsible.

responsibility for the harm their products caused to consumers and the general public. Only recently have they been facing the prospect of having to pay high punitive damages for their actions. Unfortunately, the cigarette makers are not alone in trying to evade paying for the social harms of their operations for as long as they can. Calling a halt to such actions usually hinges on (1) the effectiveness of activist social groups in publicizing the adverse consequences of a company's social irresponsibility and marshaling public opinion for something to be done, (2) the enactment of legislation or regulations to correct the inequity, and (3) decisions on the part of socially conscious buyers to take their business elsewhere.

KEY POINTS

1. Ethics concerns standards of right and wrong. Business ethics concerns the application of ethical principles to the actions and decisions of business organizations and the conduct of their personnel. Ethical principles in business are not materially different from ethical principles in general.

2. There are three schools of thought about ethical standards for companies with international operations:

    *   According to the *school of ethical universalism,* common understandings across multiple cultures and countries about what constitutes right and wrong behaviors give rise to universal ethical standards that apply to members of all societies, all companies, and all businesspeople.

    *   According to the *school of ethical relativism,* different societal cultures and customs have divergent values and standards of right and wrong. Thus, what is ethical or unethical must be judged in the light of local customs and social mores and can vary from one culture or nation to another.

    *   According to the *integrated social contracts theory,* universal ethical principles based on the collective views of multiple cultures and societies combine to form a "social contract" that all individuals in all situations have a duty to observe. Within the boundaries of this social contract, local cultures or groups can specify what additional actions are not ethically permissible. However, universal norms always take precedence over local ethical norms.

3. Apart from the "business of business is business, not ethics" kind of thinking, three other factors contribute to unethical business behavior: (1) faulty oversight that enables the unscrupulous pursuit of personal gain, (2) heavy pressures on company managers to meet or beat short-term earnings targets, and (3) a company culture that puts profitability and good business performance ahead of ethical behavior. In contrast, culture can function as a powerful mechanism for promoting ethical business conduct when high ethical principles are deeply ingrained in the corporate culture of a company.

4. Business ethics failures can result in three types of costs: (1) visible costs, such as fines, penalties, and lower stock prices; (2) internal administrative costs, such as legal costs and costs of taking corrective action; and (3) intangible costs or less visible costs, such as customer defections and damage to the company's reputation.

5. The term *corporate social responsibility* concerns a company's *duty* to operate in an honorable manner, provide good working conditions for employees, encourage workforce diversity, be a good steward of the environment, and support philanthropic endeavors in local communities where it operates and in society at large.

The particular combination of socially responsible endeavors a company elects to pursue defines its corporate social responsibility (CSR) strategy.

6. The triple bottom line refers to company performance in three realms: economic, social, and environmental, often referred to as profit, people, and planet. Increasingly, companies are reporting their performance with respect to all three performance dimensions.

7. *Sustainability* is a term that is used in various ways, but most often it concerns a firm's relationship to the environment and its use of natural resources. Sustainable business practices are those capable of meeting the needs of the present without compromising the world's ability to meet future needs. A company's environmental sustainability strategy consists of its deliberate actions to protect the environment, provide for the longevity of natural resources, maintain ecological support systems for future generations, and guard against ultimate endangerment of the planet.

8. CSR strategies and environmental sustainability strategies that both provide valuable social benefits *and* fulfill customer needs in a superior fashion can lead to competitive advantage.

9. The moral case for corporate social responsibility and environmental sustainability boils down to a simple concept: It's the right thing to do. There are also solid reasons why CSR and environmental sustainability strategies may be good business—they can be conducive to greater buyer patronage, reduce the risk of reputation-damaging incidents, provide opportunities for revenue enhancement, and lower costs. Well-crafted CSR and environmental sustainability strategies are in the best long-term interest of shareholders, for the reasons just mentioned and because they can avoid or preempt costly legal or regulatory actions.

ASSURANCE OF LEARNING EXERCISES

1. Widely known as an ethical company, Dell recently committed itself to becoming a more environmentally sustainable business. After reviewing the About Dell section of its website (www.dell.com/learn/us/en/uscorp1/about-dell), prepare a list of eight specific policies and programs that help the company achieve its vision of driving social and environmental change while still remaining innovative and profitable.   **LO 9-1, LO 9-4**

2. Prepare a one- to two-page analysis of a recent ethics scandal using your university library's resources. Your report should (1) discuss the conditions that gave rise to unethical business strategies and behavior and (2) provide an overview of the costs to the company resulting from the company's business ethics failure.   **LO 9-2, LO 9-3**

3. Based on information provided in Illustration Capsule 9.3, explain how Warby Parker's CSR strategy has contributed to its success in the marketplace. How are the company's various stakeholder groups affected by its commitment to social responsibility? How would you evaluate its triple-bottom-line performance?
LO 9-4

4. The British outdoor clothing company Páramo was a Guardian Sustainable Business Award winner in 2016. (Guardian stopped giving the award afterward.) The company's fabric technology and use of chemicals is discussed at https://www.theguardian.com/sustainable-business/2016/may/27/outdoor-clothing-paramo-toxic-pfc-greenpeace-fabric-technology. Describe how Páramo's business practices allowed it to become recognized for its bold moves. How do these initiatives help build competitive advantage?   **LO 9-4**

EXERCISES FOR SIMULATION PARTICIPANTS

LO 9-1   **1.** What factors build the business case for operating your company in an ethical manner?

LO 9-4   **2.** In what ways, if any, is your company exercising corporate social responsibility? What are the elements of your company's CSR strategy? Are there any changes to this strategy that you would suggest?

LO 9-3, LO 9-4   **3.** If some shareholders complained that you and your co-managers have been spending too little or too much on corporate social responsibility, what would you tell them?

LO 9-4   **4.** Is your company striving to conduct its business in an environmentally sustainable manner? What specific *additional* actions could your company take that would make an even greater contribution to environmental sustainability?

LO 9-4   **5.** In what ways do a company's environmental sustainability strategy in the best long-term interest of shareholders? Does it contribute to your company's competitive advantage or profitability?

ENDNOTES

[1] James E. Post, Anne T. Lawrence, and James Weber, *Business and Society: Corporate Strategy, Public Policy, Ethics,* 10th ed. (New York: McGraw-Hill, 2002).

[2] Mark S. Schwartz, "Universal Moral Values for Corporate Codes of Ethics," *Journal of Business Ethics* 59, no. 1 (June 2005), pp. 27–44.

[3] Mark S. Schwartz, "A Code of Ethics for Corporate Codes of Ethics," *Journal of Business Ethics* 41, no. 1–2 (November–December 2002), pp. 27–43.

[4] T. L. Beauchamp and N. E. Bowie, *Ethical Theory and Business* (Upper Saddle River, NJ: Prentice-Hall, 2001).

[5] www.cnn.com/2013/10/15/world/child-labor-index-2014/ (accessed February 6, 2014).

[6] U.S. Department of Labor, "The Department of Labor's 2013 Findings on the Worst Forms of Child Labor," www.dol.gov/ilab/programs/ocft/PDF/2012OCFTreport.pdf.

[7] W. M. Greenfield, "In the Name of Corporate Social Responsibility," *Business Horizons* 47, no. 1 (January–February 2004), p. 22.

[8] Rajib Sanyal, "Determinants of Bribery in International Business: The Cultural and Economic Factors," *Journal of Business Ethics* 59, no. 1 (June 2005), pp. 139–145.

[9] Transparency International, *Global Corruption Report,* www.globalcorruptionreport.org.

[10] Roger Chen and Chia-Pei Chen, "Chinese Professional Managers and the Issue of Ethical Behavior," *Ivey Business Journal* 69, no. 5 (May–June 2005), p. 1.

[11] Antonio Argandoa, "Corruption and Companies: The Use of Facilitating Payments," *Journal of Business Ethics* 60, no. 3 (September 2005), pp. 251–264.

[12] Thomas Donaldson and Thomas W. Dunfee, "Towards a Unified Conception of Business Ethics: Integrative Social Contracts Theory," *Academy of Management Review* 19, no. 2 (April 1994), pp. 252–284; Andrew Spicer, Thomas W. Dunfee, and Wendy J. Bailey, "Does National Context Matter in Ethical Decision Making? An Empirical Test of Integrative Social Contracts Theory," *Academy of Management Journal* 47, no. 4 (August 2004), p. 610.

[13] Lynn Paine, Rohit Deshpandé, Joshua D. Margolis, and Kim Eric Bettcher, "Up to Code: Does Your Company's Conduct Meet World-Class Standards?" *Harvard Business Review* 83, no. 12 (December 2005), pp. 122–133.

[14] John F. Veiga, Timothy D. Golden, and Kathleen Dechant, "Why Managers Bend Company Rules," *Academy of Management Executive* 18, no. 2 (May 2004).

[15] Lorin Berlin and Emily Peck, "National Mortgage Settlement: States, Big Banks Reach $25 Billion Deal," *Huff Post Business,* February 9, 2012, www.huffingtonpost.com/2012/02/09/-national-mortgage-settlement_n_1265292.html (accessed February 15, 2012).

[16] Ronald R. Sims and Johannes Brinkmann, "Enron Ethics (Or: Culture Matters More than Codes)," *Journal of Business Ethics* 45, no. 3 (July 2003), pp. 244–246.

[17] Kurt Eichenwald, *Conspiracy of Fools: A True Story* (New York: Broadway Books, 2005).

[18] Timothy M. Devinney, "Is the Socially Responsible Corporation a Myth? The Good, the Bad, and the Ugly of Corporate Social Responsibility," *Academy of Management Perspectives* 23, no. 2 (May 2009), pp. 44–56.

[19] Information posted at www.generalmills.com (accessed March 13, 2013).

[20] Adrian Henriques, "ISO 26000: A New Standard for Human Rights?" *Institute for Human Rights and Business,* March 23, 2010, www.institutehrb.org/blogs/guest/iso_26000_a_new_standard_for_human_rights.html?gclid=CJih7NjN2aICFVs65QodrVOdyQ (accessed July 7, 2010).

[21] Gerald I. J. M. Zetsloot and Marcel N. A. van Marrewijk, "From Quality to Sustainability," *Journal of Business Ethics* 55 (2004), pp. 79–82.

[22] Tilde Herrera, "PG&E Claims Industry First with Supply Chain Footprint Project," GreenBiz.com, June 30, 2010, www.greenbiz.com/news/2010/06/30/-pge—claims-industry-first-supply-chain-carbon-footprint-project.

[23] J. G. Speth, *The Bridge at the End of the World: Capitalism, the Environment, and Crossing from Crisis to Sustainability* (New Haven, CT: Yale University Press, 2008).

[24] Michael E. Porter and Mark R. Kramer, "Strategy & Society: The Link between Competitive Advantage and Corporate Social Responsibility," *Harvard Business Review* 84, no. 12 (December 2006), pp. 78–92.

[25] N. Craig Smith, "Corporate Responsibility: Whether and How," *California Management Review* 45, no. 4 (Summer 2003), p. 63.

[26] Jeb Brugmann and C. K. Prahalad, "Cocreating Business's New Social Compact," *Harvard Business Review* 85, no. 2 (February 2007), pp. 80–90.

[27] Wallace N. Davidson, Abuzar El-Jelly, and Dan L. Worrell, "Influencing Managers to Change Unpopular Corporate Behavior through Boycotts and Divestitures: A Stock Market Test," *Business and Society* 34, no. 2 (1995), pp. 171–196.

[28] Tom McCawley, "Racing to Improve Its Reputation: Nike Has Fought to Shed Its Image as an Exploiter of Third-World Labor Yet It Is Still a Target of Activists," *Financial Times*, December 2000, p. 14.

[29] Michael E. Porter and Mark Kramer, "Creating Shared Value," *Harvard Business Review* 89, no. 1–2 (January–February 2011).

[30] James C. Collins and Jerry I. Porras, *Built to Last: Successful Habits of Visionary Companies*, 3rd ed. (London: HarperBusiness, 2002).

[31] Joshua D. Margolis and Hillary A. Elfenbein, "Doing Well by Doing Good: Don't Count on It," *Harvard Business Review* 86, no. 1 (January 2008), pp. 19–20; Lee E. Preston, Douglas P. O'Bannon, Ronald M. Roman, Sefa Hayibor, and Bradley R. Agle, "The Relationship between Social and Financial Performance: Repainting a Portrait," *Business and Society* 38, no. 1 (March 1999), pp. 109–125.

[32] Leonard L. Berry, Ann M. Mirobito, and William B. Baun, "What's the Hard Return on Employee Wellness Programs?" *Harvard Business Review* 88, no. 12 (December 2010), p. 105.

chapter 10

Building an Organization Capable of Good Strategy Execution

People, Capabilities, and Structure

Learning Objectives

After reading this chapter, you should be able to:

LO 10-1 Understand what managers must do to execute strategy successfully.

LO 10-2 Understand why hiring, training, and retaining the right people constitute a key component of the strategy execution process.

LO 10-3 Recognize that good strategy execution requires continuously building and upgrading the organization's resources and capabilities.

LO 10-4 Identify and establish a strategy-supportive organizational structure and organize the work effort.

LO 10-5 Comprehend the pros and cons of centralized and decentralized decision making in implementing the chosen strategy.

Richard *Schneider/Getty Images*

Strategies most often fail because they aren't executed well.

Larry Bossidy and Ram Charan
Former CEO of Honeywell; Author and Consultant

I try to motivate people and align our individual incentives with organizational incentives. And then let people do their best.

John D. Liu—*CEO, Essex Equity Management*

People are not your most important asset. The right people are.

Jim Collins—*Professor and author*

Once managers have decided on a strategy, the emphasis turns to converting it into actions and good results. Putting the strategy into place and getting the organization to execute it will call for different sets of managerial skills rather than crafting strategy. Whereas crafting strategy is largely an analysis-driven activity focused on market conditions and the company's resources and capabilities, executing strategy is primarily operations-driven, revolving around the management of people, resources, business processes, and organizational structure. Successful strategy execution depends on doing a good job of working with and through others; building and strengthening competitive capabilities; creating an appropriate organizational structure; allocating resources; instituting strategy-supportive policies, processes, and systems; and instilling a discipline of getting things done. Executing strategy is an action-oriented task that tests a manager's ability to direct organizational change, achieve improvements in day-to-day operations, create and nurture a culture that supports good strategy execution, and meet or beat performance targets.

Experienced managers are well aware that it is much easier to develop a sound strategic plan than it is to execute the plan and achieve targeted outcomes. A study of 400 CEOs in the United States, Europe, and Asia found that executional excellence was the number-one challenge facing their companies.[1] According to one executive, "It's been rather easy for us to decide where we wanted to go. The hard part is to get the organization to act on the new priorities."[2] It takes adept managerial leadership to convincingly communicate the reasons for a new strategy and overcome pockets of doubt, secure the commitment of key personnel, build consensus for how to implement the strategy, and move forward to get all the pieces into place and deliver results. *Just because senior managers announce a new strategy doesn't mean that organization members will embrace it and move forward enthusiastically to implement it.* Company personnel must understand—in their heads and hearts—why a new strategic direction is necessary and where the new strategy is taking them.[3] Instituting change is, of course, easier when the problems with the old strategy have become obvious and/or the company has spiraled into a financial crisis.

But the challenge of successfully implementing new strategic initiatives goes well beyond managerial adeptness in overcoming resistance to change. What really make executing strategy a tougher, more time-consuming management challenge than crafting strategy are the wide array of managerial activities that must be attended to, the many ways to put new strategic initiatives in place and keep things moving, and the number of bedeviling issues that always crop up and have to be resolved. It takes first-rate "managerial smarts" to zero in on what exactly needs to be done and how to get good results in a timely manner. Excellent people-management skills and perseverance are needed to get a variety of initiatives underway and to integrate the efforts of many different work groups into a smoothly functioning whole. Depending on how much consensus building and organizational change is involved, the process of implementing strategy changes can take several months to several years. And executing the strategy with *real proficiency* takes even longer.

Like crafting strategy, *executing strategy is a job for a company's whole management team—not just a few senior managers.* While the chief executive officer and the heads of major units (business divisions, functional departments, and key operating units) are ultimately responsible for seeing that strategy is executed successfully, the process typically affects every part of the firm—all value chain activities and all work groups. Top-level managers must rely on the active support of middle and lower managers to institute whatever new operating practices are needed in the various operating units to achieve proficient strategy execution. Middle- and lower-level managers must ensure that frontline employees perform strategy-critical value chain activities proficiently enough to allow companywide performance targets to be met. Consequently, *all company personnel are actively involved in the strategy execution process in one way or another.*

A FRAMEWORK FOR EXECUTING STRATEGY

● **LO 10-1**

Understand what managers must do to execute strategy successfully.

The managerial approach to executing a strategy always has to be customized to fit the particulars of a company's situation. Making minor changes in an existing strategy differs from implementing radical strategy changes. The techniques for successfully executing a low-cost leader strategy are different from those for executing a high-end differentiation strategy. Implementing a new strategy for a struggling company in the midst of a financial crisis is a different job from improving strategy execution in a company that is doing relatively well. Moreover, some managers are more adept than others at using particular approaches to achieving certain kinds of organizational changes. Hence, there's no definitive managerial recipe for successful strategy execution that cuts across all company situations and strategies or that works for all managers. Rather, the specific actions required to execute a strategy— the "to-do list" that constitutes management's action agenda—always represent management's judgment about how best to proceed in light of prevailing circumstances.

The Principal Components of the Strategy Execution Process

Despite the need to tailor a company's strategy-executing approaches to the situation at hand, certain managerial bases must be covered no matter what the circumstances. These include 10 basic managerial tasks (see Figure 10.1):

1. Staffing the organization with managers and employees capable of executing the strategy well.

2. Developing the resources and organizational capabilities required for successful strategy execution.

3. Creating a strategy-supportive organizational structure.

4. Allocating sufficient resources (budgetary and otherwise) to the strategy execution effort.

5. Instituting policies and procedures that facilitate strategy execution.

6. Adopting business management processes that drive continuous improvement in how value chain activities are performed.

7. Installing information and operating systems that support strategy implementation activities.

8. Tying rewards directly to the achievement of performance objectives.

9. Fostering a corporate culture that promotes good strategy execution.

10. Exercising the leadership needed to propel strategy execution forward.

> When strategies fail, it is often because of poor execution. Strategy execution is therefore a critical managerial endeavor.

> The two best signs of good strategy execution are whether a company is meeting its performance targets and whether it has attained real proficiency in performing strategy-critical value chain activities.

How well managers perform these 10 tasks has a decisive impact on whether the outcome of the strategy execution effort is a spectacular success, a colossal failure, or something in between.

In devising an action agenda for executing strategy, managers should start by conducting *a probing assessment of what the organization must do differently to carry out the strategy successfully.* Each manager needs to ask the question "What needs to be done in my area of responsibility to implement our part of the company's strategy, and what should I do to get these things accomplished in a timely fashion?" It is then incumbent on every manager to determine *precisely how to make the necessary internal changes.* Strong managers have a knack for diagnosing what their organizations need to do to execute the chosen strategy well and figuring out how to get these things done efficiently. They are masters in promoting results-oriented behaviors on the part of company personnel and following through on making the right things happen to achieve the target outcomes.[4]

When strategies fail, it is often because of poor execution. Strategy execution is therefore a critical managerial endeavor. The two best signs of good strategy execution are whether a company is meeting its performance targets and whether it is performing value chain activities in a manner that is conducive to companywide operating excellence. In big organizations with geographically scattered operating units, senior executives' action agenda mostly involves communicating the case for change, building consensus for how to proceed, installing strong managers to move the process forward in key organizational units, directing resources to the right places, establishing deadlines and measures of progress, rewarding those who achieve implementation milestones, and personally leading the strategic change process. Thus, the bigger the organization, the more that successful strategy execution depends on the cooperation and implementation skills of operating managers who can promote needed changes at the lowest organizational levels and deliver results. In small organizations, top managers can deal directly with frontline managers and employees, personally orchestrating the action steps and implementation sequence, observing firsthand how implementation is progressing, and deciding how hard and how fast to push the process along. Whether the organization is large or small and whether strategy implementation involves sweeping or minor changes, effective leadership requires a keen grasp of what to do and how to do it in light of the organization's circumstances. Then it remains for company personnel in strategy-critical areas to step up to the plate and produce the desired results.

What's Covered in Chapters 10, 11, and 12   In the remainder of this chapter and in the next two chapters, we discuss what is involved in performing the 10 key managerial tasks that shape the process of executing strategy. This chapter explores the first three of these tasks (highlighted in blue in Figure 10.1): (1) staffing the organization with people

FIGURE 10.1   **The 10 Basic Tasks of the Strategy Execution Process**

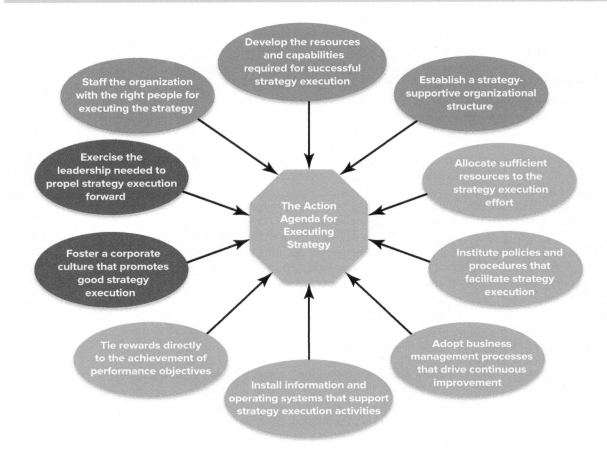

capable of executing the strategy well, (2) developing the resources and organizational capabilities needed for successful strategy execution, and (3) creating an organizational structure supportive of the strategy execution process. Chapter 11 concerns the tasks of allocating resources (budgetary and otherwise), instituting strategy-facilitating policies and procedures, employing business process management tools installing operating and information systems, and tying rewards to the achievement of good results (highlighted in green in Figure 10.1). Chapter 12 deals with the two remaining tasks: instilling a corporate culture conducive to good strategy execution, and exercising the leadership needed to drive the execution process forward (highlighted in purple).

BUILDING AN ORGANIZATION CAPABLE OF GOOD STRATEGY EXECUTION: THREE KEY ACTIONS

Proficient strategy execution depends foremost on having in place an organization capable of the tasks demanded of it. Building an execution-capable organization is thus always a top priority. As shown in Figure 10.2, three types of organization-building actions are paramount:

1. *Staffing the organization*—putting together a strong management team, and recruiting and retaining employees with the needed experience, technical skills, and intellectual capital.

2. *Acquiring, developing, and strengthening the resources and capabilities required for good strategy execution*—accumulating the required resources, developing proficiencies in performing strategy-critical value chain activities, and updating the company's capabilities to match changing market conditions and customer expectations.

3. *Structuring the organization and work effort*—organizing value chain activities and business processes, establishing lines of authority and reporting relationships, and deciding how much decision-making authority to delegate to lower-level managers and frontline employees.

Implementing a strategy depends critically on ensuring that strategy-supportive resources and Organizational capabilities are in place, ready to be deployed. These include the skills, talents, experience, and knowledge of the company's human resources (managerial and otherwise)—see Figure 10.2. Proficient strategy execution

FIGURE 10.2   Building an Organization Capable of Proficient Strategy Execution: Three Key Actions

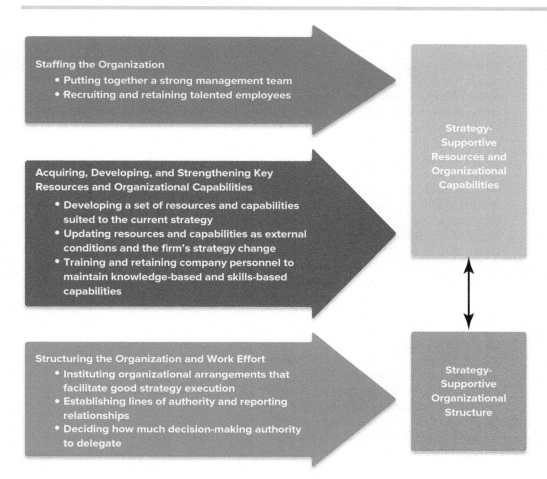

depends heavily on competent personnel of all types, but because of the many managerial tasks involved and the role of leadership in strategy execution, assembling a strong management team is especially important.

If the strategy being implemented is a new strategy, the company may need to add to its resource and capability mix in other respects as well. But renewing, upgrading, and revising the organization's resources and capabilities is a part of the strategy execution process even if the strategy is fundamentally the same, since strategic assets depreciate and conditions are always changing. Thus, augmenting and strengthening the firm's core competencies and seeing that they are suited to the current strategy are also top priorities.

Structuring the organization and work effort is another critical aspect of building an organization capable of good strategy execution. An organization structure that is well matched to the strategy can help facilitate its implementation; one that is not well suited can lead to higher bureaucratic costs and communication or coordination breakdowns.

STAFFING THE ORGANIZATION

LO 10-2

Understand why hiring, training, and retaining the right people constitute a key component of the strategy execution process.

No company can hope to perform the activities required for successful strategy execution without attracting and retaining talented managers and employees with suitable skills and *intellectual capital*.

Putting Together a Strong Management Team

Assembling a capable management team is a cornerstone of the organization-building task.[5] While different strategies and company circumstances often call for different mixes of backgrounds, experiences, management styles, and know-how, *the most important consideration is to fill key managerial slots with smart people who are clear thinkers, good at figuring out what needs to be done, skilled in managing people, and accomplished in delivering good results.*[6] The task of implementing challenging strategic initiatives must be assigned to executives who have the skills and talents to handle them and who can be counted on to get the job done well. Without a capable, results-oriented management team, the implementation process is likely to be hampered by missed deadlines, misdirected or wasteful efforts, and managerial ineptness. Weak executives are serious impediments to getting optimal results—the caliber of work done under their supervision suffers.[7] In contrast, managers with strong strategy implementation capabilities understand how to drive organizational change, and know how to motivate and lead the company down the path for first-rate strategy execution. They have a talent for asking tough, incisive questions and know enough about the details of the business to ensure the soundness of the decisions of the people around them—they can discern whether the resources people are asking for to put the strategy in place make sense. They are good at getting things done through others, partly by making sure they have the right people under them, assigned to the right jobs and partly because they know how to motivate and inspire people. They have strong social skills and high emotional intelligence. They consistently follow through on issues, monitor progress carefully, make adjustments when needed, and keep important details from slipping through the cracks.

Sometimes a company's existing management team is up to the task. At other times it may need to be strengthened by promoting qualified people from within or by bringing in outsiders whose experiences, talents, and leadership styles better suit the situation. In turnaround and rapid-growth situations, and in instances when company managers lack the requisite know-how, filling key management slots from the outside is a standard organization-building approach. In all situations, it is important to identify and replace managers who are incapable, for whatever reason, of making the required changes in a timely and cost-effective manner. For a management team to be truly effective at strategy execution, it must be composed of managers who recognize that organizational changes are needed and who are both capable and ready to get on with the process.

> Putting together a talented management team with the right mix of experiences, skills, and abilities to get things done is one of the first steps to take in launching the strategy-executing process.

The overriding aim in building a management team should be to assemble a *critical mass* of talented managers who can function as agents of change and spearhead excellent strategy execution. Every manager's success is enhanced (or limited) by the quality of his or her managerial colleagues and the degree to which they freely exchange ideas, debate ways to make operating improvements, and join forces to tackle issues and solve problems. When a first-rate manager enjoys the help and support of other first-rate managers, it's possible to create a managerial whole that is greater than the sum of individual efforts—talented managers who work well together as a team can produce organizational results that are dramatically better than what one or two star managers acting individually can achieve.[8]

Illustration Capsule 10.1 describes Deloitte's highly effective approach to developing employee talent and a top-caliber management team.

Recruiting, Training, and Retaining Capable Employees

Assembling a capable management team is not enough. Staffing the organization with the right kinds of people must extend to all kinds of company personnel for value chain activities to be performed competently. *The caliber of an organization's people is always an essential ingredient of successful strategy execution.* Companies like Mercedes-Benz, Alphabet, SAS, Boston Consulting Group, Edward Jones, Quicken Loans, Genentech, Intuit, Salesforce.com, and Goldman Sachs make a concerted effort to recruit the best and brightest people they can find and then retain them with excellent compensation packages, opportunities for rapid advancement and professional growth, and interesting assignments. Having a pool of "A players" with strong skill sets and lots of brainpower is essential to their business.

> In many industries, adding to a company's talent base and building intellectual capital are more important to good strategy execution than are additional investments in capital projects.

Facebook makes a point of hiring the very brightest and most talented programmers it can find and motivating them with both good monetary incentives and the challenge of working on cutting-edge technology projects. McKinsey & Company, one of the world's premier management consulting firms, recruits only cream-of-the-crop MBAs at the nation's top-10 business schools; such talent is essential to McKinsey's strategy of performing high-level consulting for the world's top corporations. The leading global accounting firms screen candidates not only on the basis of their accounting expertise but also on whether they possess the people skills needed to relate well with clients and colleagues. Zappos goes to considerable lengths to hire people who can have fun and be fun on the job; it has done away with traditional job postings and instead asks prospective hires to join a social network called Zappos Insiders where they will interact with current employees and have opportunities to demonstrate their passion for joining the company. Zappos is so selective about finding people who fit their culture that only about 1.5 percent of the people who apply are offered jobs.

In high-tech companies, the challenge is to staff work groups with gifted, imaginative, and energetic people who can bring life to new ideas quickly and inject into the organization what one Dell executive calls "hum."[9] The saying "People are our most important asset" may seem trite, but it fits high-technology companies precisely. Besides checking closely for functional and technical skills, Dell tests applicants for

Management Development at Deloitte Touche Tohmatsu Limited

Kent *Johansson/Shutterstock*

Hiring, retaining, and cultivating talent are critical activities at Deloitte, the world's largest professional services firm. By offering robust learning and development programs, Deloitte has been able to create a strong talent pipeline to the firm's partnership. Deloitte's emphasis on learning and development, across all stages of the employee life cycle, has led to recognitions such as being ranked number-one on *Chief Executives*'s list of "Best Private Companies for Leaders" and being listed among *Fortune*'s "100 Best Companies to Work For." The following programs contribute to Deloitte's successful execution of its talent strategy:

- *Clear path to partnership.* During the initial recruiting phase and then throughout an employee's tenure at the firm, Deloitte lays out a clear career path. The path indicates the expected timeline for promotion to each of the firm's hierarchy levels, along with the competencies and experience required. Deloitte's transparency on career paths, coupled with its in-depth performance

management process, helps employees clearly understand their performance. This serves as a motivational tool for top performers, often leading to career acceleration.

- *Formal training programs.* Like other leading organizations, Deloitte has a program to ensure that recent college graduates are equipped with the necessary training and tools for succeeding on the job. Yet Deloitte's commitment to formal training is evident at all levels within the organization. Each time an employee is promoted, he or she attends "milestone" school, a weeklong simulation that replicates true business situations employees would face as they transition to new stages of career development. In addition, Deloitte institutes mandatory training hours for all of its employees to ensure that individuals continue to further their professional development.

- *Special programs for high performers.* Deloitte also offers fellowships and programs to help employees acquire new skills and enhance their leadership development. For example, the Global Fellows program helps top performers work with senior leaders in the organization to focus on the realities of delivering client service across borders. Deloitte has also established the Emerging Leaders Development program, which utilizes skill building, 360-degree feedback, and one-on-one executive coaching to help top-performing managers and senior managers prepare for partnership.

- *Sponsorship, not mentorship.* To train the next generation of leaders, Deloitte has implemented formal mentorship programs to provide leadership development support. Deloitte, however, uses the term *sponsorship* to describe this initiative. A sponsor is tasked with taking a vested interest in an individual and advocating on his or her behalf. Sponsors help rising leaders navigate the firm, develop new competencies, expand their network, and hone the skills needed to accelerate their career.

Note: Developed with Heather Levy.

Sources: Company websites; www.accountingweb.com/article/leadership-development-community-service-integral-deloitte-university/220845 (accessed February 2014).

their tolerance of ambiguity and change, their capacity to work in teams, and their ability to learn on the fly. Companies like LinkedIn, Credit Suisse, IDEO, Amazon.com, Google, and Cisco Systems have broken new ground in recruiting, hiring, cultivating, developing, and retaining talented employees—almost all of whom are in their 20s and 30s. Cisco goes after the top 10 percent, raiding other companies and endeavoring to retain key people at the companies it acquires. Cisco executives believe that a cadre of star engineers, programmers, managers, salespeople, and support personnel is the backbone of the company's efforts to execute its strategy and remain the world's leading provider of Internet infrastructure products and technology.

In recognition of the importance of a talented and energetic workforce, companies have instituted a number of practices aimed at staffing jobs with the best people they can find:

1. Spending considerable effort on screening and evaluating job applicants—selecting only those with suitable skill sets, energy, initiative, judgment, aptitude for learning, and personality traits that mesh well with the company's work environment and culture.

2. Providing employees with training programs that continue throughout their careers.

3. Offering promising employees challenging, interesting, and skill-stretching assignments.

4. Rotating people through jobs that span functional and geographic boundaries. Providing people with opportunities to gain experience in a variety of international settings is increasingly considered an essential part of career development in multinational companies.

5. Making the work environment stimulating and engaging so that employees will consider the company a great place to work.

6. Encouraging employees to challenge existing ways of doing things, to be creative in proposing better ways of operating, and to push their ideas for new products or businesses. Progressive companies work hard at creating an environment in which employees are made to feel that their views and suggestions count.

7. Striving to retain talented, high-performing employees via promotions, salary increases, performance bonuses, stock options and equity ownership, benefit packages including health insurance and retirement packages, and other perks, such as flexible work hours and onsite day care.

8. Coaching average performers to improve their skills and capabilities, while weeding out underperformers.

> The best companies make a point of recruiting and retaining talented employees—the objective is to make the company's entire workforce (managers and rank-and-file employees) a genuine competitive asset.

DEVELOPING AND BUILDING CRITICAL RESOURCES AND ORGANIZATIONAL CAPABILITIES

High among the organization-building priorities in the strategy execution process is the need to build and strengthen the company's portfolio of resources and capabilities with which to perform strategy-critical value chain activities. As explained in Chapter 4, a company's chances of gaining a sustainable advantage over its market rivals depends on the caliber of its resource portfolio. In the course of crafting strategy, managers may well have well have identified the strategy-critical resources and capabilities it needs. But getting the strategy execution process underway requires acquiring or developing these resources and capabilities, putting them into place, upgrading them as needed, and then modifying them as market conditions evolve.

If the strategy being implemented has important new elements, company managers may have to acquire new resources, significantly broaden or deepen certain capabilities, or even add entirely new competencies in order to put the strategic initiatives in place and execute them proficiently. But even when a company's strategy has not changed materially, good strategy execution still involves continually upgrading the firm's resources and capabilities to keep them in top form and perform value chain activities ever more proficiently.

> **LO 10-3**
>
> Recognize that good strategy execution requires continuously building and upgrading the organization's resources and capabilities.

Three Approaches to Building and Strengthening Organizational Capabilities

Building the right kinds of organizational capabilities and keeping them finely honed is a time-consuming, managerially challenging exercise. While some assistance can be gotten from discovering how best-in-industry or best-in-world companies perform a particular activity, trying to replicate and then improve on the capabilities of other companies is easier said than done—for the same reasons that one is unlikely to ever become a world-class halfpipe snowboarder just by studying legendary Olympic gold medalist Shaun White.

With deliberate effort, well-orchestrated organizational actions, and continued practice, however, it is possible for a firm to become proficient at capability building despite the difficulty. Indeed, by making capability-building activities a *routine* part of their strategy execution endeavors, some firms are able to develop *dynamic capabilities* that assist them in managing resource and capability change, as discussed in Chapter 4. The most common approaches to capability building include (1) developing and strengthening capabilities internally, (2) acquiring capabilities through mergers and acquisitions, and (3) developing new organizational capabilities via collaborative partnerships.

Developing Organizational Capabilities Internally   Internal efforts to create or upgrade organizational capabilities is an evolutionary process that entails a series of deliberate and well-orchestrated steps as organizations search for solutions to their problems. The process is a complex one, since capabilities are the product of *bundles of skills and know-how that are integrated into organizational routines* and *deployed within activity systems* through the combined efforts of teams that are often cross-functional in nature, spanning a variety of departments and locations. For instance, the capability of speeding new products to market involves the *collaborative efforts* of personnel in R&D, engineering and design, purchasing, production, marketing, and distribution. Similarly, the capability to provide superior customer service is a team effort among people in customer call centers (where orders are taken and inquiries are answered), shipping and delivery, billing and accounts receivable, and after-sale support. The process of building an organizational capability begins when managers set an objective of developing a particular capability and organize activity around that objective.[10]

Because the process is incremental, the first step is to develop the *ability* to do something, however imperfectly or inefficiently. This entails selecting people with the requisite skills and experience, enabling them to upgrade their abilities as needed, and then molding the efforts of individuals into a joint effort to create an organizational ability. At this stage, progress can be fitful since it depends on experimenting, actively searching for alternative solutions, and learning through trial and error.[11]

As experience grows and company personnel learn how to perform the activities consistently well and at an acceptable cost, the ability *evolves* into a tried-and-true competence. Getting to this point requires a *continual investment* of resources and *systematic efforts* to improve processes and solve problems creatively as they arise. Improvements in the functioning of an organizational capability come from task repetition and the resulting *learning by doing* of individuals and teams. But the process can be accelerated by making learning a more deliberate endeavor and providing the incentives that will motivate company personnel to achieve the desired ends.[12] This can be critical to successful strategy execution when market conditions are changing rapidly.

It is generally much easier and less time-consuming to update and remodel a company's existing capabilities as external conditions and company strategy change than it is to create them from scratch. Maintaining organizational capabilities in top form may simply require exercising them continually and fine-tuning them as necessary. Similarly, augmenting a capability may require less effort if it involves the recombination of well-established company capabilities and draws on existing company resources. For example, Williams-Sonoma first developed the capability to expand sales beyond its brick-and-mortar location in 1970, when it launched a catalog that was sent to customers throughout the United States. The company extended its mail-order business with the acquisitions of Hold Everything, a garden products catalog, and Pottery Barn, and entered online retailing in 2000 when it launched e-commerce sites for Pottery Barn and Williams-Sonoma. The ongoing renewal of these capabilities has allowed Williams-Sonoma to generate revenues of more than $5.6 billion in 2019 and become one of the largest online retailers in the United States. Toyota, en route to overtaking General Motors as the global leader in motor vehicles, aggressively upgraded its capabilities in fuel-efficient hybrid engine technology and constantly fine-tuned its famed Toyota Production System to enhance its already proficient capabilities in manufacturing top-quality vehicles at relatively low costs.

Managerial actions to develop competitive capabilities generally take one of two forms: either strengthening the company's base of skills, knowledge, and experience or coordinating and integrating the efforts of the various work groups and departments. Actions of the first sort can be undertaken at all managerial levels, but actions of the second sort are best orchestrated by senior managers who not only appreciate the strategy-executing significance of strong capabilities but also have the clout to enforce the necessary cooperation and coordination among individuals, groups, and departments.[13]

Acquiring Capabilities through Mergers and Acquisitions   Sometimes the best way for a company to upgrade its portfolio of capabilities is by acquiring (or merging with) another company with attractive resources and capabilities.[14] An acquisition aimed at building a stronger portfolio of resources and capabilities can be every bit as valuable as an acquisition aimed at adding new products or services to the company's lineup of offerings. The advantage of this mode of acquiring new capabilities is primarily one of speed, since developing new capabilities internally can, at best, take many years of effort and, at worst, come to naught. Capabilities-motivated acquisitions are essential (1) when the company does not have the ability to create the needed capability internally (perhaps because it is too far afield from its existing capabilities) and (2) when industry conditions, technology, or competitors are moving at such a rapid clip that time is of the essence.

At the same time, acquiring capabilities in this way is not without difficulty. Capabilities involve tacit knowledge and complex routines that cannot be transferred readily from one organizational unit to another. This may limit the extent to which the new capability can be utilized. For example, Facebook acquired Oculus VR, a company that makes virtual reality headsets, to add capabilities that might enhance the social media experience. Transferring and integrating these capabilities to other parts of the Facebook organization may prove easier said than done, however, as many technology acquisitions fail to yield the hoped-for benefits. Integrating the capabilities of two companies is particularly problematic when there are underlying incompatibilities in their supporting systems or processes. Moreover, since internal fit is important, there is always the risk that under new management the acquired capabilities may not be as productive as they had been. In a worst-case scenario, the acquisition process may end up damaging or destroying the very capabilities that were the object of the acquisition in the first place.

Accessing Capabilities through Collaborative Partnerships   A third way of obtaining valuable resources and capabilities is to form collaborative partnerships with suppliers, competitors, or other companies having the cutting-edge expertise. There are three basic ways to pursue this course of action:

1. *Outsource the function in which the company's capabilities are deficient to a key supplier or another provider.* Whether this is a wise move depends on whether developing the capabilities internally are key to the company's long-term success. But if this is not the case, then outsourcing may be a good choice especially for firms that are too small and resource-constrained to execute all the parts of their strategy internally.

2. *Collaborate with a firm that has complementary resources and capabilities in a joint venture, strategic alliance, or other type of partnership established for the purpose of achieving a shared strategic objective.* This requires launching initiatives to identify the most attractive potential partners and to establish collaborative working relationships. Since the success of the venture will depend on how well the partners work together, potential partners should be selected as much for their management style, culture, and goals as for their resources and capabilities. In the past 15 years, close collaboration with suppliers to achieve mutually beneficial outcomes has become a common approach to building supply chain capabilities.

3. *Engage in a collaborative partnership for the purpose of learning how the partner does things, internalizing its methods and thereby acquiring its capabilities.* This may be a viable method when each partner has something to learn from the other and can achieve an outcome *beneficial to both partners.* For example, firms sometimes enter into collaborative marketing arrangements whereby each partner is granted access to the other's dealer network for the purpose of expanding sales in geographic areas where the firms lack dealers. But if the intended gains are only one-sided, the arrangement more likely involves an abuse of trust. In consequence, it not only puts the cooperative venture at risk but also encourages the firm's partner to treat the firm similarly or refuse further dealings with the firm.

Collaborative arrangements tend to be less risky when the partnership involves companies from different industries. In racing to develop motor vehicles with self-driving capability, most all vehicle manufacturers are supplementing their own internal efforts with collaborative partnerships with one or more of the growing number of hardware and software firms operating in the driverless vehicle space. These include those developing self-driving software (Alphabet's Waymo, Aurora Innovation, Tesla, Oxbotica, Zoox), makers of the two competing radar systems to spot road obstacles and read traffic signs and signals (RADAR, LiDAR), computing platforms (Nvidia, Qualcomm, Intel), and driverless car technology systems (Mobileye, Bosch, Aptiv).

Nike entered into a strategic partnership with Swiss company Bluesign Technologies for the purpose of making two innovative Bluesign tools available to the hundreds of textile manufacturers supplying the contract factories making Nike products. The tools enable the textile manufacturers to access more than 30,000 materials produced with chemicals that have undergone rigorous assessment for safe use in apparel products. In these types of cases, working together to achieve a capability-related outcome can be beneficial to all the partners.

The Strategic Role of Employee Training

Training and retraining are important when a company shifts to a strategy requiring different skills, competitive capabilities, and operating methods. Training is also strategically important in organizational efforts to build skill-based competencies. And it is a key activity in businesses where technical know-how is changing so rapidly that a company loses its ability to compete unless its employees have cutting-edge knowledge and expertise. Successful strategy implementation requires that the training function is both adequately funded and effective. If better execution of the chosen strategy calls for new skills, deeper technological capability, or the building and deploying of new capabilities, training efforts need to be placed near the top of the action agenda.

The strategic importance of training has not gone unnoticed. Over 4,000 companies around the world have established internal "universities" to lead the training effort, facilitate continuous organizational learning, and upgrade their company's knowledge resources. General Electric has long been known for the excellence of its management training program at Crotonville, outside of New York City. McDonald's maintains a 130,000-square-foot training facility that they call Hamburger University.

Many companies conduct orientation sessions for new employees, fund an assortment of competence-building training programs, and reimburse employees for tuition and other expenses associated with obtaining additional college education, attending professional development courses, and earning professional certification of one kind or another. A number of companies offer online training courses that are available to employees around the clock. Increasingly, companies are expecting employees at all levels are expected to take an active role in their own professional development and assume responsibility for keeping their skills up to date and in sync with the company's needs.

Strategy Execution Capabilities and Competitive Advantage

As firms get better at executing their strategies, they develop capabilities in the domain of strategy execution much as they build other organizational capabilities. Superior strategy execution capabilities allow companies to get the most from their other organizational resources and competitive capabilities. In this way they contribute to the success of a firm's business model. But excellence in strategy execution can also be a more direct source of competitive advantage, since more efficient and effective strategy execution can lower costs and permit firms to deliver more value to customers. Superior strategy execution capabilities may also enable a company to react more quickly to market changes and beat other firms to the market with new products and services. This can allow a company to profit from a period of uncontested market dominance. See Illustration Capsule 10.2 for an example of Zara's route to competitive advantage.

Because strategy execution capabilities are socially complex capabilities that develop with experience over long periods of time, they are hard to imitate. And there is no substitute for good strategy execution. (Recall the tests of resource advantage from Chapter 4.) As such, they may be as important a source of sustained competitive advantage as the core competencies that drive a firm's strategy. Indeed, they may be a far more important avenue for securing a competitive edge over rivals in situations where it is relatively easy for rivals to copy promising strategies. In such cases, the only way for firms to achieve lasting competitive advantage is to *out-execute* their competitors.

> Superior strategy execution capabilities are the only source of sustainable competitive advantage when strategies are easy for rivals to copy.

monticello/Shutterstock

Zara, a major division of Inditex Group, is a leading "fast fashion" retailer. As soon as designs are seen in high-end fashion houses such as Prada, Zara's design team sets to work altering the clothing designs so that it can produce high fashion at mass-retailing prices. Zara's strategy is clever, but by no means unique. The company's competitive advantage is in strategy execution. Every step of Zara's value chain execution is geared toward putting fashionable clothes in stores quickly, realizing high turnover, and strategically driving traffic.

The first key lever is a quick production process. Zara's design team uses inspiration from high fashion and nearly real-time feedback from stores to create up-to-the-minute pieces. Manufacturing largely occurs in factories close to headquarters in Spain, northern Africa, and Turkey, all areas considered to have a high cost of labor. Placing the factories strategically close allows for more flexibility and greater responsiveness to market needs, thereby outweighing the additional labor costs. The entire production process, from design to arrival at stores, takes only two weeks, while other retailers take six months. Whereas traditional retailers commit up to 80 percent of their lines by the start of the season, Zara commits only 50 to 60 percent, meaning that up to half of the merchandise to hit stores is designed and manufactured during the season. Zara purposefully manufactures in small lot sizes to avoid discounting later on and also to encourage impulse shopping, as a particular item could be gone in a few days. From start to finish, Zara has engineered its production process to maximize turnover and turnaround time, creating a true advantage in this step of strategy execution.

Zara also excels at driving traffic to stores. First, the small lot sizes and frequent shipments (up to twice a week per store) drive customers to visit often and purchase quickly. Zara shoppers average 17 visits per year, versus four to five for The Gap. On average, items stay in a Zara store only 11 days. Second, Zara spends no money on advertising, but it occupies some of the most expensive retail space in town, always near the high-fashion houses it imitates. Proximity reinforces the high-fashion association, while the busy street drives significant foot traffic. Overall, Zara has managed to create competitive advantage in every level of strategy execution by tightly aligning design, production, advertising, and real estate with the overall strategy of fast fashion: extremely fast and extremely flexible.

Note: Developed with Sara Paccamonti.

Sources: Suzy Hansen, "How Zara Grew into the World's Largest Fashion Retailer," *The New York Times,* November 9, 2012, www.nytimes .com/2012/11/11/magazine/how-zara-grew-into-the-worlds-largest-fashion-retailer.html?pagewanted=all (accessed February 5, 2014); Seth Stevenson, "Polka Dots Are In? Polka Dots It Is!" *Slate,* June 21, 2012, www.slate.com/articles/arts/operations/2012/06/zara_s_fast_ fashion_how_the_company_gets_new_styles_to_stores_so_quickly.html (accessed February 5, 2014).

MATCHING ORGANIZATIONAL STRUCTURE TO THE STRATEGY

● ● ● ●

While there are few hard-and-fast rules for organizing the work effort to support good strategy execution, there is one: A firm's organizational structure should be *matched* to the particular requirements of implementing the firm's strategy. Every company's strategy is grounded in its own set of organizational capabilities and value chain activities. Moreover, every firm's organizational chart is partly a product of its particular situation, reflecting prior organizational patterns, varying internal circumstances, and executive judgments about how to best structure reporting relationships. Thus, the determinants of the fine details of each firm's organizational structure are unique. But some considerations in organizing the work effort are common to all companies. These are summarized in Figure 10.3 and discussed in the following sections.

Deciding Which Value Chain Activities to Perform Internally and Which to Outsource

Aside from the fact that an outsider, because of its expertise and specialized know-how, may be able to perform certain value chain activities better or cheaper than a company can perform them internally (as discussed in Chapter 6), outsourcing can also sometimes contribute to better strategy execution. Outsourcing the performance of selected activities to outside vendors enables a company to heighten its strategic focus and *concentrate its full energies on performing those value chain activities that are at the core of its strategy, where it can create unique value.* For example, 83 percent of the top 10 pharmaceutical companies outsource tactical roles such as clinical data management and trial monitoring; they are much less likely to outsource more strategic functions, such as new product planning. Broadcom, (now part of semiconductor maker Avago Technologies) outsources the manufacture of its chips, thus freeing company personnel to focus their full energies on R&D, new chip design, and marketing. Nike concentrates on design, marketing, and distribution to retailers, while outsourcing virtually all production of its shoes and sporting apparel. Interestingly,

FIGURE 10.3   Structuring the Work Effort to Promote Successful Strategy Execution

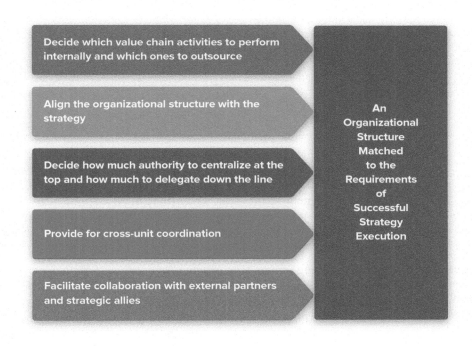

- Decide which value chain activities to perform internally and which ones to outsource
- Align the organizational structure with the strategy
- Decide how much authority to centralize at the top and how much to delegate down the line
- Provide for cross-unit coordination
- Facilitate collaboration with external partners and strategic allies

An Organizational Structure Matched to the Requirements of Successful Strategy Execution

Which Value Chain Activities Does Apple Outsource and Why?

DAVID CHANG/EPA-EFE/Shutterstock

Innovation and design are core competencies for Apple and the drivers behind the creation of winning products such as the iPod, iPhone, and iPad. In consequence, all activities directly related to new product development and product design are performed internally. For example, Apple's Industrial Design Group is responsible for creating the look and feel of all Apple products—from the MacBook Air to the iPhone, and beyond to future products.

Producing a continuing stream of great new products and product versions is key to the success of Apple's strategy. But executing this strategy takes more than innovation and design capabilities. Manufacturing flexibility and

speed are imperative in the production of Apple products to ensure that the latest ideas are reflected in the products and that the company meets the high demand for its products—especially around launch.

For these capabilities, Apple turns to outsourcing, as do the majority of its competitors in the consumer electronics space. Apple outsources the manufacturing of products like its iPhone to Asia, where contract manufacturing organizations (CMOs) create value through their vast scale, high flexibility, and low cost. Perhaps no company better epitomizes the Asian CMO value proposition than Foxconn, a company that assembles not only for Apple but for Hewlett-Packard, Motorola, Amazon.com, and Samsung as well. Foxconn's scale is incredible, with 1.3 million people on its payroll as of 2017. Such scale offers companies a significant degree of flexibility, as Foxconn has the ability to hire 3,000 employees on practically a moment's notice. Apple, more so than its competitors, is able to capture CMO value creation by leveraging its immense sales volume and strong cash position to receive preferred treatment. While outsourcing has allowed Apple to reap the benefits of lower cost and more flexible manufacturing, the lack of direct control has proven to be a challenge. Working conditions at Foxconn were so bad at one point that Foxconn installed suicide prevention nets below its windows. Apple responded by tightening its supplier standards and increasing its efforts at monitoring conditions and enforcing its standards. Apple now conducts over 700 comprehensive site audits each year to ensure compliance.

Note: Developed with Margaret W. Macauley.

Sources: Company website; Charles Duhigg and Keith Bradsher, "How the U.S. Lost Out on iPhone Work," *The New York Times,* January 21, 2012, www.nytimes.com/2012/01/22/business/apple-america-and-a-squeezed-middle-class.html?pagewanted=all&_r=0 (accessed March 5, 2012).

Wisely choosing which activities to perform internally and which to outsource can lead to several strategy-executing advantages—lower costs, heightened strategic focus, less internal bureaucracy, speedier decision making, and a better arsenal of organizational capabilities.

e-commerce powerhouse Alibaba got its start by outsourcing web development (a key function) to a U.S. firm; but this was due to the fact that China lacked sufficient development talent at the time. Illustration Capsule 10.3 describes Apple's decisions about which activities to outsource and which to perform in-house.

Such heightened focus on performing strategy-critical activities can yield three important execution-related benefits:

- *The company improves its chances for outclassing rivals in the performance of strategy-critical activities and turning a competence into a distinctive competence.* At the very least, the heightened focus on performing a select few value chain activities should promote more effective performance of those activities. This could materially enhance competitive capabilities by either lowering costs or improving product or service quality. Businesses that get a lot of inquiries from customers or that have to provide 24/7 technical support to users of their products around the world often find that it is considerably less expensive to outsource these functions to specialists (often located in foreign countries where skilled personnel are readily available and worker compensation costs are much lower) than to operate their own call centers. Many businesses also outsource IT functions such as desktop support, disaster recovery, help desk, and data center operations, which often results in cost savings due to the economies of scale available to service providers.

- *The streamlining of internal operations that flows from outsourcing often acts to decrease internal bureaucracies, flatten the organizational structure, speed internal decision making, and shorten the time it takes to respond to changing market conditions.* In consumer electronics, where advancing technology drives new product innovation, organizing the work effort in a manner that expedites getting next-generation products to market ahead of rivals is a critical competitive capability. The world's motor vehicle manufacturers have found that they can shorten the cycle time for new models by outsourcing the production of many parts and components to independent suppliers. They then work closely with the suppliers to swiftly incorporate new technology and to better integrate individual parts and components to form engine cooling systems, transmission systems, electrical systems, and so on.

- *Partnerships with outside vendors can add to a company's arsenal of capabilities and contribute to better strategy execution.* Outsourcing activities to vendors with first-rate capabilities can enable a firm to concentrate on strengthening its own complementary capabilities internally; the result will be a more powerful package of organizational capabilities that the firm can draw upon to deliver more value to customers and attain competitive success. Soft-drink and beer manufacturers cultivate their relationships with their bottlers and distributors to strengthen access to local markets and build loyalty, support, and commitment for corporate marketing programs, without which their own sales and growth would be weakened. Similarly, fast-food enterprises like Wendy's and Burger King find it essential to work hand in hand with franchisees on outlet cleanliness, consistency of product quality, in-store ambience, courtesy and friendliness of store personnel, and other aspects of store operations. Unless franchisees continuously deliver sufficient customer satisfaction to attract repeat business, a fast-food chain's reputation, sales, and competitive standing will quickly suffer. Companies like Boeing, Dell, and Apple have learned that their central R&D groups cannot begin to match the innovative capabilities of a well-managed network of supply chain partners.

However, as emphasized in Chapter 6, a company must guard against going overboard on outsourcing and becoming overly dependent on outside suppliers. A company cannot be the master of its own destiny unless it maintains expertise and resource depth in performing those value chain activities that underpin its long-term competitive success.[15]

Aligning the Firm's Organizational Structure with Its Strategy

The design of the firm's **organizational structure** is a critical aspect of the strategy execution process. The organizational structure comprises the formal and informal arrangement of tasks, responsibilities, and lines of authority and communication by which the firm is administered.[16] It specifies the linkages among parts of the

CORE CONCEPT

A firm's **organizational structure** comprises the formal and informal arrangement of tasks, responsibilities, lines of authority, and reporting relationships by which the firm is administered.

organization, the reporting relationships, the direction of information flows, and the decision-making processes. It is a key factor in strategy implementation since it exerts a strong influence on how well managers can coordinate and control the complex set of activities involved.[17]

A well-designed organizational structure is one in which the various parts (e.g., decision-making rights, communication patterns) are aligned with one another and also matched to the requirements of the strategy. With the right structure in place, managers can orchestrate the various aspects of the implementation process with an even hand and a light touch. Without a supportive structure, strategy execution is more likely to become bogged down by administrative confusion, political maneuvering, and bureaucratic waste.

Good organizational design may even contribute to the firm's ability to create value for customers and realize a profit. By enabling lower bureaucratic costs and facilitating operational efficiency, it can lower a firm's operating costs. By facilitating the coordination of activities within the firm, it can improve the capability-building process, leading to greater differentiation and/or lower costs. Moreover, by improving the speed with which information is communicated and activities are coordinated, it can enable the firm to beat rivals to the market and profit from a period of unrivaled advantage.

Making Strategy-Critical Activities the Main Building Blocks of the Organizational Structure   In any business, some activities in the value chain are always more critical to successful strategy execution than others. For instance, ski apparel companies like Sport Obermeyer, Arc'teryx, and Spyder must be good at styling and design, low-cost manufacturing, distribution (convincing an attractively large number of dealers to stock and promote the company's brand), and marketing and advertising (building a brand image that generates buzz among ski enthusiasts). For brokerage firms like Charles Schwab Corporation and TD Ameritrade, the strategy-critical activities are fast access to information, accurate order execution, efficient record keeping and transaction processing, and full-featured customer service. With respect to such core value chain activities, it is important for management to build its organizational structure around proficient performance of these activities, making them the centerpieces or main building blocks in the enterprise's organizational structure.

The rationale is compelling: If activities crucial to strategic success are to have the resources, decision-making influence, and organizational impact they need, they must be centerpieces in the enterprise's organizational scheme. Making them the focus of structuring efforts will also facilitate their coordination and promote good internal fit—an essential attribute of a winning strategy, as summarized in Chapter 1 and elaborated in Chapter 4. To the extent that implementing a new strategy entails new or altered key activities or capabilities, different organizational arrangements may be required.

Matching Type of Organizational Structure to Strategy Execution Requirements   Organizational structures can be classified into a limited number of standard types. Which type makes the most sense for a given firm depends largely on the firm's size and business makeup, but not so much on the specifics of its strategy. As firms grow and their needs for structure evolve, their structural form is likely to evolve from one type to another. The four basic types are the *simple structure,* the *functional structure,* the *multidivisional structure,* and the *matrix structure,* as described next.

1. Simple Structure   A **simple structure** is one in which a central executive (often the owner-manager) handles all major decisions and oversees the operations of the organization with the help of a small staff.[18] Simple structures are also known as *line-and-staff structures,* since a central administrative staff supervises line employees who conduct the operations of the firm, or *flat structures,* since there are few levels of hierarchy. The simple structure is characterized by limited task specialization; few rules; informal relationships; minimal use of training, planning, and liaison devices; and a lack of sophisticated support systems. It has all the advantages of simplicity, including low administrative costs, ease of coordination, flexibility, quick decision making, adaptability, and responsiveness to change. Its informality and lack of rules may foster creativity and heightened individual responsibility.

Simple organizational structures are typically employed by small firms and entrepreneurial startups. The simple structure is the most common type of organizational structure since small firms are the most prevalent type of business. As an organization grows, however, this structural form becomes inadequate to the demands that come with size and complexity. In response, growing firms tend to alter their organizational structure from a simple structure to a *functional structure.*

2. Functional Structure   A **functional structure** is one that is organized along functional lines, where a function represents a major component of the firm's value chain, such as R&D, engineering and design, manufacturing, sales and marketing, logistics, and customer service. Each functional unit is supervised by functional line managers who report to the chief executive officer and a corporate staff. This arrangement allows functional managers to focus on their area of responsibility, leaving it to the CEO and headquarters to provide direction and ensure that the activities of the functional managers are coordinated and integrated. Functional structures are also known as *departmental structures,* since the functional units are commonly called departments, and *unitary structures* or *U-forms,* since a single unit is responsible for each function.

In large organizations, functional structures lighten the load on top management, in comparison to simple structures, and enable more efficient use of managerial resources. Their primary advantage, however, is greater *task specialization,* which promotes learning, enables the realization of scale economies, and offers productivity advantages not otherwise available. Their chief disadvantage is that the departmental boundaries can inhibit the flow of information and limit the opportunities for cross-functional cooperation and coordination.

It is generally agreed that a functional structure is the best organizational arrangement when a company is in just one particular business (irrespective of which of the five generic competitive strategies it opts to pursue). For instance, a technical instruments manufacturer may be organized around research and development, engineering, supply chain management, assembly, quality control, marketing, and technical services. A discount retailer, such as Dollar General or Family Dollar, may organize around such functional units as purchasing, warehousing, distribution logistics, store operations, advertising, merchandising and promotion, and customer service. Functional structures can also be appropriate for firms with high-volume production, products that are closely related, and a limited degree of vertical integration. For example, General Motors now manages all of its brands (Cadillac, GMC, Chevrolet, Buick, etc.) under a common functional structure designed to promote technical transfer and capture economies of scale.

As firms continue to grow, they often become more diversified and complex, placing a greater burden on top management. At some point, the centralized control that

CORE CONCEPT

A **simple structure** consists of a central executive (often the owner-manager) who handles all major decisions and oversees all operations with the help of a small staff. Simple structures are also called *line-and-staff structures* or *flat structures.*

CORE CONCEPT

A **functional structure** is organized into functional departments, with departmental managers who report to the CEO and small corporate staff. Functional structures are also called *departmental structures* and *unitary structures* or *U-forms.*

The primary advantage of a functional structure is greater task specialization, which promotes learning, enables the realization of scale economies, and offers productivity advantages not otherwise available.

characterizes the functional structure becomes a liability, and the advantages of functional specialization begin to break down. To resolve these problems and address a growing need for coordination across functions, firms generally turn to the *multidivisional structure.*

<table>
<tr><td>

CORE CONCEPT

A **multidivisional structure** is a decentralized structure consisting of a set of operating divisions organized along business, product, customer group, or geographic lines and a central corporate headquarters that allocates resources, provides support functions, and monitors divisional activities. Multidivisional structures are also called *divisional structures* or *M-forms.*

</td></tr>
</table>

3. *Multidivisional Structure* A **multidivisional structure** is a decentralized structure consisting of a set of operating divisions organized along market, customer, product, or geographic lines, along with a central corporate headquarters, which monitors divisional activities, allocates resources, performs assorted support functions, and exercises overall control. Since each division is essentially a business (often called a *single business unit* or *SBU*), the divisions typically operate as independent profit centers (i.e., with profit and loss responsibility) and are organized internally along functional lines. Division managers oversee day-to-day operations and the development of business-level strategy, while corporate executives attend to overall performance and corporate strategy, the elements of which were described in Chapter 8. Multidivisional structures are also called *divisional structures* or *M-forms,* in contrast with U-form (functional) structures.

Multidivisional structures are common among companies pursuing some form of diversification strategy or international strategy, with operations in a number of businesses or countries. When the strategy is one of unrelated diversification, as in a conglomerate, the divisions generally represent businesses in separate industries. When the strategy is based on related diversification, the divisions may be organized according to industries, customer groups, product lines, geographic regions, or technologies. In this arrangement, the decision about where to draw the divisional lines depends foremost on the nature of the relatedness and the strategy-critical building blocks, in terms of which businesses have key value chain activities in common. For example, a company selling closely related products to business customers as well as two types of end consumers—online buyers and in-store buyers—may organize its divisions according to customer groups since the value chains involved in serving the three groups differ. Another company may organize by product line due to commonalities in product development and production within each product line. Multidivisional structures are also common among vertically integrated firms. There the major building blocks are often divisional units performing one or more of the major processing steps along the value chain (e.g., raw-material production, components manufacture, assembly, wholesale distribution, retail store operations).

Multidivisional structures offer significant advantages over functional structures in terms of facilitating the management of a complex and diverse set of operations.[19] Putting business-level strategy in the hands of division managers while leaving corporate strategy to top executives reduces the potential for information overload and improves the quality of decision making in each domain. This also minimizes the costs of coordinating division-wide activities while enhancing top management's ability to control a diverse and complex operation. Moreover, multidivisional structures can help align individual incentives with the goals of the corporation and spur productivity by encouraging competition for resources among the different divisions.

But a multidivisional structure can also present some problems to a company pursuing related diversification, because having independent business units—each running its own business in its own way—inhibits cross-business collaboration and the capture of cross-business synergies, which are critical for the success of a related diversification strategy, as Chapter 8 explains. To solve this type of problem, firms turn to more complex structures, such as the matrix structure.

4. Matrix Structure   A **matrix structure** is a combination structure in which the organization is organized along two or more dimensions at once (e.g., business, geographic area, value chain function) for the purpose of enhancing cross-unit communication, collaboration, and coordination. In essence, it overlays one type of structure onto another type. Matrix structures are managed through multiple reporting relationships, so a middle manager may report to several bosses. For instance, in a matrix structure based on product line, region, and function, a sales manager for plastic containers in Georgia might report to the manager of the plastics division, the head of the southeast sales region, and the head of marketing.

Matrix organizational structures have evolved from the complex, over-formalized structures that were popular in the late 20th century but often produced inefficient, unwieldy bureaucracies. The modern incarnation of the matrix structure is generally a more flexible arrangement, with a single primary reporting relationship that can be overlaid with a *temporary* secondary reporting relationship as need arises. For example, a software company that is organized into functional departments (software design, quality control, customer relations) may assign employees from those departments to different projects on a temporary basis, so an employee reports to a project manager as well as to his or her primary boss (the functional department head) for the duration of a project.

Matrix structures are also called *composite structures* or *combination structures.* They are often used for project-based, process-based, or team-based management. Such approaches are common in businesses involving projects of limited duration, such as consulting, architecture, and engineering services. The type of close cross-unit collaboration that a flexible matrix structure supports is also needed to build competitive capabilities in strategically important activities, such as speeding new products to market, that involve employees scattered across several organizational units.[20] Capabilities-based matrix structures that combine process departments (like new product development) with more traditional functional departments provide a solution.

An advantage of matrix structures is that they facilitate the sharing of plant and equipment, specialized knowledge, and other key resources. Thus, they lower costs by enabling the realization of economies of scope. They also have the advantage of flexibility in form and may allow for better oversight since supervision is provided from more than one perspective. A disadvantage is that they add another layer of management, thereby increasing bureaucratic costs and possibly decreasing response time to new situations.[21] In addition, there is a potential for confusion among employees due to dual reporting relationships and divided loyalties. While there is some controversy over the utility of matrix structures, the modern approach to matrix structures does much to minimize their disadvantages.[22]

> **CORE** CONCEPT
>
> A **matrix structure** is a combination structure that overlays one type of structure onto another type, with multiple reporting relationships. It is used to foster cross-unit collaboration. Matrix structures are also called *composite structures* or *combination structures.*

Determining How Much Authority to Delegate

Under any organizational structure, there is room for considerable variation in how much authority top-level executives retain and how much is delegated to down-the-line managers and employees. In executing strategy and conducting daily operations, companies must decide how much authority to delegate to the managers of each organizational unit—especially the heads of divisions, functional departments, plants, and other operating units—and how much decision-making latitude to give individual employees in performing their jobs. The two extremes are to *centralize decision making* at the top or to *decentralize decision making* by giving managers and employees at all levels considerable decision-making latitude in their areas of responsibility. As shown in Table 10.1, the two approaches are based on sharply different underlying principles and beliefs, with each having its pros and cons.

> **● LO 10-5**
>
> Comprehend the pros and cons of centralized and decentralized decision making in implementing the chosen strategy.

TABLE 10.1   Advantages and Disadvantages of Centralized versus Decentralized Decision Making

Centralized Organizational Structures	Decentralized Organizational Structures
Basic tenets	**Basic tenets**
• Decisions on most matters of importance should be in the hands of top-level managers who have the experience, expertise, and judgment to decide what is the best course of action. • Lower-level personnel have neither the knowledge, time, nor inclination to properly manage the tasks they are performing. • Strong control from the top is a more effective means for coordinating company actions.	• Decision-making authority should be put in the hands of the people closest to, and most familiar with, the situation. • Those with decision-making authority should be trained to exercise good judgment. • A company that draws on the combined intellectual capital of all its employees can outperform a command-and-control company.
Chief advantages	**Chief advantages**
• Fixes accountability through tight control from the top. • Eliminates potential for conflicting goals and actions on the part of lower-level managers. • Facilitates quick decision making and strong leadership under crisis situations.	• Encourages company employees to exercise initiative and act responsibly. • Promotes greater motivation and involvement in the business on the part of more company personnel. • Spurs new ideas and creative thinking. • Allows for fast response to market change. • Entails fewer layers of management.
Primary disadvantages	**Primary disadvantages**
• Lengthens response times by those closest to the market conditions because they must seek approval for their actions. • Does not encourage responsibility among lower-level managers and rank-and-file employees. • Discourages lower-level managers and rank-and-file employees from exercising any initiative.	• May result in higher-level managers being unaware of actions taken by empowered personnel under their supervision. • Can lead to inconsistent or conflicting approaches by different managers and employees. • Can impair cross-unit collaboration.

Centralized Decision Making: Pros and Cons   In a highly centralized organizational structure, *top executives retain authority for most strategic and operating decisions* and keep a tight rein on business unit heads, department heads, and the managers of key operating units. Comparatively little discretionary authority is granted to frontline supervisors and rank-and-file employees. The command-and-control paradigm of centralized decision making is based on the underlying assumptions that frontline personnel have neither the time nor the inclination to direct and properly control the work they are performing and that they lack the knowledge and judgment to make wise decisions about how best to do it—hence the need for prescribed policies and procedures for a wide range of activities, close supervision, and tight control by top executives. The thesis underlying centralized structures is that strict enforcement of detailed procedures backed by rigorous managerial oversight is the most reliable way to keep the daily execution of strategy on track.

One advantage of a centralized structure, with tight control by the manager in charge, is that it is easy to know who is accountable when things do not go well. This structure can also reduce the potential for conflicting decisions and actions among lower-level managers who may have differing perspectives and ideas about how to tackle certain tasks or resolve particular issues. For example, a manager in charge of an engineering department may be more interested in pursuing a new technology than is a marketing manager who doubts that customers will value the technology as highly. Another advantage of a command-and-control structure is that it can facilitate strong leadership from the top in a crisis situation that affects the organization as a whole and can enable a more uniform and swift response.

But there are some serious disadvantages as well. Hierarchical command-and-control structures do not encourage responsibility and initiative on the part of lower-level managers and employees. They can make a large organization with a complex structure sluggish in responding to changing market conditions because of the time it takes for the review-and-approval process to run up all the layers of the management bureaucracy. Furthermore, to work well, centralized decision making requires top-level managers to gather and process whatever information is relevant to the decision. When the relevant knowledge resides at lower organizational levels (or is technical, detailed, or hard to express in words), it is difficult and time-consuming to get all the facts in front of a high-level executive located far from the scene of the action—full understanding of the situation cannot be readily copied from one mind to another. Hence, centralized decision making is often impractical—the larger the company and the more scattered its operations, the more that decision-making authority must be delegated to managers closer to the scene of the action.

Decentralized Decision Making: Pros and Cons   In a highly decentralized organization, *decision-making authority is pushed down to the lowest organizational level capable of making timely, informed, competent decisions.* The objective is to put adequate decision-making authority in the hands of the people closest to and most familiar with the situation and train them to weigh all the factors and exercise good judgment. At Starbucks, for example, employees are encouraged to exercise initiative in promoting customer satisfaction—there's the oft-repeated story of a store employee who, when the computerized cash register system went offline, offered free coffee to waiting customers, thereby avoiding customer displeasure and damage to Starbucks's reputation.[23]

> The ultimate goal of decentralized decision making is to put authority in the hands of those persons closest to and most knowledgeable about the situation.

The case for empowering down-the-line managers and employees to make decisions related to daily operations and strategy execution is based on the belief that a company that draws on the combined intellectual capital of all its employees can outperform a command-and-control company.[24] The challenge in a decentralized system is maintaining adequate control. With decentralized decision making, top management maintains control by placing limits on the authority granted to company personnel, installing companywide strategic control systems, holding people accountable for their decisions, instituting compensation incentives that reward people for doing their jobs well, and creating a corporate culture where there's strong peer pressure on individuals to act responsibly.[25]

Decentralized organizational structures have much to recommend them. Delegating authority to subordinate managers and rank-and-file employees encourages them to take responsibility and exercise initiative. It shortens organizational response times to market changes and spurs new ideas, creative thinking, innovation, and greater involvement on the part of all company personnel. At TJX Companies Inc., parent company of T.J.Maxx, Marshalls, and five other fashion and home decor retail store chains, buyers are encouraged to be intelligent risk takers in deciding what items to purchase for TJX stores—there's the story of a buyer for a seasonal product category who cut her own budget to have dollars allocated to other categories where sales were expected to be stronger. In worker-empowered structures, jobs can be defined more broadly, several tasks can be integrated into a single job, and people can direct their own work. Fewer managers are needed because deciding how to do things becomes part of each person's or team's job. Further, today's online communication systems and smartphones make it easy and relatively inexpensive for people at all organizational levels to have direct access to data, other employees, managers, suppliers, and customers. They can access information quickly (via the Internet or company network), readily check with superiors or whomever else as needed, and take responsible action. Typically, there are genuine gains in morale and productivity when people are provided with the tools and information they need to operate in a self-directed way.

But decentralization also has some disadvantages. Top managers lose an element of control over what goes on and may thus be unaware of actions being taken by personnel under their supervision. Such lack of control can be problematic in the event that empowered employees make decisions that conflict with those of others or that serve their unit's interests at the expense of other parts of the company. Moreover, because decentralization gives organizational units the authority to act independently, there is risk of too little collaboration and coordination between different units.

Many companies have concluded that the advantages of decentralization outweigh the disadvantages. Over the past several decades, there's been a decided shift from centralized, hierarchical structures to flatter, more decentralized structures that stress employee empowerment. This shift reflects a strong and growing consensus that authoritarian, hierarchical organizational structures are not well suited to implementing and executing strategies in an era when extensive information and instant communication are the norm and when a big fraction of the organization's most valuable assets consists of intellectual capital that resides in its employees' capabilities.

Capturing Cross-Business Strategic Fit in a Decentralized Structure
Diversified companies striving to capture the benefits of synergy between separate businesses must beware of giving business unit heads full rein to operate independently. Cross-business strategic fit typically must be captured either by enforcing close cross-business collaboration or by centralizing the performance of functions requiring close coordination at the corporate level.[26] For example, if businesses with overlapping process and product technologies have their own independent R&D departments—each pursuing its own priorities, projects, and strategic agendas—it's hard for the corporate parent to prevent duplication of effort, capture either economies of scale or economies of scope, or encourage more collaborative R&D efforts. Where cross-business strategic fit with respect to R&D is important, one solution is to centralize the R&D function and have a coordinated corporate R&D effort that serves the interests of both the individual businesses and the company as a whole. Likewise, centralizing the related activities of separate businesses makes sense when there are opportunities to share a common sales force, use common distribution channels, rely on a common field service organization, use common e-commerce systems, and so on. Another structural solution to realizing the benefits of strategic fit is to create business groups consisting of those business units with common strategic-fit opportunities.

> Efforts to decentralize decision making and give company personnel some leeway in conducting operations must be tempered with the need to maintain adequate control and cross-unit coordination.

Providing for Internal Cross-Unit Coordination

Close cross-unit collaboration is usually needed to build capabilities in such strategically important activities as speeding new products to market and providing superior customer service. This is because these activities involve collaboration among the efforts of company personnel who work in different departments or organizational units (and perhaps the employees of outside strategic partners or specialty vendors). For example, being first-to-market with new products involves coordinating the efforts of personnel in R&D (to develop a stream of new products with appealing attributes), design and engineering (to prepare a cost-efficient design and set of specifications), purchasing (to obtain the needed parts and components), manufacturing (to carry out all the production activities), and sales and marketing (to secure orders, arrange for introductory advertising and the distribution of product information, and get the products on retailers' shelves). Achieving the simple strategic objective of filling customer orders accurately and promptly involves personnel from sales (to win the order); finance (to check credit terms or approve special financing); production (to produce the goods and replenish warehouse inventories as needed); and warehousing and shipping (to verify whether the items are in stock, pick the order from the warehouse, package it for shipping, and choose the best carrier to deliver the goods).

To achieve tight coordination when pieces of execution-critical tasks are performed in multiple organizational units, company executives typically emphasize the necessity of cross-unit teamwork and cooperation and the importance of frequent back-and-forth communication among key people in the various related organizational units to resolve problems, avoid delays, and keep things moving along. The executives supervising the units performing parts of the execution-critical task typically make it clear that the relevant department heads and key personnel are all *expected to work closely together and coordinate their actions.* There are meetings to discuss schedules and set deadlines, often ending with the verbal commitments of everyone involved to stick close to the agreed-upon schedule, coordinate their activities, and meet the established deadlines. Gaining such commitments is almost always imperative, along with ensuring that everyone lives up to their commitments.

Normally, the supervising executives follow up, check on progress, and, in many cases, visit the different units to personally determine how well things are going and solicit the views of numerous people about what problems exist and what they think should be done to resolve them. They seldom hesitate to intervene to make corrective adjustments and to reiterate their expectations of teamwork, close communication, effective collaboration, and cooperation to resolve issues, avoid delays, and achieve the needed degree of cross-unit coordination. Such executive interventions, together with added executive pressure on the managers of units where close collaboration and coordinated action is lacking, may suffice. If it does, then all is well and good. But if such efforts fail, execution suffers and it becomes the responsibility of executives to determine the causes and take corrective action.

In many instances, the chief cause of ineffective cross-unit coordination in building capabilities rests with departmental-level managers and other key operating personnel who, for assorted reasons, don't or won't spend the time and effort needed to partner with other organizational units in the capability-building process. But it also has to be recognized that top-executive urging that departmental managers and their staff *voluntarily* place high priority on coordinating their respective activities *poses significant challenges* in achieving effective cross-unit coordination. This is especially true in decentralized organizational structures where department heads are delegated a high degree of decision-making authority in running their respective units and, thus, have a natural tendency to place a lower priority on cooperating closely with other organizational units than on ensuring that the activities under their direct supervision are done well. The weakness of heavily depending on the largely voluntary efforts of personnel for the development of critical cross-unit capabilities has prompted many companies to supplement such efforts by forming cross-functional committees, project management teams, and centralized project management offices to forge better cross-unit working relationships and improve coordination across multiple organizational units. While these arrangements have proved helpful in a number of organizations, more effective solutions involve creating incentive compensation systems where the payouts are tied to effective group performance of cross-unit tasks.

Facilitating Collaboration with External Partners and Strategic Allies

Getting managers of execution-critical activities to live up to their commitments to coordinate closely with sister organizational unit is a *key* factor in achieving good internal cross-unit coordination.

Organizational mechanisms—whether formal or informal—are also required to ensure effective working relationships with each major outside constituency involved in strategy execution. Strategic alliances, outsourcing arrangements, joint ventures, and cooperative partnerships can contribute little of value without active management of the relationship. Unless top management sees that constructive organizational bridge building with external partners occurs and that productive working relationships emerge, the potential value of cooperative relationships is lost and the company's power to execute its strategy is weakened. For example, if close working relationships with suppliers are crucial, then supply chain management must enter into considerations of how to create an effective organizational structure. If distributor, dealer, or franchisee relationships are important, then someone must be assigned the task of nurturing the relationships with such forward-channel allies.

Building organizational bridges with external partners and strategic allies can be accomplished by appointing "relationship managers" with responsibility for making particular strategic partnerships generate the intended benefits. Relationship managers have many roles and functions: getting the right people together, promoting good rapport, facilitating the flow of information, nurturing interpersonal communication and cooperation, and ensuring effective coordination.[27] Multiple cross-organization ties have to be established and kept open to ensure proper communication and coordination. There has to be enough information sharing to make the relationship work and periodic frank discussions of conflicts, trouble spots, and changing situations.

Organizing and managing a network structure provides a mechanism for encouraging more effective collaboration and cooperation among external partners. **A network structure** is the arrangement linking a number of independent organizations involved in some common undertaking. A well-managed network structure typically includes one firm in a more central role, with the responsibility of ensuring that the right partners are included and the activities across the network are coordinated. The high-end Italian motorcycle company Ducati operates in this manner, assembling its motorcycles from parts obtained from a handpicked integrated network of parts suppliers.

CORE CONCEPT

A **network structure** is a configuration composed of a number of independent organizations engaged in some common undertaking, with one firm typically taking on a more central role.

Further Perspectives on Structuring the Work Effort

All organizational designs have their strategy-related strengths and weaknesses. To do a good job of matching structure to strategy, strategy implementers first have to pick a basic organizational design and modify it as needed to fit the company's particular business lineup. They must then (1) supplement the design with appropriate coordinating mechanisms (cross-functional task forces, special project teams, self-contained work teams, etc.) and (2) institute whatever networking and communications arrangements are necessary to support effective execution of the firm's strategy. Some companies may avoid setting up "ideal" organizational arrangements because they do not want to disturb existing reporting relationships or because they need to accommodate other situational idiosyncrasies, yet they must still work toward the goal of building a competitively capable organization.

What can be said unequivocally is that building a capable organization entails a process of consciously knitting together the efforts of individuals and groups. Organizational capabilities emerge from establishing and nurturing cooperative working relationships among people and groups to perform activities in a more efficient, value-creating fashion. While an appropriate organizational structure can facilitate this, organization building is a task in which senior management must be deeply involved. Indeed, effectively managing both internal organizational processes and external collaboration to create and develop competitively valuable organizational capabilities remains a top challenge for senior executives in today's companies.

KEY POINTS

1. Executing strategy is an action-oriented, operations-driven activity revolving around the management of people, business processes, and organizational structure. In devising an action agenda for executing strategy, managers should start by conducting a probing assessment of what the organization must do to carry out the strategy successfully. They should then consider precisely *how* to go about this.

2. Good strategy execution requires a *team effort*. All managers have strategy-executing responsibility in their areas of authority, and all employees are active participants in the strategy execution process.

3. Ten managerial tasks are part of every company effort to execute strategy: (1) staffing the organization with the right people, (2) developing and augmenting the necessary resources and organizational capabilities, (3) creating a supportive organizational structure, (4) allocating sufficient resources (budgetary and otherwise), (5) instituting supportive policies and procedures, (6) adopting processes for continuous improvement, (7) installing systems that enable proficient company operations, (8) tying incentives to the achievement of desired targets, (9) instilling the right corporate culture, and (10) exercising the leadership needed to propel strategy execution forward.

4. The two best signs of good strategy execution are that a company is meeting or beating its performance targets and is performing value chain activities in a manner that is conducive to companywide operating excellence. *Shortfalls in performance signal weak strategy, weak execution, or both.*

5. Building an organization capable of good strategy execution entails three types of actions: (1) *staffing the organization*—assembling a talented management team and recruiting and retaining employees with the needed experience, technical skills, and intellectual capital; (2) *acquiring, developing, and strengthening strategy-supportive resources and capabilities*—accumulating the required resources, developing proficiencies in performing strategy-critical value chain activities, and updating the company's capabilities to match changing market conditions and customer expectations; and (3) *structuring the organization and work effort*—instituting organizational arrangements that facilitate good strategy execution, deciding how much decision-making authority to delegate, facilitating cross-unit coordination, and managing external relationships.

6. Building competitive capabilities is a time-consuming, managerially challenging exercise that can be approached in three ways: (1) developing capabilities internally, (2) acquiring capabilities through mergers and acquisitions, and (3) accessing capabilities via collaborative partnerships.

7. In building capabilities internally, the first step is to develop the *ability* to do something, through experimenting, actively searching for alternative solutions, and learning by trial and error. As experience grows and company personnel learn how to perform the activities consistently well and at an acceptable cost, the ability evolves into a tried-and-true capability. The process can be accelerated by making learning a more deliberate endeavor and providing the incentives that will motivate company personnel to achieve the desired ends.

8. As firms get better at executing their strategies, they develop capabilities in the domain of strategy execution. Superior strategy execution capabilities allow companies to get the most from their resources and capabilities. But excellence in strategy execution can also be a more direct source of competitive advantage, since more efficient and effective strategy execution can lower costs and permit firms to deliver more value to customers. Because they are socially complex capabilities, superior strategy execution capabilities are hard to imitate and have no good substitutes. As such, they can be an important source of *sustainable* competitive advantage. Anytime rivals can readily duplicate successful strategies, making it impossible to *out-strategize* rivals, the chief way to achieve lasting competitive advantage is to *out-execute* them.

9. Structuring the organization and organizing the work effort in a strategy-supportive fashion has five aspects: (1) deciding which value chain activities to perform internally and which ones to outsource; (2) aligning the firm's organizational structure with its strategy; (3) deciding how much authority to centralize at the top and how much to delegate to down-the-line managers and employees; (4) providing for the internal cross-unit coordination needed to build and strengthen capabilities; and (5) facilitating the necessary collaboration and coordination with external partners and strategic allies.

10. To align the firm's organizational structure with its strategy, it is important to make strategy-critical activities the main building blocks. There are four basic types of organizational structures: the simple structure, the functional structure, the multidivisional structure, and the matrix structure. Which is most appropriate depends on the firm's size, complexity, and strategy.

ASSURANCE OF LEARNING EXERCISES

LO 10-1

1. The heart of Zara's strategy in the apparel industry is to outcompete rivals by putting fashionable clothes in stores quickly and maximizing the frequency of customer visits. Illustration Capsule 10.2 discusses the capabilities that the company has developed in the execution of its strategy. How do its capabilities lead to a quick production process and new apparel introductions? How do these capabilities encourage customers to visit its stores every few weeks? Does the execution of the company's site selection capability also contribute to its competitive advantage? Explain.

LO 10-2

2. Search online to read about Jeff Bezos's management of his new executives. Specifically, explore **Amazon.com's** "S-Team" meetings (**management.fortune .cnn.com/2012/11/16/jeff-bezos-amazon/**). Why does Bezos begin meetings of

senior executives with 30 minutes of silent reading? How does this focus the group? Why does Bezos insist new ideas must be written and presented in memo form? How does this reflect the founder's insistence on clear, concise, and innovative thinking in his company? And does this exercise work as a de facto crash course for new Amazon executives? Explain why this small but crucial management strategy reflects Bezos's overriding goal of cohesive and clear idea presentation.

3. Review Facebook's Careers page (www.Facebook.com/careers/). The page emphasizes Facebook's core values and explains how potential employees could fit that mold. Bold and decisive thinking and a commitment to transparency and social connectivity drive the page and the company as a whole. Then research Facebook's internal management training programs, called "employee boot camps," using a search engine like Google or Bing. How do these programs integrate the traits and stated goals on the Careers page into specific and tangible construction of employee capabilities? Boot camps are open to all Facebook employees, not just engineers. How does this internal training prepare Facebook employees of all types to "move fast and break things"?   **LO 10-2, 10-3**

4. Review Valve Corporation's company handbook online: www.valvesoftware.com/company/Valve_Handbook_LowRes.pdf. Specifically, focus on Valve's corporate structure. Valve has hundreds of employees but no managers or bosses at all. Valve's gaming success hinges on innovative and completely original experiences like Portal and Half-Life. Does it seem that Valve's corporate structure uniquely promotes this type of gaming innovation? Why or why not? How would you characterize Valve's organizational structure? Is it completely unique, or could it be characterized as a multidivisional, matrix, or functional structure? Explain your answer.   **LO 10-4**

5. Johnson & Johnson, a multinational health care company responsible for manufacturing medical, pharmaceutical, and consumer goods, has been a leader in promoting a decentralized management structure. Perform an Internet search to gain some background information on the company's products, value chain activities, and leadership. How does Johnson & Johnson exemplify (or not exemplify) a decentralized management strategy? Describe the advantages and disadvantages of a decentralized system of management in the case of Johnson & Johnson. Why was it established in the first place? Has it been an effective means of decision making for the company?   **LO 10-5**

EXERCISES FOR SIMULATION PARTICIPANTS

1. How would you describe the organization of your company's top-management team? Is some decision making decentralized and delegated to individual managers? If so, explain how the decentralization works. Or are decisions made more by consensus, with all co-managers having input? What do you see as the advantages and disadvantages of the decision-making approach your company is employing?   **LO 10-5**

2. What specific actions have you and your co-managers taken to develop core competencies or competitive capabilities that can contribute to good strategy execution and potential competitive advantage? If no actions have been taken, explain your rationale for doing nothing.   **LO 10-3**

3. What value chain activities are most crucial to good execution of your company's strategy? Does your company have the ability to outsource any value chain activities? If so, have you and your co-managers opted to engage in outsourcing? Why or why not?   **LO 10-1**

ENDNOTES

[1] Donald Sull, Rebecca Homkes, and Charles Sull, "Why Strategy Execution Unravels—and What to Do About It," *Harvard Business Review* 93, no. 3 (March 2015), p. 60.

[2] Steven W. Floyd and Bill Wooldridge, "Managing Strategic Consensus: The Foundation of Effective Implementation," *Academy of Management Executive* 6, no. 4 (November 1992), p. 27.

[3] Jack Welch with Suzy Welch, *Winning* (New York: HarperBusiness, 2005).

[4] Larry Bossidy and Ram Charan, *Execution: The Discipline of Getting Things Done* (New York: Crown Business, 2002).

[5] Christopher A. Bartlett and Sumantra Ghoshal, "Building Competitive Advantage through People," *MIT Sloan Management Review* 43, no. 2 (Winter 2002), pp. 34–41.

[6] Justin Menkes, "Hiring for Smarts," *Harvard Business Review* 83, no. 11 (November 2005), pp. 100–109; Justin Menkes, *Executive Intelligence* (New York: HarperCollins, 2005).

[7] Menkes, *Executive Intelligence*, pp. 68, 76.

[8] Jim Collins, *Good to Great* (New York: HarperBusiness, 2001).

[9] John Byrne, "The Search for the Young and Gifted," *Businessweek*, October 4, 1999, p. 108.

[10] C. Helfat and M. Peteraf, "The Dynamic Resource-Based View: Capability Lifecycles," *Strategic Management Journal* 24, no. 10 (October 2003), pp. 997–1010.

[11] G. Dosi, R. Nelson, and S. Winter (eds.), *The Nature and Dynamics of Organizational Capabilities* (Oxford, England: Oxford University Press, 2001).

[12] S. Winter, "The Satisficing Principle in Capability Learning," *Strategic Management Journal* 21, no. 10–11 (October–November 2000), pp. 981–996; M. Zollo and S. Winter, "Deliberate Learning and the Evolution of

Dynamic Capabilities," *Organization Science* 13, no. 3 (May–June 2002), pp. 339–351.

[13] Robert H. Hayes, Gary P. Pisano, and David M. Upton, *Strategic Operations: Competing through Capabilities* (New York: Free Press, 1996); Jonas Ridderstrale, "Cashing In on Corporate Competencies," *Business Strategy Review* 14, no. 1 (Spring 2003), pp. 27–38; Danny Miller, Russell Eisenstat, and Nathaniel Foote, "Strategy from the Inside Out: Building Capability-Creating Organizations," *California Management Review* 44, no. 3 (Spring 2002), pp. 37–55.

[14] S. Karim and W. Mitchell, "Path-Dependent and Path-Breaking Change: Reconfiguring Business Resources Following Acquisitions in the US Medical Sector, 1978–1995," *Strategic Management Journal* 21, no. 10–11 (October–November 2000), pp. 1061–1082; L. Capron, P. Dussauge, and W. Mitchell, "Resource Redeployment Following Horizontal Acquisitions in Europe and North America, 1988–1992," *Strategic Management Journal* 19, no. 7 (July 1998), pp. 631–662.

[15] Gary P. Pisano and Willy C. Shih, "Restoring American Competitiveness," *Harvard Business Review* 87, no. 7–8 (July–August 2009), pp. 114–125.

[16] A. Chandler, *Strategy and Structure* (Cambridge, MA: MIT Press, 1962).

[17] E. Olsen, S. Slater, and G. Hult, "The Importance of Structure and Process to Strategy Implementation," *Business Horizons* 48, no. 1 (2005), pp. 47–54; H. Barkema, J. Baum, and E. Mannix, "Management Challenges in a New Time," *Academy of Management Journal* 45, no. 5 (October 2002), pp. 916–930.

[18] H. Mintzberg, *The Structuring of Organizations* (Englewood Cliffs, NJ: Prentice Hall, 1979); C. Levicki, *The Interactive Strategy*

Workout, 2nd ed. (London: Prentice Hall, 1999).

[19] O. Williamson, *Market and Hierarchies* (New York: Free Press, 1975); R. M. Burton and B. Obel, "A Computer Simulation Test of the M-Form Hypothesis," *Administrative Science Quarterly* 25 (1980), pp. 457–476.

[20] J. Baum and S. Wally, "Strategic Decision Speed and Firm Performance," *Strategic Management Journal* 24 (2003), pp. 1107–1129.

[21] C. Bartlett and S. Ghoshal, "Matrix Management: Not a Structure, a Frame of Mind," *Harvard Business Review*, July–August 1990, pp. 138–145.

[22] M. Goold and A. Campbell, "Structured Networks: Towards the Well Designed Matrix," *Long Range Planning* 36, no. 5 (2003), pp. 427–439.

[23] Iain Somerville and John Edward Mroz, "New Competencies for a New World," in Frances Hesselbein, Marshall Goldsmith, and Richard Beckard (eds.), *The Organization of the Future* (San Francisco: Jossey-Bass, 1997), p. 70.

[24] Stanley E. Fawcett, Gary K. Rhoads, and Phillip Burnah, "People as the Bridge to Competitiveness: Benchmarking the 'ABCs' of an Empowered Workforce," *Benchmarking: An International Journal* 11, no. 4 (2004), pp. 346–360.

[25] Robert Simons, "Control in an Age of Empowerment," *Harvard Business Review* 73 (March–April 1995), pp. 80–88.

[26] Jeanne M. Liedtka, "Collaboration across Lines of Business for Competitive Advantage," *Academy of Management Executive* 10, no. 2 (May 1996), pp. 20–34.

[27] Rosabeth Moss Kanter, "Collaborative Advantage: The Art of the Alliance," *Harvard Business Review* 72, no. 4 (July–August 1994), pp. 96–108.

chapter 11

Managing Internal Operations

Actions That Promote Good Strategy Execution

Learning Objectives

After reading this chapter, you should be able to:

LO 11-1   Explain why resource allocation should always be based on strategic priorities.

LO 11-2   Comprehend how well-designed policies and procedures can facilitate good strategy execution.

LO 11-3   Understand how process management tools drive continuous improvement in the performance of value chain activities.

LO 11-4   Recognize the role of information systems and operating systems in enabling company personnel to carry out their strategic roles proficiently.

LO 11-5   Explain how and why the use of well-designed incentives can be management's single most powerful tool for promoting adept strategy execution.

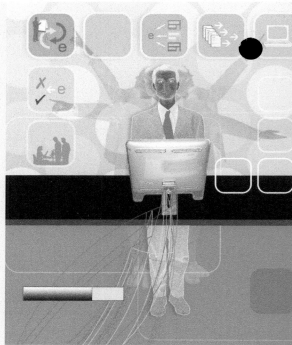

Matt Herring/Ikon Images/Media Bakery

Processes underpin business capabilities, and capabilities underpin strategy execution.

Pearl Zhu

Pay your people the least possible and you'll get the same from them.

Malcolm Forbes—late Publisher of *Forbes Magazine*

Apple is a very disciplined company, and we have great processes. But that's not what it's about. Process makes you more efficient.

Steve Jobs—*Cofounder of Apple, Inc.*

In Chapter 10, we emphasized that proficient strategy execution begins with three types of managerial actions: staffing the organization with the right people; acquiring, developing, and strengthening the firm's resources and capabilities; and structuring the organization in a manner supportive of the strategy execution effort.

In this chapter, we discuss five additional managerial actions that advance the cause of good strategy execution:

- Allocating ample resources to the strategy execution effort.

- Instituting policies and procedures that facilitate good strategy execution.
- Employing process management tools to drive continuous improvement in how value chain activities are performed.
- Installing information and operating systems that support strategy implementation activities.
- Tying rewards and incentives to the achievement of performance objectives.

ALLOCATING RESOURCES TO THE STRATEGY EXECUTION EFFORT

LO 11-1

Explain why resource allocation should always be based on strategic priorities.

A company's strategic priorities must drive how capital allocations are made and the size of each unit's operating budgets.

Early in the strategy implementation process, managers must determine what resources (in terms of funding, people, and so on) will be required and how they should be distributed across the company's various organizational units. This includes carefully screening requests for more people and new facilities and equipment, approving those that will contribute to the strategy execution effort, and turning down those that don't. Should internal cash flows prove insufficient to fund the planned strategic initiatives, then management must raise additional funds through borrowing or selling additional shares of stock to investors.

A company's ability to marshal the resources needed to support new strategic initiatives has a major impact on the strategy execution process. Too little funding and an insufficiency of other types of resources slow progress and impede the efforts of organizational units to execute their pieces of the strategic plan competently. Too much funding of particular organizational units and value chain activities wastes organizational resources and reduces financial performance. Both of these scenarios argue for managers to become deeply involved in reviewing budget proposals and directing the proper kinds and amounts of resources to strategy-critical organizational units.

A change in strategy nearly always calls for budget reallocations and resource shifting. Previously important units with a lesser role in the new strategy may need downsizing. Units that now have a bigger strategic role may need more people, new equipment, additional facilities, and above-average increases in their operating budgets. Implementing new strategy initiatives requires managers to take an active and sometimes forceful role in shifting resources, not only to better support activities now having a higher priority but also to capture opportunities to operate more cost-effectively. This requires putting enough resources behind new strategic initiatives to fuel their success and making the tough decisions to kill projects and activities that are no longer justified.

Visible actions to reallocate operating funds and move people into new organizational units signal a determined commitment to strategic change. Such actions can catalyze the implementation process and give it credibility. Microsoft has made a practice of regularly shifting hundreds of programmers to new high-priority programming initiatives within a matter of weeks or even days. Fast-moving developments in many markets are prompting companies to abandon traditional annual budgeting and resource allocation cycles in favor of resource allocation processes supportive of more rapid adjustments in strategy. In response to rapid technological change in the communications industry, AT&T has prioritized investments and acquisitions that have allowed it to offer its enterprise customers faster, more flexible networks and provide innovative new customer services, such as its Sponsored Data plan.

Merely fine-tuning the execution of a company's existing strategy seldom requires big shifts of resources from one area to another. In contrast, new strategic initiatives generally require not only big shifts in resources but a larger allocation of resources to the effort as well. However, there are times when strategy changes or new execution initiatives need to be made without adding to total company expenses. In such circumstances, managers have to work their way through the existing budget line by line and activity by activity, looking for ways to trim costs and shift resources to activities that are higher-priority in the strategy execution effort. In the event that a company needs to make significant cost cuts during the course of launching new strategic initiatives, managers must be especially creative in finding ways to do more with less. Indeed, it is common for strategy changes and the drive for good strategy execution to be aimed at achieving considerably higher levels of operating efficiency and, at the same time, making sure the most important value chain activities are performed as effectively as possible.

INSTITUTING POLICIES AND PROCEDURES THAT FACILITATE STRATEGY EXECUTION

A company's policies and procedures can either support or hinder good strategy execution. Anytime a company moves to put new strategy elements in place or improve its strategy execution capabilities, some changes in work practices are usually needed. Managers are thus well advised to carefully consider whether existing policies and procedures fully support such changes and to revise or discard those that do not.

As shown in Figure 11.1, well-conceived policies and operating procedures facilitate strategy execution in two significant ways:

LO 11-2

Comprehend how well-designed policies and procedures can facilitate good strategy execution.

1. *By providing top-down guidance regarding how things need to be done.* Policies and procedures provide company personnel with a set of guidelines for how to perform organizational activities, conduct various aspects of operations, solve problems as they arise, and accomplish particular tasks. They clarify uncertainty about how to proceed in executing strategy and align the actions and behavior of company personnel with the requirements for good strategy execution. Moreover, they place limits on ineffective independent action. When they are well matched with the requirements of the strategy implementation plan, they channel the efforts of individuals along a path that supports the plan. When existing ways of doing things pose a barrier to strategy execution initiatives, actions and behaviors have to be changed. Under these conditions, the managerial role is to establish and enforce new policies and operating practices that are more conducive to executing the strategy appropriately. Policies are a particularly useful way to counteract tendencies for some people to resist change. People generally refrain from violating company policy or going against recommended practices and procedures without gaining clearance or having strong justification.

2. *By helping ensure consistency in how execution-critical activities are performed.* Policies and procedures serve to standardize the way that activities are performed. In essence, they represent a store of organizational or managerial knowledge about efficient and effective ways of doing things—a set of well-honed routines for running the company. This can be important for ensuring the quality and reliability of the strategy execution process. It helps align and coordinate the strategy execution efforts of individuals and groups throughout the organization—a feature that is particularly beneficial when there are geographically scattered operating units. For example, eliminating significant differences in the operating practices of different plants, sales regions, or customer service centers

A company's policies and procedures provide a set of well-honed routines for running the company and executing the strategy.

FIGURE 11.1   How Policies and Procedures Facilitate Good Strategy Execution

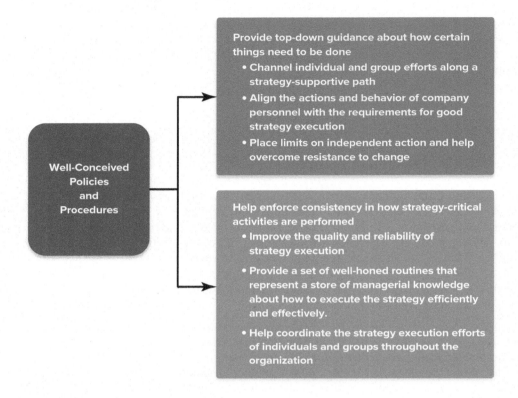

or in the individual outlets in a chain operation helps a company deliver consistent product quality and service to customers. Good strategy execution nearly always entails an ability to replicate product quality and the caliber of customer service at every location where the company does business—anything less blurs the company's image and lowers customer satisfaction.

3. *By promoting the creation of a work climate that facilitates good strategy execution.* A company's policies and procedures help set the tone of a company's work climate and contribute to a common understanding of "how we do things around here." Because abandoning old policies and procedures in favor of new ones invariably alters the internal work climate, managers can use the policy-changing process as a powerful lever for changing the corporate culture in ways that better support new strategic initiatives. The trick here, obviously, is to come up with new policies or procedures that catch the immediate attention of company personnel and prompt them to quickly shift their actions and behaviors in the desired ways.

To ensure consistency in product quality and service behavior patterns, McDonald's policy manual spells out detailed procedures that personnel in each McDonald's unit are expected to observe. For example, "Cooks must turn, never flip, hamburgers. If they haven't been purchased, Big Macs must be discarded in 10 minutes after being cooked and French fries in 7 minutes. Cashiers must make eye contact with and smile at every customer." Retail chain stores and other organizational chains (e.g., hotels, hospitals, child care centers) similarly rely on detailed policies and procedures to ensure consistency in their operations and reliable service to their customers. Video game developer Valve Corporation prides itself on a lack of rigid policies and procedures; its 37-page handbook for new employees details how things get done in such an environment—an ironic tribute to the fact that all types of companies need policies.

One of the big policy-making issues concerns what activities need to be strictly prescribed and what activities ought to allow room for independent action on the part of personnel. Few companies need thick policy manuals to prescribe exactly how daily operations are to be conducted. Too much policy can be as obstructive as wrong policy and as confusing as no policy. There is wisdom in a middle approach: *Prescribe enough policies to give organization members clear direction and to place reasonable boundaries on their actions; then empower them to act within these boundaries in pursuit of company goals.* Allowing company personnel to act with some degree of freedom is especially appropriate when individual creativity and initiative are more essential to good strategy execution than are standardization and strict conformity. Instituting policies that facilitate strategy execution can therefore mean policies more policies, fewer policies, or different policies. It can mean policies that require things be done according to a precisely defined standard or policies that give employees substantial leeway to do activities the way they think best.

> There is wisdom in a middle-ground approach: Prescribe enough policies to give organization members clear direction and to place reasonable boundaries on their actions; then empower them to act within these boundaries in pursuit of company goals.

EMPLOYING BUSINESS PROCESS MANAGEMENT TOOLS

Company managers can significantly advance the cause of competent strategy execution by using business process management tools to drive continuous improvement in how internal operations are conducted. Process management tools are used to model, control, measure, and optimize a variety of organizational activities that may span departments, functions, value chain systems, employees, customers, suppliers, and other partners in support of company goals. They also provide corrective feedback, allowing managers to change and improve company operations in an ongoing manner.

● LO 11-3

Understand how process management tools drive continuous improvement in the performance of value chain activities.

Promoting Operating Excellence: Three Powerful Business Process Management Tools

Three of the most powerful management tools for promoting operating excellence and better strategy execution are business process reengineering, total quality management (TQM) programs, and Six Sigma quality control programs. Each of these merits discussion since many companies around the world use these tools to help execute strategies tied to cost reduction, defect-free manufacture, superior product quality, superior customer service, and total customer satisfaction.

Business Process Reengineering   Companies searching for ways to improve their operations have sometimes discovered that the execution of strategy-critical activities is hampered by a disconnected organizational arrangement whereby pieces of an activity are performed in several different functional departments, with no one manager or group being accountable for optimal performance of the entire activity. This can easily occur in such inherently cross-functional activities as customer service (which can involve personnel in order filling, warehousing and shipping, invoicing, accounts receivable, after-sale repair, and technical support), particularly for companies with a functional organizational structure.

To address the suboptimal performance problems that can arise from this type of situation, a company can *reengineer the work effort,* pulling the pieces of an activity out of different departments and creating a cross-functional work group or single department (often called a *process department*) to take charge of the whole process. The use of cross-functional teams has been popularized by the practice of **business process reengineering,** which involves radically redesigning and streamlining the workflow (typically enabled by cutting-edge use of online technology and information systems), with the goal of achieving quantum gains in performance of the activity.[1]

The reengineering of value chain activities has been undertaken at many companies in many industries all over the world, with excellent results being achieved at some firms.[2] Hallmark reengineered its process for developing new greeting cards, creating teams of mixed-occupation personnel (artists, writers, lithographers, merchandisers, and administrators) to work on a single holiday or greeting card theme. The reengineered process speeded development times for new lines of greeting cards by up to 24 months, reduced costs, and increased customer satisfaction.[3] In the order-processing section of General Electric's circuit breaker division, elapsed time from order receipt to delivery was cut from three weeks to three days by consolidating six production units into one, reducing a variety of former inventory and handling steps, automating the design system to replace a human custom-design process, and cutting the organizational layers between managers and workers from three to one. Productivity rose 20 percent in one year, and unit manufacturing costs dropped 30 percent. In the health care industry, business process reengineering is being used to lower health care costs and improve patient outcomes in a variety of ways. South Africa is attempting to reengineer its primary health care system, which is in need of significant reform. Similar initiatives are ongoing in India. In the United States, exemplary health care providers, such as Mayo Clinic, are using reengineering tools on a continuous basis to achieve outcomes such as fewer hospitalizations, improved patient–physician interactions, and the delivery of lower cost health care.

While business process reengineering has been criticized as an excuse for downsizing, it has nonetheless proved itself a useful tool for streamlining a company's work effort and moving closer to operational excellence. It has also inspired more technologically based approaches to integrating and streamlining business processes, such as *enterprise resource planning,* a software-based system implemented with the help of consulting companies such as SAP (the leading provider of business software).

Total Quality Management Programs   **Total quality management (TQM)** is a management approach that emphasizes continuous improvement in all phases of operations, 100 percent accuracy in performing tasks, involvement and empowerment of employees at all levels, team-based work design, benchmarking, and total customer satisfaction.[4] While TQM concentrates on producing quality goods and fully satisfying customer expectations, it achieves its biggest successes when it is extended to employee efforts in *all departments*—human resources, billing, accounting, and information systems—that may lack pressing, customer-driven incentives to improve. It involves reforming the corporate culture and shifting to a continuous-improvement business philosophy that permeates every facet of the organization.[5] TQM aims at instilling enthusiasm and commitment to doing things right from the top to the bottom of the organization. Management's job is to kindle an organizationwide search for ways to improve that involves all company personnel exercising initiative and using their ingenuity. TQM doctrine preaches that there's no such thing as "good enough" and that everyone has a responsibility to participate in continuous improvement. TQM is thus a race without a finish. Success comes from making little steps forward each day, a process that the Japanese call *kaizen.*

TQM takes a fairly long time to show significant results—very little benefit emerges within the first six months. The long-term payoff of TQM, if it comes, depends heavily on management's success in implanting a culture within which the TQM philosophy and practices can thrive. But it is a management tool that has attracted numerous users and advocates over several decades, and it can deliver good results when used properly.

Six Sigma Quality Control Programs   **Six Sigma programs** offer another way to drive continuous improvement in quality and strategy execution. This approach entails the use of advanced statistical methods to identify and remove the causes of defects (errors) and undesirable variability in performing an activity or business process. When performance of an activity or process reaches "Six Sigma quality," there are *no more than 3.4 defects per million iterations* (equal to 99.9997 percent accuracy).[6]

> **CORE** CONCEPT
>
> **Six Sigma programs** utilize advanced statistical methods to improve quality by reducing defects and variability in the performance of business processes.

There are two important types of Six Sigma programs. The Six Sigma process of define, measure, analyze, improve, and control (DMAIC, pronounced "de-may-ic") is an improvement system for existing processes falling below specification and needing incremental improvement. The Six Sigma process of define, measure, analyze, design, and verify (DMADV, pronounced "de-mad-vee") is used to develop *new* processes or products at Six Sigma quality levels. DMADV is sometimes referred to as Design for Six Sigma, or DFSS. Both Six Sigma programs are overseen by personnel who have completed Six Sigma "master black belt" training, and they are executed by personnel who have earned Six Sigma "green belts" and Six Sigma "black belts." According to the Six Sigma Academy, personnel with black belts can save companies approximately $230,000 per project and can complete four to six projects a year.[7]

The statistical thinking underlying Six Sigma is based on the following three principles: (1) All work is a process, (2) all processes have variability, and (3) all processes create data that explain variability.[8] Six Sigma's DMAIC process is a particularly good vehicle for improving performance when there are *wide variations* in how well an activity is performed. For instance, airlines striving to improve the on-time performance of their flights have more to gain from actions to curtail the number of flights that are late by more than 30 minutes than from actions to reduce the number of flights that are late by less than five minutes. Six Sigma quality control programs are of particular interest for large companies, which are better able to shoulder the cost of the large investment required in employee training, organizational infrastructure, and consulting services. For example, to realize a cost savings of $4.4 billion from rolling out its Six Sigma program, GE had to invest $1.6 billion and suffer losses from the program during its first year.[9]

Since the programs were first introduced, thousands of companies and nonprofit organizations around the world have used Six Sigma to promote operating excellence. For companies at the forefront of this movement, such as Motorola, General Electric (GE), Ford, and Honeywell (Allied Signal), the cost savings as a percentage of revenue varied from 1.2 to 4.5 percent, according to data analysis conducted by iSixSigma (an organization that provides free articles, tools, and resources concerning Six Sigma). More recently, there has been a resurgence of interest in Six Sigma practices, with companies such as Siemens, Coca-Cola, Ocean Spray, GEICO, and Merrill Lynch turning to Six Sigma as a vehicle to improve their bottom lines. In the first five years of its adoption, Six Sigma at Bank of America helped the bank reap about $2 billion in revenue gains and cost savings; the bank holds an annual "Best of Six Sigma Expo" to celebrate the teams and the projects with the greatest contribution to the company's bottom line. GE, one of the most successful companies implementing Six Sigma training and pursuing Six Sigma perfection across the company's entire operations, estimated benefits of some $10 billion during the first five years of implementation—its Lighting division, for example, cut invoice defects and disputes by 98 percent.[10]

Six Sigma has also been used to improve processes in health care. Froedtert Hospital in Milwaukee, Wisconsin, used Six Sigma to improve the accuracy of administering the proper drug doses to patients. DMAIC analysis of the three-stage process by which prescriptions were written by doctors, filled by the hospital pharmacy, and then administered to patients by nurses revealed that most mistakes came from misreading the doctors' handwriting. The hospital implemented a program requiring doctors to enter the prescription on the hospital's computers, which slashed the number of errors dramatically. In recent years, Pfizer embarked on 85 Six Sigma projects to streamline its R&D process and lower the cost of delivering medicines to patients in its pharmaceutical sciences division.

Illustration Capsule 11.1 describes Charleston Area Medical Center's use of Six Sigma as a health care provider coping with the current challenges facing this industry.

Despite its potential benefits, Six Sigma is not without its problems. There is evidence, for example, that Six Sigma techniques can stifle innovation and creativity. The essence of Six Sigma is to reduce variability in processes, but creative processes, by nature, include quite a bit of variability. In many instances, breakthrough innovations occur only after thousands of ideas have been abandoned and promising ideas have gone through multiple iterations and extensive prototyping. Alphabet Executive Chairman of the Board Eric Schmidt has declared that applying Six Sigma measurement and control principles to creative activities at Google would choke off innovation altogether.[11]

A blended approach to Six Sigma implementation that is gaining in popularity pursues incremental improvements in operating efficiency, while R&D and other processes that allow the company to develop new ways of offering value to customers are given freer rein. Managers of these **ambidextrous organizations** are adept at employing continuous improvement in operating processes but allowing R&D to operate under a set of rules that allows for exploration and the development of breakthrough innovations. However, the two distinctly different approaches to managing employees must be carried out by tightly integrated senior managers to ensure that the separate and diversely oriented units operate with a common purpose. Ciba Vision, now part of eye care multinational Alcon, dramatically reduced operating expenses through the use of continuous-improvement programs, while simultaneously and harmoniously developing a new series of contact lens products that have allowed its revenues to increase by 300 percent over a 10-year period.[12] An enterprise that systematically and wisely applies Six Sigma methods to its value chain, activity by activity, can make major strides in improving the proficiency with which its strategy is executed without sacrificing innovation. As is the case with TQM, obtaining managerial commitment, establishing a quality culture, and fully involving employees are all of critical importance to the successful implementation of Six Sigma quality programs.[13]

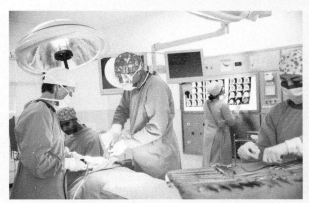

Caiaimage/Robert Daly/Getty Images

Established in 1972, Charleston Area Medical Center (CAMC) is West Virginia's largest health care provider in terms of beds, admissions, and revenues. In 2000, CAMC implemented a Six Sigma program to examine quality problems and standardize care processes. Performance improvement was important to CAMC's management for a variety of strategic reasons, including competitive positioning and cost control.

The United States has been evolving toward a pay-for-performance structure, which rewards hospitals for providing quality care. CAMC has utilized its Six Sigma program to take advantage of these changes in the health care environment. For example, to improve its performance in acute myocardial infarction (AMI), CAMC applied a Six Sigma DMAIC (define-measure-analyze-improve-control) approach. Nursing staff members were educated on AMI care processes, performance targets were posted in nursing units, and adherence to the eight Hospital Quality Alliance (HQA) indicators of quality care for AMI patients was tracked. As a result of the program, CAMC improved its compliance with HQA-recommended treatment for AMI from 50 to 95 percent. Harvard researchers identified CAMC as one of the top-performing hospitals reporting comparable data.

Controlling cost has also been an important aspect of CAMC's performance improvement initiatives due to local regulations. West Virginia is one of two states where medical services rates are set by state regulators. This forces CAMC to limit expenditures because the hospital cannot raise prices. CAMC first applied Six Sigma in an effort to control costs by managing the supply chain more effectively. The effort created a one-time $150,000 savings by working with vendors to remove outdated inventory. As a result of continuous improvement, CAMC managed to achieve supply chain management savings of $12 million in just four years.

Since CAMC introduced Six Sigma, over 100 quality improvement projects have been initiated. A key to CAMC's success has been instilling a continuous improvement mindset into the organization's culture. Dale Wood, chief quality officer at CAMC, stated: "If you have people at the top who completely support and want these changes to occur, you can still fall flat on your face. . . . You need a group of networkers who can carry change across an organization." Due to CAMC's performance improvement culture, the hospital ranks high nationally in ratings for quality of care and patient safety, as reported on the Centers for Medicare and Medicaid Services (CMS) website.

Note: Developed with Robin A. Daley.

Sources: CAMC website; Martha Hostetter, "Case Study: Improving Performance at Charleston Area Medical Center," *The Commonwealth Fund*, November–December 2007, **www.commonwealthfund.org/publications/newsletters/quality-matters/2007/november-december/ case-study-improving-performance-at-charleston-area-medical-center** (accessed January 2016); J. C. Simmons, "Using Six Sigma to Make a Difference in Health Care Quality," *The Quality Letter*, April 2002.

The Difference between Business Process Reengineering and Continuous-Improvement Programs Like Six Sigma and TQM Whereas business process reengineering aims at *quantum gains* on the order of 30 to 50 percent or more, total quality programs like TQM and Six Sigma stress *ongoing incremental progress,* striving for inch-by-inch gains again and again in a never-ending stream. The two approaches to improved performance of value chain activities and operating excellence are not mutually exclusive; it makes sense to use them in tandem. Reengineering can be used first to produce a good basic design that yields quick,

> Business process reengineering aims at one-time quantum improvement, while continuous-improvement programs like TQM and Six Sigma aim at ongoing incremental improvements.

dramatic improvements in performing a business process. TQM or Six Sigma programs can then be used as a follow-on to reengineering and/or best-practice implementation to deliver incremental improvements over a longer period of time.

Capturing the Benefits of Initiatives to Improve Operations

The biggest beneficiaries of process improvement initiatives, reengineering, TQM, and Six Sigma are companies that view such programs not as ends in themselves but as tools for implementing company strategy more effectively. The least rewarding payoffs occur when company managers seize on the programs as novel ideas that might be worth a try. In most such instances, they result in strategy-blind efforts to simply manage better.

There's an important lesson here. Business process management tools all need to be linked to a company's strategic priorities to contribute effectively to improving the strategy's execution. Only strategy can point to which value chain activities matter and what performance targets make the most sense. Without a strategic framework, managers lack the context in which to fix things that really matter to business unit performance and competitive success.

To get the most from initiatives to execute strategy more proficiently, managers must have a clear idea of what specific outcomes really matter. Is it high on-time delivery, lower overall costs, fewer customer complaints, shorter cycle times, a higher percentage of revenues coming from recently introduced products, or something else? Benchmarking best-in-industry and best-in-world performance of targeted value chain activities provides a realistic basis for setting internal performance milestones and longer-range targets. Once initiatives to improve operations are linked to the company's strategic priorities, then comes the managerial task of building a total quality culture that is genuinely committed to achieving the performance outcomes that strategic success requires.[14]

Managers can take the following action steps to realize full value from TQM, reengineering, or Six Sigma initiatives and promote a culture of operating excellence[15]:

1. Demonstrating visible, unequivocal, and unyielding commitment to total quality and continuous improvement, including specifying measurable objectives for increasing quality and making continual progress.

2. Nudging people toward quality-supportive behaviors by
   a. Screening job applicants rigorously and hiring only those with attitudes and aptitudes that are right for quality-based performance.
   b. Providing quality training for employees.
   c. Using teams and team-building exercises to reinforce and nurture individual effort. (The creation of a quality culture is facilitated when teams become more cross-functional, multitask-oriented, and increasingly self-managed.)
   d. Recognizing and rewarding individual and team efforts to improve quality regularly and systematically.
   e. Stressing prevention (doing it right the first time), not correction (instituting ways to undo or overcome mistakes).

3. Empowering employees so that authority for delivering great service or improving products is in the hands of those who do the job rather than their managers: *improving quality has to be seen as part of everyone's job.*

4. Using online systems to provide all relevant parties with the latest best practices, thereby speeding the diffusion and adoption of best practices throughout the organization. Online systems can also allow company personnel to exchange data and opinions about how to upgrade the prevailing best-in-company practices.

5. Emphasizing that performance can and must be improved, because competitors are not resting on their laurels and customers are always looking for something better.

In sum, initiatives to improve operations, like business process reengineering, TQM, and Six Sigma techniques all need to be seen and used as part of a bigger-picture effort to execute strategy proficiently. Used properly, all of these tools are capable of improving the proficiency with which an organization performs its value chain activities. Not only do improvements from such initiatives add up over time and strengthen organizational capabilities, but they also help build a culture of operating excellence. All this lays the groundwork for gaining a competitive advantage.[16] While it is relatively easy for rivals to also implement process management tools, it is much more difficult and time-consuming for them to instill a deeply ingrained culture of operating excellence (as occurs when such techniques are religiously employed and top management exhibits lasting commitment to operational excellence throughout the organization).

> The purpose of using business process management tools, such as business process reengineering, TQM, and Six Sigma programs is to improve the performance of strategy-critical activities and thereby enhance strategy execution.

INSTALLING INFORMATION AND OPERATING SYSTEMS

Company strategies can't be executed well without a number of internal systems for business operations. American Airlines, Delta, Ryanair, Lufthansa, and other successful airlines cannot hope to provide passenger-pleasing service without a user-friendly online reservation system, an accurate and speedy baggage-handling system, and a strict aircraft maintenance program that minimizes problems requiring at-the-gate service that delays departures. FedEx has internal communication systems that allow it to coordinate its over 100,000 vehicles in handling a daily average of 12.1 million shipments to more than 220 countries and territories. Its leading-edge flight operations systems allow a single controller to direct as many as 200 of FedEx's 659 aircraft simultaneously, overriding their flight plans should weather problems or other special circumstances arise. FedEx also has created a series of e-business tools for customers that allow them to ship and track packages online, create address books, review shipping history, generate custom reports, simplify customer billing, reduce internal warehousing and inventory management costs, purchase goods and services from suppliers, and respond to their own quickly changing customer demands. All of FedEx's systems support the company's strategy of providing businesses and individuals with a broad array of package delivery services and enhancing its competitiveness against United Parcel Service, DHL, and the U.S. Postal Service.

Amazon.com ships customer orders from a global network of some 707 technologically sophisticated order fulfillment and distribution centers. Using complex picking algorithms, computers initiate the order-picking process by sending signals to workers' wireless receivers, telling them which items to pick off the shelves in which order. Computers also generate data on mix-boxed items, chute backup times, line speed, worker productivity, and shipping weights on orders. Systems are upgraded regularly, and productivity improvements are aggressively pursued. Amazon has been experimenting with drone delivery in order to lower costs and speed package delivery;

> ● **LO 11-4**
>
> Recognize the role of information systems and operating systems in enabling company personnel to carry out their strategic roles proficiently.

more recently it has begun marketing a pilot project called "Seller Flex" as part of its effort to develop its own delivery service.

Otis Elevator, the world's largest manufacturer of elevators, with more than 2.6 million elevators and escalators installed worldwide, has a 24/7 remote electronic monitoring system that can detect when an elevator or escalator installed on a customer's site has any of 325 problems. If the monitoring system detects a problem, it analyzes and diagnoses the cause and location, then makes the service call to an Otis mechanic at the nearest location, and helps the mechanic (who is equipped with a web-enabled cell phone) identify the component causing the problem. The company's maintenance system helps keep outage times under three hours—the elevators are often back in service before people even realize there was a problem. All trouble-call data are relayed to design and manufacturing personnel, allowing them to quickly alter design specifications or manufacturing procedures when needed to correct recurring problems. All customers have online access to performance data on each of their Otis elevators and escalators.

Well-conceived state-of-the-art operating systems not only enable better strategy execution but also strengthen organizational capabilities—enough at times to provide a competitive edge over rivals. For example, a company with a differentiation strategy based on superior quality has added capability if it has systems for training personnel in quality techniques, tracking product quality at each production step, and ensuring that all goods shipped meet quality standards. If these quality control systems are better than those employed by rivals, they provide the company with a competitive advantage. Similarly, a company striving to be a low-cost provider is competitively stronger if it has an unrivaled benchmarking system that identifies opportunities to implement best-in-the-world practices and drive costs out of the business faster than rivals. Fast-growing companies get an important assist from having capabilities in place to recruit and train new employees in large numbers and from investing in infrastructure that gives them the capability to handle rapid growth as it occurs, rather than having to scramble to catch up to customer demand.

Instituting Adequate Information Systems, Performance Tracking, and Controls

Accurate and timely information about daily operations is essential if managers are to gauge how well the strategy execution process is proceeding. Companies everywhere are capitalizing on today's technology to install real-time data-generating capability. Most retail companies now have automated online systems that generate daily sales reports for each store and maintain up-to-the-minute inventory and sales records on each item. Manufacturing plants typically generate daily production reports and track labor productivity on every shift. Transportation companies have elaborate information systems to provide real-time arrival information for buses and trains that is automatically sent to digital message signs and platform audio address systems.

Siemens Healthcare, one of the largest suppliers to the health care industry, uses a cloud-based business activity monitoring (BAM) system to continuously monitor and improve the company's processes across more than 190 countries. Customer satisfaction is one of Siemens's most important business objectives, so the reliability of its order management and services is crucial. Caesars Entertainment, owner of casinos and hotels, uses a sophisticated customer relationship database that records detailed information about its customers' gambling habits. When a member of Caesars's Total Rewards program calls to make a reservation, the representative can review previous spending, including average bet size, to offer an upgrade or complimentary stay at

Caesars Palace or one of the company's other properties. At Uber, the popular ride-sharing service, there are systems for locating vehicles near a customer and real-time demand monitoring to price fares during high-demand periods.

Information systems need to cover five broad areas: (1) customer data, (2) operations data, (3) employee data, (4) supplier and/or strategic partner data, and (5) financial performance data. All key strategic performance indicators must be tracked and reported in real time whenever possible. Real-time information systems permit company managers to stay on top of implementation initiatives and daily operations and to intervene if things seem to be drifting off course. Tracking key performance indicators, gathering information from operating personnel, quickly identifying and diagnosing problems, and taking corrective actions are all integral pieces of the process of managing strategy execution and overseeing operations.

Statistical information gives managers a feel for the numbers, briefings and meetings provide a feel for the latest developments and emerging issues, and personal contacts add a feel for the people dimension. All are good barometers of how well things are going and what operating aspects need management attention. Managers must identify problem areas and deviations from plans before they can take action to get the organization back on course by either improving the approaches to strategy execution or fine-tuning the strategy. Jeff Bezos, Amazon.com's CEO, is an ardent proponent of managing by the numbers. As he puts it, "Math-based decisions always trump opinion and judgment. The trouble with most corporations is that they make judgment-based decisions when data-based decisions could be made."[17]

> Having state-of-the-art operating systems, information systems, and real-time data is integral to superior strategy execution and operating excellence.

Monitoring Employee Performance   Information systems also provide managers with a means for monitoring the performance of empowered workers to see that they are acting within the specified limits.[18] Leaving empowered employees to their own devices in meeting performance standards without appropriate checks and balances can expose an organization to excessive risk.[19] Instances abound of employees' decisions or behavior going awry, sometimes costing a company huge sums or producing lawsuits and reputation-damaging publicity.

Scrutinizing daily and weekly operating statistics is one of the ways in which managers can monitor the results that flow from the actions of subordinates without resorting to constant over-the-shoulder supervision; if the operating results look good, then it is reasonable to assume that empowerment is working. But close monitoring of operating performance is only one of the control tools at management's disposal. Another valuable lever of control in companies that rely on empowered employees, especially in those that use self-managed work groups or other such teams, is peer-based control. Because peer evaluation is such a powerful control device, companies organized into teams can remove some layers of the management hierarchy and rely on strong peer pressure to keep team members operating between the white lines. This is especially true when a company has the information systems capability to monitor team performance daily or in real time.

USING REWARDS AND INCENTIVES TO PROMOTE BETTER STRATEGY EXECUTION

It is essential that company personnel be enthusiastically committed to executing strategy successfully and achieving performance targets. Enlisting such commitment typically requires use of an assortment of motivational techniques and rewards.

Indeed, *an effectively designed incentive and reward structure is the single most powerful tool management has for mobilizing employee commitment to successful strategy execution.* But incentives and rewards do more than just strengthen the resolve of company personnel to succeed—they also focus employees' attention on the accomplishment of specific strategy execution objectives. Not only do they spur the efforts of individuals to achieve those aims, but they also help coordinate the activities of individuals throughout the organization by aligning their personal motives with the goals of the organization. In this manner, reward systems serve as an indirect type of control mechanism that conserves on the more costly control mechanism of supervisory oversight.

To win employees' sustained, energetic commitment to the strategy execution process, management must be resourceful in designing and using motivational incentives—*both monetary and nonmonetary.* The more a manager understands what motivates subordinates and the more he or she relies on motivational incentives as a tool for achieving the targeted strategic and financial results, the greater will be employees' commitment to good day-in, day-out strategy execution and the achievement of performance targets.[20]

A properly designed incentive and reward structure is management's single most powerful tool for gaining employee commitment to successful strategy execution and excellent operating results.

Incentives and Motivational Practices That Facilitate Good Strategy Execution

Financial incentives generally head the list of motivating tools for gaining wholehearted employee commitment to good strategy execution and focusing attention on strategic priorities. Generous financial rewards always catch employees' attention and produce *high-powered incentives* for individuals to exert their best efforts. A company's package of monetary rewards typically includes some combination of base-pay increases, performance bonuses, profit-sharing plans, stock awards, company contributions to employee 401(k) or retirement plans, and piecework incentives (in the case of production workers). But most successful companies and managers also make extensive use of nonmonetary incentives. Some of the most important nonmonetary approaches companies can use to enhance employee motivation include the following[21]:

CORE CONCEPT

Financial rewards provide **high-powered incentives** when rewards are tied to specific outcome objectives.

- *Providing attractive perks and fringe benefits.* The various options include coverage of health insurance premiums, wellness programs, college tuition reimbursement, generous paid vacation time, onsite child care, onsite fitness centers and massage services, opportunities for getaways at company-owned recreational facilities, personal concierge services, subsidized cafeterias and free lunches, casual dress every day, personal travel services, paid sabbaticals, maternity and paternity leaves, paid leaves to care for ill family members, telecommuting, compressed workweeks (four 10-hour days instead of five 8-hour days), flextime (variable work schedules that accommodate individual needs), college scholarships for children, and relocation services.

- *Giving awards and public recognition to high performers and showcasing company successes.* Many companies hold award ceremonies to honor top-performing individuals, teams, and organizational units and to celebrate important company milestones and achievements. Others make a special point of recognizing the outstanding accomplishments of individuals, teams, and organizational units at informal company gatherings or in the company newsletter. Such actions foster a positive *esprit de corps* within the organization and may also act to spur healthy competition among units and teams within the company.

- *Relying on promotion from within whenever possible.* This practice helps bind workers to their employer, and employers to their workers. Moreover, it provides strong incentives for good performance. Promoting from within also helps ensure that people in positions of responsibility have knowledge specific to the business, technology, and operations they are managing.

- *Inviting and acting on ideas and suggestions from employees.* Many companies find that their best ideas for nuts-and-bolts operating improvements come from the suggestions of employees. Moreover, research indicates that giving decision-making power to down-the-line employees increases their motivation and satisfaction as well as their productivity. The use of self-managed teams has much the same effect.

- *Creating a work atmosphere in which there is genuine caring and mutual respect among workers and between management and employees.* A "family" work environment where people are on a first-name basis and there is strong camaraderie promotes teamwork and cross-unit collaboration.

- *Stating the strategic vision in inspirational terms that make employees feel they are a part of something worthwhile in a larger social sense.* There's strong motivating power associated with giving people a chance to be part of something exciting and personally satisfying. Jobs with a noble purpose tend to inspire employees to give their all. As described in Chapter 9, this not only increases productivity but reduces turnover and lowers costs for staff recruitment and training as well.

- *Sharing information with employees about financial performance, strategy, operational measures, market conditions, and competitors' actions.* Broad disclosure and prompt communication send the message that managers trust their workers and regard them as valued partners in the enterprise. Keeping employees in the dark denies them information useful to performing their jobs, prevents them from being intellectually engaged, saps their motivation, and detracts from performance.

- *Providing an appealing working environment.* An appealing workplace environment can have decidedly positive effects on employee morale and productivity. Providing a comfortable work environment, designed with ergonomics in mind, is particularly important when workers are expected to spend long hours at work. But some companies go beyond the mundane to design exceptionally attractive work settings. The workspaces and surrounding parklands of Apple's new multibillion dollar campus headquarters were designed to inspire Apple's people, foster innovative collaboration, while also benefiting the environment. Employees have access to a 100,000 square foot fitness center, two miles of walking and running paths, an orchard, meadow, and pond as well as community bicycles, electric golf carts, and commuter shuttles for getting around. Facebook and defense contractor Oshkosh Corporation also have dramatic headquarters projects underway.

For a specific example of the motivational tactics employed by one of the best companies to work for in America, see Illustration Capsule 11.2 on the supermarket chain Wegmans.

Striking the Right Balance between Rewards and Punishment

While most approaches to motivation, compensation, and people management accentuate the positive, companies also make it clear that lackadaisical or indifferent effort and subpar performance can result in negative consequences. At General Electric,

How Wegmans Rewards and Motivates its Employees

JHVEPhoto/Shutterstock

Companies use a variety of tools and strategies designed to motivate employees and engender superior strategy execution. In this respect, Wegmans Food Markets, Inc. serves as an exemplar. With approximately 49,000 employees spread across more than 100 stores across the Northeast and Mid-Atlantic, Wegmans stands out as an organization that delivers above average results in an industry known for its low margins, low wages, and challenging employee relationships. Guided by a philosophy of *employees first,* Wegmans employs an array of programs that enables the company to attract and retain the best people.

Since the creation of its broad benefits program for full-time employees in the 1950s, Wegmans has had a strong benefits philosophy. Today, flexible or compressed schedules are common, and policies extend to same-sex partners. Regarding financial compensation, wages are above average for the grocery retail industry, which also has an added benefit of keeping its workforce nonunionized.

In addition to the traditional elements of compensation and benefits, Wegmans invests considerably in the training and education of its employees. Known for its strength in employee development, upwards of $50 million annually is spent on employee learning. Since 1984, the company has awarded nearly $110 million in tuition assistance and over $50 million in scholarships.

Another crucial aspect of employee motivation is feeling heard. Employees see their ideas put into action through a series of programs designed to capture and implement their ideas. Wegmans deploys a series of programs, including open-door days, team huddles, focus groups, and two-way Q&As with senior management.

With the recognition that employees are critical to delivering a great customer experience, Wegmans directs a considerable amount of resources to its biggest asset, its people. Its suite of programs and benefits, along with a policy of filling at least half of its open opportunities internally, lead to one of the lowest turnover rates in its industry. They have also resulted in Wegmans placing among the top five firms on Fortune's list of *The 100 Best Companies to Work For* year after year.

Note: Developed with Sadé M. Lawrence.

Sources: Company website; Boyle, M., *The Wegmans Way,* January 24, 2005, http://archive.fortune.com/magazines/fortune/fortune_archive/2005/01/24/8234048/index.htm; "Great Place to Work," *Wegmans Food Markets, Inc.—Great Place to Work Reviews,* February 14, 2018, http://reviews.greatplacetowork.com/wegmans-food-markets-inc.

McKinsey & Company, several global public accounting firms, and other companies that look for and expect top-notch individual performance, there's an "up-or-out" policy—managers and professionals whose performance is not good enough to warrant promotion are first denied bonuses and stock awards and eventually weeded out. At most companies, senior executives and key personnel in underperforming units are pressured to raise performance to acceptable levels and keep it there or risk being replaced.

As a general rule, it is unwise to take off the pressure for good performance or play down the adverse consequences of shortfalls in performance. There is scant evidence that a no-pressure, no-adverse-consequences work environment leads to superior strategy execution or operating excellence. As the CEO of a major bank put it, "There's a deliberate policy here to create a level of anxiety. Winners usually play like they're one touchdown behind."[22] A number of companies deliberately give employees heavy work-loads and tight deadlines to test their mettle—personnel are pushed hard to achieve "stretch" objectives and are expected to put in long hours (nights and weekends if need be). High-performing organizations nearly always have a cadre of ambitious people who relish the opportunity to climb the ladder of success, love a challenge, thrive in a performance-oriented environment, and find some competition and pressure useful to satisfy their own drives for personal recognition, accomplishment, and self-satisfaction.

However, if an organization's motivational approaches and reward structure induce too much stress, internal competitiveness, job insecurity, and fear of unpleasant con-sequences, the impact on workforce morale and strategy execution can be counter-productive. Evidence shows that managerial initiatives to improve strategy execution should incorporate more positive than negative motivational elements because when cooperation is positively enlisted and rewarded, rather than coerced by orders and threats (implicit or explicit), people tend to respond with more enthusiasm, dedication, creativity, and initiative.[23]

Linking Rewards to Achieving the Right Outcomes

To create a strategy-supportive system of rewards and incentives, a company must reward people for accomplishing results, not for just dutifully performing assigned tasks. Showing up for work and performing assignments do not, by themselves, guaran-tee results. To make the work environment results-oriented, managers need to focus jobholders' attention and energy on what to *achieve* as opposed to what to *do*.[24] Employee productivity among employees at Best Buy's corporate headquarters rose by 35 percent after the company began to focus on the results of each employee's work rather than on employees' willingness to come to work early and stay late.

Ideally, every organizational unit, every manager, every team or work group, and every employee should be held accountable for achieving outcomes that con-tribute to good strategy execution and business performance. If the company's strategy is to be a low-cost leader, the incentive system must reward actions and achievements that result in lower costs. If the company has a differentiation strat-egy focused on delivering superior quality and service, the incentive system must reward such outcomes as Six Sigma defect rates, infrequent customer complaints, speedy order processing and delivery, and high levels of customer satisfaction. If a company's growth is predicated on a strategy of new product innovation, incentives should be tied to such metrics as the percentages of revenues and profits coming from newly introduced products.

> Incentives must be based on accomplishing results, not on dutifully performing assigned tasks.

Incentive compensation for top executives is typically tied to such financial mea-sures as revenue and earnings growth, stock price performance, return on investment, and creditworthiness or to strategic measures such as market share growth. However, incentives for department heads, teams, and individual workers tend to be tied to per-formance outcomes more closely related to their specific area of responsibility. For instance, in manufacturing, it makes sense to tie incentive compensation to such out-comes as unit manufacturing costs, on-time production and shipping, defect rates, the number and extent of work stoppages due to equipment breakdowns, and so on. In sales and marketing, incentives tend to be based on achieving dollar sales or unit vol-ume targets, market share, sales penetration of each target customer group, the fate of newly introduced products, the frequency of customer complaints, the number of new accounts acquired, and measures of customer satisfaction. Which performance measures to base incentive compensation on depends on the situation—the priority placed on various financial and strategic objectives, the requirements for strategic and competitive success, and the specific results needed to keep strategy execution on track.

Illustration Capsule 11.3 provides a vivid example of how one company has designed incentives linked directly to outcomes reflecting good execution.

> The first principle in designing an effective incentive compensation system is to tie rewards to performance outcomes directly linked to good strategy execution and the achievement of financial and strategic objectives.

Additional Guidelines for Designing Incentive Compensation Systems   It is not enough to link incentives to the right kinds of results—performance outcomes that signal that the company's strategy and its execution are on track. For a company's reward system to truly motivate organization members, inspire their best efforts, and sustain high levels of productivity, it is also important to observe the following additional guidelines in designing and administering the reward system:

- *Make the performance payoff a major, not minor, piece of the total compensation package.* Performance bonuses must be at least 10 to 12 percent of base salary to have much impact. Incentives that amount to 20 percent or more of total compensation are big attention-getters, likely to really drive individual or team efforts. Incentives amounting to less than five percent of total compensation have a comparatively weak motivational impact. Moreover, the payoff for high-performing individuals and teams must be meaningfully greater than the payoff for average performers, and the payoff for average performers meaningfully bigger than that for below-average performers.

- *Have incentives that extend to all managers and all workers, not just top management.* It is a gross miscalculation to expect that lower-level managers and employees will work their hardest to hit performance targets if only senior executives qualify for lucrative rewards.

- *Administer the reward system with scrupulous objectivity and fairness.* If performance standards are set unrealistically high or if individual and group performance evaluations are not accurate and well documented, dissatisfaction with the system will overcome any positive benefits.

- *Ensure that the performance targets set for each individual or team involve outcomes that the individual or team can personally affect.* The role of incentives is to enhance individual commitment and channel behavior in beneficial directions. This role is not well served when the performance measures by which company personnel are judged are outside their arena of influence.

- *Keep the time between achieving the performance target and receiving the reward as short as possible.* Nucor, a leading producer of steel products, has achieved high labor productivity by paying its workers weekly bonuses based on prior-week production levels. Annual bonus payouts work best for higher-level managers and for situations where the outcome target relates to overall company profitability.

- *Avoid rewarding effort rather than results.* While it is tempting to reward people who have tried hard, gone the extra mile, and yet fallen short of achieving performance targets because of circumstances beyond their control, it is ill advised to do so. The problem with making exceptions for unknowable, uncontrollable, or unforeseeable circumstances is that once "good excuses" start to creep into justifying rewards for subpar results, the door opens to all kinds of reasons why actual performance has failed to match targeted performance. A "no excuses" standard is more evenhanded, easier to administer, and more conducive to creating a results-oriented work climate.

Nucor Corporation: Tying Incentives Directly to Strategy Execution

The strategy at Nucor Corporation, the largest steel producers in the United States, is to be *the* low-cost producer of steel products. Because labor costs are a significant fraction of total cost in the steel business, successful implementation of Nucor's low-cost leadership strategy entails achieving lower labor costs per ton of steel than competitors' costs. Nucor management uses an incentive system to promote high worker productivity and drive labor costs per ton below those of rivals. Each plant's workforce is organized into production teams (each assigned to perform particular functions), and weekly production targets are established for each team. Base-pay scales are set at levels comparable to wages for similar manufacturing jobs in the local areas where Nucor has plants, but workers can earn a one percent bonus for each one percent that their output exceeds target levels. If a production team exceeds its weekly production target by 10 percent, team members receive a 10 percent bonus in their next paycheck; if a team exceeds its quota by 20 percent, team members earn a 20 percent bonus. Bonuses, paid every two weeks, are based on the prior two weeks' actual production levels measured against the targets.

Nucor's piece-rate incentive plan has produced impressive results. The production teams put forth exceptional effort; it is not uncommon for most teams to beat their weekly production targets by 20 to 50 percent. When added to employees' base pay, the bonuses earned by Nucor workers make Nucor's workforce among the highest paid in the U.S. steel industry. From a management perspective, the incentive system has resulted in Nucor having labor productivity levels 10 to 20 percent above the average of the unionized workforces at several of its largest rivals, which in turn has given Nucor a significant labor cost advantage over most rivals.

Westend61/Getty Images

After years of record-setting profits, Nucor struggled in the last major economic downturn, along with the manufacturers and builders who buy its steel. But while bonuses dwindled, Nucor showed remarkable loyalty to its production workers, avoiding layoffs by having employees get ahead on maintenance, perform work formerly done by contractors, and search for cost savings. Morale at the company remained high, and Nucor's CEO at the time, Daniel DiMicco, was inducted into *Industry-Week* magazine's Manufacturing Hall of Fame because of his no-layoff policies. As industry growth resumed, Nucor was in the position of having a well-trained workforce, more committed than ever to achieving the kind of productivity for which Nucor is justifiably famous. DiMicco had good reason to expect Nucor to be "first out of the box" following the crisis, and although he has since stepped aside, the company's culture of making its employees think like owners has not changed.

Sources: Company website (accessed March 2012); N. Byrnes, "Pain, but No Layoffs at Nucor," *BusinessWeek*, March 26, 2009; J. McGregor, "Nucor's CEO Is Stepping Aside, but Its Culture Likely Won't," *The Washington Post* Online, November 20, 2012 (accessed April 3, 2014).

For an organization's incentive system to work well, the details of the reward structure must be communicated and explained. Everybody needs to understand how his or her incentive compensation is calculated and how individual and group performance targets contribute to organizational performance targets. The pressure to achieve the targeted financial and strategic performance objectives and continuously improve on strategy execution should be unrelenting. People at all levels must be held accountable for carrying out their assigned parts of the strategic

> The unwavering standard for judging whether individuals, teams, and organizational units have done a good job must be whether they meet or beat performance targets that reflect good strategy execution.

plan, and they must understand that their rewards are based on the caliber of results achieved. But with the pressure to perform should come meaningful rewards. Without an attractive payoff, the system breaks down, and managers are left with the less workable options of issuing orders, trying to enforce compliance, and depending on the goodwill of employees.

KEY POINTS

1. Implementing a new or different strategy calls for managers to identify the resource requirements of each new strategic initiative and then consider whether the current pattern of resource allocation and the budgets of the various subunits are suitable.

2. Company policies and procedures facilitate strategy execution when they are designed to fit the strategy and its objectives. Anytime a company alters its strategy, managers should review existing policies and operating procedures and replace those that are out of sync. Well-conceived policies and procedures aid the task of strategy execution by (1) providing top-down guidance to company personnel regarding how things need to be done and what the limits are on independent actions; (2) enforcing consistency in the performance of strategy-critical activities, thereby improving the quality of the strategy execution effort and coordinating the efforts of company personnel, however widely dispersed; and (3) promoting the creation of a work climate conducive to good strategy execution.

3. Competent strategy execution entails visible unyielding managerial commitment to continuous improvement. Business process management tools, such as reengineering, total quality management (TQM), and Six Sigma programs are important process management tools for promoting better strategy execution.

4. Company strategies can't be implemented or executed well without well-conceived internal systems to support daily operations. Real-time information systems and control systems further aid the cause of good strategy execution. In some cases, state-of-the-art operating and information systems strengthen a company's strategy execution capabilities enough to provide a competitive edge over rivals.

5. Strategy-supportive motivational practices and reward systems are powerful management tools for gaining employee commitment and focusing their attention on the strategy execution goals. The key to creating a reward system that promotes good strategy execution is to make measures of good business performance and good strategy execution the *dominating basis* for designing incentives, evaluating individual and group efforts, and handing out rewards. While financial rewards provide high-powered incentives, nonmonetary incentives are also important. For an incentive compensation system to work well, (1) the performance payoff should be a major percentage of the compensation package, (2) the use of incentives should extend to all managers and workers, (3) the system should be administered with objectivity and fairness, (4) each individual's performance targets should involve outcomes the person can personally affect, (5) rewards should promptly follow the achievement of performance targets, and (6) rewards should be given for results and not just effort.

ASSURANCE OF LEARNING EXERCISES

1. Implementing a new or different strategy calls for new resource allocations. Using your university's library resources search for recent articles that discuss how a company has revised its pattern of resource allocation and divisional budgets to support new strategic initiatives.

   LO 11-1

2. Netflix avoids the use of formal policies and procedures to better empower its employees to maximize innovation and productivity. The company goes to great lengths to hire, reward, and tolerate only what it considers mature, "A" player employees. How does the company's selection process affect its ability to operate without formal travel and expense policies, a fixed number of vacation days for employees, or a formal employee performance evaluation system?

   LO 11-2

3. Illustration Capsule 11.1 discusses Charleston Area Medical Center's use of Six Sigma practices. List three tangible benefits provided by the program. Explain why a commitment to quality control is particularly important in the hospital industry. How can the use of a Six Sigma program help medical providers survive and thrive in the current industry climate?

   connect
   LO 11-3

4. Read some of the recent Six Sigma articles posted at www.isixsigma.com. Prepare a one-page report to your instructor detailing how Six Sigma is being used in two companies and what benefits the companies are reaping as a result. Further, discuss two to three criticisms of, or potential difficulties with, Six Sigma implementation.

   LO 11-3

5. Company strategies can't be executed well without a number of support systems to carry on business operations. Using your university's library resources, search for recent articles that discuss how a company has used real-time information systems and control systems to aid the cause of good strategy execution.

   LO 11-4

6. Illustration Capsule 11.2 provides a description of the motivational practices employed by Wegmans Food Markets, a supermarket chain that is routinely listed as among the top five companies to work for in the United States. Discuss how rewards and practices at Wegman's aid in the company's strategy execution efforts.

   connect
   LO 11-5

EXERCISES FOR SIMULATION PARTICIPANTS

connect

1. What are the ways that resource allocation contributes to good strategy execution and improved company performance.

   LO 11-1

2. What actions, if any, is your company taking to pursue continuous improvement in how it performs certain value chain activities?

   LO 11-2, LO 11-3, LO 11-4

3. Are benchmarking data available in the simulation exercise in which you are participating? If so, do you and your co-managers regularly study the benchmarking data to see how well your company is doing? Do you consider the benchmarking information provided to be valuable? Why or why not? Cite three recent instances in which your examination of the benchmarking statistics has caused you and your co-managers to take corrective actions to improve operations and boost company performance.

   LO 11-3

4. What hard evidence can you cite that indicates your company's management team is doing a *better* or *worse* job of achieving operating excellence and executing strategy than are the management teams at rival companies?

   LO 11-3

LO 11-2, LO 11-3, **5.** Are you and your co-managers consciously trying to achieve operating excellence?
LO 11-4   Explain how you are doing this and how you will track the progress you are making.

LO 11-5   **6.** What are ways that incentive compensation can affect productivity gains and lower
        labor cost per unit?

ENDNOTES

[1] M. Hammer and J. Champy, *Reengineering the Corporation: A Manifesto for Business Revolution* (New York: HarperCollins, 1993).

[2] James Brian Quinn, *Intelligent Enterprise* (New York: Free Press, 1992); Ann Majchrzak and Qianwei Wang, "Breaking the Functional Mind-Set in Process Organizations," *Harvard Business Review* 74, no. 5 (September–October 1996), pp. 93–99; Stephen L. Walston, Lawton R. Burns, and John R. Kimberly, "Does Reengineering Really Work? An Examination of the Context and Outcomes of Hospital Reengineering Initiatives," *Health Services Research* 34, no. 6 (February 2000), pp. 1363–1388; Alessio Ascari, Melinda Rock, and Soumitra Dutta, "Reengineering and Organizational Change: Lessons from a Comparative Analysis of Company Experiences," *European Management Journal* 13, no. 1 (March 1995), pp. 1–13; Ronald J. Burke, "Process Reengineering: Who Embraces It and Why?" *The TQM Magazine* 16, no. 2 (2004), pp. 114–119.

[3] www.answers.com (accessed July 8, 2009); "Reengineering: Beyond the Buzzword," *Businessweek,* May 24, 1993, www.businessweek.com (accessed July 8, 2009).

[4] M. Walton, *The Deming Management Method* (New York: Pedigree, 1986); J. Juran, *Juran on Quality by Design* (New York: Free Press, 1992); Philip Crosby, *Quality Is Free: The Act of Making Quality Certain* (New York: McGraw-Hill, 1979); S. George, *The Baldrige Quality System* (New York: Wiley, 1992); Mark J. Zbaracki, "The Rhetoric and Reality of Total Quality Management," *Administrative Science Quarterly* 43, no. 3 (September 1998), pp. 602–636.

[5] Robert T. Amsden, Thomas W. Ferratt, and Davida M. Amsden, "TQM: Core Paradigm Changes," *Business Horizons* 39, no. 6 (November–December 1996), pp. 6–14.

[6] Peter S. Pande and Larry Holpp, *What Is Six Sigma?* (New York: McGraw-Hill, 2002); Jiju Antony, "Some Pros and Cons of Six Sigma: An Academic Perspective," *TQM Magazine* 16, no. 4 (2004), pp. 303–306; Peter S. Pande, Robert P. Neuman, and Roland R. Cavanagh, *The Six Sigma Way: How GE, Motorola and Other Top*

Companies Are Honing Their Performance (New York: McGraw-Hill, 2000); Joseph Gordon and M. Joseph Gordon, Jr., *Six Sigma Quality for Business and Manufacture* (New York: Elsevier, 2002); Godecke Wessel and Peter Burcher, "Six Sigma for Small and Medium-Sized Enterprises," *TQM Magazine* 16, no. 4 (2004), pp. 264–272.

[7] www.isixsigma.com (accessed November 4, 2002); www.villanovau.com/certificate-programs/six-sigma-training.aspx (accessed February 16, 2012).

[8] Kennedy Smith, "Six Sigma for the Service Sector," *Quality Digest Magazine,* May 2003; www.qualitydigest.com (accessed September 28, 2003).

[9] www.isixsigma.com/implementation/-financial-analysis/six-sigma-costs-and-savings/ (accessed February 23, 2012).

[10] Pande, Neuman, and Cavanagh, *The Six Sigma Way,* pp. 5–6.

[11] "A Dark Art No More," *The Economist* 385, no. 8550 (October 13, 2007), p. 10; Brian Hindo, "At 3M, a Struggle between Efficiency and Creativity," *Businessweek,* June 11, 2007, pp. 8–16.

[12] Charles A. O'Reilly and Michael L. Tushman, "The Ambidextrous Organization," *Harvard Business Review* 82, no. 4 (April 2004), pp. 74–81.

[13] Terry Nels Lee, Stanley E. Fawcett, and Jason Briscoe, "Benchmarking the Challenge to Quality Program Implementation," *Benchmarking: An International Journal* 9, no. 4 (2002), pp. 374–387.

[14] Milan Ambroé, "Total Quality System as a Product of the Empowered Corporate Culture," *TQM Magazine* 16, no. 2 (2004), pp. 93–104; Nick A. Dayton, "The Demise of Total Quality Management," *TQM Magazine* 15, no. 6 (2003), pp. 391–396.

[15] Judy D. Olian and Sara L. Rynes, "Making Total Quality Work: Aligning Organizational Processes, Performance Measures, and Stakeholders," *Human Resource Management* 30, no. 3 (Fall 1991), pp. 310–311; Paul S. Goodman and Eric D. Darr, "Exchanging Best Practices Information through Computer-Aided Systems," *Academy of Management Executive* 10, no. 2 (May 1996), p. 7.

[16] Thomas C. Powell, "Total Quality Management as Competitive Advantage," *Strategic Management Journal* 16 (1995), pp. 15–37; Richard M. Hodgetts, "Quality Lessons from America's Baldrige Winners," *Business Horizons* 37, no. 4 (July–August 1994), pp. 74–79; Richard Reed, David J. Lemak, and Joseph C. Montgomery, "Beyond Process: TQM Content and Firm Performance," *Academy of Management Review* 21, no. 1 (January 1996), pp. 173–202.

[17] Fred Vogelstein, "Winning the Amazon Way," *Fortune* 147, no. 10 (May 26, 2003), pp. 60–69.

[18] Robert Simons, "Control in an Age of Empowerment," *Harvard Business Review* 73 (March–April 1995), pp. 80–88.

[19] David C. Band and Gerald Scanlan, "Strategic Control through Core Competencies," *Long Range Planning* 28, no. 2 (April 1995), pp. 102–114.

[20] Stanley E. Fawcett, Gary K. Rhoads, and Phillip Burnah, "People as the Bridge to Competitiveness: Benchmarking the 'ABCs' of an Empowered Workforce," *Benchmarking: An International Journal* 11, no. 4 (2004), pp. 346–360.

[21] Jeffrey Pfeffer and John F. Veiga, "Putting People First for Organizational Success," *Academy of Management Executive* 13, no. 2 (May 1999), pp. 37–45; Linda K. Stroh and Paula M. Caliguiri, "Increasing Global Competitiveness through Effective People Management," *Journal of World Business* 33, no. 1 (Spring 1998), pp. 1–16; articles in *Fortune* on the 100 best companies to work for (various issues).

[22] As quoted in John P. Kotter and James L. Heskett, *Corporate Culture and Performance* (New York: Free Press, 1992), p. 91.

[23] Clayton M. Christensen, Matt Marx, and Howard Stevenson, "The Tools of Cooperation and Change," *Harvard Business Review* 84, no. 10 (October 2006), pp. 73–80.

[24] Steven Kerr, "On the Folly of Rewarding A While Hoping for B," *Academy of Management Executive* 9, no. 1 (February 1995), pp. 7–14; Doran Twer, "Linking Pay to Business Objectives," *Journal of Business Strategy* 15, no. 4 (July–August 1994), pp. 15–18.

chapter 12

Corporate Culture and Leadership

Keys to Good Strategy Execution

Learning Objectives

After reading this chapter, you should be able to:

LO 12-1 Understand the key features of a company's corporate culture and the role of a company's core values and ethical standards in building corporate culture.

LO 12-2 Explain how and why a company's culture can aid the drive for proficient strategy execution.

LO 12-3 Identify the kinds of actions management can take to change a problem corporate culture.

LO 12-4 Recognize what constitutes effective managerial leadership in achieving superior strategy execution.

Fanatic Studio/Alamy Stock Photo

I came to see, in my time at IBM, that culture isn't just one aspect of the game, it is the game.

    Louis Gerstner—*Former Chairman and CEO of IBM*

As we look ahead into the next century, leaders will be those who empower others.

    Bill Gates—*Cofounder and former CEO and chair of Microsoft*

A genuine leader is not a searcher for consensus but a molder of consensus.

    Martin Luther King, Jr.—*Civil Rights Leader*

In the previous two chapters, we examined eight of the managerial tasks that drive good strategy execution: staffing the organization, acquiring the needed resources and capabilities, designing the organizational structure, allocating resources, establishing policies and procedures, employing process management tools, installing operating systems, and providing the right incentives. In this chapter, we explore the two remaining managerial tasks that contribute to good strategy execution: creating a supportive corporate culture and leading the strategy execution process.

INSTILLING A CORPORATE CULTURE CONDUCIVE TO GOOD STRATEGY EXECUTION

Corporate culture refers to the shared values, ingrained attitudes, core beliefs, and company traditions that determine norms of behavior, accepted work practices, and styles of operating.

● **LO 12-1**

Understand the key features of a company's corporate culture and the role of a company's core values and ethical standards in building corporate culture.

Every company has its own unique **corporate culture**—the shared values, ingrained attitudes, and company traditions that determine norms of behavior, accepted work practices, and styles of operating.[1] The character of a company's culture is a product of the core values and beliefs that executives espouse, the standards of what is ethically acceptable and what is not, the "chemistry" and the "personality" that permeate the work environment, the company's traditions, and the stories that get told over and over to illustrate and reinforce the company's values, business practices, and traditions. In a very real sense, the culture is the company's automatic, self-replicating "operating system" that defines "how we do things around here."[2] It can be thought of as the company's psyche or *organizational DNA*.[3] A company's culture is important because it influences the organization's actions and approaches to conducting business. As such, it plays an important role in strategy execution and may have an appreciable effect on business performance as well.

Corporate cultures vary widely. For instance, the bedrock of Walmart's culture is zealous pursuit of low costs and frugal operating practices, a strong work ethic, ritualistic headquarters meetings to exchange ideas and review problems, and company executives' commitment to visiting stores, listening to customers, and soliciting suggestions from employees. The culture at Apple is customer-centered, secretive, and highly protective of company-developed technology. Apple employees share a common goal of making the best products for the consumer; the aim is to make the customer feel delight, surprise, and connection to each Apple device. The company expects creative thinking and inspired solutions from everyone—as the company puts it, "We're perfectionists. Idealists. Inventors. Forever tinkering with products and processes, always on the lookout for better." According to a former employee, "Apple is one of those companies where people work on an almost religious level of commitment." To spur innovation and creativity, the company fosters extensive collaboration and cross-pollination among different work groups. But it does so in a manner that demands secrecy—employees are expected not to reveal anything relevant about what new project they are working on, not to employees outside their immediate work group and especially not to family members or other outsiders; it is common for different employees working on the same project to be assigned different project code names. The different pieces of a new product launch often come together like a puzzle at the last minute.[4] W. L. Gore & Associates, best known for GORE-TEX, credits its unique culture for allowing the company to pursue multiple end-market applications simultaneously, enabling rapid growth from a niche business into a diversified multinational company. The company's culture is team-based and designed to foster personal initiative, with no traditional organizational charts, no chains of command, no predetermined channels of communication. The culture encourages multidiscipline teams to organize around opportunities, and in the process, leaders emerge. At Nordstrom, the corporate culture is centered on delivering exceptional service to customers, where the company's motto is "Respond to unreasonable customer requests," and each out-of-the-ordinary request is seen as an opportunity for a "heroic" act by an employee that can further the company's reputation for unparalleled customer service. Nordstrom makes a point of promoting employees noted for their heroic acts and dedication to outstanding service.

Identifying the Key Features of a Company's Corporate Culture

A company's corporate culture is mirrored in the character or "personality" of its work environment—the features that describe how the company goes about its business and the workplace behaviors that are held in high esteem. Some of these features are readily apparent, and others operate quite subtly. The chief things to look for include:

- The values, business principles, and ethical standards that management preaches and *practices*—these are the key to a company's culture, but actions speak much louder than words here.

- The company's approach to people management and the official policies, procedures, and operating practices that provide guidelines for the behavior of company personnel.

- The atmosphere and spirit that pervades the work climate—whether the workplace is competitive or cooperative, innovative or resistant to change, collegial or politicized, all business or fun-loving, and the like.

- How managers and employees interact and relate to one another—whether there is heavy or weak reliance on collaboration and teamwork, whether communications among employees are free-flowing or restrictive and infrequent, whether employees are empowered to exercise their initiative or whether actions are directed mostly by higher authority, whether co-workers spend little or lots of time together outside the workplace, and so on.

- The strength of peer pressure to do things in particular ways and conform to expected norms.

- The actions and behaviors that management explicitly encourages and rewards and those that are frowned upon.

- The company's revered traditions and oft-repeated stories about "heroic acts" and "how we do things around here."

- The manner in which the company deals with external stakeholders—whether it treats suppliers as business partners or prefers hard-nosed, arm's-length business arrangements and whether its commitment to corporate citizenship and environmental sustainability is strong and genuine.

The values, beliefs, and practices that undergird a company's culture can come from anywhere in the organizational hierarchy. Typically, key elements of the culture originate with a founder or certain strong leaders who articulated them as a set of business principles, company policies, operating approaches, and ways of dealing with employees, customers, vendors, shareholders, and local communities where the company has operations. They also stem from exemplary actions on the part of company personnel and evolving consensus about "how we ought to do things around here."[5] Over time, these cultural underpinnings take root, come to be accepted by company managers and employees alike, and become ingrained in the way the company conducts its business.

> A company's culture is grounded in and shaped by its core values and ethical standards.

The Role of Core Values and Ethics   The foundation of a company's corporate culture nearly always resides in its dedication to certain core values and the bar it sets for ethical behavior. The culture-shaping significance of core values and ethical behaviors accounts for why so many companies have developed a formal value statement and a code of ethics. Many executives want the work climate at their companies to mirror certain values and ethical standards, partly because of personal

> A company's value statement and code of ethics communicate expectations of how employees should conduct themselves in the workplace.

FIGURE 12.1   The Two Culture-Building Roles of a Company's Core Values and Ethical Standards

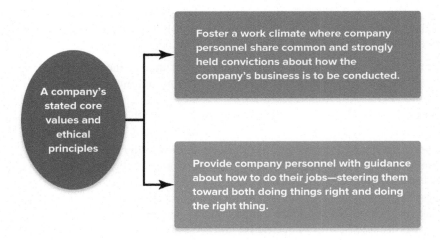

A company's stated core values and ethical principles

Foster a work climate where company personnel share common and strongly held convictions about how the company's business is to be conducted.

Provide company personnel with guidance about how to do their jobs—steering them toward both doing things right and doing the right thing.

convictions but mainly because they are convinced that adherence to such principles will promote better strategy execution, make the company a better performer, and positively impact its reputation.[6] Not incidentally, strongly ingrained values and ethical standards reduce the likelihood of lapses in ethical behavior that mar a company's public image and put its financial performance and market standing at risk.

As depicted in Figure 12.1, a company's stated core values and ethical principles have two roles in the culture-building process. First, they can foster a work climate in which company personnel share strongly held convictions about how the company's business is to be conducted. Second, they provide company personnel with guidance about the manner in which they are to do their jobs—which behaviors and ways of doing things are approved (and expected) and which are out-of-bounds. These value-based and ethics-based cultural norms serve as yardsticks for gauging the appropriateness of particular actions, decisions, and behaviors, thus helping steer company personnel toward both doing things right and doing the right thing.

Embedding Behavioral Norms in the Organization and Perpetuating the Culture
Once values and ethical standards have been formally adopted, they must be institutionalized in the company's policies and practices and embedded in the conduct of company personnel. This can be advanced in a number of different ways.[7] Tradition-steeped companies with a rich folklore rely heavily on word-of-mouth indoctrination and the power of tradition to instill values and enforce ethical conduct. But most companies employ a variety of techniques, drawing on some or all of the following:

1. Screening applicants and hiring those who will mesh well with the culture.
2. Incorporating discussions of the company's culture and behavioral norms into orientation programs for new employees and training courses for managers and employees.
3. Having senior executives frequently reiterate the importance and role of company values and ethical principles at company events and in internal communications to employees.

4. Expecting managers at all levels to be cultural role models and exhibit the advocated cultural norms in their own behavior.

5. Making the display of cultural norms a factor in evaluating each person's job performance, granting compensation increases, and offering promotions.

6. Stressing that line managers all the way down to first-level supervisors give ongoing attention to explaining the desired cultural traits and behaviors in their areas and clarifying why they are important.

7. Encouraging company personnel to exert strong peer pressure on co-workers to conform to expected cultural norms.

8. Holding periodic ceremonies to honor people who excel in displaying the company values and ethical principles.

To deeply ingrain the stated core values and high ethical standards, companies must turn them into *strictly enforced cultural norms.* They must make it unequivocally clear that living up to the company's values and ethical standards has to be "a way of life" at the company and that there will be little toleration for errant behavior.

The Role of Stories   Frequently, a significant part of a company's culture is captured in the stories that get told over and over again to illustrate to newcomers the importance of certain values and the depth of commitment that various company personnel have displayed. One of the folktales at Zappos, known for its outstanding customer service, is about a customer who ordered shoes for her ill mother from Zappos, hoping the shoes would remedy her mother's foot pain and numbness. When the shoes didn't work, the mother called the company to ask how to return them and explain why she was returning them. Two days later, she received a large bouquet of flowers from the company, along with well wishes and a customer upgrade giving her free expedited service on all future orders. Specialty food market Trader Joe's is similarly known for its culture of going beyond the call of duty for its customers. When a World War II veteran was snowed in without any food for meals, his daughter called several supermarkets to see if they offered grocery delivery. Although Trader Joe's technically doesn't offer delivery, it graciously helped the veteran, even recommending items for his low-sodium diet. When the store delivered the groceries, the veteran wasn't charged for either the groceries or the delivery. Stories of employees at Ritz Carlton going the extra mile for customers both showcase and reinforce its customer-centric culture. Recently, a family arrived at a Ritz-Carlton only to find that the specialized eggs and milk they had brought along for their son had spoiled. (The child suffered from food allergies.) When the products could not be found locally, the hotel's staff had the products flown in from Singapore, approximately 1,050 miles away!

Forces That Cause a Company's Culture to Evolve   Despite the role of time-honored stories and long-standing traditions in perpetuating a company's culture, cultures are far from static—just like strategy and organizational structure, they evolve. New challenges in the marketplace, revolutionary technologies, and shifting internal conditions—especially an internal crisis, a change in company direction, or top-executive turnover—tend to breed new ways of doing things and, in turn, drive cultural evolution. An incoming CEO who decides to shake up the existing business and take it in new directions often triggers a cultural shift, perhaps one of major proportions. Likewise, diversification into new businesses, expansion into foreign countries, rapid growth that brings an influx of new employees, and the merger with or acquisition of another company can all precipitate significant cultural change.

The Presence of Company Subcultures   Although it is common to speak about corporate culture in the singular, it is not unusual for companies to have multiple cultures (or subcultures). Values, beliefs, and practices within a company sometimes vary significantly by department, geographic location, division, or business unit. Subcultures can exist because a company has recently acquired other companies. Global and multinational companies tend to be at least partly multicultural because cross-country organization units have different operating histories and work climates, as well as members who speak different languages, have grown up under different social customs and traditions, and have different sets of values and beliefs. The problem with subcultures is that they can clash, or at least not mesh well, particularly if they embrace conflicting business philosophies or operating approaches, if key executives employ different approaches to people management, or if important differences between a company's culture and those of recently acquired companies have not yet been ironed out. On a number of occasions, companies have decided to pass on acquiring particular companies because of culture conflicts they believed would be hard to resolve.

Nonetheless, the existence of subcultures does not preclude important areas of commonality and compatibility. Company managements are quite alert to the importance of cultural compatibility in making acquisitions and the need to integrate the cultures of newly acquired companies. Indeed, cultural due diligence is often as important as financial due diligence in deciding whether to go forward on an acquisition or merger. Also, in today's globalizing world, multinational companies are learning how to make strategy-critical cultural traits travel across country boundaries and create a workably uniform culture worldwide. AES, a sustainable energy company with more than 10,000 employees and operations on four continents, has found that people in most countries readily embrace the five core values that underlie its culture—putting safety first, acting with integrity, remaining nimble, having fun through work, and striving for excellence. Moreover, AES tries to define and practice its cultural values the same way in all of its locations while still being sensitive to differences that exist among various peoples and groups around the world. Top managers at AES have expressed the view that people across the globe are more similar than different and that the company's culture is as meaningful in Brazil, Vietnam, or Kazakhstan as in the United States.

Strong versus Weak Cultures

Company cultures vary widely in strength and influence. Some are strongly embedded and have a big influence on a company's operating practices and the behavior of company personnel. Others are weakly ingrained and have little effect on behaviors and how company activities are conducted.

Strong-Culture Companies   The hallmark of a **strong-culture company** is the dominating presence of certain deeply rooted values, business principles, and behavioral norms that "regulate" the conduct of company personnel and determine the climate of the workplace.[8] In strong-culture companies, senior managers make a point of explaining and reiterating why these values, principles, norms, and operating approaches need to govern how the company conducts its business and how they ultimately lead to better business performance. Furthermore, they make a conscious effort to display these values, principles, and behavioral norms in their own actions—*they walk the talk.* An unequivocal expectation that company personnel will act and behave in accordance with the adopted values and ways of doing business leads to two important outcomes: (1) Over time, the professed values come to be widely shared by rank-and-file employees—people who dislike the culture tend to leave—and (2) individuals encounter strong peer pressure from co-workers to observe the culturally approved norms and behaviors. Hence, a strongly implanted corporate culture ends up having a powerful influence on behavior because so many company personnel are accepting of the company's culturally approved traditions and because this acceptance is reinforced by both management expectations and co-worker peer pressure to conform to cultural norms.

Strong cultures emerge only after a period of deliberate and rather intensive culture building that generally takes years (sometimes decades). Two factors contribute to the development of strong cultures: (1) a founder or strong leader who established core values, principles, and practices that are viewed as having contributed to the success of the company; and (2) a sincere, long-standing company commitment to operating the business according to these established traditions and values. Continuity of leadership, low workforce turnover, geographic concentration, and considerable organizational success all contribute to the emergence and sustainability of a strong culture.[9]

In strong-culture companies, values and behavioral norms are so ingrained that they can endure leadership changes at the top—although their strength can erode over time if new CEOs cease to nurture them or move aggressively to institute cultural adjustments. The cultural norms in a strong-culture company typically do not change much as strategy evolves, either because the culture constrains the choice of new strategies or because the dominant traits of the culture are somewhat strategy-neutral and compatible with evolving versions of the company's strategy. As a consequence, *strongly implanted cultures provide a huge assist in executing strategy* because company managers can use the traditions, beliefs, values, common bonds, or behavioral norms as levers to mobilize commitment to executing the chosen strategy.

Weak-Culture Companies   In direct contrast to strong-culture companies, weak-culture companies lack widely shared and strongly held values, principles, and behavioral norms. As a result, they also lack cultural mechanisms for aligning, constraining, and regulating the actions, decisions, and behaviors of company personnel. In the absence of any long-standing top management commitment to particular values, beliefs, operating practices, and behavioral norms, individuals encounter little pressure to do things in particular ways. Such a dearth of companywide cultural influences and revered traditions produces a work climate where there is no strong employee allegiance to what the company stands for or to operating the business in well-defined ways. While individual employees may well have some bonds of identification with and loyalty toward their department, their colleagues, their union, or their immediate boss, there's neither passion about the company nor emotional commitment to what it is trying to accomplish—a condition that often results in many employees' viewing their company as just a place to work and their job as just a way to make a living.

As a consequence, *weak cultures provide little or no assistance in executing strategy* because there are no traditions, beliefs, values, common bonds, or behavioral norms that management can use as levers to mobilize commitment to executing the chosen strategy. Without a work climate that channels organizational energy in the direction of good strategy execution, managers are left with the options of either using compensation incentives and other motivational devices to mobilize employee commitment, supervising and monitoring employee actions more closely, or trying to establish cultural roots that will in time start to nurture the strategy execution process.

Why Corporate Cultures Matter to the Strategy Execution Process

Even if a company has a strong culture, the culture and work climate may or may not be compatible with what is needed for effective implementation of the chosen strategy. When a company's present culture promotes attitudes, behaviors, and ways of doing things that are *in sync with the chosen strategy and conducive to first-rate strategy execution,* the culture functions as a valuable ally in the strategy execution process. For example, a corporate culture characterized by frugality and thrift prompts employee actions to identify cost-saving opportunities—the very behavior needed for successful execution of a low-cost leadership strategy. A culture that celebrates taking initiative, exhibiting creativity, taking risks, and embracing change is conducive to successful execution of product innovation and technological leadership strategies.[10]

A culture that is grounded in actions, behaviors, and work practices that are conducive to good strategy implementation supports the strategy execution effort in three ways:

1. *A culture that is well matched to the chosen strategy and the requirements of the strategy execution effort focuses the attention of employees on what is most important to this effort.* Moreover, it directs their behavior and serves as a guide to their decision making. In this manner, it can align the efforts and decisions of employees throughout the firm and minimize the need for direct supervision.

2. *Culture-induced peer pressure further induces company personnel to do things in a manner that aids the cause of good strategy execution.* The stronger the culture (the more widely shared and deeply held the values), the more effective peer pressure is in shaping and supporting the strategy execution effort. Research has shown that strong group norms can shape employee behavior even more powerfully than can financial incentives.

3. *A company culture that is consistent with the requirements for good strategy execution can energize employees, deepen their commitment to execute the strategy flawlessly, and enhance worker productivity in the process.* When a company's culture is grounded in many of the needed strategy-executing behaviors, employees feel genuinely better about their jobs, the company they work for, and the merits of what the company is trying to accomplish. Greater employee buy-in for what the company is trying to accomplish boosts motivation and marshals organizational energy behind the drive for good strategy execution. An energized workforce enhances the chances of achieving execution-critical performance targets and good strategy execution.

In sharp contrast, when a culture is in conflict with the chosen strategy or what is required to execute the company's strategy well, the culture becomes a stumbling block.[11] Some of the very behaviors needed to execute the strategy successfully run contrary to the attitudes, behaviors, and operating practices embedded in the prevailing culture. Such a clash poses a real dilemma for company personnel. Should they be loyal to the culture and company traditions (to which they are likely to be emotionally attached) and thus resist or be indifferent to actions that will promote better strategy execution—a choice that will certainly weaken the drive for good strategy execution? Alternatively, should they go along with management's strategy execution effort and engage in actions that run counter to the culture—a choice that will likely impair morale and lead to a less-than-enthusiastic commitment to good strategy execution? Neither choice leads to desirable outcomes. Culture-bred resistance to the actions and behaviors needed for good strategy execution, particularly if strong and widespread, poses a formidable hurdle that must be cleared for a strategy's execution to be successful.

The consequences of having—or not having—an execution-supportive corporate culture says something important about the task of managing the strategy execution process: *Closely aligning corporate culture with the requirements for proficient strategy execution merits the full attention of senior executives.* The culture-building objective is to create a work climate and style of operating that mobilize the energy of company personnel squarely behind efforts to execute strategy competently. The more deeply management can embed execution-supportive ways of doing things, the more management can rely on the culture to automatically steer company personnel toward behaviors and work practices that aid good strategy execution and veer from doing things that impede it. Moreover, culturally astute managers understand that nourishing the right cultural environment not only adds power to their push for proficient strategy execution but also promotes strong employee identification with, and commitment to, the company's vision, performance targets, and strategy.

> It is in management's best interest to dedicate considerable effort to establishing a corporate culture that encourages behaviors and work practices conducive to good strategy execution.

Healthy Cultures That Aid Good Strategy Execution

A strong culture, provided it fits the chosen strategy and embraces execution-supportive attitudes, behaviors, and work practices, is definitely a healthy culture. Two other types of cultures exist that tend to be healthy and largely supportive of good strategy execution: high-performance cultures and adaptive cultures.

High-Performance Cultures   Some companies have so-called high-performance cultures where the standout traits are a "can-do" spirit, pride in doing things right, no-excuses accountability, and a pervasive results-oriented work climate in which people go all out to meet or beat stretch objectives.[12] In high-performance cultures, there's a strong sense of involvement on the part of company personnel and emphasis on individual initiative and effort. Performance expectations are clearly delineated for the company as a whole, for each organizational unit, and for each individual. Issues and problems are promptly addressed; there's a razor-sharp focus on what needs to be done. The clear and unyielding expectation is that all company personnel, from senior executives to frontline employees, will display high-performance behaviors and a passion for making the company successful. Such a culture—permeated by a spirit of achievement and constructive pressure to achieve good results—is a valuable contributor to good strategy execution and operating excellence.[13]

Epic Systems, a company well-known by healthcare providers for the excellence of their record-keeping software, attributes much of its success to their strong, high-performance culture. By emphasizing the importance of the company's "Ten Commandments" and guiding principles, Epic has created a work climate in which employees have an overarching standard that helps guide and coordinate their actions. Epic fosters this high-performance culture from the get-go. They target top tier universities to hire entry-level talent, focusing on skills rather than personality. A rigorous training and orientation program indoctrinates each new employee. This culture positively affects Epic's strategy execution because employees are focused on the most important actions, there is peer pressure to contribute to Epic's success, and employees are genuinely excited to be involved. Epic's faith in its ability to acculturate new team members and remain true to its core values has helped sustain its status as a premier provider of healthcare IT systems over many years.

The challenge in creating a high-performance culture is to inspire high loyalty and dedication on the part of employees, such that they are energized to put forth their very best efforts. Managers have to take pains to reinforce constructive behavior, reward top performers, and purge habits and behaviors that stand in the way of high productivity

nexusby/Shutterstock

As the third largest sportswear manufacturer in the world, PUMA is racing to catch up with its competitors, Nike and Adidas. Its mission, encapsulated in the phrase "Forever Faster", speaks to its drive to out-innovate and out-pace its formidable rivals. But the more consequential driver of PUMA's speed and agility is its high performance culture.

In 2020, PUMA won Glassdoor's award for the Best Place to Work in Germany, where the company is headquartered. To inspire and energize employees at the headquarters, PUMA offers a fast-paced, fun work environment, centered on a sporting lifestyle. Employees are encouraged to enjoy the company's organic canteen, state-of-the-art gym, nature running trails, soccer fields, and basketball courts. This not only helps workers to form strong bonds with one another but it provides a kind of test lab for the company's latest innovations and designs.

As a multinational company, with nearly 15,000 employees and three international hubs outside of Germany (Hong Kong; Somerville, MA; Ho Chi Minh City, Vietnam), PUMA's challenge has been to ensure that this culture spans the entire reach of the company and unites the parts. This requires much more than ensuring that every hub has a sports driven campus like the one in Germany. It begins with hiring practices to attract and retain those people whose values, drive, and passion for sports match those of others in the company. Accordingly, PUMA is a youthful company, with the average age of its employees hovering just above 30. New employees are exposed to the company culture through learning videos and literature that support their working with "Speed and Spirit" from day one. Rookies are matched with a veteran to show them the ropes and facilitate their becoming acculturated quickly. Talent management and training at PUMA (including International Leadership Programs) contribute similarly to the company's high-performance culture. High potential and high performance individuals are identified and promoted regardless of level and across functions in the belief that successful teams and led by successful leaders.

In their annual survey of employees across many companies, Glassdoor reports that PUMA's employees rave about the speed and spirit ethos that they experience at PUMA. From its flexible hours, generous benefits, personal development opportunities, on-site recreational facilities, team-spiritedness, and commitment to work-life balance, PUMA demonstrates that it puts its people first. For that is ultimately the only sure foundation of a high-performance culture.

Sources: Glassdoor.com/employers/blog/puma-2020, by Amy Elissa Jackson, December 11, 2019; Company website, accessed 4/1/20.

and good results. They must work at knowing the strengths and weaknesses of their subordinates to better match talent with task and enable people to make meaningful contributions by doing what they do best. They have to stress learning from mistakes and must put an unrelenting emphasis on moving forward and making good progress—in effect, there has to be a disciplined, performance-focused approach to managing the organization. Illustration Capsule 12.1 describes the attention that Puma gives toward maintaining its high-performance culture.

Adaptive Cultures   The hallmark of adaptive corporate cultures is willingness on the part of organization members to accept change and take on the challenge of introducing and executing new strategies. Company personnel share a feeling of confidence that the organization can deal with whatever threats and opportunities arise; they are receptive to risk taking, experimentation, innovation, and changing strategies and practices. The work climate is supportive of managers and employees who propose or initiate useful change. Internal entrepreneurship (often called *intrapreneurship*) on the part of individuals and groups is encouraged and rewarded. Senior executives seek out, support, and promote individuals who exercise initiative, spot opportunities for improvement, and display the skills to implement them. Managers openly evaluate ideas and suggestions, fund initiatives to develop new or better products, and take prudent risks to pursue emerging market opportunities. As in high-performance cultures, the company exhibits a proactive approach to identifying issues, evaluating the implications and options, and moving ahead quickly with workable solutions. Strategies and traditional operating practices are modified as needed to adjust to, or take advantage of, changes in the business environment.

> As a company's strategy evolves, an adaptive culture is a definite ally in the strategy-implementing, strategy-executing process as compared to cultures that are resistant to change.

But why is change so willingly embraced in an adaptive culture? Why are organization members not fearful of how change will affect them? Why does an adaptive culture not break down from the force of ongoing changes in strategy, operating practices, and behavioral norms? The answers lie in two distinctive and dominant traits of an adaptive culture: (1) Changes in operating practices and behaviors must *not* compromise core values and long-standing business principles (since they are at the root of the culture); and (2) changes that are instituted must satisfy the legitimate interests of key constituencies— customers, employees, shareholders, suppliers, and the communities where the company operates. In other words, what sustains an adaptive culture is that organization members perceive the changes that management is trying to institute as *legitimate,* in keeping with the core values, and in the overall best interests of stakeholders.[14] Not surprisingly, company personnel are usually more receptive to change when their employment security is not threatened and when they view new duties or job assignments as part of the process of adapting to new conditions. Should workforce downsizing be necessary, it is important that layoffs be handled humanely and employee departures be made as painless as possible.

Technology companies, software companies, and Internet-based companies are good illustrations of organizations with adaptive cultures. Such companies thrive on change— driving it, leading it, and capitalizing on it. Companies like Amazon, Google, Apple, Facebook, Adobe, Groupon, Intel, and Yelp cultivate the capability to act and react rapidly. They are avid practitioners of entrepreneurship and innovation, with a demonstrated willingness to take bold risks to create altogether new products, new businesses, and new industries. To create and nurture a culture that can adapt rapidly to shifting business conditions, they make a point of staffing their organizations with people who are flexible, who rise to the challenge of change, and who have an aptitude for adapting well to new circumstances. Wayfair, the largest online retailer of home furnishings in the United States, attributes its rapid growth to an entrepreneurial and collaborative culture that encourages employee innovation. They hire individuals who are willing to solve problems creatively and develop new initiatives, and empower them to take measured risks.

In fast-changing business environments, a corporate culture that is receptive to altering organizational practices and behaviors is a virtual necessity. However, adaptive cultures work to the advantage of all companies, not just those in rapid-change environments. Every company operates in a market and business climate that is changing to one degree or another and that, in turn, requires internal operating responses and new behaviors on the part of organization members.

Unhealthy Cultures That Impede Good Strategy Execution

The distinctive characteristic of an unhealthy corporate culture is the presence of counterproductive cultural traits that adversely impact the work climate and company performance. Five particularly unhealthy cultural traits are hostility to change, heavily politicized decision making, insular thinking, unethical and greed-driven behaviors, and the presence of incompatible, clashing subcultures.

Change-Resistant Cultures   Change-resistant cultures—where fear of change and skepticism about the importance of new developments are the norm—place a premium on not making mistakes, prompting managers to lean toward safe, conservative options intended to maintain the status quo, protect their power base, and guard their immediate interests. When such companies encounter business environments with accelerating change, going slow on altering traditional ways of doing things can be a serious liability. Under these conditions, change-resistant cultures encourage a number of unhealthy behaviors—avoiding risks, not capitalizing on emerging opportunities, taking a lax approach to both product innovation and continuous improvement in performing value chain activities, and responding more slowly than is warranted to market change. In change-resistant cultures, proposals to do things differently face an uphill battle and people who champion them may be seen as something of a nuisance or a troublemaker. Instead, a lot of energy goes into justifying what the company is presently doing, with little discussion of what it should consider doing differently—there is strong aversion to bold action. Executives who don't value managers or employees with initiative and new ideas put a damper on product innovation, experimentation, and efforts to improve.

Hostility to change is most often found in companies with stodgy bureaucracies that have enjoyed considerable market success in years past and that are wedded to the "We have done it this way for years" syndrome. Sears, and Eastman Kodak are classic examples of companies whose change-resistant bureaucracies have damaged their market standings and financial performance; clinging to what made them successful, they were reluctant to alter operating practices and modify their business approaches when signals of market change first sounded. As strategies of "hold-the-course" won out over bold innovation, they lost market share to rivals that quickly moved to institute changes more in tune with evolving market conditions and buyer preferences. In consequence, both of these companies ultimately ended up in bankruptcy court.

Politicized Cultures   What makes a politicized internal environment so unhealthy is that political infighting consumes a great deal of organizational energy, often with the result that what's best for the company takes a backseat to political maneuvering. In companies where internal politics pervades the work climate, empire-building managers pursue their own agendas and operate the work units under their supervision as autonomous "fiefdoms." The positions they take on issues are usually aimed at protecting or expanding their own turf. Collaboration with other organizational units is viewed with suspicion, and cross-unit cooperation occurs grudgingly. The support or opposition of politically influential executives and/or coalitions among departments with vested interests in a particular outcome tends to shape what actions the company takes. All this political maneuvering takes away from efforts to execute strategy with real proficiency and frustrates company personnel who are less political and more inclined to do what is in the company's best interests.

Insular, Inwardly Focused Cultures   Sometimes a company reigns as an industry leader or enjoys great market success for so long that its personnel start to believe they have all the answers or can develop them on their own. There is a strong tendency to neglect what customers are saying and how their needs and expectations are changing. Such confidence in the correctness of how the company does things and an unflinching belief in its competitive superiority breed arrogance, prompting company personnel to discount the merits of what outsiders are doing and to see little payoff from studying best-in-class performers. Insular thinking, internally driven solutions, and a must-be-invented-here mindset come to permeate the corporate culture. An inwardly focused corporate culture gives rise to managerial inbreeding and a failure to recruit people who can offer fresh thinking and outside perspectives. The big risk of insular cultural thinking is that the company can underestimate the capabilities of rival companies while overestimating its own—all of which diminishes a company's competitiveness over time.

Unethical and Greed-Driven Cultures   Companies that have little regard for ethical standards or are run by executives driven by greed and ego gratification are scandals waiting to happen. Executives exude the negatives of arrogance, ego, greed, and an "ends-justify-the-means" mentality in pursuing overambitious revenue and profitability targets.[15] Senior managers wink at unethical behavior and may cross over the line to unethical (and sometimes criminal) behavior themselves. They are prone to adopt accounting principles that make financial performance look better than it really is. Legions of companies have fallen prey to unethical behavior and greed, most notably Turing Pharmaceuticals (whose name was changed to Vyera in the wake of scandal) and Mylan, both known for their unconscionable price hikes on life-saving medications. Notorious others include Enron, BP, AIG, Countrywide Financial, and JPMorgan Chase, Deutsche Bank, and HSBC (Europe's biggest bank) with executives being indicted and/or convicted of criminal behavior.

Incompatible, Clashing Subcultures   Company subcultures are unhealthy when they embrace conflicting business philosophies, support inconsistent approaches to strategy execution, and encourage incompatible methods of people management. Clashing subcultures can prevent a company from coordinating its efforts to craft and execute strategy and can distract company personnel from the business of business. Internal jockeying among the subcultures for cultural dominance impedes teamwork among the company's various organizational units and blocks the emergence of a collaborative approach to strategy execution. Such a lack of consensus about how to proceed is likely to result in fragmented or inconsistent approaches to implementing new strategic initiatives and in limited success in executing the company's overall strategy.

Changing a Problem Culture

When a culture is unhealthy or otherwise out of sync with the actions and behaviors needed to execute the strategy successfully, the culture must be changed as rapidly as can be managed. This means eliminating any unhealthy or dysfunctional cultural traits as fast as possible and aggressively striving to ingrain new behaviors and work practices that will enable first-rate strategy execution. The more entrenched the unhealthy or mismatched aspects of a company culture, the more likely the culture will impede strategy execution and the greater the need for change.

Changing a problem culture is among the toughest management tasks because of the heavy anchor of ingrained behaviors and attitudes. It is natural for company personnel to cling to familiar practices and to be wary of change, if not hostile to new approaches concerning how things are to be done. Consequently, it takes concerted management action over a period of time to root out unwanted behaviors and replace an unsupportive culture with more effective ways of doing things. *The single most visible factor that distinguishes successful culture-change efforts from failed attempts is competent leadership at the top.* Great power is needed to force major cultural change and overcome the stubborn resistance of entrenched cultures—and great power is possessed only by the most senior executives, especially the CEO. However, while top management must lead the change effort, the tasks of marshaling support for a new culture and

● **LO 12-3**

Identify the kinds of actions management can take to change a problem corporate culture.

FIGURE 12.2   Changing a Problem Culture

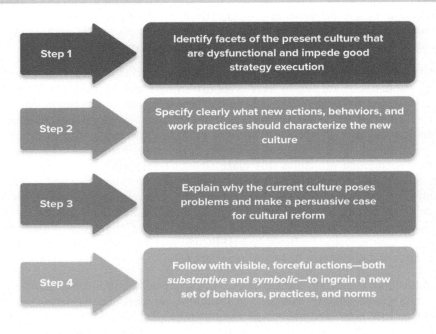

instilling the desired cultural behaviors must involve a company's whole management team. Middle managers and frontline supervisors play a key role in implementing the new work practices and operating approaches, helping win rank-and-file acceptance of and support for changes, and instilling the desired behavioral norms.

As shown in Figure 12.2, the first step in fixing a problem culture is for top management to identify those facets of the present culture that are dysfunctional and pose obstacles to executing strategic initiatives. Second, managers must clearly define the desired new behaviors and features of the culture they want to create. Third, they must convince company personnel of why the present culture poses problems and why and how new behaviors and operating approaches will improve company performance—the case for cultural reform has to be persuasive. Finally, and most important, all the talk about remodeling the present culture must be followed swiftly by visible, forceful actions to promote the desired new behaviors and work practices—actions that company personnel will interpret as a determined top-management commitment to bringing about a different work climate and new ways of operating. The actions to implant the new culture must be both substantive and symbolic.

Making a Compelling Case for Culture Change   The way for management to begin a major remodeling of the corporate culture is by selling company personnel on the need for new-style behaviors and work practices. This means making a compelling case for why the culture-remodeling efforts are in the organization's best interests and why company personnel should wholeheartedly join the effort to do things somewhat differently. This can be done by

- Explaining why and how certain behaviors and work practices in the current culture pose obstacles to good strategy execution.
- Explaining how new behaviors and work practices will be more advantageous and produce better results. Effective culture-change leaders are good at telling stories to describe the new values and desired behaviors and connect them to everyday practices.

- Citing reasons why the current strategy has to be modified, if the need for cultural change is due to a change in strategy. This includes explaining why the new strategic initiatives will bolster the company's competitiveness and performance and how a change in culture can help in executing the new strategy.

It is essential for the CEO and other top executives to talk personally to personnel all across the company about the reasons for modifying work practices and culture-related behaviors. For the culture-change effort to be successful, frontline supervisors and employee opinion leaders must be won over to the cause, which means convincing them of the merits of *practicing* and *enforcing* cultural norms at every level of the organization, from the highest to the lowest. Arguments for new ways of doing things and new work practices tend to be embraced more readily if employees understand how they will benefit company stakeholders (particularly customers, employees, and shareholders). Until a large majority of employees accept the need for a new culture and agree that different work practices and behaviors are called for, there's more work to be done in selling company personnel on the whys and wherefores of culture change. Building widespread organizational support requires taking every opportunity to repeat the message of why the new work practices, operating approaches, and behaviors are good for company stakeholders and essential for the company's future success.

Substantive Culture-Changing Actions   No culture-change effort can get very far when leaders merely talk about the need for different actions, behaviors, and work practices. Company executives must give the culture-change effort some teeth by initiating *a series of actions* that company personnel will see as unmistakably indicative of the seriousness of management's commitment to cultural change. The strongest signs that management is truly committed to instilling a new culture include

- Replacing high-profile executives and managers who are allied with the old culture and either openly or covertly oppose needed organizational and cultural changes.
- Promoting individuals who have stepped forward to spearhead the shift to a different culture and who can serve as role models for the desired cultural behavior.
- Appointing outsiders with the desired cultural attributes to influential positions— bringing in new-breed managers sends an unambiguous message that a new era is dawning.
- Screening all candidates for new positions carefully, hiring only those who appear to fit in with the new culture. For example, a company that stresses operating with integrity and fairness must hire people who themselves have integrity and place a high value on fair play. A company whose culture revolves around creativity, product innovation, and leading change must screen new hires for their ability to think outside the box, generate new ideas, and thrive in a climate of rapid change and ambiguity.
- Mandating that all company personnel attend culture-training programs to better understand the new culture-related actions and behaviors that are expected.
- Designing compensation incentives that boost the pay of teams and individuals who display the desired cultural behaviors. Company personnel are much more inclined to exhibit the desired kinds of actions and behaviors when it is in their financial best interest to do so.
- Letting word leak out that generous pay raises have been awarded to individuals who have stepped out front, led the adoption of the desired work practices, displayed the new-style behaviors, and achieved pace-setting results.
- Revising policies and procedures in ways that will help drive cultural change.

Executives must launch enough companywide culture-change actions at the outset to leave no room for doubt that management is dead serious about changing the present culture and that a cultural transformation is inevitable. Management's commitment to cultural change in the company must be made credible. The series of actions initiated by top management must command attention, get the change process off to a fast start, and be followed by unrelenting efforts to firmly establish the new work practices, desired behaviors, and style of operating as "standard."

Symbolic Culture-Changing Actions   There's also an important place for symbolic managerial actions to alter a problem culture and tighten the strategy–culture fit. The most important symbolic actions are those that top executives take to *lead by example*. For instance, if the organization's strategy involves a drive to become the industry's low-cost producer, senior managers must display frugality in their own actions and decisions. Examples include inexpensive decorations in the executive suite, conservative expense accounts and entertainment allowances, a lean staff in the corporate office, scrutiny of budget requests, few executive perks, and so on. At Walmart, all the executive offices are simply decorated; executives are habitually frugal in their own actions, and they are zealous in their efforts to control costs and promote greater efficiency. At Nucor, one of the world's low-cost producers of steel products, executives fly coach class and use taxis at airports rather than limousines. Top executives must be alert to the fact that company personnel will be watching their behavior to see if their actions match their rhetoric. Hence, they need to make sure their current decisions and actions will be construed as consistent with the new cultural values and norms.[16]

> The most important symbolic cultural-changing action that top executives can take is to *lead by example*.

Another category of symbolic actions includes holding ceremonial events to single out and honor people whose actions and performance exemplify what is called for in the new culture. Such events also provide an opportunity to celebrate each culture-change success. Executives sensitive to their role in promoting strategy–culture fit make a habit of appearing at ceremonial functions to praise individuals and groups that exemplify the desired behaviors. They show up at employee training programs to stress strategic priorities, values, ethical principles, and cultural norms. Every group gathering is seen as an opportunity to repeat and ingrain values, praise good deeds, expound on the merits of the new culture, and cite instances of how the new work practices and operating approaches have produced good results. Ceremonial events can also be used to drive home the commitment to changing culture. The late Steve Jobs, visionary co-founder of Apple, once countered resistance to change by dramatizing the death of "the old" with a coffin.

The use of symbols in culture building is widespread. Numerous businesses have employee-of-the-month awards. The military has a long-standing custom of awarding ribbons and medals for exemplary actions. Mary Kay Cosmetics awards an array of prizes ceremoniously to its beauty consultants for reaching various sales plateaus, including the iconic pink Cadillac.

How Long Does It Take to Change a Problem Culture?   Planting the seeds of a new culture and helping the culture grow strong roots require a determined, sustained effort by the chief executive and other senior managers. Changing a problem culture is never a short-term exercise; it takes time for a new culture to emerge and take root. And it takes even longer for a new culture to become deeply embedded. The bigger the organization and the greater the cultural shift needed to produce an execution-supportive fit, the longer it takes. In large companies, fixing a problem culture and instilling a new set of attitudes and behaviors can take two to five years. In fact, it is usually tougher to reform an entrenched problematic culture than it is to instill a strategy-supportive culture from scratch in a brand-new organization.

Illustration Capsule 12.2 discusses the approaches used at Goldman Sachs to change a culture that was impeding its efforts to recruit the best young talent.

Goldman Sachs was long considered one of the best financial services companies to work for, due to its prestige, high salaries, bonuses, and perks. Yet by 2014, Goldman was beginning to have trouble recruiting the best and brightest MBAs at top business schools. Part of this was due to the banking crisis of 2008–2009 and the scandals that continued to plague the industry year after year, tarnishing the industry's reputation. But another reason was a change in the values and aspirations of the younger generation that made banking culture far less appealing than that of consulting, technology, and start-up companies. Newly minted MBAs were no longer as willing to accept the grueling hours and unpredictable schedules that were the norm in investment banking. They wanted to derive meaning and purpose from their work and prized work/life balance over monetary gain. The tech industry was known for fun, youth-oriented, and collaborative working environments, while the excitement and promise of entrepreneurial ventures offered much appeal. Goldman found itself competing with Amazon, Google, Microsoft, and Facebook as well as with start-ups for the best young talent—and losing out.

Goldman's problem was compounded by the fact that its culture was regarded as stuffy and stodgy—qualities not likely to appeal to the young, particularly when contrasted with the hip cultures of tech and start-up companies. Further, it had always been slow-moving in terms of implementing organizational change. Recognizing the problem, the leadership at Goldman attempted to pivot sharply, asking its executives to think of Goldman as a tech company, complete with the associated values. The Chief Learning Office at Goldman Sachs was put in charge of the effort to transform its culture and began taking deliberate steps to enact changes. Buy-in was

JUSTIN LANE/EPA-EFE/Shutterstock

sought from the full C-suite—the leadership team at the very top of the firm. To foster a more familial atmosphere at work, the company began with small steps, such as setting up sports leagues and encouraging regular team happy hours. More significantly, they instituted more employee-friendly work schedules and policies, more accommodating of work-life balance. They liberalized their parental leave policies, provided greater flexibility in work schedules, and enacted protections for interns and junior bankers designed to limit their working hours. They also overhauled their performance review and promotion systems as well as their recruiting practices and policies regarding diversity. Although cultural change never comes swiftly, by 2017 results were apparent even to outside observers. That year, the career website Vault.com named Goldman Sachs as the best banking firm to work for, noting that when it came to workplace policies, Goldman led the industry.

Sources: http://www.goldmansachs.com/careers/blog/posts/goldman-sachs-vault-2017.html; http://sps.columbia.edu/news/how-goldman-sachs-drives-culture-change-in-the-financial-industry.

LEADING THE STRATEGY EXECUTION PROCESS

For an enterprise to execute its strategy in truly proficient fashion, top executives must take the lead in the strategy implementation process and personally drive the pace of progress. They have to be out in the field, seeing for themselves how well operations are going, gathering information firsthand, and gauging the progress being made. Proficient strategy execution requires company managers to be diligent and adept in spotting problems, learning what obstacles lay in the path of good execution, and then clearing the way for progress—the goal must be to produce better

● LO 12-4

Recognize what constitutes effective managerial leadership in achieving superior strategy execution.

results speedily and productively. There must be constructive, but unrelenting, pressure on organizational units to (1) demonstrate excellence in all dimensions of strategy execution and (2) do so on a consistent basis—ultimately, that's what will enable a well-crafted strategy to achieve the desired performance results.

The specifics of how to implement a strategy and deliver the intended results must start with understanding the requirements for good strategy execution. Afterward comes a diagnosis of the organization's preparedness to execute the strategic initiatives and decisions on how to move forward and achieve the targeted results.[17] In general, leading the drive for good strategy execution and operating excellence calls for three actions on the part of the managers in charge:

- Staying on top of what is happening and closely monitoring progress.
- Putting constructive pressure on the organization to execute the strategy well and achieve operating excellence.
- Initiating corrective actions to improve strategy execution and achieve the targeted performance results.

Staying on Top of How Well Things Are Going

To stay on top of how well the strategy execution process is going, senior executives have to tap into information from a wide range of sources. In addition to communicating regularly with key subordinates and reviewing the latest operating results, watching the competitive reactions of rival firms, and visiting with key customers and suppliers to get their perspectives, they usually visit various company facilities and talk with many different company personnel at many different organizational levels—a technique often labeled **management by walking around (MBWA).** Most managers attach great importance to spending time with people at company facilities, asking questions, listening to their opinions and concerns, and gathering firsthand information about how well aspects of the strategy execution process are going. Facilities tours and face-to-face contacts with operating-level employees give executives a good grasp of what progress is being made, what problems are being encountered, and whether additional resources or different approaches may be needed. Just as important, MBWA provides opportunities to give encouragement, lift spirits, focus attention on key priorities, and create some excitement—all of which generate positive energy and help boost strategy execution efforts.

Jeff Bezos, Amazon's CEO, is noted for his practice of MBWA, firing off a battery of questions when he tours facilities, and insisting that Amazon managers spend time in the trenches with their people to prevent getting disconnected from the reality of what's happening. Walmart executives have had a long-standing practice of spending two to three days every week visiting Walmart's stores and talking with store managers and employees. Sam Walton, Walmart's founder, insisted, "The key is to get out into the store and listen to what the associates have to say." Jack Welch, the highly effective former CEO of General Electric, not only made it a priority to personally visit GE operations and talk with major customers but also routinely spent time exchanging information and ideas with GE managers from all over the world who were attending classes at the company's leadership development center near GE's headquarters.

Many manufacturing executives make a point of strolling the factory floor to talk with workers and meeting regularly with union officials. Some managers operate out of open cubicles in big spaces filled with open cubicles for other personnel so that they can interact easily and frequently with co-workers. Managers at some companies host weekly get-togethers (often on Friday afternoons) to create a regular opportunity for information to flow freely between down-the-line employees and executives.

Mobilizing the Effort for Excellence in Strategy Execution

Part of the leadership task in mobilizing organizational energy behind the drive for good strategy execution entails nurturing a results-oriented work climate, where performance standards are high and a spirit of achievement is pervasive. Successfully leading the effort is typically characterized by such leadership actions and managerial practices as

- *Treating employees as valued partners.* Some companies symbolize the value of individual employees and the importance of their contributions by referring to them as cast members (Disney), crew members (McDonald's), job owners (Graniterock), partners (Starbucks), or associates (Walmart, LensCrafters, W. L. Gore, Edward Jones, Publix Supermarkets, and Marriott International). Very often, there is a strong company commitment to training each employee thoroughly, offering attractive compensation and benefits, emphasizing promotion from within and promising career opportunities, providing a high degree of job security, and otherwise making employees feel well treated and valued.

- *Fostering an esprit de corps that energizes organization members.* The task here is to skillfully use people-management practices calculated to build morale, foster pride in working for the company, promote teamwork and collaborative group effort, win the emotional commitment of individuals and organizational units to what the company is trying to accomplish, and inspire company personnel to do their best in achieving good results.[18]

- *Using empowerment to help create a fully engaged workforce.* Top executives—and, to some degree, the enterprise's entire management team—must seek to engage the full organization in the strategy execution effort. A fully engaged workforce, where individuals bring their best to work every day, is necessary to produce great results.[19] So is having a group of dedicated managers committed to making a difference in their organization. The two best things top-level executives can do to create a fully engaged organization are (1) delegate authority to middle and lower-level managers to get the strategy execution process moving and (2) empower rank-and-file employees to act on their own initiative. Operating excellence requires that everybody contribute ideas, exercise initiative and creativity in performing his or her work, and have a desire to do things in the best possible manner.

- *Nurturing a results-oriented work climate and clearly communicating an expectation that company personnel are to give their best in achieving performance targets.* Managers must make it abundantly clear that they expect all company personnel to put forth every effort to meet performance targets. But executives cannot expect directives to "try harder" to produce the desired outcomes in the absence of a results-oriented work climate. Nor can they expect innovative improvements in operations if they do no more than exhort people to "be creative." Rather, they must foster a strong culture with high performance standards and where innovative ideas and experimentation with new ways of doing things can blossom and thrive.

- *Using the tools of benchmarking, best practices, business process reengineering, TQM, and Six Sigma to focus attention on continuous improvement.* These are proven approaches to getting better operating results and facilitating better strategy execution.

- *Using the full range of motivational techniques and compensation incentives to inspire company personnel and reward high performance.* Individuals and groups should be strongly encouraged to brainstorm, let their imaginations fly in all directions, and come up with proposals for improving the way that things are done. This means giving company personnel enough autonomy to stand out, excel, and contribute. And it means that the rewards for successful champions of new ideas and operating improvements should be large and visible. It is particularly important that people who champion an unsuccessful idea are not punished or sidelined but, rather, encouraged to try again. Finding great ideas requires taking risks and recognizing that many ideas won't pan out.

- *Celebrating individual, group, and company successes.* Top management should miss no opportunity to express respect for individual employees and appreciation of extraordinary individual and group effort.[20] Companies like Google, Mary Kay, Tupperware, and McDonald's actively seek out reasons and opportunities to give pins, ribbons, buttons, badges, and medals for good showings by average performers—the idea being to express appreciation and give a motivational boost to people who stand out in doing ordinary jobs. At Kimpton Hotels and Restaurants, employees who create special moments for guests are rewarded with "Kimpton Moment" tokens that can be redeemed for paid days off, gift certificates to restaurants, flat-screen TVs, and other prizes. Cisco Systems and 3M Corporation make a point of ceremoniously honoring individuals who believe so strongly in their ideas that they take it on themselves to hurdle the bureaucracy, maneuver their projects through the system, and turn them into improved services, new products, or even new businesses.

While leadership efforts to instill a results-oriented, high-performance culture usually accentuate the positive, negative consequences for poor performance must be in play as well. Managers whose units consistently perform poorly must be replaced. Low-performing employees must be weeded out or at least employed in ways better suited to their aptitudes. Average performers should be candidly counseled that they have limited career potential unless they show more progress in the form of additional effort, better skills, and improved ability to execute the strategy well and deliver good results.

Leading the Process of Making Corrective Adjustments

There comes a time at every company when managers have to fine-tune or overhaul the approaches to strategy execution since no action plan for executing strategy can foresee all the problems that will arise. Clearly, when a company's strategy execution effort is not delivering good results, it is the leader's responsibility to step forward and initiate corrective actions, although sometimes it must be recognized that unsatisfactory performance may be due as much or more to flawed strategy as to weak strategy execution.[21]

Success in making corrective adjustments hinges on (1) a thorough analysis of the situation, (2) the exercise of good business judgment in deciding what actions to take, and (3) good implementation of the corrective actions that are initiated. Successful managers are skilled in getting an organization back on track rather quickly. They (and their staffs) are good at discerning what adjustments to make and in bringing them to a successful conclusion. Managers who struggle to show measurable progress in implementing corrective actions in a timely fashion are candidates for being replaced.

The *process* of making corrective adjustments in strategy execution varies according to the situation. In a crisis, taking remedial action quickly is of the essence. But it still takes time to review the situation, examine the available data, identify and evaluate options (crunching whatever numbers may be appropriate to determine which options are likely to generate the best outcomes), and decide what to do. When the situation allows managers to proceed more deliberately in deciding when to make changes and what changes to make, most managers seem to prefer a process of incrementally solidifying commitment to a particular course of action.[22] The process that managers go through in deciding on corrective adjustments is essentially the same for both proactive and reactive changes: They sense needs, gather information, broaden and deepen their understanding of the situation, develop options and explore their pros and cons, put forth action proposals, strive for a consensus, and finally formally adopt an agreed-on course of action. The time frame for deciding what corrective changes to initiate can be a few hours, a few days, a few weeks, or even a few months if the situation is particularly complicated.

The challenges of making the right corrective adjustments and leading a successful strategy execution effort are, without question, substantial.[23] There's no generic, by-the-books procedure to follow. Because each instance of executing strategy occurs under different organizational circumstances, the managerial agenda for executing strategy always needs to be situation-specific. But the job is definitely doable. Although there is no prescriptive answer to the question of exactly what to do, any of several courses of action may produce good results. As we said at the beginning of Chapter 10, executing strategy is an action-oriented task that challenges a manager's ability to lead and direct organizational change, create or reinvent business processes, manage and motivate people, and achieve performance targets. If you now better understand what the challenges are, what tasks are involved, what tools can be used to aid the managerial process of executing strategy, and why the action agenda for implementing and executing strategy sweeps across so many aspects of managerial work, then the discussions in Chapters 10, 11, and 12 have been a success.

A FINAL WORD ON LEADING THE PROCESS OF CRAFTING AND EXECUTING STRATEGY

In practice, it is hard to separate leading the process of executing strategy from leading the other pieces of the strategy process. As we emphasized in Chapter 2, the job of crafting and executing strategy consists of five interrelated and linked stages, with much looping and recycling to fine-tune and adjust the strategic vision, objectives, strategy, and implementation approaches to fit one another and to fit changing circumstances. The process is continuous, and the conceptually separate acts of crafting and executing strategy blur together in real-world situations. *The best tests of good strategic leadership are whether the company has a good strategy (given its internal and external situation), whether the strategy is being competently executed, and whether the enterprise is meeting or beating its performance targets.* If these three conditions exist, then there is every reason to conclude that the company has good strategic leadership and is a well-managed enterprise.

KEY POINTS

1. Corporate culture is the character of a company's internal work climate—the shared values, ingrained attitudes, core beliefs and company traditions that determine norms of behavior, accepted work practices, and styles of operating. A company's culture is important because it influences the organization's actions, its approaches to conducting business, and ultimately its performance in the marketplace. It can be thought of as the company's organizational DNA.

2. The key features of a company's culture include the company's values and ethical standards, its approach to people management, its work atmosphere and company spirit, how its personnel interact, the strength of peer pressure to conform to norms, the behaviors awarded through incentives (both financial and symbolic), the traditions and oft-repeated "myths," and its manner of dealing with stakeholders.

3. A company's culture is grounded in and shaped by its core values and ethical standards. Core values and ethical principles serve two roles in the culture-building process: (1) They foster a work climate in which employees share common and strongly held convictions about how company business is to be conducted; and (2) they provide company personnel with guidance about the manner in which they are to do their jobs—which behaviors and ways of doing things are approved (and expected) and which are out-of-bounds. They serve as yardsticks for gauging the appropriateness of particular actions, decisions, and behaviors.

4. Company cultures vary widely in strength and influence. Some cultures are *strong* and have a big impact on a company's practices and behavioral norms. Others are *weak* and have comparatively little influence on company operations.

5. Strong company cultures can have either positive or negative effects on strategy execution. When they are in sync with the chosen strategy and well matched to the behavioral requirements of the company's strategy implementation plan, they can be a powerful aid to strategy execution. A culture that is grounded in the types of actions and behaviors that are conducive to good strategy execution assists the effort in three ways:

   - By focusing employee attention on the actions that are most important in the strategy execution effort.

   - By inducing peer pressure for employees to contribute to the success of the strategy execution effort.

   - By energizing employees, deepening their commitment to the strategy execution effort, and increasing the productivity of their efforts

   It is thus in management's best interest to dedicate considerable effort to establishing a strongly implanted corporate culture that encourages behaviors and work practices conducive to good strategy execution.

6. Strong corporate cultures that are conducive to good strategy execution are healthy cultures. So are high-performance cultures and adaptive cultures. The latter are particularly important in dynamic environments. Strong cultures can also be unhealthy. The five types of unhealthy cultures are those that are (1) change-resistant, (2) heavily politicized, (3) insular and inwardly focused, (4) ethically unprincipled and infused with greed, and (5) composed of incompatible, clashing subcultures. All five impede good strategy execution.

7. Changing a company's culture, especially a strong one with traits that don't fit a new strategy's requirements, is a tough and often time-consuming challenge. Changing a culture requires competent leadership at the top. It requires making a compelling case for cultural change and employing both symbolic actions and substantive actions that unmistakably indicate serious and credible commitment on the part of top management. The more that culture-driven actions and behaviors fit what's needed for good strategy execution, the less managers must depend on policies, rules, procedures, and supervision to enforce what people should and should not do.

8. Leading the drive for good strategy execution and operating excellence calls for three actions on the part of the manager in charge:

   • Staying on top of what is happening and closely monitoring progress. This is often accomplished through management by walking around (MBWA).

   • Mobilizing the effort for excellence in strategy execution by putting constructive pressure on the organization to execute the strategy well.

   • Initiating corrective actions to improve strategy execution and achieve the targeted performance results.

ASSURANCE OF LEARNING EXERCISES

1. Salesforce.com earned the top spot on Fortune's list of the Best Companies to Work for in 2018, having been on the list for over 10 years. Use your university library's resources to see what their company culture and values might have to do with this. What are the key features of its culture? Do features of Salesforce.com's culture influence the company's ethical practices? If so, how?

LO 12-1

2. Based on what you learned about Salesforce.com from answering the previous question, how do you think the company's culture affects its ability to execute strategy and operate with excellence?

LO 12-2

3. Illustration Capsule 12.2 discusses culture change at Goldman Sachs. How had its organizational culture become an obstacle to its effectiveness? What substantive culture-changing actions were undertaken at Goldman Sachs? What evidence suggests that the culture change has been effective at Goldman Sachs?

LO 12-1, LO 12-2

4. If you were an executive at a company that had a pervasive yet problematic culture, what steps would you take to change it? Using Google Scholar or your university library's access to EBSCO, LexisNexis, or other databases, search for recent articles in business publications on "culture change." What role did the executives play in the culture change? How does this differ from what you would have done to change the culture?

LO 12-3

5. Leading the strategy execution process involves staying on top of the situation and monitoring progress, putting constructive pressure on the organization to achieve operating excellence, and initiating corrective actions to improve the execution effort. Using your university library's resources discuss a recent example of how a company's managers have demonstrated the kind of effective internal leadership needed for superior strategy execution.

LO 12-4

EXERCISES FOR SIMULATION PARTICIPANTS

LO 12-1, LO 12-2 1. If you were making a speech to company personnel, what would you tell employees about the kind of corporate culture you would like to have at your company? What specific cultural traits would you like your company to exhibit? Explain.

LO 12-2 2. What core values would you want to ingrain in your company's culture? Why?

LO 12-3, LO 12-4 3. Following each decision round, do you and your co-managers make corrective adjustments in either your company's strategy or the way the strategy is being executed? List at least three such adjustments you made in the most recent decision round. What hard evidence (in the form of results relating to your company's performance in the most recent year) can you cite that indicates that the various corrective adjustments you made either succeeded at improving or failed to improve your company's performance?

LO 12-4 4. What would happen to your company's performance if you and your co-managers stick with the status quo and fail to make any corrective adjustments after each decision round?

ENDNOTES

[1] Jennifer A. Chatham and Sandra E. Cha, "Leading by Leveraging Culture," *California Management Review* 45, no. 4 (Summer 2003), pp. 20–34; Edgar Shein, *Organizational Culture and Leadership: A Dynamic View* (San Francisco, CA: Jossey-Bass, 1992).

[2] T. E. Deal and A. A. Kennedy, *Corporate Cultures: The Rites and Rituals of Corporate Life* (Harmondsworth, UK: Penguin, 1982).

[3] Joanne Reid and Victoria Hubbell, "Creating a Performance Culture," *Ivey Business Journal* 69, no. 4 (March–April 2005), p. 1.

[4] Ibid.

[5] John P. Kotter and James L. Heskett, *Corporate Culture and Performance* (New York: Free Press, 1992), p. 7. See also Robert Goffee and Gareth Jones, *The Character of a Corporation* (New York: HarperCollins, 1998).

[6] Joseph L. Badaracco, *Defining Moments: When Managers Must Choose between Right and Wrong* (Boston: Harvard Business School Press, 1997); Joe Badaracco and Allen P. Webb, "Business Ethics: A View from the Trenches," *California Management Review* 37, no. 2 (Winter 1995), pp. 8–28; Patrick E. Murphy, "Corporate Ethics Statements: Current Status and Future Prospects," *Journal of Business Ethics* 14 (1995), pp. 727–740; Lynn Sharp Paine, "Managing for Organizational Integrity," *Harvard Business Review* 72, no. 2 (March–April 1994), pp. 106–117.

[7] Emily F. Carasco and Jang B. Singh, "The Content and Focus of the Codes of Ethics of the World's Largest Transnational Corporations," *Business and Society Review* 108, no. 1 (January 2003), pp. 71–94; Patrick E. Murphy, "Corporate Ethics Statements: Current Status and Future Prospects," *Journal of Business Ethics* 14 (1995), pp. 727–740; John Humble, David Jackson, and Alan Thomson, "The Strategic Power of Corporate Values," *Long Range Planning* 27, no. 6 (December 1994),

pp. 28–42; Mark S. Schwartz, "A Code of Ethics for Corporate Codes of Ethics," *Journal of Business Ethics* 41, no. 1–2 (November–December 2002), pp. 27-43.

[8] Terrence E. Deal and Allen A. Kennedy, *Corporate Cultures* (Reading, MA: Addison-Wesley, 1982); Terrence E. Deal and Allen A. Kennedy, *The New Corporate Cultures: Revitalizing the Workplace after Downsizing, Mergers, and Reengineering* (Cambridge, MA: Perseus, 1999).

[9] Vijay Sathe, *Culture and Related Corporate Realities* (Homewood, IL: Irwin, 1985).

[10] Avan R. Jassawalla and Hemant C. Sashittal, "Cultures That Support Product-Innovation Processes," *Academy of Management Executive* 16, no. 3 (August 2002), pp. 42–54.

[11] Kotter and Heskett, *Corporate Culture and Performance*, p. 5.

[12] Reid and Hubbell, "Creating a Performance Culture," pp. 1–5.

[13] Jay B. Barney and Delwyn N. Clark, *Resource-Based Theory: Creating and Sustaining Competitive Advantage* (New York: Oxford University Press, 2007), chap. 4.

[14] Rosabeth Moss Kanter, "Transforming Giants," *Harvard Business Review* 86, no. 1 (January 2008), pp. 43–52.

[15] Kurt Eichenwald, *Conspiracy of Fools: A True Story* (New York: Broadway Books, 2005).

[16] Judy D. Olian and Sara L. Rynes, "Making Total Quality Work: Aligning Organizational Processes, Performance Measures, and Stakeholders," *Human Resource Management* 30, no. 3 (Fall 1991), p. 324.

[17] Larry Bossidy and Ram Charan, *Confronting Reality: Doing What Matters to Get Things Right* (New York: Crown Business, 2004); Larry Bossidy and Ram Charan, *Execution: The Discipline of Getting Things Done* (New York: Crown Business, 2002); John P. Kotter, "Leading Change: Why Transformation Efforts Fail," *Harvard Business Review* 73,

no. 2 (March–April 1995), pp. 59–67; Thomas M. Hout and John C. Carter, "Getting It Done: New Roles for Senior Executives," *Harvard Business Review* 73, no. 6 (November–December 1995), pp. 133–145; Sumantra Ghoshal and Christopher A. Bartlett, "Changing the Role of Top Management: Beyond Structure to Processes," *Harvard Business Review* 73, no. 1 (January–February 1995), pp. 86–96.

[18] For a more in-depth discussion of the leader's role in creating a results-oriented culture that nurtures success, see Benjamin Schneider, Sarah K. Gunnarson, and Kathryn Niles-Jolly, "Creating the Climate and Culture of Success," *Organizational Dynamics,* Summer 1994, pp. 17–29.

[19] Michael T. Kanazawa and Robert H. Miles, *Big Ideas to Big Results* (Upper Saddle River, NJ: FT Press, 2008).

[20] Jeffrey Pfeffer, "Producing Sustainable Competitive Advantage through the Effective Management of People," *Academy of Management Executive* 9, no.1 (February 1995), pp. 55–69.

[21] Cynthia A. Montgomery, "Putting Leadership Back into Strategy," *Harvard Business Review* 86, no. 1 (January 2008), pp. 54–60.

[22] James Brian Quinn, *Strategies for Change: Logical Incrementalism* (Homewood, IL: Irwin, 1980).

[23] Daniel Goleman, "What Makes a Leader," *Harvard Business Review* 76, no. 6 (November–December 1998), pp. 92–102; Ronald A. Heifetz and Donald L. Laurie, "The Work of Leadership," *Harvard Business Review* 75, no. 1 (January–February 1997), pp. 124–134; Charles M. Farkas and Suzy Wetlaufer, "The Ways Chief Executive Officers Lead," *Harvard Business Review* 74, no. 3 (May–June 1996), pp. 110–122; Michael E. Porter, Jay W. Lorsch, and Nitin Nohria, "Seven Surprises for New CEOs," *Harvard Business Review* 82, no. 10 (October 2004), pp. 62–72.

PART 2

Cases in Crafting and Executing Strategy

Airbnb in 2020

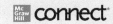

John D. Varlaro
Johnson & Wales University

John E. Gamble
Texas A&M University-Corpus Christi

Airbnb was started in 2008 when Brian Chesky and a friend decided to rent their apartment to guests for a local convention. To accommodate the guests, they used air mattresses and referred to it as the "Air Bed & Breakfast." It was that weekend when the idea—and the potential viability—of a peer-to-peer room-sharing business model was born. During its 12-year existence, Airbnb has experienced immense growth and success. With a planned IPO at some point during 2020, Airbnb had been in a strong position to continue revolutionizing the hotel and tourism industry through its business model that allowed hosts to offer spare rooms or entire homes to potential guests in a peer-reviewed digital marketplace; yet, a global pandemic in the first half of 2020 seemed ready to derail Airbnb's success.

In 2018, the room-sharing company was in approximately 190 countries with more than 4 million listed properties and had an estimated valuation of $31 billion. By 2020, Airbnb had entered over 220 countries with more than 7 million locations. Airbnb's business model has been successful by leveraging what is known as the sharing economy. As it grew, however, Airbnb's business model was met with resistance. City officials and owners and operators of hotels, motels, and bed and breakfasts complained that, unlike traditional brick-and-mortar establishments that were subject to regulations and taxation, Airbnb hosts were able to circumvent and avoid such liabilities due to participation in Airbnb's digital marketplace. In other instances, Airbnb hosts had encountered legal issues due to city and state ordinances governing hotels and apartment leases. Yet, an existential crisis for Airbnb now loomed due to the spread of the coronavirus (COVID-19). Many

hosts were using Airbnb revenue to either subsidize their mortgage payments or had purchased properties that depended solely on the revenue driven through booked accommodations. As people across the world sheltered in-place and travel restrictions were implemented to mitigate the spread of COVID-19, Airbnb and its hosts were left to navigate an uncertain travel and accommodation market with a business model that depends on everyday people sharing their own, at times, private homes.

OVERVIEW OF ACCOMMODATION MARKET

Hotels, motels, and bed and breakfasts competed within the larger, tourist accommodation market. All businesses operating within this sector offered lodging but were differentiated by their amenities. Hotels and motels were defined as larger facilities accommodating guests in single or multiple rooms. Motels specifically offered smaller rooms with direct parking lot access from the unit and amenities such as laundry facilities to travelers who were using their own transportation. Motels might also be located closer to roadways, providing guests quicker and more convenient access to highways. It was also not uncommon for motel guests to segment a longer road trip as they commuted to a vacation destination, thereby potentially staying at several motels during their travel. Hotels, however, invested heavily in additional amenities as they competed for all segments of travelers. Amenities, including on-premise spa facilities and fine dining, were often offered by the hotel. Further, properties offering spectacular views, bolstering a hotel as the vacation destination, may contribute to significant operating costs. In total, wages, property, and utilities, as well as purchases such as food, accounted for 78 percent of the industry's total costs—see Exhibit 1. The primary market segments of hotels and motels are presented in Exhibit 2.

Bed and breakfasts, however, were much smaller, usually where owner-operators offered a couple of rooms within their own home to accommodate

EXHIBIT 1   Hotel, Motel, and Bed & Breakfast Industry Estimated Costs as Percentage of Revenue, 2020

Costs	Hotels/Motels	Bed & Breakfasts
Wages	26%	28%
Purchases	18%	12%
Depreciation	9%	5%
Marketing	2%	2%
Rent and Utilities	7%	10%
Other	27%	40%

Source: www.ibisworld.com.

EXHIBIT 2   Major Market Segments for Hotels/Motels in the US, 2020

Market Segment	Hotels
Recreation	70%*
Business	18%
Other, including meetings	12%
Total	100%

*17% of recreational travel within the US was attributed to international travelers.

Source: www.ibisworld.com.

guests. The environment of the bed and breakfast—one of a cozy, home-like ambiance—was what the guest desired when booking a room. Contrasted with the hotel or motel, a bed and breakfast offered a more personalized, quieter atmosphere. Further, many bed and breakfast establishments were in rural areas where the investment to establish a larger hotel may have been cost prohibitive, yet the location itself could be an attraction to tourists. In these areas individuals invested in a home and property, possibly with a historical background, to offer a bed and breakfast with great allure and ambience for the guests' experiences. Thus, the bed and breakfast competed through offering an ambiance associated with a more rural, slower pace through which travelers connected with their hosts and the surrounding community.

While differing in size and target consumer, all hotels, motels, and bed and breakfasts were subject to city, state, and federal regulations. These regulations covered areas such as the physical property and food safety, access for persons with disabilities, and even alcohol distribution. Owners and operators were subject to paying fees for different licenses to operate. Due to operating as a business, these properties and the associated revenues were also subject to state and federal taxation.

In addition to regulations, the need to construct physical locations prevented hotels and motels from expanding quickly, especially in new international markets. Larger chains tended to expand by purchasing pre-existing physical locations or through mergers and acquisitions, such as Marriott International Inc.'s acquisition of Starwood Hotels and Resorts Worldwide in 2016.

A BUSINESS MODEL FOR THE SHARING, HEALTHY ECONOMY

Startup companies have been functioning in a space commonly referred to as the "sharing economy" for several years. According to Chesky, the previous model for the economy was based on ownership.[1] Thus, operating a business first necessitated ownership of the assets required to do business. Any spare capacity the business faced—either within production or service—was a direct result of the purchase of hard assets in the daily activity of conducting business.

Airbnb and other similar companies, however, operated through offering a technological platform, where individuals with spare capacity could offer their services. By leveraging the ubiquitous usage of smartphones and the continual decrease in technology costs, these companies provided a platform for individuals to instantly share a number of resources. Thus, a homeowner with a spare room could offer it for rent, or the car owner with spare time could offer his or her services a couple of nights a week as a taxi service. The individual simply signed up through the platform and began to offer the service or resource. The company then charged a small transaction fee as the service between both users was facilitated.

Within its business model, Airbnb received a percentage of what the host received for the room. For Airbnb, its revenues were decoupled from the considerable operating expenses of traditional lodging establishments and provided it with significantly smaller operating costs than hotels, motels, and bed and breakfasts. Rather than expenses related to owning and operating real estate properties, Airbnb's expenses were that of a technology company. Airbnb's business model, therefore, was based on the revenue-cost-margin structure of an online marketplace, rather than a lodging establishment. With an estimated 11 percent fee per room stay, it was reported that Airbnb achieved profitability for a first time in 2016,[2] and in 2017 Airbnb announced in an annual investors' meeting that the company had recorded nearly $3 billion in revenue and earned over $90 million in profit.[3]

A CHANGE IN THE CONSUMER EXPERIENCE

Airbnb, however, had not just been leveraging technology. It had also leveraged the change in how the current consumer interacted with businesses. In conjunction with this change seemed to be how the consumer had deemphasized ownership. Instead of focusing on ownership, consumers seemed to prefer sharing or renting. Other startup companies have been targeting these segments through subscription-based services and on-demand help. From luxury watches to clothing, experiencing—and not owning—assets seemed to be on the rise. Citing a more experiential-based economy, Chesky believed Airbnb guests desired a community and a closer relationship with the host—and there seemed to be support for this

assertion.[4] A recent Goldman Sachs study showed that, once someone used Airbnb, their preference for a traditional accommodation was greatly reduced.[5] The appeal of the company's value proposition with customers had allowed it to readily raise capital to support its growth, including an $850 million cash infusion in 2016 that raised its estimated valuation to $30 billion. A comparison of Airbnb's 2018 and 2020 estimated market capitalization to the world's largest hoteliers is presented in Exhibit 3.

Recognizing this shift in consumer preference, traditional brick-and-mortar operators responded. Hilton was considering offering a hostel-like option to travelers.[6] Other entrepreneurs were constructing urban properties to specifically leverage Airbnb's platform and offer rooms only to Airbnb users, such as in Japan[7] where rent and hotel costs were extremely high.

To govern the community of hosts and guests, Airbnb instituted a rating system. Popularized by companies such as Amazon, eBay, and Yelp, peer-to-peer ratings helped police quality. Both guests and hosts rated each other in Airbnb. This approach incentivized hosts to provide quality service, while encouraging guests to leave a property as they found it. Further, the peer-to-peer rating system greatly

EXHIBIT 3   Market Capitalization Comparison, 2018 to 2020 (in billions)

Competitor	Market Capitalization, 2018	Market Capitalization, 2020
Marriot International Inc.	$49	$29
Airbnb	$31	$26
Hilton Worldwide Holdings.	$25	$21
Intercontinental Hotels Group	$11	$ 8

Source: Yahoo Finance (accessed April 2018 and May 2020); "Airbnb Announces It Won't Go Public in 2018," *Business Insider,* http://www.businessinsider.com/airbnb-announces-it-wont-go-public-in-2018-2018-2 (accessed April 20, 2018); "Airbnb Raises $1 Billion to Stockpile Cash in Pandemic," *The New York Times,* https://www.nytimes.com/2020/04/06/ technology/airbnb-corona-virus-valuation.html (accessed May 21, 2020).

minimized the otherwise significant task and expense of Airbnb employees assessing and rating each individual participant within Airbnb's platform.

NOT PLAYING BY THE SAME RULES

Local and global businesses criticized Airbnb for what they claimed were unfair business practices and lobbied lawmakers to force the company to comply with lodging regulations. These concerns illuminated how, due to its business model, Airbnb and its users seemed not to abide by these same regulations. This could have been concerning on many levels. For the guest, regulations exist for protection from unsafe accommodations. Fire codes and occupation limits all exist to prevent injury and death. Laws also exist to prevent discrimination, as traditional brick-and-mortar accommodations are barred from not providing lodging to guests based on race and other protected classes, but there seemed to be evidence that Airbnb guests had faced such discrimination from hosts.[8]

Hosts might also expose themselves to legal and financial problems from accommodating guests. There had been stories of hosts needing to evict guests who would not leave, and, due to local ordinances, the guests were actually protected as apartment lessees. Other stories highlighted rooms and homes being damaged by huge parties given by Airbnb guests. Hosts might also be exposed to liability issues in the instance of an injury or even a death of a guest.

Finally, there were accusations of businesses using Airbnb's marketplace to own and operate accommodations without obtaining the proper licenses. These locations appeared to be individuals on the surface but were actually businesses. And, because of Airbnb's platform, these pseudo-businesses could operate and generate revenue without meeting regulations or claiming revenues for taxation.

Airbnb continued to respond to some of these issues. Airbnb released a report in 2015 detailing both discrimination on its platform and how it would be mitigated. Airbnb also settled its lawsuit with San Francisco in early 2017. The city was demanding Airbnb enforce a city regulation requiring host registration or incur significant fines. As part of the settlement, Airbnb agreed to offer more information on its hosts within the city.[9] And in 2018, Airbnb began partnering with local municipalities to help collect taxes automatically for rentals within their jurisdictions, helping to potentially recoup millions in lost tax revenue.[10, 11]

Recognizing that countries and local municipalities were responding to the local business owner and their constituents' concerns, Chesky and Airbnb had focused on mobilizing and advocating for consumers and business owners who utilize the app. Airbnb's website provided support for guests and hosts who wished to advocate for the site. A focal point of the advocacy emphasized how those particularly hit hard at the height of the recession in 2009 relied on Airbnb to establish a revenue stream and prevent the inevitable foreclosure and bankruptcy. "We wish to be regulated; this would legitimize us," Chesky remarked to Trevor Noah in an interview on *The Daily Show*.[12]

A BUSINESS MODEL FOR THE COVID ECONOMY

In 2019, Airbnb finally announced that the long-awaited IPO would occur during 2020, and Airbnb's revenues were estimated to reach over $2 billion—see Exhibit 4. However, Airbnb dampened expectations

EXHIBIT 4   Airbnb Estimated Revenue and Bookings Growth, 2010–2020 (in millions)

	2010	2011	2012	2013	2014	2015	2016	2017	2018	2019	2020
Estimated Revenue	$6	$44	$132	$264	$436	$675	$945	$1,229	$1,536	$1,843	$2,120
Estimated Bookings Growth	273%	666%	200%	100%	65%	55%	40%	30%	25%	20%	15%

Source: Ali Rafat, "Airbnb's Revenues Will Cross Half Billion Mark in 2015," *Analysts Estimate,* March 25, 2015, skift.com/2015/03/25/airbnbs-revenues-will-cross-half-billion-mark-in-2015-analysts-estimate/ (accessed May 21, 2020).

with the announcement that it had experienced a net loss of over $300 million through September 2019 due to increases in operating costs.[13] Then, in the spring of 2020, the pandemic and efforts by the subsequent state and local governments to stop the spread of COVID-19 presented a significant threat to Airbnb and its business model. Instead of preparing for the IPO, Airbnb had to raise $2 billion in private equity funding and debt to support operations during the pandemic.[14, 15] And in May 2020, Airbnb announced 1900 employees, or about one quarter of the workforce, would be let go.[16]

Quickly, Airbnb tried to adjust its business operations. As guests cancelled their stays with hosts, Airbnb adjusted its cancellation policy. Normally, hosts had discretion over how to handle cancellations. Due to travel restrictions imposed by state and local governments, guests were forced to cancel their stays. Yet some hosts were still charging these guests based on their own cancellation policies. In response, Airbnb adjusted the policy by offering refunds for reservations made prior to March 14, 2020, through the end of June 2020.

Airbnb also offered safety and cleaning guidelines for its hosts. Given the nature of the pandemic, it had become paramount to ensure cleanliness.

A guest or a host contracting COVID-19 due to an Airbnb stay could most certainly make people reluctant to use Airbnb in the future.

For the hosts, however, the loss of the revenue streams seemed to be the most immediate problem. Many hosts depended on their revenue from rentals to afford the properties they owned, either as private homes or as short-term rental properties. Over the years, many hosts had built their finances around the anticipated revenue from guests. Since the pandemic began, some hosts reported they had experienced monetary losses in the tens of thousands of dollars. To support hosts, Airbnb established a $17 million fund to help support hosts that had acquired long-term status with Airbnb.[17]

To confront the challenges of the pandemic, Airbnb expanded its sharing-economy model by entering the "Online Experiences" market. Virtual experiences, such as cigar tastings and virtual guided tours of cities were all being offered for patrons to book and experience from their own home–whether or not they were under stay-at-home orders. It was clear that in 2020, if Airbnb was going to successfully navigate the pandemic, it would have to consider what else people may be willing to share, albeit virtually, in a pandemic economy.

ENDNOTES

[1] Interview with Airbnb founder and CEO Brian Chesky, *The Daily Show with Trevor Noah, Comedy Central,* February 24, 2016.

[2] B. Stone and O. Zaleski, "Airbnb Enters the Land of Profitability," *Bloomberg,* January 26, 2017, https://www.bloomberg.com/news/articles/2017-01-26/airbnb-enters-the-land-of-profitability (accessed June 20, 2017).

[3] O. Zaleski, "Inside Airbnb's Battle to Stay Private," *Bloomberg.Com,* February 6, 2018, https://www.bloomberg.com/news/articles/2018-02-06/inside-airbnb-s-battle-to-stay-private (accessed April 20, 2018).

[4] Interview with Airbnb founder and CEO Brian Chesky, *The Daily Show with Trevor Noah,* Comedy Central, February 24, 2016.

[5] J. Verhage, "Goldman Sachs: More and More People Who Use Airbnb Don't Want to Go Back to Hotels," *Bloomberg,* February 26, 2016, www.bloomberg.com/news/articles/2016-02-16/goldman-sachs-more-and-more-people-who-use-airbnb-don-t-want-to-go-back-to-hotels.

[6] D. Fahmy, "Millennials Spending Power Has Hilton Weighing a 'Hostel-Like' Brand," March 8, 2016, *Bloomberg Businessweek,* www.bloomberg.com/businessweek.

[7] Y. Nakamura and M. Takahashi, "Airbnb Faces Major Threat in Japan, Its Fastest-Growing Market," *Bloomberg,* February 18, 2016,

www.bloomberg.com/news/articles/2016-02-18/fastest-growing-airbnb-market-under-threat-as-japan-cracks-down.

[8] R. Greenfield, "Study Finds Racial Discrimination by Airbnb Hosts," *Bloomberg,* December 10, 2015, www.bloomberg.com/news/articles/2015-12-10/study-finds-racial-discrimination-by-airbnb-hosts.

[9] K. Benner, "Airbnb Adopts Rules to Fight Discrimination by Its Hosts," *New York Times,* (September 8, 2016) http://www.nytimes.com/2016/09/09/technology/airbnb-anti-discrimination-rules.html (accessed June 20, 2017).

[10] S. Cameron, "New TN Agreement Ensures $13M in Airbnb Rental Taxes Collected," *wjhl.com,* April 20, 2018, http://www.wjhl.com/local/new-tn-agreement-ensures-13m-in-airbnb-rental-taxes-collected/1131192392 (accessed April 20, 2018).

[11] "Duluth, Airbnb Make Deal on Lodging Tax Collection," *TwinCitiesPioneerPress,* April 19, 2018, https://www.twincities.com/2018/04/19/duluth-airbnb-make-deal-on-lodging-tax-collection/ (accessed April 20, 2018).

[12] Interview with Airbnb founder and CEO Brian Chesky, *The Daily Show with Trevor Noah,* Comedy Central, February 24, 2016.

[13] J. Eaglesham, M. Farrell, & K. Grind. "Airbnb Swings to a Loss as Costs Climb Ahead of IPO,"

The Wall Street Journal, https://www.wsj.com/articles/airbnb-swings-to-a-loss-as-costs-climb-ahead-of-ipo-11581443123 (accessed May 21, 2020).

[14] E. Griffith. "Airbnb Raises $1 Billion to Stockpile Cash in Pandemic," *The New York Times,* April 6, 2020, https://www.nytimes.com/2020/04/06/technology/airbnb-coronavirus-valuation.html (accessed May 21, 2020).

[15] E. Wollman. "Airbnb Gets $1 Billion Loan, Bringing Coronavirus Funding to $2 Billion," *The Wall Street Journal,* April 15, 2020, https://www.wsj.com/articles/airbnb-gets-1-billion-loan-bringing-coronavirus-funding-to-2-billion-11586929819?mod=article_inline (accessed May 21, 2020).

[16] D. Bosa, & S. Rodriguez. "Airbnb to lay off nearly 1,900 people, 25% of company," *CNBC,* May 5, 2020, https://www.cnbc.com/2020/05/05/airbnb-to-lay-off-nearly-1900-people-25percent-of-company.html (accessed May 21, 2020).

[17] T. Mickle, & P. Rana. "A Bargain with the Devil–Bill Comes Due for Overextended Airbnb Hosts," *The Wall Street Journal,* April 28, 2020, https://www.wsj.com/articles/a-bargain-with-the-devilbill-comes-due-for-overextended-airbnb-hosts-11588083336 (accessed May 21, 2020).

Competition in the Craft Beer Industry in 2020

Mc Graw Hill connect

John D. Varlaro
Johnson & Wales University

John E. Gamble
Texas A&M University–Corpus Christi

Locally produced or regional craft beers caused a seismic shift in the U.S. beer industry during the early 2010s with the gains of the small, regional newcomers coming at the expense of such well-known brands as Budweiser, Miller, Coors, and Bud Light. Craft breweries, which by definition sold fewer than 6 million barrels (bbls) per year, expanded rapidly with the deregulation of intrastate alcohol distribution and retail laws and a change in consumer preferences toward unique and high-quality beers. The growing popularity of craft beers led to an approximate four percent annualized rate of growth in industry revenue between 2015 and 2020.[1]

Despite the continued growth in craft beer popularity, the overall beer industry remained flat in 2019 with total beer sales dropping by almost two percent in the United States.[2] The craft beer industry, too, had begun to show signs of a slowdown going into 2020. Annual growth for the next five years was projected to be a little over two percent; approximately half of what it had been for the past five years.[3] Part of the slowdown was due to shifting consumer trends away from beer and towards lower calorie alternatives, such as hard seltzers, or even abstaining from alcohol completely. Still, there did not seem to be a slowdown in the number of new craft brewers entering the market. In addition, consolidation continued. Led most notably by AB InBev's acquisition of several craft breweries, Grupo Modelo, and its acquisition of SABMiller—macrobrewers were continuing to battle for the craft beer market share. Established craft brewers responded in kind, as Boston Beer Company Inc. acquired Dogfish Head Brewery.

Yet, the most pressing threat to craft brewers may not have been competition, but the coronavirus (COVID-19). Beginning in early 2020, COVID-19 spread across the world, leading governments to restrict travel and to order citizens to remain at home to try to contain the spread of the virus. Within the United States, shutdowns had led to over 40 states experiencing record-setting unemployment rates.[4] For the small, local craft brewers who relied on local bars, tasting events, and other intimate settings to drive awareness and revenue, COVID-19 and social distancing could be the biggest threat in 2020.

THE BEER MARKET

The total economic impact of the beer market was estimated to be almost 2.0 percent of total U.S. GDP in 2018.[5] Total revenue for the craft beer industry was estimated at almost $8 billion in 2020[6], up almost $2 billion from $6 billion in 2017.[7] Exhibit 1 presents annual per production statistics for the United States between 2006 and 2019.

Although U.S. production had declined since 2008, consumption was increasing elsewhere in the world, resulting in a forecasted global market of over $700 billion in sales by 2022.[8] Global growth seemed to be fueled by the introduction of differing styles of beer to regions where consumers had not previously had access and the expansion of demographics not normally known for consuming beer. Thus, exported beer to both developed and developing regions helped drive future growth. As an example, China recently saw a number of domestic craft breweries producing beer as well as experimenting with locally

EXHIBIT 1 Barrels of Beer Produced in the United States, 2006–2019 (millions of barrels)

Year	Barrels produced (in millions)*
2006	198
2007	200
2008	200
2009	197
2010	195
2011	193
2012	196
2013	192
2014	193
2015	191
2016	190
2017	186
2018	183
2019	180

*Rounded to the nearest million.
Source: Alcohol and Tobacco Tax and Trade Bureau website

and regionally known flavors, enticing the domestic palette with flavors such as green tea.

The Brewers Association, a trade association for brewers, suppliers, and others within the industry, designated a brewery as a craft brewer when

EXHIBIT 2 Top 10 U.S. Breweries in 2019

Rank	Brewery
1	Anheuser-Busch, Inc
2	MolsonCoors
3	Constellation
4	Heineken USA
5	Pabst Brewing Company
6	Diageo
7	D.G. Yuengling
8	FIFCO USA
9	Boston Beer Company
10	Sierra Nevada Brewing Company

Source: Brewers Association.

output was less than 6 million barrels annually and the ownership was more than 75 percent independent of another non-craft beer producer or entity. The rapid increase in popularity for local beers led to the number of U.S. brewers to reach over 8,000 in 2019—nearly quadruple the number in 2012.[9] Of these breweries, 99 percent were identified as craft breweries with distribution ranging from local to national. While large global breweries occupied the top positions among the largest U.S. breweries, three craft breweries were ranked among the top-10 largest U.S. brewers in 2019—see Exhibit 2. Exhibit 3 shows

EXHIBIT 3 Top 10 Global Beer Producers by Volume, 2014–2018 (millions of barrels)*

Rank	Producer	2014	2015	2016	2017	2018
1	Ab InBev**	351	353	435	427	432
2	Heineken	180	186	195	200	208
3	Carlsberg	110	107	102	100	105
4	CR Snow***	N/A	N/A	100	101	96
5	Molson Coors Brewing Company	54	54	82	82	79
6	Tsingtao (Group)	78	72	67	68	68
7	Asahi	26	24	60	61	58
8	Beijing Yanjing	45	41	38	35	33
9	Castel BGI	26	26	26	26	29
10	EFES***	N/A	N/A	N/A	28	29

* Originally reported as hectoliters. Computed using 1 hL = .852 barrel for comparison; to nearest million bbl.

** Now includes SABMiller; previous volumes for SABMiller in years 2014 and 2015 prior to acquisition were 249 and 353, respectively, ranking it as second for both years.

*** Not in top 10 for years with N/A.

N/A: Not available.

Source: AB InBev 20-F SEC Document, 2015, 2016, 2017, 2018, 2019.

the production volume of the 10 largest beer producers worldwide from 2014 to 2018. The number of
craft breweries in each U.S. state in 2015, 2017, and
2019 are presented in Exhibit 4.

EXHIBIT 4   Number of Craft Brewers by State, 2015, 2017 & 2019

State	2015	2017	2019
Alabama	24	34	51
Alaska	27	36	45
Arizona	78	96	127
Arkansas	26	35	42
California	518	764	907
Colorado	284	348	425
Connecticut	35	60	104
Delaware	15	21	27
Florida	151	243	329
Georgia	45	69	111
Hawaii	13	18	24
Idaho	50	54	73
Illinois	157	200	284
Indiana	115	137	192
Iowa	58	76	105
Kansas	26	36	59
Kentucky	24	52	69
Louisiana	20	33	40
Maine	59	99	133
Maryland	60	73	112
Massachusetts	84	129	175
Michigan	205	330	400
Minnesota	105	158	196
Mississippi	8	12	14
Missouri	71	91	140
Montana	49	75	92
Nebraska	33	49	55
Nevada	34	40	45
New Hampshire	44	58	91
New Jersey	51	90	127
New Mexico	45	67	94
New York	208	329	423
North Carolina	161	257	333
North Dakota	9	12	22
Ohio	143	225	311
Oklahoma	14	27	55
Oregon	228	266	311
Pennsylvania	178	282	401

State	2015	2017	2019
Rhode Island	14	17	33
South Carolina	36	61	88
South Dakota	14	16	33
Tennessee	52	82	108
Texas	189	251	341
Utah	22	30	42
Vermont	44	55	68
Virginia	124	190	290
Washington	305	369	423
West Virginia	12	23	28
Wisconsin	121	160	205
Wyoming	23	24	41

Source: Brewers Association.

THE BEER PRODUCTION PROCESS

The beer production process involves the fermentation of grains. The cereal grain barley is the most
common grain used in the production of beer. Before
fermentation, however, barley must be malted and
milled. Malting allows the barley to germinate and
produce the sugars that would be fermented by the
yeast, yielding the sweetness of beer. By soaking the
barley in water, the barley germinates, or grows, as it
would when planted in the ground. This process is
halted through the introduction of hot air and drying
after germination has begun.

After malting, the barley is milled to break open
the husk while also cracking the inner seed that
has begun to germinate. Once milled, the barley is
mashed, or added to hot water. The addition of the
hot water produces sugar from the grain. This mixture
is then filtered, resulting in the wort. The wort is then
boiled, which sterilizes the beer. It is at this stage that
hops are added. The taste and aroma of beer depend
on the variety of hops and when the hops were added.

After boiling, the wort is cooled and then poured
into the fermenter, where yeast is added. The sugar
created in the previous stages is broken down by
the yeast through fermentation. The different styles
of beer depend on the type of yeast used, typically
either an ale or lager yeast. The time for this process
could take a couple of weeks to a couple of months.
After fermentation, the yeast is removed. The process is completed after carbon dioxide is added and
the product is packaged.

Beer is a varied and differentiated product, with over 70 styles in 15 categories. Each style is dependent on a number of variables. These variables are controlled by the brewer through the process, and could include the origin of raw materials, approach to fermentation, and yeast used. For example, Guinness referenced on its website how barley purchased by the brewer was not only grown locally, but was also toasted specifically after malting, lending to its characteristic taste and color. As another example of differentiation through raw materials, wheat beers, such as German-style *hefeweizen,* are brewed with a minimum of 50 percent wheat instead of barley grain.

DEVELOPMENT OF MICROBREWERIES AND ECONOMICS OF SCALE

Although learning the art of brewing takes time, beer production lends itself to scalability and variety. For example, an amateur, or home brewer, could brew beer for home consumption. There had been a significant increase in the interest in homebrewing, with over 1 million people pursuing the hobby in 2017.[10] It was also not uncommon for a home brewer to venture into entrepreneurship and begin brewing for commercial sales. However, beer production was highly labor intensive with much of the work done by hand. A certain level of production volume was necessary to achieve breakeven and make the microbrewery a successful commercial operation.

A small nanobrewery may brew a variety of flavor experiences and compete in niche markets, while the macrobrewery may focus on economies of scale and mass produce one style of beer. Both may attract consumers across segments and were attributed to the easily scalable yet highly variable process of brewing beer. In contrast, a global producer such as AB InBev could produce beer for millions of consumers worldwide with factory-automated processes.

LEGAL ENVIRONMENT OF BREWERIES

As beer is an alcoholic beverage, the industry is subject to much regulation. Further, these regulations can vary by state and municipality. One such regulation was regarding sales and distribution.

Distribution could be distinguished through direct sales (or self-distribution), and two-tier and three-tier systems. Regulations permitting direct sales allow the brewery to sell directly to the consumer. Growers, bottle sales, and taprooms were all forms of direct, or retail, sales. There were usually requirements concerning direct sales, including limitations on volume sold to the consumer.

Even where self-distribution was legal, the legal volumes could be very small and limited. Very few brewers were exempt from distributing through wholesalers, referred to as a three-tier distribution system. And often to be operationally viable, brewers need access to this distribution system to generate revenue. In a three-tier system, the brewery must first sell to a wholesaler—the liquor or beer distributor. This distributor then sells to the retailer, who then ultimately sells to the consumer.

This distribution structure, however, had ramifications for the consumer, as much of what was available at retail outlets and restaurants were impacted by the distributor. This was further impacted by whether a brewery bottles or cans its beer or distributes through kegs. While restaurants and bars could carry kegs, retail shelves at a local liquor store needed to have cans and bottles, as a relatively small number of consumers could accommodate kegs for home use. Thus, there may only be a few liquor stores or restaurants where a consumer may find a locally-brewed beer. In states that do not allow self-distribution or on-premise sales, distribution and exposure to consumers could represent a barrier for breweries, especially those that were small or new.

The Alcohol and Tobacco Tax and Trade Bureau (TTB) was the main federal agency for regulating this industry. As another example of regulations, breweries were required to have labels for beers approved by the federal government, ensuring they meet advertising guidelines. In some instances, the TTB may need to approve the formula used for brewing the specific beer prior to the label receiving approval. Given the approval process, and the growth of craft breweries, the length of time this takes could reach several months. For a small, microbrewery first starting, the delay in sales could potentially impact cash flow.

Employment law was another area impacting breweries. The Affordable Care Act (ACA) and changes to the Fair Labor Standards Act (FLSA) greatly affected labor cost in the industry. Where the ACA mandated health care coverage by employers, the FLSA changed overtime rules for employees previously classified as exempt or salaried. Finally, many states and municipalities passed or were considering passing, increases to minimum wage. These changes in regulations could lead to significant increases in business costs, potentially impacting a brewery's ability to remain viable or competitive.

Lawsuits might also impact breweries' operations. Trademark infringement lawsuits regarding brewery and beer names were common. Further, food-related lawsuits could occur. In 2017, there were potential lawsuits against breweries distributing in California that did not meet the May 2016 requirement of providing an additional sign warning against pregnancy and BPA (Bisphenyl-A) consumption. BPA was commonly found in both cans and bottle caps, and thus breweries were potentially legally exposed, exemplifying the potential legal exposure to any brewery.

SUPPLIERS TO BREWERIES

The main suppliers to the industry were those who supply grain and hops. Growers might sell directly to breweries or distribute through wholesalers. Brewers who wish to produce a grain-specific beer would be required to procure the specific grain. Further, recipes might call for a variety of grains, including rye, wheat, and corn. As previously mentioned, the definition of craft was changed not only to include a higher threshold for annual production, but it also changed to not exclude producers who used other grains, such as corn, in their production. Finally, origin-specific beers, such as German- or Belgian-styles might also require specific grains.

The more specialized the grain or hop, the more difficult it was to obtain. Those breweries, then, competing based on specialized brewing would be required to identify such suppliers. Conversely, larger, global producers of single-style beers were able to utilize economies of scale and demand lower prices from suppliers. Organically-grown grains and hops suppliers would also fall into this category of providing specialized ingredients, and specialty brewers tend to use such ingredients.

Hops production within the United States grew to almost $640 million in 2019, representing an approximate 10 percent increase over 2018 production,[11] which seemed to follow the growing demand due to the increased number of breweries. Hops were grown in the Pacific Northwest states of Idaho, Washington, and Oregon. Washington's Yakima Valley was probably one of the more recognizable geographic-growing regions. There were numerous varieties of hops, however, and each contributes a different aroma and flavor profile. Hop growers have also trademarked names and varieties of hops. Further, as with grains, some beer-styles require specific hops. Farmlands that were formerly known for hops have started to see a rejuvenation of this crop, such as in New England. In other areas, farmers were introducing hops as a new, cash crop. Some hops farms were also dual purpose, combining the growing operations with brewing, thus serving as both a supplier of hops to breweries while also producing their own beer for retail. Recent news reports, however, were citing current and future shortages of hops due to the increased number of breweries. Rising temperatures in Europe led to a diminished yield in 2018, further impacting hops supplies.[12] For breweries using recipes that require these specific hops, shortages could be detrimental to production. In some instances, larger beer producers had vertically integrated into hops farming to protect their supply.

Suppliers to the industry also include manufacturers and distributors of brewing equipment, such as fermentation tanks and refrigeration equipment. Purification equipment and testing tools were also necessary, given the brewing process and the need to ensure purity and safety of the product.

Depending on distribution and the distribution channel, breweries might need bottling or canning equipment. Thus, breweries might invest heavily in automated bottling capabilities to expand capacity. Recently, however, there have been shortages in the 16-ounce size of aluminum cans.

HOW BREWERIES COMPETE: INNOVATION AND QUALITY VERSUS PRICE

The consumer might seek out a specific beer or brewery's name or purchase the lower-priced globally known brand. For some, beer drinking might also be seasonal, as tastes change with the seasons. Lighter beers were consumed in hotter months, while heavier beers were consumed in the colder months. Consumers might associate beer styles with the time of year or season. Oktoberfest and German-style beers were associated with fall, following the German-traditional celebration of Oktoberfest. Finally, any one consumer might enjoy several styles, or choose to be brewery or brand loyal.

The brewing process and the multiple varieties and styles of beer allow for breweries to compete across the strategy spectrum—low price and high volume, or higher price and low volume. Industry competitors, then, might target both price-point and differentiation. The home brewer, who decided to invest several thousand dollars in a small space to produce very small quantities of their beer and start a nanobrewery, might utilize a niche competitive strategy. The consumer might patronize the brewery on location or seek it out on tap at a restaurant given the quality and the style of beer brewed. If allowed by law, the brewery might offer tastings or sell onsite to visitors. Further, the nanobrewer was free to explore and experiment with unusual flavors. To drive awareness, the brewer might enter competitions, attend beer festivals, or host tastings and "tap takeovers" at local restaurants. If successful, the brewer might invest in larger facilities and equipment to increase capacity with growing demand.

The larger, more established craft brewers, especially those considered regional breweries, might compete through marketing and distribution, while offering a higher value compared to the mass production of macrobreweries. However, the consumer might at times be sensitive to and desire the craft beer experience through smaller breweries—so much so that even craft breweries who by definition were craft might draw the ire of the consumer due to its size and scope. Boston Beer Company was one such company. Even though James Koch had started it as a microbrewery, pioneering the craft beer movement in the 1980s, some craft beer consumers do not view it as authentically craft.

Larger, macrobreweries mass produced and competed using economies of scale and established distribution systems. Thus, low cost preserves margins as lower price points drive volume sales. Many of these brands were sold en masse at sporting and entertainment venues, as well as larger restaurant chains, driving volume sales.

Companies like AB InBev possessed brands within the portfolio that were sold under the perception of craft beer, in what Boston Beer Company deems the better beer category—beer with a higher price point, but also of higher quality. For example,

Blue Moon, a Belgian-style wheat ale, was produced by MillerCoors. Blue Moon's market share had increased significantly since 2006 following the rise in craft beer popularity, competing against Boston Beer Company's Sam Adams in this better beer segment. AB InBev had also acquired larger better-known craft breweries, including Goose Island, in 2011. With a product portfolio that included both low-price and premium craft beer brands, macrobreweries were competing across the spectrum and putting pressure on breweries within the better and craft beer segments—segments demanding a higher price point due to production.

However, a lawsuit claimed the marketing of Blue Moon was misleading and its marketing obscured the ownership structure. Although the case was dismissed, it further illustrated consumer sentiment regarding what was perceived as craft beer. It also illustrated the power of marketing and how a macrobrewery might position a brand within these segments.

CONSOLIDATIONS AND ACQUISITIONS

In 2015 AB InBev offered to purchase SABMiller for $108 billion, which was approved by the European Union in May 2016 and finalized in 2016. To allow for the acquisition, many of SABMiller's brands were required to be divested. Asahi Group Holdings Ltd. purchased the European brands Peroni and Grolsch from SABMiller. Molson Coors purchased SABMiller's 58 percent ownership in MillCoors LLC—originally a joint venture between Molson Coors and SABMiller. This transaction provided Molson Coors 100 percent ownership of MillerCoors. It should be noted that AB InBev and MillerCoors represented over 80 percent of the beer produced in the United States for domestic consumption. AB InBev had also actively acquired other brands and breweries since the 1990s, including Labatt in 1995, Beck's in 2002, Anheuser-Bush in 2008, and Grupo Modelo in 2013.

Purchases of craft breweries by larger companies had also increased during the 2010s. AB InBev had purchased numerous craft breweries since 2011, including Goose Island, Blue Point and Devil's Backbone Brewing. MillerCoors—whose brands already included Killian's Irish Red, Leinenkugel's, and Foster's—acquired Saint Archer Brewing

Company. Ballast Point Brewing & Spirits was acquired by Constellations Brands. Finally, Heineken NV purchased a stake in Lagunitas Brewing Company.

In May 2019, Boston Beer Company acquired Dogfish Head Brewery. Founded in 1995 by Sam and Mariah Calagione as Delaware's first brewpub, Dogfish Head Brewery was also America's smallest brewery at the time.[13] Since its founding, Dogfish Head Brewery had become one of the best-known craft breweries in the United States. The acquisition by Boston Beer Company may have been a response to the macrobreweries push into craft beer. It would seem that craft beer and breweries had not only gained the attention of the consumer, but also the larger multinational breweries and corporations. Craft brewers, however, seemed to be taking a page out of the macrobreweries' playbook by establishing larger companies that could harness economies of scale, while maintaining the smaller, more intimate brand presence in the market.

PROFILES OF BEER PRODUCERS

Anheuser-Busch InBev

As the world's largest producer by volume, AB InBev had 170,000 employees globally. The product portfolio included the production, marketing, and distribution of over 500 beers, malt beverages, as well as soft drinks in more than 150 countries. These brands included Budweiser, Stella Artois, Leffe, and Hoegaarden.

AB InBev managed its product portfolio through three tiers. Global brands, such as Budweiser, Stella Artois, and Corona, were distributed throughout the world. International brands (Beck's, Hoegaarden, Leffe) were found in multiple countries. Local champions (i.e., local brands) represented regional or domestic brands acquired by AB InBev, such as Goose Island in the United States and Cass in South Korea. While some of the local brands were found in different countries, it was due to geographic proximity and the potential to grow the brand larger.

AB InBev reported its 2019 revenues grew four percent, with its largest growth in revenue experienced in the Middle Americas (7.2 percent) and South America (9.0 percent).[14] Its strength in brand recognition and focused marketing drove its global brands to grow by almost 10 percent outside their respective domestic markets. AB InBev had been focused on growing these brands outside of their respective home markets since 2017.

Consumer preferences towards lower calorie alcoholic beverages had bolstered the market share of the Michelob Ultra and Michelob Ultra Pure Gold brands within the United States. AB InBev, however, reported that overall market share within the United States had declined due to the change in consumer preference for hard seltzers. In response, Natural Light Seltzer was launched during August of 2019 in North America featuring two flavors, "Catalina Lime Mixer" and Aloha Beaches." Bud Light Seltzer was also launched in 2019. Pursuing the flavored malt beverage (FMB) trend, AB InBev had launched Skol Puro Malte in South American early 2019. AB InBev, however, also experienced success within the U.S. craft beer market as its craft portfolio within the United States grew more than 20 percent in 2019.

AB InBev invested heavily in sponsorships to bolster marketing and brand recognition globally. In pursuing the craft beer market outside the United States, AB InBev's Camden Town Brewery was the official beer partner in the United Kingdom and Ireland for Arsenal FC™. Non-craft beer brands continued to be heavily marketed as well. Budweiser would be a sponsor for the 2022 FIFA World Cup™, as it had been for the 2014 and 2018 competitions. Bud Light would be the official sponsor of the National Football League through 2022, as AB InBev had paid $1.4 billion for the sponsorship.[15]

Acquisitions provided AB InBev greater market share and penetration through combining marketing and operations to all brands. The reacquisition of the Oriental Brewery in 2014 was a good example of the potential synergies garnered. Cass was the leading beer in Korea and was produced by Oriental Brewery; however, while Cass represented the local brand for AB InBev in Korea, Hoegaarden was distributed in Korea along with the global brands of Budweiser, Corona, and Stella Artois. These acquisitions also allowed AB InBev to scale-up craft beer, hard seltzer, and other products within their portfolio from locally-recognized beverages to regional and globally-recognized brands.

A summary of AB InBev's financial performance from 2016 to 2019 is presented in Exhibit 5.

EXHIBIT 5   Financial Summary for AB InBev, 2016–2019 (in millions of $)

	2019	2018	2017	2016
Revenue	$52,329	$53,041	$56,444	$45,517
Cost of sales	(20,362)	(19,933)	(21,386)	(17,803)
Gross Profit	31,967	33,108	35,058	27,715
Selling, general and administrative expenses	(16,421)	(16,807)	(18,099)	(15,171)
Other operating income/expenses	875	805	854	732
Non-recurring items	(323)	(692)	(662)	(394)
Profit from operations (EBIT)	16,098	16,414	17,152	12,882
Depreciation, amortization and impairment	4,657	4,624	4,270	3,477
EBITDA	$20,755	$21,038	$21,429	$16,360

Source: AB InBev Annual Reports, 2017, 2019.

Boston Beer Company

Boston Beer Company was the second largest craft brewer by volume in the United States[16] and reported sales of more than 5 million barrels in 2019. The company had experienced a revenue decline in 2017, but experienced increases in both 2018 and 2019. Most notably, 2019 shipment volume had increased by approximately 24 percent from 2018, driven by both the acquisition of Dogfish Head in 2019, and Boston Beer's 'Beyond Beer' portfolio of hard seltzers and teas, which had been launched as early as 2001 with the Twisted Tea brand. Boston Beer had dropped from the fifth largest overall brewer in the United States in 2015 to ninth in 2017, but remained in that position through 2019—see Exhibit 2.

The company history states the recipe for Sam Adams was actually company founder Jim Koch's great-great-grandfather's recipe. The story of Boston Beer Company and Jim Koch's success was referenced at times as the beginning of the craft beer movement, often citing how Koch originally sold his beer to bars with the beer and pitching on the spot.

This beginning seemed to underpin much of Boston Beer Company's strategy as it competed in the higher value and higher price point category it refers to as the *better beer segment.* Focusing on quality and taste, Boston Beer Company marketed Samuel Adams Boston Lager as the original beer Koch first discovered. The company also produced several Sam Adams seasonal beers, such as Sam Adams Summer Ale and Sam Adams Octoberfest. Other seasonal Sam Adams beers have limited release in seasonal variety packs, including Samuel Adams Harvest Pumpkin and Samuel Adams

Holiday Porter. In addition, there was also a Samuel Adams Brewmaster's Collection, a much smaller, limited release set of beers at much higher points, including the Small Batch Collection and Barrel Room Collection. Utopia—its highest priced beer—was branded as highly experimental and under very limited release. In the spirit of craft beer and innovation, Boston Beer Company launched a craft brew incubator, Alchemy and Science.

This history also seems to have been the impetus for the acquisition of Dogfish Head Brewery, as both Boston Beer Company and Dogfish Head Brewery pride themselves as innovators and champions within the industry.[17] Both represented a formidable share of the craft beer market in the United States in 2019, as Boston Beer Company was ranked second, while Dogfish Head was ranked 13th among craft brewing companies.[18]

Boston Beer Company offered three non-beer brands. The Twisted Tea brand was launched in 2001, and the Angry Orchard originated in 2011. Truly Spiked & Sparkling is a percent alcohol sparkling water launched in 2016. As these other brands and products compete in the FMB and hard cider categories, Boston Beer Company was well positioned to compete for the changing consumer preferences during 2019.

A summary of Boston Brewing Company's financial performance from 2016 to 2019 is presented in Exhibit 6.

Craft Brew Alliance

Craft Brew Alliance was ranked thirteenth for overall brewing by volume in 2019.[19] Founded in 2008,

EXHIBIT 6 Financial Summary for Boston Brewing Company, 2016–2019 (in thousands of $)

	2019	2018	2017	2016
Revenue	$1,329,108	$1,057,495	$ 921,736	$ 968,994
Excise taxes	(79,284)	(61,846)	(58,744)	(62,548)
Cost of goods sold	(635,658)	(483,406)	(413,091)	(446,776)
Gross Profit	614,166	512,243	449,901	459,670
Advertising, promotional and selling expenses	355,613	304,853	258,649	244,213
General and administrative expenses	112,730	90,857	73,126	78,033
Impairment of assets	911	652	2,451	(235)
Operating Income	144,912	115,881	115,675	137,659
Other expense, net	(542)	405	467	(538)
Provision for income taxes	34,329	23,623	17,093	49,772
Net Income	$ 110,041	$ 92,663	$ 99,049	$ 87,349

Source: Boston Beer Company Annual Report, 2019.

it resulted from the mergers between Redhook Brewery, Widmer Brothers Brewing, and Kona Brewing Company. Each with substantial history, the decision to merge was to help assist with growth and meeting demand. In 2019, The Craft Brew Alliance was composed of eight other craft beer brands, including Omission Brewing Co., Cisco Brewers, and Square Mile Cider Company. In addition to these brands, Craft Brew Alliance operated five brewpubs. Per its annual report, there were 655 people employed at Craft Brew Alliance across its operations, including brewpubs and production. Its products included craft beer, gluten-free beer, hard ciders and seltzers.

Craft Brew Alliance utilized automated brewing equipment, contract brewing and distributed nationally through the Anheuser-Busch wholesaler network alliance, leveraging many of the logistics and thus cost advantages associated. In November 2019 Craft Brew Alliance and Anheuser-Busch announced an expansion of the partnership that would result in a merger. The merger was approved by Craft Brew Alliance's shareholders in February 2020.[20] Finalization of the merger was slated for later in 2020 and was in the process of review by the U.S. Justice Department.

A summary of Craft Brew Alliance's financial performance from 2016 to 2019 is presented in Exhibit 7.

EXHIBIT 7 Financial Summary for Craft Brew Alliance, 2016–2019 (in thousands of $)

	2019	2018	2017	2016
Revenue	$ 192,971	$ 206,186	$ 207,456	$ 202,507
Cost of sales	(130,122)	(137,863)	(142,198)	(142,908)
Gross Profit	62,849	68,323	65,258	59,599
Selling, general and administrative expenses	80,967	62,572	60,463	59,224
Operating Income	(18,118)	5,751	4,795	375
Income before provision for income taxes	(19,618)	5,429	4,041	(306)
Provision for income taxes	(6,699)	1,287	(5,482)	14
Net Income	$ (12,919)	$ 4,142	$ 9,523	$ (320)

Source: Craft Brew Alliance Annual Report, 2019.

STRATEGIC ISSUES CONFRONTING CRAFT BREWERIES IN 2020

The vast majority of the craft breweries might produce only enough beer for the local population in their area. Many of these breweries started the same way as the larger breweries—home brewers or hobbyists decided to start to brew and sell their own beer. Many obtained startup capital through their own savings or solicited investments from friends and family.

Given their entrepreneurial beginnings, these microbreweries and even smaller nanobreweries were usually located in industrial spaces. They were solely operated by the brewer-turned-entrepreneur, or a small staff of two or three. This staff would help with brewing and production, as well as potentially brewery tours and visits—probably the most common marketing and consumer relations tactic utilized by smaller breweries. While almost all breweries offered tours and tastings, these became ever more critical to the smaller brewery with limited capital for marketing and advertising. If onsite sales were available, the brewer could sell growlers to visitors.

Social media websites also offered significant exposure for free and had become a foundational element of brewery marketing. These websites helped the brewery reach the craft beer consumer, who tended to seek out and follow new and upcoming breweries. There were also mobile phone applications specific to the craft beer industry that could help a startup gain exposure. Participating in craft beer festivals, where local and regional breweries were able to offer samples to attendees, was another opportunity to gain exposure.

Some small microbreweries did not have enough employees for bottling and labeling and had been known to solicit volunteers through social media. To gain exposure and boost sales, the brewery might host events at local restaurants, such as tap-takeovers, where several of its beers are featured on draft. If enough consumers were engaged, local restaurants were enticed to purchase more beer from the distributor of the brewery. However, any number of variables—raw material shortages, tight retail competition, price-sensitive consumers—could dramatically impact future viability.

The number of beers available to the consumer throughout all segments and price points had continued to steadily climb since the mid-2000s. While the overall beer industry had seemed to plateau, the significant growth appeared to be in the craft beer, or better beer segments. Further, larger macrobreweries and regional craft breweries were seizing the opportunity to acquire other breweries as a method of obtaining distribution and branding synergies, while also mitigating the amount of direct competition. Complicating the competitive landscape were increasing availability and price fluctuations of raw materials. These sporadic shortages might impact the industry's growth and affect the production stability of breweries, especially those smaller operations that did not have capacity to purchase in bulk or outbid larger competitors.

Overall, the growth in the consumers' desire for craft beer was likely to continue to attract more entrants, while encouraging larger breweries to seek additional acquisitions of successful craft beer brands. However, the shift of consumer trends towards low-calorie alcoholic beverages and beer/wine alternatives presented not only opportunity for expansion but also a threat to those producers who either relied exclusively on beer sales or could not produce hard ciders and seltzers.

Yet, the pandemic still loomed large over the entire craft beer industry. The Brewers Association had announced almost a quarter of its staff would be laid-off, while others would experience salary cuts.[21] As craft brewers prepared to open taprooms and begin brewing under social distancing regulations, it appeared the significant growth and expansion of small and medium-sized craft breweries could come to an abrupt stop during 2020.

ENDNOTES

1 IBIS *World* Industry Report 0D4302 Craft Beer Production in the U.S., April 2020.

2 Brewers Association, National Beer Sales and Production Data, https://www.brewersassociation.org/statistics-and-data/national-beer-stats/ (accessed May 23, 2020).

3 IBIS *World* Industry Report 0D4302 Craft Beer Production in the U.S., April 2020.

4 T. Luhby. "43 States Have Record Unemployment. See Where Your State Ranks" *CNN.com*, May 22, 2020, https://www.cnn.com/2020/05/22/economy/state-unemployment-record-data-error/index.html (accessed May 23, 2020).

5 "Beer Serves America: A Study of the U.S. Beer Industry's Economic Contribution in 2018," The Beer Institute and The National Beer Wholesalers Association, May 2019, http://beerservesamerica.org/ (accessed May 23, 2020).

6 IBIS *World* Industry Report 0D4302 Craft Beer Production in the U.S., April 2020.

7 IBIS *World* Industry Report 0D4302 Craft Beer Production in the U.S., December 2017.

8 Research, Z. M. "Global Beer Market Predicted to Reach by $750.00 Billion in 2022," March 2, 2018, http://globenewswire.com/news-release/2018/03/02/1414335/0/en/Global-Beer-Market-Predicted-to-Reach-by-750-00-Billion-in-2022.html.

9 Brewers Association, National Beer Sales & Production Data, https://www.brewersassociation.org/statistics-and-data/national-beer-stats/ (accessed May 23, 2020).

10 American Homebrewers Association, Homebrewing Stats, https://www.homebrewersassociation.org/membership/homebrewing-stats/ (accessed May 23, 2020).

11 USDA, National Hop Report, https://www.usahops.org/img/blog_pdf/267.pdf (accessed May 23, 2020).

12 Deutscher Hopfenwirtschaftsverband e.V., Market Review July 2019, https://www.usahops.org/img/blog_pdf/235.pdf (accessed May 23, 2020).

13 T. Acitelli, "Dogfish Head Turns 20" *All About Beer Magazine,* May 13, 2015, http://allaboutbeer.com/dogfish-head-and-its-extreme-beers-turns-20/ (accessed May 23, 2020).

14 Anheuser-Busch InBev 2019 Annual Report.

15 D. Roberts, "Bud Light Will Remain NFL's Official Beer Until 2022" *Fortune.com*, November 4, 2015. https://fortune.com/2015/11/04/bud-light-nfl-deal/ (accessed May 23, 2020).

16 "Brewers Association Announces Top 50 Brewing Companies By Sales Volume of 2019," April 1, 2020, https://www.brewersassociation.org/press-releases/brewers-association-announces-top-50-brewing-companies-by-sales-volume-of-2019/ (accessed May 23, 2020).

17 "Boston Beer Update: The Boston Beer Company and Dogfish Head Brewery to Merge, creating the Most Dynamic American-Owned Platform for Craft Beer and Beyond," *Boston Beer Company Website,* May 9, 2019, http://www.bostonbeer.com/boston-beer-update (accessed May 23, 2020).

18 "Brewers Association Announces Top 50 Brewing Companies By Sales Volume of 2019," April 1, 2020, https://www.brewersassociation.org/press-releases/brewers-association-announces-top-50-brewing-companies-by-sales-volume-of-2019/ (accessed May 23, 2020).

19 Ibid.

20 J. Kendall., & J. Infante., "Craft Brew Alliance Shareholders Vote in Favor of Merger with Anheuser-Busch InBev," *Brewbound,* February 25, 2020, https://www.brewbound.com/news/craft-brew-alliance-shareholders-vote-in-favor-of-merger-with-anheuser-busch-inbev (accessed May 23, 2020).

21 C. Furnari., "Brewers Association Cuts 23% of Staff" *Forbes.com*, April 30, 2020, https://www.forbes.com/sites/chrisfurnari/2020/04/30/brewers-association-cuts-23-of-staff/#3fdde6044094 (accessed May 23, 2020).

Costco Wholesale in 2020: Mission, Business Model, and Strategy

Mc Graw Hill connect

Arthur A. Thompson Jr.

The University of Alabama

Eight years after turning the leadership of Costco Wholesale over to a new CEO, Jim Sinegal, Costco's co-founder and chief executive officer (CEO) from 1983 until year-end 2011, had ample reason to be pleased with the company's ongoing revenue growth and competitive standing as one of the world's biggest and best consumer goods merchandisers. Sinegal had been the driving force behind Costco's 37-year evolution from a startup entrepreneurial venture into the third largest retailer in the United States and the world (behind Wal-Mart and Amazon.com) and the undisputed leader of the discount warehouse and wholesale club segment of the North American retailing industry. Since January 2012, when then-president Craig Jelinek took the reins as Costco Wholesale's president and CEO, the company had prospered, growing from annual revenues of $89 billion and 598 membership warehouses at year-end fiscal 2011 to annual revenues of $152.7 billion and 782 membership warehouses at year-end fiscal 2019 (September 1, 2019). Costco's growth continued in the first six months of fiscal 2020; six-month revenues were $76.1 billion, up 8.0 percent over the first six months of fiscal 2019, and the company had opened five additional warehouses as of April 2020. As of March 2020, Costco had continued to maintain its ranking as the third largest retailer in both the United States and the world.

COMPANY BACKGROUND

The membership warehouse concept was pioneered by discount merchandising sage Sol Price, who opened the first Price Club in a converted airplane hangar on Morena Boulevard in San Diego in 1976.

Price Club lost $750,000 in its first year of operation, but by 1979 it had two stores, 900 employees, 200,000 members, and a $1 million profit. Years earlier, Sol Price had experimented with discount retailing at a San Diego store called Fed-Mart. Jim Sinegal got his start in retailing at the age of 18, loading mattresses for $1.25 an hour at Fed-Mart while attending San Diego Community College. When Sol Price sold Fed-Mart, Sinegal left with Price to help him start the San Diego Price Club store; within a few years, Sol Price's Price Club emerged as the unchallenged leader in member warehouse retailing, with stores operating primarily on the West Coast.

Although Price originally conceived Price Club as a place where small local businesses could obtain needed merchandise at economical prices, he soon concluded that his fledgling operation could achieve far greater sales volumes and gain buying clout with suppliers by also granting membership to individuals—a conclusion that launched the deep-discount warehouse club industry on a steep growth curve.

When Sinegal was 26, Sol Price made him the manager of the original San Diego store, which had become unprofitable. Price saw that Sinegal had a special knack for discount retailing and for spotting what a store was doing wrong (usually either not being in the right merchandise categories or not selling items at the right price points)—the very things that Sol Price was good at and that were at the root of Price Club's growing success in the marketplace. Sinegal soon got the San Diego store back into the black. Over the next several years, Sinegal continued to build his prowess and talents for discount merchandising. He mirrored Sol Price's attention to detail and absorbed all the nuances and subtleties of his mentor's style of operating—constantly improving store operations, keeping operating costs and overhead low, stocking items that moved quickly, and charging ultra-low prices that kept customers coming back to shop. Realizing that he had mastered the tricks of running a successful membership warehouse business from Sol Price, Sinegal decided to leave Price Club and form his own warehouse club operation.

Sinegal and Seattle entrepreneur Jeff Brotman founded Costco, and the first Costco store began operations in Seattle in 1983—the same year that Walmart launched its warehouse membership format, Sam's Club. By the end of 1984, there were nine Costco stores in five states serving over 200,000 members. In December 1985, Costco became a public company, selling shares to the public and raising additional capital for expansion. Costco became the first ever U.S. company to reach $1 billion in sales in less than six years. In October 1993, Costco merged with Price Club. Jim Sinegal became CEO of the merged company, presiding over 206 PriceCostco locations, with total annual sales of $16 billion. Jeff Brotman, who had functioned as Costco's chairman since the company's founding, became vice chairman of PriceCostco in 1993 and was elevated to chairman of the company's board of directors in December 1994, a position he held until his unexpected death in 2017.

In January 1997, after the spin-off of most of its non-warehouse assets to Price Enterprises Inc., PriceCostco changed its name to Costco Companies Inc. When the company reincorporated from Delaware to Washington in August 1999, the name was changed to Costco Wholesale Corporation. The company's headquarters was in Issaquah, Washington, not far from Seattle.

Jim Sinegal's Leadership Style

Sinegal was far from the stereotypical CEO. He dressed casually and unpretentiously, often going to the office or touring Costco stores wearing an open-collared cotton shirt that came from a Costco bargain rack and sporting a standard employee name tag that said, simply, "Jim." His informal dress and unimposing appearance made it easy for Costco shoppers to mistake him for a store clerk. He answered his own phone, once telling ABC News reporters, "If a customer's calling and they have a gripe, don't you think they kind of enjoy the fact that I picked up the phone and talked to them?"[1]

Sinegal spent considerable time touring Costco stores, using the company plane to fly from location to location and sometimes visiting eight to 10 stores daily (the record for a single day was 12). Treated like a celebrity when he appeared at a store (the news "Jim's in the store" spread quickly), Sinegal made a point of greeting store employees. He observed, "The employees know that I want to say hello to them, because I like them. We have said from the very beginning: 'We're going to be a company that's on a first-name basis with everyone.'"[2] Employees genuinely seemed to like Sinegal. He talked quietly, in a commonsensical manner that suggested what he was saying was no big deal.[3] He came across as kind yet stern, but he was prone to display irritation when he disagreed sharply with what people were saying to him.

In touring a Costco store with the local store manager, Sinegal was very much the person-in-charge. He functioned as producer, director, and knowledgeable critic. He cut to the chase quickly, exhibiting intense attention to detail and pricing, wandering through store aisles firing a barrage of questions at store managers about sales volumes and stock levels of particular items, critiquing merchandising displays or the position of certain products in the stores, commenting on any aspect of store operations that caught his eye, and asking managers to do further research and get back to him with more information whenever he found their answers to his questions less than satisfying. Sinegal had tremendous merchandising savvy, demanded much of store managers and employees, and definitely set the tone for how the company operated its discounted retailing business. Knowledgeable observers regarded Jim Sinegal's merchandising expertise as being on a par with Walmart's legendary founder, Sam Walton.

In September 2011, at the age of 75, Jim Sinegal informed Costco's Board of Directors of his intention to step down as CEO of the company effective January 2012. The Board elected Craig Jelinek, Costco's President and Chief Operating Officer since February 2010, to succeed Sinegal and hold the titles of both President and CEO. At the time, Jelinek was a highly experienced retail executive with 37 years in the industry, 28 of them at Costco, where he started as one of the Company's first warehouse managers in 1984. He had served in every major role related to Costco's business operations and merchandising activities during his tenure. When he stepped down as CEO, Sinegal retained his position on the company's Board of Directors and, at the age of 79, was re-elected to another three-year term on Costco's board in December 2015; he retired from Costco's Board at the end of his term in January 2018.

COSTCO WHOLESALE IN 2020

In April 2020, Costco was operating 787 warehouses, including 547 in the United States and Puerto Rico, 100 in Canada, 39 in Mexico, 29 in the United Kingdom, 26 in Japan, 16 in Korea, 13 in Taiwan, 12 in Australia, two in Spain, and one each in Iceland, France, and China. Costco also operated e-commerce sites in the United States, Canada, the United Kingdom, Mexico, Korea, Taiwan, Japan, and Australia; e-commerce sales represented about four percent of total net sales in 2019. Over 100 million cardholders were entitled to shop at Costco as of January 2020; in fiscal year 2019, membership fees generated over $3.35 billion in revenues for the company. Headed into 2020, shopper traffic at Costco's warehouse locations averaged over 3.1 million members per day. Annual sales per store averaged about $190 million ($3.7 million per week) in 2019, an amount that was 93 percent higher than the $98.2 million per year and $1.9 million per week averages for Sam's Club, Costco's chief competitor. In 2019, Costco was the only national retailer in the history of the United States that could boast of average annual revenue in excess of $190 million *per location.*

Exhibit 1 contains a financial and operating summary for Costco for fiscal years 2016 through 2019.

EXHIBIT 1   Selected Financial and Operating Data for Costco Wholesale Corp., Fiscal Years 2016–2019 ($ in millions, except for per share data)

Selected Income Statement Data	Fiscal Years Ending			
	Sept. 1, 2019	Sept. 2, 2018	Sept. 3, 2017	Aug. 28, 2016
Net sales	$149,351	$138,434	$126,172	$116,073
Membership fees	3,352	3,142	2,853	2,646
Total revenue	152,703	141,576	129,025	118,719
Operating expenses				
Merchandise costs	132,886	123,152	111,882	102,901
Selling, general and administrative	14,994	13,876	12,950	12,068
Preopening expenses	86	68	82	78
Provision for impaired assets and store closing costs	—	—	—	—
Total operating expenses	147,966	137,096	124,914	115,047
Operating income	4,737	4,480	4,111	3,672
Other income (expense)				
Interest expense	(150)	(159)	(134)	(133)
Interest income and other, net	178	121	62	80
Income before income taxes	4,765	4,442	4,039	3,619
Provision for income taxes	1,061	1,263	1,325	1,243
Net income attributable to Costco	$ 3,659	$ 3,134	$ 2,679	$ 2,350
Diluted net income per share	$ 8.26	$ 7.09	$ 6.08	$ 5.33
Dividends per share (not including special dividend of $7.00 in 2017 and $5.00 in 2015)	$ 2.44	$ 2.14	$ 1.90	$ 1.70
Millions of shares used in per share calculations	442.9	441.8	440.9	441.3

	Fiscal Years Ending			
Balance Sheet Data	**Sept. 1, 2019**	**Sept. 2, 2018**	**Sept. 3, 2017**	**Aug. 28, 2016**
Cash and cash equivalents	$ 8,384	$ 6,055	$ 4,546	$ 3,379
Merchandise inventories	11,395	11,040	9,834	8,969
Current assets	23,485	20,289	17,317	15,218
Current liabilities	23,237	19,926	17,485	15,575
Net property and equipment	20,890	19,681	18,161	17,043
Total assets	45,400	40,830	36,347	33,163
Long-term debt, excluding current portion	5,124	6,487	6,573	4,061
Stockholders' equity	15,584	13,103	10,778	12,079
Cash Flow Data				
Net cash provided by operating activities	$ 6,356	$ 5,774	$ 6,726	$ 3,292
Warehouse Operations				
Warehouses in operation at beginning of year[a]	762	741	715	686
New warehouses opened (including relocations)	25	25	28	33
Existing warehouses closed (including closures due to relocations)	(5)	(4)	(2)	(4)
Warehouses at end of year	782	762	741	715
Net sales per warehouse open at year-end (in millions)	$ 191	$ 182	$ 170	$ 162
Average annual growth at warehouses open more than a year (excluding the impact of changing gasoline prices and foreign exchange rates)	6%	7%	4%	4%
Members at year-end				
Businesses, including add-on members (000s)	11,00	10,900	10,800	10,800
Gold Star members (000s)	42,900	40,700	38,600	36,800
Total paid members	53,900	51,600	49,400	47,600
Household cardholders that both business and Gold Star members were automatically entitled to receive	44,600	42,700	40,900	39,100
Total cardholders	98,500	94,300	90,300	86,700

[a] At the beginning of Costco's 2011 fiscal year, the operations of 32 warehouses in Mexico that were part of a 50 percent-owned joint venture were consolidated and reported as part of Costco's total operations.

Note: Some totals may not add due to rounding and to not including some line items of minor significance in the company's statement of income.

Sources: Company 10-K reports for fiscal years 2017 and 2019.

COSTCO'S MISSION, BUSINESS MODEL, AND STRATEGY

Costco's stated mission in the membership warehouse business was: "To continually provide our members with quality goods and services at the lowest possible prices."[4] However, in a "Letter to Shareholders" in the company's 2011 Annual Report, Costco's three top executives—Jeff Brotman, Jim Sinegal, and Craig Jelinek—provided a more expansive view of Costco's mission, stating:

> The company will continue to pursue its mission of bringing the highest quality goods and services to market at the lowest possible prices while providing excellent customer service and adhering to a strict code of ethics that includes taking care of our employees and members, respecting our suppliers, rewarding our shareholders, and seeking to be responsible corporate citizens and environmental stewards in our operations around the world." [5]

In the company's 2017 Annual Report, Craig Jelinek elaborated on how environmental sustainability fit into Costco's mission:

> Sustainability to us is remaining a profitable business while doing the right thing. We are committed to lessening our environmental impact, decreasing our carbon footprint, sourcing our products responsibly, and working with our suppliers, manufacturers, and farmers to preserve natural resources. This will remain at the forefront of our business practices.[6]

The centerpiece of Costco's business model was a powerful value proposition that featured a combination of (1) ultra-low prices on a limited selection of nationally branded and Costco's private-label Kirkland Signature products in a wide range of merchandise categories, (2) very good to excellent product quality, and (3) intriguing product selection that included both everyday items and ongoing special purchases from a big variety of merchandise suppliers that turned shopping at Costco into a money-saving treasure hunt. Ever since the company's founding, Costco management had strived diligently to ensure that shopping at Costco delivered enough value to keep existing members returning frequently to a nearby warehouse and to spur membership growth every year, thereby generating high sales volumes and rapid inventory turnover at each warehouse and creating opportunities to open new warehouses both domestically and internationally.

Big sales volumes and rapid inventory turnover—when combined with the low operating costs achieved by volume purchasing, efficient distribution, and reduced handling of merchandise in no-frills, self-service warehouse facilities—enabled Costco to operate profitably at significantly lower gross margins than traditional wholesalers, mass merchandisers, supermarkets, and supercenters. Membership fees were a critical element of Costco's business model because they provided sufficient supplemental revenues to boost the company's overall profitability to acceptable levels. Indeed, Costco's revenues from membership fees typically exceeded 100 percent of the company's net income, meaning that the rest of Costco's worldwide business operated on a slightly below breakeven basis (see Exhibit 1)—which translated into Costco's prices being exceptionally competitive when compared to the prices that Costco members paid when shopping elsewhere.

Another important business model element was that Costco's high sales volume and rapid inventory turnover generally allowed it to sell and receive cash for inventory before it had to pay many of its merchandise vendors, even when vendor payments were made in time to take advantage of early payment discounts. Thus, Costco was able to finance a big percentage of its merchandise inventory through the payment terms provided by vendors rather than by having to maintain sizable working capital (defined as current assets minus current liabilities) to enable timely payment of suppliers.

Costco's Strategy

The key elements of Costco's strategy were ultra-low prices, a limited selection of nationally branded and top-quality Kirkland Signature products covering diverse merchandise categories, a "treasure hunt" shopping environment that stemmed from a constantly-changing inventory of about 900 "while-they-last specials," strong emphasis on low operating costs, and ongoing expansion of its geographic network of store locations.

Pricing   Costco's philosophy was to keep customers coming in to shop by wowing them with low prices and thereby generating big sales volumes. Examples of Costco's 2015 sales volumes that contributed to low prices in particular product categories included 156,000 carats of diamonds (up to 400,00 carats in 2019), meat sales of $6.4 billion, seafood sales of $1.3 billion, television sales of $1.8 billion, fresh produce sales of $5.8 billion (sourced from 44 countries), 83 million rotisserie chickens, 7.9 million tires, 41 million prescriptions, 6 million pairs of glasses, and 128 million hot dog/soda pop combinations. Costco was the world's largest seller of fine wines ($965 million out of total 2015 wine sales of $1.7 billion).

For many years, a key element of Costco's pricing strategy had been to cap its markup on brand-name merchandise at 14 percent (compared to 25 percent and higher markups for other discounters and most supermarkets and 50 percent and higher markups for department stores). Markups on Costco's private-label Kirkland Signature items were a maximum of 15 percent, but the sometimes fractionally higher mark-ups still resulted in Kirkland Signature items being priced about 20 percent below comparable name-brand items. Except for Walmart, Costco's prices for fresh foods and grocery items ranged 20 to 30 percent below of the leading supermarket chains. Aside from being lower-priced, Costco's Kirkland Signature products—which included vitamins, juice, bottled water, coffee, spices, olive oil, canned salmon and tuna, nuts, laundry detergent, baby products, dog food, luggage, cookware, trash bags, batteries, wines and spirits, paper towels and toilet paper, and clothing—were designed to be of *equal or better* quality than national brands.

As a result of its low markups, Costco's prices were just fractionally above breakeven levels, producing net sales revenues (not counting membership fees) that exceeded all operating expenses by only $1.0 billion to $1.4 billion in fiscal years 2016–2019. As can be verified from Exhibit 1, Costco's revenues from membership fees accounted for 69 to 72 percent of the company's operating profits in fiscal years 2016 to 2019 and exceeded the company's net income after taxes in every fiscal year shown in Exhibit 1 except for fiscal year 2019—outcomes that were a direct result of the company's ultra-low pricing strategy and practice of capping the margins on branded goods at 14 percent and private-label goods at 15 percent.

Jim Sinegal explained the company's approach to pricing:

> We always look to see how much of a gulf we can create between ourselves and the competition. So that the competitors eventually say, "These guys are crazy. We'll compete somewhere else." Some years ago, we were

selling a hot brand of jeans for $29.99. They were $50 in a department store. We got a great deal on them and could have sold them for a higher price but we went down to $29.99. Why? We knew it would create a riot.[7]

At another time, he said:

> We're very good merchants, and we offer value. The traditional retailer will say: "I'm selling this for $10. I wonder whether we can get $10.50 or $11." We say: "We're selling this for $9. How do we get it down to $8?" We understand that our members don't come and shop with us because of the window displays or the Santa Claus or the piano player. They come and shop with us because we offer great values.[8]

Indeed, Costco's markups and prices were so fractionally above the level needed to cover company-wide operating costs and interest expenses that Wall Street analysts had criticized Costco management for going all out to please customers at the expense of increasing profits for shareholders. One retailing analyst said, "They could probably get more money for a lot of the items they sell."[9] During his tenure as CEO, Sinegal had never been impressed with Wall Street calls for Costco to abandon its ultra-low pricing strategy, commenting: "Those people are in the business of making money between now and next Tuesday. We're trying to build an organization that's going to be here 50 years from now."[10] He went on to explain why Costco's approach to pricing would remain unaltered during his tenure:

> When I started, Sears, Roebuck was the Costco of the country, but they allowed someone else to come in under them. We don't want to be one of the casualties. We don't want to turn around and say, "We got so fancy we've raised our prices, and all of a sudden a new competitor comes in and beats our prices."[11]

Product Selection Whereas typical supermarkets stocked about 40,000 items and a Walmart Supercenter or a SuperTarget might have 125,000 to 150,000 items for shoppers to choose from, Costco's merchandising strategy was to provide members with a selection of approximately 3,700 active items that could be priced at bargain levels and thus provide members with significant cost savings. Of these, about 75 percent were quality brand-name products and 25 percent carried the company's private-label Kirkland Signature brand. The Kirkland Signature label appeared on everything from men's dress shirts to laundry detergent, pet food to toilet paper, canned foods to cookware, olive oil to beer, automotive products to health and beauty aids. According to Craig Jelinek, "The working rule followed by Costco buyers is that all Kirkland Signature products must be equal to or better than the national brands, and must offer a savings to our members." Management believed that there were opportunities to increase the number of Kirkland Signature selections and gradually build sales penetration of Kirkland-branded items to at least 30 percent of total sales—in 2018 Kirkland-brand sales exceeded 28 percent of total sales. Costco executives in charge of sourcing Kirkland Signature products constantly looked for ways to make all Kirkland Signature items better than their brand name counterparts and even more attractively priced. Costco members were very much aware that one of the great perks of shopping at Costco was the opportunity to buy top quality Kirkland Signature products at prices substantially lower than name brand products.

Costco's product range covered a broad spectrum—rotisserie chicken, all types of fresh meats, seafood, fresh and canned fruits and vegetables, paper products, cereals, coffee, dairy products, cheeses, frozen foods, flat-screen televisions, cell phones and assorted other electronics products, jewelry, fresh flowers, fine wines, baby strollers, toys and games, musical instruments, ceiling fans, vacuum cleaners, books, apparel, cleaning supplies, DVDs, light bulbs, batteries, cookware, electric toothbrushes, vitamins, office supplies, and home appliances—but the selection in each product category was deliberately limited to fast-selling models, sizes, and colors. Many consumable products like detergents, canned goods, office supplies, and soft drinks were sold only in big-container, case, carton, or multiple-pack quantities. In a few instances, the selection within a product category was restricted to a single offering. For example, Costco stocked only a 325-count bottle of Advil—a size many shoppers might find too large for their needs. Sinegal explained the reasoning behind limited selections:

> If you had 10 customers come in to buy Advil, how many are not going to buy any because you just have one size? Maybe one or two. We refer to that as the intelligent loss of sales. We are prepared to give up that one customer. But if we had four or five sizes of Advil, as most grocery stores do, it would make our business more difficult to manage. Our business can only succeed if we are efficient. You can't go on selling at these margins if you are not.[12]

In the last several years, organics had become a fast-growing category in both the fresh produce section and the grocery items section, and Costco buyers were devoting increased attention to growing the selection of organic items. In the fresh meats category, Costco was pursuing increased vertical integration, constructing a second meat plant in Illinois and a state-of-the-art poultry plant in Nebraska capable of processing 2 million chickens per week—in fiscal 2019 Costco warehouses sold almost 100 million rotisserie chickens annually at a very attractive price of $4.99. A baking commissary had been opened in Canada that supplied warehouses in much of Canada and the United States with bread and cookie dough for on-premise baking. The approximate percentage of net sales accounted for by each major category of items stocked by Costco is shown in Exhibit 2.

Management believed that Costco's ancillary offerings gave members reasons to shop at Costco

EXHIBIT 2   Costco's Sales by Major Product Category, 2016–2019

	2019	2018	2017	2016
Food and Sundries (dry foods, packaged foods, groceries, snack foods, candy, alcoholic and nonalcoholic beverages, and cleaning supplies)	40%	41%	41%	43%
Fresh Foods (fresh produce, meats and fish, bakery and deli products),	13%	14%	14%	14%
Hardlines (major appliances, electronics, health and beauty aids, hardware, office supplies, garden and patio, sporting goods, furniture, cameras, and automotive supplies)	16%	16%	16%	16%
Softlines (including apparel, domestics, jewelry, housewares, books, movie DVDs, video games and music, home furnishings, and small appliances)	11%	11%	12%	12%
Ancillary (gasoline, pharmacy, food court, optical, one-hour photo, hearing aids, and travel)	19%	18%	17%	15%

Source: Company 10-K reports, 2017 and 2019.

more frequently and make Costco more of a one-stop shopping destination. Headed into fiscal 2020, over 600 warehouses had inside food courts, pharmacies, photo centers, and optical centers. Costco's pharmacies were highly regarded by members because of the low prices. The company's practice of selling gasoline at discounted prices (often as much as 20 to 30 cents per gallon) at those store locations where there was sufficient space to install gas pumps had boosted the frequency with which nearby members shopped at Costco and made in-store purchases (only members were eligible to buy gasoline at Costco's stations). Almost all new Costco locations in the United States and Canada were opening with gas stations; globally, gas stations were being added at locations where local regulations and space permitted. Costco operated 593 gas stations as of September 2019; the steep discounts on gasoline generated about 11 percent of Costco's total net sales in fiscal 2019 (Costco did not sell gasoline in South Korea, France, or China).[13]

Treasure-Hunt Merchandising While Costco's product line consisted of approximately 3,700 active items, some 20 to 25 percent of its product offerings were constantly changing. Costco's merchandise buyers were continuously making one-time purchases of items that would appeal to the company's clientele and likely to sell out quickly. A sizable number of these featured specials were high-end or luxury-brand products that carried big price tags; examples included $1,000 to $4,500 big-screen TVs, $800 espresso machines, expensive jewelry and diamond rings (priced from $10,000 to $400,000+), Omega watches, Waterford Crystal, exotic cheeses, Coach bags, cashmere sports coats, $1,500 digital pianos, $800 treadmills, $2,500 memory foam mattresses, and Dom Perignon champagne. Many of the featured specials came and went quickly, sometimes in several days or a week—like Italian-made Hathaway shirts priced at $29.99 and $800 leather sectional sofas. The strategy was to entice shoppers to spend more than they might by offering irresistible deals on big-ticket items or name-brand specials and, further, to keep the mix of featured and treasure-hunt items constantly changing so that bargain-hunting shoppers would go to Costco more frequently rather than only for periodic "stock up" trips.

Costco members quickly learned that they needed to go ahead and buy treasure-hunt specials that interested them because the items would very likely not be available on their next shopping trip.

In many cases, Costco did not obtain its upscale treasure hunt items directly from high-end manufacturers like Calvin Klein or Waterford (who were unlikely to want their merchandise marketed at deep discounts at places like Costco); rather, Costco buyers searched for opportunities to source such items legally on the gray market from other wholesalers or distressed retailers looking to get rid of excess or slow-selling inventory.

Management believed that these practices kept its marketing expenses low relative to those at typical retailers, discounters, and supermarkets.

Low-Cost Emphasis Keeping operating costs at a bare minimum was a major element of Costco's strategy and a key to its low pricing. As first explained by Jim Sinegal and later reiterated by Craig Jelinek:

> Costco is able to offer lower prices and better values by eliminating virtually all the frills and costs historically associated with conventional wholesalers and retailers, including salespeople, fancy buildings, delivery, billing, and accounts receivable. We run a tight operation with extremely low overhead which enables us to pass on dramatic savings to our members.[14]

While Costco management made a point of locating warehouses on high-traffic routes in or near upscale suburbs that were easily accessible by small businesses and residents with above-average incomes, it avoided prime real estate sites in order to contain land costs.

Because shoppers were attracted principally by Costco's low prices and merchandise selection, most warehouses were of a metal pre-engineered design, with concrete floors and minimal interior décor. Floor plans were designed for economy and efficiency in use of selling space, the handling of merchandise, and the control of inventory. Merchandise was often stored on racks above the sales floor and/or displayed on pallets containing large quantities of each item, thereby reducing labor required for handling and stocking. In-store signage was done mostly on laser printers; there were no shopping bags at the checkout counter—merchandise was put directly into the shopping cart or sometimes loaded into empty boxes. Costco warehouses ranged in size from 73,000 to 205,000 square feet; the average size was about 146,000 square feet. Newer units were usually in the 150,000- to 205,000-square-foot range, but the world's largest Costco warehouse was a 235,000 square-foot store in Salt Lake City that opened in 2015.

Warehouses generally operated on a seven-day, 70-hour week, typically being open between 10:00 a.m. and 8:30 p.m. weekdays, with earlier closing hours on the weekend; the gasoline operations outside many stores usually had extended hours. The shorter hours of operation as compared to those of

EXHIBIT 3   Images of Costco's Warehouses

Source: Supplied by Costco and used with Costco's permission.

Image Courtesy of Costco Wholesale

Felix Mizioznikov/Shutterstock

Image Courtesy of Costco Wholesale

Image Courtesy of Costco Wholesale

Image Courtesy of Costco Wholesale

Image Courtesy of Costco Wholesale

traditional retailers, discount retailers, and super-markets resulted in lower labor costs relative to the volume of sales. By strictly controlling the entrances and exits of its warehouses and using a membership format, Costco had inventory losses (shrinkage) well below those of typical retail operations.

Growth Strategy   Costco's growth strategy was to increase sales at existing stores by five percent or more annually and to open additional warehouses, both domestically and internationally. Average annual growth at stores open at least a year was 10 percent in fiscal 2011, six percent in both fiscal 2013 and 2014, seven percent in fiscal 2015, four per-cent in 2016 and 2017, seven percent in 2018, and six percent in 2019.

Costco had been aggressive in opening new warehouses and entering new geographic areas. As of December 2000, the Company operated a chain of 349 warehouses in 32 states (251 locations), nine Canadian provinces (59 locations), the United Kingdom (11 locations, through an 80 percent-owned subsidiary), South Korea (four locations), Taiwan (three locations, through a 55 percent-owned subsidiary), and Japan (two locations), as well as 19 warehouses in Mexico through a 50 percent joint venture partner. Ten years later, in December 2010, Costco was operating 585 warehouses in 42 states (425 locations), nine Canadian provinces (80 loca-tions), Mexico (32 locations), the United Kingdom (22 locations), Japan (nine locations), South Korea (seven locations), Taiwan (six locations), and Australia (one location). Some nine years and three months later, Costco had opened an additional 203 warehouses, had 546 warehouses in 45 states, and 236 warehouses in 11 countries, including a recently-opened warehouse in Shanghai, China.

Exhibit 4 shows a breakdown of Costco's geo-graphic operations for fiscal years 2017–2019.

Marketing and Advertising

Costco's low prices and its reputation for making shopping at Costco something of a treasure-hunt made it unnecessary to engage in extensive advertis-ing or sales campaigns. Marketing and promotional activities were generally limited to monthly coupon mailers to members, periodic e-mails to members from Costco.com publicizing "hot deals" and other special promotional offerings and sales events at warehouses, occasional direct mail to prospective new members, and regular direct marketing pro-grams (such as *The Costco Connection,* a magazine published for members), in-store product sampling, and special campaigns for new warehouse openings.

For new warehouse openings, marketing teams personally contacted businesses in the area that were potential wholesale members; these contacts were supplemented with direct mailings during the period immediately prior to opening. Potential Gold Star (individual) members were contacted by direct mail or by promotions at local employee associations and businesses with large numbers of employees. After a membership base was estab-lished in an area, most new memberships came from word of mouth (existing members telling friends and acquaintances about their shopping experiences at Costco), follow-up messages distrib-uted through regular payroll or other organizational communications to employee groups, and ongoing direct solicitations to prospective business and Gold Star members.

Website Sales

Costco operated websites in the United States, Canada, Mexico, the United Kingdom, Taiwan, and South Korea—both to enable members to shop for many in-store products online and to provide mem-bers with a means of obtaining a much wider var-iety of value-priced products and services that were not practical to stock at the company's warehouses. New websites in Japan and Australia were expected to be operational by early 2020. Craig Jelinek was committed to a website strategy that provided excep-tional service and value to Costco members who wanted to shop online. In recent years, online mer-chandise offerings had expanded significantly, and the company was continuously exploring oppor-tunities to deliver added value to members via a broader array of online offerings. Examples of value-priced items that members could buy online included sofas, beds, mattresses, entertainment cen-ters and TV lift cabinets, outdoor furniture, office furniture, kitchen appliances, billiard tables, and hot tubs. Members could also use the company's websites for such services as digital photo process-ing, prescription fulfillment, travel, the Costco auto

EXHIBIT 4   Selected Geographic Operating Data, Costco Wholesale Corporation, Fiscal Years 2017–2019 ($ in millions)

	United States Operations	Canadian Operations	Other International	Total
Year Ended September 1, 2019				
Total revenue (including membership fees)	$111,751	$21,366	$19,586	$152,703
Operating income	3,063	924	750	4,737
Capital expenditures	2,186	303	509	2,998
Number of warehouses (as of September 1, 2019)	543	106	139	782
Year Ended September 2, 2018				
Total revenue (including membership fees)	$102,286	$20,689	$18,601	$141,576
Operating income	2,787	939	754	4,480
Capital expenditures	2,046	268	655	2,969
Number of warehouses (as of September 2, 2018)	527	100	135	762
Year Ended September 3, 2017				
Total revenue (including membership fees)	$ 93,889	$18,775	$16,361	$129,025
Operating income	2,644	841	626	4,111
Capital expenditures	1,714	277	511	2,502
Number of warehouses (as of September 2017)	518	98	130	746

Note: The dollar numbers shown for the "Other International" categories represent only Costco's ownership share, since all foreign operations were joint ventures (although Costco was the majority owner of these ventures). Countries with warehouses in the Other International category at the end of fiscal 2019 included Mexico, United Kingdom, Japan, South Korea, Taiwan, Australia, Spain, Iceland, France, and China; Costco's two warehouses in Puerto Rico were included in the United States Operations category.

Source: Company 10-K reports, 2017–2019.

program (for purchasing selected new vehicles with discount prices through participating dealerships), and other membership services. In 2018, Costco sold 650,000 vehicles through its 3,000 dealer partners (up 25 percent over the 520,000 vehicles sold in 2017); the big attraction to members of buying a new or used vehicle through Costco's auto program was being able to skip the hassle of bargaining with the dealer over price and, instead, paying an attractively low price pre-arranged by Costco. At Costco's online photo center, customers could upload images and pick up the prints at their local warehouse in little over an hour. Website sales accounted for four percent of Costco's total net sales in fiscal 2019, versus three percent in 2014.

In 2017, Costco made improvements in website functionality, search capability, checkout, and delivery times. New offerings were added at Costco Travel, and the company introduced hotel-only booking reservations. Costco Travel's rental car rates were consistently some of the lowest in the marketplace

and in 2017 car rentals became available to members in Canada and the United Kingdom. Additionally, the annual two percent reward for Executive members was extended to apply to Costco Travel purchases in the United States and Canada. Lastly, the company launched Costco Grocery, a two-day delivery on dry grocery items, and a same-day delivery offering both fresh and dry grocery items through partnering with Instacart.

In 2018, Costco began opening business centers in selected warehouses; at the end of fiscal 2019, it had opened 18 business centers in the United States and two in Canada. As many as 40 new business centers were planned for 2020.

Supply Chain and Distribution

Costco bought the majority of its merchandise directly from manufacturers, routing it either directly to its warehouse stores or to one of the company's cross-docking depots that served as distribution points for nearby stores and for shipping orders to members making online purchases. In 2018, Costco had more than 20 geographically-scattered cross-docking depots with a combined space exceeding 11 million square feet in the United States, Canada, and various other international locations. Depots received container-based shipments from manufacturers, transferred the goods to pallets, and then shipped full-pallet quantities of several types to goods to individual warehouses via rail or semi-trailer trucks, generally in less than 24 hours. This maximized freight volume and handling efficiencies. Depots were also used to ship bulky merchandise to members that had been ordered online; members often picked up online orders that would fit in their vehicles at nearby warehouses.

When merchandise arrived at a warehouse, forklifts moved the full pallets straight to the sales floor and onto racks and shelves (without the need for multiple employees to touch the individual packages/cartons on the pallets)—the first time most items were physically touched at a warehouse was when shoppers reached onto the shelf/rack to pick it out of a carton and put it into their shopping cart. Very little incoming merchandise was stored in locations off the sales floor in order to minimize receiving and handling costs.

Costco had direct buying relationships with many producers of national brand-name merchandise and with manufacturers that supplied its Kirkland Signature products. Costco's merchandise buyers were always alert for opportunities to add products of top quality manufacturers and vendors on a one-time or ongoing basis. No one manufacturer supplied a significant percentage of the merchandise that Costco stocked. Costco had not experienced difficulty in obtaining sufficient quantities of merchandise, and management believed that if one or more of its current sources of supply became unavailable, the company could switch its purchases to alternative manufacturers without experiencing a substantial disruption of its business.

Costco's Membership Base and Member Demographics

Costco attracted the most affluent customers in discount retailing—the average annual income of Costco members was approximately $100,000 (in 2015 Costco management believed the 8.6 million subscribers to the company's monthly *Costco Connection* magazine had an average annual income of $156,000).[15] Many members were affluent urbanites, living in nice neighborhoods not far from Costco warehouses. One loyal Executive member, a criminal defense lawyer, said, "I think I spend over $20,000 to $25,000 a year buying all my products here from food to clothing—except my suits. I have to buy them at the Armani stores."[16] Another Costco loyalist said, "This is the best place in the world. It's like going to church on Sunday. You can't get anything better than this. This is a religious experience."[17]

Costco had two primary types of memberships: Business and Gold Star (individual). Business memberships were limited to businesses, but included individuals with a business license, retail sales license, or other evidence of business existence. A business membership also included a free household card (a significant number of business members shopped at Costco for their personal needs). Business members also had the ability to purchase "add-on" membership cards for up to six partners or associates in the business. Costco's current annual fee for Business and Gold Star memberships was $60 in the United States and Canada and varied by country in its Other International operations. Individuals in the United States and Canada who did not qualify for business membership could purchase a Gold Star membership, which included a household card for another family member (additional add-on cards could not be purchased by Gold Star members). All types of members (including household card members) could shop at any Costco warehouse.

Business, Business add-on, and Gold Star members in the United States and Canada could upgrade to Executive membership for an additional $60 (an annual membership fee of $120); upgrade fees to Executive memberships elsewhere varied by country. The primary appeal of upgrading to Executive membership was eligibility for a two percent annual reward (rebate) on qualified pre-tax purchases. Reward certificates were issued annually and could be used toward purchases of most merchandise at the front-end registers of Costco warehouses—rebate awards could not be used to purchase alcohol and tobacco products, gasoline, postage stamps, and food court items. The two percent rebate for Executive members was capped at $1,000 for any 12-month period in the United States and Canada (equivalent to annual qualified pre-tax purchases of $50,000); the maximum rebate varied in other countries. Executive members also were eligible for savings and benefits on various business and consumer services offered by Costco, including merchant credit card processing, small-business loans, auto and home insurance, long-distance telephone service, check printing, and real estate and mortgage services; these services were mostly offered by third-party providers and varied by state—Executive members did not receive two percent rebate credit on purchases of these ancillary services. In fiscal 2019, Executive members represented 39 percent of Costco's cardholders (including add-ons, but not holders of household cards) and accounted for approximately two-thirds of total company sales. Costco's member renewal rate was 91 percent in the United States and Canada, and 88 percent on a worldwide basis at the end of fiscal 2019. Recent trends in membership are shown at the bottom of Exhibit 1.

In general, with variations by country, Costco members could pay for their purchases with certain debit and credit cards, co-branded Costco credit cards, cash, or checks; in the United States and Puerto Rico, members could use a co-branded Citi/Costco Visa Anywhere credit card for purchases at Costco and elsewhere, Costco Cash cards, and all Visa cards. Since the June 2016 launch of Citi/Costco Visa® Anywhere Card, 1.8 million new member accounts (approximately 2.4 million new credit cards) were opened. The enhanced cashback Visa Anywhere rewards included earning four percent on gas; three percent on restaurant, hotel, and eligible travel; two percent at Costco and Costco.com; and one percent on all other purchases, exceeding the company's previous co-branded credit card offering with American Express. Executive Members using the new Visa Anywhere card continued to earn a two percent rebate on qualified purchases.

Costco accepted merchandise returns when members were dissatisfied with their purchases. Losses associated with dishonored checks were minimal because any member whose check had been dishonored was prevented from paying by check or cashing a check at the point of sale until restitution was made. The membership format facilitated strictly controlling the entrances and exits of warehouses, resulting in limited inventory losses of less than two-tenths of one percent of net sales—well below those of typical discount retail operations.

Warehouse Management

Costco warehouse managers were delegated considerable authority over store operations. In effect, warehouse managers functioned as entrepreneurs running their own retail operation. They were responsible for coming up with new ideas about what items would sell in their stores, effectively merchandising the ever-changing lineup of treasure-hunt products, and orchestrating in-store product locations and displays to maximize sales and quick turnover. In experimenting with what items to stock and what in-store merchandising techniques to employ, warehouse managers had to know the clientele who patronized their locations—for instance, big-ticket diamonds sold well at some warehouses but not at others. Costco's best managers kept their finger on the pulse of the members who shopped their warehouse location to stay in sync with what would sell well, and they had a flair for creating a certain element of excitement, hum, and buzz in their warehouses. Such managers spurred above-average sales volumes—sales at Costco's top-volume warehouses ran about $5 million to $7 million a week, with sales exceeding $1 million on many days. Successful managers also thrived on the rat race of running a high-traffic store and solving the inevitable crises of the moment.

Compensation and Workforce Practices

As of September 2019, Costco had 149,000 full-time employees and 105,000 part-time employees. Approximately 16,000 hourly employees at locations in California, Maryland, New Jersey, and New York, as well as at one warehouse in Virginia, were represented by the International Brotherhood of Teamsters. All remaining employees were non-union.

In March 2019, Costco raised its minimum wage for hourly employees to $15 per hour and also bumped up pay scales for a variety of other jobs, including supervisory positions. Hourly pay scales for warehouse jobs ranged from $15 to $19 in the second half of 2019. The highest paid full-time warehouse employees could earn close to $25.00 per hour after four years. Front-end supervisors averaged about $26 per hour. Compensation averaged $16-$18 per hour for pharmacy technicians and $62.56 per hour for licensed pharmacists., and about $146,000 annually for pharmacy managers.[18]

Salaried Costco employees earned anywhere from $30,000 to close to $200,000 annually, depending on job type.[19] For example, salaries for merchandise managers, membership managers, and meat department managers reportedly were in the $55,000 to $85,000 range; salaries for supervisors ranged from $45,000 to $75,000; salaries for database, computer systems, and software applications developers/analysts/project managers were in the $85,000 to $125,000 range. Average salaries for pharmacy managers were in the $146,000 range. Average total compensation (including bonuses) for assistant general managers of warehouses ranged from $78,000 to $97,000 and reportedly averaged about $88,000.[20] Average total pay for general managers of warehouses ranged from $90,000 to $180,000 and reportedly averaged about $135,000.[21]

Employees enjoyed the full spectrum of benefits. Salaried employees were eligible for benefits on the first of the second month after the date of hire. Full-time hourly employees were eligible for benefits on the first day of the second month after completing 250 eligible paid hours; part-time hourly employees became benefit-eligible on the first day of the second month after completing 450 eligible paid hours. The benefit package included the following:

- Health care plans for full-time and part-time employees that included coverage for mental illness, substance abuse, and professional counseling for assorted personal and family issues.

- A choice of a core dental plan or a premium dental plan.

- A pharmacy plan that entailed (1) co-payments of $3 for generic drugs and $10 to $50 for brand-name prescriptions filled at a Costco warehouse or online pharmacy and (2) co-payments of $15 to $50 for generic or brand-name prescriptions filled at all other pharmacies.

- A vision program that paid up to $60 for a refraction eye exam (the amount charged at Costco's Optical Centers) and had $175 annual allowances for the purchase of glasses and contact lenses at Costco Optical Centers. Employees located more than 25 miles from a Costco Optical Center could visit any provider of choice for annual eye exams and could purchase eyeglasses from any in-network source and submit claim forms for reimbursement.

- A hearing aid benefit of up to $1,750 every four years (available only to employees and their eligible dependents enrolled in a Costco medical plan, and the hearing aids had to be supplied at a Costco Hearing Aid Center).

- A 401(k) plan open to all employees who had completed 90 days of employment. Costco matched hourly employee contributions by 50 cents on the dollar for the first $1,000 annually (the maximum company match was $500 per year). The company's union employees on the West Coast qualified for matching contributions of 50 cents on the dollar up to a maximum company match of $250 a year. In addition to the matching contribution, Costco also normally made a discretionary contribution to the accounts of eligible employees based on the number of years of service with the company (or in the case of union employees based on the straight-time hours worked). For other than union employees, this discretionary contribution was a percentage of the employee's compensation that ranged from a low of three percent (for employees with one to one years of service) to a high of nine percent (for employees with 25 or more years of service). Company contributions to all the various employee 410(k) plans were $489 million in 2016, $543 million in 2017, $578 million in 2018, and $614 million in 2019.

- A dependent care reimbursement plan in which Costco employees whose families qualified could pay for day care for children under 13 or adult day care with pretax dollars and realize savings of anywhere from $750 to $2,000 per year.

- Long-term and short-term disability coverage.

- Generous life insurance and accidental death and dismemberment coverage, with benefits based on years of service and whether the employee worked full-time or part-time. Employees could elect to purchase supplemental coverage for themselves, their spouses, or their children.

- An employee stock purchase plan allowing all employees to buy Costco stock via payroll deduction so as to avoid commissions and fees.

Although Costco's longstanding practice of paying good wages and good benefits was contrary to conventional wisdom in discount retailing, co-founder and former CEO Jim Sinegal, who originated the practice, firmly believed that having a well-compensated workforce was very important to executing Costco's strategy successfully. He said, "Imagine that you have 120,000 loyal ambassadors out there who are constantly saying good things about Costco. It has to be a significant advantage for you. . . . Paying good wages and keeping your people working with you is very good business."[22] When a reporter asked him about why Costco treated its workers so well compared to other retailers (particularly Walmart, which paid lower wages and had a skimpier benefits package), Sinegal replied: "Why shouldn't employees have the right to good wages and good careers. . . . It absolutely makes good business sense. Most people agree that we're the lowest-cost producer. Yet we pay the highest wages. So it must mean we get better productivity. Its axiomatic in our business—you get what you pay for."[23]

Good wages and benefits were said to be why employee turnover at Costco typically averaged about 5 percent or less after the first year of employment. Some Costco employees had been with the company since its founding in 1983. Many others had started working part-time at Costco while in high school or college and opted to make a career at the company. One Costco employee told an ABC *20/20* reporter, "It's a good place to work; they take good care of us."[24] A Costco vice president and head baker said working for Costco was a family affair: "My whole family works for Costco, my husband does, my daughter does, my new son-in-law does."[25] Another employee, a receiving clerk who made about $40,000 a year, said, "I want to retire here. I love it here."[26] An employee with over two years of service could not be fired without the approval of a senior company officer.

Selecting People for Open Positions   Costco's top management wanted employees to feel that they could have a long career at Costco. It was company policy to fill the vast majority of its higher-level openings by promotions from within; at one recent point, the percentage ran close to 98 percent, which meant that the majority of Costco's management team members (including warehouse, merchandise, administrative, membership, front end, and receiving managers) had come up through the ranks. Many of the company's vice presidents had started in entry-level jobs. According to Jim Sinegal, "We have guys who started pushing shopping carts out on the parking lot for us who are now vice presidents of our company."[27] Costco made a point of recruiting at local universities; Sinegal explained why: "These people are smarter than the average person, hardworking, and they haven't made a career choice."[28] On another occasion, he said, "If someone came to us and said he just got a master's in business at Harvard, we would say fine, would you like to start pushing carts?"[29] Those employees who demonstrated smarts and strong people management skills moved up through the ranks.

But without an aptitude for the details of discount retailing, even up-and-coming employees stood no chance of being promoted to a position of warehouse manager. Top Costco executives who oversaw warehouse operations insisted that candidates for warehouse managers be top-flight merchandisers with a gift for the details of making items fly off the shelves. Based on his experience as CEO, Sinegal said, "People who have a feel for it just start to get it. Others, you look at them and it's like staring at a blank canvas. I'm not trying to be unduly harsh, but that's the way it works."[30] Most newly appointed warehouse managers at Costco came from the ranks of assistant warehouse managers who had a track record of being shrewd merchandisers and tuned into what new or different products might sell well given the clientele that patronized their particular warehouse. Just having the requisite skills in people management, crisis management, and cost-effective warehouse operations was not enough.

Executive Compensation   Executives at Costco did not earn the outlandish salaries that had become customary over the past decade at most large corporations. In Jim Sinegal's last two years as Costco's CEO, he received a salary of $350,000 and a bonus of $190,400 in fiscal 2010 and a salary of $350,000 and a bonus of $198,400 in fiscal 2011. Craig Jelinek's salary as President and CEO in fiscal 2019 was $930,000 (which was increased to $1 million for calendar year 2019), and he received a bonus of $190,400 and a stock award worth $6.7 million; Richard Galanti's salary as Executive Vice-President and Chief Financial Officer in fiscal 2019 was

$784,146, and he received a bonus of $76,160 and a stock award worth nearly $3.2 million. Other Costco executive officers received salaries in the $662,000 to $737,000 range, bonuses of about $76,000, and stock awards worth nearly $3.2 million in fiscal 2019.

Asked why executive compensation at Costco was only a fraction of the amounts typically paid to top-level executives at other corporations with revenues and operating scale comparable to Costco's, Sinegal replied: "I figured that if I was making something like 12 times more than the typical person working on the floor, that that was a fair salary."[31] To another reporter, he said: "Listen, I'm one of the founders of this business. I've been very well rewarded. I don't require a salary that's 100 times more than the people who work on the sales floor."[32] During his tenure as CEO, Sinegal's employment contract was only a page long and provided that he could be terminated for cause.

However, while executive salaries and bonuses were modest in comparison with those at other companies Costco's size, Costco did close the gap via an equity compensation program that featured awarding restricted stock units (RSUs) to executives based on defined performance criteria. The philosophy at Costco was that equity compensation should be the largest component of compensation for all executive officers and be tied directly to achievement of pre-tax income targets.

Costco's Business Philosophy, Values, and Code of Ethics

Jim Sinegal, who was the son of a steelworker, had ingrained five simple and down-to-earth business principles into Costco's corporate culture and the manner in which the company operated. The following are excerpts of these principles and operating approaches:[33]

1. **Obey the law**—The law is irrefutable! Absent a moral imperative to challenge a law, we must conduct our business in total compliance with the laws of every community where we do business. We pledge to:
   - Comply with all laws and other legal requirements.
   - Respect all public officials and their positions.
   - Comply with safety and security standards for all products sold.
   - Exceed ecological standards required in every community where we do business.
   - Comply with all applicable wage and hour laws.
   - Comply with all applicable antitrust laws.
   - Conduct business in and with foreign countries in a manner that is legal and proper under United States and foreign laws.
   - Not offer, give, ask for, or receive any form of bribe or kickback to or from any person or pay to expedite government action or otherwise act in violation of the Foreign Corrupt Practices Act or the laws of other countries.
   - Promote fair, accurate, timely, and understandable disclosure in reports filed with the Securities and Exchange Commission and in other public communications by the Company.

2. **Take care of our members**—Costco membership is open to business owners, as well as individuals. Our members are our reason for being—the key to our success. If we don't keep our members happy, little else that we do will make a difference. There are plenty of shopping alternatives for our members, and if they fail to show up, we cannot survive. Our members have extended a trust to Costco by virtue of paying a fee to shop with us. We will succeed only if we do not violate the trust they have extended to us, and that trust extends to every area of our business. We pledge to:
   - Provide top-quality products at the best prices in the market.
   - Provide high-quality, safe, and wholesome food products by requiring that both vendors and employees be in compliance with the highest food safety standards in the industry.
   - Provide our members with a 100 percent satisfaction guaranteed warranty on every product and service we sell, including their membership fee.
   - Assure our members that every product we sell is authentic in make and in representation of performance.
   - Make our shopping environment a pleasant experience by making our members feel welcome as our guests.
   - Provide products to our members that will be ecologically sensitive.

- Provide our members with the best customer service in the retail industry.
- Give back to our communities through employee volunteerism and employee and corporate contributions to United Way and Children's Hospitals.

3. **Take care of our employees**—Our employees are our most important asset. We believe we have the very best employees in the warehouse club industry, and we are committed to providing them with rewarding challenges and ample opportunities for personal and career growth. We pledge to provide our employees with:
   - Competitive wages.
   - Great benefits.
   - A safe and healthy work environment.
   - Challenging and fun work.
   - Career opportunities.
   - An atmosphere free from harassment or discrimination.
   - An Open-Door Policy that allows access to ascending levels of management to resolve issues.
   - Opportunities to give back to their communities through volunteerism and fundraising.

4. **Respect our suppliers**—Our suppliers are our partners in business and for us to prosper as a company, they must prosper with us. To that end, we strive to:
   - Treat all suppliers and their representatives as we would expect to be treated if visiting their places of business.
   - Honor all commitments.
   - Protect all suppliers' property assigned to Costco as though it were our own.
   - Not accept gratuities of any kind from a supplier.
   - If in doubt as to what course of action to take on a business matter that is open to varying ethical interpretations, TAKE THE HIGH ROAD AND DO WHAT IS RIGHT.

If we do these four things throughout our organization, then we will achieve our ultimate goal, which is to:

5. **Reward our shareholders**—As a company with stock that is traded publicly on the NASDAQ stock exchange, our shareholders are our business partners. We can only be successful so long as we are providing them with a good return on the money they invest in our company. . . . We pledge to operate our company in such a way that our present and future stockholders, as well as our employees, will be rewarded for our efforts.

Environmental Sustainability and Responsible Sourcing of Meat and Dairy Products

In recent years, Costco management had undertaken a series of initiatives to invest in various environmental and energy saving systems, the use of packaging that could be recycled or composted, reduction of both packaging materials and food waste, greater sourcing of sustainable seafood products from wild fisheries and farmed aquaculture, working with recognized experts and suppliers to increase the percentage of cage-free eggs it sold, and compliance with best practices in dairy farming, animal care, and animal well-being. The stated objective was to ensure that the company's carbon footprint grew at a slower rate than the company's sales growth and that Costco was a responsible steward of the animals, land, and other environmental resources utilized in the products it sold.

Costco's metal warehouse design, which included use of recycled steel, was consistent with the requirements of the Silver Level LEED Standard—the certification standards of the organization Leadership in Energy and Environmental Design (LEED) were nationally accepted as a benchmark green building design and construction. Costco's recently-developed non-metal designs for warehouses had resulted in the ability to meet Gold Level LEED Standards.

All new facilities were being designed and constructed to be more energy efficient; this included using LED lighting and energy-efficient mechanical systems for heating, cooling, and refrigeration in both new and existing facilities. In 2016, Costco began retrofitting existing facilities with LED lighting; as of year-end fiscal 2018, 1,166 retrofits had been completed, resulting in a total estimated energy savings of 206 million kilowatt-hours per year.[34] All lighting in new construction utilized LED technology. At the end of fiscal 2018, Costco had rooftop solar photovoltaic systems in operation at 109 of its warehouses; some warehouses used solar power to light their parking lots. In 2017, Costco began piloting the use of fuel cells as an alternate source of electricity at a handful of locations and was continuing to evaluate their use in future facilities. So far, Costco had found the fuel cells at test sites had resulted in lower combined power and natural gas expenses. The company was also exploring use of new HVAC and refrigerant systems that were more energy efficient and increasing its use of refrigerants that further reduced global warming potential and greenhouse gas emissions.

Another energy-saving initiative had been to install Internet-based energy management systems at all Costco warehouses in North America and at some international locations, giving Costco the ability to regulate energy usage on an hourly basis. These, along with installation of LED lighting and warehouse skylights, had reduced the lighting loads on Costco's sales floors by over 50 percent since 2001. Costco had undertaken a series of initiatives at company facilities worldwide to reduce water usage, reduce or remove potential chemical harm to humans and to the environment, use recycled asphalt for paving most warehouse parking lots, and use best practices to irrigate landscapes and manage groundwater runoff. Empty store cartons were given to members to carry their purchases home. Costco had been an active member of the Environmental Protection Agency's Energy Star and Climate Protection Partnerships since 2002 and was a major retailer of Energy Star qualified compact florescent lamp (CFL) bulbs and LED light bulbs.

Costco was committed to sourcing all of the seafood it sold from responsible and environmentally sustainable sources that were certified by the Marine Stewardship Council; in no instances did Costco sell seafood species that were classified as environmentally endangered and it monitored the aquaculture practices of its suppliers that farmed seafood. The company had long been committed to enhancing the welfare and proper handling of all animals used in food products sold at Costco. According to the company's official statement on animal welfare, "This is not only the right thing to do, it is an important moral and ethical obligation we owe to our members, suppliers, and most of all to the animals we depend on for products that are sold at Costco."[35] As part of the company's commitment, Costco had established an animal welfare audit program that utilized recognized audit standards and programs conducted by trained, certified auditors and that reviewed animal welfare both on the farm and at slaughter.

COMPETITION

According to IBISWorld, the Warehouse Clubs and Supercenters industry—defined as companies that provided a range of general merchandise including food and beverages, furniture and appliances, health and wellness products, apparel and accessories, fuel and ancillary services—was expected to have sales of about $514 billion in the United States alone in 2020.[36] There were three main wholesale club competitors—Costco Wholesale, Sam's Club, and BJ's Wholesale Club. Going into 2020, these three rivals had over 1,600 warehouse locations across the United States and Canada; most every major metropolitan area had one, if not several, warehouse clubs. The combined 2019 sales of Costco, Sam's Club, and BJ's Wholesale in the United States and Canada was $224.4 billion. Costco had a 68 percent share of warehouse club sales across the United States and Canada, with Sam's Club (a division of Walmart) having just over a 26 percent share and BJ's Wholesale Club and several small warehouse club competitors close to a 6 percent share.

Competition among the warehouse clubs was based on such factors as price, merchandise quality and selection, location, and member service. However, warehouse clubs also competed with a wide range of other types of retailers, including retail discounters like Walmart and Dollar General, supermarkets, general merchandise chains, specialty chains, gasoline stations, and Internet retailers. Not only did Walmart, the world's largest retailer, compete directly with Costco via its Sam's Club subsidiary, but its Walmart Supercenters sold many of the same types of merchandise at attractively low prices as well. Target, Kohl's, Kroger, and Amazon.com had emerged as significant retail competitors in certain general merchandise categories. Low-cost operators selling a single category or narrow range of merchandise—such as Trader Joe's, Lowe's, Home Depot, Office Depot, Staples, Best Buy, PetSmart, and Barnes & Noble—had significant market shares in their respective product categories. Notwithstanding the competition from other retailers and discounters, the low prices and merchandise selection found at Costco, Sam's Club, and BJ's

Wholesale were attractive to small business owners, individual households (particularly bargain-hunters and those with large families), churches and non-profit organizations, caterers, and small restaurants. The internationally located warehouses faced similar types of competitors.

Brief profiles of Costco's two primary competitors in North America are presented in the following sections.

Sam's Club

The first Sam's Club opened in 1984, and Walmart management in the ensuing years proceeded to grow the warehouse membership club concept into a significant business and major Walmart division. The concept of the Sam's Club format was to sell merchandise at very low profit margins, resulting in low prices to members. The mission of Sam's Club was "to make savings simple for members by providing them with exciting, quality merchandise and a superior shopping experience, all at a great value."[37] The target market at Sam's Club was small businesses and suburban families with incomes of $75,000 to $125,000.

In early 2020, Sam's Club operated 599 locations in 44 states and Puerto Rico, many of which were adjacent to Walmart Supercenters, and about 100 Sam's Club locations in Mexico, Brazil, and China. (Financial and operating data for the Sam's Club locations in Mexico, Brazil, and China were not separately available because Walmart grouped its reporting of all store operations in 26 countries outside the United States into a segment called Walmart International that did not break out the international operations of Sam's Club.) In fiscal year 2020 (ending January 31, 2020), the Sam's Club locations in the United States and Puerto Rico and operations at www.samsclub.com had record revenues of $59.2 billion (including membership fees), making it the eighth largest retailer in the United States.

Sam's Clubs generally ranged between 94,000 and 168,000 square feet, with an average at the end of fiscal 2020 of approximately 134,000 square feet; several newer locations were as large as 190,000 square feet. All Sam's Club warehouses had concrete floors, sparse décor, and goods displayed on pallets, simple wooden shelves, or racks in the case of apparel. In 2009 and 2010, Sam's Club began a long-term warehouse remodeling program for its older locations. During fiscal 2018, management closed 67 underperforming Sam's Club locations.

Exhibit 5 provides financial and operating highlights for selected years from 2016 to 2020.

EXHIBIT 5   Selected Financial and Operating Data for Sam's Club, Fiscal Years 2016–2020

Sam's Club	Fiscal Years 2016–2020				
	2020	2019	2018	2017	2016
Net sales in the United States and Puerto Rico (millions of $)	$58,792	$57,839	$59,216	$57,365	$56,828
Operating income in the United States and Puerto Rico (millions of $)	1,642	1,520	982	1,671	1,820
Assets in the United States and Puerto Rico (millions of $)	13,494	12,893	13,418	14,125	13,998
Number of U.S. and Puerto Rico locations at year-end	599	599	597	660	655
Average sales per year-end U.S. and Puerto Rican location, including membership fees (in millions of $)	$98.2	$96.6	$99.2	$86.9	$86.8
Sales growth at existing U.S. and Puerto Rico warehouses open more than 12 months:					
Including gasoline sales	1.6%	(2.3)%	3.2%	0.5%	(3.2)%
Not including gasoline sales	0.9%	(3.9)%	2.2%	1.8%	1.4%
Average warehouse size in the United States and Puerto Rico (square feet)		134,000	134,100	133,900	133,700

[a] The net sales figure does not include membership fees and is only for warehouses in the United States and Puerto Rico. For financial reporting purposes, Walmart consolidates the operations of all foreign-based stores into a single "international" segment figure. Thus, separate financial information for the foreign-based Sam's Club locations in Mexico, China, and Brazil is not separately available.

Source: Walmart's 10-K reports and annual reports, fiscal years 2020, 2018, and 2016.

Merchandise Offerings

Sam's Club warehouses stocked about 4,000 items, a big fraction of which were standard and a small fraction of which represented special buys and one-time offerings. The treasure-hunt items at Sam's Club tended to be less upscale and less expensive than those at Costco. The merchandise selection included brand-name merchandise in a variety of categories and a selection of private-label items sold under the "Member's Mark," "Daily Chef," and "Sam's Club" brands. Most club locations had fresh-foods departments that included bakery, meat, produce, floral products, and a Sam's Café. Most locations also had a one-hour photo processing department, a pharmacy that filled prescriptions, hearing aid and optical departments, tire and battery centers, and self-service gasoline pumps; car wash services were available at about 40 locations. Sam's Club guaranteed it would beat any price for branded prescriptions. Members could shop for a wider assortment of merchandise (about 59,000 items) and services online at www.samsclub.com; e-commerce sales were $3.6 billion in fiscal 2020 and $2.7 billion in fiscal 2019. samsclub.com had an average of about 20.4 million unique visitors per month and provided members the option of pick-up at local Sam's Club locations or direct-to-home delivery.

The percentage composition of sales (including ecommerce sales) across major merchandise categories was:

	2020	2019	2018
Grocery and consumables (dairy, meat, bakery, deli, produce, dry, chilled or frozen packaged foods, alcoholic and nonalcoholic beverages, floral, snack foods, candy, other grocery items, health and beauty aids, paper goods, laundry and home care, baby care, pet supplies, and other consumable items)	60%	58%	58%
Fuel and other categories (gasoline, tobacco, tools and power equipment, and tire and battery centers)	19%	21%	21%
Technology, office and entertainment (electronics, wireless, software, video games, movies, books, music, toys, office supplies, office furniture, photo processing, and gift cards)	6%	6%	6%
Home and apparel (home improvement, outdoor living, grills, gardening, furniture, apparel, jewelry, housewares, toys, seasonal items, mattresses, and small appliances)	9%	9%	9%
Health and wellness (pharmacy, hearing and optical services, and over-the-counter drugs)	6%	6%	6%

Source: Walmart's fiscal year 2020 10-K report.

Membership and Hours of Operation   The annual fee for Sam's Club members was $45 for a Club membership card, with a spouse card available at no additional cost. Club members could purchase up to eight "add-on" memberships for an additional $40 each. Alternatively, members could purchase a "Plus" membership for $100, and up to 16 "add-on" memberships for $40 each. Plus members were eligible for free shipping on ecommerce orders and for Cash Rewards, a benefit that provided 2 percent back for qualifying Sam's Club purchases up to an annual maximum cash reward of $500. Cash-back rewards could be used for purchases, membership fees, or redeemed for cash. About 600,000 members shopped at Sam's Club weekly. Income from membership fees was a significant percentage of the operating income earned by Sam's Club.

Regular hours of operations were Monday through Friday from 10:00 a.m. to 8:30 p.m., Saturday from 9:00 a.m. to 8:30 p.m., and Sunday from 10:00 a.m. to 6:00 p.m.; all Plus cardholders had the ability to shop before the regular operating hours Monday through Saturday, starting at 7:00 a.m. All club members could use a variety of payment methods, including Visa credit and debit cards, American Express cards, and a co-branded Sam's Club "Cash-Back" Mastercard. Sam's Club also offered "Scan and Go," a mobile checkout and payment solution, which allowed members to bypass the checkout line. The pharmacy and optical departments accepted payments for products and services through members' health benefit plans.

Distribution Approximately 73 percent of the non-fuel merchandise at Sam's Club was shipped either from some 25 distribution facilities dedicated to Sam's Club operations that were strategically located across the continental United States or, in the case of perishable and certain other items, from nearby Walmart grocery distribution centers; the balance was shipped by suppliers direct to Sam's Club locations. Like Costco, Sam's Club distribution centers employed cross-docking techniques whereby incoming shipments were transferred immediately to outgoing trailers destined for Sam's Club locations; shipments typically spent less than 24 hours at a cross-docking facility and in some instances were there only an hour. A combination of company-owned trucks and independent trucking companies were used to transport merchandise from distribution centers to club locations. Sam's Club shipped merchandise purchased on samsclub.com and through its mobile commerce applications by a number of methods including shipments made directly from Clubs, nine dedicated eCommerce fulfillment centers, two dedicated import facilities, and other distribution centers.

Employment In early 2020, Sam's Club employed about 90,000 people across all aspects of its operations in the United States. While the people who worked at Sam's Club warehouses were in all stages of life, a sizable fraction had accepted job offers because they had minimal skill levels and were looking for their first job, or needed only a part-time job, or were wanting to start a second career. Approximately 75 percent of the management staff at Sam's Club had begun their careers at Sam's Club as hourly warehouse employees and had moved up through the ranks to their present positions.

BJ's Wholesale Club

BJ's Wholesale Club introduced the member warehouse concept to the northeastern United States in the mid-1980s and, as of April 2020, operated 218 warehouses and 145 BJ's gas locations in 17 eastern states extending from Maine to Florida. In its core New England market region, BJ's had about three times the number of locations compared to its next largest warehouse club competitor. Approximately 85 percent of BJ's warehouse clubs had at least one Costco or Sam's Club warehouse operating in their trading areas (within a distance of 10 miles or less).

Six distribution centers served BJ's existing locations and had the capacity to support up to 100 additional clubs along the East Coast of the United States. BJ's warehouse clubs ranged in size from 63,000 square feet to 163,000 square feet; newer clubs were typically about 85,000 square feet. BJ's market target was price-sensitive households with an average annual income of approximately $75,000.

In late June 2011, BJ's Wholesale agreed to a buyout offer from two private equity firms and shortly thereafter became a privately held company. However, in May 2018, the private company (recently renamed BJ's Wholesale Club Holdings) announced its intent to become a public company again and filed the necessary registration for an initial public offering of common stock with the Securities and Exchange Commission. In late June 2018, BJ's became a public company with an initial public offering of 37.5 million shares at a public offering price of $17 per share; its stock traded on the New York Stock Exchange under the ticker symbol BJ. In the next three years, BJ's hired Chris Baldwin as Chairman, President and Chief Executive Officer and made multiple senior management hires and changes to give its leadership team more experience in consumer-packaged goods, digital know-how, and consulting experience. The new management team implemented significant cultural and operational changes that included transforming how BJ's used data to improve member experience, instilling a culture of cost discipline, adopting a more proactive approach to growing its membership base, building a much more comprehensive collection of online merchandise offerings, installing the capability to deliver products to members' homes or office, and introducing a mobile app that enabled members to save coupon offers directly onto the app and self-checkout. In 2018 BJ's began same-day delivery of orders at a fixed fee. One of the new management team's strategic priorities was to make shopping at BJ's easier and more convenient for members.

Exhibit 6 shows selected financial and operating data for BJ's Wholesale Club Holdings, Inc. for the four most recent fiscal years.

Product Offerings and Merchandising Like Costco and Sam's Club, BJ's Wholesale sold high-quality, brand-name merchandise at prices that were significantly lower than the prices found at supermarkets, discount

EXHIBIT 6   Selected Financial and Operating Data, BJ's Wholesale Club Holdings, Inc., Fiscal Years 2017–2020

	Fiscal Years Ended			
	January 28, 2017	February 3, 2018	February 2, 2019	February 1, 2020
Selected Income Statement Data (in millions, except per share data)				
Net sales	$12,095.3	$12,496.0	$12,724.5	$12,888.6
Membership fees	255.2	258.6	282.9	302.2
Total revenues	12,350.5	12,754.6	13,007.4	13,190.7
Cost of sales	10,223.0	10,513.5	10,646.5	10,763.9
Selling, general and administrative expenses	1,908.8	2,017.8	2,051.3	2,059.4
Preopening expenses	2.7	3.0	6.1	15.2
Operating income	352.2	220.3	303.5	303.5
Interest expense, net	143.4	196.7	164.5	108.2
Provision for income taxes	28.0	(28.4)	11.8	56.2
Net income	$ 44.2	$ 50.3	$ 127.3	$ 187.2
Income per share attributable to common shareholders—diluted	$0.49	$0.54	$1.05	$1.35
Weighted average number of shares outstanding—diluted (in millions)	90.7	92.3	121.1	139.1
Balance Sheet and Cash Flow Data (in millions)				
Cash and cash equivalents		$ 34.9	$ 27.1	$ 30.2
Merchandise inventories		1,019.1	1,052.3	1,081.5
Total current assets		1,336.6	1,337.2	1,360.9
Property and equipment, net		758.8	748.8	760.2
Total assets		3,273.9	3,239.2	5,569.8
Total current liabilities		1,469.6	1,577.7	1,801.4
Long-term debt		2,492.6	1,546.5	1,337.3
Total stockholders' deficit		(1,029.9)	(202.1)	(54.3)
Cash flow from operations	$ 297.4	210.1	427.1	355.1
Capital expenditures	114.8	137.5	145.9	196.9
Free cash flow	182.7	72.6	281.2	158.2
Selected Operating Data				
Clubs open at end of year	214	215	216	217
Sales growth at existing clubs open more than 12 months	(2.6%)	0.8%	3.7%	0.7%
Sales growth at existing clubs open more than 12 months, excluding gasoline sales	(2.3%)	(0.9%)	2.2%	(0.9%)
Average sales per club location, including online sales	$ 56.5	$ 58.1	$ 58.9	$ 59.4
Membership renewal rate	85%	86%	87%	87%

Source: Company form S-1 registration statement, May 17, 2018; 2019 10-K report; and 2020 10-K report.

retail chains, department stores, drugstores, and specialty retail stores like Best Buy. Its merchandise lineup of about 7,200 items included consumer electronics, prerecorded media, small appliances, tires, jewelry, health and beauty aids, household products, computer software, books, greeting cards, apparel, furniture, toys, seasonal items, frozen foods, fresh meat and dairy products, beverages, dry grocery items, fresh produce, flowers, canned goods, and household products. About 70 percent of BJ's product line could be found in supermarkets. Sales of the company's two private-label brands, Wellsley Farms® and Berkley Jensen®, accounted for about 20 percent of total net sales. BJ's prices of a representative basket of 100 items were consistently about 25 percent below comparable brand name products sold by its four leading supermarket competitors. Members could purchase thousands of additional products at the company's website, **www.bjs.com**.

BJ's warehouses had a number of specialty services that were designed to enable members to complete more of their shopping at BJ's and to encourage more frequent trips to the clubs. Like Costco and Sam's Club, BJ's sold gasoline at a discounted price as a means of displaying a low-price image to prospective members and providing added value to existing members; in April 2020, there were gas station operations at 145 BJ's locations. Other specialty services included full-service optical centers; tire installation services; a propane tank filling service; home improvement services; travel services; a car rental service; cell phone kiosks; and product protection plans for appliances, electronics, and jewelry. Most of these services were provided by outside operators in space leased from BJ's. In early 2007, BJ's abandoned prescription filling and closed all of its 46 in-club pharmacies.

Membership   BJ's Wholesale Club had more than 5.5 million paid memberships as of early 2020 and a total of 10 million cardholders that generated membership fee revenues of $302 million in fiscal 2020. Individuals could become Inner Circle members for a fee of $55 per year that included a second card for a household member; cards for up to three other family members and friends could be added to an Inner Circle member's account for an additional $30 per card. A primary business membership cost $55 per year and included one free supplemental membership; business members could purchase up to eight additional supplemental business memberships at $30 each. U.S. military personnel—active and veteran—who enrolled at a BJ's club location could do so for a reduced membership fee. Individuals and businesses could upgrade to BJ's Perks/Rewards card for $110; Perks/Reward members received a free second card for a household member and could add up to three additional members for $30 each. BJ's Perks Rewards members earned two percent cash back on in-club and online purchases; cash awards were issued in $20 increments and could be used for in-store purchases; awards expired six months from the date issued. Non-members could purchase online access to **www.bjs.com** for $10 per year, which provided the benefits of member pricing for online purchases. Members could apply for a BJ's Perks Plus® or BJ's Perks Elite® credit card (MasterCard) that had no annual credit card fee and served as a membership card. The Perks Plus® card earned three percent cash back on eligible in-club and online purchases made with the credit card, while BJ's Perks Elite® cardholders earned five percent cash back on eligible in-club and online purchases made with the card. Both Plus and Elite cardholders received 10 cents off per gallon at BJ's gas stations when using their card to pay for fuel purchases, two percent cash back on non-BJ's gasoline purchases and eligible dining out purchases, and one percent cash back on all non-BJ's purchases everywhere else MasterCard was accepted. Fuel purchases made with these credit cards were not eligible for further cash back rewards; moreover, members with the $30 supplemental Business memberships had to upgrade to the $55 primary membership category to be eligible for a BJ's Plus or Elite credit card. Since fiscal year 2014, BJ's had grown co-branded Mastercard® holders by 527 percent. In fiscal year 2019, BJ's Perks Rewards members and co-branded Mastercard® members accounted for 28 percent of members and 43 percent of spend, compared to 25 percent of members and 39 percent of spend in fiscal year 2018. BJ's accepted MasterCard, Visa, Discover, and American Express cards at all locations; members could also pay for purchases by cash, check, or magnetically encoded Electronic Benefit Transfer cards (issued by state welfare departments). Manufacturer's coupons were accepted for merchandise purchased at the register in any Club where the product was sold. BJ's accepted returns of most merchandise within 30 days after purchase.

BJ's leadership team believed that members could save over ten times their $55 Inner Circle membership fee versus what they would have paid at traditional supermarket competitors if they spent $2,500 or more per year at BJ's on manufacturer-branded groceries.

Marketing and Promotion BJ's increased customer awareness of its clubs primarily through social media, direct mail, public relations efforts, community involvement programs, marketing programs for newly opened clubs, and various publications mailed to members throughout the year. BJ's also had dedicated marketing personnel who solicited potential business members and who contacted other selected organizations to increase the number of members. Periodically, it also ran free promotional membership and initially discounted membership promotions to attract new members, with the objective of converting them to paid members.

Warehouse Club Operations BJ's warehouses were located in both freestanding locations and shopping centers. Construction and site development costs for a full-sized owned BJ's club were in the $6 million to $10 million range; land acquisition costs ranged from $3 million to $10 million but could be significantly higher in some locations. Each warehouse generally had an investment of $3 to $4 million for fixtures and equipment; other pre-opening expenses at a new club were usually in the $1.0 to $2.0 million range.

Including space for parking and gas station operations, a typical full-sized BJ's club required 13 to 14 acres of land; smaller clubs typically required about eight acres.

Merchandise purchased from manufacturers was routed either to a BJ's cross-docking facility or directly to clubs. Personnel at the cross-docking facilities broke down truckload quantity shipments from manufacturers and reallocated goods for shipment to individual clubs, generally within 24 hours. BJ's worked closely with manufacturers to minimize the amount of handling required once merchandise is received at a club. BJ's contracted with a third party to operate three perishables distribution centers and deliver perishable products to its warehouse locations.

Merchandise in BJ's warehouses was generally displayed on pallets containing large quantities of each item, thereby reducing labor required for handling, stocking, and restocking. Backup merchandise was generally stored in steel racks above the sales floor. Most merchandise was pre-marked by the manufacturer so it did not require ticketing at the club. Full-sized clubs had approximately $4 million in inventory. Management was able to limit inventory shrinkage to a small fraction of one percent of net sales by strictly controlling the exits of clubs, generally limiting customers to members, and using state-of-the-art electronic article surveillance technology.

ENDNOTES

[1] As quoted in Alan B. Goldberg and Bill Ritter, "Costco CEO Finds Pro-Worker Means Profitability," an ABC News original report on *20/20*, August 2, 2006, http://abcnews.go.com/2020/Business/story?id=1362779 (accessed November 15, 2006).

[2] Ibid.

[3] As described in Nina Shapiro, "Company for the People," *Seattle Weekly,* December 15, 2004, www.seattleweekly.com (accessed November 14, 2006).

[4] See, for example, Costco's "Code of Ethics," posted in the investor relations section of Costco's website under a link entitled "Corporate Governance and Citizenship" (accessed on February 4, 2016).

[5] Costco Wholesale, 2011 Annual Report for the year ended August 28, 2011, p. 5.

[6] Costco Wholesale, 2017 Annual Report for the year ended September 3, 2017, p. 3.

[7] As quoted in ibid., pp. 128–29.

[8] Steven Greenhouse, "How Costco Became the Anti-Wal-Mart," *The New York Times,* July 17, 2005, www.wakeupwalmart.com/news (accessed November 28, 2006).

[9] As quoted in Greenhouse, "How Costco Became the Anti-Wal-Mart," *The New York Times,* July 17, 2005, www.wakeupwalmart.com/news (accessed November 28, 2006).

[10] As quoted in Shapiro, "Company for the People," *Seattle Weekly,* December 15, 2004, www.seattleweekly.com (accessed November 14, 2006).

[11] As quoted in Greenhouse, "How Costco Became the Anti-Wal-Mart," *The New York Times,* July 17, 2005, www.wakeupwalmart.com/news (accessed November 28, 2006).

[12] Boyle, "Why Costco Is So Damn Addictive," *Fortune,* October 30, 2006, p. 132.

[13] Costco 10-K Reports, 2015 and 2017.

[14] Sinegal's explanation appeared in the company's 2005 Annual Report; this same statement was also attributed to Craig Jelinek

in Costco's "Corporate Profile," posted on its Investor Relations website, accessed October 16, 2019.

[15] Jeremy Bowman, "Who Is Costco's Favorite Customer?" *The Motley Fool,* June 17, 2016, www.fool.com (accessed June 5, 2017); J. Max Robins, "Costco's Surprisingly Large-Circulation Magazine," *MediaPost,* March 6, 2015, www.mediapost.com (accessed June 5, 2017).

[16] As quoted in Goldberg and Ritter, "Costco CEO Finds Pro-Worker Means Profitability," an ABC News original report on *20/20,* August 2, 2006, http://abcnews.go.com/2020/Business/story?id=1362779 (accessed November 15, 2006).

[17] Ibid.

[18] Information posted at www.indeed.com (accessed October 16, 2019).

[19] Based on information posted at www.glassdoor.com (accessed February 28, 2012).

[20] Information posted at www.glassdoor.com (accessed October 16, 2019).

[21] Ibid.

[22] Ibid.

[23] Nina Shapiro, "Company for the People," *Seattle Weekly,* December 15, 2004, www.seattleweekly.com (accessed November 14, 2006).

[24] As quoted in Goldberg and Ritter, "Costco CEO Finds Pro-Worker Means Profitability," an ABC News original report on *20/20,* August 2, 2006, http://abcnews.go.com/2020/Business/story?id=1362779 (accessed November 15, 2006).

[25] Ibid.

[26] As quoted in Greenhouse, "How Costco Became the Anti-Wal-Mart," *The New York Times,* July 17, 2005, www.wakeupwalmart.com/news (accessed November 28, 2006).

[27] As quoted in Goldberg and Ritter, "Costco CEO Finds Pro-Worker Means Profitability," an ABC News original report on *20/20,* August 2, 2006, http://abcnews.go.com/2020/Business/story?id=1362779 (accessed November 15, 2006).

[28] Boyle, "Why Costco Is So Damn Addictive," *Fortune,* October 30, 2006, p. 132.

[29] As quoted in Shapiro, "Company for the People," *Seattle Weekly,* December 15, 2004, www.seattleweekly.com (accessed November 14, 2006).

[30] Ibid.

[31] As quoted in Goldberg and Ritter, "Costco CEO Finds Pro-Worker Means Profitability," an ABC News original report on *20/20,* August 2, 2006, http://abcnews.go.com/2020/Business/story?id=1362779 (accessed November 15, 2006).

[32] As quoted in Shapiro, "Company for the People," *Seattle Weekly,* December 15, 2004, www.seattleweekly.com (accessed November 14, 2006).

[33] Costco Code of Ethics, last updated March 2010, posted in the Governance Documents section of Costco's investor relations website, accessed October 16, 2019.

[34] Information posted in the environmental sustainability section of Costco's investor relations website, accessed October 17, 2019.

[35] Mission Statement on Animal Welfare," posted at www.costco.com in the Investor Relations section (accessed February 8, 2016).

[36] According to information in "Warehouse Clubs and Supercenters in the U.S.: Industry Statistics," posted at www.ibisworld.com, accessed June 15, 2020.

[37] Walmart 2010 Annual Report, p. 8.

CASE 4

Ford Motor Company: Will the Company's Strategic Moves Restore its Competitiveness and Financial Performance?

Marlene M. Reed
Baylor University

Rochelle R. Brunson
Baylor University

A report by Road Show on CNET, dated June 5, 2019, suggested that the Ford Fusion 2020 model would be the last car Ford would produce. The discontinuation of the Fusion was said to be a part of Ford's shifting strategic focus away from passenger cars toward crossovers and SUVs—many with electrified powertrains.[1] Observers wondered if Ford could essentially abandon the market for automobiles as car sales had been its lifeblood since 1908 when Henry Ford revolutionized passenger transportation with production of the Model T. Industry analysts also wondered if the American love affair with the SUV and trucks would continue if the price

EXHIBIT 1   History of the Ford Motor Company

1896—Henry Ford built the Quadricycle, the forerunner of the automobile.

1899—Henry Ford joins a group that founded the Detroit Automobile Company.

1901—Henry Ford defeats the top racecar driver of the era in his 26. The victory led to Sweepstakes. The victory led to Ford's second short-lived attempt at auto manufacture—the Henry Ford Company.

1903—The Ford Motor Company is incorporated with an initial 12 investors and 1,000 shares. The company had spent almost all of its $28,000 cash investment by the time it sold the first Ford Model A on July 23. By October, the company had turned a profit of $37,000.

1904—Ford Motor Company of Canada is founded. The plant was built in Windsor, Ontario, across the river from Ford's existing facilities. The company was created to sell vehicles not just in Canada but also all across the British Empire.

1907—Ford introduces the scripted typeface of its trademark.

1908—Ford introduces the Model T. Ford sold 15 million of this model before ceasing production in May 1927. It became the most famous car in the world.

1913—Ford introduces the integrative moving assembly line to auto production. This innovation reduced the Model T's chassis assembly line from 12.5 to 1.5 hours and brought about a revolution in manufacturing.

1914—Ford institutes the famous "$5 Day." This wage payment to Ford's employees was double the existing rate for factory workers. The company also reduced the workday from 9 to 8 hours. The day after this wage rate was announced, 10,000 people lined up hoping to be hired by Ford.

1917–Ford produces its first truck. The truck was called the Ford Model TT based on the Model T car but with a reinforced chassis and rear axle.

1919–Edsel Ford succeeds Henry Ford as president of the company.

1922–Ford acquires the Lincoln Motor Company.

1925–Ford begins production of the Ford Tri-Motor airplanes. The "Tin Goose" was the first airplane used by America's early commercial airlines.

1927–Ford begins selling the 1928 Model A. The company closed plants all over the world to spend six months retooling factories and perfecting the design of the car.

1936–Ford begins selling the Lincoln Zephr line. Lincoln Zephr's sleek, aerodynamic shapes helped make the brand a sales success, but when auto production ceased during World War II, the Zephr name was dropped as well.

1941–Ford begins producing Jeeps for the U.S. military.

1942–Ford halts production of automobiles in the United States to produce military equipment.

1948–Ford produces the F-Series line of trucks. The company ceased building trucks on car platforms and used a purpose-built truck platform instead.

1954–Ford introduces the Thunderbird. This car would become a classic.

1956–Ford becomes a publicly-traded company.

1959–Ford Credit is established. The company offered loans and leases to car buyers.

1964–The Ford Mustang goes on sale. The car was a huge success and has remained one of the fastest-selling vehicles in history.

1965–Ford-Philco engineers unveil the Mission Control Center used to put a man on the moon.

1976–Ford of Europe introduces the Ford Fiesta.

1986–Ford introduces the modular assembly line at its St. Louis assembly plant. This made use of automated ancillary assembly lines to produce vehicle subassemblies.

1990–Ford introduces the Explorer. With this model, Ford helped launch the SUV market. This became one of Ford's most successful models.

1996–Ford introduces the Ford Ranger Electric Vehicle. This was a forerunner of today's electric vehicles and hybrid energy systems.

1998–The Lincoln Navigator is introduced and spurs rapid growth in the luxury SUV segment.

2011–Ford discontinues the Mercury line to concentrate all of its efforts on the Ford and Lincoln brands.

2016–Ford Mobility, LLC is created. This focused on changing the way the world moves. Ford Smart Mobility was designed to take the company to the next level in connectivity, mobility, autonomous vehicles, the customer experience and data analytics.

---

of gasoline began to escalate as the United States, Russia, and the United Arab Emirates. engaged in tactics to alter energy prices around the world. Exhibit 1 below outlines key milestones in the history of the Ford Motor Company.

Ford's Strategic Situation in 2020

By 2020, Ford employed over 200,000 people worldwide in 70 plants producing midsize cars, SUVs, and pickup trucks. Since the recession of 2008, the company's revenues had rebounded due to increased disposable income levels, falling unemployment, and a renewed demand for big-ticket purchases. However, the company reported falling sales in some of its established markets in 2019 and 2020–partially due to the spread of the COVID-19 virus in early 2020. Exhibit 2 presents Ford's stock performance between April 2015 and April 2020. The company's consolidated income statements for 2017 through 2019 are presented in Exhibit 3. Ford Motor Company's consolidated balance sheets for 2018 and 2019 are presented in Exhibit 4.

EXHIBIT 2   Performance of Ford Motor Company's Stock Price, April 2015 to April 2020

(a) Trend in the Ford Motor Company's Common Stock Price

(b) Performance of the Ford Motor Company's Stock Price Versus the S&P 500 Index

Ford's New Product Strategy

William Clay Ford, Jr., Executive Chairman of Ford, suggests that 115 years ago, when the company began, the company's mission was to make people's lives better by making mobility accessible and affordable. By 2020, the company was moving toward manufacturing "smart vehicles for a smart world." The world plan focused on four pillars: (1) A winning portfolio; (2) new propulsion options; (3) a high-level autonomous business built on the most trusted self-driving systems; and (4) cloud-based mobility experiences that deliver recurring revenue.

The winning portfolio in 2020 was envisioned to be the Escape, Expedition, Explorer, Ranger, F-150 Hybrid, Bronco, and the Mustang Shelby GT500. The Ford Bronco was produced between 1966 and 1996 and was discontinued when the smaller two-door Bronco II suffered from a tipping problem. The reintroduced Bronco will be modular with a removable top and doors.

EXHIBIT 3   Consolidated Income Statements for the Ford Motor Company, 2017–2019 ($ in millions except per share amounts)

	2017	2018	2019
Revenues			
Automotive	$145,653	$148,294	$143,599
Ford Credit	11,113	12,018	12,260
Mobility	10	26	41
Total revenues	156,776	160,338	155,900
Costs and expenses			
Cost of sales	131,321	136,269	134,693
Selling, administrative, and other expenses	11,527	11,403	11,161
Ford Credit interest, operating, and other expenses	9,047	9,463	9,472
Total costs and expenses	151,895	157,135	155,326
Operating income	4,881	3,203	574
Interest expense on Automotive debt	1,133	1,171	963
Interest expense on Other debt	57	57	57
Other income/(loss), net	3,267	2,247	(226)
Equity in net income of affiliated companies	1,201	123	32
Income/(Loss) before income taxes	8,159	4,345	(640)
Provision for/(Benefit from) income taxes	402	650	(724)
Net income	7,757	3,695	84
Less: Income attributable to noncontrolling interests	26	18	37
Net income attributable to Ford Motor Company	$ 7,731	$ 3,677	$ 47
Earnings per share attributable to Ford Motor Company common and class B stock			
Basic income	$1.94	$0.93	$0.01
Diluted income	$1.93	$0.92	$0.01
Weighted-average shares used in computation of earnings per share			
Basic shares	3,975	3,974	3,972
Diluted shares	3,998	3,998	4,004

Source: Ford Motor Company 2019 10-K.

EXHIBIT 4   Ford Motor Company Consolidated Balance Sheets, 2018–2019 ($ amounts in millions)

	December 31, 2018	December 31, 2019
ASSETS		
Cash and cash equivalents	$ 16,718	$ 17,504
Marketable securities	17,233	17,147
Ford Credit finance receivables, net	54,353	53,651
Trade and other receivables, less allowances of $94 and $63	11,195	9,237
Inventories	11,220	10,786
Assets held for sale	—	2,383
Other assets	3,930	3,339
Total current assets	114,649	114,047

	December 31, 2018	December 31, 2019
Ford Credit finance receivables, net	55,544	53,703
Net investment in operating leases	29,119	29,230
Net property	36,178	36,469
Equity in net assets of affiliated companies	2,709	2,519
Deferred income taxes	10,412	11,863
Other assets	7,929	10,706
Total assets	**$ 256,540**	**$ 258,537**
LIABILITIES		
Payables	$ 21,520	$ 20,673
Other liabilities and deferred revenue	20,556	22,987
Automotive debt payable within one year	2,314	1,445
Ford Credit debt payable within one year	51,179	52,371
Other debt payable within one year	—	130
Liabilities held for sale	—	526
Total current liabilities	**95,569**	**98,132**
Other liabilities and deferred revenue	23,588	25,324
Automotive long-term debt	11,233	13,233
Ford Credit long-term debt	88,887	87,658
Other long-term debt	600	470
Deferred income taxes	597	490
Total liabilities	**220,474**	**225,307**
Redeemable noncontrolling interest	100	—
EQUITY		
Common Stock, par value $.01 per share (4,011 million shares issued of 6 billion authorized)	40	40
Class B Stock, par value $.01 per share (71 million shares issued of 530 million authorized)	1	1
Capital in excess of par value of stock	22,006	22,165
Retained earnings	22,668	20,320
Accumulated other comprehensive income/(loss)	(7,366)	(7,728)
Treasury stock	(1,417)	(1,613)
Total equity attributable to Ford Motor Company	35,932	33,185
Equity attributable to noncontrolling interests	34	45
Total equity	**35,966**	**33,230**
Total liabilities and equity	**$ 256,540**	**$ 258,537**

Source: Ford Motor Company 2019 10-K.

Two years before the Bronco was discontinued, the automobile gained a great deal of attention when Al Cowlings drove O.J. Simpson down a Los Angeles freeway after Simpson was charged with the murders of his ex-wife and her friend. More than 95 million people across the United States watched the two-hour pursuit on television while crowds gathered on overpasses to cheer on the NFL football legend.[2]

Ford Credit Company

Although the company experienced profitability difficulties in 2018 and 2019, its financial arm, Ford Credit Company, posted its best results in 2019 of the past nine years. Their profits jumped to $3 billion before taxes. The result was that this arm of the company accounted for 50 percent of Ford's profits. This was up from 15 to 20 percent in the past. Ford Motor Company had, thus, been able to subsidize Ford's losses and allowed the company to maintain a high dividend yield. Unfortunately, data released by the New York Federal Reserve Bank in late 2019, indicated that the volume of 90+ days delinquent loans had risen sharply. The value of the overall auto loan and lease balances had surged to $1.33 trillion that year. In addition, subprime loans reached $66 billion in the final quarter of 2019.[3]

There were several risks for the company in the 2020s regarding the Ford Credit Company. One risk was that this financial arm of the company could experience higher-than-expected credit losses, lower-than-anticipated residual values on higher-than-expected return volumes for leased vehicles. Another risk was that Ford Credit could face increased competition from financial institutions or other third parties seeking to increase their share of financing Ford vehicles. Finally, Ford Credit could be subject to new or increased credit regulations, consumer or data protection regulations or other types of regulations.

Challenges for 2020

The automotive industry is affected by macroeconomic conditions over which the companies have little control. Vehicles are durable goods, and consumers exert strong choices about when and if they will buy a new car. This decision is influenced by such factors as slower economic growth, geopolitical events and other factors such as the COVID-19 virus threat in 2020.

Some of the greatest challenges to Ford in 2020 identified by management included the following:

1. Acceptance of new and existing products by the market.
2. Sales of more profitable larger vehicles, especially in the United States.
3. Increased price competition resulting from industry excess capacity.
4. Fluctuations in commodity prices, foreign exchange rates, and interest rates.
5. Global macroeconomic factors such as protectionist trade policies and other events including Brexit.
6. The company's ability to maintain a competitive cost structure.
7. Pension and other post-retirement liabilities.
8. Defects that result in delays in new model launches.
9. Operational systems could be affected by cyber incidents.[4]

Ford and the Coronavirus Pandemic.

In early 2020, a new virus called the coronavirus or COVID-19 began to cause serious illness and death around the world. Because of an increasing incidence of this disease in the United States, many states declared a "shelter in place" order intended to prevent the spread of the virus by forcing people to work from home. Ford, on March 31, stated that it was delaying the restart of a car plant in Mexico as well as four truck, SUV and van plants in the United States "to help protect its workers."[5] This postponement came just two days after President Donald Trump extended the national social-distancing guidelines through the end of April 2020. The shutting down of the economy resulted in the loss of more jobs than had occurred since the Great Depression and the stoppage of purchasing non-essential goods.

Because of a shortage of ventilators to treat coronavirus patients, Ford and General Electric's Health Care Division announced on March 30 that they together planned to produce 50,000 ventilators over the next 100 days. Ford planned to use a plant in Rawsonville, Michigan, and about 500 workers to

EXHIBIT 5   Global Automobile Industry Products and Services Segmentation, 2018

Product	Percentage of Market
Cars	36.6%
Cross utility vehicles (CUVs)	32.1%
Pickup trucks	10.8%
Sports utility vehicles (SUVs)	6.9%
Other	13.6%
Total	100%

Source: Oelkan, Ediz (February 2020). Ibisworld.com, **Global Car & Automobile Mfg**.

EXHIBIT 6   2018 U.S. Retail Sales Volume Segregated by Product Type

	U.S. Retail Sales	Percentage
Trucks	1,139,079	45.6%
SUVs	872,215	34.9%
Cars	486,024	19.4%
	Total	100%

Source: Annual Report of the Ford Motor Company, 2018

make 30,000 ventilators a month. GE had licensed the design of the ventilator from Airon Corporation of Melbourne, Florida. The device works on air pressure and does not need electricity. Both Ford and GE announced that Ford would help increase production of another ventilator based on a design from GE Healthcare.[6]

Global Automobile Status

A survey of the range of products and services provided by the global automobile manufacturing industry is shown below in Exhibit 5.

Although the production of cars accounts for 36.6 percent of global industry revenue, this was lower than its production volume because cars normally sell at a lower price than SUVs and commercial vehicles. Therefore, they contribute less to revenue on a per-unit basis. The car segment had been growing as consumers opted for more fuel efficiency. Ford sales in the United States, however, showed a lower total sales of cars than trucks or SUVs—see Exhibit 6.

Generally, Germany, Japan, the United States, and Canada are expected to be the world's largest exporters of cars and automobiles (SUVs, trucks, etc.). On the other hand, Germany, China, the United Kingdom, and Belgium are expected to be the largest destinations for automobile products.[7] The historic methodology for manufacturing automotive vehicles was to assemble cars at a domestic plant and then export them to their final destinations. However, the supply chain has become more complex. The shift has been toward manufacturing cars close to their final destination to save on logistics costs. Another part of this strategy is to focus on very specific branding devices to appeal to the customer. An example of this is the logo "Made in America."

A Future Strategy

By 2020, the Ford Motor Company Board had some difficult decisions to make. Although the developing economies of the world primarily demanded smaller automobiles, the developed economies preferred the larger crossovers, SUVs, and trucks. The company had already made a decision to discontinue the Ford Fusion, its largest automobile, and the public wondered if they would drop selling all of their cars except for the Mustang in the United States.

Another question that arose was: What would happen to large vehicle sales if the price of petroleum rose to alarming rates again? That had seemed to be a remote possibility until the United States, Russia, and the United Arab Emirates decided in the spring of 2020 to limit the daily production of petroleum. There was also the question of what would happen if people began financing their vehicles at some place other than Ford Credit, and what could they do about that? The Board had much to think about as they put their strategic plan together.

ENDNOTES

[1] Ewing, Steve (June 5, 2019). All Ford Fusion models will go out of production in 2020. *Road Show* by CNET.

[2] Noble, Breanna (March 5, 2020). Ford Bronco poised to return: It's like a cult vehicle," *The Detroit News*.

[3] Singh, Ayush (March 2, 2020). Here's why Ford Motor Company still can't avoid bankruptcy, *Business News*. https://www.ccn.com/heres-why-ford-motor-company-still-cant-avoid-bankruptcy/.

[4] Annual Report of the Ford Motor Company, 2018.

[5] Wayland, Michael (March 31, 2020). Ford postpones reopening "key" plants due to coronavirus pandemic. https://www.cnbc.com/2020/03/31/ford-postpones-reopening-key-plants-due-to-coronavirus-pandemic.html.

[6] *The New York Times* (March 30, 2020). Ford joins effort to make ventilators. https://www.nytimes.com/2020/03/30/business/stock-market-today-coronavirus-html#link-310e3984/.

[7] Ozelkan, Ediz (February 2020). Global car and manufacturing, Ibisworld.com, 1999–2020.

Macy's, Inc.: Will Its Strategy Allow It to Survive in the Changing Retail Sector?

Alen Badal
University of Liverpool

John E. Gamble
Texas A&M University-Corpus Christi

The retail landscape in the United States in early 2020 may have been best characterized as rapidly changing with an uncertain future. The COVID-19 pandemic and stay-at-home orders by state and local governments had created unprecedented challenges for all retailers, but traditional brick-and-mortar retailers had under pressure for at least a decade. The convenience of shopping for nearly every type of consumer good at Amazon or other online retailer sites had radically transformed the retail industry. Consumer needs continued to allow for variations in strategy that allowed for distinctive retailer approaches to meeting customer expectations. But consumers had become to expect even the most highly differentiated retailers to have an online presence in addition to their prestigious brick-and-mortar locations.

The change in consumer shopping preferences had especially impacted mall-based department stores. Nearly all shopping malls relied on strong department store anchor tenants to draw vast numbers of shoppers, who would also patronize smaller specialized retailers during their visits to a mall. The transition to online shopping had greatly damaged the business model of many shopping malls as smaller retailers failed along with department stores, both of whom had experienced a decline in sales per square foot resulting from reduced customer traffic.

Macy's, Inc. had particularly struggled to adapt its business model to the online shopping environment with sales declining each year since its record sales of $28.1 billion generated in 2014. In 2018,

Macy's turned to 34-year company veteran Jeff Gennette to lead the company's turnaround and transformation as CEO. In early 2020, Gennette was in the second year of his five-point strategic plan designed to reinvent the company's business model and generate retail innovations. The key feature of the plan was its Growth50 initiative which strived for product and merchandising innovations in 50 stores that would establish a new retailing standard that could be rolled out to 50 to 100 additional stores per year. The company also implemented a direct vendor fulfillment model for online sales that nearly doubled the number of SKUs offered online since inventory could be maintained by vendors, not Macy's.

The third element of the turnaround plan was to allow customers to order items online and pick up merchandise in a nearby store location. Gennette also wished to expand the number of the company's off-price Macy's Backstage stores from approximately 150 to more than 200. Macy's management had determined that the off-price store locations were less vulnerable to competition from online retailers than its core Macy's stores. Expanding the company's loyalty plan to encourage repeat business, making online sales available through its new mobile app, and better utilizing its strongest product categories like housewares and women's apparel to draw customers to its stores were less sweeping changes that rounded out the plan.

As of early-2020, the plan had produced few positive results with some analysts suggesting that the strategy was better aligned with the retail environment of 2010 than of 2020. In February 2020, Macy's announced that it would close 125 store locations. By March 18, the company's COVID-19 response resulted in it closing all 775 store locations. The company began reopening stores on May 4 and expected to have 270 stores open by the 2020 Memorial Day Weekend. The combined effect of the company's ongoing poor performance and COVID-19 store closes was expected to result in a first quarter 2020 loss of $905 million to $1.1 billion.

Company Background

Headquartered in Cincinnati, Ohio, Macy's, Inc. was the second-largest department store chain with a market share of approximately 16.3 percent in 2020. The company operated about 551 Macy's department stores, 53 Bloomingdales, and 171 Bluemercury businesses in early-2020, and its retailing portfolio also included Bloomingdale's The Outlet, Macy's Backstage, and STORY and online businesses macys.com, bloomingdales.com, and bluemercury.com. The company also licensed Bloomingdale's stores in Dubai and Kuwait for operation by Al Tayer Group.

Beginning in 2018, CEO Gennette and his chief lieutenants launched a five-point turnaround plan to improve the company's performance. The Growth50 initiative was focused on 50 Macy's department stores to revitalize in 2018, including store remodels, improved customer service, and increased product assortment. The addition of STORY retail locations in 2018 supported sales growth for the company as well. STORY locations were much smaller stores with an inventory assortment that was refreshed with new items every six to eight weeks. The value proposition of the STORY business was keyed to engaging consumers through an opportunity to interact with products and collaborate. The value proposition for The Market @ Macy's was similar, but entailed departments located within select Macy's stores rather than operating as standalone locations.

Revitalization of the customer experience at Bloomingdale's and Blumercury were also important elements of the turnaround efforts. Like Bloomingdale's, the Bluemercury business operated standalone stores but also was comprised of store-within-store locations inside Macy's stores. The Bluemercury division had achieved impressive sales growth for the company and an addition of 26 stand-alone locations. Additionally, Bluemercury online sales increased by greater than 50 percent, accounting for double-digit increases in total sales. The Bluemercury division increased its private brands Lune+Aster and M-61, which accounted for greater than 10 percent of total sales at Bluemercury per company.

A focus on improvements in the online and mobile shopping experience was a second primary element of the plan and resulted in mobile representing the fastest growing channel for the company. The new practice of allowing Macy's customers to make purchases online and pick-up merchandise in the store or buy online and ship to a store for pick-up resonated with consumers. The third primary element of the company's turnaround plan included an expansion of its loyalty program to increase customer traffic and average purchase amount. In 2018, Macy's Platinum customers generated about 30 percent of store sales, shopped with more frequency, and spent 10 percent more per store visit than other customers. The company launched a new Bronze loyalty level in 2018, which yielded 3 million new customers for Macy's by year-end.

The company's off-price retail brands Backstage and Bloomingdale's The Outlet were the fourth major element of the turnaround plan because of their ability to defend against online retailers. Macy's management planned to add up to 50 Backstage locations within existing Macy's store locations and construct seven free-standing stores, all to be opened by 2020. Direct vendor fulfillment was the fifth major element of the plan and was directed at reducing distribution costs across all Macy's retail operations. Engaging customers through destination departments such as housewares, furniture, and women's apparel were additional turnaround initiatives designed to keep customers shopping once inside store locations.

Exhibit 1 presents Macy's, Inc.'s Income Statements for 2015 through 2019 and reflect the company's difficulty in sustaining a consistent improvement in performance. The company's Results of Operations shown in Exhibit 2 and Balance sheets shown in Exhibit 3 provide additional operating and financial results.

Overview of the Department Store Industry

The department store industry was under pressure not only from e-commerce, but also from discount retailers whose product lines encroached on

EXHIBIT 1 Macy's, Inc.'s Income Statements, 2015–2019
($ in millions, except per share amounts)

	2019	2018	2017*	2016	2015
Net sales	$24,560	$24,971	$24,939	$25,908	$27,079
Gross margin (a)	9,389	9,756	9,758	10,242	10,583
Operating income	970	1,738	1,864	1,371	2,028
Net income	564	1,098	1,555	619	1,070
Net income attributable to Macy's, Inc. shareholders	564	1,108	1,566	627	1,072
Basic earnings per share attributable to Macy's, Inc. shareholders	$1.82	$3.6	$5.13	$2.03	$3.26
Diluted earnings per share attributable to Macy's, Inc. shareholders	$1.81	$3.56	$5.1	$2.02	$3.22
Average number of shares outstanding	309.7	307.7	305.4	308.5	328.4
Cash dividends paid per share	$1.51	$1.51	$1.51	$1.49	$1.39
Depreciation and amortization	$ 981	$ 962	$ 991	$ 1,058	$ 1,061
Capital expenditures	$ 1,157	$ 932	$ 760	$ 912	$ 1,113
Balance Sheet Data (at year end):					
Cash and cash equivalents	$ 685	$ 1,162	$ 1,455	$ 1,297	$ 1,109
Property and equipment—net	6,633	6,637	6,672	7,017	7,616
Total assets	21,172	19,194	19,583	20,082	20,576
Short-term debt	539	43	22	309	642
Long-term debt	3,621	4,708	5,861	6,562	6,995
Total Shareholders' equity	6,377	6,436	5,733	4,375	4,253

*53 weeks

Source: Macy's, Inc. 2019 10-K.

EXHIBIT 2 Macy's, Inc.'s Results of Operations, 2017–2019
($ in millions, except per share amounts)

	2019		2018		2017	
	Amount	% to Sales	Amount	% to Sales	Amount	% to Sales
Net sales	$24,560		$24,971		$24,939	
Increase (decrease) in comparable sales	(0.8)%		1.7%		(2.2)%	
Credit card revenues, net	771	3.1%	768	3.1%	702	2.8%
Cost of sales	(15,171)	(61.8)%	(15,215)	(60.9)%	(15,181)	(60.9)%
Selling, general and administrative expenses	(8,998)	(36.6)%	(9,039)	(36.2)%	(8,954)	(35.9)%
Gains on sale of real estate	162	0.6%	389	1.5%	544	2.2%
Restructuring, impairment, store closing and other costs	(354)	(1.4)%	(136)	(0.5)%	(186)	(0.7)%
Operating income	970	3.9%	1,738	7%	1,864	7.5%
Benefit plan income, net	31		39		57	
Settlement charges	(58)		(88)		(105)	
Interest expense-net	(185)		(236)		(310)	
Gains (losses) on early retirement of debt	(30)		(33)		10	

continued

	2019		2018		2017	
	Amount	% to Sales	Amount	% to Sales	Amount	% to Sales
Income before income taxes	728		1,420		1,516	
Federal, state and local income tax benefit (expense)	(164)		(322)		39	
Net income	564		1,098		1,555	
Net loss attributable to noncontrolling interest	—		10		11	
Net income attributable to Macy's, Inc. shareholders	$ 564	2.3%	$1,108	4.4%	$1,566	6.3%
Diluted earnings per share attributable to Macy's, Inc. shareholders	$1.81		$3.56		$5.1	
Supplemental Financial Measure						
Gross margin	$ 9,389	38%	$ 9,756	39%	$ 9,758	39.1%
Digital sales as a percent of comparable sales on an owned basis	26%		23%		22%	
Supplemental Non-GAAP Financial Measures						
Increase (decrease) in comparable sales on an owned plus licensed basis	(0.7)%		2%		(1.9)%	
Adjusted diluted earnings per share attributable to Macy's, Inc. shareholders	$2.91		$4.18		$3.79	
Adjusted EBITDA	$ 2,336		$ 2,877		$ 3,109	
ROIC	17.1%		19.9%		20.8%	

Source: Macy's, Inc. 2019 10-K.

EXHIBIT 3   Macy's, Inc.'s Balance Sheets, 2018–2019 ($ in millions)

	February 1, 2020	February 2, 2019
ASSETS		
Current Assets:		
Cash and cash equivalents	$ 685	$ 1,162
Receivables	409	400
Merchandise inventories	5,188	5,263
Prepaid expenses and other current assets	528	620
Total Current Assets	6,810	7,445
Property and Equipment–net	6,633	6,637
Right of Use Assets	2,668	—
Goodwill	3,908	3,908
Other Intangible Assets–net	439	478
Other Assets	714	726
Total Assets	$21,172	$19,194
LIABILITIES AND SHAREHOLDERS' EQUITY		
Current Liabilities:		
Short-term debt	$ 539	$ 43
Merchandise accounts payable	1,682	1,655
Accounts payable and accrued liabilities	3,448	3,366
Income taxes	81	168

	February 1, 2020	February 2, 2019
Total Current Liabilities	5,750	5,232
Long-Term Debt	3,621	4,708
Long-Term Lease Liabilities	2,918	—
Deferred Income Taxes	1,169	1,238
Other Liabilities	1,337	1,580
Shareholders' Equity:		
Common stock (309.0 and 307.5 shares outstanding)	3	3
Additional paid-in capital	621	652
Accumulated equity	7,989	8,050
Treasury stock	(1,241)	(1,318)
Accumulated other comprehensive loss	(995)	(951)
Total Macy's, Inc. Shareholders' Equity	6,377	6,436
Noncontrolling interest	—	—
Total Shareholders' Equity	6,377	6,436
Total Liabilities and Shareholders' Equity	$21,172	$19,194

Source: Macy's, Inc. 2019 10-K.

traditional department store product categories. Women's clothing and footwear and home goods and appliances made up the two largest categories of products sold in department stores in 2019. Drugs and cosmetics made up the third largest category of department store sales in 2019. Men's clothing and footwear and children's clothing and footwear contributed the least to department store revenues in 2019. Most product categories sold in department stores could also be purchased at supercenter discount retailers such as Walmart and Target or wholesale clubs such as Sam's or Costco. The proliferation of such product categories both online and available in brick-and-mortar stores required mall-based department stores to offer a highly differentiated experience or distinctive product line.

The shopping mall experience. The business model of online-only retailers such as Amazon that involved low costs for land and buildings, real estate leases, inventory, store furnishings and merchandise displays, and personnel put tremendous pricing pressure on brick-and-mortar retailers. The low prices offered by many online retailers coupled with consumers' desire for the convenience of online shopping has dramatically altered the value proposition for shopping malls and resulting customer experience. Malls, which once were a popular place to visit, shop, and pass time, were challenged as the closings

of prestigious anchor stores and specialty stores made shopping at a mall less exciting for consumers.

Physical malls were also expensive to build and just as costly to remodel as many had been open for some time. The aging nature of many malls also decreased consumer desire to visit a mall. There were some locations that were characterized by extreme temperatures that made shopping indoors more appealing, such as the Mall of America in Minneapolis, Minnesota. The most viable malls in 2020 tended to be upscale outdoor lifestyle malls that featured beautiful architecture and landscaping along with a strong mix of aspirational luxury brands. The overall ambiance of such malls recreated the excitement of shopping in a mall that had been common in the 1970s and 1980s. Other malls that remained popular in 2020 were outdoor outlet malls that were located near major highways that provided deep discounts on such highly sought after brands as Gucci, North Face, Coach, Abercrombie & Fitch, Under Armour, Ralph Lauren Polo, and Tori Burch.

Changing consumer demographics. A declining birthrate in the United States and many developed countries resulted in fewer shoppers for an increasing number of goods. The peak of the baby boom in 1957 saw 122.7 births per 1,000 U.S. women, while the U.S. birth rate in 2017 had fallen to 60.3 per 1,000 women.

Baby boomers had driven sharp demand increases in industries and products such as mountain bikes, golf courses and equipment, SUVs and Harley-Davidson motorcycles in the 1980s and 1990s and still made up the largest group of consumers in 2020. By 2024, the 65 and older demographic in the United States was projected to exceed 65 million consumers. Older consumers maintained tremendous purchasing power resulting from decades of career advancements and savings. The 60+ demographic was the most highly educated generation and wealthiest generation in U.S. history. Much of baby boomer spending was on the purchase of goods and services for their children and grandchildren, which drove sales of products for all age demographics. The impact of purchases by grandparents as gifts to children and grandchildren had given rise to the term "grandparent economy" by many in the retail industry.[1]

Generation X and early- and late-Millennial shoppers were also important consumer groups with approximately 40 million to 45 million consumers in the age groups aged 25–34, 35–44, and 45–54. The focus by consumers on convenience and low prices grew stronger as age demographics declined in age. Online shopping met the discount pricing and 24-hour availability and convenience desired by Millennial shoppers. Smartphone applications greatly enhanced the ability of consumers to make purchases from any location at any time of the day. Walmart had achieved considerable success in online and mobile selling by closely studied demographics when adding services like Jetblack personal shopping, buy-online-pickup-in-store and curbside pickup services. Walmart also recognized the desire of Generation X and Millennial shoppers to focus on quality and brand prestige even though low prices remained an important consideration in purchasing decisions. The acquisitions of Bonobos, Lord & Taylor, and Bobbi Brown were made by Walmart to improve the quality of products offered in its stores and online.

Retail sector growth and the impact of COVID-19. The retail trade sector had grown at an average annual rate of 0.7 percent in the years 2015–2020 to reach $5.3 trillion in industry revenues. In 2020, the U.S. retail sector was made up of 2.8 million enterprises and employed 17.6 million Americans. Total wages in the industry exceeded $476 billion. The growth rate in retail trade had also allowed for a 3.1 percent increase in retailer profit margins in 2020

and an 8.9 percent increase in wages as a share of revenues in 2020.

The onset of the coronavirus in early-2020 was projected to lead to a 3.3 percent decline in revenues for the entire 2020 calendar year as retailers were required to temporarily close stores. Also, the spike in unemployment resulting from COVID-19 stay-at-home orders and store closures was projected to result in an overall decrease in consumer spending which would harm the U.S. department store industry and other consumer sectors. Analysts believe that the retail sector would return to a strong 1.8 percent annual growth rate for 2021 through 2025 as COVID-19 became contained and mitigated. Industry revenues were projected to increase to nearly $5.9 trillion by 2025.

The declining sales of the department store segment of the retail industry. The $100 billion department store segment of the retail sector had fared far less well than retailers such as discount supercenters, wholesale clubs, and specialty retailers during the mid-2010s. While the entire retail sector had enjoyed a 0.7 percent annual growth rate between 2015 and 2020, the department store segment of the retail sector had declined 11 percent annually during those years. The number of department stores declined 4.9 percent between 2015 and 2020, with COVID-19 hastening the decay of the industry with a projected 27.4 percent decline in department store revenues and a 3.2 percent decrease in profit margins for the industry segment. Analysts projected that the department store segment of the retail industry would continue to decline by 7.5 percent annually, falling from $100 billion in 2020 to $67.7 billion in 2025.

Profiles of the Largest U.S. Department Store Chains

Target Corporation Target Corporation was the largest U.S. department store chain in 2020 with a market share of 50.1 percent and 2019 sales of $50.1 billion. Target has achieved explosive growth between 2015 and 2020, allowing its market share to increase from approximately 34 percent in 2015 to 50 percent in 2020. The company operated 1,868 stores across the United States and recorded sales of $78.1 billion in fiscal 2020. A large portion of the company's sales was comprised of groceries, which lowered its sales of department store items to

$50.1 billion. In fact, the company's sales of department store items had declined at an annual rate of 2.2 percent between 2015 and 2020.

The company had been able to increase overall sales in its supercenter locations through a reimaging plan that included store remodeling projects and the introduction of perishable and nonperishable foods to more store locations. This introduction of grocery items produced a comparable store sales growth of 5 percent. Gains in every market category was achieved coupled with a record high earnings per share increases.

Key elements of Target Corporation's retail strategy included:

- Becoming the first U.S. retailer to offer same-day and drive-up fulfillment capabilities, coast-to-coast.
- Remodeled more than 400 store locations by 2019.
- In 2018, opened more than 24 small-store formats, with 30 more planned in 2019, in high-traffic urban locations and college campuses.
- Focused on better guest services: increased minimum wage to $12/hour; raising again in 2019 to $13/ hour, with a goal of $15/hour by the end of 2020.
- Focused on digital channels, where in 2018 comparable digital sales grew 36 percent.
- Introduction of more brands, more than doubling a goal of more than a dozen in 2017, which was one reason Target Corporation was named by Fast Company as one of the world's most innovative companies.

Nordstrom, Inc. Nordstrom Inc. was the third largest department store chain in the United States with 380 total stores in 2020. Nordstrom Inc. had a diverse mix of retailing formats with 136 fill-line Nordstrom department stores, 244 off-price Nordstrom Rack stores, and multiple e-commerce sites. The company's greatest store concentration of Nordstrom department stores was in California with 35 full-price locations followed by Texas with 10.

While Nordstrom was best known for its luxurious department stores, the company's innovative online retailing platforms accounted for 46 percent of Nordstrom Holdings' total sales of $15.1 billion. HauteLook was a rapidly growing online retailing site owned by Nordstrom Holdings that was an online private sales site. Truck Club was another personalized site that allowed men to purchase personalized clothing. The company had other small-format

online retailing sites such as The Black Tux that allowed men to order high-quality, tailored tuxes that could be tried on at home and returned for further alterations. The Black Tux rentals could also be taken to a Nordstrom department store for alterations.

The addition of specialty online retailing sites had allowed Nordstrom Holdings to achieve overall growth, its department store specific sales had declined by 5.8 percent annually between 2015 and 2020. The profitability of its department stores had also declined to less than a one percent margin in fiscal 2020.

Sears Holdings Corporation Sears Holdings Corporation resulted from the 2005 merger between Sears Roebuck and Company and Kmart Holding Corporation. The merger produced a company with a network of approximately 1,000 Sears department stores and Kmart discount stores. Sears department stores were primarily mall-based, and Kmart locations were largely standalone stores. The merger was designed to strengthen two retail brands that had each been declining rapidly for decades. For nearly 100 years, Sears held commanding market shares in nearly every department store product category, from women's, men's, and children's apparel to large appliances and even automobile tires and batteries. Sears's loss of sales in the department store industry began in the 1980s as a result of poor strategic positioning that prevented it from effectively competing with cost leaders such as Walmart and Target or with mid-tier competitors such as Macy's or J.C. Penny.

Similarly, Kmart had struggled since the 1980s to effectively compete against Walmart on price and merchandise availability. The introduction of the Walmart Supercenter in 1988 exposed problems at Kmart that included old, small store locations that were no longer located in high traffic shopping areas, supply chain inefficiencies and frequent out-of-stock store inventory, low employee morale, corrupt executive leadership, and a lack of price competitiveness.

Sears Holdings filed Chapter 11 bankruptcy in 2018 to contend with its 21 percent annual sales decline, operating losses estimated at 6.7 percent of revenues, and outstanding $5 billion debt. Sears Holdings closed more than 500 store locations in the first year of its bankruptcy protection and operated only 182 stores in 2020. The company closed all stores in April 2020 because of the COVID-19 pandemic and had reopened 25 stores in May 2020.

J.C. Penny Company, Inc.   J.C. Penny Company operated 846 store locations in the United States and Puerto Rico and achieved total revenues of $10.7 billion in fiscal 2019. The company's sales had declined steadily from a high of $20 billion in 2006 as a result of poor merchandising strategies and ineffective leadership. The company's descent accelerated during the Great Recession of the late-2000s as CEO Myron Ullman failed to adapt pricing to the diminished purchasing power of consumers suffering the effects of the recession. J.C. Penny's financial troubles grew worse under the leadership of former Apple CEO Ron Johnson who was hired in 2011 to turnaround the failing company.

CEO Johnson envisioned a J.C. Penny that would compete with more upscale retailers. His strategy was based on instinct and, without market testing, Johnson change the company's store designs, logo, advertisements, and pricing model to appeal to wealthier shoppers. Under Johnson, the company dropped its popular private label brands that were very profitable and had a loyal following among low- and middle-income customers. Johnson also ended J.C. Penny's history of using coupons and clearance sales to attract shoppers. By 2012, with sales plunging 25 percent and the company deeply in debt, it was clear that Johnson's strategy had failed to attract wealthy customers and had driven away its formerly loyal customers.

In 2013, J.C. Penny turned to former CEO Ullman in to begin a turnaround plan and, in 2015, selected Marvin Ellison as CEO. Ellison had led the appliance division at Home Depot and expected to position J.C. Penny to take advantage of the collapse of Sears to increase sales of appliances at J.C. Penny. The plan failed to achieve success, with Ellison leaving to lead Lowe's. The company continued to struggle to develop a value proposition that resonated with consumers and filed for Chapter 11 bankruptcy in May 2020. The company's restructuring plan would involve the permanent closing of 30 percent of its store locations, but analysts believe it was quite possible that J.C. Penny would be liquidated and go out of business permanently.

Macy's, Inc. Strategic Situation in Mid-2020

With the company reporting a year-over-year sales decline of more than 45 percent from approximately $5.5 billion in Q1 2019 to approximately $3 billion in Q1 2020, there was tremendous uncertainty about the effectiveness of Macy's turnaround and its ability to absorb the impact of COVID-19 on the retail industry. However, in comments to analysts following the company's announcement of its First Quarter 2020 results, CEO Gennette saw several bright spots. A portion of the company's loss in Q1 2020 was a result of a $300 million charge on inventory that would have been marked down as sale items if stores had been open. Also, CEO Gennette believed that the company would be able to right-size its inventory during the second quarter of 2020 to reduce overhead. Macy's management was particularly encouraged by the company's 80 percent increase in online sales during the month of May 2020 as consumers were forced to shop online during stay-at-home orders. Gennette had commented to analysts that while sales might not stabilize until 2021 or 2022, the company would be able to retire $1 billion in debt by 2022. With so much unpredictability, coupled with changing consumer wants and needs, the retail arena was surely one that will continue to be a challenge moving forward.

ENDNOTES

[1] Pamela N. Danziger, "Four Demographic Trends that Many Retailers Missed, but not Walmart," *Forbes,* May 5, 2019, https://www.forbes.com/sites/pamdanziger/2019/05/05/four-demographic-trends-that-many-retailers-missed-but-not-walmart/#17cc4c465c81 (accessed May 29, 2020).

TOMS Shoes: Expanding Its Successful One For One Business Model

McGraw Hill connect

Margaret A. Peteraf
Tuck School of Business at Dartmouth

Sean Zhang and Carry S. Resor
Research Assistants, Dartmouth College

While traveling in Argentina in 2006, Blake Mycoskie witnessed the hardships that children without shoes experienced and became committed to making a difference. Rather than focusing on charity work, Mycoskie sought to build an organization capable of sustainable, repeated giving, where children would be guaranteed shoes throughout their childhood. He established TOMS Shoes, with a unique business model known as "One for One". For every pair of shoes TOMS sold, TOMS would donate a pair to a child in need. By June 2020, TOMS had given away nearly 100 million pairs of shoes in over 85 different countries.[1]

The business model was a success and TOMS experienced consistent and rapid growth, despite the global recession that began in 2009. By 2015, TOMS had matured into an organization with nearly 600 employees and almost $400 million in revenues. TOMS shoes could be found in several major retail stores such as Nordstrom, Bloomingdale's, and Urban Outfitters.

Encouraged by this success and wanting to make an even greater difference in the world, Mycoskie started several new initiatives associated with the TOMS brand and the One-for-One business model.

In 2011, he launched TOMS Eyewear to help provide prescription glasses and eye surgery to those in need. In 2014, he launched TOMS Roasting Co. as a way to expand access to safe drinking water around the world. By 2020, TOMS had enabled over 780,000 sight restorations and had provided over 722,000 weeks of safe water for communities without this basic necessity. In response to the COVID-19 pandemic, the company pledged to give one-third of their net profits toward funding mental health support, handwashing, and medical supplies for those on the frontlines of the crisis. For an overview of how quickly TOMS grew, see Exhibit 1.

COMPANY BACKGROUND

While attending Southern Methodist University, Blake Mycoskie founded the first of his six start-ups, a laundry service company that encompassed seven colleges and staffed over 40 employees.[2] Four start-ups and a short stint on *The Amazing Race* later, Mycoskie found himself vacationing in Argentina where he not only learned about the Alpargata shoe

Used by permission of Tuck School of Business at Dartmouth

EXHIBIT 1 TOMS' Growth Since 2006

	2020	2016	2014	2012	2010	2008	2006
Total Employees	750	650	550	320	72	33	4
Thousands of Pairs of Shoes Sold	95,000*	60,000*	10,000	2,700	1,000	110	10

*Estimated based on shoes donated.

Source: PrivCo, Private Company Financial Report, TOMS website; craft.co, toms-shoes company profile, accessed June 4, 2020.

originally used by local peasants in the 14th century, but also witnessed the extreme poverty in rural Argentina.

Determined to make a difference, Mycoskie believed that providing shoes could more directly impact the children in these rural communities than delivering medicine or food. Aside from protecting children's feet from infections, parasites, and diseases, shoes were often required for a complete school uniform. In addition, research had shown that shoes were found to significantly increase children's self-confidence, help them develop into more active community members, and lead them to stay in school. Thus, by ensuring access to shoes, Mycoskie could effectively increase children's access to education and foster community activism, raising the overall standard of living for people living in poor Argentinian rural areas.

Dedicated to his mission, Mycoskie purchased 250 pairs of Alpargatas and returned home to Los Angeles, where he subsequently founded TOMS Shoes. He built the company on the promise of "One for One," donating a pair of shoes for every pair sold. With an initial investment of $300,000, Mycoskie's business concept of social entrepreneurship was simple: sell both the shoe and the story behind it. Building on a simple slogan that effectively communicated his goal, Mycoskie championed his personal experiences passionately and established deep and lasting relationships with customers.

Operating from his apartment with three interns he found on Craigslist, Mycoskie quickly sold out his initial inventory and expanded considerably, selling 10,000 pairs of shoes by the end of his first year. With family and friends, Mycoskie ventured back to Argentina, where they hand-delivered 10,000 pairs of shoes to children in need. Because he followed through on his mission statement, Mycoskie was able to subsequently attract investors to support his unique business model and expand his venture significantly.

In 2014, Bain Capital bought a 50 percent stake in the company, hoping to cash in on the company's success.

INDUSTRY BACKGROUND

Even though Mycoskie's vision for his company was a unique one, vying for a position in global footwear manufacturing was a risky and difficult venture. The industry was both stable and mature—one in which large and small companies competed on the basis of price, quality, and service. Competitive pressures came from foreign as well as domestic companies and new entrants needed to fight for access to downstream retailers.

Further, the cost of supplies was forecasted to increase between 2017 and 2022. Materials and wages constituted almost 80 percent of industry costs—clearly a sizable concern for competitors. Supply purchases included leather, rubber, plastic compounds, foam, nylon, canvas, laces, etc. While the price of leather rose steadily each year, the price of natural and synthetic rubber was also expected to rise over the next five years. In addition, wages as a share of revenue were expected to increase at a rate of 5.5 percent over a five-year period, from 17.1 percent in 2017 to an estimated 17.8 percent in 2022.[3]

In order to thrive in the footwear manufacturing industry, firms needed to differentiate their products in a meaningful way. Selling good quality products at a reasonable price was rarely enough; they needed to target a niche market that desired a certain image. Product innovation and advertising campaigns therefore became the most successful competitive weapons. For example, Clarks adopted a sophisticated design, appealing to a wealthier, more mature customer base. Nike, adidas, and Skechers developed athletic footwear and aggressively marketed their brands to reflect that image. Achieving economies of scale, increasing technical efficiency, and developing a cost-effective distribution system were also essential elements for success.

Despite the presence of established incumbents, global footwear manufacturing was an attractive industry to potential entrants based on the prediction of increased demand and therefore sales revenue. Moreover, the industry offered incumbents one of the highest profit margins in the fashion industry. But because competitors were likely to open new locations and expand their brands in order to discourage competition, new companies' only option was to attempt to undercut them on cost. Acquiring capital equipment and machinery to manufacture footwear on a large scale was expensive. Moreover, potential entrants also needed to launch costly large-scale marketing campaigns to promote brand awareness. Thus, successful incumbents were traditionally able to maintain an overwhelming portion of the market.

Building the TOMS Brand

Due to its humble beginnings, TOMS struggled to gain a foothold in the footwear industry. While companies like Nike had utilized high-profile athletes like Michael Jordan and Tiger Woods to establish brand recognition, TOMS had relatively limited financial resources and tried to appeal to a more socially conscious consumer. Luckily, potential buyers enjoyed a rise in disposable income over time as the economy recovered from the recession. As a result, demand for high-quality footwear increased for affluent shoppers, accompanied by a desire to act (and be *seen* acting) charitably and responsibly.

While walking through the airport one day, Mycoskie encountered a girl wearing TOMS shoes. Mycoskie recounts:

> I asked her about her shoes, and she went on to tell me this amazing story about TOMS and the model that it uses and my personal story. I realized the importance of having a story today is what really separates companies. People don't just wear our shoes, they tell our story. That's one of my favorite lessons that I learned early on.

Moving forward, TOMS focused more on selling the story behind the shoe rather than product features or celebrity endorsements. Moreover, rather than relying primarily on mainstream advertising, TOMS emphasized a grassroots approach using social media and word-of-mouth. With over 4 million Facebook "Likes" and nearly 2 million Twitter "Followers" in 2020, TOMS' social media presence eclipsed that of its much larger rivals. Based on 2020 data, TOMS had fewer "Followers" and fewer "Likes" than Skechers, Nike, and adidas. However, TOMS had more "Followers" and "Likes" per dollar of revenue. So when taking company size into account, TOMS also had a greater media presence

than the industry's leading competitors (see Exhibit 2 for more information).

TOMS' success with social media advertising can be attributed to the story crafted and championed by Mycoskie. Industry incumbents generally dedicated a substantial portion of revenue and effort to advertising since they were simply selling a product. TOMS, on the other hand, used its mission to ask customers to buy into a *cause,* limiting their need to devote resources to brand-building. TOMS lets their charitable work and social media presence generate interest for them organically. This strategy also increased the likelihood that consumers would place repeat purchases and share the story behind their purchases with family and friends. TOMS' customers took pride in supporting a grassroots cause instead of a luxury footwear supplier and encouraged others to share in the rewarding act.

A BUSINESS MODEL DEDICATED TO SOCIALLY RESPONSIBLE BEHAVIOR

Traditionally, the content of advertisements for many large apparel companies focused on the attractive aspects of the featured products. TOMS' advertising, on the other hand, showcased its charitable contributions and the story of its founder Blake Mycoskie. While the CEOs of Nike, adidas, and Clarks rarely appeared in their companies' advertisements, TOMS ran as many ads with its founder as it did without him, emphasizing the inseparability of the TOMS product from Mycoskie's story. In all of his appearances, Mycoskie was dressed in casual and friendly attire so that customers could easily relate to Blake and his mission. This advertising method conveyed

EXHIBIT 2   TOMS' Use of Social Media Compared to Selected Footwear Competitors

	2019 Revenue (Mil. of $)	Facebook "Likes"	"Likes" per Mil. of $ in revenue	Twitter "Followers"	"Followers" per mil. of $ in revenue
TOMS	$ 67.7	4,200,000	62,038	1,800,000	2,659
Skechers	185.2	6,100,000	32,937	47,800	258
adidas	597.3	37,000,000	61,945	946,700	1,585
Nike	4,053.8	34,000,000	8,387	4,600,000	1,135

Source: Author data from Facebook and Twitter May 2, 2018; revenue numbers obtained from Ecommercedb.com.

a small-company feel and encouraged consumers to connect personally with the TOMS brand. It also worked to increase buyer patronage through differentiating the TOMS product from others. Consumers were convinced that every time they purchased a pair of TOMS, they became instruments of the company's charitable work.

As a result (although statistical measures of repeating-buying and total product satisfaction among TOMS' customers were not publicly available), the volume of repeat purchases and buyer enthusiasm likely fueled TOMS' success in a critical way. One reviewer commented, "This is my third pair of TOMS and I absolutely love them!. . . I can't wait to buy more!"[4] Another wrote, "Just got my 25th pair! Love the color! They. . .are my all-time favorite shoe for comfort, looks & durability. AND they are for a great cause!! Gotta go pick out my next pair. . . ."[5]

Virtually all consumer reports on TOMS shoes shared similar themes. Though not cheap, TOMS footwear was priced lower than rivals' products, and customers overwhelmingly agreed that the value was worth the cost. Reviewers described TOMS as comfortable, true to size, lightweight, and versatile ("go with everything"). The shoes had "cute shapes and patterns" and were made of canvas and rubber that molded to customers' feet with wear. Because TOMS products were appealing and trendy yet also basic and comfortable, they were immune to changing fashion trends and consistently attracted a variety of consumers. (see Exhibit 3).

In addition to offering a high-quality product that people valued, TOMS was able to establish a positive repertoire with its customers through efficient distribution. Maintaining an online shop helped TOMS save money on retail locations but also allowed it to serve a wide geographic range. Further, the company negotiated with well-known retailers like Nordstrom and Neiman Marcus to assist in distribution. Through thoughtful planning and structured coordination, TOMS limited operation costs and provided prompt service for its customers.

Giving Partners

As it continued to grow, TOMS sought to improve its operational efficiency by teaming up with "Giving Partners," nonprofit organizations that helped to distribute the shoes that TOMS donated. By teaming up with Giving Partners, TOMS streamlined its charity operations by shifting many of its distributional responsibilities to organizations that were

EXHIBIT 3   Representative Advertisement for TOMS Shoes Company

©John M. Heller/Getty Images

often larger, more resourceful, and able to distribute TOMS shoes more efficiently. Moreover, these organizations possessed more familiarity and experience dealing with the communities that TOMS was interested in helping and could therefore better allocate shoes that suited the needs of children in the area. Giving Partners also provided feedback to help TOMS improve upon its giving and distributional efforts.

Each Giving Partner also magnified the impact of TOMS' shoes by bundling their distribution with other charity work that the organization specialized in. For example, Partners in Health, a nonprofit organization that spent almost $100 million in 2012 on providing healthcare for the poor (more than TOMS' total revenue that year), dispersed thousands of shoes to schoolchildren in Rwanda and Malawi while also screening them for malnutrition. Cooperative giving further strengthened the TOMS brand by association with well-known and highly regarded Giving Partners. Complementary services expanded the scope of TOMS' mission, enhanced the impact that each pair of TOMS had on a child's life, and increased the number of goodwill and business opportunities available to TOMS.

In order to ensure quality of service and adherence to its fundamental mission, TOMS maintained five criteria for Giving Partners:

- Repeat Giving: Giving partners must be able to work with the same communities in multi-year commitments, regularly providing shoes to the same children as they grow.
- High Impact: Shoes must aid Giving Partners with their existing goals in the areas of health and education, providing children with opportunities they would not have otherwise.
- Considerate of Local Economy: Providing shoes cannot have negative socioeconomic effects on the communities where shoes are given.
- Large Volume Shipments: Giving Partners must be able to accept large shipments of giving pairs.
- Health/Education Focused: Giving Partners must only give shoes in conjunction with health and education efforts.[6]

As of 2020, TOMS had built relationships with over 100 Giving Partners, including Save the Children, U.S. Fund for UNICEF, and IMA World Health. In order to remain accountable to their mission in these joint ventures, TOMS also performed unannounced audit reports that ensured shoes were distributed according to the One for One model.

Building a Relationship with Giving Partners

Having Giving Partners offered TOMS the valuable opportunity to shift some of its philanthropic costs onto other parties. However, TOMS also proactively maintained strong relationships with their Giving Partners. Kelly Gibson, the program director of National Relief Charities (NRC), a Giving Partner and nonprofit organization dedicated to improving the lives of Native Americans, highlighted the respect with which TOMS treated its Giving Partners:

> TOMS treats their Giving Partners (like us) and the recipients of their giveaway shoes (the Native kids in this case) like customers. We had a terrific service experience with TOMS. They were meticulous about getting our shoe order just right. They also insist that the children who receive shoes have a customer-type experience at distributions.

From customizing Giving Partners' orders to helping pick up the tab for transportation and distribution, TOMS treated its Giving Partners as valuable customers and generated a sense of goodwill that extended beyond its immediate One for One mission. By ensuring that their Giving Partners and recipients of shoes were treated respectfully, TOMS developed a unique ability to sustain business relationships that other for-profit organizations more concerned with the financial bottom line did not.

MAINTAINING A DEDICATION TO CORPORATE SOCIAL RESPONSIBILITY

Although TOMS manufactured its products in Argentina, China, and Ethiopia (countries which have all been cited as areas with a high degree of child and forced labor by the Bureau of International Labor Affairs), regular third-party factory audits and a Supplier Code of Conduct helped to ensure compliance with fair labor standards.[7] Audits were conducted on both an announced and unannounced basis while the Supplier Code of Conduct was publicly posted in the local language of every work site. The Supplier Code of Conduct enforced standards such as minimum work age, requirement of voluntary employment, non-discrimination, maximum work week hours, and right to unionize. It also protected workers from physical, sexual, verbal, or psychological harassment in accordance with a country's legally mandated standards. Workers were encouraged to report violations directly to TOMS, and suppliers found in violation of TOMS' Supplier Code of Conduct faced termination.

In addition to ensuring that suppliers met TOMS' ethical standards, TOMS also emphasized its own dedication to ethical behavior in a number of ways. TOMS was a member of the American Apparel and Footwear Association (AAFA) and was registered with the Fair Labor Association (FLA). Internally, TOMS educated its own employees on human trafficking and slavery prevention and partnered with several organizations dedicated to raising awareness about such issues, including Hand of Hope.[8]

Giving Trips

Aside from material shoe contributions, TOMS also held a series of "Giving Trips" that supported the broader notion of community service. Giving Trips were first-hand opportunities for employees of TOMS and selected TOMS customers to partake in the delivery of TOMS shoes. These trips increased the transparency of TOMS' philanthropic efforts, further engaging customers and employees. They generated greater social awareness as well, since participants on these trips often became more engaged in local community service efforts at home.

From a business standpoint, Giving Trips also represented a marketing success. First, a large number of participants were customers and journalists unassociated with TOMS who circulated their stories online through social media upon their return. Second, TOMS was able to motivate participants and candidates to become more involved in their mission by increasing public awareness. In 2013, instead of internally selecting customers to participate on the Giving Trips, TOMS opted to hold an open voting process that encouraged candidates to reach out to their known contacts and ask them to vote for their inclusion. This contest drew thousands of contestants and likely hundreds of thousands of voters, although the final vote tallies were not publicly released.

Environmental Sustainability

Dedicated to minimizing its environmental impact, TOMS pursued a number of sustainable practices that included offering vegan shoes, incorporating recycled bottles into its products, and printing with soy ink. TOMS also used a blend of organic canvas and post-consumer, recycled plastics to create shoes that were both comfortable and durable. By utilizing natural hemp and organic cotton, TOMS eliminated pesticide and insecticide use that adversely affected the environment.

In addition, TOMS supported several environmental organizations like Surfers Against Sewage, a movement that raised awareness about excess sewage discharge in the United Kingdom. Formally, TOMS was a member of the Textile Exchange, an organization dedicated to textile sustainability and protecting the environment. The company also participated actively in the AAFA's Environmental Responsibility Committee.

Creating the TOMS Workforce

When asked what makes a great employee, Mycoskie blogged,

> As TOMS has grown, we've continued to look for these same traits in the interns and employees that we hire. Are you passionate? Can you creatively solve problems? Can you be resourceful without resources? Do you have the compassion to serve others? You can teach a new hire just about any skill . . . but you absolutely cannot inspire creativity and passion in someone that doesn't have it.[9]

The company's emphasis on creativity and passion was part of the reason why TOMS relied so heavily on interns and new hires rather than experienced workers. By hiring younger, more inexperienced employees, TOMS was able to be more cost-effective in terms of personnel. The company could also recruit young and energetic individuals who were more likely to think innovatively and out of the box. These employees were placed in specialized teams under the leadership of strong, experienced managerial talent. This human intellectual capital generated a competitive advantage for the TOMS brand.

Together with these passionate individuals, Mycoskie strove to create a family-like work atmosphere where openness and collaboration were celebrated. With his cubicle located in one of the most highly-trafficked areas of the office (right next to customer service), Mycoskie made a point to interact with his employees on a daily basis, in all-staff meetings, and through weekly personal e-mails while traveling. Regarding his e-mails, Mycoskie reflected,

> I'm a very open person, so I really tell the staff what I'm struggling with and what I'm happy about. I tell them what I think the future of TOMS is. I want them to understand what I'm thinking. It's like I'm writing to a best friend.[10]

This notion of "family" was further solidified through company dinners, ski trips, and book clubs where TOMS employees were encouraged to socialize in informal settings. These casual opportunities to interact with colleagues created a "balanced" work atmosphere where employees celebrated not only their own successes, but the successes of their co-workers.

Diversity and inclusion were also emphasized at TOMS. For example, cultural traditions like the Chinese Lunar New Year were celebrated publicly on the TOMS' company blog. Moreover, as TOMS began expanding and distributing globally, the company increasingly sought to recruit a more diverse workforce by hiring multilingual individuals who were familiar with TOMS' diverse customer base and could communicate with their giving communities.[11]

The emphasis that Mycoskie placed on each individual employee was one of the key reasons why employees at TOMS often felt "lucky" to be part of the movement.[12] Coupled with the fact that TOMS employees knew their efforts fostered social justice, these "Agents of Change," as they referred to themselves, were generally quite satisfied with their work,

making TOMS Forbes's 4th Most Inspiring Company in 2014. Overall, the culture allowed TOMS to recruit and retain high-quality employees invested in achieving its social mission.

TEN YEARS OF REMARKABLE GROWTH

By 2016, global footwear manufacturing had developed into an industry worth nearly $240 billion.[13] While TOMS remained a privately held company with limited financial data, the estimated growth rate of TOMS' revenue was astounding. In the seven years after his company's inception, Mycoskie was able to turn his initial $300,000 investment into a company with over $200 million in yearly revenues. As Exhibit 4 shows, the average growth rate of TOMS on a yearly basis was 145 percent, even excluding its first major spike of 457 percent. During the same period, Nike experienced a growth rate of roughly 8.5 percent, with a *decline* in revenues from 2009 to 2010.

The fact that TOMS was able to experience consistent growth despite financial turmoil post-2008 illustrates the strength of the One for One Movement to survive times of recession. Mycoskie attributed his success during the recession to two factors: (1) As consumers became more conscious of their spending during recessions, products like TOMS that gave to others actually became *more* appealing (according to Mycoskie); (2) The giving model that TOMS employed is not "priced in." Rather than commit a percentage of profits or revenues to charity, Mycoskie noted that TOMS simply gave away a pair for every

EXHIBIT 4   **Revenue Comparison for TOMS Shoes and the Footwear Industry, 2006–2016**

	2016	2015	2014	2013	2012	2011	2010	2009	2008	2007	2006
TOMS (in Mils. of $s)											
Revenue	$416	$390	$370.9	$285	$101.8	$46.9	$25.1	$8.4	$3.1	$1.2	$0.2
Growth (%)	6.7%	5.1%	30.1%	180%	117%	86.9%	199%	171%	158.3%	500%	
Industry (in Bil. of $s)											
Revenue	$239.8	$229.4	$230.6	$221.0	$210.2	$208.1	$179.6	$162.4	$159.3	$145.8	
Growth (%)	4.5%	− 0.5%	4.3%	5.1%	1.0%	15.9%	10.6%	1.9%	9.3%	0.0%	

Source: PrivCo and "Global Footwear Manufacturing," *IBISWorld,* April 18, 2016. http://clients1.ibisworld.com/reports/gl/industry/currentperformance.aspx?entid=500.

pair it sold. This way, socially-conscious consumers knew exactly where their money was going without having to worry that TOMS would cut-back on its charity efforts in order to turn a profit.[14]

Production at TOMS

Although TOMS manufactured shoes in Argentina, Ethiopia, and China, only shoes made in China were brought to the retail market. Shoes made in Argentina and Ethiopia were strictly used for donation purposes. TOMS retailed its basic Alpargata shoes in the $50 price range, even though the cost of producing each pair was estimated at around $9.[15] Estimates for the costs of producing TOMS' more expensive lines of shoes were unknown, but they retailed for upwards of $150.

In comparison, manufacturing the average pair of Nike shoes in Indonesia cost around $20, and they were priced at around $70.[16] Factoring in the giving aspect, TOMS seemed to have a slightly smaller mark-up than companies like Nike, yet it still maintained considerable profit margins. More detailed information on trends in TOMS' production costs and practices is limited due to the private nature of the company.

Expanding the Mission

In an effort to broaden its mission and product offerings, TOMS began to expand both its consumer base and charitable-giving product lines. For its customers, TOMS started offering stylish wedges, ballet flats, and even wedding apparel in an effort to reach more customers and satisfy the special needs of current ones. For the children it sought to help, TOMS expanded past its basic black canvas shoe offerings to winter boots in order to help keep children's feet dry and warm during the winter months in cold climate countries.

On another front, TOMS entered the eyewear market in hopes of restoring vision to the 285 million blind or visually-impaired individuals around the world. For every pair of TOMS glasses sold, TOMS restored vision to one individual either through donating prescription glasses or offering medical treatment for those suffering from cataracts and eye infections. TOMS began by focusing its vision-related efforts in Nepal but by 2020 TOMS had teamed up with 16 Giving Partners to help restore sight to nearly 800,000 individuals in 14 countries.

Through TOMS' additional product launches of coffee and bags, the company has been able to expand giving efforts to the global issues of clean water and safe birth. With each pound of TOMS Roasting Co. Coffee, TOMS gives a week's supply of safe water— 140 liters—to a person in need. They have currently given over 722,000 weeks of safe water. With the sale of its bags, TOMS has supported safe birth services in parts of the world where there is dire need. This includes helping its Giving Partners with the vital materials and training necessary for a safe birth. In 2018, TOMS launched its Impact Grant program to fund short term projects with measurable goals pertaining to global issues such as gun violence and mental health. By 2020, they had awarded $6.5 million in Impact Grants to 14 of their Giving Partners.

A CHALLENGING FUTURE

In December 2019, the coronavirus now known as COVID-19 struck Wuhan, China, and swiftly spread around the world. Among the devastating effects of the pandemic were the recessionary economic consequences. The retail sector was especially hard hit as stores closed, workers lost their jobs, and discretionary spending plunged. For TOMS, this came at a particularly bad time in their corporate history. Sales had already started trending downward as the digital revolution reshaped buying behavior and new competition entered the industry with appealing storytelling that rivaled TOMS's. Moreover, the partnership with Bain failed to bring about the growth that was expected. Earnings dropped significantly in 2017 through 2019, leaving TOMS with a debt load that it was unsustainable.

Fortunately for TOMS, their creditors came to the rescue just before the coronavirus outbreak, agreeing to take over the ownership of TOMS from Bain Capital and Mycoskie in exchange for restructuring the company's debt.[17] This move gave TOMS some necessary relief at a critical time. With the right strategic moves, TOMS might yet regain its strong position in the industry. But what are the right strategic moves? Were TOMS's problems the result of the more traditional and expensive marketing strategy that Bain had advocated, as Mycoskie believed?[18] Were they due to not enough diversification or too much unrelated diversification, as TOMS entered businesses far from their strength in footwear (such as coffee roasting). Was TOMS's One-for-One business model one that could continue to be utilized successfully in a variety of industries, or was it a model that depended upon the freshness of its story? Would the uncertain trajectory of the COVID-19 pandemic present a challenge for retailers beyond the reach of even the most farsighted strategy-making? Only time would tell.

ENDNOTES

[1] TOMS Shoes company website, April 23, 2018 www.toms.com/what-we-give-shoes.

[2] Mycoskie, Blake, Web log post, *The Huffington Post,* May 26, 2013, www.huffingtonpost.com/blake-mycoskie.

[3] "Global Footwear Manufacturing," *IBISWorld.* July 2017, http://clients1.ibisworld.com/reports/gl/industry/industryoutlook.aspx?entid=500.

[4] Post by "Alexandria," *TOMS* website, June 2, 2013, www.toms.com/red-canvas-classics-shoes-1.

[5] Post by "Donna Brock," *TOMS* website, January 13, 2014, www.toms.com/women/bright-blue-womens-canvas-classics.

[6] *TOMS* website, June 2, 2013, www.toms.com/our-movement-giving-partners.

[7] Trafficking Victims Protection Reauthorization Act, *United States Department of Labor,* June 2, 2013, www.dol.gov/ilab/programs/ocft/tvpra.htm; TOMS website, June 2, 2013, www.toms.com/corporate-responsibility.

[8] Hand of Hope, "Teaming Up with TOMS Shoes," *Joyce Meyer Ministries,* June 2, 2013, www.studygs.net/citation/mla.htm.

[9] Mycoskie, Blake, "Blake Mycoskie's Blog," *Blogspot,* June 2, 2013, http://blakemycoskie.blogspot.com/.

[10] Schweitzer, Tamara, "The Way I Work: Blake Mycoskie of TOMS Shoes," *Inc.* June 2, 2013. www.inc.com/magazine/20100601/the-way-i-work-blake-mycoskie-of-toms-shoes.html.

[11] TOMS Jobs website, June 2, 2013, www.toms.com/jobs/l.

[12] Daniela, "Together We Travel," TOMS Company Blog, June 3, 2013, http://blog.toms.com/post/36075725601/together-we-travel.

[13] "Global—Footwear," *Marketline: Advantage,* April 18, 2016, http://advantage.marketline.com/Product?pid=MLIP0948-0013.

[14] Zimmerman, Mike. "The Business of Giving: TOMS Shoes," *Success,* June 2, 2013, http://www.success.com/articles/852-the-business-of-giving-toms-shoes.

[15] Fortune, Brittney, "TOMS Shoes: Popular Model with Drawbacks," *The Falcon,* June 2, 2013, http://www.thefalcononline.com/article.php?id=159.

[16] *Behind the Swoosh,* Dir. Keady, Jim, 1995. Film.

[17] https://www.cnbc.com/2019/12/30/toms-shoes-creditors-to-take-over-the-company.html

[18] https://footwearnews.com/2019/business/retail/toms-blake-mycoskie-interview-business-sales-mission-1202764082/

lululemon athletica's Strategy in 2020: Is the Recent Growth in Retail Stores, Revenues, and Profitability Sustainable?

Mc Graw Hill connect

Arthur A. Thompson
The University of Alabama

Randall D. Harris
Texas A&M University-Corpus Christi

I n May 2020, shareholders of lululemon athletica—a designer and retailer of high-tech athletic apparel sold under the lululemon athletica and ivivva athletica brand names—were highly pleased with the remarkable turnaround in the company's performance since January 2016. Calvin McDonald, who became the company's CEO in August 2018, had proven highly adept in continuing to grow the company and boost its profitability somewhat faster than his predecessor had done during 2016 and 2017. Since the end of fiscal 2016 on January 31, 2016, lululemon's revenues had almost doubled and net profits were up 243 percent. The number of company-operated stores had increased from 368 stores in 9 countries in February 2016 to 491 stores in 17 countries as of February 2020, and the company's stock price had risen from $60.75 in early February 2016 to an all-time high of $343.74 in early August 2020. Average annual sales at lululemon's retail stores open at least 12 months, which had dropped from a record high of $5.83 million per store in 2012 to $4.57 million in 2015 (a 21.6 percent decline), had climbed back to $5.2 million in fiscal 2020, ending February 2, 2020, while online sales rose from $401 million in the fiscal year ending January 31, 2016, to $1.14 billion in the fiscal year ending February 2, 2020.

Going into June 2020, the question lurking for shareholders, given the falloff in retail store sales and customer traffic that most apparel chain retailers were struggling to overcome not only during the peak months of the COVID-19 pandemic but also from the propensity of many buyers to shift their purchases of apparel and other products online, was how much longer lululemon would be able to sustain its recent rates of growth in retail stores, revenues, and profitability.

COMPANY BACKGROUND

A year after selling his eight-store surf-, skate-, and snowboard-apparel chain called Westbeach Sports, Chip Wilson took the first commercial yoga class offered in Vancouver, British Columbia, and found the result exhilarating. But he found the cotton clothing used for sweaty, stretchy power yoga completely inappropriate. Wilson's passion was form-fitting performance fabrics and in 1998 he opened a design studio for yoga clothing that also served as a yoga studio at night to help pay the rent. He designed a number of yoga apparel items made of moisture-wicking fabrics that were light, form-fitting, and comfortable and asked local yoga instructors to wear the products and give him feedback. Gratified by the positive response, Wilson opened lululemon's first real store in the beach area of Vancouver in November of 2000.

While the store featured yoga clothing designed by Chip Wilson and his wife Shannon, Chip Wilson's vision was for the store to be a community hub where people could learn and discuss the physical aspects of healthy living—from yoga and diet to running and cycling, plus the yoga-related mental aspects of living a powerful life of possibilities. But the store's clothing proved so popular that dealing with customers crowded out the community-based discussions and training about the merits of living healthy lifestyles. Nonetheless, Chip Wilson and store personnel were firmly committed to healthy, active lifestyles, and Wilson soon came to the conclusion that for the store to provide staff members with the salaries and opportunities to experience fulfilling lives, the one-store company needed to expand into a multi-store enterprise. Wilson believed that the increasing number of women participating in sports, and specifically yoga, provided ample room for expansion, and he saw lululemon athletica's yoga-inspired performance apparel as a way to address a void in the women's athletic apparel market. Wilson also saw the company's mission as one of providing people with the components to live a longer, healthier, and more fun life.

Several new stores were opened in the Vancouver area, with operations conducted through a Canadian operating company, initially named Lululemon Athletica, Inc. and later renamed lululemon Canada, Inc. In 2002, the company expanded into the United States and formed a sibling operating company, Lululemon Athletica USA Inc. (later renamed as lululemon USA, inc), to conduct its operations in the United States. Both operating companies were wholly-owned by affiliates of Chip Wilson. In 2004, the company contracted with a franchisee to open a store in Australia as a means of more quickly disseminating the lululemon athletica brand name, conserving on capital expenditures for store expansion (since the franchisee was responsible for the costs of operating and operating the store), and boosting revenues and profits. The company wound up its fiscal year ending January 31, 2005, with 14 company-owned stores, 1 franchised store, and net revenues of $40.7 million. A second franchised store was opened in Japan later in 2005. Franchisees paid lululemon a one-time franchise fee and an ongoing royalty based on a specified percentage of net revenues; lululemon supplied franchised stores with garments at a discount to the suggested retail price.

Five years after opening the first retail store, it was apparent that lululemon apparel was fast becoming something of a cult phenomenon and a status symbol among yoga fans in areas where lululemon stores had opened. Avid yoga exercisers were not hesitating to purchase $120 color-coordinated lululemon yoga outfits that felt comfortable and made them look good. Mall developers and mall operators quickly learned about lululemon's success and began actively recruiting lululemon to lease space for stores in their malls.

In December 2005, with 27 company-owned stores, 2 franchised stores, and record sales approaching $85 million annually, Chip Wilson sold 48 percent of his interest in the company's capital stock to two private equity investors: Advent International Corporation, which purchased 38.1 percent of the stock, and Highland Capital Partners, which purchased a 9.6 percent ownership interest. In connection with the transaction, the owners formed lululemon athletica inc. to serve as a holding company for all of the company's related entities, including the two operating subsidiaries, lululemon Canada Inc. and lululemon USA Inc. Robert Meers, who had 15 years' experience at Reebok and was Reebok's CEO from 1996–1999, joined lululemon as CEO in December 2005. Chip Wilson headed the company's design team and played a central role in developing the company's strategy and nurturing the company's distinctive corporate culture; he was also Chairman of the company's Board of Directors, a position he had held since founding the company in 1998. Wilson and Meers assembled a management team with a mix of retail, design, operations, product sourcing, and marketing experience from such leading apparel and retail companies as Abercrombie & Fitch, Limited Brands, Nike, and Reebok.

Brisk expansion ensued. The company ended fiscal 2006 with 41 company-owned stores, 10 franchised stores, net revenues of $149 million, and net income of $7.7 million. In 2007, the company's owners elected to take the company public. The initial public offering took place on August 2, 2007, with the company selling 2,290,909 shares to the public and various stockholders selling 15,909,091 shares of their personal holdings. Shares began trading on the NASDAQ under the symbol LULU and on the Toronto Exchange under the symbol LLL.

In 2007, the company's announced growth strategy had five key elements:

1. *Grow the company's store base in North America.* The strategic objective was to add new stores to strengthen the company's presence in locations where it had existing stores and then selectively enter new geographic markets in the United States and Canada. Management believed that the company's strong sales in U.S. stores demonstrated the portability of the lululemon brand and retail concept.

2. *Increase brand awareness.* This initiative entailed leveraging the publicity surrounding the opening of new stores with grassroots marketing programs that included organizing events and partnering with local fitness practitioners.

3. *Introduce new product technologies.* Management intended to continue to focus on developing and offering products that incorporated technology-enhanced fabrics and performance features that differentiated lululemon apparel and helped broaden the company's customer base.

4. *Broaden the appeal of lululemon products.* This initiative entailed (1) adding a number of apparel items for men, (2) expanding product offerings for women and young females in such categories as athletic bags, undergarments, outerwear, and sandals, and (3) adding products suitable for additional sports and athletic activities.

5. *Expand beyond North America.* In the near term, the company planned to expand its presence in Australia and Japan and then, over time, pursue opportunities in other Asian and European markets that offered similar, attractive demographics.

The company grew rapidly. Fitness-conscious women began flocking to the company's stores not only because of the fashionable products but also because of the store ambience and attentive, knowledgeable store personnel. Dozens of new lululemon athletic retail stores were opened annually, and the company pursued a strategy of embellishing its product offerings to create a comprehensive line of apparel and accessories designed for athletic pursuits such as yoga; running and general fitness; technical clothing for active female youths; and a selection of fitness and recreational items for men. Revenues topped $1 billion in fiscal 2011, $2 billion fiscal 2016, and $3 billion in fiscal 2018.

For fiscal year 2019, lululemon revenues grew by 21 percent over fiscal 2018 to just under $4 billion. lululemon products could be bought at its 368 retail stores in the United States and Canada, 38 stores in the People's Republic of China, 38 stores in Australia and New Zealand, and 47 stores in the rest of the world. The company's e-commerce web site, www.lululemon.com, was available to customers worldwide. In the company's most recent fiscal year ending February 2, 2020, retail store sales accounted for 62.8 percent of company revenues, web site sales accounted for 28.6 percent, and sales in all other channels (sales at outlet centers, showroom sales, sales from temporary locations, licensing revenues, and wholesale sales to premium yoga studios, health clubs, fitness centers, and a few other retailers) accounted for 8.6 percent.

Exhibit 1 presents highlights of the company's performance for fiscal years 2015–2019. Exhibit 2 shows lululemon's revenues by business segment and geographic region for the same period.

lululemon's Evolving Senior Leadership Team

In January 2008, Christine M. Day joined the company as Executive Vice President, Retail Operations. Previously, she had worked at Starbucks, functioning in a variety of capacities and positions, including President, Asia Pacific Group (July 2004- February 2007); Co-President for Starbucks Coffee International (July 2003 to October 2003); Senior Vice President, North American Finance & Administration; and Vice President of Sales and Operations for Business Alliances. In April 2008, Day was appointed as lululemon's President and Chief Operating Officer and was named Chief Executive Officer and member of the Board of Directors in July 2008. During her tenure as CEO, Day expanded and strengthened the company's management team to support its expanding operating activities and geographic scope, favoring the addition of people with relevant backgrounds and experiences at such companies as Nike, Abercrombie & Fitch, The Gap, and Speedo International. She also spent a number of hours each week in the company's stores observing how customers shopped, listening to their comments and complaints, and using the information to tweak product offerings, merchandising, and store operations.

Company founder Chip Wilson stepped down from his executive role as lululemon's Chief Innovation and Branding Officer effective January 29, 2012, and moved his family to Australia; however, he continued on in his role of Chairman of

EXHIBIT 1   Financial and Operating Highlights, lululemon athletica, Fiscal Years 2015–2019 (in millions of $, except per share data)

Selected Income Statement Data	Fiscal Year 2019 (Ending Feb. 2, 2020)	Fiscal Year 2018 (Ending Feb. 3, 2019)	Fiscal Year 2017 (Ending Jan.28,2018)	Fiscal Year 2016 (Ending Jan 29, 2017)	Fiscal Year 2015 (Ending Jan. 31, 2016)
Net revenues	$3,979.3	$3,288.3	$2,649.2	$2,344.4	$2,060.5
Cost of goods sold	1,755.9	1,472.0	1,250.4	1,144.7	1,063.4
Gross profit	2,223.4	1,816.3	1,398.8	1,199.6	997.2
Selling, general, and administrative expenses	1,334.3	1,110.5	904.3	778.5	628.1
Operating profit	889.1	705.8	456.0	421.2	369.1
Net profit (loss)	$ 645.6	$ 483.8	$ 258.7	$ 303.4	$ 266.0
Foreign currency translation adjustment	(7.8)	(73.9)	58.6	36.7	(64.8)
Comprehensive income	$ 637.8	$ 409.9	$ 317.2	$ 340.1	$ 201.3
Earnings per share—basic	$ 4.95	$ 3.63	$ 1.90	$ 2.21	$ 1.90
—diluted	$ 4.93	$ 3.61	$ 1.90	$ 2.21	$ 1.89
Balance Sheet Data					
Cash and cash equivalents	$1,093.5	$ 881.3	$ 990.5	$ 734.8	$ 501.5
Inventories	518.5	404.8	329.6	298.4	284.0
Total assets	3,281.4	2,084.7	1,998.5	1,657.5	1,314.1
Stockholders' equity	1,952.2	1,446.0	1, 597.0	1,360.0	1,027.5
Cash Flow and Other Data					
Net cash provided by operating activities	$ 669.3	$ 742.8	$ 489.3	$ 385.1	$ 298.7
Capital expenditures	283.1	225.8	157.9	149.5	143.5
Store Data					
Number of corporate-owned stores open at end of period	491	440	404	406	363
Sales per gross square foot at corporate-owned stores open at least one full year	$ 1,657	$ 1,579	$ 1,554	$ 1,521	$ 1,541
Average sales at corporate-owned stores open at least one year	$5.18 million	$4.78 million	$4.68 million	$4.47 million	$4.57 million

Source: Company 10-K reports for fiscal years 2015, 2016, 2017, 2018, and 2019.

the company's Board of Directors and focused on becoming a better Board Chairman, even going so far as to take a four-day course on board-governance at Northwestern University.[1] Christine Day promoted Sheree Waterson, who had joined the company in 2008 and had over 25 years of consumer and retail industry experience, as Chief Product Officer to assume responsibility for product design, product development, and other executive tasks that Wilson had been performing. Shortly after the quality problems with the black Luon bottoms occurred, Sheree Waterson resigned her position and left the company. In October 2013, lululemon announced that Tara Poseley had been appointed to its Senior Leadership Team as Chief Product Officer and would have responsibility for overseeing lululemon's design team, product design activities, merchandising, inventory activities, and strategic planning. Previously, Poseley held the position of Interim President at Bebe Stores, Inc, President of Disney

EXHIBIT 2   lululemon athletica's Revenues and Income from Operations, by Business Segment, Geographic Region, and Product Category. Fiscal Years 2015–2019 (dollars in millions)

Revenues by Business Segment	Fiscal Year 2019 (Ending Feb. 2, 2020)	Fiscal Year 2018 (Ending Feb. 3, 2019)	Fiscal Year 2017 (Ending Jan.28, 2018)	Fiscal Year 2016 (Ending Jan 29, 2017	Fiscal Year 2015 (Ending Jan. 31 2016)
Corporate-owned stores	$2,501.1	$2,126.4	$1,837.1	$1,704.4	$1,516.3
Direct-to-consumer (e-commerce sales)	1,137.8	858.9	577.6	453.3	401.5
All other channels*	340.4	303.1	234.5	186.7	142.7
Total	$3,979.3	$3,288.3	$2,649.2	$2,344.4	$2,060.5
Percentage Distribution of Revenues by Business Segment					
Corporate owned stores	62.9%	64.7%	69.3%	72.7%	73.6%
Direct-to-consumer (e-commerce sales)	28.6%	26.1%	21.8%	19.3%	19.5%
All other channels*	8.5%	9.2%	8.9%	8.0%	6.9%
Total	100.0%	100.0%	100.0%	100.0%	100.0%
Income from Operations (before general corporate expenses), by Business Segment					
Corporate owned stores	$ 689.3	$ 575.5	$ 464.3	$ 415.6	$ 346.8
Direct-to-consumer (e-commerce sales)	482.4	354.1	224.1	186.2	166.4
All other channels*	72.6	62.6	35.6	22.3	5.8
Total Income from Operations (before general corporate expenses)	$1,244.3	$ 992.2	$ 724.0	$ 624.1	$ 519.0
Revenues by Geographic Region					
United States	$2,854.4	$2,363.4	$1,911.8	$1,726.1	$1,508.8
Canada	649.1	565.1	491.8	447.2	416.5
Outside of North America	475.8	359.8	245.6	171.1	135.2
Total	$3,979.3	$3,288.3	$2,649.2	$2,344.4	$2,060.5
Percentage Distribution of Revenues by Geographic Region					
United States	71.7%	71.9%	72.2%	73.6%	73.2%
Canada	16.3%	17.2%	18.6%	19.1%	20.2%
Outside of North America	12.0%	10.9%	9.2%	7.3%	6.6%
Total	100.0%	100.0%	100.0%	100.0%	100.0%
Revenues by Product Category					
Women's products	$2,791.0	$2,352.8	$1,892.6	Not reported	Not reported
Men's products	933.8	694.9	526.5	Not reported	Not reported
Other categories	254.5	240.6	230.0	Not reported	Not reported

*The "All other channels" category included showroom sales, sales at lululemon outlet stores, sales from temporary store locations, licensing revenues, and wholesale sales to premium yoga studios, health clubs, fitness centers, and other wholesale accounts.

Source: Company 10-K Reports, Fiscal Years, 2017 and 2019.

Stores North America (The Children's Place), CEO of Design Within Reach (DWR), and a range of senior merchandising and design management positions during her 15-year tenure at Gap Inc.

In the aftermath of the pants recall in March 2013, the working relationship between Christine Day and Chip Wilson deteriorated. Wilson made it clear that he would have handled the product recall incident differently and that he did not think there were problems with the design of the product or the quality of the fabric. But the differences between Day and Wilson went beyond the events of March 2013, especially when some consumers began to complain about the quality of the replacement pants. Wilson returned from Australia in May 2013, and weeks later Christine Day announced she would step down as CEO when her successor was named. A lengthy search for Day's replacement ensued.

In the meantime, Chip Wilson triggered a firestorm when, in an interview with Bloomberg TV in November 2013, he defended the company's design of the black Luon bottoms, saying "Quite frankly, some women's bodies just actually don't work" with the pants. Although a few days later he publicly apologized for his remarks suggesting that the company's product quality issues back in March 2013 were actually the fault of overweight women, his apology was not well received. In December 2013, Wilson resigned his position as Chairman of lululemon's board of directors and took on the lesser role of non-executive Chairman. A few months later, Wilson announced that he intended to give up his position as non-executive Chairman prior to the company's annual stockholders meeting in June 2014 but continue on as a member of the company's Board of Directors (in 2013–2014, Wilson was the company's largest stockholder and controlled 29.2 percent of the company's common stock).

In early December 2013, lululemon announced that its Board of Directors had appointed Laurent Potdevin as the company's Chief Executive Officer and a member of its Board of Directors; Potdevin stepped into his role in January 2014, and, to help ensure a smooth transition, Christine Day remained with lululemon through the end of the company's fiscal year (February 2, 2014). Potdevin came to lululemon having most recently served as President of TOMS Shoes, a company founded on the mission that it would match every pair of shoes purchased with a pair of new shoes given to a child in need.

Prior to TOMS, Potdevin held numerous positions at Burton Snowboards for more than 15 years, including President and CEO from 2005–2010; Burton Snowboards, headquartered in Burlington, Vermont, was considered to be the world's premier snowboard company, with a product line that included snowboards and accessories (bindings, boots, socks, gloves, mitts, and beanies); men's, women's, and youth snowboarding apparel; and bags and luggage. Burton's grew significantly under Potdevin's leadership, expanding across product categories and opening additional retail stores.

Tension between Chip Wilson and lululemon's board of directors erupted at the company's annual shareholders' meeting in June 2014 when he voted his entire shares against re-election of the company's chairman and another director. In February 2015, after continuing to disagree with lululemon executives and board members over the company's strategic direction and ongoing dissatisfaction with how certain lululemon activities were being managed, Wilson resigned his position on lululemon's board of directors. In August 2014, he sold half of his ownership stake to a private equity firm. In June 2015, lululemon filed documents with the Securities and Exchange Commission enabling Wilson to sell his remaining 20.1 million shares (equal to a 14.6 percent ownership stake worth about $1.3 billion) in the event he wished to do so. As of April 2020, Chip Wilson owned 10.7 million shares of lululemon's common stock, equal to an ownership stake of about 8.1 percent. Wilson, together with his wife and son, in 2014 formed a new company, Kit and Ace, that specialized in high-end clothing for men and women made from a machine-washable, high performance, cashmere fabric; the innovative clothing line was designed for all-day wear and included a range of items suitable for running errands or attending an evening event. In 2016, there were some 60 Kit and Ace stores in the United States, Canada, Australia, Britain, and Japan; however, in 2020, the company only had 8 locations, all in Canada.

In 2018, lululemon CEO Laurent Potdevin resigned as CEO following allegations of misconduct. Potdevin was replaced by Calvin McDonald as Chief Executive Officer in August 2018. McDonald had previously served for five years as the President and CEO of Sephora America, a division of the LVMH Group. Mr. McDonald had been very successful in his previous position, a period during which Sephora America grew annually by double digits. McDonald was also an endurance athlete who had competed in both triathlons and marathons.[2] In April 2020, the Chief Financial Officer (CFO) for lululemon, Patrick Guido, resigned as CFO. Guido had not been replaced as of June 17, 2020.

THE YOGA MARKETPLACE

According to the most recent study on the practice of yoga in the United States, a "Yoga in America" study funded by the *Yoga Journal,* in 2015 there were 36.7 million people in the United States who had practiced yoga in the last six months in a group or private class setting, up from 20.4 million in 2012 and 15.8 million in 2008.[3] Worldwide, it was estimated that were about 300 million yoga practitioners.[4] About 72 percent of the people who engaged in group or class yoga exercises were women, and close to 62 percent of all yoga practitioners were in the age range of 18–49.[5] The level of yoga expertise varied considerably: 56 percent of yoga practitioners considered themselves as beginners, 42 percent considered themselves as "intermediate," and two percent considered themselves to be in the expert/advanced category. Spending on yoga classes, yoga apparel, equipment, and accessories was an estimated $16.8 billion, up from $10.3 billion in 2012, and $5.7 billion in 2008.[6]

The market for sports and fitness apparel was considerably larger, of course, than just the market for yoga apparel. The global market for all types of sportswear, activewear, and athletic apparel was estimated to be about $250 billion in 2020 and was forecast to grow at roughly five percent annually through 2026.[7] Sales of various types of sports apparel was among the fastest-growing segments in the $3 trillion global apparel market. In the United States, sales of activewear and all types of gym and fitness apparel, which included both items made with high-tech performance fabrics that wicked away moisture and items made mostly of cotton, polyester, stretch fabrics, and selected other manmade fibers that lacked moisture-wicking and other high performance features, were the fastest growing segment of the apparel industry.[8]

LULULEMON'S STRATEGY AND BUSINESS IN 2020

Lululemon athletica viewed its core mission as "creating components for people to live longer, healthier, fun lives."[9] The company's primary target customer was

> "a sophisticated and educated woman who understands the importance of an active, healthy lifestyle. She is increasingly tasked with the dual responsibilities of career and family and is constantly challenged to balance her work, life and health. We believe she pursues exercise to achieve physical fitness and inner peace."[10]

In the company's early years, lululemon's strategy was predicated on management's belief that other athletic apparel companies were not effectively addressing the unique style, fit and performance needs of women who were embracing yoga and a variety of other fitness and athletic activities. Lululemon sought to address this void in the marketplace by incorporating style, feel-good comfort, and functionality into its yoga-inspired apparel products and by building a network of lululemon retail stores, along with an online store at the company's website, to market its apparel directly to these women. However, while the company was founded to address the unique needs and preferences of women, it did not take long for management to recognize the merits of broadening the company's market target to include fitness apparel for activities other than yoga and apparel for population segments other than adult women.

In 2009, lululemon opened its first ivviva-branded store in Vancouver, British Columbia, to sell high quality, premium-priced dance-inspired apparel to female youth (ivviva was a word that lululemon made up). The Vancouver store was soon profitable, and 11 additional company-owned ivviva stores were opened in Canada and the United States during 2010–13. In 2014–15, the opening of new ivviva stores accelerated. However, in June 2019, lululemon announced the closure of all but seven of the company's ivviva stores. Sales of many ivviva branded products were moved online to the lululemon website, and sales of some ivviva products continued through other retailers, including Target and Amazon.com. In September 2019, lululemon announced it would close the seven remaining ivviva stores by mid-2020.

In 2013–14, the company began designing and marketing products for men who appreciated the technical rigor and premium quality of athletic and fitness apparel. Management also believed that participation in athletic and fitness activities was destined to climb as people over 60 years of age became increasingly focused on living longer, healthier, active lives in their retirement years and engaged in regular exercise and recreational activities. Another demand-enhancing factor was that consumer decisions to purchase athletic, fitness, and recreational apparel were being driven not only by an actual need for functional products but also by a desire to create a particular lifestyle perception through the apparel they wore. Consequently, senior executives had transitioned lululemon's strategy from one of focusing exclusively on yoga apparel for women to one aimed at designing and marketing a wider range of healthy lifestyle-inspired apparel and accessories for women and men and dance-inspired apparel for girls. In 2019, men's product lines became a major focus of growth for the company.

In early 2019, lululemon announced a new five-year "Power of Three" strategic plan featuring three growth initiatives:

- **Product Innovation.** The company sought to pursue a disruptive innovation strategy in its core apparel markets, using what management called a Science of Feel™ approach to product development that emphasized using fabrics and technologies that provided both excellent technical performance and feel-good comfort, to introduce new products with innovative features and maintain a fresh and growing lineup of yoga, running, and training products for both women and men. The plan also called for the company to continue its product collaborations, expand its popular Office/Travel/Commute line, and pursue new opportunities such as selfcare.

- **Omni Guest Experiences.** The company sought to become "an experiential brand" and use all of the company's marketing channels to grow and deepen its relationship with the guests who patronized its stores and the consumers who shopped its website, and, further, to create a series of ongoing experiential moments and opportunities where local community members striving to live the "sweatlife" and lead a healthy, mindful lifestyle could connect and come together. The company's concept of integrated "omni guest experiences" thus went beyond just the experiences customers had in shopping, purchasing, and using the company products to include creating and hosting a variety of local community events, an innovative membership program, partnerships with local yoga studios and running clubs, and unique store formats (like a 25,000 square-foot store in Chicago which had a yoga studio, meditation space, a healthy food and juice bar, and areas for community gatherings). In addition, management intended for the company's digital ecosystem to become a greater source of information and communication and a means of inspiring and igniting community building.

- **Continuing to Add lululemon Retail Stores in Both Its Core North American Market and Internationally.** Outside North America, China was the company's primary focus for new store openings, with 16 new stores added in the 2019 fiscal year and more planned for 2020. One to two new company-operated stores were being opened in several countries across Europe (notably in the United Kingdom, France, Germany, the Netherlands, and the Scandinavian countries), and in selected countries in the Asia-Pacific (Australia, Japan, Malaysia, Singapore, and South Korea).

lululemon reported significant progress on its strategic goals in early 2020, stating that the company's performance was on track to achieve its five-year strategic plan goals to double online sales, double sales of men's products, and quadruple international revenues by year-end 2023 and was well-ahead of its previously set target to reach $4 billion in annual revenue in fiscal 2020.

Product Line Strategy

In 2020, lululemon offered a diverse and growing selection of premium-priced performance apparel and accessories for women, female youths and men that were designed for healthy lifestyle activities such as yoga, swimming, running, cycling, and general fitness. Currently, the company's range of offerings included:

If you are not familiar with lululemon products, it would be useful to spend a few minutes browsing the company's e-store at www.lululemon.com.

lululemon's Strategy of Offering Only a Limited Range of Apparel Sizes.   In the months following the product recall of the too-sheer bottom pants in March 2013, lululemon officially revealed in a posting on its Facebook page that it did not offer clothing in plus-sizes because focusing on sizes 12 and below was an integral part of its business strategy;

EXHIBIT 3   lululemon athletica's Product Offerings for Women and Men, Representative Sample, 2020

Women		Men
• Sports bras	• Swimwear	• Tops
• Tanks	• Socks and underwear	• Jackets and hoodies
• Sweaters and wraps	• Scarves	• Pants and shorts
• Jackets and hoodies	• Gear bags	• Gear bags and backpacks
• Long-sleeve and short-sleeve tops and tees	• Caps and headbands	• Caps and gloves
• Pants and crops	• Sweat cuffs and gloves	• Swimwear
• Shorts	• Water bottles	• Socks and underwear
• Skirts and dresses	• Yoga mats and props	• Run accessories
• Outerwear	• Instructional yoga DVDs	• Yoga mats, props, and instructional DVDs

according to the company's posting and to the postings of lululemon personnel who responded to comments made by Facebook members who read the lululemon posting:[11]

> Our product and design strategy is built around creating products for our target guest in our size range of 2–12. While we know that doesn't work for everyone and recognize fitness and health come in all shapes and sizes, we've built our business, brand and relationship with our guests on this formula.
>
> We agree that a beautiful healthy life is not measured by the size you wear. We want to be excellent at what we do, so this means that we can't be everything to everybody and need to focus on specific areas. Our current focuses are in innovating our women's design, men's brand, and building our international market.
>
> At this time, we don't have plans to change our current sizing structure which is 2–12 for women.

In 2016, the largest size appearing in the size guide for women on lululemon's website was 12, which was said to be suitable for a 40" bust, 32.5" waist, and 43" hips. In 2020, the largest women's size appearing on the company's website was 14 (but size 12 was the largest offered for most products). Some women's products were offered in sizes ranging from XXXS (for a 21" waist, 29" bust, and 32" hips) to XXL (for a 35" waist, 42" bust, and 45" hips), but most such products were sized XS to XL.

Retail Distribution and Store Expansion Strategy

After several years of experience in establishing and working with franchised stores in the United States, Australia, Japan, and Canada, top management in 2010 determined that having franchised stores was not in lululemon's best long-term strategic interests. A strategic initiative was begun to either acquire the current stores of franchisees and operate them as company stores or convert the franchised stores to a joint venture arrangement where lululemon owned the controlling interest in the store and the former franchisee owned a minority interest. By year-end 2011, all lululemon stores were company-operated.

As of February 2020, lululemon had 491 company-operated stores in 17 countries:

- 305 stores in the United States (including 19 factory outlet stores in discount malls).

- 63 stores in Canada, including seven ivviva stores slated for closure later on in 2020.

- 38 stores in the People's Republic of China, inclusive of six stores in Hong Kong, two stores in Macau, and one store in Taiwan.

- 31 stores in Australia.

- 14 stores in the United Kingdom.

- Seven stores in Japan, seven stores in New Zealand, six stores in Germany, five stores in South Korea, four stores in Singapore, three stores in France, two stores in Malaysia, two stores in Sweden, and one store in each of the Netherlands, Ireland, Norway, and Switzerland.

In fiscal year 2020, management had announced that in new store openings would come primarily from company-operated store openings in Asia and the United States. Management reported that the company's real estate strategy going forward would be to focus on (1) the opening of new company-operated stores, and (2) expansion of the company's overall retail square footage through store expansions and store relocations.[12] With sales per square foot of $1,657 in lululemon retail stores in fiscal 2019, management believed its sales revenues per square foot of retail space were close to the best in the retail apparel sector. By way of comparison, the stores of specialty fashion retailers like Old Navy, Banana Republic, The Gap, and Abercrombie & Fitch typically had 2015 annual sales averaging less than $500 per square foot of store space.

lululemon's Retail Stores: Locations, Layout, and Merchandising.   The company's retail stores were located primarily on street locations, in upscale strip shopping centers, in lifestyle centers, and in malls. Typically, stores were leased and ranged from 2,500 to 3,500 square feet in size. Most stores included space for product display and merchandising, checkout, fitting rooms, a restroom, and an office/storage area. While the leased nature of the store spaces meant that each store had its own customized layout and arrangement of fixtures and displays, each store was carefully decorated and laid out in a manner that projected the ambience and feel of a homespun local apparel boutique rather than the more impersonal, cookie-cutter atmosphere of many apparel chain stores.

The company's merchandising strategy was to sell all of the items in its retail stores at full price.[13] Special colors and seasonal items were in stores for only a limited time—such products were on 3, 6, or 12-week life cycles so that frequent shoppers could always find something new. Store inventories of short-cycle products were deliberately limited to help foster a sense of scarcity, condition customers to buy when they saw an item rather than wait, and avoid any need to discount unsold items. In one instance, a hot-pink color that launched in December was supposed to have a two-month shelf life, but supplies sold out in the first week. However, supplies of core products that did not change much from season to season were more ample to minimize the risk of lost sales due to items being out-of-stock. Approximately 95 percent of the merchandise in lululemon stores was sold at full price.[14] When certain styles, colors, and sizes of apparel items at lululemon retail stores were selling too slowly to clear out the inventories of items ordered from contract manufacturers, lululemon typically shipped the excess inventories to one or more of the 19 lululemon Factory Outlet stores in North America to be sold at discounted prices.

One unique feature of lululemon's retail stores was that the floor space allocated to merchandising displays and customer shopping could be sufficiently cleared to enable the store to hold an in-store yoga class before or after regular shopping hours. Every store hosted a complimentary yoga class each week that was conducted by a professional yoga instructor from the local community who had been recruited to be a "store ambassador;" when the class concluded, the attendees were given a 15 percent-off coupon to use in shopping for products in the store. From time to time, each store's yoga ambassadors demonstrated their moves in the store windows and on the sales floor. Exhibit 4 shows the exteriors and interiors of representative lululemon athletica stores.

lululemon's Showroom Strategy.   Over the years, lululemon had opened "showrooms" in numerous locations both inside and outside North America as a means of introducing the lululemon brand and culture to a community, developing relationships with local fitness instructors and fitness enthusiasts, and hosting community-related fitness events, all in preparation for the grand opening of a new lululemon athletica retail store in weeks ahead. Showroom personnel:

- Hosted get-acquainted parties for fitness instructors and fitness enthusiasts.
- Recruited a few well-regarded fitness instructors in the local area to be "store ambassadors" for lululemon products and periodically conduct in-store yoga classes when the local lululemon retail store opened.
- Advised people visiting the showroom on where to find great yoga or Pilates classes, fitness centers, and health and wellness information and events.
- Solicited a select number of local yoga studios, health clubs, and fitness centers to stock and retail a small assortment of lululemon's products.

Showrooms were only open part of the week so that showroom personnel could be out in the community meeting people, building relationships with yoga and fitness instructors, participating in local yoga and fitness classes and talking with attendees before and after class, promoting attendance at local fitness and wellness events, and stimulating interest in the soon-to-open retail store. lululemon used showrooms as a means of "pre-seeding" the opening of a lululemon retail store primarily in those locations where no other lululemon retail stores were nearby.

Wholesale Sales Strategy

lululemon also marketed its products to select premium yoga studios, health clubs, and fitness centers as a way to gain the implicit endorsement of local fitness personnel for lululemon branded apparel, familiarize their customers with the lululemon brand, and give them an opportunity to conveniently purchase lululemon apparel.

lululemon management did not want to grow wholesale sales to these types of establishments into a significant revenue contributor. Rather, the strategic objective of selling lululemon apparel to yoga studios, health clubs, and fitness centers was to build brand awareness, especially in new geographic markets both in North America and other international locations where the company intended to open new stores. Wholesale sales to outlet stores were made only to dispose of excess inventories and thereby avoid in-store markdowns on slow-selling items.

lululemon had entered into license and supply arrangements with partners in the Middle East and Mexico to operate lululemon athletica branded retail locations in the United Arab Emirates, Kuwait, Qatar, Oman, Bahrain and Mexico. lululemon retained the rights to sell lululemon products through their e-commerce websites in these countries. Under the arrangement, lululemon supplied their partners with lululemon products, training, and other support. As of February 2020, there were four licensed retail locations in Mexico, three in the United Arab Emirates, and one in Qatar, none of which were included in the company-operated store numbers in Exhibit 1.

The company's wholesale sales to all these channels accounted for $340 million in sales, or 8.6 percent of total net revenues in fiscal 2019, versus 9.2 percent of total net revenues for the company in fiscal 2018.

Direct-to-Consumer Sales Strategy

In 2009, lululemon launched its e-commerce website, www.lululemon.com, to enable customers to make online purchases, supplement its already-functioning phone sales activities, and greatly extend the company's geographic market reach. Management saw online sales as having three strategic benefits: (1) providing added convenience for core customers, (2) securing sales in geographic markets where there were no lululemon stores, and (3) helping build brand awareness, especially in new markets, including those outside of North America. As of May 2020, the company website reached 6 continents and 84 separate countries in North America, South America, Africa, Asia, Europe, and the Middle East. lululemon provided free standard shipping (2–6 business day delivery) on all lululemon to customers in North America; a flat $30 shipping fee (5–10 business day delivery) was charged to buyers located in international destinations.

The merchandise selection that lululemon offered to online buyers differed somewhat from what was available in the company's retail stores. A number of the items available in stores were not sold online; a few online selections were not available in the stores. Styles and colors available for sale online were updated weekly. On occasion, the company marked down the prices of some styles and colors sold online to help clear out the inventories of items soon to be out-of-season and make way for newly-arriving merchandise—online customers could view the discounted merchandise by clicking on a "we made too much" link.

In addition to making purchases, website visitors could browse information about what yoga was, what the various types of yoga were, and their benefits; learn about fabrics and technologies used in lululemon's products; read recent posts on lululemon's yoga blog; and stay abreast of lululemon activities in their communities. The company planned to continue to develop and enhance its e-commerce websites in ways that would provide a distinctive online shopping experience and strengthen its brand reputation.

Direct-to-consumer sales at the company's websites had become an increasingly important part of the company's business, with e-commerce sales climbing from $106.3 million in fiscal 2011 (10.6 percent of total net revenues) to $1.14 billion in fiscal 2019 (28.6 percent of total revenues)—equal to a compound annual growth rate of 34.5 percent. In April 2020, when the majority of lululemon's retail stores in North America and elsewhere were closed due to COVID-19, e-commerce became a vital link between the company and the consumer. Exhibit 4 shows the growth in quarterly e-commerce sales for fiscal years 2018 and 2019 and the first quarter of 2020.

Product Design and Development Strategy

lululemon's product design efforts were led by a team of designers based in Vancouver, British Columbia partnering with various international designers.

EXHIBIT 4   lululemon's Quarterly E-commerce Sales, Q1 2018 through Q1 2020

Online Sales	Quarter 1	Quarter 2	Quarter 3	Quarter 4
2018	$157.8 million	$167.4 million	$189.4 million	$344.2 million
2019	209.8 million	217.6 million	246.7 million	463.7 million
2020	352.0 million			

Source: Quarterly Financial Results, posted in the Investor Relations section at www.lululemon.com.

The design team included athletes and users of the company's products who embraced lululemon's design philosophy and dedication to premium quality. Design team members regularly visited retail stores in a proactive effort to solicit feedback on existing products from store customers and fitness ambassadors and to gather their ideas for product improvements and new products. In addition, the design team used various market intelligence sources to identify and track market trends. On occasion, the team hosted meetings in several geographic markets to discuss the company's products with local athletes, trainers, yogis, and members of the fitness industry. The design team incorporated all of this input to make fabric selections, develop new products, and make adjustments in the fit, style, and function of existing products.

The design team worked closely with its apparel manufacturers to incorporate innovative fabrics that gave lululemon garments such characteristics as stretch ability, moisture-wicking capability, color fastness, feel-good comfort, and durability. Fabric quality was evaluated via actual wear tests and by a leading testing facility. Before bringing out new products with new fabrics, lululemon used the services of leading independent inspection, verification, testing, and certification companies to conduct a battery of tests on fabrics for such performance characteristics as pilling, shrinkage, abrasion resistance, and color-fastness. Lastly, lululemon design personnel worked with leading fabric suppliers to identify opportunities to develop fabrics that lululemon could trademark and thereby gain added brand recognition and brand differentiation.

Where appropriate, product designs incorporated convenience features, such as pockets to hold credit cards, keys, digital audio players, and clips for heart rate monitors and long sleeves that covered the hands for cold-weather exercising. Product specifications called for the use of advanced sewing techniques, such as flat seaming, that increased comfort and functionality, reduced chafing and skin irritation, and strengthened important seams. All of these design elements and fabric technologies were factors that management believed enabled lululemon to price its high-quality technical athletic apparel at prices above those of traditional athletic apparel.

Typically, it took 8 to 10 months for lululemon products to move from the design stage to availability in its retail stores; however, the company had the capability to bring select new products to market in as little as two months. Management believed its lead times were shorter than those of most apparel brands due to the company's streamlined design and development process, the real-time input received from customers and ambassadors at its store locations, and the short times it took to receive and approve samples from manufacturing suppliers. Short lead times facilitated quick responses to emerging trends or shifting market conditions.

lululemon management believed that its design process enhanced the company's capabilities to develop top quality products and was a competitive strength.

Sourcing and Manufacturing

Production was the only value chain activity that lululemon did not perform internally. Lululemon did not own or operate any manufacturing facilities to produce fabrics or make garments. In 2019, fabrics were sourced from a group of approximately 76 fabric manufacturers, with five fabric manufacturers supplying 59 percent of the total and the largest single fabric manufacturer supplying 32 percent of the fabric used. During fiscal year 2019, approximately 46 percent of the required fabrics were sourced from suppliers in Taiwan, 14 percent from suppliers in mainland China, 19 percent from manufacturers in Sri Lanka, and the remainder from other regions. Other raw materials used in lululemon products, such as content labels, elastics, buttons, clasps, and drawcords, were obtained from suppliers located predominantly in the Asia Pacific region.

Garments were sourced from approximately 39 contract manufacturers, five of which produced approximately 56 percent of the company's products in fiscal 2019, with the largest of these producing about 17 percent of the total. During fiscal 2019, approximately 33 percent of the company's products were produced in Vietnam, 16 percent in Cambodia, 15 percent in Sri Lanka, 11 percent in China (including two percent in Taiwan), and the remainder in other countries. The company deliberately refrained from entering into long-term contracts with any of its fabric suppliers or manufacturing sources, preferring instead to transact business on an order-by-order basis and rely on the close working relationships it had developed with its various suppliers over the years. lululemon maintained production relationships with several manufacturers in North America that provided the company with the capability to speed select products to market and respond quickly to changing trends and unexpectedly high buyer demand for certain products.

lululemon took great care to ensure that its manufacturing suppliers shared lululemon's commitment to quality and ethical business conduct. All manufacturers were required to adhere to a vendor code of ethics regarding quality of manufacturing, working conditions, environmental responsibility, fair wage practices, and compliance with child labor laws, among others. lululemon utilized the services of a leading inspection and verification firm to closely monitor each supplier's compliance with applicable law, lululemon's vendor code of ethics, and other business practices that could reflect badly on lululemon's choice of suppliers.

Distribution Facilities

lululemon shipped products to its stores from owned or leased distribution facilities in the United States, Canada, and Australia. The company owned a 310,000 square-foot distribution center in Columbus, Ohio and operated a leased 156,000 square-foot distribution center in Vancouver, British Columbia, a leased 250,000 square-foot distribution facility in Toronto, Ontario, and a leased 150,000 square-foot facility in Sumner, Washington. All four were modern and cost-efficient. In 2011, the company began operations at a leased 54,000 square-foot distribution center in Melbourne, Australia, to supply its stores in Australia and New Zealand. Third-party logistics providers in China and the Netherlands were used to warehouse and distribute finished products from their warehouse locations to supply the company's retail stores in China and Europe. Merchandise was typically shipped to retail stores through third-party delivery services multiple times per week, thus providing stores with a steady flow of new inventory.

lululemon's Community-Based Marketing Approach and Brand-Building Strategy

One of lululemon's differentiating characteristics was its community-based approach to building brand awareness and customer loyalty. Local fitness practitioners chosen to be ambassadors introduced their fitness class attendees to the lululemon brand, thereby leading to interest in the brand, store visits, and word-of-mouth marketing. Each yoga-instructor ambassador was also called upon to conduct a complimentary yoga class every four to six weeks at the local lululemon store they were affiliated with. In return for helping drive business to lululemon stores and conducting classes, ambassadors were periodically given bags of free products, and large portraits of each ambassador wearing lululemon products and engaging in physical activity at a local landmark were prominently displayed on the walls their local lululemon store as a means of helping ambassadors expand their clientele.

Every lululemon store had a dedicated community coordinator who developed a customized plan for organizing, sponsoring, and participating in local athletic, fitness, and philanthropic events. In addition, each store had a community events bulletin board for posting announcements of upcoming activities, providing fitness education information and brochures, and promoting the local yoga studios and fitness centers of ambassadors. There was also a chalkboard in each store's fitting room area where customers could scribble comments about lululemon products or their yoga class experiences or their appreciation of the assistance/service provided by certain store personnel; these comments were relayed to lululemon headquarters every two weeks. Customers could use a lululemon micro website to track their progress regarding fitness or progress toward life goals.

lululemon made little use of traditional advertising print or television advertisements, preferring instead to rely on its various grassroots, community-based marketing efforts and the use of social media (like Facebook and Twitter) to increase brand awareness, reinforce its premium brand image, and broaden the appeal of its products.

Store Personnel

As part of the company's commitment to providing customers with an inviting and educational store environment, lululemon's store sales associates, who the company referred to as "educators," were coached to personally engage and connect with each guest who entered the store. Educators, many of whom had prior experience as a fitness practitioner or were avid runners or yoga enthusiasts, received approximately 30 hours of in-house training within the first three months of their employment. Training was focused on (1) teaching educators about leading a healthy and balanced life, exercising self-responsibility, and setting lifestyle goals, (2) preparing them to explain the technical and innovative design aspects of all lululemon products, and (3) providing the information needed for educators to serve as knowledgeable references for customers seeking information on fitness classes, instructors, and events in the community. New hires that lacked knowledge about the intricacies of yoga were given subsidies to attend yoga classes so they could understand the activity and better explain the benefits of lululemon's yoga apparel.

People who shopped at lululemon stores were called "guests," and store personnel were expected to "educate" guests about lululemon apparel, not sell to them. To provide a personalized, welcoming, and relaxed experience, store educators referred to their guests on a first name basis in the fitting and changing area, allowed them to use store restrooms, and offered them complimentary fresh-filtered water. Management believed that such a soft-sell, customer-centric environment encouraged product trial, purchases, and repeat visits.

Core Values and Culture

Consistent with the company's mission of "providing people with the components to live a longer, healthier and more fun life," lululemon executives sought to promote and ingrain a set of core values centered on developing the highest-quality products, operating with integrity, leading a healthy balanced life, and instilling in its employees a sense of self responsibility and the value of goal setting. The company sought to provide employees with a supportive and goal-oriented work environment; all employees were encouraged to set goals aimed at reaching their full professional, health, and personal potential. The company offered personal development workshops and goal-coaching to assist employees in achieving their goals. Many lululemon employees had a written set of professional, health, and personal goals. All employees had access to a "learning library" of personal development books that included Steven Covey's *The Seven Habits of Highly Effective People,* Rhonda Byrne's *The Secret,* and Brian Tracy's *The Psychology of Achievement.*

Chip Wilson had been the principal architect of the company's culture and core values, and the company's work climate through 2013 reflected his business and lifestyle philosophy. Wilson had digested much of his philosophy about life in general and personal development into a set of statements and prescriptions that he called "the lululemon manifesto." The manifesto was considered to be a core element of lululemon's culture. Senior executives believed the company's work climate and core values helped it attract passionate and motivated employees who were driven to succeed and who would support the company's vision of "elevating the world from mediocrity to greatness"—a phrase coined by Chip Wilson in the company's early years. For a number of years, the company's shopping bags were emblazoned with a full print of the manifesto, as a means of sharing its culture and beliefs about life in general with customers, the local community, and the public at large.

In 2018, to celebrate the company's 20th year in business, lululemon's Brand Creative Director Rémi Paringaux headed an effort to create a freshly designed manifesto showcasing lululemon's long-standing brand values across nine themes: Integrity, Personal Responsibility, Social Impact, Honesty/Authenticity, Overcoming Fear, Greatness, Purpose, Elevating the World (even on hard days), and Fun + Laughter, Sweat + The Practice of Yoga. Each phrase included in the Manifesto, both the original devised by Chip Wilson and the revised version, was intentionally designed to inspire, provoke thought, and spark conversation. Excerpts from the Manifesto are shown in Exhibit 5.

EXHIBIT 5   Excepts from The lululemon Manifesto, as Revised in 2018

- Breathe deeply
- Hope is not a strategy
- Put away your phone. The real world is not on hold.
- Creativity is maximized when you are living in the moment
- Your biggest opportunity for growth is when it all hits the fan
- Gratitude is contagious
- That which matters most should never give way to that which matters least
- Reconnect with nature. The better you know it the less you take it for granted
- The most important answers will never be found in a search bar
- Open your ears, eyes and heart &Open your mind
- Jealousy works the opposite way you want it to
- Replace the word Try with Will and watch the magic happen
- The pursuit of happiness is the source of unhappiness
- Before speaking, ask yourself: Is it kind? Is it necessary? Is it true?
- You attract love when you love yourself
- Treat goals like coconuts. Hit them hard, crack them open, celebrate
- Do one thing a day that scares you
- Life is full of setbacks; success is determined by how you handle setbacks
- This is not your practice life. This is all there is
- Stress is related to 99% of all illness
- Friends are more important than money
- Vulnerability makes a good leader great

Source: The lululemon expert, "The lululemon Manifesto: The Controversies (!) and also my favorite Manifesto-printed items," www.lululemonexpert.com, September 6, 2019, accessed May 26, 2020.

COMPETITION IN ATHLETIC APPAREL

Competition in the market for athletic and fitness apparel was fierce. Companies competed principally on product quality, performance features, innovation, fit and style, distribution capabilities, brand image and recognition, and price. Rivalry among competing brands was global, vigorous, and involved both established companies who were expanding their production and marketing of performance products and recent entrants attracted by the growth opportunities.

lululemon competed with wholesalers and direct sellers of premium performance athletic apparel made of high-tech fabrics, most especially Nike, The adidas Group AG (which marketed athletic and sports apparel under its adidas and Reebok brands), and Under Armour. Nike had a powerful and well-known global brand name, an extensive and diverse line of athletic and sports apparel, and 2019 global sales of $39.1 billion ($15.9 billion in North America). Nike's sales outside of North America accounted for just over 57 percent of its worldwide revenues in fiscal 2019. Not only was Nike the world's largest seller of athletic footwear (its footwear sales exceeded $26 billion in fiscal 2019), but it was also the world's largest sports apparel brand, with 2019 sales of $11.6 billion. Sales of Nike products to women totaled $7.4 billion in 2019. The company had selling arrangements with independent distributors and licensees in over 190 countries; its retail account base for sports apparel in the United States included a mix of sporting goods stores, athletic specialty stores, department stores, and tennis and golf shops, plus it had a network of factory outlet stores (217 in the United States and 648 across the rest of the world) and Nike and NIKETOWN retail stores (29 in the United States and 57 in the rest of the world). Nike also had a strong online sales presence with websites in 46 countries; in fiscal year 2019, its Nike Direct revenues were $5.0 billion in North America and $7.1 billion worldwide.

The adidas Group, with its adidas and Reebok brands, was a global company headquartered in Germany that had worldwide sales of €23.6 billion ($26.0 billion) in 2019. Worldwide sports apparel revenues for the company were €9.0 billion ($9.9 billion) in 2019; its product lines consisted of high-tech performance garments for a wide variety of sports and fitness activities, as well as recreational sportswear. The adidas Group sold products in virtually every country of the world. In 2019, its extensive product offerings were marketed through third-party retailers (sporting goods chains, department stores, independent sporting goods retailer buying groups, lifestyle retailing chains, and Internet retailers), 2,500 company-owned adidas and Reebok retail stores, 15,000 franchised stores, and through the company's e-commerce websites at www.adidas.com and www.reebok.com.

Under Armour, an up-and-coming designer and marketer of performance sports apparel, had total sales of $5.3 billion in 2019, of which $3.58 billion was in apparel. Like lululemon, Under Armour's apparel products were made entirely of technically-advanced, high performance fabrics and were designed to be aesthetically appealing, as well as highly functional and comfortable. Under Armour regularly upgraded its products as next-generation fabrics with better performance characteristics became available. Under Armour's product line included apparel for men, women, and children. Under Armour's sales in North America unexpectedly plateaued at $4.0 in 2016, then dropped to $3.8 billion in 2017, $3.74 billion in 2018, and $3.66 billion in 2019. The company reported net losses $48.3 million in 2017 and $46.3 million in 2018. While roughly 70 percent of Under Armour's sales revenues in 2019 were in North America, the company's revenues were growing in the other regions of the world where its products were sold, particularly in the EMEA (Europe-Middle East-Africa) region and the Asia-Pacific region. The majority of Under Armour's sales were made through wholesale channels, including sporting goods stores, independent and specialty retailers, department stores, institutional athletic departments, and sports leagues and teams. However, the company also operated 169 factory outlet stores and 19 Brand House stores in North America and 104 factory outlet stores and 96 Brand House stores in international locations as of January 2020. Under Armour had direct-to-consumer sales of about $1.8 billion annually at its e-commerce website, www.underarmour.com.

Nike, The adidas Group, and Under Armour all aggressively marketed and promoted their high-performance apparel products to women and men and spent heavily to grow consumer awareness of their brands and build brand loyalty. All three sponsored numerous athletic events, provided uniforms and equipment with their logos to collegiate and professional sports teams, and paid millions of dollars annually to numerous high-profile male and female athletes to endorse their products. Like lululemon, they designed their own products but outsourced the production of their garments to contract manufacturers.

New Entrants into the Sports and Fitness Apparel Market for Women. Retailers responded to the growing market for women's sports and fitness apparel by introducing brands and product lines to compete in this segment. Entrants into this segment of the apparel market included The Gap, Nordstrom, and Victoria's Secret.

The Gap had total sales of $16.4 billion in 2019 and was the owner/operator of three well-known retail chains: The Gap, Banana Republic, and Old Navy. Product offerings at the 1,033 worldwide Gap-branded stores included a GapFit collection of fitness and lifestyle products for women. In 2008, The Gap spent $150 million to acquire Athleta, whose product line consisted of yoga, running, skiing, snowboarding, and surfing apparel that was sold online and through catalogs, and proceeded to turn it into a retail chain to compete head-on against lululemon in the market for comfortable, fashionable, high-performance women's apparel for workouts, sports, physically-active recreational activities, and leisure wear. Going into 2020, Athleta had grown to 190 retail stores in North America Athleta stores open at least 12 months had sales growth of 16 percent, 9 percent, and 5 percent in 2017, 2018, and 2019, respectively. The Gap planned to continue opening Athleta stores in 2020 and beyond. In addition to its retail stores, Athleta collected substantial revenues from sales at its e-commerce website www.athleta.gap.com. Athleta also had a social media website, www.athleta.net/chi, that connected women with interests in sports and fitness, nutrition and health, tutorials and training plans, and travel and adventure.

Athleta's expanding product line included swimwear, tops, bras, jackets, sweaters, pants, tights, shorts, tee shirt dresses, performance footwear, sneakers, sandals, bags, headwear, and gear. Items were colorful, stylish, and functional. As of May 2020, Athleta offered 391 different items under "activity" line of products at its e-commerce website. Athleta apparel items were typically available in sizes XXS, XS, S, M, L, XL, and plus sizes 1X and 2X. Athleta utilized well-known women athletes and local fitness instructors to serve as brand ambassadors by posting blogs on Athleta's website, teaching classes at local stores, and testing Athleta garments. In 2016, Athleta introduced Athleta Girl, which introduced fashion and accessories for younger women. In 2019, Athleta announced a partnership with decorated track and field athlete Allyson Felix.

A number of other national and regional retailers of women's apparel, seeking to capitalize on growing sales of activewear made of high-tech fabrics, were marketing one or more brands of fitness apparel suitable for yoga, running, gym exercise, and leisure activities. A few were selling these items under their own labels. For example, Nordstrom, a nationally-respected department store retailer, was merchandising its own Zella line of attire for yoga, cross-training, workouts, swimming, and "beyond the workout;" many of the initial products in the Zella collection were designed by a former member of lululemon's design team. Zella-branded products were offered in regular sizes (XXS, XS, S, M, L, XL, and XXL) and plus sizes (1X, 2X, and 3X). Nordstrom was also marketing several other brands of activewear for women, men, and juniors, including Nike, Under Armour, Patagonia, Reebok, and Adidas. In 2019, Nordstrom's activewear offerings could be purchased at 136 Nordstrom full-line department stores (typically 140,000 to 250,000 square-feet in size) and 242 Nordstrom Rack stores (typically 30,000 to 50,000 square-feet in size) in 36 states, at Nordstrom's website (www.nordstrom.com), and at the Nordstrom Rack website, www.nordstromrack.com.

Victoria's Secret also marketed its own line of women's fitness apparel under the Sport label. As of May 2020, Victoria's Secret offered 118 separate Sport brand items on the company's e-commerce website, www.victoriassecret.com. Offerings included sports bras, bottoms, yoga pants, sweatshirts, and hoodies.

Typically, the items in the Athleta, GapFit, Zella, and Sport collections were priced 10 percent to 25 percent below similar kinds of lululemon products. Likewise, Nike, Under Armour, adidas, and Reebok apparel items were usually less expensive than comparable lululemon-branded items.

GLOBAL PANDEMIC FORCES TEMPORARY CLOSURE OF MANY RETAIL STORES ACROSS THE WORLD

An outbreak of the COVID-19 disease, also known as the coronavirus, began in China in December 2019, spread to other countries in the first several months of 2020, and was declared a global pandemic by the World Health Organization in March 2020. Mounting concerns about the potential for the coronavirus to infect a large percentage of the population and overwhelm local hospitals and health professionals, prompted government officials in many countries during February-April 2020 to issue "stay-at-home" orders to the general public, urge companies to allow

employees to work from home where feasible, and mandate the closure of retail stores and all "non-essential" local businesses until the daily/weekly number of people in their locales being newly diagnosed with COVID-19 began to flatten out or subside. People were urged to practice "social distancing" and wear face masks when grocery-shopping, picking up to "to-go orders" from local food establishments, or otherwise venturing out beyond the confines of their homes to run errands. However, by the end of May 2020, widespread concerns about the long-term economic damage the business shutdowns were causing and signs that the spread of the virus was being contained in a growing number of locations prompted government officials to begin reopening their local economies. A growing percentage of retail stores had re-opened or partially re-opened in much of Asia, and limited re-openings were occurring in Europe and North America.

The global pandemic had a devastating impact on most apparel retailers. In North America, luxury retailer Neiman Marcus, apparel retailer J Crew, and department store retailer J.C. Penney filed for bankruptcy in May 2020. Nordstrom announced on May 5, 2020, that it would soon permanently close 16 department store locations. The Gap, Inc. was also struggling in the new environment; the price of the company's stock had plummeted since January 2020, and most of its stores in the United States remained closed as of late May 2020. Back in February 2019, The Gap announced it would close some 230 of its stores over the next two years. L Brands announced it would not be making rent payments while its Victoria's Secret and Bath and Body Works stores were closed. Many other retail and restaurant chains, also running short on cash, told landlords that they would be unable to make their rent payments until their stores and their cash flows improved. Headed into June 2020, most all chain retailers and millions of local businesses in North America, Europe, and elsewhere were wrestling with the uncertainty created by the global pandemic, store closures, how long it would take for customer traffic to return to former levels, and the extent to which consumer buying and shopping patterns would be affected both in the short term and the long term.

Retailers with robust e-commerce sales were better able to weather the global pandemic crisis. Nike, the global sports apparel leader, had a strong digital presence and was expected to experience only a modest and fairly short-lived downturn in apparel revenues. forecast to weather the storm. Further, with the re-opening of the company's Nike stores in China in May 2020, the company saw signs of sales improvement in Asia, pointing the way to a possible strong recovery in Europe and North America.[15] The adidas Group, number two globally and financially strong, was also expected to come through the pandemic in a competitively strong position. Under Armour's situation, already weakened by sales troubles in North America, was made worse by the pandemic. Many investors and industry analysts believed the near-term hit to the company's sales could be as much as 30 percent in 2020. As of May 2020, the company had announced layoffs, pay cuts for remaining employees, and the postponement of plans for an Under Armour flagship store in New York City.[16]

LOOKING AHEAD AT LULULEMON

In a March 26, 2020, conference call to discuss the company's Q4 and full-year 2019 performance with Wall Street analysts, lululemon CEO Craig McDonald commented on the impacts of the coronavirus pandemic:[17]

> . . . .we are seeing virus-related impact on performance across our markets. In North America and Europe, our stores have been closed since March 16. Stores in New Zealand are closed at this time, while Australia is operating on reduced hours. In China, all of our stores except our location in Wuhan are open with most operating on regular schedules. Our stores also remained open in other Asian markets, except for Malaysia, where our two locations are currently closed. In addition, we are closely monitoring our supply chain and staying in constant contact with our vendors as they too navigate this situation.
>
> . . . .the underlying health of our business is strong. . . . we are confident in our abilities to navigate the near-term while working to realize the opportunities over the longer term. . . we have early learnings from China which show us that our business will bounce back. We are not yet back to pre-closing volumes, but the business is getting stronger week by week.
>
> Although we do not know exactly when the current situation will pass, what we do know is that our stores will reopen. We know that initially the business will be lower than it was pre-COVID-19, but we believe that each day and each week, it will keep building. We are planning for multiple scenarios, but in any one of these we know that our brand is strong and has unique pillars of strength that will keep driving our momentum forward.

As of May 21, 2020, lululemon had reopened more than 150 stores across five continents. Plans called for reopening another 200 stores over the following two weeks. Modified store hours, store employee face coverings, physical distancing, enhanced store cleaning and sanitization, and a more relaxed return policy were being instituted at all reopened stores.

ENDNOTES

[1] Beth Kowitt and Colleen Leahey, "LULULEMON: In an Uncomfortable Position," *Fortune,* September 16, 2013, p. 118.

[2] Biography of Calvin McDonald, posted at www.investor.lululemon.com (accessed May 18, 2020).

[3] *2016 Yoga in America Study,* conducted by *Yoga Journal* and Yoga Alliance, January 2016, posted at www.yogaalliance.org in 2016 (accessed May 22, 2020 and April 29, 2016); and "Yoga in America" *Yoga Journal,* press release dated December 5, 2012, posted at www.yogajournal.com (accessed April 7, 2014).

[4] "Yoga Statistics," compiled by The Good Body and last updated in November 2018, posted at www.thegoodbody.com (accessed May 22, 2020).

[5] *2016 Yoga in America Study,* conducted by Yoga Journal and Yoga Alliance, January 2016, posted at www.yogaalliance.org (accessed April 29, 2016).

[6] Allied Market Research, "Sports Apparel Market—Report," published October 2019, www.alliedmarketresearch.com.

[7] Allied Market Research, "Sports Apparel Market—Report," published October 2019, www.alliedmarketresearch.com.

[8] Renee Frojo, "Yoga clothing retailers go to the mat for market share," *San Francisco Business Times,* December 28, 2012, posted at www.bizjournals.com/sanfrancisco (accessed April 10, 2014).

[9] As posted on www.lululemon.com (accessed May 2, 2016).

[10] Company 10-K Report for the fiscal year ending January 31, 2016, p. 1.

[11] Kim Basin, "Lululemon Admits Plus-Size Clothing Is Not Part of Its 'Formula'" posted at www.huffingtonpost.com, August 2, 2013 (accessed April 7, 2014).

[12] Company 10-K Report for fiscal year 2019.

[13] Dana Mattolli, "Lululemon's Secret Sauce," *The Wall Street Journal,* March 22, 2012, pp. B1–B2.

[14] Ibid.

[15] ValueLine, "Nike, Inc." April 24, 2020, accessed at www.valueline.com, May 19, 2020.

[16] ValueLine, "UnderArmour, Inc." April 24, 2020, accessed at www.valueline.com, May 19, 2020.

[17] Lululemon Athletica Inc. Earnings Call, March 26, 2020, posted at www.seekingalpha.com (accessed May 19, 2020).

Under Armour's Strategy in 2020: Can It Revive Sales and Profitability in Its Core North American Market?

Mc Graw Hill connect

Arthur A. Thompson,

The University of Alabama

Going into 2020, Under Armour was headed into its fifth consecutive year of sales difficulties in its core North American market which accounted for over two-thirds of the company's annual sales revenues. The troubles began in 2016 and undermined Under Armour's reputation as an up-and-coming growth company in the sports apparel business. Starting in the second-quarter of 2010 and continuing through the third-quarter of 2016, Under Armour achieved revenue growth of 20+ percent for 26 consecutive quarters. In announcing the company's 2016 third-quarter financial results, Chairman and chief executive officer (CEO) Kevin Plank said:[1]

> Over the past 20 years, we have established ourselves as a premium global brand with a track record of strong financial results. Looking back over the past nine months, it has never been more evident that we are at a pivotal moment in time, where the investments we are making today will fuel our growth and drive our industry leadership position for years to come. As a growth company with an expanding global footprint and businesses like footwear and women's each approaching a billion dollars this year, we have never been more focused on the long-term success of our Brand.

But despite Plank's optimism about Under Armour's future prospects, he went on to announce a reduced sales and earnings outlook for the fourth quarter of 2016 and weakening demand for Under Armour products in North America. So far in 2016, UA's quarterly revenue growth in North America over the same quarter of 2015 slowed from 25.7 percent in Q1 of 2016 to 21.5 percent in Q2 to 15.6 percent in Q3.

But in January 2017, Under Armour's report of its 2016 fourth quarter and full-year results rang louder alarm bells, despite record annual revenues of $4.8 billion for full-year 2016, up 22 percent over 2015, and record net profits of $259 million, up 10.5 percent over 2015. There were some obvious cracks in Under Armour's record-setting 2016 performance:

- Fourth-quarter revenues rose only 11.7 percent over fourth-quarter 2105 revenues, by far the lowest percentage fourth-quarter increase since 2010, which had ranged from a high of 35.5 percent in 2010 to a low of 25.5 percent in 2012.

- Fourth-quarter 2016 income from operations dropped 6.1 percent from the same quarter a year earlier and fourth-quarter 2016 net income dropped 0.67 percent.

- Fourth-quarter 2016 revenues in North America were up only 5.9 percent and operating income in North America dropped 15.0 percent.

- Full-year operating income in North America dropped from $461 million in 2015 to just $411.3 million in 2016.

To make matters worse, Plank said the company's outlook for full-year 2017 was gloomy—expected revenue growth of 11 to 12 percent (the lowest annual growth rate since the company became a "C" corporation in 2002) and a $97.5 million decline in operating income to approximately $320 million, attributed mainly to "strategic investments in the company's fastest growing businesses."[2] Nonetheless, Kevin Plank reiterated his confidence that the company's resources and capabilities would enable it to cope with the challenges ahead:[3]

> We are incredibly proud that in 2016, we once again posted record revenue and earnings; however, numerous challenges and disruptions in North American retail tempered our fourth quarter results. The strength of our Brand, an unparalleled connection with our consumers, and the continuation of investments in our fastest growing businesses—footwear, international and direct-to-consumer—give us great confidence in our ability to navigate the current retail environment, execute against our long-term growth strategy, and create value to our shareholders.

Under Armour's financial performance in 2017 turned out to be worse than expected. A year after growing North American sales from almost $1.0 billion in 2012 to $4.0 billion in 2016 (a compound growth rate of 41.4 percent), Under Armour's 2017 sales in North America dropped $200 million. Total revenues worldwide were up a meager 3.1 percent; operating income dropped by $290 million to just $27.8 million; and the company reported a net loss of $48.3 million. The big drops in operating income and the net loss were partly attributable to management's announcement in August 2017 that it would pursue a $140 to $150 million restructuring plan to address operating inefficiencies, transition to a product category management structure, and reengineer the company's go-to-market process (product innovation and design, vendor relationships, delivery times of seasonal products, inventory management, profit margin control, and speed of response to shifting consumer preferences and market conditions). In addition, the plan called for a global workforce reduction of about 300 people, inventory reductions and write-downs, and charges for asset impairments, facility and lease terminations, and contract terminations.

But part of Under Armour's problems in North America in 2017 stemmed from an unexpected competitive offensive by Germany-based The adidas Group. In 2015, Under Armour overtook adidas (pronounced ah-di-dahs) to become the second largest seller of sports apparel, active wear, and athletic footwear in North America.[4,5] But top executives at adidas launched an unusually strong series of strategic initiatives in 2017 to increase the company's share of the sports apparel, active wear, and athletic footwear market in North America from an estimated 10 percent to around 15 to 20 percent. The results

were impressive. Sales of adidas-branded products in North America grew by a resounding 25 percent in 2017, allowing adidas to reclaim second place in the overall North American sportswear market and dropping Under Armour back into third place.

Despite the sizable restructuring efforts undertaken at Under Armour in the last four months of 2017 and continuing into early 2018, Under Armour executives did not foresee a quick turnaround in North America. Their 2018 outlook for North American revenues was a mid-single-digit decline, although international sales were expected to grow 25 percent. Operating income was projected to be $20 million to $30 million partly because, after additional review, management decided to pursue a second restructuring plan in 2018 to further optimize operations. This plan entailed cash related charges of up to $150 million for facility and lease terminations, contract terminations, and other restructuring charges, up to $25 million in non-cash charges related to inventory write-downs and asset-related impairments that were expected to produce a minimum of $75 million in savings annually in 2019 and beyond.

But, again, Under Armour failed to achieve the modest revenue gains and return to profitability that management expected. While revenues for 2018 rose just over four percent to $5.2 billion, operating income plummeted by over $50 million, resulting in an operating loss of $25 million and a net loss of $46.3 million. A sizable portion of the decline in profitability stemmed from price discounting aimed at boosting sales volumes in North America; the price discounting failed to attract sufficient customer purchases to prevent a further two percent erosion of North American revenues. Nonetheless, Under Armour Chairman and CEO Kevin Plank put a good face on the year, saying:[6]

> Our 2018 results demonstrate significant progress against our multi-year transformation toward becoming an even stronger brand and more operationally excellent company," said Under Armour Chairman and CEO Kevin Plank. "As we look ahead to 2019, our accelerated innovation agenda, disciplined go-to-market process and powerful consumer-centric approach gives us increasingly greater confidence in our ability to deliver for Under Armour athletes, customers and shareholders."

UA management's outlook for 2019 was flat sales in North America, a low double-digit increase in international revenues, a four percent increase in total revenues, operating income in the range of $220 million to $230 million, and earnings per share of about $0.33. While closer to the mark, Under Armour's 2019 performance remained weak, Revenue was up one percent to $5.27 billion, revenues in North America declined a further $78 million to $3.66 billion, operating income was $237 million, and net income of $92 million translated in earning per share of $0.20, after special charges equal to an EPS impact of $0.14. In announcing the results, newly appointed President and CEO Patrik Frisk said:[7]

> Under Armour is an operationally better company following our transformation over the past few years, with a clearly defined and focused strategy, enhanced go-to-market process, cleaner inventories, and a stronger balance sheet. However, ongoing demand challenges and the need to drive greater efficiencies in our business requires us to further prioritize our investments to put our company in the best position possible to achieve sustainable, profitable growth over the long-term.

The company's initial 2020 outlook included an estimated negative impact of the coronavirus outbreak in China of approximately $50 million to $60 million in sales related to the first quarter of 2020. A low single-digit percentage decline in total revenues was expected, which included a high single-decline in North America revenues and a low double-digit increase in international revenues. Operating income was expected to be in the range of $105 million to $125 million, with diluted EPS of $0.10 to $0.13.

Management also announced it was currently evaluating a potential 2020 restructuring initiative to rebalance its cost base to further improve profitability and cash flow generation. In connection with this potential restructuring, the company was considering $325 million to $425 million in estimated pre-tax charges for 2020, including approximately $225 million to $250 million related to foregoing opening a flagship store in New York City while pursuing options to sublease the space under the long-term lease already in place.

Exhibit 1 shows selected financial statement data for Under Armour for 2016 through 2019.

Exhibit 2 shows Under Armour's revenues and operating income for each of its four geographic regions and its connected fitness business for 2016 through 2019.

Company Background

Founded in 1996 by former University of Maryland football player Kevin Plank, Under Armour was the originator of sports apparel made with performance-enhancing fabrics—gear engineered to wick moisture from the body, regulate body temperature, and enhance comfort regardless of weather conditions and activity levels. Plank's initial plan was to make a T-shirt that provided compression and wicked perspiration off the wearer's skin, thereby avoiding the discomfort of sweat-absorbed apparel—and sell the T-shirt to athletes and sports teams.

He worked the phone and, with a trunk full of shirts in the back of his car, visited schools and training camps in person to show his products. Plank's sales successes were soon good enough that he convinced Kip Fulks, who played lacrosse at Maryland, to become a partner in his enterprise. Operations were conducted on a shoestring budget out of the basement of Plank's grandmother's house in Georgetown, a Washington, D.C. suburb. In 1998, the company's sales revenues and growth prospects were sufficient to secure a $250,000 small-business loan, enabling the company to move operations to a facility in Baltimore. Ryan Wood, one of Plank's acquaintances from high school, joined the company in 1999 and became a partner.

KP Sports' sales grew briskly as it expanded its product line to include high-tech undergarments tailored for athletes in different sports and for cold as well as hot temperatures, plus jerseys, team uniforms, socks, and other accessories. Increasingly, the company was able to secure deals not just to provide gear for one team at a particular school but for most or all of a school's sports teams. However, the company's partners came to recognize the merits of tapping the retail market for high-performance apparel and began making sales calls on sports apparel retailers. In 2000, Scott Plank, Kevin's older brother, joined the company as Vice President of Finance and certain other operational and strategic responsibilities. When Galyan's, a large retail chain that has since been acquired by Dick's Sporting Goods, signed on to carry KP Sports' expanding line of performance apparel for men, women, and youth in 2000, sales to other sports apparel retailers began to explode. By the end of 2000, the company's products were available in some 500 retail locations.

Prompted by growing operational complexity, increased financial requirements, and plans for further geographic expansion, KP Sports revoked its "S" corporation status and became a "C" corporation on January 1, 2002. The company opened a Canadian

EXHIBIT 1   Selected Financial Data for Under Armour, Inc., 2016–2019 (in millions)

	2019	2018	2017	2016
Selected Income Statement Data				
Net revenues	$5,267.1	$5,193.2	$4,989.2	$4,833.3
Cost of goods sold	2,796.6	2,852.7	2,737.8	2,584.7
Gross profit	2,470.5	2,340.5	2,251.4	2,248.6
Selling, general and administrative expenses	2,233.8	2,182.3	2,099.5	1831.1
Restructuring and impairment charges	—	183.1	124.0	—
Income from operations	236.8	(25.0)	27.8	417.5
Interest expense, net	(21.2)	(33.6)	(34.5)	(26.4)
Other expense, net	(5.7)	(9.2)	(3.6)	(2.8)
Income (loss) before income taxes	209.8	67.8	(10.3)	388.3
Income tax expense (benefit)	70.0		38.0	131.3
Income (loss) from equity method investment	(47.7)			
Net income (loss)	92,1	(46.3)	$ (48.3)	$ 257.0
Selected Balance Sheet Data				
Cash and cash equivalents	$ 788.1	$ 557.4	$ 312.5	$ 250.5
Working capital*	1,280.2	1,277.7	1,277.3	1,279.3
Inventories at year-end	892.3	1,019.5	1,158.5	917.5
Total assets	4,843.5	4,245.0	4,006.4	3,644.3
Long-term debt, including current maturities	592.7	728.8	917.0	817.4
Total stockholders' equity	2,150.1	2,016.9	2,018.6	2,030.9
Selected Cash Flow Data				
Net cash provided by operating activities	$ 509.0	$ 628.2	$ 234.1	$ 364.4

*Working capital is defined as current assets minus current liabilities.

Note: Some totals may not add up due to rounding and to the omission of some line items in the company's income statement and consolidated balance sheet.

Source: Company 10-K report for 2019, pp. 28–29 and pp. 55–59.

EXHIBIT 2   Under Armour's Revenues and Operating Income for Its Four Geographic Regions and Its Connected Fitness Business, 2016–2019

A. Net revenues by geographic region (in millions of $)

	2019	2018	2017	2016
North America	$3,658.4	$3,735.3	$3,802.4	$4,005.3
EMEA*	621.1	591.1	470.0	330.6
Asia-Pacific	636.3	557.4	433.6	268.6
Latin America	196.1	190.8	181.3	141.8
Connected fitness	136.4	120.4	89.2	80.4
Total net revenues	$5,267.1	$5,193.2	$4,976.6	$4,833.3

*Europe–Middle East–Africa.

B. Operating income (loss) by geographic region (in millions of $)

	2019	2018	2017	2016
North America	$733.4	$718.2	$700.2	$408.4
EMEA*	53.7	30.4	26.0	11.4
Asia-Pacific	97.6	103.5	89.3	68.3
Latin America	(3.2)	(16.9)	(14.4)	(33.9)
Connected fitness	17.1	5.9	(6.5)	(36.8)
Total operating income	$236.8	$ (25.0)	$ 27.8	$417.5

*Europe–Middle East–Africa.

Note: Totals do not add because numbers for the "Corporate Other" non-operating segment were omitted; these relate to currency hedge gains and losses, restructuring charges, and various "intersegment eliminations" not directly pertinent to UA's net revenues and operating income by geographic region.

Source: Company 10-K reports, 2019 and 2018.

sales office in 2003 and began selling its products in the United Kingdom in 2005. At year-end 2005, about 90 percent of the company's revenues came from sales to some 6,000 retail stores in the United States and 2,000 stores in Canada, Japan, and the United Kingdom. In addition, sales were being made to high profile professional athletes and teams, most notably in the National Football League, Major League Baseball, the National Hockey League, and some 400 men's and women's sports teams at NCAA Division 1-A colleges and universities.

In late 2005, KP Sports changed its name to Under Armour and became a public company with an initial public offering of common stock that generated net proceeds of nearly $115 million. Under Armour immediately began pursuing a long-term strategy to grow its product line, establish a market presence in a growing number of countries across the world, and build public awareness of the Under Armour brand and its interlocking "U" and "A" logo.

Stock Price, Ownership, and Management Changes at Under Armour 2016–2020

Since early 2016 and continuing into early 2020, Under Armour's stock price remained below the $105 per share achieved in July 2015, with most of the decline coming in 2016—at year-end 2016, the price was $27, and at the end of February 2020, it was $13 per share due to the company's weak outlook for the remainder of 2020. Aside from the company's poor financial performance, the stock price declines were also a reflection of investor concerns about whether the Under Armour brand was in deep trouble in North America—the experiences of other troubled brands had demonstrated it was extremely difficult to rebuild a brand once it had fallen out of favor with the public. Investors had also been unnerved in November 2017 when analysts at 24/7 Wall St. had ranked Kevin Plank fourth on its list of "20 Worst CEOs in America 2017."[8] Plank had been under the microscope since a controversial split of the company's stock in April 2016 into Class A (vote-entitled), Class B, and Class C (no voting power) shares, that resulted in Kevin Plank having 65 percent of the total shareholder voting power on every shareholder vote taken.

Since the stock split, Plank had sold some of his Class C shares to fund the creation of Plank Industries, a privately-held investment company with ownership interests in commercial real estate, hospitality, food and beverage, venture capital, and thoroughbred horse racing. Plank's critics had claimed the new venture was absorbing too much of his time. In addition, Plank's time in dealing with UA's operating issues and sales slowdown was constrained by his involvement in helping spearhead a 25-year, $5.5 billion project (being partially financed with bonds issued by the City of Baltimore's Baltimore Development Corp.) to develop waterfront property in South Baltimore into a mini-city called Port Covington that would create thousands of jobs and drive demand for office buildings, houses, shops and restaurants. Plank Industries' Sycamore Development Co. was the lead private developer of the Port Covington project. Sycamore had completed a number of properties in the project, including a $24 million renovation of a former Sam's Club into a 170,000 square-foot facility for Under Armour, tentatively named Building 37 (Plank's number on his University of Maryland football jersey was 37). Building 37 was on acreage Under Armour had purchased for $70.3 million in 2014 and was being leased by Sycamore to Under Armour for $1.1 million annually. Building 37 was the first phase of Under Armour's plan to create a 50-acre global headquarters campus that would include a new headquarters building on the site of Building 37, additional Under Armour facilities and manufacturing space, a man-made lake, and a small stadium—a layout designed to house as many as 10,000 Under Armour employees (UA employed approximately 2,100 people in Baltimore in early 2018, some 600 of which were housed in Building 37).

To compensate for the time he was spending on outside interests, Plank engineered the appointment of Patrik Frisk, formerly CEO of the ALDO Group, a global footwear and accessories company, as President and Chief Operating Officer (COO) of Under Armour in June 2017. Frisk had 30 years of experience in the apparel, footwear, and retail industry, holding top management positions with responsibility for such brands as The North Face®, Timberland®, JanSport®, lucy®, and SmartWool®. As president and COO, Frisk was assigned responsibility for Under Armour's go-to-market strategy and the successful execution of its long-term growth plan. Kevin Plank's titles were Chairman of the Board and CEO. Then in October 2019, Under Armour announced that Frisk would become CEO, President, and a member of Under Armour's Board of Directors, effective January 1, 2020, and that Kevin Plank would become Executive Chairman of the Board and Brand Chief. Frisk would report directly to Kevin Plank.

In 2008, Plank voluntarily reduced his salary from $500,000 to $26,000,000, which was his approximate salary when he founded Under Armour. As UA's largest stockholder, Plank believed he should be compensated for his services based primarily on the company's annual incentive plan tied to the company's performance and on annual performance-based equity awards. Plank's $26,000 salary remained in place in 2020.

UNDER ARMOUR'S STRATEGY IN 2020

Until 2018, Under Armour's mission was "to make all athletes better through passion, design, and the relentless pursuit of innovation." A reworded mission—"Under Armour Makes You Better"—was publicly announced in early 2018. Kevin Plank said the new wording was meant to better convey that "in every way we connect, through the products we create, the experience we deliver and the inspiration we provide, we simply make you better."[9] In late 2018, Kevin Plank told a gathering of investors and Wall Street analysts that Under Armour's vision was "to inspire you with performance solutions you never knew you needed and can't imagine living without."

The company's principal business activities in 2020 were the development, marketing, and distribution of branded performance apparel, footwear, and related sports accessories for men, women, and youth. The brand's moisture-wicking apparel and footwear products were engineered in many designs and styles for wear in nearly every climate to provide a performance alternative to traditional products. Under Armour sports apparel was worn by athletes at all levels, from youth to professional, and by consumers with active lifestyles. The company generated revenues from the sale of its products globally through two primary channels: (1) sales to national, regional, independent and specialty wholesalers and distributors in many countries across the world and (2) direct-to-consumer sales (sales at the company's ecommerce websites in various geographic regions and at its company-owned brick-and-mortar Brand Houses and factory outlet stores).

In the company's earlier years, revenue growth was achieved primarily by growing wholesale sales to retailers of sports apparel, athletic footwear, and sports equipment and accessories in North America. Starting in 2010, Under Armour began increasing its global footprint by expanding its wholesale and online sales to countries in Europe, the Middle East, and Africa (EMEA), the Asia-Pacific, and Latin America.

In 2013, Under Armour acquired MapMyFitness, a provider of website services and mobile apps to fitness-minded consumers across the world; Under Armour used this acquisition, along with several follow-on acquisitions in 2014 and 2015, to create what it termed a "connected fitness" business offering digital fitness subscriptions and licenses, mobile apps, and other fitness-tracking and nutritional-tracking solutions to athletes and fitness-conscious individuals across the world. During 2016–2019, the company's connected fitness business experienced strong revenue growth and strategic initiative to become a major revenue driver in the years to come.

Exhibit 3 shows Under Armour's revenues for its three main product categories plus revenues associated with its licensing arrangements and its connected fitness business for 2016 through 2019.

Growth Strategy

Under Armour's growth strategy in 2020 was centered on five strategic initiatives:

- Rejuvenating sales growth and profitability in North America, via an enhanced e-commerce platform, improved shelf space visibility in retail stores, reduced price discounting, increased support of retailer efforts to merchandise Under Armour products without having to resort to off-price sales promotions, and greater emphasis on brand advertising and promotional activities that increase customer willingness to pay full price for Under Armour products and help restore UA's image as a premium-priced brand.

- Continuing to bring authenticity to the brand through innovative products and providing customers with new solutions and appealing experiences that they quickly discover are so beneficial as to merit "must have" status.

- Exerting the efforts necessary to continue to grow Under Armour's revenues in the Latin America, EMEA, and Asia-Pacific regions.

- Continued emphasis on using the endorsements of athletes and other brand influencers to enhance global awareness of the Under Armour brand name and strengthen Under Armour's image as a premium-priced provider of high-performance apparel, footwear, and accessories.

- Growing the company's connected fitness business via securing more digital subscriptions and selling additional digital advertising on its MapMyFitness, MyFitnessPal, and Endomondo platforms.

Product Line Strategy

For a number of years, expanding the company's product offerings and marketing them at multiple price points had been a key element of Under Armour's strategy. The goal for each new item added to the line-up of offerings was to provide consumers with a product that was a *superior* alternative to the traditional products of rivals—striving to always introduce a superior product would, management believed, help foster and nourish a culture of

EXHIBIT 3 Under Armour's Revenues, by Product Category 2016–2019 (in millions of $)

	2019		2018		2017		2016	
	Dollars	Percent	Dollars	Percent	Dollars	Percent	Dollars	Percent
Apparel	$3,470.3	65.9%	$3,464.1	66.7%	$3,287.1	66.4%	$3,229.1	66.1%
Footwear	1,086.6	20.6	1,063.2	20.5	1,037.8	21.0	1,010.7	20.7
Accessories	416.4	7.9	422.5	8.1	445.8	9.0	406.6	8.3
Total net sales	4,973.2	94.4%	4,949.8	95.3%	4,768.3	96.3%	$4,646.4	95.1%
License revenues	138.8	2.6	124.8	2.4	116.6	2.4	99.8	2.0
Connected fitness	136.4	2.6	120.4	2.3	101.9	2.1	88.4	1.8
Total net revenues	$5,267.1	100.0%	$5,193.2	100.0%	$4,989.2	100.0%	$4,833.3	100.0%

Note: Percentages do not add to 100% due to not including numbers for "Corporate Other" which relate to currency hedge gains and losses and various "intersegment eliminations" not directly pertinent to UA's net revenues by product category.

Source: Company 10-K reports, 2019 and 2018.

innovation among all company personnel. According to Kevin Plank, "we focus on creating products you don't know you need yet, but once you have them, you won't remember how you lived without them."[10]

Apparel   The company designed and merchandised three lines of apparel gear intended to regulate body temperature and enhance comfort, mobility, and performance regardless of weather conditions: HEATGEAR® for hot weather conditions; COLDGEAR® for cold weather conditions; and ALLSEASONGEAR® for temperature conditions between the extremes.

HeatGear. HeatGear was designed to be worn in warm to hot temperatures under equipment or as a single layer. The company's first compression T-shirt was the original HeatGear product and was still one of the company's signature styles in 2015. In sharp contrast to a sweat soaked cotton T-shirt that could weigh two to three pounds, HeatGear was engineered with a microfiber blend featuring what Under Armour termed a "Moisture Transport System" that ensured the body would stay cool, dry, and light. HeatGear was offered in a variety of tops and bottoms in a broad array of colors and styles for wear in the gym or outside in warm weather.

ColdGear. Under Armour high performance fabrics were appealing to people participating in cold-weather sports and vigorous recreational activities like snow skiing who needed both warmth and moisture-wicking protection from becoming overheated. ColdGear was designed to wick moisture from the body while circulating body heat from hotspots to maintain core body temperature. All ColdGear apparel provided dryness and warmth in a single light layer that could be worn beneath a jersey, uniform, protective gear or ski-vest, or other cold weather outerwear. ColdGear products generally were sold at higher price points than other Under Armour gear lines.

AllSeasonGear. AllSeasonGear was designed to be worn in temperatures between the extremes of hot and cold and used technical fabrics to keep the wearer cool and dry in warmer temperatures while preventing a chill in cooler temperatures.

Each of the three apparel lines contained three fit types: compression (tight fit), fitted (athletic fit), and loose (relaxed). Some of Under Armour's apparel and footwear products contained MicroThread, a fabric technology that used elastomeric (stretchable) thread to create a cool moisture-wicking microclimate, prevented clinging and chafing, and allowed

garments to dry 30 percent faster and be 70 percent more breathable than similar Lycra construction. Under Armour had also introduced a collection of workout gear, headwear, and footwear with an exclusive CoolSwitch coating on the inside of the fabric that pulled heat away from the skin, allowing the wearer to feel cooler and perform longer.

Most recently, Under Armour had introduced Rush™ or Recover™ products designed to increase blood flow.

Products within each gear line were offered in three fit types: compression (tight fit), fitted (athletic fit), and loose (relaxed). In 2016, Under Armour introduced apparel items containing MicroThread, a fabric technology that used elastomeric (stretchable) thread to create a cool moisture-wicking microclimate, prevented clinging and chafing, allowed garments to dry 30 percent faster and be 70 percent more breathable than similar Lycra construction, and were so lightweight as to "feel like nothing." It also began using a newly developed insulation called Reactor in selected ColdGear items and introduced a new apparel collection with an exclusive CoolSwitch coating on the inside of the fabric that pulled heat away from the skin, allowing the wearer to feel cooler and perform longer.

Footwear   Under Armour began marketing athletic footwear for men, women, and youth in 2006 and expanded its footwear line every year since. Its 2019 offerings included footwear models specifically designed for performance training, running, footwear, basketball, golf, and outdoor wear, plus football, baseball, lacrosse, softball, and soccer cleats. Under Armour's footwear models were light, breathable, and built with performance attributes specific to their intended use. Over the past five years, a stream of innovative technologies had been incorporated in the ongoing generations of footwear models/styles to improve stabilization, cushioning, moisture management, comfort, directional control, and performance. As of 2020, Under Armour footwear was designed with under-foot cushioning technologies labeled UA HOVR™, UA Micro G®, and Charged Cushioning®, engineered to a specific sport with advanced outsole construction.

New footwear collections for men, women, and youth were introduced annually, sometimes seasonally. Most new models and styles incorporated fresh technological features of one kind or another. Since 2012, Under Armour had more than tripled the number of footwear styles/models priced above $100 per pair. Its best-selling offerings were in the basketball and running shoe categories.

To capitalize on a recently signed long-term endorsement contract with pro basketball superstar Stephen Curry, Under Armour began marketing a Stephen Curry Signature line of basketball shoes in 2014; the so-called Curry One models had a price point of $120. This was followed by a Curry Two collection in 2015 at a price point of $130, a Curry 2.5 collection at a price point of $135 during the NBA playoffs in May and June 2016, a Curry Three collection in Fall 2016, a Curry 4 collection at a price point of $130 in Fall 2017, a Curry 5 collection at a price point of $130 at the start of the NBA playoffs in May 2018, a Curry 6 collection at a price point of $130 in December 2018, and a Curry 7 collection at a price point of $140 in November 2019.

After signing pro golfer Jordan Spieth to a 10-year endorsement contract in early 2015—Spieth had a spectacular year on the Professional Golf Association (PGA) tour in 2015 and was named 2015 PGA Tour Player of the Year—Under Armour promptly sought to leverage the signing by introducing an all-new 2016 golf shoe collection in April 2016. The collection had 3 styles, ranging in price from $160 to $220. A new Spieth One Signature collection was introduced in early 2017 with much the same price points, followed by a Spieth Two collection in early 2018, which was accompanied by a Spieth Tour™ golf glove, and a Spieth 3 collection in early 2019.

Under Armour debuted its first "smart shoe" (called the SpeedForm Gemini 2 Record Equipped) at a price point of $150 in 2016; smart shoe models were equipped with the capability to connect automatically to UA's connected fitness website and record certain activities in the wearer's fitness tracking account.

In 2018, using freshly-developed connected fitness technologies and several other innovations, Under Armour debuted a new, multi-featured HOVR™ running shoe, which Kevin Plank hailed as a new product that hit what the company called "the trifecta—style, performance, and fit." HOVR models were priced from $100 to $140; all models used compression mesh and a special molded foam that provided a "zero gravity feel," gave the runner return energy with each step to reduce impact, and claimed to deliver "unmatched comfort." The higher-priced "Connected" HOVR models had built-in Under Armour Record Sensor™ technology that could be paired with a mobile phone and used to track, analyze, and store almost every known running metric, enabling runners to know what they needed to do to get better. Plank believed the HOVR was "a home run" and a reflection of the company's growing capabilities to churn out innovative products. In 2020, HOVR models were available for running, training, basketball, golf, and casual wear; a number of the HOVR models for running had connected technology features.

Growing numbers of Under Armour's footwear models in 2019–2020 featured such recently developed technologies as Anafoam (which provided a chafe-free, body-mapped fit and lightweight structure and support) and Charged Cushioning® (which provided stabilization, directional cushioning, and moisture management, engineered to maximize comfort and control). UA's Clutch Fit® technology used in some footwear models flexed and responded "like your second skin."[11] Shoppers could also design their own customized footwear, using uploaded images, customizable patterns, an assortment of styles and technologies, and a giant array of color options. wanted

Accessories   Under Armour's accessory line in 2019 included gloves, socks, hats and headwear, belts, backpacks and bags, eyewear, protective gear, headphones, phone cases and mounts, water bottles and coolers, and an assortment of sports equipment. All of these accessories featured performance advantages and functionality similar to other Under Armour products. For instance, the company's baseball batting, football, golf, and running gloves included HEATGEAR®, COLDGEAR®, and Clutch Fit® technologies and were designed with advanced fabrics to provide various high-performance attributes that differentiated Under Armour gloves from those of rival brands.

Connected Fitness   In December 2013, Under Armour acquired MapMyFitness, which served one of the largest fitness communities in the world at its website and offered a diverse suite of websites and mobile applications under its flagship brands, MapMyRun and MapMyRide. Utilizing GPS and other advanced technologies, MapMyFitness provided users with the ability to map, record, and share their workouts. Under Armour acquired European fitness app Endomondo and food-logging app MyFitnessPal in 2015, enabling UA to create a multifaceted connected fitness dashboard that used four independently functioning apps (MapMyFitness, MyFitnessPal, Endomondo, and UA Record™) to enable subscribers to log workouts, runs, and foods eaten, and to use a digital dashboard to review measures relating to their sleep, fitness, activity, and nutrition. Next, UA introduced a Connected Fitness System called Under Armour HealthBox™ that consisted of a multifunctional wristband (that measured sleep, resting heart rate, steps taken, and workout intensity), heart rate strap, and a smart scale (that tracked bodyweight, body fat percentage, and progress toward a weight goal); the wristband was water resistant, could be worn 24/7, and had Bluetooth connectivity with UA Record.

Kevin Plank was so enthusiastic about the long-term potential of Under Armour's Connected Fitness business that he had boosted the company's team of engineers and software developers from 20 to over 350 during 2014 and 2015. In 2016, Under Armour organized all of its digital and fitness technologies and products into a new business division called Connected Fitness, under the leadership of a senior vice president of digital revenue. By December 2018, Under Armour believed it had created the world's largest digital health and fitness community. More than 250 million people had downloaded one of the company's digital fitness apps. Many users were quite active, with more than 2 million workouts and 30 million foods being logged daily across the world. Under Armour had learned that members of its digital ecosystem purchased 36 percent more Under Armour products than other consumers and that their brand preference for Under Armour products was significantly higher.[12]

While Connected Fitness sales grew rapidly, the business initially lost millions of dollars annually and achieved profitability in 2018—see Exhibits 2A and 2B. As part of the 2017 restructuring program, Under Armour merged its core connect fitness digital products, digital engineering, and digital media under the direction of a chief technology officer; this management arrangement evolved further in early 2018 with the appointment of a new senior vice president, digital product, who reported to the chief technology officer and had responsibility for leading the strategy for all digital product development in collaboration with executive management, product category heads, marketing, and creative/design. In Under Armour's February 2018 earnings announcement, the Connected Fitness business reported its first-ever positive operating income (almost $800,000) for the fourth quarter of 2017; for full-year 2018, the connected fitness business reported operating income of $5.9 million. Under Armour reported that premium subscription revenue for its Connected Fitness business grew about 56 percent during 2018. UA's MyFitnessPal was the number one grossing health and fitness app in the Apple App Store; in 2018, users of this app had over 9 billion foods and burned more than 440 billion calories. Users of various Connected Fitness apps participated in social media communities on Instagram, WeChat, Snap, YouTube, Facebook, and other platforms.

Licensing   Under Armour had licensing agreements with a number of firms to produce and market Under Armour apparel, accessories, and equipment. Under Armour product, marketing, and sales teams were actively involved in all steps of the design process for licensed products in order to maintain brand standards and consistency. During 2018–2020, licensees sold UA-branded collegiate, National Football League and National Basketball Association apparel and accessories, baby and kids' apparel, team uniforms, socks, water bottles, eyewear, and other hard goods equipment that featured performance advantages and functionality similar to Under Armour's other product offerings. Under Armour pre-approved all products manufactured and sold by its licensees, and the company's quality assurance team strived to ensure that licensed products met the same quality and compliance standards as company-sold products.

Marketing, Promotion, and Brand Management Strategies

Under Armour had an in-house marketing and promotions department that designed and produced most of its advertising campaigns to drive consumer demand for its products and build awareness of Under Armour as a leading performance athletic brand. The company's total marketing expenses were $579.0 million in 2019, $543.8 million in 2018, $565.1 million in 2017, and $477.5 million in

2016. These totals included the costs of sponsoring events and various sports teams, the costs of athlete endorsements, and ads placed in a variety of television, print, radio, and social media outlets. All were included as part of selling, general, and administrative expenses shown in Exhibit 1.

Sports Marketing   Under Armour's sports marketing and promotion strategy began with promoting the sales and use of its products to high-performing athletes and teams on the high school, collegiate, and professional levels. This strategy was executed by entering into outfitting agreements with a variety of collegiate and professional sports teams, sponsoring and hosting an assortment of collegiate and professional sports events, entering into endorsement agreements with individual athletes, and selling Under Armour products directly to team equipment managers and to individual athletes. As a result, UA products were seen on the playing field (typically with the Under Armour logo prominently displayed), giving them exposure to various consumer audiences attending live sports events or watching these events on television and through other media (pictures and videos accessed via the Internet and social media, magazines, and print). Management believed such exposure helped the company establish the on-field authenticity of the Under Armour brand with consumers. In addition, UA hosted combines, camps, and clinics for athletes in many sports at regional sites across the United States and was the title sponsor of a collection of high school All-America Games that created significant on-field and media exposure of its products and brand.

Going into 2020, Under Armour was the official outfitter of men's and women's athletic teams at such collegiate institutions as Notre Dame, UCLA, Boston College, Northwestern, Texas Tech, Maryland, South Carolina, the U.S. Naval Academy, Wisconsin, Indiana, California, Utah, and Auburn. All told, it was the official outfitter of close to 100 men's and women's collegiate athletic teams, growing numbers of high school athletic teams, and it supplied sideline apparel and fan gear for many collegiate teams as well. Under Armour had been the official supplier of competition suits, uniforms, and training resources for a number of U.S. teams in the 2014 Winter Olympics, 2016 Summer Olympics, 2018 Winter Olympics, and 2020 Summer Olympics.

Under Armour was quite active in negotiating agreements to supply products to high profile professional athletes and professional sports teams, most notably in the National Football League (NFL) and the National Basketball Association (NBA). Under Armour had been an official supplier of football cleats to all NFL teams since 2006, the official supplier of gloves to NFL teams beginning in 2011, and a supplier of training apparel for athletes attending NFL tryout camps beginning in 2012. In 2011 Under Armour became the official supplier of performance footwear to all 30 MLB teams; in 2016, Under Armour signed a 10-year deal with MLB to extend its role as official supplier for all 30 teams from just footwear to include uniforms, performance apparel, and connected fitness products and to also be an official sponsor of Major League Baseball. However, in 2018 UA exited its 2016 agreement with MLB, but retained its rights to supply performance footwear and be an MLB sponsor. In 2018, Under Armour worked with a manufacturing and distribution partner to sell MLB-licensed fan wear at retail.

Internationally, Under Armour sponsored and sold its products to several Canadian, European, and Latin American soccer and rugby teams to help drive brand awareness in various countries and regions across the world. In Canada, it had been the official supplier of performance apparel to Rugby Canada and Hockey Canada. In Europe, Under Armour was the official supplier of performance apparel to two professional soccer teams and the Welsh Rugby Union. In 2014 and 2015, Under Armour became the official match-day and training wear supplier for the Colo-Colo soccer club in Chile, the Cruz Azul soccer team in Mexico, and the São Paulo soccer team in Brazil.

In addition to sponsoring teams and events, Under Armour's brand-building strategy in the United States was to secure the endorsement of individual athletes. One facet of this strategy was to sign endorsement contracts with newly emerging sports stars—examples included Jacksonville Jaguars running back Leonard Fournette, Milwaukee Bucks point guard Brandon Jennings, Philadelphia 76ers center Joel Embiid, Charlotte Bobcats point guard Kemba Walker, 2012 National League (baseball) Most Valuable Player Buster Posey, 2012 National League Rookie of the Year Bryce Harper, tennis phenom Sloane Stephens, WBC super-welterweight boxing champion Camelo Alvarez, and PGA golfer Jordan Spieth. But the company's endorsement roster also included established stars: NFL football players Tom Brady, and Anquan Boldin; Golden State

Warriors point guard Stephen Curry; professional baseball players Ryan Zimmerman and Clayton Kershaw; U.S. Women's National Soccer Team players Heather Mitts and Lauren Cheney; U.S. Olympic and professional volleyball player Nicole Branagh; and U.S. Olympic swimmer Michael Phelps. In 2015, Under Armour negotiated 10-year extensions of its endorsement contracts with Stephen Curry and Jordan Spieth; both deals included grants of stock in the company. Recently, Under Armour had signed celebrities outside the sports world to multi-year contracts, including ballerina soloist Misty Copeland and fashion model Giselle Bündchen; wrestler, actor, and producer Dwayne "The Rock" Johnson; and rapper A$AP Rocky (Rakim Mayers). Copeland was featured in one of Under Armour's largest advertising campaigns for women's apparel offerings. Johnson was playing an integral role in promoting UA's connected fitness, apparel, footwear, and accessory products. Mayers was expected to have his own line of premium clothing in a forthcoming Under Armour Sportswear collection. In addition to signing endorsement agreements with prominent sports figures and celebrities in the United States, Under Armour had become increasingly active in using endorsement agreements with well-known athletes to help build public awareness of the Under Armour brand in those foreign countries where it was striving to build a strong market presence. As of early 2019, Under Armour had signed endorsement agreements with several hundred international athletes in a wide variety of sports.

Under Armour's strategy of signing high-profile sports figures to endorsement contracts, sponsoring a variety of sports events, and supplying products to sports teams emblazoned with the company's logo had long been used by Nike and The adidas Group. Both rivals had far larger rosters of sports figure endorsements than Under Armour and supplied their products to more collegiate and professional sports teams than Under Armour.

Nonetheless, Under Armour's aggressive entry into the market for securing such endorsement agreements had spawned intense competition among the three rivals to win the endorsement of athletes and teams with high profiles and high perceived public appeal had caused the costs of winning such agreements to spiral upward. In 2014, Under Armour reportedly offered between $265 million and $285 million to entice NBA star Kevin Durant, who

plays for the Golden State Warriors, away from Nike; Nike matched the offer and Durant elected to stay with Nike.[13] In 2015, adidas bested Nike in a bidding war to sign Houston Rockets star and runner-up NBA most valuable player James Harden to a 13-year endorsement deal, when Nike opted not to match adidas' offer of $200 million. The deal with Harden was said to be a move by adidas to reclaim its number- two spot in sports apparel sales in North America behind Nike, months after being surpassed by Under Armour.[14] In 2016, it took $280 million for Under Armour to secure a 16-year deal with UCLA to outfit all of UCLA's men's and women's athletic teams. In 2018, Under Armour enticed Joel Embiid to switch from adidas to Under Armour for a five-year apparel and footwear endorsement deal that made him the highest-earning center in the NBA (the exact terms were not disclosed).

Under Armour spent roughly $120 million for athlete and superstar endorsements, various team and league sponsorships, athletic events, and other marketing commitments, compared to about $126.2 million in 2018, $150.4 million in 2017, and $176.1 million in 2016.[15] The company was contractually obligated to spend about $350 million for endorsements, sponsorships, events, and other marketing commitments from 2020 to 2023.[16] Under Armour did not know precisely what its future endorsement and sponsorship costs would be because its contractual agreements with most athletes were subject to certain performance-based variables and because it was actively engaged in efforts to sign additional endorsement contracts and sponsor additional sports teams and athletic events.

Retail Marketing and Product Presentation The primary thrust of Under Armour's retail marketing strategy was to increase the floor space *exclusively* dedicated to Under Armour products in the stores of its major retail accounts. The key initiative here was to design and fund point of sale displays and Under Armour "concept shops"—including flooring, lighting, walls, displays, and images—within the stores of its major retail customers. This shop-in-shop approach was seen as an effective way to gain the placement of Under Armour products in prime floor space and create a more engaging and sales-producing way for consumers to shop for Under Armour products.

In stores that did not have Under Armour concept shops, Under Armour worked with retailers to establish sales-enhancing placement of its products and various point-of-sale displays. In "big-box" sporting goods stores, it was important to be sure that Under Armour's growing variety of products gained visibility in all of the various departments (hunting apparel in the hunting goods department, footwear and socks in the footwear department, and so on). Except for the retail stores with Under Armour concept shops, company personnel worked with retailers to employ in-store fixtures, life-size mannequins, and displays that highlighted the UA logo and conveyed a performance-oriented, athletic look. The merchandising strategy was not only to enhance the visibility of Under Armour products and drive sales but also grow consumer awareness that Under Armour products delivered performance-enhancing advantages.

Media and Promotion   Under Armour advertised in a variety of national digital, broadcast, and print media outlets, as well as social and mobile media. Its advertising campaigns were of varying lengths and formats and frequently included prominent athletes and personalities. Advertising and promotional campaigns in 2015–2017 featured Michael Phelps, Stephen Curry, Jordan Spieth, Tom Brady, Lindsey Vonn, Misty Copeland, and Dwayne Johnson. In 2018, UA had a digitally-led marketing approach for the launch of its UA HOVR™ running shoe models, which included a variety of content on various social media platforms.

Distribution Strategy

Under Armour products were available in roughly 17,000 retail store locations worldwide in 2018–2019. In many foreign countries, Under Armour relied on independent marketing and sales agents, instead of its own marketing staff, to recruit retail accounts and solicit orders from retailers for UA merchandise. Under Armour also sold its products directly to consumers through its own Brand House stores, factory outlet stores, and various geographic websites.

Wholesale Distribution   In 2018, Under Armour had about 13,500 points of distribution in North America, just under 40 percent of the 35,000 places that consumers could buy athletic apparel and footwear.[17] The company's biggest retail account was Dick's Sporting Goods, which in 2018 accounted for 10 percent of the company's net revenues. Until its bankruptcy and subsequent store liquidation in

2016, The Sports Authority had been UA's second largest retail account; the loss of this account was a principal factor in Under Armour's struggle to grow wholesale sales to retailers in North America. Other important retail accounts included Academy Sports and Outdoors, Hibbett Sporting Goods, Modell's Sporting Goods, Bass Pro Shops, Cabela's, Footlocker, The Army and Air Force Exchange Service, and such well-known department store chains as Macy's, Nordstrom, Belk, Dillard's, and Kohl's. In Canada, the company's important retail accounts included Sport Chek and Hudson's Bay. Roughly 75 percent of all sales made to retailers were to large-format national and regional retail chains. The remaining 25 percent of wholesale sales were to lesser-sized outdoor and specialty retailers, institutional athletic departments, leagues, teams, and fitness specialists. Independent and specialty retailers were serviced by a combination of in-house sales personnel and third-party commissioned manufacturer's representatives.

Direct-to-Consumer Sales   In 2018, about 38 percent of Under Armour's net revenues were generated through direct-to-consumer sales, versus 23 percent in 2010 and six percent in 2005; the direct-to-consumer channel included sales of discounted merchandise at Under Armour's factory outlet stores and full-price sales at Under Armour Brand Houses, and various country websites. The factory outlet stores gave Under Armour added brand exposure and helped familiarize consumers with Under Armour's product lineup while also functioning as an important channel for selling discontinued, out-of-season, and/or overstocked products at discount prices without undermining the prices of Under Armour merchandise being sold at retail stores, Brand Houses, and company websites. Going into 2020, Under Armour was operating 169 stores in factory outlet malls in North America; these stores attracted about 75 million shoppers in 2018.

During the past several years, Under Armour had opened company-owned Brand House stores in high-traffic retail locations in the United States to showcase its branded apparel and sell its products direct-to-consumers at retail prices. In early 2020, the company was operating 19 Under Armour Brand House stores in North America.

UA management's e-commerce strategy called for sales at www.underarmour.com (and 26 other in-country websites as of 2016) to be one of the company's principal vehicles for sales growth in upcoming years. To help spur e-commerce sales, the company had enhanced its efforts to drive traffic to its websites, improve its online merchandising techniques, and do a better job of storytelling about the many different Under Armour products sold on its sites. In 2017–2019, UA had made frequent use of discounted price promotions to spur online sales, but top executives decided that discount-pricing had been overdone and damaged the company's image as a premium brand. In 2020, the strategy at UA websites was to cut back on discounted price promotions and, instead, utilize marketing and advertising efforts that portrayed Under Armour as a premium brand with an attractive line-up of top-quality, high performance products well worth paying a premium price to own.

To begin reshaping its marketing approaches, in 2019 and early 2020 Under Armour started including much more user-generated content on its e-commerce website to help tell the story about UA products. This user-generated content included customer ratings and reviews, Instagram snapshots and videos of shoppers and well-known athletes wearing UA products, feedback from prelaunch "wear-testers", and quotes from athletes and spokespeople like Stephen Curry, Dwayne Johnson, and other endorsers of the company's products. Management believed that the opinions of what shoppers and athletes said about Under Armour's performance-driven products carried more weight with prospective buyers than what Under Armour said in its product descriptions.

To better compete with Amazon and other online sellers of performance sports apparel and athletic footwear, the company offered free three to five business day shipping on orders over $60 and free three business day shipping on orders over $150. From time-to-time, free limited-time shipping was offered on overstocked items. Free shipping on returns within 60 days was standard.

Distribution outside North America   Under Armour's first strategic move to gain international distribution occurred in 2002 when it established a relationship with a Japanese licensee, Dome Corporation, to be the exclusive distributor of Under Armour products in Japan. The relationship evolved, with Under Armour making a minority equity investment in Dome Corporation in 2011 and Dome gaining distribution rights for South Korea. Dome sold Under Armour

branded apparel, footwear, and accessories to professional sports teams, large sporting goods retailers, and several thousand independent retailers of sports apparel in Japan and South Korea. Under Armour worked closely with Dome to develop variations of Under Armour products to better accommodate the different sports interests and preferences of Japanese and Korean consumers.

In 2006, Under Armour opened a headquarters in Amsterdam, The Netherlands, to conduct and oversee sales, marketing, and logistics activities across Europe. The strategy was to first sell Under Armour products directly to teams and athletes and then leverage visibility in the sports segment to access broader audiences of potential consumers. By 2011, Under Armour had succeeded in selling products to Premier League Football clubs and multiple running, golf, and cricket clubs in the United Kingdom; soccer teams in France, Germany, Greece, Ireland, Italy, Spain, and Sweden; as well as First Division Rugby clubs in France, Ireland, Italy, and the United Kingdom. Sales to European retailers quickly followed on the heels of gains being made in the sports team segment. By year-end 2012, Under Armour had 4,000 retail customers in Austria, France, Germany, Ireland, and the United Kingdom and was generating revenues from sales to independent distributors who resold Under Armour products to retailers in Italy, Greece, Scandinavia, and Spain. Sales in EMEA countries in 2019 totaled $621 million (see Exhibit 2A). Adidas strongly defended its industry-leading position with European retailers, and Under Armour frequently found itself embroiled in hotly contested price-cutting battles with adidas and Nike to win orders from retailers in many EMEA locations.

In 2010 and 2011, Under Armour began selling its products in parts of Latin America and Asia. In Latin America, Under Armour sold directly to retailers in some countries and in other countries sold its products to independent distributors who then were responsible for securing sales to retailers. In 2014, Under Armour launched efforts to make Under Armour products available in over 70 of Brazil's premium points of sale and e-commerce hubs; expanded sales efforts were also initiated in Chile and Mexico. While sales were trending upward in Latin America, the company had reported operating losses in the region each of the past four years (see Exhibit 3).

In 2011, Under Armour opened a retail showroom in Shanghai, China—the first of a series of steps to begin the long-term process of introducing Chinese athletes and consumers to the Under Armour brand, showcase Under Armour products, and learn about Chinese consumers. Additional retail locations in Shanghai and Beijing soon followed (some operated by local partners). By April 2014, there were five company-owned and franchised retail locations in mainland China that merchandised Under Armour products; additionally, the Under Armour brand had been recently introduced in Hong Kong through a partnership with leading retail chain GigaSports.

Under Armour began selling its branded apparel, footwear, and accessories to independent distributors in Australia, New Zealand, and Taiwan in 2014; these distributors were responsible for securing retail accounts to merchandise Under Armour products to consumers. The distribution of Under Armour products to retail accounts across Asia was handled by a third-party logistics provider based in Hong Kong.

In 2013, Under Armour organized its international activities into four geographic regions—North America (the United States and Canada), Latin America, Asia-Pacific, and Europe/Middle East/Africa (EMEA). In the company's 2013 Annual Report, Kevin Plank said, "We are committed to being a global brand with global stories to tell, and we are on our way."[18] Sales of Under Armour products in EMEA, the Asia-Pacific, and Latin America accounted for 27.6 percent of Under Armour's total net revenues in 2019, up from 15.3 percent in 2016, and 8.7 percent in 2014 (Exhibit 2A). Under Armour saw growth in foreign sales as the company's biggest market opportunity in upcoming years, chiefly because of the sheer number of people residing outside the United States who could be attracted to patronize the Under Armour brand. In 2019 Nike generated just over 57 percent of its revenues outside North America, and adidas got about 77 percent outside of North America—these big international sales percentages for Nike and adidas were a big reason why Under Armour executives were confident that growing UA's international sales represented an enormous market opportunity for the company, despite the stiff competition it could expect from its two bigger global rivals.

One of Under Armour's chief initiatives to build international awareness of the Under Armour brand and rapidly grow its sales internationally was to open growing numbers of stores in popular factory outlet malls and to locate Brand Houses in visible, high-traffic locations in major cities. UA had 104 factory outlet stores and 96 Brand House stores in international locations as of year-end 2019, up from 37 factory outlet and 35 Brand House stores in various international locations at year-end 2017. In October 2018, UA sold its Brazilian subsidiary and entered into a license and distribution agreement with a third party to continue to sell UA products in Brazil.

Product Design and Development

Top executives believed that product innovation—as concerns both technical design and aesthetic design—was the key to driving Under Armour's sales growth and building a stronger brand name. UA products were manufactured with technically advanced specialty fabrics produced by third parties. The company's product development team collaborated closely with fabric suppliers to ensure that the fabrics and materials used in UA's products had the desired performance and fit attributes. Under Armour regularly upgraded its products as next-generation fabrics with better performance characteristics became available and as the needs of athletes changed. Product development efforts also aimed at broadening the company's product offerings in both new and existing product categories and market segments. An effort was made to design products with "visible technology," utilizing color, texture, and fabrication that would enhance customers' perception and understanding of the use and benefits of Under Armour products.

Under Armour's product development team had significant prior industry experience at leading fabric and other raw material suppliers and branded athletic apparel and footwear companies throughout the world. The team worked closely with Under Armour's sports marketing and sales teams as well as professional and collegiate athletes to identify product trends and determine market needs. Collaboration among the company's product development, sales, and sports marketing team had proved important in identifying the opportunity and market for three recently launched product lines and fabric technologies:

- CHARGED COTTON™ products, which were made from natural cotton but performed like the products made from technically advanced synthetic fabrics, drying faster and wicking moisture away from the body.

- COLDGEAR® Infrared, a ceramic print technology applied to the inside of garments that provided wearers with lightweight warmth.
- UA HOVR™, a proprietary underfoot cushioning wrapped in a mesh web, equipped with a MapMyRun powered sensor designed to deliver energy return and real-time coaching.

In 2017, Under Armour opened its newest center for footwear performance innovation located in Portland, Oregon, bringing together footwear design and development teams in a centralized location.

Sourcing, Manufacturing, and Quality Assurance

Many of the high-tech specialty fabrics and other raw materials used in UA products were developed by third parties and sourced from a limited number of pre-approved specialty fabric manufacturers; no fabrics were manufactured in-house. Under Armour executives believed outsourcing fabric production enabled the company to seek out and utilize whichever fabric suppliers were able to produce the latest and best performance-oriented fabrics to Under Armour's specifications, while also freeing more time for UA's product development staff to concentrate on upgrading the performance, styling, and overall appeal of existing products and expanding the company's overall lineup of product offerings.

In 2019, approximately 42 percent of the fabric used in UA products came from five suppliers, with primary locations in Malaysia, Taiwan, Vietnam, China, and the United States. Because a big fraction of the materials used in UA products were petroleum-based synthetics, fabric costs were subject to crude oil price fluctuations. The cotton fabrics used in the CHARGED COTTON™ products were also subject to price fluctuations and varying availability based on cotton harvests.

In 2019, substantially all UA products were made by 37 primary contract manufacturers, operating in 15 countries; 10 manufacturers produced approximately 55 percent of UA's products. Approximately 55 percent of UA's apparel and accessories products were manufactured in Jordan, Vietnam, China, and Malaysia. Under Armour's footwear products were made by six primary contract manufacturers operating primarily in Vietnam, China, and Indonesia; these five manufacturers produced approximately 96 percent of the company's footwear products.

All contract manufacturers making Under Armour apparel products purchased the fabrics they needed from fabric suppliers pre-approved by Under Armour. All of the makers of UA products across all divisions were evaluated for quality systems, social compliance, and financial strength by Under Armour's quality assurance team, prior to being selected and also on an ongoing basis. The company strived to qualify multiple manufacturers for particular product types and fabrications and to seek out contractors that could perform multiple manufacturing stages, such as procuring raw materials and providing finished products, which helped UA control its cost of goods sold. All contract manufacturers were required to adhere to a code of conduct regarding quality of manufacturing, working conditions, and other social concerns. However, the company had no long-term agreements requiring it to continue to use the services of any manufacturer, and no manufacturer was obligated to make products for UA on a long-term basis. UA had subsidiaries strategically located near its manufacturing partners to support its manufacturing, quality assurance, and sourcing efforts for its products.

Under Armour had a 17,000 square-foot Special Make-Up Shop located at one of its distribution facilities in Maryland where it had the capability to make and ship customized apparel products on tight deadlines for high-profile athletes and teams. While these apparel products represented a tiny fraction of Under Armour's revenues, management believed the facility helped provide superior service to select customers.

Inventory Management

Under Armour based the amount of inventory it needed to have on hand for each item in its product line on existing orders, anticipated sales, and the rapid delivery requirements of customers. Its inventory strategy was focused on (1) having sufficient inventory to fill incoming orders promptly and (2) putting strong systems and procedures in place to improve the efficiency with which it managed its inventories of individual products and total inventory. The amounts of seasonal products it ordered from manufacturers were based on current bookings, the need to ship seasonal items at the start of the shipping window in order to maximize the floor space productivity of retail customers, the need to adequately stock its Factory House and Brand House stores, and the need to fill customer orders. Excess inventories of particular products were either shipped to its Factory House stores or earmarked for sale to third-party liquidators.

However, the growing number of individual items in UA's product line and uncertainties surrounding upcoming consumer demand for individual items made it difficult to accurately forecast how many units to order from manufacturers and what the appropriate stocking requirements were for many items. New inventory management practices were instituted in 2012 to better cope with stocking requirements for individual items and avoid excessive inventory buildups. Year-end inventories of $1.16 billion in 2017 equated to 154.6 days of inventory and inventory turnover of 2.36 turns per year. UA's description of its restructuring plans in 2017 signaled that inventory reduction initiatives were included. Year-end inventories of $892.3 million in 2019 equated to 116.5 days of inventory and inventory turnover of 3.13 turns per year.

UNDER ARMOUR'S WEAK PERFORMANCE IN THE FIRST QUARTER OF 2020

Under Armour reported revenues of $930 million for the first quarter of 2020, down 23 percent from the first quarter of 2019, with approximately 15 percentage points of the decline related to COVID-19 impacts. North American revenues decreased 28 percent to $603 million (compared to the same quarter in 2019), but international revenues fell only 12 percent to $287 million. Revenues fell in all three product categories, with apparel revenues down 23 percent to $598 million, footwear revenues down 28 percent to $210 million, and accessories revenue down 17 percent to $68 million. The company reported an operating loss of $558 million, of which $446 million was due to the impact of the company's restructuring plan, and a net loss of $590 million, which included restructuring and other charges—the adjusted net loss was $152 million.

To counter the impact of COVID-19, which accelerated dramatically in mid-March 2020 in North America and the EMEA region (partly due to retail store closures) and the ongoing negative

impacts anticipated in the upcoming two quarters, management began a series of initiatives to reduce its planned operating expenses by $325 million; these included cutting back on marketing expenditures, temporarily laying off workers in Under Armour's retail stores, and U.S.-based distribution centers, reducing incentive compensation, postponing $60 million in planned capital expenditures, and curtailing hiring, travel and contract services.

Investors' response to the report of the company's Q1 2020 performance was understandably negative; the price of the company's Class A shares dropped from about $20 in mid-February to $7.80 in mid-May 2020. One Wall Street analyst said:[19]

> The Covid-19 crisis has exacerbated the existing problems facing the Under Armour brand. UA does not have the brand consideration or compelling product assortment necessary to reaccelerate sales post the current crisis. Elevated inventory levels should pressure the gross margin for the balance of the year and stymie UA's ability to introduce new product. UA could continue to lose market share to Nike, adidas, and others who garner greater brand consideration and have more financial flexibility.

The analyst lowered his price target for the stock price to $4 per share.

COMPETITION

The $280 billion global market for sports apparel, athletic footwear, and related accessories was fragmented among some 25 brand-name competitors with diverse product lines and varying geographic coverage and numerous small competitors with specialized-use apparel lines that usually operated within a single country or geographic region. Industry participants included athletic and leisure shoe companies, athletic and leisure apparel companies, sports equipment companies, and large companies having diversified lines of athletic and leisure shoes, apparel, and equipment. The global market for athletic footwear was projected to reach $114.8 billion by 2022, growing at a CAGR of 2.1 percent during the period 2016 to 2022.[20] The global market for sports apparel was forecast to grow about 5.1 percent annually from 2019 to 2026 and reach about $248 billion by 2020.[21] Exhibit 4 shows a representative sample of the best-known companies and brands in selected segments of the sports apparel, athletic footwear, and sports equipment industry.

In 2017–19, consumers across the world shopped for the industry's products digitally (online) or physically in stores. And they shopped either for a favorite brand or for multi-brand. The trend was for more consumers to shop digitally and for a brand deemed to be the best or their favorite. Multi-brand shoppers typically wanted to explore and compare the options, either through a dot.com experience or in stores where shoppers could view the products firsthand, get advice or personalized assistance, and/or get the product immediately.

As Exhibit 4 indicates, the sporting goods industry consisted of many distinct product categories and market segments. Because the product mixes of different companies varied considerably, it was common for the product offerings of industry participants to be extensive in some segments, moderate in others, and limited to nonexistent in still others. Consequently, the leading competitors and the intensity of competition varied significantly from market segment to market segment. Nonetheless, competition tended to be intense in almost every segment with substantial sales volume and typically revolved around performance and reliability, the breadth of product selection, new product development, price, brand name strength and identity through marketing and promotion, the ability of companies to convince retailers to stock and effectively merchandise their brands, and the capabilities of the various industry participants to sell directly to consumers through their own retail/factory outlet stores and/or at their company websites. It was common for the leading companies selling athletic footwear, sports uniforms, and sports equipment to actively sponsor sporting events and clinics and to contract with prominent and influential athletes, coaches, professional sports teams, colleges, and sports leagues to endorse their brands and use their products.

Nike was the clear global market leader in the sporting goods industry, with a global market share in athletic footwear of about 25 percent and a sports apparel share of five percent. The adidas Group, with

EXHIBIT 4   Major Competitors and Brands in Selected Segments of the Sports Apparel, Athletic Footwear, and Accessory Industry, 2019

Performance Apparel for Sports (baseball, football, basketball, softball, volleyball, hockey, lacrosse, soccer, track & field, and other action sports)	Performance-Driven Athletic Footwear	Training/Fitness Clothing
• Nike • Under Armour • adidas • Eastbay • Russell	• Nike • adidas • New Balance • Reebok • Saucony • Puma • Rockport • Converse • Ryka • Asics • Li Ning	• Nike • Under Armour • adidas • Puma • Fila • Lululemon athletica • Champion • Asics • Eastbay • SUGOI • Li Ning

Performance Activewear and Sports-Inspired Lifestyle Apparel	Performance Skiwear	Performance Golf Apparel
• Polo Ralph Lauren • Lacoste • Izod • Cutter & Buck • Timberland • Columbia • Puma • Li Ning • Many others	• Salomon • North Face • Descente • Columbia • Patagonia • Marmot • Helly Hansen • Bogner • Spyder • Many others	• Footjoy • Nike • adidas • Under Armour • Polo Golf • Ashworth • Cutter & Buck • Greg Norman • Puma • Many others

businesses that produced athletic footwear, sports uniforms, fitness apparel, sportswear, and a variety of sports equipment and marketed them across the world, was the second largest global competitor. These two major competitors of Under Armour are profiled as follows.

Nike, Inc.

Incorporated in 1968, Nike was the dominant global leader in the design, development, and worldwide marketing and selling of footwear, sports apparel, sports equipment, and accessory products. Nike was a truly global brand, with a broader and deeper portfolio of products, models, and styles than any other industry participant. The company had global sales of $39.1 billion and net income of $4.0 billion in fiscal year ending May 31, 2019. Nike was the world's largest seller of footwear with Nike-branded sales of $24.2 billion and Converse-branded sales of $1.9 billion; it held the number one market share in all markets and in all categories of athletic footwear. Nike's footwear line included some 1,500 models/styles. Nike was also the world's largest sports apparel brand, with 2019 sales of $11.6 billion. Sales of Nike products to women reached $7.4 billion in 2019.

Nike's strategy in 2019–2020 was driven by three core beliefs. One was that the growing popularity of sports and active lifestyles reflected a desire to lead healthier lives. As a result, companies like Nike were becoming more relevant for more moments in people's lives because of their growing participation in calorie-burning, wellness, and fitness activities and because active lifestyles stimulated greater interest in sports-related activities and sports events. Moreover, streaming of sports events and social media were changing the ways people consumed sports content. The NBA, for example, had over 1.3 billion social media followers across the league, teams, and player pages. The growth of watching streamed events on mobile phones was exploding. Second, in a connected, mobile-led world, consumers had become infinitely better informed and, thus, more powerful because of the information they could access in seconds and the options this opened up—"powered consumers" were prone to consult their phones (or conduct Internet searches on other devices) for price comparisons and availability before deciding where to shop or what to purchase online. Third, the world was operating at faster speeds and the numbers of powered consumers was about to explode. Nike's CEO expected over 2 billion digitally connected people in markets in China, India, and Latin America would join the middle class by 2030. In North America, Nike estimated that its primary consumer base was 50 million people, but that if population trends in China continued at the expected rate, Nike's projected consumer base in China would be more than 500 million people by 2030.

For years, the heart and soul of Nike's strategy had been creating innovative products and powerful storytelling that produced an emotional connection with consumers and caused them to gravitate to purchase Nike products. But at the same time Nike executives understood that brand strength had to be earned every day by satisfying consumer needs and meeting, if not exceeding, their expectations. Exhibit 5 shows Nike's worldwide retail and distribution network at the end of fiscal 2019.

In October 2017, Nike CEO Mark Parker provided a brief overview of the company's "Triple Double" strategy that had three components: 2X Innovation, 2X Speed, and 2X Direct:

> In 2X Innovation, we will lead with more distinct platforms, moving from seeding to scaling a lot faster. We'll . . . give consumers better choices to match their preferences. And we'll set a new expectation for style, creating a new aesthetic to wear in all moments of their lives. To the consumer, there is no trade-off between sport and style. We know that more than half of the

EXHIBIT 5 Nike's Worldwide Retail and Distribution Network, 2019

United States	Foreign Countries
• ~15,000 retail accounts	• ~15,000 retail accounts
• 217 Nike factory outlet stores	• 648 Nike factory outlet stores
• 29 Nike and NIKETOWN stores	• 57 Nike and NIKETOWN stores
• 109 Converse retail and factory outlet stores	• 63 Converse retail and factory outlet stores
• 29 Hurley stores	• —
• 6 Primary distribution centers	• 67 Distribution centers
• Company website (www.nike.com)	• Independent distributors and licensees in over 190 countries
	• Websites in 45 countries

athletic footwear and apparel is bought for non-sport activities, and we have even more room to grow in this market.

In 2X Speed, we're investing in digital end to end to serve this insatiable consumer demand for new and fresh products. To use a sports analogy, you can't run an up-tempo offense if only half your plays are designed for speed. So we're building new capabilities and analytics to deliver personalized products in real time, and we're engaging with more partners companywide to move faster against our goals. In our supply chain, we've joined forces with leading robotics and automation companies, and we're serving millions of athletes and sports fans faster through manufacturing bases that are closer to our North American consumer. 2X Speed is really all about delivering the right product in the moment, 100 percent of the time.

We never ever take the strength of our brand and premium product for granted. They are indeed our most valuable assets. With 2X Direct [to Consumer], we want as many Nike touch points as possible to live up to those expectations, and that's why we are investing heavily in our own channel and leading with digital. And with our strategic partners, we'll move resources away from undifferentiated retail and toward environments where we can better control with distinct consumer experiences.[22]

Principal Products Nike's 1,500 athletic footwear models and styles were designed primarily for specific athletic use, although many were worn for casual or leisure purposes. Running, training, basketball, soccer, sport-inspired casual shoes, and kids' shoes were the company's top-selling footwear categories. It also marketed footwear designed for baseball, football, golf, lacrosse, cricket, outdoor activities, tennis, volleyball, walking, and wrestling. The company designed and marketed Nike-branded sports apparel and accessories for most all of these same sports categories, as well as sports-inspired lifestyle apparel, athletic bags, and accessory items. Footwear, apparel, and accessories were often marketed in "collections" of similar design or for specific purposes. It also marketed apparel with licensed college and professional team and league logos. Nike-brand offerings in sports equipment included bags, socks, sport balls, eyewear, timepieces, electronic devices, bats, gloves, protective equipment, and golf clubs. Nike was also the owner of the Converse brand of athletic footwear and the Hurley brand of swimwear, assorted other apparel items, and surfing gear.

Exhibit 6 shows a breakdown of Nike's sales of footwear, apparel, and equipment by geographic region for fiscal years 2017 to 2019.

Marketing, Promotions, and Endorsements Nike responded to trends and shifts in consumer preferences by (1) adjusting the mix of existing product offerings, (2) developing new products, styles, and categories, and (3) striving to influence sports and fitness preferences through aggressive marketing, promotional activities, sponsorships, and athlete endorsements. Nike spent $3.75 billion in fiscal 2019 (as compared to $2.75 billion in 2013 for) what it

EXHIBIT 6 Nike's Sales of Nike Brand Footwear, Apparel, and Equipment, by Geographic Region and by Wholesale and Nike Direct, Fiscal Years 2017–2019

Sales Revenues and Earnings (in millions)	Fiscal Year Ending May 31		
	2019	2018	2017
North America			
Revenues—Nike Brand footwear	$10,045	$ 9,322	$ 9,684
Nike Brand apparel	5,260	4,938	4,866
Nike Brand equipment	597	595	646
Total Nike Brand revenues	$15,902	$14,855	$15,216
Sales to Wholesale Customers	10,875	10,159	10,756
Sales through Nike Direct	5,027	4,696	4,460
Earnings before interest and taxes	$ 3,925	$ 3,600	$ 3,875
Profit margin	24.7%	24.2%	25.6%

Sales Revenues and Earnings (in millions)	Fiscal Year Ending May 31		
	2019	2018	2017
Europe, Middle East, and Africa			
Revenues—Nike Brand footwear	$ 6,293	$ 5,875	$ 5,192
Nike Brand apparel	3,087	2,940	2,395
Nike Brand equipment	432	427	383
Total Nike Brand revenues	9,812	9,242	$ 7,970
Sales to Wholesale Customers	7,076	6,765	5,917
Sales through Nike Direct	2,736	2,477	2,053
Earnings before interest and taxes	1,995	1,587	$ 1,507
Profit margin	20.3%	17.2%	18.9%
Greater China			
Revenues—Nike Brand footwear	$ 4,262	$ 3,496	$ 2,920
Nike Brand apparel	1,808	1,508	1,188
Nike Brand equipment	138	130	129
Total Nike Brand revenues	$ 6,208	$ 5,134	$ 4,237
Sales to Wholesale Customers	3,726	3,216	2,774
Sales through Nike Direct	2,482	1,918	1,463
Earnings before interest and taxes	$ 2,376	$ 1,807	$ 1,507
Profit margin	44.1%	35.2%	35.6%
Asia Pacific and Latin America			
Revenues—Nike Brand footwear	$ 3,622	$ 3,575	$ 3,285
Nike Brand apparel	1,395	1,347	1,185
Nike Brand equipment	237	244	267
Total Nike Brand revenues	$ 5,254	$ 5,166	$ 4,737
Sales to Wholesale Customers	3,746	3,829	3,631
Sales through Nike Direct	1,508	1,337	1,106
Earnings before interest and taxes	$ 1,323	$ 1,189	$ 980
Profit margin	25.2%	23.0%	19.8%
All Regions			
Revenues—Nike Brand footwear	$24,222	$22,268	$21,081
Nike Brand apparel	11,550	10,733	9,654
Nike Brand equipment	1,404	1,396	1,425
Global Brand Divisions	42	88	73
Total Nike Brand revenues	$37,218	$34,485	$32,233
Sales to Wholesale Customers	25,423	23,969	23,078
Sales through Nike Direct	7,127	6,332	9,082
Corporate expenses	(1,810)	(1,456)	(724)
Total Nike earnings before interest and taxes	$ 4,850	$ 4,379	$ 4,945
Profit margin	13.0%	12.7%	15.3%
Converse			
Revenues	$ 1,906	$ 1,886	$ 2,042
Earnings before interest and taxes	303	310	477
Profit margin	15.9%	16.4%	23.4%

Note: The revenue and earnings figures for all geographic regions include the effects of currency exchange fluctuations. The Nike Brand revenues for equipment include the Hurley brand, and the Nike Brand revenues for footwear include the Jordan brand. The earnings before interest and taxes figures associated with Total Nike Brand Revenues include those for the Hurley and Jordan brands.

Source: Nike's 10-K Report for Fiscal Year 2019, pp. 727–31 and 10-K Report for Fiscal Year 2018, pp. 22, 27–31.

termed "demand creation expense" that included the costs of advertising, promotional activities, and endorsement contracts. Well over 500 professional, collegiate, club, and Olympic sports teams in football, basketball, baseball, ice hockey, soccer, rugby, speed skating, tennis, swimming, and other sports wore Nike uniforms with the Nike swoosh prominently visible. There were over 1,000 prominent professional athletes with Nike endorsement contracts in 2011–2019, including former basketball great Michael Jordan, NFL player Drew Brees, NBA players LeBron James, Kobe Bryant, Kevin Durant, and Dwayne Wade; professional golfers Tiger Woods and Michelle Wie; soccer player Cristiano Ronaldo; and professional tennis players Venus and Serena Williams, Roger Federer, and Rafael Nadal. When Tiger Woods turned pro, Nike signed him to a 5-year $100 million endorsement contract and made him the centerpiece of its campaign to make Nike a factor in the golf equipment and golf apparel marketplace. Nike's long-standing endorsement relationship with Michael Jordan led to the introduction of the highly popular line of Air Jordan footwear and, more recently, to the launch of the Jordan brand of athletic shoes, clothing, and gear. In 2003 LeBron James signed an endorsement deal with Nike worth $90 million over 7 years, and in 2015 he signed a lifetime deal with Nike. Because soccer was such a popular sport globally, Nike had more endorsement contracts with soccer athletes than with athletes in any other sport; track and field athletes had the second largest number of endorsement contracts.

Resources and Capabilities   Nike had an incredibly deep pool of valuable resources and capabilities that enhanced its competitive power in the marketplace and helped spur product innovation, shorten speed-to-market, enable customers to use digital tools to customize the colors and styling of growing numbers of Nike products, and thereby drive strong brand attachment and sales growth. Examples of these included the following:[23]

- The company's Nike APP and the SNKRS app were in more than 20 countries across North America and Europe, plus China and Japan, countries that drove close to 90 percent of Nike's growth. These apps provided easy access to Nike products and were becoming a popular way for customers to shop Nike products and make online purchases. The Nike App was the number one mono-brand retail app in the United States. Nike's apps and growing digital product ecosystem were key components of the company's 2X Speed strategy to operate faster and get innovative products in the hands of consumers faster.

- The creation and ongoing enhancement of the NikePlus membership program which in 2017 connected 100 million consumers to Nike—NikePlus members who used the company's mobile apps spent more than three times as much time on nike.com as other site visitors. Starting in 2018, NikePlus members were entitled to "reserved-for-you service" that used machine learning-powered algorithms to set aside products in a member's size that the algorithms predicted members would like. Members could also use a "reserved-by-you" service to gain guaranteed access to products they wanted; this newly developed capability was deemed especially valuable to members wanting a recently-introduced product in high demand. In 2018, Nike began accelerating invitations to NikePlus members to personalized events and experiences and extending benefits and offers from NikePlus partners like Apple Music, Headspace, and Class Pass. Special Nike Unlock offers were sent to members once a month. Nike expected that NikePlus membership would triple over the next five years. Nike executives anticipated that converting consumers into NikePlus members would heighten their relationship to and connection with Nike.

- The establishment of an Advanced Product Creation Center charged with keeping the pipeline flowing with product innovations, new digital products, and manufacturing innovations to make 2X Speed a reality. Nike was aggressively investing in 3D modeling and other related technology to quickly create prototypes of new products; with traditional technology, it often took four-to-six months to go from new idea to design to product prototype. So far, Nike had been able to go from design, to prototyping, to manufacturing, to delivery in less than months, as compared to nine to 12 months. Nike's goal was to improve its rapid prototyping capabilities to the point where 100 percent of new product innovations could be rapid-prototyped at the Advanced Product Creation Center in Portland, Oregon. Employee athletes, athletes engaged under sports marketing contracts, and other athletes wear-tested and evaluated products during the development and prototyping process.

- A relaunch of all 40+ nike.com websites in late 2017 that featured a new design with better visual appeal and functionality, more storytelling, eye-catching product displays, and better product descriptions—all aimed at generating more visitor traffic, longer shopping times, increased online sales, and achieving 2X Direct.

- Implementing robot-assisted manufacturing capabilities and other recently-developed manufacturing innovations (such as oscillating knives, laser cutting and trimming, phylon mold transfer, and computerized stitching) on a broad scale. In one instance, the use of advanced robotics and digitization techniques was generating a continuous, automated flow of the upper portion of a footwear model with 30 percent fewer steps, 50 percent less labor, and less waste in just 30 seconds per shoe—a total of 1,200 automated robots had been installed to perform an assortment of activities at various manufacturing facilities in 2017. In another instance, Nike had made manufacturing breakthroughs in producing the bottoms of its footwear (the midsoles and outsoles) using innovative techniques capable of delivering a pair of midsoles and outsoles, on average, in 2.5 minutes, compared to more than 50 minutes with previously-used techniques. This new process used 75 percent less energy, entailed 50 percent less tooling cost, and enabled a 60 percent reduction in labor.

- Revamped supply chain practices that had shortened the lead times from manufacturing to market availability from 60 days to 10 days in one instance and from six to nine months to three months in other instances.

- Creating a digital technology called Nike iD, whereby customers could go to Nike iD, design their own customized version of a product (say a pair of Free Run Flyknit shoes), view a prototype in an hour or so, have the shoes knitted to order, and get them delivered in 10 days or less.

All of Nike's competitively valuable resources and capabilities were being dynamically managed; enhancements were made as fast as ways to improve could be developed and instituted and new capabilities were being added in an effort (1) to provide customers with a better "Nike Experience" and (2) to respond faster to ongoing changes in consumer preferences and expectations. Collaborative efforts were underway in Nike's organizational units to transfer new or enhanced resources and capabilities to all seven of the company's product categories and also extend them to all of geographic regions and countries where Nike had a market presence. The goal was to mobilize Nike's resources and capabilities to produce an enduring competitive advantage over rivals and give customers the best possible experience in purchasing and using Nike products.

Manufacturing   In fiscal year 2019, Nike sourced its athletic footwear from 112 factories in 12 countries. About 93 percent of Nike's footwear was produced by independent contract manufacturers in Vietnam (49 percent), China (23 percent), and Indonesia (21 percent) but the company had manufacturing agreements with independent factories in Argentina and India, to manufacture footwear for sale primarily within those countries. Nike-branded apparel was manufactured outside of the United States by 334 independent contract manufacturers located in 36 countries; about 59 percent of the apparel production occurred in China (27 percent), Vietnam (22 percent), and Thailand (10 percent). The top five contract manufacturers accounted for approximately 49 percent of NIKE Brand apparel production.

The adidas Group

The mission of The adidas Group was to be the best sports company in the world. Headquartered in Germany, its primary businesses and brands going into 2020 consisted of:

- adidas—a designer and marketer of active sportswear, uniforms, footwear, and sports products in football, basketball, soccer, running, training, outdoor, and six other categories (91 percent of Group sales in 2019). The mission at adidas was to be the best sports brand in the world.

- Reebok—a well-known global provider of athletic footwear for multiple uses, sports and fitness apparel, and accessories (nine percent of Group sales in 2019). The mission at Reebok was to be the best fitness brand in the world.

The Group had four main objectives:

1. Grow sales significantly faster than the industry average.
2. Win additional market share across key product categories and geographic markets.

3. Substantially improve the company's profitability.

4. Increase returns to shareholders.

Exhibit 7 shows the company's financial high-lights for 2017–2019. In 2016–2017, the company divested five businesses—TaylorMade Golf, Adams Golf, Ashworth brand sports apparel, CCR Hockey, and Rockport brand shoes—to focus all of its resources on achieving faster and more profitable sales growth in both its a didas and Reebok businesses.

The company sold products in virtually every country of the world. In 2019, its extensive product offerings were marketed through thousands of third-party retailers (sporting goods chains, department stores, independent sporting goods retailer buying groups, and lifestyle retailing chains—with a combined total of 150,000 locations worldwide, and Internet retailers), 2,500 company-owned retail stores, 15,000 franchised adidas and Reebok branded stores with varying formats, adidas and Reebok e-commerce stores, and an adidas app reaching over 30 countries across all major markets that linked directly to the adidas e-commerce store.

Like Under Armour and Nike, both adidas and Reebok were actively engaged in sponsoring major sporting events, teams, and leagues and in using ath-lete endorsements to promote their products. Recent high-profile sponsorships and promotional partner-ships included numerous professional soccer and rugby teams, sports teams at the University of Miami, Arizona State University, and Texas A&M University; FIFA World Cup events; the Summer and Winter

EXHIBIT 7 Financial Highlights for The adidas Group, 2017–2019 (in millions of €)

Income Statement Data	2019	2018	2017
Net sales	€23,640	€21,915	€21,218
Gross profit	12,293	11,363	10,703
Gross profit margin	52.0%	51.8%	50.4%
Operating profit	2,660	2,360	2,070
Operating profit margin	11.3%	10.8%	9.8%
Net income	1,977	1,704	1,173
Net profit margin	8.4%	7.8%	5.5%
Balance Sheet Data			
Inventories	€ 4,805	€ 3,445	€ 3,692
Working capital	2,180	2,934	4,033
Net sales by brand			
adidas	€21,505	€19,851	€18,993
Reebok	1,748	1,687	1,843
Net sales by product			
Footwear	€13,571	€12,783	€12,427
Apparel	8,963	8,223	7,747
Equipment	1,156	910	1,044
Net sales by region			
Western Europe	€ 6,071	€ 5,885	€ 5,932
North America	5,513	4,689	4,275
Asia Pacific*	8,032	7,161	6,403
Latin America	1,660	1,634	1,907
Emerging Markets**	1,302	1,144	1,300
Russia and Commonwealth of Independent States	658	595	660

*The company redefined the countries included in the Asia Pacific Region in 2018.

**Consists mainly of countries in the Middle East and Africa.

Source: Company annual report, 2019.

Olympics; the Boston and Berlin Marathons; and the Arsenal Football Club. It was the official outfitter of items for assorted professional sports leagues and the national soccer teams of seven countries. High-profile athletes that were under contract to endorse adidas and Reebok products included NBA players James Harden, Derrick Rose, and Damian Lillard; soccer players David Beckham and Lionel Messi; NFL players Aaron Rodgers, Patrick Mahomes, and JuJu Smith-Schuster; MLB players Chase Utley, brothers B.J. and Justin Upton, Carlos Correa, Josh Harrison, and Chris Bryant; and tennis star Naomi Osaka. It had also signed non-sports celebrities Kanye West and Pharrell. In 2003, soccer star David Beckham, who had been wearing adidas products since the age of 12, signed a $160 million lifetime endorsement deal with adidas that called for an immediate payment of $80 million and subsequent payments said to be worth an average of $2 million annually for the next 40 years.[24] Adidas was anxious to sign Beckham to a lifetime deal not only to prevent Nike from trying to sign him but also because soccer was considered the world's most lucrative sport and adidas management believed that Beckham's endorsement of adidas products resulted in more sales than all of the company's other athlete endorsements combined. Companywide expenditures for marketing (advertising, event sponsorships, athlete endorsements, public relations, and point-of-sale activities) were €3.04 billion in 2019 (12.9 percent of net sales), €3.00 billion in 2018 (13.7 percent of net sales), and €2.72 billion in 2017 (12.8 percent of net sales).

In 2015–2017, adidas launched a number of initiatives to become more America-centric and regain its #2 market position lost to Under Armour in 2015. This included a campaign to sign up to 250 National Football League players and 250 Major League Baseball players over the next three years. It had secured 1,100 new retail accounts that involved prominent displays of freshly styled adidas products and newly introduced running shoes with high-tech features. The adidas brand regained its #2 position in the United States in 2017.

Research and development activities commanded considerable emphasis at The adidas Group. Management had long stressed the critical importance of innovation in improving the performance characteristics of its products. New apparel and footwear collections featuring new fabrics, colors, and the latest fashion were introduced on an ongoing basis to heighten consumer interest, as well as to provide performance enhancements—indeed, 77 percent of sales at adidas came from products launched in 2019 (versus 74 percent in 2018 and 79 percent in 2017), while only 3 percent of sales were generated by products introduced three or more years earlier; at Reebok, 67 percent of footwear sales came from products launched in both 2019 and 2018 (versus 69 percent in 2017), with only 11 percent of footwear sales being generated by products introduced three or more years earlier.

Some 1,007 people (1.8 percent of total employees) were engaged in research and development (R&D) activities in 2019; in addition, the company drew upon the services of well-regarded researchers at universities in Canada, the United States, England, and Germany. R&D expenditures in 2019 were €152 versus €153 million in 2018, €187 million in 2017, €149 million in 2016, and €139 million in 2015.

In 2019, almost 100 percent of production was outsourced to 138 independent contract manufacturers that produced in 336 manufacturing facilities; these manufacturing sites were located in China and other Asian countries (73 percent), the Americas (17 percent) and Europe, the Middle East, and Africa (9 percent). In 2019, 98 percent of the Group's production of footwear was performed in Asia (43% of total volume was sourced in Vietnam); the annual volume sourced from footwear suppliers was a record 448 million pairs in 2019, up from 409 million pairs in 2018 and 301 million pairs in 2015. In 2019, 91 percent of total apparel volume was produced in Asia, with Cambodia being the largest sourcing country (23 percent) followed by China and Vietnam with 19 percent each. In 2019, apparel production was a record 528 million units, up from 457 million units in 2018 and 364 million units in 2015. The production of hardware products was a record 127 million units in 2019, up from a range of 109 to 113 million units during 2015–2018.

The company was stepping up its investments in company-owned, robot-intensive micro-factories to speed certain products to key geographic markets in Europe and the United States much faster and to also lower production costs and boost gross profit margins. At the same time, the company had begun reengineering its existing supply chain and production processes to enable the company to respond quicker to shifts in buyer preferences, be able to reorder seasonal products and sell them to buyers within the season, and to reduce the time it took to get freshly designed products manufactured and into the marketplace.

ENDNOTES

[1] Company press release, October 25, 2016.
[2] Company press release, January 31, 2017.
[3] Ibid.
[4] Sara Germano, "Under Armour Overtakes adidas in the U.S. Sportswear Market," *Wall Street Journal,* January 8, 2015, www.wsj.com (accessed April 19, 2016).
[5] Sara Germano, "Under Armour Overtakes adidas in the U.S. Sportswear Market," *Wall Street Journal,* January 8, 2015, www.wsj.com (accessed April 19, 2016).
[6] Company press release, February 12, 2019.
[7] Company press release, February 11, 2020.
[8] Douglas A. McIntyre and Jon C. Ogg, "20 Worst CEOs in America 2017," December 26, 2017, https//247wallst.com (accessed February 22, 2017).
[9] Transcript of Quarter 4 2017 Earnings Conference Call, February 13, 2018.
[10] Under Armour's Q4 2015 Earnings Call Transcript, January 26, 2016, www.seekingalpha.com (accessed on March 30, 2016).

[11] According to the website descriptions of Under Armour products that incorporated the use of Clutch Fit® technology.
[12] Presentation by Paul Phipps, UA's Chief Technology and Digital Officer, at Under Armour's Investor Day, December 12, 2018.
[13] Dennis Green, "Kevin Durant: 'No one wants to play in Under Armour' shoes," *Business Insider,* August 30, 2017, www.businessinsider.com (accessed February 22, 2018).
[14] Nate Scott, "James Harden signs 13-year, $200 million deal with adidas after Nike opts not to match," *USA Today,* August 13, 2015, www.usatoday.com (accessed February 21, 2018).
[15] Company 10-K Reports, 2016, 2017, 2018, and 2019.
[16] Company 10-K report for 2019, p. 43.
[17] Presentation by Jason LaRose, UA's President-North America Region, at Under Armour's Investor Day, December 12, 2018.
[18] Letter to Shareholders, 2013 Annual Report.

[19] Quote attributed to market analyst Sam Poser at Susquehanna Bancshares, in a Seeking Alpha report, posted at www.seekingalpha.com/news/3573162, May 11, 2020 (accessed May 14, 2020).
[20] According to Allied Market Research, "Athletic Footwear Market—Report" published June 2016, www.alliedmarketresearch.com.
[21] Allied Market Research, "Sports Apparel Market—Report," published October 2019, www.alliedmarketresearch.com.
[22] Transcript of "Nike Investor Day 2017," October 25, 2017, posted in the Investor Relations section of www.nike.com (accessed February 24, 2018).
[23] Transcript of presentations by Nike's top executives at "Nike Investor Day 2017," October 25, 2017, posted in the Investor Relations section of www.nike.com (accessed February 24, 2018).
[24] Steve Seepersaud, "5 of the Biggest Athlete Endorsement Deals," www.askmen.com (accessed February 5, 2012).

Spotify in 2020: Can the Company Remain Competitive?

Diana R. Garza
University of the Incarnate Word

Before streaming music, many consumers may have been using file sharing services Napster, LimeWire, Pirate Bay, and other companies to download music. Using these services, cost the music industry billions each year by downloading and redistributing music (what we know as *music piracy* and, in legal terms, copyright infringement). According to the Recording Industry Association of America (RIAA), piracy of recorded music has cost the recording industry billions in lost revenues and profits (2020). It is estimated that the U.S. economy loses $12.5 billion in total output as a consequence of music theft, and approximately 71,000 jobs in the U.S. economy are lost.

Daniel Ek, one of the two founders of Spotify, has not only transformed himself in the last 14 years, his transformation is also reflective of his beloved offspring—the world's fasted growing streaming music service—*Spotify*. Ek and Spotify came to revolutionize the music industry, Daniel Ek knows well that to remain competitive, the company needs to differentiate its products and services. In the race to remain competitive, Spotify paid more than $340 million just in the past year acquiring podcast companies. Streaming services and the subscription market will continue to grow from approximately $8 billion in 2019 to over $17 billion by 2024. Spotify has entered a race where the pace is quickening with Spotify's average monthly users growing faster over the last three quarters but also other music services adding podcasts and retooling themselves to remain strong rivals.

Spotify's growth strategies include an ad-based business model allowing for both a free and paid subscription, global expansion into different markets exponentially growing its number of subscribers, multiple acquisitions that add new competencies and capabilities, and brand-name partnerships with industry leaders such as Disney, Xbox, and Samsung among others. Spotify's ongoing transformation is based on the rapid adoption of streaming music and subscription services and its leverage with smartphones, tablets, smart TVs, and high-speed internet access. As early as 2015, digital streaming became the primary revenue stream for recorded music, surpassing physical format sales of CDs.

Spotify knows its user's preferences perhaps better than subscribers themselves. The company relies on its analytical capabilities to create a competitive advantage. Through the use of analysis, machine learning algorithms, and its vast amounts of data, subscribers are presented with personalized playlists and other recommendations. The use of AI has also created value for artists allowing them to understand and visualize (through Spotify graphs) user engagement, monthly/daily listeners, metrics, and demographic details. An added advantage of using data analytics is being able to customize specific ads to different regions.

Company History

Founded in 2006, Spotify took the streaming music industry by surprise with its unprecedented growth in the last six years. Daniel Ek and Martin Lorentzon founded Spotify as a small startup in Stockholm, Sweden. Their startup music platform was in response to a growing piracy problem in the music industry. Ek and Loretzon knew there had to be a better way for artists to monetize their music and give consumers a legitimate and simpler way to listen to music. In 2008, Spotify transformed music listening when it launched its streaming service, offering listeners access to a library of music rather than making users pay for downloading albums or tracks. The music industry, which had been suffering from spending declines, resisted this new business model of offering "unlimited access," and favored the current digital download model used by Apple iTunes. Spotify began by offering its free subscription by invitation only as a way to manage growth; paid subscriptions were open to everyone. At the same time, Spotify also announced licensing deals with music labels.

In early 2009, Spotify opened its free registration tier to the public in the United Kingdom only. Due to a surge in registrations following the Spotify mobile app's release, Spotify closed its open registration in late 2009 and returned to invitation only. In 2010, Spotify integrated with Shazam to figure out who was singing a particular song and would then populate a playlist. Spotify was launched in the United States in July 2011, allowing users a six-month free ad-supported trial period to listen to unlimited music. By 2012, the trial period expired, and users were limited to ten hours of music each month and five-song replays. By March of 2012, Spotify removed all limits and introduced its free ad-supported tier.

In 2014, Spotify pushed its two-sided business model by offering a free ad-supported service to attract new users with the goal of converting them into paid subscribers. The company was able to convert 10 million users to premium subscribers from its approximately 40 million active users. At about the same time, music artist Taylor Swift pulled her music off Spotify, claiming a rapid decline in sales.

In 2017, the company announced expansion plans to move to the United States in lower Manhattan, New York City, adding approximately 1,000 jobs. In November 2018, Spotify announced a total of 13 new markets in the MENA region (the Middle East and North Africa), including a new Arabic hub and several playlists.

Spotify's success has also seen a few bumps along the way. Taylor Swift was one of the first artists to speak out against the company and its unfair compensation to artists, calling the music platform an "experiment." Three years later, the feud between Spotify and Taylor Swift ended, and the artist put

her music back on the platform. Jay Z, a hip-hop music mogul, also claimed unfair compensation to artists and launched Tidal in 2016 as his own music platform, becoming Spotify's competitor. Other artists who kept their music off Spotify included The Beatles, Adele, and Pink Floyd.

Growth Year by Year

By March of 2011, Spotify had a customer base of 1 million paid subscribers across Europe, and by the end of September of 2011, the number had doubled. By August of 2012, the company reported 15 million active users, of which 4 million were paid subscribers. By 2013, the company reported 20 million active users with one million customers in the United States. The growth for Spotify has been exponential year after year reaching 286 million users, this includes 130 million subscribers across 79 markets, with 50+ million tracks, 1 million+ podcast titles, and 4 billion+ playlists as of March 2020.

IPOs Are Too Expensive and Cumbersome

On February 28, 2018, Spotify filed a Direct Public Offering with the SEC. Barry McCarthy, Chief Financial Officer of Spotify, stated in an interview with the *Financial Times* that the company opted for a Direct Public Offering (DPO), also known as a *direct listing* instead of an IPO because "the U.S. initial public offering market is broken." A DPO is a way for companies to become public without a bank-backed initial public offering. Spotify opted for what they called a free-market approach by selling shares directly to the public without paying an underwriter. The financial benefits for Spotify were savings in underwriter fees and avoiding the IPO discount.

Growth through Acquisitions

Spotify has strengthened their competitive position through a series of targeted and timely acquisitions. Each acquisition has resulted in a stronger competitive position and new market opportunities. A list of Spotify's acquisitions between 2013 and 2020 are presented in Exhibit 1.

2014–2016. In March 2014, Spotify acquired The Echo Nest. The Echo Nest was a music intelligence and data platform for developers and media companies. The company developed and personalized music

EXHIBIT 1   Spotify's Acquisitions between 2013 and 2020

Company	Year	Company Business
Tunigo	2013	Users find, create, and share music and playlists.
The Echo Nest	2014	Music intelligence and data platform company develops music applications.
Seed Scientific	2015	Data science consulting firm
Crowd Album	2015	Company collects photos and videos of performances.
Cord Project	2016	Social messaging and sharing
Soundwave	2016	Social app focused on finding and sharing music
Preact	2016	Cloud-based service focused on helping companies acquire and retain subscribers.
Sonalytic	2017	Audio detection technology company
MIghtyTV	2017	Company provides video recommendations
MediaChain Labs	2017	Company focused on leveraging blockchain technology to solve problems with attribution.
Niland	2017	Company provides search and recommendation options for music.
Soundtrap	2017	Online Music Studio
Loudr	2018	A music licensing platform
Gimlet	2019	Podcast Network
Parcast	2019	Podcast Network
Anchor	2019	Podcast Network
SoundBetter	2019	Music and Audio production and collaboration marketplace.
The Ringer	2020	Sports and Entertainment Podcast

Source: Businesswire–https://www.businesswire.com/portal/site/home/.

applications. In June 2015, Spotify also acquired Seed Scientific, a data science consulting firm, to lead an advanced analytics unit within the company. CrowdAlbum, a startup that collected photos and videos of performances and shared them on social media, was acquired in 2016. The work created by CrowdAlbum would enhance and tighten the connection between artists and their fans. In 2016, Spotify acquired Cord Project and Soundwave, these companies focused on messaging and sharing. These acquisitions would allow users to share new music, build profiles, and message friends and followers without leaving the Spotify app. Preact was the last acquisition of 2016. Preact was acquired to find trends and behavior patterns through machine learning and analytics to grow the premium customer base.

2017. In March 2017, Spotify acquired Sonalytic. Sonalytic was an audio detection technology that identified songs, mixed content, and audio clips and tracked copyright-protected materials. This acquisition improved the company's personalized playlists and the company's publishing data system. MightyTV was a startup company focusing on video recommendations. The company was acquired and shut down. As part of the deal, MightyTV's founder and CEO Brian Adams became Spotify's VP of Technology, focusing on marketing and advertising. In the same year, Spotify acquired MediaChain, a startup that focused on leveraging blockchain technology. The goal for this company was to develop technology to connect artists and other rights holders with the tracks hosted on Spotify's service. Niland was Spotify's fourth acquisition of 2017. Niland was an A.I. company focused on providing personalized recommendations for users. SoundTrap, an online music studio startup, was Spotify's last acquisition of 2017. SoundTrap, was the maker of the freemium (paid and free) cloud-based, collaborative music podcast recording studio. Spotify's plans for the company were to assist artists by using its platform, including offering real-time streaming data through a mobile app.

2018–2019. In 2018, Spotify acquired Loudr, a music licensing platform that built products and services for content creators and digital music services to identify, track, and pay royalties to music publishers providing a more transparent and efficient music publishing industry. In 2019, Spotify acquired the podcast networks Gimlet Media and Anchor FM Inc., establishing itself as a significant player in podcasting. Gimlet added its best-in-class podcast studio, production, and advertising capabilities. Anchor added its platform of tools for podcast creators. Later that year, Spotify also acquired Parcast, a podcast that specializes in crime, mystery, and science fiction shows. Parcast added its curated library of highly produced shows and its loyal audiences. To round off the year, the company acquired SoundBetter, a music production marketplace where people in the music industry collaborate on projects and distribute music tracks for licensing. SoundBetter brought with it a strong reputation and committment to support all creators worldwide; the company joined Spotify with 180,000 registered users in 176 countries.

2020. Spotify's latest acquisition was Bill Simmon's *The Ringer* in February 2020. The Ringer was a creator of sports, entertainment, and pop culture content. The addition of *The Ringer* expanded Spotify's content offering and audience reach. This acquisition is one more example of Spotify's growth strategy.

Growth through Partnerships

Spotify's Partnerships have also strengthened the company's competitive position by expanding its market access and strategic collaborations mostly through bundling of services. A list of Spotify's partnerships between 2011 and 2020 are presented in Exhibit 2.

EXHIBIT 2   Spotify's Partnerships between 2011–2020

Company	Year	Company Collaboration Scope
Facebook	2011	Integrated into the Facebook page, users can listen simultaneously with friends.
Shazam	2011	Leading mobile discovery company
SoundHound	2011	Sound and discovery search company
Coca-Cola	2012	Global partnership to share music with consumers around the world.
Harman	2014	Premium global audio and Infotainment group.
BandPage	2014	Artists and groups engage directly with fans
Sony	2015	Added to Sony PlayStation 3 & 4 and Xperia Consoles
Starbucks	2015	Integrated into Starbucks App
Uber	2014	Riders can listen to their playlists while riding in an Uber
Adidas	2015	Integrated into the Adidas Go app where streaming music was fused with fitness metrics.
Tencent	2017	Spotify and Tencent acquired shares from each other
Microsoft	2017	Provide access to streaming music
South by Southwest	2017	Access to SXSW genre-specific curated playlists on Spotify hub
Waze	2017	Users can access Spotify playlists from Waze navigation
WNYC Studios	2017	Podcast available through Spotify
Discord	2018	Users can highlight and share music
Hulu	2018	Premium bundle of music and TV
Ellen DeGeneres	2018	Create opportunities for undiscovered talent
Samsung	2019	Spotify preinstalled in new Samsung devices
AT&T	2019	Collaboration allows AT&T Unlimited & More customers to choose Spotify Premium as an entertainment option.
Xbox	2019	Spotify can be played in the background while playing videogames
Bouygues Telecom	2019	In France, Spotify and Bouygues offered a six month free trial for customers of Bouygues.
Magalu Conecta	2019	Brazilian customers of Magalu Conecta were offered a free four-month trial of Spotify premium.
Vodafone	2019	Eligible Vodafone Australian users received a free 30-day trial of Spotify premium added to their mobile plan.
Disney	2019	Disney Playlists on Spotify aimed at boosting family memberships
ESPN	2020	Spotify created music and podcast playlists for viewers to watch after *The Last Dance* docuseries of former Chicago Bulls player Michael Jordan.
The Joe Rogan Experience	2020	Popular podcasts in diverse topics such as neuroscience, sports, comedy, health, and ever-changing culture.

Source: Various Spotify press releases. https://www.businesswire.com/portal/site/home/.

2014-2015. Spotify's partnership with Uber started in 2014. Riders were allowed to control the driver's sound system by connecting to their Spotify accounts and streaming their tunes while riding in an Uber. In 2017, Spotify considered ending its partnership with Uber after mounting scandals concerning Uber's CEO. Also, in 2014, Spotify joined forces with the musician profile service BandPage so artists and groups could engage more directly with their fans and offer concert tickets, merchandise, and VIP experiences.

In January 2015, Sony announced a new platform, PlayStation Music, a new music service with Spotify as an exclusive partner. With this partnership, Spotify was included into Sony's PlayStation 3 and PlayStation 4 gaming consoles and Sony Xperia devices. The platform was introduced in 41 markets around the world. This partnership allowed subscribers the convenience to link their accounts between PlayStation and Spotify, or sign up and subscribe.

In the same year, Spotify also partnered with Starbucks and was integrated into the Starbucks app. The Starbucks and Spotify partnership encouraged active participation among members who could create their own in-store playlists. Spotify and adidas also formed a strategic partnership to create a premium app called *Adidas go* that tracked running metrics and selected music based on running speed. At the time, the app introduced a 7-day trial period to Spotify Premium with the goal to convert runners to premium subscribers.

2017. In March 2017, Spotify partnered with South by Southwest (SXSW). Users were able to access SXSW genre-specific curated playlists on Spotify SXSW 2017 hub in "browse" on desktop and mobile devices as well as the SXSW Go App. Two more partnerships were announced in March, one with WNYC Studios and one with Waze. WNYC was the most listened to public radio station and mother station for podcasts like Radiolab, Studio 360, and Freakonomics. Waze was a navigation app that allows users to access Spotify playlists from its app. In October of the same year, Microsoft and Spotify entered into a new partnership. Microsoft ended its collaboration with Groove allowing subscribers to move their playlists and music collections to Spotify. This partnership allowed Spotify to be downloaded to Windows for P.C., including Xbox gaming consoles.

In December 2017, Spotify and China-based Tencent agreed to partner by acquiring shares from each other. Tencent operated the largest social media platform in China and provided an extensive catalog of music services to hundreds of millions of users.

2018. In April 2018, Spotify partnered with the gaming-oriented voice chat service Discord to be displayed on desktop clients. This partnership allowed users to display their currently-playing songs as a presence on their profile and invite other premium Spotify users to group "listening parties".

In April of the same year, Spotify and Hulu announced a partnership. The two companies bundled their services and offered them through a single subscription plan of $12.99-a-month bundle. This partnership was the first time Spotify partnered with streaming TV platform, and it came at a time when the company was rethinking its video offerings. With Tom Calderone, head of video and podcasts, departing the company, Spotify decided to focus on expanding video offerings on Spotify playlists. In August 2018, the company introduced an upgraded Spotify Premium for Students plan bundled with Hulu's streaming library and SHOWTIME's premium entertainment content for $4.99.

2019. A groundbreaking partnership was that of Spotify with Ellen DeGeneres in late 2019. Ellen DeGeneres is known for not only loving music but also for creating opportunities for new talent. This partnership expanded these opportunities and tapped into new markets. Also, in 2019, Spotify and Samsung announced the expansion of their collaboration. Samsung provided users with access to Spotify on Samsung mobile devices, and all new Samsung mobile devices globally would include the Spotify app preinstalled. The new devices included the Galaxy S10, S10+, S10e, S10 5G. Galaxy Fold, and select Galaxy A series. Eligible Samsung owners qualified for six months of free Spotify Premium. Following this partnership, Spotify and AT&T teamed up in a new relationship that allowed AT&T Unlimited &More Premium Wireless customers to choose Spotify Premium as their entertainment option, initially in a trial period and afterward at a rate of $9.99.

In 2019, Spotify also entered into four global partnerships; the first was with Xbox. Xbox and Spotify teamed up to deliver value in gaming and music. Spotify offered gamers in the United States and United Kingdom who joined Xbox Game Pass Ultimate or Xbox Game Pass for P.C. (Beta) for the first time a six months trial of Spotify premium. The company also entered into partnerships with French company Bouygues Telecom Broadband company; customers on mobile tariffs of > 1GB could add Spotify Premium to their existing mobile plan. A second partnership included Brazilian Magalu Conecta, a country top retailer that offered technical support, cloud storage, phone protection, and Wi-Fi spots; customers received a free four-month Spotify Premium trial. The last global partnership was with Vodafone, Australian largest mobile network; customers received a free 30-day trial of Spotify Premium.

To boost family membership, Spotify and Disney entered into a partnership that would create a Disney Hub with Disney playlists with liked soundtracks from Disney, Pixar, and Marvel movies, Star Wars instrumentals, classics, sing-alongs, and more.

2020. On May 1, 2020, Spotify, ESPN, and Netflix teamed up to curate podcasts around Netflix's *The Last Dance* docuseries of former Chicago Bulls player Michael Jordan. The partnership built on every brand's respective strengths, and for Spotify, it was on content curation and playlists. Spotify's latest partnership was with "The Joe Rogan Experience," a podcast with a loyal and engaged fanbase around the world. The podcast debuted on September 1, 2020.

The many strategic acquisitions and partnerships Spotify formed strengthen the company's competitive position as the most significant and leading music streaming global platform. Through market penetration, the company has been able to grow its number of users. Economies of scale are evident as new users and artists are added. Product development is also part of Spotify's growth strategy and can be seen in the latest acquisitions of Podcast companies.

Spotify's use of Big Data

Spotify is continuously looking for new "habits in their streaming intelligence" to learn more about how people stream. The company calls this "understanding people through music." The company's use of innovation and technology creates superior products and services to meet the growing demand of existing and potential subscribers. Spotify introduced Spotify.me, a data analytics program to capture a subscriber's listening habits. The captured data allows the company to generate content that users consider in line with their tastes, creating a unique user experience, and keeping users engaged. Spotify's

use of artificial intelligence and machine learning algorithms has been a driving force behind the company's success.

It all began in 2012 with the company's "Discover" feature, which started as a playlist of a user's favorite artists and soon became a sort of recommendation engine. In 2019, Spotify updated to "Discover Weekly," a feature that creates custom playlists unique to each listener's activity, which is curated by machine learning algorithms. The algorithm further analyzes other users' playlists to find common music themes and use that information to develop new playlists. Users also have a "taste profile" of microgenres that are used to further customize playlists. It is not only about what music users listen to, it is about the user's interaction with the song. Spotify's program is able to recognize if a user changes the track within 30 seconds giving it a thumbs down and removing it from the playlist, or, if a user adds a song to a playlist and listens to the entire song, the song is aligned with the "user's taste," a factor that helps the algorithm develop the user's overall taste profile.

Aside from "Discover Weekly," Spotify also uses a function called "Daily Mixes," these are playlists separated by genres that the user gravitated towards and includes songs the user either saved or added to a playlist, are written by the same artist, or are from new artists or albums the user does not know of yet. Spotify algorithms change the songs of these playlists as well as introduce a few extra new songs.

Not only does Spotify use analytics to understand a user's music tastes, they also use data to improve customer experiences. The data generated by consumers is used for ad campaigns and to better target consumers. The company uses what they have learned from users to develop ads that strategically target an ideal audience. The company has seen the impact of using listener data to develop ad campaigns that increase their sales and user engagement. Some examples of successful ad campaigns include a display ad in Williamsburg, New York, where the company used listening history to develop funny ads, the first ad, read "Sorry, Not Sorry Williamsburg, Bieber's hit trended highest in this zip code." This ad was displayed in a "hipster area" known for its notoriously high concentration of music snobs. Some popular campaigns included holiday ads, a set of 2018 Goal ads, and a set of "meme-inspired" ads.

As of April 2018, Spotify announced that free users would have access to explore 15 of Spotify's most popular playlists, including "RapCaviar" and "Discover Weekly." While this was great news for free users, the company had a data-driven reason behind this decision. Spotify would now generate data from the listening habits of over 124 million more users allowing for better-customized experience using data and algorithms.

Data leads the way to understand trends, and this includes the music industry. Music streaming has outranked music purchases, and the only way to understand how the public is responding to music, artists, and albums is through the use of data. Spotify understands this well and continues to focus on meeting user preferences through unique, differentiated services based on what the company has learned through user data.

Spotify's Competitors

Apple Music.   Although a newcomer, Apple music is one of Spotify's biggest rivals, with an extensive library, human-touch radio, and full integration into Apple's iOS ecosystem. Apple reached over 60 million premium subscribers worldwide as of mid-2019. The company claims to have over 60 million songs outdoing contenders such as Amazon Prime Music and Jay-Z's Tidal. With Apple Music, users can listen to local radio stations around the world, download and stream music to an Apple Watch, enjoy music in a car with CarPlay, and ask Siri (Apple's A.I.) to search for songs. Apple offers three subscriptions, a student, an individual, and a family tier. Because Apple does not have a free tier, other than its initial 3-month free trial, they have secured more exclusives with artists.

Amazon Prime Music.   Amazon Prime Music gives users access to over 60 million songs. The company has an individual, family, student plan, and a single device plan (echo or fire tv). A Prime Music subscription is free with Amazon Prime membership with access to 2 million songs, and Prime Unlimited is its paid subscription with access to up to 60 million songs.

Pandora.   Pandora is a leading music and podcast discovery platform. They are a subsidiary of Sirius XM and boast of being the largest streaming music provider in the United States with an industry-leading digital audio advertising platform. They offer their more than 70 million users a highly personalized listening experience through a proprietary Music Genome Project® and Podcast Genome Project® Technology through its mobile app. Pandora experienced a year-on-year decline in monthly active users (MAUs) between 2018 and 2019 of 8.7 percent. According to the company's quarterly financial results, Pandora has nearly 6.2 million paid subscribers, up 9.5 percent Y/Y. Pandora offers two tiers, Pandora Plus and Pandora premium with discounts for families, students, and the military. The free tier is ad-supported and asks users to view video ads, a drawback for many users.

Tidal.   Tidal is a streaming music service owned by hip-hop mogul Jay Z. Artist empowerment is a core tenant of this platform and was created in response to Spotify's perceived unfair payout to artists. The company claims to have over 60 million tracks in lossless audio quality and 250,000 videos. They offer subscribers exclusive music and videos, behind the scenes documentaries, and events including live experiences, pre-sales, and ticket giveaways. As with most companies, subscribers get a 30-day free trial. The company's subscription tiers include a premium family plan, and a student and military plan at discounted rates. The company also has HiFi subscription tiers at higher rates. The number of Tidal subscribers was not disclosed by the company.

YouTube Music.   YouTube Music is a streaming music service that allows subscribers to find albums, live performances, and remixes by searching lyrics or describing songs. Subscribers receive recommendations based on their tastes and searches. YouTube premium allows users to listen to music ad-free, offline, and while their devices' screen is locked (desktop or phone). YouTube Music has two tiers, the free ad-supported tier, and the premium music service which includes benefits like background play, ad-free music, and audio-only mode. YouTube Music is the successor to Google Play Music who decided to put its marketing emphasis on the YouTube Music platform since YouTube has billions of viewers. YouTube Music has over 20 million subscribers

Originals & Exclusives ("O&E") Content

As of June 2019, Spotify introduced a new version of its library to premium users that mixes form with functions. Users are able to get their content faster and stay up to date with podcasts on Spotify.

Podcasts can be managed in three distinct sections: episodes, downloads, and shows. The Episodes tab allows users to find or resume podcasts. The downloads tab serves as a repository for downloaded podcast episodes that users can listen to them offline. The shows tab allows for users to quickly manage podcasts they follow.

The company launched 78 Originals & Exclusives ("O&E") podcasts globally and completed its latest acquisition of The Ringer; The Ringer is a platform rich in popular sports and media podcasts. Gimlet was acquired by Spotify in early 2019; they are a Swedish digital media podcast network that focuses on narrative podcasts. The company brought with it a dedicated I.P. development team, production, and advertising capabilities. Parcast is a premier storytelling-driven podcast studio based in Los Angles, California popular for Unsolved Murders, Cult, Serial Killers, and Conspiracy podcasts. Spotify acquired Parcast in the second quarter of 2019.

Spotify now has over 1 million podcasts available on its platform, with more than 70 percent powered by Anchor. Anchor is a podcasting platform that has added its suite of tools for podcast creation, distribution, and monetization to Spotify's community of more than 200 million users. Anchor joined Spotify in early 2019 after discussions of joining forces and the similarities of their company mission statements: "to *unlock the potential of human creativity.*"

Spotify experienced a shift in listening patterns in the first quarter of 2020 due to COVID-19, but the company remained excited about its growth trajectory and adoption of podcasts at a global level. The company saw an increase of 3% from Q4'19 to Q1'20 in podcast engagement, and consumption continued to grow at triple-digit rates year after year. Spotify positioned itself to become the premier producer of podcasts and the leading platform for podcast creators.

Spotify's Web Image Matters

Spotify takes the design of their website very seriously. The company believes in *designing for belonging.* The company knows that millions of people around the globe open Spotify, so its focus is on localizing content. People in India can easily find Bollywood in India, Malay Pop in Malaysia, and Sertanejo in Brazil. While playlists may share a theme, they feature different songs in different parts of the world, so happy songs in the United States are different from those in Taiwan. Every word on Spotify is also translated into the local language(s) whenever possible. Spotify wants to "look just right" no matter where users access the app. The company spends time making sure users relate with the images, they focus on the emotional content of images, the approach to cultural sensitivities, and how they handle image localization. It is about the Spotify experience of allowing people to feel that they belong.

Music unites people and yet it is highly localized and a personal experience; therefore, Spotify's focus is on delivering a country-to-country, culture-to-culture, and person-to-person unique experience that varies but is equal in measure. A group of editors works together to minimize localization challenges. The Spotify relevance starts with translating the experience into the appropriate language(s), followed by using the same or different images based on the country. Connections are created when users open Spotify and find images that are relevant and resonate with them. For Spotify, representation matters, this could be the connection to a particular playlist and added users.

Royalties, Artist Compensation & Spotify

Spotify was created in response to protect artists from piracy and to compensate them for their work. But the road to a business model that makes sense for Labels, music producers, and recording artists has been challenging.

As of December 31, 2019, Spotify had paid more than $16 billion in royalties to labels, publishers, and collecting societies for distribution to songwriters and recording artists, an increase of 30 person from 2018. Spotify has become the biggest driver of growth in the music industry, and the biggest source of overall music revenue in many places.

Performance Royalties. Performance royalties are payments made to a songwriter or publisher for a public performance. Public performance refers to playing a song on the radio, television, in bars, nightclubs, concerts, and other public places. The Performance rights organizations collect the songwriting royalties from music users and distribute them to the legal owners. These organizations include ASCAP in North America and SACEM internationally.

Mechanical Royalties. A mechanical royalty is earned through the reproduction of a copyrighted work either in digital or physical form. The scope of mechanical reproductions covers any copyrighted audio composition that is rendered mechanically and includes: compact discs, vinyl records, tape recordings, music videos, ringtones, MIDI files, DVDs, computer games, and downloaded tracks.

By 2019, music streaming accounted for 80% of the music industry revenue and included industry leaders such as Pandora, Apple Music, Spotify, and others. The Industry Association of America reported total revenues of $5.4 billion in the first half of 2019. The increase in revenue can be traced back to more consumers signing up for subscription services and sales from downloads. Streams generate both mechanical and performance royalties.

Streaming Payouts.   Most streaming services use a "platform-centric" payout distribution model. Digital streaming providers negotiate payout rates with content owners, mainly major labels. The negotiated rate is then applied to all services revenue resulting in the total sum that the streaming service will pay to right holders. Spotify does not pay artists directly, rather they pay distribution companies and Performance Rights Organizations. Payout, however, depends on multiple factors such as how many ways the royalty is divided and in what country the stream occurred.

On average, the per-stream payout will vary depending on the types of streams the artist gets; this payout is also dependent on the artist's contracts with labels and distributors. If a stream payout is calculated at .00437, and a song has 1000 streams on Spotify, then the rights-holder(s) of the musical work will earn $4.37

Spotify.   Spotify's largest expense has been royalties paid to different companies. The company was once ranked as the worst royalty payer but increased its payments, and as of 2019, they began paying between $0.00331 and $0.00437 per stream to rights holders (Digital Music News, n.d). It has been estimated that it takes approximately 500,000 ad-supported streams to generate $100 in mechanical royalties and 180,000 premium tier streams to generate a monthly minimum wage in the United States.

Spotify for Artists and "Music for You Platform"

Supporting artists on the Spotify platform has become a focus for the company. Spotify has built a powerful suite of tools for artists to maximize their presence and help them find and connect with an audience.

The company launched "Spotify for Artists" page in 2017; it was a place where artist teams, labels, and distributors could manage their profiles, see, and analyze their data, and pitch playlists. Artists and their teams come together to make decisions about release strategies, tour schedules, and to connect with fans. Spotify Analytics was also launched for labels and distributors to access and create playlists as they support their artists. *Artist picks,* a separate tool, allows artists to know who is playing their music and where they are listening. After music is released, artists can see streams in real-time and watch their fan base grow.

Spotify's innovative ideas continue to surprise the music industry. At the end of 2019, the company announced that record companies would soon be able to pay to have their artists promoted to targeted fans within the Spotify platform via "Music For You" visual pop-up ads. The goal of the ads was to alert fans of new releases, and for Labels to manipulate which fans see what by digging into their wallets. Premium users could turn off the alerts, but free users would not have this option. Recommendations would be based on listening tastes. This paid-for promotion began as a test in the United States only. This new source of income from advertising comes from Spotify's biggest suppliers of music. Charging record companies to promote their artists on the platform increases the company's profit margin generated at the end of the year (Exhibit 3).

EXHIBIT 3   Spotify Total Monthly Active Users by Region, 2020

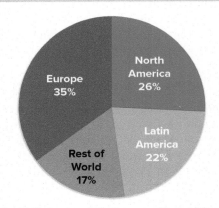

Source: Spotify Technology S.A. Announces Financial Results for First Quarter 2020. https://www.businesswire.com/news/home/20200429005216/en/Spotify-Technology-S.A.-Announces-Financial-Results-Quarter.

Spotify's Financial Performance

Despite the global uncertainty around COVID-19 in the first quarter of 2020, Spotify met or exceeded its forecast. With more than €1.8 billion in liquidity, the company remained optimistic about its underlying growth. Figure 3 shows Spotify's first quarter of 2020 growth by region. Monthly active users (MAUs) grew faster in first quarter 2020 than it did in first quarter 2019, with growth in North America showing a second consecutive quarter growth followed by Europe, Latin America, and the rest of the world. Exhibit 4 was a snapshot of the company's user and financial metrics. The decline in first quarter 2020 of MAU's was traced back to the COVID hard hit markets like Spain and Italy.

Car, Wearable, and Web platforms dropped by double digits. However, TV and game console use increased over 50 percent over the same period. Ad-supported MAUs in the United States game consoles were a top two or three platform in consumption in March and April 2020. While Car and Commute consumption had changed dramatically due to an increase of work-from-home, there was an increase in podcast listening. Two in five people surveyed in the United States stated they listened to music to manage stress, which explained the increase in podcasts related to wellness and meditation.

Monthly Active Users (MAUs). Total MAUs grew 31 percent year-over-year to 286 million between 2019 and 2020. Spotify's first quarter 2020 was the third consecutive quarter, with growth above 30 percent. North America region showed accelerated growth, with the United States being the best performer. Europe grew by 35 percent, Latin American region by 22 percent, and the Rest of the World by 17 percent–see Exhibit 4.

Premium Subscribers. At the end of first quarter2020, Spotify had 130 million premium subscribers globally; this is an increase of 31 percent Y/Y. The Spotify Family Plan was a driver for this increase. Spotify Kids, a stand-alone app designed for children, was launched in eight additional markets: Australia, the United Kingdom, Mexico, Brazil, Argentina, the United States, Canada, and France. The Duo Plan, premium plans for two people, was further introduced in three more markets: Canada, France, and Japan. This plan already existed in 23 markets (Exhibit 4).

Revenue. Total revenue of €1,848 million grew 22 percent Y/Y in first quarter 2020. Premium revenue grew 23 percent Y/Y to €1,700 million, which was in

---

EXHIBIT 4   Summary User and Financial Metrics for Spotify Technology S.A., Q1 2019, Q4 2019, and Q1 2020

USERS (M)	Q1 2019	Q4 2019	Q1 2020	% Change Y/Y	% Change Q/Q
Total Monthly Active Users ("MAUs")	217	271	286	31%	5%
Premium Subscribers	100	124	130	31%	5%
Ad-Supported MAUs	123	153	163	32%	7%
FINANCIALS					
Premium	€1,385	€1,638	€1,700	23%	4%
Ad-Supported	126	217	148	17%	(32)
Total Revenue	€1,511	€1,855	€1,848	22%	0
Gross Profit	373	474	472	27%	(1)
Gross Margin	24.7%	25.6%	25.5%	–	–
Operating (Loss) Income	€ (47)	€ (77)	€ (17)	–	–
Operating Margin	−3.1%	−4.1%	−0.9%	–	–
Net Cash Flows (used in)/from operating activities	€ 209	€ 203	€ (9)	–	–
Free Cash Flow	173	169	(21)	–	–

Source: Spotify Technology S.A. Announces Financial Results for First Quarter 2020. https://investors.spotify.com/financials/press-release-details/2020/Spotify-Technology-SA-Announces-Financial-Results-for-First-Quarter-2020/default.aspx.

EXHIBIT 5   Spotify Technology S.A. Annual Income Statements, 2015–2019
(in EUR millions, except share and per share data)

	2019	2018	2017	2016	2015
Revenue	€6,764	€5,259	€4,090	€2,952	€1,940
Cost of services	(5,042)	(3,906)	(3,241)	(2,551)	(1,714)
Gross profit	1722	1353	849	401	226
Research & development expenses	(615)	(493)	(396)	(207)	(136)
Sales & marketing expenses	(826)	(620)	(567)	(368)	(219)
General & administrative expenses	(354)	(283)	(264)	(175)	(106)
Total operating expenses	(1,795)	(1,396)	(1,227)	(750)	(461)
Operating income (loss)	(73)	(43)	(378)	(349)	(235)
Interest income	31	25	19	5	2
Finance income	275	455	118	152	36
Finance costs	(333)	(584)	(974)	(336)	(26)
Share in (losses)/earnings of associates & joint ventures	–	–	1	(2)	–
Finance income/(costs)–net	(58)	(130)	(855)	(186)	10
Profit (loss) before tax	(131)	(173)	(1,233)	(535)	(225)
Income tax (expense) benefit	55	(95)	2	4	5
Net income (loss) attributable to owners of the parent	€(186)	€(78)	€(1,235)	€(539)	€(230)
Net loss attributable to owners of the parent per share					
Basic	€(1.03)	€(0.44)	€(8.14)	€(3.63)	€(1.62)
Diluted	€(1.03)	€(0.51)	€(8.14)	€(3.63)	€(1.62)
Weighted average shares outstanding–basic	180,960,579	177,154,405	151,668,769	148,368,720	141,946,600
Weighted average shares outstanding–diluted	180,960,579	181,210,292	151,668,769	148,368,720	141,946,600
Consolidated Statement of Cash Flows Data					
Net cash flows from/(used in) operating activities	€573	€344	€179	€101	€(38)
Net cash flows used in investing activities	(218)	(22)	(435)	(827)	(67)
Net cash flows (used in)/from financing activities	(203)	92	34	916	476
Net increase/(decrease) in cash and cash equivalents	152	414	(222)	190	371
Selected Other Data (unaudited)					
EBITDA	14	(11)	(324)	(311)	(205)
Free Cash Flow	440	209	109	73	(92)
Spotify Consolidated Statement of Financial Position Data					
Cash and cash equivalents	1,065	891	477	755	597
Short term investments	692	915	1,032	830	–
Working capital	(208)	97	38	689	73
Total Assets	5,122	4,336	3,107	2,100	1,051
Convertible Notes	–	–	944	1,106	
Total Equity/(deficit) attributable to owners of the parent	2,037	2,094	238	(240)	229

Source: Spotify. Investors: Financials–Annual Report 2019 AR. https://investors.spotify.com/financials/default.aspx.

line with expectations. Ad-supported revenues grew 17 percent Y/Y but fell short of expectations, according to the company, this decline was a result of COVID-19. Ad-supported revenues of €148 million were below the company forecast by more than 20 percent. March 2020 saw several previously booked businesses cancel and buyers pulling back, leading to this decline.

Gross Margin.   Gross margin finished as 25.5 percent in quarter one, exceeding company expectations. The driver of this performance was the core royalty component due to product mix. Spotify renewed its global licensing partnership with Warner Music Group. This renewed partnership covered existing countries and a few additional ones, it was not expected that this deal would impact music economies. Premium gross margin increased to 28.3 percent in quarter one 2020 from 27.4 in quarter four 2019. Ad-supported gross margin declined to 6.6 in quarter one 2020 from 11.6 in quarter four 2019.

Operating Expenses/Income (loss). Operating expenses totaled €489 million in quarter one, an increase of 16 percent from quarter one 2019 but below expectations.

At the end of quarter one 2020, Spotify had €1.8 billion in cash, cash equivalents, restricted cash, and short-term investments on its balance sheet and no indebtedness.

In the race for market domination, Spotify has been busy hiring talent, making acquisitions and forming partnerships, and as CEO Daniel Ek stated in a Feb. 5, 2019 interview, "the company is focused on its goal of being the world's No. 1 audio platform."[1] Reid Hoffman, founder of LinkedIn and partner at Venture Capital firm Greylock Partners described Spotify's growth as "blitzscaling," a term coined by Hoffman that typically applies to young companies but as Hoffman stated, "Spotify isn't acting its age."[2]

ENDNOTES

[1] As quoted in "Why Spotify Is Still Sprinting for Maximum Market Share," *Billboard*, March 4, 2020, www.billboard.com/ articles/business/streaming/9325846/ spotify-strategy-market-share-analysis.

[2] As quoted in "Why Spotify Is Still Sprinting for Maximum Market Share," *Billboard*, March 4, 2020, www.billboard.com/ articles/business/streaming/9325846/ spotify-strategy-market-share-analysis.

Beyond Meat, Inc.

McGraw Hill **connect**

Arthur A. Thompson
The University of Alabama

Going into 2020, Beyond Meat, a producer and marketer of plant-based protein products intended as a substitute for animal-based meat products, had evolved into one of the fastest growing food companies in the United States. Company revenues had increased from $8.8 million in 2015 to $32.6 million in 2017 to $88 million in 2018 to $298 million in 2019, equal to a compound annual growth rate of 102 percent. Its portfolio of plant-based meats had expanded from just plant-based burger patties to include several varieties of Beyond Sausages, a Beyond Breakfast Sausage, one-pound packages of ground Beyond Beef, and two flavors of Beyond Beef crumbles found on the frozen meat aisle at supermarkets. The company's Beyond Chicken frozen grilled chicken strips, introduced in 2018, generated only modest customer acceptance and was quietly discontinued; however, the company immediately put a team of chefs and scientists to work on getting a better, tastier version of a Beyond Chicken product back on retail shelves and restaurant menus. In August 2019 Beyond Meat partnered with KFC, to conduct a one-day test of new "Beyond Fried Chicken" at a single Atlanta location. This taste test of what KFC advertised as "a Kentucky Fried Miracle" attracted so many customers that the store sold out of the faux chicken in less than five hours.[1] As of May 2020, Beyond Meat had not introduced a second version of its Beyond Chicken product.

Beyond Meat's brand commitment, "Eat What You Love," reflected a belief that by eating its plant-based meat offerings, consumers could enjoy more of their favorite protein dishes while helping address concerns related to human health, animal welfare, resource conservation, and climate change. As of March 31, 2020, the company's fresh and frozen plant-based protein products were being sold at some 94,000 grocery stores, restaurants, hotels, and other foodservice outlets in more than 65 countries worldwide, up from 77,000 at year-end 2019.

COMPANY BACKGROUND

Beyond Meat was founded in 2009 by Ethan Brown, and then later incorporated in Delaware in April 2011 under the name "J Green Natural Foods Co." In October 2011, the company changed its corporate name to "Savage River, Inc.," with "Beyond Meat" being its "doing business as" name. In September 2018, the corporate name was changed to "Beyond Meat, Inc." Beyond Meat's principal executive offices were located in El Segundo, California. Ethan Brown was President and Chief Executive Officer of Beyond Meat and had served in this capacity throughout all of the corporate transitions since the original company was founded. Brown grew up on a family farm in Maryland that specialized in dairy operations and became fascinated with animal agriculture, meat-raising practices, and animal protein consumption. But he also started to wrestle with a question that continued to nag him for many years to come: Do we need animals to produce meat? During the course of his business and industry career, Brown held a variety of positions in the energy business that provided him with growing familiarity about clean energy technologies, the impacts of animal meat consumption on human health, and the effects of livestock on greenhouse gas emissions, along with the related burdens on land, energy, and water.

These experiences expanded his understanding of animal meat. The key understanding he learned was that it was not necessary to limit the definition of meat to just cows, pigs, and poultry; rather, meat could just as accurately be defined in terms of its composition and structure—amino acids, lipids, trace minerals, vitamins, and water woven together in the assembly of muscle (or meat). None of these core elements of meat was exclusive to animals; they were abundant in the plant kingdom. While animals served as a bioreactor, consuming vegetation and water and using their digestive system to organize these inputs into meat, it was equally feasible to take the constituent parts of meat from plants and, together with water, organize them into the same basic architecture as animal-based meat, thereby bypassing the need for animals and the cholesterol associated with consuming animal meat.

Then, as climate change issues moved into the public spotlight, Brown became increasingly troubled by studies reporting that the livestock industry was estimated to contribute 18 to 51 percent of global greenhouse gas emissions, depending on the methodology used. And there were numerous studies in the medical journals about the adverse impacts of eating red meat on human health, which heightened his concerns about satisfying his children's protein requirements totally with animal meat. In 2009, driven by the health and environmental implications of intensive animal protein production and consumption, Brown decided to found Beyond Meat and begin the process of producing and marketing nutritious and good-tasting plant-based meat products. Brown's vision for Beyond Meat was to perfectly build a plant-based meat. Believing that there was a better way to feed the planet than by relying so heavily on animal meat, Brown's mission for Beyond Meat was "to create The Future of Protein® – delicious plant-based burgers, beef, sausage, crumbles, and more."[2] The goal was "to deliver a consumer experience that is indistinguishable from that provided by animal-based meats."[3] Brown saw four socially beneficial outcomes associated with Beyond Meat's efforts to try to shift a significant portion of the world's protein requirements from animal to plant-based meat: improving human health, positively impacting climate change, addressing global resource constraints, and improving animal welfare.

Beyond Meat's Early Successes

To begin the process of learning how to build a delicious tasting plant-based meat, Brown opened the company's first operation in a small commercial kitchen in Maryland to develop and test recipes for plant-based meat products using (1) proteins from peas, mung beans, fava beans, brown rice, and sunflower seeds, (2) various fats (cocoa butter, coconut oil, sunflower oil, and canola oil), (3) such minerals as calcium, iron, salt, and potassium chloride, and (4) beet juice extract, apple extract, and assorted other natural flavors. Ethan Brown began working extensively with two researchers at the University of Missouri's Bioengineering and Food Science Department and faculty and students in the University of Maryland's Nutrition & Food Science Department. Ultimately, the company ultimately licensed a process developed by the researchers that combined proteins from plants into a basic structure resembling animal muscle, or meat, and used this as an initial foundation for Beyond Meat products.[4] With this basic protein platform and an understanding that the balance of parts of meat, namely lipids, trace minerals, and water, were also present in abundance outside the animal, it became clear that with appropriate resources, building meat from plants was indeed possible.

The young company began selling an early plant-based product to Whole Foods Markets in the Mid-Atlantic region. It quickly discovered that traditional veggie burgers and soy-based meat had limited appeal to traditional meat eaters, who commonly criticized their inferior taste.[5] Its own market research with consumers revealed that, when choosing among plant-based meat options, taste was definitely the single most important product attribute for plant-based foods. Legacy vegetarian brands typically aimed to compensate for poor taste appeal by positioning their products as a noble sacrifice—something consumers *should* do for the benefit of their health, the environment, and/or animal welfare.

A "The Future of Protein" marketing campaign was launched in the summer of 2015.[6] The goal was to mobilize brand ambassadors to help raise brand awareness and make Beyond Meat products aspirational. A joint announcement with Leonardo DiCaprio about his becoming a Beyond Meat brand ambassador in October 2017 generated over 378 million earned media impressions, including a viral video that drew more than 8.5 million views.

Beyond Meat launched its flagship Beyond Burger in 2016 and used an unprecedented marketing approach for a vegetarian meat product.[7] Instead of marketing and merchandising The Beyond Burger to vegans and vegetarians (who represented less than five percent of the population in the United States), the company requested that the product be sold in the meat case at grocery retailers where meat-loving consumers were accustomed to shopping for center-of-plate proteins. In May 2016, the Rocky Mountain Division of Whole Foods Market became the first grocery chain to place The Beyond Burger in its meat section alongside animal-based equivalents; soon other Whole Foods Market regions followed. In April 2017, Safeway of Northern California and several Kroger divisions began to do the same. In the Southern California division of Ralph's, a Kroger subsidiary, The Beyond Burger was the number one selling packaged burger patty by unit in the meat case for the 12-week period ending August 4, 2018. Marketing personnel at Beyond Meat believed merchandising in the meat case in the retail channel had helped drive greater brand awareness with consumers.

During 2017–2019, many restaurant, hotel, and other foodservice customers choose to prominently feature the Beyond Meat/Beyond Burger name on their menu and within item descriptions, in addition to displaying Beyond Meat branded signage. Beyond Meat used its sales to foodservice businesses as a form of paid trial for its products to help drive additional retail demand and create greater brand awareness for Beyond Meat through the on-menu and in-store publicity it received.[8] Top executives believed that Beyond Meat had established its brand as one with "halo" benefits to its partners as evidenced by the speed of adoption by key partners. For example, Beyond Meat was the fastest new-product launch in the history of TGI Friday's and A&W Canada (more than 90,000 patties were sold in the first three days). In January 2018, A&W conducted concept and focus group testing to gauge consumers' appetite for The Beyond Burger. The results of the consumer testing were very positive, indicating that the concept of a plant-based burger that tasted like real meat, but without its health baggage, held strong appeal. In the taste testing, Beyond Meat's burger received high marks from surprised consumers. A&W CEO, Susan Senecal commented, "We were blown away by the flavor and taste and delicious 'burgerness' of Beyond."[9] On the strength of these results and reports from store managers that guest counts were up, A&W Canada began investing significant amounts of money across television, digital media and press to promote the addition of The Beyond Burger to its menu.

By late 2018, the Beyond Burger was being merchandised in approximately 17,000 supermarkets and retail groceries across the United States, and food service distributors were delivering the Beyond Burger to approximately 11,000 restaurant and foodservice outlets in the United States. The Beyond Burger launched in Europe in August 2018 through contracts with three major distributors, with strong expressions of interest from some of Europe's largest grocery and restaurant chains. Beyond Meat's revenues from international markets (excluding Canada) represented 13 percent of net revenues in the first half of 2019, up from 2 percent in the first half of 2018. The company expected to begin production of its plant-based products in Europe in 2020 at a new co-manufacturing facility constructed in the Netherlands by Zandbergen World's Finest Meat. In 2018, Zandbergen started distributing Beyond Meat's products throughout Europe across both foodservice and retail grocery channels. For several years, Beyond Meat had maintained a presence and generated brand awareness in Asia through a local distributor in Hong Kong. Further expansion in Asia was expected in 2020 and beyond.

Throughout 2017–18 and continuing into 2019, Beyond Meat relied primarily on its growing number of brand ambassadors (celebrities and influencers), free sampling of its products from food trucks at over 300 special events, a digital newsletter (with over 200,000 subscribers as of Sept 2018), visits to the company's website, strong social marketing, and consumer word-of-mouth as the cornerstones of a campaign to promote greater consumer awareness of the Beyond Meat brand name. As of Spring 2019, the company's website had drawn approximately 5 million visitors; the website featured packages of the company's products, provided information on where they could be purchased, highlighted nutritional facts and news about the company, and offered an assortment of recipes for using the products.

Meanwhile, Beyond Meat continued to invest heavily in research, development, and innovation—spending about 10.9 percent of net revenue of R&D in fiscal year 2019 and 6.9 percent in fiscal 2019.[10] In 2018, the company opened its state-of-the-art 30,000 square-foot Manhattan Beach Project Innovation Center as a part of its world headquarters complex in El Segundo, California. The Innovation Center included 5 laboratories, a pilot plant, and a test kitchen, staffed with a team of scientists, engineers, and cooking specialists focused on improving the company's existing products and developing new products that better replicated the sensory experience of animal meats—from the look of the package to the sizzle on grills and in skillets, and the satisfaction of eating one of the company's products. A second-version plant-based chicken product was the top new product priority following the market testing at the Atlanta KFC unit in August 2019.

As of 2018, Beyond Meat operated approximately 100,000 square feet of production space in two facilities in Columbia, Missouri, where it manufactured the woven protein that was the key ingredient of its products. This woven protein was then converted according to the company's proprietary formulas and specifications into a packaged product, either at the facilities in Columbia, Missouri, or by a network of co-manufacturers. All third-party co-manufacturers signed non-disclosure agreements to ensure that Beyond Meat's proprietary intellectual property and trade secrets were protected. Management believed that the partnering with co-manufacturers (who produced Beyond Meat products in facilities alongside their own products) was a capital efficient production model that allowed Beyond Meat to scale production more quickly and cost-effectively to supply the rapidly increasing demand for its products. Plans called for the company to continue expanding its internal production facilities domestically and abroad to produce the needed volume of woven protein while forming additional strategic relationships with co-manufacturers to complete the production of the items comprising Beyond Meat's product line.

In 2018, the United Nations officially called attention to the trailblazing accomplishments of Beyond Meat and Ethan Brown, awarding them its highest environmental accolade, "Champion of the Earth."

Beyond Meat Becomes a Public Company

Shortly after the corporate name change to Beyond Meat in September 2018, the company filed Form S-1 with the Securities and Exchange Commission in November 2018 seeking approval to conduct an initial public offering of its common stock. On May 1, 2019, the company announced (1) the pricing of its initial public offering of 9,625,000 shares of common stock at a price to the public of $25.00 per share and (2) the company's decision to grant the underwriters a 30-day option to purchase up to 1,443,750 additional shares of common stock to cover over-allotments, if any, at the initial public offering price less underwriting discounts and commissions. Beyond Meat shares began trading on the Nasdaq Global Select Market on May 2, 2019, under the ticker symbol "BYND." The opening trade for the stock was $46.00 and trading on the first day closed at $65.75, 163 percent above the IPO price. Buoyed by investor enthusiasm over the company's long-term prospects, the stock price climbed steadily higher in the ensuing weeks and months, reaching a peak of $234.90 on July 22, 2019. Various analysts estimated that the market for plant-based protein products could reach $85 billion in sales by 2030. But investor excitement and aggressive buying of Beyond Meat stock started cooling off as scrappy rival Impossible Foods announced major new grocery and restaurant chain customers for its plant-based Impossible Burger and as major meat producers Tyson Foods, Smithfield Foods, Perdue Farms, Nestlé, Hormel Foods, and Maple Leaf Foods all announced introductions of variously-formulated plant-based meat alternatives and began shipping an array of plant-based burgers, ground meat, sausage, and chicken products to their supermarket customers for display in both fresh and frozen meat sections. By late October 2019, Beyond Meat's stock price had plummeted to the low 80s and by December 2019 was trading in the mid-70s.

Exhibit 1 shows the rapid growth of Beyond Meat's quarterly revenues from 2017 forward to Q2 of 2020. Exhibit 2 shows the company's recent financial performance.

EXHIBIT 1   Beyond Meat's Quarterly Net Revenues, 2017 through Q2 2020

	2017	2018	2019	2020
Quarter 1	$ 6.2 million	$12.8 million	$ 40.2 million	$ 97.1 million
Quarter 2	$ 5.6 million	$17.4 million	$ 67.3 million	$113.3 million
Quarter 3	$ 9.4 million	$26.3 million	$ 92.0 million	
Quarter 4	$11.5 million	$31.5 million	$ 98.5 million	
Annual Total	$32.7 million	$88.0 million	$297.9 million	

Sources: Presentation at Barclay's Global Consumer Staples Conference, September 5, 2019, posted in the Investor Relations section at www.beyondmeat.com, accessed December 10, 2019; company press release, February 27, 2020; and company press release, May 5, 2020.

EXHIBIT 2   Selected Financial Data for Beyond Meat, 2016–2019 (in thousands)

	Years Ended December 31			
Selected Income Statement Data	2016	2017	2018	2019
Net Revenues	$ 16,182	$ 32,581	$ 87,934	$297,897
Cost of goods sold	22,494	34,772	70,360	198,141
Gross profit (loss)	(6,312)	(2,191)	17,574	99,756
Research and development	5,782	5,722	9,587	20,650
Selling, general, and administrative expenses	12,672	17,143	34,461	74,726
Restructuring expenses	-----	3,509	1,515	4,869
Total operating expenses	18,454	26,374	45,563	100,245
Profit (loss) from operations	(24,766)	(28,565)	(27,989)	(489)
Other income (expense), net				
Interest expense	(380)	(1,002)	(1,128)	(3,071)
Remeasurement of warrant liability			(1,120)	(12,503)
Other, net	----	(812)	352	3,629
Total other (income) expense, net	(380)	(1,814)	(1,896)	(11,945)
Loss before taxes	(25,146)	(30,379)	(29,885)	(12,434)
Income tax (benefit) expense	3	5	1	9
Net profit (loss)	$(25,149)	$(30,384)	$(29,886)	$(12,443)
Weighted average shares of common stock outstanding	6,850	8,186	6,287	42,275
Selected Balance Sheet Data				
Cash and cash equivalents	$ 16,998	$ 39,035	$ 54,271	$275,988
Inventory	6,185	8,144	30,257	81,596
Total current assets	24,499		102,826	403,594
Property, plant, and equipment, net	10,277	14,188	30,527	47,474
Total assets	34,935	66,463	133,749	451,923
Total current liabilities	5,134	12,150	25,167	47,697
Total long-term liabilities	2,570	2,032	20,136	30,792
Total stockholders' equity (deficit)	$(66,573)	$(95,913)	$(121,750)	$384,090
Selected Cash Flow Data				
Cash flows (used in) provided by operating activities	$(23,495)	$(25,273)	$ (37,721)	$ (46,995)
Capital expenditures	4,955	7,908	22,228	23,795
Net cash provided by financing activities	31,914	55,425	76,199	294,876

Sources: Beyond Meat, Form S-1, November 16, 2018, pp. F3–F8; Company 10-K Report, 2019.

BEYOND MEAT'S STRATEGY

During 2016–2019, Beyond Meat's revenue growth was driven largely by two factors: expanding its lineup of plant-based protein products and securing additional retail grocery customers to stock and merchandise its products and additional foodservice firms (chiefly restaurants) to include its Beyond Meat burgers on their menus. The company's plant-based burger patties had been its best-selling product since they were first introduced in 2016; there were two 4-ounce patties per package, and the typical retail price was about $5.99. A marbled, meatier-tasting burger patty was introduced in June 2019, replacing two earlier versions. Starting in 2020 eight-patty packages were available for $14.99. The company's second biggest seller was Beyond Sausage, introduced in 2018, which was available in two varieties, Bratwurst and Italian; four-link packages were normally priced at $8.99. Frozen Beyond Beef Crumbles, available in two flavors—Beefy and Feisty, became widely available in early 2018 and retailed for about $5.99 per 10-ounce package; these crumbles could be used in chili, tacos, spaghetti, lasagna, pizza toppings, and other recipes calling for ground meat. In mid-2019, the company introduced a one-pound plastic-sealed package of ground plant-based beef that could be used in any ground beef recipe, including chili, spaghetti sauce, meatballs, burgers, and tacos. This product was very similar in appearance to the branded one-pound ground beef packages found in the fresh meat cases at supermarkets and grocery stores. The company's Beyond Breakfast Sausage patties began hitting retail grocery shelves in March 2020. Beyond Meat's next-version plant-based chicken product was expected to be introduced sometime in 2020.

Growth Strategy

Going into 2020, Beyond Meat executives believed there was significant opportunity to expand beyond the company's current market footprint in the retail grocery and foodservice channels, both domestically and internationally. As of March 31, 2020, the company had secured 94,000 points of distribution worldwide, including 25,000 stores in the grocery channel across the United States, 34,000 foodservice outlets (chiefly restaurants), in the United States, and 18,000 outlets in the international retail grocery channel, and 17,000 international foodservice outlets. Major supermarket chains marketing Beyond Meat products in 2019–2020 included Kroger/City Market, Albertson's, Publix, Whole Foods Market, Target, Walmart, Costco, Giant, Hannaford, Stop & Shop, Safeway, Harris Teeter, Natural Grocers, Jewel-Osco, Food Lion, Ralph's, Wegmans, Sprouts Farmer's Market, The Fresh Market, Mariano's, Loblaws, and Sobeys. Restaurant and foodservice outlets offering Beyond Meat products in North America included Denny's, Dunkin Brands, Subway, Del Taco, Carl's Jr. (approximately 1,100 units),

TGI Friday's, BurgerFi, Tim Horton's, Chronic Tacos, Hello Fresh, Bareburger, WhiteSpot, A&W, Cinemark Theaters, Disney World, Marriott and Hilton hotels, and foodservice distributor Sysco. The company was aggressively developing more relationships with international partners; current customers included grocery chains Tesco (Great Britain and 6 other countries in Central Europe and Asia), Kesko (Finland), Edeka (Germany), Lidl (28 European countries), Albert (Netherlands), Coles (Australia), and Ahold Delhaize (Netherlands, Belgium, 5 other European countries, Greece, Indonesia).

McDonald's Begins Experimenting with Plant-Based Burgers Starting in 2017, McDonald's began offering McVegan® burgers, a soy-based sandwich created with Swedish vegan food company Anamma, at its restaurants in Sweden and Finland; in these two countries, vegetarianism was well entrenched, as many consumers shunned meat due to high prices and concerns about climate change. In April 2019, McDonalds introduced a Big Vegan® burger, a soy and wheat patty colored with beet juice, intended as a permanent addition to its menu offerings, at all 1,500 locations in Germany. The Big Vegan utilized a plant-based "Incredible Burger" made by Nestlé, the world's largest food and beverage company, headquartered in Switzerland.

In late September 2019, in collaboration with Beyond Meat, McDonald's began a test run of a plant-based burger called the Beyond Meat P.L.T., short for plant, lettuce, and tomato, at 28 Canada locations; McDonald's described the P.L.T. as "juicy, delicious, perfectly dressed;" it contained no artificial colors, flavors, or preservatives. Beyond Meat's CEO and Founder, Ethan Brown, said in a statement: "Being of service to McDonald's has been a central and defining goal of mine since founding Beyond Meat over a decade ago. It comes after a long and productive collaboration to make a delicious plant-based patty that fits seamlessly into McDonald's menu. . . ."[11]

In January 2020, McDonald's expanded its test run of the P.L.T. to 52 Canadian locations for a 12-week period starting January 14, 2020. Industry observers believed this more extensive market test would provide management with a clearer picture of whether the addition of a Beyond Meat plant-based burger to its menu offering would catch on sufficiently with customers to increase store traffic and drive sales growth. McDonald's announcement of the expanded test with Beyond Meat prompted management at rival Impossible Foods to discontinue efforts to persuade McDonald's to conduct a market trial of its plant-based Impossible Burger. News of the bigger test also prompted investors to bid up the price of Beyond Meat common stock by 25 percent.

In late January 2020, Denny's Corp. announced it would give away free Beyond Meat Burgers, dressed with sliced tomatoes, lettuce, onions, pickles, All-American sauce, and American cheese on a multi-grain bun, with the purchase of any beverage on January 30 from 11am to 10pm while supplies lasted. The promotion, following on the heels of a highly successful market test of the Beyond Burger in Denny's restaurants in Los Angeles, served to launch the Beyond Burger menu item nationwide at all 1,700-plus Denny's locations in the United States and Canada. Denny's announcement triggered a rush on the part of investors to purchase Beyond Meat shares, driving the stock price up another 8 percent to $129 per share.

In April 2020, Starbucks debuted a new menu in its 4,200 stores in China that included Beyond Meat's plant-based beef products in pasta and lasagna selections.

Distribution Strategy

Meat was the largest category in food. The size of the global meat category was estimated to be $1.4 trillion in 2019; the estimated size of the market for meat in the United States was $270 billion. The most common sources of meat were domesticated animal species such as cattle, pigs, poultry, and, to a lesser extent, buffaloes, sheep, and goats. In some regions of the world, other animal species such as camels, yaks, horses, ostriches and game animals, crocodiles, snakes, and lizards were also eaten as meat. Pork was the most widely eaten meat in the world accounting for roughly 36 percent of the world meat intake, followed by poultry and beef with about 35 percent and 22 percent respectively.[12]

Because the market for meat was so large, company executives saw ample room for Beyond Meat to become and remain the major disruptor in the meat category worldwide for some years to come. To achieve this role as a major disruptor and change agent in the market for meat, it was essential for Beyond Meat to sustain its efforts and successes in securing additional distribution points in the North American

and international grocery and foodservice channels in 2020 and beyond. However, because the United States had the highest level of animal meat consumption per person of any country in the world, management considered the United States as the company's core target market from a geographical standpoint and believed that over time plant-based meats could become a $35 billion food category.[13] Market research firm CFRA forecasted that the global alternative meat industry would grow to $100 billion in sales by 2030, up from about $19 billion in 2018.[14] As of October 2019, analysts had estimated that sales of plant-based meat products in the United States were only about $2.4 billion.

In the grocery channel, Beyond Meat's strategic objective was to capitalize on the company's success as the first plant-based protein offering in supermarket meat cases not only by growing the number of grocery stores carrying Beyond Meat's products but also by (1) adding more plant-based meat products to its offerings in supermarket fresh and frozen meat cases and (2) helping drive increases in the overall size of the plant-based protein category, as more consumers shifted their diets away from animal-based proteins. At the same time, it was strategically important for Beyond Meat to further disrupt the meat offerings in the restaurant channel by getting its products on more restaurant menus across an ever wider geographic area and in more dishes on these menus. This meant devoting more resources to outcompeting rival Impossible Meats and other new entrants in the plant-based meat category in convincing restaurants to use its branded products in their plant-based meat offerings rather than the brands of other makers of plant-based meats.

Growing penetration of the foodservice channel was yet another component of Beyond Meat's strategy; this channel included food distributors who supplied food products to the food operations at hospitals, schools, hotels, entertainment and hospitality vendors, country clubs, banquet facilities, sporting events, and other such venues where food was served. In 2019–20, having received significant interest from several prominent foodservice enterprises, Beyond Meat was aggressively working to expand its distribution through foodservice enterprises and food distributors in a number of different geographic locations across the world, particularly Europe, Australia, New Zealand, Israel, South Korea, Taiwan, South Africa, and parts of the Middle East.

The company had recently increased its staffing of experienced employees in sales and marketing to achieve its distribution objectives in the grocery and foodservice channels.

Shipping   Retail products sold in the grocery fresh meat sections as part of Beyond Meat's "fresh" platform, such as The Beyond Burger and Beyond Sausage, were shipped to the customer frozen. Foodservice customers were provided instructions on 'slacking,' which was typically done by moving frozen products to a refrigerator to allow them to slowly and safely thaw before being cooked. Retail grocery stores merchandising burgers and sausage in refrigerated fresh meat cases had to apply a "use by date" sticker of seven days for Beyond Sausage or ten days for The Beyond Burger. In addition to or as a substitute for their fresh meat displays of Beyond Meat products, some supermarkets and smaller groceries sold Beyond Burger patties and Beyond Sausage products in their frozen meat cases alongside various branded packages of frozen chicken and animal meat patties; this was done partly (sometimes mainly) to avoid spoilage losses of unsold products—the frozen versions required no use-by dates.

R&D Strategy

Beyond Meat had invested significant resources in building its capabilities to develop plant-based meat alternatives to popular animal-based meat products. In 2020, the company's innovation team consisted of about 40 scientists from such disciplines as chemistry, biology, materials, food science, and biophysics who collaborated with process engineers and culinary specialists in developing and testing improved versions of existing products with better taste, texture, and aroma and also discovering ways to make new plant-based meat products. New learning about taste, texture, and aroma for one product was quickly applied to the formulations of other existing product offerings and tested for use in new products under development. In addition, the innovation team devoted time and effort to exploring and testing the use of additional plant protein options, searching for ingredients that could be sourced more easily or more cheaply than current plant ingredients and that would retain and build upon the quality and appeal of current product offerings. The company sourced plant ingredients from a variety of vendors, but was heavily dependent on a single supplier, Roquette

America, for the pea protein that was the main ingredient in all of its products.[15]

Since opening the new 30,000 square foot Manhattan Beach Project Innovation Center in El Segundo, California, which was ten times the size of the company's previous lab space, Beyond Meat has increased its pipeline of products and product improvements in development and become more proficient in shortening the time it took to transition its laboratory findings, test kitchen results, and pilot plant operations into scaled production. As the company's knowledge and expertise had deepened, its pace of innovation had accelerated, allowing for reduced time between new product launches. After taking multiple years to develop the first Beyond Burger, it took less than a year to develop a second version with improved taste, texture and aroma attributes and still fewer months to develop an even better third version. Management expected that this faster pace of product introductions and meaningful enhancements to existing products would continue as ongoing R&D efforts at the Manhattan Beach Innovation Center strengthened the company's innovation capabilities.

Production Strategy

The core of Beyond Meat's production strategy was to invest in state-of-the art domestic and international production facilities and expand the capacity of these as needed to supply all of the company's requirements for woven protein, the principal ingredient of its plant-based products. Self-manufacture of woven protein allowed the company to keep the details of its manufacturing process for woven protein proprietary, thereby making it harder for rival makers of plant-based protein products to replicate the meat-like texture of Beyond Meat's products. The remainder of the manufacturing process was done by partnering with "co-manufacturers" to complete the production process in facilities they operated. While the company completed the manufacture of Beyond Burger patties that it sold to the *foodservice* channel at its production facilities in Columbia, it depended on its co-manufacturing partners to complete the production process for Beyond Burger patties sold through retail grocery channels and for all of its other products at facilities operated by the co-manufacturers. All third-party co-manufacturers signed non-disclosure agreements to ensure that Beyond Meat's proprietary intellectual property and trade secrets were protected.

In the first quarter of 2019, Beyond Meat's internal monthly production capacity was triple what it had been in the second quarter of 2018. Further increases in production capacity occurred in the remainder of 2019 and in early 2020. The company had ongoing efforts underway to evaluate and improve the company's supply chain processes for woven protein and to collaborate closely with the growing number of its co-manufacturing partners to increase manufacturing efficiencies and product quality, while reducing overall production costs.

Beyond Meat's manufacturing process for woven protein is displayed in Exhibit 3. A dry blend containing pea protein was mixed in the company's manufacturing facility in Columbia, Missouri. The dry blend then entered an extruder, where both water and steam were added. A combination of heating, cooling, and variations of pressure were used to weave together the pea protein into formed woven protein, which was used as the basis for all of the company's products.

The formed woven protein not used to produce Beyond Meat patties for foodservice customers in North America was then cut into smaller pieces to expedite the freezing process, and the frozen woven protein was shipped via third-party logistic providers to cold storage facilities or directly to production facilities operated by the company's co-manufacturers. At a co-manufacturer's production facility, thawed woven protein was further processed by adding other ingredients and flavorings, after which the final product was packaged and then shipped frozen to retail grocery stores and foodservice distributors. To control the quality of its products throughout the production process, the company utilized a type of Six Sigma quality control process called DMAIC (short for "define, measure, analyze, improve and control") that served to "improve, optimize, and stabilize" its product formulation and production processes. In-process quality checks were performed throughout the manufacturing process, including temperature, physical dimension, and weight. Specific instructions were provided to foodservice vendors and restaurants for storing and cooking the company's products. Cooking instructions for frozen Beyond Beef Crumbles, which were intended to be prepared from their frozen state, were on the packaging.

Supply Chain Practices

Raw Material Procurement Beyond Meat's products had about 20 ingredients (the Beyond Beef burger had 22)—these included pea protein isolate, canola oil, coconut oil, amino acids, lipids, trace minerals, vitamins, salt, methylcellulose (a binding agent), and assorted flavorings. The company procured raw materials for woven protein that were readily available from a number of different suppliers, except for pea protein, which in the United States as of 2018 was available only from a single supplier. A second supplier in Canada supplied yellow peas for Beyond Beef Crumbles.

All flavorings in the company's products were developed at the company's Innovation Center in collaboration with the suppliers chosen to produce the flavors, and all these flavorings were produced *exclusively* for use by Beyond Meat. Flavoring ingredients considered for use were qualified through trials at Beyond Meat's Innovation Center to ensure manufacturability. The Innovation Center staff, using only ingredients deemed manufacturable, created a

EXHIBIT 3   Beyond Meat's Manufacturing Process

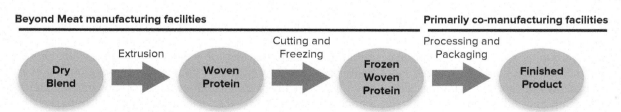

Beyond Meat manufacturing facilities   **Primarily co-manufacturing facilities**

Dry Blend → *Extrusion* → Woven Protein → *Cutting and Freezing* → Frozen Woven Protein → *Processing and Packaging* → Finished Product

Source: Beyond Meat, Form S-1, November 16, 2018, p. 92.

number of alternative formulas for each of the flavors being considered for use in one or more products. Each formula was extensively tested to identify the specific flavoring formula and the specific combination of flavorings that best impacted the final product's taste, texture, and appearance. While supplies of each ingredient in a flavoring were obtained directly by the supplier producing a specific flavoring for Beyond Meat, as new ingredient shipments arrived at a flavoring supplier's production facilities, the supplier was required to submit a Certificate of Analysis to Beyond Meat to confirm that the ingredient quality and flavoring formula used in production runs met the quality control standards previously established at the Innovation Center.

Shipping   Retail products sold in grocery store meat cases as part of Beyond Meat's "fresh" platform, such as The Beyond Burger and Beyond Sausage, were shipped to the customer frozen. Retail grocery stores merchandising burgers and sausage in refrigerated fresh meat cases as part of Beyond Meat's "fresh" platform had to apply a "use by date" sticker of seven days for Beyond Sausage or ten days for The Beyond Burger; at the end of the use-by date, unsold packages in fresh meat cases had to be discarded. In addition to or as a substitute for their fresh meat displays of Beyond Meat products, some supermarkets and smaller groceries kept incoming shipments of frozen Beyond Burger patties and Beyond Sausage products in a frozen state and placed the packages in their frozen meat cases alongside various branded packages of frozen chicken and animal meat patties; this was done partly (often mainly) to avoid spoilage losses of fresh products—the frozen versions required no use-by dates.

Foodservice customers receiving shipments of frozen Beyond Meat products were provided instructions on 'slacking,' which was typically done by moving frozen packages to a refrigerator to allow them to slowly and safely thaw before cooking.

Supplier Selection Practices   Beyond Meat did not have long-term supply agreements with most of its suppliers; this included raw materials suppliers, suppliers making flavorings, and co-manufacturers. Most all supplies of raw materials, flavorings, and final products produced and shipped by co-manufacturers were obtained on a purchase order basis. Because most of the ingredients used in its flavorings were readily available in the market from many suppliers, the company believed it could obtain needed supplies from other vendors in the event of supply interruptions from the ingredient vendors it typically used. It was the company's practice to maintain a 20-week supply of flavoring ingredients that would ultimately be shipped to producers of its flavorings.[16]

Packaging supplies were sourced in the United States with the exception of the Beyond Sausage tray which was sourced from China. The company maintained approximately 10 weeks of inventory of sausage trays to mitigate the risk of supply interruptions. The trays used for burgers sold through grocery channels were slotted for two 4-ounce patties. Packaging specifications for all products were clearly defined and provided to all packaging suppliers.

HEALTH AND ENVIRONMENTAL IMPACTS OF ANIMAL-BASED MEAT CONSUMPTION

Consumer interest in plant-based proteins, particularly among millennials and younger generations, had been driven in part by growing awareness of the health and environmental impact of animal-based meat consumption. The Internet and social media channels provided consumers with easy access to voluminous amounts of information about nutrition, the pros and cons of eating various food products, climate change, resource scarcity, and the assortment of health and environmental issues surrounding the consumption of animal meats. Management at Beyond Meat expected heightened global awareness of and concerns about these issues to have a positive impact on consumer demand for the company's products.

Health Impacts

The negative impact on health caused by certain meats has been well publicized in recent years. In 2004, the World Health Organization highlighted a paper indicating that dietary factors, including consumption of certain meats, accounted for at least 30 percent of most cancers in developed countries and up to 20 percent in developing countries. The WHO had since added processed meats such as hot dogs, ham, bacon, and sausage to its Group 1 category of carcinogens. A similar conclusion was presented at the American Heart Association, where researchers conducting a 2017 dietary study of over 15,000 adults between 2003 and 2013 highlighted that people who ate mostly a plant-based diet were associated with a 42 percent reduced risk of developing heart failure. Additionally, animals and livestock were also susceptible to various diseases such as Mad Cow (beef), Swine Flu (pork), and Avian Influenza (poultry) that may cause further health risks from consuming potentially infected animal meats. As an example of the nutritional benefits of plant-based meats, Beyond Breakfast Sausage patties had 11 grams of protein per serving with 50 percent less total fat, 35 percent less saturated fat and sodium, and 33 percent fewer calories than a leading brand of pork sausage patties, plus it was made without any genetically modified ingredients, soy, gluten, or artificially produced ingredients.

Climate Impacts

A number of research studies had indicated that the global livestock industry was responsible for about one-third of global methane emissions, with animal manure accounting for perhaps 10 percent of global nitrous oxide (carbon dioxide) emissions. According to a series of reports by the Intergovernmental Panel on Climate Control (an intergovernmental body of the United Nations which periodically compiles comprehensive "assessment reports" of published studies concerning climate change, its causes, potential impacts, and response options), there was mounting consensus among climate scientists that greenhouse gas emissions were likely to cause "severe, widespread, and irreversible impacts" on the natural environment unless carbon emissions were rapidly and sharply reduced.[17] Several studies had concluded that behavioral changes, including such dietary changes as eating less animal meat, could have a significant role in cutting carbon emissions.

Environmental Impacts

According to the Food and Agricultural Organization (FAO) of the United Nations, rising global meat consumption and livestock production had adverse impacts on the world's land and water resources.[18] According to the FAO, livestock-raising activities occupied 30 percent of the planet's land surface and accounted for 78 percent of all agricultural land use.[19] A report by the World Resources Institute (WRI) indicated that 29 percent of agriculture-related water use was directly or indirectly used for animal production.[20] The WRI also concluded that meat consumption was environmentally burdensome from the standpoint of production inputs. According to the same WRI report, beef was highly inefficient to produce because only 1 percent of the feed consumed by cattle was converted to calories that people consumed from eating beef, while pork converted approximately 10 percent and poultry converted approximately 11 percent of their feed to human-edible calories. During 2017 and 2018, Beyond Meat engaged the University of Michigan to conduct a peer-reviewed, third-party-led Life Cycle Assessment comparing the environmental impacts associated with producing a quarter-pound Beyond Burger versus a quarter-pound, standard 80 percent lean/20 percent fat beef burger.[21] The study showed that compared to the beef burger, The Beyond Burger generated 90 percent less greenhouse gas emissions, required 46 percent less energy, had 99 percent less impact on water scarcity, and 93 percent less impact on land use.

Animal Welfare

Worldwide, it was estimated in 2017 that about 60–70 billion farm animals were produced for food annually; with two out of every three being factory farmed.[22] Over the past decade, animal welfare groups had publicized a range of investigations highlighting the issues related to safety, welfare, and well-being of animals caused by mass livestock production, which Beyond Meat's management believed had prompted a consumer shift toward more plant-based alternatives.

COMPETITORS

Beyond Meat operated in a highly competitive environment that included both animal protein suppliers and plant-based meat suppliers. In North America, the leading suppliers of fresh meats (beef, pork, and poultry) and assorted branded meat products included:

• The world's largest meat supplier, JBS, a company headquartered in Brazil whose meat portfolio consisted of Swift® beef and pork products, 19 brands of fresh beef and hamburger, Butterball® brand turkey, and Pilgrim's Pride® chicken.

- Tyson Foods, a global supplier of meats with 2019 sales of more than $42 billion and a meat portfolio that consisted of Tyson® fresh and frozen chicken products, fresh beef and pork, and such meat brands as Jimmy Dean®, Hillshire Farms®, Ball Park®, Wright®, Aidells®, IBP®, and State Fair®. Tyson's plant-based meat brand, Raised & Rooted, was available in 7,000 stores as of November 2019. As of early 2020, Tyson's Raised & Rooted product line consisted of (1) frozen Nuggets—a battered chicken-like dish made of pea protein, bamboo fiber, egg whites, and golden flaxseed and (2) The Blend—burgers patties blended with Angus Beef, pea protein, dried egg white solids, and assorted flavorings and seasonings that were displayed in grocery fresh meat cases.

- China-based WH Group, whose North American brands included Smithfield pork products, Eckrich®, Nathan's®, Farmland®, John Morrell®, Armour®, Gwaltney®, and Cook's® hams. Farmland was marketing its plant-based meat under the Pure® brand.

- Cargill, one of the world's biggest global suppliers of fresh beef and poultry products with 2019 sales of over $113 billion. In April 2020, Cargill announced it would begin selling a complete line of plant-based meat products, including hamburger patties and ground meat. Shortly thereafter, three KFC restaurants in China conducted a three-day test of a plant-based fried chicken nugget supplied by Cargill.

- Hormel, a well-known company with 2019 sales of $9.5 billion, whose meat brands included Hormel® bacon and chili, Applegate® (bacon, breakfast and dinner sausage, chicken burgers and strips, hot dogs, frozen beef and turkey burgers), Jennie-O® turkey, and Columbus® deli meats.

- Maple Leaf Foods, a Canadian consumer packaged meat company with 2019 sales of about $3.5 billion, whose brands included Maple Leaf, Maple Leaf Prime, Schneiders, Greenfield, Swift, Field Roast Grain Meat, and Lightlife. Field Roast and Lightlife specialized in plant-based meat substitutes. Field Roast's product offerings were largely made of wheat and other grains; the main ingredients in Lightlife's plant-based burger patties

and ground meat were pea protein, coconut oil, and beet powder. Lightlife's other products were plant-based chicken nuggets (a menu offering at all A&W locations in Canada), chicken tenders, hot dogs, bacon, sausages, and tempeh.

There were significant variations among the various commonly available types of beef burger products regarding calorie count, total fat grams, saturated fat grams, protein grams, cholesterol, milligrams of sodium, carbohydrates, dietary fiber, and other nutritional measures—see Exhibit 4.

In addition to the above animal-protein companies, Beyond Meat confronted competition from a number of plant-based protein brands, including Kroger's Simple Truth brand of plant-based products, Impossible Foods, Boca Foods, Field Roast Grain Meat Co., Gardein, Lightlife, Morningstar Farms, and Tofurky. The products of these companies were commonly available throughout the supermarket and grocery store channel, including most national and regional supermarket chains, specialty grocer Trader Joe's, such natural foods and health food chains as Whole Foods, Natural Grocers, Sprouts Farmer Markets, Fresh Market, and Earth Fare, plus thousands of mostly local natural/health food stores.

The different brands of plant-based meat products used soy protein or pea protein or potato protein or wheat protein, or other grains as the main ingredient; lesser ingredients could include coconut oil, sunflower oil, canola oil, or some other type of vegetable oil, binding agents (food starch, potato starch, methylcellulose, xanthan gum), yeast extract, maltodextrin, beet juice extract, salt, water, and a varying assortment of spices, vitamins (C, B6, B12, niacin, thiamin, riboflavin), minerals (potassium, iron, zinc, calcium, phosphorus), and natural flavorings. There were sometimes significant variations from brand-to-brand and product-to-product regarding calorie count, total fat grams, saturated fat grams, protein grams, cholesterol, milligrams of sodium, carbohydrates, dietary fiber, and other nutritional measures— see Exhibit 5, Most plant-based meats had protein levels comparable to their animal counterparts, but had lower cholesterol, less saturated fat, higher dietary fiber, and no antibiotics or hormones. Both 4-ounce plant burger patties and 4-ounce animal burger patties typically contained about 20 grams of protein.

EXHIBIT 4   Comparative Nutrition Facts for Selected Brands of Animal Beef Burger Patties, February 2020

Grain Fed Beef 80% Lean		Grain Fed Beef 93% Lean		Ground Bison 90% Lean		Grass Fed Beef 85% Lean	
Amount per 4-oz. serving		Amount per 4-oz. serving		Amount per 4-oz. serving		Amount per 4-oz. serving	
Calories	350	Calories	170	Calories	190	Calories	240
Calories from fat	240	Calories from fat	70	Calories from fat	100	Calories from fat	150
	% of Daily Value		% of Daily Value		% of Daily Value		% of Daily Value
Total fat 27g	42%	Total fat 8%	12%	Total fat 11g	17%	Total fat 17g	26%
Saturated fat 10g	52%	Saturated fat 3.5g	17%	Saturated fat 4g	20%	Saturated fat 7g	33%
Trans fat 0g	0%	Trans fat 0g	0%	Trans fat 0g	0%	Trans fat 1g	---
Cholesterol 95mg	32%	Cholesterol 70mg	24%	Cholesterol 50mg	17%	Cholesterol 75mg	26%
Sodium 90mg	4%	Sodium 75mg	3%	Sodium 60mg	3%	Sodium 75mg	3%
Total Carbohydrate 0g	0%	Total Carbohydrate 0g	0%	Total Carbohydrate 0g	0%	Total Carbohydrate 0g	0%
Dietary fiber 0g	0%	Dietary fiber 0g	0%	Dietary fiber 0g	0%	Dietary fiber 0g	0%
Sugars 0g	0%	Sugars		Sugars 0g	0%	Sugars 0g	0%
Protein 23g	46%	Protein 24g	48%	Protein 23g	46%	Protein 21g	42%
Vitamin A	0%	Vitamin A	0%	Vitamin A	0%	Vitamin A	0%
Vitamin C	0%	Vitamin C	0%	Vitamin C	0%	Vitamin C	0%
Calcium	2%	Calcium	2%	Calcium	0%	Calcium	2%
Iron	15%	Iron	15%	Iron	10%	Iron	15%

Source: Brand labels.

Competition revolved around a host of factors:

- Taste, meat-like appearance, and texture
- Ingredients (being gluten-free and avoiding use of genetically modified ingredients) and nutritional profile (protein, carbohydrates, sugar, and fiber)
- Distribution capabilities (being able to secure a strong presence in both the retail grocery channel and the restaurant/foodservice channels, including favorable shelf and display locations in the grocery channel and menu offerings in the restaurant/foodservice channel
- Breadth of product offerings
- Competitive production costs and product prices
- Brand awareness and customer loyalty.
- Advertising/media spending
- Ability to secure intellectual property protection on products (to aid in blocking rivals' efforts to produce and market copycat products)

While Beyond Meat and other companies offering plant-based meat products were alert to all of these competitive elements, most all companies in the animal meat sector had substantially greater financial resources, more comprehensive product lines, broader market presence, longer standing relationships with distributors and suppliers, longer operating histories, greater production and distribution capabilities, stronger brand recognition, and greater marketing resources than any plant-based meat company.

EXHIBIT 5 Comparative Nutrition Facts for Selected Brands of Plant-Based Burger Patties, February 2020

Beyond Meat		Impossible Foods		Pure Foods		Kroger Simple Truth	
Amount per 4-oz. serving		Amount per 4-oz. serving		Amount per 4-oz. serving		Amount per 4-oz. serving	
Calories	250	Calories	250	Calories	240	Calories	230
Calories from fat	160	Calories from fat	160	Calories from fat		Calories from fat	160
	% of Daily Value		% of Daily Value		% of Daily Value		% of Daily Value
Total fat 18g	28%	Total fat	28%	Total fat 18g	24%	Total fat 14g	16%
Saturated fat 6g	30%	Saturated fat 6g	30%	Saturated fat 12g	60%	Saturated fat 9g	45%
Trans fat 0g	0%	Trans fat 0g	0%	Trans fat 0g	0%	Trans fat 0g	0%
Cholesterol 0mg	0%	Cholesterol 0mg	0%	Cholesterol 0mg	0%	Cholesterol 0mg	0%
Sodium 390mg	16%	Sodium 390mg	16%	Sodium 600mg	26%	Sodium 390mg	17%
Total Carbohydrate 3g	1%	Total Carbohydrate 3g		Total Carbohydrate 8g	2%	Total Carbohydrate 6g	2%
Dietary fiber 2g	8%	Dietary fiber 2g		Dietary fiber 2g	8	Dietary fiber 0g	0%
Sugars 0g		Sugars		Sugars 0g	0%	Sugars 0g	0%
Protein 20g	40%	Protein		Protein 14g	26%	Protein 20g	26%
Vitamin A	0%	Vitamin A		Vitamin D 0mcg	0%	Vitamin A	
Vitamin C	0%	Vitamin C		Potassium 374mg	8%	Potassium 136mg	2%
Calcium	8%	Calcium		Calcium 192mg	16%	Calcium 41mg	
Iron	25%	Iron		Iron 2mg	12%	Iron6 mg	35%

Source: Brand labels.

Kroger's Simple Truth Product Line. In January 2020, Kroger—one of the world's largest foot retailers with 2019 sales of about $125 billion—announced the launch of its Simple Truth® Emerge™: Plant Based Fresh Meats. Kroger's Simple Truth brand was the best-selling brand in the natural and organic foods category, and its Emerge-branded entry into plant-based meats was aimed at offering its 11 million daily customers fresh burger patties and grinds at more affordable prices.[23] Emerge patties and grinds contained 20 grams of pea-based protein per serving, and packages were located in the refrigerated meat cases alongside other plant-based and animal meat brands. Going into 2020, Kroger operated almost 2,800 supermarkets in 35 states 'under such brands as Kroger, City Market, Fred Meyer, Harris Teeter, King Soupers, Ralph's, Roundy's, Pick'n Save, Metro Market, and Mariano's Fresh Market. Kroger also operated 36 food manufacturing plants, principally to produce its private-label products.

Kroger anticipated that consumer interest in plant-based products would continue to grow in 2020 and beyond. The entire Simple Truth portfolio already included more than 1,550 natural and organic products and were located throughout Kroger grocery aisles, with new items launching monthly. Kroger expected to launch 50 additional Simple Truth plant based products in 2020 to grow sales of its Simple Truth brand, which exceeded $2.3 billion in sales in 2019.

Analysts expected that Kroger's entry into the plant-based meat segment would likely stimulate Whole Foods, Trader Joe's, and other major supermarket chains to follow Kroger's lead and introduce their own private label brands of plant-based meat alternatives.

Impossible Foods. Founded in 2011 by current CEO Pat Brown, Impossible Foods had an ambitious mission: "To drastically reduce humanity's destructive impact on the global environment by completely replacing the use of animals as a food production technology."[24] The company hoped to accomplish this mission within two decades by creating the world's most delicious, nutritious, affordable and sustainable meat, fish, and dairy foods directly from plants.

Going into 2020, Impossible Foods, whose main product was the Impossible Burger, had gained brand awareness by convincing some 15,000 restaurants to put its Impossible Burger on their menus, and by recently securing distribution of its burgers and crumbles in growing numbers of supermarkets, grocery stores, and natural food stores. In August 2019, after running market tests in several units, Burger King added the Impossible Whopper to its menu offering at all of its 7,200 Burger King locations in the United States and was featuring the Impossible Whopper in some of its national TV ads (including ads run during NFL games). The Impossible Whopper included everything that came on a regular Whopper: a quarter-pound patty, tomatoes, lettuce, mayonnaise, ketchup, pickles, and white onions on a sesame seed bun. Instead of a flame-grilled beef patty, the Impossible Whopper had a flame-grilled Impossible Burger patty consisting principally of a unique ingredient called soy leghemoglobin that made Impossible burgers taste so meat-like. Leghemoglobin was a protein found in many plants and it carried an iron-rich molecule called heme that during the cooking process caused the Impossible Burger to "bleed" and take on the product's signature blood-red color. The patties that Impossible Foods supplied to Burger King were based on the company's new 2.0 formulation that was announced in January 2019.[25] Among other upgrades, this formulation worked well in restaurant environments because version 2.0 burgers held up well in hot holding trays and could withstand the 6-inch drop at the end of Burger King's conveyor that grilled the patty for exactly 2 minutes , 35 seconds at 630 degrees Fahrenheit. The Impossible Whopper was usually priced $1 more than the regular Whopper.

In January 2020 Burger King introduced a new Impossible Sausage Croissan'wich to its breakfast menu offerings at 139 Burger King restaurants in five test locations: Savannah, Georgia; Lansing, Michigan; Springfield, Illinois; Albuquerque, New Mexico; and Montgomery, Alabama.[26] The croissan'wich featured an egg, cheese, and Impossible Sausage patty sandwiched in a toasted croissant. A raw two-ounce serving of Impossible Sausage had 7g protein, 1.69mg iron, 0mg cholesterol, 9g total fat, 4g saturated fat, and 130 calories. It was also gluten-free and designed to be both halal and kosher. Concurrent with Burger King's announcement, Impossible Foods announced its official launch of Impossible Sausage for distribution through retail grocery and foodservice/restaurants channels. In 2019, Impossible Foods had collaborated with Little Caesar's to test its new Impossible Pork product as a pizza topping. Impossible Pork was suitable for use in a wider assortment of applications and recipes for ground pork as compared to Impossible Sausage. Pork was especially popular in China, making Impossible Pork an important product for the company's global expansion. Like the Impossible Burger, both Impossible Pork and Impossible Sausage used soy leghemoglobin, a plant-based protein carrying the heme iron molecule that produced the bleeding effect, as their main ingredient. Both products were gluten free, had no animal hormones or antibiotics, and were designed for halal and kosher certification.

While burgers were an iconic part of the American diet, the founder and CEO of Impossible Foods, Pat Brown, believed that within a couple of years his company would conquer the biggest challenge in the alternative meat marketplace—plant-based steaks and that fast casual steak chains like Outback or Texas Roadhouse would put them on their menus. He thought the R&D efforts the company had put into the Impossible Burger had prepared it for the challenge, boldly stating in 2019 "I can say, with complete confidence, that we're going to nail it and not only make a great steak, but we're going to make a steak that's as good as anything that ever fell out of a cow."[27] Many observers and plant-based meat experts, familiar with plant-based proteins and the speed with which product R&D was accelerating, agreed with Pat Brown. According to Bruce Friedrich, executive director of the Good Food Institute, which championed plant- and cell-based meats, "Once we have products that taste the same or better and that cost less, plant-based and clean meat will simply take over."[28]

In early March 2020, Impossible Foods announced a 15 percent price cut on its plant-based products, and requested that its foodservice distributors pass the price cuts on to their restaurant customers. Impossible Foods CEO Patrick Brown said:[29]

Our stated goal since the founding of the company has always been to drive down prices through economies of scale, reach price parity and then undercut the price of conventional ground beef from cows.

Morningstar Farms Morningstar Farms was a division of Kellogg that produced vegetarian foods; its product line in 2020 consisted of 49 items that included veggie bacon strips, 5 varieties of breakfast sausage, 2 varieties of vegan burgers (made with 10 vegetables, grains, and seeds, with 9 grams of protein), 12 varieties of veggie burgers, 3 varieties of crumbles, vegetarian buffalo wings and parmesan garlic wings, vegetarian chicken strips, vegetarian hot dogs and corn dogs, vegetarian chicken nuggets and BBQ chicken nuggets, and 2 varieties of vegetarian chicken burgers. All products sold to the grocery channel were frozen and displayed in grocery freezer cases. Morningstar sold 26 of its products in the foodservice channel.

Until 2020, one key difference between Morningstar and the other plant-based meat brands was that most Morningstar products had egg ingredients and thus did not qualify as vegan. But in 2019 management decided to discontinue production and marketing of Morningstar egg products, abandon use of egg ingredients, and begin phasing in new vegan versions of the company's entire lineup of vegetarian products. By the end of 2020, Morningstar planned to have completed the process of transitioning all the products it sold through the retail grocery and food-service channels to vegan.

Field Roast Grain Meat Co. Since its founding in 1997 as a privately-owned company, Field Roast had been a pioneer in the plant-based industry by creating flavorful, high-quality products using fresh whole-food ingredients—grains, vegetables, legumes, and spices—to craft artisanal plant-based meats and cheeses. Its best-selling products were sausages (three varieties—apple sage, chipotle, and Italian), frankfurters, corn dogs, and Chao cheese slices, but its product line also included breakfast sausages, vegetarian deli meats, vegan field burgers, roasts (three varieties), breaded cutlets, and Fruffalo wings (apple sage sausage cut on the bias, battered and lightly fried, with buffalo sauce). Its newest product was bratwurst, which, like Field Roast sausages, came four to a package. All of the meat products were high in protein because wheat gluten was a principal ingredient. Wheat gluten was wheat flour with all the starches removed—removing the starches left pure wheat protein. Field Roast meats were soy-free and contained no GMOs. The company's products were available in most supermarket chains, medium and large natural foods stores, and a few online food retailers in both the United States and Canada.

Except for its three varieties of roasts which were displayed in grocery freezer sections, Field Roast meat products were located in the refrigerated section of grocery stores and had a "use-by" date. However, their freshness could be extended by freezing them for up to a year; once thawed, they were good for about 65 days.

Field Roast was acquired by Maple Leaf Foods in 2018.

ENDNOTES

••••

1 John Fingus, "KFC's plant-based 'chicken' sold out in five hours," posted at https://www.engadget.com/2019/08/27/kfc-beyond-fried-chicken-popular/ (accessed December 9, 2019).

2 As posted on www.beyondmeat.com (accessed December 9, 2019).

3 Beyond Meat, Form S-1, November 16, 2018, p. 82.

4 Ibid., p. 83.

5 Ibid., p. 81.

6 Ibid., p. 82.

7 Ibid., pp. 81–82.

8 Ibid., p. 82.

9 Ibid., p. 91.

10 Presentation at Barclay's Global Consumer Staples Conference, September 5, 2019, posted in the Investor Relations section at www.beyondmeat.com (accessed December 10, 2019) and Company 10-K report for 2019.

11 Jemima Webber, "McDonald's and Beyond Meat Launch Vegan 'P.L.T.' Burger," posted at https://www.livekindly.co/mcdonalds-vegan-beyond-meat-burgers/, September 26, 2019 (accessed December 30, 2019).

12 Food and Agriculture Organization of the United Nations, "Sources of Meat," http://www.fao.org/ag/againfo/themes/en/meat/backgr_sources.html (accessed January 9, 2020).

13 Beyond Meat, Form S-1, November 16, 2018, p.84.

14 Tonya Garcia, "Beyond Meat, Tyson's Raised & Rooted and other plant-based foods are officially mainstream," www.marketwatch.com, January 10, 2020 (accessed January 11, 2020).

15 Ibid., pp. 15, 71, 92.

16 Ibid., p. 92.

17 Ibid., p. 85.

18 Ibid., pp. 85–86.

19 Ibid., p. 86.

20 Ibid.

21 Ibid.

22 Ibid.

23 Company press release, January 8, 2020.

24 Posted at www.impossiblefoods.com (accessed January 2, 2020).

25 Brian Cooley, "National rollout of Burger King's Impossible Whopper is here," posted at www.cnet.com, September 1, 2019 (accessed December 30, 2019).

26 As reported in Nicole Lee, "Impossible Sausage to be in Burger King's breakfast croissants," www.engadget.com, January 6, 2020 (accessed January 9, 2020).

27 Cooley, "National rollout of Burger King's Impossible Whopper is here."

28 Ibid.

29 Company press release, March 3, 2020.

Netflix's 2020 Strategy for Battling Rivals in the Global Market for Streamed Video Subscribers

Mc Graw Hill connect

Arthur A. Thompson

The University of Alabama

Heading into 2020, Netflix was demonstrating significant competitive muscle in attracting millions of new subscribers across the world to its service for streamed internet content, despite the entry of formidable new competitors in 2019 and announcements of more to come in 2020. Netflix grew its paid membership base from 139.3 million at year-end 2018 to 167.1 million worldwide at year-end 2019; it expected to add another 7 million new paid subscribers in the first quarter of 2020. Netflix was addressing the growing competition in the global market for streamed entertainment content by increasing its releases of new original content and strengthening efforts to grow its user base in high-opportunity country markets.

Over the past nine years, the company had successfully transformed its business model from one where subscribers paid a monthly fee to receive an unlimited number of DVDs each month (delivered and returned by mail with one to three titles out at a time) to a model where subscribers paid a monthly fee to watch an unlimited number of movies and TV episodes streamed over the Internet. During the same time frame, Netflix had expanded its geographic coverage to over 190 countries, making it the world's leading Internet television network. During the past five years, Netflix had made another adjustment in its business model, shifting from a content library consisting mainly of titles licensed from the movie studios, broadcast TV networks, and other sources that produced them to a content library that increasingly consisted of its own self-produced original content (feature films, multi-episode series, and documentaries). Netflix members, as well as households subscribing to rival content providers, could not only watch as much streamed content as they wanted—anytime, anywhere, on nearly any Internet-connected screen—but they could also play, pause, and resume watching, all without commercials.

In its April 2019 report of Netflix's financial and operating results for the first quarter of 2019, management said Netflix subscribers were watching more than 165 million hours of the company's content offerings *per day.* In reporting the company's quarterly performance during the remainder of 2019, Netflix management did not disclose the total viewership hours per day, saying only that daily viewership hours worldwide were growing. The company tracked viewership of each title.

In the United States, Netflix still had 2.1 million members as of December 31, 2019 who, because of limited Internet service or just personal preference, continued to receive DVDs solely by mail (but the numbers of mail-only subscribers had been declining monthly as members transitioned to streaming).

Netflix's swift growth to 61 million paid subscribers in the United States and its promising potential for rapidly growing its base of international subscribers far past 100 million (some industry analysts believed Netflix had a clear path to 350 million subscribers worldwide by 2025) pushed the company's stock price from $270 at the beginning of 2018 to $380 in the second week of February 2020. (Netflix's all-time high stock price was $423 in July 2018). Already solidly entrenched as the global leader in paid memberships for streamed content, the principal questions for Netflix in 2020 seemed to be:

- Whether the company had sufficient competitive and financial strength to combat the efforts of larger, resource-rich rivals looking to steal subscribers away from Netflix.
- Whether the company could grow its subscriber base fast enough to (1) produce the revenues

and internal cash flows needed to finance an ever-larger annual stream of original content that would please subscribers and also (2) enable the company to be attractively profitable over the long-term.

Financial statement data for Netflix for 2015 through 2019 are shown in Exhibits 1 and 2. Netflix had never paid a dividend to its shareholders and the company had declared it had no present intention of paying any cash dividends in the foreseeable future.

EXHIBIT 1   Netflix's Consolidated Statements of Operations, 2015–2019 (in millions, except per share data)

[(g) For tables, all underlines should be the length of the longest numerical entry in each column, which may sometimes vary from column to column; align vertically on $ and ones digits; set end parenthesis to the right of the ones digit and no underline; underlines should be continuous, no breaks for commas or parentheses]

	2015	2016	2017	2018	2019
Revenues	$6,779.5	$8,830.7	$11,692.7	$15,794.3	$20,156.4
Cost of revenues (almost all of which relates to amortization of content assets)	4,591.5	6,257.5	7,659.7	9,967.5	12,440.2
Gross profit	2,188.0	2,800.8	4,033.0	5,826.8	7,716.2
Operating expenses					
Technology and development	650.8	780.2	1,052.8	1,221.8	1,545.1
Marketing	824.1	1,097.5	1,278.0	2,369.5	2,652.5
General and administrative	407.3	315.7	863.6	630.3	914.4
Total operating expenses	1,882.2	2,421.0	3,194.4	4,221.6	5,112.0
Operating income	305.8	379.8	838.7	1,605.2	2,604.3
Interest and other income (expense)	(163.9)	30.8	(591.5)	(378.80)	(542.0)
Income before income taxes	141.9	260.5	485.3	1,226.5	2,062.2
Provision for (benefit from) income taxes	19.2	73.8	(73.6)	15.2	195.3
Net income	$ 122.6	$ 186.7	$ 558.9	$ 1,211.2	1,866.9
Net income per share:					
Basic	$ 0.29	$ 0.44	$ 1.29	$ 2.78	$ 4.26
Diluted	0.28	0.43	1.25	2.68	4.13
Weighted average common shares outstanding (in millions)					
Basic	425.9	428.8	431.9	435.4	437.8
Diluted	436.5	438.7	446.8	451.2	451.8

Note 1: Some totals may not add due to rounding.

Source: Company 10-K reports for 2010, 2017, and 2019.

EXHIBIT 2   Selected Balance Sheet and Cash Flow Data for Netflix, 2015–2019 (in millions)

	2015	2016	2017	2018	2019
Selected Balance Sheet Data					
Cash and cash equivalents	$1,809.3	$ 1,467.6	$ 2,822.8	$ 3,794.5	$ 5,018.4
Current assets	5,431.8	5,720.3	7,670.0	9,694.1	6,178.5
Total current and non-current content assets	7,218.8	14,682.0	20,112.20	20,107.5	$24,504.5
Total assets	10,202.9	13,586.6	19,012.7	25,974.4	33,975.7
Current liabilities	3,529.6	4,586.7	5,466.3	6,487.3	6,855.7
Long-term debt*	2,371.4	3,364.3	6,499.4	10,360.1	14,759.3
Stockholders' equity	2,223.4	2,679.8	3,582.0	5,238.8	7,582.2
Cash Flow Data					
Net cash (used in) provided by operating activities	$ (749.4)	$(1,474.0)	$ (1,785.9)	$(2,680.5)	$ (2,887.3)
Net cash provided by (used in) investing activities	(179.2)	49.8	34.3	(339.1)	(387.1)
Net cash provided by (used in) financing activities	1,640.3	1,091.3	3,077.0	4,048.5	4,505.7

*All of Netflix's long-term debt consisted of senior unsecured notes that were issued at various points in time and had various maturity dates and various fixed rates of interest.

Sources: Company 10-K Reports 2011, 2015, 2017, and 2019.

THE FAST-CHANGING MARKET FOR STREAMED ENTERTAINMENT

In 2020, the world market for streamed entertainment (movies, episodes of TV shows, and live-streamed events) was undergoing rapid and disruptive change. There were three big change drivers:

1. Increasingly pervasive consumer access to both wired and wireless high-speed Internet connections. Worldwide rollout of 5G (fifth generation) wired and wireless digital networks promised to increase data connection speeds by 3 times those of the 3G and 4G digital networks currently serving most households and individuals across the world. Wired and wireless high-speed data connections greatly increased the ease with which households and individuals could use a TV, desktop computer, portable computer, or smartphone, coupled with a growing array of apps, to instantly connect to any Internet-accessible source/website with streaming capability and content to stream. The upcoming introduction of 5G mobile phones was widely expected to dramatically increase the time consumers used their smart phones to watch streamed content, particularly broadcasts of live sporting events, breaking news, and assorted other programs of interest.

2. A fast-moving and likely permanent shift in consumer preferences worldwide for watching content streamed directly *to whatever device they wanted to use at whatever times they wanted to watch,* rather than being locked into watching their favorite programs at the time they were broadcast on TV channels. Cable and satellite firms were losing subscribers annually, partly because these subscribers were unhappy about having to pay what they considered an outsized price for a multi-channel package containing more channels than they watched and partly because they could access their favorite programs from a growing number of streamed

sources (and also subscribe to one or more streamed content sources with sizable content libraries containing ongoing releases of new original content), thereby giving them an attractively wide variety of content selections at a lower overall cost that could be watched whenever they wished.

3. The mounting vigor with which well-known, resource-rich companies were launching strategic initiatives to (a) build bigger and more attractive content libraries—sometimes by merging with or acquiring the owners of attractive content libraries, sometimes by licensing a bigger assortment of attractive titles from various content owners, and sometimes by establishing in-house content development and production capabilities and (b) launching marketing campaigns to publicize and promote the content libraries they had assembled in an effort to secure a large enough base of paid streaming subscribers to cover the costs of their content libraries and streaming service and earn a profit.

During the past decade, the market for in-home entertainment other than broadcast and cable TV programs had evolved rapidly as households with high-speed Internet service and/or Internet-connected TVs or DVD players quickly shifted away from subscribing to Netflix's DVDs-by-mail service or else renting or buying physical DVDs with the desired content to almost exclusively watching *streamed* movies, previously broadcast episodes of TV shows, YouTube videos, and titles in the original content libraries of paid-subscriber providers, and other types of streamed content. This was because streaming had the advantage of allowing household members to access and instantly watch the movies, TV episodes, and other available content they wanted to see, which was much more convenient and often cheaper than patronizing a nearby rent-or-purchase location getting DVDs by mail from Netflix. This shift had permanently undercut the once-thriving businesses of selling movie and music DVDs and/or renting DVDs at local brick-and-mortar locations and standalone rental kiosks (like Redbox in the United States) or delivering/returning DVDs by mail (as at Netflix).

By 2020, faster internet speeds, the fast-growing and likely permanent shift in consumer preferences worldwide for watching content streamed directly to whatever device they wanted to use at whatever times they wanted to watch it, and rapid entry of new streamed content providers like AT&T's HBO Max, Disney+, Comcast's new Peacock offering, ViacomCBS, Apple TV+, and dozens of others in various geographic regions looking to compete with Netflix and Amazon's Prime Video had combined to unleash an increasingly intense competitive global battle among streaming providers to become serious contenders in the global market for subscriber-based streamed content—a market that was widely expected to be "the wave of the future," include billions of individuals and households, and be highly disruptive to the businesses of traditional cable and satellite providers, whose subscriber counts had declined annually for several years. College graduates and many millennials typically avoided subscribing to cable providers because of the "high" monthly prices and the growing availability of cheaper substitutes for viewing the programs they really wanted to watch or were satisfied with watching.

In 2019, a study by the Motion Picture Association of America (MPAA) reported that the number of streamed video subscribers grew to 613 million in 2018 (an increase of 27 percent over 2017), while the number of cable subscriptions worldwide dropped 2 percent to 551 million.[1] However, cable subscriptions generated the biggest revenues ($118 billion), followed by satellite subscriptions and streaming video subscriptions. According to the MPAA study, in 2018 80 percent of people in the United States watched cable programs, with 70 percent also watching streamed programs. The MPAA report further noted that the number of views/transactions of TV and film programs streamed from subscription-based providers, pay-per-view sources, and ad-supported sources jumped from 76.4 billion in 2014 to 182.1 billion in 2018, a four-year increase of 238 percent. The increase was partly due to an increase in the number of scripted original dramas across all sources from 390 in 2014 to 496 in 2018.

Exhibit 3 shows the percentage of Internet users, by country, who watched online video content on any device as of January 2018.

EXHIBIT 3   The Percentage of Internet Users in Selected Countries Who Watched Online Video Content on Any Device as of January 2018

Country	Percentage of Internet Users Watching Online Video Content on Any Device
Saudi Arabia	95%
China	92%
New Zealand	91%
Mexico	88%
Australia	88%
Spain	86%
India	85%
Brazil	85%
United States	85%
Canada	83%
France	81%
Germany	76%
South Korea	71%
Japan	69%

Source: Statista, www.statista.com (accessed April 10, 2018).

A SAMPLING OF NETFLIX'S COMPETITORS IN THE GLOBAL MARKET FOR STREAMED VIDEO SUBSCRIBERS

Going in 2020, Netflix' principal direct competitors included Amazon's Prime Video, AT&T (with its Warner Media and HBO Max subscription options), Disney+, Apple TV+, Comcast's new Peacock offering, and A new ViacomCBS streamin option, and AppleTV+, CBS All Access, all of whom had professed or exhibited a strategic intent to rank among the industry leaders—YouTube was not considered a direct competitor because its free and paid video content was distinctly different from the titles offered by Netflix and its direct competitors. Following is a brief description of the media resources and competitive capabilities of the chief rivals Netflix expected to battle in competing for streamed entertainment subscribers in countries across the world.

Amazon's Prime Video

Amazon competed directly with Netflix via its Amazon Prime membership service. In 2020, individuals and households could become an Amazon Prime member for a fee of $119 per year or $12.99 per month (after a one-month free trial); there was a discounted price for students of $59 per year of $6.49 per month. Membership in just Prime Video was $8.99 per month. Going into 2020, Amazon announced that it had over 150 million Amazon Prime members globally.[2] While Amazon had originally created its Amazon Prime membership program as a means of providing unlimited two-day shipping (more recently, one-day shipping in many locations and two-hour grocery delivery in 2,000 cities) on Prime-eligible items to customers who ordered merchandise from Amazon and wanted to receive their orders quickly, in 2012 Amazon began including movie and music streaming as a standard benefit of Prime membership—Amazon's video streaming service was called "Prime Video." Amazon Prime members were not, however, eligible to view every title in the Prime Video library for free; titles that were not Prime-eligible could be watched on a pay-per-view basis or else purchased. Going into 2020, many Amazon Prime members did not utilize their Prime Video membership benefit (Amazon did not disclose the overall percentage). Another video benefit of Amazon Prime membership was the ability to subscribe to over 100 premium channels with Prime Video Channels subscriptions.

In 2010, Amazon established Amazon Studios to oversee the development and production of new in-house original movies and multi-episode series; approximately 200 new original titles were released during 2015–2018. A 2019 report by *Streaming Observer,* an independent news site covering streaming industry news and reviews of movies, said that Amazon's Prime Video content library contained 17,461 titles versus 3,839 for Netflix and 2,336 for Hulu.[3] However, according to the same *Streaming Observer* report, Netflix had 592 titles that were "Certified Fresh" by Rotten Tomatoes (the leading online aggregator of movie and TV show reviews) versus 232 such films on

Prime Video and 223 on Hulu. Additionally, the report said almost 16 percent of all movies on Netflix were "critically acclaimed" compared to just 1.3 percent on Prime Video.

But in 2017 and continuing forward, Amazon began a strategic initiative to upgrade its content library, with both higher caliber new original content and licensed content. Amazon paid the National Football League $65 million a year for three seasons starting with 2017 season to live stream *Thursday Night Football* games globally to Prime Video members in 200 countries (these broadcasts attracted more than 18 million total viewers over 11 games in 2017). Amazon Studios spent a reported $250 million for licensing right to *Lord of the Rings,* with plans for spending up to $1 billion to produce 5 seasons of episodes. Amazon Studios spent an estimated $5–$6 billion on original content videos in 2019, releasing new titles monthly, including new seasons of Tom Clancy's *Jack Ryan,* Emmy-winning *The Marvelous Mrs. Maisel, Bosch, Sneaky Pete, Good Omens, Carnival Row, The Man in the High Castle, The Boys,* Emmy-winning *Fleabag, The Romanoffs, Patriot, American Gods, Preacher,* and *The Grand Tour.* Prime members watched double the hours of original movies and TV shows on Prime Video in the fourth quarter of 2019 compared to the fourth quarter of 2018, and Amazon Originals received a record 88 nominations and 26 wins at the Oscar, Emmy, and Golden Globe awards shows.[4]

The Walt Disney Company, Disney+, Hulu, and ESPN+

The Walt Disney Company in 2020 was a leading diversified international family entertainment and media enterprise with businesses that included the ABC branded broadcasting network; multiple cable channels (the ESPN family of five domestic channels and 15 international channels, three domestic Disney branded channels and approximately 100 Disney branded international channels, three FX channels, Freeform, National Geographic, and 50 percent ownership of A&E, which offered its own entertainment programming and operated four other cable channels); ABC Studios, Twentieth Century Fox Television, and Fox 21 Television which produced many of the company's TV shows; theme parks and resorts; Disney Cruise Lines; the sale of Disney-related merchandise at The Disney Stores and

assorted online sites; merchandising licensing covering a wide range of product categories and licensing of Disney's wide-ranging intellectual property; motion picture production and distribution under the Walt Disney Pictures, Twentieth Century Fox, Marvel, Lucasfilm, Pixar, Fox Searchlight Pictures, and Blue Sky Studios banners; and direct-to-consumer streaming services which included Disney+, ESPN+, Hulu, and Hotstar.

Starting in 2018, Disney made a series of strategic moves to strengthen its capabilities to enter the video streaming market by acquiring 100 percent control of streaming provider Hulu, which at the time had about 25 million subscribers in the United States. At the time, Hulu was a joint venture co-owned by Walt Disney (30 percent), Fox (30 percent), Comcast (30 percent), and Time Warner (10 percent), but Disney put a deal in place in late 2018 to buy Fox's 30 percent share of Hulu and then, months later, AT&T sold its 10 percent of Hulu to the Disney-Comcast owners of the Hulu joint venture for $1.43 billion. In May 2019, Comcast and Disney announced an agreement whereby Disney would have full 100-percent control of Hulu, starting immediately. The Disney-Comcast agreement specified that Comcast would continue to allow Hulu to carry all NBCUniversal content as well as live-stream NBCUniversal channels for Hulu's live TV service until late 2024 (Comcast was the 100-percent owner of NBCUniversal). The deal called for Comcast's ownership stake in Hulu to be officially sold to Disney starting in January 2024.

Hulu's strategy for attracting subscribers had been to attract subscribers by charging a subscription fee of $5.99 per month for regular streaming (interspersed with ads) and $11.99 per month for commercial-free streaming; new subscribers also got a one-month free trial. These two options entitled subscribers to watch *current* season episodes of popular TV shows (the day after they aired on ABC, NBC, Fox, and a few cable channels—no CBS shows were included) plus an estimated 43,000 back-season episodes of 1,650 TV shows and 2,500 movies. In addition, Hulu offered plans that included not only its video streaming service, but also packages that included 60+ live TV and cable channels (that included sports, news, and entertainment) for a monthly fee of $54.99 and options to add on HBO®, Showtime®, Starz®, and Cinemax®. In March 2020, Disney launched FX on Hulu" that featured every season of many originals that aired on FX over the past 17 years and that, going forward, would include new original scripted series by FX Productions shown exclusively to Hulu subscribers. In recent years, consumers disenchanted with the Further expansions are planned for Europe and Latin America in late 2020 through 2021, as Disney's existing international streaming distribution deals with competing services expire. Reaming prices of cable subscriptions had come to consider Hulu as their "go-to" choice, and it was widely considered the best streaming provider for watching TV shows. Nonetheless, Hulu had been a money-losing operation every year since its streaming service began operations in March 2008.

Disney debuted its new Disney+ streaming service on November 12, 2019, in the United States, Canada, and The Netherlands at low introductory prices of $69.99 per year or $6.99 per month. A week later, Disney+ was made available in Australia. New Zealand, and Puerto Rico and then further expanded to select European countries in March 2020. Additional expansions were planned for Europe and Latin America in late 2020 through 2021, as Disney's existing international streaming distribution licensing agreements with competing services expired.

Disney+ offerings centered on existing film and television content from Walt Disney Studios (including the Star Wars series), the three Disney TV channels, Pixar, Marvel, National Geographic, and 20th Century Fox, plus forthcoming new original content from these same sources. Disney's longstanding reputation for family entertainment attracted an unexpectedly large rush of new subscribers in the first three months—50 million worldwide as of April 10, 2020. This big subscription gain was partly due to the fact that, due to a deal between Disney and Verizon, whereby certain Verizon subscribers could sign up for a free one-year subscription to Disney+ until June 1, 2020, if they agreed that when the free 12-month subscription expired their Disney+ subscription would auto-renew at $6.99 per month, and they would be charged monthly on their Verizon bill unless the subscription was cancelled with Verizon. The 50 million number also included 8 million subscribers in India who were able to access Disney+ through Hotstar, a streaming service owned by Disney.

Concurrent with the launch of Disney+ in November 2019, Disney began offering a bundle of Disney+, (ad supported) Hulu, and ESPN+ for $12.99 per month with no free trial included at both the Disney+ and Hulu websites in the United States.

ESPN+ was a conglomeration of live sports programs (select live MLB, NHL, NBA, MLS, and Canadian Football League games, as well as multiple college sports games, PGA golf events, Top Rank Boxing matches, Grand Slam tennis matches, United Soccer League games, cricket and rugby games, English Football League games, and UEFA Nations League games that were *not* broadcast live on any of ESPN's family of channels (ESPN, ESPN2, ESPNU, ESPN Classic, ESPNews, ESPN Deportes, Longhorn Network, SEC Network, and ACC Network). ESPN+ was only available to viewers in the United States; the regular subscription fee for ESPN+ was $49.99 per year or $4.99 per month. ESPN+ had 7.6 million subscribers in the United States as of February 2020, up from 3.5 million paying subscribers in November 2019—the big increase was mainly due to the bundling promotion.

Disney management expected to have between 60 and 90 million Disney+ subscribers worldwide by 2024—the same year it believed the service would become profitable. The majority of those subscribers were forecast to be outside the United States.

AT&T's Two Video Streaming Subscription Options: Warner Media and HBO Max

In June 2018, AT&T completed its $108.7 billion acquisition of Time Warner, whose businesses consisted of global media and entertainment leaders Warner Bros. and WarnerMedia Entertainment. Warner Bros. business assets included the film studios and content libraries of Warner Bros. Pictures, New Line Cinema, Castle Rock Entertainment, and DC Films; a television production and syndication company; animation studios and their film libraries; and publishing company DC Comics. The WarnerMedia Communication Group included such assets as: the studios and film libraries of Home Box Office (HBO); broadcast and cable channels CNN, TBS, TNN, and TruTV; pay TV channels Cinemax, Cartoon Network, Boomerang, and Turner Classic Movies; and digital media company Otter Media. AT&T's new HBO division had 140 million subscribers who had access to HBO network's seven 24-hour multiplex channels through their cable or satellite provider (or as an add-on through Hulu); the add-on price paid to cable/satellite provider (or to Hulu) was $14.99 per month, cancellable at any time. All such HBO subscribers could download a free downloadable HBO GO app that could be used to access the HBO GO website; then, after entering their user name and password for their account at whatever provider to whom their HBO subscription fee was paid, the HBO subscriber could click on the desired HBO content and view it on mobile phones, laptops, and computers. AT&T/HBO had no interest in offering HBO GO access to people who were not already HBO subscribers because HBO's principal revenue source was a percentage of the monthly fees that its 140 million subscribers across the world paid their cable/satellite company (or Hulu) for access to HBO programming as part of their total subscription package.

AT&T executives believed Time Warner's businesses nicely complemented AT&T's core businesses in mobile, broadband, cable and satellite TV, and telephone communications in the United States, mobile services in Mexico, and pay TV services in 11 countries in South America and the Caribbean. AT&T's cable and satellite TV operations lost a combined 4 million subscribers in 2019, bringing the number of total subscribers for AT&T's various cable and satellite (DIRECTV) packages down to 19.7 million.

However, it was AT&T's strategic plan in 2020 to achieve nationwide coverage of 5G by mid-year; launch its new HBO Max streaming video service in May 2020 with a goal of securing 50 million subscribers in the United States and another 25 to 40 million international subscribers by 2025; and curtail the loss of subscribers to AT&T's cable and satellite services via simplified product packages and bundling opportunities with such other AT&T communication products as higher-speed broadband service, home security and monitoring packages, telephone services, and possibly discounted HBO Max subscriptions. The announced monthly price for the HBO Max streaming service was $14.99, the same price currently being paid by HBO Now's roughly 5 million direct subscribers. Plans were for current HBO subscribers through cable/satellite providers and direct HBO Now subscribers to be provided bundled access to HBO Max for free. AT&T expected that HBO Now subscribers would quickly migrate over to HBO Max, which would help grow total HBO Max subscriptions to 36 million by the end of 2020.

HBO Max was expected to launch with roughly 10,000 titles from the WarnerMedia film libraries of its various movie studios, all of HBO's content, a number of licensed shows, and 20+ fresh Max originals—the crown jewel of the originals was said to be *House of the Dragon,* a 10-episode story about the Targaryens centuries prior to the *Game of Thrones.*

Comcast's New Peacock Streaming Service

In January 2020, Comcast and its subsidiary NBCUniversal, jointly announced the launch of a new Peacock subscription video streaming service that would become available at no additional cost for Comcast's more than 20 million Xfinity X1 and Flex cable subscribers on April 15 and then launch July 15 for everyone else. The free tier of Peacock (Peacock Free) contained more than 7,500 hours of ad-supported programming, including next-day access to first season TV shows broadcast on NBC, a collection of Universal movies, and access to back seasons of such iconic NBC shows as *Saturday Night Live, Family Movie Night,* and *Vault.* However, Comcast subscribers and Cox cable subscriber could opt instead to subscribe to Peacock Premium, which included 15,000 hours of content, early access to NBC's 2 late night shows, live NBC sports programming, and non-televised Premier League soccer games. There were two price tiers for Peacock Premium: a $4.99 per month version that included ads and a $9.99 version with no advertising.

Steven Burke, a Comcast Executive Vice President and Chairman of NBCUniversal believed NBCUniversal was uniquely positioned to create a streaming platform that would monetize its content library and enable NBCUniversal to play a leading role in the on-demand video streaming world:[5]

Comcast management decided to use NBC's familiar peacock logo as the logo for the company's new subscription-based streaming service to remind customers that NBC was a network with great programming and to drive interest back to NBC's popular event-type TV programs (*The Masked Singer, The Last Voice, America's Got Talent*) and NBC's live sports programming, which included the *2020* Summer *Olympics.* Top management at Comcast and NBCUniversal believed that while streamed video might indeed be the future of watching TV and movies, the cable business would remain profitable for years to come (despite the likely permanent declines in the number of cable and satellite subscribers worldwide) and, further, that free ad-supported viewing was likely to remain far more prevalent and popular with consumers than subscription-supported viewing. Comcast management believed that bundling Peacock Free for customers with Comcast cable subscriptions would help reduce the number of customers dropping the company's cable service and switching to a rival streaming provider. Hence, they saw no good business reason to create a streaming platform with strategy elements that would help undermine the profitability and longevity of company's cable business.

During a Peacock Investor Day presentation on January 16, 2020, a NBCUniversal officer cited a survey where consumers were asked "Which new streaming service are you likely to try—one that is free with some ads or one that is paid with no ads?" Eighty percent responded "free with some ads," and 20 percent responded "paid with no ads." These results were a factor in convincing the Comcast-NBCUniversal management team to position Peacock as an ad-supported streamer of premium content in what they viewed as a mostly vacant market niche (among rival video streaming providers, only Hulu offered consumers a low-priced, ad-supported streaming option). Moreover, the Peacock strategy was to help secure a competitive edge by having an industry-low average of five minutes of ads per hour, which contrasted sharply with TV broadcasting where there were 16–20 minutes of ads per hour and premium video streaming where there was an average of eight minutes of ads per hour.[6] And Peacock Free's ad-supported streaming of premium content helped differentiate it from the three competitively strong subscription-based providers—Netflix, Amazon Prime Video, and HBO Max. Peacock management believed it would have little difficulty selling ads for Peacock's content, given that NBC, ABC, CBS, FOX, and some 250 other channels had advertising-based business models representing 92 percent of total viewership.[7]

NBCUniversal said it would invest $2 billion in Peacock over 2020 and 2021, with goals of reaching between 30 and 35 million active users in the United States by 2024, generating $2.5 billion in new revenues with average revenue per subscriber of $6–$7, and achieving break even on Peacock's streaming service on an earnings before interest, taxes, depreciation, and amortization (EBITDA) basis.

ViacomCBS and CBS All Access

Viacom and CBS completed their long-expected and often contentious merger in December 2019, creating a multinational media conglomerate with assets approaching $50 billion and 2019 revenues of $27.8 billion. The new company's main assets included Paramount Pictures film studio and a library of 3,600 movies; the CBS broadcasting network and its library of 140,00 TV episodes, a streaming platform called CBS All Access that provided approximately 4.5 million subscribers in the United States, Canada, and Australia with access to current and back season CBS TV shows, CBS Sports (NFL, college football, and college basketball games), other recently-aired programs on CBS broadcast properties; a number of CBS-affiliated television stations; CBS Television Studios and CBS Studios International; cable television networks MTV, Nickelodeon (watched in 600 million households around the world), BET, Comedy Central, CMT (Country Music Television), Showtime, The Movie Channel, VH1, Flix, and TEN (a high profile channel in Australia); free ad-supported video-on-demand platform Pluto TV with 100+ live TV channels and thousands of TV shows and movies; 50 percent co-ownership with AT&T's WarnerMedia subsidiary of The CW Television Network (commonly referred to as just The CW); Nickelodeon Animation Studio; an assortment of international and regional networks and operations that provided the company with the capability to engage in video streaming in many countries; and book publisher Simon & Schuster. CBS's media properties alone made it a global media titan, with some 4.3 billion watchers of its broadcast and pay TV programs in 180 countries at year-end 2019.

In early 2019, before the merger, Viacom had purchased Pluto TV for $360 million and proceeded to expand its offering of 100 ad-supported channels by adding 43 channels in the fourth quarter of 2019, including 22 Spanish and Portuguese ones that were popular in Latin America and Brazil; Pluto's subscriber base grew over 70 percent in 2019 to a total of over 20 million going into 2020. On December 20, 2019, ViacomCBS announced it was buying a 49 percent ownership stake in Miramax Pictures for an upfront payment of $150 million and an agreement to invest $225 million in Miramax for movie and television productions over the next five years. The deal also specified that ViacomCBS's Paramount Pictures would become the exclusive distributor for the Miramax library of 700+ films and have a first-look at Miramax's new content creation.

In February 2020, ViacomCBS executives were in the final stages of readying plans to launch a new video streaming service built around the CBS All Access streaming service, that would be expanded to include a broad pay "House of Brands" product offering comprised of a wide assortment of titles from Viacom's multiple libraries and selected popular shows on BET, Nickelodeon, MTV, Comedy Central, Showtime, and perhaps others. Further, the new streaming service would draw heavily upon the capabilities of Paramount's and Miramax's movie and television production studios, Nickelodeon's Animation Studio, and perhaps other ViacomCBS operations to develop and produce new original content. Going into 2020, ViacomCBS had global production studios that were currently turning out over 750 shows with 43,000 episodes.[8]

ViacomCBS said the base tier of the new streaming service would be ad-supported, but there would be two higher-end tiers: an ad-free version and a premium version that included Showtime. It was speculated that ViacomCBS's new streaming service could be the final significant streaming offering that hit the market as traditional media companies repositioned themselves and recast their strategies in preparing for a post-cable TV future.

AppleTV+

Apple launched its Apple TV+ video streaming service on November 1, 2019, in over 100 countries that could be accessed on smart TVs connected to an Apple TV box or on new TV models that had the Apple TV app already installed, or Apple devices with a downloaded Apple TV app. Pitched as Apple's strategic means of competing directly with Netflix, Amazon Prime Video and Disney+, the new Apple TV+ service streamed Apple's *original programming only* through Apple TV-capable devices. An Apple TV+ subscription could be shared with up to six family members. At $4.99 per month (or free for one year with the purchase of a new Apple device), the cost of Apple's streaming service was lower than the monthly subscription service for most of its video streaming rivals.

At launch, there were just nine Apple Originals available to view; the number had increased to a total of 20 multi-episode shows and five films as of June 2020. However, Apple had committed to adding new originals every month and 26 new original series and seven films were in development for release later in 2020 and 2021. Apple was reportedly

planning to spend about $4.2 billion on original programming by 2022.

While Apple had yet to disclose subscriber numbers for its TV+ service, an analyst at Wall Street firm at Sanford C. Bernstein had estimated that, as of February 2020, fewer than 10 million of the eligible consumers purchasing a new Apple device had opted to sign up for a free 12-month trial of Apple TV+.[9] It was speculated that Apple TV+'s failure to resonate with consumers was largely due to its unusually limited content offerings. In December 2019, one of the analysts participating on an expert panel hosted by UBS (a well-known global financial services firm) said that Apple TV+ "needs a mega-hit original series to ultimately retain subscribers," adding that the company "may likely have to ultimately also acquire an asset with a big backlog of catalog content—most of which will be very expensive at this point."[10]

YouTube TV

In April 2020, Google's YouTube subsidiary was offering a YouTube TV streamed entertainment service that included about 70 TV and movie channels for a fee of $50 per month. The service could be accessed on smart TVs, streaming boxes, computers, and mobile devices. As of early 2020, YouTube TV had over 2 million subscribers.

NETFLIX'S BUSINESS MODEL AND STRATEGY IN 2020

Since launching the company's online movie rental service in 1999, Reed Hastings, founder and CEO of Netflix, had been the chief architect of Netflix's subscription-based business model and strategy that had transformed Netflix into the world's largest online entertainment subscription service. Hastings's goals for Netflix were simple—build the world's best Internet service for entertainment content, keep improving Netflix's content offerings and services faster than rivals, attract growing numbers of subscribers every year, and grow long-term earnings per share. Hastings was a strong believer in moving early and fast to initiate strategic changes that would help Netflix outcompete rivals, strengthen its brand image and reputation, and fortify its position as the industry leader.

A Quick Overview of the Evolutionary Changes in Netflix's Subscription-Based Business Model and Strategy, 1999–2019

Netflix had employed a subscription-based business model throughout its history, with members having the option to choose from a variety of subscription plans whose prices and terms had varied over the years. Originally, all of the subscription plans were based on obtaining and returning DVDs by mail, with monthly prices dependent on the number of titles out at a time. But as more and more households began to have high-speed Internet connections, in 2007 Netflix began bundling unlimited streaming with each of its DVD-by-mail subscription options, with the long-term intent of encouraging subscribers to switch to watching instantly streamed content rather than using DVD discs delivered and returned by mail. As increasing numbers of subscribers gained access high-speed Internet connections, most quickly switched over to unlimited streaming subscription plans, enabling Netflix to avoid incurring the order fulfillment costs and postage costs associated with servicing DVD-by-mail subscribers. About two-thirds of Netflix subscribers in the United States had transitioned to streaming-only plans by year-end 2011, and fewer than four percent of Netflix's subscribers in the United States were on DVD-by-mail plans at the end of 2019.

A third major shift in Netflix's strategy began in 2010 when Netflix started to expand its streaming service internationally, beginning with Canada. Entry into other countries followed quickly, as shown in Exhibit 4, and Netflix became a truly global company in 2016. Despite dedicated efforts, going into 2020 Netflix had failed to surmount the barriers erected by the Chinese government that prevented its entry into the People's Republic of China, the world's most massive market for entertainment. For the past five years, the Chinese government had steadfastly refused to issue Netflix a license to operate in China, preferring instead to control the content its citizens were allowed to see—for example, government censors required that an entire series of a multi-episode offering had to be approved before it could begin to be shown on an online platform. Aside from the censorship issue, most observers believed the Chinese government was blocking Netflix's entry in order to

EXHIBIT 4   Netflix's Rapidly-Executed Entry into New Geographic Areas

Year	Entry into New Geographical Areas
September 2010	Canada
September 2011	42 countries in Central America, South America, and the Caribbean
January 2012	United Kingdom, Ireland
October 2012	Denmark, Sweden, Norway, Finland
September 2013	Netherlands
September 2014	Austria, Belgium, France, Germany, Luxembourg, Switzerland
March 2015	Australia, New Zealand
September 2015	Japan
October 2015	Spain, Portugal, Italy
January 2016	Rest of the world—some 130 countries (but excluding the People's Republic of China, North Korea, Syria, and Crimea)

Source: Company 2017 10-K Report, p. 21.

protect aspiring local providers of Internet-streamed content from foreign competition. Recognizing its dim entry prospects, in 2017 Netflix negotiated a licensing arrangement to exclusively provide some of its original content to a fast-growing Chinese company named iQiyi (pronounced Q wee), the leading provider of online entertainment services in China with some 106 million subscribers (as of September 30, 2019) and a reported 500 million monthly active users watching an average of 12 hours each month on the company's platforms.[11] Use of a licensing strategy was attractive to Netflix because it provided a means of gaining content distribution in China and building some awareness of the Netflix brand and Netflix content, but the licensing arrangement was expected to generate only small revenues for some years to come. The U.S. government had instituted restrictions precluding all U.S.-based companies from having operations in North Korea, Syria, and Crimea.

Netflix estimated that it usually took about two years after the initial launch in a new country or geographic region to attract sufficient subscribers to generate a positive "contribution profit"—Netflix defined "contribution profit (loss)" as revenues less cost of revenues (which consisted of amortization of content assets and expenses directly related to the acquisition, licensing, and production/delivery of such content) and marketing expenses associated with its domestic streaming and international streaming business segments (the company ceased all marketing activities related to its domestic DVD business prior to 2015).

A fourth important shift in Netflix's business model and strategy began in 2011–2012. CEO Reed Hastings and other senior Netflix executives realized that there were low barriers to entry into the subscription-based video streaming business for movie producers and TV broadcasters that had over the years amassed big libraries of attractive content. Indeed, many of the titles that Netflix was streaming to subscribers were being licensed from these very same entities, and the license fees for these titles were rising rapidly, as content owners recognized that their title libraries had significant value to Netflix, Amazon, and others who were in the streamed entertainment business and that they commanded significant bargaining power to raise licensing fees as current licenses expired. Netflix executives further foresaw that the company was likely to be put at a significant competitive disadvantage when these content owners came to the conclusion they could make bigger profits from their content libraries by starting up their own video streaming businesses to compete against Netflix for subscribers in many country markets rather than licensing titles to Netflix. Reed Hastings and his executive team believed that when content-rich rivals entered the streamed entertainment business (as they were certain to do at some point) and triggered a head-on competitive battle for subscribers that the winners would be those companies that potential subscribers viewed as having attractive and fresh content they were willing to pay monthly or annual fees to watch. Furthermore, they were certain that when these rivals emerged, they would discontinue renewing their licenses for popular programs (especially TV shows) with Netflix, preferring to use these titles to attract new subscribers to their own streamed entertainment services.

These realizations resulted in Netflix undertaking a long-term strategic initiative to change its portfolio of titles from mainly all licensed to a portfolio of titles that was increasing comprised of original content created, produced, and owned by Netflix. The company immediately moved to develop and continually strengthen its in-house content creation and production capabilities, but it also elected to supplement its internal efforts by entering into multi-year collaborative agreements with outside developers and producers not owned by its rivals to license portions of their existing titles to Netflix and to produce new original content that would be owned by Netflix or licensed to Netflix.

Netflix started streaming its first original content title, *House of Cards,* in February 2012; *House of Cards,* a political drama that ran six seasons, was a major hit with subscribers, garnered acclaim from critics and reviewers, and received 213 awards nominations (Golden Globe, Primetime Emmys, Screen Actors Guild, and others) and 35 overall wins during 2013–2018. Netflix's spending for new original content mushroomed during the ensuing years, with total spending for new content of $12 billion in 2018 and $15 billion in 2019, of which roughly 85 percent was estimated to be for original content. Spending for 2020 was projected to be $17.3 billion on a cash basis, with 85 percent or more being allocated to original content.[12] One Wall Street analyst projected that Netflix's spending for new content could rise to $26 billion by 2028.[13]

Netflix's Strategy in 2020

While over 4.5 billion (57.7 percent) of the world's population of 7.8 billion people used the Internet as of January 2020 (an increase of 298 million since January 2019)[14], Netflix viewed the size of the near-term market potential for securing streaming subscribers worldwide (including China) as being the approximately 1.1 billion people/households currently having high-speed wired and wireless internet service.[15] Surveys conducted during 2019 indicated that the worldwide average amount of time individuals spent using the internet on any device was 6 hours and 43 minutes, equal to more than 100 days of online time per year.[16] The worldwide average *fixed* internet download speed in December 2019 was 73.6 million bits per second (mbps) and the worldwide average *mobile* internet download connection speed was 32.0 mbps.[17] These speeds were expected to climb steadily toward 100 mbps (or more) by 2025, thereby making it feasible for hundreds of millions more households with fixed internet connections to watch streamed content and paving the way for a rapidly rising percentage of people worldwide to access streamed content on their smartphones or other mobile devices—going into 2020 there were some 3.5 billion users of smartphones.

Netflix's strategy going into 2020 was focused squarely on:

- Growing the number of global streaming subscribers, particularly in those countries/geographic regions with the biggest growth opportunities.
- Continuing to enhance the appeal of its library of streaming content, with growing emphasis on exclusive original movies and original series produced in-house and in collaboration with selected outside movie and TV show producers.
- Increasing partnerships with movie and television producers in specific countries to produce original content for audiences in that country's language.
- Focusing marketing and advertising on the particular countries and geographic regions deemed to have the biggest subscriber growth potential.
- Continuing to introduce mobile-only subscription plans in countries where a big percentage of the population used mobile devices to watch streaming content.

Subscription Pricing Strategy

Going into 2020, Netflix offered three types of streaming membership plans. Its basic plan, currently priced at $8.99 per month in the United States, included access to standard definition quality streaming (640 × 480 pixels) on a single screen at a time. Its standard plan, currently priced at $12.99 per month and included access to high-definition quality streaming (1080 × 720 pixels) on two screens concurrently. The company's premium plan, currently priced at $15.99 per month, included access to 4K ultra-high definition quality (3,840 × 2,160 pixels) content on four screens concurrently. Netflix recommended three mbps of download speed for standard definition streaming, five mbps for high definition and 25 mbps for 4K Ultra HD. During 2019, all three plans were attracting healthy numbers of new subscribers—none of the three clearly stood out as "most popular" worldwide. Netflix management believed this indicated "we're providing a range of options at a range of price points that allow consumers in the markets that we serve to sort of select into the right model."[18] However, over the past 5–8 years, there had been a very gradual shift towards the highest-priced premium plan, a trend likely being driven by more households purchasing big-screen ultra-high definition TVs.

As of September 2019, international pricing for the three plans ranged from approximately $3 for a mobile-only plan to $22 per month per U.S. dollar equivalent for a premium subscription plan in Switzerland; in many countries, the monthly prices of standard and premium plans were in the range of $9–$14 per U.S. dollar equivalent.[19] Netflix executives expected that the prices of the various subscription plans in each country would likely rise over time, thereby helping boost the global monthly average revenue the company received per paying subscriber above the 2019 average of $10.82.

Netflix began testing a cheaper mobile-only $3 per month plan in 2018 in India, one of its key developing markets because of the size of India's population and heavy use of mobile devices for video streaming. The $3 mobile-only plan test in India was successful in boosting subscriber growth and in increasing member retention, prompting Netflix to expand its low-priced mobile offering to Malaysia and Indonesia in 2019; the test in these countries similarly impacted subscriber growth and member retention. In December 2019, Netflix began testing subscription discounts of up to 50 percent if new subscribers signed up for three-, six- and 12-month plans; the goal was to gauge the impact of both lower prices and multi-month plans on new signups and member retention and thereby learn more about which types of mobile-only subscription plans tended to produce the biggest gains in subscriber revenues. Netflix indicated that mobile-only plans were likely to be tested in additional countries in 2020, principally in large-population countries where wired high-speed Internet connections were not widely available and where mobile devices were frequently or exclusively used for video streaming.

In January 2020, Netflix CEO Reed Hastings indicated the company had no interest in adding an ad-supported subscription plan, largely because of the difficulties in convincing advertisers to shift some of their advertising dollars to Netflix's streaming platform. In Reed Hastings view, Google, Facebook, and Amazon had tremendously powerful capabilities in online advertising because they gathered data about the browsing and purchasing habits of people while they were online (and their personal data as well) from many sources and provided it as service to their advertisers. The valuable user-related data advertisers got from Google, Facebook, and Amazon allowed them to effectively target their ads and realize a bigger return on their advertising expenditures. The detailed data that Netflix collected on every subscriber's viewing history and title preferences was of no value to advertisers and provided zero competitive benefit in taking advertising dollars away from "the big three." So, for Netflix to attract $5 to $10 billion dollars in advertising to support an ad-based subscription plan posed formidable challenges that Netflix executives firmly believed the company should not try to surmount.[20]

Netflix's Strategy to Develop and Employ Viewership Tracking and Recommendation Software to Enhance Its Engagement with Subscribers

For some time, Netflix had developed proprietary software technology that allowed members to easily scan a movie's length, appropriateness for various types of audiences (G, PG, or R), primary cast members, genre, and an average of the ratings submitted by other subscribers (based on one to five stars). With one click, members could watch a trailer previewing a movie or original series or TV show if they wished. Most importantly, perhaps, were algorithms that created a personalized "percentage match" for each title that was a composite of a subscribers' own ratings of previously viewed titles, titles the member had placed on a "watchlist" for future viewing, and the overall or average rating of all subscribers (several billion ratings had been provided by subscribers over the years).

Subscribers often began their search for titles by viewing a list of personalized recommendations that Netflix's software automatically generated for each member. Each member's list of recommended titles was also partly the product of Netflix-created algorithms that organized the company's entire content library into clusters of similar movies/TV shows and then sorted the titles in each cluster from most liked to least liked based on subscriber ratings. Those subscribers who favorably or unfavorably rated similar movies/TV shows in similar clusters were categorized as like-minded viewers. When a subscriber was online and browsing through the selections, the software was programmed to check the clusters the subscriber had previously viewed, determine which selections in each cluster the customer had yet to view or place on

watchlist, and then display those titles in each cluster in an order that started with the title that Netflix's algorithms predicted the subscriber was most likely to enjoy down to the title the subscriber was predicted to least enjoy. In other words, the subscriber's ratings of titles viewed, the titles on the subscriber's watchlist, and the title ratings of all Netflix subscribers determined the order in which the available titles in each cluster or genre were displayed to a subscriber—with one click, subscribers could see a brief profile of each title and Netflix's predicted rating (from one to five stars) for the subscriber. When subscribers came upon a title they wanted to view, that title could be watch-listed for future viewing with a single click. A member's complete watchlist of titles was immediately viewable with one click whenever the member visited Netflix's website. With one additional click, any title on a member's watchlist could be activated for immediate viewing. Netflix management saw its title recommendation software as a quick and personalized means of helping subscribers identify and then watch titles they were likely to enjoy. Netflix's subscriber tracking data indicated that 80 percent of subscribers' watch choices came from their personal recommendation engine.

Netflix invested in developing new software capabilities and refining existing capabilities every year. As of 2020, Netflix had data pertaining to:

- The titles each subscriber had viewed in the past several days, the past week, the past month, the current calendar year, the past calendar year, and the entire period the subscriber had been a member.
- The subscriber's ratings of each title.
- The titles on the subscriber's watch list.
- The number of times each title had been viewed by all subscribers *in both each country and worldwide* the past several days, the past week, the past month, the current calendar year, the past calendar year, and the entire period that title had been on Netflix.
- The total number of hours subscribers spent watching Netflix titles for each month of each year in each country and worldwide.

Content Strategy

Going into 2020, Netflix had bulked its original content offerings up to a total of 1,197 titles, but its streaming library still included 3,751 licensed movies and 1,569 television shows.[21] New seasons of five original series and sequels to two original movies had already been announced for showing in the first quarter of 2020, following an unusually heavy slate of new originals released in the last two quarters of 2019. Reed Hastings said the company's fourth quarter 2019 slate of releases "set a new bar for the variety and high quality of films we produce to appeal to our members' many diverse tastes."[22]

Three high-profile shows —*Parks and Recreation* (Peacock), *Friends* (HBO MAX), and *The Office* (Peacock)—were all set to leave Netflix and return to rivals during 2020 as current licenses expired. While the loss of these programs was a setback, Netflix management was not unduly disturbed; its chief content officer explained:[23]

> We've had, over the years, incredibly popular product come on and off the service . . . . . And typically, what happens is our members, through our incredible personalization, deep library, and broad library, are able to find their next favorite show. And [what will] will happen with *Friends* fans, [is that] some of them will find it elsewhere, and some of them will find their next favorite show [on Netflix].

To help offset the losses of these popular shows, Netflix had reportedly spent $100 million for a multi-year license to stream *Seinfeld* episodes to its subscribers.

Netflix streamed different sizes and combinations of portfolio titles to different countries. This was because its title tracking data revealed there were very big differences in the 20 to 30 most-watched titles from country to country. This was partly because of (1) the different languages spoken in different countries and the varying percentages of subscribers that understood storylines produced in one language versus another and (2) varying subscriber preferences from country-to-country for some types/ genres of movies, series, and documentaries versus others. Netflix's tracking of program viewership showed clearly that a strategy of streaming much the same number and combination of titles to all countries was inferior compared to a strategy of customizing the types of titles streamed to each country to match up well with what its tracking data showed subscribers were watching and to discontinue streaming of titles not watched or watched very infrequently. As a consequence it had become standard practice at Netflix to use its title-viewing data for each country

to guide decisions of which titles to stream to which countries and then to make changes in each country's title mix as shifts occurred in the viewing hours devoted to particular genres and the popularity of newly released titles.

However, to increase subscriber satisfaction with its streamed offering to each country, Netflix was continuing a long-term initiative to steam title offerings to more and more countries in their native languages so that subscribers could enjoy better enjoy Netflix's programs. In the last quarter of 2019, Netflix localized the language of its streaming service to Vietnam, Hungary, and the Czech Republic (Czechia). Furthermore, Netflix was engaged in an ongoing effort to license content from local producers of movies and TV shows and bundle them with the titles Netflix was streaming to that country from its own title collection. In late 2019, Netflix added new locally-bundled titles in partnership with Sky Italia, Canal+ in France, KDDI in Japan, and Izzi in Mexico.

A related shift underway in Netflix's content strategy in 2020 was the increased emphasis being placed on growing the number of titles (1) produced in languages other than English, (2) filmed in a greater number of different locations, and (3) built around local country storylines. This shift was being driven not only by the positive local subscriber response to new films and series produced in local languages and containing locally-appealing content but also by Netflix's tracking data that showed many of these titles had gained popularity in other countries. A new 2017 Brazilian science-fiction show produced in Portuguese for Brazil, to the surprise of Netflix executives, had scored well with audiences around the world—this was Netflix's first instance of a local-language program working well in locations where other languages dominated. Local language films produced in India, South Korea, Japan, Turkey, Thailand, Sweden, and the United Kingdom were among the most popular 2019 titles. An original Spanish series titled *La Casa de Papel,* which was retitled *Money Heist* in English-speaking countries and was scheduled to begin its fourth season during 2020, had developed a wide audience, appearing on the top ten most watched titles in more than 70 countries. As of January 2020, Netflix had globally released 100 seasons of local language, original scripted series from 17 countries and had plans for over 130 seasons of such programs in 2020.

As a consequence, in 2020 Reed Hastings and Netflix's other content programming executives were focused on creating a portfolio of forthcoming titles for every taste, every mood, and every region of the world. A conscious effort was being made to schedule releases of *premium* quality new original films and original series scattered fairly evenly across the year and across all genres so as to provide subscribers in all parts of the world with an ongoing stream of *fresh* new titles that looked interesting to watch and proved very enjoyable after watching them.

Netflix began ramping up its capabilities to create new original animation films in 2017. Its first big new feature, *Klaus,* was released in late 2019, and was an instant audience pleaser in countries across the world and an Oscar nominee for Best Animated Feature. Two new big theatrical-scale animated features were on tap for release in 2020; Reed Hastings believed both would be competitive with any animated films shown at movie box offices. Animated films traveled more predictably across countries than other types of titles.

Netflix management also relied heavily on its viewership tracking data for each title to guide decision-making on how to allocate upcoming expenditures for new original content. For example, if season one of a new original series was highly popular with subscribers, the series was renewed for a second season, and if a new series failed to spark widespread viewing and garnered only small audiences, with declining views of succeeding episodes, the series was canceled. If a new original series or film was viewed by 40 to 70 million subscribers in the first few weeks or months or if its viewership built significantly over a 4-to-12 month period, management was likely to invest in the development of a second season of the series and perhaps a new original series or movie in the same genre (action, suspense thriller, science fiction, or adult comedy) for release in the following year. Netflix released two romantic-comedy films in 2019 that proved quite popular with subscribers and quickly decided to follow-up with sequels to both titles in the first half of 2020. It had several action films scheduled for 2020 as follow-on releases for a much-viewed action film released in the last quarter of 2019.

Going into 2020, Netflix was continuing its efforts to upgrade the content and production quality of all new originals—the objective was to present subscribers with *premium* entertainment content calculated to please subscribers, boost subscriber retention, and help drive subscriber growth. Netflix had further learned from its viewership tracking data and subscriber growth statistics that media reports of critically-acclaimed reviews of Netflix titles, coupled with media reports of Netflix titles receiving numerous nominations and awards, were important positive factors in steering existing subscribers to watch these titles and stimulating subscriber growth. Netflix's original content programs in 2019 pulled in 24 nominations for the 2020 Academy Awards, more than any other studio. From 2013 through February 2020, Netflix original titles had received 296 nominations and 83 wins[24]—an indication of the progress the company had made in creating and producing top notch original series and films. As far as Netflix top executives were concerned, the more viewer hours spent watching Netflix originals, the more critically-acclaimed reviews of its original titles, the more award nominations, and the more award wins, the better. All contributed to improving subscribers' experiences with Netflix, higher company's revenues and operating margins, bigger internal cash flows from operations, and more funds available for creating more new original content going forward.

Content development projects announced for 2020 included a multiyear pact with Nickelodeon for animated originals; a multiyear film and TV deal with "Game of Thrones" creators David Benioff and Dan Weiss; and a three-year deal with a South Korean media conglomerate for originals and licensed titles and titles from another Korean film producer. Netflix announced in January 2020 that 30 employees in The Netherlands were being transferred to Rome, Italy, for the purpose of opening a new office to strengthen its local content creation partnerships in Italy and work on growing the number of new movies and series made in Italy.

Marketing and Advertising Strategy in 2019–2020

Netflix spent $2.65 billion on marketing and advertising in 2019, up from $2.37 billion in 2018. Netflix used multiple marketing approaches to attract subscribers, but especially online advertising (paid search listings, banner ads on social media sites, and permission-based e-mails), and ads on regional and national television. Advertising campaigns of one type or another were underway more or less continuously, with the lure of one-month free trials and announcements of new and forthcoming original titles usually being the prominent ad features. Netflix's expenditures for digital and television advertising were unreported in 2019 but were $1.8 billion in 2018 and $1.09 billion in 2017. Other marketing costs in 2019 included:

- Costs pertaining to free trial subscriptions.
- Payments to mobile operators across the world to create quick and easy-to-use procedures for smartphone users to access Netflix streamed or downloadable programming. Netflix believed it was particularly important to make mobile streaming from Netflix instantly accessible to those people who basically only wanted to have their relationship with Netflix on a mobile device.
- Promotional campaigns for new original titles to generate more density of viewing and conversation around each title. Such campaigns involved sending emails to subscribers at least weekly and often more frequently calling attention to titles highly matched to a title viewed the previous day, previous several days, or previous week. E-mails were also sent regularly to announce the availability of new releases that matched well with the subscriber's viewing history. When users were browsing various titles in various genres of interest, there was always a row of titles with the heading "Because you watched [title] just under rows of titles on the subscriber's watch list.

On several occasions, Netflix CEO Reed Hastings called attention to the growing importance of marketing efforts calling a subscriber's attention to titles closely matched to recently viewed titles or to help make certain new titles a bigger hit in a particular nation or among a particular demographic segment. These were deemed valuable contributors to heightening subscriber satisfaction with the entertainment value Netflix was providing and also aiding subscriber retention and the acquisition of new subscribers. Further, because Netflix operated in so many countries, Hastings was a big fan of experimenting with different marketing approaches in different markets and thereby learning more about what worked well in marketing Netflix's original content and differentiating Netflix from rival streaming providers.[25] Those approaches that were successful became candidates for use in other locations.

Business Segment Reporting— New Metrics for 2020

Until the fourth quarter of 2019 Netflix had reported its performance for three business segments: domestic streaming, international streaming, and domestic DVD. Management used this business segment classification for purposes of making operating decisions, assessing financial performance, and allocating resources. The company's performance in each of these three business segments for 2015 through 2019 is shown in Exhibit 5.

However, beginning with the fourth quarter of 2019 and going forward, management decided the company's operations had evolved into a single business—global streaming operations—and revealed that top management, especially the CEO, had begun making operating decisions, assessing financial performance, and allocating resources based on the performance of its streaming operations in four geographic regions: the United States and Canada (UCAN), Europe, the Middle East, and Africa (EMEA), Latin America (LATAM), and the Asia-Pacific (APAC). The company provided a breakdown of its performance in each of the four regions for 2019—see Exhibit 6.

Reed Hastings made special mention of the fact that while subscription prices were different in every country around the world and while management definitely took note of the average monthly revenues per subscriber in each country and region, Netflix was not managing its business to boost average revenue per subscriber in each country. Rather, management was managing to maximize revenues worldwide. Hastings said:[26]

> Obviously, as we have lower-priced mobile offers, that's going to bring down a blended [average revenue per subscriber] in a country or in a market. But if we're doing that in a revenue-accretive way, we think that's great for our long-term business. We're growing subscribers, and we're growing revenue.

In the first quarter of 2020, as governments in many countries instituted home confinement orders to stem the spread of coronavirus (COVID-19), Netflix's global streaming membership surged by a quarterly record 15.8 million to a total of 182.9 million paid subscribers. School-closings and work-from-home policies on the part of many organizations caused mushrooming demand for home entertainment and a jump in the average number of daily viewing hours of Netflix members. In March 2020, Internet usage became so great that a number of governments and

EXHIBIT 5   Netflix's Performance by Business Segment, 2015–2019 (in millions, except for average monthly revenues per paying member and percentages)

Domestic Streaming Segment	2015	2016	2017	2018	2019
Paid memberships at year-end	43.4	47.9	52.8	58.5	61.0
Paid net membership additions	5.6	4.7	4.9	5.7	2.6
Average monthly revenue per paying membership	$8.50	$9.21	$10.18	$11.40	$12.57*
Revenues	$4,180.3	$5,077.3	$ 6,153.0	$ 7,646.6	$ 9,243.0
Cost of Revenues (Note 1)	2,487.2	2,855.8	3,319.2	4,038.4	4,867.3
Marketing costs	313.6	412.9	603.7	1,025.4	1,063.0
Contribution profit (Note 2)	$1,375.5	$1,712.4	$ 2,078.5	$ 2,582.9	$ 3,312.6
Contribution margin	33%	34%	34%	34%	36%
International Streaming Segment					
Paid memberships at year-end	27.4	41.2	57.8	80.8	106.1
Paid net membership additions	11.7	14.3	18.5	22.9	25.3
Average monthly revenue per paying membership	$7.48	$7.81	$8.66	$9.43	Note 3
Revenues	$1,953.4	$3,211.1	$ 5,089.2	$ 7,782.1	$10,616.2
Cost of Revenues (Note 1)	1,780.4	3,042.7	4,359.6	5,776.0	7,449.7
Marketing costs	506.4	684.6	832.5	1,344.1	1,589.4
Contribution profit (Note 2)	$ (333.4)	$ (516.2)	$ (102.9)	$ 662.0	$ 1,577.1
Contribution margin	(17)%	(16)%	(2)%	9%	15%
Domestic DVD Segment					
Paid memberships at year-end	4.8	4.0	3.3	2.7	2.2
Average monthly revenue per paying membership	$10.30	$10.22	$10.17	$10.19	Note 3
Revenues	$ 645.7	$ 542.3	$ 450.5	$ 365.6	$ 297.2
Cost of Revenues (Note 1)	323.9	262.7	202.5	153.1	123.2
Marketing costs	—	—	—	—	—
Contribution profit (Note 2)	$ 321.8	$ 279.5	$ 248.0	$ 212.5	$ 174.0
Contribution margin	50%	52%	55%	58%	59%
Global Totals					
Paid memberships at year end	75.6	93.1	117.2	142.0	169.3
Global average monthly revenue per paying membership	$8.15	$8.61	$9.43	$10.31	$10.82
Revenues	$6,779.5	$8,830.7	$11,692.7	$15,794.3	$20,156.4
Operating income	305.8	379.8	838.7	1,605.2	2,604.2
Operating margin	5%	4%	7%	10%	13%
Net income	$122.6	$186.7	$558.9	$1,221.2	$1,867.0

* Includes United States and Canada, due to a Q4 2019 change in Netflix's reporting of its geographic business segments.

Note 1: Cost of revenues for the domestic and international streaming segments consist mainly of the amortization of streaming content assets, with the remainder relating to the expenses associated with the acquisition, licensing, and production of such content. Cost of revenues in the domestic DVD segment consist primarily of delivery expenses such as packaging and postage costs, content expenses, and other expenses associated with the company's DVD processing and customer service centers.

Note 2: The company defined contribution margin as revenues less cost of revenues and marketing expenses incurred by segment.

Note 3: Netflix discontinued reporting this statistic due to a change in the definitions of its geographic business segments, effective with the fourth quarter of 2019.

Source: Company 2017 10-K Report, pp. 19–22 and pp. 59–61; Company 2018 10K Report, pp. 20–22 and pp. 60–62; and p. 15 of Reed Hastings' "Letter to Shareholders," included as part of the company's Report of Fourth Quarter 2019 Earnings, January 21, 2020.

EXHIBIT 6 Netflix's Performance by Geographic Region, 2019 (in millions, except for average monthly revenues per paid subscriber)

	Three months ended				
	March 31, 2019	June 30, 2019	Sept. 30, 2019	Dec. 31, 2019	Full Year 2019
UCAN Streaming					
Revenue	$ 2,257	$ 2,501	$ 2,621	$ 2,672	$10,051.2
Paid Memberships	66.63	66.50	67.11	67.66	67.66
Paid Net Additions	1.88	−0.13	0.61	0.55	2.91
Average Monthly Revenue per Paid Subscriber	$ 11.45	$ 12.52	$ 13.08	$ 13.22	$ 12.57
EMEA Streaming					
Revenue	$ 1,233	$ 1,319	$ 1,428	$ 1,563	$ 5,543.1
Paid Memberships	42.54	44.23	47.36	51.78	51.78
Paid Net Additions	4.72	1.69	3.13	4.42	13.96
Average Monthly Revenue per Paid Subscriber	$ 10.23	$ 10.13	$ 10.40	$ 10.51	$ 10.33
LATAM Streaming					
Revenue	$ 630	$ 677	$ 741	$ 746	$ 2,795.4
Paid Memberships	27.55	27.89	29.38	31.42	31.42
Paid Net Additions	1.47	0.34	1.49	2.04	5.34
Average Monthly Revenue per Paid Subscriber	$ 7.84	$ 8.14	$ 8.63	$ 8.18	$ 8.21
APAC Streaming					
Revenue	$ 320	$ 349	$ 382	$ 418	$ 1,469.5
Paid Memberships	12.14	12.94	14.49	16.23	16.23
Paid Net Additions	1.53	0.80	1.54	1.75	5.63
Average Monthly Revenue per Paid Subscriber	$ 9.37	$ 9.29	$ 9.29	$ 9.07	$ 9.24
Total Streaming					
Revenue	$4,440.0	$4,846.0	$5,173.0	$5,399.0	$19.859.2
Paid Memberships	148,860	151,510	158,334	167,090	167,090
Paid Net Additions	9.60	3.43	6.77	8.76	27.83
Average Monthly Revenue per Paid Subscriber	Not reported	Not reported	$ 11.13	$ 11.06	$ 10.82

Source: Company website, Excel spreadsheet regional information for 2019, posted in the Investor Relations section as part of the company's report of Fourth Quarter 2019 Financial Results, www.netflix.com, accessed February 15, 2020.

internet service providers asked Netflix to temporarily reduce the network traffic of its members. According to CEO Reed Hastings,[27]

> Using our Open Connect technology, our engineering team was able to respond immediately, reducing network use by 25 percent virtually overnight in those countries, while also substantially maintaining the quality of our service, including in higher definition. We're now working with ISPs to help increase capacity so that we can lift these limitations as conditions improve.

Netflix executives expected as progress was made in containing the virus and reducing new

infections that membership growth and viewing hours would decline

The Financial Strain of Netflix's Growing Expenditures for Original Content and Other Content Acquisitions

The company's heightened strategic emphasis on original content produced in-house had resulted in multi-billion-dollar annual increases in Netflix's financial obligations to pay for streaming content and sharply higher negative cash flows from operations (see Exhibit 7). Netflix was covering these obligations with new issues of common stock and new issues of senior notes; details of Netflix's outstanding senior notes are shown in Exhibit 8.

Netflix management forecasted that the company would have a negative free cash flow deficit of about $2.5 billion in 2020 and that the company would continue to experience negative, but progressively smaller, cash flow deficits, for several more years due to growing expenditures for original content. However, executive management was confident that the company's expected growth in subscribers, subscription revenues, and operating profit margins would in the near future result in positive and growing cash flows from operations, enabling the company

EXHIBIT 7 The Growing Financial Strain of Netflix's Strategic Emphasis on Producing Original Content In-House, 2015–2019 (in millions of dollars)

	2019	2018	2017	2016	2015
Streaming content obligations at year-end	$19,490.1	$19,285.9	$17,694.6	$14,479.5	$10,902.2
Additions to streaming content assets	13,916.7	13,043.4	9,805.8	8,653.3	5,771.6
Additions to DVD content assets	Note 1	38.6	53.7	77.2	78.0
Amortization of streaming content assets	9,216.2	7,532.1	6,197.8	4,788.5	3,405.4
Amortization of DVD content assets	2.7	41.2	60.7	79.0	79.4
Net cash used in operating activities	(2,887.3)	(2,680.5)	(1,785.9)	(1,474.0)	(749.4)
Proceeds from issuance of debt	4,469.3	3,921.8	3,020.5	1,000.0	1,500.0
Proceeds from issuance of common stock	72.5	124.5	88.4	37.0	78.0
Outstanding senior notes	14,893.0	10,360.0	6,499.4	3,364.3	2,371.4

Note 1: This item was reclassified and merged into a different accounting category on the company's Cash Flow Statement.

Source: Company 10-K Reports 2019, 2018, 2017, 2016, and 2015.

EXHIBIT 8 Netflix's Outstanding Long-Term Debt as of December 31, 2019

Debt Issues	Principal Amount at Par	Issue Date	Maturity Date	Interest Due Dates
4.875% Senior Notes	$1.00 billion	October 2019	June 2030	June 15 and December 15
3.625% Senior Notes	$1.23 billion	October 2019	June 2030	June 15 and December 15
5.375% Senior Notes	$1.34 billion	April 2019	November 2029	June 15 and December 15
3.875% Senior Notes	$900 million	April 2019	November 2029	June 15 and December 15
6.375% Senior Notes	$800 million	October 2018	May 2029	May 15 and November 15
4.625% Senior Notes	$1,260 million	October 2018	May 2029	May 15 and November 15
5.875% Senior Notes	$1.9 billion	April 2018	November 2028	April 15 and November 15
4.875% Senior Notes	$1.6 billion	October 2017	April 2028	April 15 and October 15
3.625% Senior Notes	$1.561 billion	May 2017	May 2027	May 15 and November 15
4.375% Senior Notes	$1.0 billion	October 2016	November 2026	May 15 and November 15
5.500% Senior Notes	$700 million	February 2015	February 2022	April 15 and October 15
5.875% Senior Notes	$800 million	February 2015	February 2025	April 15 and October 15
5.750% Senior Notes	$400 million	February 2014	March 2024	March 1 and September 1
5.50% Senior Notes	$700 million	February 2015	February 2022	April 1 and October 1
5.375% Senior Notes	$500 million	February 2013	February 2021	February 1 and August 1

Source: Company 2019 10-K Report, p. 55.

to reduce borrowing and begin to pay down its long-term debt. In April 2018, CEO Reed Hastings said:[28]

> We will continue to raise debt as needed to fund our increase in original content. Our debt levels are quite modest as a percentage of our enterprise value, and we believe [issuing] debt is [a] lower cost of capital compared to equity.

Reed Hasting's View of the Forthcoming Globally Competitive Battle for Streamed Entertainment Subscribers

In Reed Hastings' "Letter to Shareholders" in October 16, 2019, he talked about the upcoming streaming war with all the various new competitors:[29]

> We compete broadly for entertainment time. There are many competitive activities to Netflix (from watching linear TV to playing video games, for example).

But there is also a very large market opportunity; today we believe we're less than 10% of TV screen time in the U.S. (our most mature market) and much less than that in mobile screen time. Many [industry observers] are focused on the "streaming wars," but we've been competing with streamers (Amazon, YouTube, Hulu) as well as linear TV for over a decade. The upcoming arrival of services like Disney+, Apple TV+, HBO Max, and Peacock is increased competition, but we are all small compared to linear TV. While the new competitors have some great titles (especially catalog titles), none have the variety, diversity, and quality of new original programming that we are producing around the world. The launch of these new services will be noisy. There may be some modest headwind to our near-term growth. . . In the long-term, though, we expect we'll continue to grow nicely given the strength of our service and the large market opportunity. By way of example, our growth in Canada, where Hulu does not exist, is nearly identical to our growth in the U.S. (where Hulu is very successful at about 30 million paid memberships).

ENDNOTES

[1] As reported by Andrew Liptak, "The MPAA says streaming video has surpassed cable viewing worldwide," posted at www.theverge.com, March 21, 2019 (accessed February 3, 2020).

[2] Amazon press release announcing 4th Quarter 2019 financial results, January 30, 2020.

[3] Savannah Marie, "Report: Amazon Prime Movie Library almost 5x the Size of Netflix and Nearly 7.5x the Size of Hulu," Xanjero Media, January 29, 2019, posted at www.xanjero.com (accessed February 3, 2020).

[4] Amazon press release announcing 4th Quarter 2019 financial results, January 30, 2020.

[5] Transcript of Peacock's Investor Day Presentation, January 16, 2020, posted in the Investor Relations section at www.cmcsa.com (accessed February 7, 2020).

[6] Peacock Investor Day Presentation Slides, January 16, 2020, posted in the Investor Relations section at www.cmcsa.com (accessed February 7, 2020).

[7] Transcript of Peacock's Investor Day Presentation, January 16, 2020, posted in the Investor Relations section at www.cmcsa.com (accessed February 7, 2020).

[8] ViaconCBS Factsheet, posted at www.viacbs.com (accessed February 13, 2020).

[9] Ryan Vlastelica and Bloomberg, "Apple's push in TV is 'failing to resonate', says analyst," posted at www.fortune.com, February 3, 2020 (accessed February 9, 2020).

[10] Ibid.

[11] Monthly active users and hours watched are based on information about iQiyi posted on Wikipedia (accessed January 27, 2020).

[12] Todd Spangler, "Netflix Projected to Spend Over $17 Billion on Content in 2020," Variety, January 16, 2020, posted at www.Variety.com (accessed February 11, 2020).

[13] Ibid.

[14] Digital 2020 Global Overview Report, posted at www.thenextweb.com on January 30, 2020 (accessed February 10, 2020).

[15] Transcript of remarks by David Wells, Netflix's Chief Financial Officer, at Morgan Stanley, Technology, Media & Telecom Conference, February 27, 2018, www.netflix.com (accessed April 5, 2018).

[16] Digital 2020 Global Overview Report, posted at www.thenextweb.com on January 30, 2020 (accessed February 10, 2020).

[17] According to the Speedtest Global Index, posted at www.speedtest.net (accessed February 10, 2020).

[18] From p. 7 of Netflix's 4th Quarter 2019 Earnings Call Transcript, January 21, 2020, posted in the Investor Relations section at www.netflix.com.

[19] Rebecca Moody, "Which countries pay the most and least for Netflix?" posted September 3, 2019 at www.comparitech.com (accessed February 12, 2020).

[20] For more details, see p.14 of Netflix's 4th Quarter 2019 Earnings Call Transcript, January 21, 2020, posted in the Investor Relations section at www.netflix.com.

[21] According to data from JustWatch.com, posted on January 17, 2020 and cited

in Joe Supan, "Everything You Need to Know About Netflix," Allconnect, posted at www.allconnect.com, January 17, 2020 (accessed February 11, 2020).

[22] Reed Hastings, "Letter to Shareholders," p. 3, included as part of Netflix's announcement of fourth quarter 2019 earnings, January 21, 2020, posted in the Investor Relations section at www.netflix.com.

[23] From p. 11 of Netflix's 4th Quarter 2019 Earnings Call Transcript, January 21, 2020, posted in the Investor Relations section at www.netflix.com.

[24] Wikipedia, https://en.wikipedia.org/wiki/List_of_accolades_received_by_Netflix (accessed February 14, 2020).

[25] Based on Reed Hastings' comments during the company's conference call announcing the company's financial results in the first quarter of 2018, April 16, 2018.

[26] Netflix's 4th Quarter 2019 Earnings Call Transcript, January 21, 2020, posted in the Investor Relations section at www.netflix.com.

[27] Reed Hastings, "Letter to Shareholders," p. 2, included as part of Netflix's announcement of first quarter 2020 earnings, April 21, 2020, posted in the Investor Relations section at www.netflix.com.

[28] Company press release, April 16, 2018.

[29] Reed Hastings, "Letter to Shareholders," p. 5, included as part of Netflix's announcement of third quarter 2019 earnings, October 16, 2019, posted in the Investor Relations section at www.netflix.com.

Twitter, Inc. in 2020

David L. Turnipseed
University of South Alabama

Jack Dorsey, CEO of Twitter, Inc., had breathed a slight sigh of relief when the fourth quarter, 2017 financial results showed the first profitable quarter since the company went public in 2013. One year later, the company's 2018 annual report showed net income of $1.2 billion, which was 40 percent of its revenue. Twitter had experienced rapid growth since its founding and by January 2018, there were more than 330 million active monthly users. Notables with Twitter accounts included U.S. President Donald Trump, Taylor Swift, Justin Timberlake, Ellen DeGeneres, Pope Francis, Katy Perry, and Turkish President Recep Erdogan. The first quarter, 2018 was the peak of Twitter's usage, with 336 million active monthly users: usage fell to 321 million by the year end. The first quarter, 2019 showed a small recovery to 330 million, then Twitter changed the method of reporting usage to "monetized daily users," which were 145 million in the third quarter of 2019. Twitter blamed the reduced usage over on a crackdown on bot accounts and spam (in 2017, it was estimated that 15 percent of Twitter accounts were bots). The monetized daily usage climbed a bit in 2019, and Twitter reported 152 million average daily users on December 31 of that year.

However, despite the number of users and the volume of use, Twitter had failed to provide any financial gains until the fourth quarter of 2017, and this profit had come as a result of cutting costs, not growing the business. Research and development, and sales and marketing expenses had been cut by 24 and 25 percent, respectively, and the company's annual net revenue for fiscal 2017 was down over three percent from 2016. Even more problematic was an accumulated deficit of over $2.6 billion.

Although Twitter showed its first full year profit in fiscal 2018, it was due largely to maintaining low costs, and the impact of the Tax Act. Revenue of $3.0 billion in 2018 was an increase of 24 percent over 2017, but costs for research and development, sales and marketing, and total costs and expenses were below 2016 levels, as a percent of revenue. Total costs and expenses were 11 percent lower than 2016, and research and development costs were 20 percent below 2014 levels. The accumulated deficit, which at the end of fiscal 2017 was over $2.6 billion, had been reduced to $1.5 billion.

Fiscal 2019 was another profitable year, with net income of $1.5 billion, however, a look below the surface suggested that rather than celebrate, Twitter's management should have seriously examined the company's operations. The 2019 net profit was largely due to a $1.075 billion tax benefit from loss carry forward from prior years. Although revenue increased by 14 percent from 2018, the cost of revenue increased to 33 percent of revenue, up slightly from 32 percent in 2018. More troubling, total costs and expenses increased from 85 percent of revenue in 2018 to 89 percent in 2019; consequently, the operating margin fell from 15 percent in 2018 to 11 percent in 2019. Twitter's market capitalization was $33.5 billion in November of 2019, down from $35 billion in September 2019 and $40 billion in 2014, and again there were suggestions in the media that Twitter was ripe for a buyout. Twitter, Inc.'s consolidated income statements for 2015 through 2019 are presented in Exhibit 1. The company's consolidated balance sheets for 2015 and 2019 are presented in Exhibit 2.

EXHIBIT 1   Consolidated Statements of Operations: 2015–2019 (in thousands, except per share data)

	Year Ended December 31,				
	2019	2018	2017	2016	2015
Consolidated Statement of Operations Data:					
Revenue[1]	$3,459,329	$3,042,359	$2,443,299	$2,529,619	$2,218,032
Costs and expenses[2]					
Cost of revenue	1,137,041	964,997	861,242	932,240	729,256
Research and development	682,281	553,858	542,010	713,482	806,648
Sales and marketing	913,813	771,361	717,419	957,829	871,491
General and administrative	359,821	298,818	283,888	293,276	260,673
Total costs and expenses	3,092,956	2,589,034	2,404,559	2,896,827	2,668,068
Income (loss) from operations	366,373	453,325	38,740	(367,208)	(450,036)
Interest expense	(138,180)	(132,606)	(105,237)	(99,968)	(98,178)
Interest income	157,703	111,221	44,383	24,277	9,073
Other income (expense), net	4,243	(8,396)	(73,304)	2,065	5,836
Income (loss) before income taxes	390,139	423,544	(95,418)	(440,834)	(533,305)
Provision (benefit) for income taxes	(1,075,520)	(782,052)	12,645	16,039	(12,274)
Net income (loss)	$1,465,659	$1,205,596	$ (108,063)	$ (456,873)	$ (521,031)
Net income (loss) per share attributable to common stockholders					
Basic	$1.90	$1.60	$(0.15)	$(0.65)	$(0.79)
Diluted	$1.87	$1.56	$(0.15)	$(0.65)	$(0.79)
Weighted-average shares used to compute net income (loss) per share attributable to common stockholders					
Basic	770,729	754,326	732,702	702,135	662,424
Diluted	785,531	772,686	732,702	702,135	662,424

[1] The company adopted a new revenue standard on January 1, 2018 using the modified retrospective method. Revenue for the year ended December 31, 2018 was not materially impacted by the application of the new revenue standard.

[2] Costs and expenses include stock-based compensation expense as follows:

	Year Ended December 31,				
	2019	2018	2017	2016	2015
Cost of revenue	$ 22,797	$ 17,289	$ 23,849	$ 29,502	$ 40,705
Research and development	209,063	183,799	240,833	335,498	401,537
Sales and marketing	85,739	71,305	94,135	160,935	156,904
General and administrative	60,426	53,835	74,989	89,298	82,972
Total stock-based compensation	$378,025	$326,228	$433,806	$615,233	$682,118

Source: Twitter, Inc. Annual Report 2019.

EXHIBIT 2   Consolidated Balance Sheets, 2015-2019 (in thousands)

	As of December 31,				
	2019	**2018**	**2017**	**2016**	**2015**
Consolidated Balance Sheet Data					
Cash and cash equivalents	$ 1,799,082	$ 1,894,444	$1,638,413	$ 988,598	$ 911,471
Short-term investments	4,839,970	4,314,957	2,764,689	2,785,981	2,583,877
Property and equipment, net	1,031,781	885,078	773,715	783,901	735,299
Total assets	12,703,389	10,162,572	7,412,477	6,870,365	6,442,439
Convertible notes	1,816,833	2,628,250	1,627,460	1,538,967	1,455,095
Senior notes	691,967	—	—	—	—
Total liabilities	3,999,003	3,356,978	2,365,259	2,265,430	2,074,392
Total stockholders' equity	8,704,386	6,805,594	5,047,218	4,604,935	4,368,047

Source: Twitter, Inc. Annual Report 2019.

Twitter was a giant in the industry; however, it faced serious competition from companies such as Facebook (including Instagram and WhatsApp), Snap, TikTok, Alphabet (including Google and YouTube), Microsoft (including LinkedIn), and Verizon Media Group. There were also foreign competitors that were regional social media and messaging companies, with strong positions in particular countries, including WeChat, Kakao, and Line, which posed competitive challenges. Many of these competitors were growing at a multiple of Twitter's growth—over the three-year period 2017 to 2020, Facebook had an increase of 450 million monthly active users (+35 percent), WhatsApp increased by 800 million (+67 percent) and Instagram had increases of 300 million (+43 percent). Over the two-year period 2017–2019, although there were small variations in the numbers of users, Twitter had no increase, showing 330 million monthly users in both years (Twitter stopped reporting monthly active users in the first quarter, 2019). In 2019 Twitter's share of worldwide digital ad revenue had climbed to 0.9 percent, up from 0.8 percent in 2018 (compared to Google's 32.2 percent and Facebook's 22.1).

Although Twitter had made a good profit in fiscal 2019, the company's performance failed to meet expectations during the First Quarter of 2020. The weak financial performance in early 2020 generated concerns about whether the company continue to grow revenue and operate without allowing costs and expenses to drift up and erode income. As the company entered the second quarter of 2020, Twitter's CEO and its Board were faced with three daunting questions: 1) how could they spark growth and increase the number of users, 2) what could they do to assure Twitter's continued profitability, and 3) were the two profitable years sufficient to prevent the company from being targeted as a take-over candidate?

HISTORY OF TWITTER

Founded in 2006 by Jack Dorsey, Noah Glass, Biz Stone, and Evan Williams, Twitter was an online microblogging and social networking service that allowed users to post text-based messages, known as tweets, and status updates up to 40 characters long. Jack Dorsey, a cofounder of Twitter, sent the first tweet on March 21, 2006: "just setting up my twttr"—Jack(@jack) 21 March, 2006. By the first of January 2018, Twitter had more 330 million monthly active users.

The history of Twitter began with an entrepreneur named Noah Glass who started a company named Odeo in 2005. Odeo had a product that would turn a phone message into an MP3 hosted on the Internet. One of Odeo's early investors was a former Google employee, Evan Williams, who got very involved with the company. As Odeo grew, more employees were hired, including web designer Jack Dorsey and Christopher "Biz" Stone, a friend of Odeo's new CEO Evan Williams.

Williams decided that Odeo's future was not in podcasting and directed the company's employees to develop ideas for a new direction. Jack Dorsey, who had been doing cleanup work on Odeo, proposed a product that was based on people's present status, or what they were doing at a given time. In February 2006, Glass, Dorsey, and a German contract developer proposed Dorsey's idea to others in Odeo, and over time, a group of employees gravitated to Twitter while others focused on Odeo. At one point, the entire Twitter service was run from Glass' laptop.

Noah Glass presented the Twitter idea to Odeo's Board in summer of 2006; the Board was not enthused. Williams proposed to repurchase the Odeo stock held by investors to prevent them from taking a loss, and they agreed. Five years later, the assets of Odeo that the original investors sold for about $5 million, were worth $5 billion.

After Williams repurchased Odeo, he changed the name to Obvious Corp. and fired Odeo's founder and the biggest supporter of Twitter, Noah Glass. Christopher "Biz" Stone left Twitter in 2011 and pursued an entrepreneurial venture with Obvious Corp. for six years. In mid-2017, he returned to Twitter full time. As of the second quarter, 2018, only three of the original Twitter founders remained active in the company: Biz Stone, Jack Dorsey as the company's CEO, and Evan Williams who was on the Board.

Twitter provided an almost-immediate access channel to global celebrities. The majority of the top 10 most-followed Twitter accounts were entertainers who used the service to communicate with their fans, spread news, or build a public image. The near-instant gratification through direct updates from celebrities such as Rihanna, Jimmy Fallon, Lady Gaga, and Taylor Swift and the feeling of inclusion in a specific group of fans was a major reason for social media users to use Twitter. The accounts of high-interest people such as entertainers, politicians, or others at risk of impersonation were verified by Twitter to authenticate their identity. A badge of verification was placed on confirmed accounts to indicate legitimacy. Major sporting events and industry award shows such as the Super Bowl or Academy Awards generated significant online action. The online discussion enabled users to participate in the success of celebrities who often posted behind-the-scenes photo tweets or commentaries. On-set or in-concert tweets were other methods utilized by celebrities to enhance their appeal and fan interaction.

Twitter was quite simple: tweets were limited to 140 characters until late 2017 when the limit was raised to 280. The character constraint made it easy for users to create, distribute, and discover content that was consistent across the Twitter platform as well as optimized for mobile devices. Consequently, the large volume of Tweets drove high velocity information exchange. Twitter's aim was to become an indispensable daily companion to live human experiences. The company did not have restrictions on whom a user could follow, which greatly enhanced the breadth and depth of available content and allowed users to find the content they cared about most. Also, users could be followed by hundreds of thousands, or millions of other users without requiring a reciprocal relationship, enhancing the ability of users to reach a broad audience. Twitter's public platform allowed both the company and others to extend the reach of Twitter content: media outlets distributed Tweets to complement their content by making it more timely, relevant, and comprehensive. Tweets had appeared on over one million third-party websites, and, in the second quarter of 2013, there were approximately 30 billion online impressions of Tweets. As of October 2019, there were an average of 6,000 Tweets per second, or 500 million tweets per day: these number indicate 200 billion tweets per year.

THE TWITTER BRAND IMAGE

Twitter had a powerful brand image. Its mascot bird was not chosen because birds make tweeting sounds, but rather because "whether soaring high above the earth to take in a broad view, or flocking with other birds to achieve a common purpose, a bird in flight is the ultimate representation of freedom, hope and limitless possibility."[1]

Twitter was initially named "Jitter" and "Twitch," because that is what a phone would do when it received a tweet. However, neither name evoked the image that the founders wanted. Noah Glass got a dictionary and went to "Twitch," then to subsequent words starting with "Tw" he found the word "Twitter," which in the Oxford English dictionary means a short inconsequential burst of information, and chirps from birds. Dorsey and Glass thought that "twitter" described exactly what they were doing, so they decided on that name. The name was already owned, but not being used, and the company was able to buy it very cheaply.

In 2012, the old Twitter bird was redesigned, slightly resized, changed from red to blue, and named Larry the Bird (named after NBA star Larry Bird). The lower case "t" icon and the text "twitter" were removed; the company name was no longer on the logo. The blue bird alone communicated the Twitter brand. "Twitter achieved in less than six years what Nike, Apple, and Target took decades to do: To be recognizable without a name, just an icon."[2]

According to a Twitter survey conducted to help understand the company's brand legacy, 90 percent of Twitter users worldwide recognized the Twitter brand. Twitter's 2018 ad campaign "What's happening" used only the Twitter logo and hashtag symbol. The Twitter brand was called "minimalization at its finest"[3]—an advertising campaign that did not have one word, yet delivered a powerful message from the brand.

Twitter's Global High Profile

Twitter had become very well-known because of several high-profile users and high-profile use. Several of the world's leaders had millions of followers, as shown in Exhibit 3. From May 2017 to April 2019, U.S. President Donald Trump's follow count increased from 30.1 million to 50 million. President Trump regularly used Twitter to break news, praise his friends, campaign for supporters, and feud with his enemies; consequently, Twitter had been in the daily news almost constantly since 2016.

Although the world's leaders had millions of followers, others have far more. As of June 2020, Katy Perry had over 109 million followers, Justin Bieber 112 million, former U.S. President Barack Obama 119 million, Rihanna 97 million, Ellen DeGenerres 80 million, Lady Gaga 82 million, and Justin Timberlake 65 million. Exhibit 3 presents the world leaders with the most Twitter followers in May 2017 and April 2020.

The miraculous plane crash on New York's Hudson River in 2009 was broken on Twitter, and on May 1, 2011, an IT consultant in Pakistan unknowingly live-tweeted the U.S. Navy Seal raid that killed Osama Bin Laden over nine hours before the raid was on the news. Prince William announced his engagement to Catherine Middleton in 2010 on Twitter. Whitney Houston's death and the bombing at the Boston marathon were broken on Twitter. President Obama used Twitter to declare victory in the 2012 U.S. presidential election, with a Tweet that was viewed about 25 million times on the Twitter platform and widely distributed offline in print and broadcast media. He also tweeted a goodbye message when he left office in January 2017 that garnered 794 million retweets.

TWITTER SERVICES, PRODUCTS AND REVENUE STREAMS

Twitter's primary service was the Twitter global platform for real-time public self-expression and conversation, which allowed people to create, consume, discover, and distribute content. Some of the most trusted media outlets in the world, such as CNN, Bloomberg, the Associated Press, and BBC used Twitter to distribute content. Periscope was a mobile app launched by Twitter in 2015 that enabled people to broadcast and watch live video with others. Periscope broadcasts could be viewed through Twitter and mobile or desktop web browsers.

Twitter, Inc. generated advertising and data licensing revenue as shown in Exhibit 4 by providing mobile advertising exchange services through the Twitter MoPub exchange, and offering data products

EXHIBIT 3 **World Leaders with the Most Twitter Followers, May 2017 and April 2020**

	Millions of Followers	
	2017	2020
Pope Francis, Vatican@Pontifex	34	50
Donald Trump, U.S.@RealDonaldTrump	30	77
Narendra Modi, India@NarendraModi	30	55
Prime Minster, India@PMOInd	18	33
President, U.S.@POTUS	18	29
The White House, U.S.@WhiteHouse	14	21
Recep Erdogan, Turkey@RT_Erdogan	10	15
HH Sheikh Mohammed, UAE@Jokowi	8	—
Joko Widodo, Indonesia@jokowi	7	13
Imran Khan, Pakistan@imrankhanpti	—	11
Queen Rania, Jordan@QueenRania	—	10

Source: Statista, 2018, 2020.

EXHIBIT 4   Twitter, Inc. Advertising and Data Licensing Revenue, 2017–2019 (in thousands)

	Year Ended December 31,			2018 to 2019 % Change	2017 to 2018 % Change
	2019	2018	2017		
Advertising services	$2,993,392	$2,617,397	$2,109,987	14%	24%
Data licensing and other	465,937	424,962	333,312	9%	28%
Total revenue	$3,459,329	$3,042,359	$2,443,299	14%	25%

Source: Twitter, Inc. 2019 Form 10-K.

and data licenses that allowed their data partners to search and analyze historical and real-time data on the Twitter platform, which consisted of public tweets and their content. Also, Twitter's data partners usually purchased licenses to access all or a portion of the company's data for a fixed period. The company operated a mobile ad exchange and received service fees from transactions completed on the exchange. The Twitter mobile ad exchange allowed buyers and sellers to purchase and sell advertising inventory, and it matched buyers and sellers.

TWITTER RESTRUCTURES

On June 29, 2018, Dorsey announced that he was restructuring Twitter to make the company quicker and more creative, as Ed Ho, VP of product and engineering, stepped down to a part-time position. Twitter employees would be organized in functional groups such as engineering, as opposed to the present product teams. Dorsey decided on the structural change to simplify the way the company worked and to make the organization "more straightforward." He believed that a "pure end-to-end functional organization" would help make decision making clearer, allow the company to build a stronger culture, and prepare the company for increased creativity and innovation. Dorsey believed that Twitter must enter a creativity phase to be relevant and important to the world.

Twitter restructured and merged its agency development and applications program interface departments in April 2019. Prior to the move, the agency development group focused on Twitter's relationships with major advertising agencies and the platform solutions team concentrated on

ad-tech companies such as Amobee, 4C Insights, and SocialCode Marketing which developed automated ad campaigns for digital media platforms including Twitter. There were no jobs lost due to the restructuring, rather the move showed the value that Twitter placed on its advertisers.

Twitter's Stock Performance

Twitter went public on November 7, 2013, with an IPO price of $26.00, and the stock closed up 73 percent ($44.94) on its first trading day. The stock hit its all-time high of $69.00 on January 3, 2014, and began a long down-trend, lasting until mid-April 2017. On August 21, 2015, Twitter shares dropped below the IPO price to $25.87, rebounded slightly, and then slid to $14.10 on May 13, 2016. The stock did not get above the IPO price of $26.00 until early February 2018. After a year's climb, Twitter stock hit a three year high of $47.79 in early July 2018, and then began to slide again, trading in the $28.00–$32.00 range until rebounding to $40.80 in early May 2019. Exhibit 5 tracks Twitter's market performance between May 2014 and April 2019.

Twitter, Inc. joined the S&P 500 index on June 7, 2018, replacing Monsanto. The addition of Twitter was unusual because the S&P regulations required that the sum of a member company's four most recent quarters, as well as the last quarter, were positive. In April of 2018, Twitter reported its second consecutive profitable quarter, which followed 16 consecutive quarters of losses. The addition of Twitter to the S&P 500 Index would increase the number of individual investors who owned the stock through index funds that track the large company stock gauge. Twitter's addition to the index fuelled a

EXHIBIT 5   Monthly Performance of Twitter, Inc.'s Stock Price, May 2015–June 2020

(a) Trend in Twitter, Inc.'s Common Stock Price

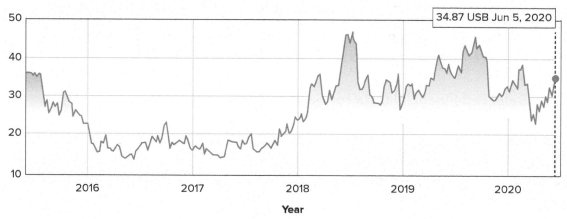

(b) Performance of Twitter, Inc.'s Stock Price Versus the S&P 500 Index, May 2015–June 2020

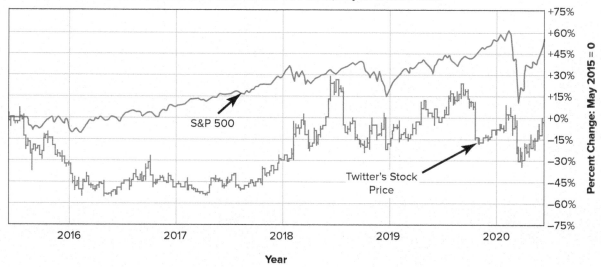

Source: Bigcharts.com.

rally that pushed the company's stock to more than $45.00/share by June 2018, which was its highest price since March of 2015.

The S&P 500 bounce was not sustained and Twitter's stock slid to $27.00 by the end of December 2018. The stock began an intermittent climb and reached $45.00 again in September 2019, and began another slide down to $23.00 on April 3, 2020. Despite negative first quarter, 2020 earnings, the share price began a choppy uptrend, closing at $34.87 on June 5, 2020.

TWITTER'S MAJOR COMPETITORS

Facebook

Facebook was the world's largest online social networking and social media company. It was founded in February 2004 by Mark Zuckerberg, Eduardo Saverin, Dustin Moskivitz, Chris Hughes, and Andrew McCollum. As was common among online social networking companies, Facebook was not immediately profitable; however, after becoming profitable in 2010, it had its IPO in 2012 at $38/share. Although the stock price dropped to under $20 in August 2012, it rebounded and was selling at $217.50/share in mid-July 2018, and then began a slide down to $124.95 in December 2018. In late December 2018, Facebook stock began a recovery and in June 2020, was trading above $230. In April 2020, Facebook had 2.6 billion users worldwide—India had the largest number of users at 280 million, the United States was second with 190 million, and Indonesia was third with 130 million.

In the first quarter 2020, Facebook had 2.6 billion average monthly users, and 90 percent of the total users were from outside the United States. Facebook's year-over-year revenue growth rate in the first quarter of 2020 was 18 percent, and net income increased 102 percent over the same period 2019. A financial summary for Facebook, Inc. for 2015 to 2019 is presented in Exhibit 6.

EXHIBIT 6   Selected Financial Data for Facebook, Inc., 2015–2019 (in millions, except per share data)

	Year Ended December 31,				
	2019	2018	2017	2016	2015
Consolidated Statements of Income Data:					
Revenue	$70,697	$55,838	$40,653	$27,638	$17,928
Total costs and expenses[1]	46,711	30,925	20,450	15,211	11,703
Income from operations	23,986	24,913	20,203	12,427	6,225
Income before provision for income taxes	24,812	25,361	20,594	12,518	6,194
Net income	18,485	22,112	15,934	10,217	3,688
Net income attributable to Class A and Class B common stockholders	18,485	22,111	15,920	10,188	3,669
Earnings per share attributable to Class A and Class B common stockholders					
Basic	$6.48	$7.65	$5.49	$3.56	$1.31
Diluted	$6.43	$7.57	$5.39	$3.49	$1.29

[1] Total costs and expenses include $4.84 billion, $4.15 billion, $3.72 billion, $3.22 billion, and $2.97 billion of share-based compensation for the years ended December 31, 2019, 2018, 2017, 2016, and 2015, respectively.

	As of December 31,				
	2019	2018	2017	2016	2015
Consolidated Balance Sheets Data:					
Cash, cash equivalents, and marketable securities	$ 54,855	$41,114	$41,711	$29,449	$18,434
Working capital	51,172	43,463	44,803	31,526	19,727
Property and equipment, net	35,323	24,683	13,721	8,591	5,687
Total assets	133,376	97,334	84,524	64,961	49,407
Operating lease liabilities[1]	10,324	—	—	—	—
Total liabilities	32,322	13,207	10,177	5,767	5,189
Additional paid-in capital	45,851	42,906	40,584	38,227	34,886
Total stockholders' equity	101,054	84,127	74,347	59,194	44,218

[1] On January 1, 2019, we adopted Accounting Standards Update No. 2016-02, *Leases (Topic 842)*. Prior period amounts have not been adjusted under the modified retrospective method.

Source: Facebook Annual Report, 2019.

WhatsApp

WhatsApp was a freeware and cross-platform messaging and IP service owned by Facebook. The company was founded in 2009 by ex-Yahoo employees Jan Koum and Brian Acton. WhatsApp used the Internet to send messages, audio, video, and images, and was similar to a text messaging service. However, because WhatsApp sent messages over the Internet, the cost for users was much less than texting. The company grew quickly and within a few months of startup, WhatsApp added a service charge to slow down its growth rate. In 2014, WhatsApp was acquired by Facebook for $21.94 billion.

In early 2018, after a long feud with Facebook founder and CEO Mark Zuckerberg about how to get additional revenue from WhatsApp, Koum and Acton resigned from Facebook. Zuckerberg was focused on using targeted ads to WhatsApp's large user base; Koum and Acton were believers in privacy and had no interest in the potential commercial applications. When WhatsApp was sold to Facebook, the founders pledged privacy of WhatsApp. Four years later, Facebook pushed WhatsApp to change its terms of service and give Facebook access to WhatsApp users' phone numbers. Facebook also wanted a unified profile that could be used for ad targeting and data mining, and a recommendation system that would suggest Facebook friends based on WhatsApp contacts. WhatsApp was the most popular messaging app in the world in 2020, with 0.2 billion more users than Facebook Messenger. WhatsApp had 1.5 billion users in 180 countries in the first quarter 2020, 68 million in the United States, with 1 billion daily active WhatsApp users and 65 billion messages, sent each day.

Snapchat

Snap Inc. was a camera company that believed that reinventing the camera was a great opportunity to improve the way that people communicated and lived. Snap, Inc.'s products empowered people to express themselves, live in the moment, learn about the world, and have fun together. The company's flagship product, Snapchat, was a camera application that helped people communicate visually with friends and family through short videos and images called snaps. Snaps were deleted by default, so there was less pressure to look good when creating and sending images on Snapchat. By reducing the friction typically associated with creating and sharing content, Snapchat became one of the most-used cameras in the world.

Snapchat had over 398 million active users worldwide, and 101 million users in the United States in January 2020. On average, 218 million people used Snapchat daily, creating over 3 billion snaps every day; however, its users were declining. A financial summary for Snap Inc. for 2015 through 2019 is presented in Exhibit 7.

Instagram

Instagram was a video and photo-sharing social network service created by Kevin Systrom and Mike Krieger in 2010. Facebook acquired the company in 2012: the agreed price was $1 billion (a mixture of case and Facebook stock), however the final price was $715 million because Facebook's share process tumbled before the deal was finalized. If Instagram were a standalone company, it would be worth more than $100 billion, which would be a 100-fold return for Facebook.

In March 2019, Instagram reached 1.1 billion monthly active users, but by April 2020, that number was down slightly to 1 billion. There were 89 percent of which are outside the United States in October 2019. The company generated $20 billion in advertising revenue in 2019, which was over 25 percent of Facebook sales, and Instagram attracted new users at a faster rate than Facebook's main site in 2018. In the second quarter 2019, at five percent per quarter growth, Instagram was ahead of Facebook, which was growing at 3.14 percent, and Snapchat, growing at 2.13 percent. The company was forecast to generate $9.5 billion in advertising revenues in 2019 and to grow 47 percent to $13.9 billion in fiscal 2020.

LinkedIn

LinkedIn was a social media service that operated through websites and mobile apps, and focused primarily on professional networking, which enabled members to create, manage, and share their professional identities online, create professional networks, share insights and knowledge, and find jobs and business opportunities. The company was founded in December 2002 by Allen Blue, Reid G. Hoffman, Jean-Luc Vaillant, Konstantin Guericke, and Eric Ly. LinkedIn was named by Forbes as one of America's Best Employers in 2016. LinkedIn was acquired by Microsoft for $26.2 billion in June 2016.

In March 2020, LinkedIn had over 660 million members, 70 percent of which were outside the

EXHIBIT 7   Selected Financial Data for Snap, Inc., 2015–2019
(in thousands, except per share amounts)

	Year Ended December 31,				
	2019	2018	2017	2016	2015
Consolidated Statements of Operations Data					
Revenue	$ 1,715,534	$ 1,180,446	$ 824,949	$ 404,482	$ 58,663
Costs and expenses:					
Cost of revenue	895,838	798,865	717,462	451,660	182,341
Research and development	883,509	772,185	1,534,863	183,676	82,235
Sales and marketing	458,598	400,824	522,605	124,371	27,216
General and administrative	580,917	477,022	1,535,595	165,160	148,600
Total costs and expenses	2,818,862	2,448,896	4,310,525	924,867	440,392
Operating loss	(1,103,328)	(1,268,450)	(3,485,576)	(520,385)	(381,729)
Interest income	36,042	27,228	21,096	4,654	1,399
Interest expense	(24,994)	(3,894)	(3,456)	(1,424)	—
Other income (expense), net	59,013	(8,248)	4,528	(4,568)	(152)
Loss before income taxes	(1,033,267)	(1,253,364)	(3,463,408)	(521,723)	(380,482)
Income tax benefit (expense)	(393)	(2,547)	18,342	7,080	7,589
Net loss	$(1,033,660)	$(1,255,911)	$(3,445,066)	$(514,643)	$(372,893)
Net loss per share attributable to Class A, Class B, and Class C common stockholders					
Basic	$(0.75)	$(0.97)	$(2.95)	$(0.64)	$(0.51)
Diluted	$(0.75)	$(0.97)	$(2.95)	$(0.64)	$(0.51)
	December 31,				
	2019	2018	2017	2016	2015
Consolidated Balance Sheet Data					
Cash, cash equivalents, and marketable securities	$2,112,805	$1,279,063	$2,043,039	$ 987,368	$ 640,810
Working capital	2,144,311	1,383,237	2,020,538	1,023,241	536,306
Total assets	4,011,924	2,714,106	3,421,566	1,722,792	938,936
Total liabilities	1,752,011	403,107	429,239	203,878	174,791
Additional paid-in capital	9,205,256	8,220,417	7,634,825	2,728,823	1,467,355
Accumulated deficit	(6,945,930)	(5,912,578)	(4,656,667)	(1,207,862)	(693,219)
Total stockholders' equity	2,259,913	2,310,999	2,992,327	1,518,914	764,145

Source: Snap Inc. Annual Report 2019.

United States, up from 575 million in March 2019: the company had revenue of $6.8 billion in 2019. The company was the number one channel that B2B marketers used to distribute content. LinkedIn had 575 million users in more than 200 countries and territories worldwide.[4]

TROUBLING SIGNS IN FIRST QUARTER—2020

Twitter's first quarter 2020 financial results took a negative turn. Although revenue was up three percent year over year to $808 million, from $787 million, it was down 20 percent from $1,007 million in the fourth quarter 2019. Twitter blamed the revenue decline on the impact of COVID-19. The quarter showed a net loss of $8.4 million, versus the $191 million net income for the first quarter 2019. The company's revenues had growth across both service areas—advertising and data licensing—but surprisingly, despite an increase in overall net revenue, international revenue was down to 42 percent in the first quarter 2020, from 45 percent in the same period in the prior year (Exhibit 8 presents Twitters first quarter, 2020 Consolidated Statements of Operations). Twitter's first quarter 2020 growth in revenue from the United States, increased by eight percent, year-over-year, from $432 million to $468 million. International revenue decreased 2.0 percent, year-over-year, from $318 million to $355 million. Twitter's first quarter 2020 Revenue by Geographic Area is provided in Exhibit 9.

Year-over-year advertising revenue increased slightly by 0.4 percent during the first quarter of 2020, from $679 million to $682 million, and data licensing revenue increased from $107 million to $125 million, year-over-year, a 17 percent increase. Cost of revenue increased to 35 percent of revenue, up from 34 percent of revenue in the same period, 2019.

EXHIBIT 8   Twitter, Inc. First Quarter, 2020 Consolidated Statement of Operations, Q1 2019 and Q1 2020

Twitter, Inc. Consolidated Statements of Operations		
	Three Months Ended March 31,	
	2020	**2019**
Revenue	$807,637	$786,890
Costs and expenses		
Cost of revenue	284,037	264,011
Research and development	200,388	146,246
Sales and marketing	221,287	205,799
General and administrative	109,368	77,176
Total costs and expenses	815,080	693,232
Income (loss) from operations	(7,443)	93,658
Interest expense	(33,270)	(37,260)
Interest income	32,897	40,541
Other expense, net	(7,719)	(436)
Income (loss) before income taxes	(15,535)	96,503
Benefit from income taxes	(7,139)	(94,301)
Net income (loss)	$(8,396)	$190,804
Net income (loss) per share attributable to common stockholders		
Basic	$(0.01)	$0.25
Diluted	$(0.01)	$0.25
Weighted-average shares used to compute net income (loss) per share attributable to common stockholders		
Basic	780,688	764,550
Diluted	780,688	777,689

EXHIBIT 9   Twitter, Inc. Revenue by Geographic Area, Q1 2019 and Q2 2020

	Three Months Ended March 31,	
	2020	**2019**
Revenue by geographic area:		
United States	$468,430	$432,356
Japan	131,132	135,571
Rest of World	208,075	218,963
Total revenue	$807,637	$786,890

Source: Facebook 10-Q, First Quarter, 2020.

Increases in operating expenses proved disastrous in the first quarter 2020: research and development expenses increased from 19 percent to 25 percent of revenue from the same period in the prior year, sales and marketing increased from 26 percent to 27 percent, and general and administrative expenses increased from 10 percent to 14 percent, as a percent of revenue. The increased expenses resulted in an operating loss of $7.4 million, down from $93.6 million (12 percent) net income in the same period 2019. The net loss of $8.4 million for the first quarter 2020 was a shocking contrast from net income of $191 million (24 percent of revenue) for the same period in the prior year.

Citing concerns about the uncertainty due to the COVID-19 pandemic, and rapidly shifting market conditions in its business environment, Twitter did not provide revenue or income guidance for the second quarter and suspended full year guidance.

Going into the second quarter of fiscal 2020, Twitter was focused on:

1. Increasing focus on revenue products, particularly performance ads beginning with MAP, with the goal of accelerating the company's long-term strategy.

2. Reducing company hiring and non-labor expenses to lower expense growth while continuing to focus investments on Engineering, Product, and Trust & Safety, ensuring that resources are allocated against the most important work.

ENDNOTES

[1] Armin, "Twitter Gives You the Bird," June 7, 2012, https://www.underconsideration.com/brandnew/archives/twitter_gives_you_the_bird.php.
[2] As quoted in "Is Twitters" logo change the most revolutionary re-branding of the Modern Era?, Gawker, June 6, 2006, http://gawker.com/5916390/is-twitters-logo-change-the-most-revolutionary-re-branding-of-the-modern-era.
[3] Sunil Singh, "How a Logo Personified the Twitter Brand," February 15, 2018, https://gulfmarketingreview.com/brands/how-a-logo-personified-the-twitter-brand/.
[4] As stated at about.linkedin.com.

Yeti in 2020: Can Brand Name and Innovation Keep it Ahead of the Competition?

Diana R. Garza
University of the Incarnate Word

David L. Turnipseed
University of South Alabama

In early 2020, Matthew Reintjes, president and CEO of Yeti, contemplated the company's fiscal 2019 operations. Although the company had shown a 17 percent increase in revenue over fiscal 2018, with sales of $914 million, and profit of over $50 million, there were uncertainties ahead for the fast-moving company. Yeti's coolers and other products had captured the number one position in the United States, and awareness in the domestic markets had risen from two percent in October 2015 to 10 percent in July 2018 according to the company's own brand tracking survey. Yeti had become a cult icon for the hunting, fishing, boating and outdoors sports communities, and was rapidly expanding beyond those groups. On almost every outing, one would see people wearing Yeti T-shirts and caps, and Yeti stickers on the rear windows of pickups and SUVs.

Yet despite the meteoric rise increase in revenues, market share, and profits, there were storm clouds on the horizon. First, the recent tariff controversy between the United States and China, and the European Union had the potential to increase prices and thus reduce sales of Yeti products. Second, the COVID-19 global pandemic that began in early 2020 and its economic fallout could certainly have a negative impact on the sales of all Yeti products, both domestically and foreign, for an extended period. Third, and perhaps most concerning, was the large and increasing number of competitors across the entire product line, ranging from large well-known brands such as Otter Box, Tervis, Igloo, and Pelican to numerous small brands.

Yeti's management was aware that although the company's products were high quality, there were many equally high-quality competitor products available in the market: the market value of Yeti appeared to be the market value of its brand. The management team recognized that the path to continued success for Yeti was to maintain and increase the value of the brand, and to position the brand to have increased value with larger numbers of consumers. Mr. Reintjes resolved to craft a strategy that would reestablish and maintain the upward trajectory of profits for the company.

Two Brothers and a Cooler: From Dream to Icon

After graduation from college, Roy (Texas Tech University) and Ryan (Texas A & M University) Seiders began searching for business plans in the outdoor field. Their father had been a successful entrepreneur in the fishing tackle industry and the boys were determined to follow his lead. Ryan started a custom fishing-rod business and Roy began building fishing boats. Roy's boats included three coolers, one of which was in the bow of the boat and used as a fishing platform. The coolers were the least satisfactory part of the boat, and Roy began looking for better options. Brother Ryan identified an imported Thai cooler at a trade show that impressed him with ruggedness (but not design or finish). He began importing the Thai coolers and marketing them to outdoor equipment retailers and fishing tackle shops, which was the market that he knew best.

The Thai cooler generated sales, but warranty costs and disappointment with improvements in the design motivated the search for another manufacturer. The brothers located a manufacturer in the Philippines that was capable of manufacturing the cooler that Ryan had envisioned. Roy believed the time had come to start a cooler business and a brand name. The result of a good cooler is ice retention–even after its usage for food or drink is complete. This feature, plus the input of family and friends resulted in the name Yeti–the Ice Monster, and the company was born in 2006. The company's mission was simple: "build the cooler you'd use every day if it existed."

Roy used the money from his Thai cooler business, and Ryan sold his fishing-rod business to fund the Yeti prototype. The cooler was designed so that anything breakable (e.g., the rope handles) could be easily replaced. The cooler was designed for durability, which came with a cost. The brothers realized that their cooler would have to be sold for about $300.00, and there was no market for a cooler in that price range. Their initial marketing and distribution plan focused on tackle shops which were offered a simple proposition: rather than compete with Wal-Mart and sell $30.00 coolers with $5.00 profit, sell $300.00 Yeti coolers with $100.00 profit.

The brothers sold majority owner in Yeti to Cortec Group Management Services, LLC, a private equity firm, in 2012. Cortec provided management services for a fee of 1 percent of sales (not to exceed $750,000 annually). With the advice of an ad agency, Yeti created a tagline 'Wildly Stronger, Keep Ice Longer' and concentrated marketing on fishermen and hunters. The young company hired influential fishermen and hunting guides as ambassadors for the brand. Brand awareness was also stoked by the inclusion of a Yeti hat or t-shirt with each cooler sold.

Over the three-year period of 2015 to 2018, Yeti's customer base progressed from nine percent to 34 percent female, and from 64 percent to 70 percent under 45 years of age. Yeti brand awareness in the U.S. cooler and drinkware markets grew from seven percent in 2015 to 24 percent in 2017. Although Yeti continued to invest in their hunting and fishing communities, their customer base dropped from 69 to 38 percent hunters during 2015–2018, as the company's appeal broadened beyond their original customer communities.

Yeti's IPO and Stock

In 2016, Yeti filed an IPO to reduce debt and cash out its private equity owners, however, a downturn in business caused the company to withdraw its filing. The young company had considerable success in the early years and grew too rapidly, with the result of pushing excess product to its retailers and overbuilding inventory in 2016. Also, a major retailer, Sports Authority, filed for bankruptcy in 2016 and a large amount of inventory was liquidated at greatly discounted prices, depressing Yeti's sales. The excessive inventory buildup resulted in the company's margins and revenue suffering a downturn. Revenue declined by 23 percent in 2017 and after-tax operating profit declined from 18 percent to seven percent. The business downturn, plus a general market selloff resulted in Yeti withdrawing its IPO plans in March 2018.

Seven months later, on October 24, 2018, Yeti went public: the company priced its public offering at $18.00, a bit less than the $19.00 to $21.00 per share price that it originally intended, and sold 16 million shares (versus the 20 million projected): the IPO brought in approximately $288 million. Yeti received only about $42.4 million of the IPO proceeds: the balance of the proceeds went to the Cortex Group, which retained its majority ownership. In November 2018, Yeti used the proceeds from the IPO, plus cash on hand to reduce its debt. The management agreement with Cortex was terminated with the 2018 IPO.

Yeti's stock had a generally upward trajectory, reaching $34.92 in April of 2019, which was its high. The stock seesawed from that point through the beginning of the COVID-19 market sell-off, during which it fell to $16.42 on March 20, 2020. The stock rode the market recovery back up and closed on May 15, 2020 at $26.93–see Exhibit 1.

Yeti's Strategy

Yeti product strategy was to expand existing product groups and enter new product categories by designing new offerings based on its consumers' visions and product knowledge. The company followed a temporal progression in expanding their product line: first was introduction of an anchor product and, second, product expansions such as new colors and sizes and then

EXHIBIT 1   Yeti Holdings, Inc. Stock Price, October 2018–May 2020

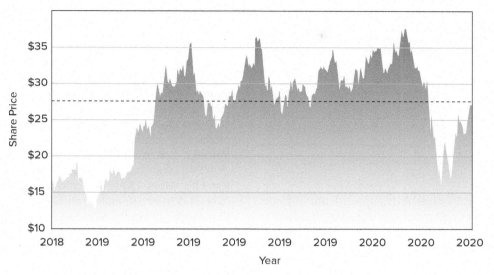

Source: nasdaq.com.

offering accessories. To ensure continued success in bringing products to market, Yeti's product development and marketing teams collaborated to identify consumer needs and wants, and then employed its research and development center to design prototypes and evaluate performance. Yeti's development process was designed to provide reliable quality control while enhancing product speed-to-market. This strategy appeared to work—a May 2018 Yeti owner study, indicated that 95 percent said they had proactively recommended Yeti products to their friends, family, and others through social media or by word-of-mouth.

Yeti collaborated with its 'YETI Ambassadors,' which was a diverse group of men and women throughout the United States and select international markets, comprised of world-class anglers, surfers, hunters, rodeo cowboys, barbecue pitmasters, and various outdoor adventurers who embodied its brand. Yeti worked hard to cultivate relationships with experts, serious enthusiasts, and everyday consumers, including a combination of traditional, digital, social media, and grass-roots initiatives to support the premium-priced brand, in addition to original short films and high-quality content for YETI.com.

Yeti learned from the 2016–17 inventory disaster and began increasing its concentration on direct-to-consumer sales through the company's direct-to-consumer strategy including its websites and Amazon

Marketplace. This strategy immediately showed positive results: the direct-to-consumer channel grew from eight percent of revenue in 2015 to 30 percent in 2017, 26 percent in 2018, and 42 percent in 2019. As comparison, Dick's Sporting Goods, Yeti's largest retail partner, accounted for 14 percent of revenue in 2017 and 15 percent in 2019. The move from brick and mortar retail outlets to increasingly direct-to-consumer sales provided Yeti with benefits beyond improved revenue. Customers dealt directly with the company rather than a retail intermediary, brand loyalty increased, the company had better ability to manage inventory, there was no retail middleman taking part of the profit, and thus gross margins were higher. In February 2020, Market Watch ranked Yeti number one in insulated coolers

Yeti's Product Line

Yeti's product portfolio comprised three categories: Coolers & Equipment; Drinkware; and Other. The company had a history of consistently broadening its premium-priced product line to meet its expanding customer base and was quite efficient at identifying customer needs and wants to drive its product line. As is shown in Exhibit 2, net sales of Coolers & Equipment, Drinkware, and Other represented 40 and 58 percent of net sales, respectively, in 2019.

EXHIBIT 2   Yeti Holdings, Inc.'s Net Sales by Category, 2017–2019 (dollars in thousands)

	2019	2018	2017
Coolers & Equipment	$368,874	$331,224	$312,237
Drinkware	526,241	424,164	310,287
Other	18,619	23,445	16,715
Total net sales	$913,734	$778,833	$639,239

Source: Yeti Holdings, Inc. Annual Report, 2019.

Coolers.   The Coolers & Equipment line included hard and soft coolers, storage, transport, outdoor living, and accessories. The Yeti hard coolers were built differently than traditional coolers, and used seamless rotationally-molded, or rotomolded, construction, making them extremely strong. To increase ice retention, Yeti pressure-injected up to two inches of polyurethane foam into the walls and lid and utilized a freezer-quality gasket to seal the lid. There were five products in Yeti's core hard cooler category: YETI Tundra (45 quart, $299.99–210 quart, $799.99), YETI TANK ($199.99–$249.99), YETI Roadie ($199.99), Tundra Haul wheeled cooler ($399.99), and YETI Silo6G ($299.99). The company also offered accessories such as cooler locks and beverage holders. In 2019, Yeti introduced a stainless-steel body YETI V Series Hard Cooler ($800.00), which combined the vacuum insulation technology used in their Tumblers with the construction of their hard coolers to produce more efficient insulation.

The Yeti Soft Cooler line was designed to be leakproof and provide superior durability and ice retention compared to competing soft coolers. The Hopper soft cooler product line included the Hopper M30 ($299.99), Hopper BackFlip ($299.99), Hopper Flip ($199.99–$299.99), and Daytrip Lunch Bag ($79.99). Yeti offered related accessories such as the SideKick Dry gear case, MOLLE Zinger lanyard, and a mountable MOLLE Bottle Opener.

Storage, Transport, and Outdoor Living.   Yeti's storage, transport, and outdoor living product category included: the Panga submersible duffel bag ($299.99–$399.99), LoadOut Bucket ($39.99), Panga Backpack ($299.99), Crossroads Backpack ($199.99), Crossroads Tote ($179.99), Camino Carryall ($149.99), SideKick Dry gear case ($49.99), Hondo Base Camp Chair ($299.99), Lowlands Blanket, Trailhead Dog Bed, and Boomer Dog Bowls. Yeti also offered several related accessories, including bottle openers, lids, and storage organizers.

Drinkware.   Yeti drinkware was manufactured with 18/8 stainless-steel, double-wall vacuum insulation, and a No Sweat design. The drinkware products kept beverages at their preferred temperature, either hot or cold, for hours at a time without condensation. Yeti's 2020 drinkware product line comprised the Rambler Colster ($29.99), Rambler Lowball ($19.99), Rambler Wine Tumbler ($24.99), Rambler Stackable Pints ($24.99–$49.99), Rambler Mugs ($24.99–$29.99), Rambler Tumblers ($34.99–$39.99), Rambler Bottles ($29.99–$49.99), and Rambler Jugs ($99.99–$129.99). There were also accessories including the Rambler Bottle Straw Cap, Rambler Tumbler Handles, Rambler Jug Mount, and Rambler Bottle Sling.

Yeti offered a broad line of YETI-branded gear and accessories including shirts, hats, bottle openers, and ice substitutes. The LoadOut GoBox, Rambler 12-ounce Bottle with Hotshot Cap, Daytrip Lunch Bag, next-generation Hopper M30 Soft Cooler, Rambler Jr. Kids Bottle, Rambler 10-ounce Stackable Mug, the Trailhead Dog Bed, Boomer 4 Dog Bowl, Crossroads 23 Backpack, Crossroads Tote Bag, Rambler 24-ounce. Mug, V Series Hard Cooler and new colorways for Drinkware, hard and soft coolers, and the Camino Carryall were all launched in 2019. Also in 2019, the company expanded distribution of its Camino Carryall to the wholesale channel.

Although Yeti products were very high quality, they were not unquestionably the best. The Strategist ranked Yeti's insulated tumbler number three, behind two little-known tumblers, the Beast and Maars Bev in 2019. In July 2019, the Chicago Tribune review also placed Yeti's Ramble tumbler number three. In April 2020, Outsidepursuits' review of camping coolers had placed the Yeti Tundra at number three behind Pelican and Engel.

Sales Channels

Yeti's gross sales to independent retail partners were 22 percent and 18 percent, in 2018 and 2019, respectively. These partners did not provide Yeti with long-term purchase commitments, and orders placed by these retail partners could be cancelled. Net channel sales are provided in Exhibit 3.

EXHIBIT 3   Yeti Holdings, Inc.'s Net Sales by Channel, 2017–2019 (dollars in thousands)

	2019	2018	2017
Wholesale	$527,634	$491,431	$444,854
Direct-to-consumer	386,100	287,402	194,385
Total net sales	$913,734	$778,833	$639,239

Source: Yeti Holdings, Inc. Annual Report, 2019.

Yeti had significant sales concentration among its retail partners. For example, Dick's Sporting Goods accounted for 16 percent and 15 percent of gross sales in 2018 and 2019 respectively. Yeti's wholesale channels sold to several large, national retailers, including Dick's Sporting Goods, Bass Pro Shops, REI, Academy Sports + Outdoors, and Ace Hardware, other retailers with a significant regional presence, and independent retail partners throughout the United States, Canada, and Australia. Yeti's network of independent retail partners included outdoor specialty, hardware, sporting goods, and farm and ranch supply stores, among others. As of the end of 2018, Yeti sold through a diverse base of nearly 4,800 independent retail partners; however, the company realized that the loss of key retail partners could be problematic. Part of the company's growth strategy was to increase the direct-to-consumer sales; however, the company had limited experience operating the retail e-commerce part of the strategy.

The company sold in a direct-to-customer channel to consumers on YETI.com, au.YETI.com, and YETI Authorized on Amazon Marketplace. Customized products with licensed brand marks and original artwork were sold through its corporate sales program and at YETIcustomshop.com. A full line of Yeti products were also sold in Austin, Texas, at the company's first retail store, which opened during fiscal 2017, and in corporate stores in Dallas, Texas; Charleston, South Carolina; and Chicago, Illinois. Yeti's direct to consumer e-commerce channel allowed the company to directly interact with customers, more effectively control its brand, better understand consumer behaviors and preferences, and offer exclusive products and customization. According to Doug Schmidt, Director of Retail Operations, the goal was to "immerse customers in the Yeti brand. The company believed its control

over its e-commerce channel provided customers the highest level of brand engagement, and built customer loyalty, while generating attractive revenues."

Yeti's global sales

Part of Yeti's strategy was international expansion, and in June 2019, the company launched its Canadian website. Also, in mid-2019, websites were opened in Europe, the United Kingdom, and New Zealand. The company showed steady increases in international sales revenue as shown in Exhibit 4.

Yeti's Innovation Center

As the company moved through the developing years, Yeti noticed that its prototyping services and testing were being outsourced, and the back and forth communication and sample development was creating long timelines for new product introductions. The company was also left vulnerable to leaks and was forced to relinquish a degree of control over product testing. In order to bring control back to the company, Yeti opened its Innovation center in August 2016. Operations were streamlined and it began prototyping, product development, and testing at its own Innovation Center. This move created greater control over its products, product innovation, and speed of development, as well as protected its intellectual property. CEO Matt Reintjes believed that their offensive strategy was to continue to be an innovation leader and stay ahead of the competition.

The Innovation Center housed 3D printers, which enabled Yeti to speed up the process of bringing products to reality through prototyping capabilities. The Innovation Center also housed machines used for rigorous product testing or as Director of

EXHIBIT 4   Yeti Holdings, Inc.'s Net Sales by Geographic Region, 2017–2019 (dollars in thousands)

	2019	2018	2017
United States	$873,867	$761,880	$635,195
International	39,867	16,953	4,044
Total net sales	$913,734	$778,833	$639,239

Source: Yeti Holdings, Inc. Annual Report, 2019.

Engineering, Scott Barbieri called it "torture tests." Prior to Yeti's products going to market, they were given to product ambassadors who were professional outdoor enthusiasts. These ambassadors provided their insights into the utility of the product, placement of zippers, straps, etc. Having a more streamlined development process allowed Yeti to involve brand ambassadors in product development discussions.

According to Category Manager Alex Baires, it was about starting from the ground up, and making a product as best the company could make it. The company products were familiar products with renewed utility that could be employed in a number of ways. The company focused on introducing new categories of products, and bringing innovation into the market through performance, durability, quality, and design. Yeti did not target a particular audience, rather it attracted new audience segments.

Yeti's Partnerships

Yeti formed several partnerships to help increase and sustain brand recognition.

Yeti became an official NASCAR partner and a sponsor of the Professional Bull Riders (PBR) in 2017. In January 2020, Yeti entered into a partnership with USA Climbing, becoming the Official Cooler and Drinkware Partner in support of the organization's sustainability efforts. The goal was to integrate Yeti in all aspects of the sport and provide support for the U.S. National team as they compete internationally. Both organizations had a commitment to sustainability and reducing single-use plastic.

Also in 2020, Yeti entered into a multiyear sponsorship agreement with Austin FC, the 27th Club Major League Soccer team. This partnership marked Yeti's formal entry into professional soccer and eSports. As official partners, Yeti was featured within Austin's FC's visual identity. The company also sponsored Austin FC's sustainability efforts to launch green initiatives that include the development of comprehensive recycling, compost, and water fill policies and practices at Austin FC's stadium.

Other Yeti partnerships included a multi-year agreement with the PGA Tour for product licensing, and the exclusive rights to sell Yeti drinkware and coolers at TOUR-operated tournament retail outlets and facilities.

Yeti's Financial Condition

Yeti's consolidated balance sheets, 2018–2019 are produced in Exhibit 5, the consolidated statement of operations in Exhibit 6, and a consolidated statement of operations data in Exhibit 7.

Yeti's Rivals in the Outdoor and Recreation Products Market

Yeti competed primarily in the large outdoor and recreation market, but also competed in other markets. According to Yeti, competition was based on product quality, performance, durability, styling, price, and brand image and recognition. In the coolers and equipment category, the company competed against Igloo and Coleman, as well as many other brands and retailers that offered similar competing products. Yeti believed that the popularity of their products, as well as their brand, had attracted numerous new competitors including Pelican, OtterBox, and others, as well as private label brands. In the Drinkware category, Yeti competed against well-known brands such as Tervis and HydroFlask, and many other brands with competing products. The outdoor and recreation market was highly fragmented and highly competitive, with low barriers to entry.

Igloo

Igloo was founded in a metalworking shop in 1947. Igloo had approximately 1200 employees and a 1.8 million square-foot, three building facility in Katy, Texas in 2019. Igloo sold more than 500 products through hundreds of retailers worldwide. The company's products included insulated coolers for personal and industrial use and insulated tumblers and growlers. In 2014, Igloo, was acquired by the private-equity firm Acon Investments.

The company's *Legacy* stainless steel tumbler line ranged from 12 ounces ($15.99) to 22 ounces ($18.99). Igloo offered stainless steel growlers in 36 ounces ($24.99) and 64 ounces ($34.99) sizes, stainless steel coffee mugs in 16-ounce ($19.99) and 20-ounce ($20.99) sizes, and a full line of tumblers, and other drinkware in double sided plastic. The company's hard side cooler offering was expansive, ranging from seven-quart coolers ($39.99) to 124-quart ($299.99) and included the very popular *Playmate* line. There were numerous Igloo soft side coolers ranging from small lunch bags ($7.99) to 46

EXHIBIT 5   Yeti Holdings, Inc.'s Consolidated Balance Sheets, 2018–2019 (in thousands, except per share data)

	December 28, 2019	December 29, 2018
ASSETS		
Current assets		
Cash	$ 72,515	$ 80,051
Accounts receivable, net	82,688	59,328
Inventory	185,700	145,423
Prepaid expenses and other current assets	19,644	12,211
Total current assets	360,547	297,013
Property and equipment, net	82,610	74,097
Operating lease right-of-use assets	37,768	—
Goodwill	54,293	54,293
Intangible assets, net	90,850	80,019
Deferred income taxes	1,082	7,777
Deferred charges and other assets	2,389	1,014
Total assets	$629,539	$514,213
LIABILITIES AND STOCKHOLDERS' EQUITY		
Current liabilities		
Accounts payable	$ 83,823	$ 68,737
Accrued expenses and other current liabilities	42,088	53,022
Taxes payable	3,329	6,390
Accrued payroll and related costs	18,119	15,551
Operating lease liabilities	7,768	—
Current maturities of long-term debt	15,185	43,638
Total current liabilities	170,312	187,338
Long-term debt, net of current portion	281,715	284,376
Operating lease liabilities, non-current	42,200	—
Other liabilities	13,307	13,528
Total liabilities	$507,534	$485,242

Source: Yeti Holdings, Inc. Annual Report, 2019.

can Tactical Duffle Bag coolers ($69.99) to 50 can coolers ($53.99).

Igloo had a very large product offering in all of the cooler and tumbler categories, which were priced very competitively, plus it had the iconic *Playmate* cooler and was a major competitor in the industry. However, its strategy moving into 2020 appeared to have the potential to significantly boost Igloo's sales revenue. In April 2019, Igloo introduced a bio-degradable cooler, the RECOOL, a 16-quart model aimed at the environmentally conscious consumer. The RECOOL, made of recycled tree pulp and paraffin wax, won Igloo multiple awards, including Best in Show from Gear Junkie, at the 2019 Outdoor Retailer and Snow Show. Following the success of the biodegradable RECOOL cooler, Igloo intro-duced the REPREVE soft side cooler made from recycled plastic bottles and announced plans to add 20 new REPREVE bag styles to the recycled plastics line in 2020.

In 2020, Igloo announced development of a bioplastic line of its *Playmate* cooler, made from sugarcane plants. The new bioplastic *Playmate* was scheduled for the consumer market in early 2021.

EXHIBIT 6   Yeti Holdings, Inc.'s Consolidated Statements of Operations, 2017–2019 (in thousands, except per share data)

	Fiscal Year Ended		
	December 28, 2019	December 29, 2018	December 30, 2017
Net sales	$913,734	$778,833	$639,239
Cost of goods sold	438,420	395,705	344,638
Gross profit	475,314	383,128	294,601
Selling, general, and administrative expenses	385,543	280,972	230,634
Operating income	89,771	102,156	63,967
Interest expense	(21,779)	(31,280)	(32,607)
Other (expense) income	734)	(1,261)	699
Income before income taxes	67,258	69,615	32,059
Income tax expense	(16,824)	(11,852)	(16,658)
Net income	$ 50,434	$ 57,763	$ 15,401
Net income per share			
Basic	$0.59	$0.71	$0.19
Diluted	$0.58	$0.69	$0.19
Weighted-average common shares outstanding			
Basic	85,088	81,777	81,479
Diluted	86,347	83,519	82,972

Source: Yeti Holdings, Inc. Annual Report, 2019.

EXHIBIT 7   Yeti Holdings, Inc.'s Consolidated Statement of Operations Data, 2015–2019 (in thousands, except per share data)

	Year Ended				
	December 28, 2019	December 29, 2018	December 30, 2017	December 31, 2016	December 31, 2015
Net sales	$913,734	$778,833	$639,239	$818,914	$468,946
Gross profit	475,314	383,128	294,601	413,961	218,701
Net Income	50,434	57,763	15,401	48,788	74,222
Net income per share—diluted	$0.58	$0.69	$0.19	$0.58	$0.92

Source: Yeti Holdings, Inc. Annual Report, 2019.

Also in 2020, Igloo partnered with BASF to engineer a new proprietary insulation foam, Thermecool, which was used for all of its hard side coolers. Igloo claimed that the new environmentally friendly insulation would have the net effect of removing over 86,000 cars from the American roads per year.

Igloo sponsored brand ambassadors who were active in outdoor sports such as fishing, running, and surfing; this group also included graphic designers whose designs were used on Igloo coolers.

Tervis

Tervis had its beginning in post WWII Detroit, Michigan, when its founders perfected the double wall cup technology to keep warm things warm and cool things cool. The name "Tervis" came from the last three letters of both founders' names: Frank Cotter and Howlett Davis. Ten years later, John Winslow bought the rights to the tumbler, moved the manufacturing to Osprey, Florida, and founded Tervis Tumbler Co. Winslow sold the cups door-to-door and dock-to-dock, and soon the tumbler became a Florida favorite. The company produced primarily state novelty cups, primarily Gulf and Atlantic coast states; however, other decals could be inserted between the two layers of plastic. Tervis made a shift from primarily state novelty cups to a national product in 1995 when it began licensing college sports and, later, major league sports logos. The company's newest products include wine glasses, sippy cups for toddlers, and metal insulated cups.

The Tervis line of drinkware was primarily plastic, however it offered several stainless-steel products, including tumblers ranging from 20 ounces ($29.99) to 30 ounces ($39.99). Tervis began a partnership with Bed, Bath, & Beyond, and launched its E-commerce site in 2008. In 2009, despite the Great Recession, Tervis's revenues rose 40 percent, from $34 million in 2008, to $47.6 million, and its employees increased from 200 to 275. In 2009, Tervis's products were sold in more than 6,000 outlets nationwide, and in company stores in Osprey, Fort Meyers, Palm Beach, and The Villages in Florida.

Otter Box

Like many start-up companies, OtterBox began with a dream. Curt Richardson started the company in a garage in 1998, and created the first OtterBox product, which was a waterproof case. Starting with a simple box, OtterBox built upon the fundamentals of hard work, taking risks, and being consumer focused to pursue its mission: "We Grow to Give." OtterBox was a seven-time honoree on the Inc. 5000 list of fastest-growing private companies in the United States. The company was also named one of 'America's Most Promising Companies' by Forbes Magazine, one of the 'Healthiest Companies to Work For in America' by Greatist, and ranked as a 'Great Place to Work' by Fortune, Forbes, and Entrepreneur Magazine. The company was headquartered in Fort Collins, Colorado, with offices in San Diego, Hong Kong, and Cork, Ireland.

Otterbox manufactured a line of coolers, drinkware and accessories that directly competed with Yeti. Their Venture coolers ranged from 25 to 65 quart capacity with prices from $229.99 to $349.99, and Otterbox Trooper soft side coolers, in 12 to 30 quart sizes, were priced from $199.99 to $299.99. The company offered a large line of insulated tumblers, ranging from small 10-ounce coffee cups (424.99), wine tumblers ($19.99), to 20-ounce tumblers ($29.99), and growlers in 28-ounce ($34.99) to 64-ounce ($69.99) sizes. There was also an expansive line of hard and soft cooler and tumbler accessories.

HydroFlask

Hydro Flask was founded in 2009 in Bend, Oregon. The company was a manufacturer of high-performance insulated products ranging from beverage and food flasks, to their Unbound Series Soft Coolers. Hydro Flask products utilized TempShield double-wall vacuum insulation and 18/8 stainless steel to maintain temperatures in their products. HydroFlask had become popular among millennials and Gen Zers due to its trendy aesthetics. There were a variety of sizes, from a 12-ounce kids' bottle to a 64-ounce jug, standard or wide mouth bottles and multiple lids to fit each. HydroFlask's stainless steel tumblers ranged from 16 ounces ($27.95) to 32 ounces ($39.95). Their large line of products included 12 ounces to 20 ounces coffee flasks priced from $29.95 to $34.95; 64-ounce. beer growlers ($64.95); drink bottles in 12-ounce to 64-ounce sizes ($29.95–$64.95); and insulated totes ($44.95–$64.95). The company's line of *Unbound* soft side coolers and totes ranged from 15 liters ($174.95) to 22 liters ($199.85). Tumblers and other drinkware carried a lifetime warranty, and coolers and totes had a five-year warranty.

Corkcicle

Corkcicle was founded in 2010 by Ben Hewitt. Hewitt, an avid chardonnay drinker, who thought there had to be a better idea to keep wine cold that did not involve a messy ice bucket. His initial idea involved putting the content of a gel pack into a test tube and covering it with a Kendall-Jackson cork. During Corkcicle's first holiday season, the company sold roughly 300,000 corkcicles. This gave way to the creation of other products such as the Chillsner that kept bottled beer cold, the Artican that would keep canned beverages chilly, and the crafted canteen that keeps beverages cool for up to 25 hours or warm for up to 12 hours. Corkcicle products included stainless steel tumblers ($27.95–$37.95), stemless wine cups ($24.95–$29.95), hybrid canteens ($39.95), coffee mugs ($39.95), lunch boxes ($39.95), and cooler bags ($129.95–$174.95). As of January 2020, Corkcicle entered into a strategic partnership with Gemline, a promotional supplier of bags, business accessories, drinkware, gifts, and writing instruments for product sales and distribution.

Coleman

Coleman had its beginning with a gas-powered lantern designed by W. C. Coleman. In 1905, the first night football game was lit by Coleman lanterns, and during WWII, Coleman camping stoves transformed the way soldiers ate in the field. Coleman designed and manufactured outdoor recreational products. Coleman's products included coolers, tents, sleeping bags, canopies, camping items, and lighting. Coleman products had been sold domestically and internationally since the 1920s. Their strong market position was attributable to its well-recognized trademarks, its broad product line, and product quality. The company did not sell direct, rather through numerous big box retailers (e.g., Bass Pro Shops, Cabela's, Home Depot, Dick's Sporting Goods, Target, and Walmart), as well as Amazon.

The large Coleman line of hard coolers ranged from small 28-quart models ($22.61) to 54-quart steel belted coolers ($119.95), and included a 52-quart Xtreme model ($51.00) that would keep drinks cold for a week in temperatures up to 90 degrees Farenheit, and a 150-quart Marine cooler that would keep 223 can cold for 6 days in 90 degree Farenheit temperatures. Coleman's soft side coolers ranged from small, 4-quart models ($11.25) to 36-quart models ($65.55), and their stainless-steel tumbler line ranged from a 13oz. *Rocks Glass* ($12.00) to a 30oz. tumbler ($19.99).

Coleman's 2019–20 partnerships included Jeep Jamboree USA, an outdoor family oriented adventure trip; Stagecoach Country Music Festival; Seven Peaks Music Festival; Great American Beer Festival; and park districts. Coleman also partnered with Team Rubicon, an organization that provided relief to those affected by natural disasters, and Convoy of Hope, a nonprofit community outreach and disaster relief organization.

Pelican

Pelican was founded in 1976 by Dave and Arline Parker in their Torrance, California garage. Dave, who had been a scuba diver since age 11, recognized the need for rugged flashlights and cases that wouldn't leak or fail and set out to build a better product than any other on the market. After years of work, Pelican Products became a reality with its first product patent, the Pelican Float™. The SabreLite™ flashlight and Protector Cases soon followed. Pelican's product line and company grew steadily over the years and, in 2004, the company was acquired by private equity firm, Behrman Capital. Shortly thereafter, the company experienced a tremendous global growth trend under its new CEO Lyndon Faulkner. The company added coolers and drinkware to its product line in 2012.

The Pelican line of *Dayventure* soft side coolers included nine-quart ($149.95) and 19-quart ($249.95) models, and its hard side cooler line ranged from 20-quart ($153.95) to 150-quart ($648.95) models. The company's hard coolers were 30 percent lighter than roto-molded coolers, and had two-inch solid wall construction, stainless-steel latches, built-in cupholders, and were guaranteed for life. Pelican's stainless steel *Dayventure* tumbler line ranged from 10oz. ($19.95) to 22oz. ($29.95), and its insulated stainless bottles ranged from 18oz. ($24.95) to 64oz. ($49.95).

Numerous Small Brands

Coolers and especially insulated tumblers and accessories were rather simple and inexpensive to manufacture and within the abilities of a large number of manufacturing companies. Consequently, many small specialty retailers contracted with manufactures for these products and competed with Yeti (and other large companies). Companies such as ORCA, Monoprice Polar Bear, RTIC, K2, Domestic, IceMule, Ozark, Titan, Frosted Frog, CaterGater, Engel, RovR, and Xspec were examples of smaller retailers competing in the insulated cooler market. The insulated tumbler market was equally crowded, with companies such as Klean Kanteen, Mira, Sunwill, Beast, Drinco, Maars Bev, RTIC, Umite Chef, Atlin, Baroon, Ozark Trail, Zojirushi, Sipworksw, Mukoko, Bugga Keg, Ultra Fyt, MalloMe, and others selling tumblers that directly competed with Yeti.

Yeti's Strategic Situation in Mid-2020

Going into mid-2020, Yeti management sought to capitalize on its financial and market success with continued growth. The company's products resonated with consumers, with sales increasing in both in the United States and internationally. There were opportunities for management to improve the company's internal operations and strategy, but external factors were among the most worrisome issues facing the company. It was imperative that the company prepare itself for the impact of unfavorable tariffs, prolonged effects of the COVID-19 pandemic, and the proliferation of rivals seeking to unseat Yeti as the leading premium brand of coolers, drinkware, and related products.

GoPro in 2020: Have its Turnaround Strategies Failed?

David L. Turnipseed
University of South Alabama

John E. Gamble
Texas A&M University–Corpus Christi

GoPro had been among the best examples of how a company could create a new market based upon product innovations that customers understood and demanded. However, by late 2015, the action camera product niche appeared saturated. The company had grown from a humble beginning as a homemade camera tether and plastic case vendor in 2004 to an action camera vendor with $350,000 in sales in 2005 (its first full year of operation) to a global seller of consumer electronics with revenue of $1.6 billion in 2015. The company's shares had traded as high as $88 in October 2014, just months after its initial public offering (IPO) in June 2014. In 2014, GoPro was ranked the number one most popular brand on YouTube with more than 640 million views, and an average of 845,000 views daily. In 2015, average daily views were up to 1.01 million.

Abruptly, in the third quarter of 2015, GoPro's magic disappeared, and, by the fourth quarter of 2015, its revenues dropped by 31 percent from the prior year. In addition, its net income fell by 128 percent to a net loss of $34.5 million. By the end of December 2015, the stock traded at less than $20. By the end of December 2016, revenues had dropped another 27 percent to $1.2 billion from $1.6 billion in 2015. In addition, the company recorded a net loss of $419 million in fiscal 2016, helping drive its share price to less than $9.00 in December 2016.

The company launched a turnaround plan in early 2017 and reduced its workforce in an effort to reverse its decline: first quarter sales in 2017 increased by 19 percent from the first quarter 2016, and its operating expenses declined by $50 million. Its adjusted EBITDA improved from an $87 million loss in the first quarter of 2016 to a $46 million loss in the first quarter of 2017. The HERO5 Black was the best-selling digital image camera in the United States in the first quarter of 2017, and GoPro's drone Karma with the HERO5 camera was the number-two selling drone priced over $1,000 in the United States.

After a recall of the Karma drone for flight failure, GoPro abandoned the drone business in early 2018. The number of camera units shipped in 2018 was flat, compared to the prior year, and the average selling price decreased which put downward pressure on the year's revenue. The company announced another restructuring in 2018, which resulted in an additional reduction in the global workforce to below 1,000 by the end of the year, and continuing reductions in operating expenses. These efforts met with mixed results, and revenue continued to fall, dropping 2.7 percent from the prior year, and gross margin fell from 32.6 percent in 2017 to 31.5 percent in 2018. Operating expense decreased from 46 percent of revenue in 2017 to 40 percent in 2018. Yet fiscal 2018 produced a loss of $109 million.

The dismal trend in financial performance continued, albeit with a four percent uptick in revenue in fiscal 2019. GoPro's 2019 gross margin increased to 35 percent, up from 31 percent in 2018, and adjusted EBITDA increased by 230 percent from 2018. Camera units shipped in 2019 were down two percent from 2018. Although the net loss in 2019 was the smallest in the past four years, it nonetheless added $14.6 million to GoPro's accumulated deficit. The continuing subpar operation took its toll on the share prices: in the fourth quarter 2019, share prices were slightly over $4.00, which was 95 percent below its $88.00 high.

In GoPro's first quarter 2020, results appeared to be the death knell for the struggling company. In the first quarter, despite GoPro.com recording record revenue, its subscription service up 69 percent year-over-year, and social followers increasing to over 44 million, GoPro's fortunes turned even more negative. The company experienced a 50 percent decrease in revenue from the same period, 2019, a decline in gross margin, a 177 percent increase in operating losses, and a 161 percent great net loss, over the same period in 2019, yet GoPro continued to be the industry leader in action cameras. The company announced another restructuring aimed at reducing expenses. Plans included trimming the remaining workforce by 20 percent, reducing operating expenses by $100 million, and cutting an additional $250 million from operating expenses in 2021. A summary of the company's financial performance for 2015 through 2019 is presented in Exhibit 1. The performance of GoPro's shares from June 2014 through May 2020 is presented in Exhibit 2.

In mid-2020, GoPro was without doubt a dominant force in the global action camera industry; however, years of net losses had resulted in an accumulated deficit of $583 million. The first quarter 2020 had produced dismal results, and although the COVID-19 pandemic could be partially to blame, the continuing losses further weakened the struggling company. The company's management was faced with the critical, time-sensitive mandate: find a way to increase revenue and restore profitability before the lack of liquidity impeded the ability to make proactive strategic moves.

Company History

GoPro began as the result of business failures. GoPro's founder, Nick Woodman, grew up in Silicon Valley, the son of wealthy parents (his father brokered the purchase of Taco Bell by Pepsi). Woodman started an online electronics store, EmpowerAll.com, which failed. He subsequently started an online gaming service, Funbug, that failed in the dot-com crash of 2001, costing investors $3.9 million. Woodman consoled himself after the failure of Funbug with an extended surfing vacation in Indonesia and Australia. While on vacation, he fashioned a wrist strap from a broken surfboard leash and rubber bands to attach a disposable Kodak camera to his wrist while on the water. Woodman's friend and current GoPro creative director Brad Schmidt joined the vacation, worked with the camera strap, and observed that Woodman needed a camera that could withstand the sea.

After his vacation, Woodman returned home and focused on developing a comprehensive camera, casing, and strap package for surfers. Originally incorporated as Woodman Labs, the company began

EXHIBIT 1   Financial Summary for GoPro, Inc., 2015–2019 (in thousands, except per share amounts)

	2019	2018	2017	2016	2015
Revenue	$1,194,651	$1,148,337	$1,179,741	$1,185,481	$1,619,971
Gross Profit	412,789	361,434	384,530	461,920	673,214
Gross Margin	34.6%	31.5%	32.6%	39.0%	41.6%
Operating income (loss)	(2,333)	(93,962)	(163,460)	(372,969)	54,748
Net Income (loss)	(14,642)	(109,034)	(182,873)	(419,003)	36,131
Net income (loss) per share:					
Basic	$(0.10)	$(0.78)	$(1.32)	$(3.01)	$0.27
Diluted	$(0.10)	$(0.78)	$(1.32)	$(3.01)	$0.25

Source: GoPro, Inc. 2019 Annual Report.

EXHIBIT 2   GoPro Stock Performance, December 2014–December 2019

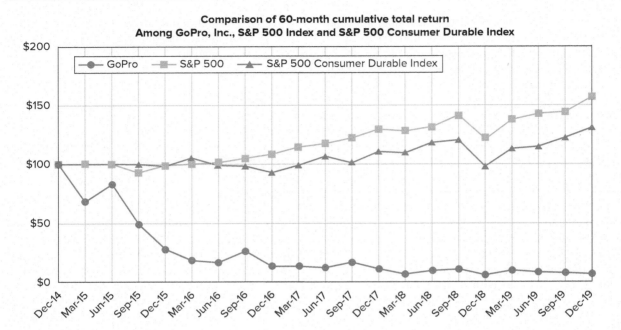

Comparison of 60-month cumulative total return
Among GoPro, Inc., S&P 500 Index and S&P 500 Consumer Durable Index

Source: GoPro, Inc. 2019 Annual Report.

doing business in 2004 as GoPro. Woodman found a 35-mm camera made in China that cost $3.05 and sent his homemade plastic case and $5,000 to an unknown company, Hotax. A few months later, Woodman received his renderings and a 3-D model from the company and sold his first GoPro camera in September 2004 at an action-sports trade show. Also that year, GoPro hired its first employee, Neil Dana, who was Woodman's college roommate.

The two-man company grossed $350,000 in 2005, the first full year of operation. Woodman wanted to keep the company private as long as possible: he invested $30,000 personally, his mother contributed $35,000, and his father added $200,000. In a fortunate coincidence for GoPro, in fall 2006 Google purchased a then-small company, YouTube, and in spring 2007, the GoPro HERO3 with VGA video was launched. According to Woodman, the competing name-brand cameras available at the time did not have good video quality. The combination of GoPro's HERO3 video quality and the increasing popularity of YouTube caused GoPro's sales to triple in 2007.

In 2007, although the company had revenues in the low seven figures, Woodman began to question his ability to take the firm further. He negotiated a deal to turn the company over to a group of outside investors, but before the deal was finalized (which was at the beginning of the 2008 financial crisis), the investors wanted to lower the valuation of the company. GoPro was profitable, and Woodman did not believe that the company was having any ill effects from the economy. He refused to negotiate the company's value down, and the company's sales were over $8 million that year. The company's growth continued and in 2010, Best Buy began carrying GoPro products, which was a clear indication that the company was accepted in the market.

In May 2011, GoPro received $88 million in investments from five venture capital firms (including Steamboat Ventures—Disney's venture capital company) which enabled Woodman, his family, and some GoPro executives to take cash from the company. Also in 2011, GoPro acquired CineForm, a small company that had developed a proprietary codex that quickly and easily converted digital video files among different formats. CineForm had used this codex in several movies including *Need for Speed* and *Slumdog Millionaire*. As part of GoPro, CineForm altered its 3-D footage tool into an editing program that became the company's first desktop application, GoPro Studio.

A Taiwanese manufacturing company, Foxconn (trading as Hone Hai Precision Industry Co.), bought 8.8 percent of GoPro for $200 million, in December 2012, which brought the value of the privately held company to about $2.25 billion, and *Forbes* reported Woodman's personal net worth to be about $1.73 billion. GoPro sold 2.3 million cameras and grossed $531 million in 2012, and, in December of that year, GoPro replaced Sony as the highest-selling camera brand at Best Buy.

Sales of GoPro cameras at snow-sports retailers increased by 50 percent for the 2012–2013 ski season. GoPro almost doubled its revenues in each of three consecutive years, from $234.2 million in 2011 to $525 million in 2012 and $985 million in 2013, according to the U.S. Securities and Exchange Commission (SEC). Although revenues increased 87 percent in 2013, in that year the decrease in revenue growth became obvious. According to its IPO filing, as of December 2013, the company had not derived any revenue from the distribution of its content on the GoPro Network; however, it announced plans to pursue new streams of revenue from the distribution of GoPro content. GoPro formed a new software division in 2013. Also in that year, the National Academy of Television Arts and Sciences recognized the company with a Technology and Engineering Emmy Award in the Inexpensive Small Rugged HD Camera category.

In June 2014, GoPro went public at an IPO price of $24.00 which valued the company at $2.7 billion. The IPO included a lockup agreement that prevented the Woodmans from selling any shares of GoPro stock for six months; four months later on October 2, 2014, the Woodmans made a donation of 5.8 million shares of GoPro stock into the Jill and Nick Woodman Foundation. A press release about the foundation stated that details about its mission would be announced at a later date, according to CNN. Share prices dropped 14 percent after the announcement and angered investors. Also, GoPro failed to meet investors' expectations when it released its first earnings report in August 2014.

GoPro increased emphasis on software and video sharing in 2015. In 2015, GoPro tied with Apple on the Google Brand Leaderboard, which measures the most popular brands on YouTube. According to Google, more than 4.6 years of content was uploaded to YouTube in 2015 with GoPro in the title, an increase of 22 percent from 2014. Also in 2015, the company launched the GoPro Channel on Amazon Fire TV and Fire TV Stick with a custom-designed streaming channel that was a one-stop destination for delivering on-demand GoPro videos to Amazon customers.

Another 2015 development was the GoPro Channel on the PlayStation Network which allowed PlayStation owners to stream GoPro content on-demand and browse GoPro cameras and accessories. PlayStation joined GoPro's growing roster of distribution partners including Amazon Fire TV, Roku, Comcast Watchable, Sky, Vessel Entertainment, Xbox, LG, and Virgin America. The GoPro Mobile App was downloaded 2.75 million times in the fourth quarter, totaling almost 24 million cumulative downloads; fourth quarter installs of GoPro Studio totaled nearly 1.7 million, totaling over 15 million cumulative installs, with average daily video exports of over 49,000. GoPro's shareholders were not impressed with the operations, and from July to the end of December 2015, the company's stock fell from $63.00 to $18.00.

GoPro purchased Kolor, a French company with experience making software for capturing and displaying virtual reality in 2016, and acquired Replay and Splice, two leading mobile video editing apps. Replay was video editing software that GoPro rebranded as Quik, and Splice was an app that promised desktop-level performance for editing video on an iPhone. The Kolor group assisted in the launch of a virtual reality social media platform that functioned both on the web and as an app. According to *The Verge* (June 2, 2016), Woodman understood that "the hardware-first chapter of GoPro" was coming to the end. He recognized that market saturation had created the problem, explaining it as "content guilt." According to Woodman, "Most people don't even watch their GoPro footage." He blamed the company for creating the problem by solving the capture side but leaving customers hanging in postproduction.

In April 2016, the investment bank Piper Jaffray reported that GoPro was gaining market share in a declining market, and that action camera ownership declined to 28 percent among teenage consumers, down from 31 percent a year previous, and 40 percent in 2013. This trend clearly indicated the need for GoPro to transform into something more than an action camera company. The GoPro brand and reputation had been made as a hardware company, and moving that reputation to a new market (i.e., software) would be difficult. Although GoPro created the market for wearable cameras, it found the content-creation software field crowded. Plus, *The Verge* (June 2, 2016) pointed out that the company had no clear way to monetize its software. According to Woodman, building the software team had been the most time-consuming project the company had undertaken. He believed that the benefits of success would be large because the amount of video being consumed was huge, and the market research company NPD Group reported that more than 80 percent of smartphone users stream video.

GoPro's third quarter 2016 performance produced large losses, leading to Woodman firing 15 percent of his workforce. The company's president, Tony Bates, announced plans to leave GoPro at year end, after little more than two years with the company. Woodman also believed in the potential of Karma, GoPro's camera drone, which was released in 2016. The Karma drone, which had been postponed several times, was eventually released in October 2016. Problems quickly became apparent with the drone— it stopped flying and crashed—that required GoPro to issue a recall on November 8, 2016, and offer full refunds.

In early 2017, GoPro announced a new 360-degree camera, Fusion, but provided few details. The company planned a pilot release of Fusion in summer 2017, and a launch with a limited release at the end of 2017. According to Woodman, professional users would be the main market for Fusion, which was a much smaller market than the traditional consumers that had bought GoPro's other cameras. The company announced another restructuring and cut an additional 270 jobs. Because of the cost reductions, CEO Woodman said that the company was on track to achieve profitability in 2017.

The Karma drone problems were corrected, and it was back on the market in February 2017. Shortly after sales resumed, Woodman claimed that the drone was "exceeding our expectations" (*Fortune,* April 27, 2017). However, GoPro CFO Brian McGee said that the bulk of Karma's sales had come from being bundled with the HERO5 camera. According to McGee, GoPro made more money from the sale of a camera than from the sale of a drone. Woodman's

forecast of profitability in 2017 was inaccurate and the company suffered a $183 million net loss.

Although the Karma's problem (battery door latch) had been corrected, and the drone was put back on the market, the damage was done. In January 2018, GoPro announced that it would exit the drone market after its existing inventory was sold, and laid off several hundred employees who worked on the drone. Attempting to garner a new niche of customers, GoPro introduced an entry level HERO, that sold for $199. The company advertised the HERO as a great first GoPro for people wishing to share experiences beyond what a phone could capture. The company's flagship HERO7 Black received numerous awards during 2018, including "Best Specialty Camera" by *Videomaker* in its 2018 Best Products of the Year awards. GoPro also received numerous awards including IEEE's ICIP "Visual Innovation" award for the HERO camera line, *Newsweek's* "America's Best Customer Service" award, and IEEE's Spectrum Consumer Electronics Hall of Fame. Despite the accolades, GoPro's sales continued to shrink in falling to $1,148 million in fiscal 2018, with losses of $109 million.

The Fusion was discontinued in 2019 and replaced by MAX. In a departure from prior operations, in 2019, GoPro stopped dropping prices on previous generation products: rather these products were discontinued. GoPro's 2019 product line continued to excel in the market with the HERO8 Black being the number one selling camera in the United States in the fourth quarter 2019 and the new 360 degree MAX capturing 54 percent of the spherical camera sales. These accolades were insufficient to rescue the struggling company. In September 2019, the company downgraded its full-year guidance for 2019 and blamed production delays for the late introduction of the HERO8 Black camera. In the later part of 2019, the industry was rife with rumors of GoPro being an acquisition target.

When GoPro exited the drone market, it pledged to continue to support the Karma drone software; however, the Karma curse continued and, at the change of the decade 2019–20, the Karma software developed a problem that resulted in grounding the drone again. According to GoPro, the problem was a GPS clock rollover occurrence. These rollovers occurred once every 1024 weeks, and most software firms avoided the problems with updates, but Karma software had not been updated since 2018. By mid

January 2020, an upgrade had been developed to correct the problem. GoPro ended 2019 with a fourth consecutive year of losses, showing a $14.6 million net loss.

As GoPro moved into 2020, the first quarter results caused many in the industry to question whether the company could continue to operate. First quarter revenue dropped by 51 percent over the same period in the prior year, and the net loss increased by 161 percent. The company's shares were selling below $3.00. The company announced another restructuring with a 20 percent employee reduction, reductions in sales and marketing expenditures, and a move to a direct sales distribution model. According to GoPro, the distribution change would cost the company between $31 million and $49 million.

Since its beginning, GoPro had been primarily an action camera and related services company, with the exception of the Karma venture; however, in May 2020, the company entered the cutthroat industry of personal lighting and released its first flashlight, the Zeus Mini, which was priced at $69.99.

The Action Camera Industry from 2014 to 2020

The global action camera market was valued at $3.13 billion in 2018, and was forecast to reach $10.3 billion by 2026, which would be a six-year CAGR of 16 percent. Much of the growth in the industry had been driven by the increasing development of the travel industry and the growing numbers of travel and adventure sports participants. Entry level pricing and the consumers' demand for the latest technology were other major driving forces in the industry. Global demand was spurred by the increased popularity and use of social networking sites such as Instagram, Twitter, and Facebook, and the trend of sharing videos and photos with friends and followers. GoPro was the market leader in the world action camera industry.

Camera unit sales increased by 38 percent in North America in 2014. However, the largest growth came from the Asia Pacific region, which was up by 114 percent. Sales of action cameras worldwide reached 10.5 million in 2017, up from 8.4 million in 2015. Although the action camera market was expected to enjoy continued sales growth through at least 2019, several factors, including lengthening replacement cycles, were expected to slow the growth rate.

Consumer sales, primarily for extreme sports, had accounted for the largest part of global demand up to mid-2015, but professional sales, primarily driven by TV production, security, and law enforcement, were expected to increase. In 2014, consumers were responsible for 86 percent of action camera sales, with the remainder coming from professional uses. Although GoPro dominated the action camera industry in mid-2015, there was increased competition from other companies, including Garmin, TomTom, Canon, JVC, Ion America, Polaroid, and Sony. Other competitors were focusing on the adjacent market of wearable cameras for security and police officers.

A defining characteristic of the action camera industry in 2019 was the increase in the number of competitors. In early 2015, the market was experiencing rapid growth and attracted many new entrants, which had the expected effect on price (lower), quality (higher), and features (more). A list of action camera brands marketed in 2020 is presented in Exhibit 3.

Another industry trend was price polarization. Sales of low-end camera models priced under $200.00 and high-end models (including GoPro's $299.00 HERO8 Black) experienced increasing growth. The action camera industry experienced significant change in early 2015. A *Futuresource* analyst reported that the 360-degree capture that had recently become available would drive virtual reality applications over the coming months, especially for sports broadcasting. The company envisioned the percentage of 360-degree video action cameras growing from one percent in 2015 to 14 percent by 2019.

EXHIBIT 3   Select Action Camera Brands in 2020

GoPro	VanTop
Sony	TomTom
Yi	DJI
Kodak	Victure
Garmin	Olfi
Activeon	Insta360
Akaso	Dragon Touch
Letscom	Vtech

Source: Compiled by case researchers from various internet retailing and product review sites.

In 2014, 95 percent of action cameras sold could take high-definition video with at least 720p resolution, and approximately 85 percent of action cameras could take HD video in 1080p. About half of cameras sold could record video in ultra-high-definition 2160p, or 4K.

In 2016, the action camera industry experienced adjustments in usage: The demand for action cameras for professional applications had grown exponentially due to the focus on better viewing of sports events. Action cameras were increasingly being used for TV production and to record closer details of sports. The National Hockey League and Fishing League Worldwide had signed major contracts with iON, GoPro, and other vendors, and the professional segment of the industry was expected to have a high growth rate. Also, Global Market Insights pointed out increasing popularity of action cameras among all age groups and advanced product features as other factors providing massive growth potential.

The security industry was also finding increasing usage for action cameras in 2016, which added more fuel to the industry growth. Action cameras and especially drone-mounted action cameras were expected to be used increasingly in security applications globally. A leading vendor in the action camera–drones, Lifeline Response, had developed a smartphone app that could fly a drone to a needed location in emergencies. According to Technavio Research, professional use of action cameras would exceed casual usage by 2020.

In addition to increased demand for action cameras for professional applications, the industry was expanding also due to demand from developing countries, with the largest growth in the Asia Pacific region. Increasing disposable income, an increase in social networking, and rapid growth in adventure sport tourism, plus an increasing number of sports leagues and tournaments were factors increasing sales in emerging countries. Several action camera vendors sponsored extreme sporting events in various emerging economies to promote their camera brands. Although European growth was predicted to be stable from 2016 to 2023, the global action camera market was projected to grow at an annual rate of 14.6 percent between 2017 and 2021, and reach 10.3 billion in by 2026. These forecasts, however, became questionable in early 2020, when the COVID-19 crises virtually stopped travel and sports around the world.

The revenue growth rate in the action camera industry was expected to be lower than the growth rate in unit sales, due to a general price decline. The average action camera price was expected to decline to $226.00 by 2020, depressed primarily by a global increase in supply. Also, young consumers were increasingly choosing smartphone cameras over traditional, which meant they were less likely to purchase an action camera.

The popularity of social networking sites was a major driver of the action camera industry, and price polarization continued as a crucial trend moving into 2020. Vendors were increasingly "bundling" their products (cameras and numerous accessories) to increase demand for cameras and accessories. Bundle packaging increased demand by offering cost-effectiveness to customers because the bundling reduced or eliminated the need to purchase additional equipment. Other industry trends moving into 2020 were increasing numbers of new entrants which reduced prices, declining prices, and increasing significance of the smartphone with enhanced quality and features which depressed demand. The saturation of the action camera market niche and the declining prices contributed to the June 2017 bankruptcy filing of iON Worldwide, a major competitor in the industry.

GoPro's Business Model and Strategy

The action camera industry was a relatively young and evolving industry, and GoPro evolved within the industry. Although the company began as an action camera company, it had rapidly evolved into a diversified lifestyle company. The company's business focus, as set out in its 2015 annual report, was to develop product solutions that enabled consumers to capture, manage, share, and enjoy some of the most important moments in their lives. In addition to selling action cameras to capture live events, the company developed GoPro Entertainment, and planned to diversify into a number of related businesses, including software and drones.

Reflecting awareness of the problems facing the company after the revenue decline and net loss in 2016, and opportunities on the horizon, GoPro set out its business strategy in its 2016 Annual Report. The core of the strategy was helping consumers capture and share experiences, and GoPro was committed to developing solutions that created an easy experience for consumers to capture, create, and enjoy personal content. The company believed that when consumers used GoPro products and services, they enabled authentic content that increased awareness for the company, and drove a self-reinforcing demand for its products. Revenue growth was expected to be driven by the introduction of new cameras, drones, accessories, and software applications. This strategy was not successful, and revenue decreased from 2016–2018, with large net losses in each of those years.

In 2018, GoPro's general strategy was unchanged from 2016: the key components of the 2010 strategy were 1) drive profitability through improved efficiency, lower costs and better execution; 2) strengthen the analytics and understanding of customer behavior to enable better business planning; 3) launch products that broadened GoPro's appeal at all price points, with greater emphasis on new customers; 4) increase the investment in marketing to grow the brand and attract new customers globally; 5) focus on the ecosystem of camera, app and cloud experiences; 6) expand the value proposition of subscription offerings to attract new consumers and engage the global user base; and 7), attract, engage, and retain top talent. Following this strategy, the company had a small four percent bounce in revenue in 2019 but continued to experience net losses.

The essence of GoPro's strategy for 2020 and beyond was to help customers capture and share their experiences in exciting ways. GoPro reiterated its belief that its revenue growth would be driven by the introduction of cameras and accessories, subscriptions, and monetizing the GoPro app. Basic to this strategy was GoPro's belief that new or better camera features would drive a replacement cycle among existing customers and attract new users.

In 2019, GoPro set out the key components of the company's 2020 strategy as the following:

1. Strengthen the core business. Focus on target customer, identify new customer segments, and deliver high-margin, high-value products which will strengthen the core business. Continued commitment and investment in consumer research. Extend GoPro's brand and products to solve problems for a broader set of customers. Leverage the GoPro brand strength and product expertise to drive a hardware upgrade cycle for existing customers and opportunistically enter complementary device segments and continue to develop cameras.

2. Maximize direct business. Increase gopro.com and direct to retailer sales which were higher margin sales than the distribution business: gopro.com was a growing percent of the company's direct revenue and therefore gross margins should increase. Focus on the direct business to improve customers' experience on gopro.com and the retail channel to improve operating results.

3. Grow the digital and subscription services. GoPro's strategy included maximizing the experience for GoPro camera customers and extending software solutions to smartphone users, thereby expanding the total addressable market. GoPro's newer cameras, GoPro Plus, and the company's apps worked together to allow users to capture, edit, and share experiences, plus back up content to the cloud. Its 2020 strategy included continuing to increase the functionality of the GoPro app for both GoPro camera owners and smartphone owners.

4. Improve efficiency and reliability. Focus on strengthening operational excellence to safeguard reliability and predictability. Operate in 2020 at a similar level of operating expenses as in 2019, and focus on generating demand, managing better and improving business predictability. GoPro recognized that future success would be partially dependent on managing operating expenses.

5. Empower employees, deepen talent development, commitment and culture. GoPro's strategy moving into 2020 included the desire to retaining committed employees. According to GoPro's strategic plan, the company intended to retain employees by leveraging its strong brand recognition; unique culture; competitive compensation and benefits; and a commitment to its diversity, inclusion, and belonging initiative.

GoPro's 2019/2020 Product Line

GoPro's 2019/2020 product line comprised the Hero line of cameras, the MAX camera, the GoPro app, and a subscription service.

HERO camera line.   The HERO8 Black, launched in Fall of 2019, was GoPro's flagship camera and sold for $299 in June 2020. The camera had enhanced HyperSmooth 2.0 image stabilization, TimeWarp Video 2.0, built-in mounting, live streaming, cloud connectivity, voice control, improved audio and touch display. The live streaming enabled users to share content in real time to their Facebook, Twitch, YouTube, Vimeo and other social media platforms. The 2019/2020 product line included three new accessories for the HERO8 Black camera, called Mods, which enabled users to transform their HERO8 Black camera into a production device. The Media Mod delivered high-quality, "shotgun"-mic performance with an integrated directional microphone, the Light Mod illuminated a scene, and the Display Mod allowed users to frame themselves perfectly during "selfie" self-capture. The company continued to offer the HERO7 Black ($299.99) and HERO7 Silver ($199.99) cameras which had been launched in the Fall, 2018.

GoPro MAX. The MAX was GoPro's newest 360-degree waterproof camera, which was launched in Fall of 2019. The MAX featured HyperSmooth image stabilization, 360-degree MAX TimeWarp Video, MAX SuperView, PowerPano, built-in mounting, high-quality audio, live streaming, voice control and a front facing touch display. The MAX SuperView provided the widest field of view ever available from a GoPro camera. There were six built-in microphones that enabled users to capture 360-degree audio, directional audio for vlogging, GoPro's best stereo sound ever. The MAX sold for $499.99 in June 2020.

GoPro App. The GoPro app was a mobile app that uploaded GoPro photos and video clips to a smartphone. The app included video editing capability, that enabled the app to better identify important moments in users' footage and suggest story compilations of photos and videos. The GoPro app cost $4.17/month on a yearly contract, or $4.99 if purchased monthly.

GoPro Plus. GoPro Plus was a subscription service that provided a camera protection plan and enabled subscribers to easily access, edit, and share content. GoPro Plus included unlimited cloud storage; supporting source video and photo quality; and discounts on accessories, camera replacement, and damage protection. The HERO5 Black and newer cameras could automatically upload photos and videos to a GoPro Plus member's account.

Manufacturing, Logistics, and Sales Channels

GoPro products were designed and developed in the United States, France, China, and Romania. The majority of the company's manufacturing was outsourced to companies in China, Mexico, Malaysia, and Japan. In 2019, GoPro moved the majority of production of its products that were to be sold in the United States from China to Mexico, due to concerns over tariffs. The company believed that outsourcing manufacturing provided greater scale and flexibility. GoPro had a strategic commodities team that managed the pricing and supply of key components of its cameras, and utilized their expertise to obtain competitive pricing.

At the end of 2019, GoPro products were sold through direct sales channels in over 100 countries and over 30,000 retail outlets. The company also sold indirectly through its distribution channel. The direct sales channel lost ground in 2019, providing 46 percent of revenue, compared to 48 percent in 2018. Gopro.com provided a significant increase in revenue, going from 16 percent in 2018 to 23 percent in 2019, and distributors increased from 52 percent in to 2018 to 54 percent in 2019.

Direct Sales

GoPro sold directly to large and small retailers in the United States and Europe, and through e-commerce channels, to consumers worldwide. The company believed that diverse direct sales channels were a key differentiator for the company, and it segregated its products among those channels. GoPro used independent specialty retailers who generally carried higher-end products, and targeted customers who were believed to be the early adopters of new technology. Big-box retailers with a national presence such as Amazon, Dixons Carphone, Walmart, Target, and Best Buy were a second component of the direct sales channel. These retailers carried a variety of GoPro products and targeted its particular end user. GoPro felt that this allowed the company to maintain in-store product differentiation between its sales channels and protected its brand image in the specialty retail markets. Point of purchase displays with video illustrating the GoPro cameras were widely employed in the direct sales channel, with about 30,00 displays globally.

Mid-market retailers with a large regional or national presence were also part of GoPro's direct sales channel. Retailers focusing on sporting goods, consumer electronics, hunting, fishing, and motor sports carried a small subset of GoPro products targeted toward its end users. The full line of GoPro products was sold directly to consumers through the company's online store, gopro.com. The company marketed its e-commerce channel through online and offline advertising. GoPro felt that its e-commerce sales provided insight into its customers' shopping behavior and provided a platform from which the company could inform and educate its customers on the GoPro brand, products, and services.

Indirect Sales/Distributors

At the end of 2019, GoPro sold to over 55 distributors who resold its products to retailers in international markets and to retailers in the United States. The company provided a sales support staff to help the distributors with planning product mix, marketing, in-store merchandising, development of marketing materials, order assistance, and education about the GoPro products. Going into 2020, GoPro, sold directly to most retailers in the United States, some retailers in Europe, and to consumers globally through its e-commerce channel.

Marketing and Advertising

GoPro's merchandising strategy focused on engaging consumers by exposing them to GoPro content and educating them about new hardware features, the power of the company's solutions for both mobile and desktop software editing, and content management with GoPro Plus. The company's marketing and advertising efforts were focused on consumer engagement by exposing them to GoPro content, believing that this approach enhanced the brand while demonstrating the performance, versatility, and durability of its products. GoPro's marketing and advertising programs spanned a wide range of consumer interests and attempted to leverage traditional consumer and lifestyle marketing.

Social media were the core of GoPro's consumer marketing. The company's customers captured and shared personal GoPro content on social media platforms such as Vimeo, YouTube, Twitter, Facebook, TikTok, and Instagram. In 2019, GoPro gained 4.3 million new followers on its social accounts for a lifetime total of 42.8 million followers. Of the 4.3 million new followers on the company's social accounts, 2.4 million were on Instagram, resulting in a lifetime total of 19.1 million on Instagram. As of the end of fiscal 2019, GoPro had reached 1.4 billion views of content tagged #GoPro on TikTok and more than 2.4 billion views on the company's YouTube channel. In the first quarter 2020, viewership of

GoPro content across all social channels reached an all-time high or 243 million views, User-generated content and GoPro originally produced content were integrated into advertising campaigns across billboards, print, television commercials, online, and other home advertising, and at consumer and trade shows. GoPro's lifestyle marketing emphasized expansion of its brand awareness by engaging consumers through relationships with influential athletes, entertainers, brands, and celebrities who used GoPro products to create and share content with their consumers and fans. The company worked directly with its lifestyle partners to create content that was leveraged to their mutual benefit across the GoPro Network.

Profiles of Select Rivals in the Action Camera Industry in 2020

Sony Sony competed in the action camera market with a lineup of nine cameras ranging in price from $199.99 to $549.99. The Sony FDR-X3000 ($549.99) was the company's top of the line and was a 4K camera with a 170 wide-angle lens, GPS, and professional quality output. The camera recorded at a high rate to give better resolution, produced better low-light pictures, and could be controlled by a remote controller. PCmag ranked the FDR-X300 best optical video stabilization in 2020. Sony's HDR-AS50 was the company's entry-level camera and produced high-definition video and still images, and included SteadyShot stabilization, low-light capabilities, and a panoramic lens. Other models included built-in stereo microphones, high-speed data transfer to capture fast action, HDMI output for sharing video on TVs, and wireless uploading to smartphones or tablets. In July 2019, Sony launched its RXO II which was the world's smallest and lightest action camera.

Nikon Camera giant Nikon announced in January 2016, that it was entering the action camera market. The company's first in its line of action cameras was the KeyMission 360, which recorded 360-degree video in 4K ultra-high-definition. The camera was dust, shock, and temperature resistant, waterproof to 100 feet, and included electronic vibration reduction to help produce sharp video. *Technowize* reported that the KeyMission 360 had the best audio quality of any action camera on the market. The KeyMission 360 was the "parent" camera in Nikon's family of action cameras. The KeyMission 360 was priced at $499.95. Nikon also offered the KeyMission 80 at $279.95 and the KeyMission 170 at $399.95 in early 2020.

Garmin International   Garmin International was far better known as a global leader in GPS navigation than for its action cameras; however, in 2013 the company released its first action camera, the VIRB. The VIRB had a color display and was manufactured in a waterproof housing so an extra protective case was unnecessary. The success of the VIRB led to two new Garmin action cameras in 2015—the VIRB X and the VIRB XE, the VIRB Ultra 30 in 2016, the VIRB 360 in 2017, and the DashCAM line in 2018. All models had GPS, Wi-Fi, and full sensor support. The new models had support for Bluetooth data streams that allowed the use of a microphone to narrate action in real time, plus a Garmin app that enabled transfer of video and photos from the camera to a smartphone and then to social media. Gauges such as altitude and speed could be applied to the video. In mid-2020, the VIRB Ultra, which sold for $309.00, was awarded the t3.com Smarter Living "Most Fully Featured" award, and the VIRB XE, which sold for $399.99 in June 2020 was recognized as number eight in the top 10 action cameras by Digital Camera World. In mid-2020, the VIRB X was priced at $299.99, the VIRB Ultra 30 at $399.99, the VIRB Elite at $349.00, the Dash Cams at $149.99 – $249.99, and the VIRB 360 was priced at $799.99.

Kodak   Kodak's PixPro SP1, priced at $170.00 in mid-2020, was rated "Best Bang for Your Buck" by *Consumer Reports* in December 2019. The PixPro had a waterproof case, produced high-quality video, could withstand drops from six feet, had an integrated display for framing shots, stereo microphones, image stabilization, a zoom lens, built-in Wi-Fi, and could be paired with iOS and Android smartphones.

Kodak extended its line to include three 360-degree models and waterproof and shockproof SPZ1. The SPZ1 was Kodak's lowest priced action camera at $65.99. The company's PixPro SP360-degree 1080p action camera was priced at $99.99, the PixPro Orbit 360 4K was $199.99, and its 360-degree 4K cameras ranged from $212.99 to $368.99 in mid-2020.

Polaroid   Polaroid entered the action camera market in 2012 by licensing a line of three low-priced cameras manufactured by C&A Marketing (a Polaroid license), and sold under the Polaroid name. The first Polaroid action cameras were the XS7, priced at $69.00; the XS20, priced at $99.00; and the XS100, priced at $199.00. The Polaroid CUBE was added to the Polaroid action camera line in 2014. The CUBE recorded up to 90 minutes of video in HD 1080p quality and sold for $18.00 in mid-2020. The Cube Act II sold for $52.99 in June 2020.

In 2015, Polaroid upgraded the CUBE to the CUBE+ which included Wi-Fi, image stabilization, HD 1440p video, and an 8.0 megapixel still capture feature. The CUBE+ was splash-resistant, shockproof, and included a microphone; numerous mountings were available for applications ranging from bikes to helmets to dogs. The CUBE+ could stream footage in real time and was compatible with both iOS and Android. A Wi-Fi enabled CUBE+ could pair with a smartphone for real-time view controls and shot framing. There was one control on the CUBE+ for on/off and to switch from video to still. The CUBE+ was priced at $59.99 in mid-2020. The upgraded POLC3BK Cube HD sold for $78.00 in May 2020.

GoPro's Financial Performance   GoPro's 2019 revenue of $1.194 billion was an increase of percent over 2018's $1.148 billion, largely due to a six percent increase in average selling price. The number of cameras sold in 2019 decreased by two percent from 4.33 million in 2018 to 4.26 million. The company reported an improved gross margin of about 35 percent for 2019, up from 31 percent in 2018. Operating expenses were down by $40 million to $415 million in 2019 (35 percent of net revenue) compared to $455 million (40 percent of net revenue) in 2018. The company attributed the decreased operating expenses to focused management of cost and the financial benefits recognized from restructuring. Despite an improvement in gross margin and operating margin, the company posted a net loss of $14.6 million, making 2019 the fourth consecutive year of losses.

GoPro's Consolidated Statements of Operations for 2017 to 2019 are presented in Exhibit 4. Its balance sheets for 2018 and 2019 are shown in Exhibit 5.

GoPro's sales were predominately from the Americas, with Europe, the Middle East, and Africa a distance second—see Exhibit 6. Revenue from outside the United States was 56 percent, 57 percent, and

EXHIBIT 4   GoPro, Inc.'s Consolidated Statements of Operations, 2017–2019 (in thousands, except per share data)

	2019	2018	2017
Revenue	$1,194,651	$1,148,337	$1,179,741
Cost of revenue	781,862	786,903	795,211
Gross profit	412,789	361,434	384,530
Operating expenses:			
Research and development	142,894	167,296	229,265
Sales and marketing	206,431	222,096	236,581
General and administrative	65,797	66,004	82,144
Total operating expenses	415,122	455,396	547,990
Operating loss	(2,333)	(93,962)	(163,460)
Other income (expense):	(19,229)	(18,683)	(13,660)
Other income, net	2,492	4,970	733
Total other expense, net	(16,737)	(13,713)	(12,927)
Loss before income taxes	(19,070)	(107,675)	(176,387)
Income tax (benefit) expense	(4,428)	1,359	6,486
Net income (loss)	$ (14,642)	$ (109,034)	$ (182,873)
Basic and diluted net income (loss) per share	$(0.10)	$(0.78)	$(1.32)
Weighted-average number of shares outstanding	144,891	139,495	138,056

Source: GoPro, Inc. 2019 Annual Report.

EXHIBIT 5   GoPro, Inc.'s Consolidated Balance Sheets, 2018–2019 (in thousands, except par values)

	December 31, 2019	December 31, 2018
Assets		
Current assets:		
Cash and cash equivalents	$150,301	$152,095
Marketable securities	14,847	45,417
Accounts receivable, net	200,634	129,216
Inventory	144,236	116,458
Prepaid expenses and other current assets	25,958	30,887
Total current assets	535,976	474,073
Property and equipment, net	36,539	46,567
Operating lease right-of-use assets	53,121	—
Intangible assets, net	5,247	13,065
Goodwill	146,459	146,459
Other long-term assets	15,461	18,195
Total assets	$792,803	$698,359

	December 31, 2019	December 31, 2018
Liabilities and Stockholders' Equity		
Current liabilities:		
Accounts payable	$160,695	$148,478
Accrued expenses and other current liabilities	141,790	135,892
Short-term operating lease liabilities	9,099	—
Deferred revenue	15,467	15,129
Total current liabilities	327,051	299,499
Long-term taxes payable	13,726	19,553
Long-term debt	148,810	138,992
Long-term operating lease liabilities	62,961	—
Other long-term liabilities	6,726	28,203
Total liabilities	559,274	486,247
Commitments, contingencies, and guarantees (Note 9)		
Stockholders' equity:		
Preferred stock, $0.0001 par value, 5,000 shares authorized; none issued	—	—
Common stock and additional paid-in capital, $0.0001 par value, 500,000 Class A shares authorized, 117,922 and 105,170 shares issued and outstanding, respectively; 150,000 Class B shares authorized, 28,897 and 35,897 shares issued and outstanding, respectively	930,875	894,755
Treasury stock, at cost, 10,710 and 10,710 shares, respectively	(113,613)	(113,613)
Accumulated deficit	(583,733)	(569,030)
Total stockholders' equity	233,529	212,112
Total liabilities and stockholders' equity	$792,803	$698,359

Source: GoPro, Inc. 2019 Annual Report.

EXHIBIT 6   GoPro, Inc. Revenue by Geographic Region, 2017–2019 (in thousands)

Geographic Region	2019	2018	2017	2019 vs 2018 % Change	2018 vs 2017 % Change
Americas	$ 523,975	$ 494,797	$ 582,917	6%	(15)%
Europe, Middle East and Africa (EMEA)	359,187	366,438	333,454	(2)	10
Asia and Pacific (APAC)	311,489	287,102	263,370	8	9
Total revenue	$1,194,651	$1,148,337	$1,179,741	4%	(3)%

Source: GoPro, Inc. 2019 Annual Report.

51 percent of the company's revenues for fiscal 2019, 2018, and 2017, respectively; and GoPro expected this portion to continue to be a significant part of revenues. Although there were no clear trends in the composition of sales revenue in the Americas, Europe, the Middle East, and Africa, there was an upward trend of revenue from outside the United States and especially from the Asia Pacific region. GoPro's supply chain partners had operations in Mexico, Hong Kong, Singapore, China, Czech Republic, the Netherlands,

and other countries in Europe and the Asia Pacific region. The company intended to expand operations in these, and perhaps other, countries as it increased its international presence.

GoPro's Performance in Early 2020

Despite a small but hopeful revenue uptick in 2019, GoPro's operations produced dismal results in early 2020. First quarter 2020 revenue was down by 51 percent year-over-year, and gross margin dropped to 32.2 percent from 33.1 percent in the same period in 2019. Operating losses increased by 177 percent to $56 million from $20 million in 2019, and net losses increased 161 percent to $64 million from $24 million the same period in 2019. The company's 2020 first quarter earnings release did not provide encouragement to investors, and GoPro's shares drifted down to a low of $2.00 in mid-March and a closing at $2.29 on April 4. Exhibit 7 presents GoPro's quarterly Statements of Operations for the first quarter of 2019 and the first quarter of 2020.

GoPro withdrew its guidance for the full year 2020, citing uncertainty due to the COVID-19 pandemic. The company announced another strategic realignment intended to concentrate on expense reduction, and an increased focus on direct-to-consumer operations. GoPro reported that it intended to reduce its workforce by more than 20 percent, cut operating expenses by $100 million, and further reduce operating expenses to $250 million in 2021. The company planned to reduce office space in five locations, reduce sales and marketing expenditures in 2020 and beyond, and curtail other expenses. GoPro Inc.'s chief hardware designer Danny Coster left the company in May 2020 after coming to GoPro from Apple's design team four years prior. Mr. Woodman's announced that he would forego the remained of his salary through the end of 2929, and the company's Board of Directors volunteered to forego the remainder of their salary through the end of 2020. Despite the financial weaknesses, GoPro remainder the leader in the action camera industry in late 2019. However, the ability of its top management to craft and execute strategies that could sustain its market leadership in action cameras while simultaneously regaining profitability would determine the success of GoPro's latest turnaround strategy and the continuing viability of the company.

EXHIBIT 7   **GoPro, Inc., Statement of Operations, Three Months Ending March 31, First Quarter 2020 Versus First Quarter 2019 (in thousands, except per share amounts)**

	2020	2019	% Change
Revenue	$119,400	$242,708	(50.8)%
Gross margin			
GAAP	32.2%	33.1%	(90) bps
Non-GAAP	34.2%	34.2%	—
Operating loss			
GAAP	$ (56,114)	$ (20,288)	176.6%
Non-GAAP	$ (46,654)	$ (8,118)	474.7%
Net loss			
GAAP	$ (63,528)	$ (24,365)	160.7%
Non-GAAP	$ (49,613)	$ (10,171)	387.8%
Diluted net loss per share			
GAAP	$ (0.43)	$ (0.17)	152.9%
Non-GAAP	$ (0.34)	$ (0.07)	385.7%
Adjusted EBITDA	$ (41,356)	$ (1,035)	3,895.7%

Source: GoPro, Inc. First Quarter 2020 10-Q.

Publix Super Markets: Its Strategy in the U.S. Supermarket and Grocery Store Industry

Gregory L. Prescott
University of West Florida

David L. Turnipseed
University of South Alabama

Moving into the decade of the 2020s, Kevin Murphy reflected back over his two years as president of Publix Super Markets, Inc. Sales and profits had maintained their positive trend, established long before Murphy's presidency, and comparable store sales continued to increase, despite the chain's expansion of the number of stores. Publix continued to enjoy excellent publicity and a great corporate image, both internally and externally: it had been on Fortune's *100 Best Companies to Work For,* and Publix's voluntary turnover rate was 5 percent, versus the industry average of 65 percent. The company was the largest employee-owned company in the United States and had never laid off an employee in its 89-year history.

Although fiscal 2019 had shown net sales of a record $38.1 billion (an increase of 5.6 percent over fiscal 2018), and net earnings of over $3 billion, or 7.9 percent of sales, Mr. Murphy was concerned about the future. The grocery industry appeared to be moving rapidly from the traditional in-person shopping experience in which the shopper visited a favorite grocery and personally chose the week's grocery items, to e-commerce with home delivery, or phone app-ordered pickup based shopping. Technology had provided the means for shoppers to select their grocery items from an app on their phones, and delivery and logistics improvements enabled quick delivery of the grocery basket to the shoppers' door. Mr. Murphy believed that Amazon's purchase of Whole Foods was a likely catalyst to cause faster than normal industry change in ecommerce grocery sales and delivery. Evolving lifestyles had resulted in a decreasing amount of food cooked at home, and an increased focus on sustainability, health, and natural organic foods. A new and powerful force that Murphy thought capable of causing significant and lasting industry effects was the COVID-19 pandemic sweeping the country. Cost control remained a major key to success, and private brands had emerged as a practical means of keeping costs low.

Murphy was concerned that the rapid change in the supermarket industry was of sufficient magnitude to cause a major disruption in Publix's positive trajectory if the company did not accurately identify the driving forces in the industry, and forecast and stay ahead of the industry's path. He resolved to accurately assess the supermarket industry and keep Publix at its forefront.

History of Publix Super Markets

The history of Publix began with its founder George Jenkins beginning his retail career in his father's general store in Harris, Georgia. In 1925, Jenkins decided that Florida's real estate boom offered better opportunities, and he moved to Tampa, Florida. Rather than working in the real estate industry, Jenkins took a job as a stock clerk in a Piggle Wiggly store. After two months, he was promoted to store manager, and a short time later, was transferred to Winter Haven, Florida, to manage the chain's largest store. Jenkins held the management position at Winter Haven from 1926 to 1930. In 1930 he resigned from Piggly Wiggly and opened his own grocery store in Winter Haven and opened a second in 1935.

Jenkins closed his first two stores, and opened his dream store, the first Publix Super Market, in November 1940. The Publix was a "food palace" of marble, stucco and glass, and included innovations such as fluorescent lighting, air conditioning, electric eye doors, and terrazzo floors at a time when these items were considered luxuries not found in competing grocery stores. He acquired a warehouse and 19 All American stores from the Lakeland Grocery Company in 1945 and began replacing the small stores with larger supermarkets. He continued his aggressive expansion and brought the Publix brand to customers throughout Florida.

The Publix Culture

From the day he opened his first grocery store, Jenkins was focused on excellent customer treatment. He thought that friendly customer service and royal treatment were crucial elements in connecting with customers and forming lasting relationships. He believed that the key to treating his customers like royalty was knowledgeable and friendly employees who provided a convenient, but lean, shopping environment. At Publix, the foundation of its first-class customer service was learning all possible about the business, and to make the shopping experience pleasurable.

Publix employees (called associates) were taught that providing the highest level of service and treating the customers like royalty, extended beyond the grocery aisles. Customers should have excellent experiences in every interaction with the company. Publix believed that its associates, who continued to embrace the philosophies set out by Jenkins, were what separated Publix from other major grocery retailers. The Company regularly recognized and rewarded its associates for their hard work, dedication, and service. Associates were recognized for many reasons, including:

- Going "above and beyond." Associates who had been a role model in embracing the Publix culture and provided premier service were eligible to receive a free sub coupon and a personalized note from their manager.
- Being dedicated to the Company. Associates received a gift and were invited to a dinner recognizing each five years of service.

Publix valued its associates and rewarded those who made a difference in the lives of others.

Although Jenkins died in 1996, his beliefs influenced the way Publix operated up to the present. Each year on September 29, the Company celebrated Jenkins's birthday. The celebrations, known as Mr. George Day, honored the man whose passion for "people first" led to Publix's beginning in 1930.

Recognition of Publix Super Markets

- *Fortune's* Best Big Companies to Work For
- *Fortune's* Best Workplaces for Parents
- Indeed's Top-Rated Workplaces for Veterans
- *Fortune's* 100 Best Companies to Work for in America for 22 consecutive years
- *Fortune's* Best Workplaces for Diversity
- *Fortune's* Best Workplaces for Women
- *Fortune's* Best Workplaces for Millennials
- *Fortune's* Best Workplaces for Retail
- *Fortune's* Most Admired Companies for 23 consecutive years
- Indeed's Top-Rated Workplaces
- Market Force's America's Favorite Grocery Chains

Publix's Mission, Commitment, Guarantee, and Key Values

Publix's mission was "*to be the premier quality food retailer in the world.*" To achieve that mission, the company focused on its customers, efficiency, employees, stockholders, and communities.

Over the years, Publix had an unwavering commitment to being:

- Passionately focused on customer value,
- Intolerant of waste,
- Dedicated to the dignity, value, and employment security of our associates,
- Devoted to the highest standards of stewardship for our stockholders, and
- Involved as responsible citizens in our communities.

The company gave its customers the guarantee that "We will never knowingly disappoint you. If for any reason your purchase does not give you complete satisfaction, the full purchase price will be cheerfully refunded immediately upon request." During the early years, Jenkins reflected on what he had learned in his business life before Publix and developed a set of values upon which he built the company.

These values were adhered to every day at Publix. These values were:

• Invest in Others	• Give Back
• Prepare for Opportunity	• Respect the Dignity of the Individual
• Be There	• Treat Customers Like Royalty

Jenkins believed in investing in others by building relationship, making connections, working collaboratively, learning, and mentoring others. Being a good community partner was requisite for organizational success in Jenkins' mind and he stressed donating time, talent and money to the cities in which Publix operated. Publix's growth required a constant increase in employees and Jenkins encouraged his people to prepare themselves for the constantly emerging opportunities in the organization. Having experienced working for a company where his thoughts and ideas were not valued, Jenkins vowed to make Publix a place where individuals were respected, communication was open, everyone had a voice, and opinions were valued. Further, he committed himself to being involved in all aspects of the company, because he wanted his customers and employees to know that he cared about them. Until his death in 1996, Jenkins regularly visited stores and other facilities, attended store openings, serving as a highly visible example of Publix connecting with its employees, customers, and stakeholders, and this practice was continued by Publix's management. Jenkins sought ways to treat customers like royalty and thereby connect with the customers and form enduring relationships. He used store presentations, personal service, and quality products to make customers feel valued. Publix attributes its high customer loyalty to unwavering focus on excellent and unmatched customer service.

Publix Super Markets' Financial Situation

As of March 2, 2020, Publix operated 1,243 supermarkets in Florida, Georgia, Alabama, South Carolina, Tennessee, North Carolina, and Virginia. In 2019, Publix ranked as the eighth largest private company in the United States. Publix's sales revenue for the five years 2015–19 increased at a compound average growth rate (CAGR) of 4.2 percent. Over the same period, gross profit had a CAGR of 3.9 percent, and net profit showed CAGR of 11.2 percent. Publix's net margin ranged from 6.1 percent in 2015 to 7.9 percent in 2019, significantly greater than the industry average—see Exhibit 1.

Publix's consolidated statement of earnings, 2017–2019, are produced in Exhibit 2, and consolidated balance sheets, 2018–2019, are provided in Exhibit 3.

EXHIBIT 1   Selected Financial Data for Publix Super Markets, Inc., 2015–2019 ($ in thousands)

	2019	2018	2017	2016	2015
Sales					
Sales	$38,116,402	36,093,907	34,558,286	33,999,921	32,362,579
Percent change	5.6%	4.4%	1.6%	5.1%	5.9%
Comparable store sales percent change	3.6%	2.1%	1.7%	1.9%	4.2%
Earnings					
Gross profit	10,375,933	9,782,516	9,428,569	9,265,616	8,902,969
Earnings before income tax expense	3,785,986	2,920,968	3,027,506	2,940,376	2,869,261
Net earnings	3,005,395	2,381,167	2,291,894	2,025,688	1,965,048
Net earnings as a percent of sales	7.9%	6.6%	6.6%	6.0%	6.1%

Source: Publix Super Markets, Inc. 2019 Annual Report.

EXHIBIT 2   Consolidated Statement of Earnings for Publix Super Markets, Inc., 2017–2019 (in thousands, except per share amounts)

	2019	2018	2017
Revenues			
Sales	$38,116,402	$36,093,907	$34,558,286
Other operating income	346,351	301,811	278,552
Total revenues	38,462,753	36,395,718	34,836,838
Costs and expenses:			
Cost of merchandise sold	27,740,469	26,311,391	25,129,717
Operating and administrative expenses	7,833,035	7,339,924	6,974,297
Total costs and expenses	35,573,504	33,651,315	32,104,014
Operating profit	2,889,249	2,744,403	2,732,824
Investment income	814,372	56,699	226,626
Other nonoperating income, net	82,365	119,866	68,056
Earnings before income tax expense	3,785,986	2,920,968	3,027,506
Income tax expense	780,591	539,801	735,612
Net earnings	$ 3,005,395	$ 2,381,167	$ 2,291,894
Weighted average shares outstanding	713,535	726,407	753,483
Earnings per share	$4.21	$3.28	$3.04

Source: Publix Super Markets, Inc. 2019 Annual Report.

EXHIBIT 3   Consolidated Balance Sheets for Publix Super Markets, Inc., 2018–2019 ($ in thousands)

	2019	2018
ASSETS		
Current assets:		
Cash and cash equivalents	$ 763,382	599,264
Short-term investments	438,105	560,992
Trade receivables	737,093	682,981
Inventories	1,913,310	1,848,735
Prepaid expenses	75,710	122,224
Total current assets	3,927,600	3,814,196
Long-term investments	7,988,280	6,016,438
Other noncurrent assets	441,938	515,265
Operating lease right-of-use assets	2,964,780	—
Property, plant and equipment:		
Land	1,984,400	1,850,718
Buildings and improvements	5,948,039	5,535,538
Furniture, fixtures and equipment	5,477,534	5,114,698
Leasehold improvements	1,660,164	1,564,243
Construction in progress	152,272	109,367
	15,222,409	14,174,564
Accumulated depreciation	(6,037,887)	(5,537,947)
Net property, plant and equipment	9,184,522	8,636,617
Total assets	$24,507,120	18,982,516

	2019	2018
LIABILITIES AND EQUITY		
Current liabilities:		
Accounts payable	$ 1,984,761	1,864,604
Accrued expenses:		
Contributions to retirement plans	581,699	540,760
Self-insurance reserves	149,082	145,241
Salaries and wages	148,662	132,916
Other	461,427	321,080
Current portion of long-term debt	39,692	4,954
Current portion of operating lease liabilities	335,391	—
Total current liabilities	3,700,714	3,009,555
Deferred income taxes	682,484	420,757
Self-insurance reserves	226,727	222,419
Accrued postretirement benefit cost	120,015	105,308
Long-term debt	131,997	162,711
Operating lease liabilities	2,603,206	—
Other noncurrent liabilities	140,633	67,102
Total liabilities	7,605,776	3,987,852
Common stock related to Employee Stock Ownership Plan (ESOP)	3,259,230	3,134,999
Stockholders' equity:		
Common stock of $1 par value. Authorized 1,000,000 shares; issued and outstanding 706,552 shares in 2019 and 715,445 shares in 2018	706,552	715,445
Additional paid-in capital	3,758,066	3,458,004
Retained earnings	12,317,478	10,840,654
Accumulated other comprehensive earnings (losses)	81,289	(55,762)
Common stock related to ESOP	(3,259,230)	(3,134,999)
Total stockholders' equity	13,604,155	11,823,342
Noncontrolling interests	37,959	36,323
Total equity	16,901,344	14,994,664
Total liabilities and shareholders' equity	$24,507,120	$ 18,982,516

Source: Publix Super Markets, Inc. 2019 Annual Report.

Stock Market Performance

Publix stock was not traded publicly: it was held only by current and former employees. Because of the lack of active trading, there was no traditional trading- or market-based daily price available. A group of independent financial analysts determined the Publix stock price based on comparison of financial performance in a "peer group" of other supermarket chains. Consequently, stock price swings in other grocers' stock price could affect Publix's share price. Exhibit 4 produces Publix's stock, compared to the S&P 500, and its peer group of supermarkets.

Supermarket and Grocery Stores Industry

The U.S. supermarket and grocery stores industry had grown during the five years 2014–19, primarily due the strong national economy, producing revenue of

EXHIBIT 4   **Comparison of Five-Year Cumulative Return Based on Fiscal Year End Price for Publix Shares, 2014–2019**

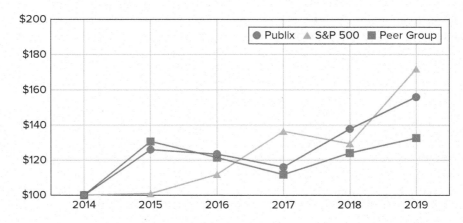

Source: Publix Super Markets, Inc. 2019 Annual Report.

$655 billion in 2019, a .9 percent increase over 2018. Annual revenue growth, 2015–20 had been 1.4 percent, and revenue was forecast to top $678 billion in 2020. There were over 66,290 grocery businesses in 2109, with industry employment of 2,772,898.

Industry Margins. The margins vary among departments in a large supermarket. The main grocery aisles margins, approximately one percent, are the lowest in the economy. Industry consolidation had resulted from the low margins: in a low margin situation, economies of scale could provide efficiency and centralization, and economic rewards. Consequently, for several decades, the grocery industry had been in the process of consolidation. New store formats pressed margins even lower as competition became more intense. The present average grocery store was a large supermarket with an average of about 45,000 square feet and annual revenue of about $14 million a year, or about $500 per square foot of sales as the industry average. New grocery formats since the 1990s changed the industry, and specialty chains like Whole Foods were earning margins of about 3.2 percent and higher, far greater than the industry average. The wholesale clubs format also undercut the larger grocery stores, putting pressure on the struggling industry.

Organic and Private Brands. During the five years 2014–19, many consumers switched to organic and all-natural food brands, and premium food brands, as per capita disposable income increased, which boosted industry revenue. However, many consumers continued purchasing private-label, or store brands due to rising food costs. Increasing generic food purchases reduced revenue growth, but increased profit margins, because store brands could be produced at less cost than national brands. Not only could private- brand foods fill inventory voids, but they also boosted the bottom line. Profit margins on third-party-branded foods were about one percent to two percent, while gross margins on private-label goods could reach between 25 percent and 30 percent. When private brands were first introduced, retailers' ideas of private labels were an afterthought. The word "Generic" was often used interchangeably with private brand, and packaging, usually black and white, was not highly desirable, and quality was also not a priority.

The Food Marketing Institute's 2019 poll reports that 46 percent of private-label brands are "very influential" in their decision of which food retailer to shop, an increase of 35 percent from three years previous. The data reflects a similar result from Coresight Research posted earlier in 2019, that suggested more than half of U.S. shoppers visit a particular retailer to purchase a private-label good. Some grocers turned their private-label brands into lines that are were as well respected as comparable options from packaged food companies like Kraft Heinz or General Mills, if not more so. Data from the Food Marketing Institute (FMI) and market research firm IRI indicated that almost half of all consumers specifically seek out a private-label product. "Food retailers should be very pleased that their brands are becoming bigger factors in how consumers shop. This gives retailers the opportunity to further drive loyalty and trips", the FMI/IRI study commented.[1] The increase in acceptance and importance of private brands offered the supermarket industry an opportunity that was far more significant than a few years previous, as the industry moved into an era in which house brands were not just the cheap alternatives, rather the private brands were increasingly the consumer's intended purchase.

Industry Challenges.   Despite the industry's revenue growth, the industry faced significant challenges. Consumer's habits had been changing–consumers expected low prices and the ability to buy almost anything, at anytime, anywhere. The largest U.S. demographic group, millennials, were the first generation to be less wealthy than their parents: they wanted deals and discounts, in addition to healthy food, socially and environmentally responsible companies, knowing where their food came from, and how it was made. They were also attracted to online shopping. According to BloomReach, a digital shopping platform, 41 percent of retailers listed improving online sale capabilities as the number one priority in 2019.[2]

The greatest challenge facing the Supermarket and Grocery Stores industry appeared to be the increase in online grocery shopping, which was between three and four percent of total industry revenue in 2019. According to many leaders in the grocery industry, that number would rapidly increase to over 20 percent, and the current industry leaders, Walmart, Kroger, Albertson's (including Safeway and others), Ahold Delhaize (Stop and Shop, Giant Food, Peapod and others), and Publix were not prepared to stay on top in online shopping. A significant problem that faced the industry as online shopping increased, was the decline in brick and mortar store profitability when 20 percent of customers no longer visited the stores, and the consequent decline in the value of supermarket real estate. In addition to developing high efficiency grocery order fulfillment

centers and controlling costs, grocers must cultivate new skills to motivate consumers. Many supermarket purchase decisions are made during a visit to the store as customers walk the aisles and make impulse purchases, motivate in some part by the attractive packaging designed by the product manufacturers. As the number of traditional grocery consumers visiting the stores decreases, consumer product companies will face pressure to develop new skills to motivate the grocery consumers.

The rapid and increasing emergence of new technologies had been quite disruptive for the retail grocery industry. Amazon and other online competitors had been successful, due partially to transparent pricing, enabled by their online environment. To compete, traditional grocers were forced to keep their prices low, even when their costs had risen. Online grocers pioneered the use of artificial intelligence, advanced analytics, and robotics far more quickly and aggressively than traditional grocers. Amazon's website, for example, has a product-recommendation search engine, over 100,000 robots moving pallets of goods through its warehouses, and innovations designed to make the online shopping experience easier and faster. Most traditional grocers were being forced to catch up.

Grocery stores were in a precarious position as they attempted to meet the millennials' expectations while maintaining low prices. Baby boomers continued to have significant buying power and remained a vital component of the industry's customer base. Boomers valued in-store customer service, they were concerned with health and wellness, were receptive to new products, and many were comfortable with technology. All demographic groups presented a huge challenge to the industry with their decreasing inclination to cook. In the United States, about 50 percent of millennials reported rarely cooking at home, and food-service revenue exceeded food-at-home sales.

Industry Reaction.   Traditional grocers reacted very slowly to the changing consumer trends, which provided entre for other types of retailers. Convenience stores, discounters, and club stores began to directly compete with traditional retailers: food service businesses seized the lunch and dinner demand. Discounters were particularly aggressive, offering a limited variety, and providing great value on all items, which provided higher earnings, than supermarkets. The discounters' low prices reduced the sector's overall revenue by about four percent.

The retail grocery industry was generally slow to respond to the changing competitive conditions, and between 2008 and 2018, sales growth of large grocery chains in North America had been only two percent, versus 8.4 percent in South America and Eastern Europe, 6.2 percent in Asia, and 9.8 percent in Africa. As labor costs and commodity prices increased between 2012 and 2017, traditional grocers had not been able to increase their prices to compensate, because of intense competition from lower priced formats such as dollar stores and discount chains. Consequently, their margins dropped dramatically.

Profile of Select Rivals in the U.S. Supermarket Industry

Kroger Co., Costco Wholesale Corporation, Albertsons, H.E. Butt Grocery Co., Meijer, Inc., and Whole Foods were Publix's close competitors for top U.S. supermarket—see Exhibit 5.

A June 2018 study of favorite grocery store chains showed that Publix Supermarkets had the second highest composite customer loyalty in the grocery/supermarket industry, scoring 76 percent, versus the leader, Wegmans (a small, privately held New England grocery chain) which was 77 percent. Among Publix's other close competitors, H-E-B was 69 percent, Costco was 65 percent, and Whole Foods 60 percent, Kroger, Albertsons, and Meijer did not make the list.[3]

Publix compared quite favorably to the top supermarket competitors in customer experience metrics, ranking first among top grocery chains in item availability, store cleanliness, and finding wanted items. Customers ranked Publix number two in checkout speed and cashier courtesy: Publix tied for number two with Whole Foods for specialty department service. Despite these high rankings, Publix placed eighth for good sales and promotions of the 22 top grocery chains surveyed, and 18th for value for the money.

The Kroger Co.

The world's largest retail grocery/supermarket chain was Kroger Co. with fiscal 2019 sales of $121,162 million. Kroger was the third-largest retailer in the world, behind Walmart Stores, Inc., and Costco Wholesale Corp. Kroger owned 18 chains of supermarkets including King Soopers', Ralph's, Smith's, City Market, and Pick'n Save, with a total of 2,764 stores, as well as price-impact stores (e.g., Food4Less), multi-department stores (e.g., Fred Meyer, Kroger Marketplace), as well as jewelry and specialty retailers. Kroger's statement of income is produced in Exhibit 6.

Kroger launched a three-year "Restock Kroger" plan, beginning in 2018, that was intended to create shareholder value by pursing its vision of serving America by food inspiration and uplift. The company reported that it delivered over $1 billion in savings in 2018 through process improvements and cost

EXHIBIT 5 Leading U.S. Supermarket and Grocery Store Chains, 2017

Global Rank	Name	U.S. Rank	2017 Revenue*	2017 Net Income*	2012–2017 Revenue CAGR
2	Costco	1	$129,025	$2,714	5.4%
3	Kroger	2	122,622	1,889	4.2%
15	Albertson's	3	59,925	46	74.4%
31	Publix	4	34,837	2,292	4.7%
37	H.E. Butt	5	24,600ᵉ	n/a	4.9%
54	Meijer		18,900ᵉ	n/a	5.3%
58	Whole Foods		16,030	245	6.5%

* In millions US $

ᵉ - estimated

Source: Deloitte, "Global Powers of Retailing 2019, https://www2.deloitte.com/content/dam/Deloitte/global/Documents/Consumer -Business/cons-global-powers-retailing-2019.pdf

EXHIBIT 6 Consolidated Statements of Operations for The Kroger Co., Fiscal 2016–Fiscal 2018 (in millions, except per share amounts)

	2018 (52 weeks)	2017 (53 weeks)	2016 (52 weeks)
Sales	$121,162	$122,662	$115,337
Operating expenses			
Merchandise costs, including advertising, warehousing, and transportation, excluding items shown separately below	94,894	95,662	89,502
Operating, general and administrative	20,305	21,041	19,162
Rent	884	911	881
Depreciation and amortization	2,465	2,436	2,340
Operating profit	2,614	2,612	3,452
Other income (expense)			
Interest expense	(620)	(601)	(522)
Non-service component of company-sponsored pension plan costs	(26)	(527)	(16)
Mark to market gain on Ocado securities	228	—	—
Gain on sale of business	1,782	—	—
Net earnings before income tax (benefit) expense	3,978	1,484	2,914
Income tax (benefit) expense	900	(405)	957
Net earnings including noncontrolling interests	3,078	1,889	1,957
Net loss attributable to noncontrolling interests	(32)	(18)	(18)
Net earnings attributable to The Kroger Co.	$ 3,110	$ 1,907	$ 1,975
Net earnings attributable to The Kroger Co. per basic common share	$3.80	$2.11	$2.08

Source: Kroger Co. 2018 Annual Report.

controls and invested in the future. One part of the Restock Kroger plan was an aggressive move toward omnichannel retailing: the Company believed that its customers did not distinguish between online and in-store purchase experiences, but rather sought the easiest and most seamless solution to their needs or problems. Kroger attempted to expand its capabilities and be available, relevant and accessible to its customers in both the physical and digital shopping environments.

The Company had been working on increasing its digital platform for several years and showed a 58 percent growth in digital sales in 2018, and a 21 percent increase in the third quarter of 2019. It was integrating its traditional brick and mortar business with its expanding digital sales platform, with the intention of serving its customers anything, anytime and anywhere. By December 2018, grocery pickup or delivery was available to 91 percent of Kroger households: in December 2019, the company

had 1,915 pickup locations and 2,326 delivery locations covering 96 percent of Kroger households.

Kroger entered into partnerships with several companies that enhanced the company's omnichannel retailing and served the rapidly evolving grocery market. The Company merged with an online meal kit company, Home Chef, which was ranked first place in online meal kit companies. Shortly after the merger, Home Chef launched the first in-store meal kit line, and at the end of 2018, they were in 700 Kroger locations, and expanding. In February 2019, Kroger announced that Home Chef retail meal kits would be added to an additional 500 Kroger stores.

Another significant partnership in 2018 was Ocado, one of the world's largest online grocery retailers, which used advanced robotics and highly efficient automated warehouses. This partnership enabled Kroger to provide faster, more organized ecommerce shopping to its customers. Customers had fresher food, delivered faster from Ocado's customer fulfillment centers initially located in central Florida, the Mid-Atlantic region, and southwest Ohio. A Wisconsin fulfillment was added in 2019.

Kroger invested heavily in private brand foods. Kroger's private brands, known as Our Brands (Kroger, Private Selection, Simple Truth, Big K, and Heritage Farms) accounted for 31 percent of Kroger's sales in 2018. In 2019, Kroger produced about 43 percent of Our Brand grocery items in Kroger owned food production plants. Kroger also debuted a Greenwise Market chain of healthy–living stores designed to be a place for customers to find products that will support their evolving lifestyles.

Greenwise locations provided a beverage bar with coffees, locally crafted beers, wines, and smoothies as well as handcrafted sandwiches, burritos, acai bowls, gourmet pizzas, bowls, sushi and sausage made in-house; local and organic produce; body care products; and natural vitamins and supplements.

Costco Wholesale Corporation

Costco was the second largest retailer in the world, with fiscal 2019 sales of $152.7 billion—see Exhibit 7. Costco operated as a Cash & Carry/Warehouse Club but was a significant competitor to grocery stores

EXHIBIT 7   Consolidated Statements of Income for Costco Wholesale Corporation, Fiscal 2017-Fiscal 2019 (amounts in millions, except per share data)

	52 Weeks Ended September 1, 2019	52 Weeks Ended September 2, 2018	53 Weeks Ended September 3, 2017
Revenue			
Net sales	$149,351	$138,434	$126,172
Membership fees	3,352	3,142	2,853
Total revenue	152,703	141,576	129,025
Operating Expenses			
Merchandise costs	132,886	123,152	111,882
Selling, general and administrative	14,994	13,876	12,950
Preopening expenses	86	68	82
Operating income	4,737	4,480	4,111
Other Income (Expense)			
Interest expense	(150)	(159)	(134)
Interest income and other, net	178	121	62
Income Before Income Taxes	4,765	4,442	4,039
Provision for income taxes	1,061	1,263	1,325
Net income including noncontrolling interests	3,704	3,179	2,714
Net income attributable to noncontrolling interests	(45)	(45)	(35)
Net Income Attributable to Costco	$ 3,659	$ 3,134	$ 2,679
Net Income Per Common Share Attributable to Costco:			
Basic	$ 8.32	$ 7.15	$ 6.11
Diluted	$ 8.26	$ 7.09	$ 6.08
Shares used in calculation (000s)			
Basic	439,755	438,515	438,437
Diluted	442,923	441,834	440,937

Source: Costco Wholesale Corporation 2019 Annual Report.

and supermarkets. The company opened its first location in 1976 as Price Club, in San Diego. The fledgling company quickly discovered that it could achieve much greater buying power by serving small businesses and a select group of non-business members. This was the beginning of the warehouse club industry. Costco's operating philosophy is "Keep costs down and pass savings on to our members." Costco focused on a best value strategy and provided a 100 percent satisfaction guarantee on the memberships and merchandise.

Costco developed its private brand Kirkland Signature as a way to support its low-cost strategy by helping to keep prices low. The Kirkland Brand included grocery items, eggs, honey, sparkling water, razor blades, tissues, wine and vodka, which sold for at least 20 percent less than national brands. Costco's strategy in private branding had been quite successful. In 2018, Kirkland Signature's revenue was $40 billion, an 11 percent increase over the prior year, and a greater amount than the revenue of Macy's and JCPenny, combined. Costco's private brand had become the powerhouse in private brands by 2019. The *Washington Post* ranked Kirkland hot dogs number one of the best-selling brands in 2019. In 2019, Costco's Kirkland brand revenue of $39 billion, and accounted for about 25 percent of the company's total sales. Kirkland accounts for about 30 percent of all U.S. private-brand grocery sales. Kirkland's numbers starkly contrast with the Private Label Manufacturers Association's report that private brands account for only 17 percent of all grocers' sales.

Costco was rather late to offer grocery delivery: its online grocery, CostcoGrocery, did not begin operations until 2017. The company was slow to adopt online shopping because its members tended to spend more money when they shopped in a physical store. Costco shoppers had one- and two-day delivery options for online groceries. Costco members in "qualifying zip codes" could order groceries, including perishable foods, meat, produce, and seafood online and have it delivered in a selected time window by Instacart, a national delivery service. The minimum order was $35.00, and prices for same-day delivery items were higher than Costco warehouse prices. Customers who were not Costco members could order online from Instacart.com but paid a higher price than Costco members. The two-day delivery could be used for cleaning supplies, organic non-perishables, tissue, detergent, and similar items. There was no separate delivery fee for two-day orders, but a minimum order of $75.00 was required.

Although many groceries and supermarkets were devoting significant resources to grocery pickup, Costco had no plans to implement pickup services as of mid-2019. Costco's CFO Richard Galanti remarked on an earnings call that despite the success that Walmart and other competitors had with grocery pickup, Costco had no plans to add pickup services. Galanti said that, "We continue to look at it, we continue to scratch our head about it, we recognize that they [Walmart] and some others are putting in a lot of financial commitment to doing this. I think what you're going to find it is like everything else in life at Costco, over time we figure out how to do it our way that makes sense for us that still works.

Albertsons

Albertsons Companies, Inc., a Boise, Idaho-based supermarket chain, was the world's 15th largest retailer. The Company family of stores includes over 2,200 supermarkets operating under 22 names in 34 states and the District of Columbia. Albertson's statement of operations, 2014–19 are produced in Exhibit 8.

Albertsons Companies' in-house brand, Own Brands, launched in 2018, comprised over 1,000 items, and was one of the most diverse private brands in the country. The Company also owned one of the nation's largest lines of USDA-certified organic products, with sales of over $1 billion yearly.

Recognizing that competitive success in the retail grocery industry required a good online grocery platform, and that omnichannel shoppers were more valuable to the Company than only traditional brick and mortar customers, Albertsons entered into three strategic digital partnerships. The partnership with BloomReach, a digital experience platform, employed artificial intelligence to provide Albertsons's online customers an enhanced search experience, quickly showed results in expanding the shopping basket. The Company partnered with Quotient Technology, which became Albertsons's exclusive digital media platform. Quotient enabled consumer packaged goods companies to work with Albertsons to direct shoppers to their branded shopping locations that allowed customers to add products directly to their carts. Although Albertsons had an existing partnership with Instacart, a grocery delivery service,

EXHIBIT 8   Consolidated Statements of Operations for Albertsons Companies, Inc., Fiscal 2014-Fiscal 2018 (in millions)

	2018	2017(2)	2016(2)	2015(2)	2014(1)(2)
Results of Operations					
Net sales and other revenue	$60,534.5	$59,924.6	$59,678.2	$58,734.0	$27,198.6
Gross Profit	16,894.6	16,361.1	16,640.5	16,061.7	7,502.8
Selling and administrative expenses	16,107.3	16,275.4	16,032.9	15,702.6	8,157.0
Goodwill impairment	—	142.3	—	—	—
Operating income (loss)	787.3	(56.6)	607.6	359.1	(654.2)
Interest expense, net	830.8	874.8	1,003.8	950.5	633.2
Loss (gain) on debt extinguishment	8.7	(4.7)	111.7	—	—
Other (income) expense	(104.4)	(9.2)	(44.3)	(49.6)	91.2
Icome (loss) before income taxes	52.2	(917.5)	(463.6)	(541.8)	(1,378.6)
Income tax benefit	(78.9)	(963.8)	(90.3)	(39.6)	(153.4)
Net income (loss)	$ 131.1	$ 46.3	$ (373.3)	$ (502.2)	$ (1,225.2)

(1) Includes results from four weeks for the stores purchased in the Safeway acquisition on January 30, 2015.

(2) These periods have been adjusted for the retrospective adoption of Accounting Standards Update ("ASU") 2017–07, *"Compensation - Retirement Benefits (Topic 715) - Improving the Presentation of Net Periodic Pension Cost and Net Periodic Postretirement Benefit Cost"* in the first quarter of fiscal 201

Source: Albertsons Companies, Inc. 2018 Annual Report.

it launched its own branded subscription delivery service in 2019, and partnered with Glympse, a location sharing technology. Glymps enabled customers to get real-time status updates for delivery and pickup orders. By the fourth quarter 2019, Albertsons's home delivery services were available in 11 of the top 15 markets across the United States.

Albertson's filed for an IPO (Initial Public Offering) in 2015 but abandoned it due to market volatility of grocery stocks. The company filed again in March of 2020, and if successful, it would be one of the largest market debuts of the year, estimated at $2 billion. However, stocks around the world were dropping sharply due to rapid spread of the coronavirus in March 2020, and the fate of Albertson's IPO was questionable.

H. E. Butt Grocery

H. E. Butt Grocery, commonly known as H-E-B, was a family-owned, regional supermarket chain in Texas and Mexico. H-E-B was founded in 1905 by Florence Butt, and had grown to 400 stores (336 domestic) in 2020. In fiscal 2018, H-E-B had $28 billion in revenue, an increase of 12 percent from the prior year. The company was the

37th largest retailer in the world in 2017, and 12th largest private company in the United States. In 2018, the company had moved up to 11th largest. The company operated as H-E-B, H-E-B Plus, Mi Tienda, Joe V's Smart Shop, and Central Market. In 2019, H-E-B was listed by Forbes as number 11 – America's largest private companies, number 23 – Best Employers for New Grads, number 32 – Best Employer for Women, and number 32 America's Best Employers by State. H-E-B tied for first in customer satisfaction in the 2019–20 survey by the American Consumer Satisfaction Index ranking.

Financial information was scarce. Annual sales were estimated to be $28 billion in fiscal 2018 (ended October 31, 2018), and $23.12 billion in fiscal 2017. These revenue amounts exclude results from Mexican operations. In fiscal 2017, Mexican operations generated sales of $1.48 billion.

H-E-B developed a family of private brands, beginning in 1991, including H-E-B, H-E-B Select Ingredients, H-E-B Organics, Hill County Products, H-E-B Buddy. Central Market, H-E-B Kitchen & Table, and ChefStyle. The company promised that the quality of H-E-B brands would always equal or exceed that of national brands. The company began grocery delivery in 1916 in a Model T Ford. A century later, in February 2018, H-E-B acquired Favor Delivery, an innovative, on-demand delivery service. Favor was the best-rated delivery service in Texas, and in 2017, had become the first U.S. on-demand company to achieve profitability at scale. According to H-E-B, the Favor and other acquisition partnerships, plus strategic investments in technology, gives H-E-B the ability to ship groceries and other merchandise to 48 states and military bases around the world.

Meijer, Inc.

Meijer, Inc. was started in 1935 as a supermarket chain in Grand Rapids, Michigan by Hendrik Meijer. The company operates over 200 stores in Michigan, Ohio, Indiana, Illinois, and Kentucky, employs over 80,000, is the 19th largest private company in the United States, and 54th largest retailer in the world in 2017. Meijer's estimated 2019 revenue was $17.8 billion. Meijer is credited for pioneering the modern supercenter concept in 1962, when it opened "Thrifty Acres," a food and general merchandise store in which customers could find everything they needed in only one trip to the store. Each Meijer supercenter has 40 departments, which sell over 120,000 products: the stores are open 24 hours daily, 364 days a year. The company has created about 10,000 private-label brands.

The Meijer corporate values are customers (customers don't need us, we need them), family (Meijer is a family business, treating each other with dignity and respect), fresh food, safety and health, and competition (Meijer is committed to keeping its competitive spirit strong and staying nimble and flexible to win in the marketplace). The manifestation of Meijer's value of competition is evidenced in Grand Rapids, Michigan, where the company is reacting to the challenge of e-commerce by piloting a micro-fulfillment center, built in repurposed footage of a supercenter. The center will employ proprietary hardware and software that will enable Meijer retail stores to pick and assemble on-line orders to meet their customers' expectations and make online grocery profitable.

Whole Foods

In 1978, John Mackey and Renee Lawson, with $45,000 borrowed from family and friends, started a natural foods store named SaferWay in Austin, Texas. Two years later, Mackey and Lawson partnered with Craig Weller and Mark Skiles, who owned Natural Grocery, and formed Whole Foods Market in 1980. The company began an expansion and acquisition strategy in 1984 and expanded into Houston and Dallas. In 1988, Whole Foods Market acquired Whole Food Company in New Orleans, and, in 1989, expanded into California. The company continued opening new stores, but the rapid growth was the result of acquisitions. Throughout the 1990s, Whole Foods Market acquired companies from California to Boston. In 2002, the company expanded into Canada, and, in 2004, entered the UK market by acquiring seven Fresh & Wild stores. Whole Foods Market was acquired by Amazon in August 2017 for $13.4 billion. Whole Foods Market statement of operations 2015–17 (prior to being acquired by Amazon) is produced in Exhibit 9. As of January 2019, Whole Foods operated 479 stores in the United States.

Amazon immediately began to work toward positioning Whole Foods Market to excel in the online grocery market. Amazon Prime members received special discount on many foods and free shipping on online grocery purchases. In many markets, Amazon Prime customers could receive their online grocery orders in as little as two hours, between 8 a.m. and 10 p.m. Cost control was a priority: Whole Foods Market centralized its procurement and operations in Austin, Texas. Amazon imposed merchandizing fees for suppliers of items that were on sale: the company offered a 10 percent Amazon Prime discount on selected items, and Whole Foods charged that 10 percent back to the vendor. It was expected that Whole Foods Market planned to focus on expanding its online grocery services and the availability of its 365 private label brands to online shoppers under Amazon managerial control.

Publix Super Markets in Mid-2020. As the industry moved into 2020, the magnitude of online sales made delivery options almost mandatory. Although delivery was necessary, it was not always profitable. For example, Walmart, which was considered one of the most successful online grocery retailers, forecast a loss of over $1 billion in 2019. Obviously, efficiency and cost control were mandatory areas for grocery retailers' attention as the rapidly changing industry moved an increasing amount of sales into ecommerce.

EXHIBIT 9   Consolidated Statements of Operations for Whole Foods Market, Inc., 2015–2017 ($ in millions)

	2017	2016	2015
Sales	$16,030	$15,724	$15,389
Cost of goods sold and occupancy costs	10,633	10,313	9,973
Gross profit	5,397	5,411	5,416
Selling, general and administrative expenses	4,627	4,477	4,472
Merger-related expenses	156	—	—
Pre-opening expenses	60	64	67
Relocation, store closure, and lease termination costs	95	13	16
Operating income	459	857	861
Interest expense	(49)	(41)	—
Investment and other income	7	11	17
Income before income taxes	417	827	878
Provision for income taxes	172	320	342
Net income	$ 245	$ 507	$ 536

Source: Whole Foods Market, Inc. 2017 Annual Report.

Profitability in the retail grocery industry had been falling due to decreasing productivity, higher costs and significantly increased price competition. According to a January 2019 McKinsey & Company report, grocers could experience a $200 billion to $700 billion in revenue shift to online, discount, and non-grocery channels. The net result was that the industry was risking more than $1 trillion in earnings (before interest and taxes), as well as the loss of about half of traditional grocery retailers.

The COVID-19 pandemic in early 2020 injected additional speed into the supermarket industry change. In 2019, about one-third of a sample of shoppers reported that they bought "almost none" of their groceries online, while 16 percent bought "some," and 12 percent bought "almost all" online. On March 13, 2020, with the COVID-19 pandemic spreading through the United States, one-third of shoppers reported purchasing groceries online during the prior week, with 41 percent being first-time online grocery shoppers.

A result of the COVID-19 crisis was that most restaurants were closed, resulting in a large swing in food sales going to supermarkets. This presented many previously reluctant online grocery shoppers with the experience of easy, convenient online shopping, which would likely accelerate the structural change in shopping with an increase in the online grocery segment. Although the large revenue increase was welcomed by the industry, it concealed e-commerce deficiencies. A looming challenge for the industry was coping with the shift from groceries purchased from store shelves to lower-profit e-commerce sales.

ENDNOTES

[1] James Brumley, "The Kirkland Brand is Costco's Secret Weapon When It Matters Most," *Motley Fool,* https://www.fool .com/investing/2019/11/19/the-kirkland-brand-is-costcos-secret-weapon-when-i .aspx.

[2] Jenna Coleman, "Three Ways Albertsons is Quietly Upping their Online Grocery Game," *Forbes,* November 8, 2019, https://www.forbes .com/sites/jennacoleman/2019/11/08/3-ways-albertsons-is-quietly-upping-their-online-grocery-game/#5c2ff0cc3827.

[3] "New Market Force Information Study Finds Wegmans is America's Favorite Grocery Store," *Market Force Information,* June 26, 2018, https://www.marketforce .com/2018-americas-favorite-grocery-stores.

Tesla's Strategy in 2020: Can It Deliver Sustained Profitability?

Mc Graw Hill **connect**

Arthur A. Thompson

The University of Alabama

Tesla shocked shareholders and Wall Street by reporting an operating loss of $521.8 million and a net loss of $702.1 million for the first quarter of 2019. But during the next three quarters of 2019, the company reported a number of significant improvements and achievements that signaled a major turning point in its prospects for competitive success and future profitability:

- Tesla delivered a record 112,095 electric vehicles to customers in Q4 of 2019. For full-year 2019, Tesla delivered a record 367,656 electric vehicles to customers, a 50 percent increase over the 245,530 vehicles delivered in 2018. Buyer demand for Tesla's models was so strong that the company spent zero dollars on advertising to achieve its record sales volumes.

- The company's automotive revenues rose from $18.5 billion in 2018 to $20.8 billion in 2019, and its free cash flows from operations (after paying for capital expenditures) jumped from –$3.35 billion in 2017 to essentially $0 in 2018 to $1.1 billion in 2019.

- In January 2020, Tesla began ramping production of a soon-to-be-introduced Model Y at the company's Fremont assembly plant in California ahead of schedule; deliveries to customers were planned to begin in late March or early April. The new Model Y, an SUV version of Tesla's best-selling Model 3 sedan, was expected to become Tesla's most popular vehicle. Tesla CEO Elon Musk said that within a few years he expected that worldwide annual demand for Model 3 and Model Y would be on the order of 750,000 and 1.25 million units, respectively.

- The company announced improvements that boosted the single-charge EPA range on the all-wheel drive Model Y from 280 miles to 315 miles.

- Tesla began producing its Model 3 electric vehicle at a new assembly plant in Shanghai less than 10 months after beginning construction; vehicles produced at the Shanghai plant were expected to be delivered to buyers in China and other Asian countries. China was by far the world's largest market for motor vehicles, and sales of electric vehicles in China, which exceeded 1.4 million units in 2019, were the fastest-growing market segment.

- Tesla's engineering team discovered ways to greatly enhance the production and assembly techniques at the new Shanghai plant compared to those currently in use at the older Fremont plant; because of the resulting efficiency gains, unit production costs were expected to be about 25 percent below those at the Fremont plant.

- The company finalized plans for constructing a third assembly plant just outside Berlin, starting in February 2020; this plant was intended to supply vehicles to customers all across Europe, Scandinavia, and the Middle East.

- The company returned to profitability in the last two quarters of 2019, with net income of $143 million in Q3 and $105 million in Q4.

- Due to continuing improvements in operating efficiencies and higher operating leverage, the company's operating profit margin went from –11.5 percent in Q1 to –2.6 percent in Q2 to 4.1 percent in Q3 to 4.9 percent in Q4.

Following the January 28, 2020 announcement of Tesla's 2019 financial results and its outlook for 2020, Tesla's stock price, which had already climbed from $480 per share on January 3 to $567 on January 28, exploded to an intra-day high of $969 on February 19, 2020. Over the next two weeks, Tesla's stock price lost some of its gains, but still was trading around $750 per share in the first week of March 2020. However, by June 2020, Tesla's stock price had surged again on prospects of a reopening of the global economy following widespread COVID-19 shutdowns, reaching an all-time high of $1,027 on June 10.

Exhibit 1 shows sales of Tesla's four models from 2012 when the Models S was first introduced through the second quarter of 2020.

Company Background

Tesla Motors was incorporated in July 2003 by Martin Eberhard and Marc Tarpenning, two Silicon Valley engineers who believed it was feasible to produce an "awesome" electric vehicle. Tesla's namesake was the genius Nikola Tesla (1856–1943), an electrical engineer and scientist known for his impressive inventions (of which more than 700 were patented) and his contributions to the design of modern alternating-current (AC) power transmission systems and electric motors. Tesla's first vehicle, the Tesla Roadster (an all-electric sports car) introduced in early 2008, was powered by an AC motor that descended directly from Nikola Tesla's original 1882 design.

Financing Early Operations.   Eberhard and Tarpenning financed the company until Tesla's first round of investor funding in February 2004. Elon Musk contributed $6.35 million of the $6.5 million in initial funding and, as the company's majority investor, assumed the position of Chairman of the company's board of directors. Martin Eberhard put up $75,000 of the initial $6.5 million, with two private equity investment groups and a number of private investors contributing the remainder.[1] Several rounds of investor funding ensued, with Elon Musk emerging as the company's biggest shareholder. Other notable investors included Google co-founders Sergey Brin and Larry Page, former eBay President Jeff Skoll, and Hyatt heir Nick Pritzker. In 2009, Germany's Daimler AG, the maker of Mercedes vehicles, acquired an equity stake of almost 10 percent in Tesla for a reported $50 million.[2] Daimler's investment was motivated by a desire to partner with Tesla to accelerate the development of Tesla's lithium-ion battery technology and electric drive train technology and to collaborate on electric cars being developed at

EXHIBIT 1   Tesla's Deliveries of the Model S, Model X, Model 3, and Model Y to Customers, 2012 through the Second Quarter of 2020

Period	Model S Deliveries	Model S plus Model X Deliveries	Model 3 Deliveries	Model 3 plus Model Y Deliveries
2012	2,653			
2013	22,477			
2014	31,655			
2015	50,332			
2016		76,230		
2017		101,420	1,734	
2018		99,475	146,055	
2019		66,771	300,885	
Q1 2020*		12,200		76,200
Q2 2020*		10,600		90,650

*Deliveries in Q1 and Q2 2020 were negatively impacted by the spread of the Coronavirus, which resulted in a government-mandated shutdown of the company's two assembly plants and a sharp falloff in buyer purchases of new motor vehicles due to stay-at-home restrictions in China, the United States, and many other countries.

Source: Company 10K reports, 2012-2019 and Tesla press releases, April 2, 2020 and July 2, 2020.

Mercedes. Later in 2009, Tesla was awarded a $465 million low-interest loan by the U.S. Department of Energy to accelerate the production of affordable, fuel-efficient electric vehicles; Tesla used $365 million for production engineering and assembly of its forthcoming Model S and $100 million for a powertrain manufacturing plant employing about 650 people that would supply all-electric powertrain solutions to other automakers and help accelerate the availability of relatively low-cost, mass-market electric vehicles.

In June 2010, Tesla Motors became a public company, raising $226 million with an initial public offering of common stock. It was the first American car company to go public since Ford Motor Company in 1956.

Management Changes at Tesla. In August 2007, with the company plagued by delays in getting its first model—the Tesla Roadster—into production, co-founder Martin Eberhard was ousted as Tesla's chief executive officer (CEO). While his successor managed to get the Tesla Roadster into production in March 2008 and begin delivering Roadsters to customers in October 2008, internal turmoil in the executive ranks prompted Elon Musk to decide it made more sense for him to take on the role as Tesla's chief executive officer—while continuing to serve as chairman of the board—because he was making all the major decisions anyway.

Elon Musk. Elon Musk was born in South Africa, taught himself computer programming, and, at age 12, made $500 by selling the computer code for a video game he invented.[3] In 1992, after spending two years at Queen's University in Ontario, Canada, Musk transferred to the University of Pennsylvania where he earned an undergraduate degree in business and a second degree in physics. During his college days, Musk spent some time thinking about two important matters that he thought merited his time and attention later in his career: one was that the world needed an environmentally clean method of transportation; the other was that it would be good if humans could colonize another planet.[4] After graduating from the University of Pennsylvania, he decided to move to California and pursue a PhD in applied physics at Stanford; however, he left the program after two days to pursue his entrepreneurial aspirations instead.

Musk's first entrepreneurial venture was to join up with his brother, Kimbal, and establish Zip2, an Internet software company that developed, hosted, and maintained some 200 websites involving "city guides" for media companies. In 1999 Zip2 was sold to a wholly-owned subsidiary of Compaq Computer for $307 million in cash and $34 million in stock options—Musk received a reported $22 million from the sale.[5]

In March 1999, Musk co-founded X.com, a Silicon Valley online financial services and e-mail payment company. One year later, X.com acquired Confinity, which operated a subsidiary called PayPal. Musk was instrumental in the development of the person-to-person payment platform and, seeing big market opportunity for such an online payment platform, decided to rename X.com as PayPal. Musk pocketed about $150 million in eBay shares when PayPal was acquired by eBay for $1.5 billion in eBay stock in October 2002.

In June 2002, Elon Musk with an investment of $100 million of his own money founded his third company, Space Exploration Technologies (SpaceX), to develop and manufacture space launch vehicles, with a goal of revolutionizing the state of rocket technology and ultimately enabling people to live on other planets. Upon hearing of Musk's new venture into the space flight business, David Sacks, one of Musk's former colleagues at PayPal, said, "Elon thinks bigger than just about anyone else I've ever met. He sets lofty goals and sets out to achieve them with great speed."[6] In 2011, Musk vowed to put a man on Mars in 10 years.[7] In May 2012, a SpaceX Dragon cargo capsule powered by a SpaceX Falcon Rocket completed a near flawless test flight to and from the International Space Station; since then, under contracts with NASA, the SpaceX Dragon had delivered cargo to and from the Space Station multiple times. In early 2020, SpaceX was working toward launching a rocket and spacecraft in May 2029 carrying two American astronauts to the International Space Station, the first visit by American astronauts on an American rocket and spacecraft since July 2011. But, more significantly, SpaceX was making rapid progress on Elon Musk's ambitious Starlink project to provide high-speed broadband service worldwide via satellite by the end of 2020. Musk envisioned it might take a network of perhaps 12,000 Starlink satellites roughly the size of an office desk and weighing about 500 pounds orbiting about 375 miles above the earth to provide dense enough coverage to provide broadband service to every nook and cranny on earth. As of April 2020, SpaceX had put up five batches of 60 satellites into orbit. Musk had tweeted after the launch of the third 60-satellite deployment that Starlink internet services would become available in the Northern United States and Canada after the completion of at least seven to nine 60-satellite deployments. After 22 launches, the company would be able to offer the service around the globe; Musk believed that if the Starlink network could capture as little as five percent of the global telecommunications market with its high-speed broadband service, SpaceX could net annual revenues of $30 billion to $50 billion. SpaceX had developed a fully and rapidly reusable Falcon rocket to power the Starlink launches (as well as other types of launches). Headquartered in Hawthorne, California, SpaceX had 7,000 employees and was owned by management, employees, and private equity firms; Elon Musk was the company's CEO and largest stockholder.

Another of Elon Musk's business ventures was SolarCity Inc., a full-service provider of solar system design, financing, solar panel installation, and ongoing system monitoring for homeowners, municipalities, businesses (including Intel, Walmart, Walgreens, and eBay), universities, nonprofit organizations, and military bases. Initially, investors were generally bullish on SolarCity's future prospects, and the company's stock price rose from about $10.50 in late December 2012 to an all-time high of $85 in March 2013. But when the company's losses continued to grow, investor sentiment cooled and SolarCity's stock price dropped to the $16-$20 range in February 2016. While Solar City had installed many solar energy systems and managed more solar systems for homes than any other solar company in the United States, its business model of recovering the capital and operating costs of the installed systems through leasing fees and power purchase agreements had resulted in negative cash flows and ever-larger net losses. In November 2016, to rescue SolarCity from probable bankruptcy, Tesla acquired the company for $2.6 billion (the deal was approved by an 85 percent shareholder vote); SolarCity's operations were folded into a new division named Tesla Energy. However, the business model was changed to one where customers financed their new solar power installations with cash and loans, thus producing a healthier mix of upfront and recurring revenue; moreover, the costs of installing solar-powered installations were declining, partly because of improvements in solar technology, greater efficiencies in manufacturing solar-generation systems, and cost savings achieved by operating Tesla's automotive and energy divisions as sister companies.

During 2008–2015, many business articles had been written about Musk's brilliant entrepreneurship in creating companies with revolutionary products that either spawned new industries or disruptively transformed existing industries. In a 2012 *Success* magazine article, Musk indicated that his commitments to his spacecraft, electric car, and solar panel businesses were long term and deeply felt.[8] The author quoted Musk as saying, "I never expect to sort of sell them off and do something else. I expect to be with those companies as far into the future as I can imagine." Musk indicated he was involved in both Tesla's motor vehicle and energy businesses "because I'm concerned about the environment," while "SpaceX is about trying to help us work toward extending life beyond Earth on a permanent basis and becoming a multiplanetary species." The same writer described Musk's approach to a business as one of rallying employees and investors without creating false hope.[9] The article quoted Musk as saying:

> You've got to communicate, particularly within the company, the true state of the company. When people really understand it's do or die but if we work hard and pull through, there's going to be a great outcome, people will give it everything they've got.

Asked if he relied more on information or instinct in making key decisions, Musk said he made no bright-line distinction between the two.

> Data informs the instinct. Generally, I wait until the data and my instincts are in alignment. And if either the data or my instincts are out of alignment, then I sort of keep working the issue until they are in alignment, either positive or negative.[10]

Musk was widely regarded as being an inspiring and visionary entrepreneur with astronomical ambition and willingness to invest his own money in risky and highly problematic business ventures. He set stretch performance targets and high product quality standards, and he pushed hard for their achievement. He exhibited perseverance, dedication, and an exceptionally strong work ethic—he typically worked 85 to 90 hours a week. Most weeks, Musk split his time between SpaceX and Tesla.

In 2019, Elon Musk's base salary as Tesla's CEO was $62,400, an amount required by California's minimum wage law; however, he was accepting only $1 in salary. The company's Board of Directors in 2017 established an executive compensation plan for Musk tied to Tesla's performance on various metrics; compensation was in the form of stock option awards subject to various vesting conditions. As of January 2020, Musk reportedly owned about 34 million shares of Tesla common stock, equal to about 19 percent of the shares outstanding.[11]

Musk's Vision and Strategy for Tesla. Elon Musk's strategic vision for the automotive segment of Tesla's operations featured three major elements:

1. Bring a full-range of affordable electric-powered vehicles to market and become the world's foremost manufacturer of premium quality, high-performance electric vehicles.

2. Convince motor vehicle owners worldwide that electric-powered motor vehicles were an appealing alternative to gasoline-powered vehicles.

3. Accelerate the world's transition from carbon-producing, gasoline-powered motor vehicles to zero-emission electric vehicles.

His strategic intent was for Tesla to be the world's biggest and most highly-regarded producer of electric-powered motor vehicles, dramatically increasing the share of electric vehicles on roads across the world and causing global use of gasoline-powered motor vehicles to fall into permanent long-term decline. At its core, therefore, Tesla's strategy was aimed squarely at utilizing the company's battery and electric drivetrain technology to disrupt the world automotive industry in ways that were sweeping and transformative. If Tesla's strategy proved to be as successful as Elon Musk believed it would be, industry observers expected that Tesla's competitive position and market standing vis-à-vis the world's best-known automotive manufacturers would be vastly stronger in 2025 than it was in 2020.

Tesla's Early Sales Successes with the Model S and Model X, 2012–2019.
In 2017 and 2018 production and sales of the company's trailblazing Model S sedan (introduced in 2012) and Model X sports utility vehicle (introduced in late 2015) were proceeding largely on plan. Combined sales of these two models were almost 101,500 units in 2017 and just under 100,000 units in 2018. Combined sales dropped to only 66,800 units in 2019, as many buyers shifted to purchasing

the lower-priced Model 3 (see Exhibit 1). Both the Model S and Model X were being sold in North America, Europe, and Asia in 2017–2020.

The Model S was a fully electric, four-door, five-passenger luxury sedan featuring all-wheel drive with dual front and rear motors (mounted on the front and rear axles), an all-glass panoramic roof, a top speed of 155 mph, the ability to accelerate from 0 to 60 mph in as little as 2.4 seconds, an estimated driving range of up to 390 miles on a single charge, a high definition backup camera, a 17-inch touchscreen that controlled most of the car's functions, keyless entry, xenon headlights, certain autopilot and self-driving capabilities, and numerous other features that were standard in most luxury vehicles.

The Model X was a sport utility vehicle with seating for up to seven adults, a top speed of 155 mph, the ability to accelerate from 0 to 60 mph in 4.4 seconds, an estimated driving range of 351 miles on a single charge, and a unique falcon wing door system for easy access to the second and third seating rows. The Model X also had an all-wheel drive dual motor system, adaptive air suspension, a premium interior and sound system, and autopilot capabilities, along with assorted other standard and optional features.

The Model S was the most-awarded car of 2013, including *Motor Trend's* 2013 Car of the Year award and *Automobile* magazine's 2013 Car of the Year award. The National Highway Traffic Safety Administration (NTSHA) in 2013, 2014, and 2015 awarded the Tesla Model S a five-star safety rating, both overall and in every subcategory (a score achieved by approximately one percent of all cars tested by the NHTSA). *Consumer Reports* gave the Model S a score of 99 out of 100 points in 2013, 2014, and 2015, saying it was "better than anything we've ever tested." However, the Tesla Model S did not make the *Consumer Reports* list of the "10 Top Picks" in 2016, 2017, and 2018, but the Model S did earn a perfect 100 score on the 2018 road test drive. In 2020 *Consumer Reports* gave the Model S a 97 on the 2020 road test drive and a #2 ranking among the top ten ultra-luxury cars; ratings for the Model X were considerably lower.

The sleek styling and politically correct power source of Tesla's Model S and Model X were thought to explain why thousands of wealthy individuals in countries where the two models were being sold—anxious to be a part of the migration from gasoline-powered vehicles to electric-powered vehicles and to publicly display support for a cleaner environment—had become early purchasers and advocates for Tesla's vehicles. Indeed, word-of-mouth praise among current owners and glowing articles in the media were so pervasive that Tesla had not yet spent any money on advertising to boost customer traffic in its showrooms. In a presentation to investors, a Tesla officer said "Tesla owners are our best salespeople."[12]

Tesla's Excruciating Struggle to Boost Production Volumes of the Model 3.

Tesla Motors began assembling the first models of its new "affordably-priced" entry-level Model 3 electric car in May 2017 and delivered the first units the last week of July. The first production vehicles, delivered to employees who had placed pre-production reservations over a year earlier, were pre-configured with rear-wheel drive and a long-range battery, had a range of 310 miles and 0 to 60 mph acceleration time of 5.1 seconds and had a sticker price starting at $44,000 with premium upgrades available for an additional $5,000 to $10,000.

Tesla unveiled six drivable prototypes of the Model 3 for public viewing and a limited number of test drives on the evening of March 31, 2016. Buyer reaction was overwhelmingly positive. Over the next two weeks, some 350,000 individuals paid a $1,000 deposit to reserve a place in line to obtain a Model 3; reportedly, the number of reservations grew to nearly 400,000 units over the next several months. Because of the tremendous amount of interest in the Model 3, Tesla advanced the schedule to begin producing the Model 3 to mid-2017 and further accelerated its efforts to expand production capacity of the Model 3.

In early August 2017, Musk said: [13]

Based on our preparedness at this time, we are confident we can produce just over 1,500 [Model 3] vehicles in Q3 and achieve a run rate of 5,000 vehicles per week by the end of 2017. We also continue to plan on increasing Model 3 production to 10,000 vehicles per week at some point in 2018.

But in his third quarter 2017 update on November 1, 2017, Musk related a host of production bottlenecks and challenges that were blocking the ramp-up of Model 3 production and delaying deliveries, saying, "this makes it difficult to predict exactly how long it will take for all bottlenecks to be cleared or when new ones will appear.[14]

Tesla's "production hell" with the Model 3 continued to haunt the company well into 2018. Many analysts believed Tesla's problems stemmed from having taken huge shortcuts in the parts approval process, production line validation, and full beta testing of the Model 3 in order to begin early assembly and production ramp-up. There were other reasons, including ongoing parts bottlenecks and reportedly inconsistent manufacturing quality. Production line employees interviewed by reporters indicated significant numbers of units coming off the assembly line had quality problems involving malfunctioning parts/components and/or faulty installation issues that required reworking. In early 2018, a big parking lot just outside the assembly plant in Fremont, California, was said to be full of Model 3s awaiting corrective attention; a few were even being junked because of the high cost of restoring them to a condition that would pass final pre-delivery inspection. On February 7, 2018, Musk reported: [15]

We continue to target weekly Model 3 production rates of 2,500 by the end of Q1 and 5,000 by the end of Q2. It is important to note that while these are the levels we are focused on hitting and we have plans in place to achieve them, our prior experience on the Model 3 ramp has demonstrated the difficulty of accurately forecasting specific production rates at specific points in time. What we can say with confidence is that we are taking many actions to systematically address bottlenecks and add capacity in places like the battery module line where we have experienced constraints, and these actions should result in our production rate significantly increasing during the rest of Q1 and through Q2.

A week or so later, Tesla shut down the Model 3 assembly line for four days to address some of the problems being encountered. Nonetheless, in early March 2018, there were reports from multiple sources that Tesla had not been able to consistently achieve a production run rate of 800 units per week. Musk's target of a weekly production rate of 2,500 Model 3s by the end of March proved unachievable. During the last week of March, Elon Musk tweeted that he had taken over the role of supervising Model 3 production for the time being.

The first week of April 2018, Tesla reported that it produced 34,494 vehicles in the first quarter of 2018 and delivered 29,980 vehicles, of which 11,730 were Model S; 10,070 were Model X; and 8,180 were Model 3. The company said that after shifting some production resources away from Model S and Model X production over to production and assembly of the Model 3 during the last week of March, it was able to produce 2,020 Model 3s in the last seven days leading up to April 3. In its production and delivery announcement, the company further said:

> Given the progress made thus far and upcoming actions for further capacity improvement, we expect that the Model 3 production rate will climb rapidly through Q2. Tesla continues to target a production rate of approximately 5,000 units per week in about three months.
>
> Finally, we would like to share two additional points about Model 3:[16]

- The quality of Model 3 coming out of production is at the highest level we have seen across all our products. This is reflected in the overwhelming delight experienced by our customers with their Model 3s. Our initial customer satisfaction score for Model 3 quality is above 93 percent, which is the highest score in Tesla's history.
- Net Model 3 reservations remained stable through Q1. The reasons for order cancellation are almost entirely due to delays in production in general and delays in availability of certain planned options, particularly dual motor AWD and the smaller battery pack.

While progress was finally being made in boosting Model 3 production volumes, Tesla still had to prove it could overcome three challenges with the potential to imperil Musk's vision for the company:

1. Gasoline prices across much of the world had dropped significantly from 2015 to early 2018 and were expected by many knowledgeable observers to remain permanently "low" because crude oil prices worldwide were expected to stay below $80 per barrel, in part due to the growing abundance of shale oil and the sharply-lower costs of extracting oil from shale deposits. Affordable gasoline prices made the purchase of electric vehicles less attractive, given that (1) electric vehicles were higher priced than vehicles with gasoline engines, (2) electric vehicles so far were limited to an upper range of about 300 miles on a single battery charge, and (3) new vehicles powered by gasoline engines were getting more miles per gallon (due to government-mandated mileage-efficiency requirements).

2. Tesla was facing the prospect of much more formidable competition from virtually all of the world's major motor vehicle manufacturers (BMW, Mercedes-Benz, Jaguar, Volkswagen-Audi, Toyota, Honda, Nissan, General Motors, and Ford) that were rushing to introduce affordable and high-end electric vehicles with features and engine configurations that would enable them to compete head-on with the Model S, Model X, and Model 3. Several vehicle makers were also pursuing the development of electric-powered semitrucks for commercial uses.

3. Tesla had yet to prove it could boost operating efficiency and lower costs enough to be both price competitive and attractively profitable in producing and marketing its vehicle models. It reported both a loss from operations and a net loss during 2013–2017, despite growing its automotive sales and leasing revenues from $2.61 billion in 2013 to $9.64 billion in 2017. In February 2018, the company did say it expected to generate a positive *quarterly* operating income before the end of 2018 (but not a positive operating income for the *year*). While Tesla's ongoing operating losses and net losses were partly, or perhaps largely, due to the sizable new product development costs associated with the Model X and Model 3 and to the required accounting treatments for both leased vehicles and Tesla's generous stock compensation plan, it was nonetheless disconcerting that Tesla's operating loss of $1.63 billion in 2017 was the largest in the company's history and its 2017 operating profit per vehicle sold was a negative $15,855.[17]

When Tesla announced its financial and operating results for the first quarter of 2018 ending March 31, Elon Musk said that after numerous adjustments in assembly methods and correcting problems with faulty and improperly designed parts Tesla was now able to sustain a production rate of 3,000 Model 3s per week. He also said that continued refinements of the assembly process and improved operational uptime of the associated machinery should lead to a production rate of "well over 5,000" vehicles per week by the end of June or beginning of July. Musk admitted that he had been wrong in mandating use of so many robots along the assembly line, and that now the assembly line had been and was still being greatly simplified, with more use being made of semi-automated and manual assembly to perform certain tasks until the company had enough time to perfect the use of robots and enable full automation to resume. Musk confidently predicted that the Model 3 would become the best-selling medium-sized premium sedan in the United States before year end and that, if Tesla executed according to plan, the company would achieve positive cash flows and positive net income (excluding non-cash stock-based compensation) in both the third and fourth quarters of 2018.[18] During the May 2, 2018 conference call with analysts to discuss Tesla's Q1 2018 financial results, Musk expressed his appreciation to the

Chinese government for its announcement that foreign companies would henceforth be allowed to have 100 percent ownership of manufacturing facilities in China and said Tesla could have a Gigafactory capable of vehicle production in China "not later than the fourth quarter" of 2018.[19]

Exhibit 2 presents selected financial statement data for Tesla for 2015 through 2019.

EXHIBIT 2   Selected Financial Data for Tesla, Inc., Years Ended December 31, 2015–2019 (in millions, except per share data)

	Years Ended December 31				
	2015	2016	2017	2018	2019
Income Statement Data:					
Revenues:					
Automotive sales	$3,432	$5,589	$ 8,535	17,632	$19,952
Automotive leasing	309	762	1,107	883	869
Total automotive revenues	3,741	6,351	9,642	18,515	20,821
Energy generation and storage	14	181	1,116	1,555	1,531
Services and other	291	468	1,001	1,391	2,226
Total revenues	4,046	7,000	11,759	21,461	24,578
Cost of revenues:					
Automotive sales	2,640	4,268	6,724.5	13,686	15,939
Automotive leasing	183	482	708	488	459
Total automotive cost of revenues	2,823	4,750	7,433	14,174	16,398
Energy generation and storage	12	178	874	1365	1,341
Services and other	287	472	1,229	1,880	2,770
Total cost of revenues	3,123	5,401	9,536	17,419	20,509
Gross profit (loss)	924	1,599	2,223	4,042	4,069
Operating expenses:					
Research and development	7,189	834	1,378	1,460	1,343
Selling, general and administrative	922	1,432.	2,477	2,834.5	2,646
Restructuring and other	—	—	—	135	149
Total operating expenses	1,640	2,267	3,855	4,430	4,138
Loss from operations	(717)	(667)	(1,632)	(388)	(69)
Interest income	2	9	19	24	44
Interest expense	(119)	(199)	(471)	(663)	(685)
Other income (expense), net	(42)	111	(125)	22	45
Loss before income taxes	(876)	(746)	(2,209)	(1,005)	(665)
Provision for income taxes	13	27	32	58	110
Net loss	$ (889)	$ (773)	$ (2,241)	$ (1,063)	$ (775)
Net loss attributable to noncontrolling interests and subsidiaries	—	(98)	(279)	(87)	87

(continue)

EXHIBIT 2   Selected Financial Data for Tesla, Inc., Years Ended December 31, 2015–2019 (in millions, except per share data)   *(continued)*

Net loss attributable to common shareholders	$ (889)	$ (675)	$ (1,962)	$ (976)	$ (862)
Net loss per share of common stock, basic and diluted	$ (6.93)	$ (4.68)	$ (11.83)	$ (5.72)	$ (4.92)
Weighted average shares used in computing net loss per share of common stock, basic and diluted	128	144	166	171	177
Selected Balance Sheet Data:					
Cash and cash equivalents	$1,197	$3,393	$ 3,368	$ 3,686	$ 6,286
Inventory	1,278	2,067	2,264	3,113	3,552
Total current assets	2,791	6,260	6,571	8,307	12,103
Property, plant, and equipment, net	3,403	5,983	10,028	11,330	10,396
Total assets	8,093	22,664	28,655	29,740	34,309
Total current liabilities	2,816	5,827	7,675	9,992	10,667
Long-term debt and capital leases, net of current portion	2,040	5,860	9,418.	9,404	11,634
Total stockholders' equity	1,089	4,753	4,237	4,923	6,618
Selected Cash Flow Data:					
Cash flows provided by (used in) operating activities	$ (524)	$ (124)	$ (61)	$ 2,098	$ 2,405
Proceeds from issuance of common stock in public offerings	730	1,702	400		848
Proceeds from issuance of convertible and other debt	319	2,853	7,138	6,176	10,669
Purchases of property and equipment excluding capital leases	(1,635)	(1,281)	(3,415)	(2,101)	(1,327)
Net cash used in investing activities	(1,674)	(1,081)	(4,196)	(2,337)	(1,436)
Net cash provided by financing activities	1,524	3,744	4,415	574	1,529

Sources: Company 10-K reports for 2015, 2017, 2018, and 2019.

Tesla in 2020

In 2020 Tesla's business consisted of designing, developing, manufacturing, and leasing high-performance fully electric vehicles, and energy generation and storage systems; it also offered services related to its products.[20] The company considered itself to be the world's first vertically integrated sustainable energy company, offering end-to-end clean energy products, including generation, storage and consumption. Tesla products were generally sold directly to customers at its website and selected retail locations and, in some cases, by an internal salesforce. To serve customers, Tesla had invested in a global network of vehicle service centers, Mobile Service technicians, body shops, Supercharger stations, and Destination Chargers to accelerate the widespread adoption of its

battery-powered electric vehicles our products and help promote the transition from gasoline-powered motor vehicles to zero emission electric vehicles.

Tesla currently offered or was planning to offer a wide range of technologically advanced, attractively styled, high-performance consumer and commercial vehicles. To differentiate its business and vehicles from other vehicle manufacturers, Tesla was aggressively striving to be the leader, or at worst among the leaders, in introducing full self-driving capability for all of its models to complement such existing features as leading mileage range on a single charge, superior acceleration, handling and safety performance, user convenience and infotainment packages, the ability to have additional features enabled through over-the-air software updates; and savings in charging, maintenance and other costs of ownership. technology for improved safety. In addition, Tesla was striving to lower the cost of ownership for our customers through continuous efforts to reduce manufacturing costs of its vehicles.

In furtherance of its mission to accelerate the world's transition to sustainable energy, Tesla had also developed an expertise in solar energy systems. It sold and leased solar energy systems for residential and commercial customers, and it offered a Solar Roof product, which featured attractive and durable glass roof tiles integrated with solar energy generation. Tesla's approach to the solar business emphasized simplicity, standardization, and accessibility to make it easy and cost-effective for customers to adopt clean energy.

Finally, Tesla had leveraged its technological expertise in batteries, energy management, power electronics, and integrated systems associated with its vehicle powertrain systems to develop and manufacture energy storage products, including Powerwall, Powerpack and Megapack. These scalable systems could be used in homes, commercial facilities, and on the utility grid, and were capable of numerous applications including backup or off-grid power, peak demand reduction, demand response, reducing intermittency of renewable energy generation, and facilitating the use of renewable energy generation over fossil fuel generation, and other grid services and wholesale electric market services. Tesla's solar business expertise enabled it to offer integrated systems that combined energy generation and energy storage. As with Tesla's vehicles, the company's energy storage products could be remotely updated over-the-air with software or firmware improvements.

Funding Its Rapidly Expanding Business Operations. During 2014–2017, Tesla raised billions of dollars via the sale of senior notes convertible into common stock, other types of long-term debt, and issues of new common stock to provide funding for research and development (R&D), the development of new models, expanded production capabilities, an ever-growing network of recharging stations, retail showrooms, vehicle service centers, and its energy product operations. Tesla's long-term debt and contractual capital lease obligations grew from $600 million at year-end 2013 to $11.6 billion at year-end 2019; and the number of shares of common stock outstanding rose from 119 million to 177 million during the same period. In recent years, Tesla burned through cash

at a torrid pace because of the heavy expenses it was incurring for design and engineering, gearing up to produce certain parts and component systems internally, constructing new facilities, equipping vehicle assembly lines with robotics technology, tools, and other machinery, and boosting its employee count from almost 6,000 employees at year-end 2013 to just over 48,000 at year-end 2019. The new Gigafactory in Shanghai, China, was being almost fully funded with local debt.

Tesla's Strategy to Become the World's Biggest and Most Highly Regarded Producer of Electric Vehicles

In 2020, Tesla's strategy and operating initiatives were focused on:

- Continuing to ramp up production of the Model 3 at both the Shanghai plant and the Fremont plant.
- Ramping up the production of the new Model Y SUV at both the Shanghai plant and the Fremont plant and beginning deliveries to customers in April 2020.
- Expanding the production capacity of certain automobile parts (battery packs, electric motors, motor controllers, cooling pipes) at the Shanghai plant to help localize its supply chain for vehicles produced in China; it was also building a second stamping line to speed up car production at the plant.
- Adding more production capacity at the Fremont plant so as to enable the production of 90,000 Model S and Model X vehicles and 400,000 Model 3 and Model Y vehicles.
- Finishing construction on the second phase of the assembly plant in Shanghai, with a goal of having 300,000 units of total production capacity (150,000 for Model 3 and 150,000 for Model Y) in place by year-end 2020 or early 2021.
- Moving quickly to construct and equip its third assembly plant in Germany in order to begin production of Model 3 and Model Y in the first quarter of 2021.
- Continuing to refine the designs and development of its next three models.
- Continuing to expand the numbers of sales and service locations, mobile service vehicles and Supercharger stations across the world.

- Continuing to develop the technologies, systems, and software to achieve full self-driving capabilities for all Tesla vehicles.
- Selecting sites in the United States for two new manufacturing and assembly plants—one for producing the Model Y and one for producing a new pickup truck.

Product Line Strategy.

A key element of Tesla's long-term strategy was to offer vehicle-buyers a full line of electric vehicle options. So far Tesla had introduced four models—the Tesla Roadster, Model S, Model X, and Model 3. Aggressive efforts were underway to get the Model Y into the marketplace in Spring 2020. along with a limited number of Tesla Semi trucks. These were scheduled to be followed by a Tesla Semi truck, a new pickup-up truck called the Cybertruck, and a fresh Roadster 2 model.

Tesla's First Vehicle—The Tesla Roadster. Following Tesla's initial funding in 2004, Musk took an active role within the company. Although he was not involved in day-to-day business operations, he nonetheless exerted strong influence in the design of the Tesla Roadster, a two-seat convertible that could accelerate from 0 to 60 miles per hour in as little as 3.7 seconds, had a maximum speed of about 120 miles per hour, could travel about 245 miles on a single charge, and had a base price of $109,000. Musk insisted from the beginning that the Roadster have a lightweight, high-strength carbon fiber body, and he influenced the design of components of the Roadster ranging from the power electronics module to the headlamps and other styling features.[21] Prototypes of the Roadster were introduced to the public in July 2006. The first "Signature One Hundred" set of fully equipped Roadsters sold out in less than three weeks; the second hundred sold out by October 2007. General production began in March 2008. New models of the Roadster were introduced in July 2009 (including the Roadster Sport with a base price of $128,500) and in July 2010. Sales of Roadster models to countries in Europe and Asia began in 2010. From 2008 through 2012, Tesla sold more than 2,450 Roadsters in 31 countries.[22] Sales of Roadster models ended in December 2012 so that the company could concentrate exclusively on producing and marketing the Model S. However, Tesla announced in early 2015 that Roadster owners would be able to obtain a Roadster 3.0 package that enabled

a 40 to 50 percent improvement in driving range to as much as 400 miles on a single charge; management indicated additional updates for Roadsters would be forthcoming. In 2017, Tesla announced it would re-introduce a new version of the Roadster in 2020 (after it began deliveries of the Tesla Semi truck and Model Y).

Tesla's Second Vehicle—The Model S. Customer deliveries of Tesla's second vehicle—the sleek, eye-catching Model S sedan—began in July 2012. Tesla introduced several new options for the Model S in 2013, including a sub-zero weather package, parking sensors, upgraded leather interior, several new wheel options, and a yacht-style center console. Later, Xenon headlights, a high definition backup camera, emergency braking, collision warning, blind-spot monitoring, and various autopilot and self-driving capabilities became standard equipment on all Model S cars. The Model S powertrain options had been modified several times. In March 2020, the Model S was being offered with two powertrains options:

- Long Range Plus — all-wheel drive with dual front and rear motors (mounted on the front and rear axles), 390-mile driving range, 0 to 60 mph in 3.7 seconds, with a standard price of $79,990 (which included adaptive air suspension, premium interior and sound, and free unlimited supercharging)
- Performance — all-wheel drive with dual front and rear motors (mounted on the front and rear axles), 348-mile driving range, 0 to 60 mph in 2.4 seconds, with a standard price of $94,990 (which included adaptive air suspension, enhanced interior styling, premium sound, and free unlimited supercharging)

Popular options included premium exterior colors (up to $2,000), 21" sonic carbon twin turbine wheels ($2,500), a full-self-driving computer, with online activation of new self-driving capabilities as regulatory approval was granted ($7,000); and third-row, rear-facing seating ($4,000). All Model S vehicles (as well as all other Tesla models) previously delivered to customers were equipped to receive software updates from Tesla that included new and updated features. Autopilot software features were updated and upgraded as fast as they were developed and tested.

To counter the "range anxiety" that Tesla owners sometimes experienced, in 2018 Tesla introduced a standard software feature called "Range Assurance," an always-running application within the car's navigation system that kept tabs on the vehicle's battery charge-level and the locations of Tesla Supercharging stations and parking-spot chargers in the vicinity. When the vehicle's battery began running low, an alert appeared on the navigation screen, along with a list of nearby Tesla Supercharger stations and public charging facilities; a second warning appeared when the vehicle was about to go beyond the radius of nearby chargers without enough juice to get to the next facility, at which point drivers were directed to the nearest charge point. There was also a Trip Planner feature that enabled drivers to plan long-distance trips based on the best locations for recharging both en route and at the destination; during travel, the software was programmed to pull in new data about every 30 seconds, updating to show which charging facilities had vacancies or were full.

In the United States, customers who purchased a Model S (or any other Tesla model) before 2019 were eligible for a federal tax credit of up to $7,500. A number of states also offered rebates on electric vehicle purchases, with states like California and New York offering rebates as high as $7,500. Customers who leased a Model S were not entitled to rebates. Legislation authorizing the federal tax credit called for the tax credits on a manufacturer's electric vehicles to expire once the manufacturer's cumulative sales of electric vehicles reached 200,000 units. Bills had been introduced in Congress to extend the credits past a cumulative sales volume of 200,000 units, but none of these had passed.

Tesla's Third Vehicle—The Model X Crossover SUV. To reduce the development costs of the Model X, Tesla had designed the Model X so that it could share about 60 percent of the Model S platform. The Model X had seating for up to 7 adults, dual electric motors that powered an all-wheel drive system, and a driving range of about 351 miles per charge. The Model X's distinctive "falcon-wing doors" provided easy access to the second and third seating rows, resulting in a profile that resembled a sedan more than an SUV. The drive train options for the Model X in 2020 were the same as for the Model S, but the driving ranges and acceleration times for the Model X were different from those of the Model S. In 2018, the standard price for the Long Range Plus Model X was $84,990; the standard price for the Performance Model X was $104,990. The options were essentially similar to the Model S

except for the seating; five-passenger seating was standard, a six-seat interior cost $6,500, and a seven-seat interior cost $3,500. Options for the Model X could boost the price to $127,990. The Model X was the first SUV ever to achieve a five-star safety rating in every category and sub-category; it had both the lowest probability of occupant injury and a rollover risk half that of any SUV on the road.

Tesla's Fourth Vehicle—The Model 3. The idea behind the Model 3 was to incorporate all the company had learned from the development and production of the Roadster, Model S, and Model X to create the world's first mass market electric vehicle priced on par with its gasoline-powered equivalents. The Model 3 was attractively styled, with seating for five adults, a driving range of 250 miles with rear-wheel drive, a driving range of up to 322 miles with dual motor all-wheel drive, 0 to 60 mph acceleration capability of 3.2 seconds to 5.3 seconds depending on the model and drive train selected, and a five-star safety rating. While the stated base price was $39,990, the range of available upgrades and options could up the price to $66,990. The average selling price of the Model 3 in 2018 exceeded $45,000 and, as of June 2019 Tesla had produced very few of the base-price Model 3 versions (since it was far more profitable to sell more fully equipped Model 3s).

In the United States, federal legislation provided that buyers of electric vehicles were eligible for a federal tax credit of up to $7,500 based on the size of the vehicle's electric battery. Buyers who leased an electric vehicle were not eligible for the tax credit (the credit went to the company offering the lease). However, there was a provision in the law stating that once the *cumulative* sales volume of a manufacturer's zero-emission vehicles in the United States reached 200,000 vehicles, the size of the $7,500 federal tax credit entered a one-year phase-out period where buyers of qualifying vehicles were "eligible for 50 percent of the credit if acquired in the first two quarters of the phase-out period and 25 percent of the credit if acquired in the third or fourth quarter of the phase-out period."[23] Purchasers of that manufacturer's vehicles were not eligible for any federal tax credit after the phase-out period. Tesla's cumulative sales in the United States exceeded 200,000 vehicles during 2018. Some states also offered tax credits for the purchases of plug-in electric vehicles. Some states also offered a variety of tax credits in addition to the federal tax credit. The governments of China,

Japan, Norway, United Kingdom, and several other European countries offered tax incentives for electric vehicle purchases as well. In 2018, Canada discontinued the use of incentives for electric vehicles with a manufacturer's suggested list price of price greater than C\$75,000 (US\$58,500) and Norway phased out its tax credits as well.

Tesla's Fifth Vehicle—The Model Y Crossover SUV. In 2017, Elon Musk announced that Tesla had begun developing plans for the development and production of an all-electric crossover SUV that would be built on the same platform as the Model 3, but like the Model X would have seating for up to 7 adults. Tesla unveiled a prototype of its Model Y SUV in March 2019. In early 2020, the Model Y vehicles being offered for sale included dual motor Long-Range and Performance versions, a driving range of about 315 miles, a top speed of 135 mph and 0 to 60 mph acceleration of 4.8 seconds for the Long Range version and a top speed of 145 mph and 0-60 mph acceleration of 3.5 seconds for the Performance version. Base prices were \$52,990 and \$60,990, respectively for the two versions, while fully equipped versions had price tags of \$67,990 and \$73,990, respectively.

In May 2018, while Tesla was struggling with all of its Model 3 production problems, Musk said he was planning for production of the Model Y to be a "manufacturing revolution," with a simplified manufacturing process and greater use of robots.[24] Because the Model Y was expected to appeal to a large market segment, Elon Musk expected that the Model Y would ultimately have higher annual sales than Model S, Model X, and Model 3 combined.

The Tesla Semi-Truck. Mention was made of a semi-truck in Tesla's 2016 master plan. But behind the scenes Tesla had moved swiftly to come up with not only a design but also prototypes. The Semi was unveiled with much fanfare at a press conference on November 16, 2017. The company described the Semi as a Class 8 semi-trailer truck prototype that would be powered by four independent electric motors on rear axles; have a driving range of either 300 miles or 500 miles on a full charge; and have a centered driver's seat in the cockpit, with touch screen controls on either side of the steering wheel. Standard equipment on all models would include Autopilot capabilities, automatic emergency braking, automatic lane keeping, forward collision warning, and ability to enter an energy-saving "convoy mode"

with other semis on the road. Elon Musk said the 500-mile version, equipped with Tesla's latest battery design, would be able to run for 400 miles after an 80 percent charge in 30 minutes using a solar-powered Tesla Megacharger charging station. He also said the Semi would be able to accelerate from 0 to 60 mph in seconds unloaded and in 20 seconds fully loaded. Tesla expected to offer a warranty for a million miles and said maintenance would be simpler than for a diesel truck.

A week later, Musk said that the regular production versions for the 300-mile range version of the Semi would be priced at \$150,000 and the 500-mile range version would be priced at \$180,000; the company also said it planned to offer a Founder's Series Semi at \$200,000. Scores of companies, including Walmart, United Parcel Service, Anheuser-Busch, J.B. Hunt Trucking Co, and PepsiCo, immediately lined up to place pre-orders for 5 to 150 Semis (at an initial reservation price of \$5,000, which was quickly raised to \$20,000 per reservation) so they could conduct tests of how well the Semi would perform in their operations. In March 2018, Tesla began testing the Semi with real cargo, hauling battery packs from Gigafactory 1 in Nevada to the Tesla Factory in Fremont, California. Pictures of the Semi being loaded with cargo at the Nevada Gigafactory and traveling on the highways were immediately publicized in the media and posted on the Internet and social media. Production of the Semi was originally scheduled to begin in 2019, but in early 2020 it appeared that production of the Semi was on pause until sometime in 2021 at best because mileage tests showed the battery pack originally planned for use in the truck was not able to achieve the targeted range of 300-to-500 miles on a single charge. More powerful battery packs capable of achieving the targeted range were under development. In June 2020, Elon Musk said getting the Tesla Semi into production was a top priority; however, the company was only in the final stage of choosing a site to construct a facility to manufacture and assemble the Semi.

The Tesla Pickup Truck. While Elon Musk began talking about Tesla making an all-electric pickup truck (and an all-electric cargo van on the same chassis) in 2016, the company had yet to finalize its design and production specifications for what it was calling the Cybertruck. Elon Musk said in a June 2019 podcast that Tesla wanted to keep the Cybertruck's starting price below \$50,000 and make sure the truck was highly functional from a load-carrying standpoint, saying:[25]

> It's going to be a truck that is more capable than other trucks. The goal is to be a better truck than a [Ford] F-150 in terms of truck-like functionality and be a better sports car than a standard [Porsche] 911. That's the aspiration.

Musk went on to say that the truck's appearance would be pretty sci-fi and not be for everyone. Further, buyers of the truck would have a range of optional extras that could push the price up close to $70,000 (on a par with current roomy, luxurious pickups with powerful engines). The Tesla Cybertruck was unveiled at the company's Tesla Design Studio in California in November 2019. Some people loved the futuristic design, others hated it, and many thought it was too far over the top. Tesla did not respond to questions about whether the truck's design would change before it went into production. In March 2020, Elon Musk announced that Tesla was in the process of evaluating sites in the central United States for a new plant to manufacture and assemble its new Cybertruck; the current plan was to begin production in late 2021.

Distribution Strategy: A Company-Owned and Operated Network of Retail Stores and Service Centers.
Tesla sold its vehicles directly to buyers and also provided them with after-sale service through a network of company-owned sales galleries and service centers. This contrasted sharply with the strategy of rival motor vehicle manufacturers, all of whom sold vehicles and replacement parts at wholesale prices to their networks of franchised dealerships that in turn handled retail sales, maintenance and service, and warranty repairs. Management believed that integrating forward into the business of traditional automobile dealers and operating its own retail sales and service network had three important advantages:

1. *The ability to create and control its own version of a compelling buying customer experience,* one that was differentiated from the buying experience consumers had with sales and service locations of franchised automobile dealers. Having customers deal directly with Tesla-employed sales and service personnel enabled Tesla to (a) engage and inform potential customers about electric vehicles in general and the advantages of owning a Tesla in particular and (b) build a more personal relationship with customers and, hopefully, instill a lasting and favorable impression of Tesla Motors, its mission, and the caliber and performance of its vehicles.

2. *The ability to achieve greater operating economies in performing sales and service activities.* Management believed that a company-operated sales and service network offered substantial opportunities to better control inventory costs of both vehicles and replacement parts, manage warranty service and pricing, maintain and strengthen the Tesla brand, and obtain rapid customer feedback.

3. *The opportunity to capture the sales and service revenues of traditional automobile dealerships.* Rival motor vehicle manufacturers sold vehicles and replacement parts at wholesale prices to their networks of franchised dealerships that in turn handled retail sales, maintenance, and service, and warranty repairs. But when Tesla buyers purchased a vehicle at a Tesla-owned sales gallery, Tesla captured the full retail sales price, roughly 10 percent greater than the wholesale price realized by vehicle manufacturers selling through franchised dealers. And, by operating its own service centers, it captured service revenues not available to vehicle manufacturers who relied upon their franchised dealers to provide needed maintenance and repairs. Furthermore, Tesla management believed that company-owned service centers avoided the conflict of interest between vehicle manufacturers and their franchised dealers where the sale of warranty parts and repairs by a dealer were a key source of revenue and profit for the dealer but where warranty-related costs were typically a substantial expense for the vehicle manufacturer.

Tesla Sales Galleries and Showrooms. Initially, Tesla's distribution strategy was to aggressively expand its network of sales galleries and service centers to broaden its geographical presence and to provide better maintenance and repair service in areas with a high concentration of Tesla owners. In 2013, Tesla began combining its sales and service activities at a single location (rather than having separate locations, as earlier had been the case); experience indicated that combination sales and service locations were more cost-efficient and facilitated faster expansion of the company's retail footprint. At the end of 2019, Tesla had 429 sales and service locations, mostly in or near major metropolitan areas in the United States, Europe, China, and selected other countries. Some were in prominent regional shopping malls and others were on highly visible sites along busy thoroughfares. Most sales locations had only several vehicles in stock that were available for immediate sale. The vast majority of Tesla buyers, however, preferred to customize their vehicle by placing an order via the Internet, frequently while in a sales gallery.

In the United States, there was a lurking threat to Tesla's strategy to bypass distributing through franchised Tesla dealers and sell directly to consumers. Going back many years, franchised automobile dealers in the United States had feared that automotive manufacturers might one day decide to integrate forward into selling and servicing the vehicles they produced. To foreclose any attempts by manufacturers to compete directly against their franchised dealers, automobile dealers in every state in the United States had formed statewide franchised dealer associations to lobby for legislation blocking motor vehicle manufacturers from becoming retailers of new and used cars and providing maintenance and repair services to vehicle owners. Legislation either forbidding or severely restricting the ability of automakers to sell vehicles directly to the public had been passed in 48 states; these laws had been in effect for many years, and franchised dealer associations were diligent in pushing for strict enforcement of these laws.

As sales of the Model S rose briskly from 2013 to 2015 and Tesla continued opening more sales galleries and service centers, both franchised dealers and statewide dealer associations became increasingly anxious about "the Tesla problem" and what actions to take to block Tesla's sell-direct strategy. Dealers and dealer trade associations in a number of states were openly vocal about their concerns and actively began lobbying state legislatures to consider either enforcement actions against Tesla or amendments to existing legislation that would bring a halt to Tesla's efforts to sell vehicles at company-owned showrooms. A host of skirmishes ensued in 12 states. In several cases, settlements were reached that allowed Tesla to open a select few sales locations, but the numbers were capped. In states where manufacturer-direct sales to consumers were expressly prohibited, Tesla was allowed to have sales galleries, service centers, and Supercharger locations—but was prevented from using its sales galleries to take orders, conduct test drives, deliver cars, or discuss pricing with potential buyers. Buyers in these states could place an order

via the Internet, specify when they would like the car to arrive, and then either have it delivered to a nearby Tesla service center for pickup or have it delivered directly to their home or business location.

Tesla Announces Sales Gallery Closures and a Shift to Online Sales. In February 2019, Tesla unexpectedly announced it was closing most of its sales galleries in malls and shopping centers and would begin to sell its cars only online. The shift was made partly to reduce employee headcount and operating expenses and partly to relax lobbying efforts in states that did not permit manufacturers to own and operate their own dealerships. As part of the shift, new owners were granted up to a week to return their newly-purchased Tesla vehicle if they were not satisfied. In the same announcement, Tesla said it would be shifting resources to improve its repair service systems, with the goal of providing same-day service to Tesla owners. However, auto dealers in several states, along with the National Automobile Dealers Association, remained dissatisfied with Tesla's online sales approach, noting that franchise laws in some states required dealers to have a physical presence in their state to sell online and that one of the main purposes of local franchising and licensing laws was promote investment in an extensive network of independent, neighborhood new-car dealers.

Tesla expected that dealer associations in some states would continue to challenge the company's efforts to sell directly to customers and to own and operate its own retail and service locations, and Tesla management intended to actively fight such efforts. To sell vehicles to residents of states where the company could not be licensed as a dealer, Tesla made arrangements to conduct the transfer of title out of the state. In these states it also opened "galleries" that served the purpose of educating prospective buyers about Tesla products and how to obtain them (but such galleries did not take any orders for vehicles or perform any title transfer services).

Tesla Service Centers and Mobile Service Technicians. Tesla Roadster owners could upload data from their vehicle and send it to a service center on a memory card; all other Tesla owners had an on-board system that could communicate directly with a service center, allowing service technicians to diagnose and remedy many problems before ever looking at the vehicle. When maintenance or service was required, a customer could schedule service by contacting a Tesla service center or, in a growing number of locations, use the Tesla mobile app to make arrangements to have service performed at their home, office, or other remote location by a Tesla Mobile Service technician who had the capability to perform a variety of services that did not require a vehicle lift. Some service locations offered valet service, where the owner's car was picked up, replaced with a well-equipped loaner car, and then returned when the service was completed—there was no additional charge for valet service. Mobile service technicians could perform most warranty repairs, but the cost of their visit was not covered under the New Vehicle Limited Warranty. Mobile service pricing was based on a per visit, per vehicle basis; there was a $100 minimum charge per visit. Tesla's mobile service fleet consisted of 743 vehicles at year-end 2019, with coverage of all of North America. In early 2018, the company reported its mobile service fleet in North America was completing 30 percent of all service jobs at a cost below the average fees charged at its service centers.

Prepaid Maintenance Program. Initially, Tesla recommended that Model S, Model X, and Model 3 owners have an inspection every 12 months or 12,500 miles, whichever came first. Owners could purchase plans covering prepaid maintenance for three years or four years; these involved simply prepaying for service inspections at a discounted rate. All Tesla vehicles were protected by a 4-year or 50,000-mile (whichever came first) New Vehicle Limited Warranty, subject to separate limited warranties for the supplemental restraint system, battery and drive unit, and body rust perforation. For the battery and drive unit on new Model S and Model X vehicles, Tesla offered an eight-year, 150,000-mile limited warranty, with minimum 70 percent retention of battery capacity over the warranty period. For the battery and drive unit on new Model 3 and Model Y vehicles, Tesla offered an eight-year or 120,000-mile limited warranty for models with a Long Range or Performance battery, with minimum 70 percent retention of battery capacity over the warranty period.

In March 2019, after a fleetwide review of maintenance and repair records, Tesla decided to do away with its recommendations for scheduled *annual* maintenance for its vehicles because they were able to withstand longer-than-usual periods of time without regular maintenance when compared with traditional gasoline-powered vehicles. Effective immediately, Tesla ceased selling extended three- and four-year

prepaid maintenance plans and began recommending that owners bring their vehicles to a service center only when a specific component needed service. Owners who had already purchased extended three- and four-year service plans could request a refund of the remaining length of the plan. However, Tesla continued to recommend service intervals for certain components of its vehicles:

- Tire Rotation, Balance, and Wheel Alignment: 10,000–12,000 miles.
- Brake Fluid Test/Flush: 2 years.
- Cabin Air Filter: 2 years.
  - High-Efficiency Particulate Air (HEPA) Filter: 3 years (if equipped).
- Air Conditioning Service: 2 years (Model S), 4 years (Model X), 6 years (Model 3).
- Winter Care: Annually or every 12,500 miles for cars in cold weather climates.

Tesla's Supercharger Network: Providing Recharging Services to Owners on Long-Distance Trips.
A major component of Tesla's strategy to build rapidly-growing long-term demand for its vehicles was to make battery recharging while driving long distances convenient and worry-free for all Tesla vehicle owners. Tesla's solution to providing owners with ample and convenient recharging opportunities was to establish an extensive geographic network of recharging stations. Tesla's Supercharger stations were strategically placed along major highways connecting city centers, usually at locations with such nearby amenities as roadside diners, cafes, and shopping centers that enabled owners to have a brief rest stop or get a quick meal during the recharging process— about 90 percent of Model S and Model X buyers opted to have their vehicle equipped with supercharging capability when they ordered their vehicle. All Model S and Model X owners were entitled to *free* supercharging service at any of Tesla's Supercharging stations; Model 3 owners had to pay a recharging fee. In March 2018, Tesla announced price increases for its Supercharging stations to about $0.25 per kWh. Tesla owners charged their vehicles at home more than 90 percent of the time and used Supercharger stations mainly for trips or when they needed extra range. A 50 percent recharge took 20 minutes, an 80 percent recharge took 40 minutes, and a 100 percent recharge took 75 minutes. As of year-end 2019, Tesla had a total of 1,821 Supercharger stations globally;

most Tesla stations had between 6 and 30 charging spaces, but newer stations in high-traffic corridors had as many as 50 spaces, a customer lounge, and a café.

Tesla executives did not expect Supercharger stations to ever become a profit center for the company; rather, they believed that the benefits of rapidly growing the size of the company's Supercharger network came from (1) relieving the "range anxiety" electric vehicle owners suffered when driving on a long-distance trip and (2) reducing the inconvenience to travelers of having to deviate from the shortest direct route and detour to the closest Supercharger station for needed recharging.

Technology and Product Development Strategy.
Heading into 2020, Tesla had spent $6.9 billion on R&D activities to design, develop, test, and refine the components and systems needed to produce top quality electric vehicles and, further, to design and develop prototypes of the Tesla Roadster, Model S, Model X, Model 3, Model Y, Cybertruck, and Tesla Semi vehicles. Tesla executives believed its R&D activities had produced core competencies in battery and powertrain engineering and manufacturing. The company's core intellectual property was contained in its work on developing self-driving technologies and capabilities and in its electric powertrain technology (the battery pack, power electronics, induction motor, gearbox, and control software) that enabled these key components to operate as a system. Tesla personnel had designed each of these major elements for the Tesla Roadster and Model S; much of this technology had been used in the powertrain systems that Tesla previously had built for other vehicle manufacturers (mainly Toyota and Mercedes) and that had been further improved and refined in the powertrain systems being used in the Model X, Model 3, Model Y, and the prototypes for the Cybertruck and Tesla Semi.

The powertrain used in Tesla vehicles in 2020 was a compact, modular system with far fewer moving parts than the powertrains of traditional gasoline-powered vehicles, a feature that enabled Tesla to implement powertrain enhancements and improvements as fast as they could be identified, designed, and tested. Tesla had incorporated its latest powertrain technology into its current models and was planning to use much of this technology in producing forthcoming electric vehicles. All models included several powertrain variants along with the latest advances in mobile computing, sensing, displays, and connectivity.

Although Tesla had more than 500 patents and pending patent applications domestically and internationally in a broad range of areas, in 2014, Tesla announced a patent policy whereby it irrevocably pledged the company would not initiate a lawsuit against any party for infringing Tesla's patents through activity relating to electric vehicles or related equipment so long as the party was acting in good faith. Elon Musk said the company made this pledge in order to encourage the advancement of a common, rapidly evolving platform for electric vehicles, thereby benefiting itself, other companies making electric vehicles, and the world. Investor reaction to this announcement was largely negative on grounds that it would negate any technology-based competitive advantage over rival manufacturers of electric vehicles.

Battery Pack.   In February 2014, Tesla announced that it and various partners, principally Panasonic—Tesla's supplier of lithium-ion batteries since 2010—would invest $4 to 5 billion through 2020 in a "gigafactory" capable of producing enough lithium-ion batteries to make battery packs for 500,000 vehicles. Tesla expected the new plant (named the Tesla Gigafactory, later changed to Gigafactory 1) to reduce the company's battery pack cost by more than 30 percent—battery packs were the most expensive component in the company's electric vehicles.

Tesla opted to locate Gigafactory 1 on a site in an industrial park east of Reno, Nevada, partly because the state of Nevada offered Tesla a lucrative incentive package said to be worth $1.25 billion over 20 years and partly because the only commercially active lithium mining operation in the United States was in a nearby Nevada county (this county was reputed to have the fifth largest deposit of lithium in the world). Construction began immediately. The facility was built in phases. In 2019, Tesla announced it would continue expanding Gigafactory 1 over the next few years so that its battery-making capacity would significantly exceed the volume needed for 500,000 vehicles per year when construction first started. Tesla had already added space at Gigafactory 1 to enable the manufacture of Tesla Energy's primary energy storage products (Powerwall, Powerpack, and Megapack) and the manufacture of Model 3 and Model Y drive units.

During 2015–2017, Tesla, in close collaboration with Panasonic, discovered ways to build an improved lithium-ion battery that would be larger, safer, and require fewer individual batteries per battery pack. The new battery was being used in the Model 3 and Model Y vehicles produced at the Fremont factory in California. However, in August 2019, Tesla agreed to purchase lithium-ion batteries from LG Chem, a South Korean firm with a battery-making plant in China about 200 miles from Shanghai, that would be used to manufacture the battery packs for the Model 3 and Model Y vehicles produced at the new Shanghai plant–LG Chem was the world's second-largest manufacturer of lithium-ion battery cells. Earlier in 2019 Tesla acquired Maxwell Technologies, a maker of ultracapacitors–energy storage devices that could charge and discharge rapidly, perform at a wide range of temperatures, had high power density, and long operational life; Maxwell's dry electrode technology could be applied to batteries of varying chemistries and offered the advantages of higher battery performance at a lower cost.

Going forward, Tesla believed it had the capabilities to quickly incorporate the latest advancements in battery technology and continue to optimize battery pack system performance and cost for its current and future vehicles. It already had proprietary technology and expertise in optimizing the design of the lithium-ion cells used in its battery packs and in achieving high energy density in its battery packs at progressively lower cost, while also maintaining safety, reliability, and long life. In addition, its proprietary technological know-how included capabilities relating to systems for high density energy storage, cooling, charge balancing, structural durability, and electronics management. Tesla had pioneered and then continuously refined its advanced manufacturing techniques to produce large quantities of high-quality battery packs at progressively lower cost per unit. Plus, it had extensive testing and R&D capabilities for battery cells, packs, and systems, along with an expansive body of knowledge on lithium-ion cell chemistry types, their performance characteristics, and lithium-ion cell vendors.

Power Electronics. The power electronics in Tesla's powertrain system had two primary functions–the control of torque generation in the electric motor while driving and the control of energy delivery back into the battery pack while charging. The first function was accomplished through the drive inverter, which converted direct current from the battery pack into alternating current to power the electric motors, provide acceleration, and enhance the overall driving performance of the vehicle. The second function was to capture kinetic energy from the wheels being in motion but being slowed down by applying the brakes and reverse the flow of energy to help recharge the battery pack–a technology called "regenerative braking." (When brakes are applied in gasoline-powered vehicles, the brake pads clamp down on the wheels to slow the vehicle (letting the kinetic energy escape as heat); but in electric vehicles (and most hybrid vehicles), the regenerative braking systems slow the vehicle by reversing the flow of electricity to the electric motors powering the wheels, while also capturing the heat from the kinetic energy to generate electrical energy for partially recharging the battery pack.) When the electric vehicle was parked, battery recharging was accomplished by the vehicle's charger, which converted alternating current (usually from a wall outlet or other electricity source) into direct current which could be accepted by the battery. The primary technological advantages to Tesla's proprietary power electronics designs included the ability to drive large amounts of electrical current into a small physical package with high efficiency and low cost, and to recharge on a wide variety of electricity sources at home, at the office or on the road, including at Tesla's network of Supercharger stations.

As of March 2020, all of Tesla's models utilized an all-wheel drive powertrain with two electric motors: one mounted on the front axle and one on the rear axle. Tesla's powertrain design digitally and independently controlled torque to the front and rear wheels, which resulted in the vehicle having a low center of gravity and enabled near-instantaneous response of the motors to the driver's placing more or less pressure on the accelerator. These design features produced greater traction control and gave drivers more control of the vehicle's performance. Tesla engineers were engaged in developing a three-motor powertrain that would provide further increases in performance.

Control and Infotainment Software. The battery pack and the performance and safety systems of Tesla vehicles required the use of numerous microprocessors and sophisticated software. For example, computer-driven software monitored the charge state of each of the cells of the battery pack and managed all of the safety systems. The flow of electricity between the battery pack and the motor had to be tightly controlled in order to deliver the best possible performance and driving experience. There were software algorithms that enabled the vehicle to mimic the "creep" feeling that drivers expected from an internal combustion engine vehicle without having to apply pressure on the accelerator. Other algorithms were used to control traction, vehicle stability, acceleration, regenerative braking, and the interior climate. Drivers used the vehicle's information and control systems to optimize performance, customize vehicle behavior, manage charging modes and times, and control all infotainment functions. Almost all of the software programs had been developed and written by Tesla personnel.

Starting in 2014, Tesla began devoting progressively larger fractions of its programming resources and expertise to developing and enhancing its software for vehicle autopilot functionality, including such features as auto-steering, traffic-aware cruise control, automated lane changing, automated parking, driver warning systems, automated braking, object detection, a Smart Summons feature that enabled vehicles to be remotely summoned over short distances in parking lots and driveways, and fully-automated self-driving. In October 2016, Tesla began equipping all models with hardware needed for full self-driving capability, including cameras that provided 360-degree visibility, updated ultrasonic sensors for object detection, a forward-facing radar with enhanced processing, and a powerful onboard computer. Wireless software updates periodically sent to the microprocessors on board each Tesla owner's vehicle, together with field data feedback loops from the onboard camera, radar, ultrasonic sensors, and GPS, enabled the autopilot system in Tesla vehicles to continually learn and improve its performance. In 2019, Elon Musk said he expected Tesla's autopilot software to be able to handle all modes of driving within two years.

Vehicle Design and Engineering.   Tesla had devoted considerable effort to creating significant in-house capabilities related to designing and engineering portions of its vehicles, and it had become knowledgeable about the design and engineering of those parts, components, and systems that it purchased from suppliers. Tesla personnel had designed and engineered the body, chassis, and interior of its current models.

As a matter of necessity, Tesla was forced to redesign the heating, cooling, and ventilation system for its electric vehicles to operate without the energy generated from an internal combustion engine and to integrate with its own battery-powered thermal management system. In addition, the low-voltage electric system that powered the radio, power windows, and heated seats had to be designed specifically for use in an electric vehicle. Tesla had developed expertise in integrating these components with the high-voltage power source in its vehicles and in designing components that significantly reduced their load on the vehicle's battery pack, so as to maximize the available driving range. All Tesla vehicles incorporated the latest advances in mobile computing, sensing, displays, and connectivity.

Tesla personnel had accumulated considerable expertise in lightweight materials, since an electric vehicle's driving range was heavily impacted by the vehicle's weight and mass. The Tesla Roadster had been built with an in-house designed carbon fiber body to provide a good balance of strength and mass. The Model S and Model X had a lightweight aluminum body and a chassis that incorporated a variety of materials and production methods to help optimize vehicle weight, strength, safety, and performance. Weight reduction was an important factor in the design of the Model 3 and Model Y. In addition, top management believed that the company's design and engineering team had core competencies in computer-aided design and crash test simulations; this expertise had reduced the development time of new models. Tesla was continuing to strengthen its capabilities for on-site crash-testing, durability testing, and validation of components from suppliers.

Manufacturing Strategy.
Tesla had contracted with Lotus Cars, Ltd. to produce Tesla Roadster "gliders" (a complete vehicle minus the electric powertrain) at a Lotus factory in Hethel, England. The Tesla gliders were then shipped to a Tesla facility in Menlo Park, California, where the battery pack, induction motors, and other powertrain components were installed as part of the final assembly process. The production of Roadster gliders ceased in January 2012.

In May 2010, Tesla purchased the major portion of a recently closed automobile plant in Fremont, California, for $42 million; months later, Tesla purchased some of the plant's equipment for $17 million.

The facility—formerly a General Motors manufacturing plant (1960–1982), then operated as a joint venture between General Motors and Toyota (1984–2010)—was closed in 2010. Tesla executives viewed the facility as one of the largest, most advanced, and cleanest automotive production plants in the world. The 5.3 million square feet of manufacturing and office space was deemed sufficient for Tesla to produce about 500,000 vehicles annually (approximately 1 percent of the total worldwide car production), thus giving Tesla room to grow its output of electric vehicles to 500,000 or more vehicles annually. The Fremont plant's location in the northern section of Silicon Valley facilitated hiring talented engineers already residing nearby and because the short distance between Fremont and Tesla's Palo Alto headquarters ensured "a tight feedback loop between vehicle engineering, manufacturing, and other divisions within the company."[26] Tesla officially took possession of the 370-acre site in October 2010, renamed it the Tesla Factory, and immediately launched efforts to get a portion of the massive facility ready to begin manufacturing components and assembling the Model S in 2012.

In late 2015, Tesla completed construction of a new high-volume paint shop and a new body shop line capable of turning out 3,500 Model S and Model X bodies per week (enough for 175,000 vehicles annually). In 2016 and 2017, Tesla made significant additional investments at the Tesla Factory, including a new body shop with space and equipment for Model 3 final assembly. Tesla expected the Fremont facility, together with a neighboring 500,000-square-foot building that Tesla had leased, would be expanded to 10 million square feet in the coming years.

In December 2012, Tesla opened a new 60,000-square-foot facility in Tilburg, Netherlands, about 50 miles from the port of Rotterdam, to serve as the final assembly and distribution point for all Tesla vehicles sold in Europe and Scandinavia. The facility, called the Tilburg Assembly Plant, received nearly complete vehicles shipped from the Tesla Factory, performed certain final assembly activities, conducted final vehicle testing, and handled the delivery to customers across Europe. It also functioned as Tesla's European service and parts headquarters. Tilburg's central location and its excellent rail and highway network to all major markets on the European continent allowed Tesla to distribute to anywhere across the continent in about 12 hours. The Tilburg

operation had been expanded to over 200,000 square feet in order to accommodate a parts distribution warehouse for service centers throughout Europe, a center for remanufacturing work, and a customer service center. A nearby facility in Amsterdam provided corporate oversight for European sales, service, and administrative functions.

Tesla's manufacturing strategy was to source a number of parts and components from outside suppliers but to design, develop, and manufacture in-house those key components where it had considerable intellectual property and core competencies (namely lithium-ion battery packs, electric motors, gearboxes, and other powertrain components) and to perform all assembly-related activities itself. In 2018–2020, the Tesla Factory contained several production-related activities, including stamping, machining, casting, plastics molding, drive unit production for the Model S and Model X, robotics-assisted body assembly, paint operations, final vehicle assembly, and end-of-line quality testing. In addition, the Tesla Factory manufactured lithium-ion battery packs, electric motors, gearboxes, and certain other components for its Model S and Model X vehicles. While some major vehicle component systems were purchased from suppliers, there was a high level of vertical integration in the manufacturing processes at the Tesla Factory in 2018–2019. From 2016 to 2019, efforts to expand production capacity at the Tesla Factory were ongoing, partly to accommodate production of the Model S and Model X but mainly to enable high volume production of the Model 3 and Model Y.

In 2014, Tesla began producing and machining various aluminum components at a 431,000-square-foot facility in Lathrop, California; an aluminum castings operation was added in 2016. Aluminum parts and components were used extensively to help reduce the weight of Tesla vehicles.

Tesla had encountered a number of unexpected quality problems in the first two to three months of manufacturing the Model X. Getting the complicated hinges on the falcon-wing doors to function properly proved to be particularly troublesome. Customers who received the first wave of Model X deliveries also reported problems with the front doors and windows and with the 17-inch dashboard touchscreen freezing (a major problem because so many functions were controlled from this screen). Most of these problems were largely resolved by mid-2016, although Model X owners rated the reliability of their vehicles significantly lower than Model S owners—the chief culprit was the falcon-wing doors, which reportedly had generated significant warranty claims and warranty costs. Weekly production volumes of the Model X rose steadily in the second half of 2016.

Musk believed Tesla had learned valuable manufacturing lessons that could be applied in ramping up the production volume of the Model 3 at the Fremont plant. These lessons had driven refinements in the production and assembly lines for the Model S, Model X, and Model 3 at the Fremont plant and had been incorporated into designing and equipping the new Shanghai Gigafactory that began construction in early 2019 and production in early 2020. The first-generation production line for the Model 3 in Shanghai was Tesla's first step in building a manufacturing platform that could be replicated quickly and cost efficiently across all vehicle types and in different geographic locations. Design and construction of a second production line in Shanghai were already underway to add Model Y manufacturing capacity, and expectations were that the second production line would be at least 50 percent cheaper per unit of capacity than the current Model 3-related assembly lines in Fremont.[27] Major gains in production efficiency and approximately 50 percent lower unit costs for the Model 3 were expected when production of the Model 3 ramped up in the new production facility in Shanghai where Tesla was installing a much-simplified production process and increasing use of robot-assisted assembly. Production costs for Model Y vehicles at the Shanghai Gigafactory were expected to be even lower than those for Model 3.

Supply Chain Strategy.

Tesla's various models used thousands of parts and components sourced from hundreds of suppliers across the world. Certain components purchased from these suppliers were either identical or very similar across the company's growing number of models, which opened opportunities for volume-based price reductions and related cost-saving efficiencies. Tesla worked to qualify multiple suppliers for each such component where it was sensible to do so, in order to reduce the bargaining power of any one supplier and to minimize production risks associated with being dependent on a single supply source. In many cases, however, components and systems were sourced from single suppliers. In such cases, the company mitigated single-source supply risk by maintaining safety stocks for key parts and assemblies and die banks for components with lengthy procurement lead times. But in some instances (like lithium-ion battery cells, battery packs, and drive trains), the company opted to produce needed parts and components internally.

Tesla's products also required purchasing such raw materials as steel, aluminum, cobalt, lithium, nickel, and copper. Pricing for these materials was governed by market supply and demand conditions, and sometimes by the activities of speculators—factors outside of the company's control. Management believed that, while the company was vulnerable to periodic spikes in the prices of particular raw materials, it nonetheless had sufficiently adequate access to supplies of raw materials to meet the needs of its operations.

Marketing Strategy.

From 2014 through year-end 2019, Tesla's principal marketing goals and functions were to:

- Work with interested buyers as needed either in sales galleries or online to arrange for a test drive, view existing inventories at nearby sites, or place an order for a custom-equipped vehicle.
- Build long-term brand awareness and manage the company's image and reputation.
- Develop and nurture brand loyalty among existing owners of Tesla vehicles and help generate customer referrals.
- Obtain feedback from the owners of Tesla vehicles and make sure their experiences and suggestions for improvement were communicated to Tesla personnel engaged in designing, developing, and/or improving the company's current and future vehicles.

As the first company to commercially produce a federally-compliant, fully electric vehicle that achieved market-leading range on a single charge, Tesla had been able to generate significant media coverage of the company and its vehicles. Management expected this would continue for some time to come. So far, the extensive media coverage, largely favorable reviews in motor vehicle publications and *Consumer Reports,* praise from owners of Tesla vehicles and admiring car enthusiasts (which enlarged Tesla's sales force at zero cost), and the decisions of many green-minded affluent individuals to help lead the movement away from gasoline-powered vehicles had all combined to drive good traffic flows at Tesla's sales galleries and create a flow of online orders and pre-production reservations. As a consequence, starting in 2012 and continuing into early 2020, Tesla had achieved a growing volume of sales without traditional advertising and at relatively low marketing costs. Nonetheless, Tesla did make use of pay-per-click advertisements on websites and mobile applications relevant to its target clientele. It also displayed and demonstrated its vehicles at such widely attended public events as the Detroit, Los Angeles, and Frankfurt auto shows.

Tesla's Leasing Activities.
Tesla, in partnership with various financial institutions, began leasing vehicles to customers in 2014; the number and percentage of customers opting to lease Model S vehicles increased substantially in 2015. By year-end 2015, Tesla was not only offering loans and leases in North America, Europe, and Asia through its various partner financial institutions, but it was also offering loans and leases directly through its own captive finance subsidiaries in certain areas of the United States, Germany, Canada, and Great Britain.

Some of Tesla's financing programs outside of North America in 2015–2017 provided customers with a resale value guarantee under which those customers had the option of selling their vehicle back to Tesla at a preset future date, generally at the end of the term of the applicable loan or financing program, for a pre-determined resale value. In certain markets, Tesla also offered vehicle buyback guarantees to financial institutions that could obligate Tesla to repurchase the vehicles for a predetermined price. These programs, when first introduced in 2015 and 2016 had been widely publicized and attracted numerous buyers, but Tesla determined in late 2016 and 2017 to back away from these offers in most countries because they were proving unprofitable, had unattractive accounting requirements, and exposed Tesla to the risk that the vehicles' resale value could be lower than its estimates and also to the risk that the volume of vehicles sold back to Tesla at the guaranteed resale price might be higher than the company's estimates—such risks had to be accounted for by establishing a contingent liability (in the current liabilities section of the balance sheet) deemed sufficient to cover these risks.

Sales of Regulatory Credits to Other Automotive Manufacturers.
Because Tesla's electric vehicles had no tailpipe emissions of greenhouse gases or other pollutants, Tesla earned zero-emission vehicle (ZEV) and greenhouse gas (GHG) credits on each vehicle sold in the United

States. Moreover, it also earned corporate average fuel economy (CAFE) credits on its sales of vehicles because of their high equivalent miles per gallon ratings. All three of these types of regulatory credits had significant market value because the manufacturers of traditional gasoline-powered vehicles were subject to assorted emission and mileage requirements set by the U.S. Environmental Protection Agency (EPA) and by certain state agencies charged with protecting the environment within their borders; automotive manufacturers whose vehicle sales did not meet prevailing emission and mileage requirements were allowed to achieve compliance by purchasing credits earned by other automotive manufacturers. Tesla had entered into contracts for the sale of ZEV and GHG credits with several automotive manufacturers, and it also routinely sold its CAFE credits. Tesla's sales of ZEV, GHG, and CAFE credits produced revenues of $594 million in 2019, $419 million in 2018, $360 million in 2017, $302 million in 2016, and $169 million in 2015. In Exhibit 2, these amounts were included on Tesla's income statement in the revenue category labeled "Automotive sales;" without these revenues, as frequently noted by Wall Street analysts, Tesla's losses in 2015 through 2019 would have been significantly higher.

Tesla and the COVID-19 Pandemic.
Tesla's deliveries of its Model 3 and Model Y vehicles in both Q1 and Q2 of 2020 were below expectations at the beginning of 2020, partly because of closure of its Gigafactory 2 in Shanghai for 2 weeks in Q1 (January 30 to February 10) that was mandated by the Chinese government as part of its campaign to limit the spread of the COVID-19 virus and partly because of California-mandated closure of the Fremont plant starting March 24 that extended until May 13, 2020, at which time limited production was allowed, provided California and Alameda County health and safety measures were strictly observed (Tesla's observance of these measures was periodically checked by Alameda County police). Tesla also experienced scaled-back battery production at its battery Gigafactory in Nevada for almost 50 percent of Q1 and then production was suspended entirely for two weeks starting March 26, which was then extended until May 4, 2020, as part of governmental efforts to contain the spread of the coronavirus. In June 2020, limited production at the Fremont plant and Nevada Gigafactory was resuming but the

wearing of masks and social distancing were required of production workers.

Tesla Energy in 2020

In 2015, Tesla formed Tesla Energy, a new subsidiary that would begin producing and selling two energy storage products in 2016—Powerwall for homeowners and Powerpack for industrial, commercial, and utility customers. Powerwall was a lithium-ion battery charged either by electricity generated from a home's solar panels or from power company sources when electric rates were low. Powerwall home batteries could also be used as a backup power source in case of unexpected power outages. Powerpack models were rechargeable lithium-ion batteries that industrial, commercial, and utility enterprises could use for energy storage or backup power.

Production and deliveries of second-generation Powerwall 2 and Powerpack 2 began in late 2016. Both products had the capability to receive over-the-air firmware and software updates that enabled additional features. In 2018–2020, these two energy storage products were being used for backup power, independence from utility grids, peak demand reduction, generating power to cover periods when solar and/or wind generating sources were unavailable, and supplying wholesale electricity to select customers.

When Solar Energy was merged into Tesla, the company arranged to lease a facility, called Gigafactory 2, in Buffalo, New York, to produce (1) solar energy systems sold to residential and commercial customers and (2) its freshly-developed Solar Roof, which used aesthetically pleasing and durable glass roofing tiles designed to complement the architecture of homes and commercial buildings, to turn sunlight into electricity. A third-generation Solar Roof was introduced in 2019 that was marketed directly to residential customers and through an assortment of distribution partners. Installation capabilities had been enhanced by training both company personnel and the installers of third-party partners. To facilitate the growth of its solar roof business, Tesla Energy had developed proprietary software to reduce solar energy system design and installation timelines and costs and had also designed the new generation of the Solar Roof to work seamlessly with its Powerwall product.

Tesla Energy's solar energy systems included solar panels that convert sunlight into electrical current, inverters that convert the electrical output from the panels to a usable current compatible with the electric grid, racking that attaches the solar panels to the roof or ground, electrical hardware that connect the solar energy system to the electric grid, and a monitoring device. The majority of the components were purchased from vendors; the company maintained multiple sources for each major component to ensure competitive pricing and adequate supplies.

Tesla Energy had an in-house engineering team that designed its energy storage products and solar roof systems. Whenever feasible, the engineering team utilized component-level technologies developed for its electric vehicles (particularly high-density energy storage, cooling, safety, charge balancing, structural durability, and electronics management) to enhance the capabilities and features of its energy storage and solar roof products. While a majority of the components in the division's energy storage and solar roof products were obtained from multiple outside sources, some solar roof components were designed and manufactured at the Gigafactory in New York.

In the United States, Tesla Energy sold its solar and energy storage products through its website and sales galleries as well as through its national sales organization, channel partner network, and customer referral program. Outside the United States, Tesla Energy used its international sales organization and a network of channel partners to market and sell Powerwall 2 to residential customers; some Powerwall 2 units were sold directly to utilities, who then installed the product in customer homes. Powerpack and Megapack systems were sold to commercial and utility customers through its international sales organization.

In December 2017, Tesla completed installation of a 100-megawatt lithium-ion battery hooked into the electricity grid in South Australia to relieve power shortages created by a tornado in 2016. Elon Musk had promised that once the contract was signed, Tesla would complete the project in 100 days or it would be furnished free of charge—Tesla completed the installation in 60 days. According to Musk, the battery was three times more powerful than the world's next biggest battery. In late 2019 Tesla Energy began selling a Megapack product, multiple units of which could be grouped together to form energy generating and energy storage installations big enough to supply the needs of large industrial customers, utilities, energy generation firms, communities, and large neighborhoods. In 2019, Tesla Energy deployed more than 1.65 Gigawatt hours of energy storage systems, an amount greater than in all previous years combined.

Tesla's revenues from energy generation and storage products were $1.1 billion in 2017, $1.6 billion in 2018, and $1.5 billion in 2019 (Exhibit 2), resulting in gross profits of $242 million in 2017, $190 million in 2018, and $190 million in 2019. Elon Musk was very optimistic about the growth opportunities for Tesla Energy, but Tesla's financial reporting did not reveal whether Tesla Energy's operations were generating positive or negative operating profit margins.

The Electric Vehicle Segment of the Global Automotive Industry

Global sales of passenger cars and SUVs totaled 79.6 million units in 2017, 78.9 million units in 2018, and 75 million units in 2019. Sales of other types of vehicles (light or pickup trucks, heavy or cargo-carrying trucks, recreational vehicles, buses, and minibuses) totaled 26.9 million in 2019 versus 26.6 million in 2018. In 2019, global sales of plug-in electric vehicles totaled 2.2 million units, up from 2.0 million in 2018. million—plug-in vehicles included both battery-only vehicles and so-called plug-in hybrid electric vehicles equipped with a gasoline or diesel engine for use when the vehicle's battery pack (rechargeable only from an external plug-in source) was depleted, usually after a distance of 20 to 50 miles. Hybrid vehicles were jointly powered by an internal combustion engine and an electric motor that ran on batteries charged by regenerative braking and the internal combustion engine; the batteries in a hybrid vehicle could not be restored to a full charge by connecting a plug to an external power source. Exhibit 3 shows the best-selling plug-in electric vehicles in the United States from 2013 through 2019. Exhibit 4 shows the world's 20 largest manufacturers of electric vehicles in 2019, along with the 20 best-selling models of electric vehicles in 2019. More electric vehicles were manufactured in China than in any other country in

EXHIBIT 3   Sales of Best-Selling Plug-in Electric Vehicles in the United States, 2014–2019

Best-Selling Models	2014	2015	2016	2017	2018	2019
Tesla Model 3*				1,764	139,782	158,925
Toyota Prius PHV/Prime	13,264	4,191	2,474	20,963	27,595	23,630
Tesla Model X*		214	18,223	21,315	26,100	19,225
Chevrolet Bolt EV*			579	23,297	18,019	16,418
Tesla Model S*	17,300	25,202	28,896	27,060	25,745	14,100
Nissan Leaf*	30,200	17,269	14,006	11,230	14,715	12,365
Honda Clarity PHEV					18,602	10,728
Ford Fusion Energi	11,550	9,750	15,938	9,632	8,074	7,524
BMW 530e				3,772	8,664	5,862
Chrysler Pacifica Hybrid				4,597	7,062	5,723
Audi e-tron*						5,369
Chevrolet Volt	18,805	15,393	24,739	20,349	18,306	4,910
Volkswagen e-Golf*			3,937	3,534	1,354	4,863
BMW i3*	6,092	11,024	7,625	6,276	6,117	4,854
Kia Nero PHEV					3,389	3,881
All Others	12,243	19,532	32,847	41,701	37,783	31,151
United States Total	123,049	116,099	158,614	199,826	361,307	329,528
Worldwide	320,713	550,297	777,497	1,227,117	2,018,247	2,209,831

*Battery-operated.
Source: Inside EVs, "Monthly Plug-in Sales Scorecard," www.insideevs.com (accessed March 5, 2018, June 4, 2019, and March 19, 2020).

EXHIBIT 4   Global Electric Vehicle Sales of Top 20 Manufacturers of Electric Vehicles and Top 20 Best-Selling Models of Electric Vehicles, 2019

Rank	Leading Manufacturers	2019 Unit Sales	Best-Selling Vehicle Models	2019 Unit Sales
1	Tesla	367,820	Tesla Model 3	300,075
2	BYD (China)	229,506	BAIC EU-Series	111,047
3	BAIC (China)	160,251	Nissan Leaf	69,873
4	SAIC (China)	137,666	BYD Yuan/52 EV	67,839
5	BMW (Germany)	128,883	SAIC Baojun E-Series	60,050
6	Volkswagen (Germany)	84,199	BMW 530e/Le	51,083
7	Nissan (Japan)	80,545	Mitsubishi Outlander PHEV	49,649
8	Geely (China)	75,869	Renault Zoe	46,839
9	Hyundai (South Korea)	72,959	Hyundai Kona EV	44,386
10	Toyota (Japan)	55,155	BMW i3	41,837
11	Kia (South Korea)	53,477	Tesla Model X	39,497
12	Mitsubishi (Japan)	52,145	Chery eQ EV	39,401
13	Renault (France)	50,609	Toyota Prius PHEV	38,201
14	Chery (China)	48,395	Volkswagen e-Golf	36,016
15	GAC (China)	46,695	BYD Tang PHEV	34,084
16	Volvo (Sweden)	45,933	GAC Aion S	32,126
17	Great Wall (China)	41,627	SAIC Roewe EIS EV	30,550
18	Dongfeng (China)	39,861	BYD e5	29,311
19	Chang'an Automobile (China)	38,793	Geely Emgrand EV	28,958
20	JAC (China)	34,494	Tesla Model S	28,248
	All others	732,769	All others	1,030,761

Source: Mark Kane, "Global EV Sales for 2019," www.insideevs.com, February 2, 2020 (accessed March 19, 2020).

the world, and China was the world's largest market for motor vehicles, with 2019 sales of 25.8 million units, down from 28.8 million units in 2017 and 28.1 million units in 2018. Europe was the world's second largest market for electric vehicles.

There was no question in 2020 and beyond that Tesla was faced with intensifying competition in the global marketplace for electric-powered vehicles. Virtually every motor vehicle manufacturer in the world was introducing new battery-powered electric vehicles, most with driving ranges of 200 miles or more. In 2018 and 2019, models with 200+ mile driving ranges had been introduced by Audi, Jaguar, Mercedes, Kia, Volvo, General Motors, and Hyundai. Fresh models from Porsche, Aston Martin, Nissan, Audi, Volkswagen, BMW, General Motors, and Ford came on the market in 2020. Sales of a second-generation Nissan Leaf with a driving range of up to 150 miles began in January 2018. At year-end 2018, there

were 43 models of electric powered vehicles being sold in the United States, with annual sales totaling just over 361,000 units. However, in the United States 2019 sales of electric vehicles dropped nearly 9 percent to 329,500 vehicles as many new vehicle buyers opted for well-equipped SUVs and pickup trucks.

In 2018 Volkswagen announced plans to equip 16 factories to produce electric vehicles by the end of 2022, compared with three currently, and to build as many as 3 million electric cars per year by 2025. In December 2017, Toyota said by around 2025, every Toyota and Lexus model sold around the world would be available either as a dedicated electrified model or have an electrified option. Additionally, Toyota expected to have annual sales of more than 5.5 million electrified vehicles by 2030 (including more than 1 million zero-emission vehicles totally powered by either batteries or fuel cells) and to halt all production of gasoline-powered vehicles by 2040. In 2018, the government of Germany launched a campaign to put one million electric cars on its roads by 2020 and to have 40 percent electric cars on its roads by 2035.

Hydrogen Fuel Cells: An Alternative to Electric Batteries.

Many of the world's major automotive manufacturers, while actively working on next-generation battery-powered electric vehicles, were nonetheless hedging their bets by also pursuing the development of hydrogen fuel cells as an alternative means of powering future vehicles. Toyota was considered the leader in developing hydrogen fuel cells and was sharing some of its fuel-cell technology patents for free with other automotive companies in an effort to spur whether there was merit in installing fuel cells and building out a hydrogen charging network. Audi, Honda, Toyota, Mercedes-Benz, and Hyundai had recently introduced first-generation models powered by hydrogen fuel cells.[28]

Hydrogen fuel cells could be refueled with hydrogen in three to five minutes. California and several states in the northeastern United States already had a number of hydrogen refueling stations. Existing gasoline stations could add hydrogen refueling capability at a cost of about $1.5 million. A full tank of hydrogen provided vehicles with a driving range of about 310 miles. While battery-powered vehicles were currently cheaper than fuel-cell powered vehicles, experts expected that cheaper materials, more efficient fuel cells, and scale economies would in upcoming years enable producers of fuel-cell vehicles to match the prices of battery-powered electric vehicles.

ENDNOTES

[1] John Reed, "Elon Musk's Groundbreaking Electric Car," *FT Magazine,* July 24, 2009, www.ft.com (accessed September 26, 2013).

[2] Tesla press release, and Michael Arrington, "Tesla Worth More Than Half a Billion After Daimler Investment," May 19, 2009, www.techcrunch.com (accessed September 30, 2013).

[3] Josh Friedman, "Entrepreneur Tries His Midas Touch in Space," *Los Angeles Times,* April 23, 2003, www.latimes.com (accessed on September 16, 2013).

[4] David Kestenbaum, "Making a Mark with Rockets and Roadsters," *National Public Radio,* August 9, 2007, www.npr.org (accessed on September 17, 2013).

[5] Ibid.

[6] Ibid.

[7] Video interview with Alan Murray, "Elon Musk: I'll Put a Man on Mars in 10 Years," *Market Watch* (New York: *The Wall Street Journal*), December 1, 2011 (accessed on September 16, 2013).

[8] Mike Seemuth, "From the Corner Office—Elon Musk," *Success,* April 10, 2011, www.success.com (accessed September 25, 2013).

[9] Ibid.

[10] Ibid.

[11] Sergei Klebnikov, "As Tesla Stock Skyrockets, Elon Musk Looks Set For $346 Million Payday," posted at www.forbes.com, January 14, 2020 (accessed May 13, 2020).

[12] Jeff Evanson, Tesla Motors Investor Presentation, September 14, 2013, www.teslamotors.com (accessed November 29, 2013).

[13] Tesla Second Quarter 2017 Shareholder Letter, August 2, 2017.

[14] Tesla Third Quarter 2017 Shareholder Letter, November 1, 2017.

[15] Tesla Fourth Quarter 2017 Shareholder Letter, February 7, 2018.

[16] Company press release, April 3, 2018.

[17] As reported in *Autoweek,* "Tesla Has to Turn Potential into Real Profits," May 5, 2017, www.autoweek.com (accessed March 7, 2018).

[18] Tesla First Quarter 2018 Shareholder Letter, May 2, 2018.

[19] Tesla Q1 2018 Results—Earnings Call Transcript, May 2, 2018, www.seekingalpha.com, (accessed May 9, 2018).

[20] Company 2019 10-K Report, p. 1.

[21] According to information in Martin Eberhard's blog titled "Lotus Position," July 25, 2006, www.teslamotors.com/blog/lotus-position (accessed September 17, 2013).

[22] 2013 10-K Report, p. 4.

[23] Company documents.

[24] Tesla First Quarter 2018 Shareholder Letter, May 2, 2018.

[25] Fred Lambert, "Tesla pickup truck to cost less than $50,000, 'be better than F150', says Elon Musk," posted June 2, 2019 at https://electrek.co/2019/06/02/tesla-pickup-truck-price-f150-elon-musk/ (accessed June 5, 2019).

[26] Company press release May 20, 2010.

[27] Tesla First Quarter 2019 Shareholder Letter, April 23, 2019.

[28] George Ghanem, "Avoid Tesla Because Hydrogen Is the New Electric," March 6, 2016, www.seekingalpha.com (accessed March 7, 2016).

Unilever's Purpose-led Brand Strategy: Can Alan Jope Balance Purpose and Profits?

Syeda Maseeha Qumer

ICFAI Business School Hyderabad

Debapratim Purkayastha

ICFAI Business School Hyderabad

In June 2019, six months after taking over as CEO of global FMCG giant Unilever, Alan Jope (Jope) warned that as part of its sustainability agenda, the company would dispose of brands that lacked a clear social or environmental purpose within a certain time frame. Unilever was undergoing seismic changes amid an increasing demand for brands to put purpose ahead of profit, he said, and added that in future, every brand in the company's portfolio would be purpose driven. Despite being profitable, Unilever's popular brands Marmite, Magnum, and Pot Noodle were left vulnerable to a cull, which potentially hurt the company's bottom line. "Principles are only principles if they cost you something,"[1] Jope said.

Jope's predecessor, Paul Polman (Polman), had transformed Unilever into an environmentally conscious and ethical organization that delivered strong financial growth. Under his leadership, Unilever launched the Unilever Sustainable Living Plan (USLP) in 2010 that aimed to halve the environmental impact of its products across the value chain by 2030 and to enhance the livelihood of millions of people by 2020. In 2018, Unilever's Sustainable Living Brands, that had a strong social or environmental purpose, grew 69 percent faster than the rest of the business and delivered 75 percent of the company's growth. After a decade as Unilever's CEO, Polman stepped down from his role in January 2019.

In succeeding Polman, Jope had big shoes to fill. He faced the tough task of building upon Polman's sustainability legacy while maintaining profits and boosting growth. Moreover, slowing sales growth, growing competition, the threat of direct-to-consumer brands, economic and political uncertainties in certain markets, and investor concerns over sustainability targets were huge challenges that he faced. With the 2020 target dates of the USLP fast approaching, analysts wondered whether Jope would be able to fulfill the targets or whether he would succumb to investors' demand for short-term profits being put ahead of purpose.

As Jope reiterated Unilever's commitment to a future focused on purpose, analysts wondered whether such an approach would work in an era of cost-cutting. How could Jope strike a balance between purpose and profits? What could he do to boost business growth through purpose-led brands while discontinuing certain other brands? In the words of Melissa Hoffmann, Content Director for PR News, "If Jope follows through on his threat to oust brands that don't have a strong purpose and mission beyond selling their products, it will set a new bar for other brands. But two questions remain: Will other brands follow this example? And in the end, will consumers demand it?"[2]

BACKGROUND NOTE

Unilever was created in 1930 through the merger of British based soapmaker Lever Brothers Ltd. and Margarine Unie, a Dutch company. In the subsequent decades, Unilever expanded and diversified into various businesses through innovation and acquisitions, setting up advertising agencies, market research companies, and packaging businesses. In the early 1980s, Unilever changed its strategy and started focusing on core product areas in strong markets with a high growth potential. The new business strategy required large acquisitions and equally large divestments, including the sale of the animal feeds, packaging, transport, and fish farming businesses. The 1990s saw a period of restructuring and consolidation, as the number of categories in which Unilever competed went down from over 50 to just 13 by the end of the decade. This included the decision to sell or withdraw many brands and concentrate on those with the biggest potential.

The 2000s were a period of great transformation for Unilever. In February 2000, the company announced a five-year restructuring plan called the 'Path to Growth' Strategy which involved changes with respect to organizational structure, brand restructuring, operational processes, and supply chain management practices. At its core was the slimming down of Unilever's portfolio from about 1,600 brands to just 400. The initiative proved to be beneficial for the company in terms of the increase in its turnover and improvement in share price. In fiscal 2001, Unilever's profits rose 34 percent to €3.7 billion and sales were up 11 percent to €53.5 billion. In 2004, Unilever became a founding member of the industry-led initiative, Roundtable on Sustainable Palm Oil.

In September 2008, Unilever appointed Polman, who was then executive vice president and zone director for the Americas at Nestlé, as its CEO. He succeeded Patrick Cescau (Cescau) and was the first outsider to lead the company since it was founded. Under Polman, Unilever eliminated quarterly reports and invested in early stage companies. In 2012, Unilever's turnover exceeded €50 billion.

By 2018, Unilever's products were being sold in over 190 countries across the globe and used by 2.5 billion consumers every day. Its business was divided into three segments: Beauty & Personal Care, Home Care, and Foods & Refreshment. In 2018, Unilever's revenue was €50.98 billion and the company had 12 brands with a turnover of over €1 billion (See Exhibit 1 and Exhibit 2). Unilever's mission was to make sustainable living commonplace with the focus on three core principles: "Brands with Purpose Grow," "Companies with Purpose Last," and "People with Purpose Thrive."

While Unilever's largest international competitors were Nestlé and Procter & Gamble, it faced competition in local markets or specific product segments from numerous companies.

EMBEDDING SUSTAINABILITY

When Polman was appointed CEO, Unilever's fiscal growth was at risk due to the global economic recession. Polman continued with the turnaround process initiated by his predecessor Cescau in 2005, which included overhauling Unilever's management structure, cutting costs, and merging its two big divisions, food and consumer products, to allow them to share marketing expertise and distribution networks. Polman's vision was to make Unilever a "truly purpose-driven company." He made sustainability the core of the company's corporate strategy, embedding it in every stage of the value chain. As part of a bold makeover, Polmon scrapped the CSR department, instructing Unilever's 169,000 employees to instead embed the company's extensive social commitments into their business targets. He began acquiring brands known for their ecological credence such as Seventh Generation and Tazo tea.

Toward the end of 2009, Polmon announced Unilever's new vision, "the Compass" strategy, which aimed to double the size of the business by 2020 while reducing the environmental impact by half. To support this strategy, he launched USLP in 2010, an initiative with three key goals: to help more than 1 billion people improve their health and well-being by 2020, to halve the environmental impact of its products across the value chain by 2030, and to enhance the livelihoods of millions of people across its supply chain by 2020. The plan covered all its brands and the 180 countries in which it operated, as well as its total supply chain, including the impact on its consumers. Polman understood that it would take years for the USLP to show concrete results, and that some of its targets could run counter to growth. So he scrapped the quarterly earnings guidance for investors in favor of a long-term vision of sustainable growth. In 2010, Unilever generated revenue of €44.2 billion, compared to €39.8 billion in 2010.

At the outset of the plan's adoption, Unilever assessed its brands and reviewed its factories to reduce waste and water and energy use. It collaborated with government entities, NGOs, and consumers to achieve its core purpose of improving the health

EXHIBIT 1   Selected Financial Data for Unilever, 2016–2018

	2018	2017	2016
Turnover growth	(5.1%)	1.9%	(1.0%)
Underlying sales growth*	2.9%^	3.1%^	3.7%
Underlying volume growth*	1.9%	0.8%	0.9%
Operating margin	24.6%	16.5%	14.8%
Underlying operating margin*	18.4%	17.5%	16.4%
Free cash flow*	€5.0 billion	€5.4 billion	€4.8 billion
Divisions:			
Beauty & Personal Care			
Turnover	€20.6 billion	€20.7 billion	€20.2 billion
Turnover growth	(0.3%)	2.6%	0.5%
Underlying sales growth	3.1%^	2.9%^	4.2%
Operating margin	20.0%	19.8%	18.4%
Underlying operating margin	21.9%	21.1%	20.0%
Foods & Refreshment			
Turnover	€20.2 billion	€22.4 billion	€22.5 billion
Turnover growth	(9.9%)	(0.4%)	(2.2%)
Underlying sales growth	2.0%^	2.7%^	2.7%
Operating margin	35.8%	16.1%	14.0%
Underlying operating margin	17.5%	16.7%	15.6%
Home Care			
Turnover	€10.1 billion	€10.6 billion	€10.0 billion
Turnover growth	(4.2%)	5.6%	(1.5%)
Underlying sales growth	4.2%^	4.4%^	4.9%
Operating margin	11.5%	10.8%	9.5%
Underlying operating margin	13.0%	12.2%	10.9%

*Key Financial Indicators.

^Wherever referenced in this document, 2018 underlying sales growth does not include price growth in Venezuela for the whole of 2018 and in Argentina from July 2018. 2017 underlying sales growth does not include Q4 price growth in Venezuela. See pages 23 and 24 on non-GAAP measures for more details.

The Group has revised its operating segments to align with the new structure under which the business is managed. Beginning 2018, operating segment information is provided based on three product areas: Beauty & Personal Care, Foods & Refreshment and Home Care.

Source: www.unilever.com/Images/unilever-annual-report-and-accounts-2018_tcm244-534881_en.pdf

and well-being of over a billion people. The company focused on sourcing 100 percent of its agricultural raw materials such as palm oil, paper and board, soy, tea, vegetables, cocoa, and sugar from sustainable sources. By 2012, Unilever was sourcing more than a third of its agricultural raw materials sustainably and more than 50 percent of its factories had achieved the goal of sending no waste to landfills.

The USLP created sustainable growth through the development of Sustainable Living Brands–brands which had a sustainable purpose and contributed to one or more of the USLP goals. Purpose took many forms among the Unilever brands. For instance, Beauty & Personal Care brand Dove's[3] campaigns focused on driving body confidence and improving women's self-esteem. Lifebuoy's mission was to improve the hygiene behavior of about 1 billion people around the world by 2020. This could prevent 600,000 child deaths annually from respiratory infections and diarrheal disease. Home Care brand Domestos was working to help 25 million people gain improved access to toilets by 2020 in partnership with UNICEF and social enterprise, eKutir. While Cif (Home Care) launched "Cif Cleans" purpose campaigns to encourage local

EXHIBIT 2 Turnover by Product and Geographical Area for Unilever, 2009–2018 (€ amounts in millions)

	2009	2010	2011	2012	2013	2014	2015	2016	2017	2018
Turnover (€ million)	€39,823	€44,262	€46,467	€51,324	€49,797	€48,436	€53,272	€52,713	€53,715	€50,982
By product area as % of total turnover(a)										
Beauty & Personal Care	30	31	33	35	36	37	38	38	38	40
Food & Refreshment	53	51	49	47	46	44	43	43	42	40
Home Care	17	18	18	18	18	19	19	19	20	20
Total	100	100	100	100	100	100	100	100	100	100
Underlying sales growth (%)	3.5%	4.1%	6.5%	6.9%	4.3%	2.9%	4.1%	3.7%	3.1%	2.9%
Underlying volume growth (%)	2.3%	5.8%	1.6%	3.4%	2.5%	1.0%	2.1%	0.9%	0.8%	1.9%
Underlying price growth (%)	1.2%	(1.6)%	4.8%	3.3%	1.8%	1.9%	1.9%	2.8%	2.3%	0.9%
By geographical area as % of total turnover										
Asia/AMET/RUB(b)	35%	38%	38%	40%	40%	41%	42%	42%	43%	45%
The Americas	32%	33%	33%	33%	33%	32%	33%	33%	33%	31%
Europe	33%	29%	29%	27%	27%	27%	25%	25%	24%	24%
Total	100%	100%	100%	100%	100%	100%	100%	100%	100%	100%

Figures are presented on the basis of continuing operations as at 31 December 2018.

(a) The Group has revised its operating segments to align with the new structure under which the business is managed. Beginning 2018, operating segment information is provided based on three product areas: Beauty & Personal Care, Foods & Refreshment and Home Care.

(b) Refers to Asia, Africa, Middle East, Turkey, Russia, Ukraine and Belarus.

Unilever Turnover (2009–2018).

Source: www.unilever.com/Images/unilever-charts-2018_tcm244-534891_en.pdf

communities to make use of their public communal areas, restore beauty to public spaces, and improve individual and community well-being. Some of the Unilever brands even took an activist stance, mobilizing citizens to change policy or create social movements. For instance, ice cream brand Ben & Jerry's campaigned for social justice and climate change while Rin's (Home Care) Career Academy worked with women across rural India through mentoring and careers fairs. Omo/Persil (Home Care) supported Outdoor Classroom Day, an initiative championed in more than 50 countries to get children all over the world, on the same day, to learn and play outdoors for at least one lesson during the school day.

Brands such as Wall's (part of Unilever's Heartbrand family of ice creams), PG Tips, and Lipton (tea brands) contributed toward reducing their environmental footprint. To help tackle climate change and reduce GHG from refrigeration, Wall's installed freezer cabinets used climate-friendly (hydrocarbon) refrigerants while PG Tips introduced fully biodegradable tea bags that used a new plant-based material that improved its environmental impact without affecting flavor. Lipton committed to sustainably sourcing 100 percent of its tea from Rainforest Alliance certified tea farms by 2020. Also, Food brand Knorr sourced 100 percent of raw agricultural materials sustainably and aimed to help more than 1 billion people improve their health and well-being by teaching them how to cook nutritiously by 2020 while popular mayonnaise brand, Hellmann's, committed to sourcing ingredients from sustainable sources by 2020, including 100 percent sustainably sourced oils and 100 percent cage free eggs.

By 2012, Unilever's initiatives to reduce disease by handwashing with soap, provide safe drinking water, promote oral health, and improve young people's self-esteem had reached 224 million people. By 2015, Unilever had 12 Sustainable Living Brands which contributed to nearly half of its growth and grew 30 percent faster than the rest of the business. In September 2016, Unilever launched a global sustainability campaign called the 'Bright Future' to highlight the social change achieved by its brands. By 2016, Unilever had helped around 482 million people to improve their health and hygiene. The company had also reached a new industry-leading achievement of sending zero non-hazardous waste to landfill across more than 600 sites in 70 countries. In 2016, Unilever's purpose-led brands grew 40 percent faster than the rest and delivered more than 60 percent of

the company's growth, as the company generated a turnover of €52.7 billion. "There is no doubt that the Unilever Sustainable Living Plan is making us more competitive by helping us to build our brands and spur innovation, strengthen our supply chain and reduce our risks, lower our costs, and build trust in our business. It is helping Unilever to serve society and our many consumers, and in doing so, create value for shareholders,"[4] said Polman.

Much like Polman, Unilever's CMO, Keith Weed (Weed), had been integral to company's focus on purposeful brands and he played a key role in developing the USLP. Under his guidance, Unilever launched the Unstereotype Alliance in June 2017 in partnership with UN Women, a UN entity which works for the empowerment of females, to eliminate stereotypical representations of gender in all advertising and brand-led content.

The strategy adopted by Polman helped bolster Unilever's reputation globally. In 2018, for the 17th consecutive year, Unilever was named the leader in the Personal Products industry in the Dow Jones Sustainability Index. As of 2018, out of 400 Unilever brands, 28 were driving the company's purpose-driven strategy at a growth rate of 69 percent and adding 75 percent to the total business. These brands accounted for more than half of the group's €51 billion sales in 2018. The company's top seven brands with the highest turnover–Dove, Knorr, Persil/Omo, Rexona, Lipton, Hellmann's, and Wall's–were among the Sustainable Living Brands line-up. According to Weed, "I am most proud that we have grown the sales line and profit every single year in the nine years I've been doing this role. We've done this while also building a more sustainable business and one with sustainability at its core. We have been able to build the business case for sustainability. A lot of people challenge if you can do both and what we've shown at Unilever is yes, you can."[5]

During his tenure, Polman delivered a total shareholder return of 290 percent, expanded the company's presence in emerging markets, and blocked a £115 billion takeover attempt by rival Kraft Heinz in 2017. However, Polman's emphasis on sustainability made him a polarizing figure at times. While some analysts lauded his efforts to promote responsible business, others were irked by his preachy style on issues such as sustainable living. Though shareholder returns were impressive during his tenure, some investors were of the view that the purpose-led approach to running the business was at their expense. "A minority of investors I speak to give two hoots about Unilever's Sustainable Living Plan. People indulged Unilever on USLP in the early years when the reporting numbers were going well. Now they want to hear more muscular language about earnings and returns,"[6] said Martin Deboo, an analyst at financial services company Jefferies.

TAKING OVER THE REINS

Polman stepped down as CEO in December 2018. The move came after he was forced to scrap a plan to move the company's headquarters from London to Rotterdam, following an investor revolt. Unilever had been operating with dual headquarters–one in London (Unilever PLC) and the other in Rotterdam (Unilever NV). In March 2018, Polman announced a plan to create a single structure for the company in the Netherlands. According to some industry observers, a failed hostile bid by Kraft Heinz played a key role in Unilever's decision to have a single headquarters in the Netherlands, as the country had stronger rules to protect companies against takeovers.

However, most of the shareholders were not supportive of the plan as it could have ended Unilever's listing on the London Stock Exchange, forcing them to sell their holdings. Polmon scrapped the plan in October 2018, but the investor revolt was viewed as a significant blow to him and to Unilever's chairman Marijn Dekkers.

Jope, who was then Unilever's President of Beauty and Personal Care, succeeded Polman on January 1, 2019. Jope had joined Unilever in the UK in 1985. Thereafter, he managed the company's business in North Asia and served as the President for Russia, Africa, and the Middle East. Jope served as President of Unilever's Personal Care business from 2014 and continued as President when the name of the division changed in 2018 to Beauty & Personal Care.

Following Polman's exit, Weed too announced his retirement from the company in December 2018 after spending close to four decades with the group. Weed's successor was yet to be announced, but according to some reports Unilever could scrap the CMO role and instead assign responsibility for the marketing functions to marketing heads within each of its three business categories.

PURPOSE BEYOND PROFIT

Jope continued with his predecessor's mission to grow the business in a purposeful and sustainable way. Outlining his vision for the company in June 2019, Jope announced that Unilever would discontinue brands that had failed to articulate a clear social or environmental purpose despite being profitable. He added that brands without a purpose would have no long-term future in Unilever and might be sold off and warned that popular brands such as Marmite, Magnum ice creams, and Pot Noodles, could face the axe. Unilever's Foods & Refreshment Business generated a turnover of €20.2 billion, accounting for 40 percent of Unilever's turnover and 58 percent of the operating profit in 2018. Magnum itself was one of the top selling ice cream brands in the world with a turnover of over €1 billion annually. Both Marmite and Pot Noodle had annual global sales in hundreds of millions of euros.

He said, going forward, even the company's acquisition strategies would target brands with purpose in high-growth spaces. Jope said, "Brands with purpose grow, companies with purpose last, and people with purpose thrive. We're proving that link and it will be our narrative for some time."[7]

Jope said that in future, every brand in Unilever's portfolio would play an active part in social change and put sustainability at the heart of all its activities. He planned to refocus the company's marketing strategy to align with that thought process. Speaking at the Cannes Lions Festival 2019, Jope said that Unilever would scrutinize marketing efforts for "woke washing" as it was polluting purpose. Besides, some brands were driving fake purpose, which could lead to consumer distrust in the advertising and marketing industry. According to him, staying relevant and aligning each brand with a specific purpose would resonate with customers, supercharge growth, and boost profits. "More and more of our brands will become explicit about the positive social and environmental impact they have. This is entirely aligned to the instincts of our people and to the expectations of our consumers. It is not about putting purpose ahead of profits, it is purpose that drives profits,"[8] said Jope. In 2018, Unilever's Sustainable Living Brands grew 69 percent faster than the rest of the business, compared to 46 percent in 2017.

Jope ordered the company's executives to assign a clear, specific mission to each brand. Unilever in association with brand consultancy Kantar undertook the service of measuring consumer perceptions around how its brands were achieving their purpose-driven goals. Those not living up to the company's expectations were likely to be disposed of. In order to measure the performance of its purpose-led brands and the impact they had, Unilever released a checklist which looked at how much investment had to go into communicating the brands' purpose and the action to be taken on the ground. Admitting that this was not an easy task, Jope said he would give brands some time to identify their purpose, should they be lacking one, and how they could take meaningful action. *"There won't be a set deadline to achieve it; it'll be a gradual process. But I would imagine in a few years' time we will look at our portfolio and the dramatic majority of our brands will be competing with a clear view on what little good they can do for society or the planet,"*[9] he added.

While Jope was committed to Unilever's brands pursuing fairness and social justice, some critics felt that the idea was risky as it would hurt the bottom line of the company. They were also worried about the future of the brands that were likely to be culled. According to Graham Hall, Co-Founder/Director of Strategy of ad agency Saturn, Jope should also make sure that these brands did not end up with an owner that did not care about sustainability. "Maybe instead he should just kill the 'bad' brands in his portfolio and retire them to the great brand graveyard in the sky? I can't see that happening as his shareholders will want him to get maximum profit from the sale of valuable brand assets,"[10] he said.

CHALLENGES AHEAD

As of September 2019, Jope faced a series of challenges including the threat posed by direct-to-consumer brands, rise of discount chains, increasing costs due to tariffs, growing competition, currency volatility and political uncertainty in some global markets, and questions over sustainable business. Moreover, regional players with innovative business models in emerging markets were finding favor with consumers. The growth in the global FMCG sector remained stagnant as consumers were trading down on their FMCG spends either by buying less or choosing private labels. The FMCG market globally grew by an anemic 1.9 percent in 2017, and there were little signs of improvement in the near future.

With the 2020 target dates of the USLP approaching, some analysts were skeptical about Unilever's ability to achieve the targets while maintaining profits and boosting growth—see Exhibit 3. One of the most pressing tasks for Jope would be to get shareholders on his side, especially after Unilever's botched attempt to move its headquarters had strained relations with them. Jope was also under pressure from the company's shareholders over slowing sales growth. Unilever's sales had slowed more than expected in the first half of 2019 with an underlying sales growth of just 2.5 percent, driven almost entirely by volume, as shown in Exhibit 4. For the first half of 2019, Unilever's underlying sales grew by a meager 3.3 percent compared to the corresponding period of the previous year led by its emerging market business, which grew by 6.2 percent. Exhibit 5 indicates turnover decreased by 0.9 percent to €26.1 billion. Some investors blamed Unilever's heavy focus on sustainability for its growth being affected. "While [Jope] certainly has the requisite skill set to do the job, the big challenge will be to generate more growth and rebuild trust with shareholders. Shareholders will want him to focus on being CEO of Unilever rather than being visible on the world stage as his predecessor was,"[11] commented Samuel Johar, Chairman of Buchanan Harvey & Co., a board advisory firm.

Jope retained the three-year plan laid out by Polman in 2017, which included targets for improving operating margins to 20 percent by 2020, while delivering three percent to five percent sales growth. Some investors felt that Jope was treading a fine line as he retained the operating margin target set by Polman that could put Unilever's brand investment under pressure while at the same time talking about discontinuing some profitable brands.

Another task for Jope would be the successful activation of purpose-led brands as aligning stakeholder behavior and decision making around these brands would be more challenging. Also, getting people to engage more on sustainability and persuading consumers to change to more sustainable behaviors would be a Herculean task as only a small number of consumers were motivated to make purchase decisions based on that alone. Moreover, with consumer activism on the rise it was no longer enough for the company's brands to claim that they were sustainable. Though Jope was committed to the strategy, there remained the risk of some brands falling short of the desired sustainable standards. This could damage Unilever's reputation and business results, opined some analysts. In the 2018 GlobeScan-Sustainability Leaders Survey[12], though Unilever continued to be the global leader on sustainability for the eighth year in a row, its 2019 ranking was down 10 points

EXHIBIT 3   Unilever Sustainable Living Plan Targets, 2016–2018

	Target	2018	2017	2016
Improving Health & Well-being Goal: By 2020 we will help more than a billion people take action to improve their health and well-being				
Health & Hygiene Target: By 2020 we will help more than a billion people to improve their health and hygiene. This will help reduce the incidence of life-threatening diseases like diarrhoea	1 billion	653 million	601 million	538 million
Nutrition Target: By 2020 we will double (i.e., up to 60%) the proportion of our portfolio that meets the highest nutritional standards, based on globally recognized dietary guidelines. This will help hundreds of millions of people to achieve a healthier diet	60%	48%	39%	35%
Reducing Environmental Impact Goal: By 2030 our goal is to halve the environmental footprint of the making and use of our products as we grow our business				
Greenhouse Gases Target: Halve the greenhouse gas impact of our products across the lifecycle (from the sourcing of the raw materials to the greenhouse gas emissions linked to people using our products) by 2030 (greenhouse gas impact per consumer use).	(50%)	6%	9%	8%
Target: By 2020 CO_2 emissions from energy from our factories will be at or below 2008 levels despite significantly higher volumes (reduction in CO_2 from energy per tonne of production since 2008).**	≤145.92	70.46	76.77	83.52
Water Target: Halve the water associated with the consumer use of our products by 2020 (water impact per consumer use).	(50%)	(2%)	(2%)	(7%)
Target: By 2020 water abstraction by our global factory network will be at or below 2008 levels despite significantly higher volumes (reduction in water abstraction per tonne of production since 2008).**	≤2.97	1.67	1.80	1.85
Waste Target: Halve the waste associated with the disposal of our products by 2020 (waste impact per consumer use)	(50%)	(31%)	(29%)	(28%)
Target: By 2020 total waste sent for disposal will be at or below 2008 levels despite significantly higher volumes (reduction in total waste per tonne of production since 2008).**	≤7.91	0.20	0.18	0.35
Sustainable Sourcing Target: By 2020 we will source 100% of our agricultural raw materials sustainably (% of tonnes purchased).	100%	56%	56%	51%
Enhancing Livelihoods Goal: By 2020 we will enhance the livelihoods of millions of people as we grow our business.				
Fairness in the Workplace Target: By 2020 we will advance human rights across our operations and extended supply chain, by:	100%	61%	55%	—
• Sourcing 100% of procurement spend from suppliers meeting the mandatory requirements of the Responsible Sourcing Policy (% of spend of suppliers meeting the Policy)				

(continue)

EXHIBIT 3 (Continue)

	Target	2018	2017	2016
• Reducing workplace injuries and accidents (Total Recordable Frequency Rate of workplace accidents per million hours worked)**		0.69	0.89	1.01
Opportunities for Women Target: By 2020 we will empower 5 million women, by:				
• Promoting safety for women in communities where we operate. • Enhancing access to training and skills (number of women). • Expanding opportunities in our value chain (number of women)	5 million	1.85 million	1.26 million	0.92 million
• Building a gender-balanced organization with a focus on management (% of managers that are women)**	50%	49%	47%	46%
Inclusive Business Target: By 2020 we will have a positive impact on the lives of 5.5 million people by:				
• Enabling small-scale retailers to access initiatives aiming to improve their income (number of small-scale retailers)	5 million	1.73 million	1.60 million	1.53 million
• Enabling smallholder farmers to access initiatives aiming to improve their agricultural practices	0.5 million	0.75 million	0.72 million	0.65 million

Baseline 2010 unless otherwise stated.

**Key Non-Financial Indicators.

() Brackets around numbers indicate a negative trend which, for environmental metrics, represents a reduction in impact.

Source: www.unilever.com/Images/unilever-annual-report-and-accounts-2018_tcm244-534881_en.pdf

EXHIBIT 4 Unilever Underlying Sales Growth and Volume Growth, 2009–2018

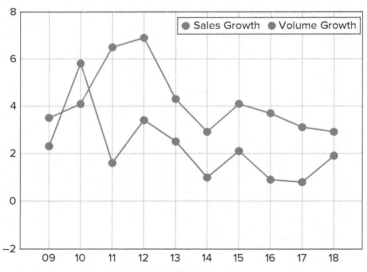

Source: www.unilever.com/Images/unilever-charts-2018_tcm244-534891_en.pdf

compared to 2018, and the gap with other top companies on the list had narrowed—see Exhibit 6.

Besides, Jope had to immediately focus on a major restructuring exercise to fuel growth as

building brand purpose would take time. In March 2019, Unilever announced changes to its leadership and organization as it continued with its transformation into a faster, leaner, and more agile company. As

EXHIBIT 5 Operational Review for Unilever, Second Quarter 2019 and First Six Months 2019 (€ amounts in billions)

	Second Quarter 2019				First Six Months 2019				
	Turnover	Underlying Sales[a] Growth (USG)	Underlying Volume Growth (UVG)	Underlying Price Growth (UPG)[a]	Turnover	USG [a]	UVG	UPG [a]	Change in underlying operating margin [b]
Unilever	€13.7	3.5%	1.2%	2.3%	€26.1	3.3%	1.2%	2.1%	50
Divisions									
Beauty & Personal Care	5.5	3.5%	1.6%	1.9%	10.7	3.3%	1.7%	1.6%	100
Home Care	2.7	8.9%	4.5%	4.3%	5.4	7.4%	2.8%	4.5%	120
Foods & Refreshment	5.5	1.0%	(0.6)%	1.6%	10.0	1.3%	(0.1)%	1.4%	(40)
Geographical Area									
Asia/AMET/RUB	6.3	6.3%	2.5%	3.7%	12.2	6.2%	2.9%	3.2%	70
The Americas	4.2	3.7%	1.3%	2.3%	8.1	2.1%	(0.1)%	2.2%	80
Europe	3.2	(1.6)%	(1.1)%	(0.5)%	5.8	(0.6)%	(0.2)%	(0.4)%	(40)

(a) Wherever referenced in this announcement, USG and UPG do not include any price growth in Venezuela and Argentina.

(b) 2018 numbers have been restated following adoption of IFRS.

Source: https://www.unilever.com/Images/ir-q2-2019-full-announcement_tcm244-538712_en.pdf

EXHIBIT 6 The 2018 GlobeScan/SustainAbility Leaders Survey: Companies Leading on Integrating Sustainable Development (*% of Experts, Total mentions, Unprompted, 2015–2019*)

	2015	2016	2017	2018	2019*
Unilever	38	43	45	47	37
Patagonia	11	17	23	23	27
IKEA	5	10	8	9	13
Interface	8	10	11	10	9
Natura	5	6	7	4	8

*Additionally for 2019, Danone (7), Nestle (6), Marks & Spencer (5), Tesla (4) and BASF (3) make up the top 10.

Adapted from https://globescan.com/category/press-release/

shown in Exhibit 7, the company reported a net profit of €3.04 billion for the six months up to June 30, 2019, down from €3.11 billion a year earlier. Jope warned that 2019 could be a tough year for Unilever in terms of sales growth as market conditions remained challenging due to the overall slowdown in emerging markets such as Asia and Latin America.

With 'Profit with Purpose' set to become the new norm for Unilever and with Jope building further on this commitment, he faced certain questions. Could he uphold Polman's sustainability legacy and live up to the expectations of the investors and the customers? What should he do with profitable brands that were not purpose-led? Should he discontinue them? If so, how? Could a purpose beyond profit drive results and long-term value? Could Jope's commitment to purpose go far enough to bring about a fundamental change in the global FMCG industry?

EXHIBIT 7   Consolidated Income Statements for Unilever, 2016-Fixt Six Months 2019

(In € million except per share data)	First Six Months 2019	2018	2017	2016
Turnover	€26,126	€50,982	€53,715	€52,713
Operating profit	4,589	12,535	8,857	7,801
After (charging)/crediting non-underlying items	(465)	3,176	(543)	(823)
Net finance costs	(351)	(481)	(877)	(563)
Finance income	86	135	157	115
Finance costs	(420)	(591)	(556)	(584)
Pensions and similar obligations	(17)	(25)	(96)	(94)
Net finance cost of non-underlying items	—	—	(382)	—
Net Monetary gain arising from Hyperinflationary economies	29	122	—	—
Share of net profit/(loss) of joint ventures and associates	85	185	155	127
After crediting non-underlying items	3	32	—	—
Other income/(loss) from non-current investments and associates	2	22	18	104
Profit before taxation	4,354	12,383	8,153	7,469
Taxation	(1,145)	(2,575)	(1,667)	(1,922)
After (charging)/crediting tax impact of non-underlying items	89	(288)	655	213
Net profit	3,209	9,808	6,486	5,547
Attributable to:				
Non-controlling interests	203	419	433	363
Shareholders' equity	3,006	9,389	6,053	5,184
Combined earnings per share				
Basic earnings per share	€1.15	€3.50	€2.16	€1.83
Diluted earnings per share	€1.14	€3.48	€2.15	€1.82

Source: www.unilever.com/investor-relations/annual-report-and-accounts/#Download

ENDNOTES

[1] Zoe Wood, "Unilever Warns it Will Sell off Brands that Hurt the Planet or Society," www.theguardian.com, July 25, 2019.

[2] Melissa Hoffmann, "Did Unilever's New CEO Just Irrevocably Change Purpose Marketing?" www.prnewsonline.com, June 21, 2019.

[3] The Dove Self-Esteem Project delivered self-esteem education to young people through lessons in schools, workshops for youth groups, and online resources for parents.

[4] "Unilever's Sustainable Living Brands Continue to Drive Higher Rates of Growth," www.unilever.com, May 18, 2017.

[5] Molly Fleming, "Keith Weed on His Biggest Success: We Proved the Business Case for Sustainability," www.marketingweek.com, December 13, 2018.

[6] Vivienne Walt, "Unilever CEO Paul Polman's Plan to Save the World," https://fortune.com, February 17, 2017.

[7] "New Unilever CEO Jope Banks on Recovery in Sales Growth," www.ft.com, June 11, 2019.

[8] "Profit Through Purpose: Eight Years of Pioneering and Learning," www.unilever.com, April 12, 2019.

[9] Stephen Lepitak, "Unilever CEO Alan Jope: 'We'll Dispose of Brands that Don't Stand for Something'," www.thedrum.com, June 19, 2019.

[10] Graham Hall, "Well Done Unilever, But Hang On. . .," www.linkedin.com, August 1, 2019.

[11] Leila Abboud, Attracta Mooney and Arash Massoudi, "Unilever Veteran Alan Jope Takes Helm at Critical Time," www.ft.com, November 30, 2018.

[12] It tracks opinions of over 800 sustainability experts in 78 countries on sustainable development leadership as well as stakeholders' views on which companies are leaders in integrating sustainability into their business strategy.

Domino's Pizza: Business Continuity Strategy during the Covid-19 Pandemic

Debapratim Purkayastha
IBS Hyderabad

Hadiya Faheem
IBS Hyderabad

> "I remain highly confident in our strategy and optimistic about the opportunity and potential of our business. Our solid, resilient business model and strong financial position will continue to serve us well in these challenging times."[1]
>
> —Ritch Allison, CEO, Domino's Pizza, US, in March 2020

> "The restaurant chain is a tech leader within the food services industry and weathering the COVID-19 crisis well."[2]
>
> —Anne Burdakin, The Motley Fool, in March 2020

On March 31, 2020, American multinational pizza giant Domino's Pizza, Inc. (Domino's) released preliminary sales results for the first quarter ended March 22, 2020—see Exhibit 1. It reported same-store sales growth of 1.6 percent for its U.S. stores and 1.5 percent for its international stores.[3] While most dine-in restaurants were grappling with the impact of the novel COVID-19[4] pandemic on their sales, Domino's was one of the few companies which had not experienced a significant downturn. This was attributed to its prowess in delivery and a new initiative—"çontactless" delivery at all its U.S. as well as international stores. Commenting on the results, Ritch Allison (Allison), CEO of Domino's, United States, said, "Across the globe, Domino's will remain focused on execution, service and value as we continue to navigate through the headwinds created by COVID-19. We are carefully managing our balance sheet, cash flow and all areas of the business to ensure we are doing what we believe will help us best

manage through the near-term and, as always, position ourselves for long-term success."[5]

The COVID-19 crisis started in December 2019 in Wuhan, China. With awareness about the virus increasing, consumers had begun taking precautions to prevent transmission of the disease. With no cure or established treatment for the infection in sight, people in many countries were forced to stay indoors. While this affected many industries, the restaurant industry was badly hit as they were no longer allowed to serve dine-in customers. Worldwide, governments only allowed the food services industry to fulfill take-out and delivery orders. Domino's too was going through disruption with its 14 international markets closed and 23 international markets experiencing partial store closures. This represented around 1,400 international stores, with key markets such as

EXHIBIT 1   Domino's Pizza Preliminary Estimated First Quarter 2020 Sales (Unaudited)

	Period 1, 2020 (Dec 30, 2019 to Jan 26, 2020)	Period 2, 2020 (Jan 27, 2020 to Feb 23, 2020	Period 3, 2020 (Feb 24, 2020 to Mar 22, 2020)	First Quarter of 2020
Same store sales growth: (versus prior year)				
U.S. Company-owned stores	+4.0%	+2.6%	+5.0%	+3.9%
U.S. franchise stores	+3.6%	+0.2%	+0.8%	+1.5%
U.S. stores	+3.6%	+0.3%	+1.0%	+1.6%
International stores (excluding foreign currency impact)	+2.3%	+2.4%	(0.2%)	+1.5%
Global retail sales growth: (versus prior year period)				
U.S. stores	+7.1%	+3.6%	+4.2%	+4.9%
International stores	+7.2%	+5.6%	(1.1%)	+3.9%
Total	+7.2%	+4.6%	+1.6%	+4.4%
Global retail sales growth: (versus prior year period, excluding foreign currency impact)				
U.S. stores	+7.1%	+3.6%	+4.2%	+4.9%
International stores	+8.3%	+8.0%	+4.2%	+6.8%
Total	+7.7%	+5.8%	+4.2%	+5.9%

Source: "Domino's Pizza® Announces Business Update," http://dominos.gcs-web.com, March 30, 2020.

France, Spain, New Zealand, and Panama accounting for nearly 900 of these temporary store closures.[6]

Analysts felt that Domino's was, however, better positioned to tackle the crisis as delivery was not new to its business. Banking on its strong delivery infrastructure, Domino's launched contactless delivery in January 2020 whereby consumers could choose the contactless delivery option while ordering food online. The delivery boy would then leave the food outside the consumer's home and wait at a distance to ensure that the order was picked up. Analysts appreciated the contactless delivery model as it was helping the pizza giant survive during the COVID-19 crisis. In fact, to cater to the increasing demand from consumers, Domino's was planning to hire 10,000 new workers in the United States.[7] However, the company also faced criticism for putting its employees at risk by expecting them to come to work at a time when most people were being asked to stay indoors.

With this being early days of the pandemic, some critics opined that it could be a tough road ahead for Domino's as the company would have to grapple with the full impact of the COVID-19 pandemic. Would it be able to come out successful from this public health crisis? Going forward, how should it balance the need for providing its service to customers with the need for keeping its employees and customers safe? How should Allison and the senior management team at Domino's ensure business continuity amidst the pandemic?

BACKGROUND NOTE

The history of Domino's Pizza (Domino's) dates back to the late 1950s, when Dominick DeVarti (DeVarti) started a small pizza store called DomiNick's Pizza on the Eastern Michigan University campus in Ypsilanti, Michigan. In 1960, two brothers who were students of the University of Michigan, Thomas S Monaghan (Thomas) and James S Monaghan (James), bought the store for US$900. In 1961, James sold his share of the business to Thomas.

The pizza business did well and by 1965, Thomas was able to open two more stores in the town—Pizza King and Pizza from the Prop. In 1966, DeVarti opened a pizza store in a neighboring town with the same name, DomiNick's Pizza. Thomas therefore decided to change the name of his store to Domino's Pizza (Domino's). The advantage of this name, Thomas felt, was that it would be listed after DomiNick in the directory. Domino's philosophy rested on two principles—a limited menu and the delivery of fresh, hot pizzas within half an hour. In 1967, it opened the first franchise store in Ypsilanti and, in 1968, a franchise store in Burlington, Vermont.

In 1982, Domino's established Domino's Pizza International (DPI) that helped in opening Domino's stores internationally. The first store was opened in Winnipeg, Canada. In 1983, DPI spread to more than 50 countries and in the same year, that is, in 1983, it inaugurated its 1000th store. Around the same time, new pizza chains like Pizza Hut and Little Caesar had appeared on the scene and begun to establish themselves in the United States. Domino's Pizza faced intense competition because its menu of traditional hand-tossed pizza had remained unchanged over the years. The other pizza chains, however, offered low-priced breadsticks, salads, and other fast food apart from pizzas. In the home delivery segment too, Domino's faced tough competition from Pizza Hut, while Little Caesar was eating into Domino's market share with its innovative marketing strategies.

By 1989, Domino's sales had fallen significantly, and its cash flows were affected due to the acquisition of assets. In 1993, Thomas decided to expand the Domino's product line in an attempt to revive the company and tackle competition. The company introduced pan pizza and breadsticks in the United States. In late 1993, it introduced the Ultimate Deep Dish Pizza and Crunchy Thin Crust Pizza. In 1994, it rolled out another non-pizza dish—Buffalo Wings. Though Domino's did not experiment with its menu for years, it had adopted innovative ways of managing a pizza store. Thomas gave about 90 percent of the franchisee agreements in the United States to people who had worked as drivers with Domino's. The company gave ownership to qualified people after they had successfully managed a pizza store for a year and had completed a training course. Domino's also gave franchises to candidates recommended by existing franchisees. Outside the United States, most of Domino's stores

were franchise-owned. Domino's was also credited for many innovations in the pizza industry and for setting standards for other pizza companies. It had developed dough trays, corrugated pizza boxes, insulated bags for delivering pizzas, and conveyor ovens.

In 1993, Domino's withdrew the guarantee of delivering pizzas within 30 minutes of ordering and started emphasizing Total Satisfaction Guarantee (TSG) which read, "If for any reason, you are dissatisfied with your Domino's Pizza dining experience, we will re-make your pizza or refund your money."

In 1996, Domino's launched its website. In 1996, it also entered India through a franchise agreement with Jubilant FoodWorks Ltd.,[8] in Delhi. With the overwhelming success of the first outlet, the company opened another outlet in Delhi. By 2000, Domino's had outlets in all the major cities in India.

In 1998, Domino's introduced a patented pizza delivery bag that was designed to keep pizzas oven hot until they were delivered to the customer.

In 2001, Domino's opened its 7000th restaurant in Brooklyn, New York. In 2002, it acquired 82 franchised restaurants in Phoenix, Arizona. This was the largest restaurant acquisition in the company's history.

In 2004, Domino's was listed on the New York Stock Exchange and became a public traded company.

In 2007, it became the first company in the Quick Service Restaurant[9] industry to offer ordering of pizzas through mobile phones. Customers could order from around 2,500 of Domino's 5,128 stores in the United States on **mobile-dominos.com**. Commenting on the launch, Rob Weisberg, Domino's vice president of precision and print marketing, said, *"With so many people living life on-the-go, Domino's mobile ordering delivers even more convenience for our customers' busy lifestyles. With the addition of yet another order-taking channel, Domino's is thrilled to lead the market with this breakthrough technology that continues to change the way people think about ordering pizza."*[10]

In 2008, Domino's started an online application called Pizza Tracker, which enabled consumers to track the delivery of their pizzas in real time.

In 2016, Domino's in cooperation with California-based self-driving robotic delivery vehicles company Starship Technologies began supplying pizzas through self-driving robots in some of Dutch and German cities. The same year, Domino's notched up another first by delivering a pizza in New Zealand using an unmanned aerial vehicle using DRU Drone by Reno, Nevada, U.S.-based drone delivery company, Flirtey. Domino's used the DRU Drone as a delivery method and integrated the drone with online ordering and GPS systems. Commenting on the initiative, Domino's Group Australia CEO and Managing Director Don Meij said, "Drones offer the promise of safer, faster deliveries to an expanded delivery area, meaning more customers can expect to receive a freshly-made order within our ultimate target of 10 minutes. This is the future."[11]

In April 2018, Domino's announced that it was adding 150,000 HotSpots to its delivery locations, which would enable pizza to be delivered to customers in a beach, park, museum, etc., without the need for a physical address.[12]

In June 2019, Domino's teamed up with California-based robotics company, Nuro, to launch a pilot for driverless pizza delivery in Houston, Texas. The pizza giant aimed to use Nuro's driverless fleet of custom-built robot cars to deliver pizzas to residents in Houston who placed online orders.

In 2019, Domino's recorded total sales of $14.3 billion, with international markets accounting for $7.3 billion—see Exhibit 2. It had more than 17,000 stores in over 90 markets. Its key international markets included Australia, India, and the United Kingdom.

EXHIBIT 2   Domino's Pizza Consolidated Statement of Profit or Loss (Dollars in thousands)

	2019	2018	2017	2016	2015
Continuing Operations:					
Revenue	$1,435,410	$1,153,952	$790,861	$705,702	$539,138
Other gains and losses	17,433	19,529	18,566	9,758	6,444
Food, equipment and packaging expenses	(451,768)	(385,675)	(354,127)	(286,069)	(213,059)
Employee benefits expense	(292,439)	(242,340)	(239,471)	(217,703)	(172,112)
Plant and equipment costs	(24,560)	(20,833)	(19,776)	(19,225)	(18,278)
Depreciation and amortisation expense	(62,785)	(53,537)	(46,369)	(38,129)	(27,480)
Occupancy expenses	(49,512)	(44,318)	(39,943)	(36,683)	(27,252)
Finance costs	(14,004)	(10,276)	(5,491)	(3,297)	(2,451)
Marketing expenses	(150,999)	(49,704)	(49,220)	(48,251)	(43,733)
Royalties expense	(68,827)	(59,564)	(52,282)	(46,655)	(37,640)
Store related expenses	(24,636)	(21,406)	(21,799)	(19,785)	(16,841)
Communication expenses	(20,666)	(17,889)	(17,760)	(15,486)	(10,927)
Acquisition, integration, conversion and legal settlement costs	(46,216)	(20,934)	(28,384)	(12,735)	—
Other expenses	(87,018)	(72,529)	(66,389)	(70,139)	(41,268)
Profit before tax	159,413	174,476	150,680	125,819	97,840
Income tax expense	(45,034)	(52,783)	(44,876)	(39,227)	(29,419)
Profit for the period from continuing operations	$ 114,379	$ 121,693	$105,804	$ 86,592	$ 68,421
Profit is Attributable to:					
Owners of the parent	115,912	121,466	102,857	82,427	64,048
Non-controlling interests	(1,533)	227	2,947	4,165	4,373
Total profit for the period	114,379	121,693	105,804	86,952	68,421
Earnings per Share from Continuing Operations:					
Basic (per share)	$1.355	$1.394	$1.16	$0.944	$0.742
Diluted (per share)	$1.354	$1.39	$1.147	$0.922	$0.728

Source: "Domino's Annual Reports, 2019, 2018, 2017, and 2016," https://investors.dominos.com.au.

Independent franchise owners accounted for 98 percent of its stores as of December 2019 as is shown in Exhibit 3.[13] In the United States, Domino's had 6,126 stores, of which 5,784 were owned by franchisees. Analysts felt that Domino's was a poster boy for globalization and franchising with 104 consecutive quarters of positive same-store sales growth. As of March 2020, Domino's and its franchisees employed around 400,000 people worldwide.[14]

THE COVID-19 PANDEMIC

COVID-19 was closely related to the severe acute respiratory syndrome (SARS) which started in China in 2002. The SARS virus infected around 8,000 people and killed 800. Another coronavirus was the Middle Eastern Respiratory Syndrome (MERS) that emerged in Saudi Arabia in 2012. There were around 2,500 infected cases and 900 deaths due to MERS.

COVID-19 was different from SARS and MERS in that 80 percent of the people affected by it reported only a mild infection. However, many people carried the disease without displaying any symptoms, which made it difficult to control its spread.

The COVID-19 outbreak started in a wet market in Wuhan, which sold fish, birds, and both live and dead animals. With live animals being kept and butchered on site, it was difficult to maintain hygiene in these markets and they posed a huge risk as viruses from these animals could easily jump onto humans. To add to the problem, the wet markets were densely packed, which meant the disease spread quickly from species to species. Though the animal source of the COVID-19 was yet to be identified, scientists believed that bats could be the original host.

Covid-19 was known to spread via droplets when an infected person coughed or sneezed. When others touched the surfaces on which the droplets had landed with their hands, they could spread the virus further. People could catch the virus if they touched their eyes, nose, or mouth with their infected hands. The single most important thing that people could do to protect themselves from the virus was to clean their hands by washing them frequently with soap and water or a hand sanitizer.

On March 11, 2020, the World Health Organization (WHO), the international public health agency of the United Nations, stated that due to the rapid increase in the number of cases outside China—over 118,000 COVID-19 cases in more than 110 countries and territories—COVID-19 could be characterized as a pandemic.[15]

While 80 percent of the people infected with COVID-19 showed mild symptoms such as cold and flu, around 14 percent displayed symptoms of pneumonia and shortness of breath. Around five percent of the patients suffered from septic shock, respiratory failure, and multiple organ failure, according to data released by the Chinese authorities.[16]

EXHIBIT 3   Domino's Pizza Preliminary Estimated First Quarter 2020 Store Counts (Unaudited)

	U.S. Company-owned Stores	U.S. Franchise Stores	Total U.S. Stores	International Stores	Total
Store counts:					
Store count at December 29, 2019	342	5,784	6,126	10,894	17,020
Openings	4	31	35	143	178
Closings*†	(1)	(4)	(5)	(104)	(109)
Store count at March 22, 2020*	345	5,811	6,156	10,933	17,089
First quarter 2020 net store growth	3	27	30	39	69

*Temporary store closures due to COVID-19 are not treated as store closures and affected stores are included in the March 22, 2020. store count.

†Unrelated to COVID-19, the South Africa market, reflecting 71 stores in total, closed in the first quarter.

Source: "Domino's Pizza® Announces Business Update," http://dominos.gcs-web.com, March 30, 2020.

Since there was no specific treatment for COVID-19, doctors were trialling existing drugs that were used in the treatment of Ebola,[17] HIV,[18] and malaria.[19] Though the early results were promising, doctors could not be certain whether the drugs were effective until full clinical trials were concluded. A vaccine for COVID-19 was also not in sight. In mid-April 2020, the WHO said that developing a vaccine for the COVID-19 pandemic might take 12 months or longer.

According to Johns Hopkins University, as of April 15, 2020, there were more than 2 million confirmed COVID-19 cases with 128,000 deaths.[20]

With no treatment options in sight, governments across the world were relying mostly on social distancing to arrest the spread of the disease. Many governments had imposed lockdowns, only allowing essential businesses to operate. This had led to massive disruptions in business. Analysts expected the restaurant business to be hit hard by the pandemic, as states in the United States and elsewhere forced restaurants to limit service to takeout and delivery in an effort to keep people from clustering together to prevent transmission of the disease. According to the National Restaurant Association, out of the 1 million restaurant locations in the United States, about three percent had already closed permanently, with another 11 percent anticipating closure by the end of April. They felt that restaurants with delivery would fare marginally better.[21]

DOMINO'S LAUNCHES 'CONTACTLESS' DELIVERY

Domino's former CEO Patrick Doyle had famously said that Domino's was a tech company that sold pizzas. However, analysts felt that it had remained true to the company's core competency: pizza.

Domino's, which accounted for a 36 percent market share in the United States, had always been an advocate of the delivery and takeout model rather than offering the dine-in facility to its consumers. As of January 2020, delivery accounted for 55 percent of its sales while carry out accounted for the remaining 45 percent of the sales.[22] The pizza chain also had an advantage as most of its consumers had the ability to order online. In the United States, Domino's garnered 65 percent of its sales through digital channels such as Facebook Messenger, Google Home, Apple Watch, Twitter, and Amazon Echo, in addition to its own ordering platform, Domino's Hotspots, that offered service to over 200,000 non-traditional delivery locations. Analysts felt that Domino's was well-positioned to tackle the COVID-19 crisis with its dedicated delivery workforce and a customer base which was accustomed to ordering online. According to R.J. Hottovy, an analyst with Morningstar, Domino's "infrastructure is set up for something like this."[23]

With health concerns growing due to the COVID-19 pandemic, Domino's decided to bank on its strong delivery infrastructure and in January 2020, it announced its plans to offer contactless delivery. This meant that the pizza chain delivery person would deliver the food to a consumer without any contact or interaction between them in a bid to ensure safety. Explaining the contactless delivery policy to its consumers, Allison said, "We also want to make sure that customers know that we will deliver any way they choose. Whether they prefer a delivery left at the front door or at a reception desk, our delivery instruction box is the place to put any special directions. We know many people would like to choose contactless delivery right now and we want customers to know we're here to deliver."[24]

Domino's ensured that all its employees were complying with the hygiene and safety protocols across all its restaurants which were open for delivery worldwide. The pizzas were cooked in an oven at 260 degree Celsius and was then packed for delivery and were not touched by human hands. In addition to this, temperature screening was done of all its employees and the delivery fleet was asked to use face masks. Domino's was constantly sanitizing its restaurants, delivery bikes, delivery bikes' boxes, and pizza delivery hot bags to assure consumers that the food delivered by them was safe.

Domino's launched contactless delivery across the majority of its U.S. as well as international stores. In India, the company's licensee, Jubilant FoodWorks Ltd (JFL), launched zero-contact delivery across all its 1,325 restaurants.[25] In addition to this, Domino's partnered with India's fastest growing FMCG company ITC Foods (ITC) to launch an initiative known as 'Domino's Essentials' wherein consumers could order groceries and other essentials by downloading the Domino's app. The service was launched after the Government of India announced a 21-day lockdown[26] in the country from March 25, 2020, to April 14, 2020, due to the COVID-19 pandemic. On April 14, the lockdown was extended till May 3,

2020, as the country reported more than 10,000 COVID-19 cases and 339 deaths, Commenting on the initiative, Pratik Pota, CEO and whole-time director, JFL, said, "We will use the Domino's supply chain and delivery network to deliver essential goods such as Aashirvaad Atta [flour], spices, etc., at people's doorstep. Customers can order using the Domino's App and their order will be delivered safely and hygienically using Zero Contact Delivery."[27]

After placing the order on the Domino's delivery app, consumers could make the payment by digital mode to complete the order. The delivery executives would follow zero-contact delivery to fulfill the order by leaving the groceries at the consumers' doorstep and waiting till the order was received. At JFL, the Safe Delivery Experts or the employees of Domino's had to undergo mandatory health screening—temperature screening was done of every employee before they entered the restaurant and the 20-second hand wash and sanitation protocol was followed every hour.

Initially, Domino's Essentials was available in Bengaluru and the company had plans to offer the service in the Indian cities of Noida, Mumbai, Kolkata, Chennai, and Hyderabad.

Allison said Domino's was taking care of its employees during the crisis. According to him, "As the single largest owner of Domino's stores in the United States [we] will be expanding paid leave for full and part time hourly employees of our company-owned stores and supply chain centers during this outbreak. All employees who are unwell are asked to stay home. Those with any possible exposure to the virus and in need of quarantine are also asked to stay home and will be paid."[28] He added, "In our corporate stores and supply chain centers, we have implemented enhanced sick pay policies, and we will provide additional compensation for our hourly team members during this crisis."[29]

Major Quick Service Restaurant chains such as McDonald's, Yum Brands (which owned Pizza Hut, KFC, and Taco Bell), Wendy's, and Dunkin' Brands, had also switched to drive-thru, takeout, and delivery only.[30] While the total restaurant transactions declined in the United States (QSR transactions down by 34 percent; full-service restaurant transaction down by 71 percent in March 2020), the average check sizes increased. This led to restaurants offering family meals/bundles. For instance, Torchy's Tacos started offering Family Packs and Black Bear Diner Family Packs and specially-priced Family Meals. KFC started offering a $30 Fill Up deal (instead of its $20 Fill Up deal) claiming that it would be enough to feed a family of four for two meals. Pizza Hut promoted the Big Dipper for $12.99; McDonald's sold a Double Big Mac with four patties instead of two, while Taco Bells promoted its massive "Tripleupa." [31]

OTHER INITIATIVES

Due to the COVID-19 pandemic, many people were working from home and several others were out of work. Thus, in April 2020, Domino's announced plans to donate 10 million slices to people most affected by the pandemic in the United States. The pizza giant aimed to donate the food to hospitals and medical centers, in addition to helping school children, grocery store workers, health departments, and 'others in need.' According to Russell Weiner, COO and president of the Americas at Domino's, "We have a long history of feeding people during times of crisis and uncertainty. When we were looking at how we could help, we knew we could use the reach of our national brand to make a difference in thousands of local neighborhoods."[32]

The pizza giant launched an initiative called 'Feeding the Need' under which all its 6,126 company-owned and franchise-owned stores across the United States aimed to donate at least 200 pizzas to people in their communities.[33] The store managers were empowered to make the call to hand out the pizzas to any local group in need.

In New Zealand, Domino's started the "Meals For Seniors" initiative under which the company distributed one free pizza meal every week during the coronavirus lockdown to New Zealanders over 70 years of age.

THE RESULTS

Domino's contactless delivery initiative helped the company thrive despite the COVID-19 lockdown across many countries worldwide. In April 2020, Domino's reported that its first-quarter sales had increased by 4.9 percent in the United States while its international stores recorded an increase in sales of 6.8 percent for the same period. Despite an increase in sales, analysts pointed out that though overall the results looked positive during the pandemic, Domino's sales had been impacted during this difficult time. The company reported that its

U.S. sales growth had fallen from 3.6 percent in January 2020 to one percent for the period February 24, 2020, to March 22, 2020. According to Allison, "U.S sales were impacted by many factors, which have varied in magnitude across the cities and towns we serve."[34] He added, "Shelter in place directives, pantry loading, university and school closures, event cancellations and the lack of televised sports have all impacted our business in ways that we cannot yet fully quantify."[35]

Domino's rivals such as Yum Brands predicted U.S. Quarter 1 (Q1) same-store sales declines in the mid-to-high single digits, while Papa John's expected an estimated 5.3 percent growth in Q1 compared to 2019.[36]

As is shown in Exhibit 4, Domino's share prices shot up 11 percent on March 19, 2020. Analysts had stated that the relative strength of Domino's shares had risen sufficiently to allow it to outperform the S&P 500.[37]

Domino's international stores were hit the hardest with China being its first market to be significantly impacted by COVID-19, according to Allison.[38] However, the company's sales were recovering and increasing in the last few weeks of the first quarter, added Allison.

Despite mixed results, several analysts appreciated Domino's for using its strong delivery infrastructure to survive amidst the COVID-19 crisis when most businesses restaurants worldwide were shutting down. "The ones that win, or relative winners, are restaurants with drive-thrus, restaurants that have big delivery business, restaurants who do a lot of take-out business—who are known for takeout. If you're mostly an in-dining room type restaurant, I think you're going to struggle,"[39] said Peter Saleh (Saleh), analyst at global financial services company BTIG.

THE CHALLENGES

Though Domino's was by and large appreciated for its contactless delivery during the COVID-19 pandemic, it faced a backlash from critics and some of its employees for keeping its stores open. A campaign started against Domino's on Change.org[40] by Domino's employee Issy Anna (Anna) accused the company of putting its employees at risk at a time when states had entered a lockdown or had urged residents to remain indoors to curb the spread of COVID-19. According to her, "We are being forced to work in cramped stores, many that are not equipped to deal with the situation at hand. Multiple employees are being forced to come in to work sick in fear of their jobs while corporate refuses to bat an eye at the situation. "Contact-less delivery" has been anything but successful, as some stores remain open for carryout with people piling into the lobbies of these establishments even in the midst of shelter-in-place

EXHIBIT 4   Domino's Pizza Stock Chart (October 2019–April 15, 2020)

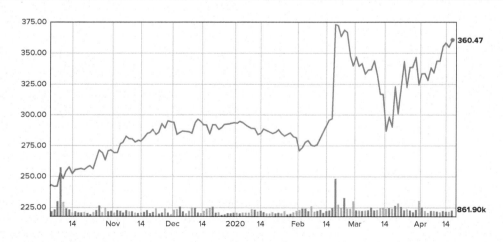

Source: https://finance.yahoo.com

orders issued by many states, customers continue to give cash which multiple employees are handling, and hardly anyone actually utilizes the contact-less system."[41] Anna further claimed that the delivery drivers did not have constant access to hand sanitizers or sanitizer sprays to properly disinfect the delivery bags. She wondered how a pizza service could be considered "essential" when there were other options such as people obtaining food from grocery stores or cooking themselves. She pointed out that American coffee company Starbucks Corporation had shut its stores temporarily and was giving each employee an option to take 30 days of paid sick leave.

In early April, Angharad Maddock, a Domino's employee in Llanelli, Carmarthenshire, UK, accused the company of dismissing her for raising concerns about lack of masks, hand sanitizers, and social distancing at the store. Domino's refuted these allegations. A spokesperson for Domino's said that in addition to introducing contactless delivery, frequent handwashing and increased sanitization, the company had stopped its collection service and cash handling. It had also put screens in place and hazard tape on the floor "to help with social distancing for team members to adhere to."[42]

The company started facing more criticism when a store worker at Domino's in Eskbank, Midlothian, Scotland, died on April 10, 2020, after contracting the coronavirus. Nina Arnott, Domino's spokesperson, offered condolences to the employee's family on his demise but stated that the stores remained opened in support of the UK government's advice that food delivery services should play an important role in keeping people at home during the COVID-19 lockdown.

In another incident on April 12, 2020, a Domino's store in Crenshaw District in Los Angeles was closed temporarily for thorough sanitizing after four of its employees tested positive for COVID-19. A group representing Domino's workers filed an emergency complaint with public health services firm Los Angeles County Public Health Department, demanding that they too shut the Domino's store. The complaint filed by delivery driver Angelica Olivares on behalf of herself and 10 co-workers stated, "Instead of closing the store temporarily and allowing exposed workers to quarantine for 14 days with pay . . . Domino's has stayed open without even providing protective equipment to workers or disinfecting the store."[43]

In mid-April, a pizza delivery boy tested positive for COVID-19 in New Delhi, India, which led to 72 homes being quarantined as a precautionary measure. Domino's issued a statement saying that this incident had nothing to do with it. The company reiterated that 100 percent of its delivery was "zero contact delivery" and that its employees in its stores were being temperature screened daily and followed hand washing protocols. Besides, the company was sanitizing restaurants, bikes, pizza boxes, and hot bags every four hours, it said.[44]

LOOKING AHEAD

Analysts appreciated Domino's strategy of gaining a larger portion of the pie during the COVID-19 lockdown. They opined that Domino's strong delivery infrastructure in addition to its having a strong digital consumer base helped it to capitalize on the contactless delivery trend. They pointed out that smaller independent pizza chains and restaurants lacking the resources stood to lose their share. According to Saleh, contactless delivery might not be a gamechanger but the service would become "table stakes and par for the course" in the pizza industry as the coronavirus was spreading continuously—see Exhibit 5. Saleh added, "If you don't have that in this environment, you are going to lose share."[45]

At a time when rivals such as The Cheesecake Factory and Union Square Hospitality were announcing furloughs and layoffs respectively, Domino's announced plans to hire 10,000 employees in its U.S. stores in March 2020 as the company was experiencing an increase in demand for its pizzas with more and more people working from home amid the pandemic. The company's UK division was also hiring more store workers and delivery drivers since more consumers were ordering online. In March 2020, the pizza giant's Australian division had already taken on over 2,000 people to serve consumers in the country.[46] "While many local, state, and federal governments [are issuing orders that close] dine-in restaurants, the opportunity to keep feeding our neighbors through delivery and carryout means that a small sense of normalcy is still available to everyone. . . Our corporate and franchise stores want to make sure they're not only feeding people but also providing an opportunity to those looking for work at this time, especially those in the heavily impacted

**EXHIBIT 5   COVID-19 Statistics—Top 25 Countries
(Data as of April 16, 2020, 12:33 GMT)**

Country	Total Cases	Total Deaths	Total Recovered	Active Cases
World	2,100,149	136,044	523,873	1,440,232
USA	644,417	28,559	48,708	567,150
Spain	182,816	19,130	74,797	88,889
Italy	165,155	21,645	38,092	105,418
France	147,863	17,167	30,955	99,741
Germany	134,753	3,804	77,000	53,949
UK	98,476	12,868	N/A	85,264
China	82,341	3,342	77,892	1,107
Iran	77,995	4,869	52,229	20,897
Turkey	69,392	1,518	5,674	62,200
Belgium	34,809	4,857	7,562	22,390
Netherlands	29,214	3,315	250	25,649
Brazil	29,015	1,760	14,026	13,229
Canada	28,379	1,010	8,979	18,390
Russia	27,938	232	2,304	25,402
Switzerland	26,422	1,269	15,400	9,753
Portugal	18,841	629	493	17,719
Austria	14,412	393	8,098	5,921
Israel	12,591	140	2,624	9,827
Ireland	12,547	444	77	12,026
Sweden	12,540	1,333	381	10,826
India	12,456	423	1,513	10,520
Peru	11,475	254	3,108	8,113
S. Korea	10,613	229	7,757	2,627
Japan	8,626	178	901	7,547
Chile	8,273	94	2,937	5,242

Adapted from www.worldometers.info/coronavirus.

restaurant industry,"[47] said Allison. Meanwhile, rivals such as Pizza Hut, Papa John's, and Jet's Pizza were also on a recruitment spree involving thousands of new employees.

Domino's was optimistic about cashing in on the trend as it borrowed $158 million in its outstanding variable funding notes in a bid to improve its strong cash position and stay operational, though the company had $300 million on hand to increase its financial flexibility.[48] Reflecting the uncertainty of the global economy, Domino's, however, withdrew its fiscal 2020 guidance.

James McCann (McCann), CEO of McCann Investments, which invested in early-stage companies in the grocery tech, food tech, and consumer goods space, opined that while contactless delivery was booming in the wake of the COVID-19 crisis for companies such as Domino's, this service would be prevalent in the future based on several factors such as how quickly employees and customers accepted the practice and how long the threat of COVID-19 remained. He added, "If we have nine months of high virus threat, then physical distancing will be normal. We will have forgotten what the pre-normal was."[49]

ENDNOTES

· ● ● ● ●

[1] Keith Nunes, "Domino's Weathering Covid-19 Storm," www.foodbusinessnews.net, March 31, 2020.

[2] Anne Burdakin, "Domino's Pizza: A Lockdown Winner Any Way You Slice It," www.fool.com, March 28, 2020.

[3] Joanna Fantozzi, "Domino's Reports Q1 Same-store Sales Growth and withdraws Financial Guidance during COVID-19," www.nrn.com, March 31, 2020.

[4] COVID-19 or coronavirus is a pandemic caused by severe acute respiratory syndrome coronavirus 2 (SARS-coV-2), which started in Wuhan, Hubei province in China, in December 2019. As of April 15, 2020, more than 2 million people affected by Covid-19 were reported with more than 128,000 deaths, according to John Hopkins University.

[5] "Domino's Pizza Announces Business Update," www.bloomberg.com, March 31, 2020.

[6] "Domino's Pizza® Announces Business Update," http://dominos.gcs-web.com, March 30, 2020.

[7] Amelia Lucas, "Domino's Expects to Hire 10,000 Workers," www.cnbc.com, March 19, 2020.

[8] In 1995, Jubilant FoodWorks Limited (JFL), part of the Jubilant Bhartia Group, was founded by two brothers Hari Bhartia and Shyam Bhartia. The Jubilant Bhartia Group has a strong presence in diverse sectors like Pharmaceuticals, Drug Discovery Services and Life Science Ingredients, Performance Polymers, Food Service (QSR), and Consulting in Aerospace and Oilfield Services.

[9] A Quick Service Restaurant is a type of restaurant which serves fast food cuisine.

[10] "Domino's Pizza First in Industry to Offer Mobile Ordering," www.webrtcworld.com, September 27, 2007.

[11] "DRU Drone by Flirtey Delivers Domino's Pizza in New Zealand," https://insideunmannedsystems.com, November 29, 2016.

[12] "Domino's Pizza Top 10 Innovations," https://aaronallen.com, May 18, 2018.

[13] "Domino's Pizza 2019 Annual Report," http://dominos.gcs-web.com.

[14] Anne Burdakin, "Domino's Pizza: A Lockdown Winner Any Way You Slice It," www.fool.com, March 28, 2020.

[15] Jamie Ducharme, "World Health Organization Declares COVID-19 a 'Pandemic.' Here's what that Means," https://time.com, March 11, 2020.

[16] Sarah Newey and Anne Gulland, "What is Coronavirus, How did it Start and How Big could it Get?" www.telegraph.co.uk, April 10, 2020.

[17] Ebola is a virus that can cause bleeding and organ failure, which can eventually lead to death.

[18] The HIV or Human Immunodeficiency virus attacks the cells in the human body that help in fighting infections and diseases.

[19] Malaria is a disease caused by the plasmodium parasite, which is transmitted by mosquito bites.

[20] "Global Coronavirus Cases Top Two Million: Johns Hopkins," www.cgtn.com, April 15, 2020.

[21] Alicia Kelso, "Why Pizza Chains are Weathering the Coronavirus Downturn Better than their Restaurant Counterparts," www.forbes.com, April 1, 2020.

[22] Alicia Kelso, "Why Domino's CFO is Confident the Pizza Chain will Gain even More Market Share in 2020," www.forbes.com, January 15, 2020.

[23] Katie Arcieri, "Pizza Chains Aim for Larger Slice of Contactless Deliveries during Coronavirus," www.spglobal.com, April 6, 2020.

[24] Daniel B Kline, "Domino's Offers Contact-Free Delivery," www.fool.com, March 17, 2020.

[25] "Coronavirus: McDonald's, Domino's Pizza Introduce Contactless Delivery," www.deccanherald.com, March 16, 2020.

[26] On March 24, 2020, the Government of India announced a complete lockdown whereby wearing masks in public places was mandatory. Educational institutions and religious places were closed during the lockdown. International and domestic flights were suspended till May 3, 2020. Only essentials such as groceries, meat shops, poultry and fish markets, vegetable and fruit shops, and milk booths were open to the public. Industries in rural areas were allowed to function from April 30, 2020 with social distancing norms. In addition to this, banks and automated teller machines (ATMs), hospital and medical facilities were also functional.

[27] Bhumika Khatri, "Domino's is now Delivering Essentials in Partnership with ITC Foods," https://inc42. com, April 11, 2020.

[28] "A Letter to Domino's Customers from Ritch Allison, CEO of Domino's Pizza, Inc.," https://biz.dominos.com.

[29] Ritch Allison, "Domino's CEO Pens a Letter Detailing the Impact of Covid-19 on Its Worldwide Business," www.franchising.com, April 2, 2020.

[30] Bill Peters, "Domino's Eyes Massive Hiring Spree While Coronavirus Ravages Restaurant Industry," www.investors.com, March 19, 2020.

[31] Alicia Kelso, "Why Pizza Chains are Weathering the Coronavirus Downturn Better than their Restaurant Counterparts," www.forbes.com, April 1, 2020.

[32] Michael Holan, "Domino's to Donate 10 Million Slices of Pizza across US," https://nypost.com, April 7, 2020.

[33] "Domino's 6,126 Stores give Communities 200 Pies each," www.pizzamarketplace.com, April 6, 2020.

[34] John Ballard, "Domino's Pizza Reports Sales Increase amid COVID-19 Pandemic," www.nasdaq.com, March 31, 2020.

[35] Jonathan Maze, "Not Even Domino's can Escape the Coronavirus Impact," www.restaurantbusinessonline.com, March 30, 2020.

[36] Alicia Kelso, "Why Pizza Chains are Weathering the Coronavirus Downturn Better than their Restaurant Counterparts," www.forbes.com, April 1, 2020.

[37] Bill Peters, "Domino's Eyes Massive Hiring Spree While Coronavirus Ravages Restaurant Industry," www.investors.com, March 19, 2020.

[38] John Ballard, "Domino's Pizza Reports Sales Increase amid COVID-19 Pandemic," www.nasdaq.com, March 31, 2020.

[39] Kate Taylor, "Dominos-Papa-Johns-and-more-Chains-Thriving-amid-Coronavirus," www.businessinsider.com, April 2, 2020.

[40] Change.org is a petition website started by California-based certified B corporation (corporations that balance profit and purpose) for-profit Change.org Inc. It aims to facilitate petitions filed by the general public. As of April 17, 2020, the website had 240 million users.

[41] Issy Anna, "Close Domino's Pizza due to COVID-19 Pandemic," www.change.org.

[42] "Coronavirus: Domino's Denies Sacking Staff over Safety Concerns," www.bbc.com, April 4, 2020.

[43] "L.A. Domino's Closed for Sanitizing after Workers say they're at Risk of Coronavirus," www.dailynews.com, April 11, 2020.

[44] "Pizza Delivery Boy Tests Positive for COVID-19: Zomato and Domino's Issue Clarification," www.dqindia.com, April 16, 2020.

[45] Katie Arcieri, "Pizza Chains Aim for Larger Slice of Contactless Deliveries during Coronavirus," www.spglobal.com, April 6, 2020.

[46] Harry Wise, "Domino's Pizza Cancels Dividend despite the Coronavirus Lockdown causing Huge Rise in Demand for Deliveries," www.thisismoney.co.uk, March 27, 2020.

[47] Anne Burdakin, "Domino's Pizza: A Lockdown Winner Any Way You Slice It," www.fool.com, March 28, 2020.

[48] Julie Littman, "Domino's US Same-store Sales Growth Drops by Half in Q1," www.restaurantdive.com, March 31, 2020.

[49] Katie Arcieri, "Pizza Chains Aim for Larger Slice of Contactless Deliveries during Coronavirus," www.spglobal.com, April 6, 2020.

Burbank Housing: Building from the Inside Out

Christy Anderson,
MBA Student, Sonoma State University

Armand Gilinsky Jr.,
Sonoma State University

On October 8, 2017, Larry Florin awoke to a phone call in the middle of the night. The call was from an employee at non-profit Burbank Housing's main office alerting him that there were massive fires ripping through Northern California, and Burbank Housing's properties were at risk. Larry scrambled to leave and drove up from Marin County to Burbank Housing's main office in Santa Rosa, California.

Just one year into Larry's new role as CEO at Burbank Housing, Northern California's housing crisis was reaching critical levels. The catastrophic fires put much more pressure on the region, but came with much needed support from federal and local government and from the community. Burbank Housing was able to take on more projects than ever.

By late 2019, two years after the 2017 devastating wildfires, Larry reflected on the company's position given the road ahead. His challenge: put Burbank Housing in a position to take on new development projects to mitigate the housing crisis while assuring that Burbank Housing could internally manage all new project growth.

For a company like ours, cash flows is everything. And this is actually not different than a for profit company. In the development world it goes up and down. There are big, big cycles. It's even worse in the affordable housing world. Because if you tax a tax credit project, our typical project, the way we make money here is off of developer fees. Which we are allowed to collect, but we cannot collect a developer fee until a project is done, and it is what is called stabilized. So, it has to have three months' worth of full occupancy and people paying rent. So, way down the line we get paid. It's really about cash flow and how you manage cash in order to keep the operation going. And that's a struggle. We do what we can with the money we have.

We currently own about 65 properties. We get a management fee. Most of that goes to our staff that work on the projects. And the costs associated with running the projects. But we could do that more efficiently. We have never here established metrics of how much per unit it should cost us. If you are a for profit management company, you live and die off the cost per unit that you incur. It is somewhere probably between $5,000 and $8,000 per unit is where our costs are. To systematize that, it would be great. The projects are pretty complex. There are sometimes four to seven funding sources for each project. The management company could really benefit from being able to systematize. And we would make money, so say if a unit cost $8,000 we could try to get to $6,000 across the board.[1]

—Larry Florin, CEO of Burbank Housing

Burbank Housing, like many affordable housing companies, was comprised of a development department, a property management department, and a resident services department as their core organizational structure. The development department was charged with constructing new projects. Property management managed the rental properties once they were completed. Resident services provided various types of support programs for renters. Reviewing these activities, Larry grappled with how to improve the coordination of these departments, manage the cash flows associated with new project developments, and systematize processes and procedures across the organization.

AFFORDABLE HOUSING SEGMENT

Affordable non-profit housing companies acted as developers in that they were able to compete for tax credits and needed to comply with certain regulations once tax credits were awarded. However, for-profit developers could also compete for tax credits. The main difference was that affordable housing companies made it their mission to provide housing for individuals below the median income levels.

According to IBISWorld, the Construction sector expanded at an annualized rate of 3.4 percent over the five years prior to 2018 and reached $2.0 trillion, including a 3.3 percent jump in 2018 alone.[2] Growth in California occurred at a faster rate. The demand for construction projects was driven by macroeconomic factors such as rising disposable income, low interest rates, mortgage interest rates, government policy measures which supported homeownership, and increased access to credit. Construction contractors additionally benefited from accommodative lending standards by banks over the five years, providing them with increased financing for operations.[2] As a result of the increased demand for construction services, the average profit margin for operators in the construction industry reached 5.9 percent of total construction revenue in 2018, up from 4.5 percent in 2013.[3] At the same time, the industry experienced severe shortages of skilled labor due to tight employment markets.

Across the United States in 2017, floods, hurricanes, wildfires, and earthquakes, among other natural disasters, acutely decreased the nation's housing supply and intensified demand for construction of single-family homes. Housing industry observers estimated that single-family housing projects had increased by 900,000 units in February 2018, the highest level since September 2007.[4] Multifamily, or apartment complex construction was also a significant driver of residential building construction from 2012–2018. Multifamily housing starts, which were generally more volatile than their single-family projects, were expected to rise at an annualized rate of 6.1 percent over the five years prior to 2018.[5] Reports from property management software solutions firm

RealPage reported "apartment completions reached a 30-year high in 2017, with 364,713 units completed in the 150 largest U.S. metro areas."[6] Investors also took note of the focus on apartment complex projects. Investors had "purchased a record-setting $19.6 billion in apartment properties in 2015, bolstering revenue for industry operators in this submarket."[7]

TAX CREDITS

Affordable housing was heavily reliant upon tax credits. The low-income housing tax credit (LIHTC) program had originally been a part of the Tax Reform Act of 1986. According to the Congressional Research Service group, the LIHTC program acted as an indirect federal subsidy used to help finance construction and rehabilitation of low-income affordable rental housing.[8] Without this incentive, affordable rental housing projects were not expected to generate sufficient profits, because housing was provided at below-market rates.

Tax credits gave investors a dollar-for-dollar decrease on their federal tax liability. At the same time, investors also accounted for depreciation or losses on housing projects. Tax credits were paid out annually over ten years. Projects that were awarded tax credits needed to be available only to low-income tenants and rents needed to be restricted for at least 30 years. There were two types of tax credits, 4 percent and 9 percent. New construction projects were generally awarded the highly sought after 9 percent tax credits, while the 4 percent credit was normally reserved for rehabilitation projects.

The general qualification required that the household made less than 50 percent of the Area Median Income (AMI). According to the Sonoma County Economic Development Board, Sonoma County had a median household income of $66,783 in 2017.[9]

HOUSING CRISIS

According to Larry, and the Congressional Research Service group, tax credits were almost non-existent during the Great Recession of 2008. The Low-Income Housing Tax Credit (LIHTC) program existed primarily because of funding from large banks. As a result, the price of LIHTCs fell, creating funding gaps in projects that had received tax credit allocations in 2007 and 2008 but had not yet sold.[10] This included thousands of projects and tens of thousands of units that would have otherwise been bought or rehabilitated. During that time Burbank Housing's focus shifted to property management. Without any affordable housing development projects to support the business during the Great Recession, property management was the only way Burbank housing could generate funds to stay afloat.

Upon its recovery from the Great Recession, California renewed its focus on trying to solve the housing crisis. "Housing [was] more expensive in California than just about anywhere else," according to the report by California's Legislative Analyst's Office (CLAO), which noted an increasing gap in supply and demand for housing in that state since the 1970s.[11] California was known for its robust economy, creating many job opportunities, often faster than the housing market could keep pace with. According to the CLAO, California maintained one of the highest median housing prices and rents in the United States. In 2015 an average California home cost $440,000, about two-and-a-half times the average national home price of $180,000, and California's average monthly rent was about $1,240, which was 50 percent higher than the rest of the country at $840 per month.[12] According to the CLAO, the main reason that homes were not built was because local communities made most decisions about housing development. How residents felt about new housing, particularly affordable housing, was another important factor. Incumbent residents concerned about new housing had the ability to bar new construction via the community's land use authority, which allowed them to effectively slow or stop housing from being built or require housing to be built in lower densities. Other important factors that prevented housing projects were the environmental impacts of new projects and a shortage of land available for development.

Larry noted how the community and local government were very much in support of new development of affordable housing projects to help solve the housing crisis, especially after the fires. The Tubbs Fire began on October 8, 2017, and quickly became the most destructive fire in California history, resulting in a loss of 4,658 homes.[13] Thirteen months later, the Camp Fire obliterated Paradise, California. In 2019, California's Governor-elect Gavin Newson called for the construction of 3.5 million new housing units over the next five years, or an average of 500,000 a year.[14] California had historically built an average of 80,000 new homes per year over the prior decade. Even to Larry, a goal of 3.5 million housing units seemed very ambitious.

COMPANY HISTORY

Burbank Housing was a 501(c)(3) charitable nonprofit with history going back 40 years. When the organization was in its first years, there was not much competition and the market itself was almost non-existent. During the Great Recession of 2008, Burbank Housing had to shift their focus to property management because of the economic factors which affected the construction industry at the time. In 2010, Burbank Housing developed a strategic plan which focused primarily on taking on tax credit projects, selling to new partnerships and updating their assets. Around this time other competitors began entering the market. In 2015, the board of directors brought in a consultant to take a deep dive into the organization and provide recommendations. Some of those changes focused on leadership, and in 2016 helped the board select Larry Florin as the new CEO.

In 2017 the Board of Directors, other organizational leaders, and a group of employees developed a strategic plan focusing on the core values of the organization. The areas of focus and goals for the strategic plan developed in 2017 can be seen in Exhibit 1. The dashboard was created (at the time of writing) to highlight in a single snapshot where the organization was with each goal from the strategic plan. When asked what his own goal was as CEO, Larry responded:

> I want us to run properties that people are going to be proud of in the community. And that's important. I want us to be known as a reputable company. So once we build it, we own it, we stay with the project, we take care of the residents. Ultimately, I think we make our mark by bringing new projects on board given the demand that is out there.

Focusing on the strategic plan allowed Burbank Housing leaders to decide which areas were considered priorities, as shown in Exhibit 1. Based on a recent review in early 2019, the leadership team color-coded where they were currently in attainment of each identified goal. Green goals were completed. Light-green goals were considered in

EXHIBIT 1   Burbank Housing's 2017 Strategic Plan, Updated Spring 2019

BURBANK HOUSING

Burbank Housing Strategic Plan Status Update
Q1 2019

Done	Done & On-going	In Process	Organizing Stage	Organizing Stages - Need Support

Organization Development	Goal #1: Develop initiatives that allow employees to work smarter.
	Goal #2: Foster strong and positive open communication between internal departments.
	Goal #3: Establish key leadership in various areas of business unit competency and implement a shared learning
	Goal #4: Provide access to a variety of learning styles.
Partnership & Collaboration	Goal #1: Pursue a minimum of 2 new partnerships in developing new communities on an annual basis.
	Goal #2: In identifying new areas of growth, focus development and partnership opportunities in Sonoma, Napa counties by developing a pipeline of projects that will maintain a continuous flow of work over the next 3 years.
	Goal #3: Cultivate 2–3 new partnership by the end of 2018 with organizations and individuals who add value to the project team, and align with our strategic plan.
	Goal #4: Strengthen existing partnerships and build new collaborations with organizations serving low-income and moderate-income populations.
	Goal #5: Burbank's primary focus will continue to be tax credit projects serving populations up to 60% AMI or homeownership projects at or below 120% AMI (minimum 40% at or below 80% AMI).
Development	Goal #1: Connect with local jurisdictions.
	Goal #2: Monitor affordable housing activities.
	Goal #3: Regularly communicate the importance of affordable housing.
Fiscal Management	Goal #1 : Portfolio Assessment.
	Goal #2: Increase cash reserves and surplus cash payments.
	Goal #3: Support fund development.
	Goal #4: Develop a corporate risk management strategy.
Resident Services	Goal #1: Strengthen resident services.
	Goal #2: Develop new collaborations and strengthen existing relationships with community partners.
	Goal #3: Build a stronger and more sustainable infrastructure of the department to better serve our residents.
	Goal #4: Increase revenue for resident services to include a fundraising strategy.
Advocacy	Goal #1: Develop policy on advocacy participation.
	Goal #2: Strengthen existing relationships and build new relationships with elected and appointed officials.
	Goal #3: Create a resident advocacy program in collaboration with Resident Services.
	Goal #4: Establish strategic coalitions.
Education & Outreach	Goal #1: Promote understanding of Burbank Housing through storytelling and by building brand loyalty.
	Goal #2: Deliver a regular flow of information to key stakeholders.
	Goal #3: Continue and update strategic communications efforts.

Source: Created by case writer based on Burbank Housing's 2017 Strategic Plan & interviews with leadership team.

completion and ongoing because much of Burbank Housing's strategic goals needed to be continuously practiced. Yellow goals were in process. Orange goals were designated as having been in beginning stages. Red goals were considered highest priority: the areas that needed more focus were cash flows, communication, standardizing processes, employee motivation and training—in order to handle the additional capacity.

As of 2019, Burbank Housing managed over 63 properties, almost 3,000 rental units, and was working on starting projects that would bring over 500 new rental units to Sonoma County. Based on 2017 financial statements, Burbank Housing reported 459 million in assets of which 385 million were property.

Burbank Housing was divided into three companies according to their Director of Human Resources.

The Development Company had 21 employees, the Property Management Company had 77, and the Resident Services Company had 66. Exhibit 2 shows the organization chart of Burbank Housing.

Development

Burbank Housing existed to develop affordable housing for the North Bay in California. The Development department was the heart of Burbank Housing.

EXHIBIT 2 Burbank Housing Leadership Team Organization Chart in 2019

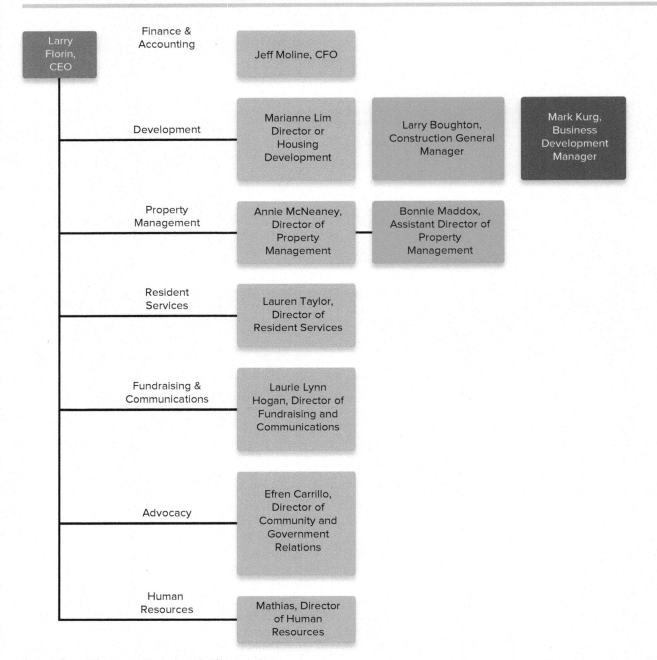

Source: Created by case writer and used with permission.

Development was also Burbank Housing's most profitable department. The development department depended on developer fees for cash flow.

Exhibits 3, 4, and 5 present financial statements for Burbank Housing from 2016 to 2018.[15] Burbank Housing had one property under construction,

EXHIBIT 3 Burbank Housing Development Corporation Statement of Activities (Change in Unrestricted Net Assets), 2016–2018

	2018	2017	2016
Support and revenue:			
Support:			
Capital grants for sale of single-family homes	$ 46,670	$ 1,276,010	$ 496,000
Donations and other grants	11,347,944	1,881,076	95,388
Total support	11,394,614	3,157,086	591,388
Revenue:			
Rental income	29,147,200	26,461,540	26,038,478
Sale proceeds - sale of single-family homes	24,860	11,271,616	10,884,565
Cost of sales - sale of single-family homes	—	(11,917,581)	(12,635,326)
Developer fees	1,438,938	2,909,714	2,282,651
Property management and accounting fees	220,542	207,469	172,017
Partnership, incentive and asset management fees	52,199	50,678	37,721
Recovery of homeownership notes	109,112	157,342	119,774
Interest income	160,000	63,116	71,667
Miscellaneous income	1,187,836	775,465	1,230,637
Total revenue	32,340,687	29,979,359	28,202,184
Total support and revenue	43,735,301	33,136,445	28,793,572
Expenses:			
Program services:			
Rental expenses	15,961,064	16,575,320	18,755,269
Project development	605,627	580,364	148,129
Property management	3,024,112	2,697,760	2,775,140
Management and general	1,852,317	2,526,425	1,550,299
Total expenses	21,443,120	22,379,869	23,228,837
Change in net assets before other expenses	22,292,181	10,756,576	5,564,735
Other expenses:			
Interest expense	9,644,746	8,964,343	5,452,411
Depreciation and amortization	14,443,728	14,223,680	14,412,960
Loss on disposal of fixed assets	837,545	555,412	337,395
Total other expenses	24,926,019	23,743,435	20,202,766
Change in net assets	(2,633,838)	(12,986,859)	(14,638,031)
Net assets—beginning of year	109,865,246	113,088,949	95,184,297
Capital contributions—net	220,080	9,763,156	745,026
Net assets—end of year	$107,451,488	$109,865,246	$81,291,292

Source: Burbank Housing's Final Combined Financial Statements, used with permission. Final audited statements for FY 2019 were not yet available at the time this case was written.

EXHIBIT 4   Burbank Housing Development Corporation Statement of Cash Flows, 2016–2018

	2018	2017	2016
Cash flows from operating activities			
Change in net assets	$ (2,633,838)	$(12,986,859)	$(15,398,575)
Adjustments to reconcile change in net assets to net cash provided by operating activities			
Depreciation	14,393,030	14,111,868	14,318,380
Amortization	50,678	111,792	94,580
Interest - amortization of permanent loan costs	174,587	101,943	88,060
Loss on retirement of fixed assets	837,545	555,412	337,395
Donation of land	—	(1,715,000)	—
(Increase) decrease in partnership activity	93,096	1,200	(20,059)
(Increase) decrease in assets:			
Contributions receivable	(858,907)	—	—
Limited partnership receivable	(28,724)	16,163	(110,651)
Property and other receivables	(81,697)	157,133	221,014
Prepaid expenses	(139,846)	(4,177)	25,151
Deposits and mortgage impounds	(41,943)	(42,583)	5,770
Notes and interest receivable from limited partnerships	(52,824)	(42,824)	(35,067)
Increase (decrease) in liabilities:			
Accounts payable and accrued expenses	(1,189,239)	335,612	1,048,104
Deferred revenue	94,500	1,404,402	(26,904)
Accrued interest on mortgages and notes payable	4,688,444	4,350,418	3,713,933
Tenant security deposits–net	(11,520)	(10,546)	32,577
Total adjustments	17,927,180	19,330,813	19,692,283
Net cash provided by operating activities	$15,293,342	$ 6,343,954	$ 4,293,708
Cash flows from investing activities:			
Net decrease (increase) in replacement, operating and other reserves	(5,487,884)	(1,398,248)	698,793
Reduction (purchase) of development in progress	(18,530,439)	(16,495,450)	5,767,299
Purchase of property and equipment	(2,469,168)	(1,769,167)	(15,245,605)
Reduction (purchase) of deferred costs	(41,533)	(66,916)	9,755
Net cash used in investing activities	(26,529,024)	(19,729,781)	(8,769,758)
Cash flows from financing activities:			
Net decrease in financing for development and progress	4,071,860	(3,273,688)	(9,477,715)
Net increase in mortgages and notes payable	9,466,330	6,840,158	8,947,241
Net increase in permanent loan costs	(530,885)	(88,912)	
Net increase (decrease) in other long-term payables	(76,522)	36,900	22,457
Proceeds from capital contributions, net of distributions and syndication costs	220,080	9,763,156	4,810,328
Net cash provided by financing activities	$13,150,863	$ 13,277,614	$ 4,302,311
Increase (decrease) in cash and cash equivalents	1,915,181	(108,213)	(173,739)
Cash and cash equivalents, beginning of year	5,532,918	5,641,131	5,814,870
Cash and cash equivalents, end of year	$ 7,448,099	$ 5,532,918	$ 5,641,131

Source: Burbank Housing's Final Combined Financial Statements, used with permission. Final audited statements for FY 2019 were not yet available at the time this case was written.

EXHIBIT 5 Map Showing Number of Units Managed by Burbank Housing in 2019, by City

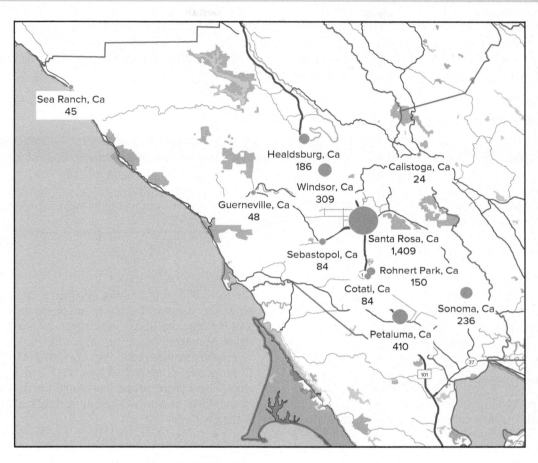

Sea Ranch, Ca
45

Healdsburg, Ca
186

Calistoga, Ca
24

Windsor, Ca
309

Guerneville, Ca
48

Santa Rosa, Ca
1,409

Sebastopol, Ca
84

Rohnert Park, Ca
150

Cotati, Ca
84

Sonoma, Ca
236

Petaluma, Ca
410

Source: Created by case writer from interview with Director of Property Management.

Stoddard West Apartments, in the city of Napa, which was 50 units of family affordable rental units. Construction started in April 2018 and was scheduled to be completed in late summer 2019.

Six projects in pre-development included:

- Redwood Grove, Napa, 34 units, ownership
- Lantana Place, Santa Rosa, 48 units, ownership
- Caritas Homes, Santa Rosa, 128 units, rental - some of which is homeless-dedicated, the rest family
- Heritage House, Napa, 66 units, rental for homeless households
- Valle Verde, Napa, 24 units, family rental
- Journey's End, Santa Rosa, 162 units, senior rental (plus another 300-450 market rental units)

Costs varied based on a host of factors but often fell into the $450,000–$550,000 per rental unit. Because ownership units tended to be modest in size, unit costs for those fell into the same range. Once a property was approved, entitled, and funding sources were secured, construction could begin. Towards the end of construction an investor or investors were locked in to take over ownership of the property. Burbank Housing usually ended up with a small portion of the ownership by entering into a limited liability partnership with an investor to transfer the management of the property over to Burbank Housing. Developer fees were not generated by Burbank Housing until, as Larry said, the project had been "stabilized." Larry explained it typically took at least three months after construction for a housing complex to reach full occupancy with pay-ing renters. These delays in revenue were a big rea-son why managing cash flows was so important for Burbank Housing.

Being a company with large development projects made managing debt important.[16] Most of the time Burbank Housing had to take on loan financing to fund development projects. Looking at debt-to-equity allows Burbank Housing insight into the level of risk they are getting taking on. Debt-to-equity ratios for a company are compared against industry ratios to see if the level of risk is higher or lower than competitors. Generally, according to Larry, a ratio of 3 or lower was acceptable in the construction industry. Table 1 highlights an overview of Burbank Housing's debt to equity ratios from 2016 to 2018.

TABLE 1   Debt-to-Equity Overview, 2016–2018

FYE 12/31	2016	2017	% Increase	2018	% Increase
Total Liabilities	$339,478,199	$349,318,958	2.9%	$366,146,306	4.8%
Total Net Assets (Shareholders' equity)	113,088,949	109,865,249	−2.9%	107,451,488	−2.2%
Debt-to-equity ratio	3.00	3.18	5.9%	3.41	7.2%

Source: Burbank Housing internal document, used with permission.

Burbank Housing's debt to equity ratio was higher in 2017 than the industry average. Larry explained a ratio of 3.2 was not alarming to him, how-ever it is something he was monitoring, and planned to reduce by increasing free cash flow.

Property management

Having developed 63 properties and counting, Burbank Housing supplied Northern California with almost 3,000 rental units. Property Management generated revenue based on management fees for running the day-to-day operations of rental prop-erties. Managing properties with more units brought in greater management fees. Looking at Table 2, 10 properties consisted of between 80 to 129 rental units. These larger properties brought in 36% of man-agement fees and at the same time only make up 16% of the portfolio.

TABLE 2   Summary of Properties Managed by Property Management, 2019

Number of Projects	Unit Count	Annual Management Fees Generated	% of Fees Generated	% of Projects Represented
19	2 to 29 Units	$ 239,188	10%	30%
20	30 to 49 Units	$ 663,490	27%	32%
14	50 to 79 Units	$ 683,723	28%	22%
10	80 to 129 Units	$ 883,881	36%	16%
	Total Fees Generated	$2,470,282		

Source: Burbank Housing internal document, used with permission.

Burbank Housing's Development Plan called out the goal to "Develop initiatives that allow employ-ees to work smarter." Annie McNeany, Director of Property Management, outlined a plan to help her staff optimize the management of their current port-folio as well as prepare them to take on more prop-erties. "Optimization of Yardi software has been a primary focus for my department." Yardi property management software was used by many affordable housing and for-profit housing companies. However, Annie and other managers agreed that Yardi had not yet been leveraged fully at Burbank Housing.

Burbank Housing implemented Yardi PAYscan paperless invoicing and Yardi Marketplace, which was to be used by Property Managers to purchase supplies. Invoicing became noticeably easier and saved costs to the organization because of a decrease in invoice processing times. Processing one invoice typically cost $35. With Yardi PAYscan, invoicing costs decreased to $5 or less per invoice. The time it took to process an invoice also dropped, from 32 to six or fewer days.

Yardi Marketplace was also implemented as a tool to help property managers purchase supplies needed for properties such as light bulbs, paint, or a refrigerator. This feature was integrated with the Yardi software used by the Finance and Property Management departments to streamline tracking costs and paying vendors. Adoption and usage of the technology remained slow, however. Some of Burbank Housing's staff indicated that additional training was needed and that it was difficult to change a workflow process with which they were already comfortable.

Yardi also had the potential to be used as a performance evaluation tool. Burbank Housing's Director of Property Management was excited about the implementation of Yardi because the performance evaluation feature allowed for greater consistency in personnel reviews, whereas previously, employee performance evaluation processes and reports had never been standardized.

For all properties, Property Management created and managed lists of people waiting to become approved for an affordable rental unit. For larger properties the lists contained hundreds of applicants. The ideal process would have been automated and/ or systematized in the Yardi software. An example: Burbank Housing purchased Parkwood Apartments, a 56-unit apartment complex, for $15 million. The City of Santa Rosa provided a loan of nearly $2.5 million to Burbank to help close the deal.[17] Often, Burbank Housing purchased an existing property to protect the current residents from having to move out with the threat of a new owner raising rent. Setting up properties like Parkwood involved a series of steps which required extensive, and often redundant, communications. When there were already residents in these apartments, they all had to apply for affordable housing through Burbank Housing. These residents' information was captured through the application processes. Then, a new person was recruited and hired to manage the property. Following that, an assessment of the property's rehabilitation needed to be done. These workflows could have been managed far more efficiently and less costly if the process of information capture and management were managed in the Yardi software.

"It [was] difficult to automate this process," said Bonnie Maddox, Assistant Director of Property Management. For each property they had to update the waiting list by sending out a letter to each applicant asking certain questions to check the status of the applicant's eligibility. Because of the time it took to manage this process, many properties had already closed waiting lists. A rental application form consisted of information that was already in the Yardi system. It has been a goal of Property Management to automate this process however specific Yardi developer experience was needed to set it up.

Director of Property Management Annie McNeany worked with a consulting company and Yardi support to try to automate processes in Yardi. Also, specific Yardi questions and issues that came up day-to-day sometimes proved challenging to solve in a timely manner. Bonnie connected with the Director of Data Governance at another large affordable housing company in Northern California to share knowledge and experience of Yardi issues and utilization. Bonnie learned that the other affordable housing company had in-house Yardi experts who assisted with issues that came up. Bonnie also learned this company was able to automate their rental applications, waitlists, and mailing lists in Yardi. Looking at Exhibit 5, we can see the geographical spread of Burbank Housing's rental properties. An in-house Yardi expert could have been added to payroll if Yardi software assistance was needed. Bonnie explained it was difficult to support all the Property Managers because of how spread out their properties were throughout Sonoma and Napa Counties, but sometimes Property Managers needed in person support. Exhibit 6 shows budget space for computer assistance and training, however this might not be enough for a full-time Yardi administrator salary.

Communication between departments was also extremely important to help Property Management

EXHIBIT 6   Burbank Housing's 2019 Budget (summarized for technology support and training-related expenses)

Burbank Housing 2019 Budget	Consolidated	Development	Property Management	Asset Management	Resident Services
Total Revenue	$ 8,399,627	$ 3,703,729	$ 3,073,071	$ 732,729	$557,734
Total Rental Expenses	57,604	—	—	—	—
Total Property Mgmt Exp.	1,912,476	—	1,648,476	—	264,000
Operating Expenses					
Computer Consultants	18,583	1,354	11,214	510	510
Computer & Software Equip.	127,895	5,336	44,182	2,008	2,008
Computer Maintenance	43,546	3,785	31,338	1,424	1,424
Training	58,500	7,000	$ 14,000	5,000	—
Other - General & Admin	2,362,892	1,762,156	(1,463,569)	386,781	252,903
Total Expenses	$ 4,581,496	$ 1,779,631	$ 285,641	$ 395,723	$520,845

Source: Burbank Housing's 2019 Budget, prepared in December 2018, used with permission.

prepare to take on more properties. Burbank Housing had a goal to "Foster strong and positive open communication between internal departments." Feedback from leadership included that communication had been an ongoing area Burbank Housing desired to improve. Some front-line staff members, such as property managers, voiced that they felt they were siloed and didn't know what was going on at the main office. Director of Fundraising and Communications, Laurie Lynn Hogan, implemented a weekly newsletter to be sent out to the entire organization with updates of new development projects. This newsletter was well received but proved to be a significant amount of work to put together. At the time of this writing, leadership was considering setting up a two-way communication process so front-line staff can communicate important information.

Employee training was also a focus Annie had in her plan for Property Management. The training plan consisted of providing employees, and possibly the entire organization, education on tax credits, affordable housing laws, and software such as Microsoft Excel. Employees had voiced that they needed more knowledge and training in those areas to do their jobs more effectively. Exhibit 6 shows the budget for 2019 allocates $58,000 for employee training, of which $14,000 is currently allocated for Property management alone. Most departments in the organization provided team development activities throughout the year. Team development activities have improved employee satisfaction and communication. Annie's opinion was that employee education and motivation would help their department efficiently take on more properties and optimize the way they managed existing properties.

MISSION AND VALUES

Burbank Housing's mission statement is as follows:

"Burbank Housing is a local nonprofit dedicated to building quality affordable housing in the North Bay. We create vibrant local communities that are carefully designed, professionally managed, and sustainable both financially and environmentally, to foster opportunities for people with limited-income of all ages, backgrounds and special needs."

Although the purchase of properties like Parkwood helps keep renters in their apartments, and generated income for Burbank Housing, this was not Burbank Housing's main *modus operandi.* CFO Jeff Moline emphasized the importance of introducing more affordable housing options into the market as their primary focus.

The organization held four core values: community, integrity, compassion, and teamwork. As stated in their strategic plan, community was defined by Burbank Housing as the desire to "actively engage with people and institutions to share information, ideas and resources in order to help others achieve their goals." Burbank Housing is a known name in the community. They have collaborated with a long list of other organizations focused on housing, homelessness, wildfire recovery, education, healthcare and politics. CEO Larry Florin and Head of Community and Government Relations Efren Carrillo, as well as other leaders of Burbank Housing, have regularly informed the community of various events. Director of Resident Services Lauren Taylor has built and maintained relationships with other housing entities in the community to share information, ideas, and resources. From almost all angles, Burbank Housing has applied their core value of community.

For integrity, Burbank Housing "delivers on our promises. Professional, ethical behavior is expected by all. We have the courage to acknowledge mistakes and do whatever is needed to address them." For compassion, Burbank Housing "values individual differences, demonstrate empathy and [works] to understand the concerns of others without judgment." Integrity and compassion are both paramount values for an organization like Burbank Housing. Being at their main office, speaking with leadership and even meeting with Burbank Housing residents, one can feel their organization is built on integrity and compassion. It is a clear part of the company's culture.

To emphasize teamwork, Burbank Housing "assumes positive intent, [practices] effective communication and collaboration to establish mutual understanding to overcome challenges and inspire others." This value relates to Goal #1 from the strategic plan: to "Develop initiatives that allow employees to work smarter." The idea is that if employees can be trained in new areas and new initiatives are implemented, then everyone in the organization can work as a more effective team. As Burbank Housing accepted new development projects and additional rental properties to manage, they acknowledged that more focus would be needed on communication, standardized processes, motivation, and training to create stronger teamwork.

FUTURE OPPORTUNITIES

Burbank Housing's leadership team concluded there were several opportunities to optimize the organization internally to handle the additional capacity in the pipeline. The team considered increasing the estimated cash flows for development projects, automating processes in Property Management, hiring a Yardi Administrator, improving internal communication, providing training and education for employees, as well as motivating employees.

Increasing Cash Flows

Increasing cash flows was not as simple as collecting cash and putting it aside for development projects. A large amount of cash came from development fees. Burbank Housing also collected management fees from managing the properties. The challenge was reaching an understanding of how much cash flows are needed for development and how much could be generated through the company without having to get funds through financing.

Yardi Administrator

According to **Glassdoor.com**, the median salary of a Yardi Administrator in California in 2019 was $63,174.[18] This figure was out of the range budgeted to Property Management for computer support. However, a Yardi Administrator could possibly pay for themselves if they automated some of the manual work currently being done by other employees. That way more of the management fee revenue earned would go to the company rather than to internal costs.

Optimize Yardi Software & Automate Processes

Opportunities to optimize processes would come from use of the Yardi software. If all property managers used Yardi marketplace, billing vendors would be easier and less costly. Waiting lists and applications processes would be automated. Currently, this is a very manual and time-consuming process. Employee performance evaluations are another process that can be optimized through consistency among the organization, if it was implemented through Yardi.

Increase Internal Communication

An increase of two-way internal communication was requested by many employees throughout the organization. Property Managers had been specifically vocal about their desire for communication concerning what was going on at the main office. Monthly newsletters had been the norm in the past. These monthly newsletters required a significant amount of time and effort. Encouraging communication would improve teamwork and provide opportunity for cross-training. Companywide informational meetings had not been done in over a year. Discussions about setting up a two-way communication process had already begun; however, the process was as of late spring 2019 not in place.

Training and Education

Property Management employees voiced a desire for Microsoft Excel training, Yardi training, as well as classes centered around learning about updated tax credits laws. Annie decided to make it her priority to create training and team-building activities to motivate and promote more effective teamwork among her staff.

NEXT STEPS

Much of Larry's time after the wildfires had been occupied talking about the housing crisis and recovery efforts. Getting support for affordable housing over the years had its up and downs, and Larry recalled a time when he was worried to be in the affordable housing industry because of the lack of funding and support. As California witnessed the effects of a shortage of supply in the housing market, affordable housing companies like Burbank Housing were receiving greater support than they had received before.[19] Consequently, much of Larry's time had shifted to focusing on opportunities on how to navigate this shortage, rather than on the difficulties.

Reviewing Burbank Housing's Strategic Plan, Larry saw that little focus had been placed on improving the organization's internal capacity to handle any future projects. Larry pondered "what is most important, and where should we start?"

ENDNOTES

[1] Case writer's interview with Larry Florin in January 2019. All subsequent quotes in this case except where noted were based on field interviews with Burbank Housing staff in 2018 and 2019 and 2020.
[2] Anon. (2019). *U.S. Construction Industry Reports*. (n.d.). Retrieved February 2, 2019, from http://clients1.ibisworld.com.sonoma.idm.oclc.org/reports/us/industry/currentperformance.aspx?entid=164#KED.
[3] Keighley, M. P. (2019). An introduction to the low-income housing tax credit. *Congressional Research Service*. Retrieved February 16, 2019, from https://crsreports.congress.gov/.
[4] Anon., Who qualifies for affordable housing assistance? (n.d.). Retrieved February 15, 2019, from https://affordablehousingonline.com/housing-help/Who-Qualifies-For-Affordable-Housing.
[5] see note 2.
[6] see note 2.
[7] Ibid.
[8] see note 3.

[9] Sonoma County Economic Development Board, (2018). *City Profile and Projections Report*. Retrieved February 15, 2019, from www.sonomaedb.org.
[10] What Works Collaborative. (2009). The disruption of the low-income housing tax credit program: causes, consequences, responses, and proposed correctives. *Joint Center for Housing Studies of Harvard University*. Retrieved March 5, 2019, from http://www.jchs.harvard.edu/sites/default/files/disruption_of_the_lihtc_program_2009_0.pdf.
[11] California Legislative Analyst Office. (2015). California's high housing costs. Retrieved February 21, 2019, from https://lao.ca.gov/reports/2015/finance/housing-costs/housing-costs.pdf.
[12] Ibid.
[13] Rossmann, R. (November 02, 2017). Cal Fire tally reveals fires' devastation. Retrieved February 9, 2019, from https://www.pressdemocrat.com/news/7588914-181/cal-fire-4658-homes-destroyed.

[14] Salam, R. (2019, February 15). Gavin Newsom's Big Idea. Retrieved February 18, 2019, from https://www.theatlantic.com/ideas/archive/2019/02/governor-newsom-addresses-californias-housing-crisis/582892/
[15] Statements for 2019 had not been audited at the time this case was written in spring 2020.
[16] Financial Ratios. (2018, February 08). Retrieved May 11, 2019, from https://www.constructionbusinessowner.com/accounting/accounting-finance/financial-ratios.
[17] Minichiello, S. (January 11, 2019). Affordable housing nonprofit buys Rincon Valley apartment complex. Retrieved February 5, 2019, from https://www.pressdemocrat.com/news/9152733-181/burbank-housing-nonproft-buys-rincon.
[18] Yardi Systems' Administrator Salaries. (n.d.). Retrieved February 20, 2019, from https://www.glassdoor.com/Salary/Yardi-Systems-Systems-Administrator-Salaries-E31057_D_KO14,35.htm.
[19] Minichiello, S. (2019), op. cit.

Boeing 737 MAX: What Response Strategy is Needed to Ensure Passenger Safety and Restore the Company's Reputation?

Rochelle R. Brunson
Baylor University

Marlene M. Reed
Baylor University

"All Boeing airplanes are certified and delivered to the highest levels of safety consistent with industry standards. Airplanes are delivered with baseline configuration, which includes a standard set of flight deck displays and alerts, crew procedures and training materials that meet industry safety norms and most customer requirements. Customers may choose additional options, such as alerts and indications, to customize their airplanes to support their individual operations or requirements."[1]

These were the words of a Boeing spokesman on March 22, 2019, a week after U.S. President Donald Trump grounded all Boeing 737 MAX planes. The reason for the grounding was the recent crash of two of these planes killing 346 people.

Following the grounding of the planes, Boeing management had to decide how to respond to this action on the part of the government, and the growing outcry that Boeing had known of certain problems with the MAX and did nothing. The MAX was scheduled to be returned to service by June or July of 2020, so the company needed to find a way to repair their faltering image by then.

History of Boeing

Commercial flight began in the early 20th Century when several engineering entrepreneurs began to build airplanes. Among those entrepreneurs were William E. Boeing, Donald Douglas, Sr., James H. "Dutch" Kindelberger, and James S. McDonnell.

The history of Boeing began in July 1916 when William Boeing incorporated the aircraft manufacturer as the Pacific Aero Products Company, which became renamed as Boeing Airplane Company in the same year. Boeing began producing aircraft for the United States military in 1917 when it produced modified Model Cs for the U.S. Navy. This began a relationship that the company would have with the military that continued through 2020.[2]

After the war ended, the first commercial craft, the B-1, began carrying mail from Seattle to Canada. In 1927, the Boeing Model 40A was designed specifically for carrying mail, and it delivered mail from San Francisco to Chicago. About this time, engineers and pilots were testing the physical limits and the durability of airplanes. The Army Air Services' "World Flyers" completed the first airplane trip around the globe in 1924. Then in 1927, Charles Lindburgh made the first solo nonstop crossing of the Atlantic. Five years later, Amelia Earhart became the first woman to fly solo across the Atlantic.

Boeing continued to develop aircraft for the U.S. military after World War I and launched the B-17 "The Flying Fortress" in 1935. The plane became a key asset in World War II, as did additional aircraft introduced by Boeing. General Carl Spaatz, who was the U.S. Air Commander in Europe, said, "Without the B-17, we may have lost the war."[3]

Commercial passenger service.   Civilian air travel grew rapidly during the 1950s and Post-War Era. The President of American Airlines, C.R. Smith, commissioned Douglas Aircraft to come up with an airplane that would carry passengers overnight. The plane the company designed was the DC-3. This plane, which was rolled out in 1936, was the first airplane that turned a profit based on commercial passenger demand. By 1939, the DC-3 and its earlier version, the DC-2, were carrying more than 90 percent of all U.S. passengers. Other versions of the DC-3 were later produced for military use during World War II. Even 70 years after its first delivery, this plane was still in use by smaller and emerging markets.[4] Boeing Commercial Airplanes, which is a unit of the Boeing Company, is headquartered in Seattle, Washington, and employed more than 60,000 people worldwide by 2020.

The Cold War and Development of Military Jet Aircraft.   During the Berlin Blockade, many countries sent the B-47 Stratojet bomber in to bring food and supplies to the divided city. Then as Cold War tensions began to escalate, the United States and the USSR raced to test new advanced jet aircraft. The U.S. F-86 Sabre Jet helped speed the end of the Korean Conflict as it dominated the skies over Korea. The F-86 destroyed so many Russian-built planes that the final air-to-air victory was 10 to 1.

The A-4 Skyhawk Light Attack Bomber gave America's allies the flexibility they needed in a light aircraft. In 1964, the first A-4s took flight in raids on North Vietnam. In addition, the F-4 Phantom II fighter was deployed in the Vietnam War and in Operation Desert Storm.[5]

Boeing's introduction of commercial jet airliners. The delivery of the four-engine Boeing 707 to Pan Am in August 1958 marked a significant advancement in commercial aviation. Pan Am made industry news later that year with its flight from New York to Paris which the 707 completed in 8 hours 41 minutes. The 707 introduced the modern era of passenger jet travel with longer flights, larger seating capacity, and faster travel times. Boeing's industry-leading commercial jet airliners dominated the 1960s through the early 21st Century with new model introductions such as the 727, 737, 747, 757, 767, 777, and 787.

Boeing 737.   The Boeing 737 became the workhorse of the airline industry soon after its introduction in 1967. Lufthansa first took delivery of the 737-100,

which had six-abreast seating, on December 28, 1967. The following day, United Airlines was the first U.S. carrier to take delivery of the plane, a 737-200 model with an increased seating capacity and range. By 1987, the 737 had become the most ordered plane in history. Boeing introduced upgraded and lengthened 737-300, −400, and −500 versions of the plane, with total orders reaching 3,100 by 1993. Boeing continued to launch advanced versions of the 737 with Next Generation −600, −700, −800, −900, and −900ER models launched between 1993 and 2005.

The Fourth Generation 737 MAX was launched in 2017 in multiple model configurations with the MAX 7 having a length of 116 feet and seating capacity of 172 passengers and the Max 10 having a length of 143 feet and seating capacity of 230. The MAX 8 and MAX 9 models fell between the two other versions of the aircraft. Key advances of the 737 MAX included improved fuel efficiency that expanded range to up to 3,850 nautical miles, innovative carbon fiber/titanium engine turbine blades, stylish cabin, improved cockpit displays and updated flight deck. The 737 MAX was Boeing's fastest-selling passenger plane in history with about 5,000 orders from carriers in more than 100 countries.

Divisions of Boeing

The Boeing Company became the world's largest producer of commercial jetliners after its merger with McDonnell Douglas in 1997 and its acquisition of the defense and space units of Rockwell International in 1996. Boeing was able to provide a selection of 23 different airplane models to serve markets that required 100 to 600 seats. They also manufactured a complete line of cargo freighters.

Boeing's divisions in 2020 were Commercial, Defense, Space, Innovation, and Services. The Commercial Division had produced such airplanes as the Next Generation 737, the 737 MAX, the 747-8, the 767, the 777, the 777X, the 787, Freighters, Boeing Business Jets, and Boeing Support and Services. By 2020, there were 10,000 Boeing commercial jetliners in service. These planes were purported to fly farther on less fuel and significantly reduce emissions.

The Defense Division produced a large number of aircraft for the government including Air Force 1, the AH-6 Light Attack Helicopter, the AH-64 Apache, and various weapons systems. Their produce line also included fighter jets, rotorcraft, cybersecurity products, surveillance suites, missile defense, and commercial aircraft derivatives.

In terms of the Space Division products in 2020, Boeing was attempting to enable critical research on the International Space Station, deep-space exploration and life on earth, and the CST-100 Starliner commercial spacecraft. The company was working on a joint venture with Lockheed Martin on a United Launch Alliance. They were also building a heavy-lift, human-rated propulsion to deep space with the Space Launch System rocket that would launch missions on a path to the Gateway Cislunar Outpost.[6]

The Services Division had two parts: The Commercial Service Division and the Government Services Division. Boeing's experience in bringing innovative service solutions to commercial, defense, and space customers had prepared them to offer customer service to those particular groups.

Finally, Boeing's organizational divisions in 2020 included an Innovation Division. This group had more than $3 billion invested annually in research and development. Some examples of Boeing's innovations were the first flights if the 737 MAX 9, the 787-10 and the T-X.

Boeing's Purpose and Mission

Connect, protect, Explore and Inspire the World through Aerospace Innovation.

At Boeing, we are committed to a set of core values that not only define who we are, but also serve as guideposts to help us become the company we would like to be. And we aspire to live these values every day.

Boeing Behaviors

Lead with courage and passion
Make customer priorities our own
Invest in our team and empower each other
Win with speed, agility and scale
Collaborate with candor and honesty
Reach higher, embrace change and learn from failure
Deliver results with excellence–Live the Enduring Values

Boeing's Aspiration

Best in Aerospace and Enduring Global Industrial Champion.

Boeing's Enterprise Strategy

Operate as One Boeing
Build Strength on Strength
Sharpen and Accelerate to Win

Boeing's 2025 Goals

Market Leadership
Top-quartile Performance and Returns
Growth Fueled by Productivity
Design, Manufacturing, Services Excellence
Accelerated Innovation
Global Scale and Depth
Best Team, Talent and Leaders
Top Corporate Citizen

The Global Aircraft Manufacturing Industry

The Boeing Company was the world's largest aerospace company in 2020. The company was also the second-largest defense contractor for the United States Government behind Lockheed Martin Corporation. Also, in 2020, Boeing was the largest exporter in the United States.

Boeing and the French company Airbus were the two largest manufacturers of commercial airplanes in the world. Boeing had developed a competitive advantage based upon its size and market diversification. The company had the ability to take on multiple projects and clients at the same time, and it leveraged its economies of scale to buy inputs in bulk.[7] Because Boeing operated in both the commercial and defense sectors, it was able to offset any decline in one division with an emphasis upon the other sector.

Over the five years leading up to 2019, Boeing's U.S. manufacturing sector revenue was expected to decline at an annual rate of 1.0 percent to $78.1 billion. A strong demand for commercial aircraft has helped soften the declining defense spending in the United States and the billions of dollars that have been committed to paying for damages caused by the recent crashes and the thousands of flight cancellations occasioned by the grounding of the 737 MAX. (See Exhibit 1 below entitled "The Boeing Company's Financial Performance 2014–19.")

EXHIBIT 1   The Boeing Company's Financial Performance 2014–2019 ($ amounts in billions)

Year	Revenue	Growth (% change)	Operating income	Growth (% change)
2014	$82.3	N/C	$4.9	N/C
2015	85.9	4.4%	4.4	−10.2%
2016	83.7	−2.6%	4.6	4.5%
2017	81.4	−2.7%	7.5	63.0%
2018	85.0	4.4%	8.4	12.0%
2019	78.1	−8.1%	8.6	2.4%

Source: IBISWorld.com

The 737 NG and 737 MAX Crashes

On February 25, 2009, a Boeing 737 NG (Next Generation), a predecessor of the 737 MAX, crashed near Amsterdam. The plane was Turkish Airlines Flight 1951, and it was carrying 128 passengers from Istanbul. The first officer guided the plane toward Runway 18R and called out changes to its speed and direction. This officer was new to the Boeing jet, so the crew included a third pilot in addition to the captain who had 13 years of experience flying this aircraft. As the plane dipped to 1,000 feet, the pilots had not completed their landing checklist. When the plane reached 450 feet, the pilots' control sticks began shaking which informed them that there was an impending stall. One of the pilots pushed the thrust lever forward to gain speed; but when he let go, the computer commanded it to idle. The captain intervened and disabled the auto-throttle. This maneuver set the thrust levers to the maximum. By this time, nine seconds had elapsed since the stall warning. Now it was too late to do anything else. The jet plunged into a field close to the airport.[8] It was later determined by an investigation of the crash that Boeing had not included information in the NG operations manual that could have helped the pilots respond when the sensor failed.

The second crash occurred on October 29, 2018, when a Lion Air Flight 610 fell into the Java Sea just 13 minutes after takeoff from Jakarta, Indonesia. In that crash, 187 people were killed. The flight crew made a distress call shortly before losing control. The aircraft had just been received by Lion Air three months earlier.[9]

The third crash, which involved a 737 MAX, occurred in March of 2019. This time Ethiopian Airlines Flight 302 crashed on takeoff from Addis Ababa killing all 157 people aboard. The plane was bound for Nairobi, Kenya. Just after takeoff, the pilot radioed a distress call and was given immediate clearance to return and land. However, before the crew could make it back to the airfield, the aircraft crashed. This aircraft was only four months old.[10]

Investigators determined that Boeing's design decisions on both the MAX and the plane involved in the 2009 crash (the 737NG) allowed a powerful computer command to be triggered by a single faulty sensor, even though each plane was equipped with two sensors. In the two MAX accidents, a sensor measuring the plane's angle to the wind prompted a flight control computer to push its nose down after takeoff. On the Turkish Airlines flight, an altitude sensor caused a different computer to cut the plane's speed just before landing.[11] (See Exhibit 2 below for a recounting of the times of the crashes entitled "Timeline of First MAX Flights and Accidents.")

What Caused the Crashes?

The 737 MAX could fly further and carry more people than any previous generation of 737s. Because the engines were bigger and because the 737 sat so low to the ground, Boeing moved the engines slightly forward and raised them higher under the wing. However, the new position of the engines changed how the aircraft handled in the air. This created a potential for the nose to pitch up during flight, and a pitched nose is a problem in flight. If it is raised too high, the aircraft can stall. To keep the nose in trim, Boeing came up with a software called the Maneuvering Characteristics Augmentation System (MCAS). With this system, when a sensor on the

EXHIBIT 2   Timeline of First MAX Flights and Accidents

Feb. 2009	**2016**
Boeing 737 NG crashes near Amsterdam	The first MAX 8 Flight
2016	**2017**
2 of Boeing's top pilots indicate problems with MCAS	The first MAX 9 Flight
2018	**Oct. 29, 2018**
The first MAX 7 Flight	Lion Air 737 MAX crashes
March 10, 2019	**March 13, 2019**
Ethiopian Airlines 737 MAX crashes	Pres. Trump grounds MAX planes
October 25, 2019	**October 28, 2019**
NTSB publishes report on Lion Air crash	Boeing's Pres. Muilenberg admits Boeing knew of pilots' concerns
December 23, 2019	
Boeing's President Muilenberg is fired by the Board of Directors	

fuselage detected the nose was too high, MCAS automatically pushed the nose down.[12]

On October 25, 2019, the Indonesian Transportation Safety Committee published its final report on the Lion Air Crash. The report largely blamed the MCAS device. Before the crash, the Lion Air pilots were unable to determine the aircraft's true airspeed and altitude and struggled to take control of the plane as it oscillated for about 10 minutes. Whenever they pulled up from a dive, MCAS pushed the nose down again. The report stated further that the MCAS function was not a fail-safe design and flight crews had not been adequately trained to use it.[13]

Boeing's Knowledge of Problems

On November 12, 2018, *The Seattle Times* reported that MAX pilots from Southwest Airlines were "kept in the dark" about the MCAS and how to respond to warnings from it. Then the *Dallas Morning News* found similar complaints from American Airlines pilots just four months later.

In April 29, 2019, shareholders' meeting, Boeing CEO Muilenberg, in response to questions about the accidents, suggested that in some cases pilots didn't completely follow the procedures that Boeing had outlined to prevent a crash in case the MCAS should happen to malfunction. On that same date, the *Wall Street Journal* reported that, even for airlines that had ordered it, the warning light was not operating.[14]

On October 17, 2019, Boeing suggested that it had turned over text messages between two of the company's top pilots which were sent in 2016. The messages revealed that the company knew about the problems with the MCAS system quite early. In fact, a former chief technical pilot for the Boeing 737 described the MCAS' habit of engaging itself "egregious."[15]

Then on December 23, 2019, the CEO of Boeing Dennis Muilenberg was fired by the Board. He was replaced by David Calhoun on January 13, 2020. Calhoun was a Boeing Board member and a former General Electric executive. In an interview on January 29, 2020, Calhoun criticized the company's prior leadership for not immediately disclosing a large amount of damning internal communications that raised safety questions about the MAX. Calhoun promised that he would be more transparent.[16]

In February of 2020, Boeing fired a midlevel executive in charge of pilots who exchanged internal emails that have embarrassed the company as it continued to struggle to get the 737 MAX flying again. Those email messages indicated that Boeing employees were mocking airline officials, aviation regulators and even their own colleagues. In one of the emails, an employee said the 7637 MAX had been "designed by clowns, who in turn are supervised by monkeys."[17]

Boeing's Dilemma

Boeing reported a loss of $1 billion in the fourth quarter of 2019 as revenue plunged 37 percent due to the grounding of the MAX (see Exhibit 3 entitled "Summary Financial Results for the Fourth Quarter of 2018 and 2019" and Exhibit 4 entitled "Commercial Airplane Deliveries in the Fourth Quarter of 2018 and 2019.") The company suspended deliveries of the plane in the early spring of 2019 and had speculated that deliveries would have been restarted by the end of the year. The company lost $636 million for all of 2019. This compared to a profit of nearly $10.5 billion in 2018. This was the first loss the company had experienced since 1997 when they were hit by parts shortages, production delays and expenses occasioned by their merger with McDonnell Douglas.[18]

The Board of Directors had to deal with the bad publicity that the company had received and the loss in revenue for the past year. Some observers speculated that it might take a rebranding of the MAX to recover the valued name of the company. Others suggested that an even more desperate act of dropping the MAX was in order. This was the dilemma the Boeing Board faced during the first quarter of 2020. There were even some observers who wondered if the coverup of the difficulties with the MCAS system might be tantamount to fraud.

EXHIBIT 3   Summary Financial Results for the Boeing, Fourth Quarter 2018 and Fourth Quarter 2019 (In millions except for share data)

	2019	2018
Revenues	$17,911	$28,341
GAAP		
(Loss) Earnings from Operations	($ 2,204)	$ 4,175
Operating Margin	(12.3)%	14.7%
Net (Loss)/Earnings	($ 1,010)	$ 3,424
(Loss)/Earnings Per Share	($ 1.79)	$ 5.93
Operating Cash Flow	($ 2,220)	$ 2,947

Source: Boeing Web Site. https://www.boeing.com

EXHIBIT 4   Commercial Airplane Deliveries in the Fourth Quarter 2018 and 2019 (Dollars in Millions)

	2019	2018
Commercial Airplane Deliveries	238	79
Revenues	$16,531	$ 7,462
(Loss)/Earnings from Operations	$ 2,600	($2,844)
Operating Margin	15.7%	(38.1)%

Source: Boeing Web Site. https://www.boeing.com

ENDNOTES

[1] German, K. (January 8, 2020). As Boeing CEO is fired, it's unclear when the 737 MAX will fly again, *CNET.* https://www.cnet.com/news/boeing-737-max-8-all-about-the-aircraft-flight-ban-and-investigations/.
[2] Boeing's website. http://www.boeing.com
[3] Boeing website. http://www.boeing.com
[4] Boeing website. http://www.boeing.com
[5] Boeing website. http://www.boeing.com
[6] Boeing website. http://www.boeing.com
[7] IBISWorld.Com. https://www.ibisworld.com
[8] Hamby, C. (January 21, 2020). How Boeing's responsibility in a deadly crash "got buried," *The New York Times.*

https://www.nytimes.com/2020/01/20/business/boeing-737-accidents.html.
[9] German, K. (January 8, 2020). As Boeing CEO is fired, it's unclear when the 737 Max will fly again. https://www.cnet.com/news/737-max-8-all-about-the-aircraft-flight-ban-ande-investigations/.
[10] Ibid.
[11] Hamby, C. (January 21, 2020). How Boeing's responsibility in a deadly crash "got buried," *The New York Times.* https://www.nytimes.com/2020/01/20/business/boeing-737-accidents.html.
[12] German, K. (January 8, 2020). As Boeing CEO is fired, it's unclear when the 737 Max will

fly again, *CNET.* https://www.cnet.com/news/boeing-737-max-8-all-about-the-aircraft-flight-ban-and-investigations/
[13] Ibid.
[14] Ibid.
[15] Ibid.
[16] Koenig, D. (January 30, 2020). Boeing posts 1st annual loss in 2 decades, *Waco Tribune-Herald.*
[17] Tangel, A. and Pasztor, A. (February 14, 2020). Boeing fired midlevel executive following embarrassing emails, *Wall Street Journal.*
[18] Ibid.

The Walt Disney Company: Its Diversification Strategy in 2020

John E. Gamble

Texas A&M University-Corpus Christi

The Walt Disney Company was a broadly diversified media and entertainment company with a business lineup that included theme parks and resorts, motion picture production and distribution, cable television networks, the ABC broadcast television network, eight local television stations, and a variety of other businesses that exploited the company's intellectual property. The company's revenues had increased from approximately $52.5 billion in fiscal 2015 to approximately $62.6 billion in fiscal 2019 and its share price had regularly outperformed the S&P 500. While struggling somewhat in the mid-1980s, the company's performance had been commendable in almost every year since Walt Disney created Mickey Mouse in 1928.

Much of the company's growth in revenues had resulted from acquisitions of leading motion picture production companies. In 2006, the Walt Disney Company completed the $7.4 billion acquisition of Pixar, the producer of *Toy Story*—the highest grossing film of 1995. In 2009, Disney acquired Marvel Entertainment for $4.2 billion, which had produced highly successful *Iron Man, Spider-Man,* and *Incredible Hulk* films. Walt Disney acquired Lucasfilm in 2012 in a $4 billion cash and stock transaction. Lucasfilm was founded by George Lucas and was best known for its *Star Wars* motion picture franchise. However, the company's 2019 acquisition of 21st Century Fox for $71.3 billion in cash and stock had the potential to radically improve its future financial performance.

The acquisition of 21st Century Fox extended Disney's impressive collection of media franchises to include 20th Century Fox, FX, National Geographic Channel, and Star India. Twenty-First Century Fox also held a 30 percent ownership interest in Hulu and a 39.1 percent stake in Sky, Europe's leading entertainment company that served nearly 23 million households in five countries. The Fox broadcast network, 29 local television stations, Fox News, and Fox Sports were not included in the merger and make up a new independent, public company named Fox Corporation.

Disney CEO Robert Iger commented on the ability of the acquisition to further boost shareholder value.

> The acquisition of 21st Century Fox will bring significant financial value to Disney and the shareholders of both companies, and after six months of integration planning we're even more enthusiastic and confident in the strategic fit of these complementary assets and the talent at Fox.
>
> The combination of Disney and 21st Century Fox is an extremely compelling proposition for consumers. It will allow us to create even more appealing high-quality content, expand our direct-to-consumer offerings and international presence, and deliver more exciting and personalized entertainment experiences to meet the growing demands of consumers worldwide.[1]

Just weeks after releasing impressive first quarter fiscal 2020 results for the combined company, Walt Disney Company announced the retirement of CEO Bob Iger—the architect of the series of acquisitions that had compounded the company's revenues and drove shareholder value for nearly 15 years. The February 25, 2020 announcement stated that Mr. Iger would remain Executive Chairman and direct the company's creative endeavors through 2021, with Mr. Bob

Chapek becoming the Walt Disney Company's seventh CEO. Mr. Chapek, a 27-year veteran of the company had most recently held the title of Chairman of Disney Parks, Experiences, and Products and would not only be required to fully integrate the 21st Century Fox creative assets and operations into the Disney organization, but would also have to contend with the effects of the novel Coronavirus (COVID-19), which were just becoming known to the world.

COMPANY HISTORY

Walt Disney's venture into animation began in 1919 when he returned to the United States from France, where he had volunteered to be an ambulance driver for the American Red Cross during World War I. Disney volunteered for the American Red Cross only after being told he was too young to enlist for the United States Army. Upon returning after the war, Disney settled in Kansas City, Missouri, and found work as an animator for Pesman Art Studio. Disney, and fellow Pesman animator, Ub Iwerks, soon left the company to found Iwerks-Disney Commercial Artists in 1920. The company lasted only briefly, but Iwerks and Disney were both able to find employment with a Kansas City company that produced short animated advertisements for local movie theaters. Disney left his job again in 1922 to found Laugh-O-Grams, where he employed Iwerks and three other animators to produce short animated cartoons. Laugh-O-Grams was able to sell its short cartoons to local Kansas City movie theaters, but its costs far exceeded its revenues—forcing Disney to declare bankruptcy in 1923. Having exhausted his savings, Disney had only enough cash to purchase a one-way train ticket to Hollywood, California, where his brother, Roy, had offered a temporary room. Once in California, Roy began to look for buyers for a finished animated-live action film he retained from Laugh-O-Grams. The film was never distributed, but New York distributors Margaret Winkler and Charles Mintz were impressed enough with the short film that they granted Disney a contract in October 1923 to produce a series of short films that blended cartoon animation with live action motion picture photography. Disney brought Ub Iwerks from Kansas City to Hollywood to work with Disney Brothers Studio (later to be named Walt Disney Productions) to produce the Alice Comedies series that would number 50-plus films by the series end in 1927. Disney followed the Alice Comedies series with a new animated cartoon for Universal Studios. After Disney's *Oswald the Lucky Rabbit* cartoons quickly became a hit, Universal terminated Disney Brothers Studio and hired most of Disney's animators to continue producing the cartoon.

In 1928, Disney and Iwerks created Mickey Mouse to replace Oswald as the feature character in Walt Disney Studios cartoons. Unlike with Oswald, Disney retained all rights over Mickey Mouse and all subsequent Disney characters. Mickey Mouse and his girlfriend, Minnie Mouse, made their cartoon debuts later in 1928 in the cartoons, *Plane Crazy, The Gallopin' Gaucho,* and *Steamboat Willie. Steamboat Willie* was the first cartoon with synchronized sound and became one of the most famous short films of all time. The animated film's historical importance was recognized in 1998 when it was added to the National Film Registry by the United States Library of Congress. Mickey Mouse's popularity exploded over the next few decades with a Mickey Mouse Club being created in 1929, new accompanying characters such as Pluto, Goofy, Donald Duck, and Daisy Duck being added to Mickey Mouse cartoon storylines, and Mickey Mouse appearing in Walt Disney's 1940 feature length film, *Fantasia*. Mickey Mouse's universal appeal reversed Walt Disney's series of failures in the animated film industry and became known as the mascot of Disney Studios, Walt Disney Productions, and The Walt Disney Company.

The success of The Walt Disney Company was sparked by Mickey Mouse, but Disney Studios also produced several other highly successful animated feature films including *Snow White and the Seven Dwarfs* in 1937, *Pinocchio* in 1940, *Dumbo* in 1941, *Bambi* in 1942, *Song of the South* in 1946, *Cinderella* in 1950, *Treasure Island* in 1950, *Peter Pan* in 1953, *Sleeping Beauty* in 1959, and *One Hundred-One Dalmatians* in 1961. What would prove to be Disney's greatest achievement began to emerge in 1954 when construction began on his Disneyland Park in Anaheim, California. Walt Disney's Disneyland resulted from an idea that Disney had many years earlier while sitting on an amusement park bench watching his young daughters play. Walt Disney thought that there should be a clean and safe park that had attractions that both parents and children alike would find entertaining. Walt Disney spent years planning the park and announced the construction of the new park to America on his *Disneyland* television show that was launched to promote the new $17 million park. The park was an instant success when it opened in 1955 and recorded revenues of more than $10 million during its first year of operation. After the success of Disneyland, Walt Disney began looking for a site in the eastern United States for a second Disney park. He settled on an area near Orlando, Florida in 1963 and acquired more than 27,000 acres for the new park by 1965.

Walt Disney died of lung cancer in 1966, but upon his death, Roy O. Disney postponed retirement to become president and CEO of Walt Disney Productions and oversee the development of Walt Disney World Resort. Walt Disney World Resort opened in October 1971—only two months before Roy O. Disney's death in December 1971. The company was led by Donn Tatum from 1971 to 1976. Tatum had been with Walt Disney Productions since 1956 and led the further development of Walt Disney World Resort and began the planning of EPCOT in Orlando and Tokyo Disneyland. Those two parks were opened during the tenure of Esmond Cardon Walker, who had been an executive at the company since 1956 and chief operating officer since Walt Disney's death in 1966. Walker also launched The Disney Channel before his retirement in 1983. Walt Disney Productions was briefly led by Ronald Miller, who was the son-in-law of Walt Disney. Miller was ineffective as Disney chief executive officer and was replaced by Michael Eisner in 1984.

Eisner formulated and oversaw the implementation of a bold strategy for Walt Disney Studios, which included the acquisitions of ABC, ESPN, Miramax Films, and the Anaheim Angels, and the Fox Family Channel; the development of Disneyland Paris, Disney-MGM Studios in Orlando, Disney California Adventure Park, Walt Disney Studios theme park in France, and Hong Kong Disneyland; and the launch of the Disney Cruise Line, the Disney Interactive game division, and the Disney Store retail chain. Eisner also restored the company's reputation for blockbuster animated feature films with the creation of *The Little Mermaid* in 1989, and *Beauty and the Beast* and *The Lion King* in 1994. Despite Eisner's successes, his tendencies toward micromanagement and skirting board approval for many of his initiatives and his involvement in a long-running derivatives suit led to his removal as chairman in 2004 and his resignation in 2005.

The Walt Disney Company's CEO in 2018, Robert (Bob) Iger, became a Disney employee in 1996 when the company acquired ABC. Iger was president and CEO of ABC at the time of its acquisition by The Walt Disney Company and remained in that position until made president of Walt Disney International by Alan Eisner in 1999. Bob Iger was promoted to president and chief operating officer of The Walt Disney Company in 2000 and was named as Eisner's replacement as CEO in 2005. Iger's first strategic moves in 2006 included the $7.4 billion acquisition of Pixar animation studios and the purchase of the rights to Disney's first cartoon character, Oswald the Lucky Rabbit, from NBCUniversal. In 2007, Robert Iger commissioned two new 340-meter ships for the Disney Cruise Lines that would double its fleet size from two ships to four. The new ships ordered by Iger were 40 percent larger than Disney's two older vessels and entered service in 2011 and 2012. Iger also engineered the $4.2 billion acquisition of Marvel Entertainment in 2009 that would enable the Disney production motion pictures featuring Marvel comic book characters such as Iron Man, Incredible Hulk, Thor, Spider-Man, and Captain America. In 2012, Walt Disney acquired Lucasfilm in a $4 billion cash and stock transaction. Lucasfilm was founded by George Lucas and was best known for its *Star Wars* motion picture franchise. The $71.3 billion acquisition of 21st Century Fox in 2019 was Iger's most ambitious merger and would create tremendous market expansion opportunities and difficult integration challenges.

Bob Chapek became The Walt Disney Company's seventh CEO on February 25, 2020. Chapek had been a Disney employee for 27 years and produced strong results in several of the company's businesses, including its Theme Parks, Disney Resorts, Consumer Products, and Walt Disney Studios Home Entertainment. His most recent position prior to being named CEO was serving as Chairman of the Parks, Experiences and Products since the segment's creation in 2018 and as Chairman of its predecessor, Parks and Resorts, since 2015. Among the most notable accomplishments of Bob Chapek was overseeing the opening of Shanghai Disney Resort, the creation of *Start Wars: Galaxy's Edge* lands at Disneyland and Walt Disney World, the expansion of Disney Cruise Line with the construction of three new ships, and the addition of Marvel-themed attractions around the world.

A financial summary for The Walt Disney Company for 2015 through 2019 is provided in Exhibit 1. Exhibit 2 tracks the performance of The Walt Disney Company's common shares between March 2013 and March 29, 2020.

EXHIBIT 1   Financial Summary for The Walt Disney Company, Fiscal Years 2015–2019 (in millions)

	2019[1]	2018[2]	2017[3]	2016[4]	2015[5]
Statements of income					
Revenues	$ 69,570	$59,434	$55,137	$55,632	$52,465
Net income from continuing operations	10,913	13,066	9,366	9,790	8,852
Net income from continuing operations attributable to Disney	10,441	12,598	8,980	9,391	8,382
Per common share					
Earnings attributable to Disney					
Continuing Operations–Diluted	$ 6.27	$ 8.36	$ 5.69	$ 5.73	$ 4.90
Continuing Operations–Basic	6.30	8.40	5.73	5.76	4.95
Dividends (6)	1.76	1.68	1.56	1.42	1.81
Balance sheets					
Total assets	$193,984	$98,598	$95,789	$92,033	$88,182
Long-term obligations	60,852	24,797	26,710	24,189	19,142
Disney shareholders' equity	88,877	48,773	41,315	43,265	44,525
Statements of cash flows					
Cash provided (used) by - continuing operations:					
Operating activities	$ 5,984	$14,295	$12,343	$13,136	$11,385
Investing activities	(15,096)	(5,336)	(4,111)	(5,758)	(4,245)
Financing activities	(464)	(8,843)	(8,959)	(7,220)	(5,801)

(1) On March 20, 2019, the Company acquired TFCF for cash and Disney shares (see Note 4 to the Consolidated Financial Statements). TFCF and Hulu's financial results have been consolidated since the date of acquisition and had a number of adverse impacts on fiscal 2019 results, the most significant of which were amortization expense related to recognition of TFCF and Hulu intangible assets and fair value step-up on film and television costs ($0.74 per diluted share), an impact from shares issued upon the TFCF acquisition ($0.74 per diluted share), restructuring and impairment charges ($0.55 per diluted share) and TFCF and Hulu operating results ($0.27 per diluted share). Additional impacts included a non-cash gain from remeasuring our initial 30% interest in Hulu to fair value ($2.22 per diluted share), equity investment impairments ($0.25 per diluted share) and a charge for the extinguishment of a portion of the debt originally assumed in the TFCF acquisition ($0.24 per diluted share). Cash provided by continuing operating activities reflected payments for tax obligations that arose from the spin-off of Fox Corporation in connection with the TFCF acquisition and the sale of the RSNs acquired with TFCF and cash used in continuing investing activities reflected a cash payment of $35.7 billion paid to acquire TFCF, offset by the $25.7 billion in cash and cash equivalents assumed in the TFCF acquisition.

(2) Fiscal 2018 results include a net benefit from the Tax Act ($1.11 per diluted share) and the benefit from a reduction in the Company's fiscal 2018 U.S. federal statutory income tax rate ($0.75 per diluted share) (see Note 10 to the Consolidated Financial Statements). In addition, fiscal 2018 included gains on the sales of real estate and property rights ($0.28 per diluted share) and an adverse impact from equity investment impairments ($0.11 per diluted share).

(3) Fiscal 2017 results include a non-cash net gain in connection with the acquisition of a controlling interest in BAMTech ($0.10 per diluted share) (see Note 4 to the Consolidated Financial Statements).

(4) Fiscal 2016 results include the Company's share of a net gain recognized by A+E in connection with an acquisition of an interest in Vice ($0.13 per diluted share).

(5) Fiscal 2015 results include the write-off of a deferred tax asset as a result of a recapitalization at Disneyland Paris ($0.23 per diluted share).

(6) In fiscal 2015, the Company began paying dividends on a semiannual basis. Accordingly, fiscal 2015 includes dividend payments related to fiscal 2014 and the first half of fiscal 2015.

Source: The Walt Disney Company 2019 10-K.

EXHIBIT 2   Performance of The Walt Disney Company's Stock Price, March 2013 to March 29, 2020

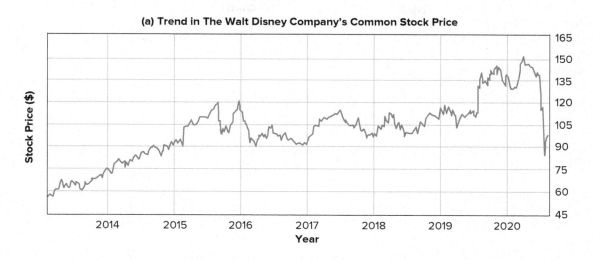

(a) Trend in The Walt Disney Company's Common Stock Price

(b) Performance of The Walt Disney Company's Stock Price Versus the S&P 500 Index

Source: Bigcharts.com

THE WALT DISNEY COMPANY'S CORPORATE STRATEGY AND BUSINESS OPERATIONS IN 2020

In 2020, The Walt Disney Company was broadly diversified into theme parks, hotels and resorts, cruise ships, cable networks, broadcast television networks, television production, television station operations, live action and animated motion picture production and distribution, music publishing, live theatrical productions, children's book publishing, interactive media, and consumer products retailing. The company's corporate strategy was centered on (1) creating high-quality content, (2) exploiting technological innovations to make entertainment experiences more memorable, and (3) international expansion. The company's 2006 acquisition of Pixar and 2009 acquisition of Marvel were executed to enhance the resources and capabilities of its core animation business with the addition of new animation skills and characters. The company's 2011 acquisition of UTV was engineered to facilitate its international expansion efforts. The acquisition of Lucasfilm's *Star Wars* franchise in 2012 not only allowed the company to produce new films in the series, but integrate *Star Wars* into its other business units, including theme park attractions. The company's 2019 acquisition of 21st Century Fox was made to further expand Disney's portfolio of high-quality branded content with new cable channels such as National Geographic, FX and accelerate its direct-to-consumer (DTC) strategy by giving the company a 60 percent controlling interest in Hulu. Hulu was made the official streaming service for FX Networks in 2020.

Disney's corporate strategy also called for sufficient capital to be allocated to its core theme parks and resorts business to sustain its advantage in the industry. The company expanded the range of attractions at its theme parks with billion-dollar plus additions such as its new *Toy Story* Land attractions opened in 2018 at Shanghai Disneyland and Disney's Hollywood Studios and its *Star Wars* Land opened in Disney's Hollywood Studios and Anaheim's Disneyland in 2019. Expansions were also underway at Tokyo Disney Resort and Hong Kong Disneyland.

The Walt Disney Company's corporate strategy also attempted to capture synergies existing between its business units. Two of the company's highest grossing films, *Pirates of the Caribbean: On Stranger Tides* and *Cars 2* were also featured at the company's Florida and California theme parks. The company had leveraged ESPN's reputation in sports by building 230-acre ESPN Wide World of Sports Complex in Orlando that could host amateur and professional events and boost occupancy in its 18 resort hotels and vacation clubs located at the Walt Disney World resort.

In 2020, the company's business units were organized into four divisions: Parks, Experiences and Products, Media Networks, Direct-to-Consumer & International, and Studio Entertainment.

Parks, Experiences and Products

The Walt Disney Company's parks and resorts division included the Walt Disney World Resort in Orlando, the Disneyland Resort in California, Disneyland Paris, the Aulani Disney Resort and Spa in Hawaii, the Disney Vacation Club, the Disney Cruise Line, and Adventures by Disney. The company also owned a 47 percent interest in Hong Kong Disneyland Resort and a 43 percent interest in Shanghai Disney Resort. Disney also licensed the operation of Tokyo Disney Resort in Japan. Revenue for the division was primarily generated through park admission fees, hotel room charges, merchandise sales, food and beverage sales, sales and rentals of vacation club properties, and fees charged for cruise vacations.

Revenues from hotel lodgings and food and beverage sales were a sizeable portion of the division's revenues. For example, at the 25,000-acre Walt Disney World Resort alone, the company operated 18 resort hotels with approximately 22,000 rooms. Walt Disney World Resort also included the 127-acre Disney Springs retail, dining, and entertainment complex where visitors could dine and shop during or after park hours. Walt Disney World Resort in Orlando also included four championship golf courses, full-service spas, tennis, sailing, water skiing, two water parks, and a 230-acre sports complex that was host to over 200 amateur and professional events each year. In 2019, Disney announced plans to build a *Star Wars*-themed hotel at Walt Disney World Resort.

Walt Disney's 486-acre resort in California included two theme parks—Disneyland and Disney California Adventure—along with three hotels and its Downtown Disney retail, dining, and entertainment complex. Disney California Adventure was opened in 2001 adjacent to the Disneyland property and included four lands—Golden State, Hollywood Pictures Backlot, Paradise Pier, and Bug's Land. The park was initially built to alleviate overcrowding at Disneyland and was expanded with the addition of World of Color in 2010 and Cars Land in 2012 to strengthen its appeal with guests.

Aulani was a 21-acre oceanfront family resort located in Oahu, Hawaii. Disneyland Paris included two theme parks, seven resort hotels, two convention centers, a 27-hole golf course, and a shopping, dining, and entertainment complex. The company's Hong Kong Disneyland, Shanghai Disney Resort, and Tokyo Disney Resort them parks were highly popular with ambitious expansion plans.

The company also offered timeshare sales and rentals in 15 resort facilities through its Disney Vacation Club. The Disney Cruise Line operated four ships out of North America and Europe. Disney's cruise activities were developed to appeal to the interests of children and families. Its Port Canaveral cruises included a visit to Disney's Castaway Cay, a 1,000-acre private island in the Bahamas. The popularity of Disney's cruise vacations allowed its fleet to be booked to full capacity year-round.

The company's consumer products division included the company's Disney Store retail chain and businesses specializing in merchandise licensing and children's book and magazine publishing. In 2020, the company owned and operated approximately 200 Disney Stores in North America, approximately 80 stores in Europe, approximately 50 stores in Japan, and two stores in China. Its publishing business included comic books, various children's book magazine titles available in print and eBook format, and smartphone and tablet computer apps designed for children. The division's sales were primarily affected by seasonal shopping trends and changes in consumer disposable income.

The division's operating results for fiscal years 2018 and 2019 are presented in Exhibit 3.

EXHIBIT 3   Operating Results for Walt Disney's Parks, Experiences and Products Business Unit, Fiscal Years 2018–2019 (in millions)

	2019	2018
Revenues		
Theme park admissions	$7,183	$6,504
Parks & Experiences merchandise, food and beverage	5,674	5,154
Resorts and vacations	5,938	5,378
Merchandise licensing and retail	4,249	4,494
Parks licensing and other	1,657	1,494
Total revenues	24,701	23,024
Operating expenses	13,326	12,455
Selling, general, administrative and other	2,930	2,896
Depreciation and amortization	2,327	2,161
Equity in the loss of investees	23	25
Operating Income	$6,095	$5,487

Source: The Walt Disney Company 2019 10-K.

Media Networks

The Walt Disney Company's media networks business unit included its domestic and international cable networks, the ABC television network, television production, and U.S. domestic television stations. The company's television production was limited to television programming for ABC and its eight local television stations were all ABC affiliates. Six of Disney's eight domestic television stations were located in the 10 largest U.S. television markets. In all, ABC had 240 affiliates in the United States.

When asked about the decline in cable television viewership, Bob Iger suggested that content delivery method was less important than the quality and appeal of content.

Well, for the most part, we've looked at channels less as channels and more as brands. And it's less important to us how people get those channels. . .but what's more important to us is the quality of the brand and intellectual property that fits under that brand umbrella. And our intention is to. . .migrate those brands and those products in the more modern direction from a distribution and consumption perspective.[2]

Exhibit 4 provides the market ranking for Disney's local stations and its number of subscribers and ownership percentage of its cable networks for 2013, 2017, and 2019. The exhibit also provides a brief description of its ABC broadcasting and television production operations. The division also included ESPN Radio, which aired sports-oriented radio programming on 400 terrestrial radio stations (4 of which were owned by Disney) in the United States. Operating results for Disney's media networks division for fiscal 2015 through fiscal 2019 are presented in Exhibit 5.

EXHIBIT 4   The Walt Disney Company's Media Network Subscribers, 2013, 2017, and 2019 (in millions)

Cable Networks	Estimated Subscribers (in millions)[1] 2013	Estimated Subscribers (in millions)[1] 2017	Estimated Subscribers (in millions)[1] 2019
ESPN			
ESPN	99	88	83
ESPN–International	n.a.	146	65
ESPN2	99	87	83
ESPNU	72	67	61
ESPNEWS	73	66	58
SEC Network[2]	n.a.	60	59
Disney Channels Worldwide			
Disney Channel–Domestic	99	92	86
Disney Channels–International[3]	141	221	227
Disney Junior–Domestic	58	72	66
Disney Junior–International[3]	n.a.	151	162
Disney XD–Domestic	78	74	68
Disney XD–International[3]	91	127	65
Freeform	n.a.	90	85
Fox			
FX	n.a.	n.a.	87
FXM	n.a.	n.a.	56
FXX	n.a.	n.a.	84
Fox International	n.a.	n.a.	220
National Geographic			
National Geographic–Domestic	n.a.	n.a.	86
National Geographic Wild	n.a.	n.a.	59
National Geographic - International	n.a.	n.a.	316
Star	n.a.	n.a.	221
A+E and Vice			
A&E	99	91	85
Lifetime	99	91	85
HISTORY	99	92	86
Lifetime Movie Network	82	73	63
FYI	n.a.	58	51
Viceland	n.a.	70	64

Broadcasting
ABC Television Network (240 local affiliates reaching nearly 100 percent of U.S. television households)

Television Production
ABC Studios, Twentieth Century Fox Television (TCFTV) and Fox 21 Television Studios (Fox21) (Daytime, primetime, late night and news television programming)

Domestic Television Stations		
Market	TV Station	Television Market Ranking[3]
New York, NY	WABC-TV	1
Los Angeles, CA	KABC-TV	2
Chicago, IL	WLS-TV	3
Philadelphia, PA	WPVI-TV	4
Houston, TX	KTRK-TV	7
San Francisco, CA	KGO-TV	8
Raleigh-Durham, NC	WTVD-TV	25
Fresno, CA	KFSN-TV	54

(1) Estimated U.S. subscriber counts according to Nielsen Media Research, except as noted below.

(2) Because Nielsen Media Research does not measure this channel, estimated subscribers are according to SNL Kagan.

(3) Based on Nielsen Media Research, U.S. Television Household Estimates, January 1, 2019.

Source: The Walt Disney Company 2019 10-K.

EXHIBIT 5   Operating Results for Walt Disney's Media Networks Business Unit, Fiscal Years 2015–2019 (in millions)

Revenues	2019	2018	2017	2016	2015
Affiliate fees	$11,907	$11,324	$12,659	$12,259	$12,029
Advertising	6,586	6,938	8,129	8,509	8,361
TV/SVOD distribution and other	3,429	3,037	2,722	2,921	2,874
Total revenues	21,922	21,299	23,510	23,689	23,264
Operating expenses	13,197	12,754	14,068	13,571	13,150
Selling, general, administrative and other	1,899	1,909	2,647	2,705	2,869
Depreciation and amortization	199	206	237	255	266
Equity in the income of investees	(711)	(766)	(344)	(597)	(814)
Operating Income	$ 7,338	$ 7,196	$ 6,902	$ 7,755	$ 7,793

Source: The Walt Disney Company 2017 and 2019 10-Ks.

Direct-to-Consumer & International

Among the most significant challenges to Disney's media networks division was the competition for viewers, which impacted advertising rates and revenues. Not only did the company compete against other broadcasters and cable networks for viewers, but it also competed against other types of entertainment and delivery platforms. For example, consumers might prefer to watch videos, movies, or other content on the Internet or Internet streaming services rather than watch cable or broadcast television. The effect of the Internet on broadcast news had been significant and the growth of streaming services had the potential to affect the advertising revenue potential of all of Disney's media businesses.

The combat competing streaming content providers and capitalize on such opportunities, Disney launched two direct-to-consumer (DTC) streaming services and Over-the-Top (OTT) services that delivered content without a distributor. Disney's ESPN+ DTC video streaming service was launched in 2018 and its Disney+ DTC subscription service that included Disney, Pixar, Marvel, Star Wars, and National Geographic branded programming was launched in the United States and four other countries in 2019. Within its first year, ESPN+ had attracted more than 3.5 million paid subscribers. The company expected Disney+ to also have strong appeal with media consumers and intended to launch Disney+ in additional countries in 2020 through 2024.

Disney+ users would have immediate access to 500 movies and 7,500 episodes of television content. Disney+ also launched with 10 original movies, and the company planned to increase Disney+ content to include 630 movies and 10,000 television episodes by 2024. Disney also planned to add 60 original series, specials and movies each year to the Disney+ library by 2024. Programming was priced at $6.99 per month for Disney+ or ESPN+ or at a $12.99 bundle price that included both DTC subscription services and ad-supported Hulu.

The company's acquisition of a controlling interest in Hulu was an integral component of its overall DTC strategy, both domestically and internationally. Hulu was planned as the official streaming service for all FX Networks programming as well as supporting ESPN+ and Disney+.

The company's international channels produced local programs or delivered Disney produced content to cable providers operating in countries throughout the world. Disney branded television channels were broadcasted in approximately 35 languages in 165 countries. Fox programming was broadcasted in 40 languages in 95 countries. National Geographic was available in 80 countries, while ESPN programming was available in 15 countries outside the United States. Star operated approximately 80 channels in ten languages in India, Asia, the United Kingdom, Europe, the Middle East, and parts of Africa. The division also operated UTC, Bindass and Hungama branded channels in India. Operating results for Disney's Direct-to-Consumer & International division for fiscal year 2018 and 2019 are presented in Exhibit 6.

Studio Entertainment

The Walt Disney Company's studio entertainment division produced live-action and animated motion pictures, direct-to-video content, musical recordings, and *Disney on Ice* and *Disney Live!* live performances. The division's motion pictures were produced and distributed under Walt Disney Pictures, 20th Century Fox, Pixar, Marvel, Lucasfilm, Fox Searchlight Pictures, and Blue Sky Studios banners. The division planned to release approximately 25 feature films in 2020 had Disney produced more than 1,000 feature films and 100 full-length animated films throughout its history. The company's complete library of Disney-produced and acquired films stood at 2,300 titles as of September 2019. Disney's most financially successful films in 2019 included *The Lion King, Toy Story 4, Frozen 2, Star Wars: The Rise of Skywalker,* and *Aladdin.* The company's largest grossing films in 2018 were the *Incredibles 2* and *Ant-Man and the Wasp.* All of the company's best-grossing films in both years were either remakes or sequels of previous Disney, Lucasfilm, or Marvel blockbusters.

Most motion pictures typically incurred losses during the theatrical distribution of the film because

EXHIBIT 6   Operating Results for Walt Disney's Direct-to-Consumer & International Business Unit, Fiscal Years 2018–2019 (in millions)

	2019	2018
Revenues		
Affiliate fees	$1,372	$1,335
Advertising	1,311	1,293
Subscription fees and other	731	447
Total revenues	3,414	3,075
Operating expenses	2,384	1,983
Selling, general, administrative and other	1,003	861
Depreciation and amortization	185	94
Equity in the income of investees	580	421
Operating Income	$ (738)	$ (284)

Source: The Walt Disney Company 2019 10-K.

of production costs and the cost of extensive advertising campaigns accompanying the launch of the film. Profits for many films did not occur until the movie became available on DVD or Blu-Ray disks for home entertainment, which usually began three to six months after the film's theatrical release. Revenue was also generated when a movie moved to pay-per-view (PPV)/video-on-demand (VOD) two months after the release of the DVD and when the motion picture became available on subscription premium cable channels such as HBO about 16 months after PPV/VOD availability. Broadcast networks such as ABC could purchase telecast rights to movies later as could basic cable channels such as Lifetime or the Hallmark Channel. Premium cable

channels such as Showtime and Starz might also purchase telecast rights to movies long after its theatrical release. Similarly, subscription video on demand (SVOD) services such as Netflix might acquire distribution rights to a film for a 12- to 19-month window. Telecast right fees decreased as the length of time from initial release increased. Operating results for the Walt Disney Company's Studio Entertainment division for fiscal 2015 through fiscal 2019 are produced in Exhibit 7.

The company's consolidated statements of income for fiscal 2017 through fiscal 2019 are presented in Exhibit 8. The Walt Disney Company's balance sheets for fiscal 2018 and fiscal 2019 are presented in Exhibit 9.

EXHIBIT 7   Operating Results for Walt Disney's Studio Entertainment Business Unit, Fiscal Years 2015–2019 (in millions)

	2019	2018	2017	2016	2015
Revenues					
Theatrical distribution	4,726	$4,303	$2,903	$3,672	$2,321
Home entertainment	1,734	1,647	1,798	2,108	1,799
TV/SVOD distribution and other	4,667	4,115	3,678	3,661	3,246
Total revenues	11,127	10,065	8,379	9,441	7,366
Operating expenses	5,187	4,449	3,667	3,991	3,050
Selling, general, administrative and other	3,119	2,493	2,242	2,622	2,204
Depreciation and amortization	135	119	115	125	139
Operating Income	$2,686	$3,004	$2,355	$2,703	$1,973

Source: The Walt Disney Company 2017 and 2019 10-Ks.

EXHIBIT 8   Consolidated Statements of Income for The Walt Disney Company, Fiscal Years 2017–2019 (in millions, except per share data)

	2019	2018	2017
Revenues			
Services	$60,542	$50,869	$46,843
Products	9,028	8,565	8,294
Total revenues	69,570	59,434	55,137
Costs and expenses:			
Cost of services (exclusive of depreciation and amortization)	36,450	27,528	25,320
Cost of products (exclusive of depreciation and amortization)	5,568	5,198	4,986
Selling, general, administrative and other	11,541	8,860	8,176
Depreciation and amortization	4,160	3,011	2,782
Total costs and expenses	57,719	(4,597)	41,264

	2019	2018	2017
Restructuring and impairment charges	1,183	33	98
Other income, net	4,357	601	78
Interest expense, net	978	574	385
Equity in the income (loss) of investees, net	(103)	(102)	320
Income from continuing operations before income taxes	13,944	14,729	13,788
Income taxes from continuing operations	3,031	1,663	4,422
Net income from continuing operations	10,913	13,066	9,366
Income from discontinued operations (includes income tax expense of $35, $0 and $0, respectively)	671	—	—
Net income	11,584	13,066	9,366
Less: Net income from continuing operations attributable to noncontrolling and redeemable noncontrolling interests	472	468	386
Less: Net income from discontinued operations attributable to noncontrolling interests	58	—	—
Net income attributable to Disney	$11,054	$12,598	$ 8,980
Earnings per share attributable to Disney:			
Diluted			
Continuing operations	$ 6.27	$ 8.36	$ 5.69
Discontinued operations	0.37	—	—
	$ 6.64	$ 8.36	$ 5.69
Basic			
Continuing operations	$ 6.30	$ 8.40	$ 5.73
Discontinued operations	0.37	—	—
	$ 6.68	$ 8.40	$ 5.73
Weighted average number of common and common equivalent shares outstanding:			
Diluted	1,666	1,507	1,578
Basic	1,656	1,499	1,568

Source: The Walt Disney Company 2019 10-K.

EXHIBIT 9   Consolidated Balance Sheets for The Walt Disney Company, Fiscal Years 2018 and 2019 (in millions, except per share data)

	September 28, 2019	September 29, 2018
ASSETS		
Current assets		
Cash and cash equivalents	$ 5,418	$ 4,150
Receivables	15,481	9,334
Inventories	1,649	1,392
Television costs and advances	4,597	1,314
Other current assets	979	635
Total current assets	28,124	16,825
Film and television costs	22,810	7,888
Investments	3,224	2,899

	September 28, 2019	September 29, 2018
Parks, resorts and other property		
Attractions, buildings and equipment	58,589	55,238
Accumulated depreciation	(32,415)	(30,764)
	26,174	24,474
Projects in progress	4,264	3,942
Land	1,165	1,124
	31,603	29,540
Intangible assets, net	23,215	6,812
Goodwill	80,293	31,269
Other assets	4,715	3,365
Total assets	$193,984	$98,598
LIABILITIES AND EQUITY		
Current liabilities		
Accounts payable and other accrued liabilities	$ 17,762	$ 9,479
Current portion of borrowings	8,857	3,790
Deferred revenue and other	4,722	4,591
Total current liabilities	31,341	17,860
Borrowings	38,129	17,084
Deferred income taxes	7,902	3,109
Other long-term liabilities	13,760	6,590
Commitments and contingencies		
Redeemable noncontrolling interests	8,963	1,123
Equity		
Preferred stock	—	—
Common stock, $.01 par value, Authorized—4.6 billion shares, Issued—1.8 billion shares at September 28, 2019 and 2.9 billion shares at September 29, 2018	53,907	36,779
Retained earnings	42,494	82,679
Accumulated other comprehensive loss	(6,617)	(3,097)
Treasury stock, at cost, 19 million shares at September 28, 2019 and 1.4 billion shares at September 29, 2018	(907)	(67,588)
Total Disney Shareholders' equity	88,877	48,773
Noncontrolling interests	5,012	4,059
Total equity	93,889	52,832
Total liabilities and equity	$193,984	$98,598

Source: The Walt Disney Company 2019 10-K.

UNCERTAINTY AS THE WALT DISNEY COMPANY ENTERS THE SECOND HALF OF 2020

The Walt Disney Company reported a revenue increase of 29 percent during its first six months of 2020 compared to the same period in 2019. However, the company's earnings per share experienced a 73 percent year-over-year decline during the first six months of 2020. The company's strong revenue growth was a result of the inclusion of 21st Century Fox business units into the company's financial reports, but the steep 73 percent decline in EPS signaled the difficulty of the effective integration of Fox businesses into the Disney organization.

The dramatic decline in net income from operations from $8.2 billion for the six months ending March 30, 2019 to $2.6 billion for the six months ending March 28, 2020, also reflected the early costs of the novel coronavirus pandemic on the company.

The greatest impact of COVID-19 on the company's divisions occurred in its Parks, Experiences and Products division, which saw a year-over-year declines in Q1 2020 revenue and operating income of 10 percent and 58 percent, respectively. Disney had closed its domestic parks and resorts, cruise line business and Disneyland Paris in mid-March 2020. The company's theme parks and resorts in Asia were closed earlier in 2020. The company estimated that approximately $1 billion of the company's operating profit decline could be attributed to the company's necessary response to the pandemic. A summary of The Walt Disney Company's second quarter revenue and operating income by division for Fiscal 2019 and Fiscal 2020 is presented in Exhibit 10.

Walt Disney Company CEO Bob Chapek, commented on the Company's Q2 2020 performance and its long-term prospects as it entered the second half of Fiscal 2020.

> While the COVID-19 pandemic has had an appreciable financial impact on a number of our businesses, we are confident in our ability to withstand this disruption and emerge from it in a strong position. Disney has repeatedly shown that it is exceptionally resilient, bolstered by the quality of our storytelling and the strong affinity consumers have for our brands.[3]

EXHIBIT 10 Revenues and Operating Income by Division for The Walt Disney Company, First Six Months 2019 and First Six Months 2020 (in millions, except per share data)

	Quarter Ended		Six Months Ended	
	March 28, 2020	March 30, 2019	March 28, 2020	March 30, 2019
Revenues				
Media Networks	$ 7,257	$ 5,683	$14,618	$11,604
Parks, Experiences and Products[1]	5,543	6,171	12,939	12,995
Studio Entertainment[1]	2,539	2,157	6,303	3,981
Direct-to-Consumer & International	4,123	1,145	8,110	2,063
Eliminations[2]	(1,453)	(234)	(3,103)	(418)
	$18,009	$14,922	$38,867	$30,225
Segment operating income (loss):				
Media Networks	$ 2,375	$ 2,230	$ 4,005	$ 3,560
Parks, Experiences and Products[1]	639	1,506	2,977	3,658
Studio Entertainment[1]	466	506	1,414	815
Direct-to-Consumer & International	(812)	(385)	(1,505)	(521)
Eliminations	(252)	(41)	(473)	(41)
	$ 2,416	$ 3,816	$ 6,418	$ 7,471

(1) The allocation of Parks, Experiences and Products revenues to Studio Entertainment was $117 million and $126 million for the quarters ended March 28, 2020 and March 30, 2019, respectively, and $301 million and $280 million for the six months ended March 28, 2020 and March 30, 2019, respectively.

Source: The Walt Disney Company Form 10-Q, March 28, 2020.

ENDNOTES

[1] As quoted by Bob Iger, Chairman and Chief Executive Officer of The Walt Disney Company, during Investor Conference Call, June 20, 2018.

[2] As quoted by Bob Iger, Chairman and Chief Executive Officer of The Walt Disney Company, during the Morgan Stanley Technology, Media and Telcom Conference, February 26, 2018.

[3] As quoted by Bob Chapek, Chief Executive Officer of The Walt Disney Company, "The Walt Disney Company Reports Secon Quarter and Six Months Earnings for Fiscal 2020," May 5, 2020.

Robin Hood

Mc Graw Hill connect

Joseph Lampel
Alliance Manchester Business School

It was in the spring of the second year of his insurrection against the High Sheriff of Nottingham that Robin Hood took a walk in Sherwood Forest. As he walked, he pondered the progress of the campaign, the disposition of his forces, the Sheriff's recent moves, and the options that confronted him.

The revolt against the Sheriff had begun as a personal crusade. It erupted out of Robin's conflict with the Sheriff and his administration. However, alone Robin Hood could do little. He therefore sought allies, men with grievances and a deep sense of justice. Later he welcomed all who came, asking few questions and demanding only a willingness to serve. Strength, he believed, lay in numbers.

He spent the first year forging the group into a disciplined band, united in enmity against the Sheriff and willing to live outside the law. The band's organization was simple. Robin ruled supreme, making all important decisions. He delegated specific tasks to his lieutenants. Will Scarlett was in charge of intelligence and scouting. His main job was to shadow the Sheriff and his men, always alert to their next move. He also collected information on the travel plans of rich merchants and tax collectors. Little John kept discipline among the men and saw to it that their archery was at the high peak that their profession demanded. Scarlett took care of the finances, converting loot to cash, paying shares of the take, and finding suitable hiding places for the surplus. Finally, Much the Miller's son had the difficult task of provisioning the ever-increasing band of Merry Men.

The increasing size of the band was a source of satisfaction for Robin, but also a source of concern. The fame of his Merry Men was spreading, and new recruits were pouring in from every corner of England. As the band grew larger, their small bivouac became a major encampment. Between raids the men milled about, talking and playing games. Vigilance was in decline, and discipline was becoming harder to enforce. "Why," Robin reflected, "I don't know half the men I run into these days."

The growing band was also beginning to exceed the food capacity of the forest. Game was becoming scarce, and supplies had to be obtained from outlying villages. The cost of buying food was beginning to drain the band's financial reserves at the very moment when revenues were in decline. Travelers, especially those with the most to lose, were now giving the forest a wide berth. This was costly and inconvenient to them, but it was preferable to having all their goods confiscated.

Robin believed that the time had come for the Merry Men to change their policy of outright confiscation of goods to one of a fixed transit tax. His lieutenants strongly resisted this idea. They were proud of the Merry Men's famous motto: "Rob the rich and give to the poor." "The farmers and the townspeople," they argued, "are our most important allies. How can we tax them, and still hope for their help in our fight against the Sheriff?"

Robin wondered how long the Merry Men could keep to the ways and methods of their early days. The Sheriff was growing stronger and becoming better organized. He now had the money and the men and was beginning to harass the band, probing for its weaknesses. The tide of events was beginning to turn against the Merry Men. Robin felt that the campaign must be decisively concluded before the Sheriff had a chance to deliver a mortal blow. "But how," he wondered, "could this be done?"

Robin had often entertained the possibility of killing the Sheriff, but the chances for this seemed increasingly remote. Besides, killing the Sheriff might satisfy his personal thirst for revenge, but it would not improve the situation. Robin had hoped that the perpetual state of unrest and the Sheriff's failure to collect taxes would lead to his removal from office. Instead, the Sheriff used his political connections to obtain reinforcement. He had powerful friends at court and was well regarded by the regent, Prince John.

Prince John was vicious and volatile. He was consumed by his unpopularity among the people, who wanted the imprisoned King Richard back. He also lived in constant fear of the barons, who had

first given him the regency but were now beginning to dispute his claim to the throne. Several of these barons had set out to collect the ransom that would release King Richard the Lionheart from his jail in Austria. Robin was invited to join the conspiracy in return for future amnesty. It was a dangerous proposition. Provincial banditry was one thing, court intrigue another. Prince John had spies everywhere, and he was known for his vindictiveness. If the conspirators' plan failed, the pursuit would be relentless and retributions swift.

The sound of the supper horn startled Robin from his thoughts. There was the smell of roasting venison in the air. Nothing was resolved or settled. Robin headed for camp promising himself that he would give these problems his utmost attention after tomorrow's raid.

Southwest Airlines in 2020: Culture, Values, and Operating Practices

Arthur A. Thompson
The University of Alabama

John E. Gamble
Texas A&M University–Corpus Christi

In 2020, Southwest Airlines was the largest U.S. domestic airline with 162.7 million passengers boarded in 2019. The company had held the title of largest U.S. air carrier since 2003, despite offering few international flights relative to major airlines, such as American Airlines, Delta Air Lines, and United Air Lines—see Exhibit 1. Southwest also had the enviable distinction of being the only major air carrier in the world that had been profitable for 46 consecutive years (1973–2019). In 2020, Southwest was named to *Fortune*'s list of the World's Most Admired Companies for the 27th consecutive year, coming in at number 11.

From humble beginnings in 1971 as a scrappy underdog with quirky practices that once flew mainly to "secondary" airports (rather than high traffic airports like Chicago O'Hare, Los Angeles International, Dallas-Fort Worth International, and Hartsfield-Jackson International Airport in Atlanta), Southwest had climbed up through the industry ranks to become a major competitive force in the domestic segment of the U.S. airline industry. It had weathered industry downturns, dramatic increases in the price of jet fuel, cataclysmic falloffs in airline traffic due to terrorist attacks and economy-wide recessions, and fare wars and other attempts by rivals to undercut its business, all the while adding more and more flights to more and more airports.

In 2019, Southwest earned after-tax profits of $2.3 billion on revenues of $22.4 billion, as airline passenger travel in the United States set a fifth consecutive record high with enplaned passengers increasing by 4.2 percent since 2018, 9.1 percent since 2017, and 12.5 percent from 2016. The grounding of the Boeing 737-MAX by President Trump on March 13, 2019 impacted Southwest Airlines' profitability for

EXHIBIT 1   Total Number of Domestic and International Passengers Traveling on Selected U.S. Airlines, 2015, 2017, 2019 (in thousands)

Carrier	Total Number of Enplaned Passengers (including both passengers paying for tickets and passengers traveling on frequent flyer awards)		
	2015	2017	2019
American Airlines			
Domestic	93,280	116,528	126,067
International	25,010	28,391	29,752
Total	118,290	144,919	155,819
Delta Air Lines			
Domestic	114,904	120,929	136,407
International	22,828	24,508	26,066
Total	137,732	145,437	162,473
Southwest Airlines			
Domestic	**142,408**	**153,859**	**158,446**
International	**2,167**	**3,868**	**4,262**
Total	**144,575**	**157,727**	**162,708**
United Air Lines			
Domestic	69,179	80,554	87,586
International	25,713	26,607	28,743
Total	94,892	107,161	116,329

Source: U.S. Department of Transportation, Bureau of Transportation Statistics, Air Carrier Statistics, Form T-100.

the year as its fleet included 34 737-MAX aircraft. The reliability of the 737 MAX had been brought into question after the crash of Lion Air Flight 610 in Jakarta, Indonesia, on October 29, 2018, which was followed by the crash of Ethiopian Airlines Flight 302 on March 10, 2019. As of mid-2020, all 737-MAX aircraft remained grounded until Boeing could develop design changes necessary to meet the Federal Aviation Administration's airworthiness directive.

More challenges to the airline industry arose in 2020 as novel Coronavirus brought about stay-at-home orders, social distancing requirements, and remote working protocols. U.S. passenger airlines experienced a combined loss of $5.2 billion for the first quarter of 2020 as a result of the impact of the COVID-19 pandemic on global air travel. The number of passengers flying on U.S. airlines had declined by 96 percent between April 2019 and April 2020 as the world focused on limiting potential exposure to the virus. Only three million passengers flew on U.S. airlines in April 2020, which was the smallest number of monthly air travelers in the United States since 1974. Between March 2020 and April 2020, airline employment had decreased by 31,000 workers to approximately 428,000—the lowest total number of full-time employees in the industry since August 2017. Southwest Airlines' strategy, commitment to excellence in operations, and strategy-supportive culture would help the company recover from the devastating effects of the pandemic on the airline industry, but few were predicting when air travel would return to pre-COVID-19 levels.

COMPANY BACKGROUND

In late 1966, Rollin King, a San Antonio entrepreneur who owned a small commuter air service, marched into Herb Kelleher's law office with a plan to start a low-cost/low-fare airline that would shuttle passengers between San Antonio, Dallas, and Houston.[1] Over the years, King had heard many Texas businessmen complain about the length of time that it took to drive between the three cities and the expense of flying the airlines currently serving these cities. His business concept for the airline was simple: Attract passengers by flying convenient schedules, get passengers to their destination on time, make sure they have a good experience, and charge fares competitive with travel by automobile. Kelleher, skeptical that King's business idea was viable, dug into the possibilities during the next few weeks and concluded a new

airline was feasible; he agreed to handle the necessary legal work and also to invest $10,000 of his own funds in the venture.

In 1967, Kelleher filed papers to incorporate the new airline and submitted an application to the Texas Aeronautics Commission for the new company to begin serving Dallas, Houston, and San Antonio.[2] But rival airlines in Texas pulled every string they could to block the new airline from commencing operations, precipitating a contentious four-year parade of legal and regulatory proceedings. Herb Kelleher led the fight on the company's behalf, eventually prevailing in June 1971 after winning two appeals to the Texas Supreme Court and a favorable ruling from U.S. Supreme Court. Kelleher recalled, "The constant proceedings had gradually come to enrage me. There was no merit to our competitors' legal assertions. They were simply trying to use their superior economic power to squeeze us dry so we would collapse before we ever got into business. I was bound and determined to show that Southwest Airlines was going to survive and was going into operation."[3]

In January 1971, Lamar Muse was brought in as the CEO to get operations underway. Muse was an aggressive and self-confident airline veteran who knew the business well and who had the entrepreneurial skills to tackle the challenges of building the airline from scratch and then competing head-on with the major carriers. Through private investors and an initial public offering of stock in June 1971, Muse raised $7 million in new capital to purchase planes and equipment and provide cash for start-up. Boeing agreed to supply three new 737s from its inventory, discounting its price from $5 million to $4 million and financing 90 percent of the $12 million deal. Muse was able to recruit a talented senior staff that included a number of veteran executives from other carriers. He particularly sought out people who were innovative, would not shirk doing things differently or unconventionally, and were motivated by the challenge of building an airline from scratch. Muse wanted his executive team to be willing to think like mavericks and not be lulled into instituting practices at Southwest that imitated what was done at other airlines.

Southwest's Struggle to Gain a Market Foothold

In June 1971, Southwest initiated its first flights with a schedule that soon included six roundtrips between

Dallas and San Antonio and 12 roundtrips between Houston and Dallas. But the introductory $20 one-way fares to fly the Golden Triangle, well below the $27 and $28 fares charged by rivals, attracted disappointingly small numbers of passengers. To try to gain market visibility and drum up more passengers, Southwest undertook some creative actions to supplement its ad campaigns publicizing its low fares:

- Taking a cue from being based at Dallas Love Field, Southwest began using the tag line "Now There's Somebody Else Up There Who Loves You." The routes between Houston, Dallas, and San Antonio became known as the Love Triangle. Southwest's planes were referred to as Love Birds, drinks became Love Potions, peanuts were called Love Bites, drink coupons were Love Stamps, and tickets were printed on Love Machines. The "love" campaign set the tone for Southwest's approach to its customers and company efforts to make flying Southwest Airlines an enjoyable, fun, and differentiating experience. (Later, when the company went public, it chose LUV as its stock-trading symbol.)

- In order to add more flights without buying more planes, the head of Southwest's ground operations came up with a plan for ground crews to off-load passengers and baggage, refuel the plane, clean the cabin and restock the galley, on-load passengers and baggage, do the necessary preflight checks and paperwork, and push away from the gate in ten minutes. The 10-minute turn became one of Southwest's signatures during the 1970s and 1980s. (In later years, as passenger volume grew and many flights were filled to capacity, the turnaround time gradually expanded to 25 minutes. Even so, the 25-minute average turnaround times at Southwest were shorter than the 30-to-50-minute turnarounds typical at other major airlines.)

- In late November 1971, Lamar Muse came up with the idea of offering a $10 fare to passengers on the Friday night Houston-Dallas flight. With no advertising, the 112-seat flight sold out. This led Muse to realize that Southwest was serving two quite distinct types of travelers in the Golden Triangle market: (1) business travelers who were more time sensitive than price sensitive and wanted weekday flights at times suitable for conducting business and (2) price-sensitive leisure travelers who wanted lower fares and had more flexibility about when to fly.[4] He came up with a two-tier on-peak and off-peak pricing structure in which all seats on weekday flights departing before 7 p.m. were priced at $26 and all seats on other flights were priced at $13. Passenger traffic increased significantly—and system-wide on-peak and off-peak pricing soon became standard across the whole airline industry.

- In 1972, the company decided to move its flights in Houston from the newly-opened Houston Intercontinental Airport (where it was losing money and where it took 45 minutes to get to downtown) to the abandoned Houston Hobby Airport located much closer to downtown Houston. Despite being the only carrier to fly into Houston Hobby, the results were spectacular—business travelers that flew to Houston frequently from Dallas and San Antonio found the Houston Hobby location far more convenient and passenger traffic doubled almost immediately.

All these moves paid off. The resulting gains in passenger traffic enabled allowed Southwest to report its first-ever annual profit in 1973.

More Legal and Regulatory Hurdles

During the rest of the 1970s, Southwest found itself embroiled in another round of legal and regulatory battles. One battle involved Southwest's refusal to move its flights from Dallas Love Field, located 10 minutes from downtown, out to the newly-opened Dallas-Fort Worth Regional Airport, which was 30 minutes from downtown Dallas. Local officials were furious because they were counting on fees from Southwest's flights in and out of DFW to help service the debt on the bonds issued to finance the construction of DFW. Southwest's position was that it was not required to move because it had not agreed to do so or been ordered to do so by the Texas Aeronautics Commission—moreover, the company's headquarters were located at Love Field. The courts eventually ruled Southwest's operations could remain at Love Field.

A second battle ensued when rival airlines protested Southwest's application to begin serving several smaller cities in Texas; their protest was based on arguments that these markets were already well-served and that Southwest's entry would result in costly overcapacity. Southwest countered that its low fares would allow more people to fly and grow the market. Again, Southwest prevailed and its views about low fares expanding the market proved accurate. In the year before Southwest initiated service, 123,000 passengers flew from Harlingen Airport in the Rio Grande Valley to Houston, Dallas, or San Antonio; in the 11 months following Southwest's initial flights, 325,000 passengers flew to the same three cities.

Believing that Braniff and Texas International were deliberately engaging in tactics to harass Southwest's operations, Southwest convinced the U.S. government to investigate what it considered predatory tactics by its chief rivals. In February 1975, Braniff and Texas International were indicted by a federal grand jury for conspiring to put Southwest out of business—a violation of the Sherman Antitrust Act. The two airlines pleaded "no contest" to the charges, signed cease-and-desist agreements, and were fined a modest $100,000 each.

When Congress passed the Airline Deregulation Act in 1978, Southwest applied to the Civil Aeronautics Board (now the Federal Aviation Agency) to fly between Houston and New Orleans. The application was vehemently opposed by local government officials and airlines operating out of DFW because of the potential for passenger traffic to be siphoned away from DFW. The opponents solicited the aid of Fort Worth congressman Jim Wright, then the majority leader of the U.S. House of Representatives, who took the matter to the floor of the House of Representatives; a rash of lobbying and maneuvering ensued. What emerged came to be known as the Wright Amendment of 1979: no airline may provide non-stop or through-plane service from Dallas Love Field to any city in any state except for locations in Texas, Louisiana, Arkansas, Oklahoma, and New Mexico. Southwest was prohibited from advertising, publishing schedules or fares, or checking baggage for travel from Dallas Love Field to any city it served outside the five-state "Wright Zone." The Wright Amendment continued in effect until 1997 when Alabama, Mississippi, and Kansas were added to the five-state "Wright Zone"; in 2005, Missouri was added to the Wright Zone. In 2006, after a heated battle in Congress, legislation was passed and signed into law that repealed the Wright Amendment beginning in October 2014. With the repeal of the Wright Amendment, Southwest

Airlines increased flight activity from Dallas Love Field by 50 percent to add 20 new nonstop destinations with 180 daily departures to a total of 50 nonstop destinations.

The Emergence of a Combative Can-Do Culture at Southwest

The legal, regulatory, and competitive battles that Southwest fought in these early years produced a strong esprit de corps among Southwest personnel and a drive to survive and prosper despite the odds. With newspaper and TV stories reporting Southwest's difficulties regularly, employees were fully aware that the airline's existence was constantly on the line. Had the company been forced to move from Love Field, it would most likely have gone under, an outcome which employees, Southwest's rivals, and local government officials understood well. According to Southwest's former president, Colleen Barrett, the obstacles thrown in Southwest's path by competitors and local officials were instrumental in building Herb Kelleher's passion for Southwest Airlines and ingraining a combative, can-do spirit into the corporate culture:[5]

> They would put twelve to fifteen lawyers on a case and on our side there was Herb. They almost wore him to the ground. But the more arrogant they were, the more determined Herb got that this airline was going to go into the air—and stay there.
>
> The warrior mentality, the very fight to survive, is truly what created our culture.

When Lamar Muse resigned in 1978, Southwest's board wanted Herb Kelleher to take over as chairman and CEO. But Kelleher enjoyed practicing law and, while he agreed to become chairman of the board, he insisted that someone else be CEO. Southwest's board appointed Howard Putnam, a group vice president of marketing services at United Airlines, as Southwest's president and CEO in July 1978. Putnam asked Kelleher to become more involved in Southwest's day-to-day operations, and over the next three years, Kelleher got to know many of the company's personnel and observe them in action. Putnam announced his resignation in Fall 1981 to become president and COO at Braniff International. This time, Southwest's board succeeded in persuading Kelleher to take on the additional duties of CEO and president.

Sustained Growth Transforms Southwest into the Domestic Market Share Leader, 1981–2019

When Herb Kelleher took over in 1981, Southwest was flying 27 planes to 14 destination cities and had $270 million in revenues and 2,100 employees. Over the next 20 years, Southwest Airlines prospered under Kelleher's leadership. When Kelleher stepped down as CEO in mid-2001, the company had 350 planes flying to 58 U.S. airports, annual revenues of $5.6 billion, over 30,000 employees, and 64 million fare-paying passengers annually.

Under the two CEOs who succeeded Kelleher, Southwest continued its march to becoming the market share leader in domestic air travel. In the process, the company won more industry Triple Crown awards for best on-time record, best baggage handling, and fewest customer complaints than any other U.S. airline. While Southwest fell short of its on-time performance and baggage handling goals in some years, it still led the domestic airline industry in Customer Satisfaction and received other awards and recognitions, including #1 U.S. Low-Cost Carrier for Customer Satisfaction by J.D. Power, Best Airline Rewards Program by *U.S. News & World Report*, 2019 Airline of the Year by Airlines Reporting Corp., #1 for Customer Satisfaction with Airline Travel Websites by J.D. Power, and the top ranking by the Freddie Awards for Best Customer Service and Best Loyalty Credit Card.

Exhibit 2 provides a five-year summary of Southwest's financial and operating performance.

HERB KELLEHER: THE CEO WHO TRANSFORMED SOUTHWEST INTO A MAJOR AIRLINE

Herb Kelleher majored in philosophy at Wesleyan University in Middletown, Connecticut, graduating with honors. He earned his law degree at New York University, again graduating with honors and also

EXHIBIT 2   Summary of Southwest Airlines' Financial and Operating Performance, 2015–2019

	Year ended December 31,				
	2019	2018	2017	2016	2015
Financial Data (in millions, except per share amounts):					
Operating revenues	$ 22,428	$ 21,965	$ 21,146	$ 20,289	$ 19,820
Operating expenses	19,471	18,759	17,739	16,767	15,821
Operating income	2,957	3,206	3,407	3,522	3,999
Other expenses (income) net	–	42	142	72	520
Income before taxes	2,957	3,164	3,265	3,450	3,479
Provision (benefit) for income taxes	657	699	(92)	1,267	1,298
Net income	$ 2,300	$ 2,465	$ 3,357	$ 2,183	$ 2,181
Net income per share, basic	$4.28	$4.30	$5.58	$3.48	$3.30
Net income per share, diluted	$4.27	$4.29	$5.57	$3.45	$3.27
Cash dividends per common share	$0.70	$0.61	$0.48	$0.38	$0.29
Total assets at period-end	25,895	26,243	25,110	23,286	21,312
Long-term obligations at period-end	1,846	2,771	3,320	2,821	2,541
Stockholders' equity at period-end	9,832	9,853	9,641	7,784	7,358
Operating Data:					
Revenue passengers carried (000s)	134,056	134,890	130,256	124,720	118,171

(continued)

	Year ended December 31,				
	2019	2018	2017	2016	2015
Enplaned passengers (000s)	162,681	163,606	157,677	151,740	144,575
Revenue passenger miles (RPMs) (in millions) (a)	131,345	133,322	129,041	124,798	117,500
Available seat miles (ASMs) (in millions) (b)	157,254	159,795	153,811	148,522	140,501
Load factor (c)	83.50%	83.40%	83.90%	84.00%	83.60%
Average length of passenger haul (miles)	980	988	991	1,001	994
Average aircraft stage length (miles)	748	757	754	760	750
Trips flown	1,367,727	1,375,030	1,347,893	1,311,149	1,267,358
Seats flown (000s) (d)	206,390	207,223	200,879	193,168	184,955
Seats per trip (e)	150.90	150.70	149.00	147.30	145.90
Average passenger fare	$154.98	$151.64	$151.73	$152.89	$154.85
Passenger revenue yield per RPM (cents) (f)	15.82	15.34	15.32	15.28	15.57
Operating revenues per ASM (cents) (g) (j)	14.26	13.75	13.75	13.66	13.98
Passenger revenue per ASM (cents) (h)	13.21	12.80	12.85	12.84	13.02
Operating expenses per ASM (cents) (i)	12.38	11.74	11.53	11.29	11.26
Operating expenses per ASM, excluding fuel (cents)	9.62	8.85	8.88	8.73	8.60
Operating expenses per ASM, excluding fuel and profitsharing (cents)	9.19	8.51	8.53	8.34	8.16
Fuel costs per gallon, including fuel tax	$2.09	$2.20	$1.99	$1.90	$1.96
Fuel consumed, in gallons (millions)	2,077	2,094	2,045	1,996	1,901
Active fulltime equivalent employees	60,767	58,803	56,110	53,536	49,583
Aircraft at end of period	747	750	706	723	704

(a) A revenue passenger mile is one paying passenger flown one mile. Also referred to as "traffic," which is a measure of demand for a given period.

(b) An available seat mile is one seat (empty or full) flown one mile. Also referred to as "capacity," which is a measure of the space available to carry passengers in a given period.

(c) Revenue passenger miles divided by available seat miles.

(d) Seats flown is calculated using total number of seats available by aircraft type multiplied by the total trips flown by the same aircraft type during a particular period.

(e) Seats per trip is calculated by dividing seats flown by trips flown.

(f) Calculated as passenger revenue divided by revenue passenger miles. Also referred to as "yield," this is the average cost paid by a paying passenger to fly one mile, which is a measure of revenue production and fares.

(g) Calculated as operating revenues divided by available seat miles. Also referred to as "operating unit revenues" or "RASM," this is a measure of operating revenue production based on the total available seat miles flown during a particular period.

(h) Calculated as passenger revenue divided by available seat miles. Also referred to as "passenger unit revenues," this is a measure of passenger revenue production based on the total available seat miles flown during a particular period.

(i) Calculated as operating expenses divided by available seat miles. Also referred to as "unit costs" or "cost per available seat mile," this is the average cost to fly an aircraft seat (empty or full) one mile, which is a measure of cost efficiencies.

(j) Year ended 2015 RASM excludes a $172 million one-time special revenue adjustment in July 2015 as a result of the Company's amendment of its co-branded credit card agreement with Chase Bank USA, N.A. and the resulting required change in accounting methodology. Including the special revenue adjustment, RASM would have been 14.11 cents for the year ended 2015.

Source: Southwest Airlines 10-K Report, 2019.

serving as a member of the law review. After graduation, he clerked for a New Jersey Supreme Court justice for two years and then joined a law firm in Newark. Upon marrying a woman from Texas and becoming enamored with Texas, he moved to San Antonio where he became a successful lawyer and came to represent Rollin King's small aviation company.

When Herb Kelleher took on the role of Southwest's CEO in 1981, he made a point of visiting with maintenance personnel to check on how well the planes were running and talking with the flight attendants. Kelleher did not do much managing from his office, preferring instead to be out among the troops as much as he could. His style was to listen and observe and to offer encouragement. Kelleher attended most graduation ceremonies of flight attendant classes, and he often appeared to help load bags on "Black Wednesday," the busy travel day before Thanksgiving. He knew the names of thousands of Southwest employees and was held in the highest regard by Southwest employees. When he attended a Southwest employee function, he was swarmed like a celebrity.

Kelleher was a strong believer in the principle that employees—not customers—came first:[6]

> You have to treat your employees like your customers. When you treat them right, then they will treat your outside customers right. That has been a very powerful competitive weapon for us. You've got to take the time to listen to people's ideas. If you just tell somebody no, that's an act of power and, in my opinion, an abuse of power. You don't want to constrain people in their thinking.

Another indication of the importance that Kelleher placed on employees was the message he had penned in 1990 that was prominently displayed in the lobby of Southwest's headquarters in Dallas:

> The people of Southwest Airlines are "the creators" of what we have become—and of what we will be.
>
> Our people transformed an idea into a legend. That legend will continue to grow only so long as it is nourished—by our people's indomitable spirit, boundless energy, immense goodwill, and burning desire to excel.
>
> Our thanks—and our love—to the people of Southwest Airlines for creating a marvelous family and a wondrous airline.

In June 2001, Herb Kelleher stepped down as CEO but continued on in his role as chairman of Southwest's Board of Directors and the head of the board's executive committee; as chairman, he played a lead role in Southwest's strategy, expansion to new cities and aircraft scheduling, and governmental and industry affairs. In May 2008, after more than 40 years of leadership at Southwest, Kelleher retired as chairman (but he remained a full-time Southwest employee until July 2013 and carried the title of Chairman Emeritus in 2016). Herb Kelleher died in Dallas, Texas at age 87 on January 3, 2019.

EXECUTIVE LEADERSHIP AT SOUTHWEST: 2001–2020

In June 2001, Southwest Airlines, responding to anxious investor concerns about the company's leadership succession plans, began an orderly transfer of power and responsibilities from Herb Kelleher, age 70, to two of his most trusted protégés. James F. Parker, 54, Southwest's general counsel and one of Kelleher's most trusted protégés, succeeded Kelleher as Southwest's CEO. Another of Kelleher's trusted protégés, Colleen Barrett, 56, Southwest's executive vice-president-customers and self-described keeper of Southwest's pep rally corporate culture, became president and chief operating officer.

James Parker, CEO from 2001–2004

James Parker's association with Herb Kelleher went back 23 years to the time when they were colleagues at Kelleher's old law firm. Parker moved over to Southwest from the law firm in February 1986. Parker's profile inside the company as Southwest's vice president and general counsel had been relatively low, but he was Southwest's chief labor negotiator and much of the credit for Southwest's good relations with employee unions belonged to Parker. Parker and Kelleher were said to think much alike, and Parker was regarded as having a good sense of humor, although he did not have as colorful and flamboyant a personality as Kelleher. Parker was seen as an honest, straight-arrow kind of person who had a strong grasp of Southwest's culture and market niche and who could be nice or tough, depending on the situation.

Parker retired unexpectedly, for personal reasons, in July 2004, stepping down as CEO and Vice Chairman of the Board and also resigning from the company's board of directors. He was succeeded by Gary C. Kelly.

Colleen Barrett, Southwest's President, 2001–2008

Barrett began working with Kelleher as his legal secretary in 1967 and had been with Southwest since 1978. As executive vice president–customers, Barrett had a high profile among Southwest employees and spent most of her time on culture-building, morale-building, and customer service; her goal was to ensure that employees felt good about what they were doing and felt empowered to serve the cause of Southwest Airlines.[7] She and Kelleher were regarded as Southwest's guiding lights, and some analysts said she was essentially functioning as the company's chief operating officer prior to her formal appointment as president. Much of the credit for the company's strong record of customer service and its strong-culture work climate belonged to Barrett.

Barrett had been the driving force behind lining the hallways at Southwest's headquarters with photos of company events and trying to create a family atmosphere at the company. Believing it was important to make employees feel cared about and important, Barrett had put together a network of contacts across the company to help her stay in touch with what was happening with employees and their families. When network members learned about events that were worthy of acknowledgment, the word quickly got to Barrett—the information went into a database and an appropriate greeting card or gift was sent. Barrett had a remarkable ability to give gifts that were individualized and connected her to the recipient.[8]

Barrett was the first woman appointed as president and COO of a major U.S. airline. In October 2001, *Fortune* included Colleen Barrett on its list of the 50 most powerful women in American business (she was ranked number 20). Barrett retired as president in July 2008.

Gary C. Kelly, Southwest's CEO, 2004-Present

Gary Kelly was appointed Vice Chairman of the Board of Directors and Chief Executive Officer of Southwest effective July 15, 2004. Prior to that time, Mr. Kelly was Executive Vice President and Chief Financial Officer from 2001 to 2004, and Vice President-Finance and Chief Financial Officer from 1989 to 2001. He joined Southwest in 1986 as its Controller. In 2008, effective with the retirement of Kelleher and Barrett, Kelly assumed the titles of Chairman of the Board, CEO, and President.

As CEO, Kelly and other top-level Southwest executives sharpened and fine-tuned Southwest's strategy in a number of areas, continued to expand operations (adding both more flights and initiating service to new airports), and worked to maintain the company's low-cost advantage over its domestic rivals.

Kelly saw four factors as keys to Southwest's recipe for success:[9]

- Hire great people, treat $$$'em like family.
- Care for our Customers warmly and personally, like they're guests in our home.
- Keep fares and operating costs lower than anybody else by being safe, efficient, and operationally excellent.
- Stay prepared for bad times with a strong balance sheet, lots of cash, and a stout fuel hedge.

To guide Southwest's efforts to be a standout performer on these four key success factors, Kelly had established five strategic objectives for the company:[10]

- Be the best place to work.
- Be the safest, most efficient, and most reliable airline in the world.
- Offer customers a convenient flight schedule with lots of flights to lots of places they want to go.
- Offer customers the best overall travel experience.
- Do all of these things in a way that maintains a low-cost structure and the ability to offer low fares.

SOUTHWEST AIRLINES' STRATEGY IN 2020

From day one, Southwest had pursued a low-cost/low-price/no-frills strategy to make air travel affordable to a wide segment of the population. While specific aspects of the strategy had evolved over the years, three strategic themes had characterized the company's strategy throughout its existence and still had high profiles in 2020:

- Offering air travelers a robust route network
- Creating compelling brand appeal through customer service, low fares, and its frequent flyer program

- Ensuring a superior financial position through a low-cost operating position

Southwest's Development of a Robust Route Network

Southwest's route network was based upon a point-to-point flight model that was more cost-efficient than the hub-and-spoke systems used by most rival airlines. Hub-and-spoke systems involved passengers on many different flights coming in from spoke locations (and sometimes another hub) to a central airport or hub within a short span of time and then connecting to an outgoing flight to their destination—a spoke location or another hub). Most flights arrived and departed a hub across a two-hour window, creating big peak-valley swings in airport personnel workloads and gate utilization—airport personnel and gate areas were very busy when hub operations were in full swing and then were underutilized in the interval awaiting the next round of inbound/outbound flights. In contrast, Southwest's point-to-point routes permitted scheduling aircraft so as to minimize the time aircraft were at the gate, currently approximately 25 minutes, thereby reducing the number of aircraft and gate facilities that would otherwise be required. Furthermore, with a relatively even flow of incoming/outgoing flights and gate traffic, Southwest could staff its terminal operations to handle a fairly steady workload across a day whereas hub-and-spoke operators had to staff their operations to serve 3-4 daily peak periods.

Expanding Daily Departure and Route Options for Passengers.   Southwest's strategy to grow its business consisted of (1) adding more daily flights to the cities/airports it currently served and (2) adding new cities/airports to its route schedule.

It was normal for customer traffic to grow at the airports Southwest served. Hence, opportunities were always emerging for Southwest to capture additional revenues by adding more flights at the airports already being served. Sometimes these opportunities entailed adding more flights to one or more of the same destinations and sometimes the opportunities entailed adding flights to a broader selection of Southwest destinations, depending on the mix of final destinations the customers departing from a particular airport were flying to.

To spur growth beyond that afforded by adding more daily flights to cities/airports currently being served, it had long been Southwest's practice to add one or more new cities/airports to its route schedule annually. In selecting new cities, Southwest looked for city pairs that could generate substantial amounts of both business and leisure traffic. Management believed that having numerous flights flying the same routes appealed to business travelers looking for convenient flight times and the ability to catch a later flight if they unexpectedly ran late.

As a general rule, Southwest did not initiate service to a city/airport unless it envisioned the potential for originating at least eight flights a day there and saw opportunities to add more flights over time—in Denver, for example, Southwest had boosted the number of daily departures from 13 in January 2006 (the month in which service to and from Denver was initiated) to 79 daily departures in 2008, 129 daily departures in 2010, and 214 daily departures in December 2019.

Creating a Compelling Brand: Southwest's Strategy to Provide a Topnotch Travel Experience

Southwest's approach to delivering good customer service and building a loyal customer clientele was predicated on presenting a happy face to passengers, displaying a fun-loving attitude, and doing things in a manner calculated to provide passengers with a positive flying experience. The company made a special effort to employ gate personnel who enjoyed interacting with customers, had good interpersonal skills, and displayed cheery, outgoing personalities. A number of Southwest's gate personnel let their wit and sense of humor show by sometimes entertaining those in the gate area with trivia questions or contests such as "who has the biggest hole in their sock." Apart from greeting passengers coming onto planes and assisting them in finding open seats and stowing baggage, flight attendants were encouraged to be engaging, converse and joke with passengers, and go about their tasks in ways that made passengers smile. On some flights, attendants sang announcements to passengers on takeoff and landing. The repertoires to amuse passengers varied from flight crew to flight crew.

Fare Structure Strategy

Southwest employed a relatively simple fare structure, displayed in ways that made it easy for customers to choose the fare they preferred. In 2020, Southwest's fares were bundled into three major categories: "Wanna Get Away," "Anytime," and "Business Select":

1. "Wanna Get Away" fares were always the lowest fares and were subject to advance purchase requirements. No fee was charged for changing a previously purchased ticket to a different time or day of travel (rival airlines charged a change fee of $75 to $550), but applicable fare differences were applied. The purchase price was non-refundable but the funds could be applied to future travel on Southwest, provided the tickets were not canceled or changed within ten minutes of a flight's scheduled departure.

2. "Anytime" fares were refundable and changeable, and funds could also be applied toward future travel on Southwest. Anytime fares also included a higher frequent flyer point multiplier under Southwest's Rapid Rewards frequent flyer program than do Wanna Get Away fares.

3. "Business Select" fares were refundable and changeable, and funds could be applied toward future travel on Southwest. Business Select fares also included additional perks such as priority boarding, a higher frequent flyer point multiplier than other Southwest fares (including twice as many points per dollar spent as compared to Wanna Get Away fares), priority security and ticket counter access in select airports, and one complimentary adult beverage coupon for the day of travel (for customers of legal drinking age). The Business Select fare had been introduced in 2007 to help attract economy-minded business travelers; Business Select customers had early boarding privileges, received extra Rapid Rewards (frequent flyer) credit, and a free cocktail.

4. No fee was charged for changing a previously-purchased ticket to a different time or day of travel, but applicable fare differences were applied. The purchase price was nonrefundable, but funds could be applied to future travel on Southwest, provided the tickets were not canceled or changed within ten minutes of a flight's scheduled departure. Also, the company's "Bags Fly Free" program that allowed passengers to check two bags at no additional charge was unmatched by all major airlines in 2020.

Southwest's Rapid Rewards Frequent Flyer Program

Southwest's Rapid Rewards frequent flyer program, launched in March 2011, linked free travel awards to the number of points members earned purchasing tickets to fly Southwest. The amount of points earned was based on the fare and fare class purchased, with higher fare products (like Business Select) earning more points than lower fare products (like Wanna Get Away). Likewise, the amount of points required to be redeemed for a flight was based on the fare and fare class purchased. Rapid Rewards members could also earn points through qualifying purchases with Southwest's Rapid Rewards Partners (which included car rental agencies, hotels, restaurants, and retail locations), and they could purchase points. Members who opted to obtain a Southwest co-branded Chase Visa credit card earned two points for every dollar spent on purchases of Southwest tickets and on purchases with Southwest's car rental and hotel partners, and they earned one point on every dollar spent everywhere else. Holders of Southwest's co-branded Chase Visa credit card could redeem credit card points for items other than travel on Southwest, including international flights on other airlines, cruises, hotel stays, rental cars, gift cards, event tickets, and more.

The most active members of Southwest's Rapid Rewards program qualified for priority check-in and security lane access (where available), standby priority, free inflight WiFi, and—provided they flew 100 qualifying flights or earned 125,000 qualifying points in a calendar year—automatically received a Companion Pass, which provided for unlimited free roundtrip travel for one year to any destination available on Southwest for a designated companion of the qualifying Rapid Rewards Member.

Rapid Rewards members could redeem their points for every available seat, every day, on every flight, with no blackout dates. Points did not expire so long as the Rapid Rewards Member had points-earning activity during the most recent 24 months.

Ensuring a Superior Financial Position: Southwest's Strategy to Create and Sustain Low-Cost Operations

Southwest management fully understood that earning attractive profits by charging low fares necessitated the use of strategy elements that would enable the company to become a low-cost provider of commercial air service. There were three main components of Southwest's strategic actions to achieve a low-cost operating structure: using a single aircraft type for all flights, creating an operationally-efficient point-to-point route structure, and striving to perform all value chain activities in a cost-efficient manner.

Use of a Single Aircraft Type   For many years, Southwest's aircraft fleets had consisted only of Boeing 737 aircraft. Operating only one type of aircraft produced many cost-saving benefits: minimizing the size of spare parts inventories, simplifying the training of maintenance and repair personnel, improving the proficiency and speed with which maintenance routines could be done, and simplifying the task of scheduling planes for particular flights. In 2019, Southwest operated the biggest fleet of Boeing 737 aircraft in the world. Exhibit 3 provides information about Southwest's aircraft fleet.

Incorporating Larger Boeing Aircraft into Southwest's Fleet   Starting in 2012, Southwest began a long-term initiative to replace older Southwest aircraft with a new generation of Boeing aircraft that had greater seating capacity, a quieter interior, LED reading and ceiling lighting, improved security features, reduced maintenance requirements, increased fuel efficiency, and the capability to fly longer distances without refueling. Southwest had consistently removed older and smaller versions of the 737, such as the Boeing 737-300 aircraft (with 143 seats and an average age of 20 years), and 15 Boeing 737-500 aircraft (with 122 seats and an average age of 22 years) from its

fleet and replaced them with new Boeing 737-700s (143 seats), 737-800s (175 seats), and 737-MAX aircraft (up to 189 seats). The company had firm orders for 30 new Boeing 737-MAX 7 and 219 MAX 8 aircraft were scheduled to be delivered in 2020–2026 (with options to take delivery on an additional 131 planes)—Southwest was Boeing's launch customer for the 737-MAX. Plans called for some of the new aircraft to be leased from third parties rather than being purchased—of the company's current fleet of 747 aircraft, 625 were owned and 122 were leased.

Southwest expected that the new Boeing 737-800 and 737-MAX aircraft would significantly enhance the company's capabilities to (1) more economically fly long-haul routes (the number of short-haul flights throughout the domestic airline industry had been declining since 2000), (2) improve scheduling flexibility and more economically serve high-demand, gate-restricted, slot-controlled airports by adding seats to such destinations without increasing the number of flights, and (3) boost overall fuel efficiency to reduce overall costs. Additionally, the aircraft would enable Southwest to profitably expand its operations to new, more distant destinations (including extended routes over water), such as Hawaii, Alaska, Canada, Mexico, and the Caribbean. Southwest management expected that the new Boeing 737-MAX planes would have the lowest operating costs of any single-aisle commercial airplane on the market.

EXHIBIT 3   Southwest's Aircraft Fleet as of December 31, 2019

Type of Aircraft	Number	Seats	Comments
Boeing 737-700	506	143	Southwest was Boeing's launch customer for this model in 1997. All were equipped with satellite-delivered broadband internet reception capability
Boeing 737-800	207	175	All were equipped with satellite-delivered broadband internet reception capability
Boeing 737 MAX 8	34	175	Southwest was Boeing's launch customer for this model in 2011. All were equipped with satellite-delivered broadband internet reception capability
TOTAL number of aircraft	747		

Other Fleet-Related Facts

Average age of aircraft fleet—approximately 11 years

Average aircraft trip length—749 miles, with an average duration of 2 hours and 4 minutes

Average aircraft utilization—more than 5 flights per day and approximately 11 hours of flight time

Fleet size—1990: 106 1995: 224 2000: 344 2009: 537

Firm orders for new aircraft—2020–2026: 380

Source: Company 10-K Report, 2019 and Southwest Corporate Fact Sheet (https://www.swamedia.com/pages/corporate-fact-sheet).

Grounding of the Boeing 737-MAX   With 189 crew and passengers lost in the Lion Air Flight 610 crash in October 29, 2018 and another 157 people killed in the March 10, 2019 crash of Ethiopian Airlines Flight 302, President Trump ordered the plane grounded on October 13, 2019 until the mechanical problems with the plane could be identified and corrected. As of mid-2020, Boeing had yet to satisfy the Federal Aviation Administration that the 737-MAX was airworthy. Southwest Airlines and other airlines who had purchased the planes were unable to utilize the equipment in their fleets until the FAA had concurred that Boeing has identified the mechanical failures of the aircraft and all planes were made safe to fly. The 737-MAX grounding resulted in $828 million in additional costs for Southwest Airlines in 2019 and continued into 2020 as planes remained grounded.

Striving to Perform All Value Chain Activities Cost Effectively   Southwest made a point of scrutinizing every aspect of its operations to find ways to trim costs. The company's strategic actions to reduce or at least contain costs were extensive and ongoing.

- Southwest was the first major airline to introduce ticketless travel.
- Southwest was also the first airline to allow customers to make reservations and purchase tickets at the company's website (thus bypassing the need to pay commissions to travel agents for handling the ticketing process and reducing staffing requirements at Southwest's reservation centers).
- For most of its history, Southwest stressed flights into and out of airports in medium-sized cities and less congested airports in major metropolitan areas (Chicago Midway, Detroit Metro, Houston Hobby, Dallas Love Field, Baltimore-Washington International, Burbank, Manchester, Oakland, San Jose, Providence, and Ft. Lauderdale-Hollywood). This strategy helped produce better-than-average on-time performance and reduce the fuel costs associated with planes sitting in line on crowded taxiways or circling airports waiting for clearance to land.
- To economize on the amount of time it took terminal personnel to check passengers in and to simplify the whole task of making reservations, Southwest dispensed with the practice of assigning each passenger a reserved seat. All passengers could check in online up to 24 hours before departure time and print out a boarding pass, thus bypassing counter check-in (unless they wished to check baggage).
- Southwest flight attendants were responsible for cleaning up trash left by deplaning passengers and otherwise getting the plane presentable for passengers to board for the next flight.
- Southwest did not have a first-class section in any of its planes and had no fancy clubs for its frequent flyers to relax in at terminals.
- Southwest did not provide passengers with baggage transfer services to other carriers—passengers with checked baggage who were connecting to other carriers to reach their destination were responsible for picking up their luggage at Southwest's baggage claim and then getting it to the check-in facilities of the connecting carrier.
- Southwest was a first-mover among major U.S. airlines in employing fuel hedging and derivative contracts to counteract rising prices for crude oil and jet fuel.
- Southwest regularly upgraded and enhanced its management information systems to speed data flows, improve operating efficiency, lower costs, and upgrade its customer service capabilities.

For many decades, Southwest's operating costs had been lower than those of rival U.S. airline carriers—see Exhibit 4 for comparative *costs per revenue passenger mile* among the five major U.S. airlines during the 2005–2019 period.

SOUTHWEST'S PEOPLE MANAGEMENT PRACTICES AND CULTURE

Whereas the litany at many companies was that customers come first, at Southwest the operative principle was that "employees come first and customers come second." The high strategic priority placed on employees reflected management's belief that delivering superior service required employees who not only were passionate about their jobs but who also knew the company was genuinely concerned for their well-being and committed to providing them with job security. Southwest's thesis was simple: Keep employees happy—then they will keep customers happy.

EXHIBIT 4   **Comparative Operating Cost Statistics per Revenue Passenger Mile, Major U.S. Airlines, 2005, 2010, 2015, 2019 (in cents)**

	Costs incurred per revenue passenger mile (in cents)							
	Total Salaries and Fringe Benefits	Fuel and Oil	Rentals	Landing Fees	Advertising	General and Administrative	Other Operating Expenses	Total Operating Expenses
American Airlines								
2005	4.65	3.67	0.41	0.32	0.10	0.95	3.66	15.18
2010	5.18	4.57	0.47	0.35	0.13	1.23	3.68	17.53
2015	5.01	3.08	0.67	0.30	0.07	2.26	3.93	17.09
2019	6.31	3.54	1.27	0.31	0.06	2.55	6.03	20.07
Delta Air Lines								
2005	4.31	3.68	0.38	0.22	0.16	0.84	6.01	16.69
2010	4.15	4.51	0.14	0.28	0.10	0.64	6.26	17.41
2015	5.55	3.45	0.18	0.27	0.12	1.38	5.08	17.50
2019	6.18	3.36	0.68	0.29	0.13	1.29	6.77	18.69
Southwest Airlines								
2005	4.70	2.44	0.31	0.34	0.29	0.73	1.23	11.21
2010	4.97	4.63	0.28	0.46	0.26	0.83	1.32	14.23
2015	5.69	3.07	0.25	0.42	0.18	1.02	1.28	13.35
2019	6.60	3.29	0.79	0.42	0.16	1.22	2.23	14.72
United Air Lines								
2005	3.72	3.53	0.35	0.30	0.16	0.60	5.09	15.35
2010	4.34	4.46	0.32	0.38	0.06	1.31	5.24	17.96
2015	5.45	3.44	0.32	0.36	0.11	1.58	5.04	17.81
2019	6.03	3.45	0.65	0.38	0.10	1.50	6.18	18.29

Note 1: Cost per revenue passenger mile for each of the cost categories in this exhibit is calculated by dividing the total costs for each cost category by the total number of revenue passenger miles flown, where a revenue passenger mile is equal to one paying passenger flown one mile. Costs incurred per revenue passenger mile thus represent the costs incurred per ticketed passenger per mile flown.

Note 2: US Airways and America West started merging operations in September 2005, and joint reporting of their operating costs began in late 2007. Effective January 2010, data for Delta Airlines includes the combined operating costs of Delta and Northwest Airlines; the merger of these two companies became official in October 2008. United Airlines acquired Continental Airlines in 2010, and the two companies began joint reporting of operating expenses in 2012.

Note 3: Southwest Airlines acquired AirTran in late 2010; starting in 2013 and continuing into 2014, AirTran flights were rebranded as Southwest Airlines flights. Southwest's first international flights began when some of AirTran's international flights were rebranded as Southwest flights in 2013.

Note 4: United Airlines acquired Continental Airlines in 2010, and the two companies began joint reporting of passenger traffic in 2012. Prior to 2012, traffic count data is only for United flights.

Source: United States Department of Transportation, Bureau of Transportation Statistics, Form 41.

Since becoming the company's CEO, Gary Kelly had continuously echoed the views of his predecessors: "Our People are our single greatest strength and our most enduring long-term competitive advantage."[11]

The company changed the personnel department's name to the People Department in 1989. Later, it was renamed the People and Leadership Development Department.

Recruiting, Screening, and Hiring

Southwest hired employees for attitude and trained for skills. Herb Kelleher explained:[12]

> We can train people to do things where skills are concerned. But there is one capability we do not have and that is to change a person's attitude. So we prefer an unskilled person with a good attitude. . . .[to] a highly skilled person with a bad attitude.

Management believed that delivering superior service came from having employees who genuinely believed that customers were important and that treating them warmly and courteously was the right thing to do, not from training employees to *act* like customers are important. The belief at Southwest was that superior, hospitable service and a fun-loving spirit flowed from the heart and soul of employees who themselves were fun-loving and spirited, who liked their jobs and the company they worked for, and who were also confident and empowered to do their jobs as they saw fit (rather than being governed by strict rules and procedures).

Screening Candidates.   In hiring for jobs that involved personal contact with passengers, the company looked for people-oriented applicants that were extroverted and had a good sense of humor. It tried to identify candidates with a knack for reading peoples' emotions and responding in a genuinely caring, empathetic manner. Southwest wanted employees to deliver the kind of service that showed they truly enjoyed meeting people, being around passengers, and doing their job, as opposed to delivering the kind of service that came across as being forced or taught. Kelleher elaborated: "We are interested in people who externalize, who focus on other people, who are motivated to help other people. We are not interested in navel gazers."[13] In addition to a "whistle while you work" attitude, Southwest was drawn to candidates who it thought would be likely to exercise initiative, work harmoniously with fellow employees, and be community-spirited.

Southwest did not use personality tests to screen job applicants nor did it ask them what they would or should do in certain hypothetical situations. Rather, the hiring staff at Southwest analyzed each job category to determine the specific behaviors, knowledge, and motivations that job holders needed and then tried to find candidates with the desired traits—a process called targeted selection. A trait common to all job categories was teamwork; a trait deemed critical for pilots and flight attendants was judgment. In exploring an applicant's aptitude for teamwork, interviewers often asked applicants to tell them about a time in a prior job when they went out of their way to help a co-worker or to explain how they had handled conflict with a co-worker. Another frequent question was "What was your most embarrassing moment?" The thesis here was that having applicants talk about their past behaviors provided good clues about their future behaviors.

To test for unselfishness, Southwest interviewing teams typically gave a group of potential employees ample time to prepare five-minute presentations about themselves; during the presentations in an informal conversational setting, interviewers watched the audience to see who was absorbed in polishing their presentations and who was listening attentively, enjoying the stories being told, and applauding the efforts of the presenters. Those who were emotionally engaged in hearing the presenters and giving encouragement were deemed more apt to be team players than those who were focused on looking good themselves. All applicants for flight attendant positions were put through such a presentation exercise before an interview panel consisting of customers, experienced flight attendants, and members of the People and Leadership Department. Flight attendant candidates that got through the group presentation interviews then had to complete a three-on-one interview conducted by a recruiter, a supervisor from the hiring section of the People and Leadership Department, and a Southwest flight attendant; following this interview, the three-person panel tried to reach a consensus on whether to recommend or drop the candidate.

Training

Apart from the FAA-mandated training for certain employees, training activities at Southwest were designed and conducted by Southwest Airlines University. The curriculum included courses for new recruits, employees, and managers. Learning was viewed as a never-ending process for all company personnel; the expectation was that each employee should be an "intentional learner," looking to grow and develop not just from occasional classes taken at Southwest Airlines University but also from their everyday on-the-job experiences.

Southwest Airlines University conducted a variety of courses offered to maintenance personnel and other employees to meet the safety and security training requirements of the Federal Aviation Administration, the U.S. Department of Transportation, the Occupational Safety and Health Administration, and other government agencies. And there were courses on written communications, public speaking, stress management, career development, performance appraisal, decision-making, leadership, customer service, corporate culture, environmental stewardship and sustainability, and employee relations to help employees advance their careers.

Leadership development courses that focused on developing people, team-building, strategic thinking, and being a change leader were keystone offerings. New supervisors attended a four-week course "Leadership Southwest Style" that emphasized coaching, empowering, and encouraging, rather than supervising or enforcing rules and regulations. New managers attended a two-and-a-half-day course on "Next-Level leadership." There were courses for employees wanting to explore whether a management career was for them and courses for high-potential employees wanting to pursue a long-term career at Southwest. From time to time supervisors and executives attended courses on corporate culture, intended to help instill, ingrain, and nurture such cultural themes as teamwork, trust, harmony, and diversity. All employees who came into contact with customers, including pilots, received customer-care training.

The OnBoarding Program for Newly-Hired Employees. Southwest had a program called OnBoarding "to welcome New Hires into the Southwest Family" and provide information and assistance from the time they were selected until the end of their first year. All new hires attended a full-day orientation course that covered the company's history, an overview of the airline industry and the competitive challenges that Southwest faced, an introduction to Southwest's culture and management practices, the expectations of employees, and demonstrations on "Living the Southwest Way." All new hires also received safety training. Anytime during their first 30 days, new employees were expected to access an interactive online tool—OnBoarding Online Orientation—to learn more about the company. During their first year of employment, new hires were invited to attend a "LUV@First Bite Luncheon" in the city where they worked; these luncheons were held on the same day as Leadership's Messages to the Field; at these

luncheons, there were opportunities to network with other new hires and talk with senior leaders.

An additional element of the Onboarding Program involved assigning each new employee to an existing Southwest employee who had volunteered to sponsor a new hire and be of assistance in acclimating the new employee to their job and Living the Southwest Way; each volunteer sponsor received training from Southwest's Onboarding Team in what was expected of a sponsor. Much of the indoctrination of new employees into the company's culture was done by the volunteer sponsor, co-workers, and the new employee's supervisor. Southwest made active use of a one-year probationary employment period to help ensure that new employees fit in with its culture and adequately embraced the company's cultural values.

Promotion

Approximately 80 to 90 percent of Southwest's supervisory positions were filled internally, reflecting management's belief that people who had "been there and done that" would be more likely to appreciate and understand the demands that people under them were experiencing and also more likely to enjoy the respect of their peers and higher-level managers. Employees could either apply for supervisory positions or be recommended by their present supervisor.

Employees being considered for managerial positions of large operations (Up and Coming Leaders) received training in every department of the company over a six-month period in which they continued to perform their current job. At the end of the six-month period, candidates were provided with 360-degree feedback from department heads, peers, and subordinates; personnel in the People and Leadership Department analyzed the feedback in deciding on the specific assignment of each candidate.[14]

Compensation and Benefits

Southwest's pay scales and fringe benefits were quite attractive compared to other major U.S. airlines (see Exhibit 4). In 2020, in addition to vacation, paid holidays, and sick leave, Southwest offered full-time and part-time Southwest employees a benefits package that included:

- A 401(k) retirement savings plan
- A profit-sharing plan

- Medical and prescription coverage
- Mental health chemical dependency coverage
- Vision coverage
- Dental coverage
- Adoption assistance
- Mental health assistance
- Life insurance
- Accidental death and dismemberment insurance
- Long-term disability insurance
- Dependent life insurance
- Dependent care flexible spending account
- Health care flexible spending account
- Employee stock purchase plan
- Wellness program
- Flight privileges
- Health care for committed partners
- Early retiree health care

Employee Relations

About 83 percent of Southwest's 60,800 employees belonged to a union. An in-house union—the Southwest Airline Pilots Association (SWAPA)—represented the company's pilots. The Teamsters Union represented Southwest's material specialists and flight simulator technicians; a local of the Transportation Workers of America represented flight attendants; another local of the Transportation Workers of America represented baggage handlers, ground crews, and provisioning employees; the International Association of Machinists and Aerospace Workers represented customer service and reservation employees, and the Aircraft Mechanics Fraternal Association represented the company's mechanics.

Management encouraged union members and negotiators to research their pressing issues and to conduct employee surveys before each contract negotiation. Southwest's contracts with the unions representing its employees were relatively free of restrictive work rules and narrow job classifications that might impede worker productivity. All of the contracts allowed any qualified employee to perform any function—thus pilots, ticket agents, and gate personnel could help load and unload baggage when needed and flight attendants could pick up trash and make flight cabins more presentable for passengers boarding the next flight.

Except for one brief strike by machinists in the early 1980s and some unusually difficult negotiations in 2000–2001, Southwest's relationships with the unions representing its employee groups had been harmonious and non-adversarial for the most part. However, the company was engaged in difficult contract negotiations with its pilots in 2016 and had been at odds with mechanics in 2019 over maintenance and safety concerns that had resulted in 40 planes being taken out of service and the company declaring an operational emergency.

The No-Layoff Policy

Southwest Airlines had never laid off or furloughed any of its employees since the company began operations in 1971. The company's no-layoff policy was seen as integral to how the company treated its employees and management efforts to sustain and nurture the culture. According to Kelleher,[15]

> Nothing kills your company's culture like layoffs. Nobody has ever been furloughed here, and that is unprecedented in the airline industry. It's been a huge strength of ours. It's certainly helped negotiate our union contracts. . .. . .We could have furloughed at various times and been more profitable, but I always thought that was shortsighted. You want to show your people you value them and you're not going to hurt them just to get a little more money in the short term. Not furloughing people breeds loyalty. It breeds a sense of security. It breeds a sense of trust.

Southwest had built up considerable goodwill with its employees and unions over the years by avoiding layoffs. Despite the impact of the Coronavirus pandemic, CEO Gary Kelly reiterated to employees in March 2020 that the company remained committed to its no-layoff policy even though small pay cuts might be necessary to protect the company's solvency. Kelly even pledged to employees that he would work for no salary if the company was forced to ask employees for large pay cuts as a result of the COVID-19 pandemic.[16]

Management Style

At Southwest, management strived to do things in a manner that would make Southwest employees proud of the company they worked for and its work force practices. Managers were expected to spend at least one-third of their time out of the office, walking around the facilities under their supervision, observing firsthand what was going on, listening to employees and being responsive to their concerns.

Company executives were very approachable, insisting on being called by their first names. At new employee orientations, people were told, "We do not call the company chairman and CEO Mr. Kelly, we call him Gary." Managers and executives had an open-door policy, actively listening to employee concerns, opinions, and suggestions for reducing costs and improving efficiency.

Employee-led initiatives were common. Southwest's pilots had been instrumental in developing new protocols for takeoffs and landings that conserved fuel. Another frontline employee had suggested not putting the company logos on trash bags, saving an estimated $250,000 annually. It was Southwest clerks that came up with the idea of doing away with paper tickets and shifting to e-tickets.

There were only four layers of management between a front-line supervisor and the CEO. Southwest's employees enjoyed substantial authority and decision-making power. From time to time, there were candid meetings of frontline employees and managers where operating problems and issues between/among workers and departments were acknowledged, openly discussed, and resolved.[17] Informal problem avoidance and rapid problem resolution were seen as managerial virtues.

Southwest's Two Big Core Values—LUV and Fun

Two core values—LUV and fun—permeated the work environment at Southwest. LUV was much more than the company's ticker symbol and a recurring theme in Southwest's advertising campaigns. Over the years, LUV grew into Southwest's codeword for treating individuals—fellow employees and customers—with dignity and respect and demonstrating a caring, loving attitude. LUV and red hearts commonly appeared on banners and posters at company facilities, as reminders of the compassion that was expected toward customers and other employees. Practicing the Golden Rule, internally and externally, was expected of all employees. Employees who struggled to live up to these expectations were subjected to considerable peer pressure and usually were asked to seek employment elsewhere if they did not soon leave on their own volition.

Fun at Southwest was exactly what the word implies and it occurred throughout the company in the form of the generally entertaining behavior of employees in performing their jobs, the ongoing pranks and jokes, and frequent company-sponsored parties and celebrations (which typically included the Southwest Shuffle). On holidays, employees were encouraged to dress in costumes. There were charity benefit games, chili cook-offs, Halloween parties, new Ronald McDonald House dedications, and other special events of one kind or another at one location or another almost every week. According to one manager, "We're kind of a big family here, and family members have fun together."

Culture-Building Efforts

Southwest executives believed that the company's growth was primarily a function of the rate at which it could hire and train people to fit into its culture and consistently display the traits and behaviors set forth in Living the Southwest Way. Kelly said. ". . ..some things at Southwest won't change. We will continue to expect our people to live what we describe as the 'Southwest Way,' which is to have a Warrior Spirit, Servant's Heart, and Fun-Loving Attitude. Those three things have defined our culture for 36 years."[18]

The Corporate Culture Committee. Southwest formed a Corporate Culture Committee in 1990 to promote "Positively Outrageous Service" and devise tributes, contests, and celebrations intended to nurture and perpetuate the Southwest Spirit and Living the Southwest Way. The Committee was composed of 100 employees that had demonstrated their commitment to Southwest's mission and values and zeal in exhibiting the Southwest Spirit and Living the Southwest Way. Members came from a cross-section of departments and locations and functioned as cultural ambassadors, missionaries, and storytellers during their two-year term.

Over the years, the Committee had sponsored and supported hundreds of ways to promote and ingrain the traits and behaviors embedded in Living the Southwest Way—examples included promoting the use of red hearts and LUV to embody the spirit of Southwest employees caring about each other and Southwest's customers, showing up at a facility to serve pizza or ice cream to employees or to remodel and decorate an employee break room. Kelleher indicated, "We're not big on Committees at Southwest, but of the committees we do have, the Culture Committee is the most important."[19]

Each major department and geographic operating unit had a Local Culture Committee charged with organizing culture-building activities and nurturing the Southwest Spirit within their unit. The company had created a new position in each of its major operating departments and largest geographic locations called Culture Ambassador; the primary function of cultural ambassadors was to nurture the Southwest Spirit by helping ensure that the Local Culture Committee had the resources needed to foster the culture at each of their locations, planning and coordinating departmental celebrations and employee appreciation events, and acting as a liaison between the local office and the corporate office on culture-related matters.

Efforts to Nurture and Sustain the Southwest Culture. Apart from the efforts of the Corporate Culture Committee, the Local Culture Committees, and the cultural ambassadors, Southwest management sought to reinforce the company's core values and culture via a series of employee recognition programs to single out and praise employees for their outstanding contributions to customer service, operational excellence, cost efficiency, and display of the Southwest Spirit. In addition to Kick Tail awards, there were "Heroes of the Heart" awards, *Spirit* magazine Star of the Month awards, President's Awards, and LUV Reports whereby one or more employees could recognize other employees for an outstanding performance or contribution.

Other culture-supportive activities included a CoHearts mentoring program, a Day in the Field program where employees spent time working in another area of the company's operations, a Helping Hands program where volunteers from around the system traveled to work two weekend shifts at other Southwest facilities that were temporarily short-handed or experiencing heavy workloads, and periodic Culture Exchange meetings to celebrate the Southwest Spirit and company milestones. Almost every event at Southwest was videotaped, which provided footage for creating such multipurpose videos as *Keepin' the Spirit Alive* that could be shown at company events all over the system and used in training courses. The concepts of LUV and fun were spotlighted in all of the company's training manuals and videos.

Southwest's monthly employee newsletter often spotlighted the experiences and deeds of particular employees, reprinted letters of praise from customers, and reported company celebrations of milestones. A quarterly news video was sent to all facilities to keep employees up to date on company happenings, provide clips of special events, and share messages from customers, employees, and executives. The company had published a book for employees describing "outrageous" acts of service.

Employee Productivity and Effectiveness

Management was convinced the company's strategy, culture, esprit de corps, and people management practices fostered high labor productivity and contributed to Southwest having low costs in comparison to the costs at its principal domestic rivals (Exhibit 4). Southwest's current CEO, Gary Kelly, had followed Kelleher's lead in pushing for operating excellence. One of Kelly's strategic objectives for Southwest was "to be the safest, most efficient, and most reliable airline in the world." Southwest managers and employees in all positions and ranks were proactive in offering suggestions for improving Southwest's practices and procedures; those with merit were quickly implemented.

Much time and effort over the years had gone into finding the most effective ways to do aircraft maintenance, to operate safely, to make baggage handling more efficient and baggage transfers more accurate, and to improve the percentage of on-time arrivals and departures. Believing that air travelers were more likely to fly Southwest if its flights were reliable and on-time, Southwest's managers constantly monitored on-time arrivals and departures, making inquiries when many flights ran behind and searching for ways to improve on-time performance. Exhibit 5 presents data comparing Southwest against its four domestic rivals on four measures of operating performance.

SOUTHWEST AIRLINES STANDING IN MID-2020

The 737-MAX grounding had affected Southwest Airlines' financial performance in the second half of 2019, but the effect of the novel coronavirus on the airline industry was a far more financially severe event and was expected to have longer term implications for the industry than even the September 11,

EXHIBIT 5   Comparative Statistics on On-Time Flights, Mishandled Baggage, Boarding Denials Due to Oversold Flights, and Passenger Complaints for Major U.S. Airlines, 2016–2020

Percentage of Scheduled Flights Arriving within 15 Minutes of the Scheduled Time (during the first quarter of each year)					
Airline	2016	2017	2018	2019	2020
American Airlines	81.7%	79.2%	78.6%	77.4%	78.4%
Delta Air Lines	87.2%	80.7%	82.1%	82.3%	83.3%
Southwest Airlines	**81.1**%	**78.7**%	**79.3**%	**78.7**%	**84.8**%
United Air Lines	80.9%	80.3%	79.7%	73.6%	78.7%

Mishandled Baggage Reports per 1,000 Passengers (in March of each year)					
Airline	2016	2017	2018	2019	2020
American Airlines	3.08	2.63	3.33	7.44	5.91
Delta Air Lines	1.56	1.63	1.81	4.39	4.09
Southwest Airlines	**2.77**	**2.36**	**2.65**	**4.23**	**3.04**
United Air Lines	2.29	2.42	2.42	6.82	4.70

Involuntary Denied Boardings per 10,000 Passengers Due to Oversold Flights (January through March of each year)					
Airline	2016	2017	2018	2019	2020
American Airlines	0.84	0.75	0.16	0.77	0.39
Delta Air Lines	0.10	0.12	0.01	0.00	0.00
Southwest Airlines	**0.91**	**0.72**	**0.18**	**0.43**	**0.04**
United Air Lines	0.49	0.44	0.02	0.01	0.00

Complaints per 100,000 Passengers Boarded (in March of each year)					
Airline	2016	2017	2018	2019	2020
American Airlines	1.99	1.45	1.05	1.46	5.15
Delta Air Lines	0.45	0.45	0.56	0.31	2.24
Southwest Airlines	**0.29**	**0.34**	**0.27**	**0.38**	**2.62**
United Air Lines	1.99	1.35	2.25	0.96	17.89

Source: Office of Aviation Enforcement and Proceedings, Air Travel Consumer Report, various years.

2001 terrorist attacks. Southwest Airlines recorded a first quarter net loss of $94 million, with operating revenues down 17.8 percent year over year. The company had obtained financial support in the amount $3.3 billion provided by the CARES Act, which protected the salaries of Southwest's 60,000+ employees and bolstered cash on hand.

CEO Gary Kelly commented in a weekly YouTube broadcast to employees that the company was in "intensive care" and the future airline competitive environment would be "a brutal, low-fare environment as there are fore more airline seats, and there will be for some time, than there are customers."[20] The company's historic focus on operational excellence, low-costs, and strategy-supportive organizational culture would likely become even more important and would be heavily relied upon during a recovery of the industry.

ENDNOTES

[1] Kevin and Jackie Freiberg, *NUTS! Southwest Airlines' Crazy Recipe for Business and Personal Success* (New York: Broadway Books, 1998), p. 15.

[2] Freiberg and Freiberg, *NUTS!*, pp. 16–18.

[3] Katrina Brooker, "The Chairman of the Board Looks Back," *Fortune,* May 28, 2001, p. 66.

[4] Feiberg and Freiberg, *NUTS,* p. 31.

[5] Freiberg and Freiberg, *NUTS!,* pp. 26–27.

[6] Ibid., p. 72.

[7] Speech at Texas Christian University, September 13, 2007; accessed at www.southwest.com on September 8, 2008.

[8] Freiberg and Freiberg, *NUTS!,* p. 163.

[9] Speech to Greater Boston Chamber of Commerce, April 23, 2008; accessed at www.southwest.com on September 5, 2008.

[10] Speech to Business Today International Conference, November 20, 2007; accessed at www.southwest.com on September 8, 2008.

[11] Statement posted in the Careers section at www.southwest.com, accessed August 18, 2010 and re-accessed on May 16, 2016. Kelly's statement had been continuously posted on www.southwest.com since 2009.

[12] As quoted in James Campbell Quick, "Crafting an Organizational Structure: Herb's Hand at Southwest Airlines," *Organizational Dynamics* 21, no. 2 (Autumn 1992), p. 51.

[13] Quick, "Crafting an Organizational Structure," p. 52.

[14] Sunoo, "How Fun Flies at Southwest Airlines," p. 72.

[15] Brooks, "The Chairman of the Board Looks Back," p. 72.

[16] Mary Schlangenstein, "With 'Virtually Zero' Air Travel, Southwest Warns of Pay Risk," *Bloomberg,* April 23, 2020, accessed at https://www.bloomberg.com/news/articles/2020-04-23/.

southwest-ceo-urges-pay-cuts-with-air-travel-at-virtually-zero.

[17] Hallowell, "Southwest Airlines: A Case Study Linking Employee Needs Satisfaction and Organizational Capabilities to Competitive Advantage," p. 524.

[18] Speech to Business Today International Conference, November 20, 2007; accessed at www.southwest.com on September 8, 2008.

[19] Freiberg and Freiberg, *NUTS!,* p. 165.

[20] As quoted in Kyle Arnold, "Southwest Airlines CEO Gary Kelly: 'It will be a brutal, low-fare environment'," *The Dallas Morning News,* May 29, 2020, accessed at https://www.dallasnews.com/business/airlines/2020/05/29/southwest-airlines-ceo-gary-kelly-it-will-be-a-brutal-low-fare-environment/.

Uber Technologies in 2020: Is the Gig Economy Labor Force Working for Uber?

Emily Farrell
MBA Candidate, Sonoma State University

Armand Gilinsky, Jr.
Sonoma State University

In the words of Travis Kalanick, founder and former CEO of Uber Technologies, "In a lot of ways, it's not the money that allows you to do new things. It's the growth and the ability to find things that people want and to use your creativity to target those."[1] When Kalanick and Garrett Camp generated the idea that became Uber in 2009, they saw an existing taxi industry that was not meeting their needs and sought to create a service that was more efficient and worked better for everyone involved. They sought out to create a service that people would want. The business model that Kalanick and Camp created saw success as the company spread internationally, but there were also many challenges. Uber had always considered as central to its business model the gig economy drivers as "customers of its mobile technology." Nonetheless, recent legislation in the State of California threatened that model as it was intended to reclassify all gig economy workers as hired and paid employees.

As of January 1, 2020, California's state legislature began to implement legislation known as Assembly Bill 5 (AB5), reclassifying many independent contractors as employees, intended to include Uber's drivers. At the time, Uber's CEO Dara Khosrowshahi faced the challenge of deciding the best course of action to handle the legal situation in California, by either agreeing to convert all California Uber drivers to payroll employees; fighting the legislation to prove that it did not apply to Uber's independent drivers; or assuming that Uber would not be impacted by the legislation and carrying on with business as usual. Each option potentially placed the company at risk. While Khosrowshahi's immediate focus was on the impact on Uber's California business model, he also needed to prepare for the possibility that other states and countries where Uber operated could follow California's example and enact similar laws challenging the labor status of gig economy workers.

THE SOFTWARE INDUSTRY

Uber Technologies often made the claim that it was not in the transportation industry as it did not own the vehicles and did not consider drivers to be its employees. Uber instead asserted itself as a technology company that supplied a software platform that allowed independent users to connect to facilitate ride sharing. The assertion that Uber was a technology company supplying software grouped it into a large and diverse industry of software developers and suppliers. The software industry was comprised of companies that design, develop, and publish software for computers, smartphones, and video games. Major industry products and services included system and application software publishing, custom application design and development, technology consulting and training, and re-sale of computer hardware and software. Total industry revenue in 2019 was $269.9 billion, but profit margins declined 28.6 percent. Annual growth from 2014 to 2019 was five percent and was projected to be 2.1 percent from 2019 to 2024. The number of businesses in the software publishing industry rose 10.8 percent from 2014 to 2019.[2]

Major Challenges

High competition was one of the major challenges of the software industry, although it had varied greatly from company to company. Because the industry was so large and broad, there has often been more external competition than competition with other companies within the industry. Competition has depended largely on the target market, with companies that produce software experiencing the highest competition.[3] Uber's direct competition within its industry sector was Lyft, another ridesharing application that had a similar business model to Uber's, while the majority of Uber's indirect competition existed within the transportation industry.

Rapid technological change was a consistent challenge for the software industry, not only in terms of changing industry standards, but also the increasing rates of adoption by and sophistication of customers. This required companies to invest significant capital in research and development for a new product. Companies had to constantly improve their performance levels while keeping prices as low as possible in order to stay competitive. Once a product was released successfully, in order to stay competitive, updates needed to be programmed and released regularly. One development that eased this stress for the industry was the trend to release software as a digital subscription rather than a physical product that must be installed on a computer. It thus became much easier for developers to provide updates that did not require the customer to return to a physical store.[4] Uber's business model allowed users to use its application free of charge, paying only for the individual ride and related charges. Its smartphone application enabled Uber to constantly improve the app performance to better support drivers and riders via periodic releases of updates to its users.

Data security was also a challenge for the software publishing industry. Many software companies retain their customers' personal and sensitive information, making them targets of cyber-attacks. With an increase in cyber hacking in the last decade, the way companies collect, store, and transmit customer data has been under scrutiny. The possibility of becoming a cyber-attack victim has been a concern for the companies' integrity and trust among consumers, not to mention the litigation and liability that comes with an attack. But it has also been a financial liability to prevent hacking, as companies must dedicate significant resources to ensure data security keeps them protected.[5] Uber's business model has allowed users to store credit card information in the application so that Uber can charge riders directly to the card on file and pay the drivers through the app as well. This has placed great responsibility on Uber to protect user financial data, as a security breach could threaten user confidence in Uber and potentially result in users no longer using Uber's technology.

Market Size and Forecasted Growth

Software is a large and diverse industry, which brought in $269.9 billion in 2019 from domestic and international sources. The United States controlled roughly 45 percent of the international software market as of 2019. Beginning in the late 1990s, the industry experienced an explosive level of growth before the recession stalled growth of sales and employment.[6] Although growth has slowed in the last decade compared to the boom of the 1990s, the software industry has forecasted to continue growing from 2020 to 2025. There has been a growing demand from businesses, individuals, and government for various types of software. Businesses have accounted for approximately 63.9 percent of industry software, while individual households have accounted for 28.6 percent and government has accounted for 7.5 percent.[7] In the ridesharing niche of the market, Uber and Lyft have been able to take control and accounted for 98 percent of market spending, which has made it a challenge for new competitors to enter the market.[8] In 2019, Uber had a total of 110 million users worldwide, and more than 200,000 in California.[9]

Industry annual growth rates were expected to slow from now through 2024, compared to the five percent annual growth from 2014 to 2019, but revenues were expected to consistently grow through 2024 as seen in Exhibit 1. In 2019, the software industry was well into the growth phase of the industry life cycle. Increases in the number of households with at least one computer, as well as increases in smartphone ownership, mobile internet connections, and government spending were expected to support continual growth in the software industry. Businesses were expected to continue to use software to improve productivity and add value to other areas of their companies. Software-as-a-service was also expected to

EXHIBIT 1   Performance Data Outlook for the Software Industry

	Revenue ($m)	Enterprises (units)	Employment (units)	Wages ($m)	Number of Mobile Internet Connections (Millions)
2019	$269,874	10,606	660,932	$117,156	366
2020	$275,864	11,257	692,231	$122,115	398
2021	$281,773	11,936	723,439	$127,042	431
2022	$287,490	12,671	756,229	$132,164	464
2023	$293,161	13,457	789,600	$137,352	497
2024	$299,084	14,290	819,270	$142,035	530
2025	$305,435	15,067	848,673	$146,717	565

Recreated from source: Cook, D. (July 2019). *IBISWorld Industry Report 51121: Software Publishing in the US.*

gain a more consistent revenue stream in the future, as it charges customers a monthly subscription fee to access software, as compared to a one-time purchase of the software.[10] As an individual company, Uber was well into the growth phase of its life cycle as well in 2019. From its early days starting in San Francisco, offering free rides in order to create buzz through word of mouth, Uber was now a well-established service provider throughout the United States, as well as worldwide. As Uber established itself in the rideshare segment, it started working on expanding its services. Uber Eats has been launched as a food delivery service, as Uber has also expanded into the trucking industry and was expected to expand into the aviation industry.[11]

Key Industry Players

The software publishing industry is very diverse, with a large number of smaller companies competing more with companies in other industries more so than with internal competition. The largest well-known companies in the industry are Apple, Microsoft, Oracle, and IBM, which only made up 37.5 percent of the market in 2019. A large number of minor players that have a narrower concentration focused only on one or two market segments, such as Uber Technologies, Square Inc., and Xcel Mobility Inc., make up the remaining 62.5 percent of the market.[12] Many companies like Uber have been considered part of the software and technology industry, but have not directly competed with many other software companies. They have instead disrupted competition in other industries, such as Uber has done in the transportation industry.

THE HISTORY OF UBER TECHNOLOGIES

In December 2008, founders Travis Kalanick and Garrett Camp could not find a ride during a snowstorm in Paris, France, which led them to create the concept of Uber. Kalanick and Camp sought out to develop a better service than the common taxi, and chose the name Uber because it is derived from the German word which means "above all the rest."[13] In March 2009, Kalanick and Camp, along with Oscar Salazar Gaitan, developed a smartphone app that allowed users to tap a button on their phone and get a car ride. UberCab officially launched in San Francisco, California, with their first ride request on July 5, 2010. Uber began hiring immediately, finding their first employee and eventual chief executive officer Ryan Graves through a Twitter post. Shortly after Graves was promoted to chief executive officer, Uber introduced UberX, the company's most well-known service, which sought to match drivers using their own vehicles to users in need of a ride. Uber's rideshare service was immediately popular with San Francisco's tech-savvy residents, many of whom did not own their own cars. They could now quickly hail a ride from the convenience of their smartphone. The founders decided in October 2010 to drop "Cab" from the company name, as they determined that their service was not a taxicab so there was no need to include it, so they opted to maintain the Uber name alone.[14]

In order to edge out competition that offers a similar service, a company must strategize a way to differentiate itself.[15] Uber has done this by continuously expanding its reach and expanding the services it offers. In May 2011, Uber launched in New York, which was met by much opposition from the city's taxi industry. Seven months later in December 2011, Uber launched internationally in Paris, the same city where the idea was first born. In August 2014, UberPool was launched, allowing rides to be coordinated so that a driver had multiple riders travelling in the same general direction. This concept allowed riders to share the cost and also aimed to decrease traffic congestion and related pollution. Uber first began to venture out of the rideshare service in April 2015 with Uber Eats, an on-demand food delivery service, which debuted in New York, Los Angeles, and Chicago. In September 2016, Uber launched a self-driving vehicle pilot program in Pittsburgh, where riders could choose to request a self-driving car to pick them up. Uber again looked to expand the services it offers in May 2017, when Uber Freight launched, offering a hassle-free platform to allow trucking companies and independent drivers to connect with shippers. Uber started as an idea that eased the way people connect through ridesharing, and over the course of time has evolved to become a multi-use platform for people in need of a variety of services to easily find someone willing to provide

such a service. In August 2017, Uber's board voted to hire Dara Khosrowshahi, former CEO of Expedia, as the new CEO. He replaced Travis Kalanick after he resigned following a series of controversies regarding Kalanick and the cultural environment of Uber.[16] As of December 2018, Uber had 91 million monthly active platform consumers and 3.9 million drivers. At this time, 10 billion trips were completed worldwide in 63 countries, with an average of 14 million trips completed each day. In May 2019, Uber went public on the New York Stock Exchange, with a share price of $45 and a market capitalization of $75.5 billion.[17] A graph depicting Uber's stock price performance since its May 10, 2019, conception date through December 30, 2019 is presented in Exhibit 2.

UBER'S BUSINESS MODEL

Target Market

As of January 2020, Uber was now a worldwide brand, but from its early days Uber sought out to serve those with busy lives in large urban cities. Many people living in large cities like San Francisco and New York often did not own cars due to the lack of parking and the high cost of available parking. Often these people relied on public transportation or taxis,

EXHIBIT 2   **Uber's Stock Price Since Going Public on May 10, 2019 through December 30, 2019**

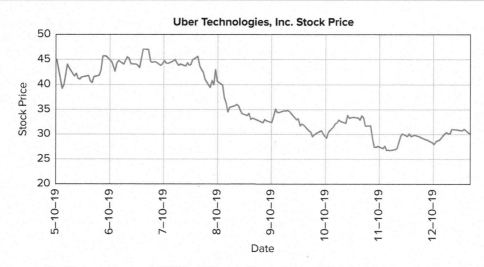

and Uber sought to provide a more efficient, lower cost means of transportation for when a ride was needed at a moment's notice. As Uber expanded, it began to offer a wide array of levels of service, aimed to serve basically every segment of society. Exhibit 3 shows a breakdown of Uber segmentation, targeting and positioning based on several demographic categories of users served worldwide in January 2020.

Uber for Business targeted the business traveler by allowing employees to use Uber and have the trip billed directly to their company's account. The aim of launching Uber for Business was to create a centralized billing system for company administrators to track and schedule rides for all members of the organization.[18]

Competition

Uber's main competition in the software industry were other gig economy companies like Lyft and DoorDash. Lyft has a seemingly similar business

EXHIBIT 3   Uber Segmentation, Target and Positioning

Type of Segmentation	Segmentation Criteria	Uber Target Customer Segment	Uber Target Customer Segment	Uber Target Customer Segment
		Uber X, Uber XI, Uber pool, Uber-MOTO, Uber Auto	**Uber Premium, Uber Go, UberEATS, UberBOAT, UberRUSH**	**Uber Access**
GEOGRAPHIC	Region	North & South America, Asia, New Zealand, Australia, Europe, Africa Uber AUTO – Bangalore and Pune only	North & South America, Asia, New Zealand, Australia, Europe, Africa	North & South America, Asia, New Zealand, Australia, Europe, Africa
DEMOGRAPHIC	Density	Urban/rural	Urban/rural	Urban/rural
	Age	18+	25–65	45–65
	Gender	Males & Females	Males & Females	Males & Females
	Life-cycle stage	Bachelor, Newly Married, Full Nest I, II, III, Empty Nest I, II, Solitary Survivor I, II	Full Nest I, II, III, Empty Nest I, II	Full Nest III, Empty Nest I, II
	Occupation	Students, employees, professionals	Employees, professionals	Retired, handicapped
BEHAVIORAL	Degree of loyalty	'Hard core loyals' 'Soft core loyals' 'Switchers'	'Hard core loyals' 'Soft core loyals' 'Switchers'	'Soft core loyals'
	Benefits sought	Cost-efficiency	Sense of achievement	Convenience
	Personality	Easygoing, determined, ambitious	Determined, ambitious	Easygoing
	User status	Non-users, potential users, first-time users, regular users	Potential users, first-time users, regular users	Non-users, potential users
PSYCHOGRAPHIC	Social class	Lower class, working class, middle class	Middle class, upper class	Working class, middle class, upper class
	Lifestyle	Struggler, mainstreamer, explorer, reformer	Aspirer, succeeder, explorer, reformer	Resigned, struggler, mainstreamer

Recreated from source: Dudovskiy, J. (2018, March 25). Uber Segmentation, Targeting and Positioning - Research-Methodology. Retrieved March 15, 2020, from https://research-methodology.net/uber-segmentation-targeting-and-positioning/.

plan that facilitates ridesharing. Both companies have recently gone public, and currently are trading for similar prices as of January 2020, although Lyft has had a higher peak in the last year at $74.99 per share and Uber's 52 week peak is only $47.08 per share.[19] Both companies' ridesharing apps offer relatively similar levels of ridesharing services that both advertise as hailing a ride with the touch of a button. Uber's meal delivery service UberEATS has competed with other similar companies like DoorDash, which offer a platform for drivers to pick up prepared food from local restaurants and deliver to the customer. Uber, Lyft, and DoorDash were facing the same controversy over how they classify their drivers, with all three gig economy companies maintaining that they do not hire employees, they have only provided the technology to facilitate the service. Uber has differentiated itself from other gig economy companies by offering a wide array of services. It has competed with Lyft in ridesharing, and its Uber Eats segment has competed with DoorDash, but as of January 2020, there are no other companies that offer the array of technology services that Uber does in every segment in which it competes.

Outside of the gig economy, the majority of Uber's competition has come from the taxi and limousine industry. From the very beginning, the taxi industry has viewed Uber as a threat and has worked to push regulations regarding how and where Uber operates. For example, in Colorado regulators working to protect the taxi industry enacted laws prohibiting Uber from operating within 100 feet of local restaurants and hotels. Limo services have also attacked Uber over its business methods. Uber has refused to back down from competition. While Travis Kalanick led Uber as CEO, the company continued to operate in mass despite many cease-and-desist letters from numerous officials in markets Uber was operating in. Kalanick was a controversial leader, but his tenaciousness earned him a reputation among Silicon Valley's elite, and earned the company high profile investors, including Jeff Bezos and Bill Gurley.[20]

Operations

As a software company, Uber has asserted that it does not employ the drivers, but rather it provides the network that connects available drivers with passengers in need of a ride. Uber has been attractive to riders as an upgraded alternative to hailing a taxi or using public transportation, while it has appealed to drivers as a flexible way to achieve a high earning potential. Uber's network orchestrator model has given it the ability to respond to market changes quickly and effectively in comparison to its competitors in the transportation industry that use a service provider network. Uber's operational strategy paid drivers based on fares rather than an hourly wage like a traditional taxi company. This has allowed revenues to be more accurately reflective of the local market share and has been useful in analyzing the markets in which Uber operates. It has also helped Uber to reduce costs, as drivers have only been paid for rides provided to passengers, rather than by the hour, regardless of the number, or lack thereof, of rides provided. Uber has offered financing options to obtain a car for people looking to drive that do not currently own their own car, but Uber's business model has depended on drivers driving their own cars. This also helped Uber to reduce costs, as Uber has not been responsible for the expense of the vehicle, insurance, gas, or maintenance cost.[21]

Controversies over the Years

Uber has not survived as a company for this long without controversy. Uber has faced much opposition in large cities, such as San Francisco and New York, from the taxi industry. In 2010, Uber received a cease and desist letter from San Francisco's Metro Transit Authority, which claimed that Uber was running a taxi service without proper licensing. After three years of regulatory litigation, a deal was reached that allowed Uber to continue to operate in San Francisco.

In February 2017, Uber faced the first of several sexual harassment charges. After news of a sexist workplace culture was exposed, Uber responded by hiring former United States Attorney General Eric Holder to investigate the claims and workplace culture issues. Founder Travis Kalanick was forced to resign as chief executive officer by strong pressure from the board of directors, and he was replaced by Dara Khosrowshahi.[22]

Uber was first met with opposition on how it classifies its drivers in December 2013, when 35,000 Uber drivers joined together to file a lawsuit against Uber. The drivers argued that they should be categorized as employees with benefits and paid time off, rather than contract workers as Uber had designated them. Uber was able to settle with the drivers outside of court, and their drivers are still considered independent contractors in most states as of January 2020.[23] Uber and other gig economy companies have faced much opposition on classifying their labor forces as independent contractors who are able to set their own flexible schedules but are not eligible for employee benefits such as paid time off, overtime, and medical coverage.

California's AB5

On January 1, 2020, a new law, AB5, took effect in California reclassifying many independent contractors as employees. The law aimed to force gig economy companies like Uber to offer their workers rights like minimum wage, overtime, and paid leave, which labor unions have been advocating for years. Uber had previously stated that it would follow AB5, but rather has so far only attempted to prove that the law's legal framework does not apply to its drivers.[24] In 2019, before the California law came into effect, Uber joined with Lyft and DoorDash to file paperwork for the Protect App-Based Drivers and Services Act, as an attempt to block the upcoming law. This initiative sought to define an app-based driver as an independent contractor based on multiple criteria. It argued that if the entity, such as Uber, did not require the driver to work or be on call for specific hours, did not require the driver to accept any specific rideshare or delivery request to remain active, and did not restrict the driver from working on other apps, that said driver should not be considered an employee. The initiative also aimed to amend certain issues that led to AB5 being passed, including requiring employers of independent contractors to provide a healthcare subsidy and a guaranteed minimum earning equal to 120 percent of the current minimum wage. The initiative also addressed a per-mile compensation to be adjusted for inflation, workers' compensation for on-the-job injuries, discrimination protections, criminal background checks for drivers, zero-tolerance drug and alcohol policies, and driver safety training. As of this time, the status of the Protect App-Based Drivers and Services Act is still pending.[25]

KHOSROWSHAHI'S DECISION

Uber had many areas to keep an eye on regarding their future operations, but as of late spring 2020,

the immediate challenges were the classification and safety of its workers. Many gig economy companies were facing the similar issues, and some had already joined with Uber to fight the pending implementation of the California legislation. Going forward, Uber's CEO Dara Khosrowshahi needed to decide how Uber should continue to operate in California, and do so safely, given the unknown ramifications and duration of the COVID-19 pandemic.

One option under consideration was to interpret AB5 as legislation that would include all Uber drivers and reclassify all California drivers as employees on their payroll. This option could be very costly to Uber, which had posted a net profit in only one fiscal year since 2016, as seen in Exhibit 4. Under this option, Uber would be required to pay for employee benefits such as paid time off and medical insurance and workers' compensation, all of which would add to the current liabilities on its balance sheet. Uber's current liabilities had already increased since 2017, as shown in Exhibit 5. This option was also not ideal for most drivers, especially those that already had another job with a set schedule and were driving to supplement their incomes. As an employer, if Uber saw it to be fit, it would have the authority to set the hours and locations that drivers were required to drive.

Khosrowshahi's second option was to ignore AB5 and continue business as usual in California. This option could be detrimental to Uber, as labor unions were adamant that the gig economy workers should be reclassified as employees with all of the benefits that would accrue to being paid workers. Ignoring AB5 could possibly result in a future court ruling that Uber drivers must be included in the umbrella of workers that California's AB5 covers. Failure to comply could also ultimately result in the termination of Uber's services in the State of California.

Khosrowshahi's third option was to hire lawyers to advocate on its behalf that Uber drivers "are independent contractors and do not fit the definition of an employee," therefore AB5 does not apply to Uber. Mindful that Uber had experienced more than a few legal and ethical controversies surrounding its operations, navigating the legal route to classifying their drivers was expected to play a major role in determining whether or not Uber would be allowed to operate in California, not to mention in other states considering similar legislation down the road.

EXHIBIT 4   Uber Technologies, Inc.'s Income Statements, 2016–2019 (in thousands)

	2019	2018	2017	2016
Total Revenue	$14,147,000	$11,270,000	$ 7,932,000	$3,845,000
Cost of Revenue	7,208,000	5,623,000	4,160,000	2,228,000
Gross Profit	6,939,000	5,647,000	3,772,000	1,617,000
Operating Expenses				
Research & Development	4,836,000	1,505,000	1,201,000	864,000
SG&A Expenses	7,925,000	5,233,000	4,787,000	2,575,000
Total Operating Expenses	15,525,000	8,680,000	7,852,000	4,640,000
Operating Income/Loss	(8,596,000)	(3,033,000)	(4,080,000)	(3,023,000)
Interest Expense	559,000	648,000	479,000	334,000
Total Other Income/Expenses Net	488,000	4,889,000	(87,000)	117,000
Income Before Tax	(8,433,000)	1,312,000	(4,575,000)	(3,218,000)
Income Tax Expense	45,000	283,000	(542,000)	28,000
Income from Cont. Operations after income taxes and before loss from equity method investment	(8,512,000)	987,000	(4,033,000)	(3,246,000)
Income (loss) from discontinued operations, net of income taxes	—	—	—	2,876,000
Net Income	$ (8,506,000)	$ 997,000	$(4,033,000)	$ (370,000)
Net Income available to common shareholders	(8,506,000)	1,938,000	(4,033,000)	(370,000)
Basic and diluted EPS	$(6.81)	—	$(9.46)	$(0.90)
Basic Average Shares	1,248,353	443,360	426,360	411,501
Diluted Average Shares	1,248,353	478,999	426,360	411,501

Source: Uber Technologies, Inc. 2019 Annual Report.

EXHIBIT 5   Uber Technologies, Inc.'s Balance Sheets, 2017–2019 (in thousands)

At December 31	2019	2018	2017
Assets			
Current Assets			
Cash and Cash Equivalents	$10,873,000	$ 6,406,000	$ 4,393,000
Other Short-Term Investments	440,000	-	-
Total Cash	11,313,000	6,406,000	4,393,000
Net Receivables	1,214,000	919,000	739,000
Other Current Assets	300,000	179,000	21,000
Total Current Assets	13,925,000	8,658,000	6,837,000
Non-Current Assets			
Property, Plant and Equipment			
Gross Property, Plant and Equipment	4,699,000	2,587,000	1,723,000
Accumulated Depreciation	(1,374,000)	(946,000)	(531,000)
Net Property, Plant and Equipment	3,325,000	1,641,000	1,192,000
Equity and Other Investments	11,891,000	11,667,000	5,969,000
Goodwill	167,000	153,000	39,000
Intangible Assets	71,000	82,000	54,000
Other Long-Term Assets	2,382,000	1,787,000	1,335,000
Total Non-Current Assets	17,836,000	15,330,000	8,589,000
Total Assets	$31,761,000	$23,988,000	$15,426,000

At December 31	2019	2018	2017
Liabilities and Stockholders' Equity			
Liabilities			
Current Liabilities			
Current Debt	$ 0	$ 0	$ 87,000
Accounts Payable	272,000	150,000	213,000
Taxes Payable	194,000	-	244,000
Accrued Liabilities	1,289,000	4,211,000	942,000
Deferred Revenues	76,000	-	38,000
Other Current Liabilities	222,000	11,000	517,000
Total Current Liabilities	5,639,000	5,313,000	3,847,000
Non-Current Liabilities			
Long Term Debt	5,707,000	4,535,000	3,048,000
Deferred Tax Liabilities	1,027,000	-	1,041,000
Other Long-Term Liabilities	315,000	1,811,000	741,000
Total Non-Current Liabilities	11,250,000	8,342,000	20,136,000
Total Liabilities	16,889,000	13,655,000	23,983,000
Stockholders' Equity			
Common Stock	-	-	-
Retained Earnings	(16,362,000)	(10,334,000)	(8,874,000)
Accumulated Other Comprehensive Income	(187,000)	(188,000)	(3,000)
Total Stockholders' Equity	14,190,000	10,333,000	(8,557,000)
Total Liabilities and Stockholders' Equity	$31,761,000	$23,988,000	$15,426,000

Source: Uber Technologies, Inc. 2019 Annual Report.

After ridership plummeted 80 percent in April 2020 due to the due to the COVID-19 pandemic, on May 4, 2020, Uber announced that it was cutting 3,700 jobs. On May 18, 2020, Uber Technologies Inc. announced in an e-mail to its staff that it was cutting thousands of additional jobs, closing more than three dozen offices, and re-evaluating big bets in areas ranging from freight to self-driving technology as Khosrowshahi attempted to steer the ride-hailing giant through the coronavirus pandemic. Through these moves, Uber planned to save more than $1 billion in fixed costs. Uber has rebuilt its app to make sure drivers and riders adhere to safety guidelines around the novel coronavirus. Before each trip, drivers and passengers will now have to agree to a "Go Online Checklist" of items, including wearing a face mask, keeping windows rolled down when possible and have no one sitting in the front seat. "Many countries around the world are moving to a new phase of recovery," Khosrowshahi was quoted in the popular business press as saying. "We've built a new product experience for a new normal." On its website, the company pledged 10 million free rides and deliveries of food for frontline healthcare workers, seniors, and people in need around the world.

As Khosrowshahi contemplated Uber's next move, he remained mindful that, while only his California drivers were currently under scrutiny, developing a California-only approach would help or hinder the company's ability to handle future legislation in the remaining 49 states and the District of Columbia.

ENDNOTES

[1] Wohlsen, M. (2018, October 5). What Uber Will Do With All That Money From Google. Retrieved April 4, 2020, from https://www.wired.com/2014/01/uber-travis-kalanick/.

[2] Cook, D. (July 2019). *IBISWorld Industry Report 51121: Software Publishing in the US.*

[3] Ibid.

[4] Ibid.

[5] Ibid.

[6] *Multimedia, graphics & publishing software - quarterly update 6/10/2019.* (2019, June 10). Fort Mill, South Carolina: Mergent. Retrieved February 20, 2020 from https://search-proquest-com.sonoma.idm.oclc.org/abicomplete/docview/2299432057/BD153144CA5F4431PQ/1?accountid=13949.

[7] Industry Profiles: Prepackaged Software. (2020, February 15). Retrieved February 22, 2020, from https://www.encyclopedia.com/economics/economics-magazines/industry-profiles-prepackaged-software-0.

[8] Cai, K. (2019, October 16). To Beat Uber And Lyft, This Startup Vows To Give Its Drivers The Full Fare. Retrieved February 15, 2020, from https://www.forbes.com/sites/kenrickcai/2019/08/22/nomad-rides-commission-free-ride-hailing/.

[9] Herrera, S. (2019, September 21). Uber, Lyft Drivers Torn as California Law Could Reclassify Them. Retrieved April 20, 2020, from https://www.wsj.com/articles/uber-lyft-drivers-torn-as-california-law-could-reclassify-them-11569063601.

[10] Cook, D. (July 2019). *IBISWorld Industry Report 51121: Software Publishing in the US.*

[11] Brown, M. (n.d.). Uber—What's Fueling Uber's Growth Engine? Retrieved February 15, 2020, from https://growthhackers.com/growth-studies/uber.

[12] Cook, D. (July 2019). *IBISWorld Industry Report 51121: Software Publishing in the US.*

[13] O'Connell, B. (2019, July 23). History of Uber: Timeline and Facts. Retrieved February 15, 2020, from https://www.thestreet.com/technology/history-of-uber-15028611.

[14] The History of Uber—Uber's Timeline: Uber Newsroom US. (n.d.). Retrieved February 22, 2020, from https://www.uber.com/newsroom/history/.

[15] Porter, M. E. (1996). What Is Strategy? *Harvard Business Review, 74*(6), pp. 61–78.

[16] Carson, B. (2017, August 30). It's Official: Dara Khosrowshahi Is Uber's New CEO. Retrieved April 15, 2020, from https://www.forbes.com/sites/bizcarson/2017/08/29/its-official-dara-khosrowshahi-is-ubers-new-ceo/.

[17] O'Connell, B. (2019, July 23). History of Uber: Timeline and Facts. Retrieved February 15, 2020, from https://www.thestreet.com/technology/history-of-uber-15028611.

[18] Donovan, F. (2014). Uber competitor Lyft targets corporate market with Lyft for work. *FierceMobileIT,* Retrieved from http://sonoma.idm.oclc.org/login?url=https://search-proquest-com.sonoma.idm.oclc.org/docview/1625154452?accountid=13949.

[19] Uber Technologies, Inc. (UBER) Stock Price, Quote, History & News. (2020, April 4). Retrieved April 4, 2020, from https://finance.yahoo.com/quote/UBER?p=UBER.

[20] Hempel, J., & Mangalindan, J. (2013). Hey, Taxi Company, You Talkin' to Me? *Fortune, 168*(6), p. 96.

[21] O'Connell, B. (2019, July 23). History of Uber: Timeline and Facts. Retrieved February 15, 2020, from https://www.thestreet.com/technology/history-of-uber-15028611.

[22] Ibid.

[23] Tamberino, R. (n.d.). Uber: A Winning Strategy. Retrieved February 29, 2020, from https://digital.hbs.edu/platform-rctom/submission/uber-a-winning-strategy/.

[24] Absher, S. (2020). California's AB5 & gig work: What now? *BenefitsPRO,* Retrieved from http://sonoma.idm.oclc.org/login?url=https://search-proquest-com.sonoma.idm.oclc.org/docview/2348119608?accountid=13949.

[25] Uber, lyft, DoorDash try end run of California's AB5 with new bill. (2019, October 30). *Benzinga Newswires* Retrieved from http://sonoma.idm.oclc.org/login?url=https://search-proquest-com.sonoma.idm.oclc.org/docview/2310418054?accountid=13949.

Starbucks in 2020: Is the Company on Track to Achieve Attractive Growth and Operational Excellence?

Mc Graw Hill **connect**

Arthur A. Thompson

The University of Alabama

Since its founding in 1987 as a modest nine-store operation in Seattle, Washington, Starbucks had become the premier roaster, marketer, and retailer of specialty coffees in the world, with just over 32,000 store locations in 78 countries as of April 2020 and annual sales of $26.5 billion in fiscal year 2019, ending September 30, 2019. In addition to its flagship Starbucks brand coffees and coffee beverages, Starbucks' other brands and products included Starbucks Reserve blends of coffee, Teavana teas, Seattle's Best Coffee, Evolution Fresh juices and smoothies, Ethos bottled waters, Torrefazione Italia Coffee, and Princi bakery products. Starbucks stores also sold baked pastries, cold and hot sandwiches, salads, salad and grain bowls, oatmeal, yogurt parfaits and fruit cups purchased from a variety of local, regional, and national suppliers. In January 2017, then CEO and company founder Howard Starbucks launched a somewhat grandiose strategic initiative to inject more innovation and fresh approaches into the company's operations and to spur growth:

- Open 20-30 Starbucks Reserve™ Roasteries and Tasting Rooms, which would showcase the theater of coffee roasting and brewing in a big, multi-level stores with amazing decorations, seating for upwards of a thousand patrons, multiple types of coffee bars with elaborate menus of innovative coffee beverages and interesting food selections, areas where friends could gather at community tables or in lounge areas with fireplaces, a mixology bar serving traditional Italian cocktails, multiple dining venues, and an upscale Princi bakery where patrons could watch chefs preparing fresh-baked artisanal Italian breads, sandwiches, and pastries being served to diners. Going into 2020, Roasteries had been opened in Seattle, Shanghai, Milan, New York, Chicago, and Tokyo—all attracted local coffee enthusiasts, partiers, nearby shoppers curious to see what the Brewery offered, and visiting sightseers looking to enjoy a very different kind of Starbucks experience.

- Open 1,000 Starbucks Reserve stores worldwide to bring premium experiences to customers and promote the company's recently-introduced Starbucks Reserve™ coffees; these locations were to offer a more intimate small-lot coffee experience and gave customers a chance to chat with a barista about all things coffee. The menu at Starbucks Reserve stores was to consist of handcrafted hot and cold Starbucks Reserve™ coffee beverages, hot and cold teas, ice cream/coffee beverages, and an assortment of small plates, sandwiches and wraps, desserts, wines, and beer. Packages of Starbucks Reserve™ whole bean coffees were to be available for purchase. Plans called for four types of brewing methods for the coffees and teas. Starbucks had 43 Starbucks Reserve locations in February 2020.

- Transform about 20 percent of the company's existing portfolio of Starbucks stores into upgraded Starbucks Reserve coffee bars.

However, shortly after announcing the initiative, Howard Schultz stepped down as Starbucks CEO, turning the role over to Kevin Johnson, Starbucks chief operating officer with whom Schultz had worked closely for the past two years—they had adjoining offices connected by a door and usually visited together multiple times a day. Shultz stayed on as chairman of the company's board of directors and focused his time on social initiatives and plans for the upscale Roastery locations and Starbucks Reserve brand. Schultz exuded confidence that Johnson was the right person to lead Starbucks in the future and that he was well prepared to meet the challenges of continuing to build the Starbucks brand, enhance the consumer experience, and manage its global operations.

Johnson fairly quickly scaled back the sizes of all three of the somewhat transformational strategic moves announced by Schultz, chiefly due to their cost and questionable profitability, and proceeded to steer Starbucks back to the strategic path the company had steadfastly pursued for most of the past decade; these included the following strategy elements:

- Maintain Starbucks standing as one of the most recognized and respected brands in the world and stay strongly focused on providing customers with a pleasing Starbucks experience that prompted them to patronize Starbucks stores frequently.
- Continue disciplined expansion of the company's store base, adding stores in both existing, developed markets and in newer, higher growth markets like China, which for several years had been singled out as Starbucks best opportunity for opening hundreds of new stores annually. During fiscal 2018 and fiscal 2019, Starbucks opened new stores in China at the rate of 1 every 15 hours; as of March 31, 2020, the company had 4,351 company-operated stores in China. Shanghai alone had over 600 Starbucks stores, more than any other city in the world. Starbucks goal was to have 5,000 stores in China by 2021.

- Optimize the mix of company-operated and licensed stores by determining which type of store was best suited to ongoing changes in business and political circumstances in various countries around the world and by recognizing that to the special situations of stores operating in big hotels, resorts, airports, hospitals, major office buildings, and on university campuses sometimes called for licensed stores and sometimes for stores owned and operated by Starbucks.

- Continue to offer consumers new coffee and other products in a variety of forms, across new categories, diverse channels, and alternative store formats.

- Continue to enhance the company's social responsibility strategy and increase the company's efforts to be a good corporate citizen, ethically source high-quality coffee, contribute positively to the communities in which it does business, be an employer of choice, and exert ever-stronger efforts to protect the planet.

Exhibit 1 provides an overview of Starbucks performance during fiscal years 2010–2019.

EXHIBIT 1   Financial and Operating Summary for Starbucks Corporation, Fiscal Years 2010–2019 ($ in millions, except for per-share amounts)

	Fiscal Years Ending				
	Sept. 29, 2019	Sept. 30, 2018	Oct. 1, 2017	Oct. 2, 2016	Oct. 3, 2010
INCOME STATEMENT DATA					
Net revenues:					
Company-operated stores	$21,544.4	$19,690.3	$17,650.7	$16,844.1	$ 8,963.5
Licensed stores	2,875.0	2,652.2	2,355.0	2,154.2	875.2
Consumer packaged goods, foodservice, and other	2,089.2	2,377.0	2,381.1	2,317.6	868.7
Total net revenues	$26,508.6	$24,719.5	$22,386.8	$21,315.9	$10,707.4

EXHIBIT 1   *(continued)*

	Fiscal Years Ending				
	Sept. 29, 2019	Sept. 30, 2018	Oct. 1, 2017	Oct. 2, 2016	Oct. 3, 2010
Cost of sales	8,526.9	$ 7,930.7	$ 8,486.8	$ 8,511.1	$ 4,458.6
Store operating expenses	10,493.6	9,472.2	7,065.8	6,064.3	3,551.4
Other operating expenses	371.0	554.9	518.0	545.4	293.2
Depreciation and amortization expenses	1,377.3	1,247.0	1,011.4	980.8	510.4
General and administrative expenses	1,824.1	1,708.2	1,408.2	1,360.6	569.5
Restructuring and impairments	135.8	224.4	153.5	---	53.0
Total operating expenses	22,728.7	21,137.4	18,643.5	17,462.2	9,436.1
Income from equity investees and other	298.0	301.2	391.4	318.2	148.1
Operating income	4,077.9	3,883.3	4,134.7	4,171.9	1,419.4
Gain resulting from acquisition of joint venture	-----	1,376.4	----	----	----
Net gain resulting from divestiture of certain operations	622.8	499.2	93.5	5.4	---
Net earnings attributable to Starbucks	$ 3,594.6	$ 4,518.0	$ 2,884.97	$ 2,817.7	$ 945.6
Net earnings per common share—diluted	$ 2.92	$ 3.24	$ 1.97	$ 1.90	$ 0.62
BALANCE SHEET DATA					
Current assets	$ 5,653.9	$12,494.2	$ 5,283.4	$ 4,757.9	$ 2,756.5
Current liabilities	6,168.7	5,684.2	4,220.7	4,546.8	2,703.6
Total assets	19,219.6	24,156.4	14,365.6	14,312.5	6,385.9
Long-term debt (including current portion)	11,167.0	9,090.2	3,932.6	3,585.2	549.4
Shareholders' equity	(6,232.0)	1,175.8	5,457.0	5,890.7	3,674.7
OTHER FINANCIAL DATA					
Net cash provided by operating activities	$ 5,047.0	$11,937.8	$ 4,251.8	$ 4,697.9	$ 1,704.9
Capital expenditures (additions to property, plant, and equipment)	1,806.6	1,976.4	1,519.4	1,440.3	440.7
STORE INFORMATION					
Stores open at year-end					
United States					
Company-operated stores	8,799	9,684	8,222	7,880	6,707
Licensed stores	6,250	7,770	5,708	6,588	4,424
International					
Company-operated stores	7,035	5,657	5,053	4,831	2,182
Licensed stores	9,172	8,356	8,356	7,082	3,545
Worldwide	31,256	29,324	27,339	25,085	16,858
Worldwide percentage change in sales at company-operated stores open 13 months or longer	5%	2%	3%	5%	7%

*Starbucks[1] fiscal year ends on the Sunday closest to September 30.

Note 1: In fiscal years 2016 and 2010, cost of sales included occupancy expenses for Starbucks company-operated stores. In fiscal years 2017, 2018 and 2019, occupancy expenses for Starbucks company-operated stores were reclassified and included in store operating expenses. This change accounts for much of the discontinuity between cost of sales for 2016 and costs of sales in 2017, 2018, and 2019, and similarly for the big jump between store operating expenses for 2017 versus store operating expenses for 2018 and 2019.

Sources: Company 10-K reports for 2011, 2017, 2018, and 2019 and data reporting Starbucks store counts by market posted in the investor relation section at www.starbucks.com (accessed November 1, 2019).

COMPANY BACKGROUND

Starbucks Coffee, Tea, and Spice

Starbucks got its start in 1971 when three academics (English teacher Jerry Baldwin, history teacher Zev Siegel, and writer Gordon Bowker—all coffee aficionados) opened Starbucks Coffee, Tea, and Spice in touristy Pike Place Market in Seattle. The three partners shared a love for fine coffees and exotic teas and believed they could build a clientele in Seattle that would appreciate the best coffees and teas. By the early 1980s, the company had four Starbucks stores in the Seattle area and had been profitable every year since opening its doors.

Howard Schultz Enters the Picture

In 1981, Howard Schultz, vice president and general manager of U.S. operations for a Swedish maker of stylish kitchen equipment and coffeemakers based in New York City, decided to pay Starbucks a visit. He was curious why Starbucks was selling so many of his company's products. When he arrived at the Pike Place store, a solo violinist was playing Mozart at the door (his violin case open for donations). Schultz was immediately taken by the coffee aroma, store décor and ambiance, and the freshly brewed cup of coffee he bought. He began asking questions about the company, the coffees from different parts of the world, and the different ways of roasting coffee.

Later, when he met with two of the owners, Schultz was struck by their knowledge about coffee, their commitment to providing customers with quality coffees, their passion for educating customers about the merits and quality of dark-roasted coffees, and their business philosophy. Top quality, fresh-roasted, whole-bean coffee was the company's differentiating feature and a bedrock value. The company depended mainly on word-of-mouth to get more people into its stores, then built customer loyalty cup by cup as buyers gained a sense of discovery and excitement about the taste of fine coffee. By the time he landed on his return trip to New York, Howard Schultz knew in his heart he wanted to go to work for Starbucks. But it took over a year and multiple meetings and discussions to convince the owners to bring in a high-powered New Yorker who had not grown up with the values of the company. In Spring 1982, Schultz was offered the job of heading marketing and overseeing Starbucks' retail stores; he assumed his new responsibilities at Starbucks in September 1982.

Starbucks and Howard Schultz: The 1982–1985 Period

In his first few months at Starbucks, Schultz spent most of his time in the four Seattle stores—working behind the counters, tasting different kinds of coffee, talking with customers, getting to know store personnel, and learning the retail aspects of the coffee business. In December, he began the final part of his training, that of actually roasting the coffee. Schultz spent a week getting an education about the colors of different coffee beans, listening for the telltale second pop of the beans during the roasting process, learning to taste the subtle differences among the various roasts, and familiarizing himself with the roasting techniques for different beans.

Schultz overflowed with ideas for the company. However, his biggest inspiration and vision for Starbucks future came during the spring of 1983 when the company sent him to Milan, Italy, to attend an international housewares show. While walking from his hotel to the convention center, he spotted an espresso bar and went inside to look around. The cashier beside the door nodded and smiled. The "barista" behind the counter greeted Schultz cheerfully and began pulling a shot of espresso for one customer and handcrafting a foamy cappuccino for another, all the while conversing merrily with patrons standing at the counter. Schultz thought the barista's performance was "great theater." Just down the way, he went to an even more crowded espresso bar where the barista was greeting customers by name, and people were laughing and talking in an atmosphere that plainly was comfortable and familiar. In the next few blocks, he saw two more espresso bars. That afternoon, Schultz walked the streets of Milan to explore more espresso bars. Some were stylish and upscale; others attracted a blue-collar clientele. Most had few chairs and it was common for Italian opera to be playing in the background. What struck Schultz was how popular and vibrant the Italian coffee bars were. Energy levels were typically high and they seemed to function as an integral community gathering place. Each one had its own unique character, but they all had a barista that performed with flair and there was camaraderie between the barista and the customers. Schultz liked it immediately, concluding that lattes should be a feature item on any coffee bar menu even though none of the coffee experts he had talked to had ever mentioned coffee lattes. Schultz was also struck by the fact that there were 1,500 coffee bars in Milan, a city about the size of Philadelphia, and a total of 200,000 in all of Italy.

Schultz's 1983 trip to Milan produced a revelation: the Starbucks stores in Seattle completely missed the point. There was much more to the coffee business than just selling beans and getting people to appreciate grinding their own beans and brewing fine coffee in their homes. What Starbucks needed to do was serve fresh-brewed coffee, espressos, and cappuccinos in its stores (in addition to beans and coffee equipment) and try to create an American version of the Italian coffee bar culture. Going to Starbucks should be an experience, a special treat, a place to meet friends and visit. Re-creating the authentic Italian coffee bar culture in the United States could be Starbucks differentiating factor.

Schultz Becomes Frustrated

On Schultz's return from Italy, he shared his revelation and ideas for modifying the format of Starbucks' stores, but the owners strongly resisted, contending that Starbucks was a retailer, not a restaurant or coffee bar. They feared serving drinks would put them in the beverage business and diminish the integrity of Starbucks' mission as a purveyor of fine coffees. They pointed out that Starbucks had been profitable every year and there was no reason to rock the boat in a small, private company like Starbucks. It took Howard Schultz nearly a year to convince them to let him test an espresso bar when Starbucks opened its sixth store in April 1984. It was the first store designed to sell beverages and it was the first store located in downtown Seattle. Schultz asked for a 1,500-square-foot space to set up a full-scale Italian-style espresso bar, but he was allocated only 300 square feet in a corner of the new store. The store opened with no fanfare as a deliberate experiment to see what happened. By closing time on the first day, some 400 customers had been served, well above the 250-customer average of Starbucks best performing stores. Within two months the store was serving 800 customers per day. The two baristas could not keep up with orders during the early morning hours, resulting in lines outside the door onto the sidewalk. Most of the business was at the

espresso counter, while sales at the regular retail counter were only adequate.

Schultz was elated at the test results, expecting that the owners' doubts about entering the beverage side of the business would be dispelled and that he would gain approval to pursue the opportunity to take Starbucks to a new level. Every day he shared the sales figures and customer counts at the new downtown store. But the lead owner was not comfortable with the success of the new store, believing that it felt wrong and that espresso drinks were a distraction from the core business of marketing fine Arabica coffees at retail.[1] While he didn't deny that the experiment was succeeding, he would not agree to go forward with introducing beverages in other Starbucks stores.

Over the next several months, Schultz made up his mind to leave Starbucks and start his own company. The two owners, knowing how frustrated Schultz had become, supported his efforts to go out on his own and agreed to let him stay in his current job and office until definitive plans were in place. Schultz left Starbucks in late 1985.

Schultz's Il Giornale Venture

Schultz spent several months raising money from investors to fund his new venture. An investor suggested naming the new company Il Giornale Coffee Company (pronounced il-jor-nahl'-ee), a suggestion that Howard accepted. The first Il Giornale store opened in April 1986. It measured 700 square feet and was located near the entrance of Seattle's tallest building. The décor was Italian and there were Italian words on the menu. Italian opera music played in the background. The baristas wore white shirts and bow ties. All service was stand up—there were no chairs. National and international papers were hung on rods on the wall. By closing time on the first day, 300 customers had been served—mostly in the morning hours. But while the core idea worked well, it soon became apparent that several aspects of the format were not appropriate for Seattle. Some customers objected to the incessant opera music, others wanted a place to sit down; many people did not understand the Italian words on the menu. These "mistakes" were quickly fixed, but an effort was made not to compromise the style and elegance of the store. Within six months, the store was serving more than 1,000 customers a day. Regular customers had learned how to pronounce the company's name. Because most customers were in a hurry, it became apparent that speedy service was essential.

Six months after opening the first store, a second store was opened in another downtown building. In April 1987, a third store was opened in Vancouver, British Columbia, to test the transferability of the company's business concept outside Seattle. By mid-1987, sales at each of the three stores were running at a rate equal to $1.5 million annually.

Il Giornale Acquires Starbucks

In March 1987, the Starbucks owners decided to sell the whole Starbucks operation in Seattle—the stores, the roasting plant, and the Starbucks name. Schultz knew immediately that he had to buy Starbucks; his board of directors agreed. Within weeks, Schultz had raised the $3.8 million needed to buy Starbucks. The acquisition was completed in August 1987. The new name of the combined companies was Starbucks Corporation. Howard Schultz, at the age of 34, became Starbucks president and CEO.

Starbucks as a Private Company: 1987–1992

The Monday morning after the deal closed, Howard Schultz returned to the Starbucks offices at the roasting plant, greeted all the familiar faces, and accepted their congratulations. Then, he called the staff together for a meeting on the roasting plant floor:[2]

> All my life I have wanted to be part of a company and a group of people who share a common vision. . . . I'm here today because I love this company. I love what it represents. . . . I know you're concerned. . . . I promise you I will not let you down. I promise you I will not leave anyone behind. . . . In five years, I want you to look back at this day and say "I was there when it started. I helped build this company into something great.

Schultz told the group that his vision was for Starbucks to become a national company with values and guiding principles that employees could be proud of. He aspired for Starbucks to become the most respected brand name in coffee and for the company to be admired for its corporate responsibility. He indicated that he wanted to include people in the decision-making process and that he would be open and honest with them. For Schultz, building a

company that valued and respected its people, that inspired them, and that shared the fruits of success with those who contributed to the company's long-term value was essential, not just an intriguing option. He made the establishment of mutual respect between employees and management a priority.

The business plan Schultz had presented investors called for the new 9-store company to open 125 stores in the next five years—15 the first year, 20 the second, 25 the third, 30 the fourth, and 35 the fifth. Revenues were projected to reach $60 million in 1992. But the company lacked experienced management. Schultz had never led a growth effort of such magnitude and was just learning what the job of CEO was all about, having been the president of a small company for barely two years. Dave Olsen, a Seattle coffee bar owner who Schultz had recruited to direct store operations at Il Giornale, was still learning the ropes in managing a multistore operation. Ron Lawrence, the company's controller, had worked as a controller for several organizations. Other Starbucks employees had only the experience of managing or being a part of a six-store organization.

Schultz instituted a number of changes in the first several months. To symbolize the merging of the two companies and the two cultures, a new logo was created that melded the designs of the Starbucks logo and the Il Giornale logo. The Starbucks stores were equipped with espresso machines and remodeled to look more Italian than old-world nautical. Il Giornale green replaced the traditional Starbucks brown. The result was a new type of store—a cross between a retail coffee bean store and an espresso bar/café—that quickly evolved into Starbucks' signature.

By December 1987, the mood at Starbucks was distinctly upbeat, with most employees buying into the changes that Schultz was making, and trust was beginning to build between management and employees. New stores were on the verge of opening in Vancouver and Chicago. One Starbucks store employee, Daryl Moore, who had started working at Starbucks in 1981 and voted against unionization in 1985, began to question the need for a union with his fellow employees. Over the next few weeks, Moore began a move to decertify the union. He got a majority of store employees to sign a de-certification letter and presented it to the National Labor Relations Board. The union representing store employees was decertified. Later, in 1992, the union representing

Starbucks roasting plant and warehouse employees was also decertified.

Market Expansion Outside the Pacific Northwest

The first Chicago store opened in October 1987 and three more stores were opened over the next six months. Initially, customer counts at the stores were substantially below expectations because Chicagoans did not take to dark-roasted coffee as fast as Schultz had anticipated. While it was more expensive to supply fresh coffee to the Chicago stores out of the Seattle warehouse, the company solved the problem of freshness and quality assurance by putting freshly roasted beans in special FlavorLock bags with a one-way valve to allow carbon dioxide to escape without allowing air and moisture in. Moreover, rents, and wage rates were higher in Chicago. The result was a squeeze on store profit margins. Gradually, customer counts improved, but Starbucks lost money on its Chicago stores until, in 1990, prices were raised to reflect higher rents and labor costs, more experienced store managers were hired, and a critical mass of customers caught on to the taste of Starbucks products.

Portland, Oregon, was the next market entered, and Portland coffee drinkers took to Starbucks products quickly. Store openings in Los Angeles and San Francisco soon followed. L.A. consumers embraced Starbucks quickly, and the *Los Angeles Times* named Starbucks the best coffee in America before the first store opened.

Starbucks's store expansion targets proved easier to meet than Schultz had originally anticipated and he upped the numbers to keep challenging the organization. Starbucks opened 15 new stores in fiscal 1988, 20 in 1989, 30 in 1990, 32 in 1991, and 53 in 1992—producing a total of 161 stores, significantly above his original 1992 target of 125 stores.

From the outset, the strategy was to open only company-owned stores; franchising was avoided so as to keep the company in full control of the quality of its products and the character and location of its stores. But company-ownership of all stores required Starbucks to raise new venture capital to cover the cost of new store expansion. In 1988, the company raised $3.9 million; in 1990, venture capitalists provided an additional $13.5 million; and in 1991, another round of venture capital financing generated $15 million.

Starbucks was able to raise the needed funds despite posting losses of $330,000 in 1987, $764,000 in 1988, and $1.2 million in 1989. While the losses were troubling to Starbucks' board of directors and investors, Schultz's business plan had forecast losses during the early years of expansion. At a particularly tense board meeting where directors sharply questioned Schultz about the lack of profitability, Schultz said:[3]

> Look, we're going to keep losing money until we can do three things. We have to attract a management team well beyond our expansion needs. We have to build a world-class roasting facility. And we need a computer information system sophisticated enough to keep track of sales in hundreds and hundreds of stores.

Schultz argued for patience as the company invested in the infrastructure to support continued growth well into the 1990s. He contended that hiring experienced executives ahead of the growth curve, building facilities far beyond current needs, and installing support systems laid a strong foundation for rapid profitable growth later on down the road. His arguments carried the day with the board and with investors, especially since revenues were growing approximately 80 percent annually and customer traffic at the stores was meeting or exceeding expectations.

Starbucks became profitable in 1990. After-tax profits had increased every year since 1990 except for fiscal year 2000 (because of $58.8 million in investment write-offs in four dot.com enterprises) and for fiscal year 2008 (when the sharp global economic downturn hit the company's bottom line very hard).

RAPID EXPANSION OF STARBUCKS LOCATIONS

In 1992 and 1993, Starbucks began concentrating its store expansion efforts in the United States on locations with favorable demographic profiles that also could be serviced and supported by the company's operations infrastructure. For each targeted region, Starbucks selected a large city to serve as a "hub;" teams of professionals were located in hub cities to support the goal of opening 20 or more stores in the hub within two years. Once a number of stores were opened in a hub, then additional stores were opened in smaller surrounding "spoke" areas in the region. To oversee the expansion process, Starbucks had zone vice presidents that oversaw the store expansion process in a geographic region and that were also responsible for instilling the Starbucks culture in the newly opened stores. For a time, Starbucks went to extremes to blanket major cities with stores, even if some stores cannibalized a nearby store's business. While a new store might draw 30 percent of the business of an existing store two or so blocks away, management believed a "Starbucks everywhere" strategy cut down on delivery and management costs, shortened customer lines at individual stores, and increased foot traffic for all the stores in an area. In 2002, new stores generated an average of $1.2 million in first-year revenues, compared to $700,000 in 1995 and only $427,000 in 1990; the increases in new-store revenues were partly due to growing popularity of premium coffee drinks, partly to Starbucks growing reputation, and partly to expanded product offerings. But by 2008-09 the strategy of saturating big metropolitan areas with stores began cannibalizing sales of existing stores to such an extent that average annual sales per store in the United States dropped to less than $1,000,000 and pushed store operating margins down from double-digit levels to mid-single-digit levels. As a consequence, Starbucks' management cut the number of metropolitan locations, closing 900 underperforming Starbucks stores in 2008–09, some 75 percent of which were within three miles of another Starbucks store.

Despite the mistake of over-saturating portions of some large metropolitan areas with stores, Starbucks was regarded as having the best real estate team in the coffee bar industry and a core competence in identifying good retailing sites for its new stores. The company's sophisticated methodology enabled it to identify not only the most attractive individual city blocks but also the exact store location that was best. It also worked hard at building good relationships with local real estate representatives in areas where it was opening multiple store locations.

Licensed Starbucks Stores. In 1995, Starbucks began entering into licensing agreements for store locations in areas in the United States where it did not have the ability to locate company-owned outlets. Two early licensing agreements were with Marriott Host International to operate Starbucks retail stores in airport locations and with Aramark Food and Services to put Starbucks stores on university campuses and other locations operated by Aramark. Very quickly, Starbucks began to make increased use of licensing, both domestically and internationally.

Starbucks preferred licensing to franchising because it permitted tighter controls over the operations of licensees, and in the case of many foreign locations licensing was much less risky.

Starbucks received a license fee and a royalty on sales at all licensed locations and supplied the coffee for resale at these locations. All licensed stores had to follow Starbucks' detailed operating procedures and all managers and employees who worked in these stores received the same training given to managers and employees in company-operated Starbucks stores.

International Expansion. In markets outside the continental United States, Starbucks had a two-pronged store expansion strategy: either open company-owned-and-operated stores or else license a reputable and capable local company with retailing know-how in the target host country to develop and operate new Starbucks stores. In most countries, Starbucks utilized a local partner/licensee to help it locate suitable store sites, set up supplier relationships, recruit talented individuals for positions as store managers, and adapt to local market conditions. Starbucks looked for partners/licensees that had strong retail/restaurant experience, had values and a corporate culture compatible with Starbucks, were committed to good customer service, possessed talented management and strong financial resources, and had demonstrated brand-building skills. In those foreign countries where business risks were deemed relatively high, most if not all Starbucks stores were licensed rather than being company-owned and operated.

Exhibit 2 shows the speed with which Starbucks grew its network of company-operated and licensed retail stores.

STORE DESIGN AND AMBIENCE: KEY ELEMENTS OF THE "STARBUCKS EXPERIENCE"

Store Design

Starting in 1991, Starbucks created its own in-house team of architects and designers to ensure that each store would convey the right image and character. Stores had to be custom-designed because the company didn't buy real estate and build its own

EXHIBIT 2 Company-Operated and Licensed Starbucks Stores

A. Number of Starbucks Store Locations Worldwide, Fiscal Years 1987–2019 and March 31, 2020

End of Fiscal Year*	Company-operated Store Locations		Licensed Store Locations		Worldwide Total
	United States	International	United States	International	
1987	17	0	0	0	17
1990	84	0	0	0	84
1995	627	0	49	0	676
2000	2,446	530	173	352	3,501
2005	4,918	1,263	2,435	1,625	10,241
2010	6,707	2,182	4,424	3,545	16,858
2015	6,764	2,198	4,364	3,309	23,043
2017	8,224	4,763	5,745	6,043	27,339
2018	8,581	6,758	6,043	7,940	29,324
2019	8,799	7,035	6,250	9,172	31,256
March 29, 2020	16,188 worldwide		15,862 worldwide		32,050

B. International Starbucks Store Locations, September 29, 2019

International Locations of Company-operated Starbucks Stores		International Locations of Licensed Starbucks Stores			
		Americas		Europe/Africa/Middle East	
Canada	1,175	Canada	432	Turkey	494
United Kingdom	288	Mexico	748	United Kingdom	707
China	4,123	17 Others	663	United Arab Emirates	211
Japan	1,379			Spain	149
All Others	70	**Asia-Pacific**		Saudi Arabia	201
		Taiwan	480	Kuwait	160
		South Korea	1,334	Germany	161
		Philippines	397	36 Others	1,135
		Malaysia	303		
		Indonesia	421		
		Thailand	392		
International Company-Operated Total	**7,035**	8 Others	784	**International Licensed Total**	**9,172**

*In the first quarter of fiscal 2018, Starbucks acquired its Chinese licensing partner's share of their joint venture in China, resulting in the transfer of all 1,477 licensed stores in China to company-operated retail stores.

Sources: Company records of store counts by market, posted in the investor relations section at www.starbucks.com (accessed May 4, 2012 and November 6, 2019); company 10-K Reports 2016, 2018, 2019; and company press release, April 28, 2020.

freestanding structures. Instead, each space was leased in an existing structure, which resulted in stores differing in size and shape. Most stores ranged in size from 1,000 to 1,500 square feet and were located in office buildings, downtown and suburban retail centers, airport terminals, university campus areas, and busy neighborhood shopping areas convenient for pedestrian foot traffic and/or drivers. A few were in suburban malls. Four store templates—each with its own color combinations, lighting scheme, and component materials—were introduced in 1996; all four were adaptable to different store sizes and settings.

But as the number of stores increased rapidly over the next 20-plus years, greater store diversity and layouts quickly became necessary. Some stores were equipped with special seating areas to help make Starbucks a desirable gathering place where customers could meet and chat or simply enjoy a peaceful interlude in their day. Flagship stores in high-traffic, high-visibility locations had fireplaces, leather chairs, newspapers, couches, and lots of ambience. Increasingly, the company began installing drive-through windows at locations where speed and convenience were important to customers and locating kiosks in high-traffic supermarkets, building lobbies, the halls of shopping malls, and other public places where passers-by could quickly and conveniently pick up a Starbucks beverage and/or something to eat.

A new global store design strategy was introduced in 2009. Core design characteristics included the celebration of local materials and craftsmanship, a focus on reused and recycled elements, the exposure of structural integrity and authentic roots, the absence of features that distracted from an emphasis on coffee, seating layouts that facilitated customer gatherings, an atmosphere that sought to engage all five customer senses (sight, smell, sound, hearing, and feel), and flexibility to meet the needs of many customer types.[4] Each new store was to be a reflection of the environment in which it operated and be environmentally friendly. In 2010, Starbucks began an effort to achieve LEED (Leadership in Energy and Environmental Design) Certification for all new company-owned stores (a LEED-certified building had to incorporate green building design, construction, operations, and maintenance solutions).[5]

To better control average store opening costs, the company centralized buying, developed standard contracts and fixed fees for certain items, and consolidated work under those contractors who displayed good cost control practices. The retail operations group outlined exactly the minimum amount of equipment each core store needed, so that standard items could be ordered in volume from vendors at 20 to 30 percent discounts, then delivered just in time to the store site either from company warehouses or the vendor. Modular designs for display cases were developed. The layouts for new and remodeled stores were developed on a computer, with software that allowed the costs to be estimated as the design evolved. All this cut store opening and remodeling costs significantly and shortened the process to about 18 weeks.

Store Ambience

Starbucks management viewed each store as a billboard for the company and as a contributor to building the company's brand and image. The company went to great lengths to make sure the store fixtures, the merchandise displays, the colors, the artwork, the banners, the music, and the aromas all blended to create a consistent, inviting, stimulating environment that evoked the romance of coffee and signaled the company's passion for coffee. To try to keep the coffee aromas in the stores pure, smoking was banned, and employees were asked to refrain from wearing perfumes or colognes. Prepared foods were kept covered so customers would smell coffee only. Colorful banners and posters were used to keep the look of the Starbucks stores fresh and in keeping with seasons and holidays. All these practices reflected a conviction that every detail mattered in making Starbucks stores a welcoming and pleasant "third place" (apart from home and work) where people could meet friends and family, enjoy a quiet moment alone with a newspaper or book, or simply spend quality time relaxing—and most importantly, have a satisfying experience.

Starting in 2002, Starbucks began providing Internet access capability and enhanced digital entertainment to patrons. The objective was to heighten the "third place" Starbucks experience, entice customers into perhaps buying a second latte or espresso while they caught up on e-mail, listened to digital music, put the finishing touches on a presentation, or surfed the Internet. Wireless Internet service and faster Internet speeds were added as fast as they became available.

STARBUCKS' STRATEGY TO EXPAND ITS PRODUCT OFFERINGS AND ENTER NEW MARKET SEGMENTS

Starting in the mid-1990s, Howard Schultz began a long-term strategic campaign to expand Starbucks product offerings beyond its retail stores and to pursue sales of Starbucks products in a wider variety of distribution channels and market segments. The strategic objectives were to capitalize on Starbucks growing brand awareness and brand-name strength and create a broader foundation for sustained long-term growth in revenues and profits.

The Strategic Initiative to Sell Starbucks Packaged Coffees Outside Its Retail Stores. Starbucks first step to expand its product offering beyond its stores involved the establishment of an in-house specialty sales group to begin marketing Starbucks coffee to restaurants, airlines, hotels, universities, hospitals, business offices, country clubs, and other select retailers. The sales group's first big success was convincing two airlines to begin serving Starbucks coffee on flights. Shortly thereafter accounts were won at five leading hotel chains, resulting in packets of Starbucks coffee being in each room with coffee-making equipment. Later, the specialty sales group began working with two leading institutional food service distributors, SYSCO Corporation and US Foodservice, to handle the distribution of Starbucks products to hotels, restaurants, office coffee distributors, educational and healthcare institutions, and other such enterprises. Sales of Starbucks packaged coffees continued to grow, with Starbucks generating revenues of $372.2 million from providing whole bean and ground coffees and assorted other Starbucks products to some 21,000 foodservice accounts in fiscal 2009.

Starbucks Partnership with PepsiCo The second initiative came in 1994 when PepsiCo and Starbucks entered into a joint venture arrangement to create new coffee-related products in bottles or cans for mass distribution through Pepsi channels. The joint venture soon introduced a bottled version of Frappuccino, a new cold coffee drink Starbucks began serving at its retail stores in the summer of 1995 that quickly became a big hot weather seller. Sales of Frappuccino ready-to-drink beverages reached $125 million in 1997 and achieved a national supermarket penetration of 80 percent. Sales of ready-to-drink Frappuccino products soon began in Japan, Taiwan, South Korea, and China chiefly through agreements with leading local distributors. In 2010, sales of Frappuccino products worldwide reached $2 billion annually.[6] Sales of Frappuccino products worldwide were continuing in 2020.

Starbucks Entry into Ice Cream In 1995, Starbucks partnered with Dreyer's Grand Ice Cream to supply coffee extracts for a new line of coffee ice cream made and distributed by Dreyer's under the Starbucks brand. Starbucks coffee-flavored ice cream became the number-one-selling super-premium brand in the coffee segment in mid-1996. In 2008, Starbucks discontinued its arrangement with Dreyer's and entered into an exclusive agreement with Unilever to manufacture, market, and distribute Starbucks-branded ice creams in the United States and Canada. Unilever was the global leader in ice cream with annual sales of about $6 billion; its ice cream brands included Ben & Jerry's, Breyers, and Good Humor. There were seven flavors of Starbucks ice cream and two flavors of novelty bars being marketed in 2010, but buyer demand eroded after several years and Starbucks-branded ice cream was discontinued in 2013. But in 2017, new premium ice cream drinks (a scoop of ice cream drowned in espresso called an "affogato," several other affogato concoctions, and tall cold brew floats and malts) became top-10 menu items at the new Starbucks Roastery and Starbucks Reserve store locations in Seattle and were rolled out to other Starbucks Roasteries and Reserve locations in 2018 and 2019.

The Licensing Agreement with Kraft Foods In 1998, Starbucks licensed Kraft Foods to market and distribute Starbucks whole bean and ground coffees in grocery and mass merchandise channels across the United States. Kraft managed all distribution, marketing, advertising, and promotions and paid a royalty to Starbucks based on a percentage of net sales. Product freshness was guaranteed by Starbucks's FlavorLock packaging, and initially the price per pound paralleled the prices in Starbucks's retail stores. Flavor selections in supermarkets were more limited than the varieties at Starbucks stores. The licensing relationship with Kraft was later expanded to include the marketing and distribution of Starbucks coffees in Canada, the United Kingdom, and other European countries. Going into 2010, Starbucks coffees were available in some 33,500 grocery and warehouse clubs in the United States and 5,500 retail outlets outside the United States; Starbucks revenues from these sales were approximately $370 million in fiscal 2009.[7] During fiscal 2011, Starbucks discontinued its distribution arrangement with Kraft and instituted its own in-house organization to handle direct sales of packaged coffees to supermarkets and to warehouse club stores (chiefly Costco, Sam's Club, and BJ's Warehouse). During 2012–2019, sales of Starbucks packaged coffees continued to grow throughout the retail grocery channel, with supermarkets stocking a wider selection of flavor selections and frequently offering promotional price discounts on Starbucks and other coffee brands to boost shopper traffic.

The Acquisition of Tazo Tea In 1999, Starbucks purchased Tazo Tea for $8.1 million. Tazo Tea, a tea manufacturer and distributor based in Portland, Oregon, was founded in 1994 and marketed its teas to restaurants, food stores, and tea houses. Starbucks proceeded to introduce hot and iced Tazo Tea drinks in its retail stores. As part of a long-term campaign to expand the distribution of its lineup of super-premium Tazo teas, Starbucks expanded its agreement with Kraft to market and distribute Tazo teas worldwide. In 2008, Starbucks entered into a licensing agreement with a partnership formed by PepsiCo and Unilever (Lipton Tea was one of Unilever's leading brands) to manufacture, market, and distribute Starbucks' super-premium Tazo Tea ready-to-drink beverages (including iced teas, juiced teas, and herbal-infused teas) in the United States and Canada—in 2012, the Pepsi/Lipton Tea partnership was the leading North American distributor of ready-to-drink teas. In fiscal 2011, when Starbucks broke off its packaged coffee distribution arrangement with Kraft, it also broke off its arrangement with Kraft for distribution of Tazo tea and began selling Tazo teas directly to supermarkets (except for Tazo Tea ready-to-drink beverages).

Introduction of the Starbucks Rewards™ Card In 2001, Starbucks introduced the Starbucks Card, a reloadable card that allowed customers to pay for their purchases with a quick swipe of their card at the cash register and also to earn "stars" and redeem rewards. Since then, Starbucks Rewards™ had evolved into one of the best retail loyalty programs in existence, aided by the introduction of Starbucks Gift Cards, the Starbucks mobile app, rewards for in-store purchases and purchases of Starbucks products in grocery stores and other retail locations where Starbucks products were sold. Rewards members earned two stars for every one dollar spent on in-store purchases; cardmembers also had the opportunity to take advantage of monthly "Double-Star Day" promotions. In April 2019, Starbucks shifted from a two-tier reward structure (green star and gold star status) to a single tier rewards structure where the various benefits/perks were linked to having earned 25, 50, 150, 250, and 400 stars. Users of the Starbucks app could easily see how many stars they currently had, place orders and make payments right from their smartphones, and find the nearest Starbucks location. Members with a Starbucks Rewards™ Visa® Card also earned one star for every four dollar

purchased with the Starbucks Visa card. When members reloaded a registered Starbucks Card using their Starbucks Rewards™ Visa® Card on the mobile app or Starbucks.com, they received one star for every dollar loaded in addition to the two stars earned for every dollar spent when using a registered Starbucks Card or the Starbucks mobile app for purchases in participating Starbucks stores. As of year-end 2019, there were 18.9 million active Starbuck Rewards™ members globally. Use of Starbucks Reward cards accounted for 40 percent of transactions in company-operated stores in the United States, and about 75 percent of Starbucks customers in North America either used a Starbucks Card or the Starbucks mobile app to pay for in-store purchases.

The Seattle's Best Coffee Acquisition In 2003, Starbucks spent $70 million to acquire Seattle's Best Coffee, an operator of 540 Seattle's Best coffee shops, 86 Seattle's Best Coffee Express espresso bars, and marketer of some 30 varieties of Seattle's Best whole bean and ground coffees. The decision was made to operate Seattle's Best as a separate subsidiary. Very quickly, Starbucks expanded its licensing arrangement with Kraft Foods to include marketing, distributing, and promoting the sales of Seattle's Best coffees and by 2009, Seattle's Best coffees were available nationwide in supermarkets and at more than 15,000 food service locations (college campuses, restaurants, hotels, airlines, and cruise lines). A new Seattle's Best line of ready-to-drink iced lattes was introduced in April 2010, with manufacture, marketing, and distribution managed by PepsiCo as part of the long-standing Starbucks–PepsiCo joint venture for ready-to-drink Frappuccino products. In 2010, Starbucks introduced new distinctive red packaging and a red logo for Seattle's Best Coffee, boosted efforts to open more franchised Seattle's Best cafés, and expanded the availability of Seattle Best coffees to 30,000 distribution points. When Starbucks licensing agreement with Kraft to handle sales and distribution of Seattle's Best coffee products was terminated in 2011, responsibility for the sales and distribution of Seattle's Best products was transitioned to the same in-house sales force that handled direct sales and distribution of Starbucks-branded coffees and Tazo tea products to supermarkets and warehouse clubs.

The Ethos™ Water Acquisition. In 2005, Starbucks Corporation acquired Ethos™ Water, a privately held bottled water company based in Santa

Monica, California, whose mission was to help children get clean water by supporting water projects in such developing countries as Bangladesh, the Democratic Republic of Congo, Ethiopia, Honduras, India, and Kenya. One of the terms of the acquisition called for Starbucks to donate $1.25 million in 2005–2006 to support these projects. In the years since the acquisition, a key element of Starbucks corporate social responsibility effort has been to donate $0.05US ($0.10CN in Canada) for every bottle of Ethos Water sold in Starbucks stores to the Ethos® Water Fund, part of the Starbucks Foundation, to fund ongoing efforts to provide clean water to children in developing countries and to support water, sanitation, and hygiene education programs in water-stressed countries.

The Introduction of New Coffee Blends In 2008, Starbucks introduced a new coffee blend called Pike Place™ Roast that would be brewed every day, all day, in every Starbucks store.[8] Before then, Starbucks rotated various coffee blends through its brewed lineup, sometimes switching them weekly, sometimes daily. While some customers liked the ever-changing variety, the feedback from a majority of customers indicated a preference for a consistent brew that customers could count on when they came into a Starbucks store. The Pike Place blend was brewed in small batches at 30-minute intervals so as to provide customers with a freshly-brewed coffee. In January 2012, after eight months of testing over 80 different recipe and roast iterations, Starbucks introduced three blends of lighter-bodied and milder-tasting Starbucks Blonde Roast® coffees to better appeal to an estimated 54 million coffee drinkers in the United States who said they liked flavorful, lighter coffees with a gentle finish. The Blonde Roast blends were available as a brewed option in Starbucks stores in the United States and in packaged form in Starbucks stores and supermarkets. Because the majority of coffee sales in supermarkets were in the light and medium roast categories, Starbucks management saw its new Blonde Roast coffees blends as being a $1 billion market opportunity in the United States alone. From time to time, Starbucks introduced new blends of its packaged whole bean and ground coffees—some of these were seasonal, but those that proved popular with buyers became standard offerings.

The Introduction of Starbucks Via® Instant Coffee In Fall 2009, Starbucks introduced Starbucks VIA® Ready Brew, packets of roasted coffee in an instant form, in an effort to attract a bigger fraction of on-the-go and at-home coffee drinkers. VIA was made with a proprietary micro-ground technology that produced an instant coffee with a rich, full-bodied taste that closely replicated the taste, quality, and flavor of traditional freshly brewed coffee. Encouraged by favorable customer response, Starbucks expanded the distribution of VIA to some 25,000 grocery, mass merchandise, and drugstore accounts, including Kroger, Safeway, Walmart, Target, Costco, and CVS. Instant coffee made up a significant fraction of coffee purchases in the United Kingdom (80 percent), Japan (53 percent), Russia (85 percent), and several other countries where Starbucks stores were located; globally, the instant and single-serve coffee category was a $23 billion market. By the end of fiscal year 2011, VIA products were available at 70,000 locations and generating annual sales of $250 million.[9]

The Introduction of Starbucks K-Cup Packs for Keurig Single-Cup Brewing Systems In fall 2011, Starbucks began selling Starbucks-branded coffee K-Cup® Portion Packs for the Keurig® Single-Cup Brewing system in its retail stores; the Keurig Brewer was produced and sold by Green Mountain Coffee Roasters. Starbucks entered into a strategic partnership with Green Mountain to manufacture the Starbucks-branded portion packs and also to be responsible for marketing, distributing, and selling them to major supermarket chains, drugstore chains, mass merchandisers and wholesale clubs, department stores, and specialty retailers throughout the United States and Canada. The partnership made good economic sense for both companies. Green Mountain could manufacture the single-cup portion packs in the same plants where it was producing its own brands of single-cup packs and then use its own internal resources and capabilities to market, distribute, and sell Starbuck-branded single-cup packs alongside its own brands of single-cup packs. It was far cheaper for Starbucks to pay Green Mountain to handle these functions than to build its own manufacturing plants and put its own in-house resources in place to market, distribute, and sell Starbucks single-cup coffee packs. Just two months after launch, shipments of Starbucks-branded single-cup portion packs had exceeded 100 million units and the packs were available in about 70 percent of the targeted retailers; company officials estimated that Starbucks had achieved an 11 percent dollar share of the market for single-cup coffee packs in the United States.[10]

Starbucks Move into Coffee-Making Equipment
In March 2012, Starbucks announced that it would begin selling its first at-home premium single cup espresso and brewed coffee machine, the Verismo™ system by Starbucks, at select Starbucks store locations, online, and in upscale specialty stores. The Verismo brewer was a high-pressure system with the capability to brew both coffee and Starbucks-quality espresso beverages, from lattes to americanos, consistently and conveniently one cup at a time; sales of the Verismo single-cup machine put Starbucks into head-to-head competition with Nestlé's Nespresso machine and, to a lesser extent, Green Mountain's popular lineup of low-pressure Keurig brewers. At the time, the global market for premium at-home espresso/coffee machines was estimated at $8 billion.[11] The Verismo introduction was the last phase of Starbucks' strategic initiative to offer coffee products covering all aspects of the single-cup coffee segment—instant coffees (with its VIA offerings), single portion coffee packs for single-cup brewers, and single-cup brewing machines.

Bigger Menu Selections at Starbucks Stores In response to customer requests for more wholesome food and beverage options and also to bring in business from non-coffee drinkers, Starbucks in 2008 altered its menu offerings in stores to include fruit cups, yogurt parfaits, skinny lattes, banana walnut bread, a 300-calorie farmer's market salad with all-natural dressing, and a line of 250-calorie "better-for-you" smoothies.[12] In 2009–11, the company continued to experiment with healthier, lower-calorie selections and by May 2012, retail store menus included a bigger assortment of hot and cold coffee and tea beverages, pastries and bakery selections, prepared breakfast and lunch sandwiches and wraps, salads, parfaits, smoothies, juices, and bottled water—at most stores in North America, food items could be warmed. A bit later, beer, wine, and other complementary food offerings were added to the menus at some stores to help them become an attractive and relaxing after-work destination. Since 2013, it has become standard practice for Starbucks to continually tweak its menu offerings, switching out whimsical and limited-edition offerings and adding/dropping certain beverages, flavorings, breakfast items, sandwiches, pastries, and snacks, both to broaden buyer appeal and respond to ongoing shifts in customer preferences. In 2018–2019, Starbucks began introducing new stores menus at the beginning of each season (spring, summer, fall, and winter), along with special Holiday menu offerings in November-December. Menu offerings at Starbucks stores were typically adapted to local cultures—for instance, the menu offerings at stores in North America included a selection of muffins, but stores in France had no muffins and instead featured locally made pastries.

The Acquisition of Evolution Fresh Starbucks purchased cold-pressed juice maker Evolution Fresh for $30 million in 2011 to use Starbucks sales and marketing resources to grow the sales of Evolution Fresh and capture a bigger share of the $3.4 billion super-premium juice segment and begin a long-term campaign to pursue growth opportunities in the $50 billion health and wellness sector of the U.S. economy. A $70 million juice making facility in California was opened in 2013 to make Evolution Fresh products. Starbucks opened four Evolution Fresh juice bars after the acquisition, but soon decided to ditch the stand-alone juice bar concept, opting to sell Evolution Fresh beverages in Starbucks stores and supermarkets. Evolution Fresh competed with PepsiCo's category leader Naked juice brand, as well as scores of other large and small bottled juice brands. As of 2017, Starbucks had secured 20,000 points of distribution for Evolution Fresh products and the brand was said to be "thriving."

The Acquisition of Teavana Tea In 2012, Starbucks paid $620 million to acquire Atlanta-based specialty tea retailer Teavana, which sold more than 100 varieties of premium loose-leaf teas and tea-related merchandise through 300 company-owned stores (usually located in upscale shopping malls) and on its website; Teavana teas were used mostly for home consumption. Howard Schultz believed Starbucks could capitalize on Teavana's world-class tea knowledge and its global sourcing and merchandising capabilities (a) to expand Teavana's domestic and global footprint, (b) to bring an elevated tea experience to the patrons of Starbucks domestic and international locations, and (c) to increase Starbucks penetration of the $40 billion world market for tea, especially in the world's high-consumption tea markets where Starbucks had stores. These strategic outcomes failed to materialize. By 2016 and 2017, sales at Teavana stores had eroded to the point where the stores were unprofitable, prompting Starbucks to begin the process of closing all 379 Teavana stores (the majority by Spring 2018). However, Starbucks continued to sell Teavana teas and beverages in

Starbucks stores because they were popular and contributed to store profitability, accounting for sales of more than $1 billion annually and growing fast enough to double over the next five years. In late 2017, Starbucks sold its Tazo Tea business to Unilever for $384 million, opting to focus its sales of tea products on the Teavana brand. In May 2019, Starbucks began selling 3 flavors of Teavana™ Sparkling Craft Iced Teas in all of its stores in the United States to complement its other Teavana bottled tea offerings.

The La Boulange Acquisition Also in 2012, Starbucks bought Bay Bread Group's La Boulange sandwich and coffee shops for $100 million. When Starbucks acquired the San Francisco chain, plans called not only for bringing La Boulange products into its stores to bolster its lineup of pastries and sandwiches but also to open new La Boulange cafes and expand the chain's geographic footprint. Three years later, however, Starbucks concluded that sales at the La Boulange cafes were growing too slowly to support its growth and profitability targets; it closed the 23 existing La Boulange cafes but retained the manufacturing facilities to stock Starbucks stores with La Boulange bakery products. Starbucks later discovered that other bakers could supply Starbucks with comparable quality products at a lower cost. In 2018, the La Boulange brand name was typically not very visible in Starbucks stores and disappeared altogether at most all locations in 2019.

THE SALES MIX AT STARBUCKS STORES IN 2019

Starbucks overall sales mix in its company-owned retail stores in fiscal 2019 was 74 percent beverages, 20 percent food, 1 percent packaged and single-serve coffees and teas, and 5 percent ready-to-drink beverages, coffee mugs, and other merchandise.[13] However, the product mix in each Starbucks store varied, depending on the size and location of each outlet. Larger stores carried a greater variety of whole coffee beans, gourmet food items, teas, coffee mugs, coffee grinders, filters, storage containers, and other accessories. Smaller stores and kiosks typically sold a full-line of coffee and tea beverages, a very limited selection of whole bean and ground coffees and Teavana teas, and a few coffee-drinking accessories.

STARBUCKS' NEW INTERNAL ORGANIZATION ARRANGEMENTS FOR OUTSIDE SALES OF STARBUCKS PRODUCTS

In 2010, Starbucks formed a new Consumer Products Group (CPG) to be responsible for sales of Starbuck products sold in all channels outside of Starbucks company-operated and licensed retail stores and to manage all of the company's distribution partnerships and joint ventures. A few years later, CPG was renamed and slightly reorganized into what was called the Channel Development segment. In 2018, management of the Channel Development segment was responsible for sales and distribution of roasted whole bean and ground coffees, Starbucks-branded single-serve products, a variety of ready-to-drink beverages (such as Frappuccino®, Starbucks Doubleshot®, Starbucks Refreshers® and Teavana™ iced tea, and Evolution juices) and other branded products sold worldwide through grocery stores, warehouse clubs, specialty retailers, convenience stores, and food service accounts. This segment accounted for sales of $2.3 billion and operating income of $927.1 million in fiscal year 2018, up from revenues of $707.4 million and operating income of $261.4 million in fiscal year 2010.

However, the Starbucks Channel Development segment, as part of a companywide effort to streamline some of Starbucks wide-ranging operations, decided to enter into a global coffee alliance with Nestlé S.A. ("Nestlé") in 2018 whereby Starbucks would agree to a licensing and distribution agreement with Nestlé that gave Nestlé the rights to market, sell, and distribute Starbucks®, Seattle's Best Coffee®, Starbucks Reserve®, Teavana™, Starbucks VIA®, and Torrefazione Italia® packaged coffees and tea in all global channels outside of Starbucks stores. In return, Nestlé was to pay Starbucks an upfront royalty payment of $7.15 billion, and Starbucks would remain as the supplier of these same branded coffee and tea products to Nestlé. The alliance agreement meant that henceforth the Channel Development segment would shift to a licensed distribution model with revenues consisting of product sales to Nestlé, royalty revenues from Nestlé, and revenues from the sales of ready-to-drink products through its distribution partnerships with PepsiCo, Anheuser-Busch InBev, and others (which sold them directly to retail grocers, warehouse clubs, specialty retail stores, and institutional food service companies). Starbucks global coffee alliance with Nestlé resulted in the Channel Development segment reporting a fiscal 2019 drop of $305 million in revenues and a drop of nearly $230 million in operating income as compared to fiscal 2018 levels. While the move resulted in weaker fiscal 2019 performance versus fiscal 2018, Starbucks expected that performance of the Channel Development segment would improve in the years to come because of Nestle's ability to significantly increase overall global sales of the packaged coffee and tea products it licensed from Starbucks.

Starbucks Advertising Strategy

Starbucks spent sparingly on advertising, preferring instead to build the brand cup by cup with customers and depend on word of mouth, the ambience of its stores, the and quality of its menu offerings, and the pleasing experience store employees delivered to customers to drive store traffic. However, from time to time Starbucks did call public attention to new Starbucks products or new things happening at Starbucks stores. The company's advertising expenses totaled $245.7 million in fiscal 2019, $260.3 million in fiscal 2018, $282.6 million in 2017, and $248.6 million in fiscal 2016.

TWO NEW DEVELOPMENTS AT STARBUCKS GOING INTO 2020

The Availability of Order Delivery

Starbucks began experimenting with a pilot program in Miami to deliver orders to customers in late 2018 via a partnership with Uber Eats, a global delivery service that partnered with over 200,000 restaurants in more than 500 cities across 36 countries. Starbucks envisioned order delivery as a means of extending its engagement with customers who currently included a Starbucks beverage as part of their morning or afternoon routines and also as a new way of extending potential engagement to new customers—delivering orders provided the ultimate Starbucks convenience.

The pilot order delivery program was enthusiastically received and repeatedly used by Starbucks customers in Miami. Starbucks management believed the pilot program suggested the existence of a strong pent-up demand for order delivery and quickly proceeded with a rollout of Starbucks® Delivers to 11 metropolitan markets in the United States and abroad in 2019 to further refine and integrate Starbucks digital ordering technology with the Uber Eats app and platform. About 95 percent of the items on Starbucks store menus were available for delivery. Customers used a downloaded Uber Eats app to place and pay for orders, which included the Uber Eats delivery fee; they also could use the Uber Eats app to track progress of their order and the location of their Uber courier. Delivery orders had splash-proof lids, delivery containers designed to keep drinks hot or cold, and tamper-proof packaging seals. In late 2019, Starbucks introduced Starbucks Delivers in five more cities in the United States, along with expanded coverage in the New York metro area. Expansion into 33 more cities in the United States. began in January 2020, and top executives expected to have Starbucks Delivers in operation in cities nationwide within four to six months.

Going into 2020, Starbucks had launched Starbucks Delivers in more than 15 global markets, including Canada, Chile, China, Colombia, Hong Kong, India, Indonesia, Japan, Mexico, Singapore, the U.K., and Vietnam. In China, where Uber did not operate, Starbucks opted to partner with Alibaba and use its Ele.me delivery platform to deliver customer orders; Alibaba's delivery drivers in China had promised to deliver orders in 30 minutes or less.

As of March 2020, Starbucks customers who placed delivery orders via the Uber Eats app were unable to receive Rewards credit for their orders and could not use the current Starbucks Mobile Order & Pay app to place delivery orders.

Starbucks indicated it had invested in voice ordering capability to enhance its delivery service, but, as of February 2020, this feature was not available in the United States.[14]

A New "Airport Strategy"

In early February, HMSHost announced it was terminating its exclusive licensing agreement to operate all Starbucks stores in airports in the United States, an agreement which had been in place since 1991; HMSHost's plan was to replace the agreement with Starbucks with new agreements to partner with local coffee companies in providing coffee service in airports. A week later, Starbucks announced that it was expanding its airport locations in partnership with airport retailer and restaurateur Paradies Lagardère and airport hospitality group OTG Management.

Starbucks and its new partners immediately announced they would be implementing a reimagined Starbucks experience for airport travelers that included (1) using mobile kiosks with digital and mobile ordering capabilities moving throughout airport terminals to provide Starbucks coffee service to travelers before boarding or upon arrival (2) widespread use of mobile ordering and payment at the counters of traditional Starbucks stores in airports where it had long been common for travelers to encounter 15- to 20-minute wait lines during peak periods to get their order. For example, OTG-operated airport locations were noted for using iPads that allowed customers to order and pay for items at their own pace without having to wait in a line. OTG had more than 5,000 iPads deployed at its retail locations in New Jersey's Newark Liberty International airport.

In November 2019, Starbucks announced the opening of its first Starbucks Pickup store in New York City's Penn Plaza. The Pickup store along with the Starbucks Dewata Coffee Sanctuary in Bali and the various Starbucks Roasters signaled that Starbucks was endeavoring to create a diverse store portfolio offering customers a variety of Starbucks experiences.

HOWARD SCHULTZ'S EFFORTS TO MAKE STARBUCKS A GREAT PLACE TO WORK, 1988–2018

Howard Schultz deeply believed that Starbucks's success was heavily dependent on customers having a very positive experience in its stores. This meant having store employees who were knowledgeable about the company's products, who paid attention to detail in preparing the company's espresso drinks, who eagerly communicated the company's passion for coffee, and who possessed the skills and personality to deliver consistent, pleasing customer service. Many of the baristas were in their 20s and worked part-time, going to college on the side or pursuing other career activities. Schultz viewed the company's challenge

as one of attracting, motivating, and rewarding store employees in a manner that would make Starbucks a company that people would want to work for and that would generate enthusiastic commitment and higher levels of customer service. Moreover, Schultz wanted to send all Starbucks employees a message that would cement the trust that had been building between management and the company's workforce.

Instituting Health Care Coverage for All Employees

One of the requests that employees had made to the prior owners of Starbucks back in the 1980s was to extend health care benefits to part-time workers. Their request had been turned down, but Schultz believed that expanding health care coverage to include part-timers was something the company needed to do. He knew from having grown up in a family that struggled to make ends meet how difficult it was to cope with rising medical costs. In 1988, Schultz went to the board of directors with his plan to expand the company's health care coverage to include part-timers who worked at least 20 hours per week. He saw the proposal not as a generous gesture but as a core strategy to win employee loyalty and commitment to the company's mission. Board members resisted because the company was then unprofitable and the added costs of the extended coverage would only worsen the company's bottom line. But Schultz argued passionately that it was the right thing to do and wouldn't be as expensive as it seemed. He observed that if the new benefit reduced turnover, which he believed was likely, then it would reduce the costs of hiring and training—which equaled about $3,000 per new hire. He further pointed out that it cost $1,500 a year to provide an employee with full benefits. Part-timers, he argued, were vital to Starbucks, constituting two-thirds of the company's workforce. Many were baristas who knew the favorite drinks of regular customers; if the barista left, that connection with the customer was broken. Moreover, many part-time employees were called upon to open the stores early, sometimes at 5:30 or 6 am; others had to work until closing, usually 9 pm or later. Providing these employees with health care benefits, he argued, would signal that the company honored their value and contribution.

The board approved Schultz's plan and part-timers working 20 or more hours were offered the same health coverage as full-time employees starting in late 1988.

Starbucks paid 75 percent of an employee's health care premium; the employee paid 25 percent. Over the years, Starbucks extended its health coverage to include preventive care, prescription drugs, dental care, eye care, mental health, and chemical dependency—see Exhibit 3 below). Coverage was also offered for unmarried partners in a committed relationship.

A Stock Option Plan for Employees

By 1991, the company's profitability had improved to the point where Schultz could pursue a stock option plan for all employees, a program he believed would

have a positive, long-term effect on the success of Starbucks.[15] Schultz wanted to turn every Starbucks employee into a partner, give them a chance to share in the success of the company, and make clear the connection between their contributions and the company's market value. Even though Starbucks was still a private company, the plan that emerged called for granting stock options to every full-time and part-time employee in proportion to their base pay. In May 1991, the plan, dubbed Bean Stock, was presented to the board. Though board members were concerned that increasing the number of shares might unduly dilute the value of the shares of investors who had put

EXHIBIT 3   Starbucks' Fringe Benefit Program, 2019

- Medical, dental, and vision coverage
- Sick pay, up to 40 hours per year
- Paid vacations (up to 120 hours annually for hourly workers with five or more years of service at retail stores and up to 200 hours annually for salaried and non-retail hourly employees with 10 or more years of service)
- Seven paid holidays
- One paid personal day every six months for salaried and non-retail hourly partners only
- Mental health and chemical dependency coverage
- 401(k) retirement savings plan—Partners age 18 or older with 90 days of service were eligible to contribute from 1 to 75 percent of their pay each pay period (up to the annual IRS dollar limit). Partners age 50 and older had a higher IRS annual limit than younger employees. Starbucks matched 100 percent of the first 5 percent of eligible pay contributed each pay period. Starbucks matching contributions to the 401(k) plans worldwide totaled $122 million in fiscal 2019, $111.7 million in fiscal 2018, and $101.4 million in fiscal 2017.
- Short- and long-term disability
- Stock purchase plan—eligible employees could buy shares at a 5 percent discount through regular payroll deductions of between 1 and 10 percent of base pay.
- Life insurance coverage equal to annual base pay for salaried and non-retail employees; coverage equal to $5,000 for store employees. Supplemental coverage could be purchased in flat dollar amounts of $10,000, $25,000, and $45,000.
- Short term disability coverage (partial replacement of lost wages/income for 26 weeks, after a short waiting period); hourly employees can purchase long-term disability coverage
- Company-paid long-term disability coverage for salaried and nonretail employees
- Accidental death and dismemberment insurance
- Adoption assistance—Reimbursement of up to $10,000 to help pay for qualified expenses related to the adoption of an eligible child
- Financial assistance program for employees that experience a financial crisis
- Stock option plan (Bean stock)—Shares were granted to eligible partners, subject to the company's achievement of specified performance targets and the employee's continued employment through the vesting period. Vesting occurred in two equal annual installments beginning two years from the grant date. The company's board of directors determined how many shares were to be granted each year and also established the specified performance targets. Pre-tax payroll deductions for work-related commuter expenses
- A free coffee or tea product each week
- An in-store discount of 30 percent on purchases of beverages, food, and merchandise
- A college achievement plan featuring full tuition reimbursement every semester for employees enrolled in Arizona State University's top ranked online degree programs. As of March 2018, some 1,282 Starbucks employees had graduated and over 10,000 were currently working toward their degrees.
- Gift-matching benefits—Starbucks matched up to $1,500 per fiscal year for individual contributions of money or volunteer time to eligible non-profit organizations

Source: Information in the Careers section at www.starbucks.com (accessed May 28, 2019); Starbucks 2018 10-K Report, pp. 80–82 and 2019 10-K Report, pp. 75–77.

up hard cash, the plan received unanimous approval. The first grant was made in October 1991, just after the end of the company's fiscal year in September; each partner was granted stock options worth 12 percent of base pay. When the Bean Stock program was initiated, Starbucks dropped the term employee and began referring to all of its people as "partners" because every member of the Starbucks workforce became eligible for stock option awards after six months of employment and 500 paid work hours.

After Starbucks went public in June 1992, starting in October 1992 and continuing through October 2004, Starbucks granted each eligible employee a stock option award with a value equal to 14 percent of base pay. Beginning in 2005, the plan was modified to tie the size of each employee's stock option awards to three factors: (1) Starbucks' success and profitability for the fiscal year, (2) the size of an employee's base wages, and (3) the price at which the stock option could be exercised. Since becoming a public company, Starbucks stock had split two-for-one on six occasions. The total intrinsic value of options exercised was $466 million, $236 million, and $181 million during fiscal 2019, 2018, and 2017, respectively. The total fair value of options vested was $31 million, $53 million, and $40 million during fiscal 2019, 2018, and 2017, respectively.

Starbucks' Stock Purchase and 401(k) Plans for Employees

In 1995, Starbucks implemented an employee stock purchase plan that gave partners who had been employed for at least 90 days an opportunity to purchase company stock through regular payroll deductions of 1 to 10 percent of their base earnings (up to an annual maximum of $25,000). At the end of each calendar quarter, each participant's contributions were used to buy Starbucks shares at a discounted price. In fiscal 2018, about 600,000 shares were purchased under this plan, and about 400,000 shares were purchased in fiscal 2019.

Later, a 401(k) plan was initiated for employees that included matching company contributions. Details of the current stock purchase plan and 401(k) plans are included in Exhibit 3.

The Workplace Environment

Starbucks management believed its competitive pay scales and comprehensive benefits for both full-time and part-time partners (employees) allowed it to attract motivated people with above-average skills and good work habits. An employee's base pay was determined by the pay scales prevailing in the geographic region where an employee worked and by the person's job, skills, experience, and job performance. About 90 percent of Starbucks' partners were full-time or part-time baristas, paid on an hourly basis. In 2020, after six months of employment, baristas at company-owned stores in the United States earned an average of -$12 per hour or about $24,240 annually, according to ZipRecruiter; the majority earned between $20,500 and $26,500 annually, but annual barista pay at some locations ranged on up to $33,500.[16] In February 2020, pay scales for shift supervisors were in the range of $11 to $16 per hour; store managers earned about $55,000, and salaries for district store managers were in the $88,000 to $134,000 range.[17]

Starbucks was named to *Fortune*'s list of the "100 Best Companies to Work For" 14 times during the 1988–2020 period.

Schultz's approach to offering employees good compensation and a comprehensive benefits package was driven by his belief that sharing the company's success with the people who made it happen helped everyone think and act like an owner, build positive long-term relationships with customers, and do things in an efficient way. Schultz's rationale, based on his father's experience of going from one low-wage, no-benefits job to another, was that if you treat your employees well, that is how they will treat customers.

Employee Training and Recognition

To accommodate its strategy of rapid store expansion, Starbucks put in systems to recruit, hire, and train baristas and store managers. Every partner/barista hired for a retail job in a Starbucks store received at least 24 hours training in their first two to four weeks. Training topics included coffee history, drink preparation, coffee knowledge, customer service, and retail skills, plus a four-hour workshop on "Brewing the Perfect Cup." Baristas spent considerable time learning about beverage preparation—grinding the beans, steaming milk, learning to pull perfect (18- to 23-second) shots of espresso, memorizing the recipes of all the different drinks, practicing making the different drinks, and learning how to customize drinks to customer specifications. There were sessions on cash register operations, how to clean the milk wand on the espresso machine, explaining the Italian drink names to unknowing customers, making eye contact with customers and interacting with them, and taking personal responsibility for the cleanliness of the store. And there were rules to be memorized: milk must be steamed to at least 150 degrees Fahrenheit but never more than 170 degrees; every espresso shot not pulled within 23 seconds must be tossed; always compensate dissatisfied customers with a Starbucks coupon that entitles them to a free drink.

There were also training programs for shift supervisors, assistant store managers, store managers, and district managers that went much deeper, covering not only coffee knowledge and information imparted to baristas but also the details of store operations, practices and procedures as set forth in the company's operating manual, information systems, and the basics of managing people. In addition, there were special career development programs, such as a coffee masters program for store employees and more advanced leadership skills training for shift supervisors and store management personnel. When Starbucks opened stores in a new market, it sent a star team of experienced managers and baristas to the area to lead the store opening effort and to conduct one-on-one training following the basic orientation and training sessions.

To recognize and reward partner contributions, Starbucks had created a partner recognition program consisting of 18 different awards and programs.[18] Examples included Partner of the Quarter Awards (for one partner per store per quarter) for significant contributions to their store and demonstrating behaviors consistent with the company's mission and values; Spirit of Starbucks awards for making exceptional contributions to partners, customers, and community while embracing the company's mission and values; a Manager of the Quarter for store manager leadership; Green Apron Awards where partners could recognize fellow partners for how they bring to life the company's mission, values, and customer commitment; and Bravo and Team Bravo! awards for above and beyond the call of duty performance and achieving exceptional results.

STARBUCKS' MISSION, BUSINESS PRINCIPLES, AND VALUES

During the early building years, Howard Schultz and other Starbucks senior executives worked to instill some values and guiding principles into the Starbucks culture. The cornerstone value in their effort "to build a company with soul" was that the company would never stop pursuing the perfect cup of coffee by buying the best beans and roasting them to perfection. Schultz was adamant about controlling the quality of Starbucks products and building a culture common to all stores. He was rigidly opposed to selling artificially flavored coffee beans—"we will not pollute our high-quality beans with chemicals;" if a customer wanted hazelnut-flavored coffee, Starbucks added hazelnut syrup to the drink.

Starbucks' management was also emphatic about the importance of employees paying attention to what pleased customers. Employees were trained to go out of their way, and to take heroic measures if necessary, to make sure customers were fully satisfied. The theme was "just say yes" to customer requests. Further, employees were encouraged to speak their minds without fear of retribution from upper management—senior executives wanted employees to be vocal about what Starbucks was doing right, what it was doing wrong, and what changes were needed. The intent was for employees to be involved in and contribute to the process of making Starbucks a better company.

Starbucks' Mission Statement

In early 1990, the senior executive team at Starbucks went to an offsite retreat to debate the company's values and beliefs and draft a mission statement. Schultz wanted the mission statement to convey a strong sense of organizational purpose and to articulate the company's fundamental beliefs and guiding principles. The draft was submitted to all employees for review and several changes were made based on employee comments. The resulting mission statement was: "Establish Starbucks as the premier purveyor of the finest coffee in the world while maintaining our uncompromising principles as we grow." It was accompanied by six guiding principles intended to help company personnel measure the appropriateness of the company's decisions:[19]

- Provide a great work environment and treat each other with respect and dignity.
- Embrace diversity as an essential component in the way we do business.
- Apply the highest standards of excellence to the purchasing, roasting, and fresh delivery of our coffee.

- Develop enthusiastically satisfied customers all of the time.
- Contribute positively to our communities and our environment.
- Recognize that profitability is essential to our future success.

In 2008, Starbucks partners from all across the company met for several months to refresh the mission statement; the revised mission statement was "To inspire and nurture the human spirit—one person, one cup, and one neighborhood at a time." That mission had endured going into 2020. But, over time, the original six guiding principles were recast into five core values that in 2020 were phrased as follows:[20]

- Creating a culture of warmth and belonging, where everyone is welcome.
- Delivering our very best in all we do, holding ourselves accountable for results.
- Acting with courage, challenging the status quo and finding new ways to grow our company and each other.
- Being present, connecting with transparency, dignity, and respect.
- We are performance-driven, through the lens of humanity.

STARBUCKS' COFFEE PURCHASING STRATEGY

Coffee beans were grown in 70 tropical countries and were the second most traded commodity in the world after petroleum. Most of the world's coffee was grown by some 25 million small farmers, most of whom lived on the edge of poverty. Starbucks personnel traveled regularly to coffee-producing countries, building relationships with growers and exporters, checking on agricultural conditions and crop yields, and searching out varieties and sources that would meet Starbucks' exacting standards of quality and flavor. The coffee-purchasing group, working with Starbucks personnel in roasting operations, tested new varieties and blends of green coffee beans from different sources. The company's supplies of green coffee beans were chiefly grown on about 1 million small family farms (less than 30 acres) located in the coffee-growing communities of countries across the world. Sourcing from multiple geographic areas

not only allowed Starbucks to offer a greater range of coffee varieties to customers but also spread its risks regarding weather, price volatility, and changing economic and political conditions in coffee-growing countries.

Starbucks' coffee sourcing strategy had three key elements:

- Make sure that the prices Starbucks paid for green (unroasted) coffee beans were high enough to ensure that small farmers were able to cover their production costs and provide for their families. The company was firmly committed to a goal of "100 percent ethically-sourced coffees"—in 2016 management believed it had reached a milestone of 99 percent ethically sourced coffee.[21] Because the company also purchased tea and cocoa for its stores and ready-to-drink beverages, it was similarly committed to 100 percent ethically sourced tea and cocoa.
- Utilize purchasing arrangements that limited Starbucks exposure to sudden spikes in green coffee prices.
- Work directly with small coffee growers, local coffee-growing cooperatives, and other types of coffee suppliers to promote coffee cultivation methods that were environmentally sustainable. Starbucks' objective was to "make coffee the world's first sustainable agricultural product."[22]

Pricing and Purchasing Arrangements

Commodity-grade coffee was traded in a highly competitive market as an undifferentiated product. However, high-altitude Arabica coffees of the quality purchased by Starbucks were bought on a negotiated basis at a premium above the "C" coffee commodity price. Both the commodity price and the prices of the top-quality coffees sourced by Starbucks depended on supply and demand conditions at the time of the purchase and were subject to considerable volatility due to weather, natural disasters, crop disease, changes in input prices and the costs of production, inventory levels, and economic and political conditions in the growing countries. Prices were also impacted by trading activities in the *arabica* coffee futures market, including the trading activities of hedge funds and commodity index funds. In addition, green coffee prices, on occasion, were influenced by the actions of certain organizations and associations to establish export quotas or restrict coffee supplies.

Starbucks bought coffee using fixed-price and price-to-be-fixed purchase commitments, depending on market conditions, to secure an adequate supply of quality green coffee. Price-to-be-fixed contracts were purchase commitments whereby the quality, quantity, delivery period, and other negotiated terms were agreed upon, but the date at which the base price component of commodity grade coffee was to be fixed was as yet unspecified. In the case of price-to-be-fixed contracts, either Starbucks or the seller had the option to select a date on which to "fix" the base price of commodity grade coffee prior to the delivery date. Starbucks also utilized forward contracts, futures contracts, and collars to hedge "C" price exposure under its price-to-be-fixed green coffee contracts and its forecasted green coffee needs for the upcoming 12 months. It was the goal of the company's coffee purchasing personnel to have sufficient purchasing and hedging agreements in place, together with its existing inventory, to provide an adequate supply of green coffee for the upcoming 11–12 months.

Purchasing of Other Needed Supplies

Products other than whole bean coffees and coffee beverages sold in Starbucks stores included tea and a number of ready-to-drink beverages that were purchased from several specialty suppliers, usually under long-term supply contracts. Food products, such as pastries, breakfast sandwiches, and lunch items, were purchased from national, regional and local sources. Starbucks purchased a broad range of paper and plastic products, such as cups and cutlery, from several manufacturers and distributors to support the needs of its retail stores and its manufacturing and distribution operations. Management believed, based on relationships established with these suppliers and manufacturers, that the risk of non-delivery of sufficient amounts of these items to its many store locations and various other operations was remote.

Starbucks' Supplier Code of Conduct

Starbucks made an effort to work with suppliers that were committed to its own principles of conducting business in a responsible and ethical manner, respecting the rights of individuals, and helping to protect the environment. All Starbucks suppliers worldwide were expected to sign an agreement pledging compliance with Starbucks Supplier Code of Conduct, which included the following:[23]

- Demonstrating commitment to the welfare, economic improvement and sustainability of the people and places that produce products and services for Starbucks.
- Adherence to local laws and international standards regarding human rights, workplace safety, and worker compensation and treatment.
- Meeting or exceeding national laws and international standards for environmental protection and minimizing negative environmental impacts of the supplier's operations.
- Commitment to measuring, monitoring, reporting and verification of compliance to this code.
- Pursuing continuous improvement of these social and environmental principles.
- There were further specified standards for manufacturers, food suppliers, and non-food suppliers pertaining to such things as anti-bribery practices, workplace harassment, quality control, hazardous materials, packing and shipping of refrigerated products, transportation and shipping modes, and customs clearance.

Verification of compliance was subject to audits by Starbucks personnel or acceptable third parties. From time to time, Starbucks had temporarily or permanently discontinued its business relationship with suppliers who failed to comply or failed to work with Starbucks to correct a non-complying situation.

COFFEE ROASTING OPERATIONS

Starbucks considered the roasting of its coffee beans to be something of an art form, entailing trial-and-error testing of different combinations of time and temperature to get the most out of each type of bean and blend. Recipes were put together by the coffee department, once all the components had been tested. Computerized roasters guaranteed consistency. Highly trained and experienced roasting personnel monitored the process, using both smell and hearing, to help check when the beans were perfectly done—coffee beans make a popping sound when ready. Roasting standards were exacting. After roasting and cooling, the coffee was immediately vacuum-sealed in bags that preserved freshness for up to 26 weeks. As a matter of policy, however, Starbucks packaged coffees were removed from retailer shelves well before the 26-week expiration date (frequently because of discounted price promotions). In the case of coffee used to prepare beverages in stores, the shelf life was limited to seven days after the bag was opened.

In 2020, Starbucks had multiple roasting plants in numerous locations, having expanded its roasting operations as its store base expanded to more geographic regions and countries. Roasting plants also had additional space for warehousing and shipping coffees. In keeping with Starbucks' corporate commitment to reduce its environmental footprint, since 2009 all newly-built roasting plants and all other newly-built company facilities had conformed to LEED (Leadership in Energy and Environment Design) standards devised by the United States Green Building Council; LEED standards were the most widely used green building rating system in the world for evaluating the environmental performance of a building and encouraging market transformation towards sustainable design. Starbucks had launched and achieved an initiative to achieve LEED Certification for all company-operated facilities built after 2010; facilities constructed prior to 2010 had been remodeled and/or retrofitted accordingly. Currently, Starbucks goal was designing, building and operating 10,000 "Greener Stores" globally by 2025.

STARBUCKS' CORPORATE SOCIAL RESPONSIBILITY STRATEGY

Howard Schultz's effort to "build a company with soul" included a long history of doing business in ways that were socially and environmentally responsible. A commitment to do the right thing and strike a balance between profitability and a social conscience was central to how Starbucks operated from the time Howard Schultz first became Starbucks CEO in 1987. The specific actions comprising Starbucks' corporate social responsibility (CSR) strategy had varied over the years but the intent of the strategy was consistently one of contributing positively to the communities in which Starbucks had stores, being a good environmental steward, and conducting the company's business in ways that earned the trust and respect of customers, partners/employees, suppliers, and the general public. Some of main elements comprising Starbucks CSR strategy over the past 30 years and some of the resulting accomplishments and beneficial outcomes include the following:

1. *Employing coffee-sourcing practices that resulted in paying fair and ethical prices to the small family farmers in low-income countries where the high-quality green coffees Starbucks purchased were being grown.* This CSR initiative, which Starbucks referred to as "ethical-sourcing, had two principal objectives. One was to ensure that small coffee growers received prices for their green coffee beans sufficiently high enough to allow them to pay fair wages to their workers, earn enough to reinvest in their farms and communities, develop the business skills needed to compete in the global market for coffee, and afford basic health care, education, and home improvements. The second was to educate these small farmers about the benefits of using sustainable agricultural practices to grow coffee and then to fund support their efforts to implement these practices—with the long-term environmentally-beneficial goal of making coffee one of the world's first products to be widely grown with sustainable agricultural practices.

   To achieve "the fair and ethical prices" objective, in 1998, Starbucks began partnering with Conservation International's Center for Environmental Leadership to develop specific guidelines (called Coffee and Farmer Equity [C.A.F.E.] Practices) covering four areas: product quality, the price received by farmers/growers, safe and humane working conditions (including compliance with minimum wage requirements and child labor provisions), and environmentally responsible cultivation practices. Top management at Starbucks set a goal that by 2015 all of the green coffee beans purchased from growers would be C.A.F.E. Practice certified, Fair Trade certified, organically certified, or certified by some other equally acceptable third party. By 2011, 86 percent of Starbucks purchases of green coffee beans were C.A.F.E. Practices–verified sources and 8 percent were from Fair Trade–certified sources, making Starbucks among the world's largest purchasers and marketers of Fair Trade–certified coffee beans. Since 2015, Starbucks coffee had been verified as 99 percent ethically sourced, and the company was committed to reaching its goal of 100 percent. It was similarly committed to 100 percent ethically sourced supplies of tea and cocoa (for its cocoa-based beverages) by 2020 and was pursuing efforts to do so.

To promote achievement of the second outcome, Starbucks created and operated farmer support centers staffed with agronomists and sustainability experts who worked with coffee farming communities to promote best practices in coffee production, implement advanced soil-management techniques, improve both coffee quality and yields, and address climate and other impacts. To complement the activities of farmer support centers, Starbucks instituted a Small Farmer Loan Program to provide funding for loans to small coffee growers since many of the small family farms lacked the money to make farming improvements and/or cover all expenses until they sold their crops. In 2010, $14.6 million was loaned to nearly 56,000 farmers who grew green coffee beans for Starbucks in 10 countries; in 2011, an additional $14.7 million was loaned to over 45,000 farmers who grew green coffee beans for Starbucks in another seven countries. Later, the company established a $50 million Starbucks Global Farmer Fund to provide loans to coffee farmers for coffee tree renovation and infrastructure improvements. Moreover, the Starbucks Foundation began partnering with organizations with local expertise to award grants to support smallholder-farming families in coffee-growing and tea-growing communities, reaching approximately 47,000 direct and indirect beneficiaries. By 2020 the Foundation planned to reach 200,000 people.

A still further ethical-sourcing initiative called the One Tree for Every Bag Commitment was launched in 2015 for the purpose of planting 20 million coffee tree seedlings to replace trees declining in productivity due to age and disease such as coffee leaf rust. The goal was exceeded in just over a year, at which time Starbucks committed to providing a total of 100 million coffee tree seedlings to farmers by 2025, particularly in coffee-growing communities being impacted by climate change.

2. *Environmental stewardship*—This CSR strategy element had taken on an ever bigger role in Starbucks overall CSR strategy over the years and was arguably the centerpiece of the company's CSR strategy in 2020. Starbucks had invested in renewable energy since 2005, and it achieved a milestone in 2015 by purchasing the equivalent of 100 percent of the electricity consumption of all company-operated stores worldwide from renewable energy sources. In North Carolina and Washington state, Starbucks had invested in a solar farm and a wind farm that delivered enough energy to power more than 700 Starbucks stores.

Beginning in 2008 and continuing thereafter, Starbucks undertook an energy-saving commitment to make all company facilities as green as possible by using environmentally friendly building materials and energy-efficient designs. Management determined that henceforth all of its new operating facilities (roasting plants, offices, manufacturing and distribution facilities) and all new company-owned retail stores globally would be constructed to achieve LEED certification (LEED stood for Leadership in Energy and Environmental Design and was a green building certification program used worldwide). LEED-certification standards were also employed in remodeling or retrofitting existing facilities and retail stores. As of 2019, Starbucks had built more than 1,600 LEED-certified retail stores in 20 countries.

Starting in 2005 and continuing until the present, Starbuck pursued actions to reduce water consumption, reduce food waste, use recycled cardboard boxes and other back-of-store items, place recycling bins in place in all company-owned locations where there were municipal recycling capabilities, use more environmentally-friendly coffee cups, and substitute paper straws for single-use plastic straws across all stores worldwide. Since 1985, Starbucks had given a $0.10 discount to customers who brought reusable cups and tumblers to stores for use in serving the beverages they ordered. An initiative was launched to empower 10,000 Starbucks employees to be "sustainability champions." Stores participated in Earth Day activities each year with in-store promotions and volunteer efforts to educate employees and customers about the impacts their actions had on the environment.

3. *Creating opportunities to help people achieve their dreams.* The chief initiatives here included partnering with some 50other employers to hire, train, and advance the careers of 100,000 youth

aged 16–24 by 2020, hiring at least 25,000 veterans and military spouses by 2025, welcoming and employing 10,000 refugees across the 75 countries in which Starbucks stores were located by 2022, and expanding partner participation in the company's college achievement plan that covered full-tuition reimbursement for admission to one of Arizona State University's online degree programs.

4. *Charitable contributions*—The Starbucks Foundation, set up in 1997, oversaw a major portion of the company's philanthropic activities; it received the majority of its funding from Starbucks Coffee Company and private donations. Over the years, the Starbucks Foundation had made to nonprofit organizations such as the American Red Cross for relief efforts to communities experiencing severe damage from earthquakes, hurricanes, tornadoes, floods, and other natural disasters, Save the Children for efforts to improve education, health, and nutrition, the Global Fund and Product (RED)™ to provide medicine to people in Africa with AIDS, and a wide assortment of community-building efforts, including youth literacy programs and jobs training programs. Donations were made in cash and in-kind contributions. In 2017-19, the foundation made "Opportunity for All" grants ranging from $10,000 to $100,000 to more than 40 nonprofits in 27 U.S. cities, plus others to various communities across the world and it donated $10 million to four Community Development Financial Institutions in Chicago to help fund loans to cash-short small business and entrepreneurs and provide borrowers with mentoring and technical assistance to help ensure the success of their projects—and thereby provide more neighborhood jobs to local area residents.[24] Water, sanitation, and hygiene education programs in water-stressed countries were supported through the Starbucks Foundation's Ethos Water Fund. For each bottle of Ethos water purchased at Starbucks stores, Starbucks donated $0.05 ($0.10 in Canada) to the Ethos© Water Fund. Since 2005, the Fund had made over $15 million in grants, benefitting more than 500,000 people around the world.

In early 2020, Starbucks CEO Kevin Johnson announced three new environmental goals for the company's CSR strategy and five strategic initiatives to pursue them. Johnson's vision was for Starbucks over a multi-decade period to become a "resource-positive" company that gave more than it took from the planet. To begin this multi-decade journey, Johnson set forth three objectives for Starbucks to achieve by 2030:

1. A 50 percent reduction in carbon emissions in Starbucks direct operations and supply chain.
2. Conserving or replenishing 50 percent of water currently being used in company operations and coffee production, with a focus on communities and basins with high water risk.
3. A 50 percent reduction in waste sent to landfill from stores and manufacturing, driven by a broader shift toward a circular plastics economy where plastics never became waste or pollution because they were 100 percent recycled.

He indicated that a comprehensive, data-driven environmental footprint of carbon emissions, water use, and waste in Starbucks global operations and supply chain had produced five strategies to prioritize the work needed to be done to reach the 2030 objectives:

1. Expanding plant-based options on Starbucks menus, thereby migrating toward a more environmentally friendly menu.
2. Shifting from single-use to reusable packaging.
3. Investing in innovative and regenerative agricultural practices, reforestation, forest conservation, and water replenishment in Starbucks supply chain.
4. Investing in better ways to manage waste, both in Starbucks stores and in its communities, to ensure more reuse, recycling, and elimination of food waste.
5. Innovating to develop more eco-friendly stores, operations, manufacturing, and delivery.

Starbucks had been named to *Corporate Responsibility Magazine*'s list of the 100 Best Corporate Citizens on numerous occasions; this list was based on more than 360 data points of publicly available information in seven categories: Environment, Climate Change, Human Rights, Philanthropy, Employee Relations, Financial Performance, and Governance. Over the years, Starbucks had received over 25 awards from a diverse group of organizations for its philanthropic, community service, and environmental activities.

LUCKIN COFFEE'S SUDDEN EMERGENCE TO CHALLENGE STARBUCKS COFFEE MARKET LEADERSHIP IN CHINA

China-based Luckin Coffee began operations in October 2017, and by March 31, 2019, had opened an astonishing 2,370 wholly-owned locations in 28 cities—a blitz rarely seen in the retail or restaurant industries. Six months later, Luckin had 3,680 store locations, of which 3,433 were pickup stores with seating for no more than 10 customers, 138 were "relax" stores with enough seating space for 25 to 50 customers, and 109 were delivery kitchens. The company's strategic intent was to become the largest network of coffee stores in China—on November 13, 2019, Luckin executives said they fully expected that Luckin Coffee would have more store locations than Starbucks by the end of 2019. Starbucks had approximately 4,292 stores in China at the end of December 2019 and was planning to add about 600 more stores in China by the end of September 2020.

In 2018, its first full year of operation, Luckin Coffee used aggressive promotions and coupons offering price discounts to achieve revenues of $125.3 million on which it reported a loss of $241.3 million. For the three months ending March 31, 2019, Luckin reported revenues of $71.3 million and a net loss of $82.2 million. Revenues during the first three months of 2019 were derived from the sale of freshly brewed drinks (75.4 percent), other products (17.6 percent), and "other" (7.0 percent). The company reported in April 2019 that it had achieved a total of 16.8 million customer transactions since inception and sold some 90 million items in 2018. Its customer repurchase rate in 2018 was just over 54 percent.

In the next six months, customer traffic at Luckin Coffee store picked up significantly. Store revenues were $208.9 million in the third quarter of 2019, up 67 percent over first quarter revenues.[25] Average monthly total items sold were 44.2 million in Q3 versus 16.3 million in Q1. The average number of customer transactions storewide in Q3 was 9.34 million versus 4.4 million in Q1. In Q3 Luckin reported its first store-level operating profit of $26.1 million, equal to 12.5 percent of store revenues in Q3. This 12.5 percent margin represented a significant improvement over the *negative store profit margins*

of 6.4 percent in Q2 and 44.3 percent in Q1. The $26 million store-level operating profit in Q3 was far short of covering corporate-level sales and marketing expenses, general administrative expenses, store pre-opening expenses, and depreciation charges, resulting in a quarterly operating loss of $82.7 million and net loss of $74.4 million. But these losses were smaller than those incurred in Q2 of 2019.

Some 2,163 of Luckin Coffee's stores (91 percent) were "pickup stores" with limited seating and were typically located in areas with high demand for coffee (office buildings, commercial areas, and university campuses); the company also had 109 "relax stores" and 98 delivery kitchens. Luckin had created mobile apps covering the entire customer purchase process, enabling it to offer app users a 100 percent cashier-free option. Luckin Coffee sourced premium Arabica coffee beans from prominent suppliers and engaged World Barista Champion teams to design its coffee recipes. Its coffee won the Gold Medal in the 2018 IIAC International Coffee Tasting Championship. The company purchased coffee machines, coffee condiments, juices, and assorted food products that were sold in its stores from reputable outside vendors at what Luckin management believed were favorable prices. Luckin had 16,645 employees as of March 31, 2019.

On April 17, 2019, Luckin Coffee filed documents with the Securities and Exchange Commission stating its desire to undertake an initial public offering (IPO) of common stock and become a public company, with its stock trading on the NASDAQ under the symbol LK. In its IPO filing, Luckin Coffee management cited four company strengths as contributing to its initial success:

- Being the leading and fastest growing player driving coffee consumption in China.
- Being the pioneer of a disruptive new retail model.
- Having strong technology capabilities.
- Offering a superior customer proposition underpinned by high quality, high affordability, and high convenience.

In May 2019, the company's IPO application received SEC approval, and Luckin quickly moved forward with its IPO. Luckin priced its IPO issue at $17 per share and raised $561 million on an upsized offering of 33 million shares, making it one of the fastest companies ever to reach a $6 billion valuation (based on all the preferred and common shares outstanding). Its common stock began trading May 17, 2019, with initial trades around $25 per share; however, the share price began a downward trend in the latter stages of the first day's trading session that continued for the next five trading days. The stock price slowly climbed back to trade in the low 20s, but then quickly jumped to over $28 per share following release of the Q3 financial results in November. Management announced it expected the company to be profitable in 2020.

On January 7, 2020, Luckin Coffee Inc. announced the launch of Luckin Pop, a smart vending machine, and Luckin Coffee Express, a smart coffee machine. Both types of vending machines were to be installed in office buildings, gas stations, bus terminals, airports, and on college campuses and various locations in residential communities. The Luckin Pop vending machines would sell bottled and canned beverages and snacks from brands like Pepsi and Nestlé that also supplied products to Luckin's retail shops. The Luckin Coffee Express vending machine enabled customers to order hot coffee drinks like those at the company's retail stores; customers used the LK App to place orders on a specific Express machine and picked up the chosen brewed coffee drink by scanning the QR code from the app after paying for it. This new strategy initiative was aimed at building a low-cost unmanned retail distribution network that would make Luckin Coffee products readily available to more customers in more locations, thereby growing the company's sales revenues while bypassing the payroll, rental costs, and other expenses associated with operating Luckin Coffee retail stores. However, some of the operating cost savings associated with vending machine sales would be offset by higher depreciation costs on the vending machines.

According to the company's January 7, 2020 announcement, the Luckin Coffee Express vending machines would contain a coffee-making machine supplied by Schaerer, a Swiss-based manufacturer of premium automated coffee machines; the cost of each installed Express vending machine was expected to be in the range of $15,000 to $20,000. Local observers believed that Luckin would employ a low-introductory pricing strategy for all the products sold in its Luckin Pop and Luckin Coffee Express vending machines. Currently, Luckin's retail stores were continuing to sell coffee products at half the posted price and were also running a special "Buy 2, get one free" promotion on top of the 50 percent discount.

To help finance its new vending machine initiative and fund capital requirements for ongoing store network expansion, sales and marketing, and other corporate activities, Luckin issued 11 million shares of common stock (realizing net proceeds of $418.3 million) and sold $460 million in convertible senior notes due 2025 (realizing net proceeds of $446.7 million) for a total capital raise of $865 million. At the end of 2019, Luckin Coffee had 4,507 self-operated stores, higher than Starbucks year-end store count of 4,292.

On April 2, 2020, Luckin Coffee disclosed that an investigation by a special committee of the Board of Directors revealed the company's chief operating officer, and several employees reporting to him, had fraudulently inflated the company's sales by approximately $310 million from the second quarter to the fourth quarter of 2019. The misconduct involved "fabricating certain transactions" and substantially inflating certain costs and expenses, thus rendering the company's financial statements unreliable; the company's auditor was Ernst & Young. The individuals involved were suspended, and the company said it intended to pursue legal actions against them. The China Securities Regulatory Commission announced it would investigate the alleged fraud; Morgan Stanley, Credit Suisse, and several other investment banks involved in preparing documents for the company's $645 million IPO and subsequent debt issues began reviewing the due diligence work they had done. Earlier in 2020, Muddy Waters Capital, a well-known short-seller located in the United States, announced it had reviewed an anonymous 69-page report alleging fraud that was circulating, found the content credible, and had initiated a short position in Luckin's common stock. When news of the fraud was publicly reported on April 2, Luckin Coffee's stock price quickly plummeted 80 percent to about $6 per share, after trading as high as $50 in the weeks following the May 2019 IPO. Trading in the company's stock on the Nasdaq was suspended on April 8, 2020; the last trade was at $4.39. On May 12, 2020, the company announced that Luckin's chief executive officer and chief operating officer had been terminated and that the company's Board of Directors had demanded and received their resignations from the Board. In addition, it was announced that six other employees, who were involved in or had knowledge of the fabricated transactions, had been placed on suspension or leave and that a Senior Vice President of the company had been appointed as the new interim CEO. In June 2020, authorities in China announced that emails had been discovered in which the company's board chairman and largest shareholder, Lu Zhengyao, instructed Luckin executives to commit fraud; Lu was expected to face criminal charges for fraud.

Back in June 2019, Jeffrey Towson, a private equity investor, author, and business professor at Peking University in Beijing, observed in a two-part article that, in China, Starbucks's most interesting competitor was not Luckin Coffee (whose coffee products were not something that many Chinese consumers drank) but rather HeyTea, an upscale Starbucks-type business focused on tea (something Chinese consumers really, really like).[26] Towson noted that HeyTea appeared to be focused on product development and continually thrilling its customers with their product offerings. He believed Hey Tea's high-priced creative tea drinks were becoming a consumer phenomenon in China because of its 220 stores operating at capacity, with people holding places in line for other people and with the average order being three drinks costing about $11.

STARBUCKS' FIRST MOVES TO COUNTER THE COMPETITIVE CHALLENGE FROM LUCKIN COFFEE

In July 2019, Starbucks opened its first Starbucks Now™ store in the central financial district of Beijing that combined the signature Starbucks café environment with Mobile Order & Pay and Starbucks Delivers™ to offer customers new levels of convenience and speed.[27] Customers entering the store were greeted by a Starbucks barista at an elevated concierge counter to assist with ordering or order pickup. They could choose from a menu of handcrafted beverage options tailored for on-the-go customers along with an assortment of popular food items. Limited seating was available for customers who chose to stay in the store and relax with their orders.

There was a dedicated area for Starbucks Delivers orders to facilitate barista-assisted quick and easy pickup by delivery drivers. Online orders that were ready for pickup were placed in an exterior wall system with designated portals for each order, which speeded drive-by pickup by delivery couriers. The Starbuck Now store also had a central kitchen where baristas could prepare handcrafted beverage orders for delivery within a certain radius. Enabling the kitchen to function as a central dispatch center at peak periods had the advantage of permitting baristas at neighboring cafes to focus on serving their in-store customers.

Starbucks had plans to open about 300 new Starbucks Now stores in high-traffic areas and business and transportation hubs in 10 cities in China.

Voice Ordering in Conjunction with Starbucks Delivery Begins in China

Two months after opening the first Starbucks Now store in Beijing, Starbucks and Alibaba, its delivery partner in China, jointly announced the launch of voice ordering within Alibaba's smart speaker, Tmall Genie, coupled with order delivery capabilities within a 30-minute timeframe.[28] Tmall Genie used cutting-edge Artificial Intelligence (AI) technology, along with voiceprint payment technology, to enable customers to place an order and pay for it using their voice and then track their order in real time during the 30-minute delivery timeframe. Starbucks®Rewards members could also earn Stars and receive Rewards membership updates, including benefits, via the Tmall Genie. Further, members were able to receive personalized recommendations when using voice commands to place orders that were tailored to previous order preferences and popular items from Starbucks seasonal menus. As yet another added benefit, Starbucks customers in China could listen to the latest Starbucks in-store playlists through Alibaba's music streaming app, Xiami Music.

An exclusive Starbucks-themed Tmall Genie was available through the Starbucks virtual store in China. This particular version of the Tmall Genie unified Starbucks offerings within Alibaba's mobile apps, including Taobao, Alipay, and Tmall.

ENDNOTES

[1] Howard Schultz and Dori Jones Yang, *Pour Your Heart Into It* (New York: Hyperion, 1997), p. 34.

[2] Ibid., pp. 101–102.

[3] Ibid., p. 142.

[4] "Starbucks Plans New Global Store Design," *Restaurants and Institutions,* June 25, 2009, accessed at www.rimag.com on December 29, 2009.

[5] Starbucks Global Responsibility Report for 2009, p. 13.

[6] As stated by Howard Schultz in an interview with *Harvard Business Review* editor-in-chief Adi Ignatius; the interview was published in the July–August 2010 issue of the *Harvard Business Review,* pp. 108–115.

[7] 2009 Annual Report, p. 5.

[8] Company press release, April 7, 2008.

[9] Company press release, April 13, 2010.

[10] Company press release, January 26, 2012.

[11] Starbucks management presentation at UBS Global Consumer Conference, March 14, 2012; accessed at www.starbucks.com on May 18, 2012.

[12] Company press release, July 14, 2008.

[13] 2018 10-K Report, p. 4.

[14] Company press release, October 22, 2019.

[15] As related in Schultz and Yang, *Pour Your Heart Into It,* pp. 131–136.

[16] Information posted at www.ziprecruiter.com, February 19, 2020.

[17] Data posted at www.indeed.com, www.pyscale.com, and www.salary.com (accessed February 19, 2020).

[18] Information posted at www.sbuxrecognition.com (accessed June 1, 2018).

[19] Company documents and postings at www.starbucks.com (accessed May 15, 2012).

[20] Posted at https://livingourvalues.starbucks.com (accessed January 31, 2020).

[21] Starbucks *2016 Global Social Impact Performance Report,* p. 4.

[22] Ibid.

[23] Information on "Doing Business with Starbucks," posted at www.starbucks.com/business/suppliers (accessed February 20, 2020).

[24] Information posted at www.starbucks.com/responsibility/community/starbucks-foundation (accessed June 5, 2018 and February 20, 2020) and company press release, October 29, 2019.

[25] Company press release announcing Q3 financial results, November 3, 2019.

[26] Jeffrey Towson, "While Luckin Fights Starbucks, HeyTea has Lines Out the Door," posted at www.jefftowson.com (accessed April 3, 2020).

[27] Company press release, July 19, 2019.

[28] Company press release, September 18, 2019.

Nucor Corporation in 2020: Pursuing Efforts to Grow Sales and Market Share Despite Tough Market Conditions McGraw Hill connect

Arthur A. Thompson

The University of Alabama

Falling steel prices, coupled with widespread customer actions to reduce their steel inventories, caused Nucor's sales to drop from a record high of $25.1 billion in 2018 down to $22.6 billion in 2019, a 10 percent decline. Net earnings suffered an even bigger 46 percent decline, from a record high of $2.36 billion in 2018 to $1.27 billion in 2019. Nucor shipped five percent fewer tons of steel, steel products, and scrap metal to outside customers in 2019 compared to 2018 and received an average percent lower price on the tons shipped. Nonetheless, during 2018–2019, Nucor Corp., already the largest manufacturer of steel and steel products in North America and the 12th largest steel company in the world based on tons shipped in 2018, continued its long-term strategy of aggressively investing in new facilities and capabilities to produce an ever-wider range of high-quality steel products, improve its cost competitiveness against rival steel producers, and serve a bigger number of the needs of steel buyers. Not only was Nucor Corp. regarded as a low-cost producer, but it also had a sterling reputation for being a global first-mover in investing in the latest steel-making technologies and production facilities and implementing the best practices to operate them very cost effectively, while at the same time developing the capabilities needed to produce more types of high-quality steel products and further diversify its already diversified product portfolio.

Heading into 2020, Nucor had 25 steel mills with the capability to produce a diverse assortment of steel shapes (steel bars, sheet steel, steel plate, and structural steel) and additional finished steel manufacturing facilities that made steel joists, steel decking, cold finish bars, steel tubing, steel buildings, steel mesh, steel grating, steel fasteners, and fabricated steel reinforcing products. The company's lineup of product offerings was the broadest of any steel producer serving steel users in North America, and top management was focused on executing strategic initiatives to further expand the range of the company's product offerings and enter even more market segments.

COMPANY BACKGROUND

Nucor began its journey from obscurity to a steel industry leader in the 1960s. Operating under the name of Nuclear Corporation of America in the 1950s and early 1960s, the company was a maker of nuclear instruments and electronics products. After suffering through several money-losing years and facing bankruptcy in 1964, Nuclear Corporation of America's board of directors opted for new leadership and appointed F. Kenneth Iverson as president and CEO. Shortly thereafter, Iverson concluded that the best way to put the company on sound footing was to exit the nuclear instrument and electronics business and rebuild the company around its profitable South Carolina-based Vulcraft subsidiary that was in the steel joist business—Iverson had been the head of Vulcraft prior to being named president. Iverson moved the company's headquarters from

Phoenix, Arizona, to Charlotte, North Carolina, in 1966 and proceeded to expand the joist business with new operations in Texas and Alabama. Then, in 1968, top management decided to integrate backward into steelmaking, partly because of the benefits of supplying its own steel requirements for producing steel joists and partly because Iverson saw opportunities to capitalize on newly-emerging technologies to produce steel more cheaply. In 1972 the company adopted the name Nucor Corporation, and Iverson initiated a long-term strategy to grow Nucor into a major player in the U.S. steel industry.

By 1985 Nucor had become the seventh largest steel company in North America, with revenues of $758 million, six joist plants, and four state-of-the-art steel mills that used electric arc furnaces to produce new steel products from recycled scrap steel. Moreover, Nucor had gained a reputation as an excellently managed company, an accomplished low-cost producer, and one of the most competitively successful manufacturing companies in the country.[1] A series of articles in *The New Yorker* related how Nucor, a relatively small American steel company, had built an enterprise that led the whole world into a new era of making steel with recycled scrap steel. Network broadcaster NBC did a business documentary that used Nucor to make the point that American manufacturers could be successful in competing against low-cost foreign manufacturers.

Under Iverson's leadership, Nucor came to be known for its aggressive pursuit of innovation and technical excellence in producing steel, rigorous quality systems, strong emphasis on workforce productivity and job security for employees, cost-conscious corporate culture, and skills in achieving low costs per ton produced. The company had a very streamlined organizational structure, incentive-based compensation systems, and steel mills that were among the most modern and efficient in the United States. Iverson proved himself as a master in crafting and executing a low-cost provider strategy, and he made a point of practicing what he preached when it came to holding down costs throughout the company. The offices of executives and division general managers were simply furnished. There were no company planes and no company cars, and executives were not provided with company-paid country club memberships, reserved parking spaces, executive dining facilities, or other perks. To save money on his own business expenses and set an example for other Nucor managers, Iverson flew coach class and took the subway when he was in New York City.

When Iverson left the company in 1998 following disagreements with the board of directors, he was succeeded briefly by John Correnti and then Dave Aycock, both of whom had worked in various roles under Iverson for a number of years. In 2000, Daniel R. DiMicco, who had joined Nucor in 1982 and risen up through the ranks to executive vice president, was named president and CEO. DiMicco was Nucor's Chairman and CEO through 2012. Like his predecessors, DiMicco continued to pursue Nucor's longstanding strategy to aggressively grow the company's production capacity and product offerings via both acquisition and new plant construction; tons sold rose from 11.2 million in 2000 to 25.2 million in 2008. Then the unexpected financial crisis in the fourth quarter of 2008 and the subsequent economic fallout caused tons sold in 2009 to plunge to 17.6 million tons and revenues to nosedive from $23.7 billion in 2008 to $11.2 billion in 2009.

Even though the steel industry remained in the doldrums until he retired in 2012, DiMicco was undeterred by the depressed market demand for steel and proceeded to expand Nucor's production capabilities and range of product offerings. It was his strong belief that Nucor should be opportunistic in initiating actions to strengthen its competitive position despite slack market demand for steel because doing so put the company in even better position to significantly boost its financial performance when market demand for steel products grew stronger. DiMicco expressed his thinking thusly:[2]

Nucor uses each economic downturn as an opportunity to grow stronger. We use the good times to prepare for the bad, and we use the bad times to prepare for the good. Emerging from downturns stronger than we enter them is how we build long-term value for our stockholders. We get stronger because our team is focused on continual improvement and because our financial strength allows us to invest in attractive growth opportunities throughout the economic cycle.

During DiMicco's 12-year tenure, Nucor completed more than 50 acquisitions, expanding Nucor's operations from 18 locations to more than 200, boosting revenues from $4.8 billion in 2000 to $19.4 billion at the end of 2012, and transforming Nucor into the undisputed leader in providing steel products to North American buyers. When DiMicco retired at the end of 2012, he was succeeded by John J. Ferriola, who had served as Nucor's President and COO since 2011. Ferriola immediately embraced Nucor's strategy of investing in down markets to better position Nucor for success when the economy strengthened and market demand for steel products became more robust. Ferriola retired at year-end 2019 and was succeeded as President and CEO by Leon J. Topalian, effective January 2020. Topalian previously served as President and Chief Operating Officer beginning in September 2019, Executive Vice President of Beam and Plate Products from 2017 to 2019, General Manager of Nucor-Yamato from 2014 to 2017, General Manager of Nucor Steel Kankakee, Inc. from 2011 to 2014, and in several other positions after beginning his career as a project engineer and then as cold mill production supervisor at Nucor Steel-Berkeley.

Going into 2020, Nucor was the biggest, most cost-efficient, and most diversified steel producer in North America. It had the capacity to produce 29 million tons of steel annually at its 25 steel mills. All of its steel mills were among the most modern and efficient mills in the United States. The breadth of Nucor's product line in steel mill products and finished steel products was unmatched; it competed in 12 distinct product categories. No other producer of steel products in North America competed in more than six of the 12 product categories in which Nucor competed.[3] Moreover, Nucor was the North American market leader in seven of the 12 product categories in which it had a market presence—merchant bar steel, structural steel, steel joists and steel decking, cold-finished bar steel, metal buildings, steel electrical conduit pipe, and steel pilings distribution.[4] It was the number two market leader in steel plate, special quality bar steel, rebar steel and fabrication, and hollow structural steel tubing. And it was the number three market leader in sheet steel (hot rolled, cold rolled, and galvanized).

With the exception of three quarters in 2009, one quarter in 2010, and the fourth quarter of 2015, Nucor earned a profit in every quarter of every year from 1966 through 2019—a truly remarkable accomplishment in a mature and cyclical business where it was common for industry members to post losses when demand for steel sagged. As of June 2020, Nucor had paid a dividend for 188 consecutive quarters and had raised the base dividend it paid to stockholders for 47 consecutive years (every year since 1973 when the company first began paying cash dividends). In years when earnings and cash flows permitted, Nucor had paid a supplemental year-end dividend in addition to the base quarterly dividend. Exhibit 1 provides highlights of Nucor's growth and performance from 1970 through 2019. Exhibit 2 shows Nucor's sales by product category for 1990–2019. Exhibit 3 contains a summary of Nucor's financial and operating performance during 2015–2019.

EXHIBIT 1   Nucor's Growing Presence in the Market for Steel, 1970–2019

Year	Total Tons Sold to Outside Customers	Average Price per Ton	Net Sales (in millions)	Earnings before Income Taxes (in millions)	Pretax Earnings per Ton	Net Earnings (in millions) Attributable to Nucor Shareholders
1970	207,000	$245	$ 50.8	$ 2.2	$ 10	$ 1.1
1975	387,000	314	121.5	11.7	30	7.6
1980	1,159,000	416	482.4	76.1	66	45.1
1985	1,902,000	399	758.5	106.2	56	58.5
1990	3,648,000	406	1,481.6	111.2	35	75.1
1995	7,943,000	436	3,462.0	432.3	62	274.5
2000	11,189,000	425	4,756.5	478.3	48	310.9
2001	12,237,000	354	4,333.7	179.4	16	113.0
2002	13,442,000	357	4,801.7	227.0	19	162.1
2003	17,473,000	359	6,265.8	70.0	4	62.8
2004	19,109,000	595	11,376.8	1,725.9	96	1,121.5
2005	20,465,000	621	12,701.0	2,027.1	104	1,310.3
2006	22,118,000	667	14,751.3	2,692.4	129	1,757.7

(continued on next page)

EXHIBIT 1   (continued)

Year	Total Tons Sold to Outside Customers	Average Price per Ton	Net Sales (in millions)	Earnings before Income Taxes (in millions)	Pretax Earnings per Ton	Net Earnings (in millions) Attributable to Nucor Shareholders
2007	22,940,000	723	16,593.0	2,253.3	104	1,471.9
2008	25,187,000	940	23,663.3	2,790.5	116	1,831.0
2009	17,576,000	637	11,190.3	(470.4)	(28)	(293.6)
2010	22,019,000	720	15,844.6	194.9	9	134.1
2011	23,044,000	869	20,023.6	1,169.9	53	778.2
2012	23,092,000	841	19,429.3	613.8	27	409.5
2013	23,730,000	803	19,052.0	714.2	31	499.4
2014	25,413,000	830	21,105.1	1,048.1	42	679.3
2015	22,680,000	725	16,439.3	129.6	6	80.7
2016	24,309,000	667	16,208.1	1,298.6	50	796.3
2017	26,492,000	764	20,252.4	1,688.1	65	1,318.7
2018	27,899,000	899	25,067.3	3,109.1	114	2,360.8
2019	26,532,000	851	22,588.9	1,683.0	65	1,271.1

Note: In 2016, Nucor changed its method of accounting for valuing certain inventories from the last-in, first-out (LIFO) method to the first-in, first out (FIFO) method. The information in this table for the years 2012–2019 reflects this change in accounting principle.

Source: Company records posted at www.nucor.com (accessed February 1, 2018 and March 23, 2020); Company 10-K Report, 2019, p. 47.

EXHIBIT 2   Nucor's Sales of Steel Mill and Finished Steel Products to Outside Customers, By Product Category, 1990–2019

	Tons Sold to Outside Customers (in thousands)									
	Steel Mill Products					Finished Steel Products				
Year	Sheet Steel (2019 capacity of ~12.1 million tons)	Steel Bars (2019 capacity of ~8.8 million tons)	Structural Steel (2019 capacity of ~3.25 million tons)	Steel Plate (2019 capacity of ~2.9 million tons)	Total (2019 capacity of ~27 million tons)	Steel Joists (2019 capacity of ~745,000 tons)	Steel Deck (2019 capacity of ~560,000 tons)	Cold Finished Steel (2019 capacity of ~1.1 million tons)	Rebar Fabrication and Other Steel Products* (2019 capacity of ~5.71 million tons)	Total Tons Sold**
2019	9,008	5,761	1,816	2,000	18,585	499	495	498	4,814	26,532
2018	9,153	6,389	2,064	2,284	19,890	490	479	569	4,846	27,889
2017	9,311	5,838	2,303	2,249	19,137	472	457	487	4,454	26,492
2016	9,119	5,304	2,319	2,023	18,160	445	442	426	3,524	24,309
2015	8,080	4,790	2,231	1,905	16,369	427	401	449	3,518	22,680
2014	8,153	5,526	2,560	2,442	17,9341	421	396	504	3,618	25,413
2013	7,491	5,184	2,695	2,363	16,976	342	334	474	3,658	23,730
2012	7,622	5,078	2,120	2,268	17,088	291	308	492	3,365	23,092
2011	7,500	4,680	2,338	2,278	17,460	288	312	494	3,073	23,044
2010	7,434	4,019	2,139	2,229	16,370	276	306	462	5,154	22,019

(continued)

EXHIBIT 2   (continued)

| | Tons Sold to Outside Customers (in thousands) | | | | | | | | | |
| | Steel Mill Products | | | | | Finished Steel Products | | | | |
Year	Sheet Steel (2019 capacity of ~12.1 million tons)	Steel Bars (2019 capacity of ~8.8 million tons)	Structural Steel (2019 capacity of ~3.25 million tons)	Steel Plate (2019 capacity of ~2.9 million tons)	Total (2019 capacity of ~27 million tons)	Steel Joists (2019 capacity of ~745,000 tons)	Steel Deck (2019 capacity of ~560,000 tons)	Cold Finished Steel (2019 capacity of ~1.1 million tons)	Rebar Fabrication and Other Steel Products* (2019 capacity of ~5.71 million tons)	Total Tons Sold**
2009	5,212	3,629	1,626	1,608	12,571	264	310	330	2,564	17,576
2008	7,505	5,266	2,934	2,480	18,696	485	498	485	2,395	25,187
2007	8,266	6,287	3,154	2,528	20,580	542	478	449	2,136	22,940
2006	8,495	6,513	3,209	2,432	20,649	570	398	327	2,883	22,118
2005	8,026	5,983	2,866	2,145	19,020	554	380	342	2,360	20,465
2000	4,456	2,209	3,094	20	9,779	613	353	250	1,351	11,189
1995	2,994	1,799	1,952	--	6,745	552	234	234	1,198	7,943
1990	420	1,382	1,002	--	2,804	443	134	163	884	3,648

*Other products include steel piling, tubular steel products, and steel fasteners (steel screws, nuts, bolts, washers, and bolt assemblies), steel mesh, steel grates, metal building systems, and light gauge steel framing.

**Includes sale of raw materials, principally scrap metal, beginning in 2008 when Nucor acquired David J. Joseph Co., a leading supplier of scrap metal.

Source: Company records posted at www.nucor.com (accessed March 23, 2020).

EXHIBIT 3   Five-Year Financial and Operating Summary, Nucor Corporation, 2015–2019 ($ in millions, except per share data and sales per employee)

	2019	2018	2017	2016	2015
FOR THE YEAR					
Net sales	$22,588.9	$25,067.3	$20,252.4	$16,208.1	$16,439.3
Costs, expenses and other:					
Cost of products sold	19,909.8	20,771.9	17,683.0	14,182.2	15,325.4
Marketing, administrative and other expenses	711.2	860.7	687.5	596.8	459.0
Equity in (earnings) losses of minority-owned enterprises	(3.3)	(40.2)	(41.7)	(38.8)	(5.3)
Impairment and losses on assets	66.9	110.0	---	---	244.8
Interest expense, net	121.4	135.5	173.6	169.2	173.5
Total	20,806.0	21,837.9	18,502.4	14,909.5	16,197.4
Earnings before income taxes and non-controlling interests	1,782.8	3,229.4	1,750.0	1,298.7	241.9
Provision for income taxes	411.9	748.3	369.4	398.2	48.8
Net earnings (loss)	1,370.9	2,481.1	1,380.6	900.4	193.0
Less earnings attributable to the minority interest partners of Nucor's joint ventures*	99.8	120.2	61.9	104.1	112.3

(continued on next page)

EXHIBIT 3 (continued)

	2019	2018	2017	2016	2015
Net earnings (loss) attributable to Nucor stockholders	$ 1,271.1	$ 2,360.8	$ 1,318.7	$ 796.3	$ 80.7
Basic	$ 4.14	$ 7.44	$ 4.11	$ 2.48	$ 0.25
Diluted	4.14	7.42	4.10	2.48	0.25
Dividends declared per share	$ 1.6025	$ 1.5400	$ 1.5125	$ 1.5025	$ 1.4925
Percentage of net earnings to net sales	5.6%	9.4%	6.5%	4.9%	0.5%
Return on average stockholders' equity	12.6%	25.5%	17.2%	10.4%	1.0%
Capital expenditures	$ 1,512	$ 997.3	$ 448.6	$ 617.7	$ 364.8
Acquisitions (net of cash acquired)	83.1	33.1	544.0	474.8	19.1
Depreciation	648.9	630.9	635.8	613.2	625.8
Sales per employee (000s)	849	986	820	690	690
AT YEAR END					
Cash, cash equivalents, and short-term investments	$ 1,834.6	$ 1,399.0	$ 999.1	$ 2,046.0	$ 2,039.5
Current assets	8,226.4	8,636.3	6,824.4	6,506.4	5,854.4
Current liabilities	2,463.8	2,806.3	2,824.8	2,390.0	1,385.2
Working capital	5,762.6	5,830.0	3,999.6	4,116.4	4,469.2
Cash provided by operating activities	2,809.4	2,394.0	1,051.3	1,737.5	2,157.0
Current ratio	3.3	3.1	2.4	2.7	4.2
Property, plant and equipment	$ 6,178.6	$ 5,334.7	$ 5,093.2	$ 5.078.7	$ 4,891.2
Total assets	18,344.7	17,920.6	15,841.3	15,223.5	14,327.0
Long-term debt (including current maturities)	4,320.6	4,233.3	3,742.2	4,339.1	4,337.1
Percentage of long-term debt to total capital**	28.6%	29.3%	29.2%	34.5%	35.6%
Stockholders' equity	10,357.9	9,792.1	8,739.0	7,879.9	7,416.9
Shares outstanding (000s)	301,812	305,592	317,962	318,737	317,962
Employees	26,800	26,300	25,100	23,900	23,700

*The principal joint venture responsible for these earnings is the Nucor-Yamato Steel Company, of which Nucor owns 51 percent. This joint venture operates a structural steel mill in Blytheville Arkansas, and it is the largest producer of structural steel beams in the Western Hemisphere.

**Total capital is defined as stockholders' equity plus long-term debt.

Note: In 2016, Nucor changed its method of accounting for valuing certain inventories from the last-in, first-out (LIFO) method to the first-in, first-out (FIFO) method. The information in this table for 2015 has been backward adjusted to reflect this change in accounting principle.

Source: Nucor's 2019 10-K, p. 23.

NUCOR'S STRATEGY TO BECOME THE BIGGEST AND MOST DIVERSIFIED STEEL PRODUCER IN NORTH AMERICA, 1967–2020

In its nearly 52-year march to become North America's biggest and most diversified steel producer, Nucor relentlessly expanded its production capabilities to include a wider range of steel shapes and more categories of finished steel products. However, most every steel product that Nucor produced was viewed by buyers as a "commodity." Indeed, the most competitively relevant feature of the various steel shapes and finished steel products made by the world's different producers was that, for any given steel item, there were very few, if any, differences in the products of rival steel producers. While some steel-makers had plants where production quality was sometimes inconsistent or on occasions failed to meet customer-specified metallurgical characteristics, most steel plants turned out products of comparable metallurgical quality—one producer's reinforcing bar was essentially the same as another producer's reinforcing bar, a particular type and grade of sheet steel made at one plant was essentially identical to the same type and grade of sheet steel made at another plant.

The commodity nature of steel products meant that steel buyers typically shopped the market for the best price, awarding their business to whichever seller offered the best deal. The ease with which buyers could switch their orders from one supplier to another forced steel producers to be very price competitive. In virtually all instances, the going market price of each particular steel product was in constant flux, rising or falling in response to shifting market circumstances (or shifts in the terms that particular buyers or sellers were willing to accept). As a consequence, spot market prices for commodity steel products bounced around on a weekly or even daily basis. Because competition among rival steel producers was so strongly focused on price, it was incumbent on all industry participants to be cost-competitive and operate their production facilities as efficiently as they could.

Nucor's success over the years stemmed largely from its across-the-board prowess in cost-efficient operations for all the product categories in which it elected to compete. Nucor's top executives were very disciplined in executing Nucor's strategy to broaden the company's product offerings; no moves to enter new steel product categories were made unless management was confident that the company had the resources and capabilities needed to operate the accompanying production facilities efficiently enough to be cost competitive.

Finished Steel Products

Nucor's first venture into steel in the late 1960s, via its Vulcraft division, was principally one of fabricating steel joists and joist girders from steel that was purchased from various steel-makers. Vulcraft expanded into the fabrication of steel decking in 1977. The division expanded its operations over the years and, as of 2018, Nucor's Vulcraft division was the largest producer and leading innovator of open-web steel joists, joist girders, and steel deck in the United States. It had seven plants with annual capacity of 745,000 tons that made steel joists and joist girders and ten plants with 545,000 tons of capacity that made steel deck; typically, about 85 percent of the steel needed to make these products was supplied by various Nucor steel-making plants. Vulcraft's joist, girder, and decking products were used mainly for roof and floor support systems in retail stores, shopping centers, warehouses, manufacturing facilities, schools, churches, hospitals, and, to a lesser extent, multi-story buildings and apartments. Customers for these products were principally nonresidential construction contractors.

In 1979, Nucor began fabricating cold finished steel products. These consisted mainly of cold drawn and turned, ground, and polished steel bars or rods of various shapes—rounds, hexagons, flats, channels, and squares—made from carbon, alloy, and leaded steels based on customer specifications or end-use requirements. Cold finished steel products were used in tens of thousands of products, including anchor bolts, hydraulic cylinders, farm machinery, air conditioner compressors, electric motors, motor vehicles, appliances, and lawn mowers. Nucor sold cold finish steel directly to large-quantity users in the automotive, farm machinery, hydraulic, appliance, and electric motor industries and to steel service centers that in turn supplied manufacturers needing only relatively small quantities. In 2017, Nucor Cold Finish was the largest producer of cold finished bar products in North America and had facilities in Missouri, Nebraska, South Carolina, Utah, Wisconsin, Ohio, Georgia, and Ontario, Canada with a capacity of about 1.1 million tons per year. It obtained most of its steel from Nucor's mills that made steel bar. This factor, along with the fact that all of Nucor's cold finished facilities employed the latest technology and were among the most modern in the world, resulted in Nucor Cold Finish having a highly competitive cost structure. It maintained sufficient inventories of cold finish products to fulfill anticipated orders.

Nucor produced metal buildings and components throughout the United States under several brands: Nucor Building Systems, American Buildings Company, Kirby Building Systems, and CBC Steel Buildings. In 2019, the Nucor Buildings Group had 9 metal buildings plants with an annual capacity of approximately 360,000 tons. Nucor's

Buildings Group began operations in 1987 and currently had the capability to supply customers with buildings ranging from fewer than 1,000 square feet to more than 1 million square feet. Complete metal building packages could be customized and combined with other materials such as glass, wood, and masonry to produce a cost-effective, aesthetically pleasing building built to a customer's particular requirements. The buildings were sold primarily through an independent builder distribution network. The primary markets served were commercial, industrial, and institutional buildings including distribution centers, automobile dealerships, retail centers, schools, warehouses, and manufacturing facilities. Nucor's Buildings Group obtained a significant portion of its steel requirements from the company's bar and sheet mills.

Another Nucor division produced steel mesh, grates, and fasteners. Various steel mesh products were made at two facilities in the United States and one in Canada that had combined annual production capacity of about 128,000 tons. Steel and aluminum bar grating, safety grating, and expanded metal products were produced at several North American locations that had combined annual production capacity of 120,000 tons. Nucor Fastener, located in Indiana, began operations in 1986 with the construction of a $25 million plant. At the time, imported steel fasteners accounted for 90 percent of the U.S. market because U.S. manufacturers were not competitive on cost and price. Iverson said "We're going to bring that business back; we can make bolts as cheaply as foreign producers." Nucor built a second fastener plant in 1995, giving it the capacity to supply about 20 percent of the U.S. market for steel fasteners. Currently, these two facilities had annual capacity of about 75,000 tons and produced carbon and alloy steel hex head cap screws, hex bolts, structural bolts, nuts and washers, finished hex nuts, and custom-engineered fasteners that were used for automotive, machine tool, farm implement, construction, military, and various other applications. Nucor Fastener obtained much of the steel it needed from Nucor's mills that made steel bar.

Beginning in 2007, Nucor—through its newly-acquired Harris Steel subsidiary—began fabricating, installing, and distributing steel reinforcing bars (rebar) for highways, bridges, schools, hospitals, airports, stadiums, office buildings, high rise residential complexes, and other structures where steel reinforcing was essential to concrete construction. Harris Steel had over 70 fabrication facilities in the United States and Canada, with each facility serving the surrounding local market. Since acquiring Harris Steel, Nucor had more than doubled its rebar fabrication capacity to over 1,650,000 tons annually. Total fabricated rebar sales in 2019 were 1,223,000 tons, up from 1,190,000 tons in 2015. Much of the steel used in making fabricated rebar products was obtained from Nucor steel plants that made steel bar. Fabricated reinforcing products were sold only on a contract bid basis.

Steel Mill Products

Nucor entered the market for steel mill products in 1968, when the decision was made to build a facility in Darlington, South Carolina, to manufacture steel bars. The Darlington mill was one of the first steel-making plants of major size in the United States to use electric arc furnace technology to melt scrap steel and cast molten metal into various shapes. Electric arc furnace technology was particularly appealing to Nucor because the labor and capital requirements to melt steel scrap and produce crude steel were far lower than those at conventional integrated steel mills where raw steel was produced using coke ovens, basic oxygen blast furnaces, ingot casters, and multiple types of finishing facilities to make crude steel from iron ore, coke, limestone, oxygen, scrap steel, and other ingredients. By 1981, Nucor had four steel mills making carbon and alloy steels in bars, angles, and light structural shapes; since then, Nucor had undertaken extensive capital projects to keep these facilities modernized and globally competitive. During 2000–2011, Nucor aggressively expanded its market presence in steel bars and by 2012 had 13 bar mills located across the United States that produced concrete reinforcing bars, hot-rolled bars, rods, light shapes, structural angles, channels, and guard rail in carbon and alloy steels; in 2019, these 13 plants had total annual capacity of approximately 8.5 million tons. Four of the 13 mills made hot-rolled special quality bar manufactured to exacting specifications. Two new bar mills, one in Florida and one in Missouri, with combined capacity of 330,000 tons per year were expected to begin production in 2020. The products of the Nucor's bar mills had wide usage and were sold primarily to customers in the agricultural, automotive, construction, energy, furniture, machinery, metal building, railroad, recreational equipment, shipbuilding, heavy truck, and trailer industries.

Expansion into Sheet Steel In the late 1980's, Nucor entered into the production of sheet steel at a newly-constructed plant in Crawfordsville, Indiana. Flat-rolled sheet steel was used in the production of motor vehicles, appliances, steel pipe and tubes, and other durable goods. The Crawfordsville plant was the first in the world to employ a revolutionary thin slab casting process that substantially reduced the capital investment and costs to produce flat-rolled sheet steel. Thin-slab casting machines had a funnel-shaped mold to squeeze molten steel down to a thickness of 1.5–2.0 inches, compared to the typically 8 to 10-inch thick slabs produced by conventional casters. It was much cheaper to then build and operate facilities to roll thin-gauge sheet steel from 1.5 to 2-inch thick slabs than from 8 to 10-inch thick slabs. When the Crawfordsville plant first opened in 1989, it was said to have cost $50 to $75 per ton below the costs of traditional sheet steel plants, a highly significant cost advantage in a commodity market where the going price at the time was $400 per ton. *Forbes* magazine described Nucor's pioneering use of thin slab casting as the most substantial, technological, industrial innovation in the past 50 years.[5] By 1996, two additional sheet steel mills that employed thin slab casting technology were constructed and a fourth mill was acquired in 2002. Nucor also operated two Castrip sheet production facilities, one built in 2002 at the Crawfordsville plant and a second built in Arkansas in 2009; these facilities used the breakthrough strip casting technology that involved the direct casting of molten steel into final shape and thickness without further hot or cold rolling. The process allowed for lower capital investment, reduced energy consumption, smaller scale plants, and improved environmental impact (because of significantly lower emissions). A fifth sheet mill with annual capacity of 1.8 million tons, strategically located on the Ohio River in Kentucky, was acquired in 2014, giving Nucor a total flat-rolled capacity of 12.1 million tons.

In May 2017, Nucor announced that it would invest approximately $176 million to build a 72-inch hot band galvanizing and pickling line at its sheet mill in Ghent, Kentucky. The new galvanizing line, which began operations in 2019, would be the widest hot-rolled galvanizing line in North America and enable Nucor to enter additional segments of the automotive market. Going into 2020, all five of Nucor's sheet mills had galvanizing lines and four of them were equipped with cold-rolling mills for the further processing of hot-rolled sheet steel.

Entry into Structural Steel Products Also in the late 1980s, Nucor added wide-flange steel beams, pilings, and heavy structural steel products to its lineup of product offerings. Structural steel products were used in buildings, bridges, overpasses, and similar such projects where strong weight-bearing support was needed. Customers included construction companies, steel fabricators, manufacturers, and steel service centers. To gain entry to the structural steel segment, in 1988 Nucor entered into a joint venture with Yamato-Kogyo, one of Japan's major producers of wide-flange beams, to build a new structural steel mill in Arkansas; a second mill was built on the same site in the 1990s that made the Nucor-Yamato venture in Arkansas the largest structural beam facility in the Western Hemisphere. In 1999, Nucor started operations at a third structural steel mill in South Carolina. The mills in Arkansas and South Carolina had combined capacity to make 3.25 million tons of structural steel products annually, and both used a special continuous casting method that was quite cost-effective.

Entry into the Market for Steel Plate Starting in 2000, Nucor began producing steel plate of various thicknesses and lengths that was sold to manufacturers of heavy equipment, ships, barges, bridges, rail cars, refinery tanks, pressure vessels, pipe and tube, wind towers, and similar products. Steel plate was made at three mills in Alabama, North Carolina, and Texas that had combined capacity of about 2.9 million tons. In 2011–2013, Nucor greatly expanded its plate product capabilities by constructing a 125,000-ton heat treating facility and a 120,000-ton normalizing line at its North Carolina plate mill. These investments yielded two big strategic benefits: (1) enabling the North Carolina mill to produce higher-margin plate products sold to companies making pressure vessels, tank cars, tubular structures for offshore oil rigs, and naval and commercial ships and (2) reducing the mill's exposure to competition from foreign producers of steel plate who lacked the capability to match the features of the steel plate Nucor produced for these end-use customers.

The Cost Efficiency of Nucor's Steel Mills All of Nucor's steel mills used electric arc furnaces to melt scrap steel and other metals which was then poured into continuous casting systems. Sophisticated rolling mills converted the billets, blooms, and slabs produced by various casting equipment into rebar, angles, rounds, channels, flats, sheet, beams, plate, and other finished steel products. Nucor's steel mill operations were highly automated, typically requiring fewer operating employees per ton produced than the mills of rival companies. High worker productivity at all Nucor steel mills resulted in labor costs roughly 50 percent lower than the labor costs at the integrated mills of companies using union labor and conventional blast furnace technology. Nucor's value chain (anchored in using electric arc furnace technology to recycle scrap steel) involved far fewer production steps, far less capital investment, and considerably less labor than the value chains of companies with integrated steel mills that made crude steel from iron ore.

Pricing and Sales

During 2012–2019, 14 to 20 percent of the steel shipped from Nucor's steel mills went to supply the steel needs of the company's finished steel operations that produced tubular products, steel joists, steel deck, rebar, fasteners, metal buildings, and cold finish products, plus the needs of its steel products distribution business. But three of Nucor's acquisitions in 2016–2017, all makers of finished steel products and tubing, began sourcing their sheet steel requirements from Nucor's steel mills, driving the percentage of steel mill shipments to internal customers to 20 percent in 2018 and 2019. The other 80 percent of the company's steel mill shipments were to external customers who placed orders monthly based on their immediate upcoming needs. It was Nucor's practice to maintain inventory levels at its steel mills that were deemed adequate to fill the expected incoming orders from customers.

Nucor marketed the output of its steel mills and steel products facilities mainly through an in-house sales force; there were salespeople located at most every Nucor production facility. Going into 2020, approximately 75 percent of Nucor's sheet steel sales were to contract customers (versus 30 percent in 2009); these contracts for sheet steel were usually for periods of 6 to 12 months, were non-cancellable, and permitted price adjustments to reflect changes in the market pricing for steel and/or raw material costs at the time of shipment. The other 25 percent of Nucor's sheet steel shipments and virtually all of the company's shipments of plate, structural, and bar steel were at the prevailing spot market price—customers not purchasing sheet steel rarely ever wanted to enter into a contract sales agreement. Nucor's spot pricing strategy was to charge external customers the going spot price on the day an order was placed. Shifting market demand-supply conditions and daily variations in spot market prices caused Nucor's average sales prices per ton to fluctuate from quarter to quarter, sometimes by considerable amounts—see Exhibit 4. It was Nucor's practice to quote the same payment terms to all external customers and for these customers to pay all shipping charges.

Nucor sold steel joists, joist girders, and steel deck on the basis of firm, fixed-price contracts that in most cases were won in competitive bidding against rival suppliers. Longer-term supply contracts for these items that were sometimes negotiated with customers contained clauses permitting price adjustments to reflect changes in prevailing raw materials costs. Steel joists, girders, and deck were manufactured to customers' specifications and shipped immediately; Nucor's plants did not maintain inventories of steel joists, girders, or steel deck. Nucor also sold fabricated reinforcing products only on a construction contract bid basis. However, cold finished steel, steel fasteners, steel grating, wire, and wire mesh were all manufactured in standard sizes, with each facility maintaining sufficient inventories of its products to fill anticipated orders; most all sales of these items were made at the prevailing spot price. The average prices Nucor received for its various finished steel products are shown in the last column of Exhibit 4.

EXHIBIT 4   Nucor's Average Quarterly Sales Prices for Steel Products, By Product Category, 2016 through Q2 2020

| Period | Sheet Steel | Steel Bars | Average Sales Prices per Net Ton | | | |
			Structural Steel	Steel Plate	All Steel Mill Products	All Finished Steel Products*
2016						
Qtr 1	$471	$505	$870	$ 545	$538	$1,271
Qtr 2	550	561	845	604	593	1,285
Qtr 3	666	567	865	661	664	1,299
Qtr 4	603	544	837	584	614	1,337
2017						
Qtr 1	661	600	738	703	657	1,201
Qtr 2	709	605	766	746	688	1,245
Qtr 3	695	624	769	749	685	1,263
Qtr 4	691	607	764	727	674	1,294
2018						
Qtr 1	723	660	798	785	717	1,270
Qtr 2	838	742	876	931	819	1,357
Qtr 3	897	781	939	988	876	1,459
Qtr 4	858	771	928	1,018	860	1,525
2019						
Qtr 1	797	762	921	1,022	826	1,480
Qtr 2	758	742	900	969	788	1,462
Qtr 3	668	695	847	839	711	1,442
Qtr 4	623	651	796	748	663	1,427
2020						
Qtr 1	650	662	787	740	680	1,372
Qtr 2	640	651	817	705	672	1,372

*An average of the steel prices for steel deck, steel joists and girders, steel buildings, cold finished steel products, steel mesh, fasteners, fabricated rebar, and other finished steel products.

Source: Company records posted in the investors section at www.nucor.com (accessed June 5, 2018, March 24, 2020, and June 12, 2020).

NUCOR'S STRATEGY TO GROW AND STRENGTHEN ITS BUSINESS AND COMPETITIVE CAPABILITIES

Starting in 2000, Nucor embarked on a five-part growth strategy that involved new acquisitions, new plant construction, continued plant upgrades and cost reduction efforts, international growth through joint ventures, and greater control over raw materials costs. Going into 2020, this same five-part strategy was still in place.

Strategic Acquisitions

Beginning in the late 1990s, Nucor management concluded that growth-minded companies like Nucor might well be better off purchasing existing plant capacity rather than building new capacity, provided the acquired plants could be bought at bargain prices, economically retrofitted with new equipment if need be, and then operated at costs comparable to (or even below) those of newly-constructed state-of-the-art plants. At the time, the steel industry world-wide had far more production capacity than was needed to meet market demand, forcing many companies to operate in the red. Nucor had not made any acquisitions since about 1990, and a team of five people was assembled in 1998 to explore acquisition possibilities that would strengthen Nucor's customer base, geographic coverage, and lineup of product offerings.

For almost three years, no acquisitions were made. But then in 2001, despite tough conditions, Nucor management concluded that oversupplied steel industry conditions and the number of belea-guered U.S. companies made it attractive to expand Nucor's production capacity via acquisition. During 2001 and continuing through 2017, the company proceeded to make a series of strategic acquisitions to strengthen Nucor's competitiveness, selectively expand its product offerings improve its ability to serve customers in particular geographic locations, and boost the company's financial performance in times when market demand for steel was strong enough to boost prices to more profitable levels:

- In 2001, Nucor paid $115 million to acquire substantially all of the assets of Auburn Steel Company's 400,000-ton steel bar facility in Auburn, New York. This acquisition gave Nucor expanded market presence in the Northeast and was seen as a good source of supply for a new Vulcraft joist plant being constructed in Chemung, New York.

- In November 2001, Nucor acquired ITEC Steel Inc. for a purchase price of $9 million. ITEC Steel had annual revenues of $10 million and pro-duced load bearing light gauge steel framing for the residential and commercial market at facilities in Texas and Georgia. Nucor was impressed with ITEC's dedication to continuous improvement and intended to grow ITEC's business via geo-graphic and product line expansion.

- In July 2002, Nucor paid $120 million to purchase Trico Steel Company, which had a 2.2 million ton sheet steel mill in Decatur, Alabama. Trico Steel was a joint venture of LTV (which owned a 50 percent interest), and two leading international steel companies—Sumitomo Metal Industries and British Steel. The joint venture partners had built the mill in 1997 at a cost of $465 million, but Trico was in Chapter 11 bankruptcy proceed-ings at the time of the acquisition and the mill was shut down. The Trico mill's capability to make thin sheet steel with a superior surface quality added competitive strength to Nucor's strategy

to gain sales and market share in the flat-rolled sheet segment. In October 2002, Nucor restarted operations at the Decatur mill and began shipping products to customers.

- In December 2002, Nucor paid $615 million to purchase substantially all of the assets of Birmingham Steel Corporation, which included four bar mills in Alabama, Illinois, Washington, and Mississippi. The four plants had capacity of approximately 2 million tons annually. Top execu-tives believed the Birmingham Steel acquisition would broaden Nucor's customer base and build profitable market share in bar steel products.

- In August 2004, Nucor acquired a cold rolling mill in Decatur, Alabama, from Worthington Industries for $80 million. This 1 million-ton mill, which opened in 1998, was located adjacent to the previously-acquired Trico mill and gave Nucor added ability to service the needs of sheet steel buyers located in the southeastern United States.

- In June 2004, Nucor paid a cash price of $80 million to acquire a plate mill owned by Britain-based Corus Steel that was located in Tuscaloosa, Alabama. The Tuscaloosa mill, which currently had capacity of 700,000 tons that Nucor manage-ment believed was expandable to 1 million tons, was the first U.S. mill to employ a special tech-nology that enabled high-quality, wide steel plate to be produced from coiled steel plate. The mill produced coiled steel plate and plate products that were cut to customer-specified lengths. Nucor intended to offer these niche products to its com-modity plate and coiled sheet customers.

- In February 2005, Nucor completed the purchase of Fort Howard Steel's operations in Oak Creek, Wisconsin, that produced cold finished bars in size ranges up to six-inch rounds and had approxi-mately 140,000 tons of annual capacity.

- In June 2005, Nucor purchased Marion Steel Company located in Marion, Ohio, for a cash price of $110 million. Marion operated a bar mill with annual capacity of about 400,000 tons; the Marion location was within close proximity to 60 percent of the steel consumption in the United States.

- In May 2006, Nucor acquired Connecticut Steel Corporation for $43 million in cash. Connecticut Steel's bar products mill in Wallingford had annual capacity to make 300,000 tons of wire rod and rebar and approximately 85,000 tons of wire mesh fabrication and structural mesh fabrication, products that complemented Nucor's present line-up of steel bar products provided to construction customers.

- In late 2006, Nucor purchased Verco Manufacturing Co for approximately $180 million; Verco produced steel floor and roof decking at one location in Arizona and two locations in California. The Verco acquisition further solidified Vulcraft's market leading position in steel decking, giving it a total annual capacity of over 500,000 tons.

- In January 2007, Nucor acquired Canada-based Harris Steel for about $1.07 billion. Harris Steel had 2005 sales of Cdn$1.0 billion and earnings of Cdn$64 million. The company's operations consisted of (1) Harris Rebar which was involved in the fabrication and placing of concrete reinforcing steel and the design and installation of concrete post-tensioning systems; (2) Laurel Steel which manufactured and distributed wire and wire products, welded wire mesh, and cold finished bar; and (3) Fisher & Ludlow which manufactured and distributed of heavy industrial steel grating, aluminum grating, and expanded metal. In Canada, Harris Steel had 24 reinforcing steel fabricating plants, two steel grating distribution centers, and one cold finished bar and wire processing plant; in the United States, it had 10 reinforcing steel fabricating plants, two steel grating manufacturing plants, and three steel grating manufacturing plants. Harris had customers throughout Canada and the United States and employed about 3,000 people. For the past three years, Harris had purchased a big percentage of its steel requirements from Nucor. Nucor management opted to operate Harris Steel as an independent subsidiary.

- Over several months in 2007 following the Harris Steel acquisition, Nucor through its new Harris Steel subsidiary acquired rebar fabricator South Pacific Steel Corporation, Consolidated Rebar, Inc., a 90 percent equity interest in rebar fabricator Barker Steel Company, and several smaller transactions—all aimed at growing its presence in the rebar fabrication marketplace.

- In August 2007, Nucor acquired LMP Steel & Wire Company for a cash purchase price of approximately $27.2 million, adding 100,000 tons of cold drawn steel capacity.

- In October 2007, Nucor completed the acquisition of Nelson Steel, Inc. for a cash purchase price of approximately $53.2 million, adding 120,000 tons of steel mesh capacity.

- In the third quarter of 2007, Nucor completed the acquisition of Magnatrax Corporation, a leading provider of custom-engineered metal buildings, for a cash purchase price of approximately $275.2 million. The Magnatrax acquisition enabled Nucor's Building System Group to become the second largest metal building producer in the United States.

- In August 2008, Nucor's Harris Steel subsidiary acquired Ambassador Steel Corporation for a cash purchase price of about $185.1 million. Ambassador Steel was one of the largest independent fabricators and distributors of concrete reinforcing steel—in 2007, Ambassador shipped 422,000 tons of fabricated rebar and distributed another 228,000 tons of reinforcing steel. Its business complemented that of Harris Steel and represented another in a series of moves to greatly strengthen Nucor's competitive position in the rebar fabrication marketplace.

- Another small rebar fabrication company, Free State Steel, was acquired in late 2009, adding to Nucor's footprint in rebar fabrication.

- In June 2012, Nucor acquired Skyline Steel, LLC and its subsidiaries for a cash price of approximately $675.4 million. Skyline was a market-leading distributor of steel pilings, and it also processed and fabricated spiral weld pipe piling, rolled and welded pipe piling, cold-formed sheet piling, and threaded bar. The Skyline acquisition paired Skyline's leadership position in the steel piling distribution market with Nucor's own Nucor-Yamato plant in Arkansas that was the market leader in steel piling manufacturing. To capitalize upon the strategic fits between Skyline's business and Nucor's business, Nucor launched a $155 million capital project at the Nucor-Yamato mill to (a) add several new sheet piling sections, (b) increase the production of single sheet widths by 22 percent, and (c) produce a lighter, stronger sheet covering more area at a lower installed cost—outcomes that would broaden the range of hot-rolled steel piling products Nucor could market through Skyline's distribution network in the United States, Canada, Mexico, and the

Caribbean. Nucor opted to operate Skyline as a subsidiary.

- In 2014, Nucor acquired Gallatin Steel Company for approximately $779 million. Gallatin produced a range of flat-rolled steel products (principally steel pipe and tube) at a mill with annual production capacity of 1.8 million tons that was located on the Ohio River in Kentucky. The Gallatin mill strengthened Nucor's position as the North American market leader in hot-rolled steel products by boosting its capacity to supply customers in the Midwest region, the largest flat-rolled consuming market region in the United States.

- In 2015, Nucor acquired Gerdau Long Steel's two facilities in Ohio and Georgia that produced cold-drawn steel bars and had combined capacity of 75,000 tons per year. These facilities, purchased for about $75 million, strengthened Nucor's already strong competitive position in cold-finished steel bars by expanding Nucor's geographic coverage and range of cold-finished product offerings.

- In October 2016, Nucor used cash on hand to acquire Independence Tube Corporation (ITC) for a purchase price of $430.1 million. ITC was a leading manufacturer of hollow structural section (HSS) tubing used primarily in nonresidential construction. ITC had the ability to produce approximately 650,000 tons of HSS tubing annually at its four facilities, two in Illinois and two in Alabama. This acquisition not only further expanded Nucor's product offerings to include a variety of tubular products but also provided a new channel for marketing Nucor's hot-rolled sheet steel, as ITC's plants (which used hot-rolled sheet steel to make tubular steel products) were located in close proximity to Nucor's sheet mills in Alabama, Indiana, and Kentucky.

- On January 9, 2017, Nucor used cash on hand to acquire Southland Tube for a purchase price of approximately $130 million. Southland Tube was also a manufacturer of HSS tubing and had one manufacturing facility in Birmingham, Alabama which shipped approximately 240,000 tons in 2016.

- Nucor further expanded its value-added product offerings to buyers of pipe and tubular products in January 2017 by purchasing Republic Conduit for a purchase price of approximately $335 million. Republic Conduit produced steel electrical conduit primarily used to protect and route electrical wiring in various nonresidential structures such as hospitals, office buildings, and stadiums. Republic had two facilities located in Kentucky and Georgia with annual shipment volume in 2015–2016 of 146,000 tons.

- In December 2019, Nucor announced the acquisition of TrueCore, LLC, a manufacturer of insulated metal panels for cold storage and other applications. TrueCore's plant in Laurens, South Carolina, was to become part of the Nucor Buildings Group, which utilized a high volume of insulated panels for buildings it designed and manufactured.

- In January 2020, Nucor and its 50–50 joint venture partner JFE Steel Corp. of Japan began operations at a newly-constructed 400,000 ton-per-year sheet steel production facility in central Mexico to produce hot-dip galvanized sheet steel for motor vehicle manufacturers who had built plants in central Mexico. Automotive production in Mexico was expected to continue to grow and the new United States-Mexico-Canada Agreement (USMCA) increased the amount of North American content required in cars and trucks to avoid tariffs imposed by the United States.

Aggressively Investing to Expand the Company's Internal Production Capabilities

Complementing Nucor's ongoing strategic efforts to grow its business via acquisitions was a strategy element to invest aggressively in (1) the construction of new plant capacity and (2) enhanced production capabilities at existing plants whenever management spotted opportunities to boost sales with an expanded range of product offerings and/or strengthen its competitive position vis-à-vis rivals by lowering costs per ton or expanding its geographic coverage. The purpose of making ongoing capital investments was to improve efficiency and lower production costs at each and every facility it operated.

This strategy element had been in place since Nucor's earliest days in the steel business. Nucor always built state-of-the-art facilities in the most economical fashion possible and then made it standard company practice to invest in plant modernization and efficiency improvements whenever cost-saving opportunities emerged.

Examples of Nucor's efforts included the following:

- In 2006, Nucor announced that it would construct a new $27 million facility to produce metal buildings systems in Brigham City, Utah. The new plant, Nucor's fourth building systems plant, had capacity of 45,000 tons and gave Nucor national market reach in building systems products.

- In 2006, Nucor initiated construction of a $230 million state-of-the-art steel mill in Memphis, Tennessee, with annual capacity to produce 850,000 tons of special quality steel bars. Management believed this mill, together with the company's other special bar quality mills in Nebraska and South Carolina, would give Nucor the broadest, highest quality, and lowest cost offering of special quality steel bar in North America.

- In 2009, Nucor opened an idle and newly-renovated $50 million wire rod and bar mill in Kingman, Arizona, that had been acquired in 2003. Production of straight-length rebar, coiled rebar, and wire rod began in mid-2010; the plant had an initial capacity of 100,000 tons, with the ability to increase annual production to 500,000 tons.

- The construction of a $150 million galvanizing facility located at the company's sheet steel mill in Decatur, Alabama, gave Nucor the ability to make 500,000 tons of 72-inch wide galvanized sheet steel, a product used by motor vehicle and appliance producers and in various steel frame and steel stud buildings. The galvanizing process entailed dipping steel in melted zinc at extremely high temperatures; the zinc coating protected the steel surface from corrosion.

- In 2013 Nucor installed caster and hot mill upgrades at its Berkeley, South Carolina, sheet mill that enabled it to roll light-gauge sheet steel to a finished width of 74 inches. This new capability (which most foreign competitors did not have) opened opportunities to sell large quantities of wide-width, flat-rolled products to customers in a variety of industries while, at the same time, providing the mill with less exposure to competition from imports of less wide, flat-rolled products.

- In 2016, Nucor initiated a project to install a $75 million cooling process at the Nucor-Yamato mill in Arkansas that was expected to generate savings on alloy costs of $12 million annually.

- In 2017, Nucor began construction of a $230 million specialty cold mill complex in Hickman, Arkansas, to produce advanced high-strength and motor lamination steel products for automotive customers. The mill began operations in October 2019.

- In 2017, Nucor initiated an $85 million project to modernize the rolling mill at Nucor's 400,000-ton steel bar mill in Marion, Ohio, that produced rebar and signposts.

- In November 2017, Nucor announced that it would construct a $250 million rebar micro mill in Sedalia, Missouri, about 90 miles from Kansas City, to give Nucor a sustained shipping cost advantage over other domestic producers in supplying rebar to customers in the Kansas City area and the upper Midwestern and Plains region. Rebar supply to customers in this geographic area currently traveled long distances, giving Nucor's micro mill a sustained shipping cost advantage. This location also allowed Nucor to take advantage of the abundant scrap supply in the immediate area provided by Nucor's scrap metal subsidiary, The David J. Joseph Co. The Sedalia mill was expected to begin production in the second quarter of 2020.

- In early 2018, Nucor initiated construction of a $185 million full-range merchant bar quality (MBQ) mill at its existing bar steel mill near Kankakee, Illinois. The MBQ mill would have an annual capacity of 500,000 tons, take approximately two years to complete, and begin production in the second quarter of 2020. Nucor executives believed the new mill's strategic location mill would enable Nucor to capture costs savings by (1) optimizing the melt capacity and infrastructure that was already in place at the existing Kankakee mill (which would continue to be a supplier of quality reinforcing bar products) and (2) taking advantage of an abundant scrap supply in the region. These cost-savings would enhance Nucor's cost-competitiveness and, in top management's opinion, position Nucor to capture a big fraction of the bar products tonnage currently being supplied by competitors outside the region and, also, fortify Nucor's market leadership in steel bars by enhancing the appeal of its product offerings of merchant bar, light shapes, structural angle bars, and channel bars used by customers in the central Midwest region of the United States—one of the largest markets for MBQ products.

- In March 2018, Nucor announced it would construct a $240 million rebar micro mill in Frostproof, Florida, with annual capacity of 350,000 tons, to complement the rebar micro mill project in Sedalia, Missouri, announced in November 2017. This second mill was in a market region with strong and growing demand, along with an abundant supply of scrap metal that could mostly be supplied by Nucor's David J. Joseph scrap metal subsidiary. Nucor management believed the Frostproof mill would have a cost advantage over competitors shipping rebar into the region from longer distances. The mill was expected to begin production in the latter part of 2020.

- In May 2018, Nucor announced it would construct a $240 million galvanizing line with annual capacity of 500,000 tons at the company's sheet mill in Arkansas to support Nucor's growth into a wider and more diverse set of advanced high-strength steel products for automotive customers. Nucor's CEO, John Ferriola, said, "This new galvanizing line, coupled with our new specialty cold mill complex, will allow us to efficiently produce products beyond the capability of any North American sheet mill."[6] The new galvanizing line was expected to be operational in the first half of 2021.

- In January 2019, Nucor announced that it would build a $1.35 billion state-of-the-art plate mill in Brandenburg, Kentucky, on the Ohio River that would be well placed to serve customers in the midwestern United States, the largest plate-consuming area in the country. The new plate mill had an annual capacity of approximately 1,200,000 tons and was expected to begin production in 2022.

- In May 2019, Nucor announced it would add vacuum degassing to its engineered bar capabilities at its bar mill in Darlington, South Carolina. Adding this capability would enable the mill to produce engineered bar products meeting some of the most stringent quality specifications in the industry and thereby growing demand in the region for higher quality automotive and other specialty steel applications. The vacuum degassing system was expected to begin operations in late 2020.

- In December 2019 Nucor announced an expansion project to add a coil paint line at the company's sheet mill in Hickman, Arkansas. The new coil paint line would have a capacity of 250,000 tons per year and was expected to start up in the first half of 2022. The new paint line further diversified the sheet mill's product and market mix by opening new sales opportunities to the makers of roofing and siding, light fixtures, and appliances, while also strengthening its product offerings to steel service centers and the makers of HVAC equipment and garage doors.

Nucor's Strategy to Be a First-Mover in Adopting the Best, Most Cost-Efficient Production Methods

The third element of Nucor's competitive strategy was to be a technology leader and first-rate operator of all its production facilities—outcomes that senior executives had pursued since the company's earliest days. Two approaches to improving and expanding Nucor's steel-making capabilities and achieving low costs per ton were utilized:

- Being quick to implement disruptive technological innovations that would give Nucor a sustainable competitive advantage because of the formidable barriers rivals would have to hurdle to match Nucor's cost competitiveness and/or product quality and/or range of products offered.

- Being quick to implement ongoing advances in production methods and install the latest and best steel-making equipment, thus providing Nucor with a path to driving down costs per ton and/or leapfrogging competitors in terms of product quality, range of product offerings, and/or market share.

Nucor's biggest success in pioneering trailblazing technology had been at its Crawfordsville, Indiana, facilities where Nucor installed the world's first facility for direct strip casting of carbon sheet steel—a process called Castrip®. The Castrip process, which Nucor tested and refined for several years before implementing it in 2005, was a major technological breakthrough for producing flat-rolled, carbon, and stainless steels in very thin gauges because (1) it involved far fewer process steps to cast metal at or very near customer-desired thicknesses and shapes and (2) the process drastically reduced capital outlays for equipment and produced sizable savings on operating expenses (by enabling the use of cheaper grades of scrap metal and requiring 90 percent less energy to process liquid metal into hot-rolled steel sheets). An important environmental benefit of the Castrip process was cutting greenhouse gas emissions by up to 80 percent. Seeing these advantages earlier than rivals, Nucor management had the foresight to acquire exclusive rights to Castrip technology in the United States and Brazil. Once it was clear that the expected benefits of the Castrip facility at Crawfordsville were indeed going to become a reality, Nucor in 2006 launched construction of a second Castrip facility on the site of its structural steel mill in Arkansas.

Since technological breakthroughs (like the Castrip process) were relatively rare, Nucor management made a point of scouring locations across the world for reports of possible cost-effective technologies, ways to improve production methods and efficiency, and new and better equipment that could be used to improve operations and/or lower costs in Nucor's facilities. All such reports were checked out thoroughly, including making trips to inspect promising new developments firsthand if circumstances warranted. Projects to improve production methods or install more efficient equipment were promptly undertaken when the investment payback was attractive.

The Drive for Improved Efficiency and Lower Production Costs When Nucor acquired plants, it drew upon its ample financial strength and cash flows from operations to immediately fund efforts to get them up to Nucor standards—a process that employees called "Nucorizing." This included not only revising production methods and installing better equipment but also striving to increase operational efficiency by reducing the amount of time, space, energy, and manpower it took to produce steel products and paying close attention to worker safety and environmental protection practices.

Simultaneously, Nucor's top-level executives insisted upon continual improvement in product quality and cost at every company facility. Most all of Nucor's production locations were ISO 9000 and ISO 14000 certified. The company had a "BESTmarking" program aimed at being the industry-wide best performer on a variety of production and efficiency measures. Managers at all Nucor plants were accountable for demonstrating that their operations were competitive on both product quality and cost vis-à-vis the plants of rival companies. A deeply embedded trait of Nucor's corporate culture was the expectation that plant-level managers would be persistent in initiating actions to improve product quality and keep costs per ton low relative to rival plants.

Nucor management viewed the task of pursuing operating excellence in its manufacturing operations as a continuous process. According to former CEO Dan DiMicco:[7]

> We talk about "climbing a mountain without a peak" to describe our constant improvements. We can take pride in what we have accomplished, but we are never satisfied.

The strength of top management's commitment to funding projects to improve plant efficiency, keep costs as low as possible, and achieve overall operating excellence was reflected in the company's capital expenditures for new technology, plant improvements, and equipment upgrades (see Exhibit 5). The beneficial outcomes of these expenditures, coupled with companywide vigilance and dedication to discovering and implementing ways to operate most cost-efficiently, were major contributors to Nucor's standing as North America's lowest-cost, most diversified provider of steel products.

EXHIBIT 5 Nucor's Capital Expenditures for New Plants, Plant Expansions, New Technology, Equipment Upgrades, and Other Operating Improvements, 2000–2019

Year	Capital Expenditures (in millions)	Year	Capital Expenditures (in millions)
2000	$ 415.0	2010	$ 345.2
2001	261.0	2011	450.6
2002	244.0	2012	1,019.3
2003	215.4	2013	1,230.4
2004	285.9	2014	568.9
2005	331.5	2015	364.8
2006	338.4	2016	617.7
2007	520.4	2017	507.1
2008	1,019.0	2018	997.3
2009	390.5	2019	1,512.1

Sources: Company records, accessed at www.nucor.com, various dates; data for 2009–2019 is from the 2013 10-K report, p. 43 and the 2019 10-K report, p. 23.

Shifting Production from Lower-End Steel Products to Value-Added Products

During 2010–2019, Nucor undertook a number of actions to shift more of the production tonnage at its steel mills and steel products facilities to "value-added products" that could command higher prices and yield better profit margins than could be had by producing lower-end or commodity steel products. Examples included:

- Adding new galvanizing capability at the Decatur, Alabama, mill that enabled Nucor to sell 500,000 tons of corrosion-resistant, galvanized sheet steel for high-end applications.

- Expanding the cut-to-length capabilities at the Tuscaloosa, Alabama mill that put the mill in position to sell as many as 200,000 additional tons per year of cut-to-length and tempered steel plate.

- Shipping 250,000 tons of new steel plate and structural steel products in 2010 that were not offered in 2009, and further increasing shipments of these same new products to 500,000 tons in 2011.

- Completing installation of a heat treating facility at the Hertford County plate mill in 2011 that gave Nucor the capability to produce as much as 125,000 tons annually of heat-treated steel plate ranging from 3/16 of an inch through 2 inches thick.

- Installing new vacuum degassers at the Hickman, Arkansas sheet mill and Hertford County, North Carolina mill to enable production of increased volumes of higher-value sheet steel, steel plate, steel piping, and tubular products.

- Investing $290 million at its three steel bar mills to enable the production of steel bars and wire rod for the most demanding engineered bar applications and also put in place state-of-the-art quality inspection capabilities. The project enabled Nucor to offer higher-value steel bars and wire rod to customers in the energy, automotive, and heavy truck and equipment markets (where the demand for steel products had been relatively strong in recent years).

- Completing installation of a new 120,000-ton "normalizing" process for making steel plate at the Hertford County mill in June 2013; the new normalizing process allowed the mill to produce a higher grade of steel plate that was less brittle and had a more uniform fine-grained structure (which permitted the plate to be machined to more precise dimensions). Steel plate with these qualities was more suitable for armor plate applications and for certain uses in the energy, transportation, and shipbuilding industries. Going into 2014, the normalizing process, coupled with the company's recent investments in a vacuum tank degasser and a heat-treating facility at this same plant, doubled the Hertford mill's capacity to produce higher-quality steel plate products that commanded a higher market price.

- Modernizing the casting, hot rolling, and downstream operations at the Berkeley, South Carolina mill in 2013 to enable the production of 72-inch wide sheet steel and lighter gauge hot-rolled and cold-rolled steel products with a finished width of 74-inches, thereby opening opportunities for Nucor to sell higher-value sheet steel products to customers in the agricultural, pipe and tube, industrial equipment, automotive, and heavy-equipment industries. In 2015, the Berkeley mill shipped 150,000 tons of wider-width products and was pursuing a goal of increasing shipments to 400,000 tons.

- Instituting a $155 million project at the Nucor-Yamato mill in 2014 to produce lighter, wider, and stronger steel pilings and a second $75 million project in 2016 to produce structural steel sections with high-strength, low-alloy grade chemistry; both projects helped Nucor grow sales of value-added structural steel products that had above-average profitability.

- Acquiring two Gerdau Long Steel facilities in 2015 that produced higher-margin, value-added cold-finished bars sold to steel service centers and other customers across the United States.

- Acquiring a specialty steel plate mill in Longview, Texas, in 2016 that was capable of producing steel plate ranging that was thicker and wider than the company's existing steel plate offerings, thereby opening opportunities for Nucor to compete for a growing share of the value-added plate market. Less than 12 months after the acquisition, production and shipments at the Longview plant had doubled.

- Investing in a $230 million specialty cold mill complex at Nucor Steel Arkansas to expand the company's capability to produce advanced high-strength, high-strength low-alloy, and motor lamination steel products for automotive customers. The project, expected to begin operations in late 2018, was expected to bring value to all of Nucor's sheet mills, mainly by broadening the automotive capability of Nucor's galvanized lines at mills in Alabama and South Carolina to include products that Nucor was currently unable to manufacture. The specialty cold mill complex in Arkansas takes Nucor into the future by enabling us to produce the high strength steel grades original equipment manufacturers are designing into future vehicles to reduce weight and improve performance and safety. The mill differentiates Nucor Steel Arkansas from its competitors; there are no other carbon mills like this in North America.

- Investing $176 million to build a 72-inch hot band galvanizing and pickling line with annual capacity of 500,000 tons at its sheet mill in Ghent, Kentucky. The 72-inch galvanizing line would be the widest hot-rolled galvanizing line in North America and would enable Nucor to enter the marketplace for such heavy-gauge, high-quality, hot-rolled galvanized steel products as frames, control arms, supports, and brackets for automotive customers, a market segment it previously was unable to serve. The new galvanizing line began operations in late 2019.

- Acquiring two plants in St. Louis, Missouri, and Monterrey, Mexico, in 2017 that produced higher-margin, value-added cold drawn rounds, hexagons, squares, and related products sold mainly to automotive and certain industrial customers in the United States and Mexico. The two facilities, with combined annual capacity of 200,000 tons, strengthened Nucor's position as the market leader in cold bar finished products by increasing the total capacity of Nucor's cold finished bar and wire facilities to more than 1.1 million tons annually, advancing Nucor's goal of growing its sales to automotive customers, and creating another channel for Nucor's existing special quality bars mills to market their products.

- Constructing a $240 million galvanizing line with annual capacity of 500,000 tons at the company's sheet mill in Arkansas in 2018 to support Nucor's growth into a wider and more diverse set of advanced high-strength steel products for automotive customers. The specialty cold mill complex in Arkansas takes Nucor into the future by enabling us to produce the high strength steel grades original equipment manufacturers are designing into future vehicles to reduce weight and improve performance and safety. The mill differentiates Nucor Steel Arkansas from its competitors; there are no other carbon mills like this in North America. With its new galvanizing line, Nucor Steel Gallatin is now positioned to supply the under-served Midwest heavy-gauge, hot-band galvanized market. The new line will enable us to grow our automotive applications to include frames, control arms, supports, and brackets. Customer feedback on the new products coming out of these two sheet mills has been excellent and now that these projects are operating, we see even more opportunities than we had anticipated.

- Adding vacuum degassing to its engineered bar capabilities at its bar mill in Darlington, South Carolina, in 2019. Adding this capability enabled the mill to produce engineered bar products meeting some of the most stringent quality specifications in the steel industry

Product upgrades had also been undertaken at several Nucor facilities making cold-finished and fastener products. Senior management believed that all of these upgrades to higher-value product offerings would boost revenues and earnings in the years ahead.

Global Growth via Joint Ventures

In 2007, Nucor management decided it was time to begin building an international growth platform. The company's strategy to grow its international revenues had two elements:

- Establishing foreign sales offices and exporting U.S.-made steel products to foreign markets. Because about 60 percent of Nucor's steel-making capacity was located on rivers with deep water transportation access, management believed that the company could be competitive in shipping U.S.-made steel products to customers in a number of foreign locations.

- Entering into joint ventures with foreign partners to invest in steel-making projects outside North America. Nucor executives believed that the success of this strategy element was finding the right partners to grow with internationally.

Nucor opened a Trading Office in Switzerland and proceeded to establish international sales offices in Mexico, Brazil, Colombia, the Middle East, and Asia. The company's Trading Office bought and sold steel and steel products that Nucor and other steel producers had manufactured. In 2010, approximately 11 percent of the shipments from Nucor's steel mills were exported. Customers in South and Central America presented the most consistent opportunities for export sales, but there was growing interest from customers in Europe and other locations.

In January 2008, Nucor entered in a 50/50 joint venture with the European-based Duferco Group to establish the production of beams and other long products in Italy, with distribution in Europe and North Africa. A few months later, Nucor acquired 50 percent of the stock of Duferdofin-Nucor S.r.l. for approximately $667 million (Duferdofin was Duferco's Italy-based steel-making subsidiary). In 2019, Duferdofin-Nucor operated a steel melt shop and bloom/billet caster with an annual capacity of 1.1 million tons and a 495,000-ton special quality merchant bar mill, and a 60,000-ton trackshoes/cutting edges mill. In May 2019, the joint venture announced it would begin construction of a new rolling mill in northern Italy to produce 1 million tons of steel beams and other rolled products using the latest technologies, with operations to begin in 2022. The new mill would be supplied by the venture's 1.1 million-ton melt shop and was expected to be a low-cost producer. The customers for the products produced by Duferdofin-Nucor were primarily steel service centers and distributors located both in Italy and throughout Europe. So far, the joint venture project had not lived up to the partners' financial expectations because all of the plants made construction-related products. The European construction industry had been hard hit by the economic events of 2008–2009 and the construction-related demand for steel products in Europe was very slowly creeping back toward pre-crisis levels. Ongoing losses at Nucor Duferdofin and revaluation of the joint venture's assets had resulted in Nucor's investment in Duferdofin Nucor being valued at $412.9 million at December 31, 2017.

In early 2010, Nucor invested $221.3 million to become a 50/50 joint venture partner with Mitsui USA to form NuMit LLC—Mitsui USA was the largest wholly-owned subsidiary of Mitsui & Co., Ltd., a diversified global trading, investment, and service enterprise headquartered in Tokyo, Japan. NuMit LLC owned 100 percent of the equity interest in Steel Technologies LLC, an operator of 26 sheet steel processing facilities throughout the United States, Canada, and Mexico. Nucor received distributions from NuMit of $6.7 million in 2013, $52.7 million in 2014, $13.1 million in 2015, $38.6 million in 2016, $48.3 million in 2017, $29.2 million in 2018, and $3.3 million in 2019 (the 2019 decrease in earnings was due to profit margin compression and lower sales volumes).

In 2016 Nucor announced a 50/50 joint venture with JFE Steel Corporation of Japan to build a $270 million galvanized sheet steel mill with a capacity of 400,000 tons in central Mexico to serve the motor vehicle manufacturers who had built or were building plants in central Mexico Automotive production in Mexico is predicted to increase from 3.4 million to 5.3 million vehicles by 2020. In January 2020, operations began at the new plant to produce hot-dip galvanized sheet steel. The recently-signed United States-Mexico-Canada Agreement (USMCA) increased the amount of North American content required in cars and trucks to avoid tariffs imposed by the United States, which enhanced the plant's competitiveness.

Nucor's Raw Materials Strategy

Scrap metal and scrap substitutes were Nucor's single biggest cost—all of Nucor's steel mills used electric arc furnaces to make steel products from recycled scrap steel, scrap iron, pig iron, hot briquetted iron (HBI), and direct reduced iron (DRI). On average, it took approximately 1.1 tons of scrap and scrap substitutes to produce a ton of steel—the proportions averaged about 70 percent scrap steel and 30 percent scrap substitutes. Nucor was the biggest user of scrap metal in North America, and it also purchased millions of tons of pig iron, HBI, DRI, and other iron products annually—top-quality scrap substitutes were especially critical in making premium grades of sheet steel, steel plate, and special bar quality steel at various Nucor mills. Scrap prices were driven by market demand-supply conditions and could fluctuate significantly—see Exhibit 6. Rising scrap prices adversely impacted the company's costs and ability to compete against steel-makers that made steel from scratch using iron ore, coke, and traditional blast furnace technology.

EXHIBIT 6   Nucor's Costs for Scrap Steel and Scrap Substitute, 2000–Q2 2020

Period	Average Cost of Scrap and Scrap Substitute per Ton Used	Period	Average Cost of Scrap and Scrap Substitute per Ton Used
2000	$120	2018 Quarter 1	$337
2005	244	Quarter 2	373
2006	246	Quarter 3	374
2007	278	Quarter 4	359
2008	438	Full-Year Average	361
2009	303		
2010	351	2019 Quarter 1	$352
2011	439	Quarter 2	330
2012	407	Quarter 3	299
2013	376	Quarter 4	275
2014	381	Full-Year Average	314
2015	270		
2016	228	2020 Quarter 1	$293
2017	307	Quarter 2	284

Source: Nucor's Annual Reports for 2007, 2009, 2011 and information posted in the investor relations section at www.nucor.com (accessed April 12, 2012, April 15, 2014, February 11, 2016, February18, 2018, and March 24, 2020).

Nucor's raw materials strategy was aimed at achieving greater control over the costs of all types of metallic inputs (both scrap metal and iron-related substitutes) used at its steel plants. A key element of this strategy was to backward integrate into the production of 6 million to 7 million tons per year of high quality scrap substitutes (chiefly pig iron and direct reduced iron) at either its own wholly-owned and operated plants or at plants jointly-owned by Nucor and other partners—integrating backward into supplying a big fraction of its own iron requirements held promise of raw material savings and less reliance on outside iron suppliers. The costs of producing pig iron and direct reduced iron (DRI) were not as subject to steep swings as was the price of scrap steel.

Nucor's first move to execute its long-term raw materials strategy came in 2002 when it partnered with The Rio Tinto Group, Mitsubishi Corporation, and Chinese steel maker Shougang Corporation to pioneer Rio Tinto's HIsmelt® technology at a new plant to be constructed in Kwinana, Western Australia. The HIsmelt technology entailed converting iron ore to liquid metal or pig iron and was both a replacement for traditional blast furnace technology and a hot metal source for electric arc furnaces. Rio Tinto had been developing the HIsmelt technology

for 10 years and believed the technology had the potential to revolutionize iron-making and provide low-cost, high quality iron for making steel. Nucor had a 25 percent ownership in the venture and had a joint global marketing agreement with Rio Tinto to license the technology to other interested steel companies. The Australian plant represented the world's first commercial application of the HIsmelt technology; it had a capacity of over 880,000 tons and was expandable to 1.65 million tons at an attractive capital cost per incremental ton. Production started in January 2006. However, the joint venture partners opted to permanently close the HIsmelt plant in December 2010 because the project, while technologically acclaimed, proved to be financially unviable. Nucor's loss in the joint venture partnership amounted to $94.8 million.

In April 2003, Nucor entered a joint venture with Companhia Vale do Rio Doce (CVRD) to construct and operate an environmentally friendly $80 million pig iron project in northern Brazil. The project, named Ferro Gusa Carajás, utilized two conventional mini-blast furnaces to produce about 418,000 tons of pig iron per year, using iron ore from CVRD's Carajás mine in northern Brazil. The charcoal fuel for the plant came exclusively from fast-growing eucalyptus trees in a cultivated forest in northern Brazil owned by a CVRD subsidiary. The cultivated forest removed more carbon dioxide from the atmosphere than the blast furnace emitted, thus counteracting global warming—an outcome that appealed to Nucor management. Nucor invested $10 million in the project and was a 22 percent owner. Production of pig iron began in the fourth quarter of 2005; the joint venture agreement called for Nucor to purchase all of the plant's production. However, Nucor sold its interest in the project to CVRD in April 2007.

Nucor's third raw-material sourcing initiative came in 2004 when it acquired an idled direct reduced iron (DRI) plant in Louisiana, relocated all of the plant assets to Trinidad (an island off the coast of South America near Venezuela), and expanded the project (named Nu-Iron Unlimited) to a capacity of 2 million tons. The plant used a proven technology that converted iron ore pellets into direct reduced iron. The Trinidad site was chosen because it had long-term and very cost-attractive supply of natural gas (large volumes of natural gas were consumed in the plant's production process), along with favorable logistics for receiving iron ore and shipping DRI to Nucor's steel mills in the United States. Nucor entered into contracts with natural gas suppliers to purchase natural gas in amounts needed to operate the Trinidad site through 2028. Production began in January 2007. Nu-Iron personnel at the Trinidad plant had recently achieved world class product quality levels in making DRI; this achievement allowed Nucor to use an even larger percentage of DRI in producing the most demanding steel products.

In September 2010, Nucor announced plans to build a $750 million DRI facility with annual capacity of 2.5 million tons on a 4,000-acre site in St. James Parish, Louisiana. This investment was expected to move Nucor two-thirds of the way to its long-term objective of being able to supply 6 to 7 million tons of its requirements for high-quality scrap substitutes. However, the new DRI facility was the first phase of a multi-phase plan that included a second 2.5 million-ton DRI facility, a coke plant, a blast furnace, an iron ore pellet plant, and a steel mill. Construction of the first DRI unit at the St. James site began in 2011, and production began in late 2013. However, the plant experienced significant operating losses in the first three quarters of 2014 and then experienced an equipment failure that shut operations down. Due to adverse market conditions that forced Nucor's

steel mills to operate well below capacity in 2015, the Louisiana DRI plant did not resume operation until early 2016. While Nucor had anticipated that its use of DRI in its steel mills would give the company an approximate $75 per ton cost advantage in producing a ton of steel over traditional integrated steel mills using conventional blast furnace technology, little if any cost-saving benefits from the $750 million investment in the Louisiana plant had seemingly been realized as of 2019, and all activities relating to a second 2.5 million ton DRI facility, a coke plant, a blast furnace, an iron ore pellet plant, and a steel mill at the St. James Parish site in Louisiana had been put on hold.[8] Nonetheless, Nucor management believed that the recent investments in its two DRI plants (in Trinidad and Tobago and Louisiana) had put the company in better position going forward to manage its overall costs of metallic materials and the associated supply-related risks.

Because producing DRI was a natural gas intensive process, Nucor pursued a number of strategic initiatives during 2011–2017 with drillers and operators of natural gas wells in Louisiana to help offset the company's exposure to future increases in the price of natural gas consumed by the DRI facility in St. James Parish. In 2020, chiefly because of highly successful exploration efforts of companies employing fracking technology in areas close to Louisiana where there were big shale deposits containing both oil and natural gas, Nucor management believed that the company's investment in the Louisiana DRI plant had little exposure to competitively-damaging increases in natural gas prices.

The Acquisition of the David J. Joseph Company In February 2008, Nucor acquired The David J. Joseph Company (DJJ) and related affiliates for a cash purchase price of approximately $1.44 billion, the largest acquisition in Nucor's history. DJJ was one of the leading scrap metal companies in the United States, with 2007 revenues of $6.4 billion. It processed about 3.5 million tons of scrap iron and steel annually at some 35 scrap yards and brokered over 20 million tons of iron and steel scrap and over 500 million pounds of non-ferrous materials in 2007. DJJ obtained scrap from industrial plants, the manufacturers of products that contained steel, independent scrap dealers, peddlers, auto junkyards, demolition firms, and other sources. The DJJ Mill and Industrial Services business provided logistics and metallurgical blending operations and offered on-site handling and trading of industrial scrap. The DJJ Rail Services business owned over 2,000 railcars dedicated to the movement of scrap metals and offered complete rail-car fleet management and leasing services. Nucor was familiar with DJJ and its various operations because it had obtained scrap from DJJ since 1969. Most importantly, though, all of DJJ's businesses had strategic value to Nucor in helping gain control over its scrap metal costs. Within months of completing the DJJ acquisition (which was operated as a separate subsidiary), the DJJ management team acquired four other scrap processing companies. Additional scrap processors were acquired during 2010–2019, and several new scrap yards were opened. As of year-end 2019, DJJ had 80 operating facilities in 18 states (along with 11 domestic and 1 foreign brokerage offices), 57 scrap yards and recycling facilities, and total annual scrap processing capacity of 5.2 million tons. And, because of DJJ's fleet of 2,500 open top railcars, Nucor could quickly and cost-efficiently deliver scrap to its steel mills.

Nucor's Commitment to Being a Global Leader in Environmental Performance

Every Nucor facility was evaluated for actions that could be taken to promote greater environmental sustainability. Measurable objectives and targets relating to such outcomes as reduced use of oil and grease, more efficient use of electricity, and site-wide recycling were in place at each plant. Computerized controls on large electric motors and pumps and energy-recovery equipment to capture and reuse energy that otherwise would be wasted had been installed throughout Nucor's facilities to lower energy usage—Nucor considered itself to be among the most energy-efficient steel companies in the world. All of Nucor's facilities had water-recycling systems. Nucor even recycled the dust from its electric arc furnaces because scrap metal contained enough zinc, lead, chrome, and other valuable metals to recycle into usable products; the dust was captured in each plant's state-of-the-art bag house air pollution control devices and then sent to a recycler that converted the dust into zinc oxide, steel slag, and pig iron. The first Nucor mill received ISO 14001 Environmental Management System certification in 2001; by year-end 2015, all of Nucor's facilities were ISO 14001 certified.

Nucor's sheet mill in Decatur, Alabama, used a measuring device called an opacity monitor, which gave precise, minute-by-minute readings of the air quality that passed through the bag house and out of the mill's exhaust system. While rival steel producers had resisted using opacity monitors (because they documented any time a mill's exhaust was out of compliance with its environmental permits, even momentarily), Nucor's personnel at the Decatur mill viewed the opacity monitor as a tool for improving environmental performance. They developed the expertise to read the monitor so well that they could pinpoint in just a few minutes the first signs of a problem in any of the nearly 7,000 bags in the bag house—before those problems resulted in increased emissions. Their early-warning system worked so well that the division applied for a patent on the process, with an eye toward licensing it to other companies.

Organization and Management Philosophy

Nucor had a simple, streamlined organizational structure to allow employees to innovate and make quick decisions. The company was highly decentralized, with most day-to-day operating decisions made by group or plant-level general managers and their staff. Each group or plant operated independently as a profit center and was headed by a general manager, who in most cases also had the title of vice president. The group manager or plant general manager had control of the day-to-day decisions that affected the group or plant's profitability.

The organizational structure at a typical plant had four layers:

- General Manager
- Department Manager
- Supervisor/Professional
- Hourly Employee

Group managers and plant managers reported to one of 5 executive vice presidents at corporate headquarters. Nucor's corporate staff was exceptionally small, consisting of about 100 people in 2019, the philosophy being that corporate headquarters should consist of a small cadre of executives who would guide a decentralized operation where liberal authority was delegated to managers in the field. Each plant had a sales manager who was responsible for selling the products made at that particular plant; such staff functions as engineering, accounting, and personnel management were performed at the group/plant level. There was a minimum of paperwork and bureaucratic systems. Each group/plant was expected to earn about a 25 percent return on total assets before corporate expenses, taxes, interest, or profit-sharing. As long as plant managers met their profit targets, they were allowed to operate with minimal restrictions and interference from corporate headquarters. There was a very friendly spirit of competition from one plant to the next to see which facility could be the best performer, but, since all of the vice presidents and general managers shared the same bonus systems, they functioned pretty much as a team despite operating their facilities individually. Top executives did not hesitate to replace group or plant managers who consistently struggled to achieve profitability and operating targets.

Workforce Compensation Practices

Nucor was a largely nonunion "pay for performance" company with an incentive compensation system that rewarded goal-oriented individuals and did not put a maximum on what they could earn. All employees, except those in the recently-acquired Harris Steel and DJJ subsidiaries that operated independently from the rest of Nucor, worked under one of four basic compensation plans, each featuring incentives related to meeting specific goals and targets:

1. *Production Incentive Plan*—Production line jobs were rated on degree of responsibility required and assigned a base wage comparable to the wages paid by other manufacturing plants in the area where a Nucor plant was located. But in addition to their base wage, operating and maintenance employees were paid weekly bonuses based on the number of tons by which the output of their production team or work group exceeded the "standard" number of tons. All operating and maintenance employees were members of a production team that included the team's production supervisor, and the tonnage produced by each work team was measured for each work shift and then totaled for all shifts during a given week. If a production team's weekly output beat the weekly standard, team members (including the team's production supervisor) earned a specified percentage bonus for each ton produced above the standard—production bonuses were paid weekly (rather than quarterly or

annually) so that workers and supervisors would be rewarded immediately for their efforts. The standard rate was calculated based on the capabilities of the equipment employed (typically at the time plant operations began), and no bonus was paid if the equipment was not operating (which gave maintenance workers a big incentive to keep a plant's equipment in good working condition)—Nucor's philosophy was that when equipment was not operating everybody suffered and the bonus for downtime ought to be zero. Production standards at Nucor plants were seldom raised unless a plant underwent significant modernization or important new pieces of equipment were installed that greatly boosted labor productivity. It was common for production incentive bonuses to run from 50 to 150 percent of an employee's base pay, thereby pushing compensation levels up well above those at other nearby manufacturing plants. Worker efforts to exceed the standard and get a bonus did not so much involve working harder as it involved good teamwork and close collaboration in resolving problems and figuring out how best to exceed the production standards.

2. *Department Manager Incentive Plan*—Department managers earned annual incentive bonuses based primarily on the percentage of net income to dollars of assets employed for their division. These bonuses could be as much as 80 percent of a department manager's base pay.

3. *Professional and Clerical Bonus Plan*—A bonus based on a division's net income return on assets was paid to employees that were not on the production worker or department manager plan.

4. *Senior Officers Annual Incentive Plan*—Nucor's senior officers did not have employment contracts and did not participate in any pension or retirement plans. Their base salaries were set at approximately 90 percent of the median base salary for comparable positions in other manufacturing companies with comparable assets, sales, and capital. The remainder of their compensation was based on Nucor's annual overall percentage of net income to stockholder's equity (ROE) and was paid out in cash and stock. Once Nucor's ROE reached a threshold of greater than three percent, senior officers earned a bonus equal to 20 percent of their base salary. If Nucor's annual ROE was 20 percent or higher, senior officers earned

a bonus equal to 225 percent of their base salary. Officers could earn an additional bonus of up to 75 percent of their base salary based on a comparison of Nucor's net sales growth with the net sales growth of members of a steel industry peer group. There was also a long-term incentive plan that provided for stock awards and stock options. The structure of these officer incentives was such that bonus compensation for Nucor officers fluctuated widely—from close to zero (in years when industry conditions were bad and Nucor's performance was sub-par) to four hundred percent (or more) of base salary (when Nucor's performance was excellent).

5. *Senior Officers Long-Term Incentive Plan*—The long-term incentive was intended to balance the short-term focus of the annual incentive plan by rewarding performance over multi-year periods. These incentives were received in the form of cash (50 percent) and restricted stock (50 percent) and covered a performance period of three years; 50 percent of the long-term award was based on how Nucor's three-year ROAIC (return on average invested capital) compared against the three-year ROAIC of the steel industry peer group and 50 percent was based on how Nucor's three-year ROAIC compared against a multi-industry group of well-respected companies in capital-intensive businesses similar to that of steel.

Nucor management had designed the company's incentive plans for employees so that bonus calculations involved no discretion on the part of a plant/division manager or top executives. This was done to eliminate any concerns on the part of workers that managers or executives might show favoritism or otherwise be unfair in calculating or awarding incentive awards.

There were two other types of extra compensation:

• *Profit Sharing*—Each year, Nucor allocated at least 10 percent of its operating profits to profit-sharing bonuses for all employees (except senior officers). Depending on company performance, the bonuses could run anywhere from 1 percent to over 20 percent of pay. Twenty percent of the bonus amount was paid to employees in the following March as a cash bonus and the remaining 80 percent was put into a trust for each employee, with each employee's share being proportional to their earnings as a percent of total earnings by all workers covered by the plan. An employee's share of profit-sharing became vested after one full year

of employment. Employees received a quarterly statement of their balance in profit sharing.

• *401(k) Plan*—Both officers and employees participated in a 401(k) plan where the company matched from 5 percent to 25 percent of each employee's first 7 percent of contributions; the amount of the match was based on how well the company was doing.

In 2020, entry-level, hourly workers at a Nucor plant could expect to earn $40,000 to $50,000 annually (including bonuses). Earnings for more experienced production, engineering, and technical personnel were normally in the $70,000 to $95,000 range. Total compensation for salaried workers ranged from $60,000 to $200,000, depending on type of job (accounting, engineering, sales, information technology), years of experience, level of management, and geographic location. It was common for worker compensation at Nucor plants to be double or more the average earned by workers at other manufacturing companies in the states where Nucor's plants were located. As a rule of thumb, production workers in Nucor's steel mills earned three times the local average manufacturing wage. Nucor management philosophy was that these workers ought to be excellently compensated because the production jobs were strenuous and the work environment in a steel mill was relatively dangerous.

Employee turnover in Nucor mills was extremely low; absenteeism and tardiness were minimal. Each employee was allowed four days of absences and could also miss work for jury duty, military leave, or the death of close relatives. After this, a day's absence cost a worker the entire performance bonus pay for that week and being more than a half-hour late to work on a given day resulted in no bonus payment for the day. When job vacancies did occur, Nucor was flooded with applications from people wanting to get a job at Nucor; plant personnel screened job candidates very carefully, seeking people with initiative and a strong work ethic.

Employee Relations and Human Resources

Employee relations at Nucor were based on four clear-cut principles:

1. Management is obligated to manage Nucor in such a way that employees will have the opportunity to earn according to their productivity.

2. Employees should feel confident that if they do their jobs properly, they will have a job tomorrow.

3. Employees have the right to be treated fairly and must believe that they will be.

4. Employees must have an avenue of appeal when they believe they are being treated unfairly.

The hallmarks of Nucor's human resources strategy were its incentive pay plan for production exceeding the standard and the job security provided to production workers—despite being in an industry with strong down-cycles, Nucor had made it a practice not to lay off workers. Instead, when market conditions were tough and production had to be cut back, workers were assigned to plant maintenance projects, cross-training programs, and other activities calculated to boost the plant's performance when market conditions improved. No Nucor employee had ever been laid off.

Nucor took an egalitarian approach to providing fringe benefits to its employees; employees had the same insurance programs, vacation schedules, and holidays as upper level management. However, certain benefits were not available to Nucor's officers. The fringe benefit package at Nucor included:

1. *Medical and Dental Plans*—The company had a flexible and comprehensive health benefit program for officers and employees that featured low premiums, no deductible, an out-of-pocket expense limit based on a percentage of the employee's earnings, a dental plan, a vision plan, healthcare spending accounts.

2. *Tuition Reimbursement*—Nucor reimbursed up to $3,500 of an employee's approved educational expenses each year and up to $1,750 of a spouse's educational expenses for two years.

3. *Service Awards*—After each five years of service with the company, Nucor employees received a service award consisting of five shares of Nucor stock.

4. *Scholarships and Educational Disbursements*—Nucor provided the children of every employee (except senior officers) with college funding of $3,500 per year for four years to be used at accredited academic institutions.

5. *Company Contributions to Profit-Sharing and Retirement Savings*—These contributions were made annually for qualified employees and were based on the company's profitability. Employees could contribute up to 4 percent of their salary to a 401(K) with Nucor matching 50 percent of the employee's contribution. The profit-sharing plan set aside at least 10 cents out of every dollar that Nucor earned before taxes. Nucor's expense for these benefits totaled $181.4 million in 2019, $307.9 million in 2018, and $169.4 million in 2017. At year-end 2018, the plan had over 20,000 active participants and net assets of $4.0 billion.[9]

6. *Other benefits*—Long-term disability, life insurance, paid vacation, paid volunteer time off, and parental leave.

Most of the changes Nucor made in work procedures came from employees. The prevailing view at Nucor was that the employees knew the problems of their jobs better than anyone else and were thus in the best position to identify ways to improve how things were done. Most plant-level managers spent considerable time in the plant, talking and meeting with frontline employees and listening carefully to suggestions. Promising ideas and suggestions were typically acted upon quickly and implemented—management was willing to take risks to try worker suggestions for doing things better and to accept the occasional failure when the results were disappointing. Teamwork, a vibrant team spirit, and a close worker-management partnership were much in evidence at Nucor plants.

Nucor plants did not utilize job descriptions. Management believed job descriptions caused more problems than they solved, given the teamwork atmosphere and the close collaboration among work group members. The company saw formal performance appraisal systems as a waste of time and added paperwork. If a Nucor employee was not performing well, the problem was dealt with directly by supervisory personnel and the peer pressure of work group members (whose bonuses were adversely affected).

Employees were kept informed about company and division performance. Charts showing the division's results in return on assets and bonus payoff were posted in prominent places in the plant. Most all employees were quite aware of the level of profits in their plant or division. Nucor had a formal grievance procedure, but grievances were few and far between. The corporate office sent all news releases to each division where they were posted on bulletin boards. Each employee received a copy of Nucor's annual report; it was company practice for the cover of the annual report to consist of the names of all Nucor employees.

All of these practices had created an egalitarian culture and a highly motivated workforce that grew out of former CEO Ken Iverson's radical insight: employees, even hourly clock punchers, would put forth extraordinary effort and be exceptionally productive if they were richly rewarded, treated with respect, and given real power to do their jobs as best they saw fit.[10] There were countless stories of occasions when managers and workers had gone beyond the call of duty to expedite equipment repairs (in many instances even using their weekends to go help personnel at other Nucor plants solve a crisis); the company's workforce was known for displaying unusual passion and company loyalty even when no personal financial stake was involved. As one Nucor worker put it, "At Nucor, we're not 'you guys' and 'us guys.' It's all of us guys. Wherever the bottleneck is, we go there, and everyone works on it."[11]

It was standard procedure for a team of Nucor veterans, including people who worked on the plant floor, to visit with their counterparts as part of the process of screening candidates for acquisition.[12] One of the purposes of such visits was to explain the Nucor compensation system and culture face-to-face, gauge reactions, and judge whether the plant would fit into "the Nucor way of doing things" if it was acquired. Shortly after making an acquisition, Nucor management moved swiftly to institute its pay-for-performance incentive system and to begin instilling the egalitarian Nucor culture and idea-sharing. Top priority was given to looking for ways to boost plant production using fewer people and without making substantial capital investments; the take-home pay of workers at newly-acquired plants typically went up rather dramatically. At the Auburn Steel plant, acquired in 2001, it took Nucor about six months to convince workers that they would be better off under Nucor's pay system; during that time Nucor paid people under the old Auburn Steel system but posted what they would have earned under Nucor's system. Pretty soon, workers were convinced to make the changeover—one worker's pay climbed from $53,000 in the year prior to the acquisition to $67,000 in 2001 and to $92,000 in 2005.[13]

New Employees. Each plant/division had a "consul" responsible for providing new employees with general advice about becoming a Nucor teammate and serving as a resource for inquiries about how things were done at Nucor, how to navigate the division and company, and how to resolve issues that might come up. Nucor provided new employees with a personalized plan that set forth who would give them feedback about how well they were doing and when and how this feedback would be given; from time to time, new employees met with the plant manager for feedback and coaching. In addition, there was a new employee orientation session that provided a hands-on look at the plant/division operations; new employees also participated in product group meetings to provide exposure to broader business and technical issues. Each year, Nucor brought all recent college hires to the Charlotte headquarters for a forum intended to give the new hires a chance to network and provide senior management with guidance on how best to leverage their talent.

THE WORLD STEEL INDUSTRY

Global production of crude steel hit a record high of 1,870 million tons in 2019—see Exhibit 7. Steel-making capacity worldwide was approximately 2,460 million tons in 2019, resulting in global excess capacity of just over 640 million tons and a 2019 capacity utilization rate of 76.0 percent (up from a historically unprecedented low of 52 percent in 2009). Overcapacity was especially pronounced in China. Nonetheless, construction of new capacity additions were underway during 2019, with more capacity additions in the planning stages; indications were that worldwide capacity would grow to about 2,570 million tons in 2021.[14] Although global demand for steel mill products had grown an average of about 3.6 percent annually during 2015-2019, going forward global demand for steel products was forecast to grow at an annual rate of 1-2 percent through 2025. The six biggest steel-producing countries in 2019 were:[15]

Country	Total Production of Crude Steel	Percent of Worldwide Production
China	996 million tons	53.3%
India	111 million tons	5.9%
Japan	99 million tons	5.3%
United States	88 million tons	4.7%
Russia	72 million tons	3.8%
South Korea	71 million tons	3.8%

Exhibit 8 shows the world's 15 largest producers of crude steel in 2018.

EXHIBIT 7   Worldwide Production of Crude Steel, with Compound Average Growth Rates, 1975–2019

Year	World Crude Steel Production (millions of tons)	Compound Average Growth Rates in World Crude Steel Production	
		Period	Compound Average Growth Rate
1975	644	1975–1980	2.17%
1980	717	1980–1985	0.06%
1985	719	1985–1990	1.38%
1990	770	1990–1995	−0.45%
1995	753	1995–2000	2.45%
2000	850	2000–2005	6.20%
2005	1,148	2005–2010	4.53%
2010	1,433	2010–2015	2.51%
2011	1,538	2015–2019	3.62%
2012	1,560		
2013	1,650		
2014	1,671		
2015	1,622		
2016	1,629		
2017	1,732		
2018	1,817		
2019	1,870		

Source: Worldsteel Association, *Steel Statistical Yearbook, 2019* (Concise Version) and Worldsteel Association press release, January 27, 2020, posted at www.worldsteel.org, accessed on March 26, 2020.

EXHIBIT 8   Top 15 Producers of Crude Steel Worldwide, 2018

Global Rank	Company (Headquarters Country)	Crude Steel Production (millions of metric tons)
1.	ArcelorMittal (Luxembourg)	96.4
2.	China Baowu Group (China)	67.4
3.	Nippon Steel Corp. (Japan)	49.2
4.	HBIS Group (China)	46.8
5.	POSCO (South Korea)	42.9
6.	Shagang Group (China)	40.7
7.	Ansteel (China)	37.4
8.	JFE Steel (Japan)	29.2
9.	Jianlong Group (China)	27.9
10.	Shougang Group (China)	27.3
11.	Tata Steel (India)	27.3
12.	Nucor (USA)	25.5
13.	Shandong Steel Group (China)	23.2
14.	Valin Group (China)	23.0
15.	Hyundai Steel (South Korea)	21.9

Source: Worldsteel Association, World Steel in Figures, 2019, posted at www.worldsteel.org, accessed on March 26, 2020.

Steel-Making Technologies

Steel was produced either by integrated steel facilities or by mills that employed electric arc furnace (EAF) technology. Integrated mills used metallurgical coal fired in coke ovens to produce coke, a fuel with low impurities and high carbon content; the coke was then used to fire blast furnaces and provide needed carbon to react with iron ore, air, and other additives at high temperatures and produce a hot metal mixture (often called molten pig iron). The hot metal was then poured into a converter where the hot metal was pretreated with magnesium and subjected to a 20-minute bath of high-purity oxygen which created a lot of heat. To cool down the reaction heat created by the oxygen bath, charges of scrap metal and lime were added. Following completion of the oxygen bath, the converter was titled and the resulting liquid crude steel was drained off. To make flat rolled steel products, liquid steel was either fed into a continuous caster machine and cast into slabs or else cooled in slab form for later processing. Slabs were further shaped or rolled at a plate mill or hot strip mill. In making certain sheet steel products, the hot strip mill process was followed by various finishing processes, including pickling, cold-rolling, annealing, tempering, galvanizing, or other coating procedures. These various processes for converting raw steel into finished steel products were often distinct steps undertaken at different times and in different on-site or off-site facilities rather than being done in a continuous process in a single plant facility—an integrated mill was thus one which had multiple facilities at a single plant site and could therefore not only produce crude (or raw) steel but also run the crude steel through various facilities and finishing processes to make hot-rolled and cold-rolled sheet steel products, steel bars and beams, stainless steel, steel wire and nails, steel pipes and tubes, and other finished steel products. But such facilities entailed high capital and energy costs and required a sizable work force to operate. The work forces at many integrated mills in Europe, the United States, and several other countries were often unionized.

Steel-making at mills using electric arc furnace technology was far simpler and quicker. High-powered electric arcs were thrust down into a vessel to melt scrap metal, scrap substitutes, and perhaps directly reduced iron pellets into molten metal which was then cast into crude steel slabs, billets, or blooms in a continuous casting process. As was the case at integrated mills, the crude steel at EAF mills was then run through various facilities and finishing processes to make hot-rolled and cold-rolled sheet steel products, steel bars and beams, stainless steel, steel wire and nails, steel pipes and tubes, and other finished steel products. EAF steel mills could accommodate short production runs and had relatively fast product change-over time. The electric arc technology employed by these mills offered two primary competitive advantages: capital investment requirements that were 75 percent lower than those of integrated mills and smaller workforce requirements (which translated into lower labor costs per ton shipped).

Initially, companies with EAF mills were able to only make low-end steel products (such as reinforcing rods and steel bars). But when thin-slab casting technology came on the scene in the 1980s, EAF mills that invested in thin-slab casting facilities were able to compete in the market for flat-rolled carbon sheet and strip products; these products sold at substantially higher prices per ton and thus were attractive and profitable market segments to enter—as Nucor proved at its plants in Indiana and elsewhere. Other EAF steel mills in the United States and across the world were quick to follow Nucor's lead in adopting thin-slab casting technology because the low capital costs of thin-slab casting facilities, often coupled with lower labor costs per ton, gave EAF-mills a cost and pricing advantage over integrated steel producers, enabling them to grab a growing share of the global market for flat-rolled sheet steel and other carbon steel products. Many integrated producers also switched to thin-slab casting as a defensive measure to protect their profit margins and market shares. But the advent of thin-slab casting was by no means the only technological

development that allowed EAF mills to enter market segments dominated by integrated mills. Since 1990, numerous production refinements and technological improvements had been introduced at various EAF mills (like those at Nucor) that permitted them to gradually invade other steel product segments and to produce higher quality steels capable of meeting the strict specifications of steel users in more and more industry categories. However, EAF mills were from time-to-time competitively challenged by rising prices for scrap metal.

In 2018, 70.8 percent of the world's steel mill production was made at large integrated mills and about 28.8 percent was made at EAF mills.[16] In China 88.4 percent of the crude steel was produced at integrated mills using the basic oxygen process; this compared with 75 percent in Japan, 67 percent in Russia, 67 percent in South Korea, and 78 percent in Brazil. In the United States, however, 68.0 percent of the crude steel was produced at EAF mills and 32.0 percent at mills using blast furnaces and basic oxygen processes.[17] Large integrated steel mills using blast furnaces, basic oxygen furnaces, and assorted casting and rolling equipment typically had the ability to manufacture a wide variety of steel mill products but faced significantly higher capital costs and higher operating costs for labor and energy. While mills using electric-arc furnaces were sometimes challenged by high prices for scrap metal, they tended to have far lower capital and operating costs compared with the integrated steel producers. However, the quality of the steel produced using basic oxygen furnace technologies tended to be superior to that of electric arc furnaces unless, like at most of Nucor's facilities, the user of electric arc furnaces invested in additional facilities and processing equipment to enable the production of upgraded steel products.

Market Conditions in the Global Steel Market, 2015–2019

The global marketplace for steel was intensely price competitive and expected to remain so unless and until the estimated 700 million tons of excess steel-making capacity across the world shrunk substantially and global demand for steel products rose sufficiently to more closely match global supplies. Approximately 150 million tons of the world's excess steel-making capacity was in China, but there were sizable pockets of excess capacity in many other countries. Companies with excess production capacity were typically active in seeking to increase their exports of steel to foreign markets. Steel producers in some countries, particularly those in the European Union, Turkey, South Korea, and Canada, were both big exporters and big importers because domestic steel makers had more capacity to make certain types and grades of steel than was needed locally (and thus strived to export such products to other countries) but lacked sufficient domestic capability to produce certain types and grades of semi-finished and finished steel products needed by domestic customers (which consequently had to be imported). In most countries of the world, the difference between steel exports and steel imports was a matter of a few million tons. But there were six countries that stood out as big *net* exporters of semi-finished and finished steel products, of which China was by far the largest (Exhibit 9).

The major Chinese steelmakers, most of which were wholly or partly government-owned, had responded to the burden of having large amounts of unused capacity by aggressively seeking out buyers for their products in other countries and securing orders by offering prices that significantly undercut the prices of local steel makers and enabled the Chinese sellers to steal away sales and market share. The low prices offered by Chinese steelmakers were partly enabled by Chinese currency devaluations initiated by the Chinese government and partly enabled by subsidies and other financial assistance the Chinese government provided to domestic steel makers. The success of Chinese steelmakers in capturing the business of foreign buyers resulted in total Chinese exports of semi-finished and finished steel products of 102.4 million tons in 2014, 123.0 million tons in 2015, 119.2 million tons in 2016, 86.4 million tons in 2017, and 75.8 million tons in 2018.[18]

A flood of steel imports from China and certain other countries into the United States and many other countries across the world in 2015–2018, powered by price discounting on the part of the sellers, resulted in governments imposing more than 130 anti-dumping tariffs and duties on Chinese steel producers (and Chinese manufacturers of aluminum and certain other metals as well) to protect their domestic steel companies from what they termed the unfair trade practices of Chinese producers to take sales away from domestic producers by selling at ultralow prices (typically enabled by subsidies from the Chinese government).[19] The average price of Chinese steel exports fell by about 50 percent between 2011 and 2016.

In 2016, the Chinese government agreed to pursue actions to reduce its domestic steel-making capacity by 150 million tons by 2020. But, while some capacity reductions had occurred, Chinese producers began pursuing ways to escape the tariffs being imposed. One method was to sell steel to buyers in a country which had not been singled out for tariffs imposed by the United States and other countries; these buyers, participants in a Chinese-engineered scheme to disguise the origin of the Chinese-made steel products, in turn shipped the steel products tariff-free to buyers in the United States and other countries. China Zhongwang Holdings, China's largest producer of aluminum flat-rolled and extrusion products, used a different tariff-evading scheme. In 2016, China Zhongwang was discovered to have stockpiled more than 500,000 metric tons of aluminum products

EXHIBIT 9 Major Net Exporters (Exports – Imports) of Semi-Finished and Finished Steel Products, By Country, 2015–2018 (in millions of metric tons)

Country	2015	2016	2017	2018
China	98.4	94.5	60.9	54.4
Japan	34.9	34.5	31.2	29.8
Russia	25.4	26.7	24.9	27.0
South Korea	9.5	7.3	12.1	15.1
Ukraine	16.9	17.1	13.8	13.5
Brazil	10.5	11.5	13.0	11.6

Source: Worldsteel Association, *Steel Statistical Yearbook, 2017* and *World Steel in Figures, 2018 and 2019.* Accessed May 31, 2018 and March 30, 2020 at www.worldsteel.org.

hidden under hay and tarpaulins in a Mexican desert just below the U.S. border, with alleged intentions of shipping them to the United States to avoid trade restrictions on Chinese exports of aluminum to the United States—provisions in the North American Free Trade Agreement allowed for aluminum products to be moved tariff-free from Mexico into the United States (reports and pictures of the stockpile in the media blew up the scheme).[20] In recent years, aluminum smelters in China had come to dominate the global aluminum market, reportedly supplying about half of the world's need for aluminum products in 2016–2017. Of the 23 aluminum smelters in operation in the United States in 2000, only 5 were still in operation in 2016, largely due to the fact that the Chinese manufacturers of aluminum products could use the subsidies they received from the Chinese government to undercut the prices of U.S. producers.

In 2018, the Trump Administration announced 25 percent tariffs on certain steel and aluminum imports from China, the European Union, Canada, and Mexico. Within weeks, there were multiple media reports that, in an effort to escape these tariffs, various Chinese steel-makers had sold steel to Chinese brokers who then shipped the steel to buyers in various countries that were not confronted tariffs on their steel exports to the United States and elsewhere; these buyers in turn promptly shipped the steel products to buyers in the United States. In 2017–2018, however, Chinese steel producers devised another way to skirt tariffs on steel. While they were shutting down some of their production in China, they had started aggressively expanding overseas, using tens of billions of dollars supplied by Chinese lenders owned by the Chinese government, to buy and build steel plants at locations around the world.[21] Already operational were plants with 3.5 million metric tons of capacity in Malaysia, 3.0 million metric tons in Indonesia, and 2.2 million metric tons in Serbia. Under construction were plants with capacity of 6.0 million metric tons in Indonesia, 2.0 million metric tons in India, and 0.5 million metric tons in Texas. And there were plants on the verge of starting construction in 2018 with capacity of 10 million metric tons in Brazil (where the Brazilian steel industry was currently operating at 70 percent of capacity), 7.5 million metric tons in Indonesia, and 2.0 million metric tons in Bangladesh.[22]

The steel plant in Serbia, owned and operated by a recently-renamed Chinese company called the Hesteel Group, had begun selling wide hot-rolled steel coil to U.S. buyers through Duferco, a Swiss trading company that was 51 percent owned by Hesteel.[23] This same plant was also reportedly exporting tariff-free steel products into the 28-nation European Union. A new 2 million metric ton steel plant built on the Indonesian island of Sulawesi by Tsingshan Group Holdings (that was funded by a $570 million loan from the government-backed China Development Bank) accounted for 4 percent of the world's stainless-steel production and had exported 300,000 metric tons to the United States through a joint venture with Pittsburgh-based stainless-steel producer Allegheny Technologies.[24]

Exhibit 10 shows the volumes of U.S. imports and exports of semi-finished and finished steel products for 2005–2018. The column showing "apparent domestic use of finished steel products" is obtained by adding up deliveries (defined as what comes out of the facility gates of domestic steel producers) minus exports of steel products plus imports of steel products; as such, it is a good approximation of total domestic consumption of steel products and is a commonly used metric in the steel industry. The last column shows the percentage of domestic steel use supplied by foreign steel producers.

NUCOR AND COMPETITION IN THE U.S. MARKET FOR STEEL

Nucor's broad product line-up meant that it was an active participant in the U.S. markets for a wide variety of unfinished and finished steel products, plus the markets for scrap steel and scrap substitutes. Nucor executives considered all the market segments and product categories in which it competed to be intensely competitive, many of which were populated with both domestic and foreign rivals. For the most part, competition for steel mill products and finished steel products was centered on price and the ability to meet customer delivery requirements. And, due to global overcapacity, many of the world's steelmakers were actively seeking new business in whatever geographic markets they could find willing buyers.

Finished steel imports into North America (the United States, Canada, and Mexico peaked in 2014 at almost 30 million tons and declined to approximately 25.7 million tons in 2017. In 2019, with section 232

EXHIBIT 10   U.S. Exports and Imports of Semi-Finished and Finished Steel Products, 2005–2018 (in millions of metric tons)

Year	U.S. Exports	U.S. Imports	Net Imports (Exports—Imports)	Apparent Domestic Use of Finished Steel Products	U.S. Imports as a Percent of Domestic Apparent Use
2005	9.4	30.2	20.8	110.3	27.4%
2006	9.6	42.2	32.6	122.4	34.5%
2007	9.8	27.7	17.9	111.2	24.9%
2008	12.0	24.6	12.6	101.1	24.3%
2009	9.2	15.3	6.1	59.3	25.8%
2010	11.8	22.5	10.7	115.8	19.4%
2011	13.3	26.6	13.3	89.2	29.8%
2012	13.6	30.9	17.3	96.2	32.1%
2013	12.5	29.8	17.3	95.7	31.1%
2014	12.0	41.4	29.4	107.0	38.7%
2015	10.0	36.5	26.5	96.1	38.0%
2016	9.2	30.9	21.7	91.9	33.6%
2017	10.2	35.4	25.2	97.7	36.2%
2018	8.6	31.7	23.1	100.2	31.6%

Source: Worldsteel Association, *Steel Statistical Yearbook, 2017* and *World Steel in Figures, 2018 and 2019,* accessed at www.worldsteel.org, May 31, 2018 and March 30, 2020; and Worldsteel Association, *Steel Statistical Yearbook, 2010,* accessed at www.steel-on-the-net.com, May 31, 2018.

(implemented in 2018) adding a 25 percent tariff on most imports outside NAFTA, finished steel imports in the United States decreased by approximately 6 million tons from the levels of 2017. As a result, import penetration in the United States fell from 23 percent in 2018 to 19 percent in 2019. Relative to other regions, imports from Canada and Mexico decreased by only about 15 percent in 2019, as section 232 tariffs were not applied after May 2019. Other countries such as Brazil, Ukraine, Australia and South Korea, though not subject to 25 percent tariffs, were subject to quotas. Imports decreased further from Turkey (down approximately 70 percent year-on-year), where its share of imports declined from 5 percent in 2018 to approximately 1 percent in 2019; the sharp Turkish decline had to do with tariffs—beginning May 16, 2019, Turkish imports were subject to a 25 percent tariff after having been subject to 50 percent tariffs since August 2018.

Many foreign steel producers had costs on a par with or sometimes below those of Nucor, although their competitiveness in the U.S. market varied significantly according to the prevailing strength of their local currencies versus the U.S. dollar, the extent to which they received government subsidies, and prevailing tariffs and trade restrictions.

In Nucor's 2017 Annual Report, CEO Ferriola reported to shareholders on the impacts that global excess capacity and unfair trade practices were having on the company:[25]

> Our industry remains greatly constrained by the impact of global overcapacity . . . . the extraordinary increase in China's steel production in the last decade, together with the excess capacity from other countries that have state-owned enterprises . . . . have exacerbated this overcapacity issue. We believe Chinese producers . . . benefit from . . . the receipt of government subsidies, which allow them to sell steel into our markets at artificially low prices.
>
> China is not only selling steel at artificially low prices into our domestic market but also across the globe. . . . Nucor has joined three other domestic steelmakers in filing a petition alleging China is circumventing previously levied duties by shipping products through third-party countries.

But conditions improved in 2019. Nucor CEO Topalian said:[26]

> As the year ended, there were a number of positive developments that led to more optimism about the

outlook for the U.S. economy in 2020. The U.S. and China signed a phase one agreement on trade issues, and the U.S. House and Senate both passed the United States-Mexico-Canada trade agreement with strong bipartisan support. The new trade deal will benefit the U.S. steel industry, especially given the revamped country of origin rules that will greatly incentivize the use of North American steel in autos, auto parts, and other products containing steel. The Section 232 steel tariffs also continued to be effective in keeping unfairly traded imports out of the U.S. market, with imports down approximately six million tons from the previous year.

Nucor's Two Largest Domestic Competitors

Consolidation of both the global and domestic steel industry into a smaller number of larger and more efficient steel producers had heightened competitive pressures for Nucor and most other steelmakers. Nucor had two major rivals in the United States—the NAFTA division of ArcelorMittal (the United States, Canada, and Mexico) and United States Steel.

ArcelorMittal NAFTA In 2020, ArcelorMittal NAFTA operated two coke-making facilities, five integrated mills, 10 EAFs at three sites, rolling and finishing facilities at about 14 sites. It had the capability to produce hot-rolled and cold-rolled coils of sheet steel, steel plate, steel bars, coated steels, high-quality wire rods, rebar, structural steel, tubular steel, and tin mill products. Much of its production was sold to customers in the automotive, trucking, off-highway, agricultural-equipment, and railway industries, with the balance being sold to steel service centers and companies in the appliance, office furniture, electrical motor, packaging, and industrial machinery sectors. The division's performance for the most recent three years is shown below: [27]

Year	Shipments (tons)	Average Price per ton	Sales Revenues	Operating Profit (Loss)
2019	20.9 million	$810	$18.6 billion	($1.3 billion)
2018	22.0 million	850	$20.3 billion	$1.9 billion
2017	23.5 million	740	$18.0 billion	$1.2 billion

Globally, ArcelorMittal was the world's largest steel producer, with steelmaking operations in 20 countries on four continents, annual production capacity of about 112 million tons of crude steel.

ArcelorMittal's performance companywide for the past three years is summarized below: [28]

Year	Shipments (tons)	Average Price per ton	Sales Revenues	Net Profit (Loss)
2019	83.9 million	$754	$70.6 billion	($2.4 billion)
2018	84.5 million	826	$76.0 billion	$5.3 billion
2017	85.2 million	736	$68.7 billion	$4.6 billion

One important cause of ArcelorMittal's spotty financial performance was the industry's massive amount of excess capacity, which had spurred steel producers in China, Japan, India, Russia, and other locations to dump steel products at artificially low prices in many of the geographic markets where ArcelorMittal had operations (and thereby push down the market prices of many steel products to unprofitable levels).

U.S. Steel U.S. Steel was an integrated steel producer of flat-rolled and tubular steel products with major production operations in the United States and Europe. Going into 2020, U.S. Steel was the third largest producer of crude steel in the United States and in 2018 the twenty-sixth largest in the world. It was widely considered to have a labor cost disadvantage versus Nucor and ArcelorMittal NAFTA, partly due to the lower productivity of its unionized workforce and partly due to its retiree pension costs.

U.S. Steel's operations were organized into three business segments: North American flat-rolled products, tubular products, and U.S. Steel Europe. The Flat-Rolled segment included four integrated steel mills in the United States, with combined crude steel capacity of 17 million tons annually, that produced slabs, strip mill plates, sheets and tin mill products, as well as iron ore and coke production facilities in the United States. These operations primarily served North American customers in the service center, conversion, transportation (including automotive), construction, container, and appliance and electrical markets.

The Tubular segment had annual production capacity of 1.9 million tons that produced seamless and electric resistance welded steel casing and tubing, standard and line pipe, and mechanical tubing primarily for customers in the oil, gas, and petrochemical markets. The European segment included coke production facilities and an integrated steel mill with annual capacity of 4.5 million tons in Slovakia that produced steel slabs, strip mill plate, sheet, tin mill products and spiral welded pipe, as well as refractory ceramic materials

EXHIBIT 11   Performance of U.S. Steel's Business Segments, 2017–2019

Year	Shipments (tons)	Average Price per ton	Sales Revenues	Operating Profit (Loss)
Flat Rolled Products				
2019	11.4 million	$ 753	$ 9.3 billion	$196 million
2018	11.9 million	811	9.7 billion	883 million
2017	10.8 million	726	1.2 billion	375 million
Tubular Products				
2019	11.4 million	$1,450	$ 1.2 billion	$(67 million)
2018	11.9 million	1,483	1.2 billion	(58 million)
2017	10.8 million	1,253	0.94 billion	(99 million)
U.S. Steel Europe				
2019	3.6 million	$652	$ 2.4 billion	$(57 million)
2018	4.5 million	693	3.2 billion	359 million
2017	4.6 million	622	2.9 billion	327 million

Source: Company 10-K Report, 2019.

to customers in Central and Western Europe in the transportation (including automotive), construction, container, appliance, electrical, service center, conversion and oil, gas and petrochemical markets.

The performance of these three business segments for the most recent three years is shown in Exhibit 11.

NUCOR CEO LEON J. TOPALIAN'S PRIORITIES GOING FORWARD

Shortly after becoming CEO on January 1, 2020, Leon Topalian in his first annual report letter to Nucor's stockholders announced what his immediate priorities were for the company:[29]

> There is no value within our culture that tells us more about ourselves than Safety. It is our cultural measuring stick. . . . Our goal is to make 2020 the safest year in our history and eventually to make Nucor the Safest steel company in the world. That means zero injuries across Nucor.

The second priority is the execution of our strategic investments. . . . These investments are focused on ensuring that Nucor is the supplier of choice in all the product areas where we compete.

The third priority is looking at how to effectively manage our portfolio of businesses to grow our earnings potential. We remain committed to, and focused on, our long-term growth strategy. We must harness Nucor's culture of continuous improvement to achieve the full return potential across our entire asset base.

Continuing to attract, hire, develop and retain future leaders of tomorrow is another priority. . . . Our focus on talent will continue to enable us to achieve the results our investors, customers and team have grown to rely on. . . . Having the right people has always driven Nucor's success.

Finally, as one of the most efficient and cleanest steel producers in the world, we will continue to focus on sustainability. We are always looking for opportunities to become even more efficient, use less energy and reduce our environmental footprint.

ENDNOTES

[1] Tom Peters and Nancy Austin, *A Passion for Excellence: The Leadership Difference,* (New York: Random House, 1985) and "Other Low-Cost Champions," *Fortune,* June 24, 1985.

[2] Nucor's 2011 Annual Report, p. 4.

[3] February 2016 Investor Presentation, posted at www.nucor.com (accessed March 21, 2016).

[4] BMO Conference Presentation, February 25, 2020, posted at www.nucor.com (accessed March 24, 2020).

[5] According to information posted at www.nucor.com (accessed October 11, 2006).

[6] Company press release, May 11, 2018.

[7] Nucor's 2008 Annual Report, p. 5.

[8] March 2014 Investor Presentation, posted at www.nucor.com, (accessed April 21, 2014).

[9] According to Form 5500 information posted at www.brightscope.com (accessed March 25, 2020).

[10] Nanette Byrnes, "The Art of Motivation," *Business Week,* May 1, 2006, p. 57.

[11] Ibid., p. 60.

[12] Ibid.

[13] Ibid.

[14] Organization for Economic Co-operation and Development, "Capacity Developments in the World Steel Industry," July 2019, posted at www.oecd.org (accessed March 27, 2020).

[15] Worldsteel Association press release, January 27, 2020, posted at www.worldsteel.org (accessed on March 26, 2020).

[16] Worldsteel Association, *World Steel in Figures, 2019,* p. 10, posted at www.worldsteel.org (accessed March 30, 2020).

[17] Ibid.

[18] Worldsteel Association, *World Steel in Figures, 2019,* posted at www.worldsteel.org (accessed March 30, 2020).

[19] Matthew Dalton and Lingling Wei, "China's Blueprint for Skirting U.S. Tariffs on Steel," *Wall Street Journal,* June 5, 2018, p. A1 and A8.

[20] Scott Patterson, Biman Mukherji, and Vu Trong Khanh, "Giant Aluminum Stockpile Was Shipped from Mexico to Vietnam," *Wall Street Journal,* December 1, 2016, posted at www.wsj.com (accessed June 8, 2018).

[21] Ibid., p. A8.

[22] Ibid.

[23] Ibid.

[24] Ibid.

[25] Nucor Annual Report, 2017, p. 24.

[26] Nucor Annual Report, 2019, p. 4.

[27] ArcelorMittal Annual Report, 2017 and 2019.

[28] Ibid.

[29] Nucor Annual Report, 2019, p. 5.

Eliminating Modern Slavery from Supply Chains: Can Nestlé Lead the Way?

Syeda Maseeha Qumer

ICFAI Business School, Hyderabad

Debapratim Purkayastha

ICFAI Business School, Hyderabad

In April 2019, a federal court in California filed a class action lawsuit against Nestlé SA (Nestlé) over claims the global chocolate manufacturer facilitated the use of forced child labor in West Africa even though it labeled its products as "sustainably sourced." Nestlé, one of the world's largest food processing companies, had been grappling with accusations of aiding and abetting child slavery on cocoa plantations in Ivory Coast[1] for more than a decade.

Earlier in 2015, Nestlé surprised many by admitting that it had found forced labor in its seafood supply chain in Thailand. Magdi Batato (Batato), Executive Vice President and Head of Operations at Nestlé, self-reported that Nestlé had uncovered child labor exploitation on fishing boats in Thailand that supplied its factories. He reported details of the investigation and also initiated a detailed action plan on how it intended to tackle the issue. The news generated a mixed response from industry observers. Hailing Nestlé's honesty, Brian Griffin, CEO of digital marketing agency Vero PR, said, "First of all, what Nestlé did was brave, and from a moral perspective, they did the right thing to let stakeholders know about this issue. They will feel some pain from this initially, particularly from a consumer standpoint, and it's not hard to imagine that sales of seafood products may decline. There is no question that the issue must be cleaned up, and that it must happen now. We should appreciate what Nestlé has done to bring even more attention to the issue."[2]

However, Nestlé's critics contended that the company had done this only to fend off growing criticism against it. It had admitted to slavery in seafood, a low-profit area of the company's business, while not doing enough to tackle this problem in its lucrative chocolate business. Critics accused Nestlé of turning a blind eye to human rights abuses by cocoa suppliers in West Africa while falsely portraying itself as a socially and ethically responsible company. Nestlé said it was committed to tackling child labor in its cocoa supply chain and had been taking action to address the issue which included increasing access to education, stepping up systems of age verification at cocoa farms, and increasing awareness about the company's own code of conduct. Despite Nestlé's assurances, the use of child labor continued and became even more prevalent in its cocoa supply chains. Though Nestlé's commitment to eliminating slavery seemed promising, lawsuits related to slavery in its core business operations questioned such promises, critics said.

The existence of modern slavery within its cocoa supply chain posed ethical and reputational risks for Nestlé. Analysts said addressing slavery would be a critical issue for the company going forward due to the complexity and limited visibility of its supply chain, its reputation for reliability among stakeholders (customers, investors, NGOs), transparency dilemmas, as well as cost and pricing pressures. However, some analysts said Nestlé being a financially sound company, it could do more to stop slave labor and take more control over its supply chain management. According to Marianne Smallwood, a diplomat for the U.S. Agency for International Development, "In initiating the public examination of its flaws, and in working with an organization like Verite, Nestlé has already gone a more honorable and transparent route than other companies have done. But while it has taken the first step toward being a more responsible company, Nestlé's commitment to funding a long-term strategy — and how it pushes beyond the inevitable roadblocks ahead — will determine its ultimate footprint and legacy."[3]

According to Batato, "Every reasonable person who has gone to Africa, gone to Asia, who has seen the farmers and factories, can tell you that [child labor] does exist. It is part of their life. Do we accept it? No. Are we going to stay quiet and do nothing? No. But making a big declaration that tomorrow morning we are going to see it disappear, sometimes the problem is bigger than us, bigger than a company even the size of Nestlé."[4] Nevertheless, the critical questions before him were: How to eliminate forced labor from Nestlé's supply chains worldover? Could he address the problem and bring real and sustained change in how the company's cocoa supply chains were managed?

BACKGROUND NOTE

Nestlé, headquartered in Vevey, Switzerland, was founded in 1866. One of the leading players in the food and beverage categories, the company had a global presence and employed more than 328,000 people as of 2017. Its sales and profits for the year 2016 were CHF 89.5 billion and CHF 8.53 billion respectively.[5]

Though Nestlé was among the world's largest food processing companies and had great consumer brands well known for their quality, critics pointed out that there seemed to be an element of arrogance in its actions.[6] The company had a history of confrontations over a range of issues.[7] There were instances of Nestlé being accused of disregarding its corporate responsibility in many countries in which it operated. The Swiss conglomerate had had its fair share of controversies and ethical dilemmas during its nearly 150-year-long history.[8] Experts pointed out that the history of Nestlé's public relations troubles began in the 1970s with allegations of unethical marketing of baby formula[9] in less developed countries.[10] Since then, Nestlé had continued to get into trouble. For instance, in 2008, it was blacklisted by the Chinese government.[11] Later, it was targeted for the misleading promotion of its bottled water brands as well as for interfering in policies that protected natural water resources.[12]

In the United Kingdom, the Ethical Consumer Research Association (ECRA)[13] gave Nestlé an ethical rating, Ethiscore[14] of 0.5 out of 20. ECRA had found the company to be linked to social ills such as child labor, slavery, rainforest destruction, water extraction, and debt perpetuation. Critics pointed out that in 2005, when it launched the 'Partners Blend' fair trade [15] coffee, Nestlé was termed as the UK's most boycotted and irresponsible corporation.[16]

MODERN SLAVERY IN GLOBAL SUPPLY CHAINS

Modern slavery could be described as control by people or organizations over vulnerable individuals in order to obtain personal gain or profit. Modern slavery included forced labor, debt-bondage, child labor, wage exploitation, human trafficking, forced marriage, involuntary domestic servitude, or any other practice wherein victims were engaged in unreasonable work through physical or mental threat. According to the 2017 Global Slavery Index, about 40.3 million people were victims of some form of modern slavery globally. Of these people, about 24.9 million were in forced labor. The rate of modern slavery was reported to be the highest in Africa, with 7.6 victims for every 1,000 people in the region—see Exhibits 1 and 2.

Modern slavery had broader social and economic costs, in terms of impeding economic development and perpetuating poverty, said experts. According to them, globalization had led companies to turn to lower-cost suppliers who sourced cheaper raw materials and used low wage labor in order to maximize profits. According to an ILO report, forced labor generated about $ 150 billion in illegal profits annually.

Analysts pointed out that slavery was an abuse of human rights in the pursuit of profits and that corporations had a moral duty not to indulge in or tolerate it. Addressing human rights and labor issues in the supply chain had become a necessity for businesses in the consumer goods industry, they said. This was partly due to rising consumer demand for ethical products. Several governments had enacted legislations which mandated that companies ensure respect for human rights in their supply chains. As shown in Exhibit 3, a number of anti-modern slavery regulations had also come into existence. The California Transparency in Supply Chains Act, signed in 2010 and enacted on January 1, 2012, was one of the first anti-modern slavery regulations. This Act aimed to ensure that "large

EXHIBIT 1   2017 Global Estimates of Modern Slavery: Prevalence of Modern Slavery (per 1,000 population), by Region and Category

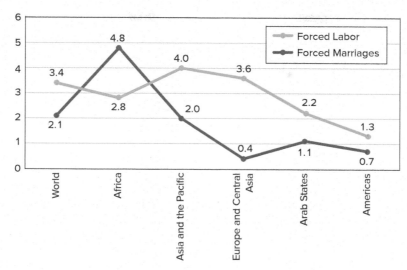

Source: https://www.alliance87.org/global_estimates_of_modern_slavery-forced_labour_and_forced_marriage.pdf

EXHIBIT 2   2017 Global Estimates of Modern Slavery: Number and Prevalence of Persons in Modern Slavery, by Category, Sex, and Age (Number in thousands and prevalence in per thousand)

| | | | Forced labor sub-categories | | | | |
		Forced labor slavery Exploitation	Forced sexual exploitation of adults and commercial sexual exploitation of children	State-imposed forced labor	Total forced labor	Forced marriage	Modern Slavery
World		Number	15,975	4,816	4,060	24,850	15,442	40,293
		Prevalence	2.2	0.7	0.5	3.4	2.1	5.4
Sex	**Male**	Number	6,766	29	2,411	9,206	2,442	11,648
		Prevalence	1.8	0	0.6	2.4	0.6	3.0
	Female	Number	9,209	4,787	1,650	15,646	13,000	28,645
		Prevalence	2.5	1.3	0.4	4.2	3.5	7.7
Age	**Adults**	Number	12,995	3,791	3,778	20,564	9,762	30,327
		Prevalence	2.5	0.7	0.7	3.9	1.9	5.8
	Children	Number	2980	1024	282	4286	5679	9965
		Prevalence	1.3	0.4	0.1	1.9	2.5	4.4

Source: https://www.alliance87.org/global_estimates_of_modern_slavery-forced_labour_and_ forced_marriage.pdf

EXHIBIT 3   Anti-Modern Slavery Regulations

Year	Regulation
2000	The United Nations passes the Protocol to Prevent, Suppress, and Punish Trafficking in Persons as part of the Convention against Transnational Organized Crime. It is the first global legally binding treaty with an internationally agreed definition of trafficking in persons.
2002	The International Cocoa Initiative is established as a joint effort of anti-slavery groups and major chocolate companies to protect children and contribute to the elimination of child labor.
2004	The United Nations appoints a Special Rapporteur on Human Trafficking.
2008	The Council of Europe Convention on Action against Trafficking in Human Beings comes into force.
2010	California enacts the California Transparency in Supply Chains Act.
2014	The ILO adopts a protocol on forced labor, bringing its 1930 Convention on Forced Labor into the modern era to address practices such as human trafficking.
2015	Britain's Modern Slavery Act comes into force.
2015	The United Nations adopts 17 Sustainable Development Goals, including a target of ending slavery and eradicating forced labor and human trafficking.

Compiled from various sources.

retailers and manufacturers provide consumers with information regarding their efforts to eradicate slavery and human trafficking from their supply chains." The United Nations Guiding Principles on Business and Human Rights (UNGPs) were endorsed by the UN Human Rights Council in June 2011. These were a set of guidelines for States and companies to prevent, address, and remedy human rights abuses committed in business operations. The UNGPs based on the three pillars "Protect, Respect, and Remedy" had since become the trusted global framework for business and human rights.

The most prominent of anti-slavery regulations was the UK Modern Slavery Act, passed on March 26, 2015. It required businesses with a turnover of more than £36 million annually to produce a 'slavery and human trafficking statement' once a year

disclosing what action they had taken to ensure their supply chains were free of slave labor. Experts felt that though the legislation did not impose financial penalties on companies that failed to comply, the adverse effects of being prosecuted for failing to do so could lead to reputational risks and could be more damaging than any fine.

CHILD SLAVERY IN Nestlé'S COCOA SUPPLY CHAIN

Nestlé was a leader in the chocolate confectionery industry and used 10 percent of the world's cocoa production. It worked directly with almost 165,000 direct suppliers and 695,000 individual farmers worldwide for procuring raw materials such as cocoa, dairy, sugar, coffee, etc. Nestlé primarily sourced cocoa from co-ops and farms in Ivory Coast and Ghana. Nestlé purchased around 414,000 tons of cocoa annually for chocolate and confectionery as well as beverages. The cocoa supply chain includes many intermediaries between the farmer and consumer. Small farmers typically sell their cocoa harvest to local middlemen for cash. The middlemen work under contract for local exporters, who, in turn, sell cocoa to international traders and the major international cocoa brands.

Allegations of child labor and human rights abuses in its cocoa and agricultural supply chains had dogged Nestlé for years. Since the late 1990s, Nestlé and its competitors had received negative publicity and media coverage over their use of child slave labor and the lack of transparency within their cocoa supply chain. Though Nestlé's Corporate Business Principles and Supplier Code prohibited both child and forced labor, Nestlé was aware that cocoa beans from Ivory Coast were produced using child labor. While Nestlé and its competitors vied for market share and profits, cocoa farmers suffered due to low income attributed to the fall in the price of cocoa beans. Cocoa bean futures on the Intercontinental Exchange in New York hit $2,052 per metric ton on February 3, 2017, compared to $3,422 per metric ton in December 2015. Many farmers felt that child labor was a viable option in order to cut production and work costs. As a result, child slavery had become extremely prevalent throughout the cocoa supply chain, and there had been minimal action taken by the chocolate manufacturing companies to stop the exploitation of these children.

The practice of child labor was rampant in the cocoa industry wherein harvesting and processing of the cocoa plant was left to children, often unpaid and living in slavery—see Exhibit 4. Some children were sold by their parents to traffickers, while many were kidnapped. Reportedly, they worked from dawn to dusk each day, were denied sufficient food, and locked in a shed at night where they were given a tiny cup in which to urinate. [17] Some children were forced to do unsafe tasks, including carrying heavy loads, using machetes and sharp tools, and applying pesticides and fertilizers. "The rules and regulations are so lax there that there is no government to step in and stop the atrocities. This horrific state of child slavery is also the perfect cheap labor for candy companies that want to sell you chocolate for dirt cheap prices. Why do you think it only costs $1 for a chocolate bar?" [18] wrote journalist LJ Vanier.

The growing awareness about child slaves working in the production of cocoa led to consumers questioning where exactly their chocolate was coming from and who was making it. In 2001, following pressure and outrage from civil society groups, media, and the general public, eight chocolate manufacturing companies in the United States including Nestlé, signed the Harkin-Engel protocol [19] to investigate the labor practices and eliminate the worst forms of child labor in the processing of cocoa in Ivory Coast and Ghana by 2005. However, when the 2005 deadline arrived, the companies had yet to eradicate child labor from their supply chains. The target was then extended to 2008. Unable to meet the new self-imposed deadline again, in 2010, the signatories of the protocol started afresh with a treaty called The Declaration of Joint Action to implement the Harkin-Engel Protocol and to reduce the worst

forms of child labor by 70 percent across the cocoa plantations of Ivory Coast by 2020.

In 2005, a lawsuit was filed against Nestlé, Archer Daniels Midland Co[20], and Cargill Inc[21] by three former child slavery victims originally from Mali in West Africa who alleged that these companies aided and abetted human rights violations through their active involvement in purchasing cocoa in Ivory Coast. The lawsuit claimed that the companies were aware of the child slavery problem and offered financial and technical assistance to local farmers to procure the cheapest source of cocoa. In court documents, the three plaintiffs claimed that they had been trafficked from their homes and put to work on plantations in Ivory Coast. They described how they had been whipped, beaten, and forced to work for 14 to 16 hours a day before being allowed to retire to their dark rooms. One plaintiff recounted how guards would slice open the feet of any child worker who tried to escape. The lawsuit accused Nestlé of making false assertions to consumers and not disclosing that its suppliers relied on child laborers to procure cocoa at the point of purchase.

Nestlé said that the claims against it should be dismissed as it was committed to the goal of eliminating child labor from its cocoa supply chain. Claiming that the lawsuit was without merit, Nestlé said that "proactive and multi-stakeholder efforts" were required to eradicate child labor, not lawsuits. "Forced child labor is a complex, global social issue in foreign countries that is not going to be solved by lawsuits in U.S. courts against the very companies that are leading the fight to help eradicate it,"[22] said Paul Bakus, President of Corporate Affairs, Nestlé USA. After a first dismissal in 2008, the case was examined again and the lawsuit was reinstated by the U.S. Court of Appeals in San Francisco in 2014 on

EXHIBIT 4   Children's Involvement in Child Labor and Hazardous Work, 2000–16

| | Children in Child Labor World (5–17 Years) | | Children in Hazardous Work World (5–17 Years) | |
	Number (000s)	Prevalence (%)	Number (000s)	Prevalence (%)
2000	245,500	16.0%	170,500	11.1%
2004	222,294	14.2%	128,381	8.2%
2008	215,209	13.6%	115,314	7.3%
2012	167,956	10.6%	85,344	5.4%
2016	151,622	9.6%	72,525	4.6%

Source: Adapted from https://www.ilo.org/wcmsp5/groups/public/@documents/publication/wcms_575541.pdf

the grounds that the plaintiffs had valid reasons to accuse Nestlé of pursuing profits more than human well-being.

In October 2009, Nestlé launched a companywide initiative called The Nestlé Cocoa Plan (TNCP) in collaboration with International Cocoa Initiative[23](ICI) in order to ensure a sustainable future for the cocoa industry worldwide and the communities depending on it. The goal of TNCP was "to help cocoa farmers run profitable farms, respect the environment, have a good quality of life and for their children to benefit from education and see cocoa farming as a respectable profession."[24] To achieve this, Nestlé committed CHF 110 million to the plan for 10 years and pledged to source 230,000 MT of cocoa through TNCP by 2020. Despite the industry's assurances, critics contended that the worst forms of child labor continued in Ivory Coast.

Amid accusations of failing to carry out checks on child labor in its cocoa supply chain, in November 2011, Nestlé commissioned Fair Labor Association (FLA)[25] to assess its cocoa supply chain in Ivory Coast. The goals of the assessment were to map stakeholders involved in Nestlé's cocoa supply chain and to analyze the associated labor risks in its cocoa supply chain. The assessment team mapped the cocoa supply chain in depth including Nestlé's headquarters in Switzerland; R&D in Abidjan; local operations in the Ivory Coast; Tier 1 suppliers of Nestlé and their subsidiaries in West Africa; processing facilities and buying centers in the Ivory Coast; third-party service providers; pisteurs[26] cooperatives; traitants[27] farmers; Métayers[28] Coxers [29] and workers—see Exhibit 5. A team of 20 local and international experts visited a total of seven suppliers, 20 co-operatives, and two co-operative unions, and 87 farms. In all, over 500 interviews were conducted with farmers and other stakeholders in the supply chain, including local community members, local governments, NGOs, suppliers, and Nestlé staff. The FLA released the results of its audit in 2012, finding continued evidence of child labor in the Ivory Coast farms supplying Nestlé. The researchers found 56 workers under the age of 18, of whom 27 were under 15. According to Steve Berman

EXHIBIT 5   Nestle's Cocoa Supply Chain Map in the Ivory Coast

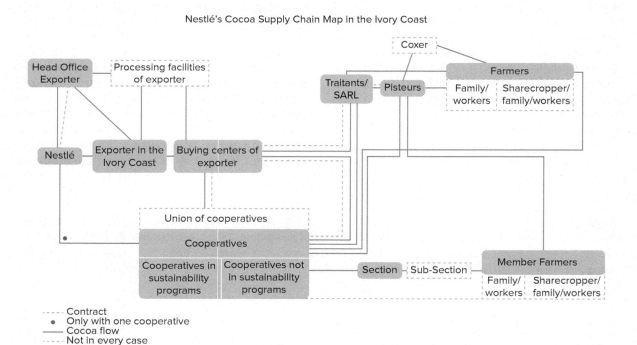

Nestlé's Cocoa Supply Chain Map in the Ivory Coast

(Berman), managing partner at law firm Hagens Berman Sobol Shapiro LLP, "They claim they've been taking steps. They partner with the Fair Labor Association to investigate, and they claim they're committed to eradicating it, but the fact is the recent reports show the number of children in the cocoa industry has increased. We doubt that Nestlé is taking this very seriously."[30]

Moreover, Nestlé's claims that it had made progress toward meeting the Harkin-Engel Protocol fell flat when a 2015 report from the Payson Center for International Development of Tulane University, sponsored by the U.S. Department of Labor, found that the number of children engaged in cocoa production in Ivory Coast had increased 51 percent to 1.4 million in 2013-14, compared to 791,181 children engaged in such work in 2008-09. However, Nestlé defended itself stating, "cocoa supply chain is long and complex – making it difficult for food companies to establish exactly where their cocoa comes from and under what conditions it was harvested."[31]

Nestlé's failure to bring transparency into its supply chain again came under the public spotlight in September when consumers filed three class-action lawsuits against Nestlé, The Hershey Co., and Mars Inc. for allegedly using child labor in chocolate production. The lawsuit stated that in violation of California law, the companies did not disclose that their suppliers in Ivory Coast relied on child laborers and instead continued to profit by tricking consumers into indirectly supporting the use of such labor. According to the complaint, "Nestlé, as one of the largest companies in the world, can dictate the terms by which cocoa beans are produced and supplied to it, including the labor conditions in the supply chain. But through its own inadequate efforts over the course of decades Nestlé is presently not able to trace all of the cocoa beans that make up its Chocolate Products back to the cocoa plantations on which they are grown, much less ensure that the cocoa beans are not the product of child or slave labor. And meanwhile Nestlé continues to profit from the child and forced labor that is used to make its Chocolate Products. This is shameful."[32]

Nestlé'S INITIATIVES TO ADDRESS THE ISSUE

Following the findings of the FLA report, Nestlé set out to address child labor by undertaking the 11

recommendations the FLA had made to it which included strengthening the Nestlé Supplier Code, increasing accountability from the various tiers of suppliers, and developing a robust and comprehensive internal monitoring and remediation system. Reiterating the promise made in 2001, Nestlé said it was taking action to progressively eliminate child labor in cocoa-growing areas by assessing individual cases and tackling the root causes. "The use of child labor is unacceptable and goes against everything Nestlé stands for. Nestlé is committed to following and respecting all international laws and is dedicated to the goal of eradicating child labor from our cocoa supply chain,"[33] the company said in a statement.

In 2012, Nestlé was the first cocoa purchaser to set up a Child Labor Monitoring and Remediation System (CLMRS) in Ivory Coast in association with ICI—see Exhibit 6. The system locally recruited 'community liaison people' and 'child labor agents' who worked to raise awareness about child labor in communities, identified children at risk, and reported their findings to Nestlé and its suppliers. By the end of 2015, the system covered 40 cooperatives and 26,000 cocoa farmers. In 2016, the CLMRS was extended to a further 29 cooperatives, taking the total to 69. As of August 2019, CLMRS covered 1,751 communities in Côte d'Ivoire compared to 1,553 in 2017[34] As shown in Exhibit 7, the number of children monitored increased from 40,728 in 2017 to 78,580 in 2019. Half of the identified children were included in CLMRS and sent to school while income generating activities were developed for their families. Nestlé built 49 schools in Ivory Coast to help end unlawful child labor. Despite this, allegations that the company was not doing enough continued. According to a spokesperson from Nestlé, "Unfortunately, the scale and complexity of the issue is such that no company sourcing cocoa from Ivory Coast can guarantee that it has completely removed the risk of child labor from its supply chain."[35]

Earlier in 2010, Nestlé entered into a partnership with the Danish Institute for Human Rights [36] (DIHR) to support its commitment to respecting human rights as stated in the company's Corporate Business Principles. As part of this commitment, Nestlé developed and implemented an 8-pillar Human Rights Due Diligence Program (HRDD) shown in Exhibit 8 with the aim of making Nestlé's approach to human rights strategic, comprehensive, and coordinated. As part of the program, Nestlé

EXHIBIT 6   Child Labor Monitoring and Remediation System

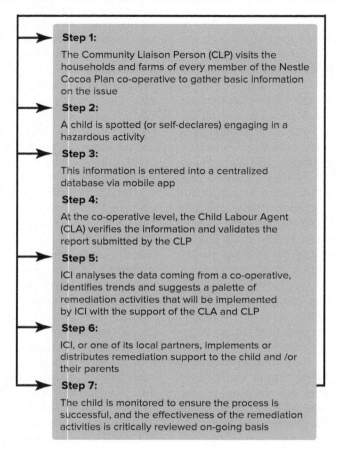

Step 1:
The Community Liaison Person (CLP) visits the households and farms of every member of the Nestle Cocoa Plan co-operative to gather basic information on the issue

Step 2:
A child is spotted (or self-declares) engaging in a hazardous activity

Step 3:
This information is entered into a centralized database via mobile app

Step 4:
At the co-operative level, the Child Labour Agent (CLA) verifies the information and validates the report submitted by the CLP

Step 5:
ICI analyses the data coming from a co-operative, identifies trends and suggests a palette of remediation activities that will be implemented by ICI with the support of the CLA and CLP

Step 6:
ICI, or one of its local partners, implements or distributes remediation support to the child and /or their parents

Step 7:
The child is monitored to ensure the process is successful, and the effectiveness of the remediation activities is critically reviewed on-going basis

Source: Adapted from www.nestle.com.

EXHIBIT 7   Growth of Child Labor Monitoring and Remediation Systems, 2017, 2019

	2017	2019
Number of co-ops in CLMRS	75	87
Number of farmers monitored by CLMRS	48,496	73,248
Communities covered by CLMRS	1,553	1,751
Community members educated about child labor	163,407 (attendees) 5,877(sessions)	593,925 (attendees) 56,183 (sessions)
Number of children aged 5–17 being monitored	40,728	78,580
Child labor rate	17%	23%
Number of children identified in child labor and existing in the system	7,002	18,283
Number of children who received atleast one form of remediation	Not measured	15,740

Source: Nestle CSV Full Report 2019.

EXHIBIT 8   Nestlé Human Rights Due Diligence Program

HRDD pillar	Components
1 Policy commitments	Revised 17 different corporate policies, standards, and commitments to incorporate the relevant human rights elements. These include Nestlé's Corporate Business Principles, Responsible Sourcing Standard, Employee Relations Policy, Consumers' Communication Policy and Privacy Policy.
2 Stakeholder engagement	Partnered with expert organizations such as the Danish Institute for Human Rights (DIHR), the Fair Labor Association (cocoa and hazelnuts) and Verité (fish and seafood, and coffee) to develop policies and procedures, and improve performance on the ground.
3 Training and awareness	Rolled out human rights training programs to raise awareness of human rights issues among employees and develop their skills in dealing with them. As of 2018, Nestlé trained about 96,599 employees.
4 Risk evaluation	Integrated human rights risks within its Enterprise Risk Management Framework and market compliance committees.
5 Salient issues	Carried out business risk and impact assessments at the corporate level and on the ground and identified 11 most salient human rights issues and developed dedicated action plans to address them.
6 Governance	Established clear roles and responsibilities at different levels of the company and set up boards and committees to assess work and lead the strategic implementation of human rights work.
7 Grievance mechanisms	Identified and enabled effective remediation across countries and industries.
8 Monitoring and reporting	Reviewed progress and performance regularly as the company was publicly accountable for its promises.

Source: http://www.nestle.com/csv/communities/respecting-human-rights

continued to tackle child labor in its cocoa supply chain in Ivory Coast by focusing on vulnerable groups, especially girls and children of migrant workers. In 2015, Nestlé was one of the early adopters of the UNGP Reporting Framework to effectively manage human rights in its operations. This Framework was based on the global standard of the UNGPs.

In October 2015, Batato[37] was appointed as Executive Vice President and Head of Operations at Nestlé. Batato controlled all 500 of Nestle's manufacturing facilities around the world He was also responsible for Nestlé's rural development activities and procurement. Nestlé operated a Child Labor and Women's Empowerment Steering Group, chaired by Batato, to identify measures, take decisions, and monitor progress.

In 2016, Nestlé increased the amount of cocoa purchased through TNCP to 140,933 tonnes at a cost of about CHF 30 million. By 2017, the company planned to source 150,000 tonnes of cocoa through TNCP and 230,000 tonnes by 2020. The company claimed that its KitKat brand had become the first global confectionery brand to be sourced from 100 percent certified cocoa. In order to strengthen its

cocoa bean supply in a responsible way, Nestlé encouraged its supplying farms to be UTZ[38] certified. The process included farm selection and farmer training in good agricultural practices, health and safety, and care for the environment. Farmer compliance was checked by both Nestlé agronomists and an external auditor.

NESTLÉ ADMITS TO FORCED LABOR

Following allegations that it was using slave labor to catch and process fish for its popular Fancy Feast cat food, in early 2015, Nestlé commissioned Verité[39], a human rights watchdog, to conduct an investigation into six of its production sites in Thailand. Verité conducted a three-month assessment into the possibility of forced labor and human trafficking in Nestlé's Thai supply chain. The investigation was targeted specifically at the vessel-to-market place shrimp and fishmeal supply chain. Verité interviewed more than 100 people, including about 80 workers from Myanmar and Cambodia, as well as boat owners, shrimp farm owners, site supervisors, and representatives of Nestlé's suppliers. It visited fishing ports, fishmeal packing plants, shrimp farms, and docked fishing boats in Thailand. Verite found indicators of forced labor, human trafficking, and child labor present in land and sea-based workers at the sites assessed. These indicators included deceptive recruitment practices, little or no employment protections for workers, restriction on the freedom of movement of workers, and instances of both verbal and physical abuse.

According to the Verité study, workers were either sold as slaves to seafood suppliers in Thailand, or trapped in the fishing industry through false promises and debt bondage. Often trafficked from Thailand's neighboring countries such as Cambodia and Myanmar, the laborers were sold to fishing boat captains needing crews to man their fishing boats, according to the report. The work was strenuous with shifts lasting up to 20 hours a day with little or no pay and refusal to work to a supervisor's satisfaction led to beatings or sometimes even death. "Sometimes, the net is too heavy and workers get pulled into the water and just disappear. When someone dies, he gets thrown into the water. Some have fallen overboard,"[40] said a Burmese worker to Verité.

While Nestlé had publicly accepted the findings of the report, Verité said this problem was not unique to Nestlé's supply chain but rather "systemic in nature" within the vulnerable migrant worker communities in Thailand.

Meanwhile, in August 2015, pet-food buyers filed a class-action lawsuit against Nestlé for importing fish-based pet food [41] from suppliers in Thailand who used slave labor. According to the lawsuit, *Nestlé* supported a system of slave labor and human trafficking to distribute and market its Purina brand Fancy Feast cat food while hiding its involvement in human rights violations from the public. Nestlé had partnered with Thai Union Frozen Products PCL to import seafood-based pet food for its Purina pet food brand. Melanie Barber, the plaintiff, alleged that Nestlé had violated consumer protection statutes by failing to disclose that some ingredients in its cat food products contained seafood which was sourced from forced labor. She argued that Nestlé was obliged to make additional disclosures at the point of sale regarding the probability that the product contained seafood sourced from forced labor.

According to Berman, "By hiding this from public view, Nestlé has effectively tricked millions of consumers into supporting and encouraging slave labor on floating prisons. It's a fact that the thousands of purchasers of its top-selling pet food products would not have bought this brand had they known the truth – that hundreds of individuals are enslaved, beaten or even murdered in the production of its pet food."[42]

The alleged violations were brought under the California Unfair Competition Law (UCL), the California Legal Remedies Act, and the California False Advertising law. Nestlé applied for the lawsuit to be dismissed, arguing that it could rely on so-called 'safe harbor' provisions, as the company had made specific disclosures on forced labor issues as required by the California Transparency in Supply Chain Acts of 2010.

After fending off allegations, in November 2015, Nestlé took observers by surprise when it publicly admitted that its seafood supply chain was tainted by modern slavery. The company emphasized that "no other company sourcing seafood from Thailand, the world's third-largest seafood exporter, could have avoided being exposed to the same risks."[43] In 2015, Batato in a brave move self-reported that Nestlé had uncovered child labor exploitation on fishing boats in Thailand that supplied its factories. According to industry observers, the disclosure came as a surprise as international companies rarely acknowledged abuses in their supply chains. Some analysts felt that Nestlé's voluntary disclosure could boost its ethical image and possibly shift the parameters of what could be expected of businesses when it came to supply chain accountability. "Nestlé's decision to conduct this investigation is to be applauded. If you've got one of the biggest brands in the world proactively coming out and admitting that they have found slavery in their business operations, then it's potentially a huge game-changer and could lead to real and sustained change in how supply chains are managed,"[44] said Nick Grono, CEO of NGO the Freedom Fund.

In December 2015, the Central District of California dismissed the lawsuit on the grounds that the California Act had created a 'safe harbor' under which companies were sheltered from liability when they accurately complied with the limited disclosure obligations that the law mandated.

Following Verité's investigation and its own admission, Nestlé launched an action plan on seafood sourced from Thailand which included a series of actions to protect workers from abuses and improve working conditions—see Exhibit 9. The plan included commitments to establish an emergency response team with various partners to remediate risks and take short-term action to protect workers,

EXHIBIT 9   Responsible Sourcing of Seafood - Thailand Action Plan 2015-2016

Objective	Action
Incorporate new business requirements into commercial relationship, based on the current signature of the Nestlé Supplier Code.	• Work closely with suppliers to ensure development and implementation of capacity building programs and business requirements that address human rights and labor standards and demonstrate compliance on an ongoing basis. • At a minimum the supplier shall run a traceability system enabling the identification of all potential origins (farms, mills, back to fishing vessels) linked with seafood and other ingredients used as part of product recipes. • Additionally the supplier shall operate a seafood responsible sourcing program to ensure that origins identified are continuously assessed and assisted in meeting business requirements detailed in the Nestlé Responsible Sourcing Guidelines.
Enforce traceable supply chains identifying all potential sources of origins as part of a comprehensive supply chain risk assessment.	• Ensure a verifiable supply chain traceability system as part of a comprehensive supply chain risk assessment that is aligned with industry partners and stakeholders within the Thailand Seafood Industry enabling traceability of seafood ingredients from fishing vessels through the complete supply chain to the receiving manufacturing sites and finished products.
Define and communicate requirements to boat owners and/or captains, including recruitment practices and living/ working conditions for boat workers.	• Building on the Marine Catch Purchasing Document, or any other industry recognized best practice, create a set of requirements for boat owners and captains. • Requirements will cover traceability, recruitment practices, fish catching system, living and working conditions for boat workers. • A toolkit composed of Employment Contract Template and rules, Worker ID cards, template to monitor worker's names, working time, salary, and associated deductions if any.
Implement a training program for boat owners and/or captains.	• In association with industry partners and stakeholders within the Thailand Seafood Industry, create a training hub to generate awareness and provide education to ensure effective worker protections in priority areas as determined by Verité. • The training hub may take the form of a "demonstration boat" or "university" where a training program will be given to electable boat owners/captains. • As reward and enabler for continuous improvement, the program will include a mechanism to apply for financial support to speed up the implementation of best practices learned. • Award financial support in the form of sponsoring or micro credit, for instance, for boat lodging and cooking facilities.
Implement an awareness raising campaign on human rights and labor conditions, targeting primarily boat workers.	• In collaboration with local authority and industry partners and stakeholders in the Thailand Seafood Industry, create an awareness raising campaign addressing the areas of labor standards & health and safety at the workplace. • Campaign to be deployed in locations identified as impactful for migrant workforce & linked with regular boat's docking, including the introduction of a grievance mechanism & providing some immediate tangible personal benefits to workers. • Campaign will incorporate an anonymous reporting system to identify the worst form of labor conditions to be addressed by the Emergency Response Team.
Enable the work of a Migrant Workforce Emergency Response team.	• Identify a third party partner (e.g., project Issara, to be considered) experienced in protecting individuals from the worst form of labor conditions. • Deploy and empower this partner organization as the Migrant Workforce Emergency Response Team in charge to deploy the necessary assessments to identify individuals in need of immediate assistance.
Create and implement a fishing vessels verification program.	• Implement, at first, an internal audit program verifying working (labor and health and safety at workplace) conditions in fishing vessels for 100 percent of the fleet used. • Along with monitoring of compliance through Key Performance Indicators, randomly select boats on a monthly basis to undergo a third-party verification audit by an independent organization, executed every quarter. • Third party verification audit should include interview of boat workers and establish the history of their working career in the region and country.

(continued)

Objective	Action
Dedicate resources.	• Appoint an executive from Nestlé to implement the action plan. His profile will include coordination with relevant parties, management of implementation activities, establishment of KPIs and dashboard, effective use of internal and financial resources, representation to relevant industry parties and stakeholders.
Collaborate and scale up	• Leverage opportunities for collaboration with industry partners and stakeholders with the Thailand Seafood Industry and seek to become a member of the Shrimp Sustainable Supply Chain Taskforce, share progress on implementation of action plan and learning, contribute to testing of innovative solutions and continuously seek to expand implementation to other supply schemes and locations in South East Asia. • Achieve similar aims as part of the Good Labor Practices Working Group, convened by Government of Thailand and supported by the International Labor Organization.
Publicly Report	• Report publicly on progress, including challenges and failures identified with how to best resolve and solutions to address. This should include ongoing monitoring of business partners' supply chain management systems by independent third party assessments and identification of risks and issues to be addressed.

Source: https://www.nestle.com/asset-library/documents/library/documents/corporate_social_ responsibility/nestle-seafood-action-plan-thailand-2015-2016.pdf

a grievance mechanism allowing anonymous reporting, a fishing vessel verification program involving regular third-party verification of randomly selected boats to assess working conditions, and a training program for boat owners and captains based on best practices. Batato, said, "As we've said consistently, forced labor and human rights abuses have no place in our supply chain. Nestlé believes that by working with suppliers we can make a positive difference to the sourcing of ingredients."[45] Batato further added that it would be neither a quick nor an easy endeavour, but the company planned to achieve significant progress going forward.

By the end of 2016, over 99 percent of the seafood ingredients that Nestlé sourced from its seafood supply chain in Thailand were traceable back to fishing vessels and farms due to actions taken as part of the plan. Nestlé worked with Verité, its supplier Thai Union, the Royal Thai Government, and the Southeast Asian Fisheries Development Center (SEAFDEC) to develop a training program to educate fishing vessel owners, captains, and crew members on living and working conditions onboard the boats, and on workers' rights. In March 2016, Nestlé partnered with the Issara Institute, a not-for-profit body focusing on worker voice and grievance mechanisms, to help workers voice their concerns.

Experts said Nestlé's disclosures and commitment to change served as an example to other

companies in industries in which labor trafficking and slavery were rampant. Praising Nestlé for self-policing and public reporting, Mark Lagon, president of nonprofit anti-trafficking organization Freedom House, said, "It's unusual and exemplary. The propensity of the PR and legal departments of companies is not to 'fess up, not to even say they are carefully looking into a problem for fear that they will get hit with lawsuits."[46]

CRITICISM

Though Nestlé was applauded for its admission of forced labor within its seafood supply chain and its move toward transparency, some analysts felt that this was just an attempt by the company to cover up bigger allegations of child labor in its profitable chocolate making business. They felt that in order to escape the charges of being an unethical company, Nestlé had admitted to slavery in seafood suppliers, a low-profit area of the company's business, in Thailand. Some critics saw Nestlé's actions as a public relations stunt to alleviate the criticism it had received for abetting child slavery in Ivory Coast. "For me there is a big issue with one part of Nestlé saying, 'OK we have been dragged along with everyone else to face the issue of slavery in Thailand and so let's take the initiative and do something about it', and at the same time fighting tooth and nail through the courts to avoid charges of child slavery in its core operations in the Ivory Coast,"[47] remarked Andrew Wallis, CEO of anti-human trafficking charity Unseen UK. Analysts said that this apparent double standard had raised doubts among civil society activists and customers regarding Nestlé's true motives. Critics said by its admission, Nestlé had left consumers falsely confident in the 'goodness' of its products.

Some anti-trafficking advocates remained highly skeptical of Nestlé's actions and saw the move toward transparency as a tactic to deflate other pending civil litigation suits in its cocoa supply chains. They said Nestlé had been falsely assuring customers that it would eliminate child and forced labor in its Ivory Coast supply chain since 2001 and in the meantime

an entire generation of children in West Africa had been suffering due to Nestlé's false promises.

Nestlé's admission that it had found slavery in its supply chain in Thailand was greeted with a negative reaction from both traditional and social media. According to the LexisNexis Newsdesk[48] analysis, mentions of Nestlé in relation to slavery rose steeply with 20 to 90 articles per week, discussing slavery in the company's supply chain. According to the sentiment chart presented in Exhibit 10, more than a third of the coverage was entirely negative, while only 2.5 percent was positive.

Some analysts contended that Nestlé's efforts to eliminate child labor from its global cocoa supply chain were not credible because of its inadequately transparent self-monitoring system. For instance,

EXHIBIT 10   Nestle's Media Coverage Related to Slavery

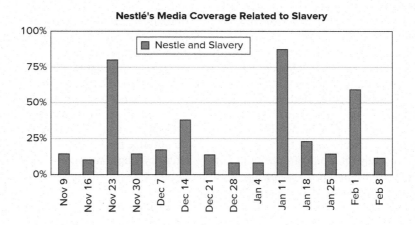

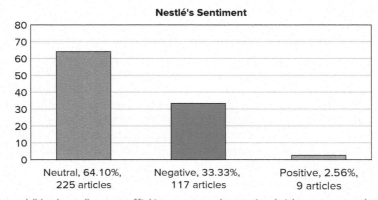

Source: https://bis.lexisnexis.co.uk/blog/posts/human-trafficking-awareness/reputational-risks-are-greater-than-ever-for-brands-associated-with-slavery

they pointed out that the company provided incomplete and insufficient information regarding the details of TNCP and its certification schemes and had omitted material information related to TNCP's distribution and progress in the rest of its global cocoa supply chain. Some analysts pointed out that the FLA investigation was not an accurate representation of the conditions on Nestlé's cocoa farms because a majority of Nestlé's cocoa farms (about 75 percent) were not part of TNCP. They also said that there was significant discrepancy between Nestlé's grand official policies and statements to combat slavery and the nominal actions it took. Nestlé had yet to develop a concrete plan outlining when it would source entirely sustainable cocoa. They said that TNCP was only a greenwashing ploy aimed at making Nestlé appear to be ethically responsible.

Nestlé received some respite in March 2017, when U.S. District Judge Stephen V. Wilson dismissed the case on child slavery in Africa on the ground that the complaint *"seeks an impermissible extraterritorial application of the Alien Tort Statute which means companies can be sued in the United States for actions outside the country but only when some conduct touches and concerns the United States with sufficient force."*[49] He said that the former child slaves could not sue in the United States over wrongdoing that had occurred in Africa. The judge said that the plaintiffs' attempt to single out CSR initiatives as evidence that Nestlé was knowingly aiding and abetting child slavery was counter-productive because it would freeze companies' speech and prevent them from taking up such initiatives in the future. He said, "Even worse, relying on corporate social responsibility programs as 'relevant conduct' would also chill corporations from creating these programs. Corporations would be incentivized to allow human rights abuses to occur without shedding light on the issue or trying to combat it out of fear they will displace the presumption and be held responsible."[50]

THE WAY FORWARD

In April 2019, a federal court in California filed a fresh class action lawsuit against Nestlé over claims the company mislabelled its products as sustainable when, in fact, it sourced its cocoa from farms that caused environmental devastation and used child slave labor. However, Nestlé said that it had prevailed in similar law suits earlier as it was committed to eliminate forced labor from its supply chain. "Forced child labor is unacceptable and has no place in our supply chain. We have explicit policies against it and are working with other stakeholders to combat this global social problem. Regrettably, in bringing such lawsuits, the plaintiffs' class action lawyers are targeting the very organizations trying to fight forced labor,"[51] said a Nestlé spokesperson.

Going forward, analysts said that identifying and tackling the menace of modern slavery in its cocoa supply chain would not be an easy task for Nestlé. Nestlé's cocoa supply chain was complex, and regulating the co-operatives and farms could be tough for the senior management, they said. It would be challenging to continually follow up on the work of co-operatives given their remote locations, they added. Though Nestlé had monitoring systems in place to communicate supplier policies and conduct audits, they often covered only tier one suppliers at the top of the value chain, while forced labor was mostly found in the bottom tiers. Moreover, cost and pricing pressures, supplier engagement, and transparency dilemmas were some of the issues Nestlé had to deal with while addressing slavery. "The problem is, we can't just stop using a supplier. People ask why we don't boycott them. We did that in the case of palm oil. We delisted suppliers. We delisted coffee suppliers in South America who were using child labor. But it doesn't always solve the bigger problem. There is no one-size fits all solution. If we took the view to delist every single supplier who is doing the wrong thing today, it will not improve the situation. It will cut the income of those who rely on this income. It is lose-lose. But, with our size, we believe we can change things over time,"[52] said Batato.

Modern slavery was considered as a criminal activity often actively hidden by perpetrators, making it difficult to detect. Third party auditors appointed by Nestlé might struggle to get full access to facilities and victims would be unwilling to speak up fearing retribution.

Another challenge would be driving workers toward community awareness-raising sessions. Some families were often resistant to change as they had few livelihood alternatives. Moreover, the isolation of some of the farms and villages was a challenge in itself. Supplying school kits and providing literacy classes to women were all the more difficult as a result. Some researchers found that though Nestlé's code of conduct prohibited the use of child labor in its supply chain, awareness of the code was low among farmers. Moreover, the farmers did not attend training sessions either due to lack of interest or lack of time. "Being a leader in our industry . . . we do understand we can influence the supply chains we work with, and that's what we do. We recognize it is a difficult issue to deal with,"[53] said Marco Goncalves, Nestlé's chief procurement officer.

Analysts said that given its global scale and financial prowess, Nestlé could play a crucial role in driving significant changes and abolishing slavery from the global cocoa supply chain. Going forward, the question before Nestlé was what more the company could do to ensure its cocoa supply chain was free from slavery. How could it assure consumers that its products did not come at the expense of innocent people who went through untold suffering. Could Nestlé have a positive impact on the chocolate industry through its honest revelations and by raising the bar on labor protection? Should the company take a clear leadership position on this issue given its influence? If so, how should Nestlé go about doing this?

ENDNOTES

[1] Ivory Coast, also known as Cote d'Ivoire, is a tropical country in southern West Africa. It is the world's largest producer of cocoa, the raw ingredient used in making chocolates.

[2] Faaez Samedi, "Nestlé Admits Forced Labor is Part of its Seafood Supply Chain," www.campaignlive.co.uk, November 27, 2015.

[3] Marianne Smallwood "Slavery Found within Nestle's Seafood Supply Chain . . . Now What?" www.triplepundit.com, December 14, 2015.

[4] Mark Hawthorne, "One Step at a Time, Nestle Slowly Changes its Ways," www.smh.com.au, February 24, 2017.

[5] "Annual Results 2016," www.nestle.com.

[6] "Nestle's 12 Dark Secrets Worldwide!" www.theequalizerpost.wordpress.com, November 18, 2010.

[7] Jon Entine, "Greenpeace and Social Media Mob Nestlé," www.blog.american.com, March 31, 2010.

[8] "Nestlé's 12 Dark Secrets Worldwide!" www.theequalizerpost.wordpress.com, November 18, 2010.

[9] Baby formula is food manufactured for supporting the adequate growth of infants.

[10] "Starbucks as Fairtrade-lite and Nestle on the Blacklist," www.faircompanies.com, October 8, 2008.

[11] "Pepsi and Nestlé Backlisted for Water Pollution in China," www.polarisinstitute .org/pepsi_and_nestle_backlisted_for_water_pollution_in_china.

[12] "Nestlé's Sinking Division," www .polarisinstitute.org/nestl%C3%A9%E2%80% 99s_sinking_division.

[13] The ECRA is a not-for-profit, multi-stakeholder co-operative, dedicated to the promotion of universal human rights, environmental sustainability, and animal welfare.

[14] The Ethiscore is a numerical rating that differentiates companies based on the level of criticism that they have attracted. Generally, an Ethiscore of 15 would be the best, while 0 would be the worst.

[15] Fair trade coffee is one that is obtained directly from the growers. It usually retails at a higher price than standard coffee.

[16] "Starbucks as Fairtrade-lite and Nestlé on the Blacklist," www.faircompanies.com, October 8, 2008.

[17] Abby Haglage, "Lawsuit: Your Candy Bar Was Made by Child Slaves," www.thedailybeast.com, September 30, 2015.

[18] LJ Vanier, "Hershey, Nestle and Mars Use Child Slaves to Make Your Chocolate," http://thespiritscience.net, October 18, 2015.

[19] In 2001, the Chocolate Manufacturers Association of the US signed the protocol for the growing and processing of cocoa beans and their derivative products in a manner that complied with ILO Convention 182 concerning the prohibition and immediate action for the elimination of the worst forms of child labor.

[20] The Archer Daniels Midland Co is a US-based global food processing and commodities trading corporation.

[21] Based in Minnesota, US, Cargill Inc is a provider of food, agriculture, financial, and industrial products and services worldwide.

[22] Daniel Fisher, "Cue The Documentary: Nestlé Still Fighting Slavery Lawsuit by Foreign Plaintiffs," www.forbes.com, October 7, 2016.

[23] Established in 2012, The International Cocoa Initiative (ICI) is a multi-stakeholder partnership between cocoa companies, labor unions, and NGOs in order to eliminate the worst forms of child labor and forced labor in the growing and processing of cocoa beans.

[24] https://www.nestle.com.au/creating-shared-value/social-impact/the-nestl%C3%A9-cocoa-plan

[25] Fair Labor Association is a non-profit multi-stakeholder initiative that works with major companies to improve working conditions in their supply chains.

[26] Pisteurs are individuals commissioned to buy cocoa beans from farmers.

[27] Traitants are middlemen, licensed by the government, who trades cocoa beans. Traitants may source beans either from cooperatives or from pisteurs.

[28] Métayers are sharecroppers who manage a cocoa farm on behalf of its owner.

[29] Coxers are individuals who live in the villages and inform pisteurs when there is a harvest ready to be collected.

[30] Abby Haglage, "Lawsuit: Your Candy Bar Was Made by Child Slaves," www.thedailybeast.com, September 30, 2015.

[31] "Nestle 'to Act over Child Labour in Cocoa Industry'," www.bbc.com, November 28, 2011.

[32] "Nestle - Truth in Advertising," www .truthinadvertising.org, September 28, 2015.

[33] Ellen Wulfhorst, "U.S. Supreme Court Gives Boost to Child Slave Labor Case Against Nestle,"www.reuters.com, January 14, 2016.

[34] Nestle CSV Full Report 2019.

[35] Joe Sandler Clarke, "Child Labour on Nestlé Farms: Chocolate Giant's Problems Continue," www.theguardian.com, September 2, 2015.

[36] The Danish Institute for Human Rights is Denmark's independent state-funded human rights institution.

[37] Previously, Batato served as the CEO and Managing Director of Nestle Pakistan Limited from June 6, 2012 to September 1, 2015 and May 25, 2012 to September 1, 2015, respectively. He has extensive experience in the manufacturing and technical area, combined with business experience in both developed and emerging markets.

[38] UTZ Certified is a program and a label for sustainable farming.

[39] Verité is a Massachusetts-based non-profit organization that advocates workers' rights worldwide.

[40] James Tennent, "Nestlé Admits Forced Labour, Trafficking, and Child Labour in its Thai Seafood Supply," www.ibtimes.co.uk, November 24, 2015.

[41] The fishmeal used to feed farmed shrimp and a prawn is made from fish caught by migrant workers. The US is the biggest customer of Thai fish, and pet food is among the fastest growing exports from Thailand. In 2014, Thai Union shipped more than 28 million pounds of seafood-based cat and dog food for some of the top brands sold in America including Iams, Meow Mix, and Fancy Feast.

[42] "Nestle Accused of Using Slave-Caught Fish in Cat Food," www.nationmultimedia.com, August 28, 2015.

[43] Annie Kelly, "Nestlé Admits Slavery in Thailand While Fighting Child Labour Lawsuit in Ivory Coast," www.theguardian.com, February 1, 2016.

[44] "Control Over Supply Chain a Must," www.pressreader.com, November 5, 2016.

[45] Annie Kelly, "Nestlé Admits Slavery in Thailand While Fighting Child Labour Lawsuit in Ivory Coast," www.theguardian.com, February 1, 2016.

[46] Marthe Mendoza, "Nestle Confirms Labor Abuse among its Thai Seafood Suppliers," www.ap.org, November 23, 2015.

[47] Claire Bernish, "Why is Nestle Finally Admitting to Using Slave Labor?" www.mintpressnews.com, February 2, 2016.

[48] LexisNexis is a global provider of legal, regulatory and business information and analytics.

[49] "Nestlé, Cargill and ADM Cocoa Child Slavery Lawsuit Dismissed," www.confectionerynews.com, March 15, 2017.

[50] Daniel Fisher, "Judge Tosses Nestlé Suit Over Child Slavery in Africa," www.forbes.com, March 13, 2017.

[51] "USA: Class Action Lawsuit Filed Against Nestle for Child Slavery on Cocoa Harvest in West African Farms, " https://www.business-humanrights.org, April 24, 2019.

[52] Mark Hawthorne, "One Step at a Time, Nestle Slowly Changes its Ways," www.smh.com.au, February 24, 2017.

[53] Katie Nguyen, "All Companies Have Slave Labour in Supply Chains but it Can be Stopped-Tesco," www.reuters.com, November 18, 2015.

Guide to Case Analysis

I keep six honest serving men
(They taught me all I knew);
Their names are What and Why and When;
And How and Where and Who.

Rudyard Kipling

In most courses in strategic management, students use cases about actual companies to practice strategic analysis and to gain some experience in the tasks of crafting and implementing strategy. A case sets forth, in a factual manner, the events and organizational circumstances surrounding a particular managerial situation. It puts readers at the scene of the action and familiarizes them with all the relevant circumstances. A case on strategic management can concern a whole industry, a single organization, or some part of an organization; the organization involved can be either profit seeking or not-for-profit. The essence of the student's role in case analysis is to diagnose and size up the situation described in the case and then to recommend appropriate action steps.

WHY USE CASES TO PRACTICE STRATEGIC MANAGEMENT?

> A student of business with tact
> Absorbed many answers he lacked.
> But acquiring a job,
> He said with a sob,
> "How does one fit answer to fact?"

The foregoing limerick was used some years ago by Professor Charles Gragg to characterize the plight of business students who had no exposure to cases.[1] The facts are that the mere act of listening to lectures and sound advice about managing does little for anyone's management skills and that the accumulated managerial wisdom cannot effectively be passed on by lectures and assigned readings alone. If anything had been learned about the practice of management, it is that a storehouse of ready-made textbook answers does not exist. Each managerial situation has unique aspects, requiring its own diagnosis, judgment, and tailor-made actions. Cases provide would-be managers with a valuable way to practice wrestling with the actual problems of actual managers in actual companies.

The case approach to strategic analysis is, first and foremost, an exercise in learning by doing. Because cases provide you with detailed information about conditions and problems of different industries and companies, your task of analyzing company after company and situation after situation has the twin benefit of boosting your analytical skills and exposing you to the ways companies and managers actually do things. Most college students have limited managerial backgrounds and only fragmented knowledge about companies and real-life strategic situations. Cases help substitute for on-the-job experience by (1) giving you broader exposure to a variety of industries, organizations, and strategic problems; (2) forcing you to assume a managerial role (as opposed to that of just an onlooker); (3) providing a test of how to apply the tools and techniques of strategic management; and (4) asking you to come up with pragmatic managerial action plans to deal with the issues at hand.

Objectives of Case Analysis

Using cases to learn about the practice of strategic management is a powerful way for you to accomplish five things:[2]

1. Increase your understanding of what managers should and should not do in guiding a business to success.

2. Build your skills in sizing up company resource strengths and weaknesses and in conducting strategic analysis in a variety of industries and competitive situations.

3. Get valuable practice in identifying strategic issues that need to be addressed, evaluating strategic alternatives, and formulating workable plans of action.

4. Enhance your sense of business judgment, as opposed to uncritically accepting the authoritative crutch of the professor or "back-of-the-book" answers.

5. Gain in-depth exposure to different industries and companies, thereby acquiring something close to actual business experience.

If you understand that these are the objectives of case analysis, you are less likely to be consumed with curiosity about "the answer to the case." Students who have grown comfortable with and accustomed to textbook statements of fact and definitive lecture notes are often frustrated when discussions about a case do not produce concrete answers. Usually, case discussions produce good arguments for more than one course of action. Differences of opinion nearly always exist. Thus, should a class discussion conclude without a strong, unambiguous consensus on what to do, don't grumble too much when you are not told what the answer is or what the company actually did. Just remember that in the business world answers don't come in conclusive black-and-white terms.

There are nearly always several feasible courses of action and approaches, each of which may work out satisfactorily. Moreover, in the business world, when one elects a particular course of action, there is no peeking at the back of a book to see if you have chosen the best thing to do and no one to turn to for a provably correct answer. The best test of whether management action is "right" or "wrong" is results. If the results of an action turn out to be "good," the decision to take it may be presumed "right." If not, then the action chosen was "wrong" in the sense that it didn't work out.

Hence, the important thing for you to understand about analyzing cases is that the managerial exercise of identifying, diagnosing, and recommending is aimed at building your skills of business judgment. Discovering what the company actually did is no more than frosting on the cake—the actions that company managers actually took may or may not be "right" or best (unless there is accompanying evidence that the results of their actions were highly positive).

The point is this: The purpose of giving you a case assignment is not to cause you to run to the library or surf the Internet to discover what the company actually did but, rather, to enhance your skills in sizing up situations and developing your managerial judgment about what needs to be done and how to do it. The aim of case analysis is for you to become actively engaged in diagnosing the business issues and managerial problems posed in the case, to propose workable solutions, and to explain and defend your assessments—this is how cases provide you with meaningful practice at being a manager.

Preparing a Case for Class Discussion

If this is your first experience with the case method, you may have to reorient your study habits. Unlike lecture courses where you can get by without preparing intensively for each class and where you have latitude to work assigned readings and reviews of lecture notes into your schedule, a case assignment requires conscientious preparation before class. You will not get much out of hearing the class discuss a case you haven't read, and you certainly won't be able to contribute anything yourself to the discussion. What you have got to do to get ready for class discussion of a case is to study the case, reflect carefully on the situation presented, and develop some reasoned thoughts.

Your goal in preparing the case should be to end up with what you think is a sound, well-supported analysis of the situation and a sound, defensible set of recommendations about which managerial actions need to be taken.

To prepare a case for class discussion, we suggest the following approach:

1. *Skim the case rather quickly to get an overview of the situation it presents.* This quick overview should give you the general flavor of the situation and indicate the kinds of issues and problems that you will need to wrestle with. If your instructor has provided you with study questions for the case, now is the time to read them carefully.

2. *Read the case thoroughly to digest the facts and circumstances.* On this reading, try to gain full command of the situation presented in the case. Begin to develop some tentative answers to the study questions your instructor has provided. If your instructor has elected not to give you assignment questions, then start forming your own picture of the overall situation being described.

3. *Carefully review all the information presented in the exhibits.* Often, there is an important story in the numbers contained in the exhibits. Expect the information in the case exhibits to be crucial enough to materially affect your diagnosis of the situation.

4. *Decide what the strategic issues are.* Until you have identified the strategic issues and problems in the case, you don't know what to analyze, which tools and analytical techniques are called for, or otherwise how to proceed. At times the strategic issues are clear—either being stated in the case or else obvious from reading the case. At other times you will have to dig them out from all the information given; if so, the study questions will guide you.

5. *Start your analysis of the issues with some number crunching.* A big majority of strategy cases call for some kind of number crunching—calculating assorted financial ratios to check out the company's financial condition and recent performance, calculating growth rates of sales or profits or unit volume, checking out profit margins and the makeup of the cost structure, and understanding whatever revenue-cost-profit relationships are present. See Table 1 for a summary of key financial ratios, how they are calculated, and what they show.

6. ***Apply the concepts and techniques of strategic analysis you have been studying.*** Strategic analysis is not just a collection of opinions; rather, it entails applying the concepts and analytical tools described in Chapters 1 through 12 to cut beneath the surface and produce sharp insight and understanding. Every case assigned is strategy related and presents you with an opportunity to usefully apply what you have learned. Your instructor is looking for you to demonstrate that you know how and when to use the material presented in the text chapters.

7. ***Check out conflicting opinions and make some judgments about the validity of all the data and information provided.*** Many times cases report views and contradictory opinions (after all, people don't always agree on things, and different people see the same things in different ways). Forcing you to evaluate the data and information presented in the case helps you develop your powers of inference and judgment. Asking you to resolve conflicting information "comes with the territory" because a great many managerial situations entail opposing points of view, conflicting trends, and sketchy information.

8. ***Support your diagnosis and opinions with reasons and evidence.*** The most important things to prepare for are your answers to the question "Why?" For instance, if after studying the case you are of the opinion that the company's managers are doing a poor job, then it is your answer to "Why?" that establishes just how good your analysis of the situation is. If your instructor has provided you with specific study questions for the case, by all means prepare answers that include all the reasons and number-crunching evidence you can muster to support your diagnosis. If you are using study questions provided by the instructor, generate at least two pages of notes!

9. ***Develop an appropriate action plan and set of recommendations.*** Diagnosis divorced from corrective action is sterile. The test of a manager is always to convert sound analysis into sound actions—actions that will produce the desired results. Hence, the final and most telling step in preparing a case is to develop an action agenda for management that lays out a set of specific recommendations on what to do. Bear in mind that proposing realistic, workable solutions is far preferable to casually tossing out off-the-top-of-your-head suggestions. Be prepared to argue why your recommendations are more attractive than other courses of action that are open.

As long as you are conscientious in preparing your analysis and recommendations, and have ample reasons, evidence, and arguments to support your views, you shouldn't fret unduly about whether what you've prepared is "the right answer" to the case. In case analysis, there is rarely just one right approach or set of recommendations. Managing companies and crafting and executing strategies are not such exact sciences that there exists a single provably correct analysis and action plan for each strategic situation. Of course, some analyses and action plans are better than others; but, in truth, there's nearly always more than one good way to analyze a situation and more than one good plan of action.

Participating in Class Discussion of a Case

Classroom discussions of cases are sharply different from attending a lecture class. In a case class, students do most of the talking. The instructor's role is to solicit student participation, keep the discussion on track, ask "Why?" often, offer alternative views, play the devil's advocate (if no students jump in to offer opposing views), and otherwise lead the discussion. The students in the class carry the burden for analyzing the situation and for being prepared to present and defend their diagnoses and recommendations. Expect a classroom environment, therefore, that calls for your size-up of the situation, your analysis, what actions you would take, and why you would take them. Do not be dismayed if, as the class discussion unfolds, some insightful things are said by your fellow classmates that you did not think of. It is normal for views and analyses to differ and for the comments of others in the class to expand your own thinking about the case. As the old adage goes, "Two heads are better than one." So it is to be expected that the class as a whole will do a more penetrating and searching job of case analysis than will any one person working alone. This is the power of group effort, and its virtues are that it will help you see more analytical applications, let you test your analyses and judgments against those of your peers, and force you to wrestle with differences of opinion and approaches.

TABLE 1   Key Financial Ratios: How to Calculate Them and What They Mean

Ratio	How Calculated	What It Shows
Profitability ratios		
1. Gross profit margin	$\dfrac{\text{Sales} - \text{Cost of goods sold}}{\text{Sales}}$	Shows the percentage of revenues available to cover operating expenses and yield a profit. Higher is better and the trend should be upward.
2. Operating profit margin (or return on sales)	$\dfrac{\text{Sales} - \text{Operating expenses}}{\text{Sales}}$ or $\dfrac{\text{Operating income}}{\text{Sales}}$	Shows the profitability of current operations without regard to interest charges and income taxes. Higher is better and the trend should be upward.
3. Net profit margin (or net return on sales)	$\dfrac{\text{Profits after taxes}}{\text{Sales}}$	Shows after-tax profits per dollar of sales. Higher is better and the trend should be upward.
4. Total return on assets	$\dfrac{\text{Profits after taxes} + \text{Interest}}{\text{Total assets}}$	A measure of the return on total monetary investment in the enterprise. Interest is added to after-tax profits to form the numerator since total assets are financed by creditors as well as by stockholders. Higher is better and the trend should be upward.
5. Net return on total assets (ROA)	$\dfrac{\text{Profits after taxes}}{\text{Total assets}}$	A measure of the return earned by stockholders on the firm's total assets. Higher is better, and the trend should be upward.
6. Return on stockholder's equity (ROE)	$\dfrac{\text{Profits after taxes}}{\text{Total stockholders' equity}}$	Shows the return stockholders are earning on their capital investment in the enterprise. A return in the 12–15% range is "average," and the trend should be upward.
7. Return on invested capital (ROIC)—sometimes referred to as return on capital employed (ROCE)	$\dfrac{\text{Profits after taxes}}{\text{Long-term debt} + \text{Total stockholders' equity}}$	A measure of the return shareholders are earning on the long-term monetary capital invested in the enterprise. A higher return reflects greater bottom-line effectiveness in the use of long-term capital, and the trend should be upward.
8. Earnings per share (EPS)	$\dfrac{\text{Profits after taxes}}{\text{Number of shares of common stock outstanding}}$	Shows the earnings for each share of common stock outstanding. The trend should be upward, and the bigger the annual percentage gains, the better.
Liquidity ratios		
1. Current ratio	$\dfrac{\text{Current assets}}{\text{Current liabilities}}$	Shows a firm's ability to pay current liabilities using assets that can be converted into cash in the near term. Ratio should definitely be higher than 1.0; ratios of 2 or higher are better still.
2. Working capital	Current assets − Current liabilities	Bigger amounts are better because the company has more internal funds available to (1) pay its current liabilities on a timely basis and (2) finance inventory expansion, additional accounts receivable, and a larger base of operations without resorting to borrowing or raising more equity capital.
Leverage ratios		
1. Total debt-to-assets ratio	$\dfrac{\text{Total liabilities}}{\text{Total assets}}$	Measures the extent to which borrowed funds have been used to finance the firm's operations. Low fractions or ratios are better—high fractions indicate overuse of debt and greater risk of bankruptcy.
2. Long-term debt-to-capital ratio	$\dfrac{\text{Long-term debt}}{\text{Long-term debt} + \text{Total stockholders' equity}}$	An important measure of creditworthiness and balance sheet strength. Indicates the percentage of capital investment that has been financed by creditors and bondholders. Fractions or ratios below .25 or 25% are usually quite satisfactory since monies invested

(Continued)

TABLE 1   (*Continued*)

Ratio	How Calculated	What It Shows
Leverage ratios (Continued)		
		by stockholders account for 75% or more of the company's total capital. The lower the ratio, the greater the capacity to borrow additional funds. Debt-to-capital ratios above 50% and certainly above 75% indicate a heavy and perhaps excessive reliance on debt, lower creditworthiness, and weak balance sheet strength.
3. Debt-to-equity ratio	$\dfrac{\text{Total liabilities}}{\text{Total stockholders' equity}}$	Should usually be less than 1.0. High ratios (especially above 1.0) signal excessive debt, lower creditworthiness, and weaker balance sheet strength.
4. Long-term debt-to-equity ratio	$\dfrac{\text{Long-term debt}}{\text{Total stockholders' equity}}$	Shows the balance between debt and equity in the firm's *long-term* capital structure. Low ratios indicate greater capacity to borrow additional funds if needed.
5. Times-interest-earned (or coverage) ratio	$\dfrac{\text{Operating income}}{\text{Interest expenses}}$	Measures the ability to pay annual interest charges. Lenders usually insist on a minimum ratio of 2.0, but ratios above 3.0 signal better creditworthiness.
Activity ratios		
1. Days of inventory	$\dfrac{\text{Inventory}}{\text{Cost of goods sold} \div 365}$	Measures inventory management efficiency. Fewer days of inventory are usually better.
2. Inventory turnover	$\dfrac{\text{Cost of goods sold}}{\text{Inventory}}$	Measures the number of inventory turns per year. Higher is better.
3. Average collection period	$\dfrac{\text{Accounts receivable}}{\text{Total sales revenues} \div 365}$ or $\dfrac{\text{Accounts receivable}}{\text{Average daily sales}}$	Indicates the average length of time the firm must wait after making a sale to receive cash payment. A shorter collection time is better.
Other important measures of financial performance		
1. Dividend yield on common stock	$\dfrac{\text{Annual dividends per share}}{\text{Current market price per share}}$	A measure of the return that shareholders receive in the form of dividends. A "typical" dividend yield is 2–3%. The dividend yield for fast-growth companies is often below 1% (maybe even 0); the dividend yield for slow-growth companies can run 4–5%.
2. Price-earnings ratio	$\dfrac{\text{Current market price per share}}{\text{Earnings per share}}$	P-E ratios above 20 indicate strong investor confidence in a firm's outlook and earnings growth; firms whose future earnings are at risk or likely to grow slowly typically have ratios below 12.
3. Dividend payout ratio	$\dfrac{\text{Annual dividends per share}}{\text{Earnings per share}}$	Indicates the percentage of after-tax profits paid out as dividends.
4. Internal cash flow	After-tax profits + Depreciation	A quick and rough estimate of the cash the business is generating after payment of operating expenses, interest, and taxes. Such amounts can be used for dividend payments or funding capital expenditures.
5. Free cash flow	After-tax profits + Depreciation − Capital expenditures − Dividends	A quick and rough estimate of the cash a company's business is generating after payment of operating expenses, interest, taxes, dividends, and desirable reinvestments in the business. The larger a company's free cash flow, the greater is its ability to internally fund new strategic initiatives, repay debt, make new acquisitions, repurchase shares of stock, or increase dividend payments.

To orient you to the classroom environment on the days a case discussion is scheduled, we compiled the following list of things to expect:

1. Expect the instructor to assume the role of extensive questioner and listener.

2. Expect students to do most of the talking. The case method enlists a maximum of individual participation in class discussion. It is not enough to be present as a silent observer; if every student took this approach, there would be no discussion. (Thus, expect a portion of your grade to be based on your participation in case discussions.)

3. Be prepared for the instructor to probe for reasons and supporting analysis.

4. Expect and tolerate challenges to the views expressed. All students have to be willing to submit their conclusions for scrutiny and rebuttal. Each student needs to learn to state his or her views without fear of disapproval and to overcome the hesitation of speaking out. Learning respect for the views and approaches of others is an integral part of case analysis exercises. But there are times when it is OK to swim against the tide of majority opinion. In the practice of management, there is always room for originality and unorthodox approaches. So while discussion of a case is a group process, there is no compulsion for you or anyone else to cave in and conform to group opinions and group consensus.

5. Don't be surprised if you change your mind about some things as the discussion unfolds. Be alert to how these changes affect your analysis and recommendations (in the event you get called on).

6. Expect to learn a lot in class as the discussion of a case progresses; furthermore, you will find that the cases build on one another—what you learn in one case helps prepare you for the next case discussion.

There are several things you can do on your own to be good and look good as a participant in class discussions:

- Although you should do your own independent work and independent thinking, don't hesitate before (and after) class to discuss the case with other students. In real life, managers often discuss the company's problems and situation with other people to refine their own thinking.

- In participating in the discussion, make a conscious effort to contribute, rather than just talk.

There is a big difference between saying something that builds the discussion and offering a long-winded, off-the-cuff remark that leaves the class wondering what the point was.

- Avoid the use of "I think," "I believe," and "I feel"; instead, say, "My analysis shows _____" and "The company should do _____ because _____." Always give supporting reasons and evidence for your views; then your instructor won't have to ask you "Why?" every time you make a comment.

- In making your points, assume that everyone has read the case and knows what it says. Avoid reciting and rehashing information in the case—instead, use the data and information to explain your assessment of the situation and to support your position.

- Bring the printouts of the work you've done on Case-TUTOR or the notes you've prepared (usually two or three pages' worth) to class and rely on them extensively when you speak. There's no way you can remember everything off the top of your head—especially the results of your number crunching. To reel off the numbers or to present all five reasons why, instead of one, you will need good notes. When you have prepared thoughtful answers to the study questions and use them as the basis for your comments, everybody in the room will know you are well prepared, and your contribution to the case discussion will stand out.

Preparing a Written Case Analysis

Preparing a written case analysis is much like preparing a case for class discussion, except that your analysis must be more complete and put in report form. Unfortunately, though, there is no ironclad procedure for doing a written case analysis. All we can offer are some general guidelines and words of wisdom—this is because company situations and management problems are so diverse that no one mechanical way to approach a written case assignment always works.

Your instructor may assign you a specific topic around which to prepare your written report. Or, alternatively, you may be asked to do a comprehensive written case analysis, where the expectation is that you will (1) identify all the pertinent issues that management needs to address, (2) perform whatever analysis and evaluation is appropriate, and (3) propose an action plan and set of recommendations addressing the issues you have identified. In going through the exercise of identify, evaluate, and recommend, keep the following pointers in mind.[3]

Identification   It is essential early on in your written report that you provide a sharply focused diagnosis of strategic issues and key problems and that you demonstrate a good grasp of the company's present situation. Make sure you can identify the firm's strategy (use the concepts and tools in Chapters 1–8 as diagnostic aids) and that you can pinpoint whatever strategy implementation issues may exist (again, consult the material in Chapters 10–12 for diagnostic help). Consult the key points we have provided at the end of each chapter for further diagnostic suggestions. Consider beginning your report with an overview of the company's situation, its strategy, and the significant problems and issues that confront management. State problems/issues as clearly and precisely as you can. Unless it is necessary to do so for emphasis, avoid recounting facts and history about the company (assume your professor has read the case and is familiar with the organization).

Analysis and Evaluation   This is usually the hardest part of the report. Analysis is hard work! Check out the firm's financial ratios, its profit margins and rates of return, and its capital structure, and decide how strong the firm is financially. Table 1 contains a summary of various financial ratios and how they are calculated. Use it to assist in your financial diagnosis. Similarly, look at marketing, production, managerial competence, and other factors underlying the organization's strategic successes and failures. Decide whether the firm has valuable resource strengths and competencies and, if so, whether it is capitalizing on them.

Check to see if the firm's strategy is producing satisfactory results and determine the reasons why or why not. Probe the nature and strength of the competitive forces confronting the company. Decide whether and why the firm's competitive position is getting stronger or weaker. Use the tools and concepts you have learned about to perform whatever analysis and evaluation is appropriate. Work through the case preparation exercise on Case-TUTOR if one is available for the case you've been assigned.

In writing your analysis and evaluation, bear in mind four things:

1. You are obliged to offer analysis and evidence to back up your conclusions. Do not rely on unsupported opinions, over-generalizations, and platitudes as a substitute for tight, logical argument backed up with facts and figures.

2. If your analysis involves some important quantitative calculations, use tables and charts to present the calculations clearly and efficiently. Don't just tack the exhibits on at the end of your report and let the reader figure out what they mean and why they were included. Instead, in the body of your report cite some of the key numbers, highlight the conclusions to be drawn from the exhibits, and refer the reader to your charts and exhibits for more details.

3. Demonstrate that you have command of the strategic concepts and analytical tools to which you have been exposed. Use them in your report.

4. Your interpretation of the evidence should be reasonable and objective. Be wary of preparing a one-sided argument that omits all aspects not favorable to your conclusions. Likewise, try not to exaggerate or overdramatize. Endeavor to inject balance into your analysis and to avoid emotional rhetoric. Strike phrases such as "I think," "I feel," and "I believe" when you edit your first draft and write in "My analysis shows" instead.

Recommendations   The final section of the written case analysis should consist of a set of definite recommendations and a plan of action. Your set of recommendations should address all of the problems/issues you identified and analyzed. If the recommendations come as a surprise or do not follow logically from the analysis, the effect is to weaken greatly your suggestions of what to do. Obviously, your recommendations for actions should offer a reasonable prospect of success. High-risk, bet-the-company recommendations should be made with caution. State how your recommendations will solve the problems you identified. Be sure the company is financially able to carry out what you recommend; also check to see if your recommendations are workable in terms of acceptance by the persons involved, the organization's competence to implement them, and prevailing market and environmental constraints. Try not to hedge or weasel on the actions you believe should be taken.

By all means state your recommendations in sufficient detail to be meaningful—get down to some definite nitty-gritty specifics. Avoid such unhelpful statements as "the organization should do more planning" or "the company should be more aggressive in marketing its product." For instance, if you determine that "the firm should improve its market position," then you need to set forth exactly how you think this should be done. Offer a definite agenda for action, stipulating a timetable and sequence for initiating actions, indicating priorities, and suggesting who should be responsible for doing what.

In proposing an action plan, remember there is a great deal of difference between, on the one hand, being responsible for a decision that may be costly if it proves in error and, on the other hand, casually suggesting courses of action that might be taken when you do not have to bear the responsibility for any of the consequences.

A good rule to follow in making your recommendations is: Avoid recommending anything you would not yourself be willing to do if you were in management's shoes. The importance of learning to develop good managerial judgment is indicated by the fact that, even though the same information and operating data may be available to every manager or executive in an organization, the quality of the judgments about what the information means and which actions need to be taken does vary from person to person.[4]

It goes without saying that your report should be well organized and well written. Great ideas amount to little unless others can be convinced of their merit—this takes tight logic, the presentation of convincing evidence, and persuasively written arguments.

Preparing an Oral Presentation

During the course of your business career it is very likely that you will be called upon to prepare and give a number of oral presentations. For this reason, it is common in courses of this nature to assign cases for oral presentation to the whole class. Such assignments give you an opportunity to hone your presentation skills.

The preparation of an oral presentation has much in common with that of a written case analysis. Both require identification of the strategic issues and problems confronting the company, analysis of industry conditions and the company's situation, and the development of a thorough, well-thought-out action plan. The substance of your analysis and quality of your recommendations in an oral presentation should be no different than in a written report. As with a written assignment, you'll need to demonstrate command of the relevant strategic concepts and tools of analysis and your recommendations should contain

sufficient detail to provide clear direction for management. The main difference between an oral presentation and a written case is in the delivery format. Oral presentations rely principally on verbalizing your diagnosis, analysis, and recommendations and visually enhancing and supporting your oral discussion with colorful, snappy slides (usually created on Microsoft's PowerPoint software).

Typically, oral presentations involve group assignments. Your instructor will provide the details of the assignment—how work should be delegated among the group members and how the presentation should be conducted. Some instructors prefer that presentations begin with issue identification, followed by analysis of the industry and company situation analysis, and conclude with a recommended action plan to improve company performance. Other instructors prefer that the presenters assume that the class has a good understanding of the external industry environment and the company's competitive position and expect the presentation to be strongly focused on the group's recommended action plan and supporting analysis and arguments. The latter approach requires cutting straight to the heart of the case and supporting each recommendation with detailed analysis and persuasive reasoning. Still other instructors may give you the latitude to structure your presentation however you and your group members see fit.

Regardless of the style preferred by your instructor, you should take great care in preparing for the presentation. A good set of slides with good content and good visual appeal is essential to a first-rate presentation. Take some care to choose a nice slide design, font size and style, and color scheme. We suggest including slides covering each of the following areas:

- An opening slide covering the "title" of the presentation and names of the presenters.
- A slide showing an outline of the presentation (perhaps with presenters' names by each topic).
- One or more slides showing the key problems and strategic issues that management needs to address.
- A series of slides covering your analysis of the company's situation.
- A series of slides containing your recommendations and the supporting arguments and reasoning for each recommendation—one slide for each recommendation and the associated reasoning will give it a lot of merit.

You and your team members should carefully plan and rehearse your slide show to maximize impact and minimize distractions. The slide show should include all of the pizzazz necessary to garner the attention of the audience, but not so much that it distracts from the content of what group members are saying to the class. You should remember that the role of slides is to help you communicate your points to the audience. Too many graphics, images, colors, and transitions may divert the audience's attention from what is being said or disrupt the flow of the presentation. Keep in mind that visually dazzling slides rarely hide a shallow or superficial or otherwise flawed case analysis from a perceptive audience. Most instructors will tell you that first-rate slides will definitely enhance a well-delivered presentation, but that impressive visual aids, if accompanied by weak analysis and poor oral delivery, still add up to a substandard presentation.

Researching Companies and Industries via the Internet and Online Data Services

Very likely, there will be occasions when you need to get additional information about some of the assignee cases, perhaps because your instructor has asked you to do further research on the industry or company or because you are simply curious about what has happened to the company since the case was written. These days, it is relatively easy to run down recent industry developments and to find out whether a company's strategic and financial situation has improved, deteriorated, or changed little since the conclusion of the case. The amount of information about companies and industries available on the Internet and through online data services is formidable and expanding rapidly.

It is a fairly simple matter to go to company websites, click on the investor information offerings and press release files, and get quickly to useful information. Most company websites allow you to view or print the company's quarterly and annual reports, its 10-K and 10-Q filings with the Securities and Exchange Commission, and various company press releases of interest. Frequently, a company's website will also provide information about its mission and vision statements, values statements, codes of ethics, and strategy information, as well as charts of the company's stock price. The company's recent press releases typically contain reliable information about what of interest has been going on—new product introductions, recent alliances and partnership agreements, recent acquisitions, summaries of the latest financial results, tidbits about the company's strategy, guidance about future revenues and earnings, and other late-breaking company developments. Some company web pages also include links to the home pages of industry trade associations where you can find information about industry size, growth, recent industry news, statistical trends, and future outlook. Thus, an early step in researching a company on the Internet is always to go to its website and see what's available.

Online Data Services LexisNexis, Bloomberg Financial News Services, and other online subscription services available in many university libraries provide access to a wide array of business reference material. For example, the web-based LexisNexis Academic Universe contains business news articles from general news sources, business publications, and industry trade publications. Broadcast transcripts from financial news programs are also available through LexisNexis, as are full-text 10-Ks, 10-Qs, annual reports, and company profiles for more than 11,000 U.S. and international companies. Your business librarian should be able to direct you to the resources available through your library that will aid you in your research.

Public and Subscription Websites with Good Information Plainly, you can use a search engine such as Google or Yahoo! or MSN to find the latest news on a company or articles written by reporters that have appeared in the business media. These can be very valuable in running down information about recent company developments. However, keep in mind that the information retrieved by a search engine is "unfiltered" and may include sources that are not reliable or that contain inaccurate or misleading information. Be wary of information provided by authors who are unaffiliated with reputable organizations or publications and articles that were published in off-beat sources or on websites with an agenda. Be especially careful in relying on the accuracy of information you find posted on various bulletin boards. Articles covering a company or issue should be copyrighted or published by a reputable source. If you are turning in a paper containing information gathered from the Internet, you should cite your sources (providing the Internet address and date visited); it is also wise to print web pages for your research file (some web pages are updated frequently).

The Wall Street Journal, Bloomberg Businessweek, Forbes, Barron's, and *Fortune* are all good sources of articles on companies. The online edition of *The Wall Street Journal* contains the same information that is available daily in its print version of the paper, but the *WSJ* website also maintains a searchable database of all *The Wall Street Journal* articles published during the past few years. *Fortune* and *Bloomberg Businessweek* also make the content of the most current issue available online to subscribers as well as provide archives sections that allow you to search for articles published during the past few years that may be related to a particular keyword.

The following publications and websites are particularly good sources of company and industry information:

Securities and Exchange Commission EDGAR database (contains company 10-Ks, 10-Qs, etc.)
http://www.sec.gov/edgar/searchedgar/companysearch
Google Finance
http://finance.google.com
CNN Money
http://money.cnn.com
Hoover's Online
http://hoovers.com
The Wall Street Journal Interactive Edition
www.wsj.com
Bloomberg Businessweek
www.businessweek.com and www.bloomberg.com
Fortune
www.fortune.com
MSN Money Central
http://moneycentral.msn.com
Yahoo! Finance
http://finance.yahoo.com/

Some of these Internet sources require subscriptions in order to access their entire databases.

You should always explore the investor relations section of every public company's website. In today's world, these websites typically have a wealth of information concerning a company's mission, core values, performance targets, strategy, recent financial performance, and latest developments (as described in company press releases).

Learning Comes Quickly   With a modest investment of time, you will learn how to use Internet sources and search engines to run down information on companies and industries quickly and efficiently. And it is a skill that will serve you well into the future. Once you become familiar with the data available at different websites mentioned above and learn how to use a search engine, you will know where to go to look for the particular information that you want. Search engines nearly always turn up too many information sources that match your request rather than too few. The trick is to learn to zero in on those most relevant to what you are looking for. Like most things, once you get a little experience under your belt on how to do company and industry research on the Internet, you will be able to readily find the information you need.

The Ten Commandments of Case Analysis

As a way of summarizing our suggestions about how to approach the task of case analysis, we have put together what we like to call "The Ten Commandments of Case Analysis." They are shown in Table 2. If you observe all or even most of these commandments faithfully as you prepare a case either for class discussion or for a written report, your chances of doing a good job on the assigned cases will be much improved. Hang in there, give it your best shot, and have some fun exploring what the real world of strategic management is all about.

TABLE 2   The Ten Commandments of Case Analysis

To be observed in written reports and oral presentations, and while participating in class discussions:

1. Go through the case twice, once for a quick overview and once to gain full command of the facts. Then take care to explore the information in every one of the case exhibits.

2. Make a complete list of the problems and issues that the company's management needs to address.

3. Be thorough in your analysis of the company's situation (make a minimum of one to two pages of notes detailing your diagnosis).

(Continued)

TABLE 2   (Continued)

4. Look for opportunities to apply the concepts and analytical tools in the text chapters—all of the cases in the book have very definite ties to the material in one or more of the text chapters!!!!

5. Do enough number crunching to discover the story told by the data presented in the case. (To help you comply with this commandment, consult Table 1 in this section to guide your probing of a company's financial condition and financial performance.)

6. Support any and all off-the-cuff opinions with well-reasoned arguments and numerical evidence. Don't stop until you can purge "I think" and "I feel" from your assessment and, instead, are able to rely completely on "My analysis shows."

7. Prioritize your recommendations and make sure they can be carried out in an acceptable time frame with the available resources.

8. Support each recommendation with persuasive argument and reasons as to why it makes sense and should result in improved company performance.

9. Review your recommended action plan to see if it addresses all of the problems and issues you identified. Any set of recommendations that does not address all of the issues and problems you identified is incomplete and insufficient.

10. Avoid recommending any course of action that could have disastrous consequences if it doesn't work out as planned. Therefore, be as alert to the downside risks of your recommendations as you are to their upside potential and appeal.

ENDNOTES

[1] Charles I. Gragg, "Because Wisdom Can't Be Told," in *The Case Method at the Harvard Business School,* ed. M. P. McNair (New York: McGraw-Hill, 1954), p. 11.
[2] Ibid., pp. 12–14; and D. R. Schoen and Philip A. Sprague, "What Is the Case Method?" in *The Case Method at the Harvard Business School,* ed. M. P. McNair, pp. 78–79.
[3] For some additional ideas and viewpoints, you may wish to consult Thomas J. Raymond, "Written Analysis of Cases," in *The Case Method at the Harvard Business School,* ed. M. P. McNair, pp. 139–63. Raymond's article includes an actual case, a sample analysis of the case, and a sample of a student's written report on the case.
[4] Gragg, "Because Wisdom Can't Be Told," p. 10.

Company Index

Name Index

Subject Index

A

ACA (Affordable Care Act), C-10
Accommodation market, overview of,
   C-2–C-3
Acquisitions and mergers
   in beer industry, C-12–C-13
   capabilities acquired through, 307
   diversifying by, 226–229
   dynamic capabilities through, 106
   international, 198
   Kraft-Heinz merger, 237
   Nucor Corporation, case, C-355–C-356,
      C-364–C-367
   Spotify, C-113–C-115
   of undervalued companies, 241
Actions defining strategy, 4
Activity, financial ratios on, 94–95
Adaptive cultures, 361, 363
Adaptive strategy adjustments, 9
Advertising. see also Marketing
   Costco Wholesale, case, C-27
   economies of scale in, 130
   GoPro, C-193
   Netflix, case, C-155–C-156
   Starbucks, Inc., case, C-340
Affordable Care Act (ACA), C-10
Alliances and partnerships
   benefits of, 179–180
   capabilities acquired through, 308
   collaboration in executing strategy, 322
   drawbacks of, 180–181
   in international markets, 191, 199–201
   Shell Oil Company, 177
   strategic, 177–179
   successful, 181–182
Arm's-length transactions, alliances advantage
   over, 181
Artificial intelligence (AI), medical applications
   of, 179
Audit committee, of corporate board of directors,
   42
Authority delegation, in strategy execution,
   317–320
Autonomous system technology, 76
Average collection period, 95

B

Backward integration
   for buyer bargaining power, 71
   difficulty of, 68
   for greater competitiveness, 171–172
   Tesla Motors, 175
Balanced scorecard, 32, 34

BAM (business activity monitoring) systems, 340
Bargaining power
   of buyers, 69–72
   for low-cost leadership, 131
   of suppliers, 67–69
Barriers to entry
   to international markets, 188, 196–201
   to strengthen competitive position, 162–163
   as test for diversification, 225, 228
   types of, 62–63
Beer industry, key success factors in, 84. see also
   Craft beer industry, competition in
Benchmarking
   competitive strength of rivals determined
     from, 116
   for continuous improvement, 372
   and ethical conduct, 113
   in solar industry, 112
   value chain, 110–112, 338
Best-cost provider strategy, 8
Best-cost (hybrid) strategies, 128–129, 146–149
Best practices, 111–114
Better-off test, for diversification, 225–226, 238
Big Data, Spotify, C-117–C-118
Biofuels, 288
Blue-ocean strategy, 160
Board of directors in strategy crafting and execution
   process, 41–44
Boeing 737 MAX, case, C-273–C-278
BPA (Bisphenyl-A) consumption, C-11
Brand management
   to increase differentiation, 138
   Nestlé, 100–101
   Procter & Gamble (P&G), 96–97
   Twitter.com, case, C-164–C-165
   Under Armour, case, C-95–C-98
Brand recognition, as entry barrier, 62
Brands, Yeti, case, C-182
Bribes and kickbacks, 270–271
BRIC countries (Brazil, Russia, India, and China),
   212
Broadcast radio industry, business models in, 13
Broad differentiation strategies
   description of, 6, 128
   pitfalls to avoid with, 141–142
   success factors for, 140–141
   superior value delivered via, 139–140
   value chain management in, 136–138
Broad low-cost strategies
   cost-efficient value chain management for,
     129–132
   description of, 128
   pitfalls to avoid with, 135
   revamping value chain for, 132–134
   successful, 134–135
Business activity monitoring (BAM) systems, 340

Business models
   Costco Wholesale Corporation, C-22
   COVID economy, C-5–C-6
   GoPro, C-190–C-191
   Netflix, case, C-149–C-160
   "power-by-the-hour" (Rolls-Royce), 12
   radio industry comparison of, 13
   sharing economy, C-3–C-4
   strategy and, 11–12
   Toms Shoes, case, C-61–C-63
   Uber Technologies, case, C-318–C-321
Business plans, C-330
Business process management tools, 333–339
Business process reengineering
   for continuous improvement, 372
   continuous improvement programs versus,
     337–339
   for cost advantage, 131
   for operating excellence, 333–334
Business risk, 173
Business strategy, 37–38
Buyers
   bargaining power and price sensitivity of, 69–72
   corporate social responsibility and, 289
   differentiation in appeal to, 139–141
   in international markets, 195–196
   value-conscious, 147
   vertical integration slowing accommodations
     to, 174

C

CAD (computer-assisted design) techniques, 131
CAFE (corporate average fuel economy) credits,
   C-233
CAFE (Coffee and Farmer Equity) Practices, of
   Starbucks, Inc., C-347
Cameras, wearable action-capture, 76
Capabilities of companies
   acquiring, developing, and strengthening,
     301–302
   collaborative partnerships to access, 308
   diversification fit with, 228
   evaluating, 100–106
   general, 231
   internal development of, 305, 307
   in international markets, 188, 207–210
   of management team, 302–305
   mergers and acquisitions to acquire, 307
   Nike, Inc., C-107–C-108
   specialized, 230–232
   strategic offensives exploiting, 158
   value chain related to, 115–116
   vertical integration requirements for, 174
Capacity-matching, 174
Capacity utilization, 131